Personality Change Due to a General Medical Condition
Mental Disorder NOS Due to a General Medical Condition

SUBSTANCE-RELATED DISORDERS

Alcohol-Related Disorders
Alcohol Use Disorders
Alcohol-Induced Disorders

Amphetamine (or Amphetamine-Like)–Related Disorders
Amphetamine Use Disorders
Amphetamine-Induced Disorders

Caffeine-Related Disorders
Caffeine-Induced Disorders

Cannabis-Related Disorders
Cannabis Use Disorders
Cannibis-Induced Disorders

Cocaine-Related Disorders
Cocaine Use Disorders
Cocaine-Induced Disorders

Hallucinogen-Related Disorders
Hallucinogen Use Disorders
Hallucinogen-Induced Disorders

Inhalant-Related Disorders
Inhalant Use Disorders
Inhalant-Induced Disorders

Nicotine-Related Disorders
Nicotine Use Disorder
Nicotine-Induced Disorder

Opioid-Related Disorders
Opioid Use Disorders
Opioid-Induced Disorders

Phencyclidine (or Phencyclidine-Like)-Related Disorders
Phencyclidine Use Disorders
Phencyclidine-Induced Disorders

Sedative-, Hypnotic-, or Anxiolytic-Related Disorders
Sedative, Hypnotic, or Anxiolytic Use Disorders
Sedative-, Hypnotic-, or Anxiolytic-Induced Disorders

Other (or Unknown) Substance-Related Disorders
Other (or Unknown) Substance Use Disorders
Other (or Unknown) Substance-Induced Disorders

SCHIZOPHRENIA AND OTHER PSYCHOTIC DISORDERS

Schizophrenia
Paranoid Type
Disorganized Type
Catatonic Type
Undifferentiated Type
Residual Type
Schizophreniform Disorder
Schizoaffective Disorder
Delusional Disorder
Brief Psychotic Disorder
Shared Psychotic Disorder
Pscychotic Disorder Due to a General Medical Condition
Substance-Induced Psychotic Disorder
Psychotic Disorder NOS

MOOD DISORDERS

Depressive Disorders
Major Depressive Disorder
Dysthymic Disorder
Depressive Disorder NOS

Bipolar Disorders
Bipolar I Disorder
Bipolar II Disorder
Cyclothymic Disorder
Bipolar Disorder NOS

Other Mood Disorders
Mood Disorder Due to a General Medical Condition
Substance-Induced Mood Disorder
Mood Disorder NOS

ANXIETY DISORDERS

Panic Disorder Without Agoraphobia
Panic Disorder With Agoraphobia
Agoraphobia Without History of Panic Disorder
Specific Phobia
Social Phobia
Obsessive-Compulsive Disorder
Posttraumatic Stress Disorder
Acute Stress Disorder

(Continued on back cover)

SEVENTH EDITION

ABNORMAL PSYCHOLOGY

CURRENT PERSPECTIVES

LAUREN B. ALLOY
Temple University

JOAN ACOCELLA

RICHARD R. BOOTZIN
University of Arizona

McGRAW-HILL, INC.

New York St. Louis San Francisco Auckland Bogotá
Caracas Lisbon London Madrid Mexico City Milan Montreal
New Delhi San Juan Singapore Sydney Tokyo Toronto

ABNORMAL PSYCHOLOGY
Current Perspectives

Credits and Acknowledgments appear on page C-1 and on this page by reference.

This book is printed on acid-free paper.

2 3 4 5 6 7 8 9 0 VNH VNH 9 0 9 8 7 6

ISBN 0-07-006615-9

This book was set in Palatino by York Graphic Services, Inc.
The editors were Roberta Meyer, Brian L. McKean,
and James R. Belser;
the designer was Joan E. O'Connor;
the production supervisor was Kathryn Porzio.
The photo editor was Barbara Salz.
Von Hoffmann Press, Inc., was printer and binder.

Cover Painting
Paul Klee: *Pomona, Overripe (slightly, inclined),*
1938/134 (J 14)
Oil on newspaper on burlap 26¼ × 20½ in.
Paul Klee Stiftung, Kunstmuseum Bern.

Library of Congress Cataloging-in-Publication Data

Alloy, Lauren B.
Abnormal psychology: current perspectives / Lauren B. Alloy, Joan Acocella, Richard R. Bootzin.—7th ed.
p. cm.
Rev. ed. of: Abnormal psychology / Richard R. Bootzin, Joan Ross Acocella, Lauren B. Alloy. 6th ed. © 1993.
Includes bibliographical references and index.
ISBN 0-07-006615-9
1. Psychology, Pathological. I. Acocella, Joan Ross. II. Bootzin, Richard R., (date). III. Bootzin, Richard R., (date). Abnormal psychology IV. Title.
[DNLM: 1. Psychopathology. WM 100 A441a 1996]
RC454.B577 1996
616.89—dc20
DNLM/DLC
for Library of Congress 95-16246

INTERNATIONAL EDITION

When ordering this title, use ISBN 0-07-114002-6.

ABOUT THE AUTHORS

Lauren B. Alloy is an internationally recognized researcher in the area of mood disorders. Her work on depression has had a major impact on the fields of clinical and social psychology. She is currently Professor of Psychology at Temple University. Previously, at Northwestern University, she became the youngest Professor in the university's history and the first woman to become Professor in the Northwestern Psychology department. She received both her B.A. and Ph.D. in psychology from the University of Pennsylvania. Dr. Alloy was awarded the American Psychological Association's Young Psychologist's Award at the XXIII International Congress of Psychology in 1984 and the Northwestern University College of Arts & Sciences Great Teacher Award in 1988 for her classroom teaching and mentoring of students. She is the author of over 65 scholarly publications, including her 1988 book entitled *Cognitive Processes in Depression.* She has served on the editorial boards of the *Journal of Abnormal Psychology, Journal of Personality and Social Psychology,* and *Cognitive Therapy and Research* and is Editor of the *Springer-Verlag Series on Psychopathology.* She regularly teaches courses on psychopathology.

Dr. Alloy's research focuses on cognitive, interpersonal, and psychosocial processes in the onset and maintenance of depression and bipolar disorder. Along with her colleagues Lyn Abramson and Gerald Metalsky, she is the author of the hopelessness theory of depression and she discovered, with Lyn Abramson, the "sadder but wiser" or "depressive realism" effect. In her leisure time, she enjoys sports, the theater, and is a movie fanatic. But most of all, she loves being with her husband, Daniel, and daughter, Adrienne.

Joan Acocella is a New York-based writer. A coauthor of *Abnormal Psychology: Current Perspectives* since its second edition in 1977, she has contributed to many textbooks in the social sciences. She also writes on the arts.

Richard R. Bootzin is a clinical psychologist and a prominent researcher in the areas of psychological treatments, sleep and sleep disorders, and mental health evaluation. Dr. Bootzin received his Bachelor's degree from the Unversity of Wisconsin at Madison and Ph.D. from Purdue University in 1968. From 1968 through 1986, he was a faculty member at Northwestern University, serving as Chairman of the Psychology Department from 1980 to 1986. Since 1987 he has been Professor of Psychology at the University of Arizona. He served as Director of the Graduate Program in Clinical Psychology from 1987 to 1992 and as Acting Head of the Psychology Department from 1994 to 1995.

Dr. Bootzin is a fellow of the American Association of Applied and Preventive Psychology, the American Psychological Association, and the American Psychological Society. He is a past-president of the Society for a Science of Clinical Psychology and he has served on a number of national committees including the steering committee of the Human Capital Initiative on Behavorial Sciences, Psychopathology, and Mental Health and the advisory committee to the National Institute of Drug Abuse on the development of behavioral treatments for substance abuse. Dr. Bootzin has published six books and more than 100 scientific papers. He has served as a reviewer or member of the editorial board for more than twenty-five journals, including *Clinical Psychology: Science and Practice*, the *Journal of Abnormal Psychology*, the *Journal of Consulting and Clinical Psychology*, and the *Archives of General Psychiatry*.

CONTENTS IN BRIEF

CONTENTS

LIST OF BOXES

PREFACE

The seventh edition of *Abnormal Psychology: Current Perspectives* preserves and improves on the strengths of the sixth edition. The multiperspective approach, which recognizes all the major viewpoints on psychological disorders, has been strengthened in three ways in this edition. First, the cognitive perspective and the neuroscience/biological perspective have been expanded and strengthened, recognizing the increasing importance of discoveries in these areas. We think that our discussion of these two perspectives, whether of cognitive styles and memory processes or of biochemical research and brain imaging, will be exciting and illuminating. Second, with the seventh edition, we have introduced the interpersonal/family perspective. Finally, we now take a more differentiated approach to the presentation of the various perspectives on psychopathology. The breadth and depth of our discussion of each perspective is proportional to its importance to the understanding of the causes and treatments of each group of mental disorders. The chapter-by-chapter overview that follows highlights the topics that have been added to the seventh edition.

The seventh edition has been thoroughly updated, consistent with the *Diagnostic and Statistical Manual of Mental Disorders–Fourth Edition (DSM-IV)*. All terminology and concepts have been revised to reflect the latest developments in *DSM-IV*.

The research orientation of the book has again been strengthened. Throughout, recent research findings have been added—many of them reflecting new discoveries about the causes of particular disorders and promising new methods of treatment. New boxes highlight controversial issues and the latest research findings.

The chapters on the major perspectives in abnormal psychology reflect the expansion of the cognitive and neuroscience/biological perspectives and include the interpersonal perspective as well. These chapters are concise, with related perspectives treated in a single chapter. Other chapters in the text have been reorganized to reflect current thinking and research (see the *Revision Overview*). Case studies have been updated and expanded. They are used consistently to introduce each disorders chapter, giving students an immediate focus for the chapter.

Finally, from studies of abnormal brain development in schizophrenia to the recent controversy over recovered memories of child sexual abuse to the latest thinking on sex differences in depression, every chapter truly reflects *current perspectives* in abnormal psychology.

Revision Overview

Chapter 1 Abnormal Behavior: Yesterday and Today offers a more thorough discussion of the meaning of "culture." The question of how abnormality is defined, by society and by *DSM-IV*, has also been expanded.

Chapter 2 The Psychodynamic and Humanistic-Existential Perspectives gives an updated review of the psychodynamic approach, emphasizing theories involving social interaction (Adler, Horney, Sullivan) and ego processes (Erikson, Kohut). The discussion of object relations theory has been expanded.

Chapter 3 The Behavioral, Cognitive, Interpersonal, and Sociocultural Perspectives has a new section on the interpersonal perspective, based on systems theories and circumplex models. The contemporary blend of cognitive, social, and learning theories is also explained in greater detail.

Chapter 4 The Biological Perspective has been updated to keep pace with the rapid advances in this field. Brain structures and synaptic transmission are explained more fully, and there are new illustrations to help the student with these complex matters. The chapter also describes new measurement techniques such as event-related potentials (ERPs) and functional magnetic resonance imaging (fMRI).

Chapter 5 Research Methods in Abnormal Psychology offers clearer, more pointed discussions of operational definitions, dependent and independent variables, and statistical variance.

Chapter 6 Diagnosis and Assessment introduces *DSM-IV* and problems associated with it, especially the high incidence of comorbidity. (This issue has a box to itself.) Criticisms of diagnosis are discussed more briefly; criticisms of IQ testing, more fully.

Chapter 7 Anxiety Disorders describes new research on the different types of panic attacks, the distinction between panic disorder and generalized anxiety disorder, the relationship between obsessive-compulsive disorder and conditions such as trichotillomania, and factors affecting risk for posttraumatic stress disorder. PTSD following rape is covered in a new box. The chapter also includes recent findings on the bearing of genes, brain structures, and serotonin functioning on the anxiety disorders.

Chapter 8 Dissociative and Somatoform Disorders contains new research on the controversial dissociative disorders. Under dissociative identity disorder (multiple personality), there are recent findings on the functions served by the alter personalities, on the possibility that primary and subordinate personalities are served by different hemispheres of the brain, and on criteria for distinguishing false cases from true. The controversy over recovered memory of childhood sexual abuse is discussed in a vivid new box.

Chapter 9 Psychological Stress and Physical Disorders presents the most current research on psychoneuroimmunology (PNI), especially as it relates to breast cancer and HIV infection. An expanded discussion of obesity presents many new findings.

Chapter 10 Mood Disorders has been reorganized. The perspectives sections on depression and suicide are integrated, to avoid redundancy. The chapter presents a wealth of new research: on bipolar subtypes, on endogenous *vs.* reactive depression, on suicide prevention (including school programs aimed at high-risk teenagers), on the relationship between depression and parenting styles. In the perspectives section, there is now less emphasis on the humanistic-existential perspective and more on behavioral/interpersonal, cognitive, and sociocultural theories. The chapter includes new findings on the genetic and biochemical correlates of depression. Theories regarding the relationship between bipolar disorder and creativity are covered in a new box.

Chapter 11 Personality Disorders offers new research on the genetics of personality disorders, on adolescence-limited *vs.* lifetime psychopathy, and on attention impairments in psychopathy. A new box describes how politics affects the framing of diagnostic categories, for example, "self-defeating personality disorder" and "sadistic personality disorder," both proposed for, and ultimately rejected from, *DSM-IV.*

Chapter 12 The Substance-Use Disorders outlines the most current research on alcohol dependence. The box on steroid use has been expanded, and there is a new box dealing with binge-drinking on campuses—how it affects both the drinkers and their classmates.

Chapter 13 Sexual and Gender Identity Disorders has been revised to reflect the *DSM-IV* classification. It presents new research on sexual exploitation: pedophilia, incest, and rape, particularly in regard to the victims. It also covers recently developed medical treatments for sexual dysfunctions and for pedophilia. There is a new box describing the findings of the 1994 "Sex in America" survey.

Chapter 14 Schizophrenia and Delusional Disorder includes the latest research on schizophrenic delusions, hallucinations, and social withdrawal, as well as the proposed positive- and negative-symptom subtypes. A new box discusses the possibility that some schizophrenics may take comfort from, and therefore not recover from, their hallucinations.

Chapter 15 Perspectives on Schizophrenia has been reorganized to reflect the currently accepted diathesis-stress model of schizophrenia. Cognitive and biological theories focusing on diathesis are followed by theories (family, psychodynamic, and also biological) that emphasize stress. Then comes a discussion of approaches (behavioral and humanistic-existential) that have to do primarily with the management of schizophrenia. Finally, a summary of the diathesis-stress position integrates these strands. The chapter includes the latest research on schizophrenia, including high-risk studies, brain-imaging studies, and findings regarding prenatal brain injury. Biological and cognitive theories now receive more attention; psychodynamic and humanistic-existential theories, less attention.

Chapter 16 Cognitive Disorders of Adulthood includes a wholly revised section on the epilepsies. Recent findings on Alzheimer's disease include a box on the problems facing Alzheimer's caregivers. The chapter gives new attention to brain trauma and includes a box on brain injury and football.

Chapter 17 Disorders of Childhood and Adolescence reflects all of *DSM-IV*'s new terminology for attention-deficit/hyperactivity disorder and the learning disorders. We discuss the conduct disorders in greater detail, with special attention to the age of onset. There is an expanded section on anorexia and a new section on bulimia, together with sociocultural theories and the eating disorders. Finally, a wholly revised box focuses on the urgent problem of child abuse.

Chapter 18 Mental Retardation and Autism features the widely reported findings of the 1994 Carnegie Report on the effects of under-stimulation on the structure of the infant brain. It also discusses the sociocultural correlates of these findings, such as the rise in teenage pregnancy, and the related infant-stimulation programs. There are expanded discussions of the relationship between drugs and mental retardation, as seen in "crack babies" and fetal alcohol syndrome.

Chapter 19 Individual Psychotherapy, in keeping with the field, places increased emphasis on accountability. Recent outcome studies are described, and there are new boxes on the effectiveness of self-help books and of paraprofessional and nonprofessional therapists. Finally, material has been added on experiential therapy and multicomponent treatments.

Chapter 20 Group, Family, and Community Therapy updates its discussion of family and marital therapies. Of special interest is a new box on the controversial issue of treatment for spouse-abusers.

Chapter 21 Biological Therapy contains the most current research on SSRI antidepressants such as Prozac, Paxil, and Zoloft. It includes a new box on Prozac, and discusses problems of withdrawal from antianxiety drugs such as Xanax and Ativan.

Chapter 22 Legal Issues in Abnormal Psychology expands its discussion of the claims of criminal law *vs.* the claims of psychology—a pressing issue today—and relates this question to the recent trials of Lorena Bobbitt and the Menendez brothers. Under patients' rights, the chapter features a new box on whether, in the age of AIDS, mental hospitals must begin monitoring their patients' sex lives.

PEDAGOGY

Each chapter begins with an outline that offers the student a concise overview of the material therein. Within each chapter, important terms are highlighted in boldface so that they can be quickly identified. These terms are defined not only in the text when they first appear but also in the glossary at the end of the book. In addition, key terms are listed at the end of each chapter. Summaries are organized around the major headings of each chapter. The references are compiled in an extensive reference section at the end of the text. This edition contains one hundred new photographs, most of which are in color.

SUPPLEMENTS

Casebook in Abnormal Psychology, Third Edition, by John Vitkus, Barnard College, contains 16 cases covering a broad range of disorders and all of the major approaches to treatment. There are 4 new cases in this edition.

Study Guide by Gary and Susan Bothe, Pensacola Junior College, is a comprehensive review of chapter objectives, key terms, fill in the blank and multiple choice questions. Flash cards of key terms and concept maps are new to this edition.

Instructor's Manual by Fred Whitford, Montana State University, is now integrated with the study guide and offers an expanded section on demonstration and discussion topics.

Test Bank by Richard Leavy of Ohio Wesleyan University is a thorough revision with 75 multiple choice and 5 essay questions in each chapter.

McGraw-Hill Overhead Transparencies

ACKNOWLEDGMENTS

We thank John Vitkus for his excellent contributions to many chapters in this book. His steadfast commitment has benefited this text in countless ways. We are also indebted to Brian McKean, psychology editor at McGraw-Hill, and Jane Vaicunas, publisher, who saw us expertly through the early planning and development of this edition; to James Belser, the editing supervisor, Susan Gottfried, the copyeditor, Barbara Salz, the photo researcher, and Joan O'Connor, the book's designer; to Susanna Nemes, who helped with Chapter 7, and Nancy Tashman, Lauren Alloy's research assistant. Finally, a book of this scope requires expert editing. We were lucky that our development editor was Roberta Meyer, with her knowledge of psychology, her long experience in textbook editing, and her unflagging good will.

CONSULTANTS

John Allen, Assistant Professor of Psychology, Cognitive Science, and Neuroscience at the University of Arizona, is a specialist in psychopathology and the psychophysiology of emotion.

Judith V. Becker, Professor of Psychology and Psychiatry at the University of Arizona, is a specialist in sexual disorders. Dr. Becker assisted with the chapter on sexual and gender identity disorders.

Richard J. Davidson, William James Professor of Psychology at the University of Wisconsin, Madison, is a specialist in brain function and psychopathology. Dr. Davidson assisted with the chapter on the biological perspective.

Carl B. Dodrill, Professor, Department of Neurological Surgery, University of Washington School of Medicine, is a specialist in the neuropsychology of epilepsy. Dr. Dodrill assisted with the chapter on cognitive disorders of adulthood.

Andrew R. Eisen, Assistant Professor of Psychology at Fairleigh Dickinson University, is a specialist in child and adolescent anxiety disorders. Dr. Eisen assisted with the chapter on the disorders of childhood and adolescence.

Steven R. Lopez, Associate Professor of Psychology at the University of California, Los Angeles, is a specialist in culture and mental health. Dr. Lopez provided advice and information on that issue.

A. Thomas McLellan, Scientific Director of the Treatment Research Institute, Philadelphia, and Professor of Psychology at the Center for Studies on Addiction at the University of Pennsylvania, is a specialist on addiction and substance abuse. Dr. McLellan assisted with the chapter on substance-use disorders.

Barry Smith, Professor of Psychology at the University of Maryland, is a specialist in psychophysiology and personality. Dr. Smith assisted with the chapter on research methods in abnormal psychology.

Arthur Stone, Professor of Psychiatry and Psychology at S.U.N.Y. Stony Brook, is a specialist in behavioral medicine. Dr. Stone assisted with the chapter on psychological stress and physical disorders.

Howard Ulan, an attorney for the Pennsylvania Department of Public Welfare, who also holds a Ph.D. in psychology, is a specialist in mental health and disability law. Dr. Ulan assisted with the chapter on legal issues in abnormal psychology.

John Vitkus, Assistant Professor of Psychology at Barnard College, is a specialist in personality theory and the interpersonal processes of depression. Dr. Vitkus assisted with the chapters on the historical and theoretical perspectives of abnormal psychology.

Lynn Waterhouse, Director of Child Behavior Study and Professor of Linguistics at Trenton State College, is a specialist in autism, language disabilities, and developmental disorders. Dr. Waterhouse assisted with the chapter on mental retardation and autism.

Thomas Widiger, Professor of Psychology at the University of Kentucky, is a specialist in diagnosis and classification. Dr. Widiger assisted with the chapters on diagnosis and assessment and the personality disorders.

Steven Zarit, Assistant Director of the Gerontology Center and Professor of Human Development at Pennsylvania State University, is a specialist in the clinical psychology of aging. Dr. Zarit assisted with the chapter on cognitive disorders of adulthood.

REVIEWERS

Serrhel G. Adams, *Department of Veterans Affairs*
Gary P. Brown, *Kellogg Community College*
Linda Flickinger, *St. Clair Community College*
Alan G. Glaros, *University of Missouri at Kansas City*
Frank Goodkin, *Castleton State College*
Caroline Keutzer, *University of Oregon*
Ann Kring, *Vanderbilt University*
Richard L. Leavy, *Ohio Wesleyan University*
John T. Long, *Mount Saint Antonio College*
Morton Marmatz, *University of Massachusetts at Amherst*
Linda Musun-Miller, *University of Arkansas at Little Rock*
Ronald Alvin Richert, *Brandon University*
Joseph Tecce, *Boston College*
Ken Vincent, *Houston Community College*
Fred Whitford, *Montana State University*

We hope that this new edition of *Abnormal Psychology* will make students not only more knowledgeable but also more understanding. For in describing what we know so far about why people act as they do, we have attempted to present this complex subject from a human perspective. "Abnormal" is a relative term, the meaning of which has changed many times over the centuries. We offer a balanced approach to the standards against which abnormality is defined. We also present the causal theories in a balanced fashion. This approach is intended to impress on the student the dynamic character of the field: its openness to dispute, to movement, and to change. We hope that the book will also encourage students to appreciate the interconnection between mind and body, which is perhaps the central theme of this book.

Lauren B. Alloy
Joan Acocella
Richard R. Bootzin

ABNORMAL PSYCHOLOGY

CURRENT PERSPECTIVES

PART ONE

HISTORICAL AND THEORETICAL PERSPECTIVES

CHAPTER 1
ABNORMAL BEHAVIOR: YESTERDAY AND TODAY

CHAPTER 2
THE PSYCHODYNAMIC AND HUMANISTIC-EXISTENTIAL PERSPECTIVES

CHAPTER 3
THE BEHAVIORAL, COGNITIVE, INTERPERSONAL, AND SOCIOCULTURAL PERSPECTIVES

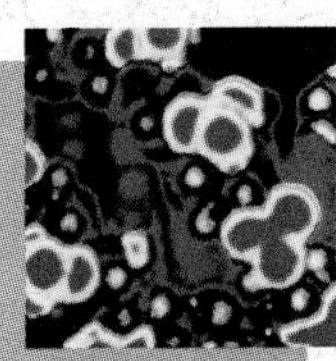

CHAPTER 4
THE BIOLOGICAL PERSPECTIVE

1

ABNORMAL BEHAVIOR: YESTERDAY AND TODAY

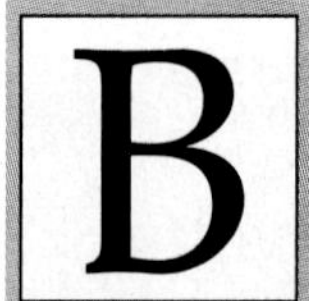

efore we can begin a study of abnormal psychology, we need to think about what kind of behavior deserves to be called "abnormal." Consider the following examples:

1 A woman becomes seriously depressed after her husband's death. She has difficulty sleeping and loses her appetite.
2 A man tries to force his woman companion to have sexual intercourse even though she says no and resists him physically.
3 A young man will not travel by airplane and insists on driving or taking buses or trains everywhere, despite considerable inconvenience.
4 An adolescent girl occasionally indulges in binge eating, after which she forces herself to vomit.
5 A woman will wear only blue clothing, although her manner of dress is appropriate otherwise.

In the first example, are we dealing with a psychological disorder or just a case of normal grieving? As for the second example, is this evidence of psychological disturbance, or is it just a crime? In the third case, do we call a behavior abnormal just because it is unusual and involves personal difficulty? Is the adolescent girl suffering from a psychological disorder, or is she responding to society's unreasonable standards for thinness? Is the woman in blue abnormal or just idiosyncratic? Does she need treatment, or is she just very fond of blue? Such questions surround most categories of abnormal behavior.

ABNORMAL BEHAVIOR AND SOCIETY

Defining Abnormal Behavior

When we ask how a society defines psychological abnormality, we are asking, first, where that society draws the line between acceptable and unacceptable behavior and, second, which unacceptable behaviors the society views as evidence of "disorder" rather than simply as undesirable. These questions are answered according to various criteria, but perhaps the most common is the society's norms.

Norm Violation Every human group lives by a set of **norms**—rules that tell us what it is "right" and "wrong" to do, and when and where and with whom. Such rules circumscribe every aspect of our existence, from our most far-reaching decisions to our most prosaic daily routines.

Consider, for example, the matter of how close we stand or sit to a person we are talking to. This is something that is taken for granted by people within a society, but it differs widely among societies. In North America, when two people who do not know one another well are conversing, they will stand about 3 feet apart, but in South America they stand much closer, and in Asia, much farther apart. In one study, Japanese, American, and Venezuelan students were asked to have a five-minute conversation with a stranger of the same sex and nationality. The Japanese sat about 40 inches apart; the Americans, 35 inches; the Venezuelans, 32 inches (Sussman & Rosenfeld, 1982). Arabs come even closer than South Americans. According to Edward Hall (1976), the primary investigator of this subject of "personal space":

> In the Arab world, you do not hold a lien on the ground underfoot. When standing on a street corner, an Arab may shove you aside if he wants to be where you are. This puts the average territorial American or German under great stress. . . . Years ago, American women in Beirut had to give up using streetcars. Their bodies were the property of all men within reach. What was happening is even reflected in the language. The Arabs have no word for trespass. (p. 66)

So the definition of personal space is a norm which differs from culture to culture. People who stand too close to us may seem to us pushy; people who stand too far away may seem cold. And while we may shrug off such social oddities, psychological professionals do not. (In a marriage counselor's office, how close a couple sit to one another will be a potentially important observation.) In other words, norm violation within one's culture tends to be viewed, in varying degrees, as abnormal. Examples 2, 3, and 5 on the first page of this chapter involve norm violation. In our culture, men are not supposed to force women to have sex; we expect people to travel on planes, and dressing in only one color seems odd.

In small, highly integrated societies, disagreement over norms is rare. In a large, complex society, on the other hand, there may be more disagreement about what is acceptable. For example, the gay liberation movement can be conceptualized as the effort of one group to persuade the society as a whole to adjust its norms so that homosexuality will fall inside rather than outside the limits of acceptability.

Since norms are so variable, they may seem a weak basis for the assessment of mental health. Furthermore, whether or not adherence to norms is an appropriate criterion for mental health, it can be called an oppressive criterion. It enthrones conformity as the ideal pattern of behavior and thereby stigmatizes the nonconformist. Nevertheless, norms remain a very important standard for defining abnormality. Though they may be relative, they are nevertheless so deeply ingrained that they *seem* absolute, and hence anyone who violates them seems abnormal.

Norms, however, are not the only standard for defining abnormal behavior. Other criteria are statistical rarity, personal discomfort, maladaptive behavior, and deviation from an ideal state.

Statistical Rarity From a statistical point of view, abnormality is any substantial deviation from a statistically calculated average. Those who fall within the "golden mean"—those, in short, who do what most other people do—are normal, while those whose behavior differs from that of the majority are abnormal.

This criterion is used in some evaluations of psychological abnormality. The diagnosis of mental retardation, for instance, is based in large part on statistical accounting. Those whose tested intelligence falls below an average range for the population (and who also have problems coping with life—which, with intelligence far lower than the average, is likely to be the case) are labeled "mentally retarded" (see Figure 1.1). Careful statistical calculations are not always considered necessary in order to establish deviance, however. In the extreme version of the statistical approach, any behavior that is unusual would be judged abnormal,

One definition of abnormal behavior has to do with violation of *norms,* or socially imposed standards of acceptable behavior. The vagueness of this definition presents problems, however. Where exactly is the line between harmless nonconformity and truly abnormal behavior?

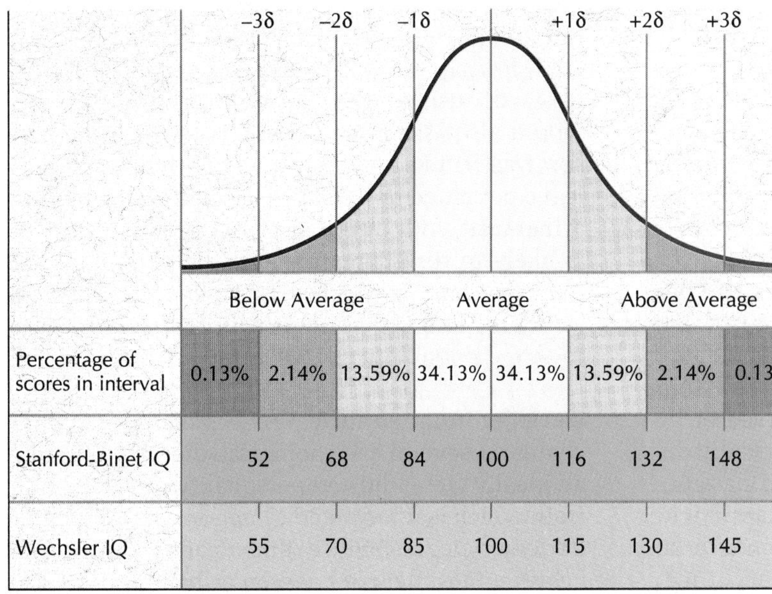

FIGURE 1.1 The distribution of IQ scores in the United States. More than 68 percent of the population scores between 84 and 116 points. Using the statistical approach to abnormality, diagnosticians designate as mentally retarded those falling below approximately 68 points. As the figure indicates, this group is statistically rare, representing only about 2 percent of the population.

even if it involves harmless eccentricity, such as wearing only blue clothing.

The statistical-rarity approach makes defining abnormality a simple task. One has only to measure the person's performance against the average performance. If it falls outside the average range, it is abnormal. There are obvious difficulties with this approach, however. As we saw earlier, the norm-violation approach can be criticized for exalting the shifting values of social groups. Yet the major weakness of the statistical-rarity approach is that it has *no* values; it lacks any system for differentiating between desirable and undesirable behaviors. In the absence of such a system, it is the average behavior that tends to be considered the ideal. Such a point of view is potentially very dangerous, since it discourages even valuable deviations. For example, not only mentally retarded people but also geniuses—and particularly geniuses with new ideas—might be considered candidates for psychological treatment. Of course, most users of the statistical-rarity approach acknowledge that not all rarities should be identified as abnormal. Still, the focus on average performance has discomforting implications.

Personal Discomfort Another criterion for defining abnormality is personal discomfort. If people are content with their lives, then their lives are of no concern to the mental health establishment. If, on the other hand, they are distressed over their thoughts or behavior—as the grieving widow mentioned at the beginning of this chapter might be—then they require treatment.

This is a more liberal approach than the two we have just discussed, in that it makes people the judges of their own normality, rather than subjecting them to the judgment of the society or the diagnostician. And this is the approach that is probably the most widely used in the case of the less severe psychological disorders. Most people in psychotherapy are there not because anyone has declared their behavior abnormal but because they themselves are unhappy with some aspect of their lives.

Reasonable as it may be in such cases, the personal-discomfort criterion has an obvious weakness in that it gives us no standard for evaluating the behavior itself. The lack of an objective standard is especially problematic in the case of behaviors that cause serious harm or are socially disruptive. Is teenage drug addiction to be classified as abnormal only if the teenager is unhappy with his or her addiction? Furthermore, even if a behavior pattern is not necessarily harmful, it may still merit psychological attention. People who believe that their brains are receiving messages from outer space may inflict no pain on others, yet most people would consider them in need of psychological treatment.

Maladaptive Behavior A fourth criterion for defining a behavior as abnormal is whether it is maladaptive. Here the question is whether the person, given that behavior pattern, is able to meet the demands of his or her life—hold down a job, deal with friends and family, pay the bills on time, and the like. If not, the pattern is abnormal. This standard overlaps somewhat with that of norm violation. After all, many norms are rules for adapting our behavior to our own and our society's requirements. (To arrive for work drunk is to violate a norm; it is also maladaptive, in that it may get you fired.) At the same time, the maladaptiveness standard is unique in that it concentrates on the practical matter of getting through life with some measure of success. If the man with the fear of flying had a job that required travel, he would be seriously inconvenienced, and his behavior could be considered maladaptive.

This practical approach makes the maladaptiveness standard a useful one. The maladaptiveness standard is also favored by many professionals for its elasticity: because it focuses on behavior *relative to life circumstances,* it can accommodate many different styles of living. But as with the personal-discomfort criterion, this liberalism is purchased at the cost of values. Are there not certain circumstances to which people should *not* adapt? In the mid-nineteenth century, for example, the diagnosis of "drapetomania" (from the Greek *drapetes,* meaning "runaway") was proposed for slaves who ran away from their masters (Cartwright, 1851/1981; Szasz, 1971). Of course, any responsible professional using the maladaptiveness standard would also assess the situation to which the person was failing to adapt. If a child whose parents leave her alone in the house at night is brought to a therapist with sleeping problems, the therapist is likely to direct treatment at the parents rather than the child. Nevertheless, the maladaptiveness standard, like the norm-violation standard, does raise the possibility of bias in favor of "fitting in."

Deviation from an Ideal As we shall see in later chapters, several psychological theories describe an ideally well-adjusted personality, any deviation from which is interpreted as abnormal to a greater or lesser degree. Since the ideal is difficult to achieve, most people are seen as being poorly adjusted at least part of the time. One may strive to achieve the ideal, but one seldom makes it.

In light of such theories, many people may judge themselves to be abnormal, or at least in need of psychological treatment, even though they have no obvious symptoms. For example, a woman may have friends and a reasonably satisfying job and yet consider herself a candidate for psychotherapy because she lacks something—an intimate relationship with another person, a sense of realizing her full potential—that is held up as a criterion for mental health by one or another theory.

The shortcomings of the deviation-from-an-ideal approach are again obvious. First, a person who falls short of an ideal does not necessarily merit the label "abnormal" or require treatment. The pursuit of ideal adjustment can add to people's troubles, making them feel seriously inadequate, whereas they may simply be imperfect, like all human beings. Second, psychological theories are as relative to time and place as social norms, and they change even more quickly. Thus if norms are a weak foundation for the evaluation of mental health, theoretical ideals are even weaker. (And at least social norms ask only for the possible.) Nevertheless, the need to achieve something more than ordinary adjustment has propelled many people into psychotherapy, especially into group therapies oriented toward what is called "personal growth."

A Combined Standard The questions raised by these different criteria for defining abnormality can be summarized as one question: Should our standard be *facts,* such as statistical rarity or a clearly dysfunctional behavior (e.g., failure to eat), or should it be *values,* such as adaptation or adherence to norms? Many professionals feel that the question cannot be decided one way or the other, but that the definition of mental disorder must rest on both facts and values. Jerome Wakefield (1992), for example, has proposed that mental disorder

> lies on the boundary between the given natural world and the constructed social world; a disorder exists when the failure of a person's internal mechanisms to perform their functions as designed by nature impinges harmfully on the person's well-being as defined by social values. (p. 373)

People diagnosed as schizophrenic, for example, often cannot think or speak coherently; their internal mechanisms, in Wakefield's terms, are failing to perform "their functions as designed by nature." And these disabilities in turn impinge on their "well-being as defined by social values"—for instance, their ability to hold down a job or raise children. As we shall see, the current *Diagnostic and Statistical Manual of Mental Disorders* also rests on a combined standard of facts and social values or norms.

However much professional dispute surrounds the definition of abnormal behavior, it should be kept in mind that most societies identify the same *categories* of behavior as indicative of mental disorder. As W. B. Maher and Maher (1985) point out, there are four basic categories:

1. Behavior that is harmful to the self or that is harmful to others without serving the interests of the self.
2. Poor reality contact—for example, beliefs that most people do not hold or sensory perceptions of things that most people do not perceive.
3. Emotional reactions inappropriate to the person's situation.
4. Erratic behavior—that is, behavior that shifts unpredictably.

Which actions fall into these categories depends, again, on the society's definitions of what is normal and appropriate, but these are the kinds of deviations that most people, worldwide, consider possible signs of mental disorder.

Explaining Abnormal Behavior

If defining abnormal behavior is difficult, explaining it is more so. Since antiquity, people have developed theories as to the causes of abnormal behavior. Not only do the theories vary with the kinds of abnormality they seek to explain; they often compete with each other to explain the same abnormality—and the entire problem of abnormal behavior. These various explanations have a common base in that they are all naturalistic. That is, in keeping with a secular and scientific age, they seek to account for abnormal behavior in terms of natural events—disturbances in the body or disturbances in human relationships. Beyond this, however, they differ greatly, and since they will figure importantly in the succeeding chapters of this book, it is worth examining them briefly at this point.

The Medical Model According to what is loosely called the **medical model** (or *disease model*), abnormal behavior is comparable to disease: each kind of abnormal behavior, like each disease, has specific *causes* and a specific *set of symptoms.* In its strictest sense, the medical model also implies that the abnormal behavior is **biogenic**—that is, it results from some malfunction within the body. However, even those who do not think that all abnormal behavior is biologically *caused* may still reflect the assumptions of the medical model if they consider "symptoms" the products of underlying causes.

Biogenic theories of abnormal behavior have been with us since ancient times. In the Middle Ages and the Renaissance they coexisted with supernatural theory, the belief that abnormal behavior was caused by God or, more often, the devil. But in the eighteenth and early nineteenth centuries, religious explanations were gradually eclipsed by biological explanations, and abnormal behavior was accordingly considered the province of medicine. It was within the framework of these assumptions that the modern discipline of abnormal psychology developed in the nineteenth century. Most of the major early theoreticians of abnormal psychology, regardless of their specific theories, were medical doctors who saw abnormality as illness.

This newly dominant medical approach was soon rewarded by a series of extremely important breakthroughs. Several previously unexplained behavior patterns were found to result from identifiable brain pathologies—infection, poisoning, and the like. Such discoveries brought immense prestige to the organic theory of abnormal behavior. Medicine, it was assumed, would ultimately conquer madness. On this assumption, madness was increasingly turned over to the medical profession.

There remained many patterns of abnormal behavior—indeed, the majority—for which no medical cause had been discovered. Yet because researchers were confident that such causes would eventually be found, and because abnormal behavior was by now the province of medicine, these patterns were treated as if they were organically based. In other words, they were treated according to a medical "model." (In scientific terms, a *model* is an analogy.) This not only meant that abnormal behavior was best handled by physicians, in hospitals, and by means of medical treatments such as drugs. It also meant that the entire problem of deviant behavior should be conceptualized in medical terms. Even those who seriously questioned the medical model still used such terms as *symptom, syndrome, pathology, mental illness, patient, diagnosis, therapy, treatment,* and *cure,* all of which are derived from the medical analogy (R. H. Price, 1978). Although this book is not based on the medical model, such terms will occur here repeatedly. They are almost unavoidable.

Not everyone accepted the medical model, however. Indeed, it was sharply criticized by many psychologists and other researchers. As these writers pointed out, biological causes had *not* been found for most patterns of abnormal behavior; therefore, it was wrong to think of such patterns as illnesses. Perhaps the most prominent critic of the medical model was the American psychiatrist Thomas Szasz. In a book called *The Myth of Mental Illness* (1961), Szasz claimed that most of what the medical model calls mental illnesses are not illnesses at all, but rather "problems in living" manifested in deviations from moral, legal, and social norms. To label these deviations "sick" is, according to Szasz, not only a falsification of the conflict between the person and the society but also a dangerous sanctification of the society's norms. As others showed, the "sick" label also deprives people of responsibility for their behavior (they can't help it—they're sick) and relegates them to a passive role that impedes their return to normal behavior. In other words, the medical model can foster serious abuses.

This controversy is not as heated today as it was in the sixties and seventies, but it is still very much alive. In response to it, many psychological professionals now take a neutral position as to the ultimate causes of abnormal behavior. (Such neutrality can be seen in the title of the American Psychiatric Association's diagnostic manual, *The Diagnostic and Statistical Manual of Mental Disorders.* These patterns are "disorders," not—or not necessarily—"illnesses.") At the same time, there have been important advances in abnormal psychology in the last two decades in the area of biological research. More and more forms of psychological disturbance have been found to also involve biological disturbance.

In the chapters that follow, we will survey some of this research, which we have grouped together as the **biological perspective** within abnormal psychology. Like the medical model, the biological perspective focuses on the physical components of abnormal behavior. Unlike the medical model, however, it does not suggest that all or even most abnormal behavior patterns are merely symptoms of biological abnormalities, or even that such patterns are best treated in a medical setting. Rather, the biological perspective simply concentrates on the physical aspects of a disorder in an effort to understand its characteristics. Consider sadness, for example. This phenomenon could be studied at many different levels of analysis. One could analyze the thoughts that accompany sadness, and that is what cognitive psychologists do (see Chapter 3). Another approach would be to use brain imaging techniques to study the biological changes that accompany reported states of sadness, and that is what neuroscientists do. Both the thoughts and the brain changes are part of sadness and may, at various levels, cause it. Neuroscientists do not claim that organic changes are the root cause, only that they constitute an important level of analysis. The biological perspective has thus retained the medical model's organic focus of study without expanding it into an all-embracing medical approach to abnormal behavior.

A Multiperspective Approach In contrast to the medical model are the psychological theories of abnormal behavior. Such theories attribute disturbed behavior patterns not to biological malfunction but to relatively intangible psychological processes resulting from the person's interaction with the environment. Thus disturbed behavior may be explained by negligent upbringing, by traumatic experiences, by inaccurate social perceptions, or by too much stress.

There are dozens of competing psychological explanations of abnormal behavior. Nevertheless, it is possible to identify a few fairly unified *perspectives*—broad schools of thought based on the same fundamental assumptions. In this book we will refer repeatedly to the following major psychological perspectives:

1 *The psychodynamic perspective,* which assumes that abnormal behavior issues from unconscious psychological conflicts originating in childhood.
2 *The behavioral perspective,* which holds that a primary cause of abnormal behavior is inappropriate learning, whereby maladaptive behaviors are rewarded and adaptive behaviors are not rewarded.
3 *The cognitive perspective,* which suggests that abnormal behavior is an outgrowth of maladaptive ways of perceiving and thinking about oneself and the environment.
4 *The humanistic-existential perspective,* which maintains that abnormal behavior results from a failure to accept oneself, to take responsibility for one's actions, and to pursue personal goals.
5 *The interpersonal perspective,* which views abnormal behavior as the product of disordered relationships.
6 *The sociocultural perspective,* which views abnormal behavior as the product of broad social forces. It also examines the biases that can influence diagnosis.

In addition to considering these psychological viewpoints, we will pay close attention to the organic approach just described:

7 *The biological perspective,* which analyzes abnormal behavior in terms of its biological components.

Each of these perspectives has made substantial contributions to the study of abnormal psychology, and each has substantial shortcomings as a comprehensive approach to human behavior. The seven perspectives will be discussed in detail in Chapters 2, 3, and 4.

Treating Abnormal Behavior

Whatever the explanation of abnormal behavior, most societies feel that something must be *done*

During the Middle Ages and the Renaissance, abnormal behavior was often believed to be caused by the devil. In this late-fifteenth-century painting, St. Catherine of Siena is casting the devil out of a possessed woman. It can be seen as a tiny imp flying from the woman's mouth.

THE MENTAL HEALTH PROFESSIONS

Psychotherapy is a relatively formal relationship between a trained professional and a person (or family) who seeks help with psychological problems.

There are four main types of mental health professionals. A **psychiatrist** is an M.D. who specializes in diagnosing and treating mental disorders. Because of their medical degree, psychiatrists can also prescribe psychoactive drugs, medications that can improve the functioning of people with mental disorders. Some psychiatrists, called *psychopharmacologists,* specialize in medical treatments. A **clinical psychologist** is a Ph.D. or Psy.D. who spent four to six years in graduate school and completed a one-year clinical internship. Clinical psychology programs emphasize training in psychological assessment and therapeutic intervention, as well as research. A **psychiatric social worker** earned an M.S.W. (master of social work), with special courses and training in psychological counseling. A **psychoanalyst** has had postgraduate training at a psychoanalytic institute and has undergone psychoanalysis himself or herself. Most psychoanalysts are psychiatrists, but other mental health professionals may undertake this training.

There are as many as 1,000 distinct forms of psychotherapy. Which approach a therapist takes depends on his or her theoretical perspective, though there are growing trends toward eclecticism, or combining techniques from different schools, and toward combining medication and therapy sessions.

about such behavior. How do human groups arrive at a way of treating the deviant in their midst?

This process depends on many factors. One is the structure and nature of the society. In a small, traditional community, where deviant persons can be looked after, they may remain at home, and their odd ways will be seen as a problem for the family rather than for the society. Typically, they will be prayed over, relieved of responsibilities, and treated with mixed kindness and ridicule. A large technological society, on the other hand, will tend to isolate deviants so as to prevent them from disrupting the functioning of the family and the community.

A second factor influencing the treatment of abnormal behavior, or at least the objective of such treatment, is the criterion by which it is identified. The standard of normality against which abnormality is defined—adherence to norms, personal satisfaction, adequate "coping"—will be the goal of treatment.

The specific treatment procedures typically follow from the society's explanation of abnormal behavior. If, as has been the case in some societies, bizarre behavior is interpreted as resulting from possession by evil spirits, then the logical treatment is to draw out such spirits—by means of prayer, special baths, special potions, or whatever. If, in keeping with the medical model, abnormal behavior is assumed to be the result of organic pathology, then the appropriate treatment is medical intervention—by means of drugs, hospitalization, or perhaps even surgery. If abnormal behavior is interpreted according to psychological theories, it will be treated via psychological therapies. As we saw above, many psychological professionals today feel that whatever its ultimate cause—if indeed ultimate causes can be found—abnormal behavior involves important psychological *and* biological components. Accordingly, in recent years there has been increased interest in *multimodal treatments,* combining two or more kinds of therapy, for example, "talk" psychotherapy and drugs. In the accompanying box we describe the kinds of therapists who provide these treatments.

How abnormal behaviors are defined, explained, and treated in our society is the subject of this book. Our modern approaches are not new, however. They are the result of centuries of trial and error. Accordingly, in the next section of this chapter we will present a brief history of Western society's interpretation of abnormal behavior. Then, in the final section, we will examine the assumptions on which this book's presentation of abnormal psychology is based.

CONCEPTIONS OF ABNORMAL BEHAVIOR: A SHORT HISTORY

Ancient Societies: Deviance and the Supernatural

We know little about the handling of deviant behavior in prehistoric and ancient societies. What we do know suggests that our early ancestors regarded deviant behavior, like most other things they did not understand, as the product of remote or supernatural forces—the movements of the stars, the vengeance of God, the operation of evil spirits. This idea seems to have endured for many centuries. References to possession can be found in the ancient records of the Chinese, the Egyptians, the Greeks, and the Hebrews. The Bible mentions demonic possession in a number of places. In the New Testament, Jesus is reported to have drawn out devils from the possessed.

The accepted cure for possession was to coax or force the evil spirits out of their victim. This practice, called **exorcism,** involved a wide variety of techniques, from the mild to the brutal. In some cases, the treatment was confined to prayer, noisemaking, and the drinking of special potions. In more difficult cases, the possessed person might be submerged in water, whipped, or starved in order to make the body a less comfortable habitation for the devil. It was once thought that some were even subjected to surgery to permit the devils to escape. (See the box below on trephining.) Not surprisingly, some people died from exorcistic treatments.

Not all ancient deviants were thought to be possessed by devils however, and not all were subjected to elaborate exorcisms. In the absence of solid evidence, it is reasonable to assume that even among highly superstitious peoples, abnormal behavior was often handled in an undramatic way. For example, the person might simply be sent home to rest and given special mention in the community's prayers. Such remedies are common in small, traditional societies today, and they were probably common in ancient societies as well.

The Greeks and the Rise of Science

Among the ancient Greeks, psychological disturbance was still widely explained in supernatural terms, as a punishment sent by the gods. However, with the Greeks and the Chinese, we begin to see the evolution of a naturalistic approach to abnormal behavior. The earliest surviving evidence of this new trend is found in the writings attributed to the Greek physician Hippocrates (c. 460–c. 360 B.C.). In opposition to current supernatural theories, Hippocrates set about to prove that all illness, including mental illness, was due to natural causes. He had little patience with supernatural explanations. For example, in his treatise on epilepsy, known at the time as the "sacred disease," Hippocrates

TREPHINING: THERAPY OR SURGERY?

Among the Stone Age skulls that have been unearthed by archeologists in Europe and South America are many that are marked by holes. Apparently the holes were purposely cut. Some of these skulls also show evidence of healing around the *trephine,* or hole, indicating that at least some Stone Age people survived this crude surgery.

Trephining, as this ancient practice is called, was long interpreted by some psychologists as evidence of supernatural theories of mental illness in prehistoric societies. According to this view, our Stone Age ancestors believed that mental illness was caused by evil spirits lodged in the head and that they would be able to escape if a hole were cut in the skull of the "possessed" person.

Recently a more prosaic explanation of trephining has been proposed: that it may have served only to remove bone splinters and blood clots resulting from blows to the head (W. B. Maher & Maher, 1985). Trephining was used for this purpose as late as the eighteenth century, and there is reason to believe that it served that purpose in the Stone Age as well.

To begin with, the Paleolithic stone axes that have survived would have been quite capable of delivering bone-crushing blows, and many of the trephined skulls do show evidence of trauma, usually fracture. Second, if trephining was performed as a ritual procedure to release evil spirits, it would be reasonable to expect trephined skulls from the same time and place to have the hole in the same location on the head, whereas in fact the placement of the hole varies, except that it seems to occur mainly in those parts of the head that would be most vulnerable to blows. Finally, if this operation was related to mental illness, we would not expect to find more trephined skulls of one sex than of the other or of any particular age group, since mental illness in the Stone Age, as in ours, presumably occurred with equal frequency in both sexes and in all age groups. But trephined skulls are usually those of adult males—in other words, the segment of the population most likely to be swinging axes at one another.

This does not mean that Stone Age societies did not attribute mental illness to possession by malevolent spirits. They well may have done so, as later societies did. But trephining is arguably not evidence of such supernatural beliefs.

The Greek physician Hippocrates rejected the supernatural theories of abnormal behavior that were prevalent in his time. Asserting that mental illness was due to natural causes, he advocated humane treatment for disturbed people.

curtly observed: "If you cut open the head, you will find the brain humid, full of sweat and smelling badly. And in this way you may see that it is not a god which injured the body, but disease" (cited in Zilboorg & Henry, 1941, p. 44).

Hippocrates' achievement was threefold. First, he set himself the novel task of actually *observing* cases of mental disturbance and of recording his observations in as objective a manner as possible. Consequently, it is in his writings that we encounter, for the first time in Western scientific literature, empirical descriptions of such mental disorders as phobia, epilepsy, and postpartum psychosis (severe depression following childbirth).

Second, Hippocrates developed one of the first biogenic theories of abnormal behavior. Though he recognized that external stress could have a damaging psychological effect, it was primarily internal processes that he held responsible for mental disturbance. To modern science some of his theories appear rather crude. Hysteria,* for example, he attributed to a wandering uterus. (The uterus at that time was thought to be unanchored in the female body and thus free to float about.) Likewise, he believed that various personality disorders were due to an imbalance among four **humors,** or vital fluids, in the body: phlegm, blood, black bile, and yellow bile. An excess of phlegm rendered people phlegmatic—indifferent and sluggish. An excess of blood gave rise to rapid shifts in mood. Too much black bile made people melancholic, and too much yellow bile made them choleric—irritable and aggressive. Primitive as some of these theories may seem, they foreshadowed today's physiological and biochemical research in abnormal psychology.

Third, Hippocrates was apparently the first Western scientist to attempt a unified classification of abnormal mental states. He classified mental disorders into three categories: mania (abnormal excitement), melancholia (abnormal dejection), and phrenitis (brain fever).

Hippocrates' contributions were in the areas of theory and methodology. He made no important advances in the cure of mental disorder. However, his treatment methods were considerably more humane than those of the exorcistic tradition, and this in itself was an advance. His treatment for melancholia, for example, involved rest, exercise, a bland diet, and abstinence from sex and alcohol. Since such a regimen could be most easily followed under supervision, he often moved patients into his home, where he could observe them.

This trend toward a gentler and more dignified treatment was supported by Hippocrates' younger contemporary, the philosopher Plato (429–347 B.C.). Though still adhering to a quasi-supernatural theory of mental disorder, Plato insisted that the care of the mentally disturbed should be a family responsibility and that they should not be held accountable or punished in any way for their irrational acts. Such thinking led to the establishment, in later Greek civilization, of retreats for the mentally ill. In Alexandria, for example, special temples dedicated to the god Saturn were set aside as asylums where the mentally ill could recover with the help of rest, exercise, music, and other therapeutic measures.

*Hysteria involves the involuntary loss or impairment of some normal function, physical or psychological (e.g., sight, sense of touch, memory), with no demonstrable organic cause. The hysterical disorders, which diagnosticians now call the somatoform and dissociative disorders, will be discussed in Chapter 8.

This painting shows Father Juan Gilabert Jofré protecting a mentally disturbed man from stones thrown by a crowd. It was reportedly this incident that inspired Father Jofré to found the world's first hospital for the insane, in Valencia, Spain, in 1410.

The Middle Ages and the Renaissance: Natural and Supernatural

With the decline of Greek civilization and the rise of the Roman Empire, the enlightened Hippocratic approach to mental disorder survived for a few more centuries. In the first century B.C., Asclepiades, a Greek physician practicing in Rome, was the first to differentiate between chronic and acute mental illness.* He also described the characteristics that distinguished hallucination, delusion, and illusion and explained how these characteristics could be used as diagnostic signs. In the second century A.D., Galen, another Greek physician who practiced in Rome, codified the organic theories of his predecessors and made significant advances in anatomical research. It was Galen, for example, who first showed that the arteries contained blood—not air, as was commonly thought. (This discovery led to the practice of bleeding the mentally disturbed, in the hope of restoring the proper balance among the humors of the body. Bleeding persisted as a treatment for emotional and physical disorders into the nineteenth century.) After the death of Galen, however, little progress was made. Eventually, with the fall of Rome to the invading tribes from northern Europe in the fifth century, the study of mental illness, together with most other branches of science, declined. It was not until the Middle Ages that Europe began to experience a revival of learning, and hence of naturalistic theories of mental illness.

*In *chronic* mental illness, symptoms are long-standing and relatively unchanging. In *acute* mental illness, symptoms appear suddenly and dramatically. See Chapter 14.

Medieval Theory and Treatment The Middle Ages was a period of ardent religiosity. Insanity, like all other things, was thought to be controlled by supernatural forces, and many of the insane were handled accordingly. Some were taken to shrines, prayed over, and sprinkled with holy water. Others were starved and flogged, to harass the devil within. Barbarous as the latter treatments may seem to us now, they were regarded as quite proper by most people, including the humane and the educated, and not only in the Middle Ages but well into the Renaissance. The wise and mild-mannered Sir Thomas More, later sainted, wrote to a friend about his handling of a lunatic: "I caused him to be taken by the constables and bound to a tree in the street before the whole town, and there striped [whipped] him until he waxed weary. Verily, God be thanked, I hear no more of him now" (cited in Deutsch, 1949, p. 13). It is impossible to know how many of the people thus treated were in fact psychologically disturbed. Obviously, some were, but others were probably local eccentrics or simply socially undesirable types.

But we do know that many cases of mental illness were approached as natural phenomena resulting from physical or emotional mishaps. For example, a search of English legal records has shown that when medieval officials examined people who were allegedly deranged, they often recorded natural, common-sense explanations for the derangement. One man, examined in 1291, was said to have lapsed into insanity after a "blow received on the head." The uncontrollable violence of another man, examined in 1366, was reportedly "induced by fear of his father" (Neugebauer, 1978).

These are the kinds of causes that might be cited today. Likewise, the *Encyclopedia of Batholomaes,* written by an English monk in the early thirteenth century and widely used in European universities for the next 300 years, traced psychological disturbance to physical and emotional sources. Most of these early diagnosticians probably did not doubt that the cause was ultimately supernatural, but the intervening, direct causes were natural causes.

Furthermore, whether insanity was attributed to natural or supernatural forces, there is evidence that once it occurred, it was often viewed as a form of illness (Kemp, 1990). Windows of medieval churches show the saints curing the insane alongside the lame and the blind. Apparently many of the insane were admitted to the same hospitals as other sufferers. For example, the deed of Trinity Hospital, founded in Salisbury, England, in the fourteenth century, provides for an institution in which, along with the treatment of other patients, "the mad are kept safe until they are restored to reason" (Allderidge, 1979, p. 322).

The Witch Hunts The Renaissance, stretching from the fifteenth to the seventeenth century, has long been regarded as a glorious chapter in the history of Western culture. Yet it is during this same period that we encounter one of the ugliest episodes in European history: the witch hunts. Ever since the eleventh century, the church had been beleaguered by heresies, demands for economic and religious reform, and other types of protest and insurrection. It is likely that some of the "witches" of the Middle Ages were simply women whose behavior caused annoyance to the local church authorities. As opposition to the church mounted during the early Renaissance, such counterattacks occurred with increasing frequency and brutality. Women (and a few men) were accused not just of being in league with the devil but of committing heinous acts—eating children, staging sexual orgies, and the like. The charges soon spread, creating a climate of fear and hysteria in which anyone who behaved strangely, or who behaved in a way that someone in power did not like, stood in danger of being executed for witchcraft.

The witch hunts soon received full endorsement from the church hierarchy in Rome. In 1484 Pope Innocent VIII issued a papal bull declaring the church's intention of rooting out the offenders. Soon afterward, he appointed church officials, called inquisitors, to seek out witches and see that they were punished. Witch hunting was embraced by the new Protestant churches as well. It is estimated that from the middle of the fifteenth century to the end of the seventeenth, 100,000 people were executed as witches (Deutsch, 1949). The hunting down of witches became a social and religious duty. Neighbors reported neighbors. Priests turned in their own parishioners. Everyone was suspect.

Renaissance Theory and Treatment It has been argued (e.g., Spanos, 1978) that the witch hunts may have had little connection with the history of mental illness, as most of the accused were probably not mentally ill. In large communities, witch hunting apparently had less to do with bizarre behavior than with political and economic interests. That is, the trials were used to eliminate political rivals, to confiscate property, and to suppress heresy. (Recall that Joan of Arc, who helped lead the French armies in their expulsion of the English invaders in 1429, was accused of witchcraft and burned at the stake. Her main crime, apparently, was to have claimed direct inspiration from God, unmediated by the church—a heresy in the eyes of the church.) In smaller communities, however, the accused were often poor, old, socially marginal women or simply socially disreputable types—"fornicators, blasphemers, thieves, ill-tempered persons, and the like" (Spanos, 1978, p. 423)—and some of the mentally ill no doubt fell into this group.

The fact that the mentally ill suffered from the witch hunts is also clear from the writings of those who protested against the craze. Among the chief arguments that these writers marshaled against the Inquisition is that many of its victims, far from being in league with the devil, were simply deranged. In 1563, for example, the German physician Johann Weyer, the first medical practitioner to have developed a special interest in mental illness, published a treatise declaring that those who were being tortured and burned as witches were actually mentally unbalanced and not responsible for their actions. Weyer was soon followed by an Englishman named Reginald Scot, who in 1584 published his *Discovery of Witchcraft,* a scholarly work pointing out, among other things, the evidence of mental illness in those being persecuted by the witch hunters.

It seems likely, then, that some of the "witches" of the Renaissance were psychologically disturbed. At the same time, the evidence suggests that the majority of the deranged were of little interest to the witch hunters. Instead, they were regarded, much as in the Middle Ages, as sick people whose problems might be explained in natural terms

(Neugebauer, 1978) and whose care, in any case, had to be seen to by the community. Some were apparently kept in almshouses (institutions for the poor), others in general hospitals. Indeed, London's Bethlem Hospital, founded in 1247, was given over almost exclusively to the insane by the fifteenth century. It is also in the Renaissance that we see, at least in England, the first major efforts to institutionalize the practice of community care (Allderidge, 1979)—that is, supervision of the mentally ill within the community but outside the hospital. The "poor laws" of seventeenth-century England required that "lunaticks," along with the aged, the blind, and other unfortunates, be provided for by their local government or parish. Such provision was not always ideal. People who were violent, for example, could be lawfully imprisoned. They could also, by law, be chained and beaten, for such treatment was considered one way of restoring their reason. But many of the approaches arrived at in Renaissance England were exactly the kinds we are using today. Some patients, for example, were kept at home, while money for their maintenance or for the relief of their families was paid out of parish funds. Homeless patients might be boarded with a succession of families in the community. The legal records of a seventeenth-century English county include an order for the care of such a person:

> It is ordered that Daniell Hancox a poore Ideott who was borne in Weston . . . and is now in the care and custody of William Mulliner gent[lemen] on[e] of the Inhabitants there shalbe forthwith Clothed by and out of the stock of money given to the Inhabitants there to that purpose. And it is further ordered that the said Daniell shalbe forthwith removed from the said Mr. Mulliner and be kept and provided for by the Inh[ab]itants of the said parish from house to house as heretofore hee hath beene there mainteyned and kept. (quoted in Allderidge, 1979, p. 327)

Community home care also existed during the fifteenth century in Belgium. Psychologically disturbed people who traveled to visit the shrine at Gheel often remained and lived with the residents. This tradition has continued; today, hundreds of psychologically disturbed people still live in private homes in Gheel (Aring, 1974). As we shall see, the practice of housing the psychologically disturbed with willing families, particularly in their own communities, is one that is being experimented with in the United States today.

The Eighteenth and Nineteenth Centuries: The Supremacy of Science

The Reform of the Asylums The practice of hospitalizing the psychologically disturbed is a very old one. In Arab countries, general hospitals provided wards for the mentally ill as early as the eighth century (Mora, 1980). As we have seen, some European hospitals of the Middle Ages and Renaissance also accepted mental patients. The first hospital exclusively for the insane opened in Muslim Spain in the early fifteenth century. This example was eventually followed elsewhere. Mental hospitals were founded in London, Paris, Vienna, Moscow, Philadelphia, and other major cities. More and more of the insane were institutionalized, if not in public hospitals, then in smaller, privately owned "madhouses," which began to flourish in the eighteenth century.

Most of these institutions were opened with the best of intentions, but the conditions in which their

These woodcuts from 1875 show male patients *(left)* let out of their rooms to "take the air" in the corridor and female patients *(right)* eating a meal in Philadelphia's Blockley Hospital.

patients lived were often terrible. London's Bethlem Hospital, mentioned earlier, became so notorious for the misery within its walls that it gave rise to the word *bedlam*, meaning "uproar." A writer in the seventeenth century described Bethlem as follows:

> It seems strange that any should recover here, the cryings, screechings, roarings, brawlings, shaking of chains, swarings, frettings, chaffing, are so many, so hideous, so great, that they are more able to drive a man that hath his witts, rather out of them, than to help one that never had them, or hath lost them, to finde them againe. (quoted in Allderidge, 1985)

Historians have produced many chilling descriptions of the early mental hospitals (Foucault, 1965; Scull, 1993), often with the suggestion or outright assertion that these institutions did not aim to cure, but only to isolate—and sometimes humiliate—the insane. Other writers have stressed a more balanced view. In a study of the archives of Bethlem, for example, Allderidge (1985) has pointed out that the bedlam therein was almost certainly due more to the difficulty of handling violent patients in the days before psychiatric medication than to any policy of abuse. As Allderidge shows, it was Bethlem's stated aim to cure, and grim though the place was, some patients were discharged as cured. The hospital had rules against beating patients, and the archives contain evidence that some patients enjoyed privileges that would not be commonly found today in a public charity, which is what Bethlem was. Indictments of Bethlem, for example, often cite the case of James Norris, who was kept in chains there for nine years in the early nineteenth century. But the records on Norris show that he was an extremely violent patient who had attacked a number of attendants and fellow patients before the staff resorted to chaining him. The records mention, furthermore, that while chained, Norris occupied himself mainly by reading books and newspapers that were given to him and by playing with his pet cat. Obviously, though he was in chains, someone on the staff remembered that he was a human being, with human needs.

The first serious efforts to improve treatment in the large hospitals began in the late eighteenth century. In 1789, Vincenzo Chiarugi, superintendent of the newly opened Ospedale di Bonifazio, a hospital for the mentally ill in Florence, published regulations stressing the need for humane treatment, ordering that the patients be provided with work and recreation, and forbidding the use of restraining devices such as chains unless absolutely necessary (B. A. Maher & Maher, 1985). But the most famous instance of reform, roughly contemporary with Chiarugi's, took place at La Bicêtre, a large hospital in Paris. This effort was due in large part to a layman with no special training, Jean-Baptiste Pussin, who was superintendent of the hospital's "incurables" ward from 1784 to 1802. Upon taking his post, Pussin laid down new rules. One was that the staff was forbidden to beat the patients. As Pussin later recalled, this innovation caused a near-insurrection: "The attendants tried to rebel against me, saying that they were not safe. . . . But, despite their clamors, I persisted in my resolve and, to reach my goal, I was forced to dismiss almost all of them in turn when they disobeyed" (quoted in D. B. Weiner, 1979, p. 1133). Pussin also gave orders to unchain a group of patients who, having been declared "furious," had lain in shackles for years—in some cases, for decades. Without their chains, these patients could now move about on the grounds, take the fresh air, and feel some sense of personal liberty. As Pussin had hoped, many of them became more manageable.

Pussin's reforms were extended by Philippe Pinel who became chief physician of La Bicêtre's ward for the mentally ill in 1793. (Pinel has usually received credit for Pussin's innovations.) Pinel's position was that the mentally ill were simply ordinary human beings who had been deprived of their reason by severe personal problems; to treat them like animals not only was inhumane but also impeded recovery. Pinel replaced the dungeons in which the patients had been kept with airy, sunny rooms and did away with violent treatments such as bleeding, purging, and cupping (blistering the skin with small hot cups). Furthermore, he spent long hours talking with the patients, listening to their problems, and giving them comfort and advice. He also kept records of these conversations and began to develop a case history for each patient. This practice of recordkeeping, introduced by Pinel, was an extremely important innovation, for it allowed practitioners to chart the characteristic *patterns* that emerge in the course of various disorders. Knowledge of these patterns has become the basis for the classification of disorders, for research into their causes, and for treatment.

Later Pinel, with the help of Pussin, reorganized the ward for the mentally ill at another large hospital in Paris, La Salpêtrière, along the same lines. After Pinel's retirement, his student and successor, Jean Esquirol, continued the reform movement, founding ten new mental hospitals in various parts

Philippe Pinel supervises the unchaining of inmates at La Salpêtrière, the hospital he directed after his work at La Bicêtre. The reforms of Pussin, Pinel, and Tuke led to a movement called moral therapy, which was widespread in the eighteenth and nineteenth centuries.

of France, all based on the humane treatment developed by Pussin and Pinel.

At the same time that Pussin and Pinel were working in Paris, a Quaker named William Tuke was attempting similar reforms in northern England. Convinced that the most therapeutic environment for the mentally ill would be a quiet and supportive religious setting, Tuke in 1796 moved a group of mental patients to a rural estate which he called York Retreat. There they talked out their problems, worked, prayed, rested, and took walks in the countryside. At York Retreat, as at almost all mental asylums of the period, restraining devices were used, but it is typical of Tuke that he specifically forbade chains, on the grounds that they were more likely to "degrade the feelings" of patients than were other means of restraint (quoted in Rosenblatt, 1984). Not surprisingly, York Retreat's recovery rate was high.

Though vigorously resisted by Pinel's and Tuke's contemporaries, these new techniques eventually became widespread, under the name of **moral therapy.** Based on the idea that the mentally ill were simply ordinary people with extraordinary problems, moral therapy aimed at restoring their "morale" by providing an environment in which they could discuss their difficulties, live in peace, and engage in some useful employment. More than anything else, moral therapy aimed at treating patients like human beings. And apparently this approach was extremely successful. Contemporary records show that during the first half of the nineteenth century, when moral therapy was the only treatment provided by mental hospitals in Europe and America, at least 70 percent of those hospitalized either improved or actually recovered (Bockoven, 1963).

The Reform Movement in America The foremost figure in the development of the American mental health establishment was Benjamin Rush (1745–1813), born in the same year as Pinel and known as the "father of American psychiatry." A remarkable man—he was a signer of the Declaration of Independence, a member of the Continental Congress, surgeon general to the Continental Army, treasurer of the United States Mint, and founder of the first free medical dispensary and the first antislavery society in America—Rush advanced the cause of mental health by writing the first American treatise on mental problems (*Medical Inquiries and Observations upon the Diseases of the Mind*, 1812), by organizing the first medical course in psychiatry, and by devoting his attention, as the foremost physician at Pennsylvania Hospital, exclusively to mental problems.

Today, some of Rush's thinking seems primitive: he believed that mental illness was due to an excess of blood in the vessels of the brain, as a result of overexcitement. The treatments to which this theory led him seem even more primitive. To relieve the pressure in the blood vessels, he relied heavily on bleeding. He also had patients dropped suddenly into ice-cold baths or strapped into a device called the "tranquilizer"—in both cases, to slow down the flow of blood to the brain. These procedures, however, were clearly intended not to torture but to cure, and were accompanied by a number of humane practices. Rush recommended that doctors regularly bring little presents such as fruit or cake to their patients. He also insisted that Pennsylvania Hospital hire kind and intelligent attendants—people who could read to patients, talk to them, and share in their activities. In sum, Rush contributed a great deal to American psychiatry, lending it his prestige and moving it in the direction of a humane therapy.

The task of extending these reforms was taken up by a Boston schoolteacher named Dorothea Dix (1802–1887). At the age of forty Dix took a job teaching Sunday school in a prison. There she had her first contact with the gruesome conditions suffered by the mentally ill. Later she went abroad, visiting York Retreat as well as other moral-therapy institutions, and became convinced of the need to reform mental health care (Rosenblatt, 1984). Soon she was traveling across the country, visiting the squalid jails and poorhouses in which the mentally ill were confined and lecturing state legislators on their duty to these people. To the Massachusetts legislature Dix spoke as follows:

> I come to place before the Legislature of Massachusetts the condition of the miserable, the desolate, the outcast. I come as the advocate of helpless, forgotten, insane and idiotic men and women . . . of beings wretched in our prisons, and more wretched in our Alms-Houses.
>
> I proceed, Gentlemen, briefly to call your attention to the state of Insane Persons confined within this Commonwealth, in *cages, closets, cellars, stalls, pens: Chained, naked, beaten with rods,* and lashed into obedience. (quoted in Deutsch, 1949, p. 165)

Dix called for the mentally ill to be removed to separate, humane facilities geared to their special needs. Carrying her campaign across the United States and eventually to Canada and Scotland as well, she was directly responsible for the founding and funding of thirty-two mental hospitals.

Hospitalization and the Decline of Moral Therapy Dix's reforms had one unfortunate result that she could not have anticipated: they contributed to the decline of moral therapy (Foucault, 1965). As hospital after hospital opened, there were simply not enough advocates of moral therapy to staff them. Indeed, there were not enough staff of any kind, for though the state governments were willing to build mental hospitals, they still did not consider mental health as important as physical health. This meant less money for mental hospitals, and less money meant fewer employees. At the same time, the patient populations of these hospitals grew year by year, so that soon the patient-staff ratio was such as to preclude altogether the sort of tranquil atmosphere and individual care essential to moral therapy. Walled off in somber isolation in rural areas, the new mental hospitals also helped the public to unlearn the lesson that Pinel and Tuke had worked so hard to teach: that the mentally ill were simply ordinary people. To the public mind, these fortresses seemed to conceal some dark horror, and the mentally disturbed were once again seen as freakish and dangerous.

But there were other reasons for the decline of moral therapy (Bockoven, 1963). To begin with, the first generation of its advocates—people such as Pussin, Pinel, and Tuke—was not succeeded by an equally powerful second generation. As a new movement, moral therapy needed strong leaders, and none came forth after the founders died. Second, by the turn of the century, many of the indigent patients who filled the mental hospitals were Irish Catholic immigrants, against whom there was considerable prejudice. The Protestant establishment might be willing to pay for these patients' hospitalization but not for the luxury of moral therapy.

Finally, the growth of the state mental hospital system occurred at the same time as the rise of the medical model. The early successes of the medical model convinced psychiatric professionals that their efforts should be directed toward biological research rather than toward creating the total therapeutic environments typical of moral therapy. The medical model also convinced them that patients should not be released until they were "cured," so as the years passed, more and more beds were occupied by chronic, long-term patients, who never got better and never left.

Thus during the second half of the nineteenth century, moral therapy was increasingly replaced by custodial care. Throughout this period, communities showed less and less support for tolerating mentally ill people as merely socially deviant (A. S. Luchins, 1993). Some became homeless; others, as before, were kept in jails and almshouses. But increasingly, they were swept into large, grim public hospitals. Recovery rates dropped (Bockoven, 1963; Dain, 1964). So the campaign for hospitalization that Dix and others pursued with such humane intentions had, in general, an inhumane result.

This situation continued until the middle of the present century, when a new class of antipsychotic drugs was introduced. Sedatives, or calming medications, had been given to mental patients for decades. But the new drugs were far more effective, and they have been the major factor in re-

This hospital for the criminally insane in Matawan, New Jersey, was one of the many state mental hospitals that were founded at the turn of the century. At the same time, abnormal behavior was attracting increased attention from scientific theorists.

ducing the number of institutionalized patients in recent years. Patients who previously might have been locked away for long periods now moved to open wards or halfway houses, or into the community itself. The use of drugs, which is proving to be a milestone in the history of treatment, will be discussed in detail in Chapter 21. It should be noted here, however, that the widespread acceptance of these drugs in recent years has lent even more support to the medical model.

Foundations of Modern Abnormal Psychology

In the late nineteenth century, as the new mental hospitals were opening throughout the United States, the study of abnormal psychology was rapidly expanding in both Europe and America. New theories were being introduced and tested, while opposing theories arose to challenge them. At the same time, theorists were developing new ways of classifying and studying abnormal behavior.

The Experimental Study of Abnormal Behavior In 1879, Wilhelm Wundt, a professor of physiology at the University of Leipzig, Germany, established a laboratory for the scientific study of psychology—that is, the application of scientific experimentation, with precise methods of measurement and control, to human thought and behavior. The opening of Wundt's laboratory is often cited as the beginning of modern psychology. It was also a critical step in the development of abnormal psychology, for the methods taught by Wundt were soon applied to abnormal as well as normal behavior.

Among Wundt's students was the German researcher Emil Kraepelin (1856–1926), who eventually established his own psychological laboratory, devoted primarily to the study of **psychopathology,** or abnormal psychology. There Kraepelin and his students investigated how psychopathology was related to movement, to fatigue, to emotion, to speech, and to memory. They also studied the effects of drugs on different kinds of psychological abnormality (B. A. Maher & Maher, 1979).

Kraepelin's example was followed elsewhere. In 1904 the first American laboratory for experimental work with mental patients opened at the McLean Hospital in Massachusetts, and other hospitals soon copied McLean's example. In 1906 Morton Prince, an American physician specializing in mental disorders, founded the first journal specializing in experimental psychopathology, the *Journal of Abnormal Psychology.* (It remains the foremost journal on this subject today.) In all, experimental abnormal psychology made substantial strides in the first two decades of the century. Thereafter, it fell behind somewhat, as a result of the rising popularity of psychodynamic theory, which, at least in its early years, did not lend itself to experimental study. But in the 1950s the experimental branch of abnormal psychology once again became influential and productive, and it has remained so, providing some of the most important current findings in the field.

Kraepelin and Biogenic Theory Biogenic theory, as we have seen, originated in ancient times and persisted, though sometimes obscured by supernaturalism, through the Middle Ages and Renaissance. Then, in the late eighteenth and early nineteenth centuries, when medical research was making rapid advances, it again became dominant. The first systematic presentation of the biogenic theory of mental disturbance was made by a German psychiatrist, Wilhelm Griesinger, in the mid-nineteenth century. But it was Kraepelin, the founder of experimental abnormal psychology, who first placed the medical model in the forefront of European psychiatric theory. In his *Textbook of Psychiatry* (1883/1923), Kraepelin not only argued for the central role of brain pathology in mental disturbance but furnished psychiatry with its first comprehensive classification system, based on the biogenic viewpoint. He claimed that mental illness, like physical illness, could be classified into separate pathologies, each of which had a different organic cause and could be recognized by a distinct cluster of symptoms, called a **syndrome.** Once the symptoms appeared, the mental disturbance could be diagnosed according to the classification system. And once it was diagnosed, its course and outcome could be expected to resemble those seen in other cases of the same illness, just as one case of measles can be expected to turn out like other cases of measles.

Kraepelin's organic theory and his classification system received wide publicity and generated high hopes that the hitherto impenetrable mysteries of mental illness might be shown to have concrete, chemically treatable organic causes. At the same time, the neurological and genetic components of psychopathology were gaining attention through the writings of another famous follower of Griesinger, Richard von Krafft-Ebing (1840–1902), who emphasized organic and hereditary causation in his *Textbook of Psychiatry* (1879/1900) and in his pioneering encyclopedia of sexual disorders, *Psychopathia Sexualis* (1886/1965). It was from the work of these early theorists that the modern medical model of mental disturbance evolved.

As we noted earlier, the medical model in its early days produced brilliant results. By the turn of the century, neurological research was progressing so rapidly that it seemed that the hopes raised by Kraepelin might at last be in the process of fulfillment. The senile psychoses, the toxic psychoses, cerebral arteriosclerosis, mental retardation—one mental syndrome after another was linked to a specific brain pathology. The most stunning success of all, however, was the discovery, through the work of Krafft-Ebing and others, that **general paresis,** a mysterious syndrome involving the gradual and irreversible breakdown of physical and mental functioning, was actually an advanced case of syphilis, in which the syphilitic microorganisms had passed through the bloodstream and into the central nervous system and the brain. This discovery had an immense impact on the mental health profession and helped to establish the medical model in the lofty position it still occupies today.

However, at the same time that neurological research was nourishing biogenic theory, other findings were laying the foundation for a comprehensive **psychogenic theory,** the theory that psychological disturbance is due primarily not to organic dysfunction but to emotional stress.

Mesmer and Hypnosis The history of modern psychogenic theory begins with a colorful and controversial figure, Franz Anton Mesmer (1733–1815). In the late eighteenth century a number of exciting discoveries were being made about magnetism and electricity. Mesmer, an Austrian physician, attemped to apply this new knowledge to the study of mental states. His theory was that the movement of the planets controlled the distribution of a universal magnetic fluid and that the shiftings of this magnetic fluid were responsible for the health or sickness of mind and body. Furthermore, he was convinced that this principle of "animal magnetism" could be used in the treatment of hysteria, a common complaint at the time, especially in women.

Mesmer's therapy for his hysterical patients was rather exotic. The patients would enter a room and seat themselves around a huge vat containing bottles of various fluids from which iron rods protruded. The lights were dimmed and soft music was played. Then Mesmer himself appeared, "magnetic" wand in hand, and passed from patient to patient, touching various parts of their bodies with his hands, with his wand, and with the rods protruding from the vat, in order to readjust the distribution of their magnetic fluids.

The most striking aspect of this treatment is that in many cases it seems to have worked. Nonetheless, Mesmer's theory of animal magnetism was investigated by a special commission and declared invalid. Yet even the investigating physicians noted in their reports what has since been recognized as Mesmer's great contribution to abnormal psychology: the discovery of the power of suggestion to cure mental disorder. Mesmer is now regarded as the first practitioner of **hypnosis** (originally known as "mesmerism"), an artificially induced trance in which the subject becomes highly susceptible to suggestion. Mesmer was eventually barred from practice in Vienna and Paris, but others continued to practice mesmerism.

The Nancy School Some years after Mesmer's death, his findings were reexamined by two enterprising French physicians, Ambrose-Auguste Liébeault (1823–1904) and Hippolyte-Marie Bernheim (1840–1919), both practicing in Nancy, in eastern France. For four years Bernheim had been treating a patient with no success. Finally, after hearing that a certain Dr. Liébeault was having considerable success with unconventional methods, Bernheim sent the patient to him. When the patient returned shortly afterward completely cured, Bernheim called on Liébeault to ask what he had done. What Liébeault had done was simple: he had hypnotized the patient and then told him, while he was under hypnosis, that when he awakened, his symptoms would be gone (Selling, 1940).

Bernheim was persuaded, and thereafter the two physicians worked as a team. Together they discovered that hysteria could be not only cured but also induced by hypnosis. For example, if a hypnotized subject were told that he or she had no feeling in the hand—as is the case in **glove anesthesia,** a form of hysteria—the hand could then be pricked with a needle without producing any response from the subject. On the basis of such findings, Liébeault and Bernheim evolved the theory that hysteria was actually a form of self-hypnosis and that other mental disorders might also be due entirely to psychological causes.

This view won a number of adherents, who became known as the "Nancy school." The Nancy school soon came under attack by a formidable challenger, Jean-Martin Charcot (1825–1893), a famous Parisian neurologist who at that time was director of La Salpêtrière Hospital. Charcot had also experimented with hypnosis, but he had abandoned it, concluding that hysteria was due to organic causes after all. The debate between the Paris school, consisting of Charcot and his supporters, and the Nancy school was one of the earliest major academic debates in the history of modern psychology. Eventually the insurgent Nancy school triumphed, and Charcot himself was later won over to the psychogenic theory of hysteria. But, the ramifications of this debate extended far beyond the specific problem of hysteria, for it raised the possibility that any number of psychological disorders might be due to emotional states rather than (or as well as) to organic causes.

Breuer and Freud: The Beginnings of Psychoanalysis One of the many students of Charcot was Sigmund Freud (1856–1939), a young Viennese physician who had gone to Paris to study under the great neurologist. Later Freud became acquainted with the methods of Liébeault and Bernheim as well, and when he returned to Vienna, he went to work with a physician named Josef Breuer (1842–1925), who at that time was also experimenting with the use of hypnosis. A few years earlier Breuer had treated a woman, later known to medical history as "Anna O.," who was troubled by

Jean-Martin Charcot, a nineteenth-century French neurologist, was active in the crucial debate over whether the origins of hysteria—and other psychological disorders—were emotional or organic.

hysterical paralysis, inability to eat, and various disturbances of sight and speech. Somewhat by chance, Breuer discovered that under hypnosis Anna O. was able to discuss her problems quite uninhibitedly, and that after doing so, she obtained some relief from her symptoms. Quick to recognize the therapeutic value of this emotional purging, Breuer called it the "cathartic method," or "talking cure."

Together Breuer and Freud experimented extensively with talking cures. They soon became convinced that hysteria and other disorders were caused by "unconscious" conflicts that could be drawn out under hypnosis; once aired, the conflicts would lose their power to maintain the symptoms. In 1895 Breuer and Freud published their findings in a volume titled *Studies in Hysteria*. This book, in which the authors put forth their theory of the unconscious, was a milestone in the history of psychology.

Later, working independently, Freud abandoned hypnosis. To begin with, not everyone could be hypnotized. Furthermore, Freud had found that he could obtain the same result—the loosening of inhibitions—by a technique that he called **free association:** patients were asked to relax on a couch and simply to pour out whatever came to mind. Freud also encouraged his patients to talk about their dreams and their childhoods. Freud then interpreted this material to the patient, based on the theories he was gradually constructing about the nature of the unconscious. To this form of therapy, in which the patient is cured through the gradual understanding of unconscious conflicts, Freud gave the name **psychoanalysis.**

The development of his theories of the unconscious (which will be explained in Chapter 2) occupied the remainder of Freud's long and fruitful career. These theories, quite radical for their time, were regarded with great skepticism by many of his contemporaries and did not become influential in the field of mental health until the 1920s. Since that time, however, they have become the basis for the psychodynamic perspective and have exerted a profound influence on twentieth-century thought.

A MULTIPERSPECTIVE APPROACH

This chapter has discussed a wide variety of perspectives on abnormal behavior. Throughout the text we continue to focus on the insights and discoveries of several perspectives. This book rests on three basic assumptions. The first is that *human behavior can be studied scientifically*. That is, scientists can observe objectively both behavior and the environment in which it occurs. From these observations they can draw conclusions about the causes of behavior, and knowing these causes, they can predict and influence behavior.

Second, this book proceeds on the assumption that *most abnormal behavior is the product of both psychological and biological processes*. The unobservable events of the mind, such as attitudes, memories, and desires, are unquestionably involved in most forms of psychopathology. And psychopathology, in turn, is connected to biological events: the secretion of hormones by the glands, the movement of electrical impulses across the brain, and so forth. How these events hook together in the web of causation—which is the primary cause, which the result, and whether the results have in turn caused other results, both psychological and biological—is, as we shall see, a maddeningly complex question.

The third assumption of this book is that *each human being is unique*. Human behavior may be discussed in general terms, and it may be traced to specific social and biological determinants. Nevertheless, it still issues from human beings, each of whom has a unique set of memories, desires, and expectations, and each of whom has some ability to control his or her behavior.

In the following chapters we will stress the perspectives on abnormal behavior that we described earlier: the psychodynamic, behavioral, cognitive, humanistic-existential, interpersonal, sociocultural, and biological perspectives. Each of these viewpoints is narrower and more specific than the broad approach we have just defined, and more often than not they disagree with one another. But taken together, they provide a comprehensive and many-faceted view of human psychology today.

KEY TERMS

biogenic (8)
biological perspective (8)
clinical psychologist (10)
exorcism (11)
free association (22)
general paresis (20)
glove anesthesia (21)
humors (12)
hypnosis (20)
medical model (7)
moral therapy (17)
norms (4)
psychiatric social worker (10)
psychiatrist (10)
psychoanalysis (22)
psychoanalyst (10)
psychogenic theory (20)
psychopathology (19)
syndrome (20)

SUMMARY

- Definitions of psychological abnormality vary from century to century and from society to society. A common criterion for psychological abnormality is a violation of social norms—behaving in a way that most people regard as wrong or improper. Behavior that is statistically rare, causes personal discomfort to the person who exhibits it, is maladaptive, or deviates from a theoretical ideal may also be considered abnormal. Most contemporary psychologists favor a combined standard of scientific facts and social values.
- Just as there are many definitions of abnormal behavior, so there are many explanations. According to the medical model, abnormal behavior is *like* a disease. Even if it is not the result of organic dysfunction, it should be diagnosed and treated as an illness. A refinement of the medical model, the modern biological perspective seeks to identify the organic components of mental disorders but does not insist that abnormal behavior is merely a symptom of underlying biological problems or that treatment must be medical.
- Psychological theories trace abnormal behavior to a person's interactions with the environment. The most prominent psychological theories include the psychodynamic approach, which emphasizes unconscious conflicts originating in childhood; the behavioral perspective, which stresses inappropriate conditioning; the cognitive perspective, which focuses on maladaptive ways of perceiving the self and the environment; the humanistic-existential perspective, which centers on the need to accept responsibility for oneself; and the interpersonal perspective, which views abnormal behavior as the product of disordered relationships.
- The sociocultural perspective examines the influence of social forces on behavior and diagnosis.
- The treatment of abnormal behavior depends on the nature of the society, the criteria used to identify abnormality, and the society's explanation of abnormal behavior.
- The earliest societies apparently viewed abnormal behavior as a product of supernatural forces. Treatment consisted of various forms of exorcism to drive away the evil spirits.
- The naturalistic approach to abnormal behavior dates to ancient Greece. Hippocrates observed and recorded cases of mental disturbance, developed an organic theory of abnormal behavior, classified disorders in terms of this theory, and recommended humane treatments.
- In the Middle Ages, supernatural explanations of abnormal behavior reappeared. Treatment of people thought to be possessed by demons ranged from prayer to flogging.
- During the Renaissance, persecution of persons alleged to be deranged reach a peak. Thousands, mostly women, were tortured and burned in witch hunts, which began in the eleventh century and continued into the seventeenth century. Many others languished in hospitals and poorhouses, under harsh conditions.
- In the eighteenth and nineteenth centuries, hospitalization of the mentally disturbed became increasingly common. But conditions in these "insane asylums" typically were cruel and degrading. Efforts to improve treatment were launched in Florence, Paris, and York in the late eighteenth century. The reform movement in nineteenth-century America advocated moral therapy, or improving the morale of the mentally ill through peaceful living, useful employment, and dignified treatment.
- The new mental hospitals of the late nineteenth century did not live up to the reformers' hopes. For a variety of reasons, moral therapy was replaced with custodial care. Increasingly, mentally disturbed people were isolated in prisonlike institutions where many remained for life—a pattern that continued into the mid-twentieth century.
- The growth of experimental psychology in Germany, biogenic theories of mental illness, and important discoveries (such as the link between general paresis and syphilis) pushed the medical model to the forefront around the turn of the century.
- At the same time, controversial work with hypnosis in France laid the groundwork for psychogenic theories, by showing that the power of suggestion could cure some mental disorders, especially hysterias. Sigmund Freud and Josef Breuer became convinced that mental disorders were caused by unconscious conflicts that, once revealed under hypnosis, could be resolved. Freud later abandoned hypnosis for free association. From the discoveries achieved through this technique, he developed his pioneering theory of psychoanalysis.
- This book is based on three basic assumptions: human behavior can be studied scientifically; most abnormal behavior is the product of *both* psychological and biological processes; and each human being is unique. We will draw on the psychodynamic, behavioral, cognitive, biological, and humanistic-existential perspectives. These perspectives offer a comprehensive and multidimensional view of abnormal psychology.

2

THE PSYCHODYNAMIC AND HUMANISTIC-EXISTENTIAL PERSPECTIVES

In this chapter we will discuss two influential schools of thought that have addressed themselves to abnormal behavior, the psychodynamic and the humanistic-existential perspectives. The psychodynamic perspective began at the turn of the century with the work of Sigmund Freud. The humanistic-existential perspective arose later, around the mid-twentieth century, in part as a reaction to the psychodynamic. Although humanistic-existential thinkers rejected the psychodynamic perspective, many of them were trained in it, and thus there is a family resemblance between the two schools. They share similar basic beliefs and employ similar therapies. The psychodynamic perspective, however, has had a far greater influence, particularly on our understanding of psychopathology, and therefore it will occupy the greater part of this chapter.

THE PSYCHODYNAMIC PERSPECTIVE

The **psychodynamic perspective** is a school of thought united by a common concern with the dynamics, or interaction, of forces lying deep within the mind. Different psychodynamic theorists emphasize different aspects of mental dynamics, but almost all agree on three basic principles. First is that of psychic determinism: that much of our behavior is not freely chosen but, on the contrary, is determined by the nature and strength of intrapsychic forces. Second is the belief that such forces operate, for the most part, unconsciously—in other words, that the true motives of our behavior are largely unknown to us. Third, most psychodynamic thinkers assume that the form these forces take is deeply affected by childhood experience, and particularly by relationships within the family.

The founding father of the psychodynamic perspective was Sigmund Freud, a neurologist who began his practice in Vienna in the 1880s. At that time the most common complaints brought to the neurologist were physical disorders—such as paralysis—for which no physical cause could be found. As we saw in Chapter 1, the idea that the origin of such disorders might be psychological rather than physiological had already been proposed. Convinced by this idea, the young Freud set himself the task of discovering the specific psychological causes involved and of working out an effective cure. Within a few years he had put forth the idea that these so-called hysterical disorders constituted a defense against unbearable thoughts or memories. (The hand may be "paralyzed," for example, to overcome an urge to strike out.) From this seed grew his theory of **psychoanalysis,** by which, ultimately, he sought to explain not just hysteria but all human behavior, normal and abnormal.

This photograph shows Sigmund Freud, the father of psychodynamic theory, in his London study soon after he and his family fled Nazi Germany in 1938.

The psychodynamic perspective is by no means bounded by Freud's theory. It is a large and living school of thought, by now a century old, built of proposals and counterproposals, propositions and refinements, contributed by many theorists besides Freud. It is impossible, however, in the space of this chapter to give appropriate coverage to the full range of psychodynamic theory.* Furthermore, Freud's theory, however much it has been revised, is still the foundation of psychodynamic thought. Therefore this chapter will give first and fullest consideration to Freud—that is, to the "classical" psychodynamic position. Then we will describe the ways in which post-Freudian theorists have expanded this view. Finally, we will discuss the arguments for and against the psychodynamic perspective.

Basic Concepts of Freudian Theory

The Depth Hypothesis The key concept of psychoanalysis, and Freud's most important contribution to psychology, is the **depth hypothesis,** the idea that almost all mental activity takes place unconsciously. According to Freud, the mind is divided

*Neither is it possible to do justice to Freud's views in one short chapter. The English edition of his collected writings, known as *The Standard Edition of the Complete Psychological Works of Sigmund Freud* (London: Hogarth Press, 1953–1974), fills twenty-four volumes. Furthermore, Freud constantly revised and refined his ideas throughout his long life. The reader should be aware that what is presented in this chapter is a condensation of a complex and extensive collection of theories.

into two levels. At the surface is the **perceptual conscious,** consisting of the narrow range of mental events of which the person is aware at any given instant. Beneath the perceptual conscious lies the **unconscious,** consisting of all the psychological materials (memories, desires, fears, etc.) that the mind is not attending to at that moment.

The unconscious, in turn, is divided into two levels, depending on the retrievability of its contents. Materials that are normally unconscious but can still be easily retrieved are said to belong to the **preconscious.** If, for example, you were asked the date of the French Revolution and said "1789," you would have called this date up from the preconscious. According to Freud, however, by far the greater part of unconscious mental contents is not readily accessible to consciousness, and it was this vast repository of hidden materials, called the *unconscious proper,* that was Freud's primary interest. Although in Freud's schema the unconscious includes both the preconscious and the unconscious proper, he tended in his writings to use the term *unconscious* to mean solely the unconscious proper. We will do the same.

It was Freud's belief that the things we forget do not in fact disappear from the mind. They simply go into the unconscious. Furthermore, much of this material is not passively forgotten. It is actively forgotten, forced out of consciousness, because it is disturbing to us—a process called *repression.* These censored materials may erupt into consciousness when psychological controls are relaxed—for example, when we are under hypnosis or when we are dreaming. But during our normal waking hours the contents of the unconscious are kept tightly sealed from our awareness. At the same time—and this is the crucial point—these unconscious materials always play some role in determining our behavior. When we choose one profession over another or marry one person rather than another, we do so not only for the reasons that we tell ourselves but also because of events from our past that are now hidden from us—a fascinating and disturbing notion.

The Necessity of Interpretation If Freud is correct that the origins of our behavior are buried deep in the psyche, then psychology cannot confine itself simply to observing surface behavior. Rather, it must engage in **interpretation,** revealing the hidden, intrapsychic motives. Interpretation was Freud's primary tool. In all human behavior—actions, dreams, jokes, works of art—he saw two layers of meaning: the **manifest content,** or surface meaning, and the **latent content,** or true, unconscious meaning. The goal of his theoretical writings and of his therapy was to reveal, via interpretation, the latent content: the unconscious forces that cause people to do what they do.

"Readings" of behavior can of course be faulty (Wolpe and Rachman, 1960). Worse yet, it is difficult to find out scientifically whether or not they *are* faulty. However, as many psychological writers have pointed out (e.g., Erdelyi & Goldberg, 1979), some decoding process, whether or not it is called "interpretation," is indispensable to human communication and is used not just by Freudian theorists but by all of us, every day. When someone you have asked for a date replies that he or she is busy for the next month, you naturally understand the message. This person does not want to go out with you. The ability to get along in human society depends on our ability to decode such statements. Interpretation, then, was not invented by Freud. What Freud invented was the idea that interpretation could be used to identify *unconscious* motives for our behavior.

The Structural Hypothesis: Id, Ego, and Superego
Some years after his formulation of the depth hypothesis, Freud constructed a second, complementary, psychic schema, the so-called **structural hypothesis.** As we have seen, the defining characteristic of psychodynamic theory, as handed down from Freud, is its concern with the interaction of forces within the mind. It is this interaction that the structural hypothesis describes. Briefly, it states that the mind can be divided into three broad forces—the id, the ego, and the superego—and that these three forces are continually interacting with one another, often in conflict.

The id At birth, according to Freud's hypothesis, the energy of the mind is bound up entirely in primitive biological drives, to which Freud gave the collective term **id.** The id is the foundation of the psychic structure and the source from which the later developments of ego and superego must borrow their energy.

The drives that make up the id are of two basic types, sexual and aggressive—the former above all.* Freud saw the sexual drive as permeating the

*On the matter of basic drives, as on other points, Freud changed his theory several times. In his early writings, he proposed that there were two basic drives, the sexual drive and the ego (or self-preservation) drive. Then, from about 1914 until 1920, he concluded that self-preservation was merely an aspect of the sexual drive, which he now felt was the sole driving force of the personality. Finally, after 1920, Freud elevated aggression to the status of a basic drive, along with sex—a position he took at least partly in response to the horrors of World War I.

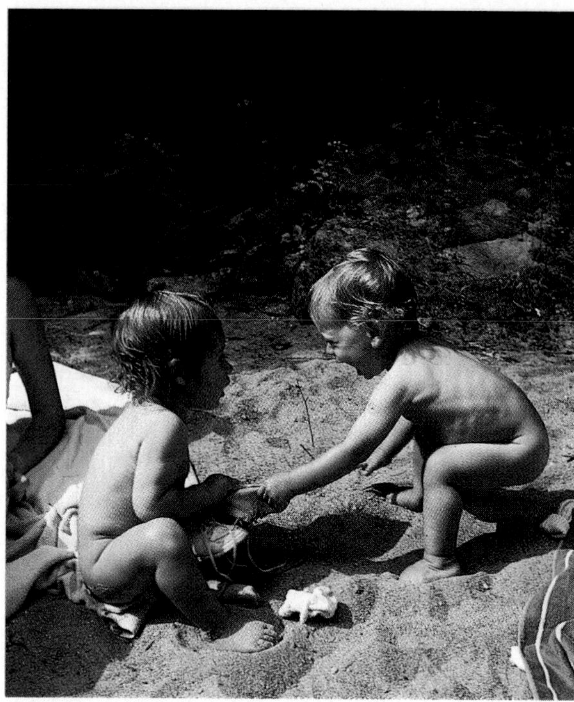
In Freud's view, small children freely use aggression to get what they want because the id is not yet under the restraint of the ego and superego.

entire personality and subsuming, in addition to actual erotic behavior, a wide range of other life-sustaining pursuits, such as the need for food and warmth, the love of friends and family, and the impulse toward creativity. These and other positive desires, in Freud's view, were extensions and transformations of a basic sexual drive, which he named the **libido** and which he saw as the major source of psychic energy.

The id operates on what Freud called the **pleasure principle.** That is, it is utterly hedonistic, seeking only its own pleasure or release from tension and taking no account of logic or reason, reality or morality. Hungry infants, for example, do not ask themselves whether it is time for their feeding or whether their mothers may be busy doing something else; they want food, and so they cry for it. According to Freud, we are all, at some level, still hungry infants.

The ego While the id can know what it wants, it has no way of determining which means of dealing with the world are practical and which are not. To fulfill these functions, the mind develops a new psychic component, the ego. The **ego** mediates between the id and the forces that restrict the id's satisfactions. Ego functions begin to develop shortly after birth and emerge slowly over a period of years.

While the id operates on the pleasure principle, the ego operates on the **reality principle**—to find what is both safe and effective. When the id signals its desire, the ego locates in reality a potential gratifier for the desire, anticipates the consequences of using that gratifier, and then either reaches out for it or, if that gratifier is ineffective or the consequences could be dangerous, delays the id's satisfaction until a more appropriate means of gratification can be found.

Imagine, for example, a three-year-old girl playing in her room. The id signals that aggressive impulses seek release, and the girl reaches for her toy hammer. The ego then goes into action, scanning the environment. The girl's baby brother is playing nearby. Should she hit him over the head with her hammer? The ego, which knows from experience that this will result in the unpleasant consequence of punishment, says no and continues the scanning process. Also nearby is a big lump of clay. The ego determines that no harm will come from pounding the clay, and so the girl hits that instead. According to Freud, it is from the ego's weighing of these considerations that the mind develops and refines all its higher functions: language, perception, learning, discrimination, memory, judgment, and planning. All these are ego functions.

The superego Imagine that three years later the same girl once again sits with hammer in hand looking for something to pound. Again she considers her brother's head, and again she rejects that possibility. This time, however, she rejects it not only because it would result in punishment but because it would be "bad." What this means is that the child has developed a superego.

The **superego** is that part of the mind that represents the moral standards of the society and the parents which the child internalizes. This superego, approximately equivalent to what we call "conscience," takes no more account of reality than the id does. Instead of considering what is realistic or possible, it embraces an abstract **ego ideal** (a composite picture of values and moral ideals) and, in keeping with that ideal, demands that the sexual and aggressive impulses of the id be stifled and that moral goals be substituted instead. It is then the job of the ego to find a way to satisfy the id without antagonizing the superego.

Thus in the fully developed psychic structure the ego has three fairly intransigent parties to deal with: the id, which seeks only the satisfaction of its irrational and amoral demands; the superego, which seeks only the satisfaction of its rigid ideals; and reality, which offers only a limited range of options.

When we consider the structural hypothesis, it is important to keep in mind that id, ego, and superego are not *things* in the mind or even parts of the mind, but simply names that Freud gave to broad categories of intrapsychic forces. It is difficult, in discussing these categories, not to speak of them as if they were actual entities—the id screaming for gratification, the superego demanding the opposite, and the ego running back and forth between them, arranging compromises. But these are metaphors, nothing more.

The Dynamics of the Mind Through ego functions, as we have seen, the mind can usually mediate conflicts among id, superego, and reality. At times, however, either the id or the superego will threaten to overwhelm the ego's controls, resulting in unacceptable feelings or behavior. In response to this threat, the person experiences anxiety.

Anxiety, akin to what most of us call "fear," is a state of psychic distress that acts as a signal to the ego that danger is at hand. Anxiety can have its source in reality, as when you confront a burglar in your bedroom. Or—and this of course was Freud's major concern—anxiety can originate in internal dynamics, in an id impulse that threatens to break through the ego's controls and cause the person to be punished, either by the superego (in the form of guilt) or by reality.

Anxiety can be managed in a number of ways. If, for example, a pregnant woman is afraid of childbirth, she can calm her fears by going to childbirth classes and learning how to cope with labor pains. However, the ego's solutions are not always so straightforward. Indeed, most anxiety is not even experienced consciously. It is kept closeted in the unconscious, and the danger is dealt with through the ego's employment of defense mechanisms.

Defense mechanisms The ego has a tendency to distort or simply deny a reality (whether external or internal) that would arouse unbearable anxiety. This tactic is called a **defense mechanism,** and as long as it works, the anxiety will not be experienced consciously. We all use defense mechanisms all the time. If we did not, we would be psychologically disabled, for the facts they conceal—of the primitive drives of the id, of the condemnations of the superego—would produce intolerable anxiety if they were constantly breaking through into the conscious mind. The defense mechanisms, then, serve an adaptive function. They allow us to avoid facing what we cannot face and thus to go on with the business of living.

If they become too rigid, however, they can defeat adjustment. When defense mechanisms force us never to leave the house or—to use a more ordinary example—to redirect onto our home life our problems at work, then we are sacrificing our adaptive capacities. Furthermore, it must be kept in mind that it is the ego that engineers these defenses. If most of the ego's energy is tied up in the job of maintaining defenses, then the ego will have little strength left for its other important functions, such as perception, reasoning, and problem solving. Defense mechanisms, then, are adaptive only up to a point. The basic defense mechanisms described by Freud and his followers (e.g., A. Freud, 1946) are as follows.

1. *Repression.* In the process of **repression,** as we have already seen, unacceptable id impulses are pushed down into the unconscious and thereby robbed of their power to disturb us consciously. Thus, for example, a girl who is sexually attracted to her father will simply remove this intolerable thought from her consciousness. It may come up in her dreams, but in disguised form, and once she wakes up, the dreams too are likely to be repressed.

One of the earliest of Freud's conceptualizations, repression is the most fundamental defense mechanism of psychodynamic theory. It is on the basis of this mechanism that Freud constructed his symbolic readings of human behavior, whereby a person's actions are viewed as masked representations of the contents of his or her unconscious. And Freud evolved his technique of psychoanalysis expressly in order to dredge up this repressed material—"to make the unconscious conscious," as he put it. Once these banished memories and desires were confronted, he believed, they would cease to cause anxiety and thus would lose their power to force the person into maladaptive behaviors in the effort to relieve that anxiety.

Repression is fundamental also in that it is the basis of all the other defense mechanisms. In every one of the defenses that we will describe below, the "forbidden" impulse is first repressed; then, instead of acting on that impulse, the person engages in some substitute behavior that serves either as an outlet for the impulse or as an additional protection against it, or both.

2. *Projection.* In the mechanism of **projection,** unacceptable impulses are first repressed, then at-

tributed to others. Thus an internal threat is converted into an external threat. For example, a man whose self-esteem is threatened by his own preoccupation with money and success may accuse others of being money-hungry. This relieves his own moral anxiety and simultaneously enables him to throw the guilt onto others.

3. *Displacement.* Like projection, **displacement** involves a transfer of emotion. In this case, however, what is switched is not the source but the object of the emotion. Afraid to display or even to experience certain feelings against whoever has aroused them, the person represses the feelings. Then, when the opportunity arises, he or she transfers them to a safer object and releases them. A good example of displacement can be found in a story by James Joyce titled "Counterparts." In it a poor man spends the day suffering humiliations for which he cannot retaliate; then he goes home, discovers that his son has let the hearth fire go out, and on that pretext gives the boy a terrible beating.

4. *Rationalization.* Most defenses occur not in isolation but in combination (Erdelyi, 1985). In the example just cited, the pretext that the man used for beating his son illustrates another defense mechanism, **rationalization.** A person who engages in rationalization offers socially acceptable reasons for something that he or she has actually done (or is going to do) for unconscious and unacceptable motives. Rationalization is one of the most common defenses. While much of our behavior may be motivated by irrational and infantile needs, as Freud claimed, we still feel required to explain it to ourselves and others in rational, grown-up terms.

5. *Isolation.* We engage in **isolation** when we avoid unacceptable feelings by cutting them off from the events to which they are attached, repressing them, and then reacting to the events in an emotionless manner. Isolation is a common refuge of patients in psychotherapy. Eager to tell the therapist what the problem is but unwilling to confront the feelings involved, patients will relate the facts in a calm, detached fashion ("Yes, my mother's death caused me considerable distress"), whereas it is actually the feelings, more than the facts, that need to be explored.

6. *Intellectualization.* Isolation is often accompanied by **intellectualization:** the person achieves further distance from the emotion in question by surrounding it with a smokescreen of abstract intellectual analysis. ("Yes, my mother's death caused me considerable distress. Young children find it difficult to endure separation, let alone final separation, from their mothers," etc.)

7. *Denial.* **Denial** is the refusal to acknowledge the existence of an external source of anxiety. In some cases, the person will actually fail to perceive something that is obvious. For example, a person who has been diagnosed as terminally ill may go on planning a lengthy trip to be taken when he or she is well again. Because it involves a drastic alteration of the facts, denial is considered a "primitive" defense. It is usually resorted to by children or by people facing a very serious threat (e.g., terminal illness or the death of a loved one).

8. *Reaction formation.* A person who engages in **reaction formation** represses the feelings that are arousing anxiety and then vehemently professes the exact opposite. Thus someone who claims to be disgusted by sexual promiscuity may be demonstrating a reaction formation against his or her own sexual impulses.

9. *Regression.* The mechanism of **regression** involves a return to a developmental stage that one has already passed through. Unable to deal with its anxiety, the ego simply abandons the scene of the conflict, reverting to an earlier, less threatening stage. Regression is a good example of the fact that defense mechanisms can vary from relatively harmless means of self-comfort to signs of severe psychological disturbance. In the extreme case, a regressed adult may be reduced to a babbling, helpless creature who has to be fed and toileted like a baby. On the other hand, well-adjusted adults often resort to minor regressive behaviors—whining, making childish demands, playing hooky from school or work—simply to take the edge off the pressures they are experiencing at the moment.

10. *Undoing.* In **undoing,** the person engages in a ritual behavior or thought in order to cancel out an unacceptable impulse. For example, people with obsessions (Chapter 7) have recurrent disturbing thoughts, often sexual or hostile in nature. Some obsessives eventually work out a little ritual, such as slapping their own faces or clapping their hands, in an attempt to dispel the disturbing thought.

11. *Identification.* **Identification**—again, widely deployed in ordinary life—involves attaching oneself psychologically to a group in order to diminish personal anxieties. Some sports fans, for example, may find added importance in their lives by experiencing their team's successes and failures as if they were their own.

According to the psychodynamic perspective, a person who engages in obsessive rituals may be resorting to the defense mechanism called *undoing,* canceling out unacceptable thoughts in order to relieve severe anxiety.

12. Sublimation. **Sublimation,** the transformation and expression of sexual or aggressive energy into more socially acceptable forms, differs from all other defense mechanisms in that it can be truly constructive. The skill of a great surgeon, for example, may represent a sublimation of aggressive impulses. Likewise, Freud hypothesized that many of the beautiful nudes created by Renaissance painters and sculptors were the expression of sublimated sexual impulses. Indeed, Freud saw civilization itself as the result of thousands of years of sublimation (Lindzey, Hall, & Manosevitz, 1973).

The Stages of Psychosexual Development In Freud's view, the development of the personality is a process of **psychosexual development,** a series of stages in which the child's central motivation is to gratify sexual and aggressive drives in various erogenous (pleasure-producing) zones of the body: the mouth, the anus, and the genitals, in that order. The characteristics of the adult personality are a consequence of the ways in which these id strivings are handled at each stage of development. For at each stage the child is forced to deal with a conflict between his or her own drive for gratification and the restrictions (in the form of weaning, toilet training, etc.) that the social environment places on that gratification. Both undergratification and overgratification can engender anxiety, and anxiety can lead to maladaptive adult behavior.

The oral stage The **oral stage** begins at birth. As the name indicates, the mouth is the primary focus of id strivings. Infants must suck in order to live. Soon, however, they are using their mouths to satisfy not only their hunger but also their libidinal and aggressive impulses. Breast, bottle, thumb, pacifier, toys—infants suck, mouth, bite, and chew whatever they can find in their search for oral stimulation. The actions involved in these oral exercises—sucking in, holding on, spitting out, and closing—serve as prototypes for later personality traits such as dependency and stubbornness.

The anal stage The **anal stage** usually begins in the second year of life. The libido shifts its focus to the anus and derives its primary gratification from the retaining and expelling of feces. In the retention of feces, the pleasurable stimulus is the pressure of the feces against the walls of the rectum, while in the expulsion of feces, the gratification is the reduction of tension as this pressure is relieved. Above all, the child takes pleasure in being able to control and regulate these functions.

The child's anal pleasures are barely established, however, before they are interfered with, through the process of toilet training. Traditionally, Freudian theorists have regarded toilet training as a crucial event, since it is children's first confrontation with an external demand that they control their impulses. Suddenly their pleasures are brought under regulation. They are told when, where, how, and so forth. Toilet training, then, is the first difficult demand on the developing ego. If problems occur, the ego may experience considerable anxiety, and as in the oral stage, such anxiety can engender personality problems.

The phallic stage In the **phallic stage,** which extends from about the third to the fifth or sixth year, the focus is shifted to the genitals, and sensual pleasure is derived from masturbation. Because of this newfound erotic self-sufficiency, the child in the phallic stage begins to develop a strong sense of self, of independence and autonomy, as opposed to the extreme dependence characteristic of earlier stages.

The phallic stage is held to be particularly crucial to psychological development because it is this stage that is the scene of the **Oedipus complex,** named after Oedipus, the legendary king of Thebes, who unknowingly killed his father and married his mother. According to Freud (1905/1953), the child's extreme dependence on the mother during infancy culminates, during the phallic stage, in sexual desire for the mother. How this is resolved depends on whether the child is a boy or a girl. In boys, the incestuous desire leads to a recognition of the father's capacity for wrath, which in turn arouses **castration anxiety:** the boy fears that his father will punish him for his forbidden wishes by cutting off the guilty organ, his penis. This worry is supposedly confirmed by the boy's observations of female anatomy. Lacking penises, girls seem to him castrated, and he fears the same fate for himself. To allay his castration anxiety, he eventually represses the incestuous desire that aroused it. Instead of competing with the father, he identifies with him, internalizing the father's—and the society's—prohibitions against incest and aggression and thus building the foundations for the superego.

In girls, the situation is more complicated. In what has been called the **Electra complex,** a girl observes that she has been born without a penis. She experiences what Freud called **penis envy,*** and this causes her to reorient her sexual interest toward her father. If she can seduce him, then at least vicariously she can obtain the desired organ. But of course her desires are as futile as the boy's, and eventually she retreats back into her earlier, dependent identification with the mother.

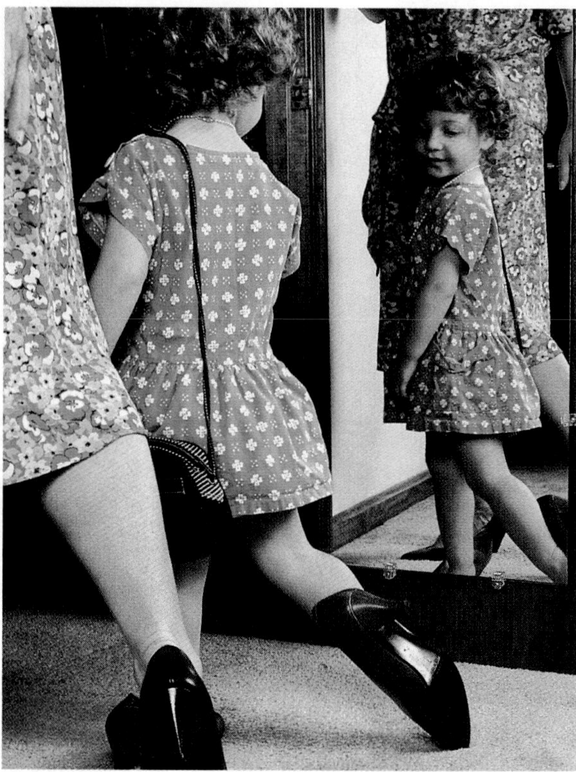

The child's identification with the same-sex parent is one of the features of the phallic stage of psychosexual development.

So eventually both boys and girls undergo identification with the parent of the same sex; in the process they incorporate that parent's values, sexual orientation, and other characteristics. And it is through incorporation of the parent's moral values that the superego develops. But according to Freud, sexual differences in the Oedipal drama give rise to sexual differences in the superego. The boy's active struggle with ambivalence toward his father supposedly endows him with greater maturity, sounder judgment, and better self-control than girls are able to develop in their passive reversion to identification with the mother. (See the box on page 33.)

Latency and the genital stage Usually between the ages of six and twelve, the child goes through the **latency** period, during which sexual impulses seem dormant. Then, as the child enters puberty, sexual strivings are reawakened. Now, however, they are directed not at the child's own body, as in earlier stages, but toward others, in a new emotion combining altruistic feeling with the primitive sexual drive. This final phase of development, called

*It has been pointed out that such concepts as castration anxiety and penis envy reflect an unjustified assumption that to be born without a penis is cause for bitter disappointment. This assumption, along with such terms as *phallic stage,* reflect the degree to which Freud's theories are based on male psychology and male anatomy—a bias that has made Freud a target of criticism from feminists. Of course, in most societies, those with penises *do* have favored status, and it is this, rather than the organ itself, that may be the focus of female envy (Horney, 1967).

PSYCHODYNAMIC THEORY AND FEMININE DEVELOPMENT

Freud, like all thinkers, reflected the values of his time. Nowhere is this more obvious than in his views on feminine development, which mirror, and in some measure defend, the inequality between the sexes in late-nineteenth-century Europe.

The Freudian theory of feminine psychology rests, basically, on the fact that a girl does not have a penis. According to Freud, the moment a child notices this basic anatomical difference, he or she begins to become, psychologically as well as biologically, a male or a female. For the little girl, the realization that she has no penis produces ineradicable jealousy, or "penis envy." As Freud (1900/1974) wrote, "The discovery that she is castrated is a turning point in a girl's growth" (p. 105). What she turns toward from that moment on is a position of inferiority.

The process may be summarized as follows: Because she lacks a penis, the girl's Oedipal conflict takes a form different from the boy's. Already "castrated," she is barred from the healthy process of experiencing and then overcoming castration anxiety. Furthermore, her choice of her father as a love object is a negative rather than a positive choice. Like the boy, she originally desired her mother, but once she discovers that her mother, like her, is castrated—and is responsible for bringing her into the world castrated—she turns instead to her father. Thus her Oedipal experience lacks both the stable heterosexual orientation and the cathartic resolution of the boy's Oedipal crisis. And as a result, her superego (the fruit of a successfully resolved Oedipus complex) is stunted. Throughout her life she remains narcissistic, vain, and, above all, envious, for she can never overcome her bitterness over her castration. Furthermore, she is culturally inferior, since the ability to contribute to the advance of civilization depends on the mechanism of sublimation, which in turn depends on a strong, mature superego—the very thing she lacks.

Thus, while men go out to do the work of justice and civilization, women remain mired in feelings of inferiority and efforts to compensate for it. If a woman is lucky, she will be rewarded with that ultimate compensation, a baby. And if the baby should turn out to be a boy, "who brings the longed-for penis with him" (S. Freud, 1974, p. 150, 154), all the better. But a baby remains a substitute. Because of their perception of themselves as castrated, women remain morally weak, culturally unproductive, and somehow "other," a deviation from the norm of masculinity.

The opposition to this theory was first put forward in 1939 by the neo-Freudian theorist Karen Horney, who retorted that it is not little girls who perceive their condition as degraded. Rather, it is little boys—and the men they eventually become—who see their penisless counterparts as deficient and who thus have created the self-fulfilling prophecy that has doomed womankind to inferiority. Horney also pointed out that if girls are envious, what they probably envy is not a penis but rather the power that in most societies is reserved for those who have penises.

More recently, psychodynamic thinkers have proposed some sharply revised ideas of feminine development. What these thinkers have in common with Freud is the notion that the young child's attachment to its mother is of crucial importance to masculine or feminine development, and that this attachment has a very different meaning for girls than for boys. Nancy Chodorow, in her book *The Reproduction of Mothering* (1978), stresses the differences between girls' and boys' early childhood environments. For both, the mother is the primary love object during early infancy. However, the girl's task is to internalize the feminine role, while the boy's task is to renounce an identification with femininity and differentiate from it in order to become masculine. Boys, therefore, place a premium on separation and individuation. Girls are less motivated to differentiate themselves and consequently have more difficulty with separation and individuation.

Another theorist in this mode is Carol Gilligan, author of *In a Different Voice* (1982), an influential book on girls' moral development. Like Chodorow, Gilligan sees boys' needs to separate from their mothers as responsible for a personality difference observable in adult men and women:

> For boys and men, separation and individuation are critically tied to gender identity since separation from the mother is essential for the development of masculinity. For girls and women, issues of femininity or feminine identity do not depend on the achievement of separation from the mother or on the progress of individuation. Since masculinity is defined through separation while femininity is defined through attachment, male gender identity is threatened by intimacy while female gender identity is threatened by separation. Thus males tend to have difficulty with relationships, while females tend to have problems with individuation. (p. 8)

In this view, the key crisis of early childhood is not the phallic conflict, but Margaret Mahler's "separation-individuation" crisis (see page 39). Girls, according to this theory, do *not* grow up into morally inferior penis enviers. They may, however, grow into adulthood with a greater need for close human attachments than many men have.

the **genital stage,** ends with the attainment of mature sexuality, which to Freud meant not only heterosexual love but also maturity in a broad sense: "loving and working," as he characterized the hallmarks of healthy functioning.

Normal and Abnormal Behavior

Normal personality functioning For centuries before Freud, people had viewed mental disorder as a loss of one's *reason:* the sane person was rational, and the insane person was irrational. In Freud's view, by contrast, both the sane and the insane are motivated by the irrational id, with its reckless drives. Some people are simply more capable of controlling these drives.

Their success in doing so depends largely on their psychosexual development, which, in the normal person, will have produced a healthy balance among the three psychic components of id, ego, and superego. While id strivings may be the generator of behavior, the form that behavior takes is dictated by the ego and superego. This does not mean that the id, ego, and superego coexist in perfect harmony. They are constantly conflicting, and power is continually shifting among them. The hallmark of a healthy personality is ego strength. Because the ego controls contact with reality, any draining of ego strength will result in an impairment of our ability to adapt to reality. Appointments will be missed; new situations will become terrifying; minor difficulties will become major calamities. In times of stress, the ego may be weakened, in which case the defenses will operate poorly, leaving us with a good deal of anxiety. Or, under the influence of alcohol or other drugs, the superego's functioning may become weak and thus allow id impulses the upper hand. Whatever the cause of the imbalance, usually the equilibrium of power among the three psychic components is eventually restored, and the person is once again able to satisfy the demands of the id without flying in the face of reality or morality.

Abnormal personality functioning Like normal functioning, abnormal functioning is motivated primarily by irrational drives and determined by childhood experiences. Indeed, one of the central principles of psychoanalytic theory is that normal and abnormal behavior lie on a continuum. Abnormality is a difference in degree, not in kind. Dreams, fantasies, works of art, psychiatric symptoms, hallucinations—these are simply different stops on the same road.

What, then, is the difference between normal and abnormal? It lies in the nature and particularly the duration of an imbalance among id, ego, and superego. Many people find themselves in such a state at some point in their lives, when they are under severe emotional stress; once the stress is lifted, the defenses are relaxed, and the ego bounces back. In some cases, however, the conflict continues, creating more and more anxiety, which in turn creates more and more rigid defenses, in the form of behaviors that seriously impede adaptive functioning. After a serious car accident, a woman who was used to driving long distances begins to feel anxious about driving and eventually stops driving altogether; a student who regularly earned A's in high school begins to have trouble studying and keeping up with his assignments, subsequently starts avoiding his classes, and by semester's end must withdraw from school. Freud called such conditions **neuroses.**

One such pathological process Freud called **fixation:** aspects of the adult personality remain fixed, or "frozen," at the anxiety-ridden stage, still acting out in symbolic fashion the impulse in question. Thus the victim of harsh toilet training may grow up "anal-retentive," that is, stingy and compulsively neat.

In extreme cases, the ego's strength may be severely depleted (or severely underdeveloped from the start), drastically curtailing adaptive functioning. Defenses break down, flooding the psyche with id impulses and attendant anxiety. Emotions are cut loose from external events. Speech loses its coherence. Inner voices are mistaken for outer voices. This condition of ego collapse, known as **psychosis,** is the furthest reach of the structural imbalance. (See the box on p. 35.)

The Descendants of Freud

As Freud's theory gained acceptance, young people came to Vienna from many different countries to be analyzed by Freud and his followers. They then took his theory back with them, disseminating it through Europe and the United States. As it spread, however, Freudian theory changed. Many of Freud's pupils and their pupils were original thinkers in their own right. On the basis of his theory, they constructed new theories, extending and modifying his principles.

In this elaboration of Freud's theory, three trends are especially noteworthy. The first is the pronounced emphasis on the ego. Freud, while by no means ignoring the ego, gave special attention to the id. In general, later contributors to psychodynamic thought shifted the spotlight to the ego.

THE PSYCHODYNAMIC PERSPECTIVE INTERPRETS PARANOIA

They're out to get me," says a man to his therapist. "They" may be the couple down the street, the police, perhaps all Catholics, Protestants, or Jews. Whoever "they" are, the patient is convinced that they want him and will pursue him until he is caught. He imagines plots against him. He is being watched and secretly manipulated by evil forces. The enemy knows his thoughts, habits, and whereabouts at all times.

People with fears and delusions of this sort are generally diagnosed as *paranoid.* Freudian analysts who encounter a person suffering from paranoia try to understand the conflicts underlying the person's fears. Consider, for example, the case of N.:

> This patient continually rails against homosexuals, whom he detests with a violent passion. After a brief, unsuccessful marriage, followed by impotence, he began to experience delusions of persecution, according to which the CIA and the FBI were continually observing him with the ultimate purpose of getting him to submit to the sexual advances of Richard Nixon. He gave up all attempts at heterosexual sex, because he "would not make love in public," i.e., in front of the lurking agents. He soon came to understand also that his impotence had been imposed on him, via laser rays, by Nixon's agents. Satellites specifically sent up for this purpose began to bombard him with homosexual messages. Finally he constructed a special protective hat fitted with a highly complex electrical jamming device. He wore this hat continually, at home and in public places, including restaurants and work (he was soon dismissed). Even so, the messages that he should submit to Nixon increased in intensity and began to "penetrate" at times. Around this period he took all his jackets to a tailor and had the tailor sew up the slits (or flaps) in the back of the jackets. He implored his male acquaintances to do likewise, lest they be taken for "slot-jacket ass panderers." He deplored tight dungarees because they revealed buttocks too openly and therefore constituted a disgraceful invitation to sodomy. He complained that the CIA was spreading rumors that he was a homosexual, indeed, they had contrived to find a "double" for himself and a friend and photographed them—the doubles—in "disgusting" homosexual acts, all for the purpose of blackmail, so that he might submit to the homosexual importunings of the "anarcho-communist sodomite" Gerald Ford, who, as he now came to realize, was really "behind" the conspiracy (Nixon, it now turned out, was just a "front"). Ford, he believed, succeeded in having his landlord evict him from his apartment, so that he would be forced to live in the local YMCA among "faggots." This was meant to be a "softening-up" tactic. (Erdelyi & Goldberg, 1979, p. 372)

What can be the meaning behind this patient's confused thoughts? Are they to be taken literally? Certainly, N. consciously hated homosexuals. He even began to talk about "destroying them." Is this simply a case of a man fearing retribution from people he hates? For the Freudian, a face-value acceptance of a patient's complaints is never enough; in fact, such a reading often contradicts the true explanation of a problem. A psychodynamic explanation of any disorder is always based on the *interpretation* of symptoms. What unconscious conflicts, then, are being masked by N.'s fear and hatred of homosexuals?

First, recall the defense mechanism known as *projection,* in which a person projects onto others his or her own unacceptable desires or impulses. Unable to entertain these thoughts or wishes in the conscious mind because of the unbearable anxiety they cause, the person attributes them to others. In this case, a psychodynamic interpretation would suggest that N. was actually *attracted* to homosexuals, but such feelings were so repulsive and anxiety-provoking that he banished them from consciousness. Instead of feeling himself attracted to men, he imagined that other men were attracted to him.

Underlying this defense mechanism, according to Freudians, lies the "true" conflict. What N. really fears is not that the homosexuals will get him, but that he will become one himself, succumbing to taboo impulses that he feels but must deny.

That is, they deemphasized sex, instincts, and determinism and emphasized goals, creativity, and self-direction. Second, the post-Freudian thinkers tended to view the child's social relationships as the central determinant of normal and abnormal development. Again, this is hardly a subject ignored by Freud; the Oedipus/Electra complex is nothing if not a social drama. Still, Freud always viewed social interactions in relation to the strivings of the id. Later thinkers, particularly the object-relations theorists, deemphasized the id and moved social interaction to center stage. Finally, later theorists tended to extend the period of critical developmental influences. Freud emphasized the phallic stage, and especially the Oedipus/Electra complex. Many subsequent thinkers have placed greater stress on infancy, while others see critical developmental junctures occurring well into adulthood.

The first and second generations of post-Freudian thinkers were often called *neo-Freudians,* a term that indicates their heavy dependence on Freud's formulations. As time and the theory have advanced, however, the elaborators of psychodynamic theory have come to be regarded simply as psychodynamic thinkers, of many different orientations. Among the post-Freudian theorists, we will consider two of Freud's students who dissented from his ideas—Carl Jung and Alfred Adler; two theorists who focused on interpersonal issues—Harry Stack Sullivan and Karen Horney; and two psychoanalysts who were pioneers in "ego psychology"—Heinz Hartmann and Erik Erikson. Finally, we will discuss Margaret Mahler and Heinz Kohut, whose theories have had a great impact on the field as it exists today.

Carl Gustav Jung Freud's most cherished pupil, the Swiss psychiatrist Carl Gustav Jung (1875–1961), broke with him early in his career, claiming that Freud's theory was unduly negative and reductive. The main focus of the disagreement was the nature of the libido. Whereas Freud saw the energy of the psyche as primarily sexual, Jung viewed the libido as a much broader force, comprising an autonomous "spiritual instinct" as well as a sexual instinct. There was a corresponding division in the two men's views of the unconscious. To Freud, the unconscious is a regressive force, pulling us back into infantile, id-directed behavior. To Jung, the unconscious is also a creative force. Jung (1935) argued, moreover, that the mind contains not just the personal unconscious (that is, biological drives and childhood memories) but also a **collective unconscious,** a repository of "archetypes," or symbols, expressive of universal human experiences. This set of symbols, shared by all humankind, is the source of mythology and art, whose unity across cultures is explained by their common origin.

Carl Gustav Jung, a student of Freud, took a broader and more positive view of the unconscious than Freud did. Jung claimed that the unconscious is creative and includes not only the personal but also the collective unconscious, a set of universal human symbols.

Jung's therapeutic practices also differed from Freud's. In Freudian therapy, the primary goal is control: the rational ego taking control of the irrational id and directing it to constructive ends. In Jungian therapy, the goal is integration: the uniting of opposing tendencies (e.g., masculinity and femininity, extroversion and introversion) within the self so that the patient can become more "whole" and thereby more creative—a view of therapy that links Jung to humanistic psychology, which we will discuss later in this chapter.

Alfred Adler Another member of Freud's inner circle who eventually broke with him was Alfred Adler (1870–1937). Like Jung, Adler believed that Freud had placed undue emphasis on sexual instincts. In Adler's view, the primary motivator of behavior is not the sexual drive but a striving to attain personal goals and overcome handicaps. (It was Adler who coined the term *inferiority complex.*) Related to his interest in power is his concept of

Alfred Adler, also a student of Freud, rejected Freud's heavy emphasis on the role of biological drives. Instead, Adler stressed the importance of viewing human beings in a social context.

masculine protest, by which Adler (1917/1988) meant the unwarranted belief that men are inherently superior to women. According to Adler, masculine protest is the product not of penis envy or the Electra crisis but simply of an unequal society. Its consequences are smugness and callousness in men and pathological feelings of inferiority in women.

Adler's most important contribution, however, was his concern with the social context of personality. Psychological disturbance, he claimed, has its roots not so much in early childhood experiences as in people's present circumstances, particularly their relationships with others. Mature people are those who can resolve their power struggle and devote themselves selflessly to others. An active socialist, Adler was concerned not just with intimate social relationships but with society in general, which he hoped to serve through psychiatric means.

Harry Stack Sullivan The study of psychological disorder as a social phenomenon was carried forward by the American psychiatrist Harry Stack Sullivan (1892–1949). Particularly crucial, in Sullivan's view, is the parent-child relationship. Children of rejecting parents develop severe anxiety about themselves—anxiety that makes it almost impossible for them, as they grow up, to weather the threats to the self that are part of almost any close relationship. (To Sullivan, an important step toward psychological health is the existence of "chumship," a close relationship with a same-sex friend, in early adolescence.) For people with disturbed family relationships, other human beings pose too great a threat. The person wards them off either by engaging in rigid self-protecting behaviors (neurosis) or by withdrawing completely from the world of other people (psychosis). But regardless of its severity, psychological disturbance is an anxiety-motivated flight from human relationships.

Aside from his elaboration of the social theory of psychopathology, Sullivan's other major contribution was in the treatment of severe mental disturbance, an area in which Freud and his early followers felt that psychoanalysis could be of little help. Sullivan was the first analyst to report significant success in the long-term psychoanalytic treatment of psychotics, and the warm, supportive approach that he developed for this purpose has served as a model for later therapies aimed at helping psychotics by placing them in a benign "milieu" (Chapter 15).

Karen Horney Another neo-Freudian thinker who focused on social relationships was Karen Horney (1885–1952). According to Horney (1937), psychological disturbance is the result of **basic anxiety,** a pervasive view of the world as impersonal and cold. This in turn is the product of a failed parent-child attachment. (Note how many neo-Freudians conceptualize anxiety as stemming from a *lack* of parent-child intimacy, as opposed to the overintimacy postulated by the Oedipus/Electra complex.) Basic anxiety, as Horney saw it, leads to one of three "neurotic trends": *moving away* (shy, withdrawn behavior), *moving toward* (dependent, needy behavior), or *moving against* (hostile, aggressive behavior—three patterns that cover most forms of psychopathology.

As the only woman among the early psychoanalytic thinkers, it was perhaps inevitable that Horney developed a theory of feminine psychology, one that departed from Freud's. (See the box on page 33.) Horney, like Freud, saw significant psychological differences between men and women, and competition between them, with men seeking to dominate women and women seeking to deceive and humiliate men. But while Freud attributed this to penis envy, Horney proposed the more direct interpretation that it is due to men's greater prestige and wider opportunities in society.

Heinz Hartmann As we saw, a critical trend in post-Freudian theory has been an increasing emphasis on ego functions. A milestone in this line of thought was Heinz Hartmann's *Ego Psychology and the Problem of Adaptation* (1939). Freud tended to regard the ego merely as the handmaiden of the id. It derives its energy from the id, and its role is to serve the id. Against this limited view of the ego's functioning, Hartmann (1894–1970) argued that the ego develops independently of the id and has its own autonomous functions—functions, in other words, that serve *ego* strivings, such as the need to adapt to reality, rather than id strivings. In particular, the mind's cognitive (mental-processing) operations, such as memory, perception, and learning, are, in Hartmann's (1939) view, "conflict-free" expressions of the ego. The id and the superego may help induce a child to go to school, for example, but only a relatively pure ego motivation can explain how the child learns to solve an algebra problem. From this proposition it follows that Freud overemphasized the role of conflict in mental life. If, in many of its basic operations, the ego is working for itself rather than mediating battles between the id and its opponents, then the life of the mind also has a "conflict-free sphere."

Hartmann's ideas were instrumental in the founding of a whole new school of **ego psychology,** which has had a huge influence on psychoanalytic theory since World War II. Today many psychoanalytic writers focus on the ego and the interplay between its conflict-solving functions and its conflict-free functions, particularly cognitive processes. This shift has had the effect of bringing psychoanalysis closer to other branches of psychology, where cognitive processes have been commanding more attention in the past few decades.

Erik Erikson An important extension of the new ego psychology and of the social analysis of personality was the developmental theory put forth

Stage	1	2	3	4	5	6	7	8
Maturity								Ego Integrity vs. Despair
Adulthood							Generativity vs. Stagnation	
Young Adulthood						Intimacy vs. Isolation		
Puberty and Adolescence					Identity vs. Role Confusion			
Latency				Industry vs. Inferiority				
Locomotor-Genital			Initiative vs. Guilt					
Muscular-Anal		Autonomy vs. Shame, Doubt						
Oral Sensory	Basic Trust vs. Mistrust							

FIGURE 2.1 Erikson viewed life as a succession of biological stages, each having its own developmental conflict whose resolution has lasting effects on personality. Erikson's psychosocial stages represent an extension and expansion of Freud's psychosexual stages, with parallels between the first four stages of each theory.

by Erik Erikson (1902–1994). To Erikson, the major drama of development is the formation of the **ego identity,** an integrated, unique, and autonomous sense of self. The ego identity is the product of what Erikson called **psychosocial development.** Like Freud's theory of psychosexual development, of which it is a deliberate revision, Erikson's psychosocial development proceeds through a series of chronological stages. But these stages differ from Freud's (see Figure 2.1). In the first place, there are more of them. To Freud, the personality is essentially formed by the age of six or seven; to Erikson, personality development extends from birth to death. The second difference is the pronounced social emphasis of Erikson's theory, proclaimed in the term *psychosocial.* While Freud saw the individual psyche in near isolation (except for the influence of parents and siblings), Erikson saw personality development as deeply affected not only by the family but also by teachers, friends, spouses, and many other social agents.

Third and most important is the central role of the ego in Erikson's developmental progression. Freud's stages have to do with challenges to id strivings; Erikson's stages have more to do with challenges to the ego. At each stage there is a crisis—a conflict between the individual and the expectations now imposed by society. The ego is then called upon to resolve the crisis by learning new adaptive tasks. In the second year, for example, the child is faced with toilet training, a challenge that may lead to a new sense of self-reliance or, if the training is poorly handled, to feelings of shame and self-doubt. Likewise, from the third to the fifth

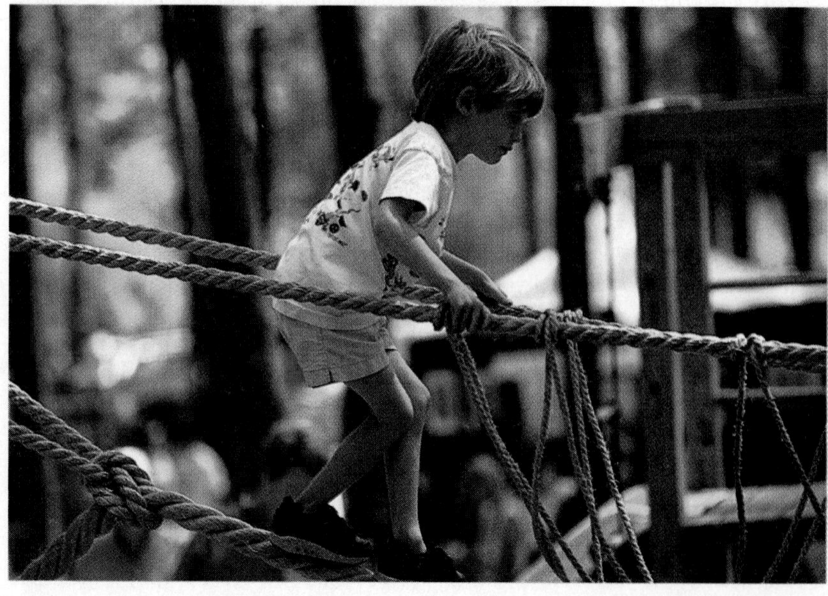

In Erikson's theory of psychosocial development, the primary task of the preschool child is to separate his or her identity from that of the mother. If successful, the child acquires the initiative to master a variety of skills.

years, when the challenge confronting the child is that of separating from the mother, a successful resolution will lead to a new sense of initiative, whereas a troubled separation will foster guilt.

Through this process of conflict resolution, the ego identity—the image of oneself as a unique, competent, and self-determining individual—is gradually formed. Or, if the ego fails to master the crisis, this failure will hamper identity formation and may generate psychological disorders. Erikson believed, however, that a failure at one stage does not guarantee failure at future stages. In his scheme, the ego is a resilient force, and there is always a second chance. Erikson's theory is thus more hopeful than Freud's scheme, where a serious childhood trauma can handicap a person for life. In general, recent psychoanalytic thinking, because of its emphasis on the adaptive, problem-solving ego, is more optimistic than earlier psychoanalytic formulations.

Margaret Mahler Certainly the most influential concept in contemporary psychodynamic thought is that of **object relations.** In psychodynamic terminology, "objects" are the people to whom one is attached by strong emotional ties. For the child, obviously, the chief object is the primary caretaker, usually the mother. And according to the *object-relations theorists,* the most powerful determinant of psychological development is the child's interaction with the mother.

A very influential member of this school was Margaret Mahler (1897–1985). As she indicated when she titled her book *The Psychological Birth of the Human Infant* (Mahler, Pine, & Bergman, 1975), Mahler was concerned primarily with charting the process by which infants separate themselves psychologically from their mothers. Mahler saw newborns as having no sense of their own existence apart from their mothers. Then, at around five months, begins the long and sometimes wrenching process of **separation-individuation.** As conceptualized by Mahler, separation-individuation involves several stages, each marked by greater independence and greater ambivalence, as the child vacillates between pleasure and terror over his or her new separateness from the mother. This ambivalence is finally resolved between the ages of two and three, when children achieve *object constancy:* they internalize the image of the mother—fix her in their minds so that she is no longer losable—and are thereby freed to consolidate a separate identity.

This, however, is the ideal scenario. Separation-individuation can be disturbed by many factors,

Margaret Mahler, like other object-relations theorists, was interested in the process by which children gradually separate themselves psychologically from their mothers and become individuals in their own right.

above all by the mother, if she either hurries or resists the toddler's move toward independence. In any case, Mahler felt that the success with which the separation-individuation process is navigated determines the child's psychological future, since the features of this first, crucial relationship will be repeated in later intimate relationships.

Heinz Kohut Like Mahler, Heinz Kohut (1913–1981) was interested primarily in the psychological consequences of the parent-child relationship. In his practice as a therapist Kohut encountered a great many patients who, though they shared similar problems—extreme demandingness and self-importance covering a very fragile self-esteem—seemed to fit no diagnostic category. He referred to this syndrome as *narcissistic personality disorder* (see Chapter 11), and from his work with these patients he built his so-called **self psychology.**

Kohut proposed that the development of the *self,* or core of the personality, depends on the child's receiving two essential psychological supports from the parents. One is the confirmation of the child's sense of vigor and "greatness." The other is a sense of calmness and infallibility: the feeling that there is nothing that the child can't handle. Parents communicate these things through the most ordinary daily behavior—by exclaiming over the artworks that their children bring home from school, by assuring them, when they are nervous over a test, that they can surely pass it. "If the parents are at peace with their own needs to shine and succeed," Kohut wrote, "then the proud exhibitionism of the budding self of their child will be responded to acceptingly" (Kohut & Wolf, 1978, p. 417), and the child will develop a "healthy narcissism." But some parents cannot provide this support, and the result, for the child, is a damaged self. Thus Kohut's theory, like Mahler's, differs

The surrealist painters were heavily influenced by Freudian theory, depicting dream-inspired symbols and sexual imagery. Reproduced here is Ives Tanguy's *Mama, Papa Is Wounded!* (1927).

from Freud's both in its interpersonal character and in its emphasis on cognitive and emotional rather than biological needs. Kohut and Mahler also place the critical events of early childhood well before the phallic stage, and this is the general trend in psychodynamic theory today.

Evaluating the Psychodynamic Perspective

Psychodynamic Theory versus the Medical Model Since Freud was trained in medicine, it is no surprise that the theoretical perspective he founded has ties to the medical model. The Freudian view of behavioral abnormalities as the symptoms of an underlying psychic disturbance is close to the medical model's approach to maladaptive behavior patterns as the symptoms of an underlying organic dysfunction. However, Freud went to great pains to differentiate his theory from the medical view. He claimed that a medical education was of no use to the psychoanalyst—"The analyst's experience lies in another world from that of pathology, with other phenomena and other laws" (S. Freud, 1926/1953, p. 119)—and he urged the training of lay (nonphysician) analysts. Furthermore, he insisted that psychoanalysis could offer nothing comparable to a medical cure. Actually, despite its parallels with medicine, the psychodynamic perspective was the first of the purely psychological approaches to abnormal behavior—the first, that is, to regard abnormal behavior not as a moral, religious, or organic problem, but as a problem in the history of the individual's emotional life.

Criticisms of Psychodynamic Theory and Responses

Lack of experimental support The most common criticism of the psychodynamic position is that most of its claims have never been tested in scientifically controlled experiments. Freud evolved his theories on the basis of **clinical evidence**—that is, observations of patients in therapy—and today psychodynamic writers still tend to rely on case studies to support their formulations. The problem with case studies is that they are open to bias. We can never know to what degree psychodynamic therapists' expectations color the patient's responses or their reporting of those responses.

The reason psychodynamic writers have depended on clinical evidence rather than controlled experiments is that most of the phenomena they deal with are too complex to be testable by current experimental techniques (Erdelyi & Goldberg, 1979). Furthermore, most of these phenomena are unconscious, and hence inaccessible to direct testing. Nevertheless, some of Freud's most basic claims have been subjected to research and have been validated (Fisher & Greenberg, 1977; D. S. Holmes, 1978). Experiments have shown, for example, that dreams do allow people to vent emotional tension; that children do go through a period of erotic interest in the parent of the opposite sex, accompanied by hostile feelings toward the same-sex parent; and that people who experience unusual anxiety over anal imagery do tend to show what Freud regarded as the "anal" traits of orderliness and stinginess. Likewise, recent research has shown that many of the basic methods of psychodynamic "insight" therapy do have the intended result of revealing core issues and fostering positive change (Luborsky, Barber, & Crits-Christoph, 1990; Luborsky, Crits-Christoph, Mintz, et al., 1988).

In other cases, the evidence contradicts Freudian theory. For example, there is little or no support for Freud's claim that dreams represent wish fulfillment or that women regard their bodies as inferior to men's because they lack penises. (Most of Freud's conclusions regarding specifically female sexuality have been contradicted by research [Fisher & Greenberg, 1977].) However, the important point is that psychodynamic theory is not altogether closed to empirical testing and that in some cases it holds up well under such testing. Indeed, even without the intention of testing psychodynamic theory, experimental psychologists have turned up evidence in support of many of Freud's positions—for example, that most of our mental contents are unconscious (G. Miller, 1956); that under normal conditions some of our unconscious mental contents are accessible to us while others are not (Kihlstrom, 1987; Schacter, 1987); and that most of the causes of our behavior are inaccessible to us (Nisbett & Ross, 1980; Nisbett & Wilson, 1977).

Dependence on inference A second, related criticism of the psychodynamic approach is that because it assumes that most mental processes are unconscious, it must depend on inference, and inference can easily be mistaken. Indeed, the psychodynamic view of the relationship between behavior and mental processes is so complicated and indirect that behaviors could conceivably be taken to mean whatever the psychodynamic interpreter wants them to mean. If a six-year-old boy expresses great love for his mother, this could be interpreted as a sign of Oedipal attachment. However, if the same six-year-old boy expresses hatred for his mother, this too could be interpreted as an expression of Oedipal attachment, via reaction formation. It should be added, however, that responsible analysts rarely, if ever, draw conclusions on the basis of one piece of evidence alone.

Unrepresentative sampling and cultural bias Another point on which psychodynamic theory has been criticized is that it is based on the study of a very limited sample of humanity. In most of Freud's published cases, the patients were upper-middle-class Viennese women between the ages of twenty and forty-four (Fisher & Greenberg, 1977). Though these people were adults, Freud drew from them his theories regarding the child's psyche. (He never studied children in any systematic way.) Though they had serious emotional problems, he drew from them his theories regarding normal development. Though they lived in a time and place where overt expressions of sexuality, especially by women, were frowned upon, he concluded that their sexual preoccupations were typical of all human beings.

There is also the matter of Freud's own life circumstances and his consequent personal biases. Freud lived in a highly repressive society where social-class distinctions were rigidly observed, where the family was dominated by the father, and where women's opportunities were strictly limited. That these social facts influenced his patients' thoughts is unquestionable. In addition, as Erich Fromm (1980) pointed out, they may have influenced Freud's interpretation of that evidence, leading him to see more repression, more sexual motivation, and more "penis envy" than are actually universal properties of the human psyche.

Reductive interpretation of life Finally, it has been argued that psychodynamic theory has handed down to the twentieth century an exceedingly dismal vision of human life—a vision in which the human being is a creature driven by animal instincts beyond his or her conscious control; in which people are virtually helpless to change themselves after the die is cast in early childhood; in which acts of heroism or generosity are actually disguised outgrowths of baser motives; and in which all that most people can know of their own minds is the surface, while the true causes of their behavior remain sealed up in the dark chambers of the unconscious.

Many of these positions, it should be recalled, have been substantially modified by later psychodynamic theorists. Furthermore, even if that were not the case, it is not the duty of science to produce a comforting picture of life, only a true one. Freud, as it happens, found much to admire in the human psyche he envisioned. If the ego could fashion civilization out of the base materials provided by the id, then the ego was a heroic force indeed. Furthermore, if psychodynamic theory is deterministic, so (as we shall see) are most other schools of psychology. And the psychodynamic perspective does hold out the hope that by acquainting ourselves with our inner lives, we can exercise greater control over our destinies. In short, it has pointed out the adaptive value of self-knowledge.

The Contributions of Psychodynamic Theory Whatever the criticisms, psychodynamic theory has made enormous contributions to the study of abnormal behavior. To begin with, it has helped to demythologize mental disorder. By arguing that the most "crazy" behaviors have their roots in the same mental processes as the most "sane" behaviors, Freud contributed greatly to the modern effort to treat the mentally disturbed as human beings rather than as freaks. Furthermore, by pointing out what he called the "psychopathology of everyday life"—the ways in which irrational and unconscious impulses emerge in dreams, in jokes, in slips of the tongue, in our ways of forgetting what we want to forget—Freud showed that the mentally disturbed have no monopoly on irrationality. This aspect of psychodynamic theory helped to establish the concept of mental health as a continuum ranging from adaptive to maladaptive rather than as a dichotomy of "sick" and "healthy."

Second, to the treatment of mental problems Freud contributed the technique of psychoanalysis, which helps patients to confront and understand their unconscious impulses and thus to gain greater mastery over their actions. Actually, Freud's major contribution to modern psychological treatment is probably not orthodox psychoanalysis, which is now relatively rare, but rather the wide variety of other therapies that grew out of psychoanalysis. Even therapists who reject Freud's theory altogether reveal his influence in the consulting room. The now-traditional technique of a one-to-one patient-therapist relationship aimed at increasing the patient's self-knowledge—a technique that underlies almost every known form of psychotherapy—was essentially a Freudian invention.

While modern thinkers are still arguing with Freud, no one can deny his impact on the contemporary conceptualization, assessment, and treatment of abnormal behavior. It is Freudian theory that is responsible for the widespread assumption that abnormal behavior stems from events in the individual's past and that it occurs in response to unconscious and uncontrollable impulses. In terms of psychological assessment, the popular "projective" tests (e.g., inkblot tests), in which the person is asked to respond to various ambiguous pictures and symbols, are interpreted according to the Freudian notion that behavior is symbolic and that what a person reads into a picture or an event is actually a reading of his or her own psyche.

The impact of psychodynamic theory has been felt far beyond the field of professional psychology. Freud directed the attention of the twentieth century to the gap between the outer life and the inner life—to dreams, to fantasies, to memory, and to the subterranean influence of these factors on our daily behavior. In doing so, he changed not only psychology but art, literature, history, and education. Indeed, he altered popular thinking. Today, people who have never read a word by Freud show no hesitation in explaining their problems in terms of their childhood experience, in viewing their own children's development as crucial prefigurations of their adult lives, or in using such terms as *repressed, rationalization,* and *ego*—terms coined by Freud to explain the human psyche. In truth, Freud radically altered the Western conception of the human mind. The same cannot be said of any other psychological theorist.

THE HUMANISTIC-EXISTENTIAL PERSPECTIVE

As we said earlier, the **humanistic-existential perspective** is both an outgrowth of and a reaction to the psychodynamic perspective. Indeed, many early humanistic and existential thinkers were trained as psychoanalysts. For these thinkers, however, psychodynamic theory came to seem inadequate. Many were repelled by the conservatism of Freud's thinking—the idea that good adjustment meant adapting to one's society, however questionable its values. Others quarreled with its tendency to break down thought and behavior into discrete components, while ignoring the "whole" person. Above all, humanistic and existential thinkers took exception to the determinism of the psychodynamic approach—the idea that human action is the product of forces beyond the control (indeed, often beyond the knowledge) of the individual.

While it is convenient for the purpose of clarity to speak of a unified humanistic-existential perspective, humanistic and existential psychology can only loosely be defined as a single school of thought, or even as two schools of thought. Rather, what we are dealing with in this section is a group of highly individual theorists. To do justice to the individualism that marks this perspective, our discussion will focus on the views of five representative theorists: the humanists Carl Rogers and Abraham Maslow and the existentialists Rollo May, Viktor Frankl, and R. D. Laing.

Underlying Assumptions

To subject such ideas as *authenticity* and *becoming* to scientific study may seem a difficult matter, but according to the humanists and existentialists, science must adapt its methods to its subject matter—in this case, human life—rather than vice versa. Early in the twentieth century the German philosopher Wilhelm Dilthey emphasized the distinction between the *natural sciences,* which treat their subject matter as material "things," and the *human sciences,* which treat their subject matter as subjective, dynamic processes. The humanists and existentialists argue that psychology should be converted into a human science, by focusing on specifically human characteristics. This implies a set of assumptions different from that of psychological theories based more on natural science. Though with differing emphases, the humanists and existentialists would agree on four basic premises.

The Phenomenological Approach "Can we be sure . . . that we are seeing the patient as he really is, knowing him in his own reality; or are we seeing merely a projection of our own theories about him?" This question, posed by the existential theorist Rollo May (1959, p. 3), points to one of the central assumptions of humanistic and existential psychology: that the therapist must enter into the patient's world. This method, known as the **phenomenological approach,** means listening with maximum empathy to everything that patients communicate about their experiences. To do this, therapists must avoid attending only to evidence that fits their own theoretical biases. Nor should they necessarily try to dig below the patient's statements in order to drag up the "real" truth. Their primary duty is to "tune in" to the patient's mental life, to see the world through the patient's eyes.

It must be stressed that humanistic-existential theorists embrace the phenomenological method not because they are warm, sympathetic people but because they have a firm philosophical and indeed scientific conviction that this is the only authentic approach to human experience. Phenomenology was an important philosophical movement of the early twentieth century, and its basic discovery—that all knowledge is subjective and therefore cannot be considered apart from the mind doing the "knowing"—has been incorporated into much of modern culture.

The Uniqueness of the Individual Because each person perceives the world in a special way and participates in his or her own "self-creation," each person is unique. According to the humanistic-existential perspective, to reduce the individual to a set of formulas, whether behavioral or psychodynamic, is to see only a very limited portion of his or her being. While human behavior may follow certain rules, such rules can never define a human life.

Human Potential The humanists, like the existentialists, see the individual as a process rather than a product. For both, human life is a matter of growth through experience. Hence the humanistic-existential perspective places great emphasis on human potential—the ability of individuals to become what they want to be, to fulfill their capabilities.

Freedom and Responsibility The humanistic-existential perspective is unique in its insistence on the freedom of the individual. The lives of human animals, like those of all other animals, are affected by external events beyond their control. But unlike other animals, human beings are gifted (and burdened) with self-awareness. Their self-awareness allows them to transcend their impulses and to *choose* what they will make of the "givens" of their existence. By so doing, they make their own destinies. The corollary of this freedom is that people are also responsible for their destinies. Authentic or inauthentic, our lives are the result of our own free choosing.

Humanistic Psychology

As we have seen, humanistic psychology is based on an emphatically positive vision of the human being. Whereas Freud saw the individual as motivated, at bottom, by the selfish and irrational id, which had to be constantly checked, humanists hold that if people are allowed to develop freely, without undue constraints, they will become rational, socialized beings. Furthermore, they will become *constructive* beings, intent on fulfilling not only their biological needs but also some higher vision of their capabilities. Of the humanists who have built their theories on this optimistic foundation, the most influential have been Carl Rogers and Abraham Maslow.

Rogers: The Organism and the Self Unlike psychodynamic theorists, who see behavior as a compromise among three opposing forces in the personality, Carl Rogers (1902–1987) saw all behavior as motivated by a single overriding factor, the *actualizing tendency.* The actualizing tendency is the desire to preserve and enhance oneself. On one level, it includes the drive simply to stay alive, by eating, keeping warm, and avoiding physical danger. On a higher level, the actualizing tendency also includes people's desire to test and fulfill their capabilities: to seek out new experiences, to master new skills, to quit boring jobs and find more exciting ones, and so on. This process of exploring and fulfilling one's potential is called **self-actualization.**

In the course of pursuing self-actualization, people engage in what Rogers called the **valuing process.** Experiences that are perceived as enhancing to oneself are valued as good and are therefore sought after. Experiences perceived as not enhancing are valued as bad and avoided. In other words, people know what is good for them.

Whether people will actually trust the valuing process and *do* what is good for them depends on the interaction of two factors that Rogers saw as the basic units of the personality: the organism and the self. The *organism* is our total perception of our experience, both internal and external. The *self* is our image of ourselves, akin to what others call the self-concept. And the degree of self-actualization that we achieve depends on *the degree of congruence between the self and the organism.* If the image of the self is flexible and realistic enough to allow us to acknowledge and evaluate all the experiences of the organism, then we are in an excellent position to pursue those experiences that are most enhancing. The nature of the self is thus the crucial factor in self-actualization.

What determines whether we will become self-actualizing? The decisive factor is childhood experience. As children become aware of themselves, they automatically develop the need for what Rogers called **positive regard**—that is, affection and approval from the important people in their lives, particularly their parents. Invariably, however, positive regard comes with strings attached: to be loved, the child must be mild-mannered, assertive, boyish, girlish, or whatever. These extraneous values, dictating which of the child's self-experiences are "good" and which are "bad," are incorporated as **conditions of worth.** If the conditions are few and reasonable, then the child will entertain a variety of experiences. If, however, the conditions of worth are severely limiting, screening out large portions of the experience of the organism, then they will seriously impede self-actualization.

The latter situation is, according to Rogers, the source of abnormal behavior. As external conditions of worth come to control more and more of a person's behavior, a gap opens between the person's actions and his or her true self. The person automatically covers over this split with perceptual distortions, denying the conflict between self and reality. As in the case of Freudian defense, such distortions can lead to personality breakdown. Rogers (1980) cited the case of a woman who, raised to be gentle and docile, grew up denying to herself that she ever felt angry. When at last she discovered angry feelings in herself, it was as if an "alien" had taken over her consciousness; in fact, the alien was a screened-out part of herself.

To undo such damage, Rogers developed a technique that he called **client-centered therapy** (Chapter 19).* Briefly, what the client-centered therapist does is create for the patient a warm and accepting atmosphere, by mirroring whatever feelings the patient expresses, by attempting to perceive the patient's world as he or she does, and most of all by offering the patient *unconditional positive regard*—respect and approval, with no conditions of worth. In this accepting atmosphere, the patient can at last confront feelings and experiences that are inconsistent with the self—a process that will result in the broadening of the self to include the total experience of the organism. The self and the organism are thereby brought back into congruence, and the patient is free to "*be*, in a more unified fashion, what he organismically *is*" (Rogers, 1955, p. 269). Thus freed, the patient can once again proceed with self-actualization.

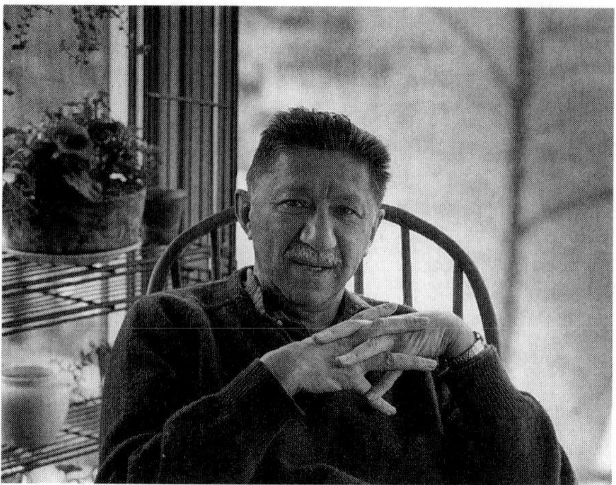

Abraham Maslow denounced the existing formulations of psychology as pessimistic, negative, and limited because they did not view human beings as dynamic, creative, holistic organisms.

Maslow: The Hierarchy of Needs Like Rogers, Abraham Maslow (1908–1970) started out with the premises that human beings are basically good and that all their behavior issues from a single master motive, the drive toward self-actualization. Maslow's special contribution to the humanistic program was his concept of the **hierarchy of needs,** a series of needs that must be met in the process of development before the adult can begin to pursue self-actualization. (See Figure 2.2.)

**Client-centered* was Rogers' original term for his therapy, and since it is the familiar term, it is the one that will appear in this book. Rogers later began to call his approach *person*-centered rather than *client*-centered to indicate his belief that the same principles apply in all human interaction, not just in the relations between therapist and client.

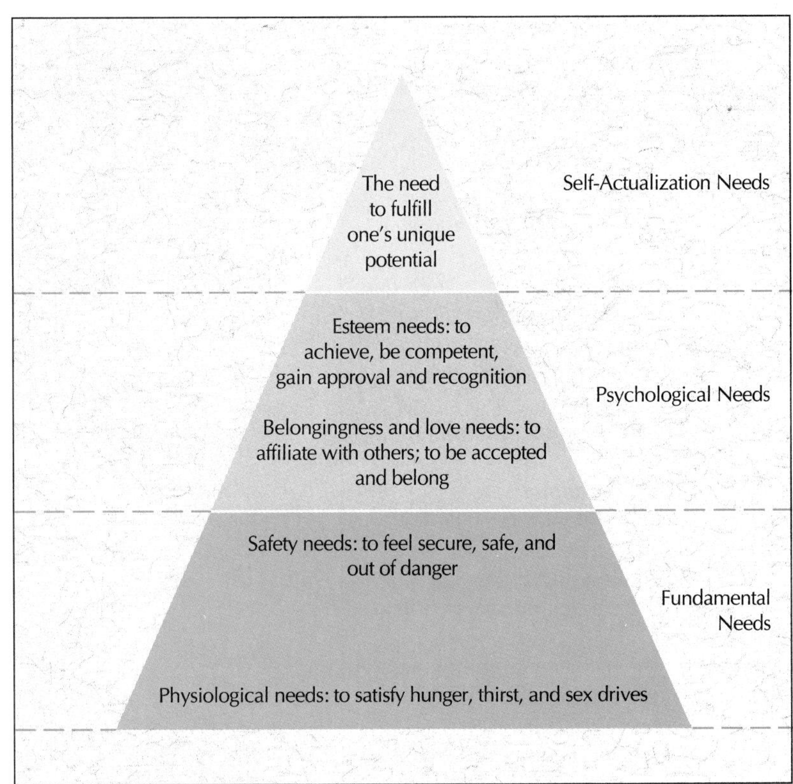

FIGURE 2.2 Maslow's hierarchy of needs. According to Maslow, fundamental needs must be satisfied before a person is free to progress to psychological needs, and these in turn must be satisfied before a person can turn to self-actualization needs.

Maslow proposed five levels of needs, each of which must be satisfied before a person can proceed to the next level. First are the *biological* needs, the need for physical comfort and survival. Second are the *safety* needs, the need for a stable and predictable environment. The third level is the need for *belongingness and love*—that is, warm relationships with friends and family. At the fourth level are the *esteem* needs, which impel the person to seek the respect of others and eventually to create an internal fund of self-esteem. Finally, having fulfilled these prior needs, the person can proceed to the fifth level and begin fulfilling the need for *self-actualization.* "People who are at this level of motivational development . . . are in a very high degree spontaneous, guileless, open, self-disclosing, and unedited and therefore expressive" (Maslow, 1987, p. 66). Maslow also identified fourteen characteristics, called *B-values* (*B* for "being"), that he felt defined self-actualized people. (See Table 2.1.) For Maslow, as for Rogers, abnormality consists essentially of being blocked in the drive toward self-actualization.

This represents a unique outlook on psychopathology. What both Rogers and Maslow were concerned with was not really abnormality, but rather the failure to progress beyond the minimum acceptable standards of normality. According to Maslow, a man might hold down a job, take care of his children, differentiate between the real and the imaginary, and yet still feel lonely, alienated, and ineffectual—a situation Maslow called "the psychopathology of the normal." Human beings, Maslow argued, require a great deal more than mere "adjustment." Hence psychology should address itself not just to repairing "breakdowns" but also to helping people live rich, creative lives. This preoccupation with self-fulfillment, more than anything else, sets the humanistic school apart from other schools of abnormal psychology, most of which are chiefly concerned with repairing actual damage.

Existential Psychology

As we have seen, existential psychology is an outgrowth of European existential philosophy, with its emphasis on the difficulty of living authentically in the modern world. In the existentialist view, human beings, in their rush to obtain the material comforts offered by modern technology, have abandoned their values and lost their sense of personal responsibility. They do not choose; they follow. And the result is the denial of the true self. According to the existentialists, this condition, which they call *alienation,* is a sort of spiritual

TABLE 2.1
MASLOW'S 14 B-VALUES

1 Aliveness	The desire to be part of the surrounding world and appreciate life
2 Autonomy	The need to direct one's own life
3 Beauty	The tendency to surround oneself with aesthetical, pleasing environments
4 Completion	The desire to persevere and see projects through to their end
5 Effortlessness	The preference for adopting straightforward, pragmatic solutions to problems
6 Goodness	A tolerance for others and a belief in the worth of all individuals
7 Humor	The ability to laugh at oneself and life's circumstances rather than belittling others
8 Justice	A belief in fairness and democratic principles
9 Perfection	The desire to do a task right, not to make do or settle for mediocrity
10 Simplicity	A preference for unpretentious, genuine life styles
11 Totality	A need to place oneself in a social context; a nonegotistical interest in others
12 Truth	An openness to novel ideas; a greater tolerance for ambiguity
13 Uniqueness	A desire to lead one's own life rather than follow social conventions or fads
14 Wholeness	The ability to accept the good with the bad and to accept all aspects of self

death, in which the person is haunted by a sense of the meaninglessness of life and by terror over the nothingness that will come with death.

As a means of ministering to this anguish of the spirit, existential psychology gained considerable attention during the 1960s and 1970s. We will focus here on the theories of three of its major contributors, the American psychologist Rollo May and the Europeans Viktor Frankl and R. D. Laing.

May: The Ontological Context The existential perspective was introduced into the United States by Rollo May (1909–1994), and, until his death, he remained its foremost interpreter. May accepted many basic principles of the psychodynamic perspective, such as neurosis, repression, and defense. His unique contribution was his insistence that such facts have meaning only in the *ontological context.* That is, the person can be understood not in

The humanistic-existential perspective affirms the ability of all human beings to fulfill their potential, sometimes despite apparently overwhelming obstacles.

terms of externally imposed theoretical models or diagnostic lists but only in terms of his or her subjective sense of self, which May called the *center.* Abnormality, he argued, is often merely a stratagem for protecting that center against perceived threats. The person gives up on new risks and challenges—and therefore self-growth—and instead retreats to the secure, known center. As May (1961) put it, this is "a way of accepting *nonbeing* . . . in order that some little *being* may be preserved" (p. 75)—a formulation similar to Rogers'.

To minister to this problem, the therapist must appeal to another ontological characteristic, self-transcendence, the ability to see oneself as a responsible, growing individual. By affirming the person completely and also approaching the person from his or her own perspective, the existential therapist fights for the full emergence of the person's potential. This is a halting and fear-laden process, for there is much that we would rather not know. Furthermore, seeing ourselves as having a world that is purely our own means accepting responsibility, will, and even aloneness (May, 1990).

As this method suggests, May was in the forefront of the humanistic-existential campaign to make psychology deal with the whole person rather than with isolated functions. He cited, for example, the case of a highly "repressed" patient of his who suffered from hysterical tenseness of the larynx, a problem that conveniently inhibited her speech (May, 1961). A previous therapist had told her that she was too proper, too controlled:

> She reacted with great upset and immediately broke off the treatment. Now, technically speaking, he was entirely correct; existentially, he was entirely wrong. What he did not see . . . was that this very properness, this overcontrol, far from being things that Mrs. Hutchens wanted to get over, were part of her desperate attempt to preserve what precarious center she had. As though she were saying, "If I opened up, if I communicated, I would lose what little space in life I have." (p. 75)

Frankl: The Will-to-Meaning A student of Freud, the Austrian-born psychiatrist Viktor Frankl (b. 1905) spent the years 1942 to 1945 in Nazi concentration camps. Imprisoned along with him were his parents, his brother, and his wife, all of whom died in the camps. From this harrowing experience Frankl evolved the basic tenets of his theory. In the camps, he observed that those prisoners who were able to resist despair were those who could find some spiritual meaning in their suffering. This observation led Frankl to the conclusion that traditional psychology, in dealing with human beings only in their biological and psychological dimensions, was omitting an all-important third dimension: the spiritual life.

It is this emphasis on spiritual meaning that is the central feature of Frankl's existential theory. According to Frankl, the prime motive of human behavior is not the will-to-pleasure or the will-to-power, as psychodynamic theory would have it, but rather the **will-to-meaning**—the struggle of human beings to find some reason for their troubled, complicated, and finite existence. They can discover such meaning only through *values.* And they discover values through work, through love of other people and of the world, and through confrontation with their own suffering.

Frankl (1962) views this process of pursuing values as a moral duty: "Ultimately, man should not ask what the meaning of life is, but rather he must recognize that it is *he* who is asked. In a word, each man is questioned by life, and he can only respond by being responsible" (p. 101). For those blocked in this process, Frankl has evolved a treatment strategy that he calls **logotherapy** (from the Greek word *logos,* meaning "word" or "thought"). The role of the therapist in logotherapy is to confront patients with their responsibility for their existence and help them choose values. This demanding process is softened by the nature of the patient-therapist relationship. As Frankl views it, this relationship is an existential partnership in which the therapist, by intuiting the patient's world, explores that world with him or her. The two of them then work together to correct the flaws in the patient's approach toward life so that he or she can once again take up the task of seeking meaning through values (Frankl, 1975b).

Laing: The False and the True Self For the British psychiatrist R. D. Laing (1927–1989) the central fact of our being-in-the-world is our interpersonal experience—or "interexperience," as he calls it—much of which, in his view, is damaging. The existential conceptualization of the modern mind as a divided entity—the false self covering the true, unexpressed inner self—is essentially Laing's, and he blamed the split on the falseness of modern social communication. The family in particular, by surrounding us with "double messages" and by requiring us to stifle our feelings and pursue meaningless goals, consistently discourages authentic behavior. By the time we reach adulthood, we are cut off from our true selves. Seemingly normal, we are actually deeply impaired—"half-crazed creatures more or less adjusted to a mad world" (Laing, 1967, p. 58).

Like "normal" behavior, abnormal behavior, according to Laing, is a function of relationships. Laing concentrated on schizophrenia, one of the severest forms of psychological disturbance. Schizophrenia, he wrote, is not so much a disorder as "a special strategy that a person invents in order to live in an unlivable situation" (Laing, 1979, p. 115). Certain people, when faced with extraordinary interpersonal stresses—perhaps combined, as Laing conceded, with a biochemical handicap (Sedgwick, 1982)—find themselves no longer able to maintain the false self that society requires of them. Hence they retreat from reality, plunging into their own inner worlds.

The Impact of the Humanistic-Existential Perspective

Humanistic-existential theorists have had only a limited impact on the field of abnormal psychology, partly because, as highly independent thinkers, they have been less interested than others in organizing themselves into a "movement" and pushing for power within the profession. Nevertheless, their ideas have clearly affected the field, particularly in the area of therapy. Today, therapists from many perspectives show their patients more overt empathy, focus more on the present and less on the past, and are more concerned with growth, as opposed to mere adjustment, than therapists of twenty or thirty years ago—a shift that is unquestionably due in part to humanistic-existential writings.

During the 1960s and 1970s humanistic-existential psychology provided a stimulus to the so-called human potential movement, in which people sought to contact untapped parts of themselves through such means as meditation, yoga, biofeedback, hypnosis, and hallucinogenic drugs. Although that wave has now receded, one aspect of it is still practiced—encounter groups, which can take any number of forms—Gestalt therapy, sensitivity training, psychodrama, marathon groups, and so on (Chapter 20).

Comparing the Humanistic-Existential and Psychodynamic Perspectives

Many humanistic and existential theorists began as psychodynamic therapists and have retained certain basic assumptions of psychodynamic theory. Rogers' and May's idea that abnormality is the result of the screening out of experience in order to preserve some psychological anchor (the "self," the "center") is an obvious adaptation of Freud's theory of defense. Likewise, the humanistic-existential theorists, like their psychodynamic counterparts, believe that the key to therapeutic change is insight (London, 1964). In psychodynamic therapy, however, the insights are provided mainly by the therapist and are presumably interpretations of repressed material. In humanistic-existential therapy, on the other hand, the insights are supposed to come from patients themselves. Patients' statements, while they may not always be taken at face value, are seen as important in their own right. Finally, the goal of insight is not merely to cope better with inevitable anxiety but rather to fill in the missing pieces of a self which can then follow its natural drive toward positive goals.

Evaluating the Humanistic-Existential Perspective

The primary criticism of the humanistic-existential perspective is that it is unscientific, even antiscientific. The main source of information in humanistic therapy, for example, is simply what the therapist thinks about what the patient thinks about his or her own life. The existentialists, with their philosophical inquiries, are perhaps even less scientifically precise. In some cases, the perspective seems actually to scorn scientific methodology. Another questionable matter is whether therapists can verify that they are in fact perceiving the patient's inner world—or, even if they are, that such empathy is actually of therapeutic value.

To these charges humanistic-existential theorists reply that the scientific methods being demanded of them are borrowed from natural science and therefore are inadequate for the study of human behavior (Giorgi, 1970). What psychology needs is a new, "human" science—one that can take into account such fundamental human matters as will, values, goals, and meaning. Their argument, in other words, is that they are being scolded for failing to use the wrong tool. They would add (and many would agree) that it is questionable whether the therapeutic situation can actually be judged by scientific standards. At the same time, humanistic-existential thinkers have not utterly turned their backs on research. Carl Rogers was one of the first psychotherapists to test his theories scientifically (Chapter 19). Studies of terminally ill patients (P. Reed, 1987), suicide attempters (T. J. Young, 1985), and anorexics (Dittmar & Bates, 1987) have also verified the existentialists' claim that mental health depends on spiritual values and self-transcendence.

KEY TERMS

anal stage (31)
anxiety (29)
basic anxiety (37)
castration anxiety (32)
client-centered therapy (44)
clinical evidence (40)
collective unconscious (36)
conditions of worth (44)
defense mechanism (29)
denial (30)
depth hypothesis (26)
displacement (30)
ego (28)
ego ideal (28)
ego identity (38)
ego psychology (37)
Electra complex (32)
fixation (34)
genital stage (34)
hierarchy of needs (44)
humanistic-existential perspective (42)
id (27)
identification (30)
intellectualization (30)
interpretation (27)
isolation (30)
latency (32)
latent content (27)
libido (28)
logotherapy (47)
manifest content (27)
masculine protest (36)
neuroses (34)
object relations (39)
Oedipus complex (32)
oral stage (31)
penis envy (32)
perceptual conscious (27)
phallic stage (32)
phenomenological approach (43)
pleasure principle (28)
positive regard (44)
preconscious (27)
projection (29)
psychoanalysis (26)
psychodynamic perspective (26)
psychosexual development (31)
psychosis (34)
psychosocial development (38)
rationalization (30)
reaction formation (30)
reality principle (28)
regression (30)
repression (29)
self-actualization (43)
self psychology (39)
separation-individuation (39)
structural hypothesis (27)
sublimation (31)
superego (28)
unconscious (27)
undoing (30)
valuing process (43)
will-to-meaning (47)

SUMMARY

- The psychodynamic perspective holds that much of our behavior is not the result of conscious choice but is driven by unconscious, internal forces which often reflect our childhood experiences and family relationships.
- Sigmund Freud's theory of psychoanalysis laid the foundation for the psychodynamic perspective. The key concept in Freud's theory is the depth hypothesis, the idea that almost all mental activity takes place outside conscious awareness. The preconscious consists of information that can be easily retrieved, but the unconscious contains material that has been actively forgotten, or repressed.
- Freud held that psychology cannot limit itself to observations but must use interpretation to probe beneath manifest (surface) reasoning to identify latent (unconscious) motivations. The goal of psychoanalysis, in Freud's words, is "to make the unconscious conscious."
- Freud later proposed the structural hypothesis, which divides the mind into three forces—the id, ego, and superego. Present from birth, the id consists of primitive biological drives, the most powerful of which are sex and aggression. The id operates on the pleasure principle, ignoring reason, reality, and morality. The ego develops later and operates on the reality principle, seeking ways to gratify the id that are both safe and effective. The superego, which develops last, represents the moral standards of society and parents that the child internalizes. Rigid and uncompromising, the superego demands perfection. The ego's task is to satisfy the id without provoking the superego.
- The id, ego, and superego coexist in a state of dynamic tension, which may explode at any time. Anxiety results when the ego senses danger. Most anxiety is not experienced consciously but is held in check by defense mechanisms, including repression, projection, displacement, rationalization, isolation, intellectualization, denial, reaction formation, regression, undoing, identification, and sublimation. Though often adaptive, overuse of defense mechanisms may interfere with thought processes and everyday functioning.
- Freud viewed personality as the product of childhood psychosexual development, from the oral and anal stages to the phallic, latency, and genital stages. At each stage the child is forced to resolve conflicts between his or her biological urges and social restraints. Under- or overgratification at any stage may create anxiety and lead to maladaptive adult behavior.
- Freud believed that both normal and abnormal behavior result from interactions among the id, ego, and superego. A healthy adult has the ego strength to balance conflicting demands by the id and the superego. When the ego expends too much energy on defense mechanisms, however, it is weakened. This produces rigid behavior patterns, called neuroses. In extreme cases, the ego collapses and adaptive functioning ceases, a condition known as psychosis.
- Freud's theories were extended and modified by a number of other thinkers. Post-Freudian theorists

tended to put less emphasis on the id and more on the ego; to focus less on sexual drives, or libido, and more on personal fulfillment and social relationships; and to pay less attention to childhood traumas and more to present circumstances and ongoing development.

- Among the most influential post-Freudian theorists, many of whom were Freud's students, are Carl Jung, who developed the concept of a collective unconscious, a set of symbols shared by all humankind that is a source of creativity and wholeness; Alfred Adler, who saw the failure to achieve goals, and corresponding feelings of inferiority, as a major source of psychological problems; Harry Stack Sullivan, who focused on interpersonal relationships, not only between parents and child, man and woman, but also between same-sex friends; Karen Horney, for whom basic anxiety caused weak parent-child attachment, led to interpersonal neurotic trends; Heinz Hartmann, whose ego psychology created a bridge between psychoanalytic theory and cognitive psychology; and Erik Erikson, who saw the development of ego identity as the product of lifelong psychosocial development. One of the most influential schools in contemporary psychodynamic psychology is object-relations theory (in which "objects" are the people to whom an individual is emotionally attached). Margaret Mahler studied the processes whereby children establish psychological separation from their mothers, or individuation; Heinz Kohut developed self psychology and identified narcissistic personality disorder.
- The psychodynamic perspective has been criticized for lack of experimental support, dependence on inference, unrepresentative sampling, cultural biases (especially relating to gender differences), and a negative portrait of human nature. But psychodynamic theory played a major role in demystifying abnormal behavior by exposing the irrationality of everyday life and showing that normal and abnormal behavior are not so much distinct categories as points on a continuum. Psychodynamic theory has also had an enormous impact on Western culture by calling attention to the inner world of dreams and fantasies.
- Humanistic-existential psychology is both an outgrowth of and a reaction to psychodynamic theory. Humanistic and existential thinkers reject the determinism of psychodynamic theory and the passivity this implies. Rather they emphasize the human capacity for growth, freedom to choose one's fate, and responsibility for one's decisions. Although similar in many ways, humanistic psychology is more concerned with individuality, and existential psychology, with the human condition.
- Humanistic psychology sees people as basically good, rational, and social beings. Human beings are distinguished from other animals by their drive toward self-actualization, the fulfillment of one's capacities. Abnormal behavior occurs when this drive is blocked, either because of incongruence between a person's behavior and his or her true self (Carl Rogers' theory) or because of a failure to satisfy basic needs (Abraham Maslow's theory). Both theorists held that psychotherapy should aim not only to help people with damaged psyches but also to help people who are functioning adequately to lead richer lives.
- Existentialist psychology focuses on alienation, or feelings of meaninglessness, and on the struggle to live authentically, by one's own principles and values. It stresses the importance of the present and future as opposed to the past. Rollo May concentrates on the ontological context and the individual's subjective sense of self, or center; Victor Frankl, on the struggle to find meaning through values; and R. D. Laing, on the hypocracies of contemporary society and the "insanity" of attempting to adapt to a "mad world."
- The humanistic-existential perspective has not had the impact of the psychodynamic approach. Rather, its influence is seen in the greater emphasis on empathy with patients and clients and a concern with personal growth rather than mere adjustment.

FIRST
PLACE

3

THE BEHAVIORAL, INTERPERSONAL, COGNITIVE, AND SOCIOCULTURAL PERSPECTIVES

In the last chapter we considered two perspectives, the psychodynamic and humanistic-existential, whose primary interest is the subjective experience of the individual, something that, because it cannot be observed, is difficult to study. In the present chapter we turn to four perspectives that concern themselves with experience in its more observable aspects. For the behavioral perspective, the primary focus is behavior itself: observable action. For adherents of the cognitive perspective, subjective experience is more important—their subject is cognition, or mental processing—but only insofar as such experience can be studied objectively, as measurable behavior. For the interpersonal and sociocultural perspectives, the main concern is the individual's social environment, again a matter of observable phenomena. Given these concerns, these four perspectives are more empirical, less intuitive, than the psychodynamic and humanistic-existential schools.

All four are products of the twentieth century, and arose in reaction to prior philosophies of behavior—behaviorism as a reaction to psychodynamic theory and to the introspective method; cognitive theory as a reaction, in some measure, to the extreme focus on observable behavior of classical behavioral theory; and interpersonal and sociocultural theories as a reaction to psychology itself, with its habit of viewing abnormal behavior as a problem in the person rather than in the social context.

THE BEHAVIORAL PERSPECTIVE

Perhaps the most fundamental assumption of psychodynamic theory is that what you see is not what you've got. Behavior and even thought, insofar as it is conscious, are only the surface of mental functioning; its substance lies beneath, in remote, unconscious processes. It is on this point that the **behavioral perspective,** which views behavior as the result of learning, departs most radically from psychodynamic thought. For the behaviorists, the most important causes of behavior are *proximal* causes, causes that lie close to the behavior itself and can therefore be readily identified (Bandura, 1986; Bootzin & Max, 1980). Faced with a student who is depressed after failing an exam, a psychodynamic theorist would take the exam as a jumping-off point for more fundamental explorations: How did failure during childhood affect his relationship with his parents? And what are the chances that perhaps his true emotion is not depression but something that the depression is covering—anger at his parents, for example. Faced with the same student, the behavioral theorist would be more interested in current experiences: What did the student say to himself before the exam and after? What circumstances in his environment may have caused the failure, and what current circumstances may now be operating to encourage the response of depression?

This difference in focus between psychodynamic and behavioral theorists is reflected in their methods. Psychodynamic theorists, interested in the inner reaches of the psyche, must frequently forgo scientific verifiability. The behaviorists' proximal focus, by contrast, is in part the result of their insistence on scientific method.

The Background of Behaviorism

An important component of many psychological theories in the late nineteenth century was *introspection,* the study of the mind by analysis of one's own thought processes. It was in reaction to this trend that behaviorism arose, claiming that the causes of behavior need not be sought in the depths of the mind but could be observed in the immediate environment, in stimuli that elicited, reinforced, and punished certain responses. The explanation, in other words, lay in **learning,** the process whereby behavior changes in response to the environment.

Actually, learning had long been recognized as an important influence on human character. But it was not until the early twentieth century that scientists began to uncover the actual mechanisms of learning, thereby laying the theoretical foundation for behaviorism. The contributions of four particular scientists—Ivan Pavlov, John B. Watson, Edward Lee Thorndike, and B. F. Skinner—were especially crucial.

Pavlov: The Conditioned Reflex In conducting research with dogs, Ivan Pavlov (1849–1936), a Russian neurophysiologist, found that if he consistently sounded a tone at the same time that he gave a dog food, the dog would eventually salivate to the sound of the tone alone. Thus Pavlov discovered a basic mechanism of learning, the **conditioned reflex:** if a neutral stimulus (e.g., the tone) is paired with a nonneutral stimulus (e.g., the food), the organism will eventually respond to the neutral stimulus as it does to the nonneutral stimulus.

The implications of this discovery were revolutionary. Whereas it had always been assumed that

Ivan Pavlov won the Nobel prize in 1904 for his work on the physiology of the digestive system in dogs, but he is better remembered today for his discovery of the conditioned reflex.

human beings' reactions to their environment were the result of complicated subjective processes, Pavlov's finding raised the possibility that many of our responses, like those of the dogs, were the result of a simple learning process. In other words, our loves and hates, our tastes and distastes might be the consequences of nothing more mysterious than a conditioning process whereby various things in our environment became "linked" in our minds to other things that we responded to instinctively, such as food, warmth, and pain. Along with this greatly simplified view of psychology came the possibility of testing such processes empirically, under controlled conditions.

Watson: The Founding of Behaviorism It is John B. Watson (1878–1958), an American psychologist, who is credited with founding the behavioral movement. This is not because Watson made major contributions to the theory of behaviorism but rather because he publicized the empirical method and made it the battle cry for a new school of psychology, aggressively opposed to subjective approaches.

In a now-famous article, "Psychology as the Behaviorist Views It," Watson (1913) made his position clear: "Psychology, as the behaviorist views it, is a purely objective, experimental branch of natural science which needs introspection as little as do the sciences of chemistry and physics" (p. 176). Watson argued that introspection was, if anything, the province of theology. The province of psychology was behavior—that is, observable and measurable responses to specific stimuli. And the goal of psychology was the prediction and control of behavior.

Watson supported his rejection of the introspective method by demonstrating, in a classic experiment, that a supposedly subjective emotion such as fear could, like the salivation response of Pavlov's dogs, result from a simple, objective conditioning process. With the help of a colleague, Rosalie Rayner, Watson conditioned a fear of rats in an eleven-month-old boy, Albert B. (J. B. Watson & Rayner, 1920). Before the experiment, Albert had no fear of tame laboratory rats. On the first day of the experiment, the boy was shown a white rat. Watson then struck an iron bar with a hammer, producing a very loud noise. The first time this happened, Albert was simply startled. As it happened again and again, he began to show signs of fright—crying, falling over, crawling away from the rat. After seven pairings of the rat and the noise, Albert showed these reactions in response to the rat alone, without the noise. Thus a conditioned fear reaction had been established. Later tests showed that without further conditioning, Albert produced these sorts of behaviors in re-

Left: John B. Watson founded the behaviorist movement. He argued for an empirical approach to the study of human behavior. In his experiment with Albert B., he demonstrated that human emotions could be generated through observable conditioning processes.

Right: Edward L. Thorndike's major contribution to behavioral theory was the law of effect, which established the importance of consequences in the learning process.

sponse to a variety of stimuli similar to the rat: a rabbit, a dog, a sealskin coat, a bearded Santa Claus mask. Commenting on these results, Watson argued that many of our "unreasonable" fears are established in the same way that Albert's was—through conditioning.

Thorndike: The Law of Effect Another psychologist of Watson's time was Edward Lee Thorndike (1874–1949), whose early experiments with animals had a decisive influence on learning theory. Unlike Pavlov and Watson, who had studied the relationship between stimuli that preceded behavior, Thorndike was interested in the impact of such stimuli as *consequences* of behavior. If an organism is repeatedly presented with a pleasant or painful stimulus after making a given response, how will this affect the response?

In one experiment Thorndike placed a hungry cat in a box equipped in such a way that if the cat pulled a cord or pressed a lever, the door of the chamber flew open. When the cat escaped, it was given a piece of salmon to eat. In early trials the cat often took a long time to get out of the box. Gradually, however, the escape time grew shorter and shorter until finally the cat was no sooner placed in the box than it exited and collected its reward. Thorndike concluded that the reason the cat learned the proper escape response was that this response had become associated with the food, which was the consequence of escaping. From this conclusion Thorndike formulated what he called the **law of effect,** which stated that responses that lead to "satisfying" consequences are strengthened and therefore are likely to be repeated, while responses that lead to "unsatisfying" consequences are weakened and therefore are unlikely to be repeated.

Though Thorndike used objective methods in his experiments, Watson did not consider him a behaviorist, for he used subjective terms such as *satisfying* and *unsatisfying* to describe his observations. For the early behaviorists, all references to inferred mental states were unscientific and therefore to be avoided. Yet despite its subjective wording, Thorndike's law of effect had laid down another fundamental principle of learning: the importance of reward in the learning process.

Skinner: The Control of Behavior Following the pioneering discoveries of Pavlov and Thorndike, many prominent psychologists—including Edwin Guthrie, Edward Chase Tolman, Clark Hull, and B. F. Skinner—contributed to the development of learning theory. Of these, the one who has had the most decisive influence on the behavioral perspective was B. F. Skinner (1904–1990).

B. F. Skinner refined and extended earlier behavioral theories, demonstrating their applicability to everyday life.

Skinner's major contribution was to refine Thorndike's discoveries and to demonstrate their application to everyday life. Like Watson, Skinner was interested in the control of behavior, and he saw in Thorndike's law, which he renamed the *principle of reinforcement,* the basic mechanism for predicting and controlling human behavior. Skinner (1965) pointed out that our social environment is filled with reinforcing consequences, which mold our behavior as surely as the piece of salmon molded the behavior of Thorndike's cat. Our friends and families control us with their approval or disapproval. Our jobs control us by offering or withholding money. Our schools control us by passing us or failing us and thus affecting our access to jobs. Thus Skinner stated outright what Pavlov had merely suggested: that much of our behavior is based not on internal contingencies but on external contingencies. Furthermore, precisely because they *are* external, these contingencies can be altered to change our behavior. As we shall see, this is a fundamental principle of behavioral treatment in abnormal psychology.

The Assumptions of Behavioral Psychology

Before we go on to discuss the mechanisms of learning, we will review the basic assumptions of behaviorism as it developed in the hands of the scientists whose work we just discussed.

The first assumption is that the task of psychology is, as Watson claimed, the study of behavior—

that is, the study of the responses that an organism makes to the stimuli in its environment. Such stimuli may come from outside us—from the people, objects, and events in our external environment. They can also be internal, such as back pain, which may elicit the response of taking a pill. Likewise, responses may be external (e.g., pounding a table in anger) or internal (e.g., the thought "I'm not going to show her I'm angry").

A second basic assumption has to do with methodology. According to classical behaviorism, both stimuli and responses are objective, empirical events that can be observed and measured, and that *must* be observed and measured in order to qualify as scientific evidence. Hence behavioral studies since the time of Pavlov have always attempted to include careful measurement of responses.

A third assumption, again formulated by Watson, is that the goal of psychology is the prediction and control of behavior. In declaring this goal, Watson aligned behavioral psychology with the natural sciences, whose object is to discover and apply general laws. For the behaviorist working in a laboratory, under controlled environmental circumstances and with experimental animals whose conditioning history is known, prediction and control are realistic goals. But when the behaviorist moves out of the laboratory into the world at large and attempts to deal with human beings, prediction and control become more difficult. The environmental stimuli of everyday life are infinitely more varied, complex, and uncontrollable than those of the laboratory. Furthermore, the responses of human beings are far more complicated—and their conditioning histories far less knowable—than those of the white rat. One might predict, for example, that a hungry boy, when called to dinner, might go directly to the dinner table. But if the boy has come to associate dinnertime with his parents' quarreling, then he may be just as likely to lock himself in his room. Many behaviorists would now argue that these more nebulous variables—associations, feelings—can also be pinpointed, just like the dinner call. Finally, ethical considerations greatly limit the scientist's control over human subjects. (Today, for example, Watson's experiment with Albert B. would not be considered ethically permissible.) Still, the behavioral position is that human responses to various kinds of stimuli can be stated as general laws and that when a response is interfering with a person's adjustment, that response can be changed by changing the stimuli in question.

The final basic assumption of behaviorism is that the major ingredient in behavior is learning. As we have seen, behavioral psychology was founded on learning theory. The two are not synonymous, for behaviorism is method as well as theory. Behavioral psychology might best be defined as the application of learning theory and other experimentally derived principles to human behavior (Bootzin, 1975). Nevertheless, the behaviorists do regard learning as the central component of behavior, and it is primarily in terms of learning theory that they try to explain both normal and abnormal behavior.

The Basic Mechanisms of Learning

Respondent Conditioning According to traditional behavioral theory, all behavior falls into two categories, respondent and operant. **Respondent behavior**—behavior that occurs reflexively, or automatically, in response to specific stimuli—consists of *unconditioned responses* and *conditioned responses*. Unconditioned responses are simple responses, such as blinking or salivation, that occur automatically when elicited by certain stimuli. It is possible, however, through the pairing of stimuli, to condition an organism so that it will show a similar response to a neutral stimulus, one that would not naturally have elicited the response. The learning of such a conditioned response is called **respondent conditioning** (or *classical conditioning*). An excellent example is one we discussed above: Pavlov's dog experiment. As we saw, Pavlov presented the dog with the food and the tone together, and eventually the dog salivated to the tone alone. Since a hungry dog will salivate naturally, that is, without conditioning, when presented with food, the food is designated as an **unconditioned stimulus** (UCS) and the natural response of salivation as the **unconditioned response** (UCR). And since the dog's salivation to the tone was the result of conditioning, the tone is called the **conditioned stimulus** (CS) and the salivation to the tone alone, without the food, the **conditioned response** (CR).

Operant Conditioning In respondent behavior, the organism responds to the environment; in **operant behavior,** as the name suggests, the organism operates on the environment—in short, *does* something—in order to achieve a desired result. Unlike respondent behavior, all operant behavior is the result of conditioning. In **operant conditioning** (also called *instrumental conditioning*), the likelihood of a response is increased or decreased by virtue of its consequences. Having taken a certain action, the organism learns to associate that action with certain consequences. This perceived association between action and consequence is called a **contingency,** and it will direct the organism's behavior in the future: the organism will repeat the behavior, or cease to engage in it, in order to obtain or avoid the consequence. This, of course, is Thorndike's law of effect, and a good example is Thorndike's cat. After a few accidental pressings of the lever, resulting in an open door and piece of fish, the cat eventually learned to associate these consequences with the pressing of the lever. Consequently, it began to press the lever as soon as it was put in the box. According to behavioral theory, human beings, like the cat, learn to do things that will bring them the results they want.

Reinforcement and Punishment Were it not for the fish, Thorndike's cat would not have learned to press the lever. Were it not for the paycheck, most people would not go to work. Operant conditioning depends on **reinforcement,** whereby behavior is increased or maintained by rewarding consequences. As Skinner pointed out, the world is full of reinforcers. The simplest type, the **primary reinforcer,** is one to which we respond instinctively, without learning—for example, food, water, warmth, and sex. Most of the reinforcers to which we respond, however, are not the simple primary reinforcers but rather **conditioned reinforcers** (also called *secondary reinforcers*), stimuli to which we have learned to respond by associating them with primary reinforcers. Money is a good example of a conditioned reinforcer. We respond to it positively not because we have an instinctive liking for green pieces of paper printed with symbols but because those pieces of paper are associated with past reinforcers and signal the future delivery of further reinforcers.

Modes of reinforcement Reinforcement operates on behavior in four basic ways. In **positive reinforcement** a response is followed by a positive reinforcer, with the result that the response *increases* in frequency. Suppose a child dresses herself for school for the first time. Her parents reward her by saying, "Good girl!" and giving her pancakes for breakfast in the hope that she will dress herself the next morning. If she does, we can say that positive reinforcement has occurred.

A second type of reinforcement that increases the frequency of behavior is **negative reinforcement.** In this case, however, what promotes the response is *the avoidance or removal of an aversive stimulus.* (Negative reinforcement should not be confused with punishment, the suppression of a response through the presentation of an aversive stimulus. This mechanism will be discussed shortly.) To understand negative reinforcement, let us imagine that a student fails to study for an exam and consequently is exposed to the aversive stimulus of receiving an F. If he or she then studies for the next exam, avoids an F, and in consequence goes on studying for exams in the future, negative reinforcement has taken place.

This process, also called *avoidance learning,* can teach us some very useful behaviors, as in the example just cited. However, behaviorists feel that it may also be responsible for many patterns of abnormal behavior. For example, the little boy who is bitten by a dog may afterward simply run the other way whenever he sees a dog, and every time he flees, the reduction of his fear will reinforce the escape response. As a result, the dog phobia will be maintained indefinitely.

While reinforcement has the effect of promoting a response, **punishment** acts to suppress responses. *Positive punishment* occurs when an organism, in order to obtain some consequence, stops performing a behavior. Modern agriculture provides a good example. To stabilize crop prices, the government often limits farm production by giving farmers subsidies for *not* growing crops. So, to gain the subsidy (positive), the farmers decrease their farming (punishment, because a behavior is being suppressed).

Positive punishment is rare, however. Far more common is *negative punishment,* in which the organism, in order to avoid a consequence, stops performing a behavior. For example, when we strike a dog with a newspaper for chewing on the furniture or scold a child for hitting another child, we are trying to use negative punishment, and if the dog and the child therefore indulge less frequently in these behaviors, we have succeeded.

So operant conditioning is defined along two dimensions: whether the consequence is being sought or avoided, and whether the target behavior thereby increases or decreases in frequency. This scheme produces the four kinds of operant conditioning shown in Figure 3.1. The different categories are sometimes confused, for a number of reasons. First, similar consequences do not have similar effects on all people. For example, we think of scolding as a punishment, and when we scold a child for aggressive behavior, we would expect the aggression to decrease. But in some troubled families, parental scolding actually results in *increased* aggression, a phenomenon called the *nega-*

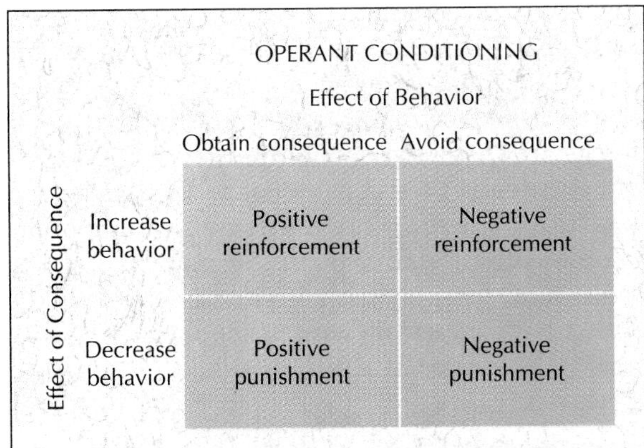

FIGURE 3.1 The four mechanisms of operant conditioning produced by crossing the likely effect of the target behavior *(obtain versus avoid consequences)* with the likely effect of the consequence *(increase versus decrease of target behavior).*

tive spiral (Patterson, 1982). So while the parent is trying to produce negative punishment, the child doesn't perceive it as such, and what is actually occurring is positive reinforcement. Another reason for confusion among the categories is that people find it hard to think of reinforcement as negative or punishment as positive, so they just call "pleasant" situations reinforcement and "unpleasant" situations punishment. Keep in mind that traditional behaviorists avoid referring to subjective concepts such as "pleasantness"; they are concerned only with observable behavior. Reinforcement increases the likelihood of a response; punishment decreases the likelihood of a response. Finally, the definition of a conditioning event does shift, legitimately, depending on which behaviors and consequences are targeted. Consider once again the farm subsidies. If the target behavior is crop production, then punishment has occurred, for crop production has decreased. But if the target behavior is cooperation with the government, then reinforcement has occurred, for cooperation has increased. To keep the categories clear when analyzing a situation, follow three steps. First, pinpoint the target behavior and the target consequence. Second, decide whether the frequency of the target behavior was increased (reinforcement) or decreased (punishment). Third, determine whether the effect of this change was to obtain the target consequence (positive) or avoid it (negative).

Other Mechanisms Associated with Learning

In addition to defining respondent and operant conditioning, psychologists have identified a number of other mechanisms associated with learning. These mechanisms don't explain how learning occurs, but they help to explain its scope and complexity, as well as the conditions under which it occurs.

Extinction The most important of these mechanisms is **extinction,** the elimination of a response by ending the conditioning that created it. In respondent conditioning, as we saw, a CS comes to be paired with a UCS, creating a CR. By the same token, the CR will extinguish if the UCS is unpaired, that is, repeatedly presented *without* the CS. Take, for example, the case of the dog-phobic child. Just as his fear was created by the pairing of the dog (CS) with the bite (UCS), so it will dissipate if he repeatedly encounters dogs who don't bite. (And that is how dog phobias are generally treated by behavioral therapists. The trick is to get the phobic person to play with friendly dogs so that extinction can take place.) As for operant behaviors, here extinction simply requires the removal of the reinforcement that is maintaining the response. Such a process is probably involved in the normal child's gradual abandonment of infantile behaviors. When temper tantrums are no longer rewarded by parental attention, they are likely to extinguish. Similarly, behavior will extinguish if punishment is withdrawn. When a child is no longer scolded for crossing a street unattended, this behavior will no longer be avoided.

Generalization Another important aspect of learning is the process of **generalization,** whereby once an organism has been conditioned to respond in a certain way to a particular stimulus, it will respond in the same way to similar stimuli without further conditioning. In other words, the conditioned response automatically "spreads," or generalizes, to things that resemble the conditioned stimulus. Once again, we have already seen an example: Albert B.'s spontaneous fear of rabbits, dogs, sealskin coats, and Santa Claus masks once he was conditioned to fear the white rat.

Discrimination The opposite side of the coin from generalization is **discrimination**—that is, learning to distinguish among similar stimuli and to respond only to the appropriate one. Pavlov, for instance, found at first that a number of different tones, close in frequency, would elicit his dogs' salivation response, but when only one of those tones was consistently accompanied by food, the dogs learned to salivate to that tone only. Likewise, people learn to discriminate between similar stim-

Researchers often use the mechanism of habituation to study the behavior and abilities of preverbal infants. Babies reveal what they already expect, or know, by looking at familiar items for briefer intervals. According to Karen Wynn of the University of Arizona, infants, once they are habituated to correct combinations of Mickey Mouse dolls, look longer at incorrect ones (such as 2 + 1 = 2), thus demonstrating that they understand the rudiments of addition and subtraction.

uli—between a friendly smile and a malicious grin—when one turns out to have reinforcing consequences and the other does not.

Habituation A mechanism that modifies the effects of respondent conditioning is **habituation,** whereby repeated exposure to a stimulus results in the lessening of the organism's response to the stimulus. Cavalry horses, for example, must be trained not to start at the sound of gunfire, and this is done by exposing them to it again and again. At first they start and rear; in time, they ignore the sound. Likewise, people who have just moved to a big city will often be kept up all night by the sounds of the traffic—horns honking, tires screeching—but eventually they take no notice. Certain behavioral treatment programs are based on habituation. People with morbid fears of dirt may be asked to make mud pies; people with dog phobias will be shown videotapes of German shepherds. As with noise, the response tends to exhaust itself over time.

Shaping A process critical to operant conditioning is **shaping,** the reinforcement of *successive approximations* of a desired response until it finally achieves the desired form. Shaping is involved in the development of many of our skills. Imagine a child learning to dive. First she sits on the edge of the pool, puts her head down, and just sort of falls into the water. For this first step she receives a pat on the back (positive reinforcement) from the swimming teacher. Then she may start from a standing position and even hazard a little push as she takes off. This effort will be reinforced by further approval from the teacher, by the pleasure of a smoother descent into the water, and by her own feelings of achievement. Soon she will be ready for the diving board and then for fancier and fancier dives, with external and internal rewards at every step of the way. Thus throughout the process there is positive reinforcement of successive approximations of the diving response.

Modeling Actually, it is unlikely that the swimming teacher would ask the child to learn by trial and error. Instead, the teacher would dive into the

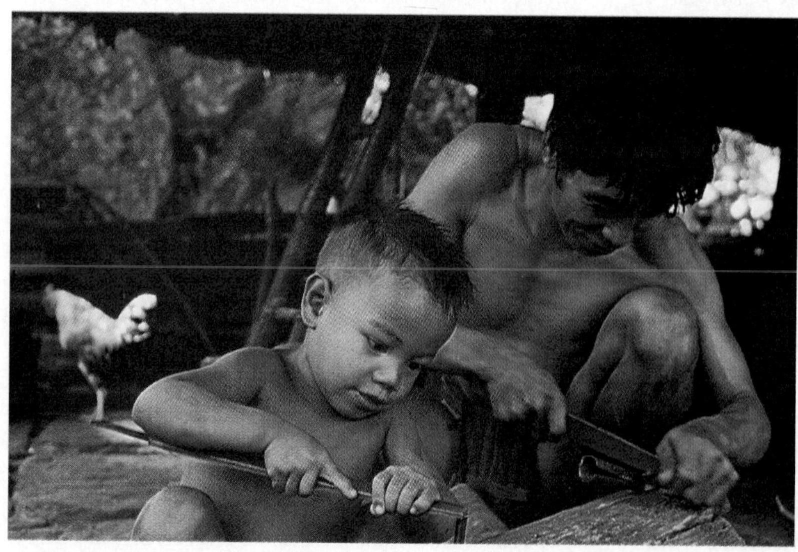

Modeling, which is controlled by internal processes, can occur without reinforcement: in order to be reproduced, a behavior simply has to be observed. Thus, by watching his father use woodworking tools, this boy in the Philippines develops his own skills.

pool to show the child the proper technique and would then reward her with approval for imitating the performance. This type of learning—learning through imitation—is known as **modeling** (Bandura & Walters, 1963; T. Rosenthal & Bandura, 1978).

As in the diving lesson, so in human development in general, modeling normally accompanies shaping—that is, we are rewarded for successive approximations of a modeled response. But the converse is not necessarily true. Many children get no pats on the back as they are learning how to dive; they simply watch someone else do it, and suddenly they too are doing it. A striking characteristic of modeling is that unlike many other forms of learning, it can—and often does—occur without any obvious external reinforcement (T. Rosenthal & Bandura, 1978). The discovery of this fact gave an immense push to the cognitive position within behaviorism. Clearly, if modeling is not controlled by external reinforcements, then it must be controlled by internal processes, processes occurring within the mind. And by extension, the same might well be true of other kinds of learning.

A summary of the various learning mechanisms is presented in the box on page 62.

Abnormal Behavior as a Product of Learning

Personality development, in the behavioral view, is simply the result of the interaction between our genetic endowment and the types of learning to which we are exposed by our environment. And according to the behaviorists, this is as true of abnormal development as it is of normal development. We have already seen, for example, how a dog phobia could develop through respondent conditioning and be maintained through negative reinforcement. Similarly, depression may be due in part to extinction: if significant positive reinforcements are withdrawn—a job lost, a marriage ended—many of a person's behaviors will simply extinguish, and he or she will become inactive, withdrawn, and dejected—in short, depressed.

These theories stress stimulus-response (S-R) mechanisms alone, but contemporary behaviorists are more likely to support theories that combine S-R mechanisms with cognitive processes and other factors to produce a complex picture of causality. The extinction theory of depression, for example, arose in the 1970s, with P. M. Lewinsohn as its leading proponent. Today Lewinsohn claims that extinction theory is no longer sufficient to account for depression. Instead, Lewinsohn and his colleagues have put forth a vicious-cycle theory involving many components, with stress leading to a disruption of ordinary behavior patterns, leading to reduced positive reinforcement (extinction theory), leading to increased self-awareness and self-criticism (cognitive processing), leading to feelings of hopelessness, leading to self-defeating behaviors that occasion further stress, thus taking the person through the cycle again (Lewinsohn, Hoberman, Teri, et al., 1985). Such explanations, favoring complexity over simplicity and attempting to incorporate all recent experimental findings, represent the coming of age of behavioral theory of abnormal behavior.

Despite their complexity, it is important to note that such theories still concentrate on proximal causes. In the behavioral view, psychopathology need not be explained by any "underlying" condition; it is the product of the same learned behaviors and cognitions that lead to normal behavior. As a corollary, behaviorists avoid using such terms as *normal* and *abnormal,* since these terms imply a clear distinction between something healthy and something sick. Instead, behaviorists see the range of human responses as a continuum, with all the responses being united by the same principles of learning. At one end of the continuum we can indeed identify responses that make it difficult for people to conduct their lives successfully, but these responses do not differ qualitatively from more adaptive responses. Hopelessness, as we just saw, may develop through the same mechanisms as hopefulness. Hence behaviorists, instead of designating such patterns *abnormal,* prefer the term *maladaptive.*

Likewise, behaviorists have traditionally been skeptical of the usefulness of labeling people according to diagnostic categories (e.g., phobia, schizophrenia, paranoia), since these categories, with their resemblance to medical diagnoses (e.g., pneumonia, cancer), seem to imply the medical model. That is, they suggest disease states—a suggestion that runs directly counter to the behaviorists' belief in the continuity of normal and abnormal. To the behaviorists, what is needed is not to put diagnostic labels on people but simply to specify as clearly as possible what the maladaptive behavior is, what contingencies may be eliciting and maintaining it, and how these contingencies may be rearranged in order to alter it (Hersen & Turner, 1984; Widiger & Costa, 1994).

In applying this sort of analysis to psychological abnormalities, the behaviorists do not claim that all such abnormalities are the result of learning alone, but only that learning may be an important

THE MECHANISMS OF LEARNING

	DEFINITION	EXAMPLE
RESPONDENT CONDITIONING	Pairing a neutral stimulus with a nonneutral stimulus until the organism learns to respond to the neutral stimulus as it would to the nonneutral stimulus	A child who has seen a taxicab strike a pedestrian learns to fear all taxis.
OPERANT CONDITIONING	Rewarding or punishing a certain response until the organism learns to repeat or avoid that response in anticipation of the positive or negative consequences	See specific examples below.
Positive reinforcement	Increasing the frequency of a behavior by rewarding it with consequences the organism wishes to obtain	Students praised by parents for studying study more and do better in school. AA programs reward alcoholics with praise, hugs, and certificates when they meet sobriety goals.
Negative reinforcement	Increasing the frequency of a behavior by removing a stimulus the organism wishes to avoid	A claustrophobic person goes on taking the stairs rather than the elevator, because he thereby avoids anxiety.
Positive punishment	Decreasing the frequency of a behavior by offering a consequence the organism wishes to obtain	A violent psychotic patient, offered extra privileges for every week that he does not get into a fight, becomes less aggressive.
Negative punishment	Decreasing the frequency of a behavior by offering a consequence the organism wishes to avoid	A child molester, in treatment, views pictures of naked children, becomes aroused, then inhales ammonia and learns not to be aroused by this stimulus.
EXTINCTION	Decreasing the frequency of a behavior by unpairing UCS and CS or behavior and reinforcement	A teacher decides to ignore an autistic child's disruptions in class, and the disruptions decrease.
GENERALIZATION	Spontaneously transferring a conditioned response from the conditioned stimulus to similar stimuli	A woman, after having been raped, begins to fear all men.
DISCRIMINATION	Learning to confine a response only to particular stimuli	In therapy, a hopeless depressed person learns to distinguish situations that can be changed from situations that cannot.
HABITUATION	Decreasing the frequency of response via repeated exposure to the stimulus	A person with severe anxiety about public speaking learns to control this by joining a group in which she is required to give a short speech to the members twice a week.
SHAPING	Reinforcing successive approximations of a desired response until that response is gradually achieved	A mentally retarded person is taught to make his bed by being praised first for pulling up the sheets and smoothing them down, then for pulling up the covers and smoothing them down, then for tucking them in.
MODELING	Learning by imitation	A person with a phobia for heights watches a model climb a fire escape and gradually learns to climb one herself.

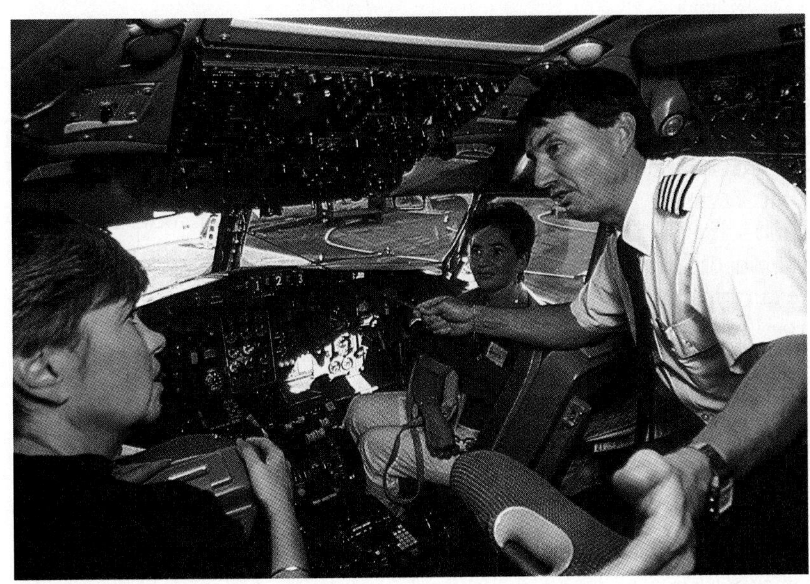

Programs to help people overcome their fear of flying use the principles of systematic desensitization. Here, a pilot explains the cockpit controls, thus removing some of the frightening mystery from air travel.

contribution and that, *whatever the cause,* relearning may help to alter the behavior. For example, no one would claim that the basic cause of mental retardation is faulty learning, yet many mentally retarded people have been greatly helped by behavior therapies.

Behavior Therapy The most decisive influence of the behavioral perspective has been in the area of treatment. The techniques that behaviorists have used to treat specific problems will be brought up in the chapters dealing with those problems, and the subject of **behavior therapy** as a whole will be discussed in Chapter 19. Here, however, we can introduce the topic by saying that behavior therapy concentrates on the behavior itself and attempts to alter it via the same types of learning that presumably engender behavior in the first place—reinforcement, punishment, extinction, discrimination, generalization, modeling, and so forth.

One of the earliest attempts at behavior therapy was a now-famous experiment by Mary Cover Jones (1924). What Jones did was essentially the reverse of Watson's respondent-conditioning experiment with Albert B. Whereas Watson had instilled a fear of furry animals in Albert by pairing the animals with an aversive stimulus, Jones eliminated a fear of furry animals in a boy named Peter by pairing the feared animals with a pleasant stimulus. She first got the child busy eating candy and then introduced a rabbit into the room at some distance from where the boy was sitting. On successive occasions the rabbit was brought closer and closer, again while the child was eating, and eventually he was able to touch it without exhibiting any fear. The rabbit was thus paired with the pleasant stimulus of the candy so that eventually it took on pleasant associations. At the same time, whatever unpleasant consequences the child expected from his encounter with the rabbit did not take place, with the result that the fear, lacking reinforcement, was extinguished.

The most widely discussed treatment via respondent conditioning is *systematic desensitization,* a technique developed by the psychiatrist Joseph Wolpe (1958, 1973) for relieving anxiety. In this procedure, patients imagine their anxiety-eliciting stimuli (e.g., dogs, exams, heights) under conditions that inhibit the development of anxiety—usually a state of deep muscle relaxation. Through repeated pairings of the stimulus with the relaxed state, the stimulus gradually loses its power to arouse anxiety. This technique has had a major influence on the development of behavior therapy and has now been incorporated into behavioral treatments for a vast range of problems, from sexual dysfunction to alcoholism—indeed, any problem in which anxiety is thought to play an important role.

Operant conditioning has also been widely used in behavior therapy. Through shaping, schizophrenics have been taught to start speaking again after years of muteness (Isaacs, Thomas, & Goldiamond, 1960). Children with autism, a severe developmental disability, have also been taught to speak, as well as to reduce self-harming behavior, such as head banging, through operant conditioning (Carr & Durand, 1985; Lovaas, 1977, 1987). Such techniques have also helped Alzheimer's disease patients in nursing homes learn self-care and other skills (Carstensen & Fisher, 1991).

Evaluating Behaviorism

Behavioral Theory versus Other Theories For reasons outlined above, behaviorists have forthrightly opposed competing theories of abnormal behavior: the medical model, the psychodynamic perspective, the humanistic-existential perspective. But these other theories are not just scientific constructs; they are outgrowths of some of our most deeply ingrained beliefs—for example, the belief that the psychologically disturbed are "different" from the rest of us (medical model) and that psychological disturbance has its roots deep in the psyche (psychodynamic and humanistic-existential theory). Hence the disagreements between behaviorism and these other schools are not just quibbles over details. Though the behaviorists shy away from grand philosophical claims, the fact remains that their theory of behavior constitutes a drastic revision of Western thought on the subject of human life. As such, it has been severely criticized.

Criticisms of Behaviorism

Oversimplification A primary objection to behaviorial theory is that it oversimplifies human life. In particular, the behaviorists' technique of reducing human existence to small, measurable units of behavior has been criticized as a naive simplification, one that distorts the very data they are measuring. Furthermore, critics claim that by excluding the inner life from consideration, classical behaviorists have chosen to ignore everything that distinguishes a human being from an experimental animal. From the standpoint of introspective theories, they ignore the deeper workings of the mind. Introspective theories sacrifice rigor for the sake of these intangibles; behaviorists sacrifice the intangibles for the sake of rigor.

Determinism The second major focus of criticism is the deterministic emphasis of behaviorism. According to behaviorists, most human behavior is the product of respondent and operant conditioning. Thus it is not free will but rather the stimuli in our environments that determine what we will do with our lives.

Skinner (1965), for example, argued that the notion of human freedom was simply obsolete:

> The free inner man who is held responsible for the behavior of the external biological organism is only a prescientific substitute for the kinds of causes which are discovered in the course of a scientific analysis. All these alternative causes lie *outside* the individual. . . . These are the things that make the individual behave as he does. For them he is not responsible, and for them it is useless to praise or blame him. (pp. 447–448)

If we follow this idea to its conclusion, there is no foundation for any kind of legal system, for any religious belief, or for any moral code. Law, religion, and morality are all based on the notion that we are capable of choosing between right and wrong, whereas according to Skinner, whatever we do—whether we treat other people kindly or brutally, whether we behave ourselves or lie, cheat, and steal—we do these things because our conditioning history has programmed us to do them. Needless to say, such ideas have been coldly received by humanistic and existential theorists, who emphasize free will and moral responsibility.

The issue of "control" Finally, the word *control,* as used by the behaviorists, often makes people uneasy. Skinner in particular aroused fears with his descriptions of how all behavior is controlled by environmental reinforcers and how we could lead happier lives if we simply admitted we were controlled and set about designing better reinforcement programs. Such "behavioral engineering," as critics noted, could conceivably become the basis of a totalitarian regime in which people were coerced not by force but by reinforcement.

Actually, the term *control,* in the behavioral vocabulary, does not mean coercion. It means predictability and adherence to scientific laws. Still, the mere fact that behaviorists feel they can identify the factors that control our behavior has caused some critics to worry that such knowledge, in irresponsible hands, might lead to coercion. Actually, psychology in general could arouse the same concern, for all psychologists attempt to identify the factors that cause human beings to behave as they do. It is only because the behaviorists have focused on external variables—those, in other words, that can be manipulated—that they have been the primary object of "mad scientist" suspicions.

It should be added that Skinner's belief in the power of reinforcement alone, exclusive of mental processes, has not been validated by research. Results of behavioral therapy, and particularly the high relapse rates among substance abusers (Nicolosi, Molinari, Musicco, et al., 1991), show that behavioral techniques are futile without the cooperation of the patient. Free or not, will is a critical factor in therapy, even behavioral therapy.

The Contributions of Behaviorism There is much

that can justly be said in favor of behaviorism. In the first place, the objectivity of behavioral research is not a virtue to be slighted. Indeed, a major problem with most of the other psychological perspectives is that their statements on human behavior are often vague, based more on inference than on fact, and open to the charge of bias. In contrast, the behaviorists' findings are expressed much more concisely and as much as possible are based on actual, measurable evidence, with the result that they can easily be retested by other professionals. The value of such precision has not gone unnoticed. Almost all psychological research is now behavioral in method. That is, it is based on experimentation and on objective measurement. If inferred constructs are used, they are "operationalized," that is, defined in terms of concrete behaviors.

Second, while the behaviorists are accused of doing away with individualism, it can be argued that individualism is safer with the behaviorists than it is with psychologists of other schools of thought. For unlike many other psychologists, the behaviorists recognize a broad range of responses as legitimate and are very sensitive to the adverse effects of labeling people as "abnormal."

Finally, the treatment methods developed by the behaviorists have produced some promising results, and with a wide range of disorders: phobia, depression, insomnia, conduct disorders (delinquency), and such health-related problems as overeating, smoking, and hypertension. Behavior therapy takes less time, is less expensive, and in many cases has been found more effective than other forms of treatment. In addition, substantial contributions have been made in education, business, and sports physiology through the application of behavioral principles. Such successes do not necessarily support the behaviorists' claim that learning is the source of abnormal behavior: the fact that conditioning can eliminate a response does not prove that the response was acquired through conditioning. Nevertheless, even if they tell us nothing about cause, such treatments still constitute an achievement—one that no psychological perspective can afford to do without, no matter how intriguing its theories.

The success of behavior therapy may be due in part to the modesty of its stated goals. While a psychodynamic or humanistic-existential therapist may try to help patients find meaning in life or achieve self-knowledge, the behavioral therapist will typically try to help them achieve limited behavioral goals: fewer nights of insomnia, fewer anxiety attacks, fewer cigarettes smoked, and so on. As both cause and result of these differing goals, behavior therapy is more optimistic in tone than most insight therapies (Messer & Winokur, 1984). Psychoanalysis and existential therapies in particular tend to side with the "tragic" view of life; they see happiness as elusive, existence as a struggle. Behavioral therapists tend to believe in happy endings, as well they might, given the practical nature of the endings they seek.

THE COGNITIVE PERSPECTIVE

Although the **cognitive perspective,** which views abnormal behavior as the product of mental processing, did not become important in abnormal psychology until the 1970s, cognitive functions such as memory, reasoning, and problem solving had been of interest to psychologists ever since psychology began. Cognition is important to abnormal psychology for two reasons. First, many psychological disorders involve serious cognitive disturbances. For example, severely depressed people usually cannot concentrate—a condition that makes them fail at tasks and thus feel more depressed. Schizophrenics too have severe cognitive problems; typically, they cannot think or use language clearly. Second, it is believed that certain cognitive patterns may not be symptoms but actual causes of their associated disorders—a possibility that has given considerable impetus to cognitive research in the last few decades.

The Background of the Cognitive Perspective

At a time when the stimulus-response position was endorsed by most learning theorists, other theorists questioned the exclusion of such mental processes as emotion, thought, expectation, and interpretation. How is it, they asked, that the same stimulus can produce different responses in different human beings? For example, an avid golfer would find a tournament broadcast on TV exciting, but a nongolfer would find the same event utterly boring. Some other factor, in addition to the stimulus, must be influencing the response. Presumably, that other factor was **cognition,** or the mental processing of stimuli.

Given the variability of responses, some behaviorists questioned not only S-R theory but also the very principle of reinforcement. For example, Edward Tolman (1948) held that human beings learn not by reinforcement of trial-and-error responses but by perceiving the relationship among various elements of the task. Reinforcement, Tolman argued, affected learning by creating expectancies, inner "predictions" as to which responses would lead to rewards and punishments in which situations. As for the responses themselves, they were learned through mental processes independent of reinforcement. Tolman and Honzig (1930) demonstrated this principle by showing that if rats were given a chance to explore a maze, without reinforcement, then later, when reinforcement was available, these rats would run the maze faster than other rats that had not had an opportunity to explore the apparatus. In other words, the rats had learned something without being rewarded for it.

Cognitive Behaviorism

Thus behaviorism no sooner developed S-R theory than it produced a cognitive challenge to that theory. As we shall see, an alliance between these two, called **cognitive behaviorism,** has produced valuable results in the form of refined theories and treatments. The central claim of the cognitive behaviorists is that people's actions are often responses not so much to external stimuli as to their own individual mental processing of those stimuli. These theorists claim that though cognitive events are not objectively observable, they are learned responses and thus are subject to the same laws as other behavior. Ultimately, theory and research on cognitive factors and their role in influencing behavior developed into a broader movement within psychology known as the cognitive perspective.

As the term *cognitive behaviorism* suggests, the two perspectives share certain assumptions. Cognitive theorists emphasize observation and measurement of behavior. Most cognitive theorists are thus to some extent cognitive behaviorists, even though the cognitive perspective is now highly influential in its own right.

Besides its importance in providing new theories about behavior, the cognitive perspective has had a decided influence on the process of psychotherapy. We shall consider cognitive therapies in more detail in Chapter 19, but here we will note how two of the most influential thinkers within the cognitive perspective, Albert Ellis and Aaron T. Beck, developed their ideas about the role of cognition in abnormal behavior from working with clients in therapy.

Albert Ellis: Irrational Beliefs Albert Ellis (b. 1913) developed what has come to be known as *rational-emotive therapy,* which is based on the idea that psychological problems are caused not by events in the outside world but by people's reacting to such events on the basis of irrational beliefs. Ellis (1962) has proposed an ABC system to explain how this process works: A is the activating experience; B, the beliefs or thoughts that irrationally follow; and C, the consequences for the person, both emotional and behavioral. Ellis (1980) suggests that most problems stem from certain core irrational beliefs, such as:

1 I must do well and win approval, or I rate as a rotten person.
2 Others must treat me considerately and kindly, or society and the universe should punish them.
3 I should be able to get all the things I want easily and quickly.

Most people, when they see these beliefs stated so bluntly, are able to recognize their irrationality. Yet they react to many events as if such statements were entirely true and reasonable. For example, a person may become extremely upset and depressed about some minor failing (reflecting irrational thought number 1) or angry at some slight (reflecting irrational thought number 2). Ellis' therapy involves confronting and disrupting the irrational beliefs (B) so that the emotional and behavioral consequences (C) will change accordingly.

Aaron T. Beck: Cognitive Distortions In a number of influential books and articles, Aaron T. Beck (1921–) has pointed out that psychological disorders are often associated with specific patterns of distorted thinking (1963, 1967, 1976; Beck, Emery, & Greenberg, 1985; Beck, Rush, Shaw, et al., 1979). In depression, for example, the distorted thoughts center on a pessimistic view of the self, the world, and the future—the "negative triad," as Beck calls it. In anxiety, the distorted thoughts center on threats of danger. The cognitive distortions Beck has identified include magnification (seeing minor events as far more important than they are), overgeneralization (drawing a broad conclusion from little evidence), and selective abstraction (paying attention only to certain kinds of evidence while ignoring other equally relevant information). These distortions operate automatically, without a person's being aware of them. Thus, a person who becomes extremely depressed at not receiving a birthday card from one family member, while receiving cards from many other relatives and friends, would probably be engaging in all three kinds of cognitive distortion. In Beck's therapy, clients are led to discover their distorted thoughts and to replace them with more reasonable and valid thoughts.

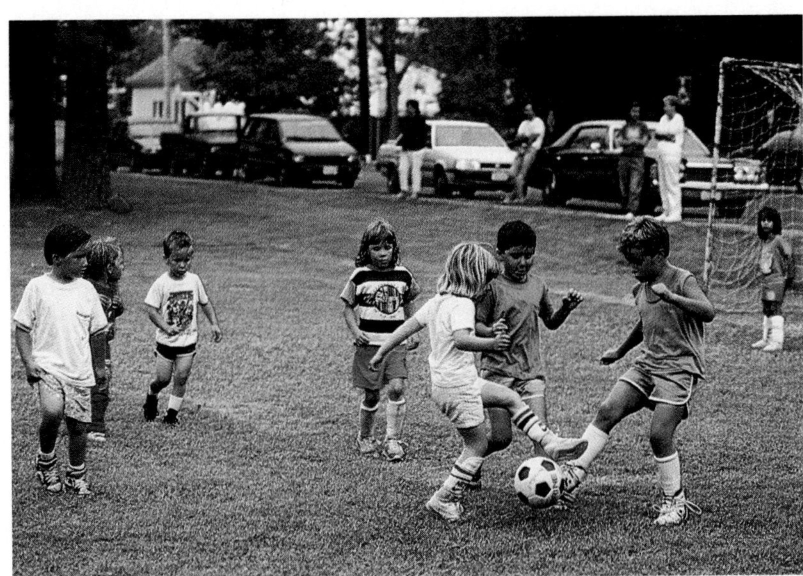

Cognitive behaviorists believe that our cognitive appraisal of our competence affects our behavior in relevant situations. People who learn athletic skills in childhood are likely to feel confident about participating in sports—and perhaps other group activities—later in life.

We shall refer to Ellis and Beck in other chapters in this book. Now let us consider some of the cognitive processes that they and other thinkers within this perspective have identified as crucial to abnormal behavior.

Cognitive Appraisal

Cognitive theorists have disputed the behaviorists' tight link between stimulus and response. In between, they claim, comes the all-important process of **cognitive appraisal.** In this process, the person, before reacting, evaluates the stimulus in light of his or her own memories, beliefs, and expectations. It is this internal mental activity that accounts for the wide differences in individual responses to the same external stimulus. Faced with a banana split, one person may attack it with gusto; a second person, in whom this stimulus calls up thoughts regarding the social desirability of being thin, may pick at the sundae more delicately; a third person, for whom the stimulus arouses fears regarding the medical dangers of butterfat and refined sugar, may extract the banana, eat that, and walk away. Likewise, two people giving a lecture may react quite differently to the stimulus of seeing several members of the audience get up and walk out in the middle of the talk. One may say to himself, "Oh, I must be boring them to tears. I knew I would make a bad lecturer." And to this cognitive appraisal he will respond by becoming anxious, perspiring, and perhaps stumbling over his words. Another lecturer, with a more positive view of herself and her speaking skills, interprets the people's departure as due to circumstances external to herself: "They must have a class to catch. Too bad they have to leave; they will miss a good talk" (Meichenbaum, 1975, p. 358). And she will proceed, unruffled, with her lecture.

In other words, what determines the response is not the stimulus itself but the person's interpretation of the stimulus. As the Greek philosopher Epictetus put it, "Men are disturbed not by things but by the views they take of them"—a maxim that cognitive theorists are fond of quoting.

Attributions One form of cognitive appraisal that has attracted a number of researchers is **attribution,** our beliefs about the causes of life events (B. Weiner, Frieze, Kokla, et al., 1971). Research in this area has focused on three dimensions of attribution: global/specific, stable/unstable, and internal/external. Consider, for example, a woman who was recently fired. How she explains this event to herself will affect her emotional state. Internal attributions ("I can't handle pressure") are much more damaging to self-esteem than external attributions ("My boss was impossible to work for!"). Likewise, broad-based or global attributions ("I'm incompetent") are more destructive than specific attributions ("I don't belong in sales") and long-term or stable attributions ("I'll never get ahead") are more harmful than unstable attributions ("I picked the wrong job"). As we will see in Chapter 10, people who habitually attribute failures to global, stable, internal faults have an attributional style that makes them more vulnerable to feelings of hopelessness and helplessness, and ultimately more susceptible to depression (Abramson, Metalsky, & Alloy, 1989; Abramson, Seligman, & Teasdale, 1978).

Cognitive Variables Affecting Behavior What types of processes are involved in cognitive appraisal? Walter Mischel (1973, 1979) has proposed five basic categories of cognitive variables that help to determine individual responses to a given stimulus:

1 *Competencies*. Each of us has a unique set of skills, acquired through past learning, for dealing with various situations. If one person has learned to respond to pushiness by standing up for himself and another person has not, these two people will react differently when someone cuts in front of them in the checkout line at the supermarket.
2 *Encoding strategies*. Each of us has a special way of perceiving and categorizing experience. One woman, upon finding a copy of *Playboy* under her teenage son's mattress, may have a talk with the boy on the injustice of viewing women as sex objects. Another woman may think of the magazine as a normal sign of male puberty and just push it back under the mattress.
3 *Expectancies*. Through learning, each of us forms different expectations as to which circumstances are likely to lead to rewards and punishments. A student who has had very supportive teachers in math courses and one who has had very critical teachers will have different expectations about whether math courses are likely to be reinforcing.
4 *Values*. Each of us places different values on different stimuli. A person who values outdoor activities will find an invitation to go hiking more appealing than will someone who prefers watching TV.
5 *Plans and goals*. As a result of different learning histories, we also formulate different plans and goals, which then guide our behavior. If a store employee who hopes to become floor manager finds out that other employees are pilfering, he might report this to his boss, whereas an employee who hates the store and intends to quit soon might keep quiet.

Albert Bandura (1977, 1982, 1986) also sees behavior as regulated primarily by cognition, but whereas Mischel divides the cognitive territory into five categories of variables, Bandura has concentrated on one category, expectancies. Bandura distinguishes between two types of expectancies: (1) *outcome expectancies*, expectations that a given behavior will produce a certain result, and (2) *efficacy expectancies*, expectations that one will be able to execute that behavior successfully. Bandura claims that efficacy expectancies are the chief determinant of coping behavior, and that they in turn are determined primarily by performance feedback from prior experience. Imagine, for example, that a woman who is afraid of flying must fly to a distant city for a job interview. Here the outcome expectancy is the woman's judgment as to how likely it is that the plane will get her to her destination. In this case, the outcome expectancy is quite high. But whether or not she will actually make the reservation depends more on her efficacy expectancy, her confidence as to whether she will actually be able to get on the plane and make the trip without incident. That confidence depends on how well she has managed similar stressful situations in the past.

Self-Reinforcement

Cognitive theorists agree with the behavioral position that behavior is molded by reinforcement and punishment, but they claim that the most potent rewards and punishments come not from the external environment but from the mind—in the form of self-approval and self-criticism. In some cases this cognitive reinforcement can lead to external reinforcement ("I just made it through that frightening plane trip—I'll go buy myself a steak"), but more often it remains on the cognitive level, in the form of self-congratulation ("I did just fine") and increased self-esteem. This mechanism of cognitive self-reinforcement may account for the fact that modeling often occurs without external reinforcement. Conceivably, the prospect of being like the admired model—teacher, mother, older brother, local football star—is sufficiently rewarding to fuel the response of imitation.

Information Processing

Information processing is a broad area of cognitive research concerned with how the human mind takes in, stores, interprets, and uses information from the environment. Cognitive researchers have learned, for example, to make a distinction between what they call automatic and controlled processing of information. *Automatic processing* requires little attention and yields quick, well-learned responses that remain stable over time. *Controlled processing*, on the other hand, requires logic and consideration as the mind integrates new information and devises a response. When a child with a skinned knee comes crying to a parent, for example, the parent will engage in automatic processing—not a lot of thought, but rather a quick succession of responses: consoling words, soap and water, bandage. But when, at age fourteen, the same child begins moping, coming in late from school, and spending time locked in his room, the parent, lacking any "formula" for this new problem, will have to engage in controlled processing. Many abnormal behavior patterns, such as phobias and other anxiety responses, can be viewed as the result of inappropriate automatic processing, and therapists have had some success in teaching people with these problems to convert to controlled processing (Kanfer & Hagerman, 1985).

As this talk of information processing suggests, many cognitive thinkers now take the computer as their model for the human mind. One great difference, however, between the computer and the human mind is that the former takes in information passively; whatever is put into it, it absorbs. The human mind, on the other hand, actively selects, and at times distorts, the information that it takes in. This fact makes cognitive research rather more slippery than computer studies.

Attention Human beings cannot possibly attend to, let alone process, all the information that bombards their senses at any given moment. So they take in only some information, the information that seems to them most important, and filter out the rest. This mechanism, an indispensable adaptive function, is called **selective attention.**

Some forms of psychopathology may be due to a failure in selective attention. It has been proposed, for example, that many of the symptoms of schizophrenia, such as distorted perceptions and unwanted thoughts, stem from a breakdown in selective attention, with the result that the mind is flooded with information (B. D. Cohen, Nachmani, & Rosenberg, 1974). Attention may be an important factor in other disorders as well. Depressives have been found to pay more attention to negative stimuli than do nondepressed people (Kuiper, Olinger, & MacDonald, 1988). Furthermore, most psychiatric disorders involve increased self-focused attention (Ingram, 1990). That is, people with these disorders spend an inordinate amount of time brooding about themselves and their problems. In part, this is undoubtedly a result of their problems—they are experiencing anxiety attacks or sexual dysfunction or whatever, and therefore they worry about themselves—but it may also be a cause, in that it seems to reduce their flexibility in considering how to solve their problems.

Organizing Structures The mind doesn't just choose what information it will take in. It also arranges that information in lasting and meaningful patterns, which then affect how other information will be taken in.

Schemas In the vocabulary of cognitive psychology, a **schema** is an organized structure of information about a particular domain of life—a structure that serves the person as a pattern for selecting and processing new information (Markus, 1977). Of particular interest to abnormal psychology are the *self-schemas,* the schemas that relate to our self-concept and identity. Most people have positive self-schemas—they see themselves as successful, talented, and well liked—and such a view is adaptive. It motivates people to pursue goals; it also protects them psychologically, causing them to focus on their successes and dismiss their failures as due to outside factors such as bad luck. By the same token, negative self-schemas are maladaptive, eroding motivation and causing people to focus on their failures. According to Aaron Beck, whose theories we discussed earlier, depression is due primarily to self-schemas dominated by themes of worthlessness, guilt, and deprivation. Beck believes that anxiety too is caused by distorted self-schemas, in this case dominated by themes of threat and uncertainty.

Beliefs A related cognitive theory is Albert Ellis' view that anxiety and depression are due to irrational beliefs. If, for example, a woman believes that she must be approved of by everyone, she will spend inordinate amounts of time trying to please others, even to her own detriment. As a result, her behavior will appear odd and inappropriate. Furthermore, it will allow no expression of her true preferences and interests—a sacrifice that will eventually give rise to feelings of acute frustration.

This is where treatment comes in, with cognitive therapists trying to induce patients to change their schemas and beliefs. A popular method, and one that is now often included in behavioral treatment, is *cognitive restructuring,* whereby the therapist teaches patients to revise their schemas by revising their interpretation of events—for example, by admitting to themselves that if a wished-for phone call hasn't come, its absence doesn't necessarily mean that they are worthless or unlovable. This chipping away at negative schemas will ultimately result in the formation of new schemas and more adaptive behavior (Nasby & Kihlstrom, 1986).

Evaluating the Cognitive Perspective

Criticisms of Cognitive Psychology Cognitive theory is open to the same criticism as any other theory depending on inference: that it is unscientific, because we can't actually observe the forces under discussion. And as critics have pointed out, the history of cognitive theory—memory theory in particular—has been one in which hypothesized factors claimed to be central are eventually replaced by other hypothesized factors claimed to be central (Skinner, 1990; Watkins, 1990), inviting the question of how central they actually are, if they are so changeable. Whatever the hypothesized factors, noncognitive theorists are likely to deny not so much their existence as their centrality. According to behaviorists (e.g., Skinner, 1990), cognitions may be there, but they are only a product of reinforcement history; therefore what we have to study is not the former but the latter. Likewise, psychodynamic theorists would certainly not deny the existence of cognitions or negative self-schemas, but they would say that these were the product of early family relationships, and that it is those relationships, not their cognitive consequences, that constitute the root problem.

Finally, many psychological theorists, the humanists above all, balk at the use of something as cold and mechanical as the computer as a model for the experience of the human mind. However many concessions cognitive theorists may make about how the mind, unlike the computer, engages in active, not passive, processing, the use of any machine model is objectionable to those who view individuality, creativity, and choice as major aspects of human experience.

The Contributions of Cognitive Psychology The cognitive approach shares the basic virtues of behaviorism: the focus on specific, operationalized variables and the insistence on empirical evidence. At the same time, cognitive psychology goes beyond behaviorism in considering intangible, yet still measurable, factors. This is logically consistent with behaviorism, for despite the protests of radical behaviorists such as Skinner, behaviorism at its heart relies on cognitive mechanisms. Respondent conditioning involves an *association* between stimuli; operant conditioning requires the *memory* of past consequences and the *anticipation* of future consequences. Furthermore, cognitive researchers have accumulated a large body of empirically based findings, with many useful models of the causes of abnormal behavior. They have also developed very useful and effective therapies for depression, anxiety disorders, and other problems.

THE INTERPERSONAL PERSPECTIVE

The **interpersonal perspective** is devoted to analyzing behavior as a function of the person's relationships with others. According to this perspective, psychological disorders are not necessarily problems of the person; many result from disorders of relationships. The primary concern of interpersonal theorists, therefore, is the person's *social environment,* particularly his or her current relationships. Like behaviors and cognitions, interpersonal processes are subjected to careful empirical study, in keeping with the standards of modern psychological research.

Systems Theories

In the 1950s researchers began formulating **systems theories,** in which abnormal behavior is seen as the product of habitual relationship patterns, usu-

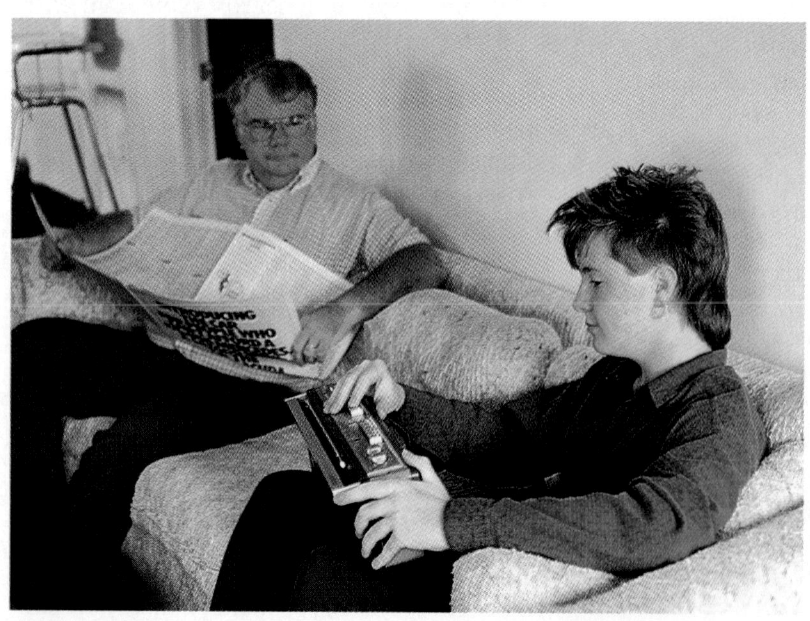

Systems theories of abnormal behavior see it as stemming from flaws in the particular social system (usually the family) that the person inhabits. Thus, communication theory holds that serious disturbances in a family's patterns of communication can give rise to psychopathology in one or more members of that family.

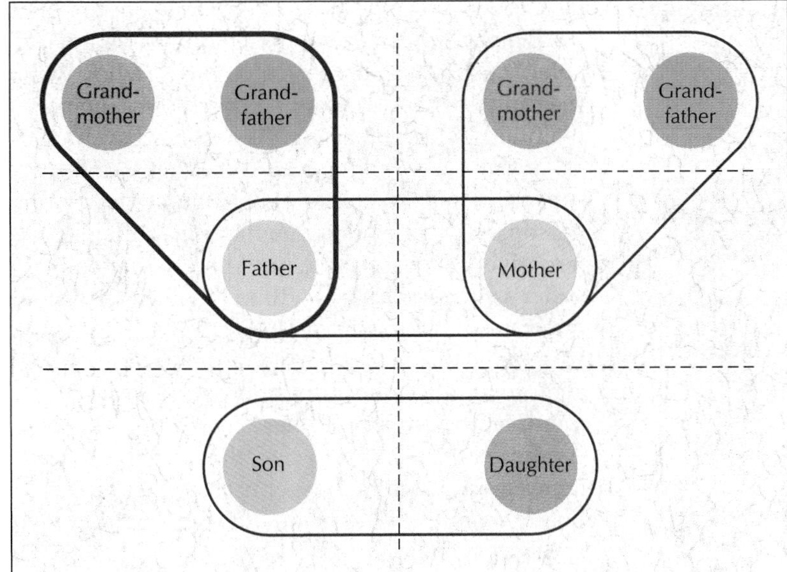

FIGURE 3.2 An "enmeshed" relationship. Minuchin's structural theory views the family in terms of units (solid lines) and boundaries (broken lines). In the above family, the boundary between the father and his parents has weakened, resulting in an enmeshed relationship that isolates him from the rest of the family.

ally within the family. According to one approach, *communication theory,* psychopathology results from faulty communications, which can take a number of different forms (Bateson, Jackson, Haley, et al., 1956; Watzlawick, Beavin, & Jackson, 1967). In *double-bind communication,* one person presents another with a contradictory message; no matter how the other person responds, he or she is "wrong." For example, a mother may ask a child to kiss her but turn away when he tries to do so. Other patterns proposed by the communications theorists are ambiguous messages, in which one person makes a demand without indicating how it might be met; *hostile, runaway* exchanges, in which disagreement, instead of being negotiated, simply escalates from hostility to greater hostility, like a runaway train; and silent schisms, in which the family splits into factions, always engaged in an unacknowledged war.

Another systems theory, formulated somewhat later by Salvador Minuchin (1972, 1974), is *structural theory,* which conceptualizes relationships in terms of *units,* individuals and alliances that serve some function within the group, and the *boundaries,* or psychological "fences," between them. According to Minuchin, problems within the family result from problems with its structural balance. Weak boundaries lead to "enmeshed" relationships: units that are supposed to have some distance from one another become too close, thereby disturbing their relationships with other units (see Figure 3.2). Overly rigid boundaries, on the other hand, create disengaged relationships between units, as, for example, in the "generation gap," where a wall is erected between the parents and the children.

The Interpersonal Circle

While systems theories were being developed, another research team was working on a different organizational model (M. B. Freeman, Leary, Ossorio, et al., 1951; Leary, 1957). According to these researchers, every interpersonal behavior has two essential dimensions: *control* (ranging from dominance to submissiveness) and *affiliation* (ranging from hostility to friendliness). By plotting a particular behavior in terms of these two dimensions, researchers constructed the so-called *interpersonal circle* (D. J. Kiesler, 1983, 1992; LaForge & Suczek, 1955). Where a behavior falls on control and affiliation predicts where the response will fall: a behavior and its likely response tend to be similar in affiliation (friendly elicits friendly; hostile elicits hostile) and opposite in control (dominant elicits submissive, and vice versa)—a pattern described as *complementarity* (Carson, 1969). (See Figure 3.3.)

FIGURE 3.3 Two examples of complementary behavior pairs plotted on a simplified interpersonal circle.

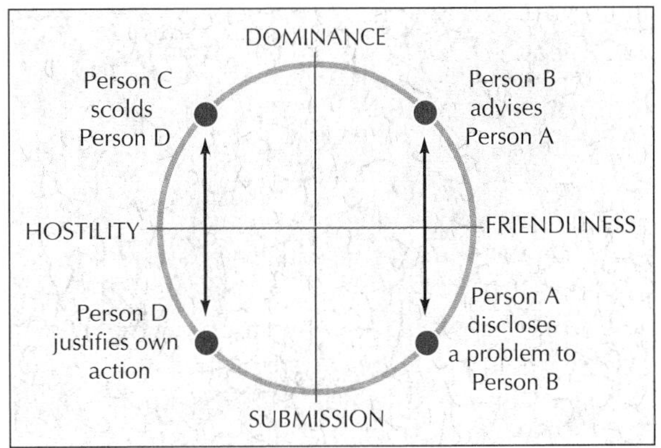

Interpersonal Theory and Abnormal Behavior

By the seventies these theories began being applied to specific patterns of abnormal behavior. Coyne (1976b) and D. J. Kiesler (1983), for example, suggested that depression might be the product of a spiral of complementary dominance and submission responses. Drawing on this work, Horowitz and Vitkus (1986) proposed the following five-step process:

1 The depressed person feels hopeless and inept.
2 The depressed person seeks reassurance from others, often through self-critical statements.
3 Others respond with complementary controlling statements (e.g., offering advice).
4 These controlling responses evoke further submissive behavior from the depressed person.
5 Others become frustrated with the depressed person's continued (or increased) negativity.

In other words, even though others may be sincerely trying to help the depressed person, they are unwittingly encouraging his or her symptoms via their complementary controlling behavior.

Other interpersonal research has focused on the interplay of social roles with psychological symptoms. For example, an aspect of nonassertiveness, the inability to refuse unreasonable requests, has been explained by behaviorists as a skills deficit: the person simply doesn't know how to refuse such requests and needs to be taught this skill. But interpersonal researchers have found that the problem is caused not by lack of skill but by the social context in which the skill is required. Nonassertive people are actually good at turning down unreasonable requests on behalf of other people; it is only when they themselves are the target of the request that they become unable to refuse (R.M. Schwartz & Gottman, 1976). A number of other psychological problems have also been found to appear and disappear depending on the role the person occupies in relation to the other person (Gottman, 1979; Patterson, 1982; Sim & Romney, 1990; Vitkus & Horowitz, 1987).

This suggests that the psychological problem is as much in the relationship as in the person, and that is the guiding principle of interpersonal therapy. Many interpersonal theorists go so far as to label the person seeking treatment as the "identified patient." In other words, he or she is merely the one who has been identified by the others as sick, whereas in truth it is the interpersonal structure—in most cases, the couple or the family—that is "sick." For example, it is widely acknowledged by experts on substance abuse and obesity that people with these problems tend to have an "enabler," usually a parent or spouse, who, while seeming to be put upon, nevertheless helps to maintain the problem and has strong psychological reasons for doing so. Accordingly, interpersonal therapists prefer to treat the network, not the person, lest the network sabotages treatment or, alternatively, lest someone in the network begins to suffer psychologically as the person in treatment improves. G. Greenberg (1977) cites the case of a woman who was in therapy for depression. As her symptoms lifted, her husband began phoning the therapist to complain of her worsening condition. As she continued to improve, the husband became increasingly distressed, eventually lost his job, and finally committed suicide. Obviously, the husband's psychological well-being was dependent on the wife's continued pathology.

Evaluating the Interpersonal Perspective

The interpersonal perspective appeals to psychodynamic theorists because both emphasize underlying dynamics (Goodman, 1992; Grey, 1988). Yet it is also consistent with cognitive behaviorism because it focuses on observable exchanges and can therefore be tested empirically (Safran, 1990a, 1990b). Some theorists look to interpersonal theory as a way of integrating the often quarrelsome perspectives in abnormal psychology (D. J. Kiesler, 1992). In the meantime, those perspectives have learned from interpersonal theory, particularly in the area of treatment. Therapists from most perspectives now agree that for many problems the best approach is to treat the couple or the family rather than just the "identified" patient.

Another contribution that interpersonal theory has made to psychotherapy in general is its analysis of the subtle and sometimes counterproductive workings of the patient-therapist relationship (Henry, Schacht, & Strupp, 1990; Horowitz & Vitkus, 1986). Many practitioners of insight therapy, in the effort not to influence what the patient is saying, confine themselves to minimal feedback; in psychoanalysis, they may even seat themselves out of the patient's field of vision. In effect, they try to disappear. But as interpersonal research has shown, therapists never disappear from their patients' awareness, and when their responses are ambiguous—for example, when they are silent—patients are likely to interpret this in a manner consistent with their symptoms (P. L. Wachtel, 1973). For example, a depressed patient will think, "He disapproves of what I'm saying," and will become

Sociocultural theorists maintain that social conditions such as poverty and racial discrimination can lead to psychological disorders.

more depressed. Such research has had its effect. In recent years, therapists have become more empathetic and responsive, less interested in attempting to establish "objectivity" and more interested in giving the patient hope.

The interpersonal perspective has been criticized on two counts. First, some of its findings have not stood up under later research. For example, while friendly interactions do seem to follow the rule of complementarity, hostile interactions often do not. On the contrary, hostile assertions of control tend to provoke hostile assertions of control—a "negative spiral" that has repeatedly been observed in troubled marriages (Gottman, 1979) and in families with rebellious children (Patterson, 1982). Interpersonal theorists counter that a disruption of complementarity is in fact a sign of a disordered relationship. A second criticism is that interpersonal theory is limited in scope. Most current researchers in this area conceptualize the interpersonal relationship as a factor that maintains, or even aggravates, psychological disorders, but not as the root cause, and it is partly for this reason—the modesty of its claims—that interpersonal theory has yet to become a major, unified perspective. Rather, it has shared the fate of the humanistic-existential perspective: it has contributed to other, more dominant perspectives, particularly in the area of treatment, rather than taking a place alongside them.

THE SOCIOCULTURAL PERSPECTIVE

Like interpersonal theory, the sociocultural perspective studies abnormal behavior in an interactive context. But whereas interpersonal theorists confine their attention to small groups such as the family, the **sociocultural perspective** views abnormal behavior as the product of broad social forces. This view is based on epidemiological research that shows that rates of mental illness are higher among people in poor urban areas than among other segments of the population. The sociocultural perspective embraces two interrelated theories—one straightforward, one more subtle.

Mental Illness and Social Ills

The more straightforward position is that psychological ills are the result of social ills. While we may single out this or that person as being psychologically disturbed, such individual disturbances are merely symptoms of general disturbances in the society. Recent periods of economic recession have provided abundant evidence for this hypothesis. As unemployment rose in the late 1970s and early 1980s, admissions to mental hospitals, suicides, and deaths from stress-related ailments such as heart disease and cirrhosis of the liver rose significantly as well (Pines, 1982b).

Sociocultural theorists have also pointed to the many injustices built into our society—poverty, the lack of any respected role for the aged, discrimination against minority groups and women, and condemnation of AIDS sufferers—as further instances of the cultural provocation of psychological disturbance. According to the sociocultural view, it should come as no surprise if a poor, ill-educated, and jobless teenager acts "wild" or if a lonely and idle eighty-five-year-old woman is depressed. And rather than probe their psyches for an underlying psychological cause, we should address ourselves to the obvious social causes. Above all, poverty should be looked at as a significant risk factor for psychopathology. In addition to experiencing more stress, the poor are less likely to have the personal resources and social support to cope with stress (Dohrenwend & Dohrenwend, 1981). Two recent epidemiological studies (Bruce, Takeuchi, & Leaf, 1991; Kessler, McGonagle, Zhao, et al., 1994) found that people in the lowest income groups had about *twice* the risk of developing an episode of a psychiatric disorder as people who were not poor. Furthermore, cultural and subcultural values influence assessments of mental illness (see Chapter 6).

Mental Illness and Labeling

As we saw in Chapter 1, the definition of abnormal behavior depends upon who is doing the defining. It is on this fact that the second sociocultural theory rests. Adherents of this theory claim that we may label people "mentally ill" not because of anything intrinsically pathological in their behavior but simply because they have violated social norms—a situation that the society cannot tolerate and that it handles by labeling and treating the people in question as if they were "sick." This theory has generated some interest in the process whereby people become labeled as mentally ill. How does the society choose which deviants it will designate as sick? And why do the people accept the label?

One theorist who has considered these questions at length is Thomas Scheff (1966, 1975). His analysis of the labeling process is as follows. Deviant behavior, whatever its cause, is extremely common. Most of it is transitory and is ignored by the society. However, certain forms of deviance, for one reason or another, come to the attention of the mental health establishment and are singled out as "mental disorders." Once singled out and labeled in this way, the person is placed in the *social role* of the "mentally ill" person. And it is extremely likely that he or she will accept that role, for as with any other social role (e.g., teacher, student, wife, husband), the society provides strong rewards for behavior consistent with the role and strong punishments for behavior inconsistent with the role. If, for example, a man who has once been labeled "mentally ill" tries to rejoin the world of the sane, he will find much to deter him—rejections from employment agencies, raised eyebrows from people who know about his "past," and so forth. Thus, according to Scheff, most people who are designated mentally ill ultimately embrace the role and settle back into what has been called the "career" of the mental patient (Goffman, 1959a). In short, the label becomes a self-fulfilling prophecy.

Class, Race, and Diagnosis What *kinds* of behavior are most likely to identify a person as mentally ill? What do those socially learned stereotypes of mental illness consist of? A famous group of studies, the so-called New Haven studies (Hollingshead & Redlich, 1958; Myers & Bean, 1968), throws some light on this question, suggesting not only that psychological disturbance is a social phenomenon but that it is closely related to social class.

What the New Haven studies found was that when people of lower socioeconomic levels suffered from behavior disturbances, they were more likely than middle-class people to be placed in state mental hospitals. The reasons were twofold. First, the lower-class people could not afford private outpatient care. Second, they tended to express their unhappiness in aggressive and rebellious behaviors. And these behaviors, while acceptable to other lower-class people as "normal" signs of frustration, appeared unacceptable—indeed, bizarre—to the mental health professionals who were diagnosing them, since those professionals came from higher socioeconomic brackets and accordingly had different ideas about what constituted normal responses to stress. Hence people with lower socioeconomic backgrounds were more likely to be labeled as psychotic and to be hospitalized as a result. In contrast, people of higher socioeconomic levels tended not to be hospitalized, not only because they could pay for outpatient care but also because their "style" of deviance (e.g., withdrawal and self-deprecation) seemed to the doctors, coming from the same social class, less bizarre. Consequently, these people were diagnosed as having "neurotic" disorders—diagnoses that carry much less stigma—and with the help of regular therapy were able to return to their daily lives. Unlike the hospitalized and "psychotic" poor, they were given less of a "sick" role to fill and thus were more likely to improve.

In a recent review of research findings, Lopez (1989) showed that this principle applies to race as well as to class. In one study (Luepnitz, Randolph, & Gutsch 1982), experienced therapists were given sets of hypothetical patient profiles and asked to provide diagnoses. From therapist to therapist, the profiles were the same except for one factor: race. Patients identified as white in one set were said to be black in another. The study found that with *the same symptoms*, blacks were more likely to be diagnosed as alcoholic or schizophrenic, whereas whites were more likely to be diagnosed as depressed. As in the New Haven studies, these different disorders carry different levels of stigma, have different prognoses, and lead to different treatments. Differences in race and class not only determine who is considered severely abnormal but, by doing so, affect the person's chances for improvement (Braginsky, Braginsky, & Ring, 1969).

Those charged with developing diagnostic criteria have not ignored these problems. One proposal, which we will discuss in Chapter 6, is to replace the current diagnostic system with a dimensional system, classifying patients not according to disorders but simply on how they rate on variables such as depression or anxiety. Presumably, this would discourage stereotyping. Another possible solution, which has already been implemented in *DSM-IV*, is to inform diagnosticians about cultural variations in normal and abnormal behavior and to warn them against specific biases. Both dimensional diagnosis and the *DSM* treatment of cultural variation will be discussed in Chapter 6.

Evaluating the Sociocultural Perspective

Almost no one in the mental health field would dispute the first theory outlined above: socioeconomic conditions *do* contribute to psychological disturbance. What distinguishes the sociocultural perspective, like most other perspectives, from competing theories is a matter of emphasis. Whereas sociocultural theorists claim that socially engendered stress is the primary cause, other theorists say that it is secondary to other factors, such as personal resources or family conflict. In turn, most sociocultural theorists readily concede the influence of personal resources and family discord but argue that these are often the result of social disadvantage.

The second theory—that psychological abnormality is a cultural artifact, maintained through labeling—is far more controversial. Differential labeling is not the only possible explanation for the disproportionate numbers of lower-class people who are diagnosed as psychotic. The phenomenon could be accounted for more simply via the socioeconomic-stress theory: since the poor have to cope with more serious stresses, they have more serious breakdowns. Another possible explanation is that severely disturbed people slip downward on the socioeconomic ladder—they tend to lose their jobs, for example—so that whatever their original socioeconomic status, they are members of the lower class by the time they are diagnosed (Dunham, 1965; Kohn, 1973).

A third hypothesis has to do with differing attitudes toward psychological disturbance. There is evidence that lower-class people are more resistant than the middle class to the idea that they are psychologically disturbed and therefore are more likely to reach a diagnostician only after their symptoms have become severe enough to be described as psychotic (Gove, 1982). In short, labeling is only one of several possible factors underlying the correlation between diagnosis and social class.

KEY TERMS

attribution (67)
behavior therapy (63)
behavioral perspective (54)
cognition (65)
cognitive appraisal (67)
cognitive behaviorism (66)
cognitive perspective (65)
conditioned reflex (54)
conditioned reinforcers (58)
conditioned response (57)
conditioned stimulus (57)
contingency (58)
discrimination (59)
extinction (59)
generalization (59)
habituation (60)
interpersonal perspective (70)
law of effect (56)
learning (54)
modeling (61)
negative reinforcement (58)
operant behavior (57)
operant conditioning (57)
positive reinforcement (58)
primary reinforcer (58)
punishment (58)
reinforcement (58)
respondent behavior (57)
respondent conditioning (57)
schema (69)
selective attention (69)
shaping (60)
sociocultural perspective (73)
systems theories (70)
unconditioned response (57)
unconditioned stimulus (57)

SUMMARY

- The psychodynamic and humanistic-existential perspectives described in the preceding chapter are primarily concerned with subjective experience, revealed through introspection and interpretation. Other theories, discussed in this chapter, focus more on observable behavior and empirical research.
- The behaviorist perspective stresses immediate causes of behavior, rather than deep-seated, unconscious ones. Behaviorism was developed in the early twentieth century as a result of discoveries about the mechanisms of learning. Most important were Ivan Pavlov's demonstration that learning could be the result of the conditioned reflex, or simple association; John B. Watson's belief that psychology should be a natural, empirical science; Edward Lee Thorndike's law of effect (responses that lead to "satisfying" consequences are strengthened and likely to be repeated, while responses that lead to "unsatisfying" consequences have the opposite effect); and B. F. Skinner's view that the law of reinforcement could predict and control behavior.
- The basic assumptions of behaviorism are that psychology's task is to study behavior, or the responses an organism makes to the stimuli in its environment; that psychological research should be empirical, based on measurement; that behavior can be controlled and predicted; and that the major component of behavior is learning.
- According to behaviorists, there are two basic ways of learning: respondent conditioning (an organism's responding to a neutral stimulus as it would to a nonneutral one) and operant conditioning (an organism's operating on the environment to obtain or avoid consequences). The frequency of behavior may be increased by positive or negative reinforcements or decreased through positive or negative punishments.
- Related learning mechanisms include extinction (unpairing stimulus and response); generalization (responding to related stimuli in similar ways); discrimination (learning to differentiate among related stimuli); habituation (experiencing a weakened response due to repeated exposure); shaping (reinforcing successive approximations to a desired response); and modeling (learning vicariously through observation).
- Behaviorists see both normal and abnormal behavior as the product of the same processes of learning. They hold that if maladaptive behavior can be learned, it can also be *un*learned. An example is systematic desensitization, in which anxiety is reduced by pairing the anxiety-producing stimulus with a relaxed state.
- Behaviorism challenges not only other theories of abnormal behavior but basic Western cultural notions. It has been criticized as oversimplified and deterministic and as a possible means of political coercion. At the same time, behaviorism has made important contributions by promoting objective research and experimentation; destigmatizing abnormal behavior; and offering effective treatments, especially for limited goals.
- The cognitive perspective is both an outgrowth of and a reaction to behaviorism. The early cognitive behaviorists argued that variations in responses to the same stimuli could be explained only in terms of cognitive events. They argued that psychological problems arise from irrational beliefs (Ellis) or distorted thinking (Beck).
- The cognitive perspective holds that a person's response to a stimulus reflects the way he or she processes or appraises the stimulus, not the stimulus itself. Some attribution styles are more adaptive than others.
- The cognitive perspective has been criticized for being unscientific, mistaking secondary for primary causes, and reducing the human heart and mind to a mere computer. At the same time, the cognitive perspective has produced useful therapies as well as empirical measures of such intangibles as memory, association, and anticipation.
- The interpersonal perspective concentrates on current relationships. According to this view, the causes of abnormal behavior lie not in the person but in habitual relationship patterns, ambiguous or negative communication styles, imbalanced alliances, and an interpersonal cycle that encourages or allows problem behavior. In other words, the troubled person's behavior is the symptom of problems in the group (usually the family).
- The interpersonal perspective has been criticized for its limited scope. At the same time, the interpersonal perspective has encouraged therapists to treat couples and families, not just individual persons, and to pay closer attention to their own relationships with patients.
- The sociocultural perspective argues that the root cause of abnormal behavior lies not in the individual mind but in society. One theory is that social ills such as poverty and discrimination push people into psychopathology. Another theory holds that labeling people as "mentally ill" tends to become a self-fulfilling prophecy. Additional research indicates that people's

class and race influence how their problems are diagnosed and what treatment they receive.

- No one disputes that socioeconomic factors and cultural variables may contribute to psychological disturbance, but whether these are causes or effects of abnormal behavior is controversial.

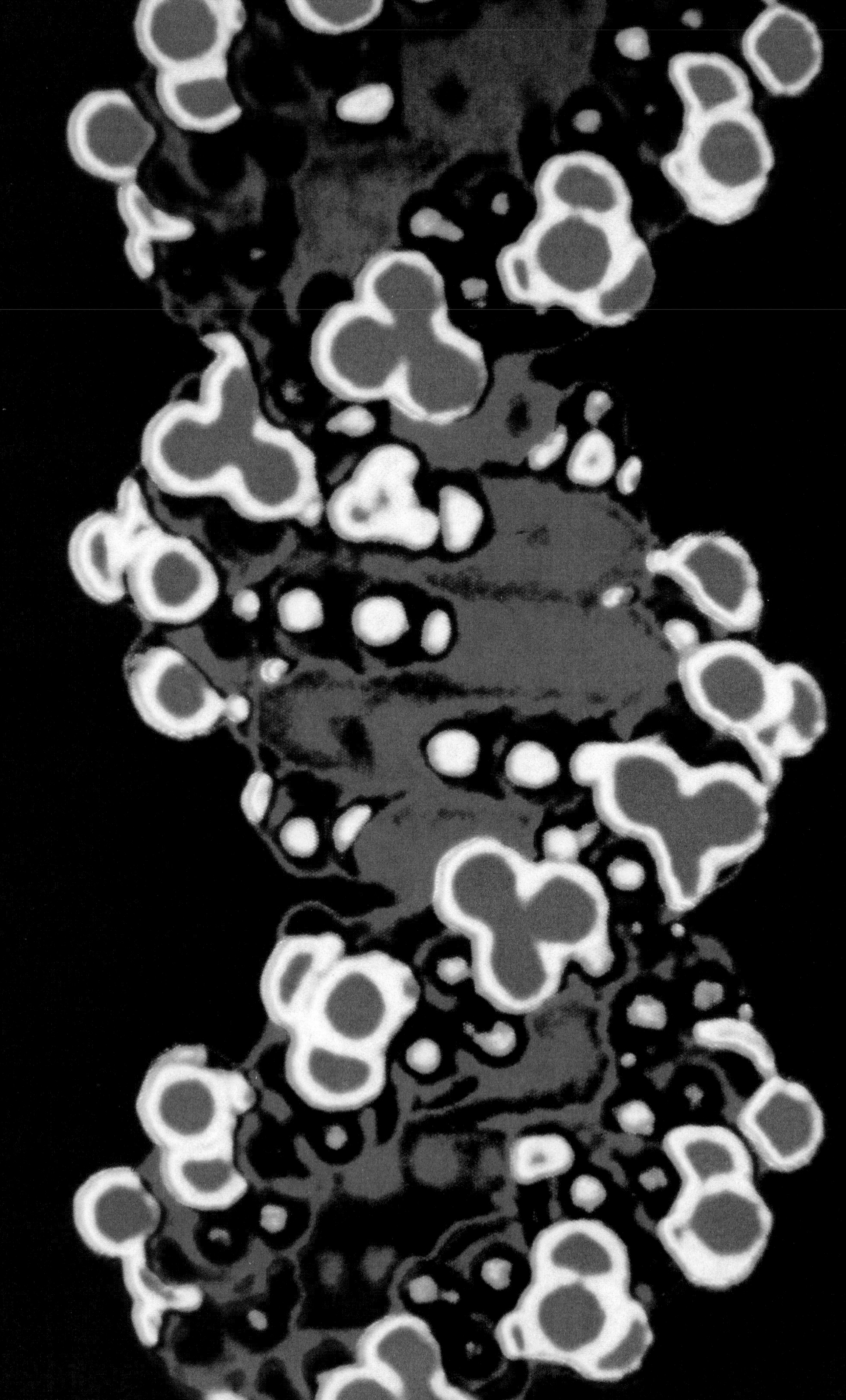

4

THE BIOLOGICAL PERSPECTIVE

Long before recorded history, people associated abnormal behavior with things going on inside the head. But the brain does not permit easy access, and therefore theories about the organic bases of abnormal behavior remained for centuries in the realm of speculation. Today such theories are being built with concrete evidence. With the help of advanced technology, researchers can now flip a switch, see a moving picture of a living brain as it is functioning, and search such pictures for blood clots, tumors, and other possible causes of behavioral problems.

The brain, then, is no longer the dark territory that it used to be. The same is true of other biological functions that affect our thoughts and emotions. Perhaps the greatest source of optimism and excitement in the field of abnormal psychology in the last thirty years has been the tremendous advance in the study of the biological bases of behavior. And this advance in turn has led to a tremendous rise in prestige for the biological perspective.

The biological perspective focuses on the interaction between behavior and organic functions. It is not a single, general theory but rather a collection of specific theories about specific pathologies. Most of these theories will be dealt with in the chapters that discuss those syndromes. The purpose of the present chapter is to describe the kinds of biological mechanisms—the genes, the nervous system, the endocrine system—now being investigated by neuroscientists and to give some picture of their research methods. This will lay the groundwork for the theories we will consider in later chapters.

THE BIOLOGICAL BASES OF BEHAVIOR

Fundamental to the biological perspective is the issue of the relationship between the physical and psychological aspects of our functioning—the so-called *mind-body problem.* While the psychological perspectives we have examined so far regard human behavior primarily as a function of the relationship between the mind and the social environment, biological researchers focus on the relationship between the mind and its *organic* environment, the body. In this view they are certainly justified. Though most of us tend to regard our minds as things apart from our bodies, the two are really aspects of a single, complex entity. What the mind experiences affects the body. A stressful job can contribute to hypertension; a death in the family can alter the survivors' immune systems, making them illness-prone. Conversely, alterations in body chemistry can have massive effects on emotion and behavior. Physical and mental functioning cannot realistically be considered apart from each other.

Actually, it has long been recognized that certain abnormal behavior patterns are caused by organic factors. Two chapters of this book—Chapter 16, "Cognitive Disorders of Adulthood," and Chapter 18, "Mental Retardation and Autism"—are devoted largely to such patterns. But in recent years researchers have come increasingly to suspect—indeed, to show—that organic factors are involved in, and possibly important causes of, disorders *not* traditionally considered organic, such as anxiety and depression. The reverse is also true: researchers are discovering more and more ways in which what used to be regarded as purely organic illness is in fact related to psychological stress—a matter that is the subject of Chapter 9, "Psychological Stress and Physical Disorders." It is on the biological factors involved in this new research that we will concentrate in this chapter.

Behavior Genetics

Every cell in the human body contains a mass of threadlike structures known as **chromosomes.** Coded on the chromosomes are all the instructions, inherited from the parents at the moment of conception, as to what proteins the body should produce. The proteins in turn determine what the body will become: brown-eyed or blue-eyed, tall or short, male or female. The individual units in which this information is carried are called **genes,** and there are more than 2,000 genes on a single chromosome. In some cases, a given trait is controlled by a single gene. But the vast majority of human traits are **polygenic,** the products of the interaction of many genes.

It has long been known that genetic inheritance influences not only physical traits, such as eye color, but also behavior. What is not known is the *extent* to which genes control behavior. This is the famous nature-nurture question, and it is as unresolved in abnormal psychology as it is in any other branch of psychology. Researchers in **behavior genetics,** as this subfield is called, have methods of determining whether a behavioral abnormality is subject to genetic influence. But establishing the degree of genetic influence is a much thornier matter. As we just saw, most traits are controlled by the subtle interaction of many genes—and affected, furthermore, by other factors in the body

Family studies are an important avenue of investigation into the genetic aspects of psychological disorder. Such research explores the extent to which the shared genes of parents, children, cousins, and other relatives affect the likelihood that any one member of a family will develop a disorder.

chemistry, as well as by experience. Thus the relationship of genes to traits is not a single link but a vast net of influences.

Because of these complexities, it is only in the past three decades that researchers have begun to make any genuine progress in relating genetics to behavior disturbances. To date, genetic defects have been shown to be directly responsible for a few forms of abnormality—for example, Down syndrome, a form of mental retardation. But the research suggests that such clear-cut cases of direct genetic causation are rare. Instead, most genetically influenced disorders seem to fit what is called the **diathesis-stress model.** According to this model, certain genes or gene combinations produce a **diathesis,** or constitutional predisposition, to a disorder. If this diathesis is then combined with certain kinds of environmental stress, abnormal behavior will result. Studies within the past thirty years seem to indicate that just as a tendency to develop diabetes, heart disease, and certain types of cancer can be genetically transmitted, so can a predisposition to certain psychological disturbances. It is possible, for example, that some people are genetically predisposed to be unusually responsive to stress, thus putting them at risk for a range of psychological (and physical) disorders. Or, in the case of the mood disorders, some people may have regulatory systems that take longer to return to a balanced state after a spell of depression. It is on schizophrenia, however, that most of the diathesis-stress research has concentrated. As we shall see in Chapter 15, we now have firm evidence that genes do in fact play a role in the development of this form of psychosis.

The Mechanics of Genetic Studies To understand the genetic evidence, one must understand the methods by which it is obtained. Every human being is born with a unique **genotype**—that is, a highly individual combination of genes representing the biological inheritance from the parents. This genotype interacts with the person's environment to determine the **phenotype**—that is, the person's equally unique combination of observable characteristics. The entire purpose of behavior genetics is to discover to what extent different psychological disorders are due to genetic inheritance rather than environmental influence. This is done via three basic types of studies: family studies, twin studies, and adoption studies.

Family studies Family studies are based on our knowledge that different types of family relationships involve different degrees of genetic similarity. All children receive half their genes from one parent and half from the other. Thus parents and children are 50 percent identical genetically. On average, any two siblings have approximately 50 percent of their genes in common. Aunts and uncles, one step further removed, are approximately 25 percent identical genetically to a given niece or nephew. And first cousins, yet another step removed, have approximately 12.5 percent of their genes in common.

With these percentages in mind, the genetic researcher puts together a substantial sample of families containing one diagnosed case, referred to as the **index case,** or *proband case,* of the disorder in question. Then the researcher studies the other members of each family—grandparents, parents,

Twin studies are revealing the concordance rate of various disorders in both MZ (identical) and DZ (fraternal) twins. Even when identical twins do not grow up in the same household, they are likely to have a great deal in common. These twins, separated at birth and reunited at age thirty-one, had both become fire fighters. Unfortunately, some twins also share a greater vulnerability to psychological disorders such as schizophrenia.

children, grandchildren, siblings, aunts and uncles, cousins—to determine what percentage of persons in each of these relationship groups merits the same diagnosis as the index case. When all the families have been examined in this way, the percentages for each relationship group are averaged, so the researcher ends up with an average percentage of siblings sharing the index case's disorder, an average percentage of aunts and uncles bearing the index case's disorder, and so on down the line. If it should turn out that these percentages roughly parallel the percentages of shared genes—if, for example, siblings prove approximately twice as likely as aunts and uncles to share the index case's disorder—then this evidence would strongly suggest that predisposition to the disorder in question might be transmitted genetically. If you turn ahead to Figure 15.1 (page 382), you will see a graph summarizing family studies of schizophrenia. The figures clearly suggest that the more closely one is related to a schizophrenic, the more likely one is to develop schizophrenia.

Such evidence, however, only suggests—it does not prove—genetic transmission. While a person has more genes in common with siblings than with aunts and uncles, he or she also has much more of the environment in common with siblings than with aunts and uncles. Therefore, if a person is more likely to share a psychological disorder with siblings than with aunts and uncles, this differential could be the result of shared environment (same parents, same schools, same neighborhood) rather than shared genes.

Twin studies The genes-versus-environment confusion is less troublesome in twin studies. Here the basic technique is to compare monozygotic and dizygotic twins. **Monozygotic (MZ) twins,** also called *identical twins,* develop from a single fertilized egg and therefore have exactly the same genotype. They are always of the same sex, have the same eye color, share the same blood type, and so on. In contrast, **dizygotic (DZ) twins,** also called *fraternal twins,* develop from two eggs fertilized by two different sperm. Therefore DZ twins, like any pair of siblings, have only approximately 50 percent of their genes in common. Like ordinary siblings, one may be female and the other male, one blue-eyed and one brown-eyed, and so forth. Thus while monozygotic twins are as likely as dizygotic twins to share the same environment, they have approximately twice as many genes in common.

From this configuration one can guess the research design. The researcher assembles one group of index cases, each of whom is an MZ twin, and a second group of index cases, each of whom is a DZ twin. All the **co-twins** (the twins of the index cases) are then examined to determine how many of them are **concordant**—that is, share the same disorder—with their index twin. If the researcher should discover that the concordance rate for the MZ twins is considerably greater than that for the DZ twins, then this would be substantial evidence that predisposition to the disorder is genetically transmitted. And that in fact is what has been discovered in the case of schizophrenia: a concordance rate three to five times higher for MZ twins than for DZ twins. Even more than the family studies, this is strong evidence for a hereditary factor in schizophrenia.

THE MINNESOTA STUDY OF TWINS REARED APART

One of the most extensive studies of twins reared apart began in 1979 at the University of Minnesota. Since that time, the Minnesota researchers have studied more than 100 sets of monozygotic and dizygotic twins from across the United States and as far away as New Zealand and China. The twins were all separated early in life, reared apart in their formative years, and reunited as adults. The researchers located the twin pairs through such means as adoption officials, friends and relatives of the twins, and the twins themselves, many of whom volunteered for the project hoping to be reunited with a separated twin.

The idea behind the project is to collect information about the medical and social histories of each twin, assess each twin's current medical and psychological states, and then compare any differences or similarities within each twin pair. Each participant in the study agrees to undergo about fifty hours of medical and psychological assessment during a week's stay at the research center. The psychological assessment includes a psychophysiological test battery, individual ability testing, measurement of special mental abilities, personality inventories, psychomotor assessment, a life stress interview, a life history interview, a twin relationship survey, a test of emotional responsiveness, and measurement of interests, values, and expressive style. By the end of the week, each subject has answered more than 15,000 questions (N. L. Segal, 1984). In addition, the researchers thoroughly examine significant aspects of the twins' rearing environments.

This study has so far yielded two unmistakable conclusions: genetic factors account for a large part of behavioral variability, and being reared in the same environment has only a negligible effect on the development of similar psychological traits (Bouchard, Lykken, McGue, et al., 1990). Of all the traits tested, IQ shows the highest correlation between monozygotic twins reared apart: a heritability factor of about 0.70. But other psychological traits, such as personality variables, social attitudes, and interests, have also showed strong correlations. In one case, a twin who was reared in Trinidad by a Jewish father had a nearly identical personality profile with the other twin, who was reared in Germany by a Catholic mother (N. L. Segal, 1984). The researchers have also begun to evaluate the degree of heritability for abnormal behavior, such as alcohol and drug abuse and antisocial behavior. Initial results have found a genetic component for drug abuse and for both child and adult antisocial behavior but not for alcohol abuse (Grove, Eckert, Heston, et al., 1990).

In sum, the study of twins at the Minnesota Center has found that correlations for monozygotic twins reared apart are about the same as those for monozygotic twins reared together. According to Bouchard and his associates, "Being reared by the same parents in the same physical environment does not, on average, make siblings more alike as adults than they would have been if reared separately in adoptive homes" (Bouchard, Lykken, McGue, et al., 1990, p. 227).

The twin studies, however, do not discount environment altogether. That is because people with the same genotype tend to seek out or be exposed to the same type of environment. Each of us wants to live in a congenial environment, and what we find congenial is influenced by our genetic individuality. In this way an energetic toddler will have different learning experiences from a passive toddler. An outgoing child will elicit different reactions from people than will a shy child. These varying experiences will certainly have an effect on psychological variability among people, but it is important to remember that many of these experiences are self-selected, a process directed by our genetic predispositions. Bouchard has shown that monozygotic twins reared apart tend to select very similar environments, and to the extent that these experiences have an impact on their behavior, there is an interaction between heredity and environment. The old nature-versus-nurture argument should probably give way to a new understanding of nature *via* nurture.

Source: Based on Bouchard, Lykken, McGue, et al. (1990).

Twin studies are beautifully simple in design but not in practice, the chief problem being that MZ twins are rare. It is no easy task, for example, to assemble an adequate sample of paranoid schizophrenics all of whom are MZ twins. Furthermore, the question of environmental influence cannot be altogether eliminated from twin studies, since MZ twins, so similar physically and always of the same sex, may be raised in ways that are different from the ways that DZ twins are raised.

Adoption studies Adoption studies represent an attempt at decisively separating the evidence of genetic influence from that of environmental influence. As we have seen, as long as two relatives share the same environment—live under the same roof, pet the same dog, fight the same family fights—the fact that they share the same psychological disorder cannot be attributed with certainty to genetic influence. But if, through adoption, the environmental tie were broken, then any significant similarities in psychological history should be entirely the result of the genetic tie. For example, if infants who were born of severely disturbed mothers and adopted into other families at birth developed that same psychological disorder at approximately the same rate as infants born of *and* raised by mothers suffering from that disorder, then the disorder must, to a large extent, be in the genes. Likewise, if a pair of MZ twins who were separated at birth and raised in different homes still showed a substantially higher concordance rate for a given disorder than did DZ twins raised together or separately, then this would constitute the firmest possible evidence for genetic transmission. (See the box on page 83 for a large-scale study of separated twins, though this research focused on personality in general.)

It is just such mother-child pairs and twin pairs that are the object of adoption studies. The adopted-twin studies are the less important of the two, because the samples are so small. (If it is difficult to assemble a group of MZ twins all of whom are paranoid schizophrenic, imagine the difficulty of putting together a group of MZ twins all of whom are paranoid schizophrenic *and* have been raised apart from their co-twins.) The mother-child adoption studies are somewhat easier to do, since a severely disturbed mother is likely to give up her child for adoption. Several such studies have been done, and as we shall see in Chapter 15, they now constitute our best evidence for the genetic transmission of a tendency toward schizophrenia.

The Central Nervous System

If behavioral abnormalities do result from some form of biological malfunction, then the likely place to look for such malfunction is the nervous system. The **nervous system** is a vast electrochemical conducting network that extends from the brain through the rest of the body. Its function is to transmit information, in the form of electrochemical impulses, among various cells throughout the body.

The nervous system has many divisions (see Figure 4.1), but its headquarters is the **central nervous system (CNS),** consisting of the brain and spinal cord. Of all the parts of the nervous system, the CNS is the one primarily responsible for the storage and transmission of information.

Logically, when there is a problem in the CNS, there is a problem in behavior. As we shall see in Chapter 16, any damage to the brain, whether from injury or disease, can cause a massive revolution in the personality. Recent research, however, has concentrated more on subtle chemical changes that may be implicated in psychopathology.

Neurons Like every other part of the body, the nervous system is made up of cells specifically adapted for its functions. Nerve cells, called **neurons,** have the following characteristic structural features (see Figure 4.2):

1 The *cell body,* which contains the nucleus. The chemical reactions that take place in the cell body provide the energy and the chemicals needed for the transmission of impulses.
2 The *dendrites,* short fibers branching out from the cell body. In most neurons, it is the dendrites that receive impulses from other neurons.
3 The *axon,* a long fiber stretching outward from the cell body. This is the passageway through which impulses are transmitted along the neu-

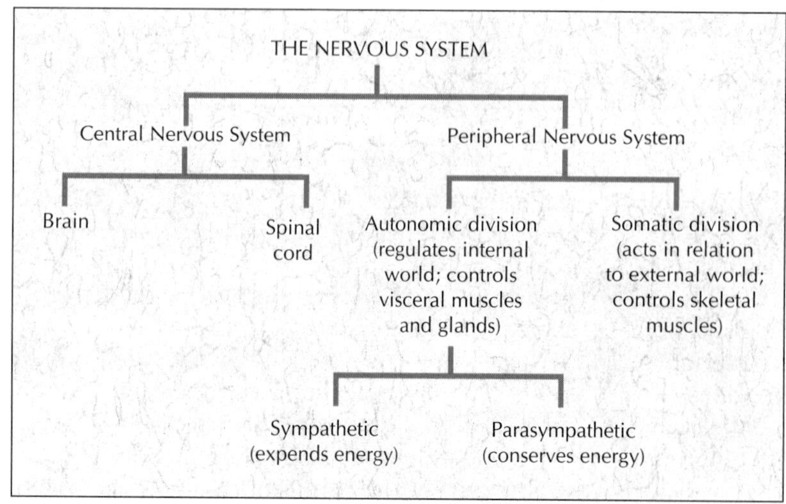

FIGURE 4.1 Diagram of the relationships among the parts of the nervous system.

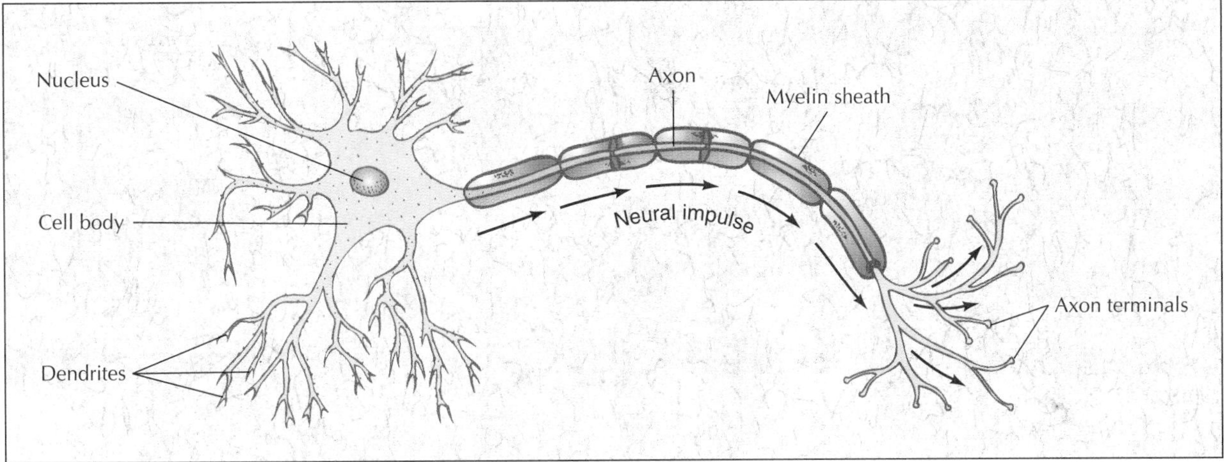

FIGURE 4.2 The structure of this motor neuron is typical of many other neurons. The dendrites, short fibers branching out from the cell body, receive impulses from other neurons and transmit them along the axon to the axon terminals. Impulses cross the gap at the end of each axon terminal, moving on to the next group of dendrites. In many neurons, a myelin sheath wrapped around the axon speeds the transmission of the impulses.

ron on their way to other neurons or to the muscles and glands.

4 The *axon terminals,* the axon's branchlike endings, each with a buttonlike structure at its tip. It is through these buttons at the ends of the axon terminals that the impulse is transmitted to the next neuron.

5 In some neurons, a *myelin sheath,* which is made up of fatty cells wrapped around the axon in segments. The myelin sheath speeds neural transmission by insulating the axon and limiting the connections to other cells, much like traffic on an interstate is sped along by limiting the access of other roadways.

This is a false-color scanning electron micrograph of neurons from the cerebral cortex. It clearly shows the large central cell body of each neuron, with a single axon extending from one end and one or more smaller dendrites from the other.

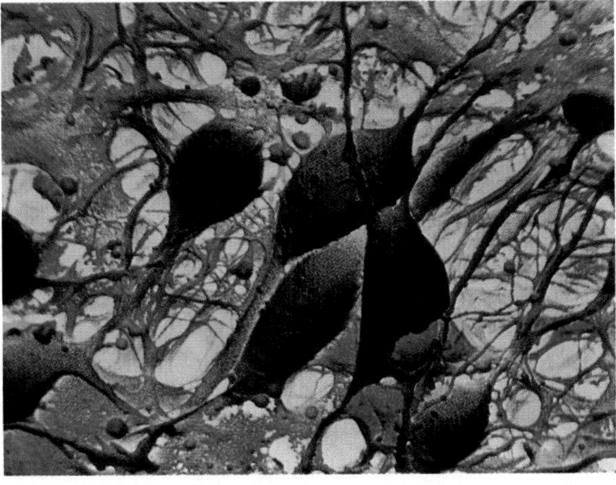

The typical pathway is as follows. Through its dendrites, a neuron receives an impulse from a neighboring neuron. The number of neighboring neurons may range from one to several thousand. The neuron then passes that impulse along its axon to the axon terminals. At the terminal, the impulse must leap a small gap, called the **synapse,** between the terminal button and the neuron that is to receive the impulse. This leap is accomplished by a chemical known as a **neurotransmitter.** If a sufficient amount of neurotransmitter crosses the synapse, the receiving neuron will "fire"—that is, send on the impulse.

It is important to note that firing is an all-or-nothing response: if enough neurotransmitter is received, the neuron fires; if not, it doesn't. This is important because changing the amount of neurotransmitter available in the synapse, even by a little bit, may determine whether the receiving neuron fires or not. In fact, most psychoactive drugs do exactly this: they affect the amount of neural activity by altering the amount of neurotransmitter in the synapse.

It is also important to note that not all impulses stimulate the nerve to fire. Some may inhibit transmission; that is, the impulse makes the receiving neuron *less* likely to fire. In a typical case, a receiving neuron is stimulated by both excitatory

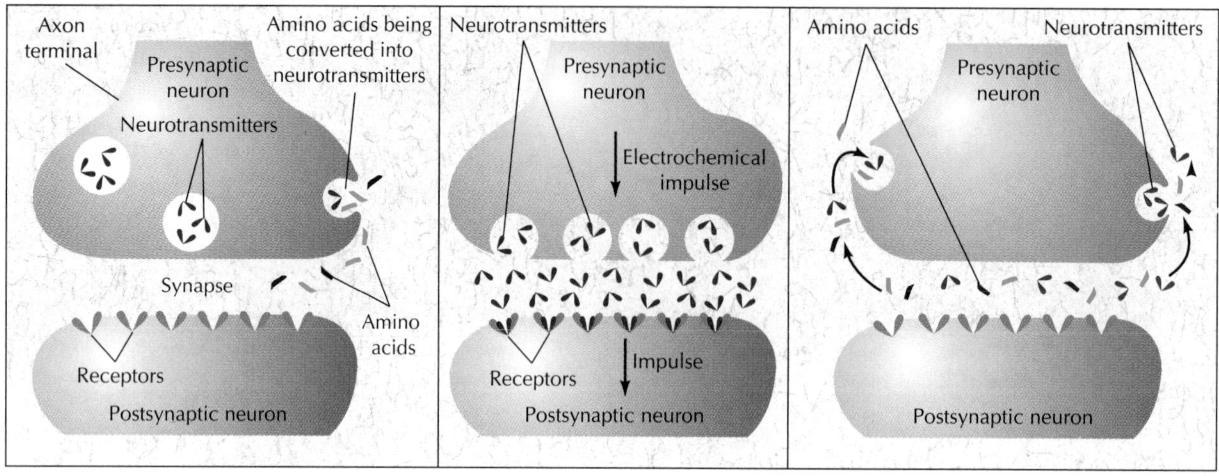

FIGURE 4.3
Stage 1: Amino acids from the protein we eat are taken up by the axon terminals, where they are converted into neurotransmitters.

Stage 2: An electrochemical impulse passing through the presynaptic neuron causes the neurotransmitter to be released into the synapse, where it bonds with the receptors of the postsynaptic neuron, transmitting the impulse.

Stage 3: Some of the neurotransmitter breaks down into its original amino acids. Some is taken back up into the presynaptic neuron (reuptake). The remainder circulates in the extracellular environment.

and inhibitory impulses. It will then tally the excitatory and inhibitory input and will or will not fire. For example, consider neural activity during rapid-eye-movement (REM) sleep, which is also called *paradoxical sleep.* REM sleep gets this name because the brain is very active while the skeletal muscles are virtually paralyzed. It's not that the brain is receiving impulses while the body is not; rather, the majority of the impulses routed to the brain are excitatory, while the majority that affect the skeletal muscles are inhibitory.

So we see that the information that our nervous system receives, and how it will be acted on, is regulated by synaptic transmission. Synaptic transmission, in turn, is determined by the action of neurotransmitters. It is thus no surprise that the neurotransmitters have been a major focus of biological research in abnormal psychology.

Neurotransmitters Look at Figure 4.3, which shows the life cycle of neurotransmitters. Neurotransmitters are made in the axon terminals and are stored there in small sacs *(stage 1).* When an impulse reaches the axon terminal, the neurotransmitter is squirted into the synapse, where it floods the gap and makes contact with special proteins called **receptors** on the surface of the receiving neuron. Molecules in the neurotransmitter fit into the receptors like a key into a lock, and this reaction causes a change in voltage in the receiving neuron, which will then either fire or not fire *(stage 2).* The neurotransmitter may then break down into its component amino acids, be reincorporated into the axon terminal through a process called **reuptake,** or remain circulating in the synapse *(stage 3).*

Scientists have been aware of the existence of neurotransmitters only since the 1920s, and the study of their relation to psychological disorders is more recent still, beginning in the 1950s. This is now one of the most exciting areas of neuroscience research. It is not yet known how many kinds of neurotransmitters exist in the human body—probably more than fifty. The ones that seem to have important roles in psychopathology are the following (McGeer, Eccles, & McGeer, 1987; S. H. Snyder, 1980):

1 *Acetylcholine.* The first neurotransmitter discovered, acetylcholine is involved in transmitting nerve impulses to the muscles throughout the body. In the central nervous system it may also be involved in sleep disorders and in Alzheimer's disease.
2 *Dopamine.* This substance seems to be crucially involved in the regulation of motor behavior and

in reward-related activities. Certain frequently abused drugs, such as stimulants, act on the dopamine system. Excess dopamine activity is thought to be related to schizophrenia, as we shall see in Chapter 15.

3 *Enkephalins.* These substances seem able to act upon the opiate receptors in the brain (the parts that are affected by opium or related drugs). As such, they may be the body's "natural drugs."
4 *GABA* (gamma-amino-butyric acid). GABA is a neurotransmitter that works almost exclusively in the brain, inhibiting neurons from firing. Tranquilizing drugs that inhibit anxiety work by increasing the activity of GABA, as we shall discuss in Chapter 7.
5 *Norepinephrine.* In the autonomic nervous system this substance is involved in producing "fight or flight" responses, such as increased heart rate and blood pressure. In the central nervous system norepinephrine activates alertness to danger.
6 *Serotonin.* This neurotransmitter has an important role in constraint. Imbalances in serotonin and norepinephrine may be involved in severe depression, a theory we shall examine in Chapter 10.

In treating those disorders in which neurotransmitter imbalances seem to be involved, physicians have tried to correct those imbalances with drugs that interfere with the neurotransmitter at any one of several stages. As we saw (Figure 4.3), neurotransmitters begin as amino acids in the bloodstream; they are then converted into neurotransmitters in the axon terminal before they are used in firing. Thus, if the goal is to increase the action of a neurotransmitter, drugs may be used to increase the level of the neurotransmitter in the synapse—for example, by slowing down its reuptake. If the goal is to suppress the action of a neurotransmitter, drugs may be used to attach to the receptors in place of the neurotransmitters, thus blocking them. But these are very delicate manipulations, still in the experimental stages. Indeed, as we shall see, in some cases researchers still do not know whether the neurotransmitter in question needs to be enhanced or suppressed.

The Anatomy of the Brain While behavior may be affected by chemical reactions at the finest level of brain activity, we also know that many behavioral abnormalities are related to the gross structure of the brain. Therefore a knowledge of the anatomy of the brain is essential to an understanding of psychopathology.

The outermost part of the brain is an intricate, convoluted layer of "gray matter" called the *cerebral cortex* (see Figures 4.4A and 4.4B). The external surface of the cerebral cortex has many *sulci* (fissures) and *gyri* (ridges between sulci), which are "landmarks" in studying the brain. A major sulcus called the *longitudinal fissure* divides the brain along the midline into two hemispheres, the right and left brain, connected by the *corpus callosum,* a band of nerve fibers. Each hemisphere is further divided into four lobes. The *central sulcus* (or *fissure of Rolando*) divides the cortex into the *frontal lobe* and the receptive cortex, made up of the *parietal, temporal,* and *occipital lobes.* Another major fissure, the *lateral sulcus* (or *fissure of Sylvius*), runs along the side of each hemisphere, separat-

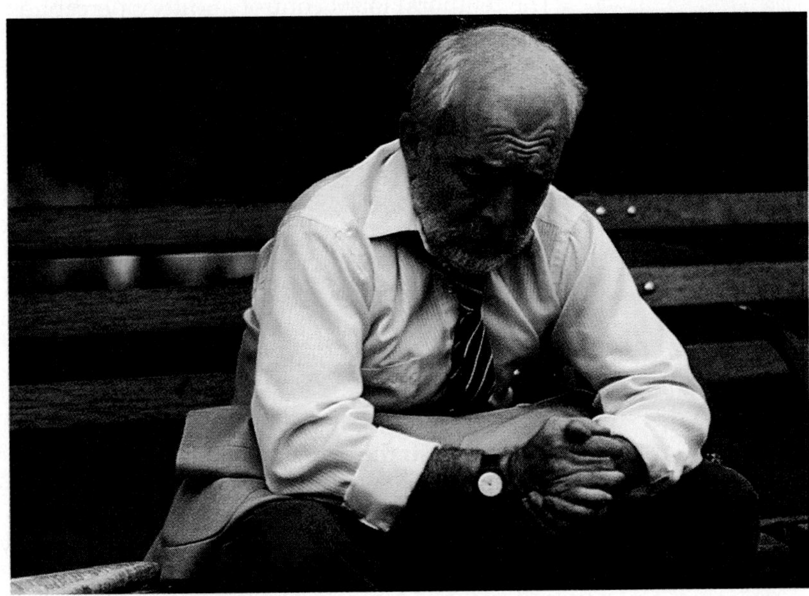

Neurotransmitters may have a profound effect on our emotional as well as physical well-being. Many researchers believe that an imbalance in the neurotransmitter serotonin plays a role in severe depression.

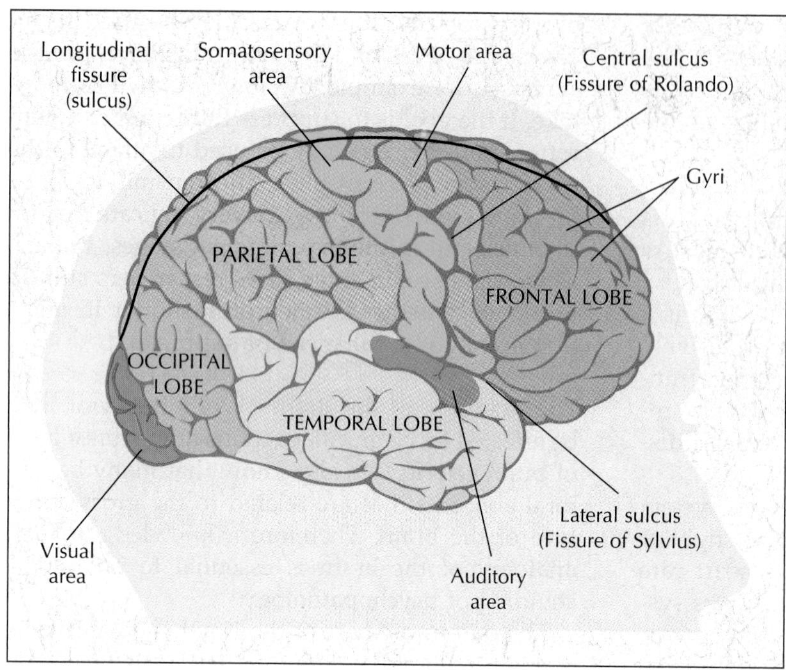

FIGURE 4.4A The four lobes of the cortex and the major fissures that separate them.

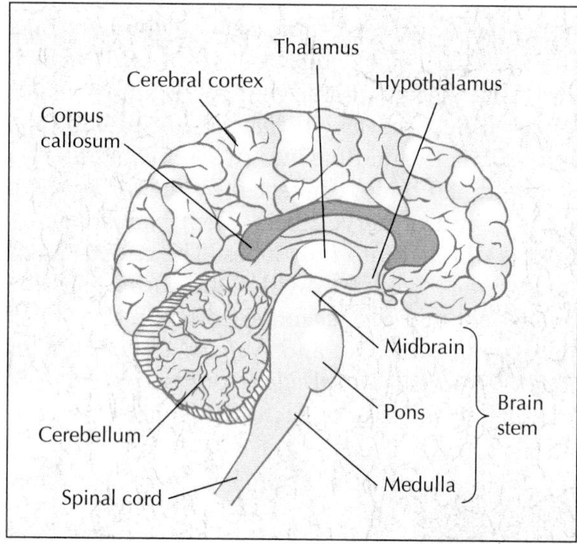

FIGURE 4.4B A cross section of the brain.

ing the temporal lobe from the frontal and parietal lobes.

The functions of these different lobes have been the subject of much research and debate. The frontal lobes are a particular enigma, but at present it appears that they are related essentially to language ability, to the regulation of fine voluntary movements, and to higher cognitive functions such as judgment, planning, the ordering of stimuli, and the sorting out of information. In addition, the frontal lobes serve as a comparator organ—that is, they somehow allow us to look at our behavior and evaluate its appropriateness by seeing how it is perceived by others. This enables us to change our behavior when feedback suggests the need. The frontal lobes also serve to overcome psychological inertia (that is, they help tell us when to start and stop an action). Knowing the proper time to stop or change course is crucial to socially appropriate behavior. Finally, the frontal lobes, because they have two-way connections between the perception-processing centers and the emotion-processing centers, are key to the integration of emotion and cognition (Fuster, 1989), which in turn is critical to mental health. Many mental disorders—depression, for example—involve a disruption of that relationship.

The temporal lobes control auditory perception and some part of visual perception. Furthermore, they clearly have some role in memory, for damage to the temporal lobes generally involves memory loss. The parietal lobes are the center of intersensory integration (e.g., the ability to visualize a cow upon hearing a "moo") and of motor and sensory-somatic functions. Damage to the parietal lobes frequently results in spatial disorientation and in loss of control over gross-motor behavior (e.g., walking). Finally, the occipital lobes appear to control visual discrimination and visual memory. Although the four lobes have been described separately, in fact they are intricately connected to one another, so the functions of each are affected by the functions of the others.

A cross section of the brain reveals other important structural features (see Figure 4.5). Particularly important in emotional functioning are the

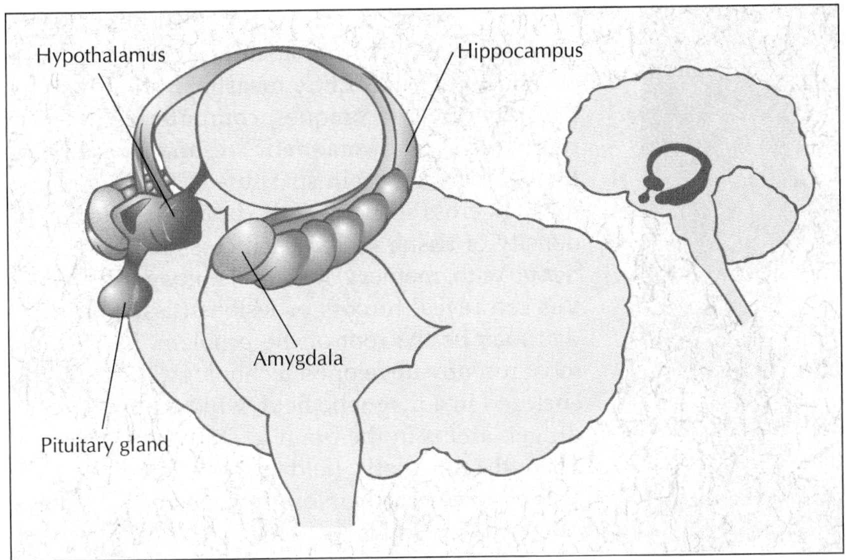

FIGURE 4.5 The limbic structures and hypothalamus. Coming from the Latin word for "border," *limbus,* the limbic structures, including the amygdala and the hippocampus, form a kind of dividing line between the cerebral cortex above and the midbrain and cerebellum below.

hypothalamus and the limbic structures. The *hypothalamus* controls hunger, thirst, and sexual desire; regulates body temperature; and is involved in states of emotional arousal. The *limbic structures,* interacting with the hypothalamus, control behaviors such as mating, fighting, and experiencing pleasure (LeDoux, 1986). The *amygdala,* one of the limbic structures, is involved in emotional responses, both positive, such as romantic attraction, and negative, such as "fight or flight" reactions. The *hippocampus,* another limbic structure, operates on memory as well as emotion, which may help to explain why we remember emotionally charged experiences more clearly than neutral ones.

Buried in the middle of the brain is the *thalamus,* which relays input from the peripheral nervous system to other brain structures, including the frontal lobe and the limbic structures. Scientists have recently discovered direct connections between the thalamus and the amygdala, which may help to account for "automatic" emotional reactions such as phobias (Aggleton, 1992). Other brain structures include the *basal ganglia,* which are involved in carrying out planned, programmed behaviors; the *cerebellum,* which is involved in posture, physical balance, and fine-motor coordination; the *pons,* a relay station connecting the cerebellum with other areas of the brain and with the spinal cord; and the *medulla,* which regulates such vital functions as heartbeat, breathing, and blood pressure. The *brainstem* includes the pons, the medulla, and the *reticular activating system,* which extends through the center of the brainstem and regulates sleep and arousal. Within the brain there are *ventricles,* cavities filled with cerebrospinal fluid.

Several of these brain structures are now the focus of intense study by researchers in abnormal psychology. Schizophrenia has been associated with abnormalities of size in various parts of the brain: enlarged ventricles, smaller frontal lobes, cerebrums, and craniums (skulls). Temporal-lobe malfunction may be responsible for the memory loss seen in Alzheimer's disease. The appetite-control function of the hypothalamus is being investigated in relation to obesity and bulimia. Basal ganglia abnormalities have been linked to conditions involving ritualistic behavior, such as obsessive-compulsive disorder. Damage to the limbic structures may lead to emotional problems and personality disturbance. These theories will be discussed in later chapters.

Measuring the Brain For years, much of what was known about the relationship between structure and function in the brain was inferred from the behavior of brain-damaged patients. It was found, for example, that patients with damaged parietal lobes often could no longer walk, and therefore it was concluded that the parietal lobes had some control over gross-motor behavior. Or, on rare occasions, the functioning of the brain could be observed and tested in the course of brain surgery. Today, however, there are techniques that allow researchers to see inside the brain without surgically invading it.

A test that has been used for decades is **electroencephalography (EEG).** In EEG, electrodes are attached to the head with tape. The electrodes then pick up electrical activity within the brain and record it in oscillating patterns known as *brain waves.* EEG can be used to measure general brain activity, such as sleep patterns in people with in-

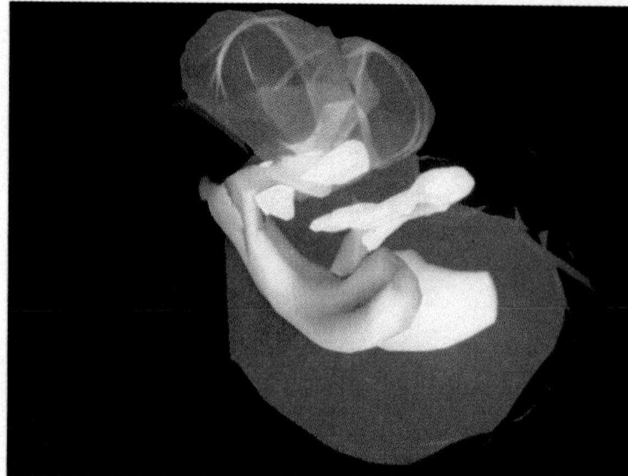

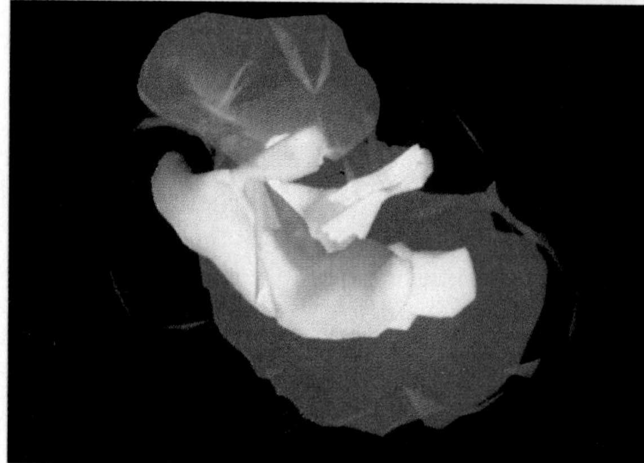

The magnetic resonance imaging (MRI) technique provides unparalleled views of brain structure. The three-dimensional MRI image of a normal adult brain *(above)* contrasts with that of a schizophrenic patient *(below),* in whom the hippocampus (in yellow) is shrunken and the fluid-filled ventricles (in gray) are enlarged.

somnia. It can also give a picture of the brain's responses to specific external events. People suffering from depression, for example, have been given EEGs to determine their reactions to pleasant and unpleasant stimuli. A variation on EEG is the newer *magnetoencephalography (MEG),* which measures the magnetic fields caused by the brain's electrical reactions. MEG is better than EEG at specifying the location of brain activity.

In recent years, however, scientists have invented a number of extremely sophisticated techniques that produce an actual image of the brain, like a photograph. One such technique is **positron emission tomography (PET).** In a PET scan radioactive water molecules are injected into the bloodstream. Then a computerized scanner tracks the molecules on a screen as they are metabolized by the brain. Differences in metabolism in different parts of the brain show up as color contrasts on the screen, and these can point to brain damage—for example, from a stroke.

While PET, like EEG, measures brain activity, two other new techniques, **computerized tomography (CT)** and **magnetic resonance imaging (MRI),** focus on brain structure. CT passes x-rays through cross sections of the brain, measuring the density of tissue within each cross section. In patients with memory loss or language disorders, this can reveal tumors or lesions (tissue damage) that may be the root of the problem. In MRI, the most recently developed technology, the subject is enclosed in a magnetic field, which causes the hydrogen atoms in the brain to shift their positions. Then the magnetic field is turned off, and the atoms return to their original positions, leaving electromagnetic tracks which, read by the computer, produce an image of the brain tissue. MRI thus works at a subatomic level. (It was originally called "nuclear magnetic resonance imaging," but the name was changed because the word *nuclear* frightened many patients [Raiche, 1994].) Because it works with such minute particles, MRI yields very precise images, like photographic negatives. A recently developed variation, *functional MRI (fMRI),* measures the magnetic action of blood oxygen and thus—like PET, but again far more precisely—produces images of brain metabolism.

Each of these techniques has its strengths and weaknesses. EEG and MEG, because they measure electrical activity, are far more precise at specifying the *timing* of brain activity. Indeed, they can record events in the brain within milliseconds of neuron firing. They are also inexpensive and completely noninvasive, with no radioactive tracers (PET), no x-rays (CT), no powerful magnetic fields (MRI). CT, PET, and MRI are more expensive and more invasive, and they give less information about the timing of brain functions. Their great virtue is their ability to reveal brain structure and, in the case of PET and fMRI, the location of brain activity. The choice of technique usually depends on the purposes of the test—what the testers are trying to find—and, to a large extent, on financial resources.

Neuroscientists are now using these technologies to test hypotheses about various psychological disorders—schizophrenia, for example. As we mentioned above, schizophrenia has been linked to abnormalities in the size of various parts of the brain: enlarged ventricles, smaller frontal lobes, and so on. These findings, which will be discussed in Chapter 15, are largely the product of CT, PET, and MRI scans.

Lateralization: Effects on Language and Emotion

One aspect of brain functioning that researchers are now studying is **lateralization,** the differences between the right and the left hemispheres of the brain. Though the two hemispheres appear similar, they have pronounced differences in structure and function. To begin with, neuron connections between the brain and the peripheral nervous system are crossed, so each hemisphere controls the opposite side of the body. Damage to the right hemisphere will disrupt the functioning of the left side of the body, and vice versa. This lateralization is most pronounced in right-handed males, but it is also seen in females and in left-handed males.

In the past it was popular to assign neat "function" labels to the two sides of the brain. The left brain handled language; the right brain, visual-spatial skills. The left brain was "logical"; the right brain, "emotional." Today we know that these generalizations do not hold. Pronounced lateralization is seen for only very limited functions, and in those cases the link is to a specific brain location. Complex cognitive processes such as language and emotion require interplay among various parts of the brain, on both sides. Nevertheless, different *aspects* of these processes do seem to be localized on the left or right.

In the case of language, the left brain has long been recognized as the center of language production. Recently, however, areas in the right hemisphere have been found to affect "pragmatic" aspects of language, such as the understanding of context and the use of metaphors and humor (H. H. Brownell, Simpson, Bihrle, et al., 1990; Gardner, 1990; Hough, 1990). Thus while damage to the left hemisphere creates problems in producing and understanding language—these conditions are called *aphasias* (Chapter 16)—damage to the right hemisphere seems to produce more subtle difficulties in "getting the point."

As for emotion, many studies have shown that the perception of emotion is a right-hemisphere activity (Hellige, 1993). Indeed, it seems to be controlled by the area where the right temporal lobe meets the right parietal lobe. But this does not mean that emotion in general is headquartered in the right brain. Actually, it now appears that different emotions may be controlled by the right *and* left hemispheres. Patients whose left hemisphere has been anesthetized often have bouts of sadness and crying, whereas patients whose right hemisphere has been anesthetized tend to feel tranquillity, even joviality (G. P. Lee, Loring, Meader, et al., 1990)—a pattern that has been confirmed by EEG studies (R. J. Davidson, 1992). A corresponding EEG finding is that people with a history of depression tend to have reduced electrical activity in left-hemisphere emotion centers (Henriques & Davidson, 1990, 1991). As we shall see in Chapter 10, researchers now believe that some people are biologically predisposed to depression. Possibly, the predisposition involves the disabling of protective mechanisms in the left brain. On the other hand, such abnormalities might be the result rather than the cause of depression.

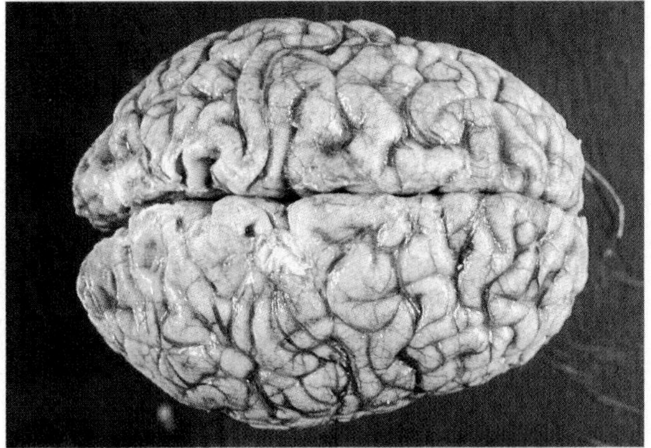

The two hemispheres of the brain, while symmetrical in appearance, do not divide so neatly when it comes to various brain functions. Strict lateralization is limited to just a few brain processes.

The Peripheral Nervous System: Somatic and Autonomic

While the central nervous system is the high command of the body's information network, the **peripheral nervous system,** a network of nerve fibers leading from the CNS to all parts of the body, is what carries out the commands. The peripheral nervous system has two branches. One is the **somatic nervous system,** which senses and acts on the external world. The somatic nervous system relays to the brain information picked up through the sense organs, and it also transmits the brain's messages to the skeletal muscles, which move the body. The actions mediated by the somatic nervous system are actions that we think of as voluntary: picking up a telephone, crossing a street, tying one's shoes.

The second branch of the peripheral nervous system is the autonomic nervous system, and it is this branch that is of special interest to abnormal psychology.

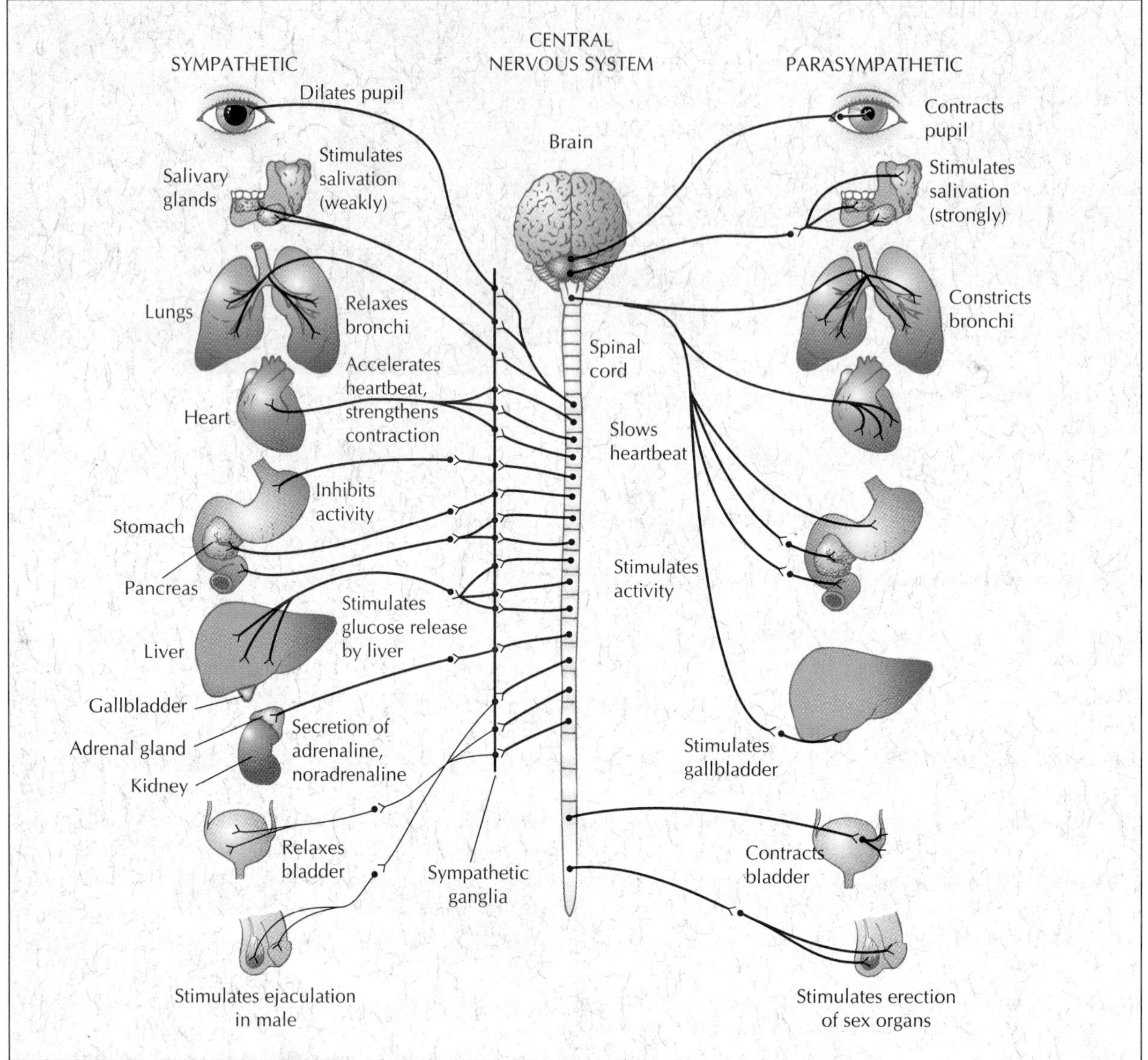

FIGURE 4.6 The autonomic nervous system. The fibers of the autonomic nervous system connect the central nervous system to the smooth muscles, glands, and internal organs. The ANS has two branches, *sympathetic* and *parasympathetic*. The sympathetic division's fibers emerge from the middle of the spinal cord, and pass through a number of nerve fibers and cell bodies known as the sympathetic ganglia. They govern mobilization for activity. The parasympathetic division's fibers emerge from the medulla region of the brainstem and from the bottom of the spinal cord. They govern metabolic slowdown and energy replenishment. Together, the two divisions innervate most of the internal organs and regulate those functions that tend to be automatic—pupil dilation, for example, and saliva flow.

The Autonomic Nervous System While the somatic nervous system activates the skeletal muscles, the **autonomic nervous system (ANS)** controls the smooth muscles, the glands, and the internal organs. Thus while the somatic division directs our more purposeful responses to environmental stimuli, such as crossing a street when the light turns green, the autonomic division mediates our more automatic responses, such as increased heart rate if we come close to being run over as we cross the street. Because the functions of the ANS tend to be automatic, it used to be known as the "involuntary" nervous system. And though we now know that many autonomic functions can be brought under voluntary control, it is still true that these functions—the regulation of heartbeat, respiration, blood pressure, pupil dilation, bladder contraction, perspiration, salivation, adrenaline secretion, and gastric-acid production, to name only a few—are generally carried out without our thinking about them.

The role of the ANS is to adjust the internal workings of the body to the demands of the environment. Like the central and the peripheral nervous systems, the ANS is subdivided into two branches—the sympathetic division and the parasympathetic division—which are structurally and functionally distinct (Figure 4.6).

The sympathetic division The **sympathetic division,** consisting of the nerve fibers that emanate from the middle of the spinal cord, mobilizes the body to meet emergencies. To return to the example of crossing the street, if you were to see a car speeding toward you, you would automatically experience a sudden increase in sympathetic activity, which in turn produces a number of physiological changes. The heart beats faster and pumps out more blood with each beat. The blood vessels near the skin and those that lead to the gastrointestinal tract constrict, increasing blood pressure and slowing digestion. At the same time, the blood vessels serving the large muscles—the muscles that will be needed for action—dilate, so they receive more blood. The pupils of the eyes also dilate, making vision more acute. Adrenaline is pumped into the blood, and this in turn releases blood sugar from the liver so that it can be used by the muscles. Breathing becomes faster and deeper so as to take in more oxygen. All these changes prepare the body for quick action. Of course, sympathetic arousal is not always so intense, but regardless of its intensity, the result is an adjustment of internal conditions so that the organism can make maximum use of whatever energy it has stored within it.

The parasympathetic division The **parasympathetic division,** which consists of nerve fibers emerging from the top and bottom of the spinal cord (Figure 4.6), is essentially opposite in function to the sympathetic division. While the latter generally gears up the body to use its energy, the parasympathetic division slows down metabolism and regulates the organs in such a way that they can do the work of rebuilding their energy supply. Thus, while sympathetic activity increases heart rate, parasympathetic activity decreases it; while sympathetic activity inhibits digestion, parasympathetic activity promotes it; and so on. The relationship between the two systems is complex, however, and sometimes they work together rather than in opposition (Bernston, Cacioppo, & Quigley, 1991). For example, the orienting response—when an infant instinctively turns toward its mother—involves a slowing of heart rate (parasympathetic activity) in combination with pupil dilation and increased sweating (sympathetic activity).

Because of its connection to arousal, the ANS is critically important in regard to stress-related disorders such as headaches, hypertension, and insomnia. As we shall see in Chapter 9, an important theory in the study of these disorders is that something has gone wrong in the regulation of the cycle connecting the brain to the ANS to the organ in question as they operate together in response to the environment.

The Endocrine System

Closely integrated with the central nervous system is the **endocrine system,** which is responsible for the production of **hormones,** chemical messengers that are released into the bloodstream by the endocrine glands and that affect sexual functioning, appetite, sleep, physical growth and development, the availability of energy, and also emotional responses. For example, chronically low levels of thyroid activity result in anxietylike symptoms—feeling tense, nervous, and irritable, whereas low levels of pituitary activity result in depressionlike symptoms—feeling fatigued, apathetic, and lethargic (Morley & Krahn, 1987). Interest in the interplay between hormones, neurochemistry, and behavior has stimulated the formation of a new field of study: psychoneuroendocrinology.

The headquarters of the endocrine system is the hypothalamus, which, as we saw, lies at the center of the brain. Just below the hypothalamus is the pituitary gland, called the "master gland" because it regulates hormone secretion by the other glands of the body.

Hormones may be involved in certain highly specific psychological disorders. One is antisocial personality disorder, which involves reckless and predatory behavior. Unlike ordinary criminals, antisocial personalities do not seem to experience fear. This may be due to deficiencies in adrenaline, which promotes anxiety (S. Schacter & Latané, 1964). We will examine the hormonal theories of antisocial personality in Chapter 11. Hormones have also received prominent attention in studies of depression and bipolar disorder (Chapter 10), stress (Chapter 9), and eating disorders (Chapter 17).

EVALUATING THE BIOLOGICAL PERSPECTIVE

The biological perspective is intuitively appealing. If the causes of psychological disturbance are understood as even partly organic, this would help to relieve the stigma that still attaches to psychopathology. And if psychopathology is biologically caused, then it might be biologically cured, through treatments quicker and less expensive than psychological therapy. But the greatest argument in favor of this perspective is simply its record of achievement. In the past few decades, neuroscientists have made immense strides in understanding the relationship between physiological systems and psychological disorders. Such breakthroughs *have* led to the development of some effective drugs and to the invention of remarkable diagnostic tools such as CT, PET, and MRI. These, in turn, have provided the foundation for further discoveries.

But we must not embrace this approach uncritically. It cannot be assumed, for example, that if a psychological disorder is linked to biochemical abnormalities, such abnormalities are the cause of the disorder. As we saw earlier, they might be the result of the disorder. (Or both might be due to a third, unknown factor.) Similarly, we cannot infer the cause of a disorder from an effective treatment for it. Aspirin may relieve headaches, but that does not mean that headaches are caused by a lack of aspirin. Finally, not all biological treatments are successful. From medieval bleeding to modern psychosurgery, the history of abnormal psychology provides numerous examples of widely accepted biological treatments that later turned out to be ineffective or even dangerous. With these facts in mind, neuroscience researchers are careful to acknowledge the limitations and risks of any biological treatment.

Neuroscience research also raises ethical questions. In the case of disorders that are linked to genes, such as schizophrenia, should we attempt to "repair" the defective genes if and when technology makes this possible? In the meantime, should we prohibit people with these disorders from having children? Can we even require that they be cautioned about the risk of passing the disorder on?

Another ethical problem has to do with symptom reduction and its consequences. Since the 1950s, for example, drugs have been available that control schizophrenia. While they do not cure the disorder, they eliminate its most dramatic symptoms, with the result that thousands of mental patients have been released from hospitals. But what have they been released to? Many of them end up on the street or in squalid shelters. Have drugs been used as a "quick fix," enabling us to put off the more complex challenge of developing long-term community care for psychotic patients?

But it is not the fault of the biological perspective if its discoveries raise ethical problems. Einstein's theory of relativity also raised ethical problems, in the form of nuclear arms. It is up to societies to solve these problems. As for hasty conclusions about organic causation, it is rarely the researchers who make one-cause claims. As we saw, they tend to espouse the diathesis-stress model, acknowledging both organic and environmental

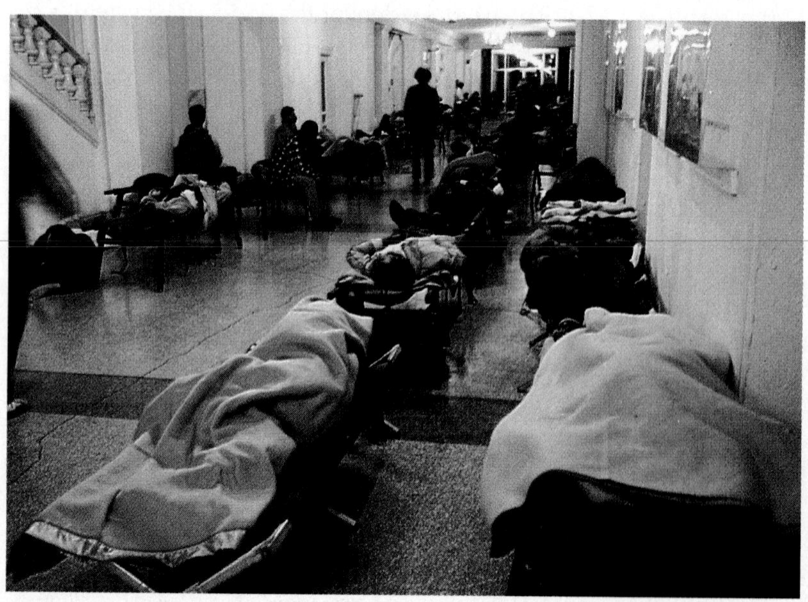

One of the unforeseen consequences of advances in neuroscience research has raised ethical questions: The release of disturbed people from hospitals with prescriptions for the drugs they need but without provisions for adequate follow-up care meant that many of these discharged patients would end up living on the streets and sleeping in public shelters.

causes. In recent years the prestige of this model has been greatly boosted by the evidence for brain plasticity. Before, we knew that the environment worked together with brain chemistry to mold behavior. Now we know that the environment can actually alter brain chemistry—indeed, even brain structure. Given this kind of interaction, it is no longer possible to consider biogenic and psychogenic causation as an either-or proposition. As a result, one may argue with this or that neuroscience finding, but the biological perspective itself cannot be dismissed.

KEY TERMS

autonomic nervous system (ANS) (92)
behavior genetics (80)
central nervous system (CNS) (84)
chromosomes (80)
computerized tomography (CT) (90)
concordant (81)
co-twins (81)
diathesis (81)
diathesis-stress model (81)
dizygotic (DZ) twins (82)
electroencephalography (EEG) (89)
endocrine system (93)
genes (80)
genotype (81)
hormones (93)
index case (81)
lateralization (91)
magnetic resonance imaging (MRI) (90)
monozygotic (MZ) twins (82)
nervous system (84)
neurons (84)
neurotransmitters (85)
parasympathetic division (93)
peripheral nervous system (91)
phenotype (81)
polygenic (80)
positron emission tomography (PET) (90)
receptors (86)
reuptake (86)
somatic nervous system (91)
sympathetic division (93)
synapse (85)

SUMMARY

- The biological perspective focuses on the interaction between behavior and organic functions. The mind and body are two aspects of a single complex entity. Psychological stress and physical illness often influence each other.
- Behavior genetics is a subfield of psychology that attempts to determine the degree to which specific psychological disorders are genetically inherited. Only a few psychological disorders have a clear-cut genetic cause, but many disorders, including schizophrenia, apparently result from the interaction of environmental stressors and an inherited diathesis, or predisposition, to the disorder. A person's observable characteristics, or phenotype, are the product of experience combined with his or her genotype, or genetic endowment. Through family, twin, and adoption studies, behavior geneticists try to assess heritability.
- The central nervous system (CNS), consisting of the brain and spinal cord, controls behavior by processing, transmitting, and storing information. Neurotransmitters mediate the transmission of impulses across the synapse between two neurons, or nerve cells. Six neurotransmitters are implicated in psychopathology: acetylcholine, dopamine, enkephalins, GABA, norepinephrine, and serotonin. Drugs intended to alleviate a disorder by increasing the action of a given neurotransmitter may do so by slowing down its reuptake into the neurons' axon terminals, where it is made. A neurotransmitter's action may be suppressed by using a drug to attach to receptors on the neurons in the neurotransmitter's place.
- A major focus of neuroscience research has been brain anatomy. The external surface of the cerebral cortex shows many fissures (sulci) and ridges (gyri). The longitudinal fissure divides the brain along the midline into two hemispheres, each containing four lobes with differentiated functions. Regulatory structures include the hypothalamus, limbic structures, thalamus, basal ganglia, cerebellum, and brainstem, a structure containing the pons, medulla, and reticular activating system. Psychological disorders have been traced to dysfunctions in many of these structures.
- Research on the relationship between brain anatomy and psychological functioning has been greatly aided by electroencephalography (EEG), magnetoencephalography (MEG), positron emission tomography (PET), computerized tomography (CT), and magnetic resonance imaging (MRI).
- Lateralization is the localization of functions in one hemisphere of the brain or the other. Only a few, very limited functions are completely lateralized. Complex cognitive processes, such as language and emotion, involve interplay among parts of the brain on both hemispheres, although *aspects* of these processes are apparently lateralized. For example, in most people, the left hemisphere seems to control language production; the right hemisphere seems to be specialized for the subtle interpretation of language.
- The peripheral nervous system consists of the somatic nervous system and the autonomic nervous system (ANS). The somatic nervous system activates skeletal muscles and controls purposeful behavior. The autonomic nervous system activates smooth muscles, glands, and internal organs and controls such automatic responses as heart rate, respiration, and the release of adrenaline. The ANS functions to adjust the body to changing environmental demands through its sympathetic and parasympathetic branches. Sympa-

thetic arousal prepares us for quick action in emergencies—for example, increasing heart rate, respiration, and blood sugar. The parasympathetic division slows metabolism and helps to restore the system to equilibrium. The ANS is associated with such stress-related disorders as hypertension and insomnia.

- The endocrine system influences emotional states, sexual functioning, energy availability, and physical growth and development by releasing hormones into the bloodstream from the hypothalamus, pituitary gland, and other endocrine glands. Glandular dysfunction may be involved in certain psychological disorders.
- The biological perspective presents problems of both causality and ethics. Finding that a genetic predisposition or chemical imbalance accompanies a given disorder does not mean that the organic factor is the only or even the principal cause of the disorder. Ethical concerns involve genetic engineering and the sometimes negative consequences of symptom reduction without adequate follow-up care. Neuroscientists have made great strides in developing diagnostic tools and discovering effective drug treatments for some disorders. Even for these disorders, however, researchers favor the diathesis-stress model, which studies the combined influences of environmental stress and biochemical factors.

PART TWO

RESEARCH METHODS AND DIAGNOSIS

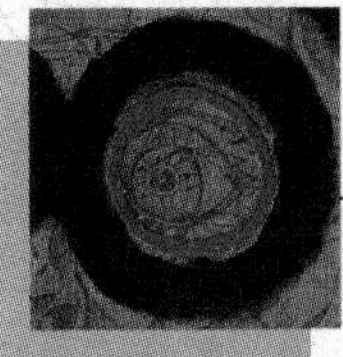

5

RESEARCH METHODS IN ABNORMAL PSYCHOLOGY

Though it is doubtful that Isaac Newton really stumbled on the law of gravitation by being hit on the head by a falling apple, the principle behind the story is sound. Scientific discovery sometimes occurs in a very unmethodical way, through accidents, hunches, and intuition. The earliest antipsychotic drug, for example, was developed by accident. Called chlorpromazine, it was first introduced as a treatment for surgical shock. Actually it did little to reduce surgical patients' risk of going into shock, but strange to say, it made them calm. The drug was then tested, quite successfully, with schizophrenics. It reduced these patients' hallucinations and thought disorders. Chlorpromazine is still used today, and its discovery has led to the development of other, even more effective, treatments for schizophrenia.

Discovery, then, is sometimes a process of groping that is creative and disorderly. However, far more often, important scientific discoveries follow from meticulous, systematic research conducted over long periods of time, and even the occasional "accidental" discovery must be verified through careful scientific investigation. This chapter describes the general principles of scientific research. First we will examine the characteristics of the scientific method. Then we will look at the research designs that scientists have found most useful in the study of abnormal behavior.

CHARACTERISTICS OF THE SCIENTIFIC METHOD

Skeptical Attitude

More than anything else, scientists are skeptical. Not only do they want to see it before they believe it; they want to see it again and again, under conditions of their own choosing. Scientists come to be skeptical because they recognize two important facts. First, they know that behavior is complex: that there are often many factors behind any psychological phenomenon. They also know that it is usually quite difficult to identify those factors. Explanations are often premature; not enough factors may have been considered. While it may seem that a child's asthma attacks always follow an emotional upset, for example, it is possible that cat hair, pollen levels, and the child's history of respiratory infection are also involved. Single-cause explanations, because they are simple, are inherently appealing, but in the study of behavior they are rarely accurate.

The second reason for skepticism is that science is a human endeavor. People make mistakes. The powers of human reasoning are not always to be trusted. Therefore, scientists are almost always skeptical of "new discoveries" and extraordinary claims—until they can be repeated under controlled conditions.

Objectives

The scientific method is intended to meet four objectives: description, prediction, control, and understanding (Figure 5.1). **Description** is the defining and classifying of events and their relationships. To be useful, a description must have **reliability**—that is, it must be stable over time and under different testing conditions. Suppose, for example, that a person is given an IQ test and scores very high; then he is given the same IQ test two days later and scores very low. Since IQ is unlikely to change in the course of two days, we would assume that the test was unreliable. A useful description must also have **validity**—that is, it must measure what it claims to be measuring. If that IQ test was actually measuring social skills rather than intelligence, then it would not be valid. (Reliability and validity will be examined more closely in Chapter 6.) Assessment techniques have been developed to provide reliable and valid descriptions of a wide range of concepts, from extroversion to depression.

A description of events and their relationships often serves as a basis for **prediction.** If a description of schizophrenia notes that children of schizophrenic parents are ten times more likely to become schizophrenic than children of nonschizophrenic parents, it can reasonably be predicted that there is a causal relationship between the two factors.

However, successful prediction doesn't always depend on the ability to pinpoint a cause. In the case of schizophrenia, for example, the fact that children of schizophrenic parents are at risk for schizophrenia does not tell us whether this relationship is due to genes, to nongenetic biological dysfunction, or to family dynamics. Nevertheless, it is still useful to know that these children are at risk, for such knowledge can serve as a basis for research that will help to determine the causes of schizophrenia and can also give us a basis for developing treatments and preventive measures.

Indeed, it is the development of treatment and preventive strategies that forms the basis of the third goal of science—**control.** When scientists can control behavior, they can change it for the better.

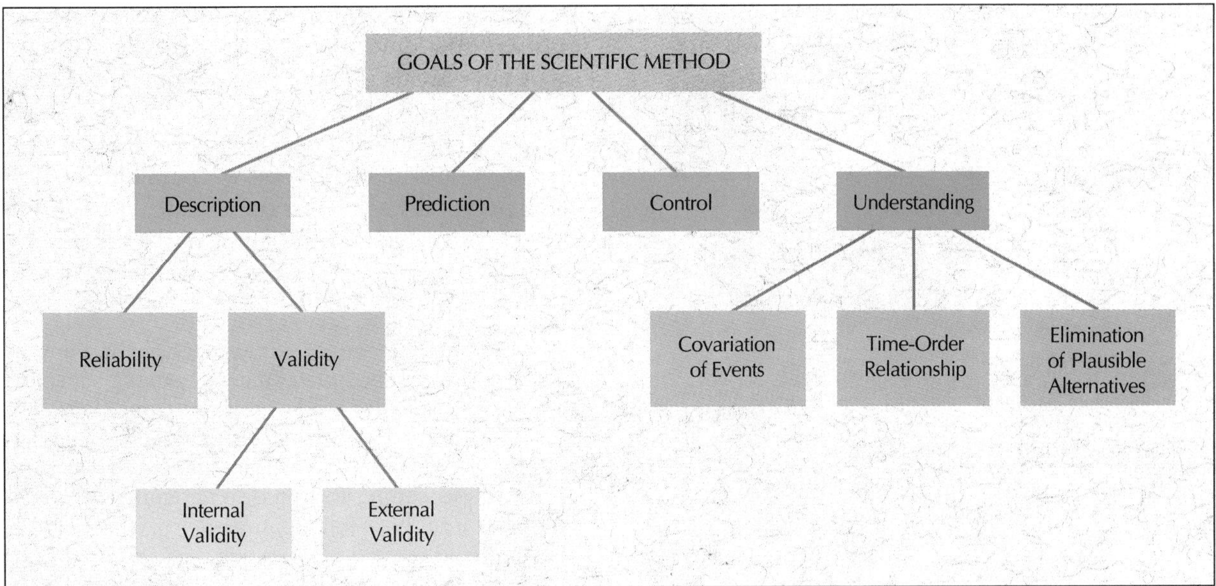

FIGURE 5.1 The four objectives of the scientific method, together with their individual requirements.

For example, psychologists may attempt to teach schizophrenic parents better communication skills in an effort to prevent the development of schizophrenia in their children.

If we ever find out how much responsibility can be assigned to each of the factors thought to lead to schizophrenia, we will have achieved the fourth goal of the scientific method: **understanding,** the identification of the cause or causes of a phenomenon. Before causality can be demonstrated, three conditions must be met. First is the **covariation of events:** if one event is to be accepted as the cause of another, the two events must vary together—that is, when one changes, the other must also change. Second is a **time-order relationship:** the presumed cause must occur *before* the presumed effect. The final condition is the **elimination of plausible alternative causes:** the proposed causal relationship can be accepted only after other likely causes have been ruled out.

Covariation and time order are sometimes difficult to establish. But it is usually far harder to determine that changes in behavior are the result *solely* of changes in the proposed causal factor.

Internal and External Validity In trying to eliminate plausible alternative explanations, a scientist is often faced with a problem called *confounding.* **Confounding** occurs when two or more causal factors are exerting an effect on the same thing at the same time, thus interfering with accurate measurement of the causal role of either one. For example, suppose a group of researchers is trying to understand the mental confusion that characterizes schizophrenia. They might compare the word associations of hospitalized schizophrenic patients with the word associations of people chosen from the general population, in the hope of linking to schizophrenia any important differences between the linguistic patterns of the two groups. However, the patient population in this study would probably differ from the nonpatient population in many ways other than mental condition. For example, the patients would probably be receiving drug treatment. Drug differences between the two groups thus *confound* the patient-nonpatient difference. That is, any differences in word associations between the patients and the nonpatients could be caused by the mental disorder, the drugs, some combination of these factors, or even some other difference between the groups. When factors are confounded, it is generally impossible to determine the one factor that is responsible for differences in performance. When *no* confounding takes place, a research study is said to have **internal validity.**

The internal validity of a study can be distinguished from its external validity. **External validity** is the extent to which research results can be generalized. **Generalizability**—the ability of a finding to be applied to different populations, settings, and conditions—in turn depends on the **representativeness** of the sample from which the findings were gathered: the degree to which this sample's essential characteristics match those of the population we want to generalize about. An internally

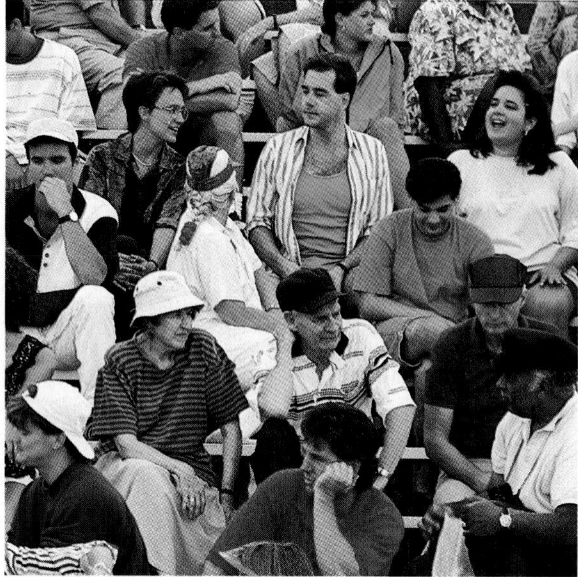

Most natural populations show demographic differences—variations in age, sex, race, and so on. Random sampling is the best technique available for ensuring that the various characteristics of the population as a whole are adequately reflected in the research sample. This representativeness, in turn, helps ensure a study's external validity.

valid study may show, for example, that schizophrenic patients at a certain hospital respond better to one drug than to another. But if the schizophrenic patients in that hospital are not representative of schizophrenic patients in general—if, let's say, they are less severely ill than patients at other hospitals—then the findings cannot be generalized.

The representativeness of a sample depends on how carefully the subjects, settings, and conditions of the study have been selected. The best way to achieve a representative sample is to use random sampling. A **random sample** is one in which every element of the population has an equal likelihood of being included. Given that the sample is large enough, random sampling makes it likely that the characteristics of the sample will generally match the characteristics of the population.

Experimental Procedures

The scientific method is put to use—or should be—every time researchers perform an experiment. In any well-conducted experiment, the key elements are the development of a hypothesis, the formulation of operational definitions, and the establishment of methods of control.

Development of a Hypothesis Research often begins with the development of a testable hypothesis. A **hypothesis** is a tentative explanation for behavior; it attempts to answer the questions "How?" and "Why?" Hypotheses are the result of discovery, and discovery, as we pointed out, is a creative process—perhaps the one area of scientific endeavor in which skepticism is out of place. Psychologist Neal Miller (1972) has described the state of mind required:

> During the discovery or exploratory phase, I am interested in finding a phenomenon, gaining some understanding of the most significant conditions that affect it, and manipulating those conditions to maximize the phenomenon and minimize the "noise" that obscures it. During this phase I am quite freewheeling and intuitive—follow hunches, vary procedures, try out wild ideas, and take shortcuts. During it, I am usually not interested in elaborate controls; in fact, I have learned to my sorrow that one can waste a lot of time on designing and executing elaborate controls for something that is not there. (p. 348)

But as we also noted, the romance of discovery is followed by the rigors of testing. For a hypothesis to be scientifically useful, it must be possible to *disconfirm* it—that is, to show that it is *not* true. This aspect of a hypothesis is called *testability* (also *falsifiability*).

Operational Definitions If a hypothesis is to be testable, the concepts involved must be "operationalized," or given **operational definitions**—that is, they must be defined in terms of operations that can be observed and measured. "Depression," for example, could be operationalized by defining it in terms of the Beck Depression Inventory, a test in which subjects circle, as applicable or inapplicable to themselves, statements about sadness, discouragement, sleeping problems, and so forth. Their endorsement of these statements is an observable operation. It is also measurable. Subjects receive a score based on which statements they circle. A very low score indicates no depression, and a very high score means severe depression. The score serves as the operational definition of depression. So in a study of nondepressed versus severely depressed people, the researchers might operationally define these two conditions as Beck Inventory 9-or-below (no depression) and Beck Inventory 24-and-over (severe depression), respectively. In doing so, they would be ensuring that everyone involved in that research, and everyone reading about it, understood these concepts in the same way.

Methods of Control In setting up experiments to test their hypotheses, researchers often need to control events that might influence the behavior they are studying. An experiment usually involves the *manipulation* (deliberate changing) of one or more factors and the *measurement* of the effects of that manipulation on behavior.

Independent and dependent variables The **independent variable** is the factor that is manipulated by the experimenters in the effort to measure its effects. The **dependent variable** is the factor (or, in psychological research, the behavior) that will presumably be affected by the manipulation of the independent variable and whose changes the experiment aims to measure. If a hypothesis is to receive a fair trial, the experiment must be internally valid; that is, the only possible cause for any obtained outcome must be the independent variable. The internal validity of a study is ensured if **control techniques** are used properly. The three methods of control are manipulating, holding conditions constant, and balancing. These three methods can be illustrated by a hypothetical experiment. Let us say that we are going to examine the effect of alcohol consumption on tension.

In the simplest of experiments, the independent variable is *manipulated* at two levels. These two levels usually represent the presence and absence of some treatment. The condition in which the treatment is *present* is commonly called the *experimental* condition; the condition in which the treatment is *absent* is called the *control* condition. In the experimental condition in our hypothetical research project, subjects are given 0.5 gram of alcohol per kilogram of body weight. The alcohol is administered as a mixture of vodka and tonic water. In the control condition, subjects are given the tonic water plain—no vodka. The alcohol is thus the independent variable; its presence or absence is manipulated by the researcher. The dependent variable is the subject's heart rate, which is the operational definition of tension in this study.

Other factors in the experiment that could influence the subjects' performance are controlled by *being held constant*. For instance, the instructions given for performing the tasks in the experiment, the tone of voice used by the experimenter in giving these instructions, the setting and the length of time in which the subjects are allowed to consume the drink, and other factors that can be held constant are identical in the two conditions. When factors that could be independent variables are held constant, no confounding is possible. Therefore, the researcher can be reasonably sure that the experiment has only one independent variable.

At least one set of factors cannot be held constant in this or any other experiment—namely, the characteristics of the subjects tested. Researchers control factors that cannot be held constant by *balancing* the influence of these factors among the different experimental conditions. The most important balancing technique, **random assignment,** involves assigning subjects randomly to the different groups in the experiment. For example, if our hypothetical researchers assigned all the male subjects to the vodka group and all the female subjects to the no-vodka group, sex differences would confound the experiment. If, however, the subjects were assigned randomly—by drawing lots, for example—then the researchers could assume that the two groups were equivalent on all measures other than the independent variable. (Note the difference between random assignment and random sampling, described earlier. In random sampling, subjects are chosen at random from a population, the goal being representativeness. In random assignment, already-chosen subjects are sorted at random into different experimental groups, the goal being balance among the groups.)

In a properly conducted experiment, then, all variables other than the independent variable are either held constant or balanced. If it were not for the manipulation of the independent variable (the presence or absence of alcohol in the drink), the groups would be expected to perform similarly. Therefore, if the groups perform *differently,* the researchers can assume that the independent variable is responsible for the difference.

Minimizing the effects of expectations A further problem in conducting experiments is that both the experimenter and the subjects may *expect* a certain outcome and may act accordingly. For example, if subjects know that they are drinking alcohol, they are likely to expect certain effects: that they will feel relaxed, giddy, and so on. If subjects respond according to these expectations, called **demand characteristics,** it will be difficult to determine the effect of the alcohol. Similarly, the experimenters may have expectations and may consequently treat the subjects who have received alcohol differently from those who are drinking plain tonic. For example, the experimenter may read the instructions more slowly to the "drinkers." The experimenter's observations of behavioral results may also be biased by the knowledge of the experimental conditions. For instance, the experi-

In a double-blind study, the experimental substance and the placebo control are administered from coded containers. This procedure keeps both the experimenters and the subjects from knowing until afterward which subjects received which substance. The purpose is to prevent the expectations of the experimenter and of the subjects from affecting the study's results.

menter, in observing the "drinking" group, may be more likely to notice any unusual motor movements or slurred speech. The term used to describe these biases is **experimenter effects.**

Researchers have developed procedures to control for both demand characteristics and experimenter effects. One is the use of a **placebo control group.** A *placebo* (Latin for "I shall please") is a substance that looks like a drug or other active substance but that is actually an inert, or inactive, substance. In our alcohol example, a placebo control group would receive a drink that would look, smell, and taste like the alcoholic drink but would contain no alcohol. Thus if "alcoholic" effects could be noted in these subjects' behavior after they had had their drinks, the experimenters would know that the subjects' expectations played an important role in their behavior.

Placebo control groups are traditionally used for evaluating drug treatments, but they have also been used to assess various forms of psychotherapy. While other groups will undergo specific therapies, the placebo control group will receive a "theoretically inert" treatment (Hibbs, 1993; S. Taylor & McLean, 1993). That is, they will be taken through some procedure that, while sufficiently complicated to seem like a form of psychotherapy, is nevertheless unrelated to any recognized form of therapeutic intervention. If, as has happened, this group shows improvement comparable to that of subjects receiving recognized treatments, experimenters will at least be alerted to the fact that therapeutic outcome is being affected by nonspecific (non-theory-related) factors, such as attention from the therapist or expectations of improvement.

Another way to minimize the influence of subjects' and experimenters' expectations is to use a **double-blind** procedure. In this technique, both the subject and the observer are kept unaware (blind) as to what treatment is being administered. In our alcohol study, we could achieve double-blind control by having two researchers: one to prepare the drinks and to code the glasses, and a second researcher to pass them out, recording which subject got which glass. As long as the first researcher did not know who got what drink and the second researcher did not understand the coding system, neither of them would know, when they go to the stage of observing the subjects' behavior, who was a "drinker" and who was not. The drinkers would be identified only later, when the code was compared with the record of who received what. In addition, the drinkers would have no way of knowing whether they were receiving the alcohol or the placebo. Thus, the double-blind.

Statistical inference Suppose we have conducted our alcohol study on a random sample of college students in California. Can we reasonably generalize the results to all California college students? To all college students in the United States? To all people over the age of eighteen? To answer questions of generalizability, researchers use a technique called **statistical inference.** Statistical inference is inductive and indirect. It is inductive because we draw *general* conclusions about populations on the basis of *specific* samples we test in our experiments. It is indirect because it begins by assuming the **null hypothesis**—which, as the name implies, is the assumption that the independent variable *has had no effect.* Then we use probability theory to determine the likelihood of obtaining the results of our experiment if the null hypothesis were true (that is, the likelihood of obtaining these results if the independent variable had had no effect). If this likelihood is small (conventionally, less than 5 times out of 100, or 0.05), we judge the result to be "statistically significant," reject the null hypothesis, and conclude that the independent variable did have an effect.

You can appreciate the process of statistical inference by considering the following situation: You and a friend have dinner together once a week, and you always toss a coin to see who will pay the bill. Curiously, your friend always has a coin ready, and so he always does the tossing. Now, it would be convenient if you could examine the coin to see if it is unfairly weighted. But since this might cause a problem in your relationship, the best you can do is test his coin indirectly by using the null hypothesis. That is, you assume that the coin is unbiased and then wait to see the results. If, over time, the coin tossing deviates from the expected 50-50 split of heads and tails more than chance would predict, you might conclude that there is something funny about your friend's coin. You don't know for sure that his coin is unfairly weighted, but you do know that the likelihood of your losing that often with a fair coin is less than 5 out of 100, or 0.05. Similarly, researchers would like to test any obtained result directly for significance, but usually the best they can do is compare their outcome to the expected outcome under conditions involving chance variation alone.

Statistical inference, like any tool, can be and is misused and sometimes is misleading. A good example is the famous "executive monkey" study of vulnerability to ulcers (J. V. Brady, 1958). In this study four pairs of monkeys were wired to receive electric shocks every twenty seconds. In each pair, however, one monkey, the so-called executive monkey, could turn off the coming shock if at any time in the intervening twenty seconds it pressed a lever near its hand. The second monkey in each pair, called the "yoked" monkey, had no such control. It simply received whatever shocks the executive received. The results of this study were not only statistically significant, they were dramatic. All four executive monkeys developed ulcers and died, while the yoked monkeys showed no signs of ulcer. The conclusion seemed clear: being in charge is stressful and can be hazardous to health.

After several attempts to replicate this finding had failed, however, researchers began to look more closely at the procedures followed in the original experiment. Rather than being randomly assigned, the four executive monkeys had been selected because, on a preliminary test, they had shown higher rates of responding than their yoked partners—a factor that, as it turned out, had confounded the experiment. Subsequent research has shown that animals with higher response rates have an increased likelihood of developing ulcers (J. M. Weiss, 1977). In fact, the more recent research findings suggest that being in charge *decreases* the likelihood of developing ulcers.

Another problem with statistical inference is that it is always possible to produce statistically significant findings merely by controlling procedures in such a way that a large number of factors are held constant. In "sensitive" experiments of this kind, very small average differences may be statistically significant. At the same time, the external validity of such findings may be so small as to render them useless in practical terms. A therapist reading about a new treatment wants to know not just whether the effect on his or her patients will be statistically significant but whether it will be *substantial*. Thus information about the strength of a treatment is more important for the clinician than is the treatment's statistical significance (Yeaton & Sechrest, 1981). This does not mean that tests of statistical significance are a waste of time. In some cases, they are a crucial protection against mistaking chance conjunctions for important relationships. But statistical significance is a minimum standard, beyond which the finding's *clinical significance*—can it be used? will it work?—remains to be shown.

For example, a clinician is treating patients with high anxiety. She reads a hypothetical study showing that fifteen therapy sessions of two hours each reduce self-rated anxiety significantly more than do fifteen sessions of the usual one-hour length. However, the greater reduction is actually only 5 additional points on a 100-point anxiety rating scale. Although the result is statistically significant, it would probably not be considered *clinically* significant enough to justify doubling the length of therapy.

RESEARCH DESIGNS

Research designs are the tools experimenters use to test hypotheses. Each design has its advantages and disadvantages. Asking a researcher whether one design is better than another is like asking a carpenter whether a screwdriver is better than a hammer. Which tool is best depends on the job to be done.

The Case Study

Psychology, as a *nomothetic* (law-establishing) discipline, seeks to develop broad generalizations, universal "laws" that apply to wide populations. In consequence, psychological research frequently involves the study of large groups and emphasizes the average performance of the group. Such studies, however, cannot capture the actual feel of human life: vivid, concrete, and personal. This shortcoming

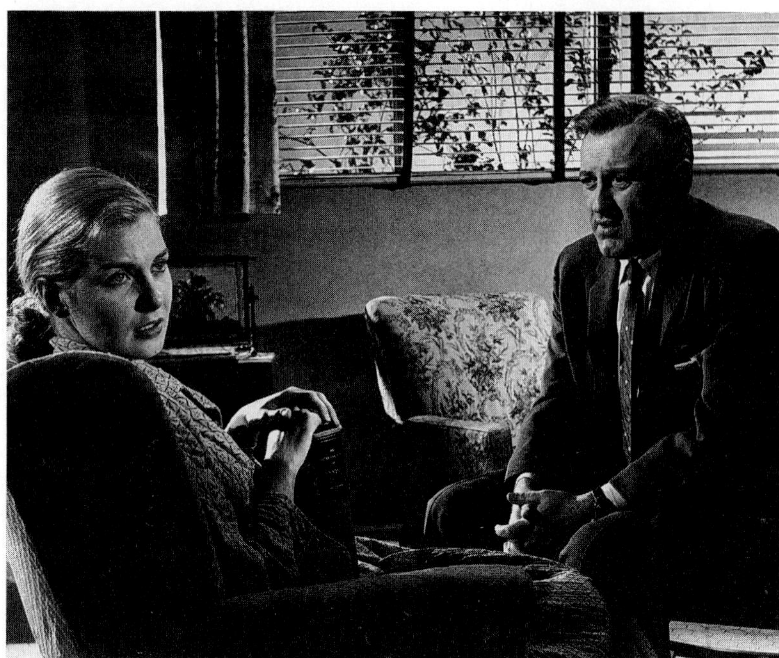

Joanne Woodward, as the patient, and Lee J. Cobb, as her psychiatrist, are shown in a scene from *The Three Faces of Eve,* a 1957 film dramatization of an actual case study of multiple personality.

has led some psychologists, notably Gordon Allport (1961), to argue that research based on groups must be supplemented by **idiographic research,** research built on the individual. A major form of idiographic research is the case study method, a **case study** being an intensive description and analysis of a single individual.

In its classic form, the case study begins with a detailed description of the subject, including test results, interview impressions, and physical and psychological history. Then it goes on to describe the psychological treatment of that person and the treatment outcome. Such studies have been instrumental in encouraging clinical innovation. The vividness of the case study is itself inviting—clinicians can imagine themselves implementing the same procedure—and the amount of detail included in the typical case study instructs clinicians as to how, exactly, the treatment is applied. Freud's famous case studies—Little Hans (1909/1962), about a child with a phobia; Anna O. (1895/1962), about a woman with "hysteria"; the Rat-Man (1909/1962), about a man with obsessional thoughts—did as much as his general writings to gain followers for his new psychoanalytic method. The same has been true of behavioral treatment. One of the crucial factors in the spread of behavioral therapy in the sixties and seventies was the publication, in 1965, of Leonard Ullmann and Leonard Krasner's *Case Studies in Behavior Modification,* a collection of accounts of single-case applications of what were then relatively new behavioral treatments.

The case study is also an effective means of describing rare phenomena. Certain kinds of psychopathology occur so infrequently that assembling a group to study becomes impossible—hence the case study. Multiple personality, a condition in which the person alternates between two or more separate personalities, is a rarity of this sort, and we have learned much from famous case studies such as *Sybil* (Schreiber, 1974) and *The Three Faces of Eve* (Thigpen & Cleckley, 1957).

Case studies can also advance scientific thinking by providing a *counterinstance,* a case that violates a widely accepted principle (Kazdin, 1980). Twenty-five years ago, for example, it was generally agreed that the human brain acted as a single unit—an assumption that was then challenged by the results of an operation on a patient suffering from uncontrollable epilepsy (Bogen, Fisher & Vogel, 1965). In an attempt to alleviate this patient's violent seizures, surgeons severed the corpus callosum, the major brain pathway between the two hemispheres, thus disrupting the unity of the patient's normal consciousness. The outcome of this "split brain" was, in the words of one researcher, a "patient with two minds" (Gazzaniga, 1972, p. 311). Although the patient behaved normally, careful testing revealed that it was literally possible for the right brain to know something that the left brain did not, and vice versa.

GENIE: A TRAGIC TEST CASE OF THE EFFECTS OF DEPRIVATION

The case study of Genie, a modern-day "wild child," offers both testimony to the strength of the human spirit and insight into the consequences to a child of untreated parental psychopathology. Genie's birth had been unwanted by her father, who had a history of violence toward his family. Before Genie, he and his wife had had another child who died of exposure at two and a half months after the father, irritated by the baby's crying, had placed it in the garage.

The mother, who was going blind and who feared that her husband might kill her, felt helpless to intervene on behalf of her children. Excerpts from Genie's case study reveal the extreme cruelty of the father's actions and the degree of her social isolation:

> In the house Genie was confined to a small bedroom, harnessed to an infant's potty seat. Genie's father sewed the harness, himself; unclad except for the harness, Genie was left to sit on that chair. Unable to move anything except her fingers and hands, feet and toes, Genie was left to sit, tied-up, hour after hour, often into the night, day after day, month after month, year after year. At night, when Genie was not forgotten, she was removed from her harness only to be placed into another restraining garment—a sleeping bag which her father had fashioned to hold Genie's arms stationary (allegedly to prevent her from taking it off). In effect, it was a straitjacket. Therein constrained, Genie was put into an infant's crib with wire mesh sides and a wire mesh cover overhead. Caged by night, harnessed by day, Genie was left to somehow endure the hours and years of her life.
>
> Hungry and forgotten, Genie would sometimes attempt to attract attention by making noise. Angered, her father would often beat her for doing so. In fact, there was a large piece of wood left in the corner of Genie's room which her father used solely to beat her whenever she made any sound. Genie learned to keep silent and to suppress all vocalization; but sometimes, desperate for attention or food, Genie would use her body or some object to make noise. Her father would not tolerate this either, and he often beat her with his wooden stick on these occasions as well. During these times, and on all other occasions that her father dealt with Genie, he never spoke to her. Instead, he acted like a wild dog. He made barking sounds, he growled at her, he let his nails grow long and scratched her, he bared his teeth at her; and if he wished to merely threaten her with his presence, he stood outside the door and made his doglike noises—to warn her that he was there and that if she persisted in whatever she was doing, he would come in and beat her. That terrible noise, the sound of her father standing outside her door growling or barking or both, was almost the only sound Genie heard during those years she was imprisoned in her room.
>
> This was Genie's life—isolated, often forgotten, frequently abused (many details of horrible abuse are omitted here), physically restrained, starved for sensory stimulation. Thus minimally exposed to humanity, and most of that the most hideous of human behavior, Genie grew into a pitiful creature.
>
> Finally, when Genie was thirteen and a half years old, Genie's mother . . . took Genie and left her home and her husband.
>
> They escaped to the grandmother's home, where she and Genie stayed for three more weeks. During the third week, Genie's mother was advised to apply for aid to the blind. Taking Genie with her, she inadvertently went to the family aids building, where an eligibility worker, upon seeing Genie, sensed that something was terribly wrong. The worker alerted her supervisor immediately, and the two of them questioned the mother. What they saw and heard caused them to call the police. The police took Genie into custody; charges were brought against the parents. On the day of the trial the father killed himself. He left a suicide note stating, "The world will never understand."
>
> Genie was admitted into the hospital for extreme malnutrition. She had been discovered, at last. (Curtiss, 1977, pp. 5–6)

Among the many skills that Genie lacked, probably the most serious was language. Though she could apparently understand a few simple words, she had never learned to speak. Therefore her case offered a test of the critical-period hypothesis of language development, which holds that human beings cannot acquire normal language skills after they have passed a critical period ending at some point before adolescence (Lenneberg, 1967). The evidence of Genie's later development supported that hypothesis. After much time and work, she showed some progress in language acquisition, but never developed anything resembling normal speech.

While case studies sometimes disconfirm assumptions, in other instances they offer tentative support for a theory under debate. Particularly convincing are case studies that provide an "extreme test" of a theory. Consider, for example, the theory that human language develops through exposure to normal speech during a "critical period" of childhood, extending from about age two to the onset of puberty (Lenneberg, 1967). In this view, natural language acquisition cannot take place after puberty. Of course, most human beings acquire language long before puberty, and no researcher would try to test this theory by isolating a child until puberty. However, a "natural" test of this theory was provided by the discovery of a child called Genie, who had been subjected to extreme isolation from birth to age thirteen (Curtiss, 1977). Genie's history and its relevance to the critical-period hypothesis are summarized in the box above.

The limitations of the case study method are

quite obvious. Because numerous variables are not controlled, cause-and-effect conclusions can rarely be drawn; too many plausible alternative causes remain uneliminated. Likewise, it is impossible to generalize safely from one person. Who can say that the progress of a dog phobia in patient *X* is representative of phobics in general? Yet, case studies do have the unique advantage of vividness. In reading a case study—especially an account of a "textbook case," a person who sums up the characteristics of a disorder—one can actually form a mental picture of what that condition is like. In view of these strengths and weaknesses, case studies are generally regarded as most valuable when they are used to *complement* other, specifically nomothetic research (Kazdin, 1980). That is the way they will be used in this book.

Correlational Research

In abnormal psychology, both ethical and practical considerations influence our choice of research method. For example, if we were interested in whether a traumatic event such as physical assault can cause depression, we could not assault a randomly selected group of people and compare them with another, unmolested group to see which group was more likely to get depressed. Similarly, if we were interested in the relationship between divorce and emotional disorders, we could not randomly assign some people to get divorced.

A common approach to this research dilemma is to examine groups that have been "treated naturally." That is, people who have been assaulted can be compared with those who have not; people who are divorced can be compared with those who have remained married. Because subjects in these studies are selected from existing, natural groups, the designs are called **natural group designs.** The purpose of such studies is to see whether these natural treatments result in other differences between the groups. For example, studies have shown that people who are separated or divorced are much more likely to become depressed than are those who are married (Bruce & Kim, 1992). Since such designs involve looking for correlations, or relationships, between subjects' characteristics and their performance, they are also called **correlational research designs.**

One type of correlational design frequently used in research on psychopathology is the **case-control design,** in which people diagnosed as having some kind of mental disorder—these are the *cases*—are compared with *controls,* or people who have not been diagnosed as having the disorder. We have already seen an example of this: the hypothetical study in which word associations of schizophrenics are compared with those of people chosen from the general population. If cases and controls differ in their word associations, this may be attributable to schizophrenia as long as other characteristics are balanced across the two groups.

Correlational research designs are highly effective in meeting the first two objectives of the scientific method, description and prediction. Unfortunately, serious problems arise when the results of correlational studies are used as a basis of causal inference. People have a tendency to assume that all three conditions for a causal inference (covariation of events, a time-order relationship, and elimination of plausible alternative causes) have been met when really only the first condition, covariation, has been met. For instance, the finding that divorced people are more likely than married people to become depressed shows that these two factors are correlated. This finding could be taken to mean that divorce causes depression. Before reaching this conclusion, however, we must be sure that the time-order condition has been met—namely, that divorce *preceded* the depression. Perhaps depressed people are more likely to get divorced, because of the strain placed on the relationship by the depression. In other words, a demonstration of covariation offers no indication of the *direction* of a causal relationship. (For a discussion of the most common measure of covariation, the *correlation coefficient,* see the box on page 109.)

Nor does covariation eliminate plausible alternative causes. The fact that two factors covary does not mean that one is the cause of the other. Perhaps they are both dependent on another factor altogether—a situation called the **third-variable problem.** In our sample, perhaps the situation is not that divorce causes depression or vice versa but rather that both are caused by the stresses of poverty. The directionality and third-variable problems make it a treacherous enterprise to infer causation from correlations.

One possible solution to the third-variable problem is *matching,* whereby the subjects are matched on potentially relevant factors other than the factor of interest. The divorced and nondivorced subjects could be matched, for example, on income level. The idea, of course, is to end up with two groups that differ only in the matter of divorce. In a sense, matching is an application of the control technique of holding conditions constant. One problem with this approach is that matching may lead to such a restriction of the people included in the study that the groups may no longer be rep-

THE CORRELATION COEFFICIENT: A MEASURE OF PREDICTIVE STRENGTH

The correlation coefficient (*r*) is a measure of how well we can predict one variable if we know the value of another variable. For example, we might want to know how accurately we could predict students' success in college on the basis of their SAT scores. The correlation coefficient has two characteristics, a direction and a magnitude.

The *direction* can be either positive or negative. A positive correlation indicates that as the value of one variable (*X*) increases, the value of the other variable (*Y*) also increases (see diagram *A*). The correlation between SAT scores and success in college should be a positive one. In a negative correlation, as the value of *X* increases, the value of *Y* decreases (see diagram *B*). The higher a person's social class, the *less* likely that person is to be admitted to a mental hospital; social class and admission to mental hospitals are negatively correlated. Diagram *C* shows what happens when two variables are neither positively nor negatively correlated: as the value of *X* increases, the value of *Y* changes unpredictably. Because we have no ability to predict *Y* on the basis of *X*, the correlation coefficient in this situation is zero. The relationship between eye color and mental illness represents a zero correlation; we could not predict the likelihood that a person would become mentally ill by knowing the person's eye color.

The *magnitude* of the correlation coefficient can range from 0 to 1.00. A value of +1.00 indicates a perfect positive correlation, and a value of −1.00 indicates a perfect negative correlation. Values between 0 and 1.00 indicate predictive relationships of intermediate strength. Remember, the sign of the correlation signifies only its direction. An *r* value of −0.46 indicates a stronger relationship than an *r* of +0.20.

One final word of caution: The correlation coefficient represents only the *linear* relationship between two variables. The linear correlation of *X* and *Y* in diagram *D* is zero, but the two variables are obviously related. A curvilinear relationship like that shown in diagram *D* exists between level of arousal and performance. Performance first increases with increasing arousal but then declines when arousal exceeds an optimal level.

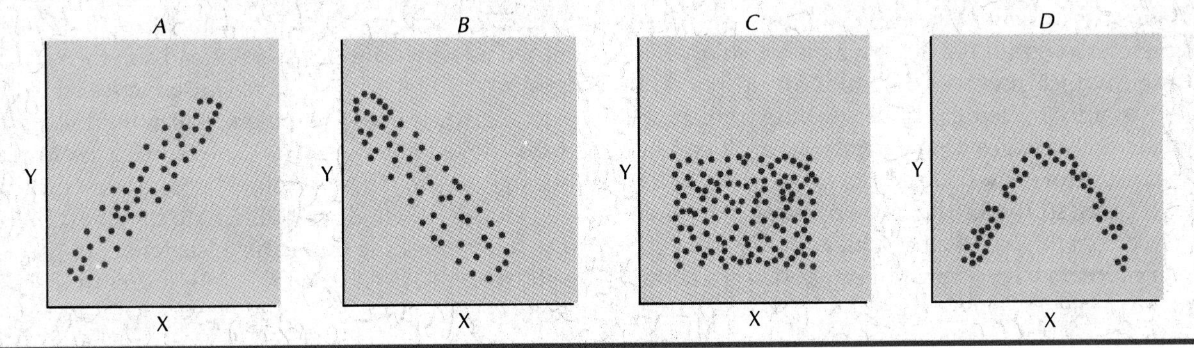

resentative of the general population. If you were to compare the emotional disorders of college students with those of elderly people who had been matched with the students for general health and amount of education, you would probably be studying a very unrepresentative group of elderly people. A more serious problem with matching, however, is that the number of potentially relevant factors is usually so large that it is impossible to select two or more groups equal in all characteristics except the one of interest. In the divorce study, one might want to control many factors besides income—for example, educational level, religion, ethnic origin, number of children. Nonetheless, matching can be useful. If a relationship between divorce and depression persisted after divorced and married groups were matched on income level, then the researcher could reasonably conclude that income level alone was not responsible for the difference. Alternatively, the researcher could revert to random selection. When there are many potentially confounding factors, the best choice is usually careful random selection or random selection within certain broad restrictions—in this case, for example, married people with family incomes of $50,000 to $100,000 *versus* divorced people whose predivorce family income was $50,000 to $100,000.

Sometimes the best way to eliminate a potentially confounding factor is to go ahead and test it. For instance, a correlational study of biochemical differences between patients and nonpatients might show that the patient group had more of one particular enzyme in their bodies. This finding could be used to support a biochemical explanation of their disorder. On the other hand, the enzyme difference could be the result not of biochemical malfunction but of diet or drug differences between the two groups. To eliminate this question, the researchers could have patients and nonpatients follow a special diet so that the influence of diet on the enzyme difference between the two groups could be evaluated. If differences in diet had contributed to the *original* enzyme difference, then the enzyme difference between patients and nonpatients should vary with changes in diet. If it does not, then the researchers can probably assume that diet is not confounding their findings.

Longitudinal Studies One type of correlational research design is sufficiently distinct to warrant separate discussion. In these studies, called **longitudinal studies** (or *prospective studies*), the behaviors of the same subjects are studied on several different occasions over what is usually an extended period of time. Because the same people are tested several times, it is possible to specify more precisely the time-order relationship between factors that covary.

High-risk designs One of the most important forms of longitudinal research is the **high-risk design,** which involves the study of people who have a high probability of developing a disorder. For several decades now, Sarnoff Mednick and his research team (e.g., T. D. Cannon & Mednick, 1993) have been studying the development of people who are at high risk for schizophrenia because their mothers were schizophrenic and because this disorder seems to have a strong genetic component. The findings of Mednick's team will be discussed in detail in Chapter 15, but two points are worth noting here, as examples of what high-risk research can produce. First, schizophrenic mothers whose children also became schizophrenic were more severely disturbed than were schizophrenic mothers whose children did not become schizophrenic. Second, the mothers of the high-risk children who became schizophrenic were hospitalized—and thus separated from their families—while their children were young.

Mednick's longitudinal studies are an example of *genetic high-risk design:* the subjects are chosen because they are thought to be genetically predisposed to the disorder. Another type of high-risk design that has been used increasingly in psychopathology research in the last ten years is the *behavioral high-risk design.* Here, subjects are chosen for longitudinal study not because of genetic vulnerability but because they show some behavioral or psychological characteristic, of whatever origin, that is thought to make them vulnerable to a disorder. A good example of this design is the research of Loren and Jean Chapman and their associates (Allen, Chapman, Chapman, et al., 1987; Chapman & Chapman, 1987). The Chapmans selected a group of young people who, by virtue of their unusual thought processes as identified on a test, were considered to be prone to psychosis. After only a two-year follow-up, the sixty people in their high-risk group had more psychotic and psychotic-like episodes than did those in the low-risk group (Chapman & Chapman, 1987). Three high-risk subjects had actually developed full-blown psychotic disorders, whereas none of the low-risk subjects had developed a psychotic disorder.

Although longitudinal designs are more powerful than conventional correlational designs, they too present problems when it comes to inferring causation. For example, in Mednick's study, to say that the child's schizophrenia is related to the severity of the mother's schizophrenia and to the timing of her hospitalization is not necessarily to say that separation from the mother or the degree of her psychopathology caused the disorder in the child. Perhaps the children who were later diagnosed as schizophrenic were already, in their early years, sufficiently affected to cause increased emotional distress in their mothers, which in turn could have caused these mothers to be more severely disturbed and to be hospitalized sooner. Longitudinal studies, then, do not eliminate the question of causality, but they do enable researchers to gain a more complete picture of the time course of the development they are investigating.

Epidemiological Studies

Epidemiology is the study of the frequency and distribution of disorders within specific populations. Key concepts in epidemiology are **incidence,** the number of new cases of the disorder in question within a given time period, such as a year; **prevalence,** the percentage of the population that has the disorder at a particular time; and duration, simply the average length of a given disorder. The simple formula is prevalence = incidence × duration. Thus acute depression is a brief disorder with a high incidence, while schizophrenia is a lengthy disorder with a low incidence. Both have fairly high prevalence but for different reasons. Epidemiological data, then tell us, to begin with, how common a disorder is. They may also point researchers to significant relationships between the

These children have spent their early years amid random violence in Belfast, Northern Ireland. Epidemiological studies would reveal the incidence of depression and anxiety disorders among children in this community. Such studies might also identify the kinds of buffers that are common to children who cope well with extreme stress.

disorder and other variables, such as age, sex, or the prevalence of *another* disorder. Such findings, in turn, may lead us to causes. For example, the epidemiological finding that depressed people have higher rates of negative life events than do nondepressed people (e.g., Paykel, 1979b) has led to what is now the widely held hypothesis that life stresses may trigger depressive episodes in vulnerable people.

Epidemiological surveys, like other research designs, are prone to certain pitfalls. The most serious concern is that descriptions of a population based on a sample are dependent on the representativeness of the sample. Random sampling is the best technique currently available to ensure representativeness, but random sampling produces representativeness only when all the selected respondents take part in the survey. In one study, for example, a random sample of Canadian women was surveyed in order to obtain information on the prevalence of fears and phobias in women (Costello, 1982), but as the research report points out, 16 percent of the women selected refused to participate. We have no way of knowing whether these women would be more likely or less likely to have fears and phobias than were the women who agreed to participate. Perhaps the nonparticipants were generally more fearful and therefore unwilling to talk to a stranger. Or perhaps they were generally *less* fearful and thus able to be assertive in refusing to be questioned. Although the representativeness of a survey is compromised whenever the response rate falls below 100 percent, the fact is that the usual response rate is about 50 to 60 percent, and, however short of the ideal, this is generally considered acceptable in psychological research.

Experimental Designs

A true experimental design is one in which an independent variable is manipulated by the experimenter and a dependent variable is measured. For example, researchers might identify a group of people with dog phobias. Each person could be randomly assigned to one of three treatment conditions (the independent variable): medication, Freudian psychoanalysis, or behavioral treatment. The dependent variable might be a scale measuring the severity of dog phobia that would be administered before and after the treatment to determine the most effective form of therapy.

Analogue Experiments One type of true experimental design often used in psychopathology research is the **analogue experiment.** In this approach, the researcher designs an experimental situation that is analogous to "real life" and may therefore serve as a model for how psychopathology develops and how it can be alleviated. Watson and Rayner's (1920) conditioning of a phobia in Little Albert (Chapter 3) was an analogue experiment—the first attempt to induce psychopathology in a human subject under laboratory conditions (Abramson & Seligman, 1977). By demonstrating that the pairing of the rat with a very loud noise resulted in a fear of white rats, Watson and Rayner provided evidence that naturally occurring phobias could be acquired through respondent conditioning.

The critical advantage of multigroup and analogue experiments is that they permit the kinds of control necessary to identify causal relationships and therefore have high internal validity. Hiroto and Seligman (1975), for instance, presented one group of college students with solvable cognitive problems and another group with unsolvable problems; then they measured all the students' mood and performance on some unrelated tasks. Students who had been given the unsolvable problems became sad and did not do as well on the later tasks as did the students who had worked with the solvable problems. Similar mood and performance deficits have been observed in people diagnosed as depressed. Therefore the findings of this analogue experiment can be viewed as supporting the theory that depression is a form of "learned helplessness" (Nolen, Girgus, & Seligman, 1992).

Another important advantage of analogue research is that in the "artificial" analogue setting the experimenter can test variables that could not be manipulated with genuinely distressed subjects. To cause ordinary college students to become briefly depressed, as was done in the experiment just described, is ethically permissible, but one cannot risk making depressed people more depressed. On the other hand, the kinds of psychological problems that one can ethically induce in an experiment may *not* be analogous to mental disorders (Suomi, 1982). In general, the more ethical an analogue experiment in abnormal psychology, the less analogous it is likely to be, but one cannot, for that reason, ignore ethics. To state the problem more concretely, failure to complete a set of unsolvable laboratory problems may not be comparable to real precursors of depression, such as the death of a close friend, but researchers cannot kill people's friends in order to produce a better analogue. This problem can be partially solved by development of animal models of psychopathology. For example, uncontrollable electric shock has been used with animal subjects as an analogue of the types of stressful experiences that are thought to cause ulcers and depression (J. M. Weiss, 1977, 1982). We saw this technique in the executive monkey experiment.

Animal models offer several advantages (Suomi, 1982). Not only can researchers more closely mimic the severity of naturally occurring events; they can also gain almost complete control over the subject's developmental history (e.g., diet and living conditions) and even, through controlled breeding, its genetic endowment. Many important variables, therefore, can be held constant and thus eliminated as possible explanations for behavior change. Further, many behavioral and physiological procedures considered too intrusive to be used with human subjects (e.g., sampling brain neurotransmitters or cerebrospinal fluid) can be performed on animals. And since laboratory animals develop more rapidly and have shorter life spans than do human subjects, the long-term consequences of pathology and effectiveness of treatment can be assessed quickly. Animal models have been developed for drug addiction, anxiety disorders, and various other forms of psychopathology (King, Campbell, &

The baby macaque on the left exhibits normal curiosity, while the one on the right, suffering from induced fetal alcohol syndrome, is listless and unresponsive. Such animal models of human pathology can make valuable contributions to our understanding of various disorders. They present special ethical problems and have become controversial. However, animal research will remain an essential tool in determining the causes of psychopathology.

Edwards, 1993). It should be added, however, that experimentation with animals has also become increasingly controversial on ethical grounds.

Though analogue experiments cannot be exactly like the real thing, they can come close to it, and it is on the degree of likeness that they are evaluated: How close to reality did they come? This evaluation in turn depends on how much we currently know about the real thing in question (Suomi, 1982). We still do not know the causes of many psychological disorders, let alone the cures. (This is what the researchers are trying to find out.) Consequently, many models can be validated only partially—in terms of the symptoms they reproduce, for instance. Yet even though experimenters may, by manipulating certain variables, reproduce the symptoms of a naturally occurring disorder, they still have not proved that the naturally occurring disorder issues from those same variables (Abramson & Seligman, 1977). When animal subjects are used, a nagging question is always present: Just how similar is the behavior of any other animal species to that of the human species? In addition, it is unlikely that all forms of human psychopathology can be induced in animals.

The internal validity provided by analogue experiments must be weighed against the cost to external validity. As a general rule, experimental procedures that increase internal validity tend to decrease or limit external validity (Kazdin & Rogers, 1978). Nevertheless, the search for causal relationships is best served by the tightly controlled investigations that tend to increase internal validity.

The Single-Case Study

Experiments with multiple groups, particularly those in which subjects are randomly assigned to experimental conditions, are often considered the best means of establishing cause-and-effect relationships. Nevertheless, they have certain disadvantages for research in abnormal psychology (Hersen & Barlow, 1976). For example, ethical problems arise when researchers withhold treatment from subjects in order to provide a "control" group. Furthermore, it is sometimes difficult to assemble enough appropriate subjects for a group experiment. Finally, the average response of a group of subjects may not be representative of any one subject. These problems have led some researchers to turn to single-case experiments.

The **single-case experiment** resembles its cousin the case study in focusing on behavior change in one person. However, it differs from the traditional case study in that it methodically varies the conditions surrounding the person's behavior and continuously monitors the behavior under those changing conditions. When properly carried out, the single-case experimental design has considerable internal validity.

The first stage of a single-case experiment is usually an observation, or *baseline,* stage. During this stage, a record is made of the subject's behavior before any intervention. A typical measure is frequency of behavior over some period of time, such as an hour, a day, or a week. For example, a record might be made of the number of tantrums thrown by a child or the number of panic attacks reported by a person with an anxiety disorder. (A potential drawback to this approach is that the mere fact of observation can change the behavior if the subject knows he or she is being observed, a problem known as Hawthorne effect.) Once behavior is shown to be relatively stable—that is, once there is little fluctuation between recording intervals—a treatment is introduced. The effect of the treatment is ordinarily evaluated by comparing baseline behavior with after-intervention behavior. Single-case designs are most often carried out by practitioners of behavior modification (Chapter 3), and interventions are therefore usually based on learning principles.

While several different experimental designs are available to the researcher (Kazdin, 1980), the most commonly used are the ABAB and multiple-baseline designs.

ABAB Design In the **ABAB design,** an initial baseline stage (A) is followed by a treatment stage (B), a return to baseline (A), and another treatment stage (B). Because treatment is removed during the second A stage and any improvement in behavior is likely to be reversed, this design is also referred to as a *reversal design.* If behavior, after improving in the first treatment stage, reverts to baseline when the treatment is withdrawn and then improves again in the final treatment stage, it is fair to assume that the treatment was responsible for the behavior change. On the other hand, if only one baseline and one treatment stage were used (an AB design), any improvement in the B stage might reasonably be seen as a coincidence, reflecting perhaps a spontaneous change occurring at the same time the treatment was introduced.

Kelly and Drabman (1977) used an ABAB design when they tried to modify a socially undesirable behavior in a three-year-old mentally retarded girl named Susan. For most of her life, Susan had had a habit of repeatedly sticking out her tongue. The clinicians were concerned that, left untreated, this behavior would become even more persistent and would make it difficult for Susan to be accepted by other people.

Baseline observations were made of the frequency of Susan's tongue thrusts during daily ten-minute sessions. Then came the treatment: a mildly aversive stimulus, lemon juice, was squirted on Susan's tongue whenever she stuck it out. Treatments lasted ten minutes and continued for nine sessions. Treatment was then withdrawn for sixteen sessions. Finally, a second treatment stage was instituted, for another sixteen sessions. A follow-up was conducted six months after the end of the ABAB treatment. Figure 5.2 shows the changes in Susan's behavior through alternating baseline and treatment conditions. As the graph shows, the lemon juice was successful in eliminating tongue thrusting, and the six-month follow-up revealed no recurrence.

The withdrawing of treatment in the ABAB design may pose certain ethical problems. Although Susan's behavior would not be judged as life threatening or particularly debilitating, there are certain behaviors—such as head banging in severely disturbed children—for which it would not be appropriate to halt treatment once its effectiveness had been demonstrated. In such cases, other single-case experimental designs must be considered.

Multiple-Baseline Design An experimental design that does not depend on removing treatment or reversing a positive effect is the **multiple-baseline design.** In this procedure, the same treatment is aimed successively at several targets—usually several subjects, or several behaviors in one subject, or several situational variants for one behavior. When the design is used across subjects, for example, a baseline is first established for each subject; then the intervention is introduced first for one subject, then for the next, and so on. If the intervention is responsible for changing behavior, then presumably an effect will be observed in each subject immediately following treatment. Like the ABAB design, the multiple-baseline design rules out alternative explanations for behavior change by demonstrating that behavior responds *systematically* to the introduction of the treatment.

Dyer, Christian, and Luce (1982) used a multiple-baseline design to see whether children suffering from autism (Chapter 18) could be taught to "look before they leaped" in performing discrimination-learning tasks. Teachers of autistic children have often observed that many such children seem to begin a task without paying any attention to its requirements. It was felt that this tendency could be remedied by use of a *response-delay* procedure, which requires the child to wait a predetermined amount of time before responding. The procedure was tried on three autistic children. In practical terms it generally meant holding the child's hands for several seconds after he or she was presented with a discrimination problem.

Multiple baselines for performance on the dis-

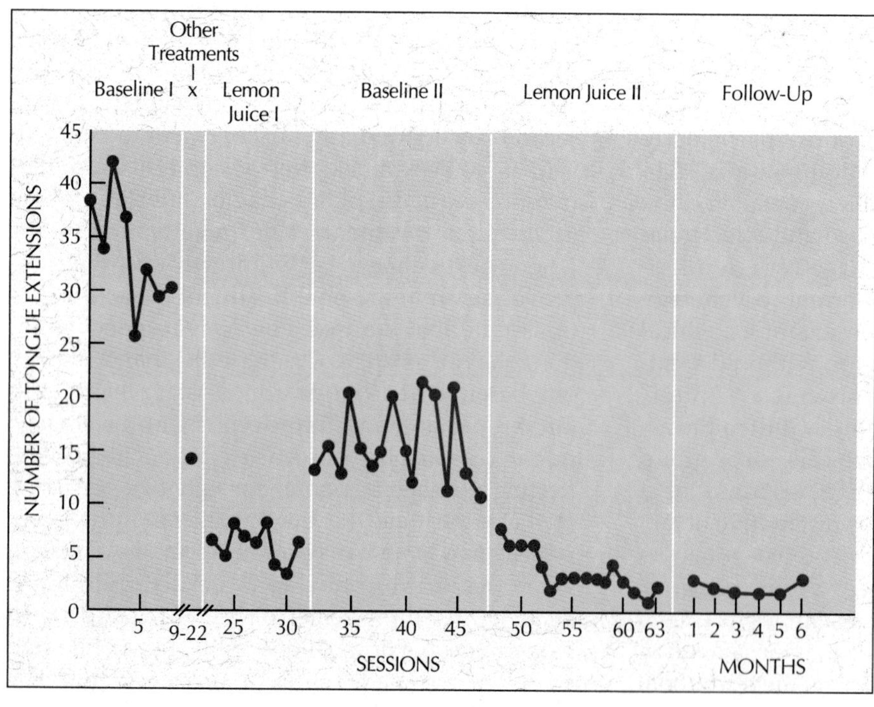

FIGURE 5.2 The ABAB procedure helped Susan, a retarded three-year-old, learn to stop sticking out her tongue. As the graph shows, squirting lemon juice on her tongue discouraged her habit. When the lemon juice treatment was temporarily halted (Baseline II), her tongue thrusting started up again. (During sessions 9 through 22, several treatment strategies were explored "without lasting success" before lemon juice was used [J. A. Kelly & Drabman, 1977].)

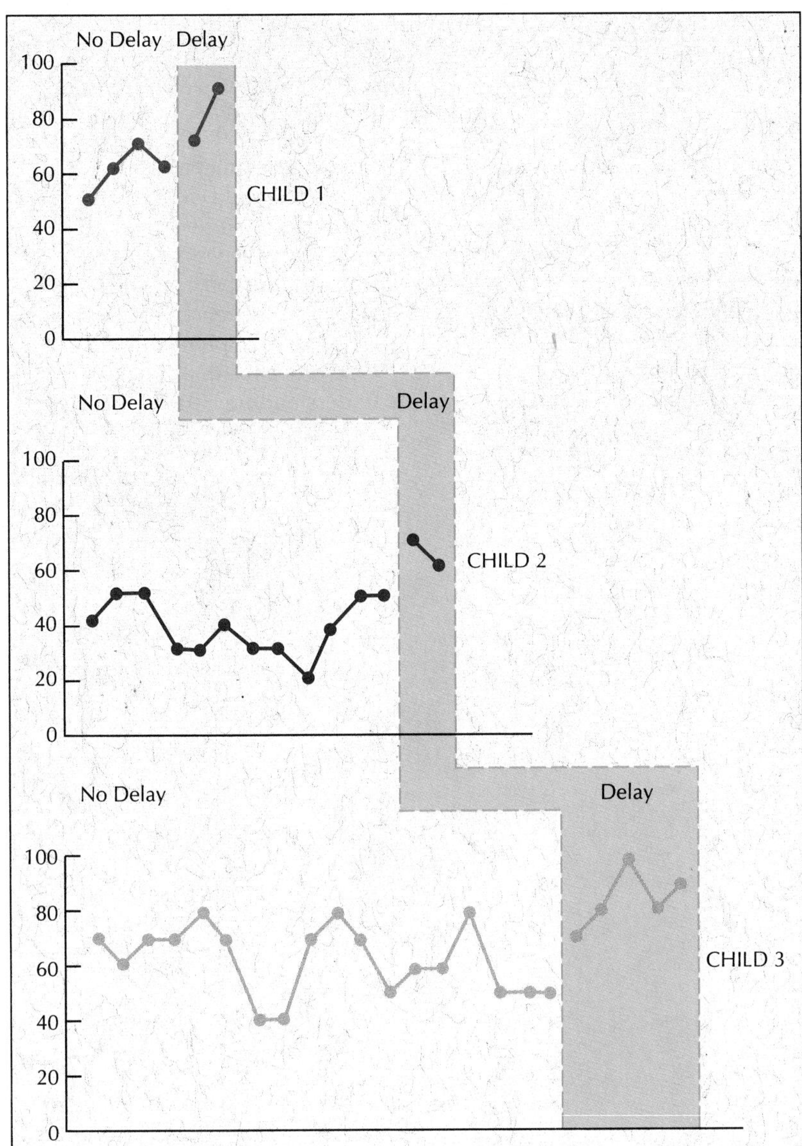

FIGURE 5.3 The multiple-baseline design was employed to see whether encouraging autistic children to pay attention to instructions before performing a discrimination-learning task would help them do better on the task (Dyer, Christian, & Luce, 1982). The multiple-baseline design has an important advantage over the ABAB design: it does not require the experimenter to interrupt a treatment that seems to be helpful.

crimination-learning tasks were established for the three children. Intervention was introduced first with one child, then with the second, and finally with the third. An examination of the behavioral records (Figure 5.3) shows that each child's discrimination learning immediately improved with the response-delay treatment.

Limitations of the Single-Case Design Like the traditional case study, the single-case experiment design is weak in external validity. As each person is unique, it can be argued that there is no way of knowing whether the effect of a particular treatment on one person can predict its effect on other people. This problem may not be as serious as it appears, because the efficiency with which data can be collected from one subject often makes it easy to repeat the procedures with other subjects (Kazdin, 1978). Therefore while generalizability is in no way guaranteed by the single-case design, it can easily be tested. Moreover, external validity can be enhanced by use of a single *group* of subjects in a single-case experimental design, such as ABAB. Then it is possible to draw conclusions about the effect of the experimental variable not just on the individual subjects but on the population from which the sample was drawn.

KEY TERMS

ABAB design (113)
analogue experiments (111)
case-control design (108)
case study (106)
confounding (101)
control (100)
control techniques (103)
correlational research designs (108)
covariation of events (101)
demand characteristics (103)
dependent variable (103)
description (100)
double-blind (104)
elimination of plausible alternative causes (101)
epidemiology (110)
experimenter effects (104)
external validity (101)
generalizability (101)
high-risk design (110)
hypothesis (102)
idiographic research (106)
incidence (110)
independent variable (103)
internal validity (101)
longitudinal studies (110)
multiple-baseline design (114)
natural group designs (108)
null hypothesis (104)
operational definitions (102)
placebo control group (104)
prediction (100)
prevalence (110)
random assignment (103)
random sample (102)
reliability (100)
representativeness (101)
single-case experiment (113)
statistical inference (104)
third-variable problem (108)
time-order relationship (101)
understanding (101)
validity (100)

SUMMARY

- The scientific method is characterized by the skeptical attitude of those who use it, by the objectives it is intended to meet (namely, reliable and valid description, prediction, control, and understanding of behavior), and by the specific procedures used to meet those objectives (hypothesis testing, definition formulation, and methods of control).
- Research that fails to eliminate alternative explanations of a phenomenon is said to be confounded. Only when no confounding is present is a study internally valid. The external validity of research depends on whether the findings can be generalized, or applied, to different populations, settings, and conditions. External validity increases as the representativeness of a sample increases. The best way to achieve a representative sample is to use a random sampling procedure.

  Research often begins with the development of a testable, or falsifiable, hypothesis. To be testable, a hypothesis must be formulated in terms of concepts that have been given operational definitions so that they can be observed and measured.
- Generally, a hypothesis is tested in an experiment, in which three control techniques are used: manipulating the independent variable in order to measure its effects on the dependent variable; holding all other variables constant; and balancing uncontrollable factors—the personal characteristics of the subjects being tested—among all conditions.
- Many different research designs are used to investigate abnormal behavior. A case study is the intensive description and analysis of a single person. Case studies encourage clinical innovation, describe rare phenomena, and can either disconfirm a general scientific principle or offer tentative support for a psychological theory. The usefulness of the case study is limited because investigators usually cannot draw cause-and-effect conclusions from it or apply their findings to other individuals.

  Correlational or natural group designs examine whether systematic differences exist between groups of people who have been treated "naturally." A serious problem in evaluating the results of correlational studies is to determine the direction of the causal relationship and to eliminate possible third variables that may cause differences between groups.
- Longitudinal studies examine the behavior of people over time. Although this design does not solve the problem of causality, it is more powerful than a correlational design because assumptions of covariation and time-order relationships can be more easily tested.
- The high-risk design is a type of longitudinal research that follows persons who are thought to be vulnerable to developing a disorder in the future.
- Epidemiological studies examine the incidence and prevalence of a behavioral disorder in a population. Such studies can help to determine whether the frequency of a particular disorder is related to other variables, which may be causes. A major concern in epidemiological surveys is the representativeness of the sample.
- In experimental designs an independent variable is manipulated by the experimenter and a dependent variable is measured.
- Single-case experimental designs monitor behavior change in an individual following an intervention that was introduced after a baseline (no-treatment) observation. Evidence for a causal relationship is obtained if the person's behavior changes systematically with the introduction of the treatment.

6

DIAGNOSIS AND ASSESSMENT

Most of this book is devoted to the common categories of abnormal behavior. As categories, such disorders are relatively easy to discuss. We chart the symptoms, give illustrative case histories, weigh the possible causes, and review the suggested treatments. It is only in the vocabulary of psychology, however, that abnormal behaviors exist as categories. In reality, they are the complex and ambiguous things that people do and say. And the first job of the mental health profession is to look at what the person says and does and to make some sense out of it. This process is called **psychological assessment,** which may be defined as the collection, organization, and interpretation of information about a person and his or her situation.

Psychological assessment is not a recent invention. Throughout history people have been developing systems for sorting people into categories so as to predict how they will behave. The first assessment system was probably astrology, developed by the ancient Babylonians and later disseminated to Egypt, Greece, India, and China (McReynolds, 1975). Initially the stars were read only for clues about matters of public concern—wars, floods, crop failure. By the fifth century B.C., however, astrology was also being used as the basis of personal horoscopes, revelations of individual character and destiny.

Around the same time, ancient Greece produced another assessment procedure—physiognomy, the interpretation of character according to physique and bearing. Physiognomy may have been responsible for the first psychological test. It is reported that the Greek philosopher Pythagoras (sixth century B.C.) screened candidates for his religious society not just by questioning them verbally but also by subjecting them to a physiognomic examination, in which the form and bearing of their bodies, along with their facial features and expressions, were "read" as indicators of their character. The Chinese probably had the first written assessment procedures. In the late Qin or early Han dynasty, around the second century B.C., the emperor used written tests of literacy, verbal cleverness, and knowledge of geography and law to select civil servants (Bowman, 1989; Matarazzo, 1990).

Other societies produced their own systems of assessment, from Hippocrates' four humors to Kraepelin's medical classification scheme (Chapter 1). An important thing to note about all these assessment systems is that each is based on a theory of human behavior. To the astrologists, behavior was determined not by will, learning, or parentage but by the positions of the stars at one's birth. To the physiognomists, behavior was the product of a consistent underlying personality—one that could be determined on the basis of physical features. Similarly, modern assessment procedures are outgrowths of psychological theories, which, like all theories, are revised from decade to decade. Thus with assessment—as with the definition, explanation, and treatment of abnormal behavior—we are looking at something that is relative and changing, the product of each generation's efforts to make sense of human behavior.

This eighteenth-century cartoon lampoons the pseudoscience of craniology, one of the many systems for categorizing behavior—in this case, on the basis of the size and shape of the skull—that have been developed throughout history.

In this chapter we will first discuss the issues surrounding assessment: what it aims to do, how well it succeeds, and what can cause it to fail. Then we will describe the most commonly used assessment techniques and their relation to the major psychological perspectives.

ASSESSMENT: THE ISSUES

Why do people undergo psychological assessment? In what cases, and why, does such assessment involve diagnostic labeling? How useful are diagnostic labels? How can we tell a good assessment technique from a bad one? What extraneous factors can influence assessment? These questions have no easy answers. The entire enterprise of assessment—to say nothing of individual assessment methods—is surrounded by controversy.

Why Assessment?

All psychological assessment has two goals. The first is **description,** the rendering of an accurate portrait of personality, cognitive functioning, mood, and behavior. This goal would be important even if there were no such thing as abnormal psychology. Science aims to describe, and psychology, the science of human personality and behavior, aims to describe personality and behavior, simply for the sake of increasing our understanding of reality. However, such descriptions may also be needed for decision-making purposes, and this is definitely the case in abnormal psychology.

This brings us to the second goal of psychological assessment: **prediction.** Again, prediction need serve no practical purpose. The mere desire to advance human knowledge could motivate a psychologist to try to predict, for example, whether children of divorced parents are likely to become divorced themselves. Such predictions are scientific hypotheses, and assessment is our only method of testing them.

But predictions based on psychological assessment also have important practical applications. People are given psychological tests to determine who will go to which college, who is best for a given job, and so forth. Within the *clinical* context—that is, the context of abnormal behavior—people are assessed to determine what kind of behavior they might be likely to display and what kind of treatment they require. Should this child be put in a special-education program? Is this person psychologically fit to stand trial? Would that patient benefit from drugs? Should he be hospitalized—even against his will? These are critical questions, the answers to which may determine the direction of the person's entire future. Patients must also be reassessed to determine which treatments actually work.

The Diagnosis of Mental Disorders

In nonclinical contexts, assessment may involve no labeling. One person is chosen for the job or admitted to the college, the others are not, and that is all. Clinical assessment, however, often includes **diagnosis,** in which the person's problem is classified within one of a set of recognized categories of abnormal behavior and labeled accordingly.

The Classification of Abnormal Behavior All sciences classify—that is, they order the objects of their study by identifying crucial similarities among them and sorting them into groups according to those similarities. Botanists classify plants according to species. Astronomers classify heavenly bodies according to color, size, and temperature. Physicians classify diseases according to the organ or system affected. And mental health professionals classify mental disorders according to patterns of behavior, thought, and emotion.

As we saw in Chapter 1, the classification of abnormal behavior appears to have begun with Hippocrates. But the first truly comprehensive classification system for severe mental disorders was developed by Kraepelin in the late nineteenth century. All later systems were influenced by Kraepelin's. Eventually, in 1952, the American Psychiatric Association (APA) published its own version of the system, under the title *Diagnostic and Statistical Manual of Mental Disorders,* or *DSM.* Since that time, the *DSM* has undergone several revisions. There was a *DSM-II,* followed in turn by *DSM-III, DSM-III-R* (revised), and, most recently, *DSM-IV,* which was published in 1994.* *DSM-IV*'s listing of diagnostic categories may be seen inside the cover of this book.

The Practice of Diagnosis It is the *DSM* that provides the foundation for diagnosing mental disorders. Each of the *DSM* categories is accompanied by a description of the disorder in question, together with a set of specific criteria for diagnosis. Faced with a patient, the assessor decides which diagnosis seems most likely, consults the criteria for that disorder, and then determines which criteria the patient actually meets. If the patient satisfies the minimum number of criteria specified by the *DSM* for that disorder, then that is the patient's diagnosis. The purpose is to supply a description of the patient's problem, along with a **prognosis,** or prediction of its future course.

As the term *diagnosis* suggests, this procedure is analogous to medical evaluation, and in the minds of some, it implies the medical model, the practice of treating abnormal behaviors as if they were

*Another classification system that should be noted is the mental disorders section of the *International Classification of Diseases (ICD),* published by the World Health Organization (WHO). All members of the WHO, including the United States, use the *ICD,* though each member can revise the *ICD* criteria for disorders to reflect diagnostic practices within that country. Most revisions of the *DSM* have been coordinated with revisions of the *ICD. DSM-IV* is consistent with the *ICD*'s current, tenth edition, *ICD-10.*

symptoms of organic dysfunction. Yet mental health professionals of all persuasions, including those who strongly object to the medical model, use diagnosis, and for good reasons.

To begin with, research depends on diagnosis. In order, for example, to find out the causes of schizophrenia, researchers need to have groups of schizophrenics to study, and it is only through diagnosis—that is, labeling certain people schizophrenic—that they can gather such groups. But even apart from research requirements, mental health professionals, like other professionals, need a vocabulary in order to discuss their subject. If they did not establish a common vocabulary, such as that provided by the *DSM,* they would develop their own, idiosyncratic terms and definitions, with much resulting confusion. Finally, psychology is tied in with many other institutions in our society, and all of these institutions require the use of diagnostic labels. To get funding for its special-education program, a school system has to say how many mentally retarded or autistic children it is handling. When hospitals apply for funds, they have to list the number of schizophrenics, alcoholics, and so on, that they are treating. Insurance companies require a diagnosis before they will pay the bills. And so diagnosis is practiced, and its vocabulary—that of the *DSM*—has become our society's primary means of communicating about abnormal behavior.

Criticisms of Diagnosis The major criticism of diagnosis has to do with what some perceive as its tie to the medical model. As we noted in Chapter 1, Szasz (1961) and many other writers have vigorously attacked the medical model, and they have attacked the diagnosis of mental disorders on the same grounds—namely, that its purpose is to give psychiatrists control over other people's lives. In addition to this argument, four other criticisms of diagnosis merit consideration.

The first is that diagnosis falsifies reality by implying that most abnormal behavior is qualitatively different from normal behavior. *DSM-IV,* for example, lists a condition called "nightmare disorder," with, as usual, specific criteria for diagnosis: the person's nightmares must be "extended and extremely frightening"; they must occur repeatedly; and so on. One person with nightmares will meet these criteria, while another will not. But the application of the diagnosis to one and not the other suggests that there is a difference in kind between their two conditions, whereas, to all appearances, the difference is simply one of degree. Likewise, most forms of psychopathology are the far end of a long continuum from normal to abnormal, with many gradations in between.

If diagnosis discounts the gradations between normal and abnormal, it is even more likely to discount the gradations between different forms of abnormality—a second major criticism. Many "depressives" suffer the same problems as "schizophrenics"; others have much in common with "anxiety disorder" patients. In other words, behavior is far less clear-cut than the diagnostic system, and in imposing this artificial clarity, critics claim, diagnosis distorts human truth.

A third criticism is that diagnosis gives the illusion of explanation. For example, the statement "He is hallucinating because he is schizophrenic" *seems* to have explanatory value. In fact, it has none. "Schizophrenic" is simply a term that was made up to describe a certain behavior pattern involving hallucinations—a behavior pattern of which the cause is still largely unknown. Likewise, "depression," "phobia," "paranoia," and other diagnostic labels are not explanations but terms used so that researchers can do the work necessary to find explanations. This fact is often forgotten.

A fourth criticism is that diagnostic labeling can be harmful to people. As humanistic-existential theorists have argued, the label obscures the person's individuality, inviting mental health professionals to attend to the "phobia" or "depression" rather than the human being—or, for that matter, the family or the society, which may be the true seat of the disorder. In addition, diagnostic labels can do concrete harm, damaging people's personal relationships, making it hard for them to get jobs, and in some cases depriving them of their civil rights. (In many states, people classified as psychotic may be hospitalized against their will, and once committed, they forfeit many of their legal rights.) Furthermore, as we saw in Chapter 3, sociocultural theorists such as Scheff (1975) claim that diagnostic labels encourage people to settle back into the "sick" role and embark upon careers as mental patients.

These criticisms can be applied to any diagnostic method—indeed, to most assessment methods. But because the diagnosis of mental disorders interacts with social values, it is at that system that they are most often directed. According to some writers, the shortcomings of *DSM*-based diagnosis are so serious that the system should be abandoned altogether. In a much-discussed 1975 paper, for example, Rosenhan argued that a diagnostic system must demonstrate that its benefits (in indicating appropriate treatments, for instance, or leading researchers to causes) outweigh its liabilities in order to justify its use. Since causes and effective treatments had not yet been discovered for so many of the *DSM* categories, there was no justification, as Rosenhan saw it, for continuing to use these labels. (For further discussion of Rosenhan's position, see the box on page 124.)

Such criticisms have not gone unheeded. For disorders that the diagnostic system seems to have cut up into overly simple categories—the childhood disorders and the personality disorders (Chapter 11) are notorious problem areas in this regard—it has been suggested that classification be done not by category but by dimensional analysis (McReynolds, 1989; Widiger & Trull, 1991). In this method, the diagnostician would not seek to pinpoint the person's dominant, "defining" pathology; instead, people would be classified according to how they score on a number of different dimensions of pathology (e.g., depression, anxiety), with the possibility that they might score high on several. It has also been suggested that certain categories be left "fuzzy": a prototype, or most characteristic case, would be described, and then patients would be rated on how close they came to this prototype (Cantor & Genero, 1986). At the same time, the recent revision of the diagnostic manual involved a painstaking review of research in order to strengthen the descriptions of the disorders (Frances, Widiger, & Pincus, 1989).

Experienced diagnosticians harbor no hopes that *DSM-IV* is foolproof, yet most mental health professionals today would not side with the arguments that Rosenhan mounted against the *DSM* system in the seventies. The crucial point is, again, that research depends on diagnosis. As Spitzer (1976) wrote in response to Rosenhan's challenge:

> Is Rosenhan suggesting that prior to the development of effective treatments for syphilis and cancer, he would have decried the use of these diagnostic labels? Should we eliminate the diagnoses of antisocial personality, drug abuse, and alcoholism until we have treatments for these conditions whose benefits exceed the potential liabilities associated with the diagnosis? How do we study the effectiveness of treatments for these conditions if we are enjoined from using the diagnostic categories until we have effective treatments for them? (p. 469)

Such arguments have had their effect. Since the seventies, *DSM*-based diagnosis has become more widely used and, with successive improvements in the manual, less controversial.

In order to aid research, however, diagnosis must be consistent and meaningful. It must *mean* something—and it must mean the same thing to everyone—that a patient is labeled "schizophrenic" or "phobic." In this respect, diagnosis made a poor showing in the past. Earlier editions of the *DSM* offered relatively brief and vague descriptions of the disorders listed. As a result, there was a good deal of inconsistency in diagnosis, with the further result that diagnostic groups were disappointingly heterogeneous. That is, the symptoms of the patients assigned to many of the categories were not similar enough to make the label truly useful. Furthermore, the early editions of the manual explicitly or implicitly ascribed numerous disorders to causes that had not been definitely established, thus further complicating diagnosis and impeding research.

DSM-IV Beginning with *DSM-III* in 1980, the recent revisions of the manual have been, in large part, an effort to remedy these problems. Let us look at the latest edition, ***DSM-IV.***

Specific diagnostic criteria First, the criteria for diagnosis are highly detailed and specific, including the following:

1 *Essential features* of the disorder: those that "define" it.
2 *Associated features:* those that are usually present.
3 *Diagnostic criteria:* a list of symptoms (taken from the lists of essential and associated features) that *must* be present for the patient to be given this diagnostic label.
4 Information on *differential diagnosis:* data that explain how to distinguish this disorder from other, similar disorders.

In addition, the descriptions offer information on the course of the disorder, age at onset, degree of impairment, complications, predisposing factors, prevalence, family pattern (that is, whether the disorder tends to run in families), laboratory and physical-exam findings, and the relationship of the disorder to gender, age, and culture. The most important feature of the descriptions, however, is the highly specific quality of the diagnostic criteria.

Five axes of diagnosis A second important feature of *DSM-IV* is that it requires the diagnostician to give a substantial amount of information about patients, evaluating them on five different "axes," or areas of functioning:

> *Axis I—Clinical syndrome:* the diagnostic label for the patient's most serious psychological problem, the problem for which he or she is being diagnosed.

ON BEING SANE IN INSANE PLACES

Can the sane be distinguished from the insane via *DSM*-based diagnosis? In the early 1970s, D. L. Rosenhan (1973) set up an experiment whereby eight psychologically stable people, with no history of mental disorder, would try to get themselves admitted to mental hospitals. The eight "pseudopatients"—three psychologists, a psychiatrist, a graduate student in psychology, a pediatrician, a painter, and a housewife—presented themselves at separate hospitals in five states. They all went under assumed names, and those involved in mental health lied about their professions. Otherwise they gave completely accurate histories, adding only one false detail: each of them claimed that he or she had been hearing voices that seemed to say something like "hollow," "empty," or "thud."

The pseudopatients' greatest fear in embarking on their experiment was that they would be unmasked as frauds and thrown out of the hospital. As it happened, they were diagnosed as schizophrenic, and without exception they were all admitted as mental patients.

Once admitted, the pseudopatients made no further reference to the voices. They behaved completely normally, except that they made special efforts to be courteous and cooperative. Yet none of them was ever exposed as a fraud. In Rosenhan's opinion, the staff simply assumed that because these people were in a mental hospital, they were disturbed. This assumption persisted despite the fact that all the pseudopatients spent a good part of the day taking notes on what went on in the ward. The staff either ignored the note taking or interpreted it as an indication of pathology. On one pseudopatient's hospital record the nurse, day after day, noted this same symptom: "Patient engages in writing behavior" (Rosenhan, 1973, p. 253). The genuine mental patients were apparently not so easy to fool. According to Rosenhan, they regularly accused the pseudopatients of being sane and speculated out loud that they were journalists sent in to check up on the hospital.

All the patients were eventually discharged. Their stays ranged from seven to fifty-two days, with an average of nineteen days. Upon discharge, they were classified not as being "cured" or as showing no behavior to support the original diagnosis but rather as having psychosis "in remission." In other words, their "insanity" was still in them and might reappear.

The evidence of this study led Rosenhan to conclude that while there might in fact be a genuine difference between sanity and insanity, those whose business it was to distinguish between them were unable to do so with any accuracy. The focus of his criticism was the fact that once the pseudopatients were admitted and began behaving normally, their normality was not detected. In his view, the reason for this was that in diagnosis the initial evaluation—which, as in this case, may be based on a single symptom—distorts all future evaluations of the patient, making it impossible for diagnosticians to see the person otherwise than in the role of "schizophrenic" or whatever he or she has been labeled. As a result, the sane cannot be distinguished from the insane.

Rosenhan's conclusion has been contested by a number of other investigators. Spitzer (1976), for example, argued that the fact that the pseudopatients were able to lie their way into the hospital was no proof that the diagnostic system was invalid. (If a person swallows a cup of blood and then goes to an emergency room and spits it up, and if the physician on duty diagnoses the person's condition as a bleeding ulcer, does this mean that the diagnostic criteria for bleeding ulcer are invalid?) As for the hospital staffs' failure to detect the pseudopatients' normality once they were in the hospital, Spitzer again argued that this was no reflection on the diagnostic system. People are not diagnosed solely on the basis of how they are behaving at the moment but also on the basis of their past behavior. If a person reports having repeated hallucinations and then reports no further hallucinations for two weeks, this does not necessarily—or even probably—mean that no psychiatric abnormality exists, much less that none ever existed. In the absence of alcoholism or other drug abuse, hallucination is ordinarily a sign of severe psychological disturbance; for a diagnostician to discount this symptom simply because it had not appeared for a few weeks would be extremely careless. Indeed, as Spitzer pointed out, the fact that the hospitals released the pseudopatients in an average of nineteen days actually shows a rather rapid response to their failure to produce any further symptoms. And the fact that they were released as being "in remission," an extremely rare diagnosis, suggests that the hospital staff recognized that they were atypical, if not faked, cases; in any case, they were not just lumped together with all other diagnosed schizophrenics.

Rosenhan's study was widely debated in the 1970s. Whatever the validity of its conclusions, it added to the general dissatisfaction with *DSM-II* which led to the continuing tightening of the diagnostic criteria and the effort to base those criteria on empirical evidence.

Axis II—Personality disorders (adults) or mental retardation (children and adolescents): any accompanying long-term disorder not covered by the Axis I label.*

Axis III—General medical disorders: any medical problem that may be relevant to the psychological problem.

Axis IV—Psychosocial and environmental problems: current social, occupational, environmental, or other problems that may have contributed to or are resulting from the psychological problem.

Axis V—Global assessment of functioning: a rating, on a scale of 1 to 100, of the patient's current adjustment (work performance, social relationships, use of leisure time) and of his or her adjustment during the past year.

A hypothetical patient's diagnosis might be as follows:

Axis I: Major depressive episode

Axis II: Avoidant personality disorder

Axis III: Diabetes

Axis IV: Occupational (loss of job)

Axis V: Current—major impairment (40). In past year—moderate difficulty (60)

Thus instead of simply writing down "depression," today's diagnostician must create a little portrait, the features of which may then be useful in devising a treatment program. Furthermore, it is hoped that this five-part diagnosis will help researchers in their explorations of connections between psychological disorders and other factors, such as stress and physical illness.

Unspecified etiology A final important feature of *DSM-IV* is that it avoids any suggestion as to the cause of a disorder unless the cause has been definitely established. This feature, introduced with *DSM-III* in 1980, necessitated substantial changes in the classification system. The term *neurosis,* for example, was dropped altogether, as it implies a Freudian theory of causation (i.e., that the disorder is due to unconscious conflict). Since 1980, the manual has simply named the disorders and described them as clearly and specifically as possible. Their causes, if they are not known, are not speculated upon.

The major goal of the 1980 revision was to improve the reliability and validity of psychiatric diagnosis. Reliability and validity have already been discussed briefly in Chapter 5. They are important criteria to be met by *any* assessment procedure, but we will examine these two concepts by considering how they apply to the diagnosis of mental disorders.

Assessing the Assessment: Reliability and Validity

Reliability The **reliability** of any measurement device is the degree to which its findings can stand the test of repeated measurements. Thus, in its simplest sense, reliability is a measure of the consistency of such a device under varying conditions. A 12-inch ruler is expected to produce the same measurements whether it is used today or tomorrow, in Salt Lake City or New Orleans, by you or by me. Likewise, a psychological assessment technique, to be considered reliable, must produce the same results under a variety of circumstances.

There are three criteria for reliability in psychological assessment:

1 **Internal consistency.** Do different parts of the test yield the same results?
2 **Test-retest reliability.** Does the test yield the same results when administered to the same person at different times?
3 **Interjudge reliability.** Does the test yield the same results when scored or interpreted by different judges?

Each of these three criteria applies with particular force to certain kinds of tests. Test-retest reliability is most important in assessments of stable individual-difference characteristics—for example, IQ tests. Internal consistency is most important in tests that use many items to measure a single characteristic—for example, a sixty-item test for anxiety. In the diagnosis of mental disorders the most crucial criterion is interjudge reliability, the degree of agreement among different diagnosticians as to what specific disorder any given patient has.

As we indicated earlier, in the past this rate of

*Axis II is confined to disorders that generally date from childhood. They are separated from the Axis I "clinical syndromes" to give the diagnostician a chance to note not just the primary problem (Axis I) but also any other, chronic condition (Axis II) that accompanies the primary problem and perhaps contributes to it. In some instances, a chronic condition *is* the patient's primary problem, in which case it is still listed on Axis II but is marked "principal diagnosis."

agreement has been extremely low. Indeed, Spitzer and Fleiss (1974), in a review of research on the reliability of psychiatric diagnosis, found that interjudge reliability was satisfactory in only *three* diagnostic categories: mental retardation, organic brain syndrome, and alcoholism. And these are broad categories. When diagnosticians were called upon to make finer distinctions—assigning patients not only to "schizophrenia," for example, but also to subcategories within that category—the degree of agreement fell even lower. In one study, a number of psychologists and psychiatrists were asked to evaluate a series of simulated patient profiles and to assign each "patient" to a subtype of schizophrenia. The resulting rate of agreement between any two judges assigned the same profile was a dismally low 25 percent (Blashfield, 1973).

When detailed, specific diagnostic criteria were introduced in *DSM-III,* this problem was solved to some degree. In one study, with diagnosticians trained beforehand in the use of *DSM-III,* the rate of overall agreement was 74 percent, a comparatively good score (Webb, Gold, Johnstone, et al., 1981). Yet for certain *DSM-III* categories, notably the personality disorders, interjudge reliability was still poor (Drake & Vaillant, 1985; Mellsop, Varghere, Joshua, et al., 1982). This is one area of weakness that later editions of the *DSM* have tried to address. As we shall see when we examine the personality disorders, the criteria for these diagnoses are now highly specific.

Increased interjudge reliability is not achieved without costs, however. As Blashfield and Draguns (1976) have pointed out, reliability is not the only consideration in creating a diagnostic system. Ideally, the system should also have high "coverage"—that is, most cases of abnormal behavior should qualify for one or another of its categories. Earlier editions of the *DSM* achieved high coverage by having loose diagnostic criteria; because the behavioral descriptions were so broad, almost any patient could be made to fit somewhere. The later editions, with their stricter criteria, have lower coverage, with the result that more patients are swept into residual categories such as "psychotic disorder not otherwise specified." This problem, in turn, has been addressed by adding new categories. The number of categories has more than tripled since the introduction of the diagnostic manual. Even so, the diagnostic criteria are so strict that many patients still end up with "not otherwise specified" (NOS) diagnoses. In certain categories, such as the dissociative disorders (Chapter 8), the *majority* of patients are given NOS diagnoses (Mezzich, Fabrega, Coffman et al., 1989; Saxena & Prasad, 1989). So as diagnostic groups have become purer, they have become smaller, leaving researchers less to work with.

Validity Whereas *reliability* refers to the consistency of a measuring instrument under varying conditions, **validity** refers to the extent to which the test measures what it is supposed to measure. Do people who score high on a typing test really type better than people who score low? If so, the test is valid.

As with reliability, there are several kinds of validity. Because the major purpose of any assessment system is to describe and predict behavior, we will discuss the two kinds of validity that are most relevant to the diagnosis of mental disorders: descriptive validity and predictive validity (Blashfield & Draguns, 1976).

Descriptive validity The **descriptive validity** of an assessment device is the degree to which it provides significant information about the current behavior of the people being assessed. A frequent criticism of the diagnosis of mental disorders is that it has little descriptive validity—that it does not tell us much about the people diagnosed. Proponents of this view point to the fact, mentioned earlier, that people assigned to the same diagnostic group may actually behave quite differently, while people assigned to different diagnostic groups may show many of the same behavioral oddities (Zigler & Phillips, 1961). But diagnosis does not claim to produce groups that are completely homogeneous; this would be impossible, for no two people, normal or abnormal, behave exactly alike. Nor does it claim that a symptom typical of one diagnostic group will not be found in other groups. In all of abnormal psychology, there are very few *pathognomic symptoms,* symptoms that accompany all cases of a given disorder and that never accompany any other disorder. Like any other scientific classification system, diagnosis groups cases not according to individual characteristics but according to *patterns* of characteristics—patterns in which there is invariably some duplication of individual characteristics (Spitzer, 1976). Three people may have high fevers, yet if their symptom pictures differ in other ways—one having a runny nose, another being covered with red spots, another having swollen cheeks—they will be diagnosed as having different diseases. Likewise, three people may have hallucinations, yet if they differ in other important respects—one having a long history of alcohol abuse, the second showing severe depression, and the third believ-

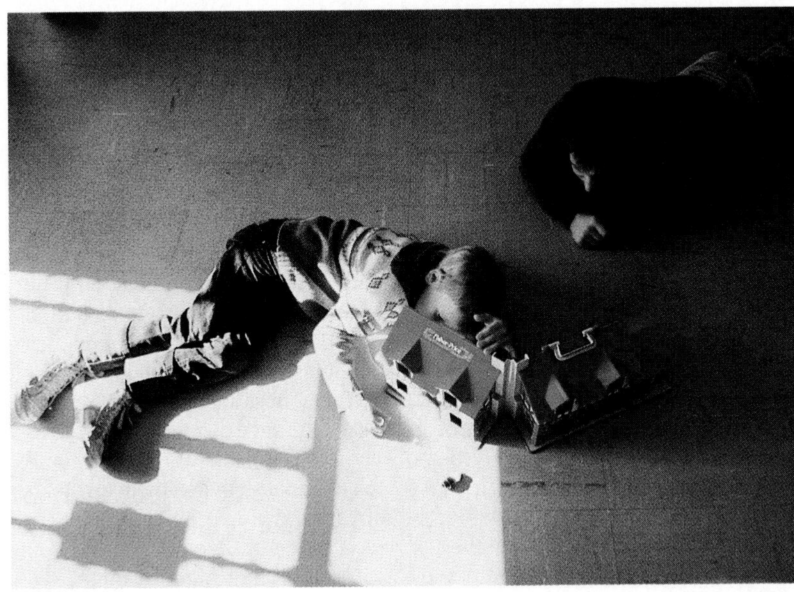

Assessment techniques must be geared to the capabilities of the subject. Some children, for example, will not respond well to a formal interview. The assessor may find it more effective to let the child's concerns emerge through play in an informal setting.

ing that his thoughts are being broadcast so that everyone in the room can hear them—then they are likely to be given three different diagnoses: alcoholism, depression, and schizophrenia, respectively. In other words, research would have to show that the *pattern* of symptoms—not just individual symptoms—is substantially different within categories and substantially similar between categories before the diagnosis of mental disorders could be said to have poor descriptive validity.

A more serious challenge to the descriptive validity of diagnosis is the fact that many patients—indeed, most patients (Kessler, McGonagle, Zhao, et al., 1994)—show **cormorbidity.** That is, they meet the diagnostic criteria for more than one Axis I disorder. In such cases, the person is usually given more than one diagnosis, but such multiple diagnoses, implying that the person has two (or more) independent disorders, may not be an accurate description of the case. Comorbid conditions generally have a more chronic course, a poorer response to treatment, and a poorer prognosis than single disorders. In other words, they may represent a different, unrecognized disorder, rather than a combination of recognized disorders. (See the box on page 128.) Recent editions of the *DSM* have struggled with the question of comorbidity—some of the newly added categories cover what, earlier, would have been called comorbid conditions—but this problem will remain an issue for those revising the manual in the future.

Predictive validity An assessment tool with high descriptive validity is one that helps us describe the person's current behavior. An assessment method with high **predictive validity** is one that helps us answer important questions about that behavior. In abnormal psychology, the most important questions are cause, prognosis, and treatment. The extent to which a diagnosis answers those questions is the extent of its predictive validity.

Some diagnostic labels have high predictive validity in some respects. We know, for example, that people diagnosed as manic or schizophrenic are likely to respond to certain drugs (Chapter 21). Likewise, we know that many people diagnosed as either manic or depressive will probably recover within a short time—and that they will probably have further episodes of mood disturbance. Diagnostic labels offer less information, however, as to the course of milder disturbances or the treatment they will respond to.

It is possible that the limited predictive validity of diagnosis is due primarily to its limited reliability. While an assessment technique that has high reliability may have low validity,* the reverse is not true. To have high validity, a system must have high reliability. The improved reliability of the recent editions of the *DSM* may result in improved validity. In one study, for example, the records of 134 patients, all potential candidates for a diagnosis of schizophrenia, were examined. The patients were diagnosed according to four different sets of criteria, one of which was *DSM-III.* Follow-up

*For example, astrology has high reliability. People can be grouped according to birth date with great consistency and accuracy. But in order to have high validity as well, these groupings would have to reflect what the astrologers claim they reflect—namely, individual personality traits. Since there is no evidence that they do, the system has low validity.

COMORBIDITY: DISTURBANCE AS A PACKAGE

One out of every two people in this country has had or will have a serious psychological disorder, and one out of three has had to cope with such a disorder within the last year. These sobering figures were the product of a recent survey of over 8,000 people, ages fifteen to fifty-four—the first survey, ever, to administer a structured, face-to-face mental health interview to a representative sample of the population of the United States (Kessler, McGonagle, Zhao, et al., 1994).

The subjects were questioned as to whether they had suffered any one of fourteen major disorders described in the *DSM* and, if so, what treatment they had received. Leading the list were major depression, alcohol dependence, and phobias. (Remember that the prevalence rate of 50 percent was for only fourteen disorders. What would the rate have been if the researchers had inquired about all the *DSM* disorders?) As surprising as the prevalence was the rate of treatment. Less than 40 percent of those who reported having had a disorder had ever sought or received treatment.

The primary focus of this study was comorbidity—two or more disorders occurring simultaneously—and the results were eye-opening. The National Comorbidity Survey (NCS) discovered that having two or more psychological disorders at the same time is more common than having just one. Almost 80 percent of the disorders reported to the NCS coexisted with at least one other disorder. Interestingly, these comorbid disorders tended to be concentrated in a relatively small sector of the population. More than 50 percent of all the reported disorders occurred in the 14 percent of the subjects who had a history of three or more comorbid disorders. This group—which also tended to have the most serious disorders—tended to be urban, low-income, poorly educated, white, female, and ages twenty to forty. (In general, the more years, the more money, and the more education a subject had, the less likely he or she was to report a current disorder.) If nothing else, we now know which segment of the population is most in need of psychological services.

Only recently has comorbidity come to be a pressing issue in abnormal psychology. Now, in view of the NCS findings, it will surely be more discussed. Perhaps the most important question about cases of comorbidity is whether in fact they represent comorbidity. When a person shows symptoms of two different disorders, does he or she really have two disorders—or just one complex disorder that our diagnostic system is wrongly separating into two?

Consider the relationship between antisocial personality disorder (a long-standing pattern of violating the rights of others—see Chapter 11) and substance dependence. These two disorders often turn up in the same person—so often, indeed, that each is mentioned in the *DSM*'s description of the other. But *are* they two different disorders? Sometimes it is possible, from the person's history, to see how one seemed to give rise to the other—how, for example, a heroin addiction eventually led the person into antisocial acts (theft, betrayal of friends, abandonment of children) or, conversely, how a long-standing pattern of antisocial behavior eventually came to include heroin addiction. But very often the two patterns develop simultaneously. Furthermore, even if one precedes the other, this does not prove that it caused the other. Possibly, both were caused by something else altogether. (As we will see in Chapter 12, antisocial behavior and one pattern of alcohol dependence seem to be related to the same genetic factor.)

The comorbidity question, then, has to do with more than terminology. How we define a disorder affects our theories of causation. It also affects treatment decisions. Consider, for example, the second scenario above: a person whose heroin dependence developed as part of a long-standing pattern of antisocial behavior. If he is diagnosed as having two comorbid disorders—substance dependence and antisocial personality disorder—this may obscure the fact that what he really needs to be treated for is antisocial personality disorder and that without such treatment any therapy for the drug problem is likely to be a waste of time.

On the other hand, it might still be useful to provide both diagnoses, for each condition, whether or not it represents a separate disorder, may require separate treatment. In the above case, the fact that the drug dependence seemed to develop as a consequence of the antisocial personality disorder does not mean that it will automatically clear up if the person is treated for antisocial personality disorder. By that point, the drug habit may have developed a life of its own, creating the conditions for its continuance. Furthermore, any drug problem will seriously affect the person's chances of responding to treatment for antisocial personality disorder (just as, conversely, antisocial tendencies will undermine drug treatment).

Antisocial personality disorder and drug dependence are not the only pair of disorders involved in the comorbidity question. There are a number of such pairings, and the list will no doubt lengthen as research continues. In light of the NCS finding that most cases of psychological disorder are actually cases of more than one disorder, our current way of viewing psychological abnormality—as a matter of discrete syndromes—may have to be revised. Even if the syndromes remain separate, we will need to study them not in isolation but in interaction.

records were also available in which the patients were interviewed on an average of six and a half years after the initial interview. Of the four sets of criteria, *DSM-III* was the most accurate in predicting which of the patients continued to show poor adjustment (Helzer, Brockington, & Kendell, 1981).

Problems in Assessment

The reliability and validity of any assessment tool can be affected by a number of problems, some having to do with the administration of the measure, others with its interpretation. One such problem is the assessor—his or her personal manner and how it affects the person being assessed (Masling, 1960; Mischel, 1968). If a diagnostician tends to be very formal and businesslike during a diagnostic interview, the subject—particularly a child or a troubled adult—may respond in a guarded and apprehensive way. If the diagnostician interprets this behavior as a reflection of paranoid or depressive leanings and diagnoses accordingly, how are the people who later treat the patient to know that the "paranoia" or "depression" was, in part, a response to the diagnostician? Even attributes that the examiner cannot control, such as physical appearance, race, and sex, may affect the subject's performance.

Assessors affect examination results more directly through their interpretation of the evidence. Subjects present many different sorts of information; diagnosticians must filter all of it through their own minds, selecting what seems most important. In the selection process, they are bound to be guided to some extent by their own biases. For example, some diagnosticians favor certain diagnoses over others. Indeed, there have often been marked differences in diagnosis between hospitals, between communities, and between countries. For years, what was called depression in England was often called schizophrenia in the United States (J. E. Cooper, Kendell, Gurland, et al., 1972). Likewise, one hospital may have long experience treating manic episodes, while a neighboring hospital has equally long experience with paranoid schizophrenia—largely because those are the diagnostic labels favored by their respective staffs. On a more comprehensive level, many critics feel that diagnosticians in general have a "pathological bias"—a tendency to see sickness instead of health. Diagnosticians often have neither the tools nor the training to assess areas of strength, whereas they are carefully trained to spot signs of weakness or deviance (Harlage, Howard, & Ostror, 1984). Consequently, it is weakness and deviance that they tend to find. (See the box on page 124.)

Finally, pragmatic considerations may interfere with accurate evaluation. When psychological treatment is paid for through company insurance, word of the patient's "condition" may reach the ears of his or her co-workers. Anticipating such gossip, diagnosticians may apply a label that indicates a milder disturbance than they feel the patient actually has. In other instances, they may exaggerate a patient's disturbance—again for practical reasons. The Veterans Administration, for example, pays higher benefits to veterans diagnosed as psychotic than to those with less severe diagnoses. Thus, when a patient's financial circumstances are particularly bad, psychiatrists may favor the evidence for psychosis.

Recent editions of the *DSM* have tried to minimize these interferences in various ways, principally by making the criteria for a diagnosis very specific and by establishing for each disorder a fixed "decision rule," or minimum number of symptoms that must be present for a patient to receive that diagnosis. Under "major depressive episode," for example, the manual lists nine different symptoms (they will be discussed in Chapter 10) and then specifies that, for that diagnosis to be given, the person must have shown five of the symptoms during the same two-week period. Such a rule is harder to interpret freely than the vaguer descriptions in earlier editions of the manual.

Another suggestion that has been offered for minimizing assessment interferences is that diagnosticians should rely more on statistical relationships, or *actuarial judgment,* than on their own clinical judgment. Insurance companies, for example, use actuarial judgment to calculate risks. Given an applicant who is male, fifty years old, married, and the survivor of one heart attack, they will use tables based on the histories of other such people to calculate what this person's life expectancy is and what his medical expenses are likely to be. Since research has shown that actuarial judgment is superior to clinical judgment (Dawes, Faust, & Meehl, 1989), it has been proposed that particularly in making treatment decisions—whether a patient should be given psychotherapy, or put on drugs, or hospitalized—diagnosticians should turn to the actuarial method. One problem with the actuarial approach is that diagnosticians sometimes confront rare situations for which statistical data are not available—for example, whether a particular type of person is likely to commit random acts of unprovoked violence.

Even if the diagnostic system were flawless, however, there would still be a problem, because a certain percentage of diagnosticians simply do not follow the rules. A study of *DSM-III* diagnoses made by psychiatrists and graduating psychiatric residents found that 48 percent of the psychiatrists' patients and 36 percent of the residents' patients did not satisfy the diagnostic criteria for the disorders ascribed to them (Jampala, Sierles, & Taylor, 1986). Many therapists whose patients tend to have the normal run of middle-class sorrows fall back repeatedly on certain diagnoses (anxiety disorder and adjustment disorder are particular favorites) that they feel are specific enough to satisfy the insurance company but "harmless" and vague enough not to invade the patient's privacy. Consequently they will seldom even open the diagnostic manual.

METHODS OF ASSESSMENT

Current assessment techniques fall into four general categories: the interview, psychological tests, laboratory tests, and observation in natural settings.

The Interview

Of all the methods of assessment, the **interview,** consisting of a face-to-face conversation between subject and examiner, is the oldest, the most commonly used, and the most versatile. It may be highly structured, with the subject answering a prearranged sequence of questions, or it may be unstructured, giving subjects the chance to describe their problem in their own way. The evaluation method also varies from structured to unstructured. Even after a highly structured question-and-answer session, examiners may rely primarily on their own subjective impressions in evaluating subjects. Alternatively, they may follow a detailed manual to score subjects' responses, giving 1 point for one type of response, 2 points for another type of response, and so forth.

The degree of structure in the interview and the questions asked will depend on the interviewer's purpose. If the aim is simply to put the client at ease, in an effort to promote trust and candor, then the structure will be loose. This is usually the case, for example, with the intake interview at the beginning of psychotherapy. However, interviewers often have a clear idea of what kind of information they need and cannot waste too much time obtaining it. Therefore, most interviews have some definable structure.

The major pitfall of assessment by interview is that it can give uncontrolled play to interviewers' subjectivity and biases, both as they conduct the interview and as they evaluate it. Political, cultural, and even personal biases are likely sources of interference. Interviewers, like most of the rest of us, have feelings about blacks and whites, women and men, handsome people and plain people, even short people and tall people, and such feelings can influence the results of the interview.

For this reason, a fairly structured interview and scoring system are often recommended, even though the subject's responses and the interviewer's intuitive powers are thereby restricted. When the purpose of the interview is diagnosis, and particularly when the diagnosis is to be used in research—for example, to assemble a study group—researchers use highly structured inter-

The interview between subject and examiner is the most common and most versatile method of psychological assessment.

views. One such interview is the Schedule for Affective Disorders and Schizophrenia, or SADS (Endicott & Spitzer, 1978), which, with its own special scoring system, has proved highly reliable (Andreasen, McDonald-Scott, Grove, et al., 1982). Another is the Structured Clinical Interview for *DSM-IV* or SCID, widely used by clinicians to help in providing *DSM*-based diagnoses. A third is the Diagnostic Interview Schedule, or DIS, of the National Institute of Mental Health (L. N. Robins, Helzer, Croughan, et al., 1981), which yields diagnoses by computer. Such diagnostic tools do not have high coverage, but that is not their purpose. Their goal is to give diagnoses as precisely as possible, so that when a team of researchers says that the new drug worked or didn't work with a group of schizophrenics, they can be fairly certain that it was in fact tested on a group of schizophrenics.

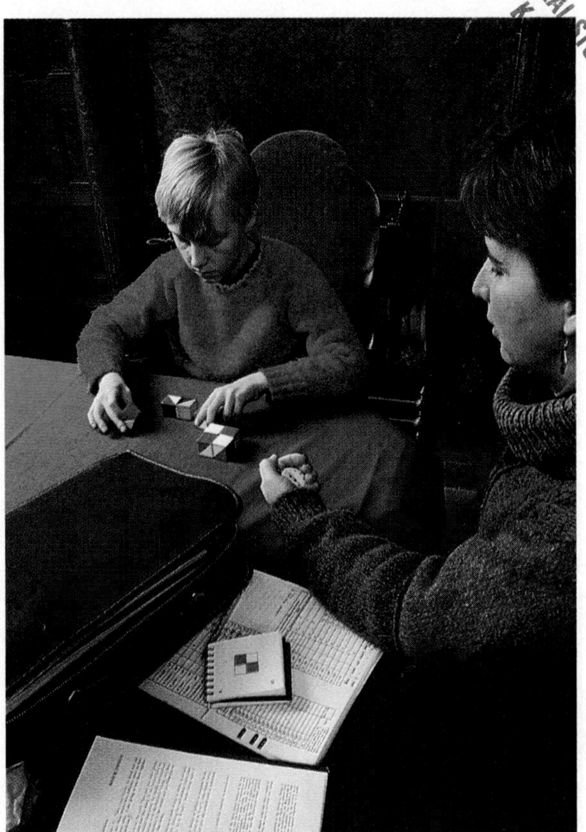

The Wechsler Intelligence Scales measure a number of dimensions of intelligence, including Performance IQ. In the segment of that test shown here, the subject is being timed as he tries to reproduce a pattern of blocks.

Psychological Tests

More structured than the normal interview, the **psychological test** is a standard procedure in which persons are presented with a series of stimuli to which they are asked to respond. Such a test, like the highly structured interview, gives the subject little freedom in responding, but because of its restrictive quality, the psychological test can be scored more easily and more objectively. In fact, many psychological tests are scored by computer.

For decades the dominant method of psychological testing has been the **psychometric approach.** The aim of this method is to locate stable underlying characteristics, or **traits** (e.g., anxiety, passivity, aggression, intelligence), that presumably exist in differing degrees in everyone. Because it assumes the existence of stable traits and aims to measure them, the psychometric method considers response variability due to situational influences to be simply a source of error and makes every effort to screen out such influences. For example, instead of leaving it to examiners to give the test instructions in their own words—words that might vary in substance and tone from one examiner to the next—most psychological tests now provide extremely precise directions that the examiner reads aloud to the subjects, just as with the Scholastic Aptitude Test (SAT).

There are many different kinds of psychological tests. We will examine only the most important categories: intelligence tests, projective personality tests, self-report personality inventories, and tests for organic impairment.

Intelligence Tests **Intelligence tests** were the first of the psychological assessment techniques to be widely used. Modern intelligence tests are based on the work of Alfred Binet, the French psychologist who in 1905 introduced the first intelligence test into the French school system to help teachers determine which children would require special education. Later revised by Lewis Terman of Stanford University and now known as the Stanford-Binet Intelligence Scale, the test measures a child's ability to recognize objects in a picture, to remember a series of digits, to define simple words, to complete sentences in a logical fashion, and so forth. There is also an adult version of the test, with comparable tasks scaled to adult abilities. The subject's final score on the test is rendered as an **intelligence quotient,** or **IQ.**

Another widely used series of intelligence tests is the Wechsler Intelligence Scales. Developed by the American psychologist David Wechsler, these tests, unlike the Stanford-Binet tests, yield not only a general IQ but also a Verbal IQ, measuring verbal ability, knowledge, and comprehension, and a Performance IQ, measuring problem solving and

Paraphrased Wechslerlike Questions

General Information
1. How many wings does a bird have?
2. How many nickels make a dime?
3. What is steam made of?
4. Who wrote "Paradise Lost"?
5. What is pepper?

General Comprehension
1. What should you do if you see someone forget his book when he leaves his seat in a restaurant?
2. What is the advantage of keeping money in a bank?
3. Why is copper often used in electrical wires?

Arithmetic
1. Sam had three pieces of candy and Joe gave him four more. How many pieces of candy did Sam have altogether?
2. Three men divided eighteen golf balls equally among themselves. How many golf balls did each man receive?
3. If two apples cost 15¢, what will be the cost of a dozen apples?

Similarities
1. In what way are a lion and a tiger alike?
2. In what way are a saw and hammer alike?
3. In what way are an hour and a week alike?
4. In what way are a circle and a traingle alike?

Vocabulary
This test consists simply of asking, "What is a ______?" or "What does ______ mean?" The words cover a wide range of difficulty or familarity.

intelligence in a manner that does not depend upon verbal ability (see Figure 6.1). When Verbal IQ is being assessed, adults might be asked how many days there are in a year or how many state capitals there are in the United States. When Performance IQ is being assessed, they might be asked to transcribe a code or to reproduce a design with colored blocks. There are three Wechsler tests, each geared to a different age group: the Wechsler Adult Intelligence Scale–Revised (WAIS-R), the Wechsler Intelligence Scale for Children (WISC-III), and the Wechsler Preschool and Primary Scale of Intelligence (WPPSI).

Evaluation of intelligence tests The potential influence of intelligence tests is very great. Not only do they play an important part in the diagnosis of mental retardation and brain damage, but unlike all other psychological tests, they are routinely given to schoolchildren across the country, often with serious consequences. Ability tests can determine whether students are placed in special-education or "gifted" classes, what high schools and colleges they will attend, and in turn what kind of education they will receive.

Because of their importance, intelligence tests are very carefully designed. They have been shown to have high internal consistency: a given person will do approximately the same on different items measuring the same kind of ability. They also have high test-retest reliability: a person who takes the same IQ test twice, several years apart, will score approximately the same both times (L. T. Brown & Weiner, 1979; Lindemann & Matarazzo, 1990). Finally, the validity of the major IQ tests has been shown to be relatively high in the sense that there is a strong correlation between children's IQ scores and their later performance in school (Anastasi, 1982; Matarazzo, 1972).

But is the ability to do well in our school systems the most important measure of intelligence? As Wechsler (1958) himself pointed out, intelligence is not an existing *thing,* such as heart rate or blood pressure, that can be objectively quantified. Rather, it is an inferred construct. We infer what we call intelligence from what we consider correct behavior in response to various problems. For a number of years it has been charged that both our schools and our IQ tests are culturally biased—that they interpret as intelligence what is actually just familiarity with middle-class culture (Lampley & Rust, 1986; Puente, 1990). A test question that asks whether a cup goes with a bowl, a spoon, or a saucer will not be easy for a lower-income child who has never seen a saucer. In recent years efforts have been made to remove inadvertent cultural bias from the major IQ tests.

A more general challenge to IQ testing is whether it reflects too narrow a view of mental ability. Psychologist Howard Gardner (Gardner & Hatch, 1989) has argued that traditional IQ tests measure only three components of intelligence: verbal ability, mathematical-logical reasoning, and spatial-perceptual skills. In Gardner's view there are at least four other important kinds of intelligence: musical ability, physical skill, interpersonal ability (the capacity to understand others), and intrapersonal ability (the capacity to understand oneself). The empathy of a friend, the skills of Mikhail Baryshnikov or Michael Jordan—in our culture these are not considered components of "intelligence," and they are not what IQ tests aim to measure. According to Gardner, they should be, for they are controlled by the brain and help to determine people's success in life.

FIGURE 6.1 These test items are similar to those included in the various Wechsler Intelligence Scales. *(Top left)* A sampling of questions from five of the verbal subtests. *(Top right)* A problem in block design—the subject is asked to arrange the blocks to match a pattern on a card. *(Bottom)* Another example of a performance subtest—the subject is required to put together puzzle pieces to form an object such as a duck. (Reproduced by permission of the Psychological Corporation, New York)

Projective Personality Tests **Projective personality tests** are based on the psychodynamic assumption that people's true motives, because they are largely unconscious, must be drawn out indirectly. Accordingly, projective tests expose subjects to ambiguous stimuli into which they must "read" meaning. Whatever meaning they give to the stimulus is thought to contain clues to their unconscious processes—clues that the interviewer must interpret.

The Rorschach Most famous of the projective tests is the **Rorschach Psychodiagnostic Inkblot Test** (Rorschach, 1942), in which subjects are asked to respond to ten cards, each showing a symmetrical inkblot design. The designs vary in complexity and coloring. The test is administered in two phases. In the first phase, the *free-association* phase, subjects are asked to describe as specifically as possible what each card reminds them of. In the second phase, called the *inquiry* phase, subjects are

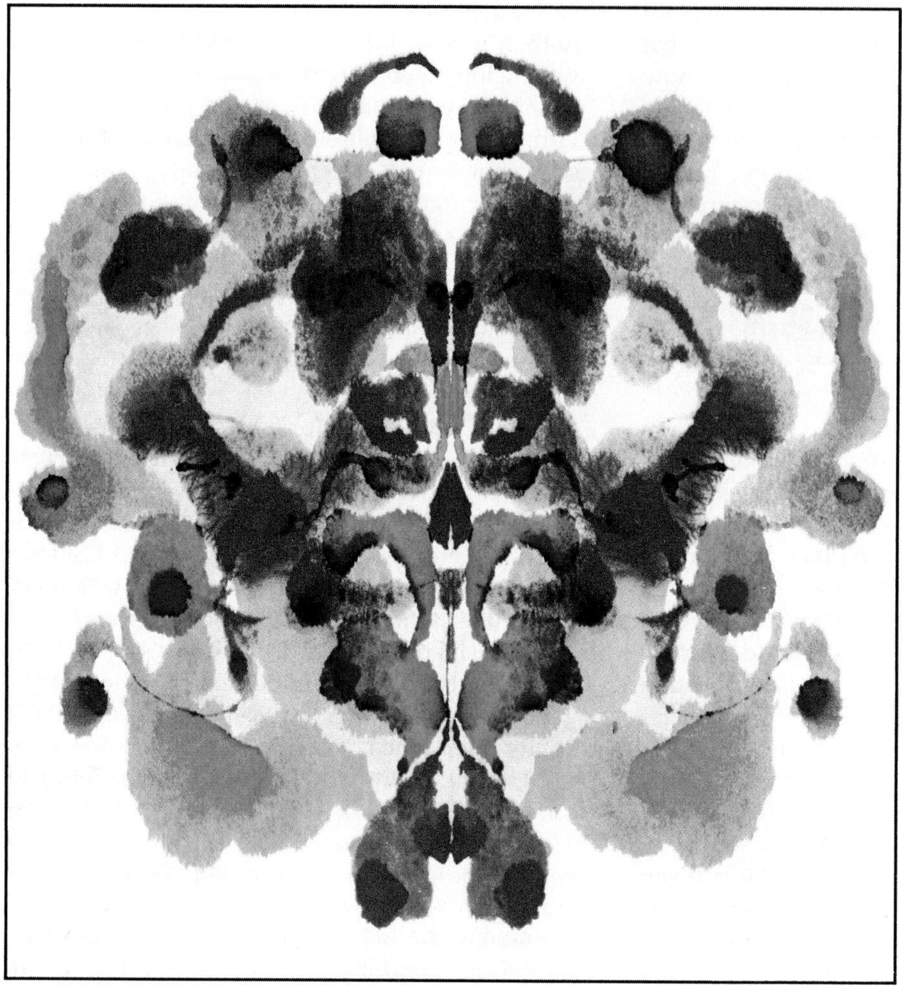

FIGURE 6.2 An inkblot card similar to those used in the Rorschach test. In this test, the subject is asked to describe what he or she "sees" in the design, and why.

asked which characteristics of each inkblot contributed to the formation of their impression of that inkblot.

As we pointed out earlier, highly unstructured interviewing methods may be combined with highly structured scoring methods. This is the case with the Rorschach. The subjective material elicited by the inkblots is generally evaluated according to a detailed manual indicating how specific responses are to be interpreted (S. J. Beck, 1961; Exner, 1978, 1982, 1986). For example, an important aspect of the evaluation depends on the extent to which the subject's responses represent what is called "good form"—that is, how plausible the subject's interpretation of a picture is in view of the shapes contained in it and how closely the subject's interpretation matches that of most other people in response to that picture. Consider, for example, the inkblot in Figure 6.2, which might reasonably be interpreted as an elaborate flower or insect. Many other readings are plausible as well, but if a subject claimed that what he or she saw in this picture was a small boy crouching in a corner—something that actually contradicts the form of the inkblot—then the interviewer might conclude that the response reflected an inner conflict and distortion of reality (or that the subject was not taking the test seriously).

The examiner also weighs the content of the subject's responses. If a certain theme keeps reappearing in the subject's interpretations, then, depending on the nature of the theme, the examiner may take it as a clue to underlying conflicts. Water, for example, may be interpreted as a sign of alcoholism; eyes as indicative of paranoid suspicion; and so forth.

The TAT and CAT A second popular projective technique is the **Thematic Apperception Test,** or **TAT.** In this test the subject is presented with a series of pictures. Unlike the ambiguous inkblots of the Rorschach, most of the TAT pictures show a person, or possibly two or three people, doing something. The scenes are ambiguous enough to allow for a variety of interpretations, yet they nudge the subject in the direction of certain kinds of associations. For example, the picture at the far left in Figure 6.3, showing a man in a business suit coming through a door, might tap the subject's feelings about his or her father. Some researchers (e.g., Rapaport, Gill, & Schaefer, 1968) claim that certain cards are particularly useful in eliciting specific kinds of information, such as the presence of underlying depression, suicidal thoughts, or strong aggressive impulses.

As with the Rorschach, subjects go through the cards one by one. With each card they are asked to describe what has led up to the scene presented in the picture, what is going on in the picture itself, what the characters are thinking and feeling, and what the outcome will be. Like the Rorschach, the TAT includes an inquiry phase to clarify ambiguous responses. Then, through a complex scoring system, the subject's responses are converted into an interpretation of his or her unconscious conflicts and motivations. A children's version of this test, the *Children's Apperception Test,* or *CAT* (Bellak, 1954), follows the same principles as the TAT except that the scenes focus on situations particularly relevant to children, such as feeding, toileting, and rivalry.

Evaluation of projective tests Of all forms of psychological testing, the projective techniques allow subjects the greatest freedom in expressing themselves. However, these tests also allow the interviewer the greatest freedom in interpreting the subject's responses, and herein lies their major problem. Opponents of the projective tests claim that the chain of inference leading from the subject's response to the interviewer's report is simply too long, too complex, and too subjective, with the result that the report may tell more about the interviewer than about the subject. This argument has been supported by numerous studies (e.g., Datel & Gengerelli, 1955; Howard, 1962; Little & Shneidman, 1959) showing poor interjudge reliability for the projective tests. And as may be expected when a method lends itself to many different clinical interpretations, many researchers have found the validity of the projective tests to be disturbingly low (Chapman & Chapman, 1969; Mischel, 1968; Nunnally, 1978). It was partly in response to such findings that empirically based scoring systems were developed for the projective tests. The Exner scoring system for the Rorschach is a highly detailed procedure in which the subject's responses are reduced to a numerical pattern, which is then compared with patterns derived from a variety of normative groups; however, validity still remains low (Nezworski & Wood, 1995).

Whatever the scientific standing of projective testing, its supporters claim that this is the only assessment method open and flexible enough to provide information about the subject's unconscious processes and, even if its validity is hard to document, it is still useful to the clinician. Many clearly agree, for both the Rorschach and the TAT are among the ten most frequently used psychological tests (Lubin, Larsen, & Matarazzo, 1984).

FIGURE 6.3 Pictures similar to those used in the Thematic Apperception Test (TAT). In this test, the subject is asked to tell a story about what is being shown in the pictures.

Self-Report Personality Inventories Unlike projective tests, **self-report personality inventories** ask the subjects direct questions about themselves. Such a test may instruct subjects to rate a long list of descriptive statements—such as "I am afraid of the dark" or "I prefer to be alone most of the time"—according to their applicability to themselves. Or the test may consist of a list of things or situations that subjects are asked to rate according to whether they are appealing or frightening. In any case, in the self-report inventory, as the name indicates, subjects assess themselves. This self-assessment may not be taken at face value by the testers, but it is given some weight.

The MMPI The most widely used self-report personality inventory is the **Minnesota Multiphasic Personality Inventory–2,** or **MMPI-2** (Hathaway & McKinley, 1943, 1989). The purpose of the MMPI-2 is to simplify differential diagnosis by comparing self-descriptive statements endorsed by new patients to those endorsed by groups of people already diagnosed as schizophrenic, depressive, and so forth. Thus it is important to note that an evaluation produced by the MMPI-2 is not derived directly from the subject's self-description. A person who answers yes to such statements as "Someone is pouring dirty thoughts into my head" is not automatically judged to be schizophrenic. Rather, the evaluation depends on whether responses to these and other statements show a *pattern* similar to that seen in the MMPI-2 responses of already diagnosed schizophrenics.

The test items range from statements of ordinary vocational and recreational preferences to descriptions of bizarre thoughts and behaviors. We have already given one example of the latter. Other items similar to those on the MMPI-2 checklist would be:

"I go to a party every week."

"I am afraid of picking up germs when I shake hands."

"I forgive people easily."

"I sometimes enjoy breaking the law."

The test items were originally compiled from a variety of sources—psychiatry textbooks, directions for psychiatric and medical interviews, and previously published personality tests (Hathaway & McKinley, 1940). These items were tried out on groups of patients hospitalized for schizophrenia, depression, and so on, and then given to normal subjects. Only those items on which the pathological groups substantially diverged from the normal groups were retained. In the end, the test was made up of over 500 statements, yielding a rating of the subject on ten clinical scales. The following are the ten scales, along with the characteristics that might be inferred from a high score on any one of them:

Hypochondriasis: anxious over bodily functioning

Depression: hopeless

Hysteria: immature, suggestible, demanding

Psychopathic deviate: amoral, unscrupulous, rebellious

Masculinity-femininity: characterized by traits and interests typically associated with the opposite sex

Paranoia: suspicious, jealous

Psychasthenia: fearful, unconfident

Schizophrenia: withdrawn, disorganized in thought processes

Hypomania: impulsive, distractible

Social introversion: shy, self-effacing

In addition to the clinical scales, the MMPI-2 uses a number of control scales designed to measure the validity of the subject's responses. The L (Lie) scale indicates the degree to which the subject appears to be falsifying responses in a naive way in order to "look good." For example, if the subject checks "false" next to a statement such as "I do not always tell the truth," this will boost his or her score on the L scale. The K (Subtle Defensiveness) scale measures less obvious kinds of defensiveness. Most educated people would know better than to claim on a psychological test that they never told a lie, but if, for example, they were involved in a child-custody case, they might be motivated to distort the truth about their moral character in subtler ways. This is what the K scale is designed to detect. Roughly the opposite of the L and K scales is the F (Infrequency) scale, which measures the subject's tendency to *exaggerate* his or her psychological problems. Included on the MMPI-2 are a number of statements (e.g., "Someone has been trying to rob me," "Evil spirits possess me at times") that are very infrequently endorsed by normal subjects and that people with mental disorders endorse only selectively, in a manner consistent with their symptoms. Subjects who frequently and unselectively endorse these statements receive a high F-scale score, which may mean that they are trying to fake mental illness—for example, for the sake of a lawsuit claiming psychological injury—or that they are very distressed and trying to get help. (Alternatively, it may mean that they have reading problems or are responding randomly.) When the MMPI was revised in 1989, several additional control scales were added. One measures whether the subject, partway through the test, has begun responding to it differently (e.g., stopped taking it seriously). There are also two new scales that measure whether the subject is responding consistently. These new scales can be helpful in interpreting the other scales. High scores on consistency combined with a high F-scale score suggest that the person is not having reading problems, let alone responding at random, but is in fact exaggerating his or her psychological problems (Butcher, 1990).

The usual procedure for evaluating an MMPI-2 is to arrange the subject's scores on the various scales in numerical order, from the highest to the lowest score, and then to interpret the pattern of scores by comparison with patterns seen in normal and pathological groups, rather than to interpret any one scale separately. Some clinicians do draw diagnostic conclusions from scores on individual scales. A clinician may assume, for example, that a person who scores high on the depression scale is a good candidate for the psychiatric diagnosis of depression—that is, that he or she will show not only sadness but also guilt, lack of motivation, sleeping and eating problems, and other symptoms of depression. Such one-scale diagnoses are apparently not very meaningful, however. In a review of several studies on the relationship between specific symptoms and individual MMPI scales, Hedlund (1977) found that although many of the scales were related to the expected symptoms, these symptoms were usually related to several (in some cases, almost all) of the other scales as well. Thus scores on individual scales cannot, in general, yield sound diagnoses. Indeed, there is some doubt as to whether even the pattern of scores is a valid source of diagnostic information. The major value of the MMPI-2 is probably in communicating the degree of overall disturbance (mildly troubled, deeply troubled, etc.) rather than in pinpointing the exact nature of the disturbance.

Evaluation of the MMPI-2 Even as a measure of the degree of disturbance, the MMPI-2 is not an infallible instrument. A concern about the original edition of the test was the narrowness of the group of normal subjects on whom it was standardized. All were white, and most were young married people living in small towns or rural areas near Minneapolis. With the revision, the test was standardized on a much more representative sample (J. R. Graham, 1990) and modernized in other ways as well. Sexist language was removed, as were test items that seemed aimed at identifying people's religious beliefs.

But however updated, the test still has many of its original shortcomings (Helmes & Reddon, 1993). Most important, it is still a self-report test and is thus faced with the problem that many people do not give accurate reports about themselves. Some will lie; others will fall into what are called **response sets,** test-taking attitudes that lead them to shade their responses one way or another, often unconsciously. One such response set is the *social desirability set,* the tendency to try to make oneself look good; another is the *acquiescence set,* the tendency to agree with statements whether they apply to oneself or not (D. N. Jackson & Messick, 1961). The control scales, as we saw, were designed to detect such distortions, but no one pretends that they eliminate all inaccuracy. In clinical settings, where people are usually taking the MMPI-2 because they have problems and want help, deliberate falsification is less likely, but it can easily occur in other situations, such as the screening of job applicants. As for unconscious falsification, it is probably common in all settings.

The major argument in support of the MMPI-2 is that since it can be scored by computer, it enables examiners to measure a given subject against previously tested subjects with great precision (Butcher, 1978)—and also with great speed. The computers that now analyze the answer sheets and make up the profiles can do so in less than one and a half seconds. Furthermore, although the test is not immune to error, it has been found to agree substantially with personality descriptions derived from elaborate case histories (Little & Shneidman, 1954).

The MCMI-II While the MMPI-2 is used in a wide variety of contexts, another self-report test, the *Millon Clinical Multiaxial Inventory,* or *MCMI-II* (Millon, 1987), is intended specifically to aid in the diagnosis of disorders in the *DSM,* particularly the personality disorders. The personality disorders (Chapter 11) are long-standing patterns of maladaptive thought and behavior. Unlike most other disorders, they do not disrupt the person's life; they are part of that life—and as such, they are hard to diagnose. The MCMI-II is an effort to solve this problem. The test is a 175-item true-false inventory that yields ratings on twenty clinical scales, all of which correspond to *DSM* categories, including the personality disorders. The correspondence between the *DSM* criteria and the MCMI-II is not exact. Millon has relied on his own theories, especially with regard to the personality disorders, as well as on the diagnostic manual. But as intended, the MCMI-II does a better job than other self-report inventories in identifying the patterns described in the *DSM* (Millon, 1985a, 1985b).

Psychological Tests for Organic Impairment As we have seen in earlier chapters, psychological disturbance may be due to neurological problems rather than, or as well as, "life" problems. Thus a major task of psychological assessment is to distinguish biogenic from psychogenic cases and, in biogenic cases, to determine what the neurological problem is.

Certain pencil-and-paper tests have proved valid measures of neurological damage. One device that is widely used to screen patients for "organicity" (i.e., neurological malfunction) is the *Bender Visual-Motor Gestalt Test* (Bender, 1938). Here the subject is shown nine simple designs, each printed on a separate card, and is asked to reproduce the designs on a piece of paper. If certain errors, such as rotation of the figures or rounding of the corners, consistently appear in the subject's drawings, the examiner is likely to suspect neurological impairment. (See Figure 6.4.) In some cases the test involves a second phase, in which the examiner asks the subject to reproduce the designs from memory. Failure to reproduce more than two designs is generally viewed as further evidence of impairment.

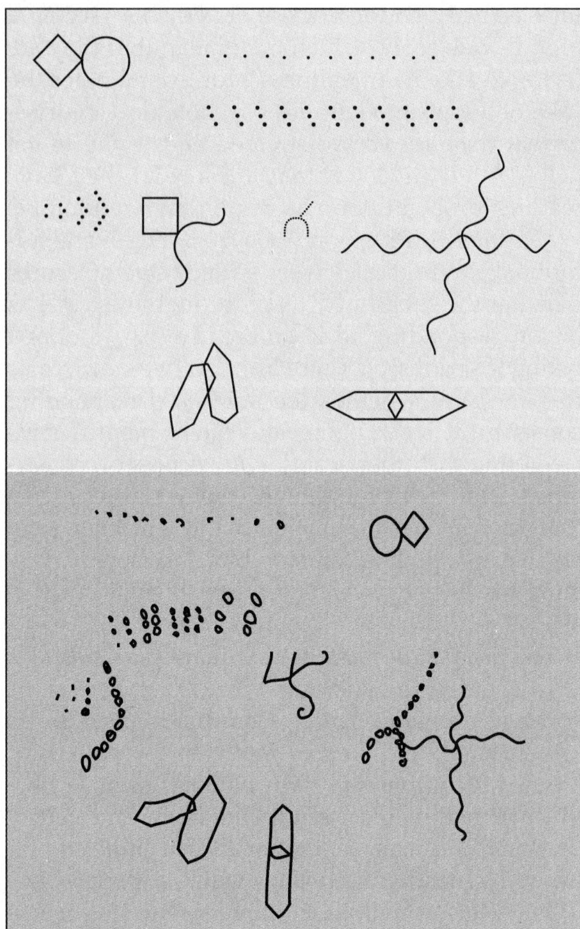

FIGURE 6.4 *(Top)* The nine figures of the Bender Visual-Motor Gestalt Test. *(Bottom)* Reproductions of the Bender drawings done by a ten-year-old boy. Certain characteristics of the boy's drawings, such as the reversal of the square and the circle in the first figure and the rotation of the last figure, strongly suggest organic impairment.

More helpful in providing specific information is a coordinated group of tests called the *Halstead-Reitan Neuropsychological Battery.* These tests are based on our (still imperfect) knowledge of which areas of the brain control which intellectual and motor functions. The subject is confronted with a variety of tasks—several performance measures, including those of the Wechsler Adult Intelligence Scale, along with tests of perception and rhythm, a test measuring the subject's ability to fit various wooden forms into receptacles of the same shapes while blindfolded, and so forth. Each of these tasks was originally designed to assess the functioning of a specific area of the brain. So failure at any one task can presumably help the diagnostician pinpoint the site of the neurological damage. However, given the complex crisscrossings of the neural pathways—together with the equally complex interaction between the brain and behavior—such decisions are still not easily made with any psychological test.

Laboratory Tests

While psychological measures can be of help in diagnosing organicity, the primary means of detecting such problems is direct testing of the structure and function of the nervous system through laboratory methods. A standard test is the **electroencephalogram (EEG),** in which the electrical activity in the brain cells is picked up by electrodes attached to the skull and recorded in oscillating patterns called *brain waves.* The EEG can detect tumors and injuries in the brain. As we saw in Chapter 4, researchers have recently developed more sophisticated means of testing for organicity, such as *computerized tomography (CT),* which is essentially a series of computer-enhanced x-rays of the brain, and *positron emission tomography (PET),* which involves tracing the progress of radioactive particles through the brain. Both techniques have already produced new findings with regard to schizophrenia. An even newer method is *magnetic resonance imaging (MRI).* Through the use of magnetic fields, MRI yields a highly precise picture of the brain from more vantage points than other methods.

Laboratory tests can also be used to identify psychogenic disorders. There is an intimate relationship between emotion and physiological functioning. When a person's hostility level rises, so may the blood pressure. When a person's anxiety level rises, so may the activation level of the sweat glands. Such changes can be monitored by physiological recording devices such as the **polygraph,** a machine equipped with a number of sensors, which, when attached to the body, can pick up subtle physiological changes. These fluctuations, in the form of electrical impulses, are amplified within the polygraph and activate pens that then record the changes on a continuously moving roll of paper. When sensors are attached to the scalp, the result is an EEG. When the sensor measures changes in the electrical resistance of the skin—an indication of sweat gland activity—the result is a reading of **galvanic skin response (GSR).** When the sensor is used to pick up subtle changes in the electrical activity of muscles, the result is an **electromyogram (EMG).** The polygraph can also measure a number of other physiological responses, such as heart rate, blood volume, and blood pressure. (The polygraph is the standard lie-detector test, the assumption being that in persons who are lying, anxiety over being discovered will produce the kinds of autonomic arousal that the machine records.)

Either the polygraph as a whole or its separate measures can be used as indicators of emotional responses to specific stimuli and thus can aid in assessment. For example, patients with high blood pressure may be fitted with a portable blood-pressure recorder so that they can take their own blood pressure at regular intervals during the day, at the same time recording in a notebook what they are doing at the time of each reading. When the two records are compared and elevations in blood pressure correlate consistently with some specific environmental stimulus, such as the family dinner hour, then the diagnostician has at least some preliminary clue as to the source of the patient's stress.

In other cases, physiological measures may be required to pinpoint the actual *nature* of the patient's problem. **Polysomnography,** the all-night employment of a variety of measures including EEG, EMG, and respiration, can be invaluable in determining whether patients who complain of insomnia do in fact have what psychologists and physicians call insomnia or whether they are suffering from some other sleep disorder. For example, people who complain of insomnia may actually have *sleep apnea,* a respiratory disorder in which breathing repeatedly stops for ten seconds or more during the night. Since sleep apnea causes extreme daytime tiredness, both patient and doctor may assume that the problem is insomnia. Often it is only by means of polysomnography that sleep apnea can be detected.

Observation in Natural Settings

As we noted earlier, the psychometric approach aims to measure what are presumed to be the person's stable personality characteristics. Supporters of this approach would not deny that behavior is influenced by **situational variables,** the environmental stimuli that precede and follow any given action. No one disputes, for example, that children who are coddled by their parents after temper tantrums are likely to have more temper tantrums. Nevertheless, adherents of the psychometric approach assume that behavior issues primarily from **person variables,** the person's stable traits.

In the last few decades this theory has been challenged by a number of behavioral psychologists, who take essentially the reverse position. They acknowledge that human actions are determined in part by person variables (which they see as learned patterns of thought and behavior rather than as "traits"). But they claim that the major determinants of behavior are the situational variables—the physical and social settings in which the behavior takes place. From this point of view, it follows that abnormal behavior cannot be accurately assessed in a clinician's office. People must be observed in their natural settings—the classroom, the home, wherever the diagnostician can unobtrusively follow them—so that the connections between behavior and situation will be revealed.

Actually, a diagnostician need not subscribe to behavioral theory in order to value this method of assessment. It has been used for a very long time by clinicians of many persuasions, especially in treating children. Its value is that it allows the diagnostician to pinpoint circumstances that elicit the problem behavior—information that is useful

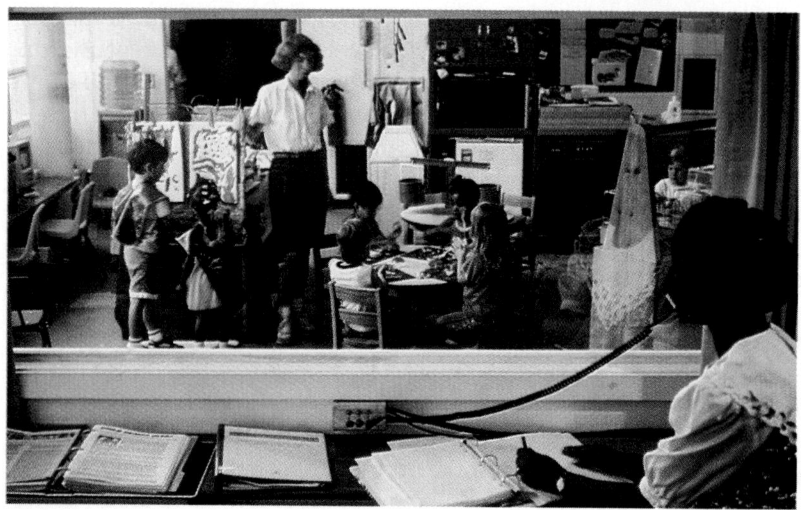

A one-way window can be useful in assessing behavior in natural settings. Subjects are usually informed that they are being watched; but they are less aware of being observed, and thus behave more naturally, because they cannot see the assessor.

no matter what the behavior is ultimately ascribed to. Consider, for example, a child who is having discipline problems in school. An observer may be sent into the classroom to analyze precisely what environmental conditions provoke her outbursts—teasing by other children, difficult academic tasks, or whatever. Once this information is collected, the diagnostician is in a better position to determine what the child's problem actually is.

Direct observation has a number of advantages over other assessment techniques. For one thing, it does not depend on self-report, which, as we have seen, may be inaccurate. While the parents of an aggressive boy may state that he is *always* making trouble, and while the child may report that he makes trouble only when someone hits him or takes his things, the observer has a better chance of finding out where the truth lies. Second, observation cuts down on assessment errors caused by the subject's response to the examiner or by the examiner's overly subjective interpretations. Finally, observation tends to provide *workable* answers to behavioral problems. Whereas a projective test may show that a child's aggressive behavior is due to unconscious conflicts, situational observation may reveal that his aggression surfaces only during certain kinds of interaction with his mother—a variable that is much easier to deal with than unconscious conflict. Furthermore, if an underlying conflict does exist, it is possible that adjustment of the mother-child interaction will help resolve it.

Observation is not without its problems. In the first place, it requires a great investment of time. Second, the presence of observers may be "reactive." That is, the person being observed may act differently because he or she is being observed. "Problem" children (and "problem" parents and teachers) often show speedy improvement once they realize they are being watched by a person with a clipboard. Sometimes this problem can be solved through surreptitious observation. Either the assessor can watch through a one-way mirror, or, in the case of a classroom, he or she can be introduced as the "teacher's helper" for the day. However, such teacher's helpers often fool nobody, and surreptitious observation is ethically questionable in any case. An alternative, though it too presents ethical problems, is to use recording equipment rather than human beings to do the observing. Unlike a human observer, a video camera can be set up to operate continuously, with the result that the people being observed eventually forget its presence and resume their accustomed behavior.

THEORETICAL PERSPECTIVES ON ASSESSMENT

As we have seen in preceding chapters, the various psychological perspectives, while acknowledging that abnormal behavior may have many different types of causes, nevertheless have clear ideas as to which is the most *important* type of cause. And not surprisingly, each perspective favors assessment methods that focus on that sort of cause.

The Psychodynamic Approach

As we saw in Chapter 2, two basic assumptions of classical psychodynamic theory, as derived from Freud, are (1) that people's behavior is determined primarily not by their will or by their current environment but by motivations and conflicts established in childhood, and (2) that these latter factors, kept in check by defenses, operate unconsciously in motivating behavior. Proceeding on these two assumptions, psychodynamic assessment procedures attempt to place the subject in a free atmosphere, so that defenses will be relaxed and unconscious material will reveal itself.

This assessment strategy involves two basic techniques. The first is the **depth interview,** in which subjects are encouraged to talk about their childhood and also about their current lives as candidly as possible. The second major psychodynamic assessment tool is the projective test, in which it is hoped that subjects will project onto the Rorschach's or TAT's ambiguous images whatever is foremost in their unconscious.

These psychodynamic assessment techniques have the same virtues and vices as psychodynamic theory itself. On the one hand, they represent one method of tapping the inner reaches of the personality, levels that lie below the person's surface behaviors. On the other hand, they tend to accord the status of fact to assumptions that are difficult to validate empirically—for example, that the unconscious is the prime motivator of behavior. Furthermore, like psychodynamic theory, they assume that most responses are interpretable in terms of unconscious motivation.

What these criticisms come down to is a concern regarding the faith that psychodynamic assessment places in the clinician's judgment. As we saw in our discussion of actuarial *versus* clinical judgment, research has found the predictive validity of clinical judgment to be low. An interesting example is a follow-up study of psychiatric predictions about the future adjustment of four successive classes (1946–1949) of first-year medical students at the University of Chicago. On the basis of psychiatric interviews, each student was rated as having a good, guarded, or poor prognosis with regard to academic, professional, and personal adjustment. Then, thirty-five years later, the subjects were tracked down, and on the basis of a detailed questionnaire, they were rated on current adjustment. How well were the predictions borne out? Not very well. Overall, those who had been rated as having a poor prognosis had not fared as well in life as those with good prognoses, but actually most of the subjects had fared very well indeed and showed little sign of emotional impairment. C. K. Aldrich (1986), who conducted this study, concludes that the original interviewers paid too much attention to signs of possible disturbance—a good example of the "pathological bias" mentioned earlier—and too little attention to the students' capacity for change and coping.

The problem of clinical judgment plagues mental health workers of all persuasions. But of all the psychological perspectives, the psychodynamic is the most vulnerable on this score, for it is the one that relies most heavily on inference and interpretation. What the psychodynamic theorists reply is that whatever the problems with inference, it is the only way of getting at essential information. Indeed, many psychodynamic theorists feel that the problem with current *DSM*-based diagnosis, particularly in its recent form, with the highly specific criteria, is that it depends not too much but too *little* on clinical judgment—that in its effort to banish vagueness and subjectivity, it has fallen into the opposite error of focusing only on the superficial (T. Shapiro, 1989a).

The Behavioral Approach

Behaviorists, as we saw in Chapter 3, regard behavior as issuing primarily from people's interaction with their environment. Thus, in assessing a psychological problem, the behaviorist will concentrate on determining with the greatest possible accuracy what it is in the environment that is reinforcing the maladaptive response.

Because they see behavior as changing in relation to the environment, behaviorists are skeptical about such stable-trait-oriented assessment methods as the projective tests and the MMPI. Indeed, behaviorists are generally not interested in interpreting human actions as *signs* of anything else—underlying traits, intrapsychic conflicts, or even psychological disorders (hence their distrust of diagnostic labeling). Rather, they view behaviors as *samples,* specimens of a particular person's responses in particular situations. In dealing with a patient who complains of shyness, for example, a behavioral clinician would not care greatly whether such behavior was a sign that the trait "introversion" was particularly pronounced in this person. The behaviorist would simply regard the patient's social behavior as a sample of a particular response pattern and would concentrate on finding out what concrete stimuli—and, in keeping with the new cognitive behaviorism, what thoughts—were eliciting and maintaining that response pattern (Kendall, 1992). The main tools for obtaining such information are interviews, self-monitoring diaries, and direct observation.

An assessment interview conducted by a behaviorist bears little resemblance to the psychodynamic depth interview. Generally, it will take the form of a **functional analysis,** or systematic dissection of the person's complaint: what precisely the problem behavior is, how it developed, what the person has done to try to combat it, and—most important of all—the changes in the environment that precede, accompany, and follow the behavior. In addition, the interviewer will try to get some idea of the person's strengths and preferences, since such elements help in designing an appropriate treatment program. In such an interchange, the subject's remarks are assumed to be fairly accurate statements of the problem rather than veiled clues to its underlying dynamics.

To supplement information gathered in the interview, many behavioral examiners will ask subjects to keep a self-monitoring diary of their problem behaviors. For example, a woman who is afflicted with vague anxieties would be asked to note down when her anxiety occurs and what circumstances surround the episodes. If the diary should reveal, for instance, that her anxiety regularly escalates when she is taking the bus home from work, then this correlation will provide a starting point for determining the stimuli that are maintaining the anxiety in this and other situations.

Finally, a widely used behavioral assessment method is direct observation of the problem behavior. The behaviorist may observe the subject in the school, work, or home environment in order to identify the stimuli that trigger the maladaptive responses. Or the behavior sampling may take place in the clinical situation itself, as when married couples are asked to discuss points of disagreement in front of the therapist.

In evaluating the behavioral approach to assessment, we should note first of all that this approach generally fulfills its stated objective—that is, the detailed and concrete analysis of the problem behavior and the environmental conditions that support the behavior. On the negative side, behavioral assessment is subject to the same objection that has been leveled at behavioral theory in general, that it is reductive and superficial: that it treats human beings as if they were on a par with laboratory animals and that it attends only to the symptoms, ignoring the underlying causes. In answer to this criticism, behavioral clinicians argue that a technique that works for human beings should not be discarded because it also works for laboratory animals and that if problems can be solved by attention to environmental contingencies, then there is no need for speculation as to unverifiable underlying causes.

The Cognitive Approach

Cognitive theorists, as we have seen, interest themselves in cognitive processes, such as attention, memory, and problem solving, together with cognitive "products," such as self-defeating thoughts. Accordingly, their assessment methods are aimed at highlighting these matters as they relate to psychopathology.

To get at self-defeating thoughts, questionnaires are often used. One is the Hopelessness Scale (A. T. Beck, Weissman, Lester, et al., 1974), which measures the subject's expectations for the future. Another is the Attributional Style Questionnaire (Peterson, Semmel, von Baeyer, et al., 1982), which aims to find out how subjects explain negative and positive events to themselves—whether, for example, they tend to blame themselves for misfortunes or to blame others or circumstances beyond their control. Both these scales were developed on the basis of the cognitive theory that depression is the product of pessimistic and self-castigating thoughts.

Another way of getting at self-defeating thoughts is to have subjects record them. For example, in the self-monitoring diary described above, under behavioral assessment, the woman with anxiety problems would be asked to record not just the external circumstances surrounding her episodes of anxiety but also the thoughts that went through her head at those moments (Kendall & Hollon, 1981). Armed with this information, the cognitive therapist would then know which of her thoughts needed to be reexamined.

The cognitive perspective is still a relatively new approach, and while its assessment methods have added to our knowledge of how the mind works, its findings are still largely preliminary. Most of the cognitive assessment techniques now in use are aimed at dysfunctional thoughts (Nasby & Kihlstrom, 1986). What is needed is more testing of how the deeper cognitive processes, such as attention and memory, are involved in abnormal behavior.

The Sociocultural Approach

A major concern of sociocultural theorists is cultural bias in assessment. We have already considered this matter in relation to IQ testing, and in Chapter 3 we discussed various studies revealing such bias—for example, when diagnosticians are shown case studies identical in every respect except race, blacks are more likely to be labeled alcoholic or schizophrenic while whites tend to receive the less stigmatizing diagnosis of depression.

These, however, are only the most blatant examples of cultural bias in assessment. Researchers have revealed subtler distortions as well. For instance, several studies have shown that diagnoses received by bilingual patients can vary drastically depending on whether the interview is conducted in the patient's first or second language. Del Castillo (1970), the first researcher to raise this problem, and a Spanish speaker, described the following case:

> R. A. was a 28-year-old Cuban patient charged with murder. During his rather lengthy hospitalization he was under the care of a Spanish-speaking physician who found him to be psychotic, suffering from terrifying imaginary experiences. Occasionally he was interviewed by an English-speaking psychiatrist, in whose judgment the patient was coherent, factual, and free from overt psychotic manifestations. I was asked to evaluate his mental status on a few different occasions and encountered exactly what the other Spanish-speaking physician had found. (p. 161)

Later researchers (C. Price & Cuellar, 1981) have likewise shown that diagnosticians find less pathology in patients speaking a second language, and they explain the phenomenon as Del Castillo did: that using the second language requires patients to organize their thinking better, with the result that their thoughts seem less disturbed. Curiously, other researchers have found the opposite effect, that diagnosticians find *more* pathology in patients speaking a second language (Marcos, Urcuyo, & Kesselman, 1973). (They explain this as the diagnostician's response to the patient's language problems—misunderstood questions, misused words, speech hesitations, etc.) How can we evaluate such contradictory evidence? For Lopez (1988), the opposing findings suggest that several kinds of distortion can affect the assessment of bilingual patients. If you consider that most diagnostic interviews with nonnative English speakers are conducted in English, this could be a serious problem.

The broader matter of cultural bias was acknowledged in the latest revision of the *DSM*. Earlier editions of the manual contained very little information on how behaviors thought normal in one ethnic group or age group or gender might be misinterpreted as abnormal by a diagnostician of a different sex, age, or ethnic background. Now, in *DSM-IV*, most of the diagnostic categories include such information. For example, the diagnostic criteria for "conduct disorder" (a pattern of antisocial behavior—aggression, destructiveness, deceitfulness—beginning in adolescence [Chapter 17]) are accompanied by a warning that this diagnosis may be "misapplied to individuals in settings where patterns of undesirable behavior are sometimes viewed as protective (e.g., threatening, impoverished, high-crime)" (American Psychiatric Association, 1994, p. 88). In other words, gang members in ghetto neighborhoods may have social, more than psychological, reasons for delinquency. Likewise, under "schizophrenia," the manual cautions that "in some cultures, visual or auditory hallucinations with a religious content may be a normal part of religious experience (e.g., seeing the Virgin Mary or hearing God's voice)" (p. 281) and therefore should not automatically be taken as symptoms of psychosis. The manual also has a new "Glossary of Culture-Bound Syndromes," including conditions such as "ghost sickness" ("a preoccupation with death . . . observed among members of many American Indian tribes" [p. 846]) and the "evil eye" ("a concept widely found in Mediterranean cultures" [p. 847]) that may or may not warrant diagnosis.

Such cautionary information may help people from various subgroups to receive less biased diagnoses. Or, ironically, it may not. Remember that the best diagnosis is not the mildest diagnosis but the most accurate diagnosis, which will presumably lead to the most appropriate treatment. In a large-scale study of California clinicians, Lopez and Hernandez (1986) found that some of these therapists, in an attempt to be sensitive to "cultural diversity," underestimated the seriousness of their patients' symptoms. One clinician, for example, had a patient who was hallucinating, but he did not consider the diagnosis of schizophrenia because the patient was black and black people, he reasoned, were culturally more prone to hallucinations than white people. His conclusion was not inconsistent with *DSM-IV*'s warning that hallucinations are a normal part of religious experience in "some cultures." Nevertheless, as the researchers point out, the woman may indeed have been schizophrenic—and deprived of appropriate treatment as a result of her therapist's watchfulness regarding cultural bias.

Still, as with the conflicting evidence about assessments in a second language, this does not mean that diagnosticians should give up trying to correct bias. Fifty years ago, many diagnostic practices were patently racist. If, today, the effort to solve that problem involves some error and overcompensation, the effort is still necessary.

The Interpersonal Approach

We have already seen how the interpersonal perspective tends to cut across other perspectives, borrowing from them and contributing to them. This is true of its assessment techniques as well. Like psychodynamic therapists, interpersonal therapists rely on interviews. They may also use questionnaires, as cognitive therapists do. But whatever the instrument, the focus is interpersonal: the aim is to assess relationships rather than persons. In the interview process, for example, patients will be asked who the important people are in their lives, what conflicts they have with those people, and what conditions seem to make the conflicts escalate. Following such an interview, the interpersonal clinician will want to interview the patient *with* those others. As we've noted, many interpersonal therapists see the person seeking treatment as merely the "identified patient." The real patient is the relationship—usually, the family relationship—and that is what the clinician will want to assess.

With the interpersonal perspective, as with all the others, the assessment approach is subject to the same criticisms as the assumptions on which it is based—in this case, that it rests not so much on a theory as on a collection of subtheories and that it does not uncover the causes of psychological problems but just factors maintaining those problems. A more practical weakness of interpersonal assessment is that the patient's "others" may have no interest whatsoever in becoming involved in the diagnostic process and may strongly resent the implication that they are contributing to what they see as someone else's pathology. But neither this pitfall nor the other objections take anything from the general usefulness of interpersonal assessment, and as usual, other perspectives have learned from it. It is the rare clinician today who, in treating a troubled child or adolescent, will not ask the parents to come in for an interview, preferably with the patient.

The Humanistic-Existential Approach

Like behaviorists, humanists and existentialists avoid labeling in the assessment process, but for a different reason: they consider diagnostic labels an affront to the patient's individuality. As we saw in Chapter 2, humanistic-existential theorists see psychopathology, in large measure, as a *loss* of individuality. This is what they are trying to restore—a goal that will not be served by diagnosis.

Accordingly, humanistic-existential assessment procedures are aimed at helping both the therapist and the patient become more fully aware of what the patient's self really is. Any assessment instrument may be employed, but it will be used primarily to encourage patients to reveal their subjective world (Dana, 1982). Not everything the patient says will be taken as the whole truth—these therapists believe strongly in the power of denial and "inauthenticity"—but it will be accepted as a version of the truth and then used as an avenue to deeper truths. This procedure, like humanistic-existential theory in general, has been criticized as unscientific. Its defenders argue that natural science itself has limited value as a tool for understanding the human experience.

The Biological Approach

Given its focus on the organic components of behavior, the biological perspective naturally favors assessment methods that reveal organic structure and function. A good deal of the excitement that has surrounded this perspective in recent years has been due to the development of more sophisticated organic tests, particularly such imaging procedures as the CT and PET scans and MRI. For years the brain was unexplored territory; one might speculate on its functions and malfunctions, but with little empirical support. Now, with such things as PET scan images of the actual itinerary that glucose takes as it travels through a given brain, there is ground for theory building, and therefore theories and research have proliferated.

Progress is slow, however, and despite the new procedures, our knowledge of the brain and its relation to behavior is still very elementary. Therefore neuropsychological assessment still depends heavily on psychological tests, such as the Halstead-Reitan Battery, that reveal performance deficits.

KEY TERMS

comorbidity (127)
depth interview (141)
description (121)
descriptive validity (126)
diagnosis (121)
DSM-IV (123)
electroencephalogram (EEG) (138)
electromyogram (EMG) (139)
functional analysis (142)
galvanic skin response (GSR) (139)
intelligence quotient (IQ) (131)
intelligence tests (131)
interjudge reliability (125)
internal consistency (125)
interview (130)
Minnesota Multiphasic Personality Inventory–2 (MMPI-2) (136)
person variables (139)
polygraph (139)
polysomnography (139)
prediction (121)
predictive validity (127)
prognosis (121)
projective personality tests (133)
psychological assessment (120)
psychological test (131)
psychometric approach (131)
reliability (125)
response sets (137)
Rorschach Psychodiagnostic Inkblot Test (133)
self-report personality inventories (136)
situational variables (139)
test-retest reliability (125)
Thematic Apperception Test (TAT) (134)
traits (131)
validity (126)

SUMMARY

- Psychological assessment has two goals. The first is to describe the personality and behavior of the person being assessed. The second is to predict that person's psychological functioning in the future. Psychological assessment is used for such practical purposes as school placement and job screening; in the clinical context, it helps clinicians determine the most effective treatment.
- Clinical assessment is a form of diagnosis, in which mental health professionals label an individual's problems according to criteria specified in the *DSM* and suggest his or her prognosis. This classification provides an essential common vocabulary for researchers, practitioners, and public health officials. Critics argue that psychiatric diagnosis falsely implies that abnormal behavior is qualitatively different from normal behavior; that there are clear-cut differences between different diagnostic categories; that diagnostic labels may be mistaken for explanations; and that the person may be stigmatized.
- *DSM-IV* attempts to remedy these problems by offering detailed, specific criteria and by requiring data on five dimensions or axes: the specific clinical syndrome being diagnosed; long-standing personality disorders (or, for children, mental retardation); relevant medical problems; psychosocial and environmental problems; and a numerical assessment of the patient's recent levels of adjustment and of the current degree of impairment. Like *DMS-III, DMS-IV* deliberately avoids reference to the causes of a disorder. Ideally, the result of assessment is a portrait, not a label.
- The usefulness of an assessment depends on reliability, or the consistency of measurement under varying conditions, and validity, or whether the assessment tool measures what it is supposed to measure. Diagnoses based on early editions of the *DSM* have shown low interjudge reliability and, perhaps for this reason, poor predictive validity. The more detailed, specific criteria and categories of recent editions of the *DSM* have corrected these problems to some degree. But growing recognition of comorbidity (in which one person exhibits symptoms of more than one disorder) have complicated the picture.
- Other problems relate to the assessor. The influence of the clinician's behavior and appearance on the subject's behavior and responses, the assessor's personal and professional biases, and pragmatic considerations all may interfere with accurate psychological assessment. The stricter criteria of recent editions of the *DSM* correct some problems but may also encourage clinicians to overuse residual diagnoses (such as anxiety disorder).
- There are four common methods of assessment. The first is the interview, which may be structured or unstructured.
- A second method is psychological testing. Intelligence tests (e.g., the Stanford-Binet and Wechsler scales) have high internal consistency and reliably predict performance in school, but they may be culturally biased and measure too narrow a range of mental abilities. Projective personality tests (e.g., the Rorschach and TAT) allow subjects freedom of expression but also permit variable interpretations, which led to the development of empirical scoring. Self-report personality inventories such as the MMPI-2, likewise, are scored against norms (how people with known disorders responded). Despite controls against false answers, these tests are not foolproof. The MCMI-II, created to identify personality disorders, is one of the most accurate.
- A third type of assessment is designed to detect neurological impairment. Today pen-and-pencil tests are supplemented by sophisticated laboratory tests which produce detailed pictures of the brain at work and physiological measures of emotional arousal (the polygraph) and sleeping patterns.

- A fourth method of assessment is observation of subjects in real-life settings, either directly or surreptitiously, with one-way mirrors or video cameras.
- As a rule, an examiner's choice of assessment technique reflects his or her theoretical orientation. Psychodynamic therapists tend to favor depth interviews and projective tests to probe the unconscious. Critics argue that these methods rely too heavily on interpretation, and follow-up studies suggest a pathological bias. Psychodynamic clinicians counter that other assessment techniques are superficial.
- Behavioral assessment, in contrast, avoids subjective interpretations and relies instead on functional analysis, self-monitoring, and situational observation. To the criticism that their assessments are limited, behaviorists respond that their treatments work. Cognitive therapists use laboratory tests to identify perceptual distortions and use questionnaires and self-monitoring to identify self-defeating thought patterns. This approach is too new to evaluate.
- Interpersonal therapists, like psychodynamic therapists, rely heavily on interviews, but they focus on the patient's current relationships with others and generally want to see the patient *with* those others in therapy. Humanistic-existential therapists also use interviews, but to uncover the patient's individuality, his or her authentic self.
- Neuroscientists test for organic problems, either directly with CT and PET scans and MRI or indirectly with psychological tests.

PART THREE

EMOTIONAL AND BEHAVIORAL DISORDERS

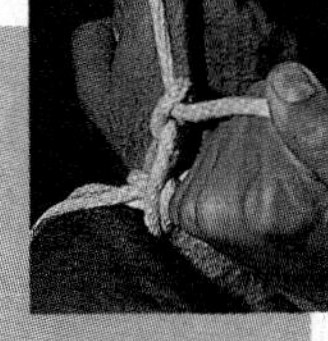

7

ANXIETY DISORDERS

ANXIETY DISORDER SYNDROMES

- Panic Disorder
- Generalized Anxiety Disorder
- Phobias
- Obsessive-Compulsive Disorder
- Posttraumatic Stress Disorder

PERSPECTIVES ON THE ANXIETY DISORDERS

- The Psychodynamic Perspective: Neurosis
- The Humanistic-Existential Perspective: The Individual and Society
- The Behavioral Perspective: Learning to Be Anxious
- The Cognitive Perspective: Misperception of Threat
- The Biological Perspective: Heredity and Biochemistry

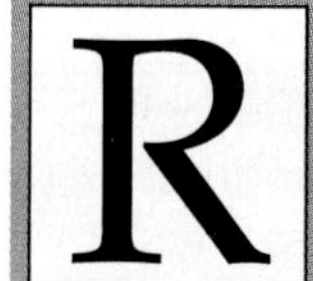ichard Benson, age thirty-eight, applied to a psychiatrist for therapy because he was suffering from severe and overwhelming anxiety which sometimes escalated to a panic attack. . . . During the times when he was experiencing intense anxiety, it often seemed as if he were having a heart seizure. He experienced chest pains and heart palpitations, numbness, shortness of breath. . . .

The intensity of the anxiety symptoms was very frightening to him and on two occasions his wife had rushed him to a local hospital because he was in a state of panic, sure that his heart was going to stop beating and he would die. . . .

Mr. Benson had had a chronic problem of bladder and kidney infections when he was a child [when suffering from these infections, he had great difficulty controlling his bladder; furthermore, urination was intensely painful], but he had had no further infections since the age of eleven. Nevertheless, he had continued his childhood practice of always making sure that he knew exactly where a bathroom was located whenever he was in an unfamiliar place. He indicated a fear that he would wet his pants if he could not find a bathroom immediately when he had an urge to urinate. The client stated that he still felt extremely anxious when he did not have direct access to a bathroom, but over the past few months [since his promotion to a new job] his anxiety had become more intense and had generalized to many other circumstances. . . .

[In the new job] he was no longer able to spend most of the working day at his desk. He had to meet with persons in their offices and he was sometimes involved in conferences in unfamiliar buildings that lasted an hour or more. It was more difficult for him to find a bathroom in his immediate vicinity and if he did not locate a rest room before he began conferring with someone, he felt an overwhelming need to urinate. He was extremely fearful that he would embarrass himself by wetting his pants and he eventually had to make some excuse in order to leave the conference and urinate in a rest room. The client revealed that he had also begun to feel trapped when someone engaged him in conversation, and he occasionally experienced a sensation of panic. Even if he knew the location of a bathroom, he did not feel that he was free to leave the room as long as someone was talking to him. He also feared that he would be trapped in his car by heavy traffic, or that his car would stall in a tunnel or on a bridge. . . .

Mr. Benson reported that he had derived great enjoyment from bicycle riding with his children on the weekend. However, he became more and more reluctant to go cycling because many of the trails the children urged him to go on did not have bathroom or medical facilities available. . . . [Since the advent of the panic attacks, he had become as concerned about availability of a doctor as about bathrooms.] He eventually gave up cycling even on familiar trails with hospitals nearby, because he was afraid that the rest room facilities would be in use if he had a sudden urge to urinate. . . .

After suffering through an episode of severe anxiety, the client said that he was unable to eat and he could not go to work the next day. He took a sick leave from his job five weeks after the anxiety attacks began, because he was intensely anxious in most interpersonal situations. He found it difficult to be out of the house even during the short time it took to do an errand at a neighborhood store and he therefore tried to stay home as much as possible. (Leon, 1977, pp. 113–188)

At the heart of Richard Benson's problem is **anxiety,** a state of fear and apprehension that affects many areas of functioning. Anxiety involves three basic components:

1 *Subjective reports* of tension, apprehension, dread, and expectations of inability to cope.
2 *Behavioral responses* such as avoidance of the feared situation, impaired speech and motor functioning, and impaired performance on complex cognitive tasks.
3 *Physiological responses* including muscle tension, increased heart rate and blood pressure, rapid breathing, dry mouth, nausea, diarrhea, and dizziness.

Anxiety is part and parcel of human existence. All people feel it in moderate degrees, and in moderate degrees it is an adaptive response. In the words of one researcher, "Without it, we would probably all be asleep at our desks" (Stephen M. Paul, quoted in Schmeck, 1982). We would also expose ourselves to danger. It is anxiety that impels us to go for medical checkups, to slow down on a slippery road, to study for exams, and thus to lead longer and more productive lives. But while most people feel anxiety some of the time, some people feel anxiety most of the time. For these people it is not an adaptive response. It is a source of extreme distress, relievable only by strategies that limit freedom and flexibility.

In this chapter we will focus on the **anxiety disorders,** characterized either by manifest anxiety or by behavior patterns aimed at warding off anxiety. Until recently, the anxiety disorders were grouped with the somatoform and dissociative disorders (Chapter 8) under the single diagnostic heading of *neurosis.* This term was coined in the eighteenth century by a Scottish physician, William Cullen, to describe a general affliction of the nervous system that produced "nervous" behavior. Throughout the nineteenth century, people who were "sane" but nevertheless engaged in rigid and self-defeating behaviors were labeled neurotic and were thought to be the victims of some unidentified neurological dysfunction. Then, beginning around the turn of the century, this biogenic view was gradually replaced by Freud's psychogenic view. To Freud, neurosis was due not to organic causes but rather to anxiety. As repressed memories and desires threatened to break through into the conscious mind, anxiety occurred as a "danger signal" to the ego. And neurotic behavior was either the expression of that anxiety or a defense against it.

The early editions of the *DSM* implicitly endorsed Freud's view by gathering all the so-called neurotic disorders into a single, anxiety-based category. Many people objected to this, however. The diagnostic manual, as they pointed out, was meant to be used by mental health professionals of all theoretical persuasions; therefore, to use a term that implied a psychodynamic interpretation (and one that remained to be proved) was inappropriate. In response to these criticisms, *DSM-III* (1980) eliminated the "neurosis" heading and broke the "neurotic disorders" up into separate categories, based on the behavior patterns they involved—a practice that has survived into *DSM-IV*. Nevertheless, the term *neurosis* is still widely used in psychodynamic writings. And mental health professionals of many persuasions continue to use it as an indication of the *severity* of a psychological disorder, "neurotic" indicating the milder disturbances and "psychotic" the more debilitating ones.

In that sense of severity, the anxiety disorders are "neurotic" conditions. They do not destroy reality contact. People with anxiety disorders may misinterpret or overreact to certain stimuli related to their psychological problems, but in general they see the same world as the rest of us. And in most cases they still go about their daily rounds, studying or working, carrying on fairly reasonable conversations, engaging in relationships with other people, and so on. They may cope poorly, but they cope.

Though the anxiety disorders as a group may not be crippling, they still represent the single largest mental health problem in the United States (Kessler, McGonagle, Zhao, et al., 1994). They are more common than any other psychological disorder, and they can lead to more severe disorders, such as depression and alcoholism. They may also lead to physical disorders such as heart disease (Barlow, 1988; Wells, Golding, & Burnam, 1989).

In this chapter we will describe the various syndromes that fall under the heading of "anxiety disorders." Then we will examine the different theoretical perspectives on the anxiety disorders.

ANXIETY DISORDER SYNDROMES

Anxiety can be experienced in a variety of ways. There are three basic patterns, however. In panic disorder and generalized anxiety disorder, the anxiety is unfocused; either it is with the person continually or it seems to descend "out of nowhere," unconnected to any special stimulus. In phobias, on the other hand, the fear is aroused by an identifiable object or situation. Finally, in obsessive-compulsive disorder, anxiety occurs if the person does *not* engage in some thought or behavior that otherwise serves no purpose and may in fact be unpleasant, embarrassing, and inconvenient.

Panic Disorder

We have already seen the general features of a panic attack in the case of Richard Benson. In a **panic attack,** anxiety begins suddenly and unexpectedly and soon mounts to an almost unbearable level. The person sweats, feels dizzy, trembles, and gasps for breath. The pulse quickens and the heart pounds. Nausea, chest pains, choking, feelings of numbness, and hot flashes or chills are also common. To people in the grip of such an attack, the world may suddenly seem unreal *(derealization)*, or they may seem unreal to themselves *(depersonalization)*. Above all, they have a sense of inescapable doom—that they are going to lose control, go crazy, or even die. Indeed, patients are often first recognized as having panic disorder when they turn up in hospital emergency rooms claiming, despite evidence of good health, that they are dying of a heart attack (H. I. Kaplan & Sadock, 1991). Such catastrophic thoughts are central to panic disorder and help to distinguish it from other anxiety disorders (Noyes, Woodman, Garvey, et al., 1992). A panic attack usually lasts several minutes, though it may continue for hours. When it subsides, the person feels exhausted, as if he or she had survived a traumatic experience—which is in fact the case. Between panic attacks, the person may have periods of no anxiety, although he or she will often worry about having another attack.

There are two kinds of panic attacks. In *unexpected* or *uncued* attacks, the attack seems to the person to come "out of the blue," unconnected to any specific stimulus. In *situationally bound* or *cued*

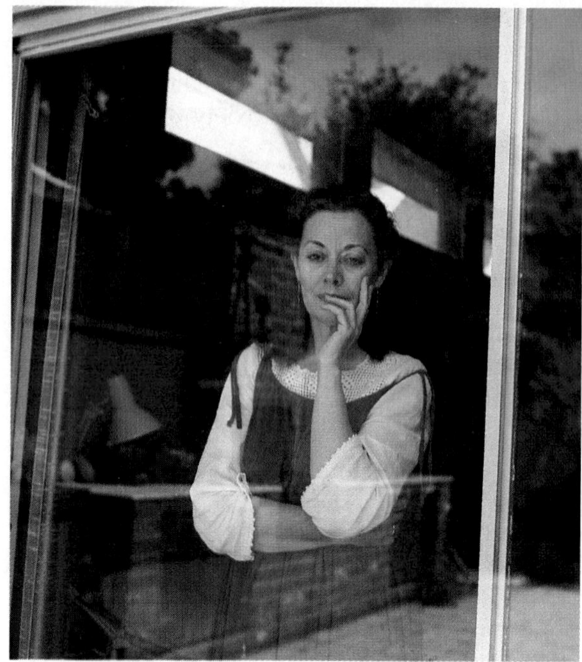

Agoraphobia can become so severe that the person does not dare to venture outside the home for months—sometimes even years—at a time.

attacks, the attack occurs in response to some situational trigger, such as seeing a snake. This distinction is used in differential diagnosis, for although panic attacks may occur in all the anxiety disorders, situationally bound attacks are more characteristic of phobias, while unexpected attacks are by definition present in panic disorder. According to *DSM-IV*, a person has **panic disorder** when he or she has had recurrent unexpected panic attacks, followed by psychological or behavioral problems—that is, persistent fear of future attacks, worry about the implications or consequences of the attacks, or significant changes in behavior (e.g., staying home from work) as a result of the attacks.

There remains some question, however, as to whether even in panic disorder the attacks are truly uncued. While people diagnosed as having panic disorder usually cannot point to any precipitating event—hence the diagnosis of panic disorder—they also generally report one or more stressful events in the year before the first attack (Katon, 1989; Pollard, Pollard, & Corn, 1989). Experts in this area now believe that most panic attacks do have precipitating events—subtle changes, such as physical exercise, that cause some alteration in body chemistry (Craske, 1991). Nevertheless, when victims report that their attacks are unexpected, this in itself is important, for it helps to account for the victims' catastrophic feelings, their sense of going out of control. People with panic disorder cannot go anywhere—to work, the movies, the supermarket—without fearing that they may have an attack in front of everyone, and with help nowhere in sight.

Consequently, some may in fact cease to go anywhere—a complication of panic disorder called agoraphobia. Literally, **agoraphobia** means "fear of the marketplace." Actually, what the agoraphobic fears is being in any situation from which escape might be difficult, and in which help would be unavailable, in the event of panic symptoms. Agoraphobia is often preceded by a phase of panic attacks, the first of which is likely to have occurred outside the home. (Only 9 percent of first attacks occur at home [Lelliott, Marks, McNamee, et al., 1989].) Eventually, the person becomes so afraid of having an attack, especially in a public place, that he or she begins to stay closer and closer to home. Some agoraphobics refuse to leave home unless someone goes with them; some are able to leave home to go to places in which they feel safe; and others refuse to leave home at all. At the end of the case of Richard Benson we saw agoraphobia beginning to develop, preceded by panic attacks and based on a fear of further attacks.

Because so many panic disorder victims are also agoraphobic, *DSM-IV* lists agoraphobia as a complication of panic disorder; but it also classifies agoraphobia as a disorder in its own right, for many agoraphobics—indeed, two-thirds, according to one estimate—have no history of panic disorder (Eaton & Keyl, 1990). Conversely, many victims of panic disorder do not become agoraphobic. Finally, in a sample of panic disorder patients with agoraphobia, 90 percent were found to have reported agoraphobic avoidance *before* the first panic attack (Fava, Grandi, Rafanelli, et al., 1992). So while panic attacks often lead to agoraphobia, they are by no means a prerequisite.

What predicts whether a person with panic attacks will develop agoraphobic avoidance? One might guess that the determining factors would be the frequency and severity of the attacks, but this is apparently not the case. Instead, avoidance seems to be linked to cognitive factors. Among panic disorder victims, those who believe that their attacks will be beyond their ability to cope and will lead to negative consequences are the ones most likely to become agoraphobic (Clum & Knowles, 1991).

Women are more likely than men to develop panic disorder, and they are far more likely than men to develop agoraphobia. (Approximately 75 percent of agoraphobics are women.) Panic disorder, with or without agoraphobia, tends to make its appearance in late adolescence or early adulthood—the median age of onset is twenty-four (Burke, Burke, Regier, et al., 1990). Whether children, too, have panic attacks is controversial (Moreau, Weissman, & Warner, 1989; Nelles & Barlow, 1988). Panic disorder is a common condition, affecting about 3.5 percent of Americans during their lifetime; agoraphobia is more common, with a prevalence of 5.3 percent (Eaton, Kessler, Wittchen, et al., 1994; Kessler, McGonagle, Zhao, et al., 1994). Also common is the occasional panic attack, experienced by over 7 percent of Americans in their lifetime (Eaton, Kessler, Wittchen, et al., 1994), though occasional panic attacks are generally less severe, and less likely to involve catastrophic thoughts, than the attacks of people who actually meet the diagnostic criteria for panic disorder (Telch, Lucas, & Nelson, 1989).

An interesting fact about panic attacks is that they can be induced under laboratory conditions, with results closely resembling those of natural attacks. Furthermore, they can be induced in many different ways: by pharmacological agents such as sodium lactate, yohimbine, and caffeine; by breathing-related procedures such as exercise, hyperventilation, and carbon dioxide inhalation; and by behavioral procedures such as relaxation exercises or confrontation with a phobic stimulus. The panic-provoking agent that has been most extensively studied is sodium lactate, which produces panic attacks in 70 to 80 percent of panic disorder patients, compared with 0 to 10 percent of normal controls (T. A. Aronson, Carasiti, McBane, et al., 1989). It seems also to produce panic attacks in patients who have had panic attacks before, even though they have diagnoses other than panic disorder.

Generalized Anxiety Disorder

As the name suggests, the main feature of **generalized anxiety disorder** is a chronic state of diffuse anxiety. *DSM-IV* defines the syndrome as excessive worry, over a period of at least six months, about several life circumstances. The most common areas of worry are family, money, work, and health (Rapee & Barlow, 1993). Many normal people worry about such things, but it is the excessiveness and uncontrollability of the worrying that makes it a disorder. People with generalized anxiety disorder are continually waiting for something dreadful to happen, either to themselves or to those they care about, and this subjective condition spills over into their cognitive and physiological functioning. They feel restless and irritable; they have difficulty concentrating; they tire easily. Typically, they also suffer from chronic muscle tension and insomnia. And in response to symptoms, many of them develop secondary anxiety—that is, anxiety about their anxiety—fearing that their condition will cause them to develop ulcers, lose their jobs, alienate their spouses, and so forth. Most people with generalized anxiety disorder develop the condition fairly early in life; many report that they have always felt anxious. It is a common disorder, affecting as much as 4 to 5 percent of the U.S. population, and it is twice as common in women as in men (Kessler, McGonagle, Zhao, et al., 1994; Rapee, 1991). The rates are similar across a variety of cultures (Anderson, 1994).

Generalized anxiety disorder sounds as though it might be the "resting state" of panic disorder, and some researchers believe that this is the case—that these syndromes are two phases of a single disorder (Barlow, 1988). At the same time, there are strong grounds for separating them. In a recent comparison, Noyes and his colleagues found three major differences between the two syndromes. First, their symptom profiles differ. The symptoms of generalized anxiety disorder suggest hyperarousal of the central nervous system (insomnia, restlessness, inability to concentrate), whereas the symptoms of panic disorder seem connected to hyperarousal of the autonomic nervous system (pounding heart, rapid breathing, dizziness, nausea). Second, generalized anxiety disorder usually has a more gradual onset and a more chronic course than panic disorder. Finally, when these disorders run in families, they tend to run separately. First-degree relatives of people with generalized anxiety disorder are more likely to have generalized anxiety disorder than panic disorder; first-degree relatives of panic disorder patients are more likely to have panic disorder than generalized anxiety disorder (Noyes, Woodman, Garvey, et al., 1992).

Phobias

A **phobia** involves two factors: (1) an intense and persistent fear of some object or situation which, as the person realizes, actually poses no real threat; and (2) avoidance of the phobic stimulus. In some cases, the phobic stimulus is something that seems utterly harmless. Often, however, the stimulus is one that carries a slight suggestion of danger—something that a child, for example, might be afraid of, such as dogs, insects, snakes, or high places. (Many phobias do in fact begin in childhood. The mean age of onset is between ages eleven and seventeen [Boyd, Rae, Thompson, et al., 1990].) Nonphobic people may also avoid these things. Many people, for example, distinctly prefer not to step out onto a fire escape and would never touch a snake, no matter how harmless. The difference between these reactions and a phobic reaction is, first, one of severity. While the normal person may feel apprehension at the sight of a snake, the snake-phobic person will show intense anxiety, along with its usual physiological signs: escalated heart rate, sweating, and so forth. Second, because of the severity of the anxiety response, phobic people, unlike others, must design their lives so that they avoid the thing they fear. Phobias are divided into two types, specific phobias and social phobias.

The fear of speaking before a group is a common social phobia. Hours of effortless rehearsal in front of the mirror at home can go to waste as the person gives way to severe stage fright at the prospect of facing an audience.

Specific Phobia **Specific phobia** is fairly common, affecting up to 11 percent of the general population, and it is twice as common in women as in men (Kessler, McGonagle, Zhao, et al., 1994). It is also more common in African-Americans than in Caucasians (Neal & Turner, 1991). Among the more frequently seen types are **acrophobia,** fear of heights; **claustrophobia,** fear of enclosed places (e.g., elevators, subways); phobias of body injury; and animal phobias, particularly for dogs, snakes, mice, and insects. The most common specific phobias are the animal phobias (Costello, 1982), but many people with these conditions do not seek help, for they can manage, without much difficulty, to avoid the animal in question. In general, the degree of impairment in phobia cases depends on the degree to which the phobic stimulus is a usual factor in the person's normal round of activities. Dog-phobic people are in a bad position, for dogs are a common sight. Fear of air travel might be more debilitating to a business executive than to a suburban homemaker. In other cases, the phobic stimulus is so rare a factor in the person's environment that it has little or no effect on daily activities. For example, a city dweller with a phobia for snakes need only avoid going to the zoo.

Social Phobia People suffering from **social phobia** avoid performing certain actions in front of other people, for fear of embarrassing or humiliating themselves. Common objects of social phobia are public speaking, eating in public, and using public bathrooms. Social phobia erodes self-confidence: to have to plan one's life in order to avoid encountering a stranger in the lavatory is a humiliating experience. But the basic problem with this phobia is that it restricts people's choices, forcing them into rigid and narrow channels of behavior. Social phobia may also interfere seriously with work, as the following case shows:

> The patient was a 33-year-old man who . . . had been employed as a salesperson for an insurance company since graduating from college. . . .
>
> His initial training (attending lectures, completing reading assignments) proceeded smoothly, but as soon as he began to take on clients, his anxiety returned. He became extremely nervous when anticipating phone calls from clients. When his business phone rang, he would begin to tremble and sometimes would not answer. Eventually, he avoided becoming anxious by not scheduling appointments and by not contacting clients whom he was expected to see.
>
> When asked what it was about these situations that made him nervous, he said that he was concerned about what the client would think of him. "The client might sense that I am nervous and might ask me questions that I don't know the answers to, and I would feel foolish." As a result, he would repeatedly rewrite and reword sales scripts for telephone conversations because he was "so concerned about saying the right thing. I guess I'm just very concerned about being judged." . . .
>
> Although financial constraints were a burden, the patient and his wife entertained guests at their home regularly and enjoyed socializing with friends. . . . The patient lamented, "It's just when I'm expected to do

something. Then, it's like I'm on stage, all alone, with everyone watching me." (H. I. Kaplan & Sadock, 1991, pp. 401–402)

In social phobia, the person's fears are more realistic than those of other phobia sufferers. Agoraphobics are not very likely to collapse or have a heart attack in a public place, but social phobics, precisely because they are fearful of social blunders, are likely to commit them. People with this disorder generally have low self-esteem. They often engage in cognitive distortions in which they magnify their personal imperfections. Finally, as part of their anxiety response, they are prone to blush, sweat, and tremble (Uhde, Tancer, Black, et al., 1991). All these handicaps tend to interfere with their social performance and thus increase their anxiety—a vicious cycle (Schneier, 1991; C. B. Taylor & Arnow, 1988).

Social phobia affects about 13 percent of Americans at some time in their lives (Kessler, McGonagle, Zhao, et al., 1994), and unlike panic disorder, agoraphobia, and specific phobia, this disorder strikes men and women equally. Its onset is usually in early adolescence (S. M. Turner & Beidel, 1989), which seems logical, for that is believed to be the developmental stage at which children become acutely aware of how they are impressing others, and hence prone to embarrassment.

Is social phobia just a specific phobia for social situations? Researchers think not. To begin with, social phobias are more pervasive than specific phobias. Rare is the social phobic who is afraid of only one situation. Usually, the anxiety spreads over many situations (S. M. Turner, Beidel, Dancu, et al., 1986). Indeed, what social phobics often fear is the disapproval of others in general, and this is not a phobic stimulus that can easily be avoided.

In consequence, social phobics are generally more impaired than people with specific phobias. In one survey of social phobics (S. M. Turner, Beidel, Dancu, et al., 1986), 92 percent reported that anxiety had interfered with their careers, 64 percent said that it prevented them from attending social functions, and 50 percent admitted that they used alcohol or tranquilizers to calm themselves in social situations. (The risk for alcohol and drug abuse in social phobia has been reported by other researchers as well [M. R. Fyer, 1990; Liebowitz, Gorman, Fyer, et al., 1985].) Finally, social phobics report more distress than people with specific phobias (S. M. Turner & Beidel, 1989).

Distinguishing social phobia from other syndromes, such as agoraphobia, is sometimes difficult. Still, according to the research, there is a difference. Agoraphobics are afraid of the actual symptoms of acute anxiety—afraid that they will scream, pass out, or have a heart attack. For social phobics, the fear is social. It is not the symptoms that scare them but the idea that someone will witness the symptoms and think poorly of them as a result. Furthermore, agoraphobics tend to seek out others for comfort; social phobics are comforted by avoiding others (Schneier, 1991; S. M. Turner & Beidel, 1989).

Shyness tends to run in families and probably has some genetic underpinning (Plomin & Daniels, 1986). As for social phobia, there have been no genetic studies as yet, but there are a number of theories about high-risk parenting styles. Many social phobics remember their parents as being overprotective and emotionally unsupportive (Arrindell, Emmelkamp, Monsma, et al., 1983; G. Parker, 1979). Another parental attitude that seems likely to foster social phobia is overconcern about dress, grooming, and manners (Buss, 1980, 1986). Finally, some researchers suspect that parents who discourage children from socializing—and thus prevent them from learning social skills and extinguishing social fears—can lay the groundwork for social phobia (D. Daniels & Plomin, 1985).

Obsessive-Compulsive Disorder

An **obsession** is a thought or image that keeps intruding into a person's consciousness; the person finds the thought inappropriate and distressing and tries to suppress it, but still it returns. Similarly, a **compulsion** is an action that a person feels compelled to repeat again and again, in a stereotyped fashion, though he or she has no conscious desire to do so. People suffering from either obsessions or compulsions—or, as is usually the case, from both—are said to have **obsessive-compulsive disorder.**

Mild obsessions strike many of us from time to time. A song may keep playing in our minds; our thoughts may return again and again to a story we read in the paper or to the question of whether we fed the cat before going to work. But these minor obsessions pass, and we go on about our business. Pathological obsessions, on the other hand, do not pass; though the person tries to suppress them, they recur day after day. Furthermore, they often involve scandalous or violent themes—most obsessions revolve around contamination, violence, sex, or religious transgression, which makes them even more demoralizing to the people who have them.

Compulsions, though they may be as irrational

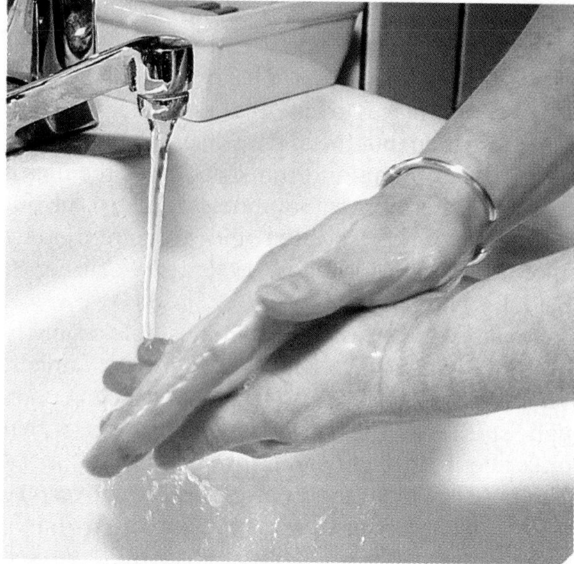

The cleaning rituals that often characterize obsessive-compulsive disorder go far beyond the requirements of ordinary hygiene. The need to, say, wash his or her hands dozen of times a day interferes with the person's ability to enjoy life.

and disruptive as obsessions, tend to have more neutral content. Indeed, they are often responses to obsessions—responses aimed at warding off the danger posed by the obsession—and as such, they generally have overtones of duty and caution. The most common compulsions fall into two categories, cleaning rituals and checking rituals (Khanna & Mukherjee, 1992; S. J. Rachman & Hodgson, 1980). People with cleaning rituals are compelled again and again to stop whatever they are doing and go through some hygiene procedure—typically, hand washing. People with checking rituals are forced, with equal frequency, to interrupt their activities and go make sure they have done something that they were supposed to do. Some people, for example, no sooner get into bed than they have to get up and make certain they have locked the front door or, worse yet, all the doors and windows in the house—a process that may be repeated seven or eight times until, exhausted and still uncertain, they at last fall asleep. Checking rituals are often responses to obsessions about harm to loved ones, while cleaning rituals often accompany obsessions about contamination. Whatever their routine, compulsives become extremely anxious if they are prevented, or try to prevent themselves, from engaging in it. They recognize that their compulsions are excessive, unreasonable, and perhaps even humiliating. Nevertheless, they give in to them to relieve their mounting anxiety.

At its worst, obsessive-compulsive disorder can be completely disabling, as the person's life is given over to obeying the compulsion. Such was the situation in the following case. The patient was nineteen years old, and the account was provided by his father:

> When George wakes in the morning. . . . he feels that his hands are contaminated and so he cannot touch his clothing. He won't wash in the bathroom because he feels that the carpet is contaminated and he won't go downstairs until he is dressed. Consequently, I have to dress him, having first cleaned his shoes and got out a clean shirt, underclothes, socks and trousers. He holds his hands above his head while I pull on his underpants and trousers and we both make sure, by proceeding very cautiously, that he doesn't contaminate the outside of his clothing. . . . George then goes downstairs, washes his hands in the kitchen and thereafter spends about twenty minutes in the toilet. . . . I then have to stand in the doorway and supervise him, my main function being to give reassurance that he has not done anything silly to contaminate his clothing. Thankfully he is now managing on some occasions to cope in the toilet without my close supervision but I still have to be on call so that I can help him if he starts to panic for any reason. Incidentally, I have to put newspapers down on the floor of the toilet and change them daily to make sure that his trousers never come into contact with any contaminating substances. If he only wants to urinate then my task is made easier. I simply have to check his trousers and boots for splashes, sometimes getting down on my hands and knees with a [flashlight].
>
> . . . Recently he has been checking that there are no pubic hairs on the floor and he asks me to get down on my hands and knees to check the floor meticulously. Basically he has to be completely sure that there is no contamination around because if he is not sure then he will start to worry and ruminate about it later on. He has to be completely sure and therefore needs a second opinion. As soon as he has zipped up his trousers I have to march in with a pad soaked in antiseptic and give the zip a quick once-over. When he washes his hands after toileting, he meticulously scrubs each finger and methodically works his way up as far as his elbow. I used to have to watch him at every step of the way but now he only calls me in occasionally. Sometimes he will have washed and dried his hands and then decides that he is not sure whether he washed properly. At this stage I usually have to supervise him so that when he is finished he is absolutely certain that the job has been done perfectly without missing a square inch of contamination. (S. J. Rachman & Hodgson, 1980, pp. 66–67)

This was just the patient's morning routine. The rest of the day followed a similar course.

Obsessive-compulsive disorder was once thought to be very rare, but recent estimates suggest that it affects 2 to 3 percent of the population (Karno, Golding, Sorenson, et al., 1988). People who are separated, divorced, or unemployed are at greater risk (Karno, Golding, Sorenson, et al., 1988). Men and women are equally at risk (S. A. Rasmussen & Eisen, 1992), though there is a curious sex differential in the nature of compulsions: young, single men are more likely to have checking rituals, whereas married women are more likely to have cleaning rituals (Khanna & Mukherjee, 1992; Sturgis, 1993). Obsessive-compulsive disorder usually appears in late adolescence or early adulthood—the median age of onset is twenty-three (Burke, Burke, Regier, et al., 1990)—but it may also begin in childhood (Swedo, Leonard, & Rapoport, 1992). In about 50 to 70 percent of patients, the onset of obsessions and compulsions begins after some stressful event, such as a pregnancy or the death of a relative (H. I. Kaplan & Sadock, 1991).

Traditionally, it has been assumed that obsessive-compulsive disorder was related to what is called obsessive-compulsive personality disorder, a personality type characterized by rigidity, overconscientiousness, and overconcern with detail. (The personality disorders will be the subject of Chapter 11.) This view was heavily influenced by the psychoanalytic theory that both syndromes were rooted in conflicts over toilet training and the associated issues of control and autonomy—in other words, in anal fixation. But recent well-controlled studies (Steketee, 1990) indicate that people with obsessive-compulsive disorder generally do not show the traits associated with obsessive-compulsive personality disorder. Instead, they are more likely to show traits associated with other personality disorders, such as withdrawal (avoidant personality disorder), dependency (dependent personality disorder), or self-dramatization (histrionic personality disorder) (Baer & Jenike, 1992; Steketee, 1990).

Obsessive-compulsive disorder should not be confused with the far more common problems of excessive drinking, eating, or gambling. We often hear people speak, for example, of "compulsive gamblers" or "compulsive eaters." These activities, however, are not compulsions. By definition, a compulsion is engaged in not as an end in itself but as a means of relieving the distress attendant upon *not* engaging in it. "Compulsive eaters" and "compulsive gamblers," while they may be pained by the *consequences* of these excesses, do nevertheless pursue eating and gambling as ends in themselves.

Another syndrome that may, however, be related to obsessive-compulsive disorder is **trichotillomania,** the compulsive pulling out of one's own hair. Trichotillomania has long been considered rare, but this may be because those who suffer from it tend to hide it. In a recent survey of over 2,500 college freshmen, 1.5 percent of males and 3.4 percent of females reported this problem (Christenson, Pyle, & Mitchell, 1991). Most trichotillomanics pull out the hairs on their heads—in severe cases, this can produce large bald spots—but they may also pull at their eyebrows, eyelashes, pubic hair, and facial hair. Over the years, trichotillomania has been classified in various ways, but there is reason to believe that it is a variant of obsessive-compulsive disorder. Like people with compulsions, trichotillomanics recognize that their behavior is senseless, try to resist it, eventually succumb, and, once they succumb, obtain tension relief until the urge strikes again. There is also some evidence for a biological connection between the two syndromes. First-degree relatives of trichotillomanics are at increased risk for obsessive-compulsive disorder. Furthermore, trichotillomania, like obsessive-compulsive disorder, responds to certain antidepressant drugs—those that block serotonin reuptake—and not to other antidepressants.

If obsessive-compulsive patients can be helped by antidepressant drugs, is their problem a mood disorder (Chapter 10) rather than an anxiety disorder? Perhaps so, for obsessive-compulsive patients sometimes show depressive reactions—guilt, dejection, feelings of helplessness—as strongly as they show anxiety. It is possible that obsessive-compulsives belong in an intermediate category, overlapping both the anxiety and mood disorders (Insel, Zahn, & Murphy, 1985; Sturgis, 1993).

Posttraumatic Stress Disorder

Posttraumatic stress disorder is a severe psychological reaction, lasting at least one month, to intensely traumatic events—events involving actual or threatened death or serious injury to oneself or others. Such events include assault, rape, natural disasters such as earthquakes and floods, accidents such as airplane crashes and fires, and wartime traumas. Predictably, most of our knowledge of posttraumatic stress disorder comes from war survivors—people who survived Nazi concentration camps, the bombing of Hiroshima, or the daily agonies of combat during wars.

Posttraumatic stress disorder differs from other anxiety disorders in that the source of stress is an external event of an overwhelmingly painful nature, so the person's reaction, though it may resemble other anxiety disorders, seems to some degree understandable. Understandable or not, however, posttraumatic stress disorder can be extremely debilitating. The person may go on for weeks, months, or years reexperiencing the traumatic event, either in painful recollection or in nightmares. In some cases, stimuli reminiscent of the event may cause the patient to return psychologically to the scene of the disaster and go through it, in his or her mind, all over again. Consequently, victims of posttraumatic stress disorder usually go out of their way to avoid being reminded of the trauma. At the same time, they seem to numb themselves to their present surroundings. They may find it difficult, for example, to respond to affection—a source of great pain to families of returning soldiers—or to interest themselves in things that they cared for before the trauma. Typically, they also show symptoms of heightened arousal, such as insomnia and irritability. They may also show strong physiological responses to any reminder of the trauma. In one study of two groups of Vietnam veterans—the first diagnosed as having posttraumatic stress disorder, the second as suffering from other anxiety disorders—each of the subjects heard a taped account of his own war experiences. The change in heart rate in the posttraumatic stress disorder group was almost double that of the second group (Pitman, Orr, Forgue, et al., 1990).

Posttraumatic stress disorder is fairly common. In a random sample of close to 3,000 North Carolina residents, 1.3 percent had had this disorder at some time in their lives, though women, younger people (under forty-five), and nonwhites were more at risk (Davidson, Hughes, Blazer, et al., 1991). Among subgroups exposed to traumatic events, the incidence, of course, is much higher. After disasters such as plane crashes, somewhere between one-third and one-half of the survivors may develop posttraumatic stress disorder (B. L. Green, Lindy, Grace, et al., 1990; E. M. Smith, North, McColl, et al., 1990).

As these figures show, however, not all people are disabled by traumatic experiences. Many soldiers, for example, go through grueling combat experiences and emerge with nothing more than a few bad dreams. What determines the severity of the response? As Table 7.1 indicates, the severity of the trauma is a significant factor. Among soldiers, for example, the greater the combat exposure and the threat of death, the greater the likelihood of posttraumatic stress disorder (Fairbank, Schlenger, Caddell, et al., 1993). The person's psychological strength before the trauma may be more important. In a study of volunteer fire fighters who survived the huge wave of bushfires that hit southern Australia in 1983, Alexander McFarlane (1988, 1989) found that the intensity of exposure to the fire, the degree of perceived threat, and even the extent of personal losses did not predict posttraumatic stress disorder; what did predict it was pretrauma adjustment and family psychiatric history. Those who had been chronically distressed, especially in their personal relationships, and those with a greater family history of psychopathology were the most likely to develop posttraumatic stress disorder. Related to this finding are the long-term studies by Zahava Solomon and her colleagues of Israeli soldiers who fought in the 1982 Lebanon war (Mikulincer & Solomon, 1988; Z. Solomon, Mikulincer, & Benbenishty, 1989b; Z. Solomon, Mikulincer, & Flum, 1988). These researchers found that coping styles and attributional styles (styles of assigning causes to life events) had an important relationship to the soldiers' posttraumatic state. "Problem-focused coping," the effort to analyze problems or get help in dealing with them—as opposed to "emotion-focused coping" (wishful thinking, denial, emotional venting)—apparently served as good protection against posttraumatic stress disorder, as

TABLE 7.1
FACTORS AFFECTING THE LIKELIHOOD OF POSTTRAUMATIC STRESS DISORDER

Features of the Trauma	Features of the Person
Intensity of exposure to trauma	Pretrauma psychological adjustment
Duration of exposure to trauma	Family history of psychopathology
Extent of threat posed by trauma	Cognitive and coping styles
Nature of trauma: caused by humans or natural disaster	Feelings of guilt

More than other American conflicts, the Vietnam War is associated with lingering cases of posttraumatic stress disorder. Public acknowledgments of the courage and sacrifice of those who served, such as this memorial wall in New York City, were belated attempts to ease the veterans' return to civilian life.

did a tendency to attribute events to controllable causes. As cognitive theorists would predict, those who felt (and acted) most helpless were the most vulnerable to long-term psychiatric effects.

Finally, the likelihood of posttraumatic stress disorder also depends on the nature of the trauma. Traumas caused by human actions, such as rape, tend to precipitate more severe reactions than natural disasters such as floods, earthquakes, or hurricanes. Apparently the nature of the symptoms also depends on the nature of the trauma. Studies of Vietnam veterans (Laufer, Brett, & Gallops, 1985) and of survivors of civil and terrorist violence in Northern Ireland (Loughrey, Bell, Kee, et al., 1988) indicate that *reexperiencing symptoms* (intrusive memories, nightmares, startle reactions) are most common in those who have witnessed or suffered acts of abusive violence, whereas *denial symptoms* (emotional numbing, difficulty in concentrating) are most common in those who have themselves participated in acts of abusive violence.

Symptoms of posttraumatic stress disorder generally appear shortly after the trauma. In some cases, however, there is an "incubation period." For days or even months after the event the person is symptom-free, and then, inexplicably, the traumatic reaction begins to surface. In many cases, symptoms clear up by themselves within about six months; some, however, may linger for years. In a study of 147 Dutch veterans who had fought in the Resistance against the Nazis in World War II, it was found that, forty years after the end of the war, over half these people were still suffering from posttraumatic stress disorder, and only 4 percent showed no symptoms at all (Hovens, Falger, Op den Velde, et al., 1992).

Combat Since the time of World War I, traumatic reactions to combat have been known by a succession of names: "shell shock," "combat fatigue," "combat exhaustion," and so forth. Actually, no one term is fitting, for stress reactions to combat differ markedly from one person to another. Some soldiers become depressed and curl up in their bunks, unable to move. Others experience anxiety, which escalates to panic attacks. Whatever the response, the precipitating stimulus is usually the same: a close escape from death, often with the added horror of seeing one's companions killed. Such traumas, however, are usually preceded by months or years of accumulated stress: fear, sleep deprivation, cold, heat, and numerous brushes with death. Many soldiers seem to succumb not so much to a single trauma as to this constant piling up of stress. Indeed, many show no effects until they have returned to civilian life and are suddenly surprised by nightmares and nervous tremors. Their symptoms may be a problem not just for them but for their families as well. One study found that Vietnam posttraumatic stress disorder patients had more difficulty communicating with their partners and were more likely to be physically abusive toward them than other people seeking treatment (Carroll, Rueger, Foy, et al., 1985).

The Vietnam war seems to have left its soldiers especially traumatized. In one survey, 15 percent of male veterans and 8.5 percent of female veterans were still suffering from posttraumatic stress disorder fifteen or more years after the war (Schlenger, Kulka, Fairbank, et al., 1992; D. S. Weiss, Marmar, Schlenger, et al., 1992). Why should this war have been more stressful than other wars? According to one study (Figley, 1979),

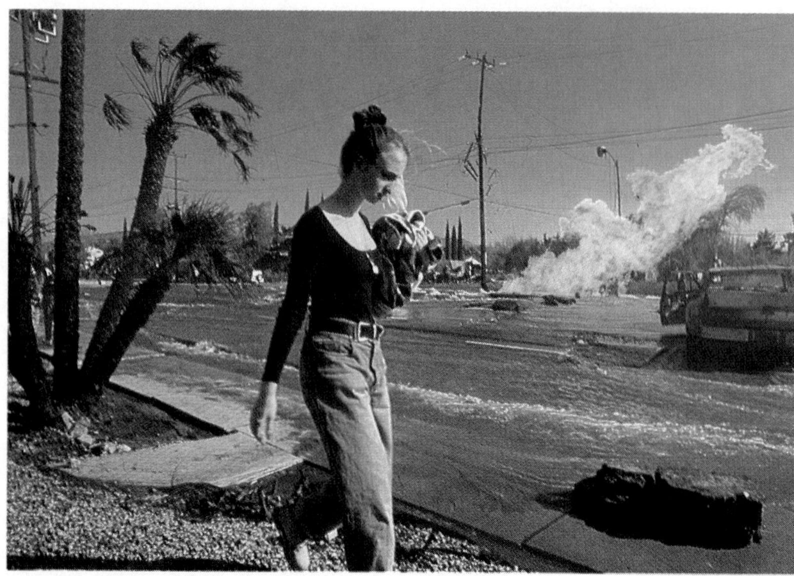

Natural catastrophes, such as the recent series of earthquakes in California, can trigger in survivors a form of posttraumatic stress disorder called the disaster syndrome, which begins with a stage of dazed shock.

certain characteristics of the Vietnam conflict made it particularly damaging psychologically. To begin with, soldiers were shipped to Vietnam simply as masses of recruits, rather than as members of specific units. As a result, they had less chance to develop a sense of group identity, which provides psychological protection against stress. Second, opposition to the war by growing numbers of Americans bred feelings of purposelessness in the soldiers. Third, the lack of an all-out attempt to win the war aggravated the troops' confusion and sense of purposelessness. Finally, removal from combat was extremely abrupt. Some soldiers went from the firing lines to their living rooms in a matter of two or three days, with no chance to make a reasonable transition to civilian life.

Civilian Catastrophe Disaster is not confined to wartime. There are "civilian catastrophes" as well. Victims of a plane crash, earthquake, fire, or flood, of assault or rape or hijacking, are also subject to posttraumatic stress disorder.

According to some writers, victims of severe physical trauma show a definite pattern of response known as the **disaster syndrome.** In the first phase, the *shock stage,* they are stunned and dazed, frequently to the point of immobility. In extreme cases, there may be disorientation and memory loss as well. During the second stage, the *suggestibility stage,* they become passive and are willing to take orders from almost anyone. At this point, they may begin to express concern for other people involved in the incident. During the *recovery stage,* they begin to pull themselves together and to approach their situation in a more rational way. However, they may still show signs of generalized anxiety and may go on recounting their experience to others again and again (Raker, Wallace, & Raymer, 1956). The psychological effects of a disaster may persist for many months. Among the survivors of the Mount St. Helens eruption in 1980, most of those diagnosed with posttraumatic stress disorder still had this condition three years later (Shore, Tatum, & Vollmer, 1986).

Another important component of the survivor's psychology is guilt. Many people, having barely escaped some disaster, begin to feel deep remorse that their lives were spared, as if by taking up a place on the survivor list, they had caused others to die. This guilt was a theme reiterated by the survivors of a devastating flood in 1972 at Buffalo Creek, West Virginia:

> One of our very close friends stayed drunk for almost five months because he could still hear his brother and sister screaming for their mother and his mother screaming "God help us" when the water hit them. Sometimes he talks with me about it and I get the impression that he feels bad because he lived through it all. He is only twenty years of age, but I guess sometimes he feels like a thousand years old. (quoted in K. T. Erikson, 1976, p. 171)

A similar sense of guilt has been observed in Hiroshima and concentration-camp survivors and in combat troops.

The responses of the survivors of Hiroshima and the Nazi death camps are the extreme case, for these people suffered not only extreme physical peril but also the deaths of their families and friends, the loss of their homes, the obliteration of their whole world. Survivors of less complete disasters (e.g., near-death in a fire or automobile accident), who can go home to their families and their accustomed surroundings, tend to recover more quickly and more completely. Yet even these people, after getting over the acute phase of the traumatic reaction, may suffer irritability and have difficulty concentrating and resuming their former daily routine. Of all the traumas that may affect civilians, perhaps the most likely to lead to posttraumatic stress disorder is rape. The box on page 162 describes the serious consequences of rape (see also the discussion of rape in Chapter 13).

Problems in the Classification of Posttraumatic Stress Disorder There are a number of questions about posttraumatic stress disorder as a diagnostic category (Davidson & Foa, 1991). To begin with, *DSM-IV* defines the disorder as a response to an event that involves "actual or threatened death or serious injury, or a threat to the physical integrity of oneself or others." But studies have found that more usual events, such as a miscarriage or the discovery of a spouse's affair, can also precipitate the symptoms of posttraumatic stress disorder (Helzer, Robins, & McEvoy, 1987). Currently, severe reactions to these more ordinary traumas are classified separately as *adjustment disorders*. But it is possible that they too should be called posttraumatic stress disorder.

A second problem with this diagnostic category is whether it should be grouped with the anxiety disorders. There are grounds for doing so. Not only is anxiety one of the foremost symptoms of posttraumatic stress disorder; the disorder shares additional symptoms, such as fear-based avoidance, with the other anxiety syndromes (Davidson & Foa, 1991; Rothbaum, Foa, Murdock, et al., 1990). Furthermore, first-degree relatives of posttraumatic patients show a high rate of anxiety disorders (Davidson, Smith, & Kudler, 1989). But there is also an argument for placing posttraumatic stress disorder among the dissociative disorders, for the defining characteristic of that group—the dissociation or splitting off of some part of experience or personality—is also seen in the "psychic numbing" and other denial symptoms of posttraumatic stress disorder patients. According to some researchers, however, posttraumatic stress disorder should not be classified with either the anxiety or the dissociative disorders. They argue that since posttraumatic stress disorder is defined in large measure by its precipitating event, the trauma, it should be placed in a separate category of stress-related disorders (Davidson & Foa, 1991).

PERSPECTIVES ON THE ANXIETY DISORDERS

In Chapters 2, 3, and 4 we presented a general overview of the psychodynamic, humanistic-existential, behavioral, cognitive, and biological approaches to abnormal behavior. In the present section, we shall see how adherents of each of these perspectives would interpret and treat the anxiety disorders. (Since treatment will be discussed in detail in Part Six, our coverage of the treatments for these disorders will be brief.)

The Psychodynamic Perspective: Neurosis

The psychodynamic view of the anxiety disorders—or neuroses,* as psychodynamic writers call them—is difficult to summarize, for these disorders have been the major focus of psychodynamic theory. Psychodynamic writings on neurosis could, and do, fill whole libraries. Our discussion here is only an outline.

The Roots of Neurosis Freud argued that anxiety stemmed not just from external threats but also from internal ones, in the form of id impulses attempting to break through into consciousness. It is this latter type of anxiety that psychodynamic theory sees as the root of neurosis. In the mind of the neurotic, the id is pushing in one direction, toward the enactment of its sexual or aggressive impulse. Meanwhile, the ego, knowing that the id impulse is unacceptable in terms of both reality and the superego's ideals, is working in the opposite direction, pushing the impulse back into the unconscious through repression and other defense mechanisms. As we noted in Chapter 2, this push and counterpush goes on all the time in normal lives and usually works well enough so that anxiety over the id impulse is never experienced consciously. In some cases, however, the anxiety is so intense that it *is* experienced consciously, with debilitating results. Or it is kept at bay only through the employment of extremely rigid defense mechanisms. It is these situations that, according to psychodynamic theory, constitute neurotic behavior.

In cases where anxiety is experienced chronically and directly, without elaborate defense, what we see is generalized anxiety disorder. The cause

*Since psychodynamic writers call these disorders "neuroses" and those who have them "neurotics," we shall do the same in discussing the psychodynamic perspective.

RAPE AND ITS AFTERMATH

A 29-year-old attorney, Laura, was assaulted several years ago. She had just graduated from law school and was serving as a law clerk in a large city. One hot summer night she was alone in the house she shared with five other women when she went to bed wearing no clothes. At 1:30 A.M. she awoke to see a figure by her bed going through her wallet. Refusing to answer any of Laura's questions, the figure suddenly jumped on top of her. . . . She began to struggle. However, when the man held a silvery metal object to her throat, Laura ceased resisting physically and attempted to talk her way out of the assault. The man told her to "shut up" . . . and then attempted unsuccessfully to penetrate her vaginally. After about 15 minutes he stopped and put her in the closet.

Laura . . . continues to experience great fears related to the assault and is very ashamed of her fears. She insists that she live on a high floor in a building with a doorman. She continues to feel compelled to check every room in her apartment before she locks the door. Every night she puts large boxes in front of her door to make it more difficult for an intruder to enter. Additionally, she insists upon having two telephones with lighted push-button dials in her apartment.

Laura said that all her activities are planned around safety issues. She feels she must be able to take taxicabs or she is unable to go somewhere. She has great difficulty sleeping alone in her apartment and continues to experience insomnia and nightmares. (Becker, Skinner, & Abel, 1983, pp. 252–253)

Of all the calamities that people can encounter in ordinary life, one that is especially likely to have lasting psychological consequences is rape. A large study involving 3,132 adults in two Los Angeles communities found that those who had been raped at some time in their lives—13.2 percent of the sample—were two and a half times more likely than others to develop major depression, alcoholism, and drug abuse and four times more likely to develop phobia, panic disorder, and obsessive-compulsive disorder after the assault (Burnam, Stein, Golding, et al., 1988). Not surprisingly, sexual dysfunction—low desire, low arousal—is also a problem for many rape victims (Becker, Skinner, Abel, et al., 1986). But the psychological disorder most likely to follow upon rape is probably posttraumatic stress disorder. In a recent study of ninety-five rape victims by Barbara Rothbaum and her colleagues, two-thirds of the subjects had posttraumatic stress disorder one month after the rape, with symptoms including flashbacks, nightmares, insomnia, hyperalertness, blunted emotions, concentration problems, and continuing feelings of fear and guilt (Rothbaum, Foa, Riggs, et al., 1992). Interestingly, rape is more likely than many other serious traumas—robbery, assault, natural disasters, the death of a family member or a close friend—to precipitate posttraumatic stress disorder (Norris, 1992). This may be due, in part, to the particular nature of this assault and to the stigma that is still attached to rape. Robbery victims will tell their friends about their experience; rape victims, out of shame, tend to keep silent, and thus have less chance to vent their feelings (Koss, Woodruff, & Koss, 1991). They also tend not to seek treatment (Koss, 1988). Nor, until recently, was there much treatment available to them. It was not until the 1970s, with the rise of the women's movement, that rape crisis centers came into being. Typically, rape victims simply go back to their normal routines and "try not to think about it."

For many of them, this works. But for almost as many, apparently, it does not—or not soon. In the study by Rothbaum and her team, as we saw, two-thirds of the rape victims showed posttraumatic stress disorder one month postrape. Three months postrape, more than half still had not recovered (Rothbaum, Foa, Riggs, et al., 1992). Are there certain responses to rape that predict how fast a person will get over it? Most studies are in a poor position to answer this question, because they are retrospective studies, with victims being interviewed long after the rape and trying to piece together their reactions from memory. But the study by Rothbaum's team was a longitudinal study, in which the victims were first interviewed soon after the rape (twelve days, on average) and then reinterviewed weekly for three months. In this way the researchers were able to pinpoint factors that seemed to affect recovery. What they found was that the women least likely to improve spontaneously were those who, at the first interview, reported the most distress and the most "intrusion" symptoms: flashbacks, nightmares, involuntary relivings of the trauma.

Other studies, combining victims of rape and victims of nonsexual assault, have linked three additional factors with the likelihood and severity of posttraumatic stress disorder: feelings of guilt, feelings of threat, and bodily injury during the assault (Kilpatrick, Saunders, Amick-McMullan, et al., 1989; Riggs, Foa, Rothbaum, et al., 1991). One group of researchers claims that anger too can be crucial in slowing the victim's return to normal functioning (Riggs, Dancu, Gershuny, et al., 1992). According to Rothbaum's team, rape victims who have not recovered from posttraumatic stress disorder two months after the assault are not likely to recover spontaneously; they need treatment (Rothbaum, Foa, Riggs, et al., 1992).

Rape shatters many of its victims' most fundamental and comforting beliefs: the belief in one's safety, in one's personal efficacy, in the goodness of other human beings. It may also create an intense, easily reactivated fear memory, which then triggers further anxiety. According to many experts, the key to relieving rape-induced posttraumatic stress disorder is to reverse this cognitive process. The victim's fear memory must be confronted and then challenged by new, fear-incompatible information: that she can in fact protect herself against future assaults, that this does not require staying home every night, that not all men are potential rapists, and so forth (Foa, Steketee, & Rothbaum, 1989). Most of the treatments that have been effective for rape victims, such as systematic desensitization and cognitive therapy, involve this scenario of activating and then challenging the fear memory. Some experts, however, believe that the best treatment for rape victims is group therapy, on the grounds that women who have survived the same trauma are the best suited to listen, validate feelings, share grief, counteract guilt, and rebuild self-esteem (Koss & Harvey, 1991).

is repressed, but the anxiety leaks through. In the panic attack, the cause—that is, the id impulse—moves closer to the boundaries of the conscious mind, resulting in the rapid buildup of anxiety. The ego responds with desperate efforts at repression, and a state of maximum conflict ensues. Once the ego regains the upper hand and the impulse is once again safely repressed, the attack passes.

Usually, however, the defenses marshaled against anxiety are considerably more elaborate than repression, and it is these defenses that appear as the symptoms of neurotic disorder. In phobias, for example, displacement may be at work, as in Freud's classic case of "Little Hans" (1909/1962). Hans was a five-year-old Viennese boy who refused to go out into the street for fear that a horse from one of the city's many horse-drawn carriages would bite him. Freud's interpretation of the phobia was that Hans was caught up in a fierce Oedipal struggle, in which his strong attachment to his mother was accompanied by extreme hostility toward his father. As usual in Oedipal conflicts, the hostility was accompanied by intense anxiety that the father would retaliate by castrating the boy. Therefore Hans displaced his fear and hostility onto horses—a logical substitution, since his father would sometimes play "horsie" with him and had black glasses and a moustache reminiscent of the horses' black blinders and muzzles. Having made this displacement, Hans could then relieve his anxiety by avoiding horses—a strategy which, however, left him agoraphobic.

Psychodynamic thinkers may interpret obsessive-compulsive disorder in a number of ways, depending on the nature of the obsession or compulsion. In the case of a man who is obsessed with the fear that he will kill his wife in her sleep, for example, psychodynamic theory would suggest that the unconscious aggressive impulse has in fact made its way into the conscious mind. On the other hand, cleanliness rituals and obsessions with germs would be interpreted as a combination of fixation and reaction formation occurring during the anal stage, the ego defending itself against the id's desire to soil, to play with feces, and to be generally messy and destructive.

To psychodynamic theorists, then, the anxiety disorders really differ only in the choice of defense, and some preliminary research supports this view. In a study of anxiety disorder patients (C. Pollock & Andrews, 1989), those with panic disorder were most likely to employ displacement, reaction formation, and somatization (preoccupation with physical symptoms); those with social phobia tended to use displacement and devaluation (criticism of self and others); and those with obsessive-compulsive disorder relied on projection, acting out (childish, impulsive behavior), and undoing (making amends for a negative thought or action by some compensatory action). This theory that "defense style" determines the nature of the disorder is one of the strengths of the psychodynamic position. Other perspectives, as we shall see, also tend to explain all the anxiety disorders by a single theory, but some of them are far less clear on why a given patient ends up, for example, with social phobia rather than a hand-washing compulsion. In psychodynamic theory, the nature of the disorder points to the defense, and the nature of the defense points to the underlying conflict.

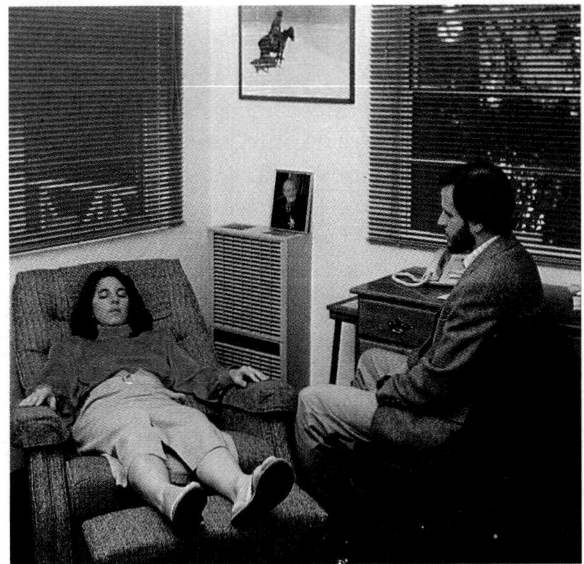

When used in the treatment of neurosis, hypnosis can furnish access to the unconscious conflicts against which the patient has erected defense mechanisms.

Treating Neurosis We have seen that according to psychodynamic theory the job of maintaining elaborate defenses monopolizes and exhausts the ego. The goal of psychodynamic therapy is to remedy this situation by exposing and neutralizing the material that the ego is wasting its energy trying to repress. The assumption is that if patients can face and understand their buried conflicts, the ego will be liberated from the all-consuming task of masking these conflicts and can devote itself to more useful and creative tasks.

Orthodox psychoanalysis uses two basic techniques to achieve this goal. The first is **free association.** Here the patient lies back on a couch and simply says whatever comes to mind, without the censorship of reason, logic, or "decency." Unconscious material will eventually surface, at which point it will be interpreted—that is, the therapist will point out how the patient's remarks indicate this or that unconscious preoccupation. The second technique is **dream interpretation,** whereby patients report their dreams as accurately as possible and the therapist explores with the patient the latent content of the dream. Free association is traditionally a part of dream interpretation; the patient free-associates to the content of the dream. In other forms of psychodynamic therapy—far more common today than classical psychoanalysis—underlying conflicts are excavated in a more conventional manner, with patients sitting face to face with the therapist and simply discussing their problems as frankly as possible.

It is assumed that when the therapist begins to reach sensitive parts of the patient's unconscious, the patient will begin to show **resistance,** arguing with the therapist, changing the subject, missing appointments, and so forth. Because resistance is an unconscious process, this too must be interpreted to the patient. A final and critical component of psychodynamic therapy is analysis of **transference.** Presumably, patients transfer to their therapists the love and also the hostility that as children they felt for their parents. These emotions, again, are interpreted to the patient, in the effort to clarify conflicts left over from the parent-child relationship.

The Humanistic-Existential Perspective: The Individual and Society

Like psychodynamic theorists, humanistic-existential theorists see the disorders we have discussed in this chapter as stemming from anxiety over intrapsychic conflicts. What is unique about the humanistic-existential approach is that it conceptualizes this anxiety not simply as an individual problem but as the predictable outcome of conflicts between the individual and the society.

The Impaired Self-Concept According to the humanists, the seat of anxiety is the self-concept. Humanistic psychologists have found that patients entering therapy tend to have lofty notions of what they would like to be and negative views of what they actually are. In other words, they experience a gap between the self-concept and the ideal self—the result of overrestrictive "conditions of worth" in childhood. Yet they still strive for self-actualization, and the conflict between this effort and the negative self-concept is what produces anxiety. More important, it retards self-actualization by preventing the integration of new experiences. Basically, according to the humanists, "neurotics" are people who are blocked in their growth.

Existential theorists would emphasize not so much the drive for self-actualization as the drive for authenticity. According to this view, "neurotics" are simply people who are not as successful as others in being inauthentic. While others have actually forgotten their true selves, "neurotics" are still aware of the split between the true self and the false, conforming self that society forces them to adopt. Awareness of this division between the true and false selves leads to anxiety.

Rebuilding the Damaged Self One of the most popular humanistic treatment approaches is **client-centered therapy,** designed by Carl Rogers (1951). According to Rogers (1980), what psychologically troubled people need is not to be analyzed or advised but simply to be "heard"—that is, to be truly understood and respected by another human being. Therefore, client-centered therapists apply all their powers of attention and empathy to grasping what the client is actually feeling. To show that they have understood, they "mirror" the feelings, restating them to the client. This gives clients the sense that their inner life has validity. It also helps them expand their self-concept, incorporating into it *all* their feelings and experiences. Rogers (1951) demonstrated that this mirroring, along with the "unconditional positive regard" that the therapist gives the client, does in fact improve the self-concept.

Existential therapies for "neurotic" patients are perhaps even less directive than humanistic therapies. In recent years there has been a push toward a completely phenomenological approach, with therapists attempting to exclude from the therapeutic situation all their own preconceptions, even their convictions about authenticity and other central tenets of existential theory. As for specific procedures, the existentialists, like the humanists, are less concerned with symptoms than with restoring the patient's sense of wholeness and freedom. For example, in a technique called **paradoxical intention,** originated by Viktor Frankl (1975a), patients are told to indulge their symptoms, even exaggerate them. A person with a checking compulsion, for example, might be encouraged to spend an entire day doing nothing but checking. In this way, the person comes to learn that the behavior can be controlled; if it can be performed more frequently, it can be performed less frequently. Furthermore, through deliberate enactment, the person masters his or her *fear* of the symptom.

The Behavioral Perspective: Learning to Be Anxious

Behavioral researchers have challenged the psychodynamic argument that the anxiety disorders stem from unconscious conflict. In their view, these disorders arise from faulty learning.

How We Learn Anxiety One important theory of anxiety disorders is that they are engendered through avoidance learning (Mowrer, 1948). This theory, already described briefly in Chapter 3, involves a two-stage process:

> *Stage 1.* In the course of the person's experience, some neutral stimulus is paired with an aversive stimulus and thus, through respondent conditioning, becomes anxiety-arousing.
>
> *Stage 2.* The person avoids the conditioned stimulus, and since this avoidance results in relief from anxiety (i.e., negative reinforcement), the avoidance response, via operant conditioning, becomes habitual.

Imagine, for example, a man who periodically gets drunk and beats his young daughter. Soon the signs of the father's drinking (CS) will become paired in the child's mind with the pain of the beating (UCS), and she will experience anxiety (CR) at the first sign that her father has been drinking. Eventually this anxiety may generalize to the father as a whole, drunk or sober, in which case he himself becomes the CS. She therefore avoids him, and every time she does so, her anxiety is relieved, thus reinforcing the avoidance response. In time, the anxiety may generalize further—for example, to men in general. Again she responds with avoidance, and again avoidance produces negative reinforcement in the form of anxiety relief. Ultimately, this process may leave her, as an adult, with serious social problems.

In the view of many behaviorists, the disorders that we have discussed in this chapter are variations on avoidance-reinforced anxiety. Panic attacks, for example, are seen as extreme conditioned fear reactions to internal physiological sensations (Wolpe & Rowan, 1988); agoraphobia, which, as we have seen, often develops as a way of avoiding having a panic attack in public, is thus the product of stage 2. In specific phobias, the avoidance strategy is less global—one need not become housebound in order to avoid elevators, for example—but the process is the same: the object becomes aversive through respondent conditioning

What do you feel when you look at this picture? One intriguing theory about the origins of anxiety is that natural selection may have predisposed humans to fear certain stimuli, such as heights, that our prehistoric ancestors would have had to avoid in order to survive.

(e.g., a childhood experience of feeling smothered in a confined space), and then avoidance is learned through negative reinforcement. In obsessive-compulsive disorder, the anxious person has found that some action, such as hand washing, reduces his or her anxiety; the action thus becomes a form of avoidance, strengthened once again through negative reinforcement. In posttraumatic stress disorder, the psychological distress and heightened arousal that patients show in response to reminders of the trauma are the products of respondent conditioning, and their "psychic numbing" and amnesia for the event would be the avoidance strategy.

This two-stage avoidance-learning theory has been buttressed by a number of studies. However, it has at least three problems. First is the fact that many features of the anxiety disorders are simply not explainable by the theory. For example, while some anxiety patients do report traumatic conditioning experiences (Merckelbach, DeRuiter, Van

Den Hout, et al., 1989), others do not. Many phobics, for example, cannot remember any formative encounter with the object of their phobia. Second, traditional learning theory is hard put to explain why only very select, nonrandom types of stimuli typically become phobic objects. Guns, knives, and electrical outlets, for example, should be at least as likely as animals, heights, and enclosed spaces to be associated with traumatic conditioning experiences, yet the former are rare as phobic objects while the latter are common. Why? Seligman (1971) proposed that via natural selection human beings may be "prepared" to fear certain stimuli that would have been threatening to our evolutionary ancestors—as snakes, for example, would have been, and as electrical outlets would not. This is an ingenious theory that has been supported by some experimental evidence, though it is contradicted by other evidence (Davey, in press; McNally, 1987; Tomarken, Mineka, & Cook, 1989).

A third and very serious problem with the avoidance-learning theory is that it focuses entirely on concrete stimuli and observable responses without concern for the *thoughts* that may be involved in anxiety. Many studies indicate that such an explanation is insufficient. To begin with, a painful stimulus need not be concrete in order to arouse anxiety. Cognitive events such as mental images and verbal self-statements can also engender anxiety responses. Furthermore, the stimulus need not be experienced directly. People can also acquire anxiety responses vicariously, by watching others react with pain to a given stimulus. Even monkeys can learn to be afraid just by watching other monkeys respond with fear to an unfamiliar object (Cook, Mineka, Wolkenstein, et al., 1985; Mineka, Davidson, Cook, et al., 1984). In human beings, not even observation is required. To feel fear while walking through a high-crime neighborhood, you do not have to have seen someone mugged in that part of town. You need only have heard or read that that neighborhood is dangerous (Bootzin & Max, 1980).

What all this suggests is that cognitive processes play an important role in the acquisition of anxiety responses. And indeed, recent research indicates that for most people suffering from agoraphobia, specific phobias, and social phobia, the fear was acquired through a combination of direct learning and cognitive processes such as observation and exposure to negative information (Merckelbach, DeRuiter, Van Den Hout, et al., 1989). Cognitive processes may also determine the behavioral *response* to anxiety. Albert Bandura (1977, 1982) has shown that the best predictor of avoidance behavior is not the amount of anxiety experienced but rather *efficacy expectations*—people's expectations, based on past performance, as to how well they will be able to cope with the situation. Many actors and dancers, for example, suffer intense stage fright, some to the point of vomiting before performances. Yet they still go onstage, presumably because they know from experience that they can perform well despite their anxiety.

A recent theory related to efficacy expectations is the *fear-of-fear* interpretation of panic disorder (Barlow, 1988). In this view, the physiological changes that accompany the panic attack—increased heart rate, sweating, and so forth—become conditioned stimuli for further panic attacks: when these changes start to occur, even for ordinary reasons, the person begins to feel afraid of a coming attack, and in a classic spiral, the fear intensifies the physiological reactions and vice versa until the attack occurs. For example, many panic patients avoid exercise or sexual activity because the increased physiological arousal produces fear of an impending attack (Barlow, 1988). This fear of fear can be seen in many kinds of anxiety disorder, but above all in panic disorder (Reiss, Peterson, Gursky, et al., 1986).

Unlearning Anxiety For the anxiety disorders behaviorists have evolved a set of related techniques aimed at reducing anxiety through graduated exposure to the feared stimulus. One classic technique is **systematic desensitization** (Wolpe, 1973), already described briefly in Chapter 3. In this technique, patients draw up a "hierarchy of fears"—a list of increasingly anxiety-arousing situations culminating in the situation they most fear (e.g., holding a snake). Then they are taught to engage in deep muscle relaxation, and in this state of relaxation they imagine the situations in their hierarchy one by one, progressing from the least to the most feared over a number of therapy sessions. By the end of the treatment, if it is successful, they are able to imagine their most anxiety-arousing stimulus and still remain relaxed—a response that ideally will generalize to the real-life situation.

A variation on this technique, called **in vivo desensitization,** involves leading patients through their hierarchies in real life. For example, a dog-phobic person, usually in the company of the therapist, will first look at pictures of dogs, then enter a room where there is a caged dog, then go near the dog, and so on, until at last he or she is able to remain relaxed in the presence of dogs.

In the treatment of phobias and obsessive compulsive disorder, the therapist will often combine modeling with the sort of exposure just described. With a compulsive hand washer, for example, the therapist would first model the act of touching something "unclean," then encourage the patient to do it as well. With repetition, this procedure desensitizes the patient to the fear and makes the ritual unnecessary (S. J. Rachman & Hodgson, 1980).

Modeling also provides an opportunity for therapists to teach patients new cognitive strategies, by alerting them to their self-defeating thoughts and showing them how to combat such thoughts. For instance, in the procedure just described, the therapist might say out loud, while touching the "unclean" matter, "I can't do this. This problem has been with me for years, and there's no way of solving it now." Then the therapist would "answer" such thoughts: "If other people can do it, so can I. There's nothing lethal about this stuff." Later, when patients are on their own and are assailed by self-defeating thoughts, they will have some way of answering them (Meichenbaum, 1977).

While the last method addresses cognitive processes directly, cognitive factors such as attitudes, personal goals, and mental images are involved in the other techniques as well. On a more concrete level, all these treatment strategies depend both on respondent conditioning (the pairing of the feared stimulus with a new, relaxed response) and on operant conditioning, in the form of extinction (the removal of the reward of anxiety relief via avoidance) and in the form of positive reinforcement (praise from the therapist plus the simple and potent reward of success).

Reinforcement can also be manipulated more directly. For some people, an anxiety disorder may be maintained in part by positive reinforcers, in which case the disorder might be eliminated by eliminating these reinforcing elements. In the case of George, the obsessive-compulsive, the elaborate anticontamination ritual obviously depended on the father's collaboration, which was probably reinforcing to the patient. With such a situation, the behavioral therapist might well begin by instructing the father not to participate in the ritual.

The Cognitive Perspective: Misperception of Threat

As we have just seen, cognitive processes play some role in the development of anxiety disorders. To cognitive theorists, that role is central. According to their theory, the problem with anxiety disorder patients is that they misperceive or misinterpret stimuli, internal and external. What is not really threatening, these people *see* as threatening—hence their symptoms (see the box on page 168). Although cognitive models have been proposed for each of the anxiety disorders, we will focus here primarily on the cognitive explanation of panic disorder. This is because cognitive approaches and therapies for panic disorder have been especially successful and influential.

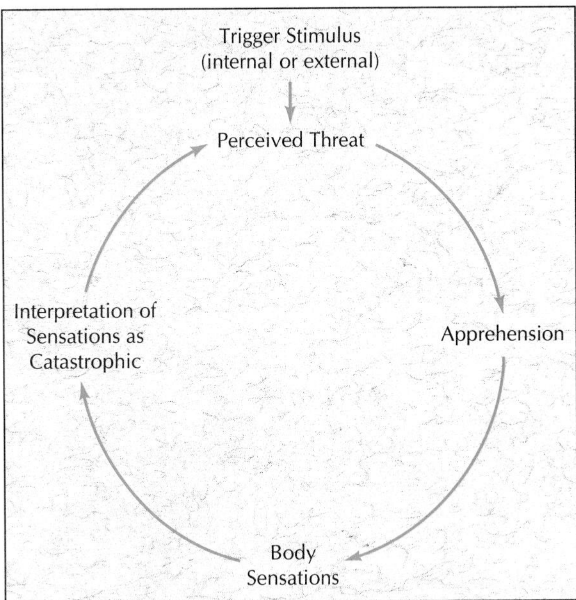

FIGURE 7.1 A cognitive model of a panic attack.

Anxiety as Misperception We noted earlier that many different kinds of stimuli—sodium lactate, hyperventilation, carbon dioxide inhalation, confrontation with phobic stimuli—have been found to provoke panic attacks. No single biological mechanism can account for the fact that all these different things produce panic. But there is a single cognitive mechanism that can explain it. If a person, upon experiencing unusual bodily sensations (which all these panic-inducing agents do produce), interprets such sensations catastrophically, as a signal that he or she is about to pass out or have a heart attack, then panic could result. (See Figure 7.1.)

That, fundamentally, is the cognitive interpretation of panic disorder. As we noted, most experts do not believe that panic attacks come "out of the blue." Often, upon investigation, an attack is found to have been preceded by an event that altered the person's physiological state in some way—for example, exercising, having sexual relations, drinking a beverage containing caffeine, or even getting up quickly from a seated position. Most of us, when we do these things, experience some internal adjustments—the heart skips a beat, breathing may become momentarily labored—but

ANXIETY AND SELECTIVE ATTENTION

Cognitive theorists believe that people with anxiety disorders have distorted perceptions of the world around them, and a number of recent studies suggest that this is the case. Not only do people with anxiety disorders pay more attention to threatening stimuli than to neutral or positive stimuli, but they choose their threatening stimuli according to the type of anxiety disorder they have.

The studies that produced these findings were ingeniously designed. Some rely on the so-called Stroop paradigm (Stroop, 1935), which asks subjects to name, as quickly and accurately as possible, the colors of the ink in which a series of words is presented. Subjects are not supposed to pay attention to the meaning of the words, only to their colors. In one study, however, people with generalized anxiety disorder took significantly longer to identify the colors of "threat" words than the colors of "nonthreat" words such as *holiday* and *contented.* Subjects whose concerns were predominantly physical hesitated over "physical threat" words such as *disease* and *mutilated.* Those whose anxiety was primarily social paused for "social threat" words such as *failure* and *inadequate* (Mogg, Mathews, & Weinman, 1989).

In another study, Vietnam combat veterans with posttraumatic stress disorder were slower than control subjects to name the colors of words such as *bodybags, 'Nam,* and *firefight* (McNally, Kaspi, Riemann, et al., 1990). They also took more time on Vietnam-related words than on other words that were emotionally charged, either positively (*love, pleasant, loyal*) or negatively (*germs, filthy, urine*—words selected because they relate to another anxiety disorder, obsessive-compulsive disorder).

Similarly, in subjects with panic disorder, "fear" words (*panic, fear, anxiety*), "bodily sensation" words (*dizzy, heartbeat, faintness*), and "catastrophe" words (*death, heart attack, insane*) produced progressively greater interference with the speed of color naming than did neutral words (*polite, moderate, clever*). Control subjects experienced a similar *pattern* of delay in naming the colors, especially of the "catastrophe" words; but the *magnitude* of interference for these and the other threat cues was much less for them (McNally, Riemann, & Kim, 1990).

Another paradigm used to measure this attentional bias involves homophones, words that sound alike but are spelled differently and mean different things. In one homophone study, anxious subjects listened to a tape recording of words that might or might not be threatening, depending on which way they were spelled (*die/dye, slay/sleigh, foul/fowl*). After they heard each word, they were asked to spell it. The clinically anxious subjects tended to choose the more threatening of the two possible spellings—to write *moan* instead of *mown* and *pain* instead of *pane,* for example (Mathews, Richards, & Eysenck, 1989). Presumably, these subjects interpreted the world in the same way: a phone ringing in the night meant a death in the family; a boss's bad mood meant the person was going to be fired. And so, by attentional bias, they created the dangers they feared.

we ignore these sensations. Panic disorder patients do not ignore them; they interpret them as dangerous, which of course aggravates the sensations. As the sensations become more extreme, so does the interpretation, mounting eventually to the conviction of impending doom that characterizes a panic attack (A. T. Beck, 1988; Clark, 1988). Note that this formulation is related to, but slightly different from, the fear-of-fear theory. In fear of fear, the internal changes become a conditioned stimulus for the panic attack. In the cognitive model, the internal changes must be followed by an *interpretation* of those changes, a catastrophic interpretation, for the attack to ensue. Having developed the catastrophic interpretation, the person begins to pay even closer attention to internal sensations that might mean "danger"—which makes further attacks more likely.

There is considerable experimental support for this model. Research has shown that panic disorder patients are more likely to misinterpret bodily sensations than are other anxiety disorder patients or normal controls (Clark, Salkovskis, Gelder, et al., 1988; Foa, 1988). In addition, activating negative interpretations of bodily sensations has been found to produce panic attacks in panic disorder patients. For example, in one study panic patients and controls were asked to read aloud a series of word pairs, some of which linked internal sensations with catastrophic experiences (e.g., *breathlessness/suffocate; palpitations/dying; collapse/insane*). Ten out of twelve of the panic patients, but no recovered patients or normal controls, had a panic attack while reading these words (Clark, Salkovskis, Gelder, et al., 1988).

Finally, some studies have shown that panic attacks can be prevented by decreasing patients' tendency to misinterpret internal sensations as catastrophic (Clark, Gelder, Salkovskis, et al., 1991; Sanderson, Rapee, & Barlow, 1989). In one experiment twenty panic disorder patients were asked to inhale carbon dioxide, which they knew might produce a panic attack, and they were all told that when a light in front of them went on, they could use a dial attached to their chairs to adjust the carbon dioxide level. In fact, the dial did nothing; all the subjects received the same amount of carbon dioxide, but under differing cognitive conditions, since, as it turned out, the light went on for only half the subjects. So the subjects in this experiment differed not in their actual control but in their sense of control. At the end of the experiment, the "controlling" subjects reported significantly fewer panic symptoms than those who had no sense of control (Sanderson, Rapee, & Barlow, 1989).

This theory is not airtight, however. It does not explain, for example, why panic attacks that occur during sleep are often unconnected with dreams of any sort, let alone dreams of catastrophe (Ley, 1988a, 1988b). Furthermore, certain studies have found that some panic disorder patients either do not report catastrophic cognitions until *after* the attack (Wolpe & Rowan, 1988) or do not report them at all (S. Rachman, Levitt, & Lopatka, 1987; S. Rachman, Lopatka, & Levitt, 1988). And the theory does not explain how such catastrophic interpretations of bodily sensations develop in the first place.

The cognitive theorists' view of agoraphobia is simply an expansion of their view of panic disorder. For agoraphobia to develop out of panic disorder, what is needed is one further cognitive appraisal: that one cannot cope with the panic. In a study comparing panic disorder patients with and without agoraphobia, the agoraphobics, predictably, scored much lower on the perception of self-efficacy in coping with panic (Telch, Brouillard, Telch, et al., 1989). Similarly, agoraphobic avoidance in the absence of panic attacks is seen as a consequence of the belief that one will not be able to cope if some symptom occurs away from home. It has also been found that prior history of mastery and control experiences is a predictor of agoraphobic avoidance. Not surprisingly, people who have faced difficulties and overcome them are less likely to deal with panic attacks by avoidance, as happens in agoraphobia (Craske & Barlow, 1988). A final factor that may predict agoraphobia is social demand: the degree to which the person is required to go to work, meet responsibilities, and generally deal with the world. The higher the social demand, the lower the probability of agoraphobia. This may help to explain why three-fourths of agoraphobics are women. It is more "acceptable" for a woman to stay home. Men are likely to turn to other anxiety relievers, notably alcohol and drugs, before they will confine themselves to their homes (Barlow, 1988).

The remaining anxiety disorders are seen by cognitive theorists as variations on this misinterpretation-of-threat theme. In specific phobia, it is the threat of the phobic object that is misinterpreted; in social phobia, it is the threat of disapproval from others; in posttraumatic stress disorder, it is the threat of things in the environment associated with the remembered trauma; in obsessive-compulsive disorder, it is the threat of certain thoughts, which, in the person's eyes, will have catastrophic consequences if such consequences are not forestalled by the compulsive ritual.

Reducing Perceptions of Threat Under behavioral therapy we have already seen, in general, how a therapist would attack self-defeating thoughts such as misperceived threat. For panic disorder, David Clark and his colleagues have designed a cognitive treatment that has three main parts: identifying patients' negative interpretations of bodily sensations; suggesting alternative, noncatastrophic interpretations; and helping patients test the validity of these alternative explanations (Clark, Salkovskis, & Chalkley, 1985; Clark, Salkovskis, Gelder, et al., 1988; Salkovskis & Clark, in press). For example, patients may be taught an alternative interpretation for the bodily sensations they respond to with such fear, namely, that the sensations are the result of something they can control: breathing. Patients are asked to hyperventilate. Then, when they begin to experience the same sensations that have triggered their panic attacks, this similarity is pointed out to them, and they are taught how to do slow, shallow breathing that reduces the symptoms. For many patients, this is their first experience of controlling a panic attack—a lesson which is then buttressed by the therapist's teaching them new cognitions to use in combating the misperception of threat when an attack occurs outside the office. Together, patient and therapist will also try to identify what the patient's attack "triggers" are. When the triggers are identified, the attacks seem more understandable, less terrifying. (The patient may also be able to avoid some of them.)

This therapy has proved highly successful. In five controlled studies, between 75 and 95 percent of panic disorder patients became free of panic attacks after three months of cognitive therapy, and these improvements were maintained at one- and two-year follow-ups (Clark, 1991). Moreover, cognitive therapy compares favorably with behavioral and drug treatments for panic disorder, and compared with these other forms of treatment, it appears to decrease the likelihood of relapse (Clark,

1991). Similar cognitive treatments have been designed for other anxiety disorders. Some of these treatments also include the same graduated-exposure techniques that we saw under behavioral therapy, but the focus is slightly different: to challenge and change the patient's cognitions at each stage of exposure.

The Biological Perspective: Heredity and Biochemistry

Genetic Research Of all the anxiety disorders, the one that seems most likely to have a genetic basis is panic disorder (Crowe, 1991). One study of patients hospitalized for panic disorder found that the risk of panic disorder in their first-degree relatives (that is, immediate family: parents, siblings, and children) was 25 percent, as opposed to 2 percent for the first-degree relatives of normal controls (Crowe, Noyes, Pauls, et al., 1983). As we have seen, family studies offer the weakest form of genetic evidence, for they cannot separate environmental from genetic influence. But twin studies, which are more informative, have also implicated genes in panic disorder. In a Norwegian study, the concordance rate for panic disorder in MZ twins was 31 percent, as opposed to 0 percent for DZ twins (Torgersen, 1983).

For the other anxiety disorders, the genetic evidence is weaker but still significant. Studies of obsessive-compulsive children and adolescents have found that about one-third of their parents also have either a full-scale obsessive-compulsive disorder or some symptoms, compared with 2 to 3 percent of the general population (Lenane, Swedo, Leonard, et al., 1990; Riddle, Schaill, King, et al., 1990). Of course, the children could be imitating their parents, but the fact that the children's obsessions and compulsions usually differed in focus from the parents' suggests otherwise. Twin studies also indicate some genetic basis for obsessive-compulsive disorder: the concordance rate for compulsive behaviors has been found to be about twice as high in MZ twins as in DZ twins (G. Carey & Gottesman, 1981). As for specific phobias, a study of the first-degree relatives of phobics found them to be three times more likely to have phobias than first-degree relatives of normal controls (A. J. Fyer, Mannuzza, Gallops, et al., 1990). For social phobia, the evidence is sketchier, though here too there are indications that the disorder runs in families (Reich & Yates, 1988; S. M. Turner & Beidel, 1989). Posttraumatic stress disorder also seems to involve some genetic predisposition, if only toward psychological disturbance in general. Earlier in this chapter we saw that a family history of psychopathology predicted which of the Australian fire fighters succumbed to posttraumatic stress disorder after the 1983 bushfires (McFarlane, 1988, 1989). In a study of war veterans, it was found that when combat exposure was high, a family history of psychopathology seemed to have no effect on whether a person would develop a posttraumatic syndrome; it was when combat exposure was low that the soldiers with a family history of psychopathology were at greater risk (Foy, Resnick, Sipprelle, et al., 1987). The anxiety disorder for which there is the weakest evidence of genetic influence is generalized anxiety disorder. One family study found that one-fifth of the first-degree relatives of people with generalized anxiety disorder had the same condition, compared with 4 to 5 percent of the general population (Noyes, Clarkson, Crowe, et al., 1987), but this may be the product of learning rather than genes, for there seems to be no difference between MZ and DZ twins in concordance rates for this syndrome (Torgersen, 1983).

If anxiety disorders are inherited, *what* exactly is inherited? Probably a diathesis, or vulnerability, toward anxiety disorders in general rather than toward a specific syndrome. Rats can be bred for "nervousness" (Barlow, 1988); apparently, so can human beings. As for what this nervousness consists of, that is an open question. Possibly it is an overly responsive autonomic nervous system (Eysenck, 1967) or an attentional bias for threat. (See the box on page 168.) Whatever it is, however, one should keep in mind that it is only a predisposition. Recall the Norwegian twin studies, where there was a 31 percent concordance rate between MZ twins for panic disorder. This is an impressive figure, but it means that more than two-thirds of the MZ twins, people with exactly the same genetic endowment, were not concordant. Obviously, environment plays an important role.

The Role of Neurotransmitters For years it was known that anxiety can often be relieved by such drugs as Valium and Librium, which belong to a chemical group called the benzodiazepines. But how the benzodiazepines actually affect the brain's chemistry remained a mystery. Then, in 1977, it was discovered that the benzodiazepines attach to certain specific receptors on the neurons of the brain. This finding suggests that the brain may have a natural chemical, similar to the benzodiazepines, that regulates anxiety. It follows, then, that abnormalities in this chemical—too high a level or too low a level—may underlie the anxiety disorders.

Whatever the chemical process in question, we know that it involves a neurotransmitter called GABA (gamma-aminobutyric acid), for it is GABA that is activated by the benzodiazepines (Costa & Guidotti, 1985). GABA is an inhibitory neurotransmitter; that is, once it is activated, it turns *off* the affected neurons. This, presumably, is the chemical basis of the benzodiazepines' ability to control anxiety: they signal GABA to shut off a certain measure of the brain's activity.

It is doubtful, however, that this process underlies all anxiety conditions, for certain types of anxiety, those experienced as generalized tension, are more responsive to the benzodiazepines than are other anxiety conditions, such as panic disorder, which are more responsive to antidepressant drugs. This finding points to two conclusions. First, the chemical basis of panic disorder is probably different from that of generalized anxiety—a conclusion already suggested by the genetic evidence. In other words, there is apparently more than one kind of anxiety, at least biochemically. Second, panic disorder may be more closely related to depression biochemically than to generalized anxiety. We know that the antidepressants in question affect the neurotransmitters norepinephrine and serotonin, which have been repeatedly implicated in depression. Presumably, norepinephrine and serotonin are also involved in panic disorder (Hoehn-Saric, 1982)—a theory bolstered by the finding that panic disorder patients often show abnormalities in the functioning of those two neurotransmitters (J. Butler, O'Halloran, & Leonard, 1992).

One hypothesis as to the biochemistry of panic disorder (Gorman, Liebowitz, Fyer, et al., 1989) is that panic attacks are triggered by increased neurological firing in a section of the brainstem known as the locus ceruleus, a major norepinephrine center. Several lines of evidence point to this specific location. First, as we saw earlier, panic attacks can be provoked in the laboratory by an infusion of the drug yohimbine, and we know that yohimbine raises the firing rate in the locus ceruleus. Second, studies have shown that monkeys will have paniclike reactions in response to electrical stimulation of the locus ceruleus and that if the locus ceruleus is removed, they will become less vulnerable to anxiety-provoking stimuli (Redmond, 1977, 1979). Third, substances that reduce the locus ceruleus firing rate—and these include the drugs currently used for panic disorder—do prevent panic attacks. Nevertheless, these findings have been challenged by conflicting results. Furthermore, yohimbine is far from the only stimulus that produces panic attacks. Researchers in the laboratory have now provoked panic attacks with a wide range of stimuli, not all of which are clearly connected even to the brainstem, let alone to the locus ceruleus, and several of which seem to have opposite biological effects. (For further discussion of the relation between anxiety and the locus ceruleus, see the box on page 172.)

Obsessive-compulsive disorder has also been the object of intense biochemical study in recent years. There is a growing consensus that obsessive-compulsive disorder is connected to serotonin abnormalities, for drugs that selectively inhibit serotonin reuptake do relieve the symptoms of this disorder (L. C. Barr, Goodman, Price, et al., 1992; Zohar & Zohar-Kadouch, 1991). At the same time, some dysfunction of the frontal lobe of the brain may also be involved, for PET scans of the brains of obsessive-compulsive patients in the process of glucose metabolism show abnormalities. Furthermore, when, in rare cases, obsessive-compulsive disorder has been treated by surgical disconnection of the frontal lobe, this has relieved the disorder (Mindus & Jenike, 1992).

Yet another line of research has to do with the basal ganglia, a region of the brain known to be involved with movement. Researchers have turned up a number of connections between obsessive-compulsive disorder and movement disorders thought to be caused by basal ganglia abnormalities. One such movement disorder is Tourette's syndrome, which produces tics—involuntary movements and verbalizations. Tourette's patients show a disproportionately high rate of obsessive-compulsive disorder, as do their relatives; conversely, obsessive-compulsive patients and their relatives are disproportionately likely to have tics (Pauls, 1990; Pitman, Green, Jenike, et al., 1987). Meanwhile, PET scans of obsessive-compulsive patients have found abnormalities in the basal ganglia, and specifically in the caudate nucleus, which is thought to be the cognitive section of the basal ganglia (Baxter, Phelps, Mazziotta, et al., 1987). So perhaps obsessions are a sort of cognitive tic.

Even the anxiety disorder with the greatest "environmental" aspect is now being probed for biochemical underpinnings. Roger Pitman (1988, 1989) has put forth a hormonal theory of posttraumatic stress disorder. We know that hormones and neurotransmitters are involved in memory processes. According to Pitman, they may therefore be responsible for the intrusive memories that afflict posttraumatic patients. That is, the trauma may overstimulate stress-responsive hormones and

ANXIETY AND THE MIDDLE-AGED BRAIN

When is brain deterioration good news? According to some researchers, the decreased incidence of anxiety disorders in middle-aged people may be the result of deterioration in the locus ceruleus, a portion of the medulla oblongata, which in turn is part of the brainstem.

The medulla oblongata has long been known to control such functions as breathing and heart rate and to produce the neurotransmitters epinephrine (adrenaline) and norepinephrine. The locus ceruleus in particular appears to be responsible for norepinephrine production—some 70 percent of all cells with receptors for this neurotransmitter are located there. Although the locus ceruleus is a tiny mass at the base of the brain, it has extensive connections to many other parts of the nervous system.

Normally the locus ceruleus acts as a sort of alarm system, producing increased amounts of norepinephrine in the face of stress and of real or imagined danger. High activity levels in the locus ceruleus are characteristic of panic attacks, for example, and low activity levels may be associated with reckless behavior.

As the body ages, however, the locus ceruleus apparently undergoes changes that reduce the amount of anxiety the person experiences. Autopsies of people aged forty to sixty indicate that the cells of the locus ceruleus begin to lose their bluish color after forty. The cells of the locus ceruleus also become clogged in middle age with neuromelanin, thought to be a waste product of norepinephrine. This excess of neuromelanin slows the cells' functioning and eventually kills them. As a result, norepinephrine production declines sharply in middle age. At the same time, there is an increase in the production of monoamine oxidase, an enzyme that breaks down norepinephrine, thereby reducing further the amount of norepinephrine available to the brain.

As norepinephrine declines, so does anxiety. Many middle-aged people report feeling less worried and more self-assured than when they were younger. Of particular interest to psychotherapists is the decline of drug addiction, bulimia, and anxiety disorders such as panic attacks in patients over age forty. According to Dr. Stephen Roose, a psychiatrist at the New York State Psychiatric Institute, "As these cells [of the locus ceruleus] die, diseases that are pathologies of this brain system seem to burn out."

neurotransmitters, with the result that the memory of the trauma becomes "overconsolidated" and cannot fade.

Whatever the specific biochemical processes involved in the anxiety disorders, these recent findings have given new impetus to research on neurotransmitters. And the newfound connection between neurotransmitters and anxiety states has generated renewed interest in the possible role of drugs in treating these disorders. As we shall see in Chapter 21, there are now several promising drug treatments for the anxiety disorders.

KEY TERMS

acrophobia (154)
agoraphobia (152)
anxiety (150)
anxiety disorders (150)
claustrophobia (154)
client-centered therapy (164)
compulsion (155)
disaster syndrome (160)
dream interpretation (164)
free association (163)
generalized anxiety disorder (153)
in vivo desensitization (166)
obsession (155)
obsessive-compulsive disorder (155)
panic attack (151)
panic disorder (152)
paradoxical intention (164)
phobia (153)
posttraumatic stress disorder (157)
resistance (164)
social phobia (154)
specific phobia (154)
systematic desensitization (166)
transference (164)
trichotillomania (157)

SUMMARY

- Anxiety disorders are characterized either by manifest anxiety or by behavior patterns aimed at warding off anxiety. Whatever its form, anxiety involves a subjective sense of tension and fear, behavioral responses such as avoidance of a feared situation, and physiological responses such as increased heart rate and respiration.
- In a panic disorder a person experiences and/or intensely fears a series of panic attacks, sudden and unexpected onsets of severe anxiety. Physical sensations such as dizziness, trembling, and shortness of breath give rise to a feeling of impending catastrophe. Panic disorder can lead to agoraphobia, a fear of leaving the safety of home.

- In generalized anxiety disorder, a person experiences a chronic state of excessive and uncontrollable worry, including the expectation that catastrophic events are impending.
- A person with a phobia intensely fears some object or situation and persistently tries to avoid that stimulus. Persons with a specific phobia react to a particular object (such as a rat) or situation (such as an enclosed space). Social phobia is aroused by a social situation (such as public speaking) that calls on a person to perform in front of others, at the risk of embarrassment or humiliation.
- People suffering from obsessive-compulsive disorder are bothered by recurring thoughts (obsessions) and/or actions (compulsions) that they seem unable to control. A related syndrome is trichotillomania, the compulsive pulling out of one's own hair.
- Posttraumatic stress disorder is a severe reaction to traumatic events that pose mortal danger to a person, such as natural disaster, assault, and combat. Victims typically reexperience the event for long periods of time, show diminished responsiveness to their surroundings, develop physical symptoms, and may suffer from depression, anxiety, and irritability.
- Psychodynamic theorists view the anxiety disorders as neuroses resulting from unconscious conflicts between id impulses and ego actions. The neurotic individual experiences conscious anxiety over these conflicts or keeps the anxiety at bay through rigid defense mechanisms. Treatment focuses on uncovering what the ego is trying to suppress and involves the techniques of free association, dream interpretation, and analysis of resistance and transference.
- Humanistic-existential theorists also ascribe the anxiety disorders to intrapsychic conflicts. However, they see anxiety not just as an individual problem but as the outcome of conflicts between the person's self-concept and society's ideal. If how we perceive ourselves varies greatly from how we would like to be, we feel inadequate for meeting life's challenges, and anxiety results. Humanistic-existential therapies strive to improve the patient's self-concept and restore a sense of wholeness and freedom.
- Behaviorists attribute anxiety disorders to faulty learning, not unconscious conflicts. In the process of learning to avoid anxiety, people may also learn to associate a neutral stimulus with the anxiety-producing stimulus and then be conditioned to habitually avoid that stimulus. Behavioral therapy is directed at removing the symptoms of a disorder through such techniques as desensitization, modeling, and operant conditioning.
- According to the cognitive perspective, people with anxiety disorders misperceive or misinterpret internal and external stimuli. Events and sensations that are not really threatening are interpreted as threatening, and anxiety results. Cognitive therapy aims at helping the patient to interpret bodily sensations in a noncatastrophic way.
- The biological perspective seeks genetic and biochemical links to anxiety. Some anxiety disorders, especially panic disorder, appear to have a genetic component. Recent evidence also suggests that brain chemistry and neurotransmitters influence some forms of anxiety.

8

DISSOCIATIVE AND SOMATOFORM DISORDERS

A well-dressed woman in her early thirties was brought to the hospital by the police after she was found wandering on an interstate highway. She had no identification with her. She spoke coherently but slowly and was apparently traumatized, but not psychotic. On the ward she seldom spoke, and she ate only when she was coaxed. When asked who she was, she would stare into space or shrug her shoulders with a gesture of despair. She was given the temporary name of Jane Doe, and after four weeks of futile attempts to establish her identity, she was moved to a ward for chronic patients.

Jane was taken to the psychologist's office every day, but she barely responded to him, and she could not be hypnotized, because she would not close her eyes or concentrate on the procedure. Eventually the psychologist tried progressive relaxation, to which Jane responded well. After each relaxation session, the psychologist would pick up his office telephone and pretend to call a friend or relative. Then he would give Jane the phone and suggest that she make a call, but she always said that she didn't remember anyone's number. Finally, one day, after Jane had achieved a state of deep relaxation, the psychologist gave her the phone again and asked her just to punch in numbers at random. She did so, and after a while she was consistently punching the same area code and phone number, though she never waited for the ring. But the psychologist wrote down the number, and taking the phone from Jane, he called it himself and gave the phone back to Jane, whereupon she got to speak to her mother in Detroit, 400 miles away. As it turned out, Jane was a highly skilled engineer who had wandered away from her home in Boston on the day when the movers came to move her household to another state, where she was supposed to be relocating. Jane's family arrived to pick her up the next day. (adapted from Lyon, 1985)

DB was a thirty-three-year-old man who had a clerical job and lived with his parents. Seven years earlier, during military training, he had been hit in the right eye by a rifle butt. Thereafter he claimed that he was blind in that eye, though medical examinations indicated that the eye was functioning normally.

To find out whether DB was in fact receiving no information through his right eye, he was given a test during which his left eye was completely covered. The test involved a machine that emitted a buzz. The machine had three switches, only one of which could turn off the buzz, and with each trial the controlling switch changed at random. DB's hands were placed on the machine, and he was told that on each trial he was to try to turn off the buzz. What he was not told was that the machine also had a visual component: a screen showing three triangles, one of which was always pointed in a direction different from the other two. On each trial the controlling switch was the one under the twisted triangle. So the machine gave its user the right answer—if the user could see.

DB had twenty-one sessions with the machine. Four of those were control sessions: the screen was turned off, so that there were no visual cues. On these control sessions, DB pulled the right switch 39 percent of the time, roughly what one would expect by chance. But in the seventeen experimental sessions, when the screen was on, he pulled the right switch 74 percent of the time—far greater than a chance percentage. Furthermore, when the visual cue was present, he took twice as long to pull the switch, indicating that he was processing information. DB's "blind" eye was clearly seeing, and he was reclassified as having a psychological, not a physical disorder. (adapted from Bryant & McConkey, 1989)

According to current psychiatric terminology, these two cases represent different disorders. Jane Doe has dissociative amnesia, one of the dissociative disorders, which are disturbances of higher cognitive functions such as memory or identity. DB, on the other hand, has a conversion disorder, which is one of the somatoform disorders, characterized by physical complaints or disabilities for which there is no apparent organic cause.

Despite their different labels, however, conversion disorder and the dissociative disorders have much in common (Kihlstrom, Tataryn, & Hoyt, 1993). First, both of them mimic actual neurological disorders—amnesia in the case of Jane Doe, blindness in the case of DB. Second, in both cases, the problem is not a neurological disability but a disruption of conscious awareness. Jane Doe knew her mother's telephone number, and DB could see with his right eye. In each case the ability affected behavior, but neither Jane Doe nor DB was consciously aware of that ability.

Because of these similarities, conversion disorder and the dissociative disorders were grouped together for a long time in a broad category called "hysterical neurosis," **hysteria** being a psychogenic disorder that mimics a biogenic disorder. But when the *DSM* abandoned the concepts of neurosis and hysteria in 1980, the dissociative disorders and conversion disorder became separated. The dissociative disorders now include only disturbances of higher cognitive functions. Conversion disorder, since it affects not cognitive functions but sensory functions (as in blindness) or motor functions (as in paralysis), has been removed to the category of "somatoform disorders," psychological disorders that take somatic, or physical, form. But in view of their shared features and their historical connection, the present chapter will consider these two categories, and their theories and treatments, together. We will first discuss the dissociative disorders and then the somatoform disorders.

DISSOCIATIVE DISORDERS

As the name indicates, the **dissociative disorders** involve the dissociation, or splitting apart, of components of the personality that are normally integrated. As a result, some psychological function—identity, memory, perception of oneself or the environment—is screened out of consciousness. Many people, especially children and adolescents, have dissociative experiences—feelings of "strangeness," brief spells of memory loss or identity confusion—in the course of normal life (C. A. Ross, Joshi, & Currie, 1991; Vanderlinden, Van Dyck, Vandereycken, et al., 1991). In some measure, dissociation is an adaptive skill. For example, when we drive a car while having a conversation, what we attend to is the conversation, all the while screening out the psychological and motor functions involved in driving the car. However, if we have to attend to these functions—if, for example, the road suddenly becomes dangerous—we can do so. What was screened out can be called back. In the dissociative disorders, the screened-out function is not accessible to conscious awareness. Furthermore, it is a critical function, such as our memory of past events or of who we are.

The dissociative disorders occur without any demonstrable damage to the brain. Instead, as we shall see, they have their origin in severe psychological stress and develop as a way of coping with that stress. In this regard they are like posttraumatic stress disorder (Chapter 7), which often includes dissociative symptoms such as amnesia. We will discuss four syndromes: dissociative amnesia, dissociative fugue, dissociative identity disorder, and depersonalization disorder.

Dissociative Amnesia

Amnesia, the partial or total forgetting of past experiences, may be caused by a blow to the head or by any one of a number of brain disorders. Some amnesias, however, occur without any apparent organic cause, as a response to psychological stress. In addition to medical tests for organic pathology, there are several ways of distinguishing between organic and **dissociative amnesia** (Sackeim & Devanand, 1991). First, dissociative amnesia is almost always *anterograde,* blotting out a period of time after the precipitating stress, whereas organic amnesia, particularly from a head injury, is usually *retrograde,* erasing a period of time prior to the precipitating event. Second, dissociative amnesia is often selective; the "blank" period tends to include events that most people would want to forget—either a trauma or perhaps an unacceptable action such as an extramarital affair. Third, people with dissociative amnesia are often much less disturbed than those around them over their condition—an indifference that suggests relief from conflict. Finally, because the events forgotten in dissociative amnesia are simply screened out of consciousness rather than lost altogether (as is the case in organic amnesia), they can often be re-

Dissociative amnesia is a popular plot device for Hollywood movies. In this scene from Alfred Hitchcock's *Spellbound* (1945), psychiatrist Ingrid Bergman tries to help Gregory Peck recover his memory.

covered under hypnosis or with the aid of sodium amytal, a barbiturate (Ruedrich, Chu, & Wadle, 1985).

Patterns of Memory Loss There are five broad patterns of dissociative amnesia. First and most common is *localized amnesia,* in which all events occurring during a circumscribed period of time are blocked out. For example, a man who has survived a fire in which the rest of his family died might have no memory of anything that happened from the time of the fire until three days later. Second is *selective amnesia,* in which the person makes "spot" erasures, forgetting only certain events that occurred during a circumscribed period of time. In the above case, for example, the man might recall the fire engines coming and the ambulance taking him to the hospital, but forget seeing his children carried out of the house or identifying their bodies the next day. Third is *generalized amnesia,* in which, as in the case of Jane Doe, the person forgets his or her entire past life. Though this is the kind that tends to turn up in novels and movies, it is actually rare. A fourth pattern, also rare, is *continuous amnesia,* in which the person forgets all events that occur after a specific period up to the present, including events that occur *after* the onset of amnesia. For example, if the amnesia begins on Monday, the person will not know on Wednesday what he or she did on Tuesday, let alone prior events. Finally, in *systematized amnesia,* the person forgets only certain categories of information (e.g., all information about his or her family); other memories remain intact. While some patterns are more common than others, amnesia in general is rare. However, its incidence tends to spiral among victims of war and natural disasters. Indeed, many of the reported cases of amnesia were soldiers in World War I and World War II (Loewenstein, 1991).

Predictably, confusion and disorientation tend to accompany amnesia, especially generalized and continuous amnesia, in which all or much of the person's past is blocked out. Patients with these forms of amnesia do not know who or where they are, do not recognize family or friends, and cannot tell you their name, address, or anything else about themselves. In other words, their *episodic memory,* or memory of personal experience, is lost. Typically, however, their *semantic memory,* or general knowledge, is spared. A patient who cannot identify a picture of his wife will still be able to identify a picture of John Kennedy (Schacter, Wang, Tulving, et al., 1982). *Procedural memory,* or memory for skills, is also usually intact. Amnesia victims can read and write, add and subtract.

In most cases, though, even episodic memory is only partially erased. **Explicit memories,** memories we are aware of, may be gone, but often the person shows evidence of **implicit memories,** memories that he or she cannot call into conscious awareness but that still affect behavior. At the beginning of this chapter we saw an example of this: Jane Doe's dialing the telephone number of the mother she didn't remember she had. Under the influence of implicit memory, many victims of amnesia show strong reactions to things that recall the initiating trauma. In one reported case the patient, a victim of male rape, had no conscious memory of the rape but clearly had unconscious knowledge of it. When shown a TAT card that depicted a person attacking another person from behind, he became extremely upset. Then he left the testing session to go to his room, where he attempted suicide (Kaszniak, Nussbaum, Berren, et al., 1988).

When dissociative amnesia occurs in novels and movies, it appears suddenly and dramatically, as the only symptom; it also disappears suddenly, with the person gratefully resuming his or her former life. This, apparently, is not the usual pattern. Many amnesias do remit suddenly, without treatment—others become chronic—but even when they remit, they tend to recur. In a recent survey of twenty-five patients, almost half had had more than one episode of amnesia. Furthermore, their memory loss was accompanied by a wide range of other symptoms, above all, depression, headaches, and sexual dysfunction (typically, decreased sexual desire). Indeed, in most cases the amnesia was discovered only on questioning; the presenting complaint was usually depression. As for what precipitated the first amnesic episode, this was retrospective evidence, which is always questionable—and more so, needless to say, in people with memory disorders—but 60 percent named childhood sexual abuse; 24 percent, marital trouble; 16 percent, a suicide attempt; 16 percent, disavowed sexual behavior such as adultery or promiscuity (Coons & Milstein, 1992).

Amnesia and Crime Amnesia has created difficulties for the legal system (Kihlstrom, Tataryn, & Hoyt, 1993). Crime victims who cannot consciously recall the crime are unable to offer what would be valuable testimony in court. A worse problem is that people *accused* of crimes often do not remember the event. One researcher (Schacter, 1986a, 1986b) found that between 23 and 65 percent of people charged with or convicted of homicide claim to have no memory of the crime. In such cases alcohol or other drugs are often involved, so some of these amnesias may be drug-induced "blackouts." Others may be faked. But others are probably true dissociative amnesias, responses to the extreme emotional arousal surrounding the crime. Whatever the source, defendants claiming amnesia may be judged incapable of assisting in their own defense, in which case they may be judged incompetent to stand trial. So if they are tried, they may qualify for the insanity defense, on the grounds that they committed the crime in an altered state of consciousness, in which they did not know what they were doing or that it was wrong (D. O. Lewis & Bard, 1991). Such was the case in the 1993 trial of Lorena Bobbitt (Chapter 22), who claimed to have no memory of cutting off her husband's penis, and Bobbitt was acquitted on the grounds of temporary insanity. For other legal problems posed by the dissociative disorders, see the box on page 180.

Dissociative Fugue

A condition related to amnesia is **dissociative fugue,** in which the person not only forgets all or most of his or her past but also takes a sudden, unexpected trip away from home. Fugue, then, is a sort of traveling amnesia, but it is more elaborate than amnesia. While people with amnesia, in their confusion, may wander about aimlessly, fugue patients are purposeful in their movements. Furthermore, while amnesia patients may also forget their identity, many fugue patients go one step further and manufacture a new one.

The length and elaborateness of fugues vary considerably. Some people may go no farther than the next town, spend the day in a movie house, check into a hotel under an assumed name, and recover by morning. Such relatively subdued adventures are the usual pattern. In rare cases, however, patients will travel to foreign countries, assume a new identity, fabricate a detailed past history, and pursue an altogether new life for months or even years. During the fugue, they will appear fairly normal to observers. Finally, however, they "wake up," often after some jolting reminder of their former life or, as it appears in some cases, simply when they once again feel psychologically safe (Riether & Stoudemire, 1988). Fugue usually remits suddenly, and when fugue victims wake up, they are completely amnesic for the events that occurred during the fugue. The last thing they may remember is leaving home one morning. This second-stage amnesia is what usually brings fugue victims to professional attention. Apparently normal during the fugue period, they seek professional help only once the fugue ends, partly because they want to find out what they did during the fugue.

Like amnesia, fugue is generally rare, but more common in wartime and after natural disasters. Again like amnesia, it tends to occur after a severe psychological trauma and—as the term (derived from the Latin word for "flight") suggests—seems to function as an escape from psychological stress. The following case shows both the precipitating trauma and the escape motivation. It is also a good example of implicit memory:

> Bernice L., a middle-aged housewife, had been raised in a stern, loveless, and extremely religious home. She grew up shy and anxious, but when she went away to college, she began to "bloom" a bit. This was largely the work of her roommate, a vivacious girl by the name of Rose P., who introduced Bernice to her friends, encouraged her to develop her talent for the piano, and in general drew her out. In their junior year, however, their friendship suffered a crisis. Rose became engaged to a young man with whom Bernice too promptly fell in love. When the man married Rose, Bernice fell into a severe depression. She returned home for a while, but at her parents' insistence, she eventually went back to school.
>
> Upon graduation, Bernice married a young clergyman for whom she felt little attraction but whom her parents approved of. They had two children and eventually settled in a small town not unlike her childhood home. Bernice had few satisfactions in life other than her children and her happy memories of her first two years in college. Then, when she was thirty-seven years old, her younger child, a musically talented boy, died. The next day she disappeared, and for four years she could not be found.
>
> Later, with the help of a therapist, Bernice recalled some of the events of those four years. Totally amnesic for her past life, she had returned to her old college town. There, under the name of Rose P., she began giving piano lessons, and within two years she became assistant director of the local conservatory of music. She made a few friends, but she never spoke of her past life, for it was still a complete blank to her. Then one day she was recognized by a woman who had known both her and Rose P. during college. Bernice's husband, now a minister in Chicago, was located, and reluctantly she was returned to him.
>
> In therapy, Bernice's amnesia was finally dispelled. She resumed her old identity, readjusted to her husband, who proved patient and sympathetic, and settled down to life in Chicago. (adapted from Masserman, 1961, pp. 35–37)

Dissociative Identity Disorder

Perhaps the most bizarre of the dissociative disorders is **dissociative identity disorder,** also known as *multiple personality.* In this pattern the personality breaks up into two or more distinct personali-

WHO COMMITTED THE CRIME? SUBORDINATE PERSONALITIES AND THE LAW

In 1977, a man named William Stanley Milligan was arrested for the rape of three women in Columbus, Ohio. Two of the women positively identified him as the Ohio State University "campus rapist," and fingerprints found at the scene of one of the crimes matched his. It seemed to be an open-and-shut case. Not until Milligan twice tried to commit suicide in jail while awaiting trial did it occur to his lawyers that he might need psychiatric help.

The report of the examining psychologists and psychiatrists profoundly altered the nature of the case. At the time of the trial they had identified at least ten different personalities somehow coexisting within Milligan. These included the core personality, "Billy"; Arthur, an emotionless, self-taught Englishman, who dominated the other personalities; Ragen, a Yugoslavian of extraordinary strength, an associate of criminals and addicts, who was known as the protector of women and children and the "keeper of hate"; Allen, an eighteen-year-old manipulator and con artist; Tommy, a sixteen-year-old antisocial personality, who was also a landscape painter and escape artist; Danny, fourteen, a timid painter of still lifes; eight-year-old David, who "absorbed" the pain and suffering of the others; Christene, a three-year-old English girl; Christopher, her troubled thirteen-year-old brother; and Adalane, nineteen, an introverted lesbian.

The astonishing range of talents and dispositions manifested by these personalities showed up from time to time in Milligan's jail experience. For instance, after his second suicide attempt he was placed in solitary confinement in a straitjacket. When his jailers looked in on him, they found him fast asleep with the straitjacket under his head as a pillow. Presumably, Tommy, the escape artist, had effected his release.

Milligan was eventually found not guilty by reason of insanity—the first case of dissociative identity disorder to be acquitted of a major crime under that plea. Accordingly, he was sent to a mental hospital near Columbus, where he was placed under the care of David Caul, a psychiatrist who had experience in treating dissociative identity disorder.

Caul soon discovered more personalities. In addition to the ten already identified, there were thirteen "undesirables." (Arthur called them this because they rebelled against his control.) One of the undesirables was the Teacher—the fusion of all twenty-three alter egos. Described as "Billy all in one piece," the Teacher had total recall of the events in Milligan's life. In his sessions with Caul, Milligan's personalities fused more and more into one competent person. Soon he was allowed unattended trips into town and weekend furloughs. These privileges, however, provoked anger among the people of Columbus, who still feared Milligan's potential for violent behavior.

Under the glare of unfavorable publicity and open public hostility, Milligan's personalities once again split apart. Aggressive personalities came to the fore, causing Milligan to be sent to a maximum-security institution. Eventually, after years of treatment, his personalities seemed to fuse, and he was released. He established a child-abuse prevention agency, worked as a farmer, and developed a career as an artist (Kihlstrom, Tataryn, & Hoyt, 1993).

Even though several experienced psychiatrists testified that Milligan's disorder was dissociative identity disorder, traceable to traumatic abuse he suffered in childhood at the hands of his stepfather, many professionals and laypeople alike still suspect that Billy Milligan was faking. This disorder typically arouses such skepticism, sometimes justifiably. But it is difficult to see how one person could carry off the impersonation of so many roles so convincingly, so consistently, for so long.

In another case soon after Milligan's, Kenneth Bianchi, a man accused of a number of rape-murders in the Los Angeles area, claimed in an insanity defense that the crimes he was accused of were committed by one of his personalities, Steve Walker. The defense was undermined, however, by evidence that he was faking. (His alter egos were not consistent, for example.) Bianchi was convicted of multiple counts of murder.

In another twist, a Wisconsin man named Mark Peterson was accused of sexual assault by a dissociative identity disorder patient who said that only one of her personalities gave consent. (Another watched the event and another went to the police.) Peterson was eventually convicted under a law that makes it equivalent to rape to have sexual intercourse with a mental patient (Kihlstrom, Tataryn, & Hoyt, 1993).

These cases raise fascinating and difficult questions for the legal system. Should a person be held responsible for crimes committed by a subordinate personality? Is a person the victim of a crime if one personality gives consent? Since our laws assume that a person has only one personality, not several, each such case must be considered individually.

ties, each well integrated and well developed, which then take turns controlling the person's behavior. (Sometimes called "split personality," dissociative identity disorder should not be confused with schizophrenia, which is an altogether different syndrome. See Chapter 14.) Amnesia is part of the pattern. At least one of the personalities will be amnesic for the experiences of the other or others. The first case of dissociative identity disorder to receive extensive professional attention—the case of "Miss Beauchamp," who may have had as many as seventeen personalities—was reported by Morton Prince in 1905. Ever since, this disorder has held a certain fascination for the public, as shown by the immense popularity of Thigpen and Cleckley's *The Three Faces of Eve* (1957), both book and movie, and by the best-seller *Sybil* (Schreiber, 1974), about a girl with sixteen personalities.

There are many different forms of dissociative identity disorder, and they become more complicated as the number of personalities increases (Putnam, 1989). In the simplest form, called **alternating personality,** two identities take turns controlling behavior, each having amnesia for the thoughts and actions of the other. A second pattern involves one or more dominant personalities and one or more subordinate ones. While the dominant personality is directing the person's behavior, the subordinate personality, fully aware of the thoughts and actions of the dominant personality, continues to operate covertly and to make its presence felt now and then. In such cases, the subordinate personality is said to be **coconscious** (M. Prince, 1905) with the dominant personality. When the coconscious personality finally surfaces, it can discuss in detail the interesting problems of the dominant personality. Meanwhile, the dominant personality only gradually becomes aware of the existence of the subordinate personality, usually by encountering the evidence of his or her activities. In one case (Osgood, Luria, Jeans, et al., 1976), the dominant personality, "Gina," first learned of the existence of a subordinate personality, "Mary Sunshine," when she began waking up in the morning to find cups with leftover hot chocolate in the kitchen sink. "Gina" did not drink hot chocolate.

This pattern of the initially ignorant dominant personality and the coconscious subordinate personality was illustrated in the famous case described in *The Three Faces of Eve* (Thigpen & Cleckley, 1957):

> Eve White was the original dominant personality. She had no knowledge of the existence of her second personality, Eve Black, although Eve Black had been alternating with Eve White for some years. Whenever Eve Black surfaced, all that Eve White could report was that she had "blackouts." Eve Black, on the other hand, was coconscious with Eve White, knew everything that she did, and would talk about her with contempt. Eve White was bland, quiet, and serious—a rather dull personality. Eve Black, on the other hand,

Chris Sizemore was the subject of *The Three Faces of Eve,* first a book and then a film about her dissociative identity disorder.

was carefree, mischievous, and uninhibited. She would "come out" at the most inappropriate times, leaving Eve White with hangovers, bills, and a reputation in local bars that she could not explain. During treatment, there emerged a third personality, Jane, who was coconscious with both Eve White and Eve Black, though she had no memory of their activities prior to her appearance. More mature than the other two, Jane seemed to have emerged as the result of the therapeutic process.

Eve's problems with dissociative identity disorder did not stop in 1957 with the publication of *The Three Faces of Eve*. In 1975, a woman called Chris Sizemore, an apparently unremarkable middle-aged housewife from Fairfax, Virginia, revealed that she was "Eve" and that Eve Black, Eve White, and Jane were only three of the many personalities with which she had struggled throughout her life. Indeed, Mrs. Sizemore had manifested twenty-one separate identities, each with its own speech patterns, habits, preferences, and moral code. The personalities invariably came in sets of three, with considerable conflict among them. "If I had learned to sew as one personality and then tried to sew as another, I couldn't do it. Driving a car was the same. Some of my personalities couldn't drive" (Nunes, 1975, p. 4).

In the early years, a particular personality would dominate for a period of several days. Later, Mrs. Sizemore's personality would change at least once a day. The transition from one personality to another was usually marked by a sudden and very painful headache. The headache would last for about ten seconds, during which Mrs. Sizemore was conscious of nothing. When the pain disappeared, a new personality would be in control.

In 1977 Mrs. Sizemore reported that she was cured (Sizemore & Pittillo, 1977), a fact she ascribed to the eventual realization that all of her different personalities were truly parts of herself, not invaders from the outside. "You don't know how wonderful it is," she said, "to go to bed at night and know that it will be you that wakes up the next day" (Nunes, 1975, p. 4).

Patterns of Personalities As with Eve, many cases of dissociative identity disorder involve personalities that are polar opposites: one conformist, duty-doing, "nice" personality and one rebellious, impulsive, badly behaved personality. In this respect, multiple personalities seem to be extreme cases of the normal conflict between self-indulgence and restraint—or, as the Freudians would put it, between id and superego. In surveys of dissociative identity patients by two teams of researchers, at least 50 percent of the patients reported drug abuse by an alternate personality; 20 percent claimed that an alternate personality had been involved in a sexual assault on another person; and 29 percent reported that one of their alternates was homicidal (Putnam, Guroff, Silberman, et al., 1986; C. A. Ross, Miller, Reagor, et al., 1990). Dissociative identity patients may do violence to themselves when one personality tries to kill another. Such "internal homicide" attempts were reported by more than half the people in the above surveys.

But "good" versus "bad" is not the only pattern. In some cases, one personality will encapsulate a traumatic memory while the others are unaware of it. In other cases, the personalities may divide up the emotional life, one dealing with anger, another handling sadness, and so on. Often the personalities will specialize in different areas of functioning, one for family relations, one for sex life, one for work, others for specific skills. And these patterns may overlap. For example, a personality that embodies the memory of an abusive father may also be the only one who can solve complex mathematical problems (Loewenstein & Ross, 1992). Most patients—85 percent in the Putnam survey—have at least one personality who is a child, and more than half of Putnam's subjects had at least one personality of the opposite sex. Recent surveys have found an average of about thirteen subordinate personalities per patient (Kluft, 1984b; Putnam, Guroff, Silberman, et al., 1986). The younger the patient was when the first subordinate personality appeared, the more subordinates he or she is likely to have.

Childhood Abuse In any given constellation of personalities, the theme of abuse is likely to be present, and it usually matches the patient's reported history. In the Putnam survey only 3 out of 100 patients did not report some significant trauma in childhood. The most common was sexual abuse, reported by 83 percent of the patients, and in 68 percent of the patients this sexual abuse involved incest. Three-fourths of the patients also claimed to have suffered repeated physical abuse in childhood, and almost half reported having witnessed a violent death, usually of a parent or sibling, during their early years (Putnam, Guroff, Silberman, et al., 1986). The Putnam findings have been roughly duplicated by other studies (Boon & Draijer, 1993; C. A. Ross, Miller, Reagor, et al., 1990).

These nearly unanimous testimonies of abuse suggest that dissociative identity disorder may be a stratagem that terrified children use to distance themselves from the realities of their lives. In support of this view, most patients report that the disorder began in childhood, at a time of severe trauma. (In the Putnam survey, 89 percent reported onset before the age of twelve.) It should be kept in mind, however, that almost all the evidence of childhood abuse is based on retrospective surveys of the patients or their therapists. Some experts (Frankel, 1990; Kihlstrom, Tataryn, & Hoyt, 1993) are concerned that claims of abuse may be biased by the patients' or clinicians' theories of multiple personality. More important, there have been no prospective studies examining the outcomes of children who have been abused. Thus, we do not know whether abused children are more likely to develop dissociative identity disorder than are nonabused children. Finally, we do not know whether the incidence or severity of childhood abuse is any greater for dissociative identity than for other psychological disorders, such as depression or borderline personality disorder (Chapter 11), for which childhood abuse has also been reported to be common. The recall of childhood sexual abuse is itself a highly controversial issue today. (See the box on pages 184–186.)

Even if a connection between childhood abuse and dissociative identity disorder becomes established in the future, researchers will still be left with the task of identifying the mechanism by which the one leads to the other. Many, many children are abused. Why do only some of them—the minority of them—develop multiple identities? Certain studies (E. L. Bliss, 1984, 1986; Spiegel, 1984) have found that people with dissociative identity disorder are easier to hypnotize and in general more suggestible than either the general population or other psychiatric patients. Thus it is possible that hypnotic susceptibility or something related to it, such as proneness to fantasy or the ability to focus attention narrowly, may make some people vulnerable to subdividing their personalities under stress (Kihlstrom, Glisky, & Angiulo, 1994).

Problems in Diagnosis While dissociative identity disorder was once considered very rare, it is now reported much more frequently. In the words of one research team, writing in 1986, "More cases of MPD [multiple-personality disorder] have been reported within the last five years than in the preceding two centuries" (Putnam, Guroff, Silberman, et al., 1986, p. 285). And most of them have been reported in the United States, where public interest in this disorder—aroused by books, movies, and magazine articles on cases such as Eve, Sybil, and Billy Milligan (see the box on page 180)—seems to run highest. Such circumstances, together with the fact that therapists have often used hypnosis in getting dissociative identity disorder patients to switch from one personality to another, raise the possibility that the power of suggestion may be influencing some patients to convert severe but common disorders into more interesting "multiple personalities" (Fahy, 1988; Merskey, 1992).

Alternatively, the rise in the numbers of reported cases may reflect better recognition and diagnosis of the syndrome (C. A. Ross, 1991). People with dissociative identity disorder suffer a wide variety of symptoms besides alternating personalities (Putnam, Guroff, Silberman, et al., 1986; C. A. Ross, Miller, Reagor, et al., 1990). Depression, suicidal behavior, insomnia, amnesia, sexual dysfunction, and panic attacks were all reported by more than half the people in the Putnam and Ross surveys. Many of these patients also "hear voices," the voices of their other personalities (Boon & Draijer, 1993). When such patients first come before a diagnostician, they will report all these symptoms, and if the diagnostician is unfamiliar with or skeptical about dissociative identity disorder, the patient may easily be diagnosed as suffering from some other disorder, such as schizophrenia or depression. Indeed, in the Putnam and Ross surveys, an average of seven years passed between the time the subjects first contacted a mental health professional about symptoms related to dissociative identity disorder and the time when that diagnosis was applied.

In distinguishing false from true cases of multiple personality, one useful criterion is the nature of the accompanying amnesia (Eich, 1986). In false dissociative identity disorder cases, the "amnesia" is usually symmetrical—that is, material learned by one personality is unknown to the other personalities. In true cases, the amnesia is usually asymmetrical: material learned by the primary personality is remembered by all the secondary personalities, but material learned by a secondary personality is not known to the other secondary personalities or to the primary personality. In a discussion of courtroom diagnoses, Coons (1991) lists a number of other criteria. Patients whose subpersonalities change over relatively short periods of time; patients who manifest subpersonalities only under hypnosis; patients whose personality switches are not accompanied by the usual signs (headache, altered appearance); patients who do not show the multiple symptomatology (depression, panic attacks, etc.) typical of dissociative identity disorder—in these cases, according to Coons, the diagnostician should strongly consider the possibility of **malingering,** the conscious faking of symptoms in order to avoid responsibility.

Another interesting finding about dissociative

RECOVERED MEMORY OF CHILDHOOD ABUSE: A MODERN DILEMMA

One day in 1989 Eileen Franklin Lipsker, a twenty-eight-year-old California woman, was at home watching her red-haired, blue-eyed daughter Jessica draw pictures. Jessica twisted her head sideways and looked up at her mother. Suddenly, Lipsker said, she remembered another red-haired, blue-eyed girl who had twisted her head to look up at her. It was Susan Nason, her childhood friend, who had been murdered at age eight—a crime that had never been solved. But Lipsker didn't just see Susan. In the days that followed, she claimed, the memory expanded. Now she saw a man standing over Susan with a rock in his hands, about to bring it down on the girl's head. After twenty years, Lipsker claimed, she remembered witnessing Susan's murder, and the murderer—who, as Lipsker also allegedly recalled, had raped Susan before killing her and had assaulted Lipsker too—was Lipsker's own father, George Franklin. Lipsker went to the police, and Franklin was arrested. In 1990, on the basis of Lipsker's account, together with a child psychiatrist's testimony that people could indeed repress and later recover memories of childhood trauma, Franklin was found guilty of first-degree murder and sentenced to life (Terr, 1994) convicted in prison.

This was only the most sensational of hundreds of recent cases of so-called *recovered memory*—memories of childhood abuse, particularly sexual abuse, that according to the rememberers were repressed and then eventually returned to consciousness. At the same time, "recovery specialists," therapists expert in excavating such memories, have published best-selling books claiming that many, many people with psychological problems are suffering from buried memories of abuse.

*In 1995, Franklin conviction was reversed on appeal.

Eileen Franklin Lipsker testifies about her recovered memory of having seen her father sexually abuse and murder her playmate twenty years before, when she was eight years old. Her testimony resulted in her father's conviction and imprisonment.

In the past five years, recovered memory has generated huge public interest, stimulated by magazine articles and television talk shows. This fascination, in turn, has prompted a wave of skepticism. According to some observers, many recovered memories of abuse are nothing more than the product of suggestion—and hypnosis—by irresponsible therapists. Such skepticism, however, is mild compared with the outrage of parents who say they have been wrongly accused. Some are fighting back in court, and not just against their children but against the therapists in whose offices these alleged memories have surfaced. In 1994 a California court awarded one man $500,000 in damages from the therapists under whose care his daughter claimed to recall that he had molested her.

How can false memories be distinguished from true ones? This question has prompted a flurry of research, which so far has established a few principles. First, it is apparently possible to forget and then remember a childhood sexual trauma. In one study, researchers asked a national sample of psychologists whether they had been sexually abused as children and, if so, whether they had ever forgotten this. Almost one-quarter of those in the sample responded that they had been abused. Of these, 40 percent reported that during some period of their lives they had forgotten all or part of the abuse (Feldman-Summers & Pope, 1994).

That study, however, relied on self-report. Another researcher, L. M. Williams (1994), began her study with records of documented abuse. Using one hospital's files on 206 girls, ages 10 months to 12 years, who had received medical treatment following verified sexual abuse in the early 1970s, Williams tracked down as many of those girls, now women, as she could and asked them if they would participate in a survey about women treated at that hospital. More than half consented, and in the course of a three-hour interview, they were asked about many things. But when the question of childhood sexual abuse was put to them, 38 percent did not report the incident for which the hospital records showed they had been treated. Perhaps they were simply withholding this information, out of a sense of privacy. Probably not, says Williams, for 68 percent of these "nonreporters" told the interviewer about *other* episodes of childhood abuse.

So apparently people can forget true episodes of abuse. And according to other recent research, they can remember false episodes of abuse. The latter process seems to hinge on what is called *source amnesia.* In storing a memory, the brain distributes it among various areas—the sounds of the memory in one part, the sight of it in another part, and so on. Information as to the *source* of a memory, when and where the thing happened—in life, in a movie, in a story told to the person—seems to be stored primarily in the frontal cortex, and this information is more fragile than other parts of memory. People often remember things but forget the source (e.g., recalling a face but forgetting where they know it from). Or they misidentify the source (claiming, e.g., that they remember an event from childhood when in fact they have only been told about it).

According to some researchers, source amnesia is what is happening in many cases of recovered memory. The rememberers are not inventing the memory; they are simply misattributing it—to their own lives. Where, then, does it come from?

One possibility is the media: the talk shows, magazine articles, and books mentioned earlier. An item of special interest to researchers is Ellen Bass and Laura Davis' *The Courage to Heal,* the so-called bible of recovery specialists. This 1988 book, which has no doubt given needed comfort to numerous survivors of childhood abuse, may also have confused many other people. One of its main premises is that a great number of people are victims of incest but don't realize they were abused. For readers who are in doubt, the book offers a list of things they might recall, ranging from the relatively harmless, such as being held in a way that made them uneasy, to the clearly criminal, such as rape. Then readers are told, "If you are unable to remember any specific instances like the ones mentioned above but still feel that something abusive happened to you, it probably did" (p. 21). Abuse can also be deduced from psychological symptoms, the authors claim, and they list the symptoms, including depression, self-destructive thoughts, low self-esteem, and sexual dysfunction—in other words, "symptoms" experienced by many, many people, including the children of irreproachable parents. In a recent survey of several hundred families involved in recovered-memory accusations, *The Courage to Heal* was implicated "in almost all the cases" (H. Wakefield & Underwager, 1992, p. 486).

Another possible source of suggestion is therapists. Psychologist Elizabeth Loftus recently reported a case in which a man, whose daughter claimed to have recovered memories of his molesting her, hired a private investigator to go to the daughter's therapist. The investigator pretended that she was seeking psychological help; her complaint was nightmares and insomnia. By the fourth session the therapist had declared the investigator a probable incest survivor, a diagnosis she said was "confirmed on the basis of the 'classic symptoms' of body memory and sleep disorders. When the patient insisted that she had no memory of such events, the therapist assured her that this was often the case" (Loftus, 1993, p. 530). The therapist recommended that she read *The Courage to Heal.*

The fact that therapists specializing in recovered memory often unearth such memories through hypnosis and hypnotic age regression (telling the patient, under hypnosis, that he or she is now a child) only increases people's concerns about such therapy, for the research on memories obtained through hypnosis seriously questions their accuracy (Nash, 1987; Smith, 1983). Under hypnosis, for example, people have remembered being abducted by aliens (Gordon, 1991).

But can the memory of a traumatic event actually be planted in a person's brain? According to several recent studies, the answer is yes. In one experiment (Loftus & Coan, in press) the researchers were reluctant to instill a memory of sexual abuse, so they chose instead the widespread childhood fear of getting lost in a store. One fourteen-year-old subject, Chris, was told by his older brother, Jim, that their mother had lost Chris in a shopping mall when he was five. Jim told Chris the story briefly, with few details. Then, for several days afterward, Chris was questioned about the episode, and he began to recover the memory. On the second day he recalled how he felt when he was lost; on the fourth day he reported what his mother had said to him when she found him. Within a few weeks he remembered a great deal more:

> I was with you guys for a second and then I think I went over to look at the toy store, the Kay-bee toy and uh, we got lost and I was looking around and I thought, "Uh-oh. I'm in trouble now." . . . I thought I was never going to see my family again. I was really scared you know. And then this old man, I think he was wearing a blue flannel, came up to me . . . he was kind of old. He was kind of bald on top . . . he had like a ring of gray hair . . . and he had glasses. (Loftus, 1993, p. 532)

When Chris was finally debriefed, he was incredulous. By that time, he remembered the "episode" very well.

But being lost is not the same as being molested. As noted, the researchers in this case did not feel it was safe to implant a memory of abuse, but such an experiment took place informally in the widely publicized case of Paul Ingram. Ingram, a county sheriff in Olympia, Washington, was arrested in 1988 after his two daughters, ages eighteen and twenty-two, claimed to have retrieved memories of being abused by him. Ingram was at first bewildered by the accusations, but gradually he claimed that he remembered episodes in which he had assaulted the girls. Soon the accusations escalated. One daughter, who had read books on satanic ritual abuse and had seen "satanic abuse" survivors on *Geraldo,* now remembered that Ingram had forced her to take part in satanic rituals—she estimated that she had attended 850 such events—in which babies were chopped up. Under prodding by police investigators, Ingram remembered the satanic rituals too.

Social psychologist Richard Ofshe, an authority on cults and mind control, was brought in by the prosecution to question Ingram. To determine how suggestible Ingram was, Ofshe told him a lie: that one of his daughters and one of his sons were now claiming that he had forced them to have sex with each other. At first, as before, Ingram seemed puzzled, but by his third meeting with Ofshe, he proudly produced a three-page confession, describing how he had forced the two children to have sex and how he had watched and including numerous details of their intercourse. Ofshe eventually concluded that all of Ingram's memories of the abuse he had inflicted were fantasies, the product of suggestion by the investigators questioning him. Ingram concluded the same thing—too late to retract his guilty plea. He was convicted of rape and sentenced to twenty years in prison (L. Wright, 1994).

No one involved in the recovered-memory controversy denies that children are sexually abused (including many whose memories of abuse require no recovery). Nor, in the face of the studies cited above, would most experts claim that all recovered memories of abuse are false. Clearly, some that are called true are false, with terrible consequences for the accused, and some that are called false are true, with the equally traumatic consequences for the accusers. What would be possible, however, is a commitment on the part of therapists to search for confirming physical evidence whenever possible. Such evidence can help to separate false charges from the true.

identity disorder patients, and another possible aid in separating true from false cases, is that their physiology—brain waves, pain sensitivity, and skin conductance—may vary significantly depending on which personality is in charge (S. D. Miller & Triggiano, 1992). For example, in a study of evoked brain potentials—that is, the brain waves elicited by various stimuli—Putnam (1984) compared eleven dissociative identity disorder patients with ten controls who had been asked to simulate the disorder. In the true patients, the brain waves varied much more from personality to personality than they did in the controls. The different personalities of a single patient may also score very differently on standardized personality tests. Even handedness and eyeglass prescription may shift from personality to personality within a single patient (Putnam, 1991a).

The same person—a dissociative disorder patient—produced these dramatically different handwriting samples under the influence of different personalities.

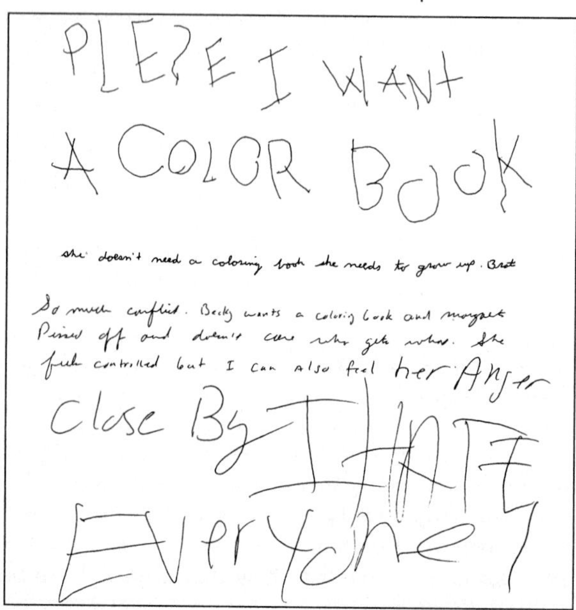

Dissociative identity disorder is anywhere from three to nine times more common in women than in men (G. Peterson, 1991; Putnam, Guroff, Silberman, et al., 1986). Though, as noted, it is said by its victims to begin in childhood—and some cases have been identified in childhood (G. Peterson, 1991; Putnam, 1991b)—most cases are not diagnosed until late adolescence or early adulthood, after repeated misdiagnosis. The disorder tends to be chronic, though the frequency of personality switches decreases over time.

Depersonalization Disorder

Like fugue and dissociative identity disorder, **depersonalization disorder** involves a disruption of personal identity. Here, though, the disruption occurs without amnesia. The central feature of this syndrome is depersonalization, a sense of strangeness or unreality in oneself. People with depersonalization disorder feel as though they have become cut off from themselves and are viewing themselves from the outside, or that they are functioning like robots or living in a dream. The sense of strangeness usually extends to the body. Patients may feel as though their extremities have grown or shrunk, as though their bodies were operating mechanically, as though they were dead, or as though they were imprisoned inside the body of somebody else.

These feelings of strangeness in the self are often accompanied by **derealization,** a feeling of strangeness about the world: other people, like oneself, seem robotic or dead or somehow unreal, like actors in a play. People experiencing depersonalization or derealization may also have episodes of *déjà vu* (French for "already seen"), the sense of having been in a place or situation before, when one knows that this is not the case. Or they may have the opposite experience, *jamais vu*, (French for "never seen"), the sense, when one is in a familiar place or situation, of never having encountered it before. In the view of cognitive psychology, depersonalization and derealization constitute a failure of recognition memory. The person is unable to match current experience with past experience, as might happen on entering a familiar room that has been redecorated (G. Reed, 1988). Depersonalization often involves reduced emotional responsiveness, a loss of interest in others and in the world in general. People afflicted with depersonalization do not lose touch with reality. They know that their perceptions of strangeness are wrong. Nevertheless, the perceptions are frightening. The person may feel that he or she is going insane.

Depersonalization can occur briefly in the course of normal life. When people wake up from sleep or when they have had a bad scare or when they are very tired or practicing meditation, they may have a brief spell of depersonalization. Depersonalization also occurs as a component of other psychological disorders, particularly anxiety disorders, depression, and schizophrenia, and it is a common symptom of the other dissociative disorders (Simeon & Hollander, 1993). Finally, depersonalization often occurs after "near-death experiences," in which people are rescued at the last moment from drowning or other accidents. In a study of people who survived an airplane crash landing, 54 percent felt detached and estranged from themselves (Sloan, 1988). Some research indicates that the experience of depersonalization *during* a traumatic event is adaptive—that it decreases the risk of depression and anxiety after the event (Shilony & Grossman, 1993). Possibly, the sense that this is happening in a dream or to someone else protects the person from suffering the full impact of the trauma. At the same time, other evidence (McFarlane, 1986; Solomon, Mikulincer, & Benbenishty, 1989a) suggests that people who develop pronounced feelings of depersonalization *after* a trauma are more likely to succumb to a full-blown posttraumatic stress disorder (Chapter 7).

A brief spell of depersonalization connected with a trauma does not, however, constitute depersonalization disorder. The diagnosis is made only when depersonalization (with or without a trauma) is severe and persistent enough to disrupt the person's life. The syndrome is apparently rare (Steinberg, 1991). It tends to strike people in their teens or twenties (Simeon & Hollander, 1993), and onset may be rapid. Recovery, on the other hand, tends to be slow, and a chronic condition may develop. The following case illustrates the basic features of the disorder:

> A 20-year-old male college student sought psychiatric consultation because he was worried that he might be going insane. For the past two years he had experienced increasingly frequent episodes of feeling "outside" himself. These episodes were accompanied by a sense of deadness in his body. In addition, during these periods he was uncertain of his balance and frequently stumbled into furniture. . . . His thoughts seemed "foggy" as well, in a way that reminded him of having received intravenous anesthetic agents for an appendectomy some five years previously.
>
> The patient's subjective sense of lack of control was especially troublesome, and he would fight it by shaking his head and saying "stop" to himself. This would momentarily clear his mind and restore his sense of autonomy, but only temporarily, as the feelings of deadness and of being outside himself would return. . . .
>
> At the time the patient came for treatment, he was experiencing these symptoms about twice a week, and each incident lasted from three to four hours. On several occasions the episodes had occurred while he was driving his car and was alone; worried that he might have an accident, he had stopped driving unless someone accompanied him. Increasingly he had begun to discuss this problem with his girl friend, and eventually she had become less affectionate toward him, complaining that he had lost his sense of humor and was almost totally self-preoccupied. . . .
>
> Because he had had a cousin hospitalized for many years with severe mental illness, the patient had begun to wonder if a similar fate might befall him. (Spitzer, Skodol, Gibbon, et al., 1981, pp. 112–113)

PERSPECTIVES ON THE DISSOCIATIVE DISORDERS

Almost all theories of the dissociative disorders begin with the assumption that dissociation is a way in which people escape from situations that are beyond their coping powers. As for how the process occurs, and how the resulting disorders should be treated, these questions receive different answers.

The Psychodynamic Perspective: Defense against Anxiety

It was in the late nineteenth century that the dissociative disorders were first extensively studied. A pioneer in this research was the French psychologist Pierre Janet (1929), who originated the idea of mental dissociation. Under certain circumstances, Janet claimed, one or more divisions of mental functioning could become split off from the others and operate outside conscious awareness. Janet called this phenomenon *désagrégation*, which was translated into English as "dissociation." (Hence the name of this category.) Janet and others considered the dissociative disorders a subdivision of the hysterical neuroses, disabilities that appeared to be neurologically based when in fact they were psychologically based. But it was left to Janet's contemporary Sigmund Freud to enunciate a *cause* of dissociation, in the theory of hysteria that was to become the basis for his entire theory of the mind.

Dissociation as Defense Freud, as we have seen, believed that many basic human wishes were in direct conflict with either reality or the superego and that the result of this conflict was painful anxiety. To protect the mind against the anxiety, the ego repressed the wish and mounted defenses against it. The dissociative disorders—indeed, all the neuroses—were simply extreme and maladaptive defenses. Classical psychodynamic theory still holds to this position on the dissociative disorders. Dissociative amnesia, for example, is regarded by Freudian theorists as a simple case of repression. Fugue and dissociative identity disorder are more complicated in that the person also acts out the repressed wish directly or symbolically—the fugue patient goes off and has adventures, the person with dissociative identity disorder becomes a different, "forbidden" self—while the ego maintains amnesia for the episode, thus protecting the mind against the strictures of the superego.

This theory has on its side the observation that dissociative disorders do appear to operate in such a way as to grant wishes that the person could not otherwise satisfy (as illustrated in the above case histories). But with its strict division between conscious and unconscious, the Freudian model does not seem to offer an adequate explanation of dissociative identity disorder, in which the "forbidden" self does not in fact remain unconscious but instead seizes the consciousness. Several writers (B. G. Braun & Sachs, 1985; Kluft, 1987, 1991; Putnam, 1989) have put forth more complex theories of dissociative identity disorder, in line with current psychodynamic thinking. Kluft's hypothesis is that this condition develops when a child with a special capacity to dissociate—that is, to focus intensely on one thing, to the exclusion of others—is exposed to overwhelming stress. Imagine, for example, a young girl who has an imaginary companion (as many dissociative identity disorder patients report having had [Sanders, 1992]). If she were sexually abused and no adult were available to minister to her distress, she might expand the imaginary companion to contain the abuse experience, thus walling it off from herself. (This would help to account for the frequent reports of child subordinates in multiple personality.) She might also develop a third, punitive personality, based on the abuser, as a refraction of her guilt feelings, and also a "protector" personality, in answer to her need for protection. Over time, this constellation could be expanded to contain and enclose other upsetting experiences. The subpersonalities might remain dormant for years, but under the stress of later traumas they could emerge as overt, alternating personalities—in other words, dissociative identity disorder.

Treating Dissociation Psychodynamic therapy is the most common treatment for the dissociative disorders. Since, according to this perspective, the dissociative disorders arise through the same mechanism as the anxiety disorders—conflict, anxiety, defense—the treatment is basically the same as for the anxiety disorders: to expose and "work through" the traumatic material that the ego is defending against. With the dissociative disorders the therapist's special task is to show patients that the split-off material is not "other" or "outside" but, on the contrary, a part of them, which must be reintegrated into the self (Marmer, 1991).

Exposing the repressed material may be no easy task, however. After all, the whole thrust of the dissociative disorders is to protect that material from exposure. In amnesia, fugue, and dissociative identity disorder, the traditional method of bringing forth the lost material has been hypnosis. (Barbiturates may achieve the same effect.) Under hypnosis, fugue and amnesia patients will often reveal the events covered by the amnesia, and people with dissociative identity disorder will bring forth subordinate personalities. Indeed, many cases of dissociative identity disorder are *discovered* through hypnosis. A disadvantage of hypnosis is that in some cases it seems to bring on or exacerbate dissociative symptoms. But since it also uncovers dissociated material, most treatments for dissociative

Hypnosis has been shown to be helpful in treating amnesia, fugue, and dissociative identity disorder, allowing some patients to recover the material that had been lost to their memories.

identity disorder still rely on this method (Putnam & Loewenstein, 1993). After the material is uncovered, the therapist will try, through gentle, supportive discussion, to get the patient to confront and integrate the banished portions of his or her experience.

Therapeutic outcome studies (Coons, 1986; Kluft, 1988) indicate that this may be a long process. As we pointed out earlier, fugue tends to remit without treatment, and dissociative amnesia may also. Hence the usual goal of therapy in these disorders is to recover and integrate the lost material so that the patient doesn't suffer a relapse. But dissociative identity disorder is far more stubborn. The more personalities, the more difficult the integration (Kluft, 1986), and when integration is achieved, it can crumble if the person experiences stress or if, as sometimes happens, another, previously undetected personality surfaces.

The Behavioral and Sociocultural Perspectives: Dissociation as a Social Role

Learning to Dissociate The dissociative disorders constitute a problem for learning theory, for it is almost impossible to discuss these disorders without invoking concepts such as awareness and identity—indeed, they are fundamentally disorders of awareness and identity—and such concepts are not part of the behaviorist's vocabulary (Sackeim & Devanand, 1991). What the behaviorists have done is to conceptualize the dissociative disorders as a form of learned coping response, the production of symptoms in order to obtain rewards or relief from stress.

According to the behaviorists, the dissociative disorders, like many other psychological disorders, are the result of a person's adopting a social role that is reinforced by its consequences (Ullmann & Krasner, 1975). In amnesia, fugue, and dissociative identity disorder, the rewarding consequence is protection from stressful events. Fugue, for example, gets its victims away from situations painful to them, and amnesia for the fugue protects them from painful consequences of their actions during the fugue. Note the similarity between this interpretation and the psychodynamic view: in both cases, the focus is on motivation, and the motivation is escape. The difference is that in the psychodynamic view the process is unconscious, whereas in the behavioral view dissociative behavior is maintained by reinforcement like any other behavior.

Like the behaviorists, sociocultural theorists see dissociative symptoms as the product of social reinforcement. In a theory put forth by Spanos (1994), for example, dissociative identity disorder is a strategy that people use to evoke sympathy and escape responsibility for certain of their actions. Those actions, they say, were performed by some other, nonresponsible part of themselves. According to Spanos, this process is aided by hypnosis: patients learn the "hypnotic role" and in that role produce the kind of behavior that the clinician hypnotizing them seems to want. Once they produce it, the clinician validates it with an "expert" diagnosis, and that diagnosis results in a number of possible rewards: relief from distress, an ability to control others, permission for misbehavior, and even, in some cases, avoidance of criminal pro-

Kenneth Bianchi, the "Hillside Strangler," made an unsuccessful attempt to prove that he was not guilty by reason of insanity, in the form of dissociative identity disorder.

ceedings. The clinician is rewarded too, by attention: he or she has uncovered another case of this celebrated disorder. So, having created the disorder, both therapist and patient come to believe in its existence, for they have good reason to do so.

To test this hypothesis, Spanos and his colleagues designed an experiment based on the case of Kenneth Bianchi, the so-called Hillside strangler, who raped and murdered several women in the Los Angeles area during the early 1980s. Upon arrest, Bianchi claimed he was innocent, and he was sent for a psychiatric evaluation, during which he supposedly showed evidence of dissociative identity disorder. What happened was as follows. First Bianchi was hypnotized. Then the clinician described the situation to him as one in which another, hidden "part" of him might emerge. Bianchi was given an easy way to signal the arrival of that part. The clinician said to him:

> I've talked a bit to Ken but I think that perhaps there might be another part of Ken that I haven't talked to. And I would like to communicate with that other part. And I would like that other part to come to talk to me. . . . And when you're here, lift the left hand off the chair to signal to me that you are here. Would you please come, Part, so I can talk to you. . . . Part, would you come and lift Ken's hand to indicate to me that you are here. . . . Would you talk to me, Part, by saying "I'm here"? (Schwarz, 1981, pp. 142–143)

Bianchi answered yes and then had the following exchange with the clinician (B = Bianchi; C = clinician):

> C: Part, are you the same as Ken or are you different in any way?
> B: I'm not him.
> C: You're not him. Who are you? Do you have a name?
> B: I'm not Ken.
> C: You're not him? Okay. Who are you? Tell me about yourself. Do you have a name I can call you by?
> B: Steve. You can call me Steve.
>
> (Schwarz, 1981, pp. 139–140)

"Steve" went on to say that he hated Ken because Ken was so nice; that with the help of a cousin, he had murdered a number of women; and that Ken knew nothing either about him (Steve) or about the murders. When he was released from his hypnotic state, Bianchi was "amnesic" for all that Steve had said. He then pleaded not guilty by reason of insanity, the insanity being dissociative identity disorder. (The defense failed. See the box on page 180.)

What Spanos and his colleagues did was to subject a number of college students to variations on the procedure Bianchi went through. The students were instructed to play the role of accused murderers, and they were divided among three experimental conditions. In the "Bianchi condition" the subjects were hypnotized and then put through an interview taken almost verbatim from the Bianchi interview. In a second, "hidden-part condition" the subjects were also hypnotized, after which they were told that under hypnosis people often reveal a hidden part of themselves. However, in contrast to the Bianchi condition, that hidden part was not directly addressed, nor was it asked whether it was different from the subject. In the third, control condition, the subjects were not hypnotized, and they were given only vague information about hidden parts of the self.

After these experimental conditions were set up, all the subjects were questioned about whether they had a second personality. They were also asked about the murders. In the Bianchi condition 81 percent of the subjects came up with second personalities that had different names from themselves, and in the majority of cases this second personality admitted guilt for the murders. In the hidden-part condition only 31 percent revealed second personalities with new names, though here again the majority of second personalities confessed to the murders. In the control condition only 13 percent confessed to the murders, and no one produced a new personality with a different name.

Of course, these students were only playing the role of murderers. Even so, it appears that when the situation demands, people who are given appropriate cues can manufacture a subordinate personality and will shift blame onto the subordinate. Furthermore, in keeping with Spanos' theory, those students who produced a second personality in some measure came to believe in it, or at least knew how to design it skillfully. When, in a second session, these "multiple-personality" subjects were given the same personality test twice, one time for each personality, their new subordinate personalities tested very differently from their dominant personalities even though most of these subjects claimed to have amnesia for what they had said under hypnosis (Spanos, Weekes, & Bertrand, 1985).

What this suggests, according to Spanos (1994), is that most cases of dissociative identity disorder are strategic enactments. Many of these patients are described by their therapists as highly imaginative people, with rich fantasy lives. And as we saw, they are very susceptible to hypnosis. If such people were placed in difficult circumstances from which "multiple personality" would help them escape and if they were hypnotized and, under hypnosis, essentially told *how* to produce a subordinate personality, they could in fact develop one and come to believe in it.

Nonreinforcement According to behavioral and sociocultural theory, the way to treat dissociative symptoms is to stop reinforcing them. In a case of dissociative identity disorder, for example, therapists, friends, and family members would express no interest in subordinate personalities. At the same time, they would expect the patient to take responsibility for actions supposedly produced by subordinate personalities. Using such an approach with a woman who reported three subordinate personalities, Kohlenberg (1973) found that the subordinates' behaviors became less frequent when they were not reinforced. The therapist may also help patients deal with emotions that they are presumably pushing off onto subordinate personalities. In one case a passive patient, L, had a very aggressive subordinate personality, "Toni." Once L was given assertiveness training and taught how to express anger, Toni disappeared (J. Price & Hess, 1979).

The Cognitive Perspective: Memory Dysfunction

Cognitive theorists view the dissociative syndromes as fundamentally disorders of memory. In each case, what has been dissociated is all or part of the patient's "autobiography." As we have seen, the patient's skills (procedural memory) and general knowledge (semantic memory) are usually intact. What is impaired is the patient's episodic memory, or record of personal experience. As we have also seen, it is only partially impaired. Patients may still show evidence that they have implicit memory of their past. What they don't have is explicit memory for the dissociated material, the ability to retrieve it into consciousness.

Retrieval Failure What causes this selective impairment of explicit episodic memory? Three different cognitive theories have been proposed. One has to do with what is called *state-dependent memory.* A number of studies have shown that people have an easier time recalling an event if they are in the same mood state as the one they were in when the event occurred (Blaney, 1986; G. H. Bower, 1981). Hence memories established in an extreme emotional state—for example, the kind of severe traumatic reaction that is thought to set off dissociative amnesia and fugue—may be "lost" simply because they are linked to a mood that is not likely to recur. A dramatic case of state-dependent memory is that of Sirhan Sirhan, the man convicted of killing Robert F. Kennedy. In the waking state, Sirhan claimed amnesia for the crime, but under hypnosis his mood became more and more agitated, as it had been during the crime, and in this state he not only recalled the murder but reenacted parts of it (G. H. Bower, 1981).

Such a mechanism may also help to explain dissociative identity disorder. Typically, the different personalities are characterized by different mood states. Therefore, state dependency may lead one personality to have amnesia for the experiences of another. By the same token, situations that produce strong emotion may cause a shift from one personality to a different personality, one with moods and memories consistent with that emotion. For example, if a quiet-tempered patient is made angry, this may cause a sudden shift to a hostile subordinate personality, for that is the personality that can process and express the anger.

A second cognitive theory of dissociation has to do with *control elements,* facts about oneself which other information is categorized under and which

Sirhan Sirhan gave dramatic evidence of state-dependent memory: awake, he said he did not remember having killed Senator Robert F. Kennedy; but in an agitated state under hypnosis he remembered and even reenacted the murder.

therefore can activate or inhibit the retrieval of that other information. According to Schacter and his colleagues, a person's name may be the ultimate control element of episodic memory. If the name is forgotten, the life is forgotten. Schacter and his team, for example, described a case in which a patient hospitalized for amnesia had almost no episodic memory. He knew, however, that he had a nickname, "Lumberjack," and also that he had worked for a messenger service. As it turned out, it was his coworkers at the messenger service who had given him that nickname. So, remembering the name he had at work, he could remember his work, but not remembering his real name, he could not remember the rest of his life (Schacter, Wang, Tulving, et al., 1982). This theory is supported by the finding that in some cases, but not all, amnesia remits once the person is confronted with his or her name (Kaszniak, Nussbaum, Berren, et al., 1988).

A third hypothesis concerns *self-reference.* According to Kihlstrom (1987, 1990), the originator of this theory, the way we retrieve autobiographical memories is by linking them to our representation of the self. We don't just remember our high school prom; we remember it as something that happened to *us.* Other kinds of memory, on the other hand, are more independent of self-reference. When we think that two and two make four, we don't think of this as involving us. According to Kihlstrom, this difference in self-reference between the different categories of memory may help to account for dissociative amnesia and fugue. In these states, what is lost is the representation of the self, and therefore episodic memory, for it depends on self-reference. But semantic memory and procedural memory remain in place, for they are not based on self-reference.

Improving Memory Retrieval To date, there has been little work on cognitive therapy for dissociative disorders. Nevertheless, many therapists use cognitive mechanisms in treating dissociative patients. For example, in the case of Jane Doe at the beginning of this chapter, the therapist was appealing to her implicit memory when he asked her to punch in telephone numbers at random. Other patients have been asked to state the first name that comes to mind or to say which of a list of cities "rings a bell," the hope being that the name or city will be the patient's own, arising from implicit memory. There is also the possibility that retrieved facts will act as control elements, releasing the information stored under them. State dependency has also been appealed to. As in the case of Sirhan Sirhan, many therapists have tried to reinstate strong emotions in their patients, first under hypnosis and then in the waking state, in order to spring the lock on state-dependent memories.

The Biological Perspective: Brain Dysfunction

The dissociative disorders, as we have pointed out, involve psychiatric symptoms that look like the product of neurological disease but are thought instead to be the result of psychological processes. Are they? According to neuroscience researchers, some so-called dissociative disorders may be neurological disorders after all. According to one theory (Mesulam, 1981; Schenk & Bear, 1981), the dissociative syndromes may be a byproduct of undiagnosed epilepsy (Chapter 16). Epileptic-type seizures have been associated with dissociative identity disorder ever since the disorder was first described (Charcot & Marie, 1892). Conversely, some victims of epilepsy have reported dissociative experiences such as depersonalization, déja vu, and feelings of demonic possession following seizures. This theory may apply to certain dissociative conditions, but it is unlikely to explain dissociative identity disorder, where the symptoms are far more elaborate than the dissociative experiences reported by epileptics.

A second, more radical hypothesis, is that we all have within us rebellious subparts—parts that know a different reality, live a different life—but that the normal brain knows how to suppress these subparts. Dissociative symptoms arise when some damage or other change in the brain releases the neurological mechanisms suppressing these subparts, thus allowing them to express themselves. This view is supported by studies of patients who have undergone corpus callostomy, an operation that severs the connection between the right and left hemispheres of the brain, to relieve uncontrollable epilepsy. One such patient, described by Gur (1982), found after the operation that her left hand was continually doing things she disapproved of. It stole money, pushed her against walls, unbuttoned her blouse in public. The patient began using the name "Lefty" to refer to the part of herself that was doing these things, a situation not unlike dissociative identity disorder.

The part-suppression hypothesis is also supported by evidence that in dissociative identity patients the primary personality and the main subordinate personality are controlled by opposite hemispheres of the brain. For example, Henninger (1992) studied a nineteen-year-old woman whose main subordinate personality was a nine-year-old girl. On dichotic listening tests, in which different sounds are presented to the right and left ears, the nineteen-year-old depended mainly on right-hemisphere processing. When the nine-year-old subordinate was in control, however, she relied chiefly on left-hemisphere processing.

The part-suppression theory is even more tentative than the epilepsy theory. Furthermore, neither of them rules out psychological causation. What these neuroscience researchers are speculating about is the neurological processes underlying dissociative states. Such processes, in their view, could be activated by psychological stress as well as by neurological disease or injury (Sackeim & Devanand, 1991).

SOMATOFORM DISORDERS

The primary feature of the **somatoform disorders** is, as the name suggests, that psychological conflicts take on a somatic, or physical, form. Some patients complain of physical discomfort—stomach pains, breathing problems, and so forth. Others show an actual loss or impairment of some normal physiological function: suddenly they can no longer see or swallow or move their right leg. In either case, there is no organic evidence to explain the symptom, while there *is* evidence (or at least a strong suspicion) that the symptom is linked to psychological factors. We will discuss four syndromes: body dysmorphic disorder, hypochondriasis, somatization disorder, and conversion disorder.

Body Dysmorphic Disorder

Many of us are preoccupied with our appearance. We worry that we are too fat or too thin, that we have too little hair or too much (in the wrong places), that our noses are too big, our ears too prominent, and so on. Such concerns are normal, particularly during adolescence. Some people, however, are so distressed over how they look that they can no longer function normally. Such people are said to have **body dysmorphic disorder,** defined as preoccupation with an imagined or grossly exaggerated defect in appearance.

Most people with this condition complain of facial flaws, such as the quality of the skin or the shape of the nose. Another common complaint is thinning hair. But any part of the body, or several parts at once, may be the focus of the concern. People with this disorder are not delusional (though they may eventually become so). If confronted, they will usually admit that they are exaggerating. Nevertheless, they suffer great unhappiness. They may spend several hours a day looking in mirrors and trying to correct the defect—recombing the hair, picking the skin. In one reported case, a woman spent hours each day cutting her hair to try to make it symmetrical (Hollander, Liebowitz, Winchel, et al., 1989). People with this disorder may try to camouflage the imagined defect—for example, by growing a beard to cover "scars." Some resort to plastic surgery, which, however, rarely satisfies them. Many of them repeatedly seek reassurance. (Again, this does not reassure.) To avoid being seen, they may drop out of school, quit their jobs, avoid dating, and become housebound. In severe cases, the person may contemplate or even attempt suicide.

Body dysmorphic disorder is a relatively new *DSM* category, and there are no reliable figures on its prevalence. Such figures may be slow in coming, for according to some researchers victims are ashamed of the disorder and tend not to seek treatment. Most patients are unmarried, and the average age of onset is fifteen (K. A. Phillips, McElroy, Keck, et al., 1993).

Not surprisingly, the disorder is associated with social phobia; it is also associated with depression and can sometimes be treated with antidepressant drugs. But the syndrome most closely associated with body dysmorphic disorder is obsessive-compulsive disorder. Both conditions involve obsessional thinking as well as compulsive behaviors (e.g., mirror checking); both tend to appear in adolescence and to be chronic; both may respond to the same drugs, such as Prozac; in some cases, both occur in the same families; finally, both may coexist in the same patient (K. A. Phillips, 1991; K. A. Phillips, McElroy, Keck, et al., 1993). It is possible that body dysmorphic disorder is a form of obsessive-compulsive disorder. This and other questions about the syndrome will not be answered until more cases are studied.

Hypochondriasis

The primary feature of **hypochondriasis** is a gnawing fear of disease—a fear maintained by constant misinterpretation of physical signs and sensations as abnormal. Hypochondriacs have no real physical disability; what they have is a conviction that a disability is about to appear. Hence they spend each day watching for the first signs, and they soon find them. One day the heart will skip a beat, or the body will register some new pain. This is then interpreted as the onset of the disease. Often, when they appear at the doctor's office, hypochondriacs have already diagnosed their condition, for they are usually avid readers of articles on health in popular magazines. And when the medical examination reveals that they are perfectly healthy, they are typically incredulous. Soon they will be back in the doctor's office with reports of further symptoms, or they may simply change doctors. Some go through several doctors a year. Others will resort to "miracle" cures, or they will try to cure themselves, either with strenuous health regimens or with pills, of which they typically have large collections.

It should be emphasized that hypochondriacs do not fake their "symptoms." They truly feel the pains they report; they are sincerely afraid that they are about to succumb to some grave disease; and in consequence they suffer terribly, not just from anxiety but also from depression (Kellner, 1992). Insofar as they cannot be reassured by the medical evidence, their fears are irrational. However, these fears do not have the bizarre quality of the disease delusions experienced by psychotics, who will report that their feet are about to fall off or that their brains are shriveling. Hypochondriacs tend to confine their anxieties to more ordinary syndromes, such as heart disease or cancer. Hypochondriac fears are also different from obsessive-compulsive fears of contamination and disease. Obsessive-compulsives know that their fears are groundless, and they try to resist them. Hypochondriacs find their fears quite reasonable and don't see why others question them (Barsky, 1992a; Salkovskis & Warwick, 1986).

Several developmental factors may predispose a person to hypochondriasis. Hypochondriacs are more likely than others to have suffered, or to have had a family member who suffered, a true organic disease, thus making their fears, however unfounded, at least understandable (Barsky, Wool, Barnett, et al., 1994; Kellner, 1985). And if the sick

Molière's comedy *The Imaginary Invalid* was written in the seventeenth century, a time when hypochondriasis was widely regarded as an unsurprisingly common, inevitable disease of civilization.

person in their past was a parent, their symptoms will often resemble the parent's (Kellner, 1985). Finally, there is some evidence that people who had overprotective mothers are more likely to be hypochondriacs (B. Baker & Merskey, 1982; G. Parker & Lipscombe, 1980).

Somatization Disorder

A third somatoform pattern is **somatization disorder,** characterized by numerous and recurrent physical complaints that begin by age thirty, persist for several years, and cause the person to seek medical treatment but cannot be explained medically. Somatization disorder resembles hypochondriasis in that it involves symptoms with no demonstrable physical cause. Yet the two disorders differ in the focus of the patient's distress. What motivates the hypochondriac is the fear of disease, usually a specific disease; the "symptoms" are troubling not so much in themselves but because they indicate the presence of that disease. In contrast, what bothers the victim of somatization disorder is actually the "symptoms" themselves. There is also a difference in their approach to the symptoms. Whereas hypochondriacs may try to be scientific, measuring their blood pressure several times a day and carefully reporting the results, victims of somatization disorder usually describe their symptoms in a vague, dramatic, and exaggerated fashion. Finally, the two disorders differ in the number of complaints. Hypochondriacs often fear one particular disease, and therefore their complaints tend to be limited. In somatization disorder, on the other hand, the complaints are many and varied. Indeed, *DSM-IV* requires that the patient present with at least four pain symptoms, two gastrointestinal symptoms, one sexual symptom, and one symptom that mimics neurological disorder, such as blindness, dizziness, or seizures, before this diagnosis can be made. Like hypochondriacs, somatization patients tend to engage in "doctor shopping," going from one physician to the next in search of the one who will finally diagnose their ailments (Escobar, Burnam, Karno, et al., 1987).

Though the complaints for which they are diagnosed are not organically based, somatization patients may develop actual organic disorders, as a result of unnecessary hospitalization, surgery, and medication. In one case, (Pitman & Moffett, 1981) a patient had averaged one hospitalization per year for the preceding thirty-nine years.

In contrast to hypochondriasis, which affects men and women equally, somatization disorder is much more common in women than in men (Golding, Smith, & Kashner, 1991). Even among women it is rare, affecting only one woman per thousand (Regier, Boyd, Burke, et al., 1988), though less severe forms of somatization are more common, occurring in 4 percent of the population (Katon, Lin, Von Korff, et al., 1991). Full-scale somatization disorder occurs more frequently among less educated people (Swartz, Blazer, George, et al., 1986) and in cultures where the verbal expression of emotional distress is frowned upon (Escobar & Canino, 1989), suggesting that sociocultural factors may play a role in the disorder. Like hypochondriasis, somatization disorder is often accompanied by depression and anxiety (Iezzi & Adams, 1993). In other respects, somatization patients resemble dissociative patients. They too are highly hypnotizable (E. L. Bliss, 1984), and like dissociative identity patients, they tend to report histories of sexual abuse (J. Morrison, 1989).

Conversion Disorder

In hypochondriasis and somatization disorder, there is no physical disability, only fear of or complaints about illness or disability. In **conversion disorder,** there *is* an actual disability: the loss or impairment of some motor or sensory function, although again, there is no organic pathology that would explain the disability. Conversion symptoms vary considerably, but among the most common are blindness, deafness, paralysis, and anesthesia (loss of sensation)—often partial but sometimes total (S. M. Turner, Jacob, & Morrison, 1985). Also common are conversion symptoms that mimic other physical illnesses, such as epilepsy or cancer. For example, some men in non-Western cultures show couvade, a condition in which they experience pains similar to their wives' labor pains during childbirth (Iezzi & Adams, 1993). Like the "symptoms" involved in hypochondriasis and somatization disorder, conversion symptoms are not supported by the medical evidence, but neither are they faked. They are involuntary responses, independent of the person's conscious control. At the same time, they contradict the medical facts. Upon examination, for example, the eyes will be found to be perfectly free from defect or damage, and yet the person is unable to see.

Conversion disorder, formerly known as "hysteria," has played a central role in the history of psychology. As we saw in Chapter 1, it was named and described by Hippocrates, who believed that it was confined to women, particularly childless women (still today, the disorder is at least twice as common in women as in men.) In Hippocrates' view, hysteria was caused by the wanderings of a uterus that was not being put to its proper use. Idle and frustrated, the uterus traveled around inside the body, creating havoc in various organ systems. The Greek word for uterus is *hystera*. Hence the term *hysteria*.

In the nineteenth century, hysteria served as the focal point for debate between psychogenic and biogenic theory. It was the cure of this disorder through hypnosis that laid the foundation for Freud's theory of the unconscious. Interestingly, Freud's explanation of hysteria stressed the same factor as Hippocrates': sexual conflict. Today, many psychologists reject the sexual interpretation, but it is generally agreed that conversion disorders are the result of *some* psychological conflict. According to this view, the conversion symptom serves two important psychological purposes. First, it blocks the person's awareness of internal conflict; this is called the **primary gain.** In addition, it confers the **secondary gain** of excusing the person from responsibilities and attracting sympathy and attention.

One reason psychologists tend to accept the conflict-resolution hypothesis is that many conversion patients (about one-third) seem completely unperturbed by their symptoms—a response known as **la belle indifférence,** or "beautiful indifference." Whereas most people would react with horror to the discovery that they were suddenly half-blind or could no longer walk, "indifferent" conversion patients are undismayed. Typically, they are eager to discuss their symptoms, and will describe them in the most vivid terms, but they do not seem eager to part with them. This paradoxical reaction, like the equanimity of people suffering from dissociative amnesia, has been interpreted by psychodynamic theorists as a sign of relief once the newfound disability supplies a defense against unconscious conflicts and thereby reduces anxiety.

Conversion disorders represent something of a philosophical paradox. On the one hand, the patient's body appears to be in good health. Biologically, conversion patients *can* do whatever it is that they say they can't do. And often they can be made to do it, either by trickery or under hypnosis or drugs. Further evidence for their lack of organic pathology is that the symptoms are often selective. Conversion "epileptics," for example, seldom injure themselves or lose bladder control during attacks, as true epileptics do. Likewise, in conversion blindness, patients rarely bump into things. Furthermore, victims of conversion blindness, when given visual discrimination tests, will often perform either much better or much worse than if they had answered merely at random—a result indicating that they *are* receiving visual input (Kihlstrom, Barnhardt, & Tataryn, 1991; Sackeim, Nordlie, & Gur, 1979). In short, all evidence points to the conclusion that the patient's body is capable of functioning properly. On the other hand, conversion patients by definition are *not* consciously refusing to use parts of their body. The response is involuntary.

This situation is something like the memory problem in dissociative disorders. Just as dissociative patients lose explicit memory but retain implicit memory, so conversion patients lose explicit perception but still show implicit perception. As in the case of DB at the opening of the chapter, these patients show clear evidence that their supposedly disabled organs are in fact operating normally, but they are not aware of those operations. The organ's functioning has been dissociated, as it were, from the patient's conscious awareness (Kihlstrom, Barnhardt, & Tataryn, 1991).

The following case illustrates some characteristic features of this disorder:

> After a minor industrial accident, Ari, a twenty-seven-year-old Israeli, developed paralysis in both legs—a condition for which no organic cause could be found. The paralysis seemed genuine. When pins were pushed into Ari's legs at various points up to the groin, he showed no response whatsoever. Nevertheless, he moved his legs during sleep.
>
> There were several possible explanations for this case. Ari was due shortly to report for military service, and unlike the army, the hospital was an extremely pleasant place. Patients were offered movies, television, and excellent food, and after dinner there was much socializing, which Ari seemed to enjoy. Finally, as a disabled person, Ari would be entitled to a government pension.
>
> Ari's therapists began treatment by making the disability less rewarding. They informed him that because his condition was not organic, he would not be entitled to a pension. They then told him that for the next several weeks he would have to go to bed at eight o'clock, since they were going to give him a drug that required a great deal of sleep. The core of the treatment, however, was the "drug." They told him that it was a new medication that had been very successful in curing paralyzed Vietnam veterans. Actually, it was a placebo, which the doctors were hoping would work by the power of suggestion and at the same time provide a face-saving mechanism—a way of getting well without having to face the charge that he had been well all along.
>
> As the investigators relate, the drug did its job: "Ap-

proximately one hour after his first treatment, a nurse excitedly called us to Ari's room. We rushed to his bedside, where we found that a crowd of staff and patients had gathered. Ari was sitting up, smiling, beads of perspiration on his forehead, tears rolling down his face; he had what appeared to be a look of genuine euphoria. He stated that he was in pain, kept pointing to his toes, and then moved them slightly" (Goldblatt & Munitz, 1976, p. 261). On the second day he could move his toes easily. On the fourth day he could walk without crutches. On the sixth day he could do cartwheels. On the seventh day he was discharged from the hospital. (adapted from Goldblatt & Munitz, 1976)

Conversion, Malingering, or Organic Disorder? With conversion disorder, differential diagnosis is both important and tricky. First, malingering must be ruled out, which is often hard to do. However, malingerers are usually cautious and defensive when questioned about their symptoms, since they are afraid of being caught in a lie. Conversion patients, on the other hand, are typically candid and naive and, as we noted, will sometimes talk eagerly and at length about their disabilities. Furthermore, precisely *because* they are unaware that their organs are functioning normally, conversion patients will sometimes innocently reveal this. Most malingerers, for example, would not be foolish enough to claim blindness and then catch a ball thrown in their direction, but a conversion patient might do this (Kihlstrom, Barnhardt, & Tataryn, 1991).

Second and more difficult is the task of ruling out an actual organic disorder. In some cases, the symptoms constitute "neurological nonsense," as Charcot put it—that is, they directly contradict what we know about the nervous system. For example, in *glove anesthesia,* patients report that the entire hand is numb, from the tips of the fingers to a clear cutoff point at the wrist (see Figure 8.1)—in other words, the area covered by a short glove—whereas if they were suffering from a true neurological impairment, the area of numbness would run in a narrow stripe from the lower arm through one or two of the fingers. Furthermore, the line of demarcation between sensitive and insensitive areas would be much less precise, with some intermediate areas of semisensitivity.

These, however, are the easier cases. In others, the symptoms are uncannily similar to those of true organic disorders. Nevertheless, there may still be certain signs that suggest conversion disorder. (Note the similarity between these criteria and those for distinguishing dissociative from organic amnesia.) These include:

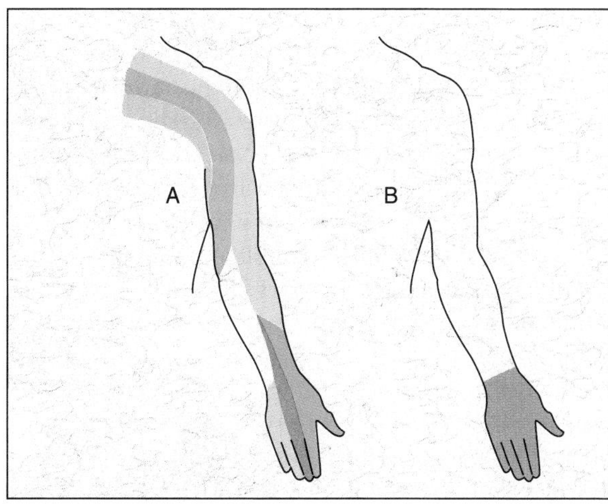

FIGURE 8.1 A patient with glove anesthesia—that is, numbness in the whole hand, ending at the wrist—will be suspected of having conversion disorder. The skin areas served by nerves in the arm are shown in A. Glove anesthesia, shown in B, cannot result from damage to these nerves.

1 *Rapid appearance of symptoms, especially after some psychological trauma.* Organic disorders tend to surface more gradually.
2 *La belle indifférence.* Organic patients are more likely to be upset over their symptoms.
3 *Selective symptoms.* If "paralyzed" legs move during sleep, the paralysis is presumably not organic.

These criteria, in addition to specialized medical tests, are usually the basis for the diagnosis of conversion disorder. However, they are not foolproof—a fact that research has made embarrassingly clear. In one study, the later medical records of fifty-six patients diagnosed as having conversion disorder were compared with the records of fifty-six patients diagnosed as suffering from anxiety or depression. In the "conversion" group, 62.5 percent had since developed signs of organic brain disorder, compared with only 5.3 percent of the anxiety-depression group (Whitlock, 1967). In a more recent study (Gould, Miller, Goldberg, et al., 1986), involving thirty patients, 80 percent were eventually found to have a diagnosable medical disorder as the underlying cause of symptoms originally diagnosed as conversion. Clearly, a substantial proportion of "conversion disorders" are in fact neurological disorders in their early stages, when they are hardest to detect (Marsden, 1986).

Conversion disorder is usually described as rare. It is possible, however, that what is rare is merely the *diagnosis* of conversion disorder. Conversion patients, after all, believe they have a medical problem. Therefore they go to physicians, not to psychotherapists. As we have noted, differential diagnosis is quite tricky. Furthermore, many physicians may associate conversion disorder with the more bizarre symptoms of late-nineteenth-century hysteria—glove anesthesia, inability to swallow, paralysis—thus allowing the more ordinary cases, such as back trouble or blurred vision, to slip by unnoticed. In short, it seems likely that while many "conversion disorders" are actually organic, many conditions diagnosed as organic are actually conversion disorders (M. M. Jones, 1980). Indeed, it is estimated that between 5 and 14 percent of all consultations in a general medical setting are for conversion symptoms (Iezzi & Adams, 1993).

Freud believed that conversion disorder was rare among the poor. Today the reverse is true. The poorer, the less educated, and the less psychologically sophisticated a community, the greater the prevalence of conversion disorder (and also somatization disorder). Rural rather than urban populations also tend to produce conversion cases (Folks, Ford, & Regan, 1984). Not surprisingly, patients in such communities tend to report more bizarre symptoms, whereas more sophisticated patients generally report symptoms that resemble true organic diseases (M. M. Jones, 1980).

PERSPECTIVES ON THE SOMATOFORM DISORDERS

The Psychodynamic Perspective: Defense against Anxiety

Somatizing as Conflict Resolution As we saw in Chapter 1, Freud and Josef Breuer found that if hysterical patients could be induced under hypnosis to talk uninhibitedly about their childhoods and their present problems, their symptoms subsided somewhat. Out of this treatment Freud independently evolved his theory of the "conservation of energy," which stated that strong emotions that were not expressed would lead to somatic symptoms. The distressing memories that Freud's patients revealed to him were often of childhood seduction. In the beginning, Freud assumed that these seductions had actually occurred. Later, he came to believe that they were usually fantasies generated during the Oedipal period. Real or imagined, however, the episode seemed to be reawakened in the mind by the sexual feelings accompanying puberty. The result was anxiety, leading in turn to repression of the memory, leading in turn to the conversion of the forbidden sexual wishes into physical symptoms, which both expressed the wish and prevented its fulfillment. For example, a person with glove anesthesia might be reacting to guilt over masturbation, particularly masturbation associated with Oedipal eroticism. But sexual feelings were not the only cause; hostility too could lead to hysteria. A hysterical paralysis, for instance, could be a defense against the expression of murderous anger. (A person who cannot move cannot kill.) The effectiveness of this mechanism in blocking both the impulse and the person's awareness of the impulse accounted, in Freud's opinion, for *la belle indifférence.* Inconvenient though the symptoms might seem, they relieved the anxiety, and therefore the person was not in a hurry to get rid of them.

In the psychoanalytic view, hypochondriasis and somatization disorder are also defenses against the anxiety produced by unacceptable wishes. Hypochondriacs, Freud reasoned, were people who, deterred by the superego from directing sexual energy onto external objects, redirected it onto themselves. Eventually, this self-directed sexual energy overflowed, transforming itself into physical symptoms. Other psychoanalytic thinkers have blamed hostility rather than sexual desire. In one theory (H. N. Brown & Vaillant, 1981) hypochondriacs are angry over having been unloved or hurt. Rather than express their grievances, they displace them onto the body, imagining *it* to be hurt. Similar conflict-resolution theories have been offered for somatization disorder (Kellner, 1990; Steckel, 1943). In all of the somatoform disorders, psychodynamic theorists also see a strong element of regression. Beset by anxiety, the person regresses to the state of a sick child, in which he or she hopes to receive attention, "babying," and relief from responsibilities—in other words, secondary gains. The primary gain is the relief of anxiety through the use of the defense mechanism.

This conflict-resolution model of somatoform disorders is an old and famous theory, intuitively appealing. But as usual with psychodynamic theories, it is hard to test. Furthermore, there is some evidence against it. For example, as noted earlier, only about one-third of conversion patients seem to show *la belle indifférence.* One study, comparing conversion patients to a group of anxiety disorder patients and a group of normal controls, found that the anxiety levels in the conversion patients, as measured by self-report and tests of autonomic arousal, exceeded the anxiety not only of the controls but also of the anxiety disorder patients (Lader & Sartorius, 1968). Other studies of "somatizing" patients have also found a strong correlation between reports of physical distress and reports of psychological distress (Simon, 1991). If the function of the somatoform disorders is to relieve psychological suffering, they do not seem to be doing a good job—a fact which casts some doubt on the psychodynamic interpretation.

Uncovering Conflict Psychodynamic treatment for the somatoform disorders involves roughly the same "talking cure" that led to Freud's theory of these syndromes. As usual in psychodynamic therapy, the patient is induced to release the repression, thus bringing into consciousness the forbidden thoughts and memories. Presumably, the somatic symptoms will then subside, and the ego's energy, formerly tied up in maintaining the symptoms, will be free to pursue more constructive ends. With the dissociative disorders, as we saw, hypnosis is typically used to bring forth the repressed material. With the somatoform disorders, the therapist is more likely to ask the patient to produce this material in his or her normal conscious state, either through free association or simply through candid discussion.

There is no evidence, however, that this psychodynamic approach is any more effective than other therapies for somatoform disorders. In general, the somatoform disorders are not particularly responsive to treatment, nor do they generally improve without treatment. One study found that 80 to 90 percent of diagnosed conversion patients still merited that diagnosis six to eight years later (Guze, Cloninger, Martin, et al., 1986). Somatization disorder also tends to persist. One study suggests that the best treatment for somatization patients is simply low-level medical care: brief physical examinations, supportive talks. This does not cure the disorder, but it helps to prevent patients from seeking more invasive cures and thus harming themselves with unnecessary surgery or drugs (G. R. Smith, Monson, & Ray, 1986a).

Did Elizabeth Barrett Browning (1806–1861) suffer from a somatoform disorder? Behavioral and sociocultural theorists might say that she adopted the "sick role." Following a minor accident at the age of fifteen, she spent twenty-five years as an invalid, cared for at home by her family. She experienced a rapid and nearly total recovery when she married fellow-poet Robert Browning.

The Behavioral and Sociocultural Perspectives: The Sick Role

Illness is not just a biological dysfunction. It also has social components (Mechanic, 1962; Parsons, 1951). People who are ill are justified in adopting the "sick role." They can stay home from work or school; they are relieved of their normal duties; others are expected to be sympathetic and attentive to them. According to behavioral and sociocultural theorists, somatoform disorders are inappropriate adoptions of the sick role (Pilowsky, 1990).

Learning to Adopt the Sick Role The sick role also involves sacrifices: loss of power, loss of pleasurable activities. Why would people want to give up these things for long? Probably, the behaviorists say, because their learning histories have made the rewards of the sick role more reinforcing than the rewards of illness-free life. According to Ullmann and Krasner (1975), two conditions increase the chances that a healthy person will adopt the sick role. First, the person must have had some experience with the role, either directly, by being ill, or indirectly, by having the sick role modeled. Many people with somatoform disorders meet this condition. Hypochondriasis, somatization, and conversion patients are all likely to have early personal or family histories of physical illness or somatic symptoms (Kellner, 1985; E. Miller, 1987). The second condition, according to Ullmann and Krasner, is that the adoption of the sick role must be reinforced. This too has been found to be the case with somatoform patients. Many have childhood histories of receiving attention and sympathy during illness, and according to the behavioral scenario, this operant-conditioning process predisposes them to adopt the sick role as a coping style in adult life. Respondent conditioning may also play a part. The autonomic nervous system, which controls breathing, heart rate, and numerous other bodily functions (Chapter 4), is subject to conditioning. So if anxiety is paired, for example, with minor heartbeat irregularities, as it may be in an illness-preoccupied household, then anxiety can come to *trigger* that symptom, which in turn will cause further anxiety, then further symptoms—in other words, the beginning of hypochondriasis (Kellner, 1985).

Sociocultural theorists also regard somatoform disorders as a case of role adoption, but they focus less on the family than on larger cultural forces. In the sociocultural view, the likelihood of people's using the sick role as a coping style depends on their culture's attitudes toward unexplained somatic symptoms. If this theory is correct, then rates of somatoform disorder should vary from culture to culture. They do, and in ways consistent with cultural values. Somatization and conversion disorder are more prevalent in non-Western cultures and in less industrialized cultures—China, Nigeria, Libya, Mexico—cultures in which the expression of emotional distress in psychological terms is less accepted (Escobar & Canino, 1989; D. P. Goldberg & Bridges, 1988). And in the United States, as we saw, conversion and somatization disorder are more common in rural communities and in lower socioeconomic groups, in which again psychological expressions of emotional problems may be frowned on. So people in these communities and groups may be encouraged to somaticize unhappiness rather than psychologize it (D. P. Goldberg & Bridges, 1988).

Treatment by Nonreinforcement As with dissociative disorders, the behavioral treatment of somatoform disorders is usually two-pronged. First, the therapist withdraws reinforcement for illness behavior. Second, the therapist tries to build up the patient's coping skills, a lack of which is presumably part of the reason for resorting to the sick role. A recently described short-term treatment for seventeen people with hypochondriasis and illness phobia (disabling fear of illness) emphasized the withdrawal of reinforcement, particularly the negative reinforcement (via anxiety relief) that the patients derived through reassurance seeking. When they sought reassurance from the therapist, they were given none, and their families were instructed to give them none. In a five-year follow-up, about half the patients located were symptom-free (Warwick & Marks, 1988).

As for building coping skills, behavioral treatments often include social-skills training, in which patients are taught how to deal effectively with other people, and assertiveness training, which teaches patients how to show strength—how to make requests, how to refuse requests, how to show anger when necessary. For many people, the sick role may be a way of making demands on others, and of evading their demands, without taking responsibility for such actions. ("Because I am sick, you have to do things for me and I don't have to do things for you.") Behaviorists try to teach people how to manage social give-and-take without such blackmail.

In treating conversion disorders, the therapist will often try to provide some face-saving mechanism so that patients can give up the "illness" without having to face the accusation that they were never ill to begin with. This mechanism may be a placebo drug, as in the case of Ari, described earlier, or it may be some sort of physical therapy. In any case, the placebo is there to provide a socially acceptable reason for the cure; the cure, meanwhile, is effected through a change in reinforcement.

The Cognitive Perspective: Misinterpreting Bodily Sensations

Overattention to the Body Recall the cognitive interpretation of panic disorder (Chapter 7): that it is essentially a problem of misinterpretation. The cognitive view of hypochondriasis and somatization disorder is roughly the same. According to several theorists, people with these disorders have a "cognitive style" predisposing them to exaggerate normal bodily sensations and catastrophize over minor symptoms. Given these tendencies, they misinterpret minor physiological changes as major health problems (Barsky, 1992b; Warwick & Salkovskis, 1990). When, for example, these patients are under stress and feel their heart rate speed up, they will say, "I am having a heart attack" rather than "I am nervous." In support of this idea, it has been shown that hypochondriacs focus more attention on bodily sensations, catastrophize more readily about symptoms, hold more false beliefs about disease, and fear aging and death more than nonhypochondriac psychiatric patients or normal controls (Barsky & Wyshak, 1989; Barsky, Wyshak, & Klerman, 1990). It has also been found that "somatizers," or people with a high rate of medically unexplainable somatic complaints, have correspondingly high rates of negative affect: pessimism, self-blame, general unhappiness (Pennebaker & Watson, 1991). If this negative affect were combined with difficulty in expressing emotion, a trait that apparently runs high in somatization disorder patients (Shipko, 1982), then the person would be all the more likely to redirect distress onto the body—an explanation consistent with Freud's.

Treatment: Hypothesis Testing Recent reports show that hypochondriacs can be helped by a combination of cognitive therapy (revising thinking habits) and behavioral therapy (change in reinforcement) (Visser & Bouman, 1992). Salkovskis and Warwick (1986), for example, have described their cognitive-behavioral treatment of a thirty-two-year-old man who, because he had developed a harmless rash was convinced that he had leukemia. He inspected the rash constantly, spent hours reading medical textbooks in order to find out the true, undiagnosed cause of his disorder, and talked of this problem incessantly with his wife and friends. Racked with worry, he eventually became suicidal and was hospitalized. The therapists, using a cognitive approach, got the patient to agree on two competing hypotheses to explain his condition: (1) that he was suffering from a deadly illness, not yet diagnosed, and (2) that he had a problem with anxiety, maintained by incessant checking and reassurance seeking. The therapists reviewed with the patient the evidence for the two hypotheses, and in view of the strong evidence for the second one, he agreed to test it by altering the conditions that might be maintaining his anxiety. This meant that he would stop reading the medical books, stop checking the rash, and stop seeking reassurance. The hospital staff, the family doctor, and the family were also instructed to stop giving reassurance. His hypochondriacal anxieties swiftly declined. Discussing this case, the therapists stress the role of reassurance in maintaining anxiety via negative reinforcement. In their view, the *DSM's* description of hypochondriasis as a fear of disease that persists "despite medical reassurance" should possibly be changed to "because of repeated medical reassurance" (Salkovskis & Warwick, 1986, p. 601).

The Biological Perspective: Genetics and Brain Dysfunction

Genetic Studies We have already discussed the fact that people with somatoform disorders tend to have family histories of somatic complaints. Is it possible that this is the product not of learning but of genes? Guze and his colleagues have conducted several family studies of somatization disorder, with intriguing results. First, it appears that among the first-degree relatives of patients with somatization disorder, the women show an increased frequency of somatization disorder, while the men show an increased frequency not of somatization disorder but of antisocial personality disorder, a personality pattern characterized by chronic indifference to the rights of others (Chapter 11). Women with somatization disorder also tend to marry men with antisocial personality disorder. Furthermore, somatization disorder and antisocial personality are seen together in the same person much more frequently than we would expect by chance. These findings have led to the hypothesis that somatization disorder and antisocial personality disorder may be the product of similar genetic endowment and that what determines whether a person with this endowment will be a somatizer or an antisocial personality is his or her sex (Guze, Cloninger, Martin, et al., 1986; Guze, Woodruff, & Clayton, 1971; see also Coryell, 1980; Lilienfeld, 1992).

Of course, the basis of these family patterns need not be genetic. It could be environmental. To document the genetic factor more clearly, twin and adoption studies are needed. One twin study (Torgersen, 1986b), conducted in Norway, found that MZ twins had a higher concordance rate for somatoform disorders than DZ twins, but the sample was small, and there was reason to believe that the MZ twins in this study shared not only more similar genotypes but also more similar environments than the DZ twins. In an adoption study conducted in Sweden, the researchers tracked down the medical and criminal histories of the biological and adoptive parents of 859 women with somatization disorder. The results seemed to show not one but two patterns, depending on whether the woman was a "high-frequency somatizer" (frequent somatic complaints, but few kinds of complaints) or a "diversiform somatizer" (less frequent complaints, but of a more diverse nature). The biological fathers of the high-frequency somatizers showed disproportionately high rates of alcoholism, the biological fathers of the diversiform somatizers showed disproportionately high rates of violent crime (Bohman, Cloninger, von Knorring, et al., 1984; Cloninger, Sigvardsson, von Knorring, et al., 1984). These findings, though preliminary, support the suggestion that there is a genetic factor in somatization disorder and that the factor is somehow linked to antisocial behavior (Lilienfeld, 1992).

Brain Dysfunction and Somatoform Disorders The essential mystery of conversion disorder—that while the body is functioning normally, the consciousness does not know this—has been the subject of some neuroscience research. Tests of brain waves in people with conversion anesthesias, blindness, and deafness clearly indicate that these patients' brains are receiving normal sensory input from their "disabled" organs. If you prick the finger of a person with glove anesthesia, this message does arrive in the cerebral cortex, as it is supposed to. Likewise, electrical stimulation of the movement centers of the brain does produce normal movement in patients with conversion paralysis. In other words, there seems to be no blockage of the neural pathways between the brain and the peripheral organs. Why then can't conversion patients consciously feel sensations or initiate movement? Presumably the problem lies in the *processing* of sensory signals in the cerebral cortex, for it is that processing that would bring the signal into conscious awareness. Conversion patients seem to have suppressed some stage of cerebral processing (Marsden, 1986). In support of this hypothesis, several studies of conversion patients with loss of sensory function have revealed high levels of inhibitory (transmission-suppressing) action in the cerebral cortex in the response to sensory stimuli (Hernandez-Peon, Chavez-Ibarra, & Aguilar-Figueroa, 1963; Levy & Behrman, 1970; Levy & Mushin, 1973). Such a slowdown in processing might be caused by a shock to the brain. Some evidence indicates that hypoxia (oxygen deprivation) and hypoglycemia (low blood sugar) can bring on conversion symptoms (Eames, 1992).

Another interesting finding has to do with lateralization, the difference between the right and left hemispheres of the brain (Chapter 4). In a study of 430 patients with conversion disorder, somatization disorder, and other psychological disorders involving somatic complaints, it was found that 70 percent had their symptoms on the left side of the body (Bishop, Mobley, & Farr, 1978). Since the left side of the body is controlled by the right side of the brain, this suggests that somatoform disorders may stem from some dysfunction in the right cerebral hemisphere, a possibility that has since been supported by other neurological studies (Flor-Henry, Fromm-Auch, Tapper, et al., 1981; L. James, Singer, Zurynski, et al., 1987).

At present, these findings, like the genetic evidence, amount to little more than intriguing suggestions, but with the expansion of neuroscience research, they should eventually lead to more solid conclusions. It should be reemphasized, however, that the discovery of a neurological basis for a psychological disorder does not rule out a psychological basis. If the brains of conversion patients are inhibiting sensory input, they may be doing so for psychological reasons.

KEY TERMS

alternating personality (181)
amnesia (177)
body dysmorphic disorder (193)
conversion disorder (195)
depersonalization disorder (186)
derealization (186)
dissociative amnesia (177)
dissociative disorders (177)
dissociative fugue (179)
dissociative identity disorder (179)
explicit memories (178)
hypochondriasis (194)
hysteria (176)
implicit memories (178)
la belle indifférence (196)
malingering (183)
primary gain (196)
secondary gain (196)
somatization disorder (195)
somatoform disorders (193)

SUMMARY

- Dissociative disorders occur when stress causes components of the personality that are normally integrated to split apart, or dissociate. As a result, some critical psychological function is screened out of consciousness. These disorders disturb only higher cognitive functions, not sensory or motor functions.
- In dissociative amnesia, psychological stress screens out the memory function. The loss of memory typically applies to a period of time *after* the precipitating stressful event, is selective, is not disturbing to the amnesiac, and is recoverable.
- A related condition is dissociative fugue, in which a person not only forgets all or some of the past but also takes a sudden, unexpected trip and often assumes a new identity.
- In dissociative identity disorder, also known as multiple personality, a person develops two or more distinct personalities that take turns controlling the person's behavior. At least one of the personalities will be amnesic of the other(s). In some cases, the various personalities display significant physiological differences.
- Depersonalization disorder involves a persistent sense of strangeness or unreality about one's identity. The person may feel like a robot or an actor in a dream. Such feelings are often accompanied by dere-

alization, a sense of strangeness about the world and other people. Those suffering with this disorder recognize the strangeness of their feelings and may fear they are going insane.

- Almost all theories of the dissociative disorders assume they are means of escape from situations beyond the patient's coping power. In the psychodynamic view, dissociative disorders are extreme and maladaptive defenses against the anxiety produced by repressed wishes. Psychodynamic therapy—the most common treatment for these disorders—aims at identifying the repressed material and reintegrating it into the personality.
- Both behaviorists and socioculturalists hold that a person adopts the symptoms of a dissociative disorder in order to get the reward of protection or relief from stress. These theorists believe that reinforcement maintains the dissociative behavior. Accordingly, the way to treat dissociative symptoms is to stop reinforcing them.
- Cognitive theorists view these disorders as impairments of episodic memory, or one's record of personal experience. Cognitive therapy uses various cognitive techniques to trigger and release memories.
- Neuroscience researchers hypothesize that the dissociative disorders are a byproduct of undiagnosed epilepsy or of damage to neurological mechanisms that normally suppress rebellious subparts of the brain.
- The primary feature of the somatoform disorders is that psychological conflicts take on a somatic, or physical, form.
- A person with a body dysmorphic disorder is so preoccupied with an imagined or grossly exaggerated defect in appearance that he or she cannot function normally. This syndrome is closely associated with obsessive-compulsive disorder.
- In hypochondriasis, a person maintains a chronic fear of disease by misinterpreting physical signs and sensations as abnormal. Hypochondriacs do not fake their symptoms; they are genuinely convinced they are ill.
- In somatization disorder, a person has physical complaints that begin by age thirty, persist for several years, and cannot be medically explained. The complaints are many, varied, and dramatic and are not focused on one particular disease, as in hypochondriasis.
- In conversion disorder, an actual disability, such as blindness or paralysis, exists with no medical basis. The condition is produced involuntarily, but it is generally agreed that conversion disorders provide relief for some internal conflict.
- From the psychodynamic perspective, the somatoform disorders are defenses against the anxiety caused by unacceptable wishes. All also contain a strong element of regression, or return to a childlike state that will elicit care from others. As with other disorders, psychodynamic treatment aims at uncovering what is repressed and resolving the conflicts the repression is creating.
- From the behavioral and sociocultural perspectives, the somatoform disorders represent inappropriate adoptions of the "sick role" in order to reap its rewards (attention, relief from responsibility, etc.). Treatment calls for not reinforcing illness behavior and for developing the patient's coping skills.
- Cognitive theorists attribute the somatoform disorders to a cognitive style that exaggerates normal bodily sensations and makes catastrophic interpretations of minor symptoms. Cognitive therapy calls on patients to test their faulty hypotheses and on others to cease providing reassurance to patients, which only serves to give negative reinforcement to their claims.
- The neuroscience perspective has found evidence for a genetic role in somatization disorder and some evidence of brain dysfunction in conversion disorder.

9

PSYCHOLOGICAL STRESS AND PHYSICAL DISORDERS

In a recent experiment Sheldon Cohen and his colleagues asked 420 volunteers to fill out questionnaires about the amount of stress they had been coping with during the preceding year. Then 394 of the subjects were given nose drops containing cold viruses and the remaining 26 were given placebo drops. They were quarantined and watched, to see who caught colds. Some of the experimental subjects came down with colds, while others did not. That was to be expected—people's immune responses differ. What was not expected, however, was how clearly these people's immune responses reflected the psychological pressures they had been under. The more stress a subject had reported on the pretest questionnaire, the more likely he or she was to catch the cold (S. Cohen, Tyrrell, & Smith, 1991).

This was a watershed study. For years psychology had acknowledged the existence of **psychophysiological disorders** (also called *psychosomatic disorders*), that is, illnesses influenced by emotional factors. But it was generally believed that there were only a few such illnesses. These conditions, including asthma, ulcer, hypertension, and migraine headaches, were listed in the *DSM* as "psychophysiological disorders," the assumption being that all other illnesses were purely organic. Increasingly, this assumption came under attack, as evidence accumulated that widely diverse medical conditions were affected, if not caused, by psychological factors. Accordingly, in the 1980s *DSM-III* dropped the list of psychophysiological disorders in favor of a comprehensive category—"psychological factors affecting physical condition"—that could be applied to any illness. Still, the importance of such factors was bitterly contested. In June 1985 the highly respected *New England Journal of Medicine* published an editorial dismissing most reports of psychological influence on physical health as "anecdotal." "It is time to acknowledge that our belief in disease as a direct reflection of mental state is largely folklore," the editorial concluded (quoted in Kiecolt-Glaser & Glaser, 1991). Particularly in the case of cancer and also infectious diseases such as colds, theories of psychological influence were viewed with great skepticism. Then, four years after the *New England Journal of Medicine* editorial, a competing journal published the results of a carefully controlled study showing that breast cancer patients who were given supportive group therapy in addition to their medical care survived almost twice as long, after the beginning of treatment, as those not receiving group therapy (Spiegel, Bloom, Kraemer, et al., 1989). Two years after that, the Cohen group's findings about stress and the common cold were published—in the *New England Journal of Medicine.* Today, there are very few experts who still doubt that the workings of the mind influence the health of the body. In the words of *DSM-IV,* "Psychological . . . factors play a potential role in the presentation or treatment of almost every general medical condition" (American Psychiatric Association, 1994, p. 676).

The conceptualization of the role of stress in physical illness has not only broadened in recent years; it has become far more complex. Researchers now recognize that even if an illness is caused by a purely physical factor, that illness in turn *causes* emotional stress. Surveys have found that about 20 percent of people in the hospital, for whatever illness, have a diagnosable depressive syndrome (G. Rodin & Voshort, 1986). There is no question that these emotional factors in turn affect the course of the illness—how serious it will become, whether and how quickly the patient will recover. In sum, many professionals are coming to believe that physical illness can no longer be studied apart from psychological factors.

This more *holistic,* or unified, concept of body and mind has led to the development of a new research discipline, **health psychology** (also called *behavioral medicine*). Three major historical trends have met in health psychology. The first is the above-mentioned trend toward holistic thinking: the recognition that our way of living and state of mind affect our physical well-being. The second is the recognition that psychological and life-style factors can be used to prevent, as well as treat, illness. The third is the discovery that certain treatments pioneered by behavioral psychology, such as biofeedback and relaxation training, can relieve stress-related physical ailments. One branch of health psychology in which research has truly exploded in the past decade is psychoneuroimmunology, the study of the relationship between physical stress and the immune system.

In this chapter we will first review the history of the concept of mind *versus* body. Then we will discuss psychological stress: how it is defined and how it influences illness, particularly via the immune system. Finally we will examine the interaction of mind and body in certain specific illnesses, and we will describe the current psychological perspectives on the nature of that interaction.

MIND AND BODY

What is the relationship between the mind and the body? This question—the **mind-body problem**—has been under debate for centuries. Logically, it would seem that mind and body are essentially the same thing. *Mind,* after all, is simply an abstract term for the workings of the brain. And the brain not only is part of the body but is directly connected by nerves to all other parts of the body. Therefore whatever is going on "mentally" inside a person is also going on physically, and vice versa. Most of the time, however, we are unaware of the activity going on in our brains. We are conscious only of the *effects* of that activity—effects that we think of as "mental," not physical. This is undoubtedly one reason why we tend to regard the mind as something apart from the body (G. E. Schwartz, 1978).

Whatever the reason, the prevailing opinion for centuries has been that mind and body are separate entities—interrelated, perhaps, but still independent. This *dualism* of mind and body is often said to have originated with the Greek philosopher Plato, in the fifth century B.C., but it undoubtedly reaches much further back, to prehistoric peoples' efforts to explain death. In death, they observed, the body remained, yet it was no longer alive. Something, then, must have departed from it. That something—the mind or soul or spirit—was clearly separate from the body.

Incorporated into the Jewish and Christian religions, mind-body dualism was handed down from ancient times to the Middle Ages and the Renaissance. In the early seventeenth century, the French philosopher René Descartes described mind and body as altogether independent entities—the mind spiritual, the body physical. Descartes' influential theories, together with the discoveries of Galileo and Sir Isaac Newton, laid the foundation of modern scientific rationalism. In this view, nature was a vast, self-powered machine. To explain its operations, one need not—indeed, should not—resort to philosophical or religious concepts. Nature could be explained only by reference to its internal parts—that is, only through empirical evidence, things that could be observed and measured. Actually, many nonempirical factors, such as norms and values—also philosophical beliefs, as we just saw with Descartes—had a huge impact on science, but such factors usually operated unconsciously. Scientists, as they saw it, were drawing the line between matters that could be studied scientifically and matters that could not. The mind fell on one side of this line, the body on the other, and physicians were trained to confine themselves to the latter.

Of course there were many illnesses whose empirical causes were not known. Might they involve factors that could not be observed? The question was sometimes asked. But in the late nineteenth century, with the discovery by Louis Pasteur and others that germs caused disease, such doubts were largely dispelled. The causes of illness were indeed observable; all we needed were better microscopes. Some exceptions were still recognized. Over the years, physicians repeatedly noted a connection between certain disorders, such as high blood pressure and psychological tension. And so the list of "psychophysiological disorders" was drawn up. They were the exceptions, though. Organic causation was the rule.

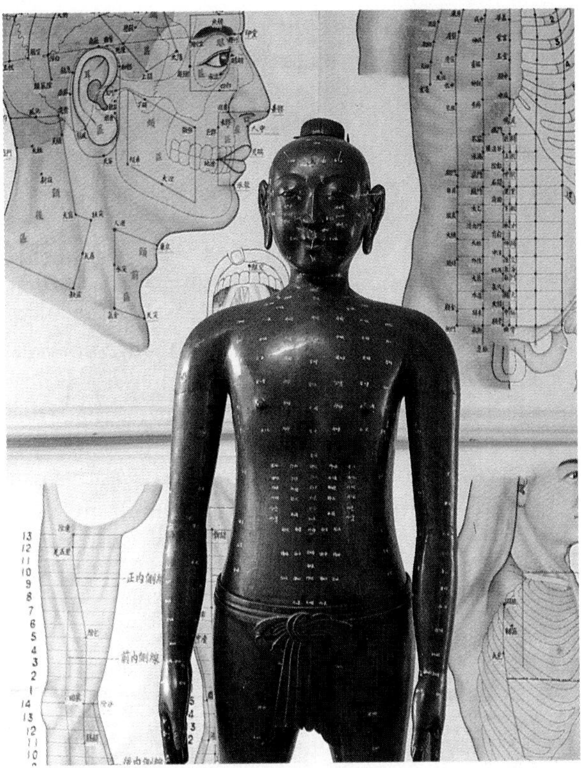

While Western philosophy and medicine separated the mind from the body, Eastern cultures, such as the Chinese, have always joined them. This Sung Dynasty (tenth through thirteenth centuries) bronze statue was used to teach acupuncture, a pain-relieving technique based on the connections between the brain and the rest of the nervous system.

Only in the last half-century has this assumption been called into serious question. In the sixties it was discovered that physiological functions such as blood pressure and heart rate, which were once considered completely involuntary (i.e., the province of the body, not of the mind), could be influenced voluntarily. And if the mind could affect the beating of the heart or the dilation of blood vessels, why could it not also affect such processes as the growth of cancer cells? The remainder of this story was told at the beginning of the chapter. As recent research has demonstrated, psychological factors *can* affect the growth of cancer cells, as well as many other disease processes, down to the common cold. The list of "psychophysiological disorders" is now gone from the *DSM; all* illnesses are considered potentially psychophysiological. Kept apart for centuries, mind and body are increasingly being considered as one.

In this chapter we will take the position that mind and body are, in fact, one. What people experience as a mental event, such as sadness, is also, whether they realize it or not, a physical event. Likewise, physical events, such as the firing of neurons in the brain, trigger mental events. It is not so much that the one causes the other as that they cannot, in truth, be separated. As one researcher explained, the words *psychological* and *physical* refer not to different phenomena but to different ways of talking about the same phenomenon (D. T. Graham, 1967, p. 52).

PSYCHOLOGICAL STRESS

Stress and the Autonomic Nervous System

What are the physiological changes associated with stress? To attempt an answer we must look again at the autonomic nervous system (ANS). As we saw in Chapter 4, the ANS controls the smooth muscles, the glands, and the internal organs, regulating a wide variety of functions—among them heartbeat, respiration, blood pressure, bladder contraction, perspiration, salivation, adrenaline secretion, and gastric-acid production—to allow the body to cope with the ebb and flow of environmental demands. In general, the sympathetic division mobilizes the body to meet such demands by speeding up heart rate, constricting the blood vessels near the skin (and thereby raising blood pressure), increasing adrenaline flow, and so forth. And in general, the parasympathetic division reverses these processes, returning the body to a resting state so that it can rebuild the energy supply depleted by sympathetic activity (see Figure 4.6, page 92).

Several decades ago, W. B. Cannon (1936) proposed that stress results in a massive activation of the entire sympathetic division: increased heart rate and blood pressure, fast breathing, heavy adrenaline flow, dilated pupils, inhibited salivation and digestion. Regardless of the nature of the stress or of the person, the physiological response, according to Cannon, was the same generalized sympathetic arousal. That hypothesis has been confirmed in broad outline. On the basis of extensive research, Hans Selye (1956, 1974) described a "general adaptation syndrome" which divides the body's reaction into three successive stages: (1) alarm and mobilization—a state of rapid, general arousal in which the body's defenses are mobilized; (2) resistance—the state of optimal biological adaptation to environmental demands; and (3) exhaustion and disintegration—a stage reached when the body loses its ability to cope with prolonged demands.

Defining Stress

In these discussions, the definition of **stress** tends to shift. Some writers, such as W. B. Cannon (1936), define it as a *stimulus:* stress consists of environmental demands that lead to autonomic responses. This definition has been adopted by many later researchers and has generated a number of studies on how various life events, such as divorce or losing a job, affect people. An interesting question in this line of research has to do with positive life events. According to some researchers, not just divorce but also marriage, not just losing a job but also taking one, can be stressful enough to tax one's health (T. H. Holmes & Rahe, 1967). Other researchers have pointed to the usefulness of minor positive events such as gossiping with friends or getting a good night's sleep as buffers against stress. (See the box on page 209.)

A second definition holds that stress is a *response*—primarily ANS activation, as described above. This was Selye's view, and it has stimulated other lines of research, focusing on physiological reactions. Finally, some cognitive theorists define stress not as stimulus or response but as the *interaction between the stimulus and the person's appraisal of it,* a process that will determine the person's response (Lazarus & Folkman, 1984). This theory will be discussed later, under the cognitive perspective.

What Determines Responses to Stress?

Regardless of whether stress is a response, a stimulus, or an appraisal of a stimulus, the fact remains that different people experience it differently. Why do some people cope well with stress and others fall ill? And why do some people fall ill with migraines, others with hypertension or backaches?

Stimulus Specificity One of the earliest indications that people's responses to stress are keyed to the type of stress involved came from a rather bizarre experiment (S. Wolf & Wolff, 1947). In 1947 a patient named Tom who had experienced severe

MINOR STRESSES AND ILLNESS

In exploring the links between psychological stress and physical illness, researchers have tended to concentrate on the impact that major stressors have on the human body. Divorce, a death in the family, losing a job, moving to a distant city—these and other major life events cause tremendous stress and put the person at increased risk of becoming ill (T. H. Holmes & Rahe, 1967; Selye, 1976). Happy occasions—getting married, receiving a promotion, going on vacation—may also cause stress, but they are much less likely to result in illness.

More recently, researchers have begun to look into the role that less dramatic events play in the stress-disease connection. Surprisingly, the daily hassles of life—getting caught in traffic jams, waiting in lines, losing the car keys—may be more stressful than major unpleasant events (Lazarus, 1980). In fact, continual mild stress has been found to be a better predictor of declines in physical health—and of depression and anxiety—than major life events (DeLongis, Coyne, Dakof, et al., 1982). Whether daily hassles have a cumulative effect, simply wearing people down, or whether they make people more vulnerable when a big event comes along is uncertain. Perhaps both effects are involved.

Since only unpleasant stress has been connected with illness, Richard Lazarus and his colleagues have been exploring the possibility that everyday pleasures, or "uplifts"—listening to music, working on a hobby, taking a walk in the country—have positive effects, perhaps by acting as buffers against stress (Lazarus, Kanner, & Folkman, 1980). This research team has devised "hassles" and "uplifts" scales that make it possible to trace the connections from pleasurable and irritating events to stress and changes in health. Sample items from both scales are given below. A high total score on the "hassles" scale does not necessarily mean that a person will become ill, but the risk of illness is likely to be greater. A high score on the "uplifts" scale indicates that the person may be better equipped to fend off stress and avoid illness.

Sample Items from the "Hassles" Scale	Sample Items from the "Uplifts" Scale
1. Misplacing or losing things	1. Practicing your hobby
2. Troublesome neighbors	2. Being lucky
3. Social obligations	3. Saving money
4. Inconsiderate smokers	4. Liking fellow workers
5. Thoughts about death	5. Gossiping; "shooting the bull"
6. Health of a family member	6. Successful financial dealings
7. Not enough money for clothing	7. Being rested
8. Concerns about owing money	8. Feeling healthy
	9. Finding something presumed lost

SOURCE: A. D. Kanner, Coyne, Schaeffer, and Lazarus (1981).

gastrointestinal damage underwent surgery, and with his permission the surgeon installed a plastic window over his stomach so that its internal workings could be observed. In subsequent sessions with Tom, the investigators found that his flow of gastric juices decreased when he was exposed to anxiety-producing stimuli and increased when he was exposed to anger-producing stimuli. This experiment not only showed that gastric activity (and by extension ulcer) was related to emotional states, as researchers had long suspected. It also established the principle of **stimulus specificity**—that different kinds of stress produce different kinds of physiological response. This principle has since been confirmed by other investigators. Different emotions—fear, anger, disgust, sadness, happiness—have been shown to have significantly different effects not only on gastric activity but also on heart rate, blood pressure, muscle tension, respiration rate, and other physiological functions (Levenson, 1992; G. E. Schwartz, Weinberger, & Singer, 1981). Researchers have pinpointed subtler distinctions as well. Apparently, the physiological reaction differs depending on whether we are anticipating a stressful event or actually undergoing it, as students may verify in the case of final exams. It also differs according to whether the stress is short-term or long-term (H. Weiner, 1994). Finally, the reactions in question are extraordinarily complex. It is not just a matter of changes in heart rate or breathing. Different stressors produce whole, distinctive *patterns* of physiological response, involving not just autonomic activity but also different facial expressions, brain-wave changes, and hormone secretions (H. Weiner, 1994).

Individual Response Specificity Physiological responses to stress depend not only on the kind of stress. They also depend on the person responding. Whether as a result of genes or learning (probably both), people appear to have characteristic patterns of physiological response, which carry over from one type of stress to another—a phenomenon called **individual response specificity.** The first hint of this fact came in an experiment in which a group of people with histories of cardiovascular complaints (e.g., high blood pressure) and a group of people with histories of muscular complaints (e.g., backache) were both exposed to the same painful stimulus. Though the stressor was the same, the cardiovascular group responded with greater changes in heart rate than the muscular group, while the muscular group showed greater changes in muscle tension than the cardiovascular group (Malmo & Shagass, 1949). What this suggested—and it has since been confirmed—is that in responding to stress people tend to favor one or another physiological system.

It also appears that some people respond more intensely to stress in general. In an intriguing experiment it was found that whether or not a ten-month-old baby would cry when its mother left the room could be predicted from the baby's EEG brain-wave pattern as tested earlier, when the mother was in the room. Infants whose EEGs showed *hemispheric asymmetry*, or more activity on one side of the brain than on the other—in this case, more activity in the right frontal area than in the left—were the most likely to cry when their mothers exited (R. J. Davidson & Fox, 1989). This same pattern of asymmetry has also been observed in shy three-year-olds and in depressed adults (R. J. Davidson, 1992). Possibly, it reflects an innate hypersensitivity to stress.

Stimulus versus Individual There is an apparent contradiction between individual response specificity and stimulus specificity. If people have characteristic patterns of response that carry over from stressor to stressor, how can patterns of response vary with changes in the stressor? This seems improbable only if we think of physiological response to stress as a simple process. But as we saw, it is an extremely complex process, and many different variables influence the final response. The two variables we are considering—the person and the stressor—operate simultaneously (B. T. Engel, 1960; B. T. Engel & Bickford, 1961). As described, the flow of gastric juices tends to increase with anger and decrease with anxiety; here we see stimulus specificity. The *degree* of increase and decrease, however, will be subject to individual response specificity. That is, "gastric reactors" may show extreme increases and decreases; "cardiac reactors," on the other hand, may show only mild gastric changes, concentrating instead on heart-rate changes. And if, as the hemispheric asymmetry research suggests, some people are generally heavy reactors to stress, then this factor too will influence the response.

HOW STRESS INFLUENCES ILLNESS

Over the years, more and more research has established a connection between stress and illness. The study discussed at the opening of this chapter—the Cohen group's investigation of colds—is a good example, and it has been built upon by later researchers. For example, the Cohen group found that levels of stress predicted not only who developed cold symptoms but also who became infected (as revealed by levels of antibodies in the blood), whether or not they developed symptoms (S. Cohen, Tyrrell, & Smith, 1991). Later, another research group (Stone, Bovberg, Neale, et al., 1992) found much the same thing. They exposed seventeen subjects to a cold virus, and all seventeen became infected, but only twelve went on to show cold symptoms. As in the Cohen study, the subjects had filled out stress questionnaires, and what the questionnaires revealed was that those who came down with the colds were those who had experienced the most "major life events," both positive and negative, in the preceding year. So if, as we have so often been told, colds strike when we are "run-down," there is more to this than staying up late. Even positive changes in our lives can run us down.

A more dramatic example has to do with sudden cardiac death (SCD), a form of heart attack that kills 450,000 people per year in the United States alone. Most people who die of SCD are found to have an underlying heart disease, but only about one-third show evidence of the coronary occlusion (blockage in the arteries of the heart) that causes most heart attacks. Rather, SCD is primarily an electrical accident that occurs when the heart's large, steady contractions give way to rapid, irregular contractions known as fibrillations. Vulnerability to SCD seems to be associated with long-term psychological stress (Kamarck & Jennings, 1991). Furthermore, in about 20 percent of cases, SCD is connected to an experience of great emotion, such as sudden surprise, anger, grief, or even happiness (Lane & Jennings, 1995). Other kinds of heart disease are also associated with stress. Heart patients often show constriction of the coronary arteries and reduced blood flow during acute stress; these effects can also be produced by laboratory stressors such as having to solve difficult arithmetic problems or give a speech about one's personal life (Lane & Jennings, 1995). Conversely, some people who are especially reactive to stress, the so-called Type A personalities, seem to be at high risk for heart disease—a subject that we will come to later in this chapter.

So stress and illness are clearly related, but what is it that mediates the relationship? How are thought and emotion translated into physical breakdown?

Changes in Physiological Functioning

You have already read part of the answer. Stress produces direct physiological effects, and those effects have other effects. The body's various functions—digestion, respiration, circulation—are not single-component operations. They are systems of many parts, each of which sends the others **feedback,** or information about regulating the system. Especially important in theories of stress and illness is **negative feedback,** in which the turning *on* of one component in a system leads to the turning *off* of another component. According to Gary Schwartz's (1977) *disregulation model*, stress-related illness occurs when there is some disruption in the negative-feedback cycle. Consider the case of blood pressure. In response to threats in the environment, the brain causes the arteries to constrict. In doing so, it depends on the *baroreceptors*, pressure-sensitive cells surrounding the arteries, to signal when blood pressure is running too high. But various circumstances, such as chronic stress or genetic predisposition, may blunt the responsiveness of the baroreceptors, so they fail to provide this crucial negative feedback. When that happens, a regulated system becomes a disregulated system, and the result is illness—in this case, hypertension, or chronically high blood pressure.

Another influential theory, developed by Herbert Weiner (1994), concerns the **oscillations,** or rhythmic back-and-forth cycles, of the various systems in the body. Such oscillating cycles control almost all bodily functions. Breathing, blood pressure, heartbeat, temperature, digestion, menstruation, sleep, the production of hormones, neurotransmitters, immune cells—all go up and down on a number of time scales, whether second by second, day by day, or month by month. These cycles too are controlled by negative feedback. Indeed that is what keeps them oscillating: turning on in one cycle leads to turning off in another, and vice versa. (For example, the turning off of sleep results in the turning on of stomach contractions, so we want breakfast.) According to Weiner, stress may throw a system out of rhythm, in which case the other systems will also be affected. After the disruption, the system may find a new rhythm, or it may become chronically irregular. In either case, the result may be a disease process. For example, people who work late shifts suffer chronic disruptions of their sleep cycle. On workdays they wake up in the afternoon; on days off, if they want to see their families and friends, they wake up in the morning. This irregularity apparently takes its toll, and not just on sleep. Long-term night-shift workers have more gastrointestinal problems and more illness than people who work day shifts (Rutenfrantz, Haider, & Koller, 1985).

Medical interns once epitomized the kind of chronic irregularities in work schedule—many hours on duty alternating with a few hours off—that can result in stress-related illness. Now that such fatigue has been shown to interfere with patient care, many teaching hospitals are scheduling shorter and more regular shifts for their interns.

Schwartz's model, then, focuses more on the failure of a single component, which then disregulates the system as a whole. Weiner's model concentrates from the beginning on the system—indeed, on the whole body as a finely tuned network of oscillating systems, all vulnerable to stress.

Changes in High-Risk Behavior

Schwartz's and Weiner's theories are models—comprehensive, abstract descriptions. On a more concrete level, stress may contribute to illness by causing people to behave in a way that puts them at risk for illness. For example, people with adult-onset diabetes can usually maintain their health by taking medication and following a special diet. As studies (e.g., Brantley & Garrett, 1993) have shown, however, diabetics who are under stress are likely to stray from their diets and forget their pills, with the result that they may fall ill. But in order to see the chain leading from stress to high-risk behavior to illness, it is hardly necessary to look to diabetics. As anyone knows, stress may lead to smoking, drug use, sleep loss, overeating, and undereating, and any of these will increase the risk of illness.

Changes in Illness Reporting

Stress may also encourage its victims to report illness. People whose lives are going smoothly tend to overlook health problems; people who are under pressure are more likely to call the doctor. This is one reason for the association between stress and illness—which is not to say that such reports of illness are exaggerated. On the contrary, this connection illustrates one of the few beneficial effects of stress: it causes people who are at risk to seek help earlier, with the possibility that they may receive needed treatment or learn to change their behavior, for example, by eating more healthfully or starting an exercise regimen.

Changes in the Immune System

In the studies of colds, as we saw, not all the people who were exposed to the virus became infected, and not all the people who became infected developed symptoms—only those, in both cases, who had been under greater stress. Clearly the factor mediating this connection was the **immune system,** the body's system of defense against infectious disease and cancer. The job of the immune system is to distinguish between "self" and "nonself" within the body and then to eliminate "nonself." The primary agents of the immune system are small white blood cells called *lymphocytes* that patrol the body, identifying foreign substances and either attacking them or producing specially adapted proteins called *antibodies* that undertake the attack. In either case, the first stage of attack involves the immune particle's attaching itself to the foreign particle, which it can do only if its chemical structure fits that of the invader. As a result, the body, in order to stay healthy, has to circulate a vast number of different lymphocytes, each adapted for a different virus, bacterium, or other invader.

Scientists have only just begun their inventory of the immune system, but this research has accelerated rapidly in the last decade. One reason is the AIDS epidemic. The AIDS virus kills its victims by destroying immune cells and thus leaving the body undefended against illness. Obviously, if we knew more about the immune system, we might find a cure for AIDS. Another stimulus to research on immune functions has been the effort to save lives through organ transplants. A major frustration in organ transplant surgery is that the immune system often perceives the new organ as "nonself" and rejects it. Again, if we had more detailed knowledge of the immune system, we would be in a better position to control this response. Finally, a critical factor in the stepping up of research on immune functions has been the research on stress and illness. As mentioned earlier, the study of the immune system as a link between stress and illness has evolved into a new subspecialty of health medicine, **psychoneuroimmunology,** or **PNI.**

In most PNI research immune responses are studied by means of blood samples. Blood is taken from the subjects; then white blood cells are isolated and exposed to *mitogens,* compounds that mimic the action of foreign substances in the body. Healthy white blood cells, upon encountering mitogens, will begin multiplying and secreting attack compounds. Less healthy white blood cells will do this less efficiently. Thus, by recording the number and behavior of white blood cells in people who are under stress and then comparing those results with white-blood-cell action in the same people when they are under less stress or in control subjects, researchers can draw conclusions about the relationship between stress and immune function.

In this research, then, immune function is the dependent variable, stress the independent variable. PNI research has focused on three broad categories of stressors: naturalistic major events, naturalistic minor events, and laboratory stressors.

Naturalistic Major Events Needless to say, the major real-life events that are most likely to produce stress—divorce, a death in the family—cannot be arranged for experimental purposes. Nor, in most cases, can they be studied prospectively; they are too infrequent and unpredictable. But by assembling and studying subjects after the event, researchers have been able to establish that major life stresses do indeed penetrate to the immune system.

One of the earliest studies to demonstrate this principle involved twenty-six people whose spouses had recently died. The subjects' blood was tested two weeks after the death of the spouse and then again six weeks after the death. On the second trial it was found that the responsiveness of these people's white blood cells to mitogens was significantly lower than that of controls (Bartrop, Luckhurst, Lazarus, et al., 1977). Most of us have heard of people dying of a "broken heart" after the death of a loved one, and this phenomenon has been documented by research (Lynch, 1977). Possibly one of the avenues by which the heart is broken is the immune system.

For many of the subjects in the study just cited, the spouse's death was sudden. What is the immune response to the long-term stress of watching a family member die slowly? A major health problem in the United States today is Alzheimer's disease, an organic brain disorder that strikes the elderly and causes *dementia,* a progressive breakdown of mental functioning involving memory loss, agitation, and irrational behavior (Chapter 16). There is no cure for Alzheimer's, nor, in most cases, is there a speedy end. Patients may survive for twenty years. Many are placed in nursing homes, but some are cared for by their families, a situation that is often extremely stressful for the caregivers. Day by day, they watch the personality of a spouse or father or mother disintegrate. This process has been described by caregivers as a "living bereavement," and like ordinary bereavement, it taxes the immune system, as a recent study showed. Janice Kiecolt-Glaser and her colleagues studied a group of sixty-nine men and women who had been taking care of a spouse with Alzheimer's dementia for an average of five years. During the year-long interval between the beginning of the study and the follow-up, the caregivers, compared with controls, showed decreases in three different measures of cellular immunity. They were also ill for more days with respiratory infections (Kiecolt-Glaser, Dura, Speicher, et al., 1991). This study was the first good evidence that chronic stress leads to chronically depleted immune function.

Naturalistic Minor Events Interesting as these studies are, they have limited bearing on the question of how the immune system responds to ordinary, daily stress: traffic jams, family arguments, bounced checks. Typically, until recently these "naturalistic minor events" were rarely studied by PNI researchers. (Indeed, human beings were rarely studied by PNI researchers. Most experiments involved rodents.) Then in 1982 Kiecolt-Glaser and her coworkers began looking at the immune responses of Ohio State University medical students during final examinations. The students' blood was tested periodically throughout the academic year, including the tense three-day final-exam period. On every measure of response studied—the numbers of different kinds of immune cells, the cells' activity, their secretions—immune functioning decreased during the exam period. On one measure, the production of chemicals that activate the so-called natural-killer (NK) cells, which fight tumors and viruses, immune activity dropped by as much as 90 percent during the exam period. In a later study, the medical students' blood showed increased levels of the stress-response hormones adrenaline and noradrenaline during both waking and sleeping hours over the course of the exam period. It is possible that these hormone changes were responsible in part for the immune-function changes (Glaser, Pearson, Bonneau, et al., 1993; Kiecolt-Glaser & Glaser, 1991).

Other studies have shown that stress affects the body's defenses against herpes viruses. Unlike most other common viruses, which the immune system actually eliminates from the body, herpes viruses, once they enter the system, remain there for life. Most of the time, they are inactive, but they may flare up now and then, producing cold sores, genital herpes, mononucleosis, or other illnesses, depending on which herpes virus is involved. In medical students who have been infected with herpes viruses, immune activity against the virus has been shown to drop during final exams and then to rise again during summer vacation (Glaser, Pearson, Bonneau, et al., 1993). Indeed, stress apparently affects not only one's defenses against already present herpes viruses but also one's risk of being infected in the first place. In a recent experiment, a group of West Point cadets were tracked for four years after they entered the academy. None of these students had been infected with the Epstein-Barr virus, which causes mononucleosis, before coming to West Point. But in the course of the four years a number of them became infected. Those who did—and those who spent longest in the infirmary—tended to be the ones who, on an earlier test, had shown three risk factors for stress: high motivation for a military career, poor grades, and fathers who were "overachievers" (Kiecolt-Glaser & Glaser, 1991).

Laboratory Stressors When researchers study real-life stressors, there are many factors they can't control. Perhaps some third variable was affecting the immune functions of the West Point cadets or the Alzheimer's patients' caregivers. Out of respect for such possibilities, experimenters studying real-life stress have to be cautious in drawing cause-and-effect conclusions. By using laboratory stressors, on the other hand, researchers can control conditions in such a way as to eliminate confounding variables. They can also observe the response to stress *as it occurs* and thus study its internal dynamics.

In an interesting recent study thirty subjects were given two hard tasks to perform. One was an arithmetic problem. Starting with a four-digit number (e.g., 4,269), the subjects had to subtract 13 repeatedly in their heads and announce the results ($4,256, 4,243, 4,230, . . ."). All the while, an experimenter urged them to work faster. The second task was the so-called Stroop color-word test, in which subjects are shown, on a video monitor, the names of colors appearing in a different color. (For example, the word *blue* might appear printed in red.) Subjects are asked to ignore the word on the screen and just report the color that the word is printed in (here, red)—a difficult task that is made even harder by the fact that each presentation is accompanied by a taped voice naming various colors randomly connected to the one on the screen. The subjects in the PNI experiment worked at these tasks for twenty minutes, after which blood samples were taken. The samples showed significantly reduced immune functioning compared with that of controls who did not perform the tasks. An hour later, blood was taken again, and again it showed depleted immune activity. So immune responses to stress are not necessarily brief, transient effects (Stone, Valdimarsdottir, Katkin, et al., 1993).

For all its advantages, laboratory research has the disadvantage that its conditions are not those of ordinary life. The Stroop color-word task is not among the trials that most people endure in their daily existence. However, one recent experiment, again by the Kiecolt-Glaser team, went fairly far in duplicating an important source of real-life stress: marital conflict. Ninety recently married couples were admitted to a hospital research unit for twenty-four hours. By means of an interview and questionnaire, two or three topics of conflict were identified for each couple. Then the couples were asked to discuss these problems and try to resolve them during a thirty-minute session. The session was videotaped, and blood samples were taken several times in the course of it. (The couples had been outfitted with catheters.) The videotapes were later rated on various measures—negative behavior, positive behavior, problem-solving behavior, avoidant behavior—by independent raters, and these results were compared with the results of immune-function tests on the blood samples. What the researchers found, in general, was that the more negative behavior, such as arguing or accusing, a subject showed, the more likely he or she was to show reduced immune functioning. Interestingly, immune changes were not found to be related to positive, problem-solving, or avoidant behaviors, only to negative behaviors. Another curious finding was that women were more likely than men to show negative immune changes. As in the stress-task experiment, the immune effects were not transient. They were still present twenty-four hours after the taped session (Kiecolt-Glaser, Malarkey, Chee, et al., 1993).

PSYCHOLOGICAL FACTORS AND PHYSICAL DISORDERS

Psychological factors, as we saw, can affect any physical disorder. We will discuss only a few conditions in which the influence of mental processes has been of special concern to researchers.

Essential Hypertension

Of all the physical disorders commonly associated with psychological stress, chronically high blood pressure, known as **hypertension,** is the most common and the most dangerous. An estimated 15 percent of the population of the United States suffers from this cardiovascular disorder, which in turn predisposes them to two other, deadly cardiovascular disorders: heart attack and "stroke" (MacMahon, Peto, Cutter, et al., 1990). Untreated hypertensives have an average life expectancy of between fifty and sixty years, compared with seventy-one years for the population at large.

We saw earlier how hypertension illustrates the principle of disregulation (G. E. Schwartz, 1977): breakdown in one component leads to breakdown in the system as a whole. The function of the cardiovascular system, consisting of the heart and the peripheral blood vessels, is to pump blood through

Even for young people, the stress of living in a dangerous, drug-ridden neighborhood like New York City's south Bronx, raises the risk for developing essential hypertension.

the body, carrying nutrients where they are needed and carrying wastes where they can be disposed of. Every heartbeat represents a contraction of the heart; with each contraction, blood is pushed out of the heart and through the blood vessels. At the same time, the blood vessels are contracting and dilating in response to internal and external stimuli. The blood pressure—that is, the pressure that blood exerts on the walls of the blood vessels—is a function of several variables, but one of the most important, at least in chronic hypertension, seems to be the degree of constriction in the blood vessels (Forsyth, 1974). When a normal person's blood pressure rises too high, the baroreceptors convey this information to the brain, and in response to this negative feedback, the brain then relaxes the constricted vessel walls. In hypertensives, however, the regulatory mechanism somehow fails to work, with the result that the blood vessels remain chronically constricted and hence the blood pressure chronically high.

Why does this happen? In a small percentage of cases, approximately 10 to 15 percent, hypertension is linked to an identifiable organic cause, usually kidney dysfunction (D. Shapiro & Goldstein, 1982). In the remaining cases, known as **essential hypertension,** there is no known organic cause. Many different factors have been suggested.

One is environment. It may be that some essential hypertensives live in environments that are particularly rich in the kinds of stressors that increase blood pressure—danger, for example. Researchers have noted that people have bouts of high blood pressure when they are in situations requiring constant alertness against danger (Gutmann & Benson, 1971). In light of these findings, it is interesting to note that essential hypertension is twice as common among blacks as it is among whites. While this disparity may be a function of genes, diet, or other factors, one might also hypothesize that blacks as a group are exposed to greater stress than whites. A study of black people in Detroit found that those living in high-stress areas—neighborhoods with lower income, higher unemployment, higher divorce rate, higher crime rate—had higher blood pressure than those living in low-stress areas (Harburg, 1978).

Essential hypertension may also be due in part to individual response specificity. In other words, genes or experience may have programmed the brain to respond to different kinds of stress with increases in blood pressure. Recent research has focused on subjects assumed to be at risk for hypertension, including people with at least one hypertensive parent and people who have had mildly elevated blood pressure in childhood or early adulthood. When confronted with demanding behavioral and cognitive tasks, such people do experience greater cardiovascular reactions than people without a family history of hypertension (Fredrikson, 1990; Steptoe, 1984). Some research suggests that hypertension may be associated with certain personality traits, above all, the tendency to suppress anger.

Because high blood pressure produces no immediate discomfort, many hypertensives are unaware of their condition, with the result that it may go untreated for years. Furthermore, those who are aware that they have hypertension are often unaware that circumstances in their family life or work environment may be aggravating it. Like the aforementioned baroreceptors, they have adapted to the stress and no longer see it as stressful. Often it takes some kind of crisis—a situation in which blood pressure and environmental pressures simultaneously increase dramatically—before such patients will take seriously the connection between their blood pressure and their way of life, and consider changing the latter. In many cases, family and work circumstances are not all that need changing. A number of physical factors—above all, smoking, obesity, and high salt intake—have been shown to aggravate hypertension. Obese people are three times more likely to be hypertensive than people who are not overweight (Van Itallie, 1985). As for smoking, it apparently combines synergistically with hypertension to create a high risk of heart disease (Wilhelmsen, 1988).

Headache

Stress has long been thought to be implicated in chronic headaches, including the very severe form known as **migraine headache.** Migraines differ from ordinary headaches—often called **muscle-contraction headaches,** or *tension headaches*—in that they are usually localized on one side of the head and are far more intense. A migraine attack further differs from a tension headache in that it is sometimes preceded by an *aura,* or spell of perceptual distortion, often involving strange visual sensations such as flashing lights or blind spots. Finally, in migraine, unlike tension headaches, head pain is typically accompanied by other symptoms: physical (nausea, vomiting), cognitive (confusion), and affective (depression, irritability). Intolerance to light and sound are also common. Migraine attacks range from bearable discomfort to complete immobilization. They may last from several hours to several days and may occur as frequently as every day or as infrequently as once every few months.

In recent years theories of migraine have shown a dramatic shift from psychological to organic causation. For the last half-century migraine was thought to be the product of a stress-induced cardiovascular process involving the constriction and dilation of the blood vessels in the head (Wolff, 1948). As for the psychological causes behind this cardiovascular quirk, there were various theories, ranging from descriptions of a "migraine personality" to speculations about female emotional instability. (Migraine is twice as common in women as in men.)

Recently, however, these theories have been essentially scrapped, together with the idea that migraine is a cardiovascular disorder. According to newer findings (Raskin, Hosobuchi, & Lamb, 1987), migraine is a neurological disorder involving some dysfunction in the operation of the neurotransmitter serotonin. A number of different signs pointed researchers in this direction. For one thing, the most effective drugs for migraine are all connected to serotonin, whereas they are not directly connected to blood-vessel function. Furthermore, serotonin and its chemical counterpart norepi-

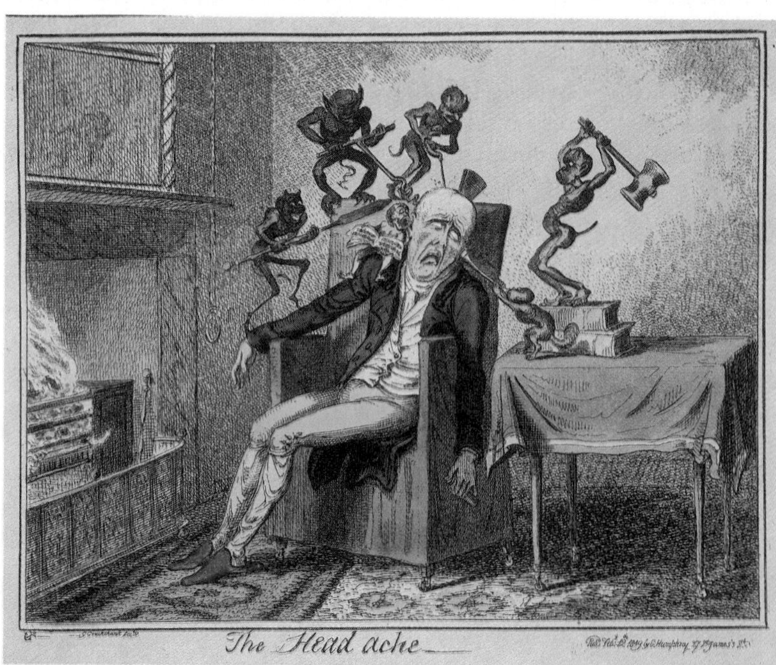

This nineteenth-century etching by George Cruikshank conveys the intense misery caused by a head-splitting migraine headache.

nephrine are both linked to depression and sleep disturbances, which in turn are linked to migraine and are commonly seen in families with a susceptibility to migraine. The connection between migraine and serotonin was also signaled by a curious accidental experiment. Fifteen people with no history of migraine, but with intractable back pain, were given electrode implants in their brains as a treatment for their back problems. All of them developed severe migraine. According to Raskin and colleagues (1987), the site of the electrode implantation was near the region of the brain where serotonin is most active.

No one knows as yet the precise nature of the presumed serotonin dysfunction. Perhaps, in migraine sufferers, the body simply produces too little serotonin. Or perhaps the available serotonin is destroyed too quickly by enzymes as it crosses the synapses between the nerve cells. Another possibility is that the receptors responsible for taking up serotonin are not accepting enough of it. In any case, the serotonin hypothesis has unleashed a great flurry of research, and more refined hypotheses are expected shortly.

If effective drugs are developed, they will be welcome, for migraine is a common disorder, afflicting approximately 18 million people in the United States alone. The fact that two-thirds of these people are women—and that their attacks tend to appear in adolescence and disappear after menopause—suggests that hormonal changes associated with the menstrual cycle are also involved in migraine. And underlying all these organic factors is presumably some measure of genetic causation, for as many as 90 percent of migraine sufferers have a family history of the disorder.

None of this means that stress is not involved in migraine. Many different stimuli—bright lights, red wine, changes in atmospheric pressure—can precipitate a migraine, but one of the most common triggers is minor stress (Brantley & Jones, 1993). In one study it was found that the best predictor of migraines was stress one to three days prior to the headache. For muscle-contraction headaches, the best predictor was stress on the same day (Mosley, Penizen, Johnson, et al., 1991). What the serotonin research suggests is simply that migraine is one of many physical disorders involving both organic and environmental causes.

Obesity

Eating behavior, like most other bodily functions, is regulated by feedback loops. In highly simplified terms, the sequence is as follows. When the body is in need of nourishment, it sends hunger signals to the brain. Then, as we eat, other internal signals alert the brain that the body is satiated, at which point we put down our forks. This is the normal regulatory cycle. It too can succumb to disregulation, however. The feedback may fail to reach the brain, or the brain may receive the feedback but still respond inappropriately. In either case, the cycle is thrown off, and the person either fails to eat when the stomach signals hunger or goes on eating when the stomach signals satiety.

The line that separates obesity from normal weight varies across cultures and centuries. More than a few of today's Americans wish they could have lived in seventeenth-century Europe, when Rubens's voluptuous nudes represented the ideal of female beauty. (Men have had their turn in other ages—in the early decades of this century, for example, when a protruding abdomen was a sign of a man's success and prosperity.)

The first of these two patterns of disregulation—chronic failure to eat, to the point of extreme malnutrition—is known as *anorexia nervosa*. Because it normally begins in adolescence, we will discuss it under childhood and adolescent disorders (Chapter 17). We turn our attention now to the second and far more familiar pattern, obesity.

Obesity is a socially defined condition. Strictly speaking, the term refers to an excessive amount of fat on the body, but every culture has its own idea of what is excessive. What would have been regarded as a healthy adult in the nineteenth century would now be called a fat person; conversely, to nineteenth-century eyes, the thinness of today's fashion models would seem grotesque. Our society, actually, is caught in a curious paradox. Perhaps in no other culture has thinness been so highly prized, and obesity so prevalent. Somewhere between 15 and 50 percent of American adults are more than 20 percent overweight. The prevalence of obesity increases with age and is highest among lower socioeconomic groups (K. D. Brownell, 1982).

Obesity is not good for the body. It increases the likelihood of digestive disease, cardiovascular disease, adult-onset diabetes, and cancer (Brantley & Garrett, 1993; Bray, 1984). But does this make an "abnormal" condition? Certainly not by the statistical-rarity criterion, as we have just seen. However, it might be defined as such according to the norm-violation criterion, the norm being thinness. Above all, the "abnormality" of obesity would be related to the personal-discomfort criterion. In many sectors of our society, obesity is viewed as "a state verging on crime" (J. Rodin, 1977a). As a result, the obese not only suffer the consequences of their socially defined unattractiveness—consequences ranging from a mild sense of inferiority to extreme social and sexual maladjustment—but they must suffer shame as well. This is personal discomfort indeed, and it brings many people into therapy.

What causes obesity? In part, the reasons are directly physiological. Excess weight is not necessarily due to excess eating. Many obese people eat moderately and still remain fat, while many thin people can "eat anything" and still stay thin—an injustice of which overweight people often complain. In such cases, the controlling variables are apparently activity level and metabolic rate, the rate at which the body converts food into energy (J. K. Thompson, Jarvie, Lahey, et al., 1982). And while activity level can be altered by exercise programs, metabolic rate is in large measure genetically determined. Furthermore, once a person becomes overweight, the added pounds *further* lower the metabolic rate. (That is, once the weight is gained, fewer calories are needed to keep it on than were needed to put it on.) To make matters worse, dieting also tends to lower the metabolic rate, with the result, ruefully noted by many dieters, that one can count calories religiously and still not lose weight (J. Rodin, 1981). In sum, certain bodies are apparently born to carry more fat than others.

Yet obesity is due not to physiology alone but to an interaction of physiological and psychological factors. A number of studies indicate that obese people are far more responsive than others to any food-relevant stimulus: the taste of food (Nisbett, 1968), the sight and smell of food (J. Rodin, 1981; Schachter, 1971), the clock indicating that it is mealtime (Schachter & Gross, 1968), and, presumably, television commercials and magazine advertisements. Other experiments suggest that overweight people may also have a problem with the transmission of feedback from the stomach to the brain. When normal people are asked how hungry they are, their answers correlate strongly with the frequency of their stomach contractions. When overweight people are put to the same test, the correlation is much weaker (Stunkard & Koch, 1964).

It is hard to say, however, whether the disregulation observed in these experiments was actually due to obesity. Most overweight people are dieters, and whatever disregulation they show may be the result not of excess weight but of dieting. Several experiments have found that obese people who are not dieters do not show overresponsiveness to food cues (C. P. Herman & Mack, 1975; Ruderman & Wilson, 1979). On the other hand, overresponsiveness and many of the other peculiarities said to characterize the eating behavior of the obese *are* found in people who are of normal weight but are chronic dieters (Klajner, Herman, Polivy, et al., 1981). There is now solid evidence that chronic dieting may lead to disregulation. People who, whether or not they are overweight, have been kept from their normal eating pattern are more likely to engage in binge eating (Wardle, 1980), are more likely to eat in response to stress (Cools, Schotte, & McNally, 1992; Heatherton, Herman, & Polivy, 1991), and are more likely to go on eating once they have violated the dietary restraint (Ruderman, 1986)—facts that will sound familiar to anyone who has been on a diet. This disregulation may eventually lead to the chronic pattern of binge eating known as bulimia (Polivy & Herman, 1985). Bulimia will be discussed, with anorexia, in Chapter 17.

Such findings, together with the physiological evidence described above, have caused many weight-reduction programs to shift their emphasis from dieting to exercise. Exercise presumably does not interfere with the regulatory cycle that controls eating. On the other hand, it does burn up calories, suppress the appetite, and increase the metabolic rate, so even when one is not exercising, calories are being burned faster. But exercise alone may not be enough. Recent research indicates that the most effective weight-reduction programs are those that focus on several components—typically, dietary changes, problem solving, and peer support as well as exercise—and that extend over a long period, such as a year. As for the maintenance of weight loss, those who go on exercising are the most likely to keep the pounds off (Craighead & Agras, 1991).

In addition to advocating weight reduction for the obese, many experts feel that what our society needs is a broader definition of physical attractiveness, so that beauty is not confined to the thinnest end of the spectrum of human body types. Many moderately heavy people have nothing wrong with them, either physically or psychologically. On the other hand, it is possible that dieting has acquired an undeservedly bad name in recent years. "The 1990s are taking shape as an antidieting decade," weight expert Kelly Brownell has written (1993, p. 339). Popular magazines regularly publish articles critical of weight consciousness, and antidieting books are appearing. A statistic often cited in such writings is that 95 percent of all diets fail. That figure, however, is over thirty years old (Stunkard & McLaren-Hume, cited in K. D. Brownell, 1993) and was derived from people in university-based treatment programs—people who were heavier, showed more psychological disorders, and were more likely to be binge eaters than overweight people in general (K. D. Brownell, 1993). In fact, it is not at all clear how successful most diets are; research is badly needed on this question. In the meantime, it appears that the perils of dieting have been exaggerated. According to a recent review (French & Jeffrey, 1994), dieting is not usually associated with nutritional deficiencies, adverse physiological reactions, severe psychological reactions, or the development of eating disorders. Such problems can arise, but ordinarily they don't.

Asthma

Asthma has been the focus of considerable attention, not only because of its high prevalence—about 5 percent of the general American population suffers from it—but also because it is one of the few stress-related physical disorders common in young children. About 8 percent of children between the ages of six and eleven suffer from asthma (M. R. Sears, 1991).

Asthma is a disorder of the respiratory system, the function of which is to bring air into and out of the lungs, so that the body can take in oxygen and give off carbon dioxide. During an asthma attack the body's air passageways narrow, and the constriction causes coughing, wheezing, and general difficulty in breathing. Asthma attacks may last for only a few minutes or for several hours. They also vary considerably in their intensity. Some attacks are mild; in others, bronchial spasms constrict the air passageways to the point where the person has immense difficulty getting air into and out of the lungs. Wheezing and coughing uncontrollably, the asthmatic feels that he or she is suffocating, literally at the point of death. This is a terrifying experience. It may also be a dangerous one. A series of severe attacks can cause a progressive deterioration of the bronchial system, so mucus accumulates and the muscles lose their elasticity. In such a weakened condition, the bronchial system loses its ability to fight back, and any further attack may indeed prove fatal. Very few asthmatics die of the disorder, however.

Asthma is normally divided into two classes: allergic and nonallergic. Some asthmas are, at least in part, allergies—reactions to specific irritants such as pollen, molds, and animal dander. Nonallergic asthmas may stem from a variety of organic disorders, the most common causes being respiratory infections such as pneumonia and whooping cough. Indeed, the first asthma attack usually follows closely upon a respiratory infection (A. B. Alexander, 1981). However, there are many cases for which no organic cause, allergic or otherwise, can be found and for which no medical therapy proves truly effective. Such cases are often suspected to be psychogenic.

The psychogenic theory of asthma is quite old. Indeed, asthma was one of the cornerstones of "psychosomatic" theory in general, particularly in psychodynamic quarters. But as with migraine, the recent trend in asthma theory has been away from psychogenic causation, for research has repeatedly failed to establish psychological factors as a primary cause. There is even some doubt about psychological stress as a secondary cause—that is, as a trigger for attacks, whatever the original cause of the condition. Attempts to induce attacks in asthma sufferers by exposing them to emotion- and stress-inducing stimuli have resulted in slightly decreased airflow but no actual attacks (e.g., J. M. Weiss, Glazer, & Pohorecky, 1976).

The best evidence for a psychological factor in asthma is an experiment by Luparello, McFadden, Lyons, and Bleecker (1971). In what the researchers claimed was a study of air pollution, each of forty asthmatics and forty normal subjects was given five substances to inhale. The asthmatics were told that they were inhaling irritants known to be related to their previous attacks. The normal subjects were told that they were inhaling five progressively stronger concentrations of air pollutants and that they might respond with breathing problems. Actually, all of the subjects were inhaling nonallergenic saline vapors. The normal subjects proved quite resistant to the power of suggestion; none of them showed any pathological reactions. By contrast, one-third of the asthmatic group developed constricted airways, and twelve of the forty proceeded to have full-scale attacks.

Still, this does not prove that in those cases the asthma was entirely or even largely psychogenic. More likely, the subjects were showing a short-term conditioning effect. That is, since in the past their expectation of having an attack was followed by an attack, the raising of that expectation by the experimenters was sufficient to bring on the attack. (If so, the response would probably have extinguished after a few trials.) Conditioned stimuli can produce elaborate physiological responses, but that does not mean that those responses are *typically* elicited by those stimuli, let alone that they were first established by those stimuli.

This is not to say that psychological problems are not associated with asthma. The disorder itself may lead to psychological problems, particularly in children who are overprotected because of their condition. And even if the disorder is clearly biogenic, such psychological ramifications may aggravate it.

Sleep Disorders

Insomnia **Insomnia,** the chronic inability to sleep, is rarely discussed in textbooks on abnormal psychology except as a symptom of other disorders, such as depression. Yet for an extremely large number of people, sleeplessness is the sole complaint, and one that causes severe physical and psychological distress. Sleeping problems affect an estimated 14 to 25 percent of the population. Women are at higher risk than men, and older people are at considerably higher risk than younger people.

There are three broad patterns of insomnia. Some people take an extremely long time to fall asleep; others fall asleep easily but awaken repeatedly during the night; others fall asleep easily but wake up much too early in the morning (e.g., 3 or 4 A.M.) and are unable to fall asleep again. At some point in our lives, each of us has probably experienced one or another of these difficulties. The term *insomnia* is applied only if the problem persists and the person's daily functioning is clearly disturbed—by fatigue, irritability, inability to concentrate, and so forth—as a result.

Sleep disturbance is almost always a source of concern for the person experiencing it, and this concern leads to what is called *anticipatory anxiety.* The minute the person gets into bed, or even while undressing, he or she begins to worry: Will I be able to sleep? Will it be like last night? And since worry of any kind impedes sleep, the person probably *will* have another night like last night. Hence insomnia is a classic example of the vicious cycle.

Insomnia can stem from many factors, including drugs, alcohol, caffeine, nicotine, stress and anxiety, physical illness, psychological disturbance, inactivity, poor sleep environment, and poor sleep habits (Bootzin & Perlis, 1992). It may also be a subjective matter in part. Many insomniacs underestimate the amount of sleep they get, at least as measured by instruments such as EEGs. When the gap between reported and measured sleep is extreme, this condition is called *sleep-state misperception.* Some cases of sleep-state misperception seem to be due to an inability to distinguish between sleep states and going-to-sleep states. People who go on thinking, during sleep, about problems that were on their minds during the day are likely to believe that they weren't sleeping but were still in that twilight stage between waking and sleep (Engle-Friedman, Baker, & Bootzin, 1985). Actually, what insomnia experts call sleep, based on EEG brain-wave patterns, is simply an operational definition. People who are "asleep" by EEG criteria will often, if you wake them up, say that they were awake. Still, this happens far more often with insomniacs than with good sleepers (Borkovec, Lane & VanOot, 1981). And by measures other than the EEG, some of these insomniacs *are* awake. In one experiment, a group of insomniacs "slept" (by EEG criteria) while, every four or five minutes, a voice on a tape, speaking at normal volume, said a letter of the alphabet. If awakened and asked to repeat the last letter spoken, some of the subjects were able to give the right answer (Engle-Friedman, Baker, & Bootzin, 1985). Such evidence suggests that at least for some insomniacs, the critical problem may be hypervigilance. That is, they are less able to turn off the sounds of the night while asleep than the rest of us.

Most sleep-inducing drugs are ineffective when used over a long period, and many of them have undesirable side effects. (We shall discuss sleeping pills in Chapter 21.) Hence there is a great need for treatments that can compete with drugs. Insight therapy may be helpful for those whose insomnia is part of a larger psychological problem, but for those whose major or only problem is insomnia, the best route now available is probably behavioral therapy, which typically combines relaxation training with procedures to strengthen the habit of falling asleep at bedtime (Bootzin & Perlis, 1992).

Circadian Rhythm Disorders Circadian rhythm disorders occur when people try to sleep at times that are inconsistent with Circadian rhythms, the cycles dictated by their "biological clocks." Sometimes the disorder is due to work shifts. We noted earlier that many late-shift workers try, on their days off, to wake up at the same time as their friends and families, thus derailing their sleep cycles. Other workers' cycles are disturbed by rotating shifts. In both cases, the result is often reduced sleep, drowsiness on the job, and health problems. But circadian rhythm disorders are not limited to shift workers. Many people, for no external reason, fall asleep earlier or later than seems to them normal or desirable. They get a good night's sleep, but not when they want to. Age is often a factor in this pattern. Many young people lie awake at 2 A.M., while old people fall asleep after dinner and then wake up at 3 A.M. Such problems, which can be very distressing, are sometimes treated by *chronotherapy,* which involves moving bedtime later and later in regular increments. For example, a "night person" who regularly goes to sleep at 3 A.M. will be told to put off going to sleep until 6 A.M., then the next day till 9 A.M., and so on, until, by moving bedtime around the clock, he or she reaches the desired bedtime. Once the target bedtime is reached, however, it must be adhered to strictly, for there is a tendency to drift back to the former pattern (Czeisler, Richardson, Coleman, et al., 1981). Another therapy that appears promising for circadian rhythm disorders is light treatment. To move bedtime earlier, the person is exposed to bright light in the morning; to move bedtime later, lights are used in the evening. This treatment is still new, but it has been shown to help shift workers, jet-lag sufferers, "night people," and elderly people suffering from early-morning waking (Bootzin, Manber, Perlis, et al., 1993; Czeisler, Kronauer, Allen, et al., 1989).

Common sleep disorders also include nightmares, night terrors, and sleepwalking. All three tend to afflict children, and therefore they will be discussed under childhood disorders in Chapter 17.

Cancer

Cancer is one of the greatest challenges that the human body has ever posed to medical science. This disease accounts for almost one-quarter of all deaths in the United States, and it is gaining ground. Death rates from other major killers such as heart disease and strokes have been decreasing, but death rates due to cancer have actually risen 20 percent in the past three decades (American Cancer Society, 1994).

For a long time it was believed that whatever physical disorders might be associated with psychological stress, cancer was not one of them. Now, as recent studies have established, cancer *is* one of them. At the beginning of this chapter we mentioned one such study, involving breast cancer patients who, in addition to their medical treatment, attended weekly group therapy for a year (Spiegel, Bloom, Kraemer, et al., 1989). The therapy sessions addressed various matters. The women were taught by the group leaders how to control pain through self-hypnosis; they were also advised on how to communicate with their families and how to be assertive with their doctors. But the main function of the group was to give the women a chance to express their feelings and support one another. They discussed their family problems, their physical distress as a result of chemotherapy and radiation, their fear of dying. Eventually they developed strong bonds. They visited one another in the hospital, wrote poems together, and even, at one point, moved their meeting to the home of a dying member. As we saw, these women were found, on follow-up, to have survived twice as long as controls after the beginning of treatment. What kept them alive? The experimenters speculate that the advice and sympathy the subjects received may have influenced them to follow health regimens better—eat, exercise, take medication—and thus live longer. But in the experimenters' opinion a major factor was simply social support. It is a well-established fact that married cancer patients survive longer than unmarried cancer patients (Goodwin, Hunt, Key, et al., 1987), but even families, out of worry and grief, may be of limited use, psychologically, to a dying member. The women in this study had each other, and apparently that helped them to fight breast cancer.

Other researchers have found the same thing with people suffering from malignant melanoma, a form of skin cancer that can be cured in its early stages but tends to recur. In a study of sixty-eight patients, thirty-four controls were given medical treatment only; the remaining thirty-four subjects were given medical treatment and group therapy—in this case, only six sessions—focused on education, stress management, coping skills, and psychological support. Recontacted five to six years later, the two groups showed widely different health records. Twice as many of the controls had had a recurrence of malignant melanoma, and three times as many of the controls had died (Fawzy, Fawzy, Hyun, et al., 1993).

So group therapy seems to help some cancer patients. Possibly one of its crucial benefits is that it encourages active coping as opposed to helplessness. Animal studies have shown a close correlation between helplessness and the growth of cancer cells. In one study, Sklar and Anisman (1979) implanted tumor cells in rats and then divided the rats into three groups. One group received electric shocks that they could escape by pressing a bar. The second group received inescapable shocks, and the third group, no shocks. The experimenters found that the tumors grew more quickly in the rats given inescapable shocks than in either of the other groups. In a later study, with much the same design, the cancer cells were implanted in smaller doses, so that the animals' immune systems could conceivably combat them. The results were quite striking: the rats given the inescapable shocks were only half as likely to reject the cancer and were twice as likely to die of it as the escapable-shock and no-shock groups (Visintainer, Volpicelli, & Seligman, 1982). Generalizing from rats to human beings is always problematic, but it is likely that helplessness will be a major concern of future PNI research on cancer.

Whatever the relationship between cancer and life stress, cancer itself—finding out one has it, dealing with the family, going through treatments—is a major life stress, one that can affect behavior in a way that influences the person's chance of survival. Eating habits, alcohol consumption, the taking of medication—all of these behaviors are vulnerable to stress. Psychological treatment for cancer patients is still in its early stages. (As noted, it was only recently recognized that psychological treatment helps cancer patients.) But in the future such treatment should probably place more emphasis on these practical issues (B. L. Anderson, Kiecolt-Glaser, & Glaser, 1994).

AIDS

Acquired immune deficiency syndrome, or **AIDS,** was first identified in 1981. It is caused by the **human immunodeficiency virus (HIV),** which is communicated via the blood, semen, vaginal secretions, or breast milk of an infected person, either during unprotected sex, through a shared hypodermic needle, from a contaminated blood transfusion, or (in the case of a newborn whose mother is infected) in the womb. Once the virus becomes active, it attacks the immune system, leaving the person open to various infections, including Kaposi's sarcoma, a form of cancer rare in people unexposed to HIV. But HIV can remain dormant for a long time before becoming active. Some people are said to have been HIV-positive for twenty years before developing symptoms. To date, almost 356,000 Americans have been diagnosed with AIDS—the epidemic is far worse in other countries—and 217,917 Americans have died of AIDS (Center for Disease Control, 1993). More will die in the years to come. Between 1 and 2 million Americans are estimated to be HIV-positive, but this figure may be unrealistically low, for many people have not yet been tested. Indeed, the largest risk group, heterosexual men and women having unprotected sex with multiple partners, has a testing rate of only 35 percent (Berrios, Hearst, Coates, et al., 1993).

The "Aliveness Project" in Minneapolis helps AIDS patients reduce stress, in an effort to relieve some of their symptoms.

In view of the evidence that psychological stress affects the immune system, we might assume that stress would speed the course of AIDS, a disease centered in the immune system. The findings are contradictory, however. Some studies have found no relationship between stress and the progress of HIV infection (Kessler, Foster, Joseph, et al., 1991; Rabkin, Williams, Remien, et al., 1991). Others have found more vigorous immune responses in HIV-positive men with more active coping styles (Goodkin, Blaney, Feasler, et al., 1992). As for the medical benefits of psychological treatment, most efforts have been focused on one potential benefit, the avoidance of high-risk behavior. There have been a number of cognitive-behavioral skills-training programs designed to discourage unsafe sex. Typically, these programs include several components: instructions about safe and unsafe sex; assertiveness training (to enable people to say no to unsafe sex); problem-solving training (to teach people to anticipate and avoid risk factors such as alcohol or drug use); and reinforcement of behavior change. Such programs, so far aimed primarily at homosexual men (Kelly & Murphy, 1992) and sexually active teenagers (Rotheram-Borus, Koopman, & Haignere, 1991), have reported good results.

PERSPECTIVES ON STRESS AND ILLNESS

The Behavioral Perspective

Respondent versus Operant For years it was generally accepted that autonomic responses were involuntary. Therefore, if conditioning were involved in the disregulation of these responses, it would have to be respondent conditioning, for operant conditioning requires that the organism be capable of voluntarily modifying responses in order to obtain rewards or avoid punishments. We now know that respondent conditioning can have a powerful effect on physiological responses. A problem with cancer patients, for example, is that in response to chemotherapy they develop conditioned nausea and immune dysfunction. In a study of twenty women receiving chemotherapy for ovarian cancer, the women were tested first at home and then at the hospital. Even though the hospital tests were done before the chemotherapy, the women still showed an increase in nausea and a decrease in immune activity—clearly a conditioned response, and one that does not aid in recovery (Bovjberg, Redd, Maier, et al., 1990).

Until about thirty years ago, such respondent behaviors were all that behaviorists could point to as an explanation for stress-related illness, and they were not a very comprehensive explanation. Then, in the sixties, a series of breakthrough experiments with rats showed that not only heart rate but also blood pressure and urine formation could be modified through operant conditioning (N. E. Miller, 1969). One rat was even taught to dilate the blood vessels in one ear and at the same time to constrict the blood vessels in the other ear in response to a cue (Di Cara & Miller, 1968). Clearly, some autonomic responses could not only be controlled but controlled with great precision.

This discovery had two important consequences. First, it helped to explain how learning could operate in the development of physical disorders: if the disorder had any rewarding consequences, then these consequences might be maintaining the disorder through operant conditioning. Second, whether or not voluntary control was involved in the development of the disorder, it could be enlisted to relieve disorder.

Biofeedback, Relaxation, and Exercise Since these early experiments, it has been found that the physiological responses underlying many physical disorders can be partially controlled if patients are first trained to recognize these responses in their bodies—to know what it "feels like" when their heart rate or blood pressure, for example, goes up and down. Given this information, the patient can then *make* it go up and down. This training is known as **biofeedback training.** Migraine patients, for example, will be hooked up to a machine that gives them feedback on temperature and blood flow in their hands. (Whatever the implications of the serotonin hypothesis, many migraine patients obtain relief when blood flows away from the head toward the periphery [Blanchard & Andrasik, 1985].) The patients, in other words, are given immediate feedback on their bodily functioning, and then somehow, through a process that we do not yet understand, they begin to exert control over this functioning—a control that it is hoped will extend beyond the biofeedback laboratory, into their daily lives. Indeed, biofeedback has proved quite helpful with headaches (Olton & Noonberg, 1980).

Another technique that behaviorists have used extensively in stress-relief programs is **relaxation training.** There are several procedures for inducing deep muscle relaxation, but perhaps the most popular is *progressive relaxation,* developed by E. Jacobson (1938). In this technique, the client, going from muscle group to muscle group within the body, is instructed to contract the muscles, to hold them that way for about ten seconds, and then to release them, thus achieving a state of relaxation. The object is to teach the person, first, how to distinguish between tension and relaxation and, second, how to achieve the latter. With practice in this technique, many people, as soon as they feel themselves going tense, can relax their bodies—a great aid in combating stress. Relaxation training has been used for years, successfully, in treating a wide variety of conditions—depression, anxiety disorders, insomnia—that involve stress. Recently, researchers have found that it can also stimulate immune functioning, as has been shown in studies of older people (Kiecolt-Glaser, Glaser, Williger, et al., 1985) and of HIV patients (Rutenfanz, Haider, & Koller, 1985).

Finally, exercise can relieve stress, as was shown in an interesting experiment with men who had signed up for HIV testing. Half these men were assigned to a five-week aerobic exercise program, the other half to no intervention. Then they waited for their HIV status results. Their immune functions were tested a week before they received their results and again a week after. Not surprisingly, many of the men who were found to be HIV-positive showed decreased immune activity, together with anxiety and depression, but as it turned out, these were the men in the no-intervention group. The results for the HIV-positive men in the exercise group were roughly the same as for the men who were HIV-negative: no emotional or immunological change (LaPerriere, Antoni, Schneiderman, et al., 1990).

The Cognitive Perspective

Predictability and Control With stress, as with anxiety, the cognitive theorists have pointed out that there is more to the process than simply stimulus and response. Two cognitive variables that seem to be particularly important in stress reactions are the person's ability to predict the stressful stimulus and his or her sense of control over the stimulus. As research has shown, predictable stimuli are less stressful than unpredictable stimuli. This principle was borne out during the London blitz of World War II. Londoners, who were bombed regularly and frequently, experienced very few serious stress reactions, whereas people in the countryside, who were bombed far less frequently but unpredictably, often responded with severe anxiety (Vernon, 1941).

Even more important than predictability, however, seems to be the sense of control. Remember the rats who were implanted with the cancer cells. Remarkably, the rats who were able to control the shock were as likely to reject the cancer as those who received no shock (Visintainer, Volpicelli, & Seligman, 1982). This phenomenon is presumably related to Bandura's theory of "efficacy expectations" and their effect on anxiety levels (Chapters 3 and 7). In any case, its applicability to humans as well has been shown experimentally. The point is not just that by coping we can actually solve the problems that create stress; coping also affects our physiological responses to stress. Researchers have found that decreased catecholamine levels, which are associated with depression, are also associated with subjective judgments of inability to cope, and that as people's sense of their coping ability increases, so does their catecholamine level (Bandura, Taylor, & Williams, 1985). According to PNI researchers, coping also affects the immune system. Poor coping suppresses immune responses; good coping enhances them (Kiecolt-Glaser, Fisher, Ogrocki, et al., 1987). So effective coping not only keeps people healthy; it probably also helps them get better once they fall ill (J. Rodin & Salovey, 1989).

In all cases, however, according to cognitive researchers, coping is connected back to cognitive processes and determined by cognitive styles. This interaction is the focus of the model of stress developed by Richard Lazarus and his research group (Folkman, Lazarus, Dunkel-Schetter, et al., 1986; Lazarus & Folkman, 1984). The model describes stress not as something in the person or something in the environment but as a dynamic, mutually reciprocal, bidirectional relationship between the two, involving six basic stages. The first stage is the *environmental event.* Second comes *primary appraisal,* in which the person decides whether he or she has anything at stake in the event. The third stage is *secondary appraisal:* having decided that there is something at stake, the person determines whether he or she can influence the situation. This is where efficacy expectations come into play. The fourth stage is *coping,* which may be either problem-focused (taking action to change the situation) or emotion-focused (e.g., seeking social support). Coping and appraisal, however, are not really two successive stages but a constant back-and-forth dynamic: the person appraises, copes, appraises the feedback, copes again, and so on. The fifth stage involves the *outcomes of coping.* These may be physiological (ANS arousal, immune system activation), behavioral (changes in high-risk behaviors), and cognitive (changed goals or beliefs). Finally, the sixth stage consists of *health outcomes,* such as illness or, if one copes effectively, prevention, illness reporting, and/or recovery. Conceptually, the value of this model is its interactive nature, but it also has a practical benefit: because it is broken down into multiple stages, with multiple reappraisals, it offers second and third chances for improved coping.

Cognitive principles have been put into practice in so-called stress management programs (Meichenbaum & Jaremko, 1983). The goal of such programs is to pinpoint the cognitive and environmental sources of the patient's stress and then to build up the skills that he or she needs in order to cope with those stressors. If the person complains of being pushed around by others, for example, assertiveness training can help the person avoid being pushed around. Likewise, people who feel overwhelmed by demands on their time may be given help with time management. Most patients are also instructed in muscle relaxation, either through the contracting-and-relaxing technique or through meditation. The newer psychological treatments for people with serious illnesses often involve such training. Stress management was part of the Fawzy team's group therapy for malignant melanoma patients, for example (Fawzy, Fawzy, Hyun, et al., 1993).

The Psychodynamic Perspective

Psychodynamic theorists, as we have seen, regard most behavior as symptomatic of buried emotional content. Thus it comes as no surprise that the psychodynamic school was the first to recognize that psychological difficulties might contribute significantly to physical illness. Traditionally psychodynamic theorists have referred to stress-related physical disorders as *organ neuroses*. As the term suggests, psychodynamic theory regards these disorders as caused by the same mechanisms—repression, anxiety, defense—as the anxiety, somatoform, and dissociative disorders. Accordingly, they would be treated by the same therapy: excavation of the repressed material, catharsis, the working out of better defenses. Where a serious physical illness is involved, however, a psychodynamic therapist would also insist on the patient's receiving medical treatment at the same time.

Psychodynamic theorists regard family interactions as central to stress-related physical disorders, as to all other psychological disorders. And they may be correct, for these disorders tend to run in families. Migraine, hypertension, and asthma are all more common in families of people with these disorders than in the population at large, though this might be a function of shared genes rather than, or as well as, shared emotional distress.

The Value of Catharsis A psychodynamic principle that has been confirmed by PNI research is the value of emotional catharsis to physical health. In one experiment fifty undergraduates at Southern Methodist University were asked to keep journals for twenty minutes a day over a period of four days. Half the students agreed to write about personal or traumatic events, and some of the entries they produced were quite painful: accounts of homesickness, family quarrels, family violence. The other half of the students were asked to write on trivial topics, which were assigned each day. (On one day they were asked to describe the shoes they were wearing; on another, to tell about a party they had recently attended.) At the beginning of the experiment there were no differences in immune function between the two groups, but there were by the end. The immune cells of the traumatic-journal students were more active than those of the trivial-journal students, and these differences had an impact on health. Six weeks after the journal keeping, the experimenters checked the students' health center records for the period before and after the journal assignment. Compared with the trivial-journal students, the traumatic-journal students showed a significant drop in clinic visits after the experiment (Pennebaker, Kiecolt-Glaser, & Glaser, 1988).

These results have been supported by experiments with other groups of students (Esterling, Antoni, Kuman, et al., 1990) and with working adults, who showed a reduction in sick days after keeping "traumatic" journals (Pennebaker, 1990). For many people, clearly, expressing emotion is a healthy activity. According to James Pennebaker (1993), the originator of this research, what is most crucial is the expression of *negative* emotion. This was confirmed by the Fawzy group's malignant melanoma study. In that experiment, the group-therapy patients who showed the best outcomes in terms of recurrence and survival were those who had expressed the most emotional distress before beginning the therapy (Fawzy, Fawzy, Hyun, et al., 1993).

Personality Theories

Several decades ago, psychodynamic theorists attempted to link "symptom choice" to personality type—an approach that appealed to many other theorists as well. Dunbar (1935), on the basis of interviews with patients, sketched a number of such personality portraits. Eczema sufferers were self-punitive, frustrated, hungry for affection. Migraine patients were hardworking, conscientious,

Some research on the link between stress and illness has found that people with "Type A" personalities—who are impatient, striving, and, above all, hostile and aggressive—are predisposed to heart disease.

perfectionistic, and committed to "good causes." Similarly, F. Alexander (1939) described hypertensives as inhibited in the expression of aggressive feelings—a handicap that made them envious, ineffective, and self-demeaning. Later studies, however, tended to discredit this trait-cluster approach. Though classic cases do turn up—perfectionistic migraine sufferers, anger-inhibiting hypertensives—the population of patients with each of these disorders seems to be quite heterogeneous.

Type A Behavior Despite these setbacks, the search for traits and attitudes that may predispose people to specific illnesses continues. An example is the book *Type A Behavior and Your Heart* (1974), by M. Friedman and Rosenman. The thesis of this book is that hypertension, along with other cardiovascular disorders, tends to strike a specific kind of personality, which the authors call **Type A.** Unlike Alexander's inhibited hypertensives, Friedman and Rosenman's Type A people are aggressive achievers. They talk, walk, and eat rapidly and are highly impatient. They fidget in frustration if kept waiting by an elevator or a traffic light. They finish other people's sentences for them. They pride themselves on getting things done in less time than other people, and they measure their own performance by rigorous standards. In short, they keep themselves under heavy pressure—pressure that eventually takes a toll on their cardiovascular systems.

In an impressive longitudinal study, 2,249 male executives between the ages of thirty-nine and fifty-nine were evaluated and followed for nine years (Rosenman, Brand, Jenkins, et al., 1975). Approximately half of them were identified as Type A and the other half as Type B (the more relaxed, patient executive). Of the 257 men who had heart attacks during the nine years, 178 were Type A while only 79 were Type B—a striking 2-to-1 differential. Soon, however, conflicting findings began to appear. In one study of heart-attack survivors, the Type A's actually lived longer than the Type B's (Ragland & Brand, 1988). Other studies have also indicated that workaholic Type A's are not in as much danger as was once thought. There seems to be no correlation between heart disease and the impatient struggle to accomplish ever more work. There is, however, a correlation between heart disease (together with depression) and high levels of anger, hostility, and aggression—qualities that are often seen in Type A people (Booth-Kewley & Friedman, 1987). Other research has confirmed the link between heart disease and hostility (Matthews, 1988; T. W. Smith, 1992). In exploring why the hostility of Type A's predisposes them to heart disease, researchers have found that Type A's have an extremely responsive physiology. When exposed to stress, their bodies respond with exceptionally high levels of sympathetic nervous system activity, which, it is safe to assume, eventually weakens the heart (Lyness, 1993).

These findings have led to the development of therapies aimed at teaching Type A's how to cope with stress more effectively. In one such program, for example, a group of Type A's who had survived one heart attack were trained in relaxation, self-control, and goal setting. Over a three-year period, only 7 percent of these subjects suffered a second heart attack, compared with 13 percent of a control group that received only the customary medical treatment (M. Friedman, Thoresen, Gill, et al., 1984).

The Sociocultural Perspective

Several theorists claim that a major source of physical illness is the stresses imposed by modern industrial societies. One such stress is the disruption of marriage and the family. The number of single-person households in the United States has multiplied many times in the last century. And according to an impressive array of findings, people living alone, if they have no regular social support, are depriving themselves of potent protection against illness. As we saw earlier, married cancer patients survive longer than the unmarried, and there is good evidence that social support also helps people combat many other illnesses, as well as injuries (S. Cohen & Wills, 1985; Meyerowitz, 1980; Silver & Wortman, 1980; Sklar & Anisman, 1981). There is also strong evidence that people without social support are more prone to disease. Among the leading causes of premature death in our society are heart disease, cancer, strokes, cirrhosis of the liver, hypertension, and pneumonia. For every one of these disorders, without exception, premature death rates are significantly higher in the unmarried than in the married. In the case of heart disease, our society's major killer, the death rate, depending on age group, is anywhere from two to five times higher among the unmarried (Lynch, 1977). While the lack of an intimate relationship may predispose people to disease, the *loss* of such a relationship may be an even greater health hazard. In a study of 400 cancer patients it was found that 72 percent had suffered the loss of an important personal relationship within eight years prior to the diagnosis of cancer, compared with 10 percent of a control group for a comparable period (LeShan, 1966a).

In addition to the breakup of the family, other broad changes in our society appear to be affecting the susceptibility of certain groups to particular illnesses. For example, ulcers were once four times as prevalent among men as among women. This ratio has now been reduced to about 2 to 1, presumably because more women are now doing the same work as men and are therefore exposed to the same stressors. As this change in the workplace continues, it is possible that the sex differential for ulcers will disappear altogether. Likewise, if the fact that blacks are twice as likely as whites to develop hypertension is due to the stresses of being a disadvantaged minority rather than to genes (or to a salt-heavy diet, another possibility), this ratio too may be equalized as opportunities are equalized.

The Biological Perspective

Genetic Predisposition As we have seen, stress-related physical disorders tend to run in families—a fact that suggests genetic risk. This is true of migraine and also of hypertension. As we saw earlier, people with at least one hypertensive parent show greater cardiovascular reactions to stress than people without a family history of hypertension. This evidence is supported by twin studies, which have found exaggerated reactivity to be more commonly shared between MZ twins than between DZ twins or siblings (R. J. Rose & Chesney, 1986). Since we know from longitudinal studies that people with heightened cardiovascular reactivity are at risk for hypertension (Falkner, Kushner, Onesti, et al., 1981), early identification and treatment of stress-reactive people should help to prevent this disorder. The Type A hypothesis may also help in early intervention. Type A's tend to breed Type A's (Plomin & Rende, 1991), so it is possible to identify and help them before they develop the heart problems to which some of them are clearly predisposed.

PNI and Interactive Theories Apart from genetic risk, the major concern of recent biological research has been a matter that we have already discussed at length in this chapter: the immune system. The new PNI findings, combined with interactive models such as those of Schwartz, Weiner, and Lazarus, have basically overturned our conceptualization of stress and illness. In other chapters of this book, there may be close ties between the various perspectives, but in this chapter the division into perspectives indicates nothing more than slight differences of focus. No one in the field claims that there is one cause, or even one kind of cause. The subject itself—stress and illness—is interactive, and the most promising theories are all cat's cradles of intersecting causes. Consider the diagrams on page 228, adapted from the work of Sheldon Cohen (of the cold research) and Gail Williamson. Figure 9.1 shows the relationship between stress and the onset of infectious disease. Figure 9.2 shows the relationship between stress and the reactivation of latent pathogens (disease-causing

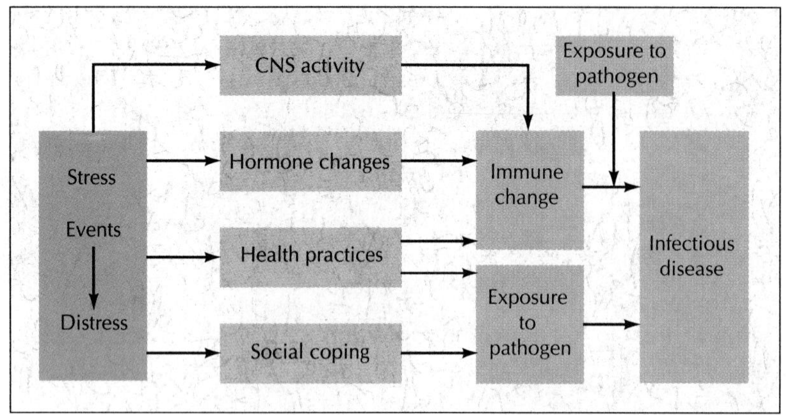

FIGURE 9.1 Model for the relationship between stress and the onset of infectious disease. (Adapted from S. Cohen & Williamson, 1991, p. 8)

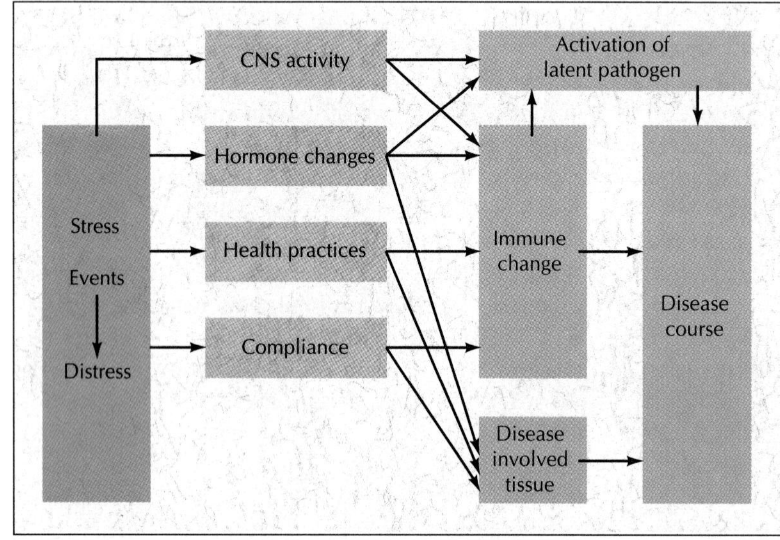

FIGURE 9.2 Model linking stress to the reactivation of latent pathogens and to the severity of the ongoing disease. (Adapted from S. Cohen & Williamson, 1991, p. 8)

agents), such as HIV or a herpes virus. For purposes of clarity, feedback loops are not indicated, but even in this simplified form, what the figures show are highly intricate systems, including physical, behavioral, and emotional causes. Researchers on stress and illness face a complicated problem, but by accepting this fact, they have begun producing very exciting findings.

KEY TERMS

acquired immune deficiency disorder (AIDS) (222)
asthma (219)
biofeedback training (223)
circadian rhythm disorders (221)
essential hypertension (215)
feedback (211)
health psychology (206)
human immunodeficiency virus (HIV) (222)
hypertension (214)
immune system (212)
individual response specificity (210)
insomnia (220)
migraine headache (216)
mind-body problem (206)
muscle-contraction headaches (216)
negative feedback (211)
obesity (217)
oscillations (211)
psychoneuroimmunology (PNI) (212)
psychophysiological disorders (206)
relaxation training (223)
stimulus specificity (209)
stress (208)
Type A (226)

SUMMARY

- The mind-body problem—the relationship between mental and physical processes—has been debated for centuries. Until recently, science endorsed dualism, drawing a sharp line between physical and psychological disorders. Stress-related illnesses were regarded as exceptions to the rule. However, new research has demonstrated that state of mind influences diseases ranging from the common cold to cancer. Health psychology, or behavioral medicine, takes the holistic view that mind and body are one and that *all* illnesses are potentially psychophysiological.

- Researchers who study the physiological changes associated with emotion focus on the autonomic nervous system (ANS), which mobilizes the body to meet environmental challenges and then (usually) reverses these processes to permit the body to build energy resources. Stress can be defined in terms of the stimulus, the person's response, or the person's appraisal of the stimulus. Physiological reaction to stress depends on the specific type of stress, the person's characteristic mode of responding to stress, and his or her general level of reactivity. According to Schwartz's negative-feedback or disregulation model, stress-related illness occurs when the "on switch" that mobilizes the body to cope with stress functions but the "off switch" that restores equilibrium malfunctions. Weiner's oscillation model holds that stress interferes with the regular, rhythmic on-and-off cycles of various body systems.
- Some of the most interesting new research comes from the subfield of psychoneuroimmunology (PNI). The immune system defends the body against "invaders" by circulating a large and varied number of small white blood cells called lymphocytes that identify foreign bodies and either attack them directly or produce antibodies to do so. When the immune system is not functioning properly, health is compromised.
- PNI research has shown that immune functioning may decline after major events, whether sudden shock (the death of a spouse) or chronic stress (caring for a spouse with Alzheimer's); minor events (such as final exams); and laboratory stressors (frustrating tests, induced marital conflict).

Researchers who study essential hypertension, headaches, obesity, asthma, sleep disorders, and, most recently, cancer have paid special attention to psychological factors. Hypertension (or high blood pressure) and obesity seem to fit the disregulation model of stress-related disorders: hereditary and environmental factors interact to disrupt feedback loops. Migraine headaches and asthma, once thought to arise from psychological causes, are now thought to be largely biogenic. There is no single explanation of sleep disorders (insomnia and circadian rhythm problems), but behavioral therapies often are the most effective treatment. Cancer may not be caused by stress, but several studies have found that cancer patients who participate in group therapy, as well as receive medical treatment, live longer than controls, perhaps because they are better able to overcome feelings of hopelessness. With AIDS, however, therapy may be more successful in preventing risky behavior than slowing progress of the disease.

- The behaviorist perspective emphasizes the role of respondent and operant conditioning in the disregulation of ANS responses. Behavioral therapists treat many disorders with biofeedback, relaxation training, and exercise, which can stimulate the immune system.
- The cognitive perspective emphasizes the person's ability to predict stressful events and his or her sense of efficacy. Lazarus' dynamic model identifies six stages of coping with stress, from the event to the health outcome. Stress management programs help people to pinpoint the stage at which they experience stress and to develop appropriate coping skills.
- Psychodynamic theorists emphasize the role of unconscious conflicts and family interactions; the goal of psychodynamic therapy is catharsis. Research shows that catharsis, in "traumatic" journals or group therapy, can boost immune function and aid recovery, even from cancer.
- Personality theories, in which clusters of personality traits are linked to specific disorders, have largely been discredited. However, there is evidence that the aggressive, highly reactive component of Type A behavior is linked to heart disease and can be treated through relaxation therapies.
- The sociocultural perspective focuses on the role of social change—especially family breakdown and women's entry into the work force—in stress-related physical disorders.
- The biological perspective emphasizes the role of heredity and, increasingly, the immune system in stress and illness. It highlights complex patterns of interaction between psychological and biological factors.

10

MOOD DISORDERS

CHARACTERISTICS OF DEPRESSIVE AND MANIC EPISODES

- Major Depressive Episode
- Manic Episode

MOOD DISORDER SYNDROMES

- Major Depressive Disorder
- Bipolar Disorder
- Dysthymic Disorder and Cyclothymic Disorder
- Dimensions of Mood Disorder
- Comorbidity: Mixed Anxiety-Depression

SUICIDE

- The Prevalence of Suicide
- Who Commits Suicide?
- Myths about Suicide
- Suicide Prediction
- Suicide Prevention

PERSPECTIVES ON THE MOOD DISORDERS AND SUICIDE

- The Psychodynamic Perspective
- The Humanistic-Existential Perspective
- The Behavioral Perspective
- The Cognitive Perspective
- The Sociocultural Perspective
- The Biological Perspective

aula Stansky was a 57-year-old woman, widow and mother of four children, who was hospitalized . . . because, according to her children, she was refusing to eat and take care of herself.

> The patient . . . was described as a usually cheerful, friendly woman who took meticulous care of her home. . . . About two months prior to her hospitalization, however, her younger children reported a change in their mother's usual disposition, for no apparent reason. She appeared more easily fatigued, not as cheerful, and lackadaisical about her housework. Over the course of the next few weeks, she stopped going to church and canceled her usual weekly bingo outing with neighborhood women. As the house became increasingly neglected and their mother began to spend more time sleeping or rocking in her favorite chair, apparently preoccupied, the younger children called their married brother and sister for advice. . . .
>
> When her son, in response to the telephone call, arrived at her house, Ms. Stansky denied that anything was wrong. She claimed to be only tired, "possibly the flu." For the ensuing week, her children tried to "cheer her up," but with no success. After several days had gone by without her taking a bath, changing her clothes, or eating any food, her children put her in the car and drove her to the hospital. . . .
>
> On admission, Ms. Stansky was mostly mute, answering virtually no questions except correctly identifying the hospital and the day of the week. She cried periodically throughout the interview, but only shook her head back and forth when asked if she could tell the interviewer what she was feeling or thinking about. She was agitated, frequently wringing her hands, rolling her head toward the ceiling, and rocking in her chair. . . . Her children indicated that during the past week she had been waking up at 3:00 A.M., unable to fall back to sleep. She also seemed to them to have lost considerable weight. (Spitzer, Skodol, Gibbon, et al., 1983, p. 118)

Some of us respond to stress by going into a "down"—becoming inactive, feeling dejected, and thinking that nothing seems worthwhile, least of all ourselves. Many of us have also known the opposite state, a mood of excitement and recklessness in which we become feverishly active and think we can accomplish anything. In other words, **depression** and **mania,** in mild and temporary forms, are part of ordinary existence. In some cases, however, such mood swings become so prolonged and extreme that the person's life is completely disrupted. These conditions are known as the **mood disorders,** or *affective disorders, affect* meaning "emotion."

The mood disorders have been recognized and written about since the beginning of the history of medicine. Both depression and mania were described in detail by Hippocrates in the fourth century B.C. As early as the first century A.D., the Greek physician Aretaeus observed that manic and depressive behaviors sometimes occurred in the same person and seemed to stem from a single disorder. In the early nineteenth century, Philippe Pinel (1801/1967), the reformer of Paris' mental hospitals (Chapter 1), wrote a compelling account of depression, using the Roman emperor Tiberius and the French king Louis XI as illustrations. Depression has also been vividly described by some of its more famous victims. In one of his recurring episodes of depression, Abraham Lincoln wrote, "If what I feel were equally distributed to the whole human family, there would not be one cheerful face on earth."

Though they have been scrutinized for centuries, however, these debilitating extremes of mood still remain something of a mystery. What is known about them will be outlined in the first section of this chapter. In the second section we will turn our attention to suicide, which is often the result of depression.

CHARACTERISTICS OF DEPRESSIVE AND MANIC EPISODES

One of the most striking features of the mood disorders is their episodic quality. Within a few weeks, or sometimes within a few days, a person who has been functioning normally is plunged into despair or scaling the heights of mania. Once the episode has run its course, the person may return to normal or near-normal functioning, though he or she is likely to have further episodes of mood disturbance. The nature of the episode (whether it is depressive or manic), its severity, and its duration determine the diagnosis and often the treatment too—matters that we will discuss below. For now, let us examine more closely the typical features of severe depressive and manic episodes.

Major Depressive Episode

In some cases a psychological trauma may plunge a person into a **major depressive episode** overnight, but usually the onset of depression is gradual, occurring over a period of several weeks or several months. The episode itself typically lasts several months and then ends, as it began, gradually (Coryell, Akiskal, Leon, et al., 1994).

The person entering a depressive episode undergoes profound changes in most aspects of his or her functioning—not just mood but also motivation, thinking, and physical and motor functioning. The following are the characteristic features of the major depressive episode as described by *DSM-IV:*

1 *Depressed mood.* Almost all severely depressed adults report some degree of unhappiness, ranging from a mild melancholy to total hopelessness. This dejection may be described by the person as utter despair, loneliness, or simply boredom. Mildly or moderately depressed people may have frequent crying spells; more severely depressed patients often say they feel like crying but cannot. Deeply depressed people generally regard their condition as irreversible; they cannot help themselves, nor can anyone help them. This way of thinking has been characterized as the **helplessness-hopelessness syndrome.**
2 *Loss of pleasure or interest in usual activities.* Aside from depressed mood, the most common characteristic of a major depressive episode is loss of pleasure, and therefore lack of interest, in one's accustomed activities. This loss of pleasure, known as **anhedonia,** is generally far-reaching. Whatever the person once liked to do—in the above case, for example, keep house, play bingo, go to church—no longer seems worth doing. To depressives, food no longer tastes good, sex no longer feels good, friends are no longer interesting to talk to. Severely depressed patients may experience a complete "paralysis of the will"—an inability even to get out of bed in the morning.
3 *Disturbance of appetite.* Most depressives have poor appetite and lose weight. Some, however, react by eating more and putting on weight. Whatever the weight change, whether loss or gain, that same change will tend to recur with each depressive episode (Stunkard, Fernstrom, Price, et al., 1990).
4 *Sleep disturbance.* Insomnia is an extremely common feature of depression. Awakening too early and then being unable to get back to sleep is the most characteristic pattern, but depressed people may also have trouble falling asleep initially, or they may awaken repeatedly throughout the night. As with eating, however, the sleep disturbance may take the form of excess rather than deficiency, with the patient sleeping fifteen hours a day or more.
5 *Psychomotor retardation or agitation.* Depression can usually be "read" immediately in the person's motor behavior and physical bearing. In the most common pattern, **retarded depression,** the patient seems overcome by a massive fatigue. Posture is stooped, movement is slow and deliberate, gestures are kept to a minimum, and speech is low and halting, with long pauses before answering. In severe cases, depressives may fall into a mute stupor. More rarely, the symptoms may take the opposite form, **agitated depression,** marked by incessant activity and restlessness—hand wringing, pacing, and moaning.

Abraham Lincoln, whom many historians consider the greatest U.S. president, was subject to recurring bouts of severe depression.

6 *Loss of energy.* The depressive's reduced motivation is usually accompanied by a sharply reduced energy level. Without having done anything, he or she may feel exhausted all the time.
7 *Feelings of worthlessness and guilt.* Depressives are dismayed not only by life but also by themselves. Typically, they see themselves as deficient in whatever attributes they value most: intelligence, beauty, popularity, health. Their frequent complaints about loss—whether of love, material goods, money, or prestige—may also reflect their sense of personal inadequacy. Such feelings of worthlessness are often accompanied by a profound sense of guilt. Depressives seem to search the environment for evidence of problems that they have created. If a child has trouble with schoolwork or the car has a flat tire, it is their fault.
8 *Difficulties in thinking.* In depression, mental processes, like physical processes, are usually

slowed down. Depressives tend to be indecisive, and they often report difficulties in thinking, concentrating, and remembering. The harder a mental task and the more attentional resources it requires, the more difficulty they will have (Hartlage, Alloy, Vázquez, et al., 1993).

9 *Recurrent thoughts of death or suicide.* Not surprisingly, many depressives have recurrent thoughts of death and suicide. Often they will say that they (and everyone else) would be better off if they were dead. As we shall see, some depressed people do in fact kill themselves.

Manic Episode

The typical **manic episode** begins rather suddenly, over the course of a few days, and is usually shorter than a depressive episode. A manic episode may last from several days to several months and then usually ends as abruptly as it began. *DSM-IV* describes the prominent features of the manic episode as follows:

1 *Elevated, expansive, or irritable mood.* The mood change is the essential, "diagnostic" feature of a manic episode. Typically, manics feel wonderful, see the world as an excellent place, and have limitless enthusiasm for whatever they are doing or plan to do. This expansiveness is usually mixed with irritability. From the heights of their euphoria, manics often see other people as slow, doltish spoilsports and can become quite hostile, especially when someone tries to interfere with their behavior. In some cases irritability may be the manic's dominant mood, with euphoria either intermittent or simply absent.

2 *Inflated self-esteem.* Manics tend to see themselves as extremely attractive, important, and powerful people, capable of great achievements in fields for which they may in fact have no aptitude whatsoever. They may begin composing symphonies, designing nuclear weapons, or calling the White House with advice on how to run the country.

3 *Sleeplessness.* The manic episode is almost always marked by a decreased need for sleep. Manics may sleep only two or three hours a night and yet have twice as much energy as those around them.

4 *Talkativeness.* Manics tend to talk loudly, rapidly, and constantly. Their speech is often full of puns, irrelevant details, and jokes that they alone find funny.

5 *Flight of ideas.* Manics often have racing thoughts. This is one reason why they speak so rapidly—to keep up with the flow of their ideas. Manic speech also tends to shift abruptly from one topic to the next.

6 *Distractibility.* Manics are easily distracted. While doing or discussing one thing, they will notice something else in the environment and abruptly turn their attention to that instead.

7 *Hyperactivity.* The expansive mood is usually accompanied by restlessness and increased goal-directed activity—physical, social, occupational, and often sexual.

8 *Reckless behavior.* The euphoria and grandiose self-image of manics often lead them into impulsive and ill-advised actions: buying sprees, reckless driving, careless business investments, sexual indiscretions, and so forth. They are typically indifferent to the needs of others and think nothing of yelling in restaurants, calling friends in the middle of the night, or spending the family savings on a Cadillac.

The following is a clear-cut case:

> Terrence O'Reilly, a single 39-year-old transit authority clerk, was brought to the hospital in May, 1973, by the police after his increasingly hyperactive and bizarre behavior and nonstop talking alarmed his family. He loudly proclaimed that he was not in need of treatment, and threatened legal action against the hospital and police.
>
> The family reported that a month prior to admission Mr. O'Reilly took a leave of absence from his civil service job, purchased a large number of cuckoo clocks and then an expensive car which he planned to use as a mobile showroom for his wares, anticipating that he would make a great deal of money.
>
> He proceeded to "tear around town" buying and selling the clocks and other merchandise, and when he was not out, he was continuously on the phone making "deals." He rarely slept and, uncharacteristically, spent every evening in neighborhood bars drinking heavily and, according to him, "wheeling and dealing." Two weeks before admission his mother died suddenly of a heart attack. He cried for two days, but then his mood began to soar again. At the time of admission he was $3000 in debt and had driven his family to exhaustion. . . . He said, however, that he felt "on top of the world." (Spitzer, Skodol, Gibbon, et al., 1983, p. 115)

For a condition to be diagnosed as a manic episode, it must have lasted at least a week (or less if hospitalization is required) and seriously interfered with the person's functioning. A briefer and less severe manic condition is called a **hypomanic**

episode. On occasion patients will meet the diagnostic criteria for both manic episode and major depressive episode simultaneously. (For example, they will show manic grandiosity and hyperactivity, yet weep and threaten suicide.) This combined pattern is called a **mixed episode.**

MOOD DISORDER SYNDROMES

Major Depressive Disorder

People who undergo one or more major depressive episodes, with no intervening periods of mania, are said to have **major depressive disorder.** This disorder is one of our society's greatest mental health problems. Its prevalence in the United States during any given month is close to 4 percent for men and 6 percent for women. The lifetime risk—that is, the percentage of Americans who will experience major depression at some point in their lives—is about 17 percent (Blazer, Kessler, McGonagle, et al., 1994). Depression is second only to schizophrenia (Chapter 14) in frequency of first and second admissions to American mental hospitals. As for the nonhospitalized, private physicians report that as many as 12 to 48 percent of their patients suffer from depression (J. E. Barrett, Barrett, Oxman, et al., 1988), and those patients are more debilitated—lose more workdays, spend more time in bed—than patients with many chronic medical conditions, such as diabetes or arthritis (Wells, Stewart, Hays, et al., 1989). Grave as the situation is, it is getting worse. Each successive generation born since World War II has shown higher rates of depression (Burke, Burke, Roe, et al., 1991; Klerman, 1988). According to some experts, we are embarking on an "age of depression."

Certain groups within the population are more susceptible than others. People who are separated or divorced show a disproportionately high prevalence of major depression (Blazer, Kessler, McGonagle, et al., 1994). So do women. Their risk is one and a half to three times higher than men's—a fact that investigators have tried to explain with theories ranging from hormonal differences to the changing social role of women. One promising theory has to do with differences in the way men and women respond to depressed moods. According to Susan Nolen-Hoeksema (1987, 1991), women, when they are "down," tend to ruminate on this, focusing on the depression, wondering why it is happening and what it will lead to. Men take the opposite tack: they try to distract themselves. Since the evidence indicates that rumination prolongs depression and distraction relieves it, women are likely to have longer and more serious depressions. For a more comprehensive theory of the female disadvantage with regard to depression, see the box on page 254.

It was once thought that susceptibility to mood disorders also varied with age, the middle-aged and the elderly being the high-risk groups. Today it seems that if any group is most susceptible, it is the young. The peak age at onset for major depression is now fifteen to nineteen years for women and twenty-five to twenty-nine years for men (Burke, Burke, Regier, et al., 1990), though the disorder may strike at any age, even in infancy.

The symptom picture differs somewhat depending on age group (Harrington, 1993). In depressed infants, the most striking and alarming sign is failure to eat. In older children, depression may manifest itself primarily as apathy and inactivity. Alternatively, it may take the form of severe separation anxiety, in which the child clings frantically to parents, refuses to leave them long enough to go to school, and is haunted by fears of death (or of the parents' death). In adolescents, the most prominent symptoms may be sulkiness, negativism, withdrawal complaints of not being understood or appreciated, and perhaps antisocial behavior and drug abuse as well (Cantwell, 1982; Goodyer, 1992)—in other words, an exaggeration of normal adolescent problems. (See Chapter 17 for further discussion of depression in childhood.) In the elderly, lack of pleasure and motivation, expressions of hopelessness, and psychomotor retardation or agitation are common signs, as are delusions and hallucinations (Brodaty, Peters, Boyce, et al., 1991).

In about 50 percent of all cases of major depression, the first episode is also the last, though some experts argue that this figure is simply the result of inadequate follow-up (A. S. Lee & Murray, 1988). In any case, at least half of all first episodes are followed by a second episode, and perhaps many more (Shea, Elkin, Imber, et al., 1992). Further episodes are more likely the more previous episodes a person has had, the younger the person was when the first episode struck, the more painful events he or she has endured recently, the less supportive his or her family has been, and the more negative cognitions he or she has (Belsher & Costello, 1988; Lewinsohn, Roberts, Seeley, et al., 1994).

The course of recurrent depression varies considerably. For some people, the episodes come in clusters. For others, they are separated by years of normal functioning. As for the quality of the normal functioning, that too varies. Some people do return to their **premorbid adjustment**—that is, their level of functioning prior to the onset of the disorder. As for the others, one study of people who had been symptom-free for two years found that they still showed serious impairment in job status, income, marital adjustment, social relationships, and recreational activities (Coryell, Scheftner, Keller, et al., 1993). Depression also affects the immune system, leaving its victims more susceptible to illness (D. L. Evans, Folds, Petitto, et al., 1992). All of these effects make it difficult for people coming out of a depressive episode to resume their former lives. Indeed, some research indicates that the symptoms and behaviors characteristic of a depressive episode actually generate stressful life events, which in turn can maintain the depression and produce a cycle of chronic stress and impairment (Hammen, 1991; S. M. Monroe & Simons, 1991). So people snap back, but many of them do not snap back entirely, just as scar tissue is not the same as the original tissue. Not surprisingly, the longer a depressive episode lasts, the less likely it is that the person will fully recover (Keller, Lavori, Mueller, et al., 1992).

Bipolar Disorder

Whereas major depression is confined to depressive episodes, **bipolar disorder,** as the name suggests, involves both manic and depressive phases. In the usual case, bipolar disorder will first appear in late adolescence in the form of a manic episode. The subsequent episodes may occur in any of a variety of patterns. The initial manic episode may be followed by a normal period, then by a depressed episode, then a normal period, and so forth. Or one episode may be followed immediately by its opposite, with normal intervals occurring only between such manic-depressive pairs. In a relatively rare pattern called the *rapid-cycling type,* the person (usually a woman) switches back and forth between depressive and manic or mixed episodes over a long period, with little or no "normal" functioning between. This pattern tends to have a poor prognosis (Bauer, Calabrese, Dunner, et al., 1994).

The addition of manic episodes is not the only characteristic that differentiates bipolar disorder from major depression. The two syndromes differ in many important respects (Depue & Monroe, 1978; F. K. Goodwin & Jamison, 1990). First, bipolar disorder is much less common than major depression, affecting an estimated 0.8 to 1.6 percent of the adult population (Kessler, McGonagle, Zhao, et al., 1994). Second, the two disorders show different demographic profiles. Unlike major depression, bipolar disorder occurs in the two sexes with approximately equal frequency, and bipolar disorder is more prevalent among higher socioeconomic groups. Third, people who are married or have intimate relationships are less prone to major depression but have no advantage with respect to bipolar disorder. Fourth, people with major depression tend to have histories of low self-esteem, dependency, and obsessional thinking, whereas people with bipolar disorder are more likely to have a history of hyperactivity (Winokur, Coryell, Endicott, et al., 1993). Fifth, the depressive episodes in bipolar disorder are more likely to involve a pervasive slowing down—psychomotor retardation, excess sleep—than are those in major depression. Sixth, the course of the two disorders is somewhat different. Episodes in bipolar disorder are generally briefer and more frequent than are those in major depression. Finally, bipolar disorder is more likely to run in families than is major depression. On the basis of these clues, many researchers think that the two disorders, similar as they may appear, spring from different causes. (The genetic evidence for this view will be examined at the end of the chapter.)

We may, however, be looking at more than two disorders. Some patients have a manic or mixed episode—or a series of such episodes—with no subsequent depressive episode. Such cases, though they involve only one "pole," are nevertheless classified as bipolar disorder, since apart from the absence of depressive episodes they resemble the classic bipolar disorder. (Some researchers suspect that they are simply cases of insufficient follow-up.) Alternatively, some patients have both depressive and manic phases but in the latter are hypomanic rather than fully manic. In recognition of these two patterns—and the need to assemble research groups to test whether they are different disorders—*DSM-IV* has now divided bipolar disorder into two types. In *bipolar I disorder* the person has had at least one manic (or mixed) episode and usually, but not necessarily, at least one major depressive episode as well. In *bipolar II disorder* the person has had at least one major depressive episode and at least one hypomanic episode but has never met the diagnostic criteria for manic or mixed episode.

The following is a case of bipolar I disorder, in this instance involving both full-blown manic and depressive episodes:

At 17 [Mrs. M. had] suffered from a depression that

rendered her unable to work for several months. . . . At 33, shortly before the birth of her first child, the patient was greatly depressed. For a period of four days she appeared in coma. About a month after the birth of the baby she "became excited" and . . . signed a year's lease on an apartment, bought furniture, and became heavily involved in debt. Shortly thereafter, Mrs. M. became depressed and returned to the hospital in which she had previously been a patient. After several months she recovered and . . . remained well for approximately two years.

She then became overactive and exuberant in spirits and visited her friends, to whom she outlined her plans for reestablishing different forms of lucrative business. She purchased many clothes, bought furniture, pawned her rings, and wrote checks without funds. She was returned to a hospital. Gradually her manic symptoms subsided, and after four months she was discharged. For a period thereafter she was mildly depressed. In a little less than a year Mrs. M. again became overactive. . . . Contrary to her usual habits, she swore frequently and loudly, created a disturbance in a club to which she did not belong, and instituted divorce proceedings. On the day prior to her second admission to the hospital she purchased 57 hats.

During the past 18 years this patient has been admitted and dismissed from the hospital on many occasions. At times, with the onset of a depressed period, she has returned to the hospital seeking admission. At such times she complained that her "brain just won't work." She would say, "I have no energy, am unable to do my housework. I have let my family down; I am living from day to day. There is no one to blame but myself." During one of her manic periods, she sent the following telegram to a physician of whom she had become much enamored: "To: You; Street and No.: Everywhere; Place: the remains at peace! We did our best, but God's will be done! I am so very sorry for all of us. To brave it through thus far. Yes, Darling—from Hello Handsome. Handsome is as Handsome does, thinks, lives and breathes. It takes clear air. Brother of Mine, in a girl's hour of need. All my love to the Best Inspiration one ever had." (Kolb, 1982, pp. 376–377)

Dysthymic Disorder and Cyclothymic Disorder

There are many people who are chronically depressed or who chronically pass through depressed and expansive periods but whose condition is nevertheless not debilitating enough to merit the diagnosis of major depressive disorder or bipolar disorder. Such patterns, if they last for two years or more, are classified as dysthymic disorder and cyclothymic disorder, respectively.

Dysthymic disorder involves a mild, persistent depression. Dysthymics are typically morose, introverted, overconscientious, and incapable of fun (Akiskal, 1983). In addition, they often show the low energy level, low self-esteem, suicidal ideation, and disturbances of eating, sleeping, and thinking that are associated with major depression, though their symptoms are not so severe or so numerous. The syndrome is about half as common as major depressive disorder.

Cyclothymic disorder, like dysthymic disorder, is chronic. For years, the person never goes longer than a few months without a phase of hypomanic or depressive behavior. Because the pattern is mild and persistent, as in dysthymia, it becomes a way of life. In their hypomanic periods, which they come to depend on, cyclothymics will work long hours without fatigue—indeed, with their mental powers newly sharpened—before lapsing back into a normal or depressed state. It has been suggested that cyclothymia and bipolar disorder are especially common in creative people and help them get their work done. (See the box on pages 238–239.)

Both dysthymia and cyclothymia have a slow, insidious onset in adolescence and may persist for a lifetime. In this sense they are like the personality disorders, the subject of our next chapter. Far closer, however, is the link with the major mood disorders. Like persons with major depressive disorder or bipolar disorder, dysthymics and cyclothymics have relatives with higher-than-normal rates of mood disorders. Also, dysthymia and cyclothymia show the same sex distribution as their graver counterparts. Dysthymic disorder, like major depression, is one and a half to three times more common in women, whereas in cyclothymic disorder, as in bipolar disorder, the two sexes are at equal risk (Kessler, McGonagle, Zhao, et al., 1994). In some cases, these disorders *are* the early stages of major mood disorders. About 10 percent of dysthymics go on to develop major depressive disorder, and 15 to 50 percent of cyclothymics eventually show bipolar disorder.

Dimensions of Mood Disorder

In addition to the important distinction between bipolar disorder and depressive disorder, there are certain *dimensions,* or points of differentiation, that researchers and clinicians have found useful in classifying mood disorders. We shall discuss three dimensions: psychotic-neurotic, endogenous-reactive, and early-late onset.

Psychotic versus Neurotic As we saw in Chap-

STREAMS OF FIRE: BIPOLAR DISORDER AND CREATIVITY

The "mad genius" is an ancient idea, but recently it has been restated by Kay Jamison, a professor of psychiatry at Johns Hopkins School of Medicine. In her 1992 book, *Touched with Fire: Manic-Depressive Illness and the Artistic Temperament,* Jamison argues that artists show an unusually high rate of mood disorder and that this is part of what makes them creative. To assemble her evidence, Jamison studied the lives of a large group of British and Irish poets born between 1705 and 1805. Her conclusion was that they were thirty times more likely to have suffered manic-depressive illness, twenty times more likely to have been committed to an asylum, and five times more likely to have killed themselves than were members of the general population. Jamison studied not just poets but artists in many media: Baudelaire, Blake, Byron, Coleridge, Dickinson, Shelley, Tennyson, Whitman, Balzac, Conrad, Dickens, Zola, Handel, Berlioz, Schumann, Tchaikovsky, Michelangelo, van Gogh, Gauguin—all these, Jamison believes, probably suffered from serious mood disorders.

Nor is the evidence confined to the past. Jamison provides a list of major American poets of the twentieth century: Hart Crane, Theodore Roethke, Delmore Schwartz, John Berryman, Randall Jarrell, Robert Lowell, Anne Sexton, and Sylvia Plath. Of these, five won the Pulitzer prize, and five committed suicide. All eight were treated for depression, and all but one were treated for mania. Many of Jamison's creative manic-depressives also had family histories of mood disorder. Lord Byron, who once described his brain as "a whirling gulf of fantasy and flame," had a great-uncle known as "Mad Lord Byron" and a father known as "Mad Jack Byron." His mother had violent mood swings; his maternal grandfather, a depressive, committed suicide.

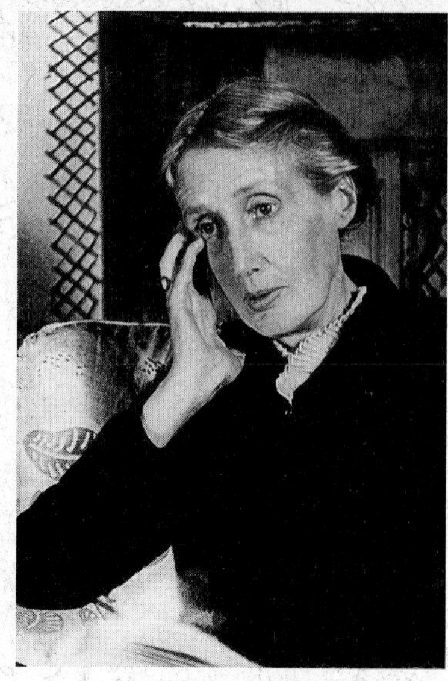

Left: *Virginia Woolf (1882–1941), a prolific novelist and literary critic and an innovator in the stream-of-consciousness technique in fiction, struggled with mental illness for years and drowned herself in the Thames River.*
Right: *Peter Ilyich Tchaikovsky (1840–1893) was one of the most popular and influential Russian composers of the nineteenth century. He is believed to have had a severe mood disorder.*

Together with these sad histories,

ter 7, psychological disorders may be described, in terms of severity, as either psychotic or neurotic—a distinction that has traditionally hinged on the matter of reality contact. Neurotics, as we noted, do not lose their ability to interact with their environment in a reasonably efficient manner. Psychotics do, partly because their thinking processes are often disturbed by *hallucinations,* or false sensory perceptions, and *delusions,* or false beliefs. This same neurotic-psychotic distinction is often applied to depression. In psychotic depression, hallucinations, delusions, or extreme withdrawal effectively cut the tie between the person and the environment. Manic episodes can also have psychotic features. Mrs. M.'s letter to her doctor (page 237) qualifies as evidence of psychotic-level thought disturbance. Neurotic-level mood disorders may also wreak havoc on people's lives, yet people with these disorders still know what is going on around them and can function to some degree. Many cases of major depression and bipolar disorder remain at this level, and dysthymia and cyclothymia are by definition nonpsychotic.

Are neurotic- and psychotic-level mood disorders, then, two different entities altogether? The traditional position is that they are. For example, Kraepelin (Chapter 1), in his original classification system, listed all incapacitating mood disorders under the heading "manic-depressive psychosis," which he considered an organic illness quite dis-

Jamison describes the creative benefits of mania. For one thing, it instills confidence. It also allows its victims to work uninterruptedly for long hours. (Earlier studies of outstanding artists and scientists have shown that, whatever their mental status, they have one trait in common: the ability to work hard for many hours at a time [Roe, 1952].) But above all, the euphoria, the hyperintense perceptions, the feeling of bursting inspiration that accompanies mania provides rich material for art. "I am almost sick and giddy with the quantity of things in my head," wrote the great art historian John Ruskin. The composer Hugo Wolf described his blood as "changed into streams of fire." The novelist Virginia Woolf wrote, "As an experience madness is terrific . . . and in its lava I still find most of the things I write about."

"These are people who have had emotional experiences that most of us have not had," says Jamison, and in their work they give us the benefit of what they discover through those experiences: "We ask artists to go over the edge emotionally on our behalf" (quoted in Keiger, 1993, p. 40).

Some observers find Jamison's conclusions more romantic than scientific, particularly insofar as they involve "diagnosing the dead" on the basis of the anecdotal (and often apocryphal) evidence of biographies. There were no *DSM* criteria in the nineteenth century, let alone before, and consequently it is hard to know whether the eccentricities of people such as "Mad Jack Byron" constitute the same condition that we call bipolar disorder. Also, famous artists' lives have been very heavily scrutinized, and this may lead to distortion:

> The more we know about anyone, the easier it becomes to discern neurotic traits. . . . The famous and successful are usually less able to conceal whatever vagaries of character they may possess because biographers or Ph.D. students will not let them rest in peace (Storr, quoted in F. K. Goodwin & Jamison, 1990, p. 335)

Schoolteachers and bus drivers may also feel, now and then, that their brains are licked with fire, but because they are not artists, they are less likely to interest the public in this fact. Partly because of the "mad genius" stereotype—and also because mad geniuses make lively reading—artists' biographers have a tendency to stress the extravagant and the pathological.

Yet Jamison's findings have been supported in some measure by studies of living people. Andreasen (1987) surveyed thirty writers taking part in the University of Iowa's Writer's Workshop and found that fully 80 percent had met the *DSM* criteria for a major affective disorder. In a later study, Richards and her colleagues found that bipolar and cyclothymic patients and their normal first-degree relatives scored significantly higher on creativity than either normal controls or people with psychiatric diagnoses other than mood disorder. An interesting aspect of this study was that the research team used a much broader and more "normal" definition of creativity than other researchers have. Subjects who were involved in social and political causes, who showed a special flair for business, who worked at hobbies—they too got points for creativity. The researchers concluded that the most creative people were not those with or without bipolar disorder but those in between, the cyclothymics and the even milder, "subclinical" moody types, together with the normal first-degree relatives of people with pronounced mood disorders (Richards, Kinney, Lunde, et al., 1988).

tinct from the less extreme mood disturbances that we would now call neurotic. Many theorists still hold to this position, and there is some evidence to support it. Psychotic depressives tend to differ from nonpsychotic depressives not just in reality contact but also in psychomotor symptoms, biological signs, family history, and response to various treatments (Schatzberg & Rothschild, 1992).

Other theorists argue that the distinction between neurotic and psychotic depression is quantitative rather than qualitative. This theory, known as the **continuity hypothesis,** rests on the idea that depression appears, above all, to be an exaggerated form of everyday sadness (Vrendenberg, Flett, & Krames, 1993; but see also Coyne, 1994). According to the proponents of the continuity hypothesis, psychotic depression, neurotic depression, dysthymia, and normal "blues" are simply different points on a single continuum. The finding that dysthymics and cyclothymics are at risk for more severe mood disorders gives some support to the continuity hypothesis. And *DSM-IV* in some measure reflects this position. Though diagnosticians are expected to note whether a patient's behavior is psychotic, all mood disorders, whether neurotic or psychotic, are grouped together.

Endogenous versus Reactive Many proponents of the continuity hypothesis believe that all mood disorders are in large part psychogenic. Those who hold to the Kraepelin tradition, on the other hand, generally believe that only the neurotic forms are psychogenic. The psychotic forms they regard as biogenic.

Basic to the latter point of view is a second dimension of mood disorder: the endogenous-versus-reactive dimension. Originally, the terms *endogenous* and *reactive* were intended to indicate whether or not a depression was preceded by a precipitating event, such as a death in the family or the loss of a job. Those that were linked to such an event were called **reactive;** those that were not were called **endogenous** (literally, "coming from within"). According to adherents of Kraepelin's position, neurotic depressions were generally reactive and therefore psychogenic, while psychotic depressions were generally endogenous and therefore biogenic.

As it turns out, however, the distinction is not so easily made. It is often difficult to determine whether a depression has been triggered by a specific event. Furthermore, even when there is a trigger, this factor may change as the disorder develops. There are often clear precipitating events for a first episode of major depressive disorder but not for later episodes (G. W. Brown, Harris, & Hepworth, 1994; E. Frank, Anderson, Reynolds, et al., 1994). As a result of these confusions, the terms *endogenous* and *reactive,* despite their dictionary meanings, are now generally used not to indicate the absence or presence of precipitating events but to describe different patterns of symptoms. Patients who show pronounced anhedonia together with the more *vegetative,* or physical, symptoms (e.g., early-morning awakening, weight loss, psychomotor changes) and who describe their depression as different in quality from what they would feel after the death of a loved one are classified as endogenous, or, in *DSM-IV*'s terminology, as having "melancholic features." Those whose disturbance is primarily emotional or cognitive are called reactive, or without melancholic features.

The endogenous-reactive distinction made on the basis of symptoms does seem to describe a genuine difference. Endogenous patients differ from reactive patients in their sleep patterns. They are also more likely than reactive patients to show the biological abnormalities that we will describe later in this chapter, and to respond to biological treatments, such as electroconvulsive ("shock") therapy (Rush & Weissenburger, 1994). Accordingly, some researchers still suspect that endogenous cases are more biogenic, but this has not been established, and there is some evidence to the contrary. For example, if endogenous depression were more biochemically based, then we would expect endogenous patients to have a greater family history of depression than reactives, but numerous studies have shown that they do not (Rush & Weissenburger, 1994). Researchers are still investigating this question intensively, and it is partly to help them assemble research groups that the *DSM* requires diagnoses of major depression to specify the presence or absence of melancholic features.

When depression is preceded by a clear precipitating event, that event is usually some kind of uncontrollable loss—being laid off from work, losing one's home—and particularly interpersonal loss (Shrout, Link, Dohrenwend, et al., 1989). "Exit events"—death, separation, divorce, a child's leaving home—rank high among stressors associated with the onset of depression (Paykel & Cooper, 1992). By the same token, if a person has a close relationship, and therefore someone to confide in, he or she is less likely to succumb to depression in the face of stressful life events (G. W. Brown, 1979; Holahan & Moos, 1991). The same principles hold for people recovering from depression. Stress, particularly stress connected with exit events and other losses, is associated with relapses, while social support, particularly in the form of a confidant, is associated with continued recovery, even in the face of stress (Lewinsohn, Hoberman, & Rosenbaum, 1988; Paykel & Cooper, 1992).

Early versus Late Onset In the last few years there has been steadily accumulating evidence that age of onset constitutes an important dimension of mood disorder. Studies of people with major depressive disorder, bipolar disorder, and dysthymic disorder have all shown that the earlier the onset of the disorder, the more likely it is that the person's relatives will have, or have had, mood disorders. Some of the findings are quite remarkable. In a study of children of people with major depression, it was found that when the parent's age at onset was under twenty, the lifetime risk of major depression in the child was almost twice as great as the risk when the parent's age at onset was over thirty—57.8 percent compared with 32.4 percent (Weissman, Warner, Wickramaratne, et al., 1988)—and this approximately 2-to-1 ratio has been duplicated by later investigators (Kupfer, Frank, Carpenter, et al., 1989). Another study found that when onset occurred after forty, relatives were at no greater risk than the general population (R. A. Price, Kidd, & Weissman, 1987).

Early onset also seems to predict whether the person and the family will develop other, related

Research indicates that both genetics and environment—that is, family history and home situation—affect a child's risk of early-onset mood disorder.

disorders. In a study of dysthymics, 94 percent of the early-onset group graduated to major depression, compared with 55 percent of the late-onset group—again, something like a 2-to-1 ratio (D. N. Klein, Taylor, Dickstein, et al., 1988). In a study of recurrent depressives, not just depression but also alcoholism was significantly more common in relatives of the people whose age at onset was under twenty (Kupfer, Frank, Carpenter, et al., 1989).

In general, then, the earlier the onset, the harder the road, both for the person and for the relatives. These findings may suggest that early-onset patients have a higher "genetic loading" for mood disorder. Alternatively, the higher rates of depression in the relatives of early-onset patients could be due to environmental effects. Relatives of early-onset cases have lived with a depressed person for a longer period of time. In particular, children of an early-onset depressed parent have had greater opportunity to learn depressive behaviors from the parent.

Comorbidity: Mixed Anxiety-Depression

One important trend in the study of depression is the increasing evidence of the **comorbidity,** or co-occurrence, of depressive and anxiety disorders (Alloy, Kelly, Mineka, et al., 1990; Klerman, 1990). The symptomatologies of the two disorders show considerable overlap (see Table 10.1), such that people diagnosed as having one are likely to meet the diagnostic criteria for the other as well, either simultaneously (*intraepisode comorbidity*) or at different times in their lives (*lifetime comorbidity*). People in these two diagnostic groups also tend to respond to the same antidepressant drugs (A. J. Fyer, Liebowitz, & Klein, 1990), share similar endocrine abnormalities (Heninger, 1990), and have family histories of both anxiety and depressive disorders (Merikangus, 1990; Weissman, 1990). These new findings have reignited an old debate over whether depression and anxiety are in fact two distinct entities or whether they are somewhat different manifestations of the same underlying disorder.

The comorbidity findings have also led to a proposal that a new category, "mixed anxiety-depression," be included in future *DSM*s. This would make the *DSM* consistent with the World Health Organization's *ICD-10,* which has such a category. More important, it would provide a diagnostic label for people who have mixed symptoms of anxiety and depression but who do not meet the *DSM-IV* criteria for either disorder alone. There are many such people, and they may be at risk for more severe mood and anxiety disorders, especially if they are not given appropriate treatment (Katon & Roy-Byrne, 1991; Zinbarg, Barlow, Liebowitz, et al., 1994). Having no diagnostic label for them makes appropriate treatment less likely; and, of course, if these people do represent an important category of psychopathology, then having no diagnostic label gives us a false picture of the field.

SUICIDE

Any consideration of the mood disorders must include some discussion of suicide. People take their lives for many reasons, but a very common reason

TABLE 10.1
SUMMARY OF SYMPTOMS UNIQUE AND COMMON TO DEPRESSION AND ANXIETY

Type of Symptoms	Unique to Depression	Unique to Anxiety	Overlap Both Syndromes
Affective	Severe sadness and despair Low positive affect	Severe fear and tension	Negative affect Crying Irritability
Behavioral	Psychomotor retardation Anhedonia Loss of interest Suicidal acts (and ideation)	Increased activity Behavioral agitation	Decreased activity Lowered initiation of responses Decreased energy Behavioral disorganization and performance deficits Increased dependency Poor social skills
Somatic	Decreased sympathetic arousal Decreased appetite Reduced sexual desire	Increased sympathetic arousal	Restless sleep Initial insomnia Panic attacks
Cognitive	Hopelessness Perceived loss	Perceived danger and threat Uncertainty Hypervigilance (watchfulness)	Helplessness Repetitive rumination and obsessions Worry Low self-confidence Negative self-evaluation Self-criticism Self-preoccupation Indecisiveness Poor concentration

SOURCE: Adapted from Alloy, Kelly, Mineka, & Clements (1990), p. 507.

is depression. The lifetime risk of suicide among people with mood disorders is estimated at 19 percent (F. K. Goodwin & Jamison, 1990). In a sample of adolescents who had committed suicide, it was found that almost half had been depressed before the fatal attempt (Marttunen, Aro, Henriksson, et al., 1991).

The Prevalence of Suicide

Accurate statistics on the prevalence of suicide are difficult to obtain, since many people who commit suicide prefer to make their deaths look accidental. It has been estimated that at least 15 percent of all fatal automobile accidents are actually suicides, for example (Finch, Smith, & Pokorny, 1970). In 1986, the last year for which census statistics are available, there were just over 30,000 suicides reported in the United States (U.S. Bureau of the Census, 1990). In the general population, it has been estimated that eight people attempt suicide for every one who commits suicide (Leenaars & Wenckstern, 1991), which would mean that each year perhaps a quarter of a million people in the United States attempt suicide. Many statisticians and public health experts would consider these figures far too low. Other countries, such as France and Denmark, have far higher rates; Austria's is almost double the U.S. rate (U.S. Bureau of the Census, 1990). But even at 30,000 per year, suicide is the tenth most common cause of death in this country.

Who Commits Suicide?

Certain demographic variables are strongly correlated with suicide. Twice as many single people as married people kill themselves, and childless women are more likely to commit suicide than those with children (Hoyer & Lund, 1993). In general the likelihood of a person's committing suicide increases as a function of age, especially for men. Three times as many women as men attempt suicide, and three times as many men as women succeed in killing themselves. The fact that men choose more lethal methods, such as shooting themselves, is one of the reasons more men die (Garland & Zigler, 1993). In addition to the depressed, people who abuse drugs or alcohol are more likely to commit suicide (Lesage, Boyer, Grunberg, et al., 1994; N. S. Miller, Mahler, & Gold, 1991).

According to a demographic summary put together by Shneidman and Farberow in 1970, the *modal suicide attempter* (i.e., the person who most commonly attempts suicide and survives) is a native-born Caucasian female, a housewife in her twenties or thirties, who attempts to kill herself by swallowing barbiturates and gives as her reason either marital difficulties or depression. In contrast, the *modal suicide committer* (i.e., the person who succeeds in taking his or her own life) is a native-born Caucasian male in his forties or older who, for reasons of ill health, depression, or marital difficulties, commits suicide by shooting or hanging himself or by poisoning himself with carbon monoxide (see Figures 10.1 and 10.2).

According to later research, these generalizations still hold (Maris, 1992), but there have been some recent shifts in suicide-related variables, particularly regarding age. Perhaps the most striking shift is the decrease, over the past sixty years, in suicide rates among men over sixty (E. Murphy, Lindesay, & Grundy, 1986)—a heartening change that may be due to improved economic and social conditions for retirees. On the other hand, suicide rates among men aged fifteen to thirty-four have increased in the past few decades (G. E. Murphy & Wetzel, 1980). Older men are still more likely than younger men to kill themselves, but the gap is narrowing. (See the box on page 244.)

Is there a type of personality that is predisposed toward suicide? Apparently not. Suicide may be undertaken by any type of person in any of a variety of moods, ranging from the most frenzied to the most sober and calculating. Even so formidable a psychological intelligence as Freud's was not immune to suicidal thoughts. At age twenty-nine, in the throes of love, Freud wrote to his fiancée: "I have long since resolved on a decision [i.e., suicide], the thought of which is in no way painful, in the event of losing you" (quoted in E. Jones, 1963, p. 85).

Myths about Suicide

Common as it is, suicide is still surrounded by an aura of mystery and by a number of popular misconceptions. One of the most unfortunate myths about suicide is that people who threaten to kill themselves will not carry out the threat—that only

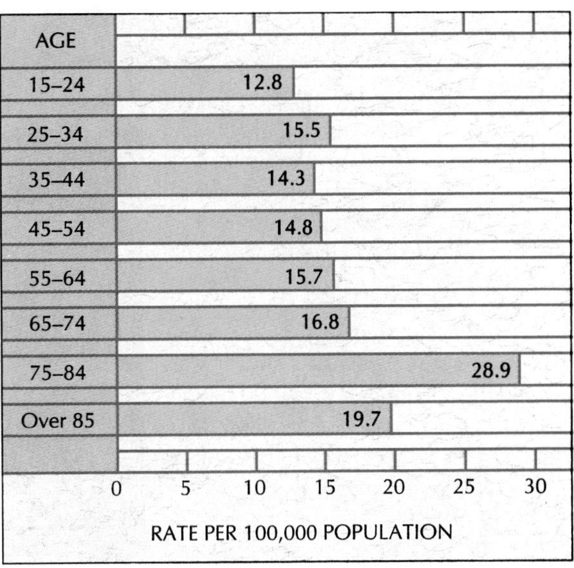

FIGURE 10.1 Suicide rates by age. The largest number of suicides occurs in people between seventy-five and eighty-four years of age; in this group there are 28.9 deaths per 100,000 of population. (U.S. Bureau of the Census, 1990)

the "silent type" will pull it off. This is quite untrue. In a recent study of seventy-one completed suicides, more than half the victims had clearly communicated their suicidal intent within three months before the fatal act (Isometsä, Henriksson, Aro, et al., 1994). In other words, when people threaten suicide, they should be taken seriously.

Another myth is that people who attempt suicide and fail are not serious about ending their lives—they are just looking for sympathy. On the contrary, about 40 percent of all suicides have

FIGURE 10.2 Suicide rates by race and sex. Suicide occurs most frequently among white males, least frequently among nonwhite females. (U.S. Bureau of the Census, 1990)

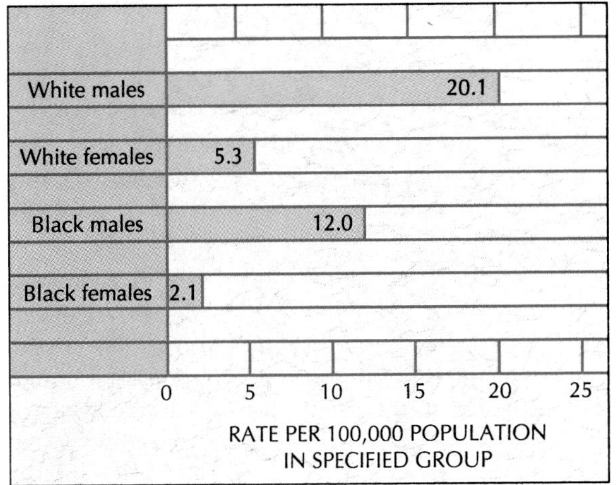

TEENAGE SUICIDE

Since 1960, the suicide rate among teenagers has risen 200 percent. In 1987 suicide became the second leading cause of death (after accidents) among fifteen- to nineteen-year-olds (M. S. Gould, Shaffer, Fisher, et al., 1992). As many as 8 to 9 percent of high school students have made at least one suicide attempt (J. A. Andrews & Lewinsohn, 1992; Harkavy-Friedman, Asnis, Boeck, et al., 1987). For many of their elders, this is hard to understand. How can people who "have their whole lives ahead of them" want to take those lives?

Apparently, the answer often lies in the family. One study compared 505 suicide attempters who came to the emergency room of a large children's hospital between 1970 and 1977 with 505 sex- and age-matched controls who were treated at the emergency room but not for a suicide attempt. In comparison with the controls, the suicide attempters had more experience with substance abuse, more history of psychiatric disorder, and more prior psychotherapy. But in addition, the families of the attempters had more psychiatric disorder (primarily alcohol and drug abuse), more history of suicide, more paternal unemployment, and more parental absence—whether through death or divorce (B. D. Garfinkel, Froese, & Hood, 1982). A more recent study found that there was more family turmoil among those who had committed suicide (versus attempters) as well as more social instability, such as changes in residence and school (de Wilde, Kienhorst, Diekstra, et al., 1992).

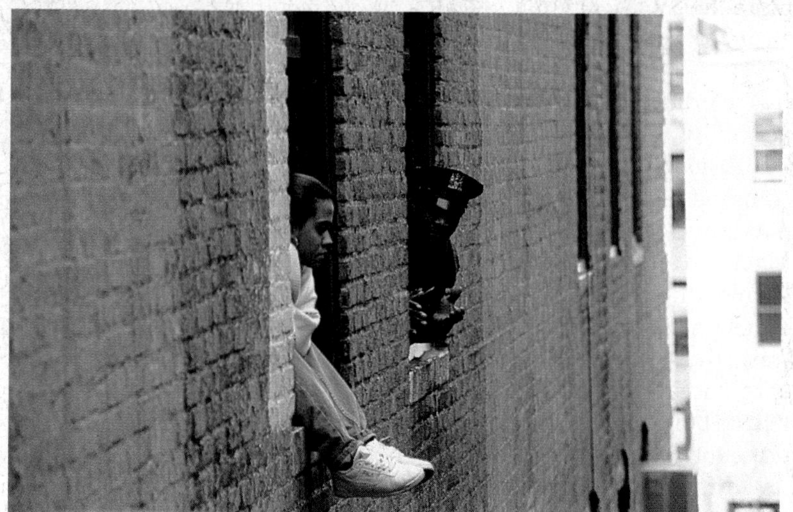

Teenage suicide has reached epidemic proportions in the United States. The episode shown here ended well, with the guard talking the young woman back into the building.

Thus the problems of suicidal teenagers are often rooted in their parents' problems. But for the teenagers, the difficulties are multiplied: they are still dependent on their families for love and support that may not be forthcoming, and they are often too young to seek out professional help for themselves. Sadly, only a third of the teenagers who commit suicide have ever had even one contact for professional treatment (Brent, Perper, Goldstein, et al., 1988). These young people may indeed feel that there is no one to turn to—no solution.

made a previous attempt or threat (Maris, 1992), and the more prior attempts, the greater the likelihood of a completed suicide (R. B. Goldstein, Black, Nasrallah, et al., 1991). Among 1,959 suicide attempters in England who were followed up for eight years, the number who eventually did commit suicide was twenty-seven times higher than the number who would be expected to die during this eight-year period (Hawton & Fagg, 1988).

As we have mentioned, the issue of suicide is often obscured by a cloud of mystery. Our emotional reactions to this phenomenon—fear, horror, curiosity, incomprehension—give suicide the status of "unmentionable" in the minds of many people, a taboo that is strengthened by the Judeo-Christian prohibition against taking one's own life. Connected with this response is a third myth about suicide: that in conversation with depressed people, suicide is an unmentionable topic. According to this notion, questioning depressives about whether they have suicidal thoughts will either put the idea into their heads or, if it is already there, give it greater force. In opposition to this belief, almost all clinicians agree that encouraging patients to talk about suicidal wishes helps them to overcome such wishes.

Suicide Prediction

When someone commits suicide, family and friends are often astonished. Such comments as "He seemed to be in such good spirits" or "But she had everything to live for" are typical reactions. These responses reveal how frequently those in the immediate social environment of a potential suicide are oblivious to the signs. As we just saw, most suicidal people clearly communicate their intent. For example, they may say, "I don't want to go on living" or "I know I'm a burden to everyone." But even those who don't announce their plans usually give signals (Shneidman, 1992). Some withdraw into an almost contemplative state. Others act as if they were going on a long trip. Others give away their most valued possessions. Sometimes the expression of suicidal intent is less direct, however clear in retrospect. For example, a depressed patient leaving the hospital on a weekend pass may say, "I want to thank you for trying so hard to help me."

Since a period of calm may follow a decision to commit suicide (Keith-Spiegel & Spiegel, 1967), the sudden tranquility of a previously agitated patient is a danger signal, but it is often misinterpreted as a sign of improvement. Since such people seem better, they may be watched less carefully. And not uncommonly they will use this new freedom to carry out the suicide. In this connection, it should be pointed out that depressives who commit suicide tend to do so as they are coming out of their depression. It is not clear whether they seem less depressed because they have made the decision to commit suicide or whether, being less depressed, they at last have the energy to act upon their suicidal wishes.

Predictably, suicide is often directly related to stress. There is some evidence that the nature of the stress may vary over the life cycle. One study found that interpersonal conflicts, rejections, and separations most often precede suicide in younger people, whereas economic problems are more critical in middle age and illness in old age (Rich, Warsradt, Nemiroff, et al., 1991). Like the onset of depression, suicide attempts are frequently preceded by "exit" events. Unlike depressions, however, suicide attempts also tend to be preceded by "entrance" events, such as births, marriages, or the return of a family member (Paykel, 1979a).

Cognitive variables may be among the most useful predictors of who will attempt suicide. Not surprisingly, the cognitive variable most frequently associated with serious suicidal intent is hopelessness (Weishaar & Beck, 1992). In a ten-year follow-up study of hospitalized patients who expressed suicidal thoughts, hopelessness turned out to be the best single predictor of who would eventually kill themselves (A. T. Beck, Steer, Kovacs, et al., 1985), and this has proved true with outpatients as well (A. T. Beck, Brown, Berchick, et al., 1990). From accounts of people who survived suicide attempts, together with research on those who died, suicide expert Edwin Shneidman (1992) put together a "suicidal scenario," a summary of elements that are usually present in the decision to take one's own life:

> **1** A sense of unbearable psychological *pain*, which is directly related to thwarted psychological *needs*.
> **2** Traumatizing *self-denigration*—a self-image that will not include tolerating intense psychological pain.
> **3** A marked *constriction* of the mind and an unrealistic narrowing of life's actions.
> **4** A sense of *isolation*—a feeling of desertion and the loss of support of significant others.
> **5** An overwhelmingly desperate feeling of *hopelessness*—a sense that nothing effective can be done.
> **6** A conscious decision that *egression*—leaving, exiting, or stopping life—is the *only* (or at least the best possible) solution to the problem of unbearable pain. (pp. 51–52)

As this summary shows, many people who commit suicide imagine that it is the only way out of an unbearably painful situation—a conviction that is often clear in the notes they leave. In a study comparing real suicide notes with simulated notes written by a well-matched control group, Shneidman and Farberow (1970) found that the writers of the genuine notes expressed significantly more suffering than the control group. Truly suicidal anguish is evidently hard to feign. Interestingly, though, the genuine suicide notes also contained a greater number of neutral statements—instructions, admonitions, lists of things to be done after the suicide has taken place, and so forth. Both the ring of authentic hopelessness and the neutral content are illustrated in the following two notes:

> Barbara,
> I'm sorry. I love you bunches. Would you please do a couple of things for me. Don't tell the kids what I did. When Theresa gets a little older, if she wants to cut her hair please let her. Don't make her wear it long just because you like it that way. Ask your Mom what kind and how much clothes the kids need and then buy double what she says. I love you and the kids very much please try and remember that. I'm just not any good for you. I never learned how to tell you no. You will be much better off without me. Just try and find someone who will love Theresa and Donny.
> Love Bunches—Charlie
> P.S. Donny is down at Linda's
> Put Donny in a nursery school

> Dear Steve:
> I have been steadily getting worse in spite of everything and did not want to be a burden the rest of my life.
> All my love,
> Dad
> My brown suit is the only one that fits me.

Not all suicides experience unqualified despair, however. According to Farberow and Litman (1970), only about 3 to 5 percent of people who attempt suicide are truly determined to die. Another 30 percent fall into what the researchers call the "to be or not to be" group—those who are ambivalent about dying. Finally, about two-thirds of suicide attempters do not really wish to die but instead are trying, through the gesture of a suicide attempt, to communicate the intensity of their suffering to family and friends. Regarding the last two groups, it bears repeating that their mixed feelings do not mean that they are not in danger. As we saw above, many of those who are not determined this time will be more determined next time.

Suicide Prevention

As we just pointed out, most people who attempt suicide do not absolutely wish to die. It was on the basis of this finding, together with the fact that suicide attempters are often reacting to crises in their lives, that the first telephone "hot lines" for potential suicides were established in the late 1950s (Shneidman & Farberow, 1957). Hot-line staffers, often volunteers, try to "tune in" to the caller's distress, at the same time presenting arguments against suicide and telling the caller where he or she can go for professional help. (Hot lines will be discussed further in Chapter 20.) Another preventive effort, this one aimed specifically at the newly high-risk adolescent population, involves school-based programs. Here, teachers, parents, and the teenagers themselves are given workshops in which they are informed of the "warning signs" of suicide and told how and where to refer someone who seems to be in danger.

Unfortunately, neither of these efforts has been especially successful. Communities with suicide hot lines appear to have lower suicide rates only for one group—young white women, the most frequent hot-line users—and even for them the decrease is slight (H. L. Miller, Coombs, & Leeper, 1984; Shaffer, Garland, Fisher, et al., 1990). As for the school-based programs, they seem to be minimally effective in changing attitudes and coping behavior, particularly in boys (Shaffer, Garland, & Vieland, 1991), who are less likely than girls to turn to the kind of social and professional support that such workshops recommend (Overholser, Evans, & Spirito, 1990). It is probable, furthermore, that school-based programs are not reaching their target population. The adolescents most at risk for suicide—delinquents, substance abusers, runaways, incarcerated teenagers—are the ones least likely to be in school, let alone paying close attention to a suicide-prevention workshop.

A recent review of such programs suggests that efforts might be better spent attacking the social problems most closely associated with suicide: delinquency, truancy, substance abuse, teen pregnancy, family distress (Garland & Zigler, 1993). Several researchers have also called for stricter gun-control laws (D. Lester & Murrell, 1980) and for educating journalists about the possible imitative effects of suicide coverage. There is some evidence, though mixed, that highly publicized suicides may inspire teenagers to follow suit. In 1977, for example, there was a significant increase in suicide by gunshot in Los Angeles County during the week following comedian Freddie Prinze's suicide by gunshot (Berman, 1988).

PERSPECTIVES ON THE MOOD DISORDERS AND SUICIDE

Since depression is far more common than mania and since many theorists regard mania as a secondary reaction to depression, most theories of mood disorder have concentrated on depression alone. (The biological perspective is the exception.) We will discuss theories of suicide together with interpretations of depression.

The Psychodynamic Perspective

Reactivated Loss The first serious challenge to Kraepelin's biogenic theory of mood disorder came from Freud and other early psychoanalytic theorists, who argued that depression was not a symptom of organic dysfunction but a massive defense mounted by the ego against intrapsychic conflict. In his now-classic paper "Mourning and Melancholia" (1917/1957) Freud described depression as a response to loss (real or symbolic), but one in which the person's sorrow and rage in the face of that loss are not vented but remain unconscious, thus weakening the ego. This formulation was actually an elaboration of a theory put forth by one of Freud's students, Karl Abraham (1911/1948, 1916/1948). Abraham had suggested that depression arises when one loses a love object toward whom one had ambivalent feelings, positive and negative. In the face of the love object's desertion, the negative feelings turn to intense anger. At the same time, the positive feelings give rise to guilt, a feeling that one failed to behave properly toward the now-lost love object. Because of this guilt—and also because of early memories in which the

Severe stress and feelings of hopelessness drive some people to attempt suicide. This desperate man seized a gun and threatened suicide from the back seat of a police car. He later surrendered.

primary love object was symbolically "eaten up," or incorporated, by the infant—the grieving person turns his or her anger inward rather than outward, thus producing the self-hatred and despair that we call depression. In the case of suicide, the person is actually trying to kill the incorporated love object. "Anger in" has escalated to "murder in."

While "anger in" still figures importantly in traditional psychoanalytic discussions of depression and suicide, modern theorists have expanded and revised this early position. There are now many psychodynamic theories of depression, yet they do share a certain number of core assumptions (Bemporad, 1988; Stricker, 1983). First, it is generally believed that depression is rooted in some very early defect, often the loss or threatened loss of a parent (Bowlby, 1973). Second, the primal wound is reactivated by some recent blow, such as a divorce or job loss. Whatever the precipitating event, the person is plunged back into the infantile trauma. Third, a major consequence of this regression is a sense of helplessness and hopelessness—a reflection of what was the infant's actual powerlessness in the face of harm. Feeling incapable of controlling his or her world, the depressive simply withdraws from it. Fourth, many theorists, while perhaps no longer regarding anger as the hub of depression, do feel that ambivalence toward introjected objects (i.e., love objects who have been "taken in" to the self) is fundamental to the depressive's emotional quandary. Fifth, it is widely agreed that loss of self-esteem is a primary feature of depression. Otto Fenichel (1945) described depressives as "love addicts," trying continually to compensate for their own depleted self-worth by seeking comfort and reassurance from others. This leads to the sixth common psychodynamic assumption about depression: that it has a functional role. It is not just something that people feel but something that they *use,* particularly in the form of dependency, in their relationships with others.

Like most psychodynamic theories, these assumptions are not fully open to empirical validation, but two claims have been tested. First, a high level of dependency on others does appear to characterize some depressed persons, and these highly dependent people are more likely to become depressed when they experience social rejections (Nietzel & Harris, 1990). Second, research has examined the role of parental loss, though here the results are mixed. There is evidence for the link. Women who have lost their mothers in childhood through either death or separation are apparently more likely to succumb to depression (Harris, Brown, & Bifulco, 1990), and depressed patients who have suffered a serious childhood loss, particularly separation from a parent, are more likely to attempt suicide (Bron, Strack, & Rudolph, 1991). But many researchers now believe that the crucial risk factor, at least for depression, is not so much parental loss as poor parenting (Kendler, Neale, Kessler, et al., 1992; Tennant, 1988). Recent research has focused especially on a parenting pattern called *affectionless control*—that is, too much protectiveness combined with too little real care. This pattern may leave children feeling chronically helpless and overdependent. When, as adults, they encounter stress, they are more vulnerable to depression because they feel helpless (Blatt & Homann, 1992; G. Parker, 1992).

Repairing the Loss Long-term psychodynamic treatment generally strives to uncover the presumed childhood roots of the current depression and to unknot and explore the ambivalent feelings toward the lost object, both primal and current. As we have noted, however, today's psychodynamic therapists tend to be more directive than their predecessors, and more concerned with the patient's present circumstances as opposed to the past. Hence many of them will focus less on childhood trauma than on the current cause of the depression and on how the patient uses the depression in his or her dealings with others. This pragmatic approach is even more pronounced in short-term therapy. Klerman and his coworkers have produced a manual for a twelve- to sixteen-session treatment in which therapist and patient identify the core problem—the four most common categories being grief, interpersonal disputes (e.g., a failing marriage), role transition (e.g., retirement), and lack of social skills—and then actively attack that problem together (Klerman, Weissman, Rounsaville, et al., 1984). Recent studies indicate that this form of dynamic, interpersonal therapy is effective in preventing relapse of depression among patients who have discontinued drug treatment (E. Frank, Kupfer, Perel, et al., 1990; E. Frank, Kupfer, Wagner, et al., 1991).

Psychodynamic treatment of the suicidal patient tends to follow the same lines as treatment for depression, though with special emphasis on emotional support. With potential suicides, therapists are careful to avoid doing or saying anything that could be viewed as rejection. In their analysis of the patient's behavior, they are likely to interpret suicidal threats as an appeal for love, whether from the therapist or from others.

The Humanistic-Existential Perspective

Depression as a Response to Inauthenticity Existentialists would interpret depression as a response to a sense of "nonbeing," resulting from a failure to live completely and authentically. If depressives speak of their guilt feelings, the existentialist, along with the humanist, would say that they *are* guilty, because they are failing to make choices, fulfill their potential, and take responsibility for their lives (May, 1958). In sum, depression is an understandable reaction to an inauthentic existence. Suicide is interpreted as a sort of culmination of inauthentic choices. Indeed, Boss (1976) claims that all suicides are preceded by "an existential partial suicide" in which the person withdraws from others, abrogates responsibilities, and ceases to pursue genuine values.

One aspect of this inauthenticity may be fear of aloneness. As we have seen, depressives are often highly dependent people—"love addicts" as Fenichel called them. Thus loneliness may be an important constituent of depression. From the existential point of view (Moustakas, 1961, 1972, 1975), loneliness is not something to be avoided or treated. On the contrary, it is the human condition and should be accepted. Just as depressives must be confronted with aloneness, suicidal patients should be made to understand the importance of death. According to Rollo May (1958), death is what gives life absolute value. It is our knowledge of the inevitability of death that makes us take life seriously, as an opportunity for action.

Confronting Existence Humanistic-existential therapists try to help depressed and suicidal patients to see that their emotional pain is an authentic reaction, which they should accept and learn from. What is to be learned is that one can never attain personal satisfaction by being overdependent on others. An authentic life means pursuing one's *own* goals. It is by leading depressed and suicidal patients to discover such goals that humanistic-existential therapists hope to give them a better reason for living. In the process, however, these therapists will also try very hard, in keeping with Carl Rogers' principles, to "tune in" to their patients, to "hear" them, a technique that, like other humanistic-existential tactics, has been widely adopted by other therapists. Indeed, the approach taken by volunteers on suicide hot lines—that of just listening, uncritically—is basically the Rogerian technique.

The Behavioral Perspective

Like the psychodynamic perspective, the behavioral perspective on depression and suicide is a collection of theories. We shall discuss the two major approaches, one focusing on external reinforcers and the other on interpersonal processes.

Extinction Many behaviorists regard depression as the result of extinction (Ferster, 1965, 1973; Lewinsohn, 1974). As one proponent of this view puts it, depression is "a function of inadequate or insufficient reinforcers" (A. A. Lazarus, 1968, p. 84). That is, once behaviors are no longer rewarded, people cease to perform them. They become inactive and withdrawn—in short, depressed.

What causes the reduction in reinforcement?

Lewinsohn (1974) has pointed out that the amount of positive reinforcement a person receives depends on three broad factors: (1) the number and range of stimuli that are reinforcing to that person; (2) the availability of such reinforcers in the environment; and (3) the person's skill in obtaining reinforcement. Sudden changes in a person's environment may affect any one of these factors. A new and reluctant retiree, for example, may find that the world outside the office holds few things that are truly reinforcing. Or a man whose wife has recently died may find that whereas he had the social skills to make a success of marriage, he is at a loss in the dating situation. In their new circumstances, these people simply do not know how to obtain reinforcement, and therefore they withdraw into themselves. Eventually the depressed person may come to see death as more reinforcing than life, in that it will make others feel sorry or guilty. In such a case, depression may lead to a suicide attempt (Ullmann & Krasner, 1975).

A number of studies by Lewinsohn and his colleagues have produced results consistent with the extinction hypothesis. For example, one objection to this hypothesis has been the widely held assumption that depressives are *resistant* to reinforcement; it is not that they lack sources of pleasure but rather that they have lost the ability to experience pleasure. It has been found, however, that even severely depressed people will, like nondepressed people, show an elevation of mood if they learn to decrease the frequency of unpleasant events and increase the frequency of pleasant activities (Lewinsohn, Sullivan, & Grosscup, 1980). Depressives also lack skill in obtaining reinforcement, as Lewinsohn suggested. Depressed people are much less adept than nondepressed people at interacting with others (Belsher & Costello, 1991; Gotlib & Robinson, 1982). They are also less skillful at coping with the impediments to reinforcement. Not surprisingly, this is all the more true of suicide attempters. When a group of teenagers, hospitalized after a suicide attempt, was compared with a group of distressed but nonsuicidal teenagers, the suicidal subjects were far more likely to use social isolation as their way of coping with problems (Spirito, Overholser, & Stark, 1989). Suicidal adolescents are also likely to avoid problems, to see them inaccurately, and to respond to them in a more emotional fashion (Sadowski & Kelley, 1993). Of course, poor coping and avoidance of problems mean that these people are less likely to get help.

Aversive Social Behavior Some research has found that depressives are more likely than nondepressives to elicit negative reactions from people they interact with (Coyne, 1976a; Marcus & Nardone, 1992), and this finding has formed the basis of interpersonal theories of depression. According to one theory, depressives have an aversive behavioral style in which, by constantly seeking reassurance, they try to force "caring" behavior from people who, they feel, no longer care enough. Instead of love, however, what depressives are likely to get from their put-upon families and friends is shallow reassurance of the "now, now" variety or, worse, rejection, which simply aggravates their depression (Coyne, 1976b; Joiner, Alfano, & Metalsky, 1992). Depression, then, is a cry for help, but one that rarely works. An alternative interpersonal theory is that depressives actually seek out rejection, for this is more familiar and predictable to them than positive feedback (Swann, Wenzlaff, Krull, et al., 1992).

Consistent with these interpersonal hypotheses, some studies have found that rejecting responses from friends and family do tend to maintain or exacerbate depression (Hokanson, Rubert, Welker, et al., 1989; Swann, Wenzlaff, Krull, et al., 1992). For example, Hooley and Teasdale (1989) found that depressed patients whose spouses were critical toward them were more likely to suffer a relapse of depression in the next nine months than were those with more accepting spouses. However, it is not clear that depressives' interpersonal style predates the onset of their depression. Some evidence suggests that this style is only present during the depressed episode and goes away when the depressed person recovers (Rohde, Lewinsohn, & Seeley, 1990). Whether or not it predates the depression, though, depressives' poor interpersonal skills may contribute to maintaining their depression.

Increasing Reinforcement and Social Skills In keeping with the extinction theory of depression, behavioral treatment usually focuses on increasing the patient's rate of reinforcement. Fensterheim (1975), for example, describes what is essentially a project for the relearning of pleasure. First, patients are urged to imagine a gratifying action—eating an ice cream cone, reading a detective story, anything that seems remotely appealing to them. Then they must make an "appointment" with themselves to perform this action, and when the time of the appointment arrives, they must perform the action, whether or not they feel like it. Patients repeat this process a number of times, all the while keeping a record of their responses to their "plea-

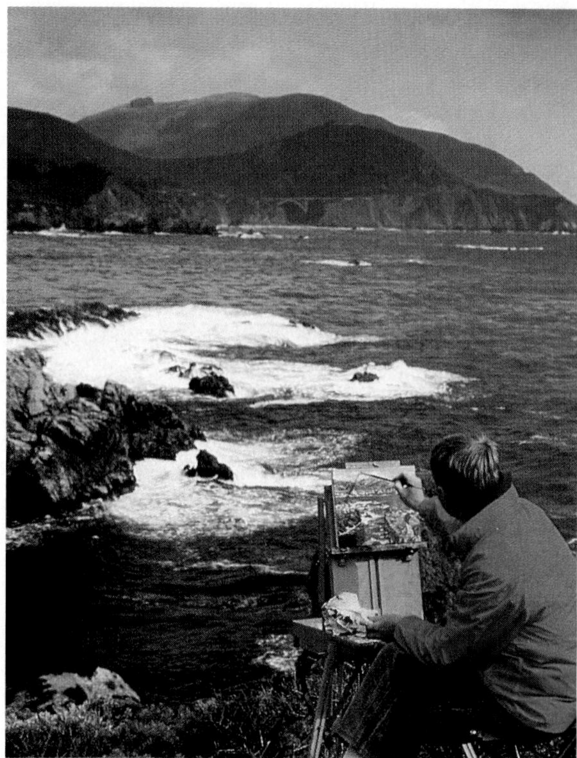

A program of regularly performed pleasurable activities may be useful in treating depression as well as warding it off.

sure excursions." The goal is not only to increase the patients' contact with reinforcers but also to retrain them in the experience of pleasure.

Another important thrust in the behavioral treatment of depression is **social-skills training.** As we have seen, depressives are not popular with others—a problem that social-skills training aims to remedy directly by teaching basic techniques for engaging in satisfying social interactions. Patients are shown how to initiate a conversation, how to keep eye contact, how to make small talk, how to end a conversation—in other words, the nuts and bolts of socializing. Such behaviors are often modeled for patients, after which they are practiced through role playing. The therapist, for example, might pretend to be a guest at a party with whom the patient must open a conversation.

Most behavioral treatments for depression are multifaceted, using the techniques described above, together with others, in combination. For example, Lewinsohn and his colleagues have put together a treatment that includes self-monitoring of mood and activities, instruction in positive coping self-statements, and training in a variety of areas—coping skills, social skills, parenting skills, time management—with the aim of decreasing unpleasant experiences and increasing pleasant experiences (Lewinsohn, Sullivan, & Grosscup, 1980). Similar multifaceted programs have been used with suicidal patients. For example, Liberman and Eckman (1981) have reported a successful evaluation of a behavioral program for repeated suicide attempters that comprises social-skills training, anxiety management, and contingency contracting (Chapter 20) with family members regarding family disputes.

The Cognitive Perspective

As we saw earlier in this chapter, depression involves a number of changes: emotional, motivational, cognitive, and physical. Cognitive theorists hold that the critical variable is the cognitive change. In all cognitive formulations, it is the way people *think* about themselves, the world, and the future that gives rise to the other factors involved in depression.

Helplessness and Hopelessness In a cognitive-learning model of depression, Martin Seligman (1975) has suggested that depression may be understood as analogous to the phenomenon of **learned helplessness** in animals. This phenomenon was first demonstrated with laboratory dogs. After exposing a number of dogs to inescapable electric shocks, Seligman and his colleagues found that when the same dogs were later subjected to escapable shocks, they either did not initiate escape responses or were slow and inept at escaping. The investigators concluded that during the first phase of the experiment, when the shocks were inescapable, the dogs had learned that the shock was *uncontrollable*—a lesson that they continued to act upon even in the second phase of the experiment, when it was possible to escape the shocks (Maier, Seligman, & Solomon, 1969).

After further research on learned helplessness in animals and humans, Seligman noted that this phenomenon closely resembled depression. He therefore proposed that depression, like learned helplessness, was a reaction to inescapable or seemingly inescapable stressors, which undermined adaptive responses by teaching the person that he or she lacked control over reinforcement. This formulation is consistent with the finding, noted earlier, that when there is a clear precipitating event for a depression, it is often some kind of uncontrollable loss. Learned helplessness also fits nicely with certain neuroscience findings. For example, depressed patients who see themselves as helpless tend to show higher levels of MHPG, a product of norepinephrine metabolism (Samson, Mirin, Hauser, et al., 1992). As we shall see, norepinephrine abnormalities are heavily implicated in the biochemistry of depression.

Note the difference between the learned-helplessness theory and extinction theory. In extinction theory, the crucial factor is an objective environmental condition, a lack of positive reinforcement; in learned-helplessness theory, the crucial factor is a subjective cognitive process, the *expectation* of lack of control over reinforcement. One should also note the connection between learned helplessness theory and the psychodynamic theory of early loss. The evidence for the psychodynamic theory—for example, that women who lost their mothers in childhood tend to show greater helplessness—is also evidence for the learned-helplessness theory.

When it was originally formulated, the learned-helplessness model had certain weaknesses. As Seligman and his colleagues themselves pointed out, the model explained the passivity characteristic of depression but it did not explain the equally characteristic sadness, guilt, and suicidal thoughts. Nor did it account for the fact that different cases of depression vary considerably in intensity and duration. To fill these gaps, Abramson and her colleagues, adapted the model from a helplessness to a hopelessness theory. According to their view, depression depends not just on the belief that there is a lack of control over reinforcement (a *helplessness expectancy*) but also on the belief that negative events will persist or recur (a *negative outcome expectancy*). When a person holds these two expectations—that bad things will happen and that there is nothing one can do about it—he or she becomes hopeless, and it is this hopelessness that is the immediate cause of the depression (Abramson, Metalsky, & Alloy, 1989).

But what is the source of the expectations of helplessness and negative outcomes? According to the researchers, these expectations stem from the *attributions* and *inferences* that people make regarding stressful life events—that is, the perceived causes and consequences of such events. People who see negative life events as due to causes that are (1) permanent rather than temporary, (2) generalized over many areas of their life rather than specific to one area of their functioning, and (3) internal, or part of their personality, rather than external, or part of the environment, are at greatest risk for developing hopelessness and, in turn, severe and persistent depression. Likewise, people who infer that stressful events will have negative consequences and implications for themselves will be more likely to become hopeless and depressed. In fact, Abramson and her coworkers have proposed that "hopelessness depression" constitutes a distinct subtype of depression, with its own set of causes (negative inferential styles combined with stress), symptoms (passivity, sadness, suicidal tendencies, low self-esteem), and appropriate treatments. Thus what was once a cognitive-learning formulation has been refined in this theory to an explicitly cognitive formulation. This theory also applies to suicide. Hopelessness is the best single predictor of suicide—even better than depression (Spirito, Brown, Overholser, et al., 1989).

In the past few years, the revised hopelessness theory has begun to be tested, with mixed results. On the positive side, it has been found that depressives are more likely than controls to explain negative events by means of the kind of attributions listed above (Sweeney, Anderson, & Bailey, 1986). Moreover, attributional style can help predict who, in a given sample, has been depressed in the past (Alloy, Lipman, & Abramson, 1992) and who will become depressed in the future when exposed to stress (Abramson, Alloy, & Metalsky, 1994; Alloy, Abramson, Whitehouse, et al., 1994; Nolen-Hoeksema, Girgus, & Seligman, 1992). It also predicts who, in a group of depressed people, will recover when exposed to positive events (Needles & Abramson, 1990). Other studies have shown that the reason a combination of stress and negative attributional style predicts depression is because that combination predicts hopelessness. It is hopelessness which, in turn, predicts depression (Metalsky, Joiner, Hardin, et al., 1993). Finally, people who show this combination also exhibit many of the symptoms said to be part of the hopelessness-depression subtype (Alloy, Just, & Panzarella, 1994; Spangler, Simons, Monroe, et al., 1993). At the same time, there is conflicting evidence. For example, some researchers have found that the stress-plus-negative-attributions combination did not necessarily lead to depression (Hammen, Adrian, & Hiroto, 1988; Parry & Brewin, 1988). To summarize, most of the evidence does argue that attributional style and hopelessness play a role in depression. What is not clear is whether they actually help to *cause* the depression.

Negative Self-Schema A second major cognitive theory of depression, Aaron Beck's negative self-schema model, evolved from his findings that the hallucinations, delusions, and dreams of depressed patients often contain themes of self-punishment, loss, and deprivation. According to Beck, this negative bias—the tendency to see oneself as a "loser"—is the fundamental cause of depression.

If a person, because of childhood experiences, develops a cognitive "schema" in which the self, the world, and the future are viewed in a negative light, that person is then predisposed to depression. Stress can easily activate the negative schema, and the consequent negative perceptions merely serve to strengthen the schema (A. T. Beck, 1987; Haaga, Dyck, & Ernst, 1991).

Recent research supports Beck's claim that depressives have an idiosyncratically negative schema, at least as regards the self (Roberts & Monroe, 1994; Z. V. Segal, 1988). In one study, three groups of people—a clinically depressed group, a group with other psychological disorders, and a normal group—were asked to rate a series of words on how closely each word applied to them. Later, when asked to recall as many of the words as possible, the depressed group remembered more of the negative words that they had earlier judged to be self-descriptive than did the other two groups (Derry & Kuiper, 1981). Other studies indicate that depressives selectively attend to and remember more negative than positive information about themselves (Z. V. Segal & Moran, 1993). Still other research suggests that depressives may have two distinct negative self-schemas, one centered on dependency, the other on self-criticism (Nietzel & Harris, 1990). For those with dependency self-schemas, it is stressful social events—in other words, situations in which their dependency would be most keenly felt—that, according to this view, lead to depression. For those with self-criticism schemas, it is failure that should trigger depression. Researchers testing this hypothesis have found that it works better for dependency self-schemas and social events than for self-criticism schemas and failure (Barnett & Gotlib, 1990; Rude & Burnham, 1993; Z. V. Segal, Shaw, Vella, et al., 1992).

An interesting finding is that while depressives may be more pessimistic than the rest of us, their pessimism is sometimes more realistic than our optimism. Lewinsohn and his colleagues put a group of depressives and two control groups through a series of social interactions and then asked the subjects (1) how positively or negatively they reacted to the others and (2) how positively or negatively they thought the others reacted to them. As it turned out, the depressives' evaluations of the impression they had made were more accurate than those of the other two groups, both of whom thought they had made more positive impressions than in fact they had (Lewinsohn, Mischel, Chaplin, et al., 1980). To quote the report of another Lewinsohn research team, "To feel good about ourselves we may have to judge ourselves more kindly than we are judged" (Lewinsohn, Sullivan, & Grosscup, 1980, p. 212).

We may also have to judge ourselves more capable than we are. Alloy and Abramson (1979) found that depressives, in doing an experimental task, were far more accurate in judging how much control they had than nondepressed subjects, who tended to overestimate their control when they were doing well and to underestimate it when they were doing poorly. Thus, in certain respects it may be that normal people, not depressives, are cognitively biased—and that such bias is essential for psychological health (Alloy & Abramson, 1988). Research supports this view. Alloy and Clements (1992), for example, tested a group for bias in judging personal control. They found that the subjects who had been inaccurately optimistic about their personal control when they were first tested were less likely than more realistic subjects to become depressed a month later in the face of stress.

Perhaps the best evidence for the cognitive underpinnings of depression comes from studies showing that depressed states can be induced by cognitive manipulation. Velten (1968), for example, found that a person would become depressed by simply reading a list of depressing statements aloud. Alloy and her colleagues found that when euphoric moods were induced in depressed subjects through cognitive means, the subjects developed the same "illusion of control" that was seen in the normal subjects in the Alloy and Abramson (1979) experiment, described above. By the same token, when depressed moods were induced in nondepressed subjects, the subjects showed the same "depressive realism" that depressed subjects showed in that experiment (Alloy, Abramson, & Viscusi, 1981).

Again, while these studies strongly suggest that cognitive variables play a role in depression, it is by no means clear that this role is causal (Haaga, Dyck, & Ernst, 1991). As we have seen before, however, a factor need not be causal in order to be useful in treatment.

Changing Negative Cognitions Aaron Beck and his coworkers have developed a multifaceted therapy that includes both behavioral assignments and cognitive retraining. In the cognitive retraining, destructive thoughts are first identified. Then the client learns to "answer" them with more realistic thoughts. Sometimes clients are asked to write down their negative thoughts—when they occur, how they feel when such thoughts come to mind, and so on—according to a list such as the following:

1 Briefly describe an upsetting situation.
2 Identify the emotions associated with it.
3 List the corresponding automatic thoughts.
4 Provide rational responses to the dysfunctional ideation.

(Bedrosian & Beck, 1980, p. 142)

A refinement of cognitive retraining is *reattribution training*, which aims to correct negative attributional styles (A. T. Beck, Rush, Shaw, et al., 1979). In this approach, patients are taught to explain their difficulties to themselves in more constructive ways ("It wasn't my fault—it was the circumstances," "It's not my whole personality that's wrong—it's just my way of reacting to strangers") and to seek out information consistent with these more hopeful attributions (Alloy, Clements, & Kolden, 1985). A similar approach has been used with suicidal patients. Beck and his colleagues see this as a way of correcting negative bias. As the research cited above suggests, it may also be a way of instilling positive bias. In any case, it seems to combat hopelessness.

In some encouraging evaluations, cognitive therapies have been shown to be more effective than drug therapy alone, both at the end of treatment and at a one-year follow-up (Dobson, 1989; Hollon, Shelton, & Davis, 1993), although combined cognitive and drug treatment for depression appears to work best of all (Hollon, DeRubeis, Evans, et al., 1992). Moreover, cognitive therapy has been found to be more effective than drug therapy in preventing relapse of depression (M. D. Evans, Hollon, DeRubeis, et al., 1992; Hollon, Shelton, Loosen, et al., 1991). Some studies have found, however, that very severely depressed patients do not show as much improvement with cognitive therapy as those who are less severely ill (Sotsky, Glass, Shea, et al., 1991; Thase, Simons, Calahane, et al., 1991). Cognitive therapy and its effectiveness relative to drugs will be discussed further in Chapters 19 and 21.

The Sociocultural Perspective

One of the first scholars to study suicide scientifically was the French sociologist Émile Durkheim, writing in the late nineteenth century (1897/1951). Durkheim saw suicide as an act that occured *within a society* and, in some measure, under the control of that society. Today, it is widely recognized that socioeconomic factors affect suicide rates. In 1932, at the height of the Depression, the suicide rate in the United States almost doubled in one year. During the recession of the 1970s, it rose again (Wekstein, 1979).

An even more dramatic indicator of social determinants of hopelessness is the rise in rates of depression in the last century. The first clear evidence of this phenomenon came from a study conducted in the mid-eighties (L. N. Robins, Helzer, Weissman, et al., 1984). The researchers surveyed 9,500 people randomly selected from urban and rural areas to see how many had had an episode of serious depression in their lives. In the twenty- to twenty-five-year-old group, 5 to 6 percent had had at least one episode; in the twenty-five- to forty-four-year-old group, the rate was higher: 8 to 9 percent. That made sense—the longer you have lived, the greater your chance of having experienced depression. But what were the researchers to make of the fact that the seventy-year-olds in the survey showed a rate of only 1 percent? The people who had lived the *longest* had the least experience of depression. These results were essentially duplicated by a study of close relatives of depressed patients (G. L. Klerman, Lavori, Rice, et al., 1985). Even among people at risk for depression, the young adults were six times as likely as the over-sixty-five group to have had a depressive episode, and these findings too have been confirmed (Blazer, Kessler, McGonagle, et al., 1994; Lewinsohn, Rohde, Seeley, et al., 1993). The inescapable conclusion is that the prevalence of depression in the United States has increased steadily, and the age of onset dropped precipitously, in the last hundred years.

Why? Presumably, social change has something to do with it. We know, for example, that rates of depression tend to be lower in highly traditional social groups. Depression does not seem to exist, for instance, in a New Guinea tribe called the Kaluli (Scheiffelin, 1984). Among the Amish living in Pennsylvania, the incidence of major depression is one-fifth to one-tenth the rate of depression among people living in Baltimore, only 100 miles away (Egeland & Hostetter, 1983). The common denominator of the Kaluli and the Amish is that each is a traditional, tight-knit, nonindustrialized community with stable families, a stable social structure, and long-held customs and beliefs. In our society, on the other hand, what we see predominantly is change, as people move away from their families, away from their birthplaces, and up and down the socioeconomic ladder. As Martin Seligman (1988) notes, "The modern individual is not the peasant of yore with a fixed future yawning ahead. He (and now she, effectively doubling the market) is a battleground of decisions and preferences" (p. 91). What this means is that young people today cannot rely on the support systems

WHY DO SEX DIFFERENCES IN DEPRESSION EMERGE IN ADOLESCENCE?

Women are twice as likely as men to develop a serious depression, but curiously, the same is not true of boys and girls. Prior to age fourteen or fifteen, the two sexes are at equal risk. (If anything, boys show a slightly higher risk.) What happens to girls in adolescence to make them so much more prone to depression?

To answer that question, Susan Nolen-Hoeksema and Joan Girgus (1994) have tentatively proposed an interactive model. According to this model, girls already carry a heavier load of risk factors for depression from childhood, but it is not until those factors are activated by the special challenges of adolescence that they crystallize into a greater vulnerability to depression. In defense of this theory, the researchers list a number of characteristics associated with depression: a negative attributional style, a tendency to ruminate on depression, helplessness, avoidance of aggression, avoidance of dominance in groups. Though all these characteristics correlate with depression in both males and females, girls show them to a greater extent than boys long before adolescence.

Then, in adolescence, new risk factors arise, and it is the combination of these with the prior risks that tips the balance. One new risk, for example, is shame about one's body. Research has shown that boys value the physical changes associated with puberty more than girls do (Brooks-Gunn, 1988). Boys like their newly muscled shoulders; girls, on the other hand, tend to be distressed by the gain in body fat, and they often find menstruation embarrassing. Such "body dissatisfaction" is associated with depression (Allgood-Merten, Lewinsohn, & Hops, 1990). So is sexual abuse and rape, another puberty-connected risk factor that is far more serious for girls than for boys. It is estimated that girls aged fourteen to fifteen have a higher risk of being raped than any other age or sex group (Hayman, Stewart, Lewis, et al., 1968).

Finally, it is in adolescence that girls begin to confront most directly the restricted role carved out for them by their society. Many adopt the role quickly. Youngsters of both sexes show less interest in school as they pass from sixth to seventh grade, but girls show a sharper drop in academic ambition (Hirsch & Rapkin, 1987). By the time they enter college, women are sorting themselves into less lucrative, less competitive fields. In 1986 to 1987, American women received only 15 percent of the bachelor's degrees awarded in engineering, whereas they took 76 and 84 percent of the bachelor's degrees in education and nursing, respectively (National Center for Education Statistics, 1989). In many cases, women actively choose these fields—that is the work they truly want. In other cases, however, it is probable that the choice is made because these are "women's fields," with less competition from men.

Apparently, girls who accept the narrowed role prescribed for women are at higher risk for depression (Girgus, Nolen-Hoeksema, Paul, et al., 1991). According to studies done in the 1970s, girls who defied such role expectations were *also* more prone to depression (Gove & Herb, 1974)—a reflection, no doubt, of the widespread disapproval of assertive women. That standard is surely changing, but not overnight. In a recent study, female leaders, especially those who behaved in stereotypically masculine aggressive ways, were still rated more negatively and viewed as less normal than equally assertive male leaders (Eagly, Makhijani, & Klonsky, 1992).

If they encountered the challenges of adolescence with no disadvantage, girls might weather them well enough. But since they are already handicapped by a higher load of risk factors, they are less likely to cope well. And so, according to Nolen-Hoeksema and Girgus (1994), they may develop the patterns that will make them, from then on, twice as vulnerable to depression as men.

that were in place in their grandparents' day: the family, the church, the traditions and customs that once dictated choices. People must rely on themselves, and if the answer is not there, apparently, a sense of helplessness sets in, greatly increasing the risk of depression. (For sociocultural factors that may contribute to women's increased vulnerability to depression, see the box above.)

The Biological Perspective

Recent genetic studies along with biochemical and neurophysiological research, suggest that, whatever the contribution of environmental stress, organic dysfunction also plays an important role in mood disorders.

Genetic Research Family studies have shown that first-degree relatives of people with major mood disorders are much more likely than other people to develop these disorders. For major depression, their risk is one and a half to three times higher, and for bipolar disorder it is fully ten times higher, than that of the general population (Strober, Morrell, Burroughs, et al., 1988). As we have seen, the family risk for bipolar disorder is even greater when the index case had an early onset. Although unipolar patients are found among the relatives of bipolar patients, the reverse seldom occurs (Depue & Monroe, 1978)—further support for the theory that the two syndromes spring from different causes. Finally, suicide also runs in families (Egeland & Sussex, 1985; Roy, 1992).

As we know, it is difficult in family studies to separate environmental from genetic influence. However, twin studies also support the role of genetic inheritance in the mood disorders and suicide. In a review of genetic research on mood disorders in twins, M. G. Allen (1976) found that the concordance rate for bipolar disorder was 72 percent among monozygotic twins as compared with 14 percent among dizygotic twins. The concordance rate for unipolar disorder was 40 percent among monozygotic twins as compared with 11 percent among dizygotic twins. In this study, the difference between the bipolar and unipolar concordance rates among monozygotic twins (72 percent versus 40 percent) suggested that genetic factors were more important in bipolar disorder than in depression. But according to more recent twin studies by Kendler and his colleagues, genes play a crucial role in major depression as well. According to these researchers, 40 to 45 percent of the difference they found in depression rates between MZ and DZ twins was attributable solely to genes. The rest of the difference, their results indicated, was due to individual-specific environment—in other words, life events specific to each member of the twin pair—and not at all to shared environmental factors such as social class, parental child-rearing practices, or early parental loss (Kendler, Neale, Kessler, et al., 1992, 1993).

But the most impressive evidence for heritability comes from adoption studies. In a study of the biological and adoptive parents of bipolar adoptees as compared with the biological and adoptive parents of normal adoptees, Mendlewicz and Rainer (1977) found a 31 percent prevalence of mood disorders in the biological parents of the bipolar adoptees as opposed to 2 percent in the biological parents of normal adoptees—a striking difference. A more recent study (Wender, Kety, Rosenthal, et al., 1986), this time of the biological and adoptive parents, siblings, and half-siblings of adoptees with a broad range of mood disorders, found that the prevalence of unipolar depression was eight times greater—and the suicide rate *fifteen* times greater—in the biological relatives of the mood disorder cases than in the biological relatives of normal adoptees. Taken together, these two studies constitute firm support for a genetic component in both bipolar and unipolar mood disorder.

An important new direction in the genetic study of mood disorders is *linkage analysis* (Faraone, Kremen, & Tsuang, 1990). In linkage analysis, a *genetic marker* (a gene with a known location on the human chromosome set) is used as a clue to the location of a gene controlling a disease. Genes that are in close physical proximity tend to be "linked," or inherited together. Therefore, if bipolar disorder were unusually common in people who are color-blind—a characteristic whose controlling gene has been located—we could reasonably assume that a gene related to bipolar disorder was located near the "color-blind gene," on the same chromosome. In an intriguing study, blood samples were taken from every person in an eighty-one member Amish clan. Then, for each subject, the researchers iso-

Research among the Amish has turned up a linkage between a chromosomal characteristic and bipolar disorder. Such studies can shed light on the heritability of mood disorders.

lated the DNA molecule and searched the molecule for evidence of a characteristic that they knew tended to be inherited with bipolar disorder. They found what appeared to be the characteristic on chromosome 11. Furthermore, when they compared the chromosomes of the nineteen family members diagnosed as suffering from psychiatric disorders (primarily bipolar disorder) with those of the sixty-two members considered psychiatrically well, they consistently found a difference at chromosome 11 (Egeland, Gerhard, Pauls, et al., 1987).

Unfortunately, other studies have failed to show linkage between bipolar disorder and markers on chromosome 11 (Gill, McKeon, & Humphries, 1988; Hodgkinson, Sherrington, Gurling, et al., 1987). Rather than viewing these results as a negation of the Amish study, however, many scientists see them as an indication that bipolar disorder is not a single disease but a group of related diseases, with a variety of genetic (and environmental) causes that await identification. In the 1990s, the National Institute of Health is sponsoring a project to map the entire human chromosome set, most of which remains unexplored. As this project proceeds, we may well see the emergence of genes that are consistently linked to bipolar disorder.

Neurophysiological Research Given that organic factors are implicated in the mood disorders, the next question is: *What* organic factors? According to neurophysiological researchers, the problem may have to do with biological rhythms. As we have seen, sleep disturbance is one of the most common symptoms of depression. Depressives also consistently show abnormalities in their progress through the various stages of sleep (Benca, Obermeyer, Thisted, et al., 1992). One such abnormality is shortened rapid-eye-movement (REM) latency—that is, in depressives the time between the onset of sleep and the onset of REM sleep, the stage of sleep in which dreams occur, is unusually short. And this particular characteristic may indicate a biological vulnerability to depression, for depressives who have shortened REM latency (1) are more likely to have the endogenous symptom pattern and to respond to antidepressant drugs, (2) tend to go on showing shortened REM latency, even after the depressive episode has passed, (3) are likely to have first-degree relatives who also have shortened REM latency, and (4) are more likely to relapse (Buysse & Kupfer, 1993; Giles, Biggs, Rush, et al., 1988).

These sleep disturbances, together with the hormonal abnormalities associated with depression (see below), suggest that in depressives the "biological clock" has somehow gone out of order—a hypothesis that Ehlers and her colleagues have combined with the findings on loss and depression to produce an integrated biopsychosocial theory. According to this theory, our lives are filled with social "zeitgebers" (literally, "time givers"): personal relationships, jobs, and other responsibilities and routines that help to activate and regulate our biological rhythms. Having someone with whom you sleep, for example, helps to enforce your sleep rhythms. When he or she goes to bed, so do you. Consequently, when an important social zeitgeber is removed from a person's life—when a spouse dies, for example—the removal may not only produce an important loss but also disrupt the body's circadian rhythms, or biological cycles, leading to a range of consequences (sleep disturbance, eating disturbance, mood disturbance, hormonal imbalance) that we call depression (Ehlers, Frank, & Kupfer, 1988). In keeping with this disrupted-rhythm theory, some evidence suggests that depriving a depressed patient of sleep, particularly of REM sleep, may have a therapeutic effect (Liebenluft & Wehr, 1992; Wehr, 1990).

Seasonal affective disorder (SAD) One specific form of depression that may be closely related to the body's biological rhythms is **seasonal affective disorder,** or **SAD.** Beginning with Hippocrates, physicians over the centuries have noted that many depressions come on in wintertime. In the late nineteenth century the surgeon and Arctic explorer Frederick Cook made the connection between this phenomenon and light exposure. In the Eskimos, and also in the members of his expeditionary team, Cook observed a depressed mood, together with fatigue and decreased sexual desire, during the long, dark Arctic winter. Recently this seasonal depression has been added to the *DSM.* Many people experience it in a mild degree. In order for the diagnosis of SAD to be made, however, the patient must meet the criteria for major depressive episode; remission as well as onset must be keyed to the seasons; and the pattern must have lasted for at least two years. There is a summer version of SAD, but the winter version is much more common. Women are at far higher risk—60 to 90 percent of patients are female—and so are the young. The average age of onset is twenty-three (Oren & Rosenthal, 1992).

The most promising current theory of SAD is that it is caused by a lag in circadian rhythms, with the result that the person experiences during the day the kind of physical slowdown he or she should be undergoing at night. About three-quarters

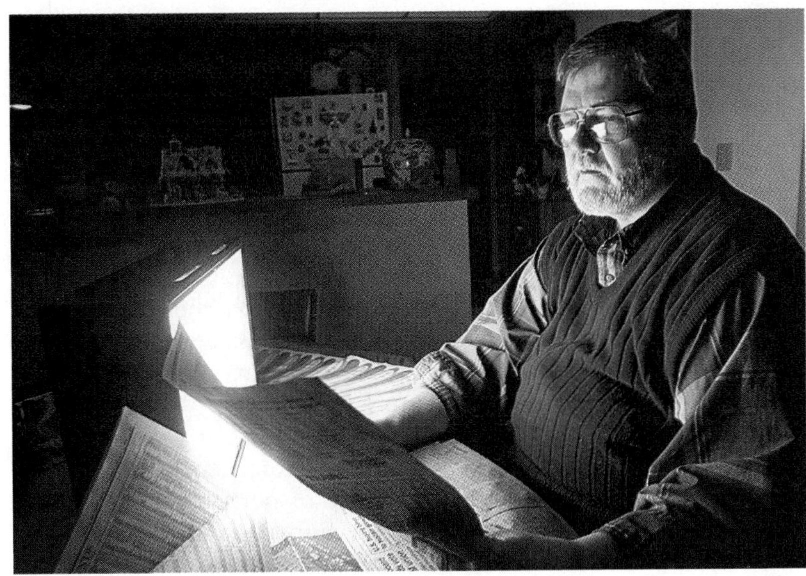

Sometimes the treatment for a troubling disorder is as blessedly simple as a few extra hours of sunshine each day. Many people with the aptly named SAD, or seasonal affective disorder, benefit from sitting in front of an ultraviolet light box for a prescribed amount of time during the short days of winter.

of SAD patients improve when given the same kind of light therapy that is used for circadian rhythm sleep disorders (Chapter 9): exposure to bright artificial light for several hours a day (Oren & Rosenthal, 1992). In some cases, light therapy, if it is applied at the first sign of symptoms, can actually prevent a full-blown episode (Meesters, Jansen, Beersma, et al., 1993). Some studies (e.g., Sack, Lewy, White, et al., 1990) have found—and others have not (Wirz-Justice, Graw, Kräuchi, et al., 1993)—that light therapy works better if it is applied in the morning rather than the evening. If this turns out to be true, then it is good evidence for the circadian rhythm theory, for morning light advances circadian rhythms, whereas extra evening light does not.

Biochemical Research If there is something neurologically wrong with depressives, the problem may be biochemical. At present there are two major biochemical theories.

Hormone imbalance One theory is that depression is due to a malfunction of the hypothalamus, a portion of the brain known to regulate mood. Since the hypothalamus affects not only mood but also many other functions that are typically disrupted in the course of a depression, such as appetite and sexual interest, some researchers (e.g., Holsboer, 1992) suggest that the hypothalamus may be the key to depressive disorders. If so, the abnormality may have to do with the control of hormone production. The hypothalamus regulates the pituitary gland, and both the hypothalamus and the pituitary control the production of hormones by the gonads and the adrenal and thyroid glands. There is substantial evidence that in depressives there is some irregularity in this process. In the first place, depressives often show abnormal hormone levels. Second, people with abnormal hormone activity often show depression as a side effect. Third, CT scans show that many depressives have enlarged adrenal glands (Nemeroff, Krishnan, Reed, et al., 1992). But perhaps the best evidence is that depression can sometimes be effectively treated by altering hormone levels. In certain cases, for example, induced changes in thyroid output have aided in recovery from depression; in others, estrogen, a sex hormone, has proved an effective treatment (Bauer & Whybrow, 1990; Prange, Lipton, Nemeroff, et al., 1977).

Hormone imbalances appear to be particularly characteristic of endogenous depressions. Indeed, such imbalances can be used to help differentiate between endogenous and reactive cases, via a technique called the **dexamethasone suppression test (DST).** Dexamethasone is a drug that in normal people suppresses the secretion of the hormone cortisol for at least twenty-four hours. However, endogenously depressed patients, who seem to secrete abnormally high levels of cortisol (Holsboer, 1992), manage to resist the drug's effect as long as they are in the depressive episode. This is the basis for the DST. Depressed patients are given dexamethasone, and then their blood is tested at regular intervals for cortisol. The nonsuppressors—those whose cortisol levels return to high levels within twenty-four hours despite the drug—are classed as endogenous (Carroll et al., 1981). Since the DST was developed, researchers have discovered other interesting things about nonsuppressors. They tend not to respond to psychotherapy (or placebos); they tend to show nonsuppression in later depressive episodes as well; if they continue to show nonsuppression after treatment, this predicts relapse. All these facts support the notion that DST nonsuppression is a marker of a more endogenous depression (Ribeiro, Tandon, Grunhaus, et al., 1993).

An important finding in the research on hormone imbalances is that such imbalances occur both in major depression and in depressive episodes of bipolar disorder. Genetic research, as we noted, suggests that major depression and bipolar disorder are two distinct syndromes, with different causes. For this reason, it seems unlikely that the hormonal abnormalities common to both syndromes constitute a *primary* cause. (A good possibility is that they are caused by the neurotransmitter imbalances that we will discuss next [Delgado, Price, Heninger, et al., 1992; Holsboer, 1992].) Nor does the stubborn cortisol production of the DST nonsuppressors seem to be a primary cause of depression, for DST nonsuppression is also seen in many other disorders, including schizophrenia, obsessive-compulsive disorder, eating disorders, and alcoholism (Thase, Frank, & Kupfer, 1985). At the same time, the fact that hormones can sometimes relieve depression suggests that in certain, perhaps atypical, cases, hormone imbalance may in fact play a causal role.

Neurotransmitter imbalance The second important area of biochemical research has to do with the neurotransmitters norepinephrine and serotonin. According to one theory, called the **catecholamine hypothesis,*** increased levels of norepinephrine produce mania, while decreased levels produce depression (Schildkraut, 1965). The only way to test this hypothesis directly would be to analyze brain-tissue samples of manics and depressives to determine whether their norepinephrine levels are in fact abnormally high and low, respectively. Since this cannot be done without damage to the brain, we have to rely on indirect evidence. That evidence consists of animal-research findings that drugs and other treatments that relieve depression or produce mania increase the level of norepinephrine in the brain, while drugs that produce depression or alleviate mania reduce the level of norepinephrine in the brain (Schildkraut, 1972).

*This theory is so called because norepinephrine belongs to a group of structurally similar molecules called the *catecholamines.*

This research is spurred by the hope that the action of the drugs will tell us something about the process by which mood disorders develop in the first place. As we saw in Chapter 4, when an impulse travels down a neuron and reaches its end, this neuron, the so-called *presynaptic* neuron, releases the neurotransmitter into the synapse that lies between it and the next, or *postsynaptic,* neuron. The neurotransmitter bonds with the receptors of the postsynaptic neuron, thereby transmitting the impulse. Some of the neurotransmitter is taken back up into the presynaptic neuron (reuptake). (See Figure 4.3, page 86).

The **tricyclics** (Chapter 21), a class of drugs widely used for depression, generally work by blocking the reuptake of norepinephrine by the presynaptic neuron. Superficially, this suggests that depression may be due to too-rapid reuptake, or perhaps to inadequate secretion. However, the picture is probably more complicated than that. First of all, recent research indicates that if depressives have a problem with norepinephrine function, it has to do not with the presynaptic receptors, which appear to operate normally, but with the postsynaptic receptors, which appear to be undersensitive to norepinephrine (Halper, Brown, Sweeney, et al., 1988; Heninger, Charney, & Price, 1988). Second, some newer (and effective) tricyclics do not work by blocking reuptake; they increase norepinephrine levels by more subtle means (McNeal & Cimbolic, 1986). The fact that tricyclics generally take two weeks to start relieving symptoms suggests that their success has to do not with immediate effects, such as blocking reuptake, but with long-term effects—specifically, the readjustment of regulatory mechanisms (Delgado, Price, Heninger, et al., 1992).

Nor, as the research suggests, does the system have to do with norepinephrine alone. Serotonin is probably involved as well. It has been shown, for example, that L-tryptophan, an amino acid that increases serotonin levels, is an effective treatment for *both* mania and depression. Furthermore, when recovered depressives are put through a procedure that depletes their tryptophan levels, their depressive symptoms return within twenty-four hours (Delgado, Charney, Price, et al., 1990). So serotonin and norepinephrine are probably both involved. Prange and his colleagues have put forth a combined norepinephrine-serotonin hypothesis with two premises: (1) that a deficiency of serotonin creates a predisposition to mood disorder; and (2) that given the serotonin deficiency, too high a level of norepinephrine will produce mania, while too low a level of norepinephrine will produce depression (Prange, Wilson, Lynn, et al., 1974).

Serotonin has been implicated not just in depression but specifically in suicide. As we saw in the discussion of adoption studies, the biological relatives of adoptees with mood disorders appear to be fifteen times more likely to commit suicide than the biological relatives of control adoptees. This argues very strongly for an inheritable risk for suicide, even apart from depression. It has been proposed that a decreased flow of serotonin from the brainstem to the frontal cortex may be associated with suicide, independent of depression—indeed, with impulsive, aggressive behavior as well. In support of this hypothesis, tests of the cerebrospinal fluid of suicide attempters, particularly those who have chosen violent methods, have found evidence of abnormally low serotonin activity (Mann, McBride, Brown, et al., 1992; Roy, DeJong, & Linnoila, 1989). In addition, postmortem analyses of suicides have found subnormal amounts of serotonin and also impaired serotonin receptors in the brainstem and frontal cortex (e.g., Nordström & Asberg, 1992). Should this hypothesis gain further support, it is possible that in the future we will have special drug therapies for people who attempt suicide.

We can summarize the biochemical findings as follows. At this point it seems indisputable that norepinephrine, serotonin, and hormone abnormalities are all involved in the mood disorders, and the most compelling current theories differ only in the emphasis they give to each of these three factors. No doubt they are all involved. Indeed, what is most likely is that mood disorders are due to a complex interaction of genetic, neurophysiological, biochemical, developmental, cognitive, and situational variables (Kendler, Kessler, Neale, et al., 1993; Whybrow, Akiskal, & McKinney, 1984).

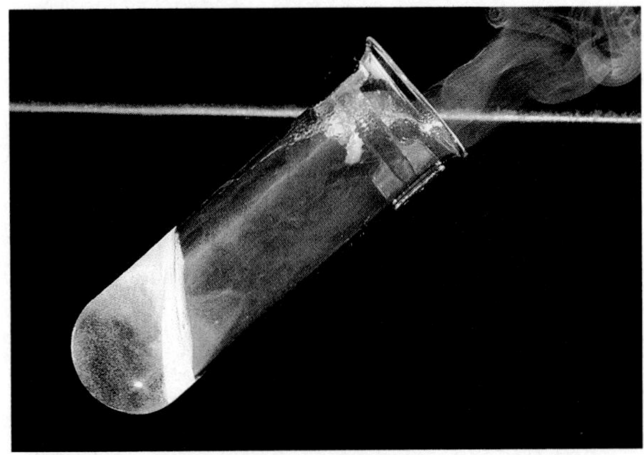

Lithium carbonate is the drug treatment of choice for bipolar disorder.

Whatever the biological perspective ultimately contributes to uncovering the cause of mood disorders, it has already contributed heavily to their treatment. The most common therapy for patients with mood disorders, whether or not they are receiving other kinds of therapy, is drugs. For bipolar disorder, lithium carbonate is generally prescribed; for major depression, either the tricyclic antidepressants or Prozac, which blocks serotonin reuptake. Another physical treatment, though less widely used, is electroconvulsive therapy. These treatments will be described more fully in Chapter 21.

KEY TERMS

agitated depression (233)
anhedonia (233)
bipolar disorder (236)
catecholamine hypothesis (258)
comorbidity (241)
continuity hypothesis (239)
cyclothymic disorder (237)
depression (232)
dexamethasone suppression test (DST) (257)
dysthymic disorder (237)
endogenous (240)
helplessness-hopelessness syndrome (233)
hypomanic episode (234)
learned helplessness (250)
major depressive disorder (235)
major depressive episode (232)
mania (232)
manic episode (234)
mixed episode (235)
mood disorders (232)
premorbid adjustment (236)
reactive (240)
retarded depression (233)
seasonal affective disorder (SAD) (256)
social-skills training (250)
tricyclics (258)

SUMMARY

- People who suffer from the major mood disorders—disorders of affect, or emotions—experience exaggerations of the same kinds of highs and lows all human beings experience. Mood disorders are episodic: the depressive or manic episode often begins suddenly, runs its course, and may or may not recur. Thinking, feeling, motivation, and physiological functioning are all affected.
- A major depressive episode is characterized by depressed mood (the helplessness-hopelessness syndrome), loss of pleasure in usual activities, disturbance of appetite and sleep, psychomotor retardation or agitation, loss of energy, feelings of worthlessness and guilt, difficulty remembering or thinking clearly, and recurrent thoughts of death or suicide.
- A major manic episode is characterized by an elated, expansive, or irritable mood combined with inflated self-esteem, sleeplessness, talkativeness, flight of ideas, distractibility, hyperactivity, and recklessness.
- Major depressive disorder is one of the most common mental health problems in the United States, affects women more often than men, and seems to be increasing in younger generations. People with bipolar disorder experience mixed or alternating manic and depressive episodes. Many others suffer from dysthymic disorder (milder but chronic depression) or cyclothymic disorder (recurrent depressive and hypomanic episodes). Demographic, family, and individual case patterns suggest that different mood disorders may have different etiologies.
- Mood disorders differ along several dimensions, including psychotic versus neurotic; endogenous (from within) versus reactive (a response to loss); and early versus late onset. Evidence of comorbidity, especially mixed anxiety-depression, is increasing.
- People suffering from depression are at high risk for suicide. Single people are more likely to kill themselves than married people, and although more women than men attempt suicide, more men succeed in killing themselves. Contrary to popular beliefs, people who threaten to commit suicide often attempt to do so; people who attempt suicide, but fail, often try again; and encouraging people to talk about suicidal thoughts often helps them overcome these wishes. Among factors that predict suicide, hopelessness—the belief that there is no other escape from psychological pain—stands out. Sadly, suicide hot lines and school-based prevention programs often do not appeal to the people who need them most.
- Most theories of mood disorders focus on depression (not mania) and suicide. Psychodynamic theorists, beginning with Freud, trace depression to an early trauma that has been reactivated by a recent loss, bringing back infantile feelings of powerlessness. Some see depressives as "love addicts" who attempt to compensate for their low self-esteem by seeking reassurance from others. But dependency on a loved one can turn to anger and guilt. According to this view, suicidal persons are attempting to destroy another person whom they have incorporated into their own psyches. Empirical studies lend some support to the association of depression with dependency and with early loss of a parent or poor parenting. Psychodynamic treatment of depression aims not only to unearth the early trauma but also to examine how the patient may be using depression to get what he or she wants from others.
- The humanistic-existential perspective traces depression and suicide to an inauthentic life, to failure to make choices and take responsibility for oneself. Suicide is seen as the ultimate "inauthentic" choice. Therapists in this school encourage patients to "listen" to their pain and thus discover their true goals.
- There are two prominent behaviorist perspectives on depression and suicide. According to one view, the extinction hypothesis, depression results from a loss of reinforcement, often exacerbated by a lack of skill in seeking interpersonal rewards. According to a second view, depressives elicit negative responses by demanding too much reinforcement in inappropriate ways. However, which comes first, depression or aversive behavior, is debatable. Behaviorist therapies focus on increasing self-reinforcement and on teaching social and other skills.
- The cognitive perspective also has two main theories of depression and suicide. One focuses on learned helplessness (the belief that one cannot control or avoid aversive events) combined with hopelessness (the feeling that negative events will continue and even increase). Hopelessness, in particular, is a predictor of suicide. A second cognitive theory traces depression and suicide to negative schemas or images of the self, the world, and the future. But again, whether these feelings are a cause or consequence of depression is debatable. Cognitive therapists seek to correct negative thoughts and attributions.
- The sociocultural perspective attempts to explain historical changes and cross-cultural differences in the rates of depression and suicide. One view is that rapid social change, one of the defining characteristics of modern life, deprives people of necessary social supports.
- The biological perspective holds that, whatever the contribution of early or current emotional and/or social stress, mood disorders are at least partly organic. Some neuroscientists study families, twins, and adopted children and their biological and adoptive parents to discover the degree to which mood dis-

orders are inherited. There is strong evidence that vulnerability to mood disorders and suicide runs in families. Some neuroscientists look at seasonal fluctuations in mood. And some focus on biochemistry, especially hormonal imbalances and the neurotransmitters norepinephrine and serotonin. Today treatment of major depression and bipolar disorder nearly always combines medication (either tricyclic antidepressants or serotonin reuptake blockers such as Prozac for depression; lithium carbonate for bipolar disorder) with psychotherapy.

American Challenge
HIGH SPIRIT

11

PERSONALITY DISORDERS

r. X is a 43-year-old bachelor who lives alone and seeks psychiatric help because he fears the second half of his life will be no different from the first—boring and unrewarding. . . .

Mr. X's view of his life makes sense. It is indeed very dull, uneventful, and unchanging. Timid and easily daunted, he avoids new experiences in order to avoid feeling inadequate, embarrassed, or even slightly uncomfortable. He would like to date. Through his work with the Library Association he has contact with many single women (perhaps with similar problems) who would probably be most delighted by an invitation, but he lacks the courage to ask someone out. He would be terrified if the woman said yes, and humiliated if she said no. . . .

Mr. X's professional life is also in a rut. He would advance to a more stimulating and responsible position at a university library if he were more productive, but for 10 years he has worked and reworked his master's thesis for eventual publication in book form. Each time he has written a "final draft" the fears about exposing his work prevent his moving the project forward, and he decides to make one more revision. Even if the thesis were published, he realizes that he might be once again passed over for a promotion because his supervisors have openly stated that he lacks the air of authority to supervise others. Mr. X does not deny their assessment. . . .

Mr. X's life away from the library is as regimented as his life among the stacks. Because any new experience feels risky, he is a creature of habit. He has the same breakfast in the same coffee shop at the same time every morning (including days off) and is somewhat annoyed if his customary booth is occupied. . . .

[According to Mr. X's family, he was] a timid, easily startled baby from birth and, unlike his siblings, was upset by any minor changes in the nursery or dietary routine. He had difficulty adjusting to babysitters, playgroups, and kindergarten. Whereas many of the first graders were more excited than frightened about entering school, Mr. X cried piteously each morning his mother left him with the teacher. . . .

Later in grade school, Mr. X was regarded as an outsider and was teased by the other boys for being a "scaredycat." To relieve the loneliness, Mr. X would usually be able to find a close friend—sometimes a boy, sometimes a girl—who was also outside the "in groups" and who also felt frightened. Along with this capacity to always find at least one close friend, Mr. X's other saving grace has been his ability to perform research by doggedly pursuing every small reference until a given subject has been thoroughly mastered. Because of this ability, he was an exceptionally fine graduate student and was encouraged to go on for a doctorate degree. He declined on the grounds that doctoral candidates were too competitive (i.e., intimidating) and that he would be comfortable living at a level that was more relaxed. He now realizes that in seeking comfort he has found boredom and loneliness. (S. Perry, Frances, & Clarkin, 1990, pp. 324–326)

Many of the psychological disorders that we have discussed so far arise like physical disorders in the sense that their sufferers, having once been "well," find themselves "ill," and in a specific way. They can no longer look at a dog without fear; they can no longer find reason to be happy. By contrast, the personality disorders are conditions that have generally been with the person for many years and have to do not so much with a specific problem, such as dog phobia or depression, as with the entire personality. To quote the *DSM-IV* definition, a **personality disorder** is "an enduring pattern of inner experience and behavior that deviates markedly from the expectations of the individual's culture, is pervasive and inflexible, has an onset in adolescence or early adulthood, is stable over time, and leads to distress or impairment" (American Psychiatric Association, 1994, p. 629). This disorder, then, has to do with stable traits. To quote *DSM-IV* again, "*Personality traits* are enduring patterns of perceiving, relating to, and thinking about the environment and oneself that are exhibited in a wide range of social and personal contexts. Only when personality traits are inflexible and maladaptive and cause significant functional impairment or subjective distress do they constitute Personality Disorders" (American Psychiatric Association, 1994, p. 630). Because personality disorders are so generalized and of such long standing, people with these disorders may not see their condition as a problem that can be treated; it is just who they *are*. Typically, they are very unhappy, though in some cases they may give less pain to themselves than to those who have to deal with them—their families, coworkers, and so forth.

There is considerable debate over the value of the personality disorders as diagnostic categories. In the first place, most of these categories are not particularly reliable. Though diagnosticians generally agree that a given case is one of personality disorder (as opposed to obsessive-compulsive disorder or schizophrenia, e.g.), they frequently disagree on *which* personality disorder they are confronting. What one calls "schizoid personality disorder" another may call "avoidant personality disorder" or something else. Furthermore, in the past the diagnostic criteria for the personality disorders had narrow boundaries. While not specific enough to ensure high reliability, the criteria were too specific to cover many of the people thought to have personality disorders, and so these people were shunted into relatively meaningless residual categories such as "mixed" or "atypical" personality disorder. In the 1987 revision of the *DSM*, the diagnostic categories were broadened, with the result that their coverage increased—together with their overlap (Morey, 1988). In turn, the next revision, the recent *DSM-IV*, has made the diagnostic criteria more specific (Gunderson, 1992). It is hoped that this will control the overlap.

Such diagnostic problems have led some experts to propose that people with personality disorders be classed not by diagnostic categories but by dimensional ratings, somewhat as people are scored on the MMPI (Chapter 6). In other words, people would be rated on such things as dominance *versus* submission or novelty seeking *versus* novelty avoiding. Mr. X, for example, would be identified not as being an "avoidant personality" (which would be his current diagnosis) but simply as having a high score on introversion and neuroticism, plus other ratings that might be relevant to his problem (P. T. Costa & Widiger, 1994). While such a system would no doubt increase reliability, it would also create difficulties in communication among psychological professionals and probably in treatment decisions as well.

Another problem has to do with the assumption, clearly stated in the *DSM-IV* definition, that human beings have stable personality traits. This assumption has been vigorously attacked by behaviorists, who have argued that human behavior is influenced as much by the situation the person is in at the moment as by his or her presumed traits (Mischel & Peake, 1982). Other experts (Epstein, 1983; Kenrick & Funder, 1988), while acknowledging situational influence, have shown that people do tend to act in certain ways with a relatively high frequency over time. (A student who cheats on one test is more likely than others to cheat on the next test, though the situation will also influence that decision.) Indeed, some people act in certain ways with an extraordinarily high frequency—in other words, they are rigid—and these are precisely the people who are said to have personality disorders. Nevertheless, the problem of situation specificity, like that of diagnostic overlap, was addressed in *DSM-IV*, and one diagnostic category, "passive-aggressive disorder," was removed because of evidence that this pattern was often a situational reaction rather than a stable personality disposition (Gunderson, 1992).

DSM-IV now lists ten personality disorders. We will discuss all of them but will give the most space to antisocial personality disorder, which has the most harmful consequences.

PERSONALITY DISORDERS: INDIVIDUAL SYNDROMES

Paranoid Personality Disorder

The defining trait of **paranoid personality disorder** is suspiciousness. We all feel suspicious in certain situations and with certain people, often for good reasons. However, paranoid personalities feel suspicious in almost all situations and with almost all people, usually for very poor reasons. And when they are confronted with evidence that their mistrust is unfounded, they will typically begin to mistrust the person who brought them the evidence: "So he's against me too!"

Such an attitude of course reflects an impairment in cognitive functioning. Paranoid personalities are constantly scanning the environment for evidence to support their suspicions—and constantly finding such evidence. If two people are talking together near the coffee machine, or if the mail is late, or if the neighbors are blaring music at midnight, this is taken as evidence of personal hostility.

Emotional adjustment is equally hampered. Friendship and love are based on trust—the very thing that paranoid personalities lack. Hence they typically have few friends. They may have an "ally," usually a person in a subordinate position, but eventually they begin to suspect the ally too and switch to another ally. This process repeats itself time after time. Despite these interpersonal problems, paranoid personalities rarely turn up in the offices of psychologists and psychiatrists, for they see their difficulties as coming from without rather than within. For this reason it is difficult to estimate the prevalence of this disorder.

Despite similarities in name and in the defining trait of suspiciousness, paranoid personality disorder should not be confused with paranoia or paranoid schizophrenia, which are psychoses (see Chapter 14)—that is, severely disabling disorders, involving loss of reality contact. Paranoid personality disorder is not as disabling. It should be added, however, that researchers have found paranoid personality disorder to be significantly more common among the biological relatives of schizophrenics than in the population at large (Nigg & Goldsmith, 1994). Therefore, different as the two disorders are, there may be some genetic relationship between them.

Schizotypal Personality Disorder

The person with **schizotypal personality disorder** will seem odd in his or her speech, behavior, thinking, and/or perception, but not odd enough for a diagnosis of schizophrenia. For example, speech may ramble, but never to the point of actual incoherence, as is often the case with schizophrenics. Or the person may report recurrent illusions such as feeling as if his dead mother were in the room—a situation nevertheless different from that of the schizophrenic, who is more likely to report that his dead mother *was* in the room. Schizotypal personalities may also show magical thinking, claiming that they can predict the future, read the thoughts of others, and so on. Partly, no doubt, because of the disbelief inspired by such claims, they tend to be suspicious, aloof, and withdrawn.

Schizotypal personality disorder was added to the *DSM* in 1980 as part of an effort to improve the reliability of the diagnosis of schizophrenia and to study its relation (if any) to other conditions. In schizophrenia, diagnostic lines are often hard to draw. In the "classic" case, the person will appear decidedly odd in many respects: speech, thought, perception, emotion, social behavior, motor behavior, and so on. Yet many cases are not classic ones. For example, the person will seem only marginally odd in a number of respects or very odd but in only one respect, social withdrawal. These two patterns, classified in the past as subtypes of schizophrenia, are now labeled as personality disorders: schizotypal personality disorder and schizoid personality disorder, respectively.

A further distinction between these two disorders is susceptibility to schizophrenia. There is evidence that schizotypal personality disorder is more common in the families of diagnosed schizophrenics than in the population at large (Nigg & Goldsmith, 1994). Furthermore, schizotypal personalities tend to respond to the same medications as schizophrenics (Schulz, Schulz, & Wilson, 1988), a tendency suggesting a biological relationship between the two disorders. Thus, schizotypal personalities may be at risk, genetically or otherwise, for schizophrenia, but this is apparently not as likely with schizoid personalities (Nigg & Goldsmith, 1994).

Schizoid Personality Disorder

As we have seen, schizotypal personality disorder involves a range of eccentricities, while **schizoid personality disorder** is defined by one fundamental eccentricity, a preference for being alone. According to current thinking, schizoids are deficient in the capacity to experience social warmth or any deep feelings and are unable to form attachments. Schizoid personalities rarely marry, have few (if any) friends, and seem indifferent to praise or criticism from others. Because of their self-absorption, they may appear absentminded—"out of it," so to speak. However, they do not show the unusual thoughts, behaviors, or speech patterns that one sees in the schizotypal personality. And unlike schizotypal personalities, they may be quite successful in their work if it requires little social contact.

Avoidant Personality Disorder

Like schizoid personality disorder, **avoidant personality disorder** is marked by social withdrawal. However, the avoidant personality withdraws not out of inability to experience interpersonal warmth or closeness but out of fear of rejection. This category, based primarily on research by Millon (1981), has as its essential feature a hypersensitivity to any possibility of rejection, humiliation, or shame. For most of us, making friends with a new person is somewhat difficult; for avoidant personalities, it is supremely difficult, because, though they want to be loved and accepted, they expect not to be. Therefore they tend to avoid relationships unless they are reassured again and again of the other's uncritical affection. Even then, they remain watchful for any hint of disapproval. Not surprisingly, avoidant personalities generally have low self-esteem. They typically feel depressed and angry at themselves for their social failure. The case of Mr. X at the opening of the chapter illustrates avoidant personality disorder.

Dependent Personality Disorder

The defining characteristic of **dependent personality disorder,** as the name indicates, is dependence on others. Fearful or incapable of making their own decisions, dependent personalities turn over to one or two others—for example, a spouse or a parent—the responsibility for deciding what work they will do, where they will go on vacation, how they will handle the children, what people they will associate with, even what they will wear. Underlying this self-effacement is a fear of abandonment. For most of us, waiting for a friend who is late is an inconvenience or annoyance. For the dependent personality, it is an emotional catastrophe: the long-dreaded sign that the friend no longer cares. Because of the fear of abandonment,

A person with avoidant personality disorder is more than just shy; he or she is hypersensitive to any form of disapproval or rejection, needing constant reassurance about being liked.

the dependent personality, often a woman, will tolerate her husband's infidelities, drunkenness, even physical abusiveness for fear that, should she protest, he will leave her. This passivity breeds a vicious cycle. The more the dependent personality lets others control and abuse her, the more helpless she feels, and these feelings in turn further discourage her from taking any self-respecting action.

The following history—in this case, a man—illustrates the basic features of dependent personality:

> Matthew is a 34-year-old single man who lives with his mother and works as an accountant. He seeks treatment because he is very unhappy after having just broken up with his girl friend. His mother had disapproved of his marriage plans, ostensibly because the woman was of a different religion. Matthew felt trapped and forced to choose between his mother and his girl friend, and since "blood is thicker than water," he had decided not to go against his mother's wishes. Nonetheless, he is angry at himself and at her and believes that she will never let him marry. . . .
>
> Matthew works at a job several grades below what his education and talent would permit. On several occasions he has turned down promotions. . . . He has two very close friends, whom he has had since early childhood. He has lunch with one of them every single workday and feels lost if his friend is sick and misses a day.
>
> Matthew is the youngest of four children and the only boy. He was "babied and spoiled" by his mother and elder sisters. He had considerable separation anxiety as a child—difficulty falling asleep unless his mother stayed in the room, mild school refusal, and unbearable homesickness when he occasionally tried "sleep-overs." . . . He has lived at home his whole life except for one year of college, from which he returned because of homesickness. (Spitzer, Gibbon, Skodol, et al., 1989, pp. 123–124)

Borderline Personality Disorder

First proposed by psychodynamic theorists (e.g., O. F. Kernberg, 1975)—and still questioned by some other theorists (e.g., Siever & Davis, 1991)—the category of **borderline personality disorder** has received a great deal of attention in recent years (Clarkin, Marziali, & Monroe-Blum, 1991; Gunderson & Phillips, 1991). Morey (1991) describes the disorder as a syndrome involving four core elements:

1. *Difficulties in establishing a secure self-identity.* Borderline personalities have an unstable sense of self and are therefore heavily dependent on their relationships with others in order to achieve a sense of identity, of self-hood. Hence they have a hard time being alone and tend to be devastated when a close relationship comes to an end. The character played by Glenn Close in the movie *Fatal Attraction* resembles borderline personality and in particular exemplifies this catastrophic response to the end of a relationship.
2. *Distrust.* As dependent as they are on other people, borderline personalities are also suspicious of those people and expect to be abandoned or victimized by them. Given their difficult behavior, they may well be (Kroll, 1988). This combination of dependence and mistrust creates a profound ambivalence in the borderline personality's feel-

ings for others. A friend who is idolized one moment may be attacked the next.

3 *Impulsive and self-destructive behavior.* Borderline personalities are typically impulsive and unpredictable in their actions. When they cut loose, they will often engage in self-destructive behavior such as drug abuse, reckless driving, fighting, and promiscuity. They are also given to making manipulative suicide threats.

4 *Difficulty in controlling anger and other emotions.* This is a very prominent feature of borderline personalities. They exist in a state of perpetual emotional crisis, the primary emotions being grief and anger. This has led some researchers to suggest that borderline personality, like mood disorders, may be due to abnormalities in the limbic system, the part of the brain that regulates emotions (Kling, Kellner, Post, et al., 1987). Many theorists have raised the question of whether borderline personality is not a form of depression. A number of patients meet the diagnostic criteria for both disorders, and there is some evidence, though not conclusive, that mood disorders may be more prevalent in the families of borderline personalities (Gunderson & Elliott, 1985). Like victims of dissociative identity disorder, borderline patients tend to report childhood histories of physical and sexual abuse (J. L. Herman, Perry, & van der Kolk, 1989). In view of the borderline patient's general conviction of victimization, however, these reports may be exaggerated.

Histrionic Personality Disorder

The essential feature of **histrionic personality disorder** is self-dramatization—the exaggerated display of emotion. Such emotional displays are often clearly manipulative, aimed at attracting attention and sympathy. Histrionic personalities will "faint" at the sight of blood, will dominate an entire dinner party with the tale of their recent faith healing, will be so "overcome" with emotion during a sad movie that they have to be taken home immediately (thus spoiling their companions' evening), will threaten suicide if a lover's interest cools, and so forth. To themselves, they seem sensitive; to others, after the first impression has worn off, they usually seem shallow and insincere.

Their interpersonal relationships, then, are usually fragile. Initially, upon meeting a new person, they will seem warm and affectionate. Once the friendship is established, however, they become oppressively demanding, needing their friends to come right over if they are having an emotional crisis, wondering piteously why no one called them after a traumatic visit to the dentist, and generally taking without giving. They are typically flirtatious and sexually provocative, but their characteristic self-absorption prevents them from establishing any lasting sexual bond.

The histrionic personality resembles a hostile caricature of femininity—vain, shallow, self-dramatizing, immature, overdependent, and selfish. The disorder is diagnosed more often in women than in men. (See the box on pages 270-271 for a discussion of the possibility of bias against women in *DSM* criteria for personality disorders.)

Narcissistic Personality Disorder

The personality syndrome most commonly diagnosed in a number of psychoanalytic centers in recent years has been the so-called narcissistic personality (Millon, 1981). Largely because of the interest of the psychoanalytic community (Lion, 1981), this category was added to the *DSM* in 1980. The essential feature of **narcissistic personality disorder** is a grandiose sense of self-importance, often combined with periodic feelings of inferiority (O. F. Kernberg, 1975; Kohut, 1966). Narcissistic personalities will brag of their talents and achievements, predict for themselves great successes—a Pulitzer prize, a meteoric rise through the company ranks—and expect from others the sort of attention and adulation due to one so gifted. Yet this apparent self-love is often accompanied by a very fragile self-esteem, causing the person to "check" constantly on how he or she is regarded by others and to react to criticism with rage or despair. (Alternatively, in keeping with their sense of self-importance, narcissistic personalities may respond to personal defeats with cool nonchalance.)

Narcissistic personalities are poorly equipped for friendship or love. They characteristically demand a great deal from others—affection, sympathy, favors. Yet they give little in return, and tend to show a striking lack of empathy. If a friend calls to say that he has had an automobile accident and cannot go to the party that night, the narcissistic personality is likely to be more concerned over the missed party than over the friend's well-being. Narcissistic personalities are also given to exploitation, choosing friends on the basis of what they can get from them. Their feelings about such friends tend to alternate between opposite poles of idealization and contempt, often depending on how flattering the friend has been lately. Not surprisingly, in view of these facts, narcissistic personalities tend to have long histories of erratic interpersonal relationships, and it is usually failures in this area that bring them into therapy.

In the past decade or two, a number of articles and books have been written about narcissistic personality disorder from two opposite perspectives: the psychoanalytic and social learning points of view. Psychoanalytic theory suggests that such personalities are compensating for inadequate affection and approval from their parents in early childhood (O. F. Kernberg, 1975; Kohut, 1972). The social learning perspective (Millon, 1969, 1981) sees this disorder as created by parents who have inflated views of their children's talents and therefore unrealistic expectations.

Obsessive-Compulsive Personality Disorder

The defining characteristic of **obsessive-compulsive personality disorder** is excessive preoccupation with trivial details, at the cost of both spontaneity and effectiveness. Obsessive-compulsive personalities are so taken up with the mechanics of efficiency—organizing, following rules, making lists and schedules—that they cease to be efficient, for they never get anything important done. In addition, they are generally stiff and formal in their dealings with others and find it hard to take genuine pleasure in anything. For example, they may spend weeks or months planning a family vacation, deciding what the family will see and where they will eat and sleep each day and night, and then derive no enjoyment whatsoever from the vacation itself. Typically, they will spoil it for the others as well by refusing to deviate from the itinerary, worrying that the restaurant will give away their table, and so forth.

This personality disorder should not be confused with obsessive-compulsive disorder (Chapter 7). Though a superficial similarity—the shared emphasis on rituals and propriety—has led to their bearing similar names, the two syndromes are quite different. In the personality disorder, compulsiveness is not confined to a single sequence of bizarre behaviors, such as constant hand washing, but is milder and more pervasive, affecting many aspects of life. Furthermore, while obsessive-compulsive disorder is not common, obsessive-compulsive personality disorder is fairly common (more so in men than in women). Finally, as we saw in Chapter 7, people suffering from obsessive-compulsive disorder generally do not also show obsessive-compulsive personality disorder.

Though some jobs would seem to require a degree of "compulsiveness," people with obsessive-compulsive personality disorder rarely do well in their occupations because they are too preoccupied with trivia to get anything accomplished. Furthermore, because of their concern over doing things "just right," they generally have tremendous difficulty making decisions and meeting deadlines.

"Let me make a little note of that. I never seem to get anything done around here unless I make little notes."

Obsessive-compulsive personality disorder makes it impossible for the person to accomplish any meaningful work.

ANTISOCIAL PERSONALITY DISORDER

People suffering from the personality disorders that we have studied so far may inconvenience their families and friends considerably, but usually they harm themselves more than they harm others. The defining trait of **antisocial personality disorder,** by contrast, is a predatory attitude toward other people—a chronic indifference to and violation of the rights of one's fellow human beings.

Antisocial personality disorder is by no means an unusual phenomenon. It affects about 1 percent of females and 3 to 5 percent of males in their teens and twenties among the general population, according to *DSM-IV* and epidemiological research (Kessler, McGonagle, Zhao, et al., 1994; Robins, Tipp, & Przybeck, 1991). Furthermore, since antisocial behavior often involves criminal behavior, this disorder raises the whole issue of the relationship between abnormal psychology and crime. For these reasons—and because it is the most reliably diagnosed of the personality syndromes—we will discuss this disorder in considerable detail.

POLITICS AND PERSONALITY DISORDERS

Certain personality disorders—histrionic, dependent, and borderline—are diagnosed more frequently in women, while others, such as obsessive-compulsive and antisocial, are diagnosed more frequently in men. Such sex imbalances are seen in many psychological disorders: schizophrenia (more common in men), major depressive disorder (more common in women), dissociative identity disorder (far more common in women), alcohol abuse (far more common in men). In the case of the personality disorders, however, some observers feel that the imbalance lies less in psychological than in political facts.

M. Kaplan (1983), for example, has pointed out that the *DSM* criteria for histrionic personality disorder—emotionalism, attention seeking, seductiveness, suggestibility—resemble an age-old stereotype of women. (*The Penguin Dictionary of Proverbs,* 1983, in its section on women, lists 104 old sayings on the subject of the female character, including its emotionalism ["Early rain and a woman's tears are soon over"]; shallowness ["Women have long hair, and short brains"]; deceitfulness ["Women naturally deceive, weep and spin"]; and capriciousness ["Because is a woman's reason"]. The dictionary offers no section on the qualities of the male sex.) In other words, the society defines women as histrionic and then, when they act histrionic, diagnoses them as disturbed. In Kaplan's view, the same situation pertains to dependent personality disorder: the society places women in a position of dependency and then labels them disturbed when they show dependency.

When *DSM-III* was being revised in the eighties and nineties, such political questions were hotly debated, and not just apropos of the histrionic and dependent personality disorders. It was proposed, for example, that the manual add a new category: self-defeating personality disorder, characterized by chronic pessimism and self-destructive behavior. Actually, this was just a variant of the "masochistic personality disorder" that had been mentioned in passing, and without a formal listing, in *DSM-III.* When it was suggested that masochistic personality disorder be formally listed in *DSM-IV,* many people objected: first, because such a category might give renewed credence to the old psychoanalytic idea that many people, particularly women, wish to be abused (Caplan, 1984), and second, because the diagnosis could be used to blame victims of abuse—again, particularly women—for their victimization (Walker, 1984).

Partly in answer to these concerns, the name of the proposed syndrome was changed from "masochistic" to "self-defeating" personality disorder, but that did not settle the dispute. There were protest demonstrations, threats of legal action (Coalition Against Misdiagnosis, 1986; Rosewater, 1986), and angry articles in the press. Finally, self-defeating personality disorder was dropped from consideration for *DSM-IV.*

At the same time that this controversy was going on, there was a parallel dispute over another proposed syndrome, "sadistic personality disorder." Basically, this proposal was a response to the debate over self-defeating personality disorder. If some people were abused because they had personality traits that invited abuse, then presumably some people *inflicted* abuse because they had personality traits tending in that direction—hence, sadistic personality disorder. However, this category too was opposed on the grounds of potential misuse against women. If "self-defeating personality disorder" could be invoked to excuse abusers on the grounds that they were simply responding to the masochistic needs of their victims, "sadistic personality disorder" could be used to excuse abusers on the grounds that they couldn't help it—they had a personality disorder that made them assault people. Eventually, this category too was dropped.

Did the framers of *DSM-IV* simply cave in to political pressure? According to some research, a significant proportion of abused women do show a long-standing pattern, if not of placing themselves in harm's way, then at least of failing to get out of the way. In a study of 119 women in a battered women's shelter, Snyder and Fruchtman (1981)

Antisocial Behavior and Abnormal Psychology

The question of the relationship between psychological disturbance and **antisocial behavior,** behavior that violates the rights of others, forms an interesting chapter in the history of psychology.*

*It is important to remember that antisocial behavior is not identical with antisocial personality disorder. Just as anxiety is the defining characteristic of anxiety disorder but is not limited to people with this disorder, so antisocial behavior is the defining characteristic of antisocial personality disorder but is not limited to antisocial personalities. Psychologically normal people also lie, cheat, and steal.

Until about 200 years ago, criminals were generally treated as criminals, with little thought as to their psychological well-being. Then in the eighteenth and nineteenth centuries, clinicians such as Philippe Pinel and Benjamin Rush began to speculate that certain cases of immoral and criminal behavior might be subtle forms of mental illness. In 1835 an English psychiatrist, J. C. Prichard, identified a condition that he called "moral insanity," which he described as "a form of mental derangement in which the intellectual functions appear to have sustained little or no injury, while the . . . moral or active principles of the mind are strangely identified four patterns of abuse, at least one of which seemed to suggest a personality disorder. All the women in this group had suffered substantial neglect and abuse as children. As adults, almost half of them had been abused by people other than their current abuser, and 27 percent of them had been abused by their husbands *before* marrying them. Finally, 60 percent of this group rejected the shelter's offers of intervention and returned home to their assailants. As was detailed in a recent article on controversies over the *DSM-IV* personality disorders (Widiger, in press), many investigators have concluded that a history of victimization in childhood can produce chronic, pervasive attitudes of self-blame, together with an expectation of abuse and behaviors that make abuse more likely—in other words, an overall cognitive-emotional-behavioral pattern that we would call a personality disorder. Likewise, there is evidence that some abusers (again, people likely to have been abused in childhood) show a long-standing, pervasive pattern of sadistic thought and behavior (Gay, in press; Spitzer, Fiester, Gay, et al., 1991). Such evidence might have been enough to obtain listings for these categories if sensitive political issues had not been involved (Walker, 1989).

But domestic violence is now an exceedingly sensitive political issue, and the publicity surrounding the 1995 trial of football star O. J. Simpson, accused of killing his former wife, has made it even more pressing. When a behavior is designated as the product of psychological disturbance, people tend to regard it as a problem merely in the person rather than in the society—a point that sociocultural theorists have repeatedly stressed. Furthermore, the person showing the behavior tends to be *excused* from both moral and criminal responsibility. (See Chapter 22, "Legal Issues in Abnormal Psychology.") For both these reasons, many observers feel that to describe proneness toward violence (seen more frequently in men) and proneness toward submitting to violence (seen more frequently in women) as psychological syndromes will simply perpetuate those problems.

Whatever the "right" answer, this dispute illustrates a point we have made before: Diagnosis, like any other social institution, is influenced by politics—by shifting power relations among social groups. It is no accident that it was in the eighties, in the wake of the gay rights movement, that homosexuality was deleted from the *DSM*'s list of sexual deviations. Nor is it surprising that feminist issues are now at the forefront of diagnostic controversy. In such debates, however, it is not always easy to determine where a group's best interests lie. If a diagnostic category describes a behavior specific to your subgroup, is this good or bad for you? On the one hand, it may stigmatize your group. (This, obviously, was the argument with regard to homosexuality.) On the other hand, it may encourage the study and treatment of a condition that is in fact a cause of suffering to many in your group. This was the argument for listing self-defeating personality disorder. If such a disorder exists, most commonly in women, then preventing its recognition and treatment is a serious disservice to women (Widiger, in press).

Finally, however, the question that must be asked about any diagnostic category is not whether it is good for one group or another but whether it is good for science—whether it describes a condition that actually exists. The fact that a diagnostic category has a high potential for misuse does not mean that it is scientifically invalid (Fiester, 1991). This is not to say that the self-defeating and sadistic personality disorders were known to be valid. The research on both was preliminary. Nor should it be thought that politically disadvantaged groups are the only ones with political agendas. If some women have nonscientific reasons for rejecting "self-defeating personality disorder," some men may have nonscientific reasons for endorsing it. In any case, it is not just research but also social conflicts such as these that make the establishment of diagnostic categories a permanently shifting process.

perverted or depraved" (cited in Preu, 1944, p. 923).

In the late nineteenth century such people came to be called "psychopaths," and in keeping with the biogenic thinking of the period, it was assumed that their problem was a hereditary defect. This "bad seed" theory was widely accepted for many decades. Then, with the rise of sociology in the twentieth century, researchers began instead to stress the influence of social conditions. Accordingly, "psychopaths" were relabeled "sociopaths" (Birnbaum, 1914), the implication being that the problem lay not in the person but in the person's relationship to society.

Thus, while its causes were still being disputed, antisocial behavior was absorbed into abnormal psychology. In the beginning, however, perhaps too much was absorbed. Once psychologists learned to see some antisocial behavior as "sick," some of them began to see *all* antisocial behavior as "sick." There were no longer any criminals, just disturbed people. Yet many criminals seem to commit their crimes for simple and relatively understandable reasons—to supplement their incomes, to punish someone who has done them wrong, and so forth. Are these people also to be regarded as psychologically disturbed? In early editions of the

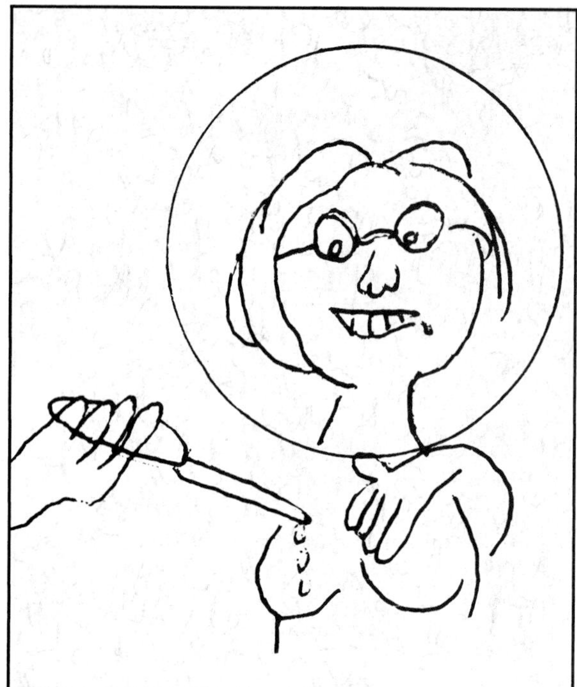

FIGURE 11.1 A hostile, sociopathic patient made this doodle of a bloody knife being plunged into a female breast. On a subsequent occasion only the face within the circle was shown to the patient, and he identified it as his mother's. (Courtesy of C. Scott Moss)

DSM there was some hedging on this point. In more recent editions there is not. *DSM-IV* offers two distinct categories, one pathological and one normal. The first is "antisocial personality disorder," described above, in which antisocial behavior is presumed to be a function of psychological disturbance. The second is "adult antisocial behavior," listed in the back of the manual under "other conditions that may be a focus of clinical attention" but reserved for those whose antisocial activities do not seem to be linked to any psychological disturbance.

Thus the pendulum, having swung from one direction to the other, has now settled in the middle. Some people who engage in antisocial behavior are psychologically "normal," and others are not. We shall confine our attention to the second group.

Characteristics of the Antisocial Personality

DSM-IV's list of criteria for the diagnosis of antisocial personality disorder can be summarized as five basic points:

1 *A history of illegal or socially disapproved activity beginning before age fifteen and continuing into adulthood.* Usually by the time of puberty—or, in the case of boys, earlier—the person has begun his or her career of antisocial behavior, in the form of truancy, delinquency, theft, vandalism, lying, drug abuse, running away from home, and/or chronic misbehavior in school. As adults, antisocial personalities may graduate to prostitution, pimping, drug selling, and other crimes.
2 *Failure to show constancy and responsibility in work, sexual relationships, parenthood, or financial obligations.* Antisocial personalities lack steadiness and a sense of obligation. They tend to walk out on jobs, spouses, children, and creditors.

At the turn of this century, when government offered fewer social welfare programs than is the case now, poor children sometimes committed crimes such as theft and truancy out of need. Today such behavior is likely to be labeled antisocial.

The antisocial personality, with its pattern of irritability and aggressiveness, is often associated with spousal abuse, but domestic-violence experts stress the sociocultural factors that influence this behavior.

3 *Irritability and aggressiveness.* Antisocial personalities are easily riled, and they express their anger not just in street brawls but often in abuse of mates and children.
4 *Reckless and impulsive behavior.* Unlike most "normal" criminals, antisocial personalities rarely engage in planning. Instead, they tend to operate in an aimless, thrill-seeking fashion, traveling from town to town with no goal in mind, falling into bed with anyone available, stealing a pack of cigarettes or a car, depending on what seems easiest and most gratifying at the moment. (For other disorders involving impulse control, see the box on page 274.)
5 *Disregard for the truth.* Antisocial personalities lie frequently and easily. Cleckley (1976) offered the following example:

> In a letter to his wife, at last seeking divorce and in another city, one patient set down dignified, fair appraisals of the situation and referred to sensible plans he had outlined for her security. He then added that specified insurance policies and annuities providing for the three children (including their tuition at college) had been mailed under separate cover and would, if she had not already received them, soon be in her hands. He had not taken even the first step to obtain insurance or to make any other provision, and, once he had made these statements in his letter, he apparently gave the matter no further thought. (p. 342)

As is almost always the case with the *DSM* criteria, only some, not all, of these characteristics need be present in order for the case to be diagnosed as antisocial personality disorder. However, a history of antisocial behavior during both adolescence and adulthood must be present.

In keeping with the policies of the diagnostic manual, this list confines itself to verifiable behaviors. Other writers, going further, have created more subjective portraits of the antisocial personality. For example, Cleckley, who treated antisocial personalities for many years, devoted an entire book, *The Mask of Sanity* (1976), to a description of this disorder. (His conceptualization, updated and expanded by Hare and his colleagues, formed the basis, in part, for *DSM-IV*'s discussion of the disorder [Hare, Hart, & Harpur, 1991].) According to Cleckley, antisocial personalities differ from normal people, including "normal" criminals, not only in their actions but also in their emotions, motivations, and thought processes. First, their misdeeds are not just impulsive but almost unmotivated—or rather, not motivated by any understandable purpose. Their behavior, therefore, often has a perverse or irrational quality. Cleckley cites the case of a teenager whose exploits included "defecation into the stringed intricacies of the school piano, the removal from his uncle's automobile of a carburetor for which he got 75 cents, and the selling of his father's overcoat to a passing buyer of scrap materials" (p. 65). This lack of purposefulness, Cleckley claims, is what makes most antisocial personalities unsuccessful criminals.

Second, according to Cleckley, antisocial personalities have only the shallowest emotions. Through lack of love, of loyalty, and, above all, of empathy—an inability to imagine what might be the feelings of the child they have left alone all day in an empty house, the friend whose credit cards they have stolen, and so forth—they are able to ignore what most people would regard as obligations. Nor do they feel anxiety or remorse over such actions, for

IMPULSE-CONTROL DISORDERS: PATHOLOGICAL GAMBLING

Antisocial personality disorder, along with other syndromes that we will describe in this book, such as drug dependence, involve a failure to resist harmful impulses. But there are certain patterns of impulsive behavior that seem to exist not as part of another major syndrome but independently. *DSM-IV* calls these the **impulse-control disorders,** their essential feature being the failure to resist impulses to act in a way harmful to oneself or others. The disorders included in this category, together with the behavior involved, are *intermittent explosive disorder* (destructiveness), *kleptomania* (theft of objects not needed for personal use or monetary value), *pyromania* (setting fires for pleasure or tension relief), *trichotillomania* (pulling out one's own hair—see Chapter 7), and *pathological gambling.* For the first four, prevalence, where it is known, is low. (Kleptomania, for example, seems to occur in only about 5 percent of identified shoplifters.) Pathological gambling, however, is not rare. Estimates in this country range from 1.1 million (Blume, 1987) to 9 million people (Gamblers Anonymous), and therefore it deserves special discussion.

Pathological gamblers are more likely to be men than women, and they seem to share certain personality characteristics: above-average intelligence and education; competitiveness; and a need for challenge, stimulation, and risk taking (Peck, 1986). Interestingly, this personality pattern may be connected to a central nervous system dysfunction. Some compulsive gamblers have been found to have abnormalities in their noradrenergic system, a part of the central nervous system that is related to extroversion and impulse control (Roy, Adinoff, Roehrich, et al., 1988; Roy, DeJong, & Linnoila, 1989b).

Like other disorders, pathological gambling seems to develop in stages, with predictable crises. In the earliest phase, the person tends to win—and continues to win as beginner's luck is replaced by increasingly skillful betting and playing. The gambler becomes more and more confident and excited. Eventually, the "big win" occurs, in an amount that may exceed a year's salary. In the typical case, this sets off the compulsion (Custer & Custer, 1978).

Now the winning phase gives way to the second phase, losing. The gambler begins betting compulsively and "chasing," or betting more and more to get back the money lost. Skilled bettors know that chasing is a novice's strategy, or in any case a losing strategy, but pathological gamblers cannot resist it. Now betting poorly and heavily, they fall deeply into debt. Having run through their income and savings, they begin borrowing, buoyed by the irrational belief that they will soon win and repay the debt. Most report that the initial experience of borrowing is not depressing. On the contrary, it feels like the big win.

As debts mount, so do personal consequences. Like alcohol-dependent people who hide bottles around the house, pathological gamblers often try to conceal their losses from their families. At the same time, they may manipulate family and friends to pay off pressing debts. When legal sources dry up, the gambler may turn to loan sharks. Divorce, imprisonment, and job loss become increasing threats. At this point, pathological gamblers may become paranoid. Some confess their problem to family members and are "bailed out." Like the first stage of borrowing, however, the bailout generally does not rein in the gambler. Rather, it is exhilarating, like the big win.

Now the gambler enters the final phase—desperation. Gambling continues with "all-consuming intensity and apparent disregard for family, friends, and employment" (Moran, 1970). In the typical pattern, the person begins having problems eating and sleeping. Depression, irritability, hypersensitivity, and restlessness are other common symptoms.

Many compulsive gamblers recover in self-help groups such as Gamblers Anonymous, but mental health professionals have taken little interest in the problem. With treatment facilities almost nonexistent and compulsive gambling so widespread, people who suffer from this ruinous disorder do not get the help they need—despite the fact that it can be treated (Blume, 1987).

---

they are as deficient in guilt as in other basic emotions. Zax and Stricker (1963) report the case of a boy who killed a neighborhood child by shooting her in the head:

> He spoke of the incident . . . in a nonchalant, unfeeling way, and was very suave and unnaturally composed in explaining why he was on the ward. He said, "I was showing her the gun. I didn't know it was loaded. She turned her head and it got her in the temple. I told the police that I was very sorry. You're to find out if there is anything mentally wrong with me. I thought I'd have to go to reform school." (p. 240)

A third aspect of Cleckley's portrait is poor judgment and failure to learn from experience. Antisocial personalities, he argues, do not make the connection between their actions and the consequences of those actions. Or, as later theorists (Newman, Patterson, Howland, et al., 1990) have refined the concept, antisocial personalities are bad at **passive avoidance learning,** learning to stop making a response that results in punishment. Once punished for some action, normal people learn either not to repeat the action or to repeat it in such a way that they will not be caught. In contrast, antisocial personalities may repeat the same offense again and again, and in the same manner, even though they have been punished for doing so.

Finally, according to Cleckley, most antisocial personalities are able to maintain a pleasant and convincing exterior. Because of their lack of anxiety and guilt, they can lie, cheat, and steal with remarkable poise. Therefore, despite repeated offenses, they are still able to convince people of their goodwill.

The Case of Roberta

Though no single human being will conform in every detail to the pattern outlined above, the following case comes close. In Roberta's history, reported by Cleckley (1976), we see most of the features outlined by *DSM-IV* as well as those listed by Cleckley:

> "I can't understand the girl, no matter how hard I try," said the father, shaking his head in genuine perplexity.
>
> He had related, in a rambling but impressive account, how Roberta at the age of ten stole her aunt's silver hairbrush, how she repeatedly made off with small articles from the dime store, the drug store, and from her own home. "At first it seemed just the mischievous doings of a little girl," he said, "a sort of play. . . . You know how children sometimes tell a lot of fanciful stories without thinking of it as lying."
>
> Neither the father nor the mother seemed a severe parent. . . . However, there was nothing to suggest that this girl had been spoiled. The parents had, so far as could be determined, consistently let her find that lying and stealing and truancy brought censure and punishment.
>
> As she grew into her teens this girl began to buy dresses, cosmetics, candy, perfume, and other articles, charging them to her father. He had no warning that these bills would come. Roberta acted without saying a word to him, and no matter what he said or did she went on in the same way. For many of these things she had little or no use; some of them she distributed among her acquaintances. . . .
>
> In school Roberta's work was mediocre. She studied little and her truancy was spectacular and persistent. No one regarded her as dull and she seemed to learn easily when she made any effort at all. (Her I.Q. was found to be 135.) She often expressed ambitions and talked of plans for the future. . . . For short periods she sometimes applied herself and made excellent grades, but would inevitably return to truancy.

Roberta was expelled from three successive schools. She then went to work for her father's business, embezzling funds on a regular basis. Periodically she would disappear from home for days or weeks. On one such occasion she took off with the intention of finding a soldier friend, whom, as she later explained, she was thinking of marrying. Unable to locate him, she ended up at nightfall in a strange town, and there she had her first sexual experience:

> Not having concluded plans for her next step, she sat for a while in a hotel lobby. Soon she was approached by a middle-aged man. . . . He soon offered to pay for her overnight accommodations at the hotel. She realized that he meant to share the bed with her but made no objection. As well as one can tell by discussing this experience with Roberta, she was neither excited, frightened, repulsed, nor attracted by a prospect that most [adolescent girls] would certainly have regarded with anything but indifference. . . .
>
> Next morning she reached her soldier friend by telephone. . . . He discouraged her vigorously against coming, refused to send money, and urged her to return home. She was not, it seems, greatly upset by this turn of events, and, with little serious consideration of the matter, decided to go to Charlotte, which was approximately 150 miles distant.

Short of funds during her stay in Charlotte, Roberta drifted into prostitution. Finally, after three weeks, she was located by her parents, whom she greeted with great affection. But her behavior did not change. Indeed, she went on for years in exactly the same way, with intervals in which her parents would have her hospitalized for psychiatric observation:

> She returned for psychiatric treatment on several occasions, always saying she had been helped and expressing simple but complete confidence that it was impossible for her to have further trouble. Despite her prompt failures she would, in her letters to us at the hospital, write as if she had been miraculously cured:
>
> "You and Doctor —— have given me a new outlook and a new life. This time we have got to the very root of my trouble and I see the whole story in a different light. I don't mean to use such words lightly and, of all things, I want to avoid even the appearance of flattery, but I must tell you how grateful I am, how deeply I admire the wonderful work you are doing. . . . If, in your whole life you had never succeeded with one other patient, what you have done for me should make your practice worthwhile. . . . I wish I could tell you how different I feel. How different I am!" . . .
>
> Though she realized I had been informed of recent episodes quite as bad as those in the past, on several occasions she wrote requesting letters of recommen-

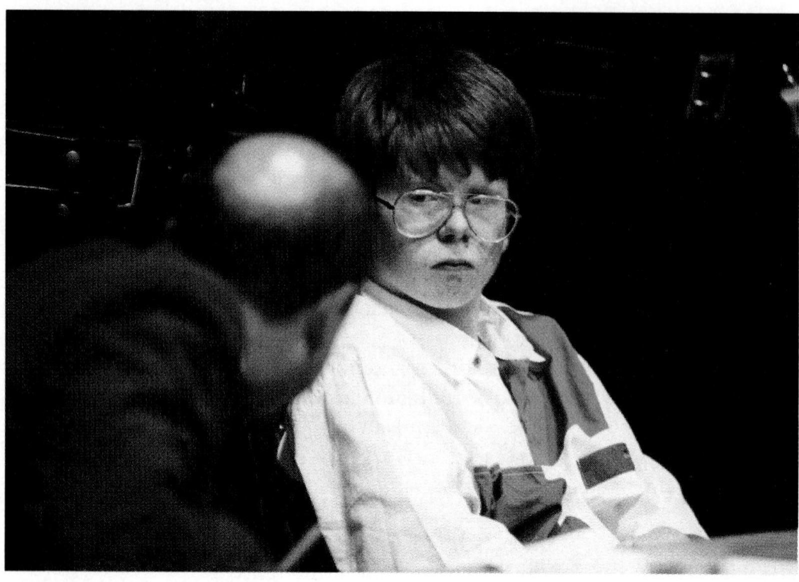

Juveniles account for an increasing proportion of arrests for serious crimes. Eric Smith, age fourteen, was tried as an adult and found guilty in 1994 of bludgeoning and strangling a preschooler.

dation for various positions she had applied for or was considering. . . . Roberta seemed sweetly free of any doubt that such recommendations would be given without qualification. (Cleckley, 1976, pp. 46–55)

Antisocial Behavior in Juveniles: The Conduct Disorders

Antisocial behavior is not confined to adults. Almost 30 percent of all arrests for serious crimes involve juveniles (U.S. Department of Commerce, 1993), and many arrested juveniles are actually preadolescent. In a widely publicized 1993 case in Liverpool, England, two ten-year-old boys abducted a two-year-old boy named James Bulger from a shopping mall, walked him 2½ miles to a railroad track, stoned him to death, and then laid his body on the track, where it was cut in half by the next train. The boys then went home, stopping in at their favorite video store on the way.

Juvenile delinquency comes under the heading of "conduct disorders" in *DSM-IV* and is grouped not with the personality disorders but with the disorders of childhood and adolescence. Therefore we will deal with this subject more fully when we come to the childhood disturbances (Chapter 17).

Juvenile delinquency raises some very urgent psychological issues. First is the question of cause. What is it that "hardens" children to the point where they can engage in antisocial acts? Second is the matter of psychological intervention. Conduct disorders have a well-established connection with antisocial personality and with adult antisocial behavior in general. In one important study Robins (1966) followed a number of children who exhibited antisocial behavior. She found that such behavior was a good predictor of adult antisocial personality, and later research (Loeber & Dishion, 1983) has supported her findings. It was such research that led to the inclusion of childhood antisocial behavior among the criteria for adult antisocial personality. According to the current definition, as we saw, antisocial personality disorder begins before age fifteen. Therefore all antisocial personalities, by definition, were once teenagers with conduct disorders. It is important to remember, however, that the reverse is not true: most teenagers with conduct disorders do *not* grow up to have antisocial personalities or even to engage in "normal" antisocial behavior (Moffitt, 1993). With continuing research, we may discover what distinguishes juveniles with "normal" antisocial behavior from those who will have continuing conduct disorders.

PERSPECTIVES ON THE PERSONALITY DISORDERS

The Psychodynamic Perspective

Character Disorders Psychodynamic theorists interpret personality disorders, which they call "character disorders," as stemming from disturbances in the parent-child relationship. The more severe syndromes, such as antisocial personality, are thought to originate in the early, pre-Oedipal relationship between infant and mother (or other caretaker), and particularly in what Mahler called the *separation-individuation* process (Chapter 2), in which children learn to separate from their mothers and regard themselves, and others, as individual persons. A troubled separation-individuation could lead to a poorly defined sense of self, as in borderline personality, or a difficulty in relating to others as human beings, as in antisocial personality.

Whatever the root of the problem, the final result, as in all psychological disorders according to the psychodynamic view, is a weakened ego and therefore poor adaptive functioning. Psychodynamic theorists see people with character disorders as falling somewhere between neurotics and psychotics in terms of ego strength. (In other words, they function better than psychotics and worse than neurotics.) In all the character disorders, normal "coping" behavior, the province of the ego, has to some extent broken down and been replaced by erratic, distorted, or deviant behavior. The borderline personality falls apart in times of stress; the antisocial personality cannot delay gratification; the dependent personality is constantly ceding adaptive decisions to others. These breakdowns in coping behavior affect the broad range of ego functions—perception, memory, language, learning. Antisocial personalities cannot learn from experience; obsessive-compulsive personalities shift all mental energy into planning; paranoid personalities shift all energy into perception, scanning the environment for signs of who is against them.

Narcissistic personality disorder has recently been the subject of much study and controversy in psychodynamic circles. Otto Kernberg (1975), along with *DSM-IV*, sees the basic pattern as a combination of grandiosity and feelings of inferiority. In his view, however, it is the sense of inferiority that is primary; the grandiosity is merely a defense against childhood feelings of rage and inferiority. Heinz Kohut (1966, 1972, 1977), on the other hand, sees the grandiosity as primary—the expression of a "narcissistic libido" that for various reasons has evaded the neutralizing efforts of the ego. When the narcissistic personality shows rage and wounded self-esteem, these are reactions to blows to the grandiose self-image.

Predictably, psychodynamic theorists attribute antisocial personality disorder to superego failure. For some reason, the person has failed to acquire adequate superego controls and consequently cannot resist the temptation of instant gratification. Why the failure? As we saw in Chapter 2, the emergence of the superego depends on the child's identification with the parent of the same sex at the end of the Oedipal stage. Presumably, if there is some serious disturbance in the parent-child relationship at this point, or if there *is* no parent-child relationship at this point, such identification may never occur.

What kinds of family problems could give rise to antisocial personality? Some theorists hold that the crucial predisposing factor is parental deprivation. It has been demonstrated time and again (Greer, 1964; Oltman & Friedman, 1967; Robins, 1966) that the antisocial personality is much more likely than the average person to have suffered, as a child, the loss of a parent through death, separation, or simple abandonment. Other writers (e.g., McCord & McCord, 1964) claim that the crucial determinant is parental rejection. It should be remembered, however, that these family problems—divorce, separation from parents, rejection by parents—have also been implicated in the etiology of anxiety disorders, depression, schizophrenia, autism, alcoholism, and a host of other disorders. Furthermore, many children of rejecting parents grow up to be altogether normal. Conversely, many antisocial personalities, such as Roberta, come from apparently normal homes. Robins (1966, 1979), attempting to sort through this confusion, proposes that the critical variable is not family disruption but the presence of an antisocial parent, and particularly an antisocial father. It is this parent's antisocial behavior, causing him or her to be rejecting or absent, that results in family disruption.

Psychotherapy for Personality Disorders Since people with personality disorders are often not distressed by their behavior, they tend not to seek treatment. When they do end up in a therapist's office, it is often not on their own initiative but rather because they have been induced into marriage counseling or family therapy because of a spouse's complaints or a child's emotional problems. In such situations, they are generally resistant to treatment. And even when they do experience sufficient unhappiness to enter treatment on their own, they tend to see the problem as external to them rather than internal—an attitude that bodes ill for insight-oriented therapy.

The treatment of antisocial personality disorder has yielded particularly unimpressive results, and hence the prognosis for antisocial personalities is poor. Characteristically lacking both insight and the desire to change, they are poor candidates for the insight-oriented psychotherapies. Furthermore, whatever the form of therapy, the antisocial personality's emotional poverty and lack of motivation place immense demands on the patience of the therapist. Antisocial personalities are most unlikely to enter psychotherapy voluntarily, and when they are treated involuntarily—in prisons, for example—they show little improvement (A. Ellis, 1977; Palmer, 1984).

In treating patients with personality disorders, psychodynamic therapists will often take a more directive, more parental approach than that taken with other patients. Waldinger and Gunderson (1987) list a number of basic tenets common to the psychodynamic treatment of borderline personality: the therapist is more active, more likely to block acting-out behavior, more focused on the present than on the past, and more concerned with connecting feelings and actions than is the case in the usual insight therapy. The adoption of this forthright, ego-strengthening approach shows how modern psychodynamic therapists have learned to tailor their traditional concepts to the needs of individual patients.

The Behavioral Perspective

Many behaviorists, as we saw, object to the very concept of personality disorder, because it implies fixed personality traits. However, as was pointed out in a review of behavioral work in this area (Turkat & Levin, 1984), the personality disorders can be usefully addressed by behaviorists if the diagnostic terms are understood as "descriptors of classes of behavior that have been learned and can be changed" (p. 497). This position is actually not so different from the behaviorists' approach to other, less trait-bound disorders. As for how these "classes of behavior" are learned, the behaviorists point as usual to eliciting stimuli and reinforcing consequences.

Skills Acquisition, Modeling, and Reinforcement In a study of borderline personality, for example, Linehan (1987) claims that many borderline patients come from families that show "invalidating syndrome," "the tendency to invalidate affective experiences and to oversimplify the ease of solving life's problems" (p. 264). These are families that expect children to be cheerful and to understand that if they fail, it is their fault. Such parents do not coddle. As a result the child is never able to obtain sympathy for minor upsets. The only thing that will get such parents' attention is a major emotional display, and so that is what the child learns to produce. Furthermore, because these parents will not address minor sorrows, their children never learn the emotional skills that other children do when they take their problems to their parents: how to calm themselves down, how to comfort themselves. Such children, Linehan argues, may logically grow to show the kind of constant and uncontrollable emotional turbulence that we call borderline personality.

With cases of antisocial personality, behaviorists focus on other mechanisms. Modeling, as research has demonstrated, can both teach aggressive behavior and trigger specific aggressive acts (Bandura, 1976). The crucial models are undoubtedly parents and peers. Many antisocial personalities do have fathers who are themselves antisocial personalities. However, the entertainment media probably do their part as well. Many studies indicate that when children watch aggressive acts on film or television, they may initiate the violence they have seen if an appropriate situation arises shortly thereafter. The horror movie *Child's Play 3* was implicated in the murder of James Bulger, described above. In the climax of that movie, Chucky, the homicidal doll, has his face stained with blue paint. Apparently, both of James Bulger's ten-year-old murderers saw *Child's Play 3* on video shortly before they abducted him, and as they walked him to the railroad tracks, they stopped off to buy a can of blue paint, which they threw at him while throwing the bricks that killed him.

In addition to modeling, reinforcement and skills acquisition—or failure of skills acquisition—may also play a role in the development of antisocial personality, as well as of borderline personality. Studies of children who seldom engage in antisocial behavior have shown that the parents of these children consistently reinforce prosocial behavior (e.g., helpfulness, cooperation, affection) and ignore or punish antisocial behavior (S. M. Johnson, Wahl, Martin, et al., 1973; J. J. Snyder, 1977). In the case of parents whose children have conduct disorders, a different pattern emerges. First, when such parents respond to their child, the response tends to be a punishing one. Second, the reinforcement that the parents provide is generally **noncontingent reinforcement.** That is, the nature of the parents' response is not related to whether the child's behavior was prosocial or antisocial; it is simply arbitrary (J. J. Snyder, 1977). Both these factors—overuse of aversive consequences and noncontingent reinforcement—are vividly illustrated in the following statement by Albert DeSalvo, who came to be known as the Boston Strangler:

> My father . . . we used to have to stand in front of him, my brother Frank and me, every night and be beaten with his belt. I can still to this very moment tell you the color of the belt and just how long it was—

Behaviorists maintain that children often learn antisocial behavior from adult models. These young men are not only the fathers of young children but, as their hand signals indicate, members of a gang in Culver City, California.

> two inches by 36—a belt with a big buckle on it. We used to stand in front of him every night and get beaten with that damn thing—every night, whether we did anything wrong or not. We were only in the fourth or fifth grade. (quoted in G. Frank, 1966, p. 316)

Such parents, according to the behaviorists, not only serve as models for aggression but also teach children that there is no connection tween their behavior and the treatment they will receive. Consequently, the children become desensitized to social stimuli such as rules and laws that indicate to people what the consequences of their behavior will be. Rather than heed these stimuli, they do as they please, assuming that the outcome of their behavior will be determined not by the nature of that behavior but by some arbitrary force such as luck.

Antisocial behavior may also be learned through direct positive reinforcement. It may win approval from peers and attention from parents and school authorities, while prosocial behavior goes unnoticed by elders and is ridiculed by peers.

Behaviorists analyze other personality disorders in the same straightforward fashion. For example, dependent personality disorder might result from a childhood in which assertiveness was repeatedly punished; histrionic personality disorder, from parental indulgence of temper tantrums obsessive-compulsive personality disorder, from consistent rewards for neatness, rule following, and other "goody-goody" behaviors (Millon, 1981). Or, as with antisocial personality disorder, parental modeling of the behaviors in question might be as important as rewards and punishments.

New Learning In handling personality disorders, behaviorists have operated on the assumption that since most of these disorders can be seen as inappropriate social behavior, what the patients need is social-skills training. Some histrionic patients have been given social-skills training, with special attention paid to skill in interacting with the opposite sex, since most of them complain of troubled romances (Kass, Silver, & Abrams, 1972). Behavioral techniques have also been used to teach empathic behavior to histrionic patients (Woolson & Swanson, 1972).

With borderline patients, Linehan (1987) has employed a more comprehensive skills-acquisition treatment, involving social-skills training together with training in regulating emotions and tolerating distress and grief. These "grieving skills" are necessary since borderline patients, as we saw, tend to respond with utter devastation when they are abandoned by the people to whom they show such neediness and such hostility. Linehan calls this approach "dialectical behavior therapy." It is behavior therapy in that it aims at skill enhancement; it is "dialectical" in that, while teaching skills, the therapist has to cope with the many tensions presented by these desperately unhappy patients, and does so by means of empathy and acceptance. In other words, behaviorists too will tailor the treatment approach to the needs of the individual patient. Linehan reports that this therapy has so far been successful in reducing suicidal threats and self-destructive behavior in the women patients that she and her colleagues have treated (Linehan, Heard, & Armstrong, 1993).

The Cognitive Perspective

Faulty Schemas Cognitive theory holds that our thoughts, emotions, and behavior are organized by underlying schemas, structures of information that we have in our minds about various domains of life (Chapter 3). In keeping with this assumption, cognitive theorists interpret the personality disorders as the product of distortions or exaggerations in the schemas. Since faulty schemas are "structuralized," or woven into a person's normal cognitive processes (A. T. Beck, Freeman, Pretzer, et al., 1990), the person does not recognize them as faulty. On the contrary, the distortions generate perceptions, and even situations, that confirm the schemas. They may also help someone to survive in a job or marriage, which in turn would increase his or her investment in the schemas.

Consider, for example, obsessive-compulsive personality. For people who fit this label, a central belief of the self-schema may be "I am basically overwhelmed, so I need strict systems and rules in order to function." This belief, in turn, will generate the view that others who do not show the same system-bound behavior are incompetent or irresponsible, and their incompetence will make the obsessive-compulsive personality even more insistent on rules.

Other common beliefs of the obsessive-compulsive personality are "I have to drive myself and others relentlessly" and "Everything must be done perfectly." And when, life being what it is, things are not done perfectly, the obsessive-compulsive personality's response is guilt over his or her own failures and anger over others' derelictions. This produces a constant state of tension, stifling pleasure, affection, and spontaneity. So the final result is emotional distress and ineffective behavior, all traceable to the faulty beliefs.

According to cognitive theorists, such beliefs are acquired through learning—often through modeling—and may be a response to developmental conditions. (Perfectionistic parents, for example, could breed obsessive-compulsive personality.) What distinguishes the beliefs peculiar to personality disorder, however, is not just their dysfunctional character—for many of us hold unhelpful beliefs—but their rigid character. In the cognitive view, schemas normally exist on a continuum from compelling to noncompelling. Many of us, for example, have schemas about nutrition that are on the relaxed end of the scale, whereas our schemas about child rearing are likely to be much more compelling—that is, based on firmly held beliefs. In personality disorder patients, most schemas are pushed to the compelling end of the range. The beliefs are rigid and admit no exceptions.

Altering Schemas Since the schema is seen as the root of the problem, the goal of cognitive therapy is to induce the patient to alter the schema. A very ambitious goal is to tear down the schema altogether, but in the case of personality disorders, in which habits are old and deeply ingrained, many therapists opt for the more practicable goal of getting the patient to modify, reinterpret, or camouflage the schema (A. T. Beck, Freeman, Pretzer, et al., 1990; H. Freeman, 1989; A. Freeman & Leaf, 1989).

With obsessive-compulsive personality, for example, modifying the schema might mean inducing the patient to confine his or her perfectionism to the job and not let it spill over into the home, where the patient might be destroying family harmony over such relatively trivial matters as the proper way to make a bed or rake a lawn. Reinterpreting a schema means putting it to more functional use. Thus the therapist might guide an obsessive-compulsive personality into a line of work in which perfectionism would be more appropriate and less of a nuisance to others. Finally, "schematic camouflage" involves teaching patients socially acceptable behaviors that they can use simply to ease their way in situations in which their habitual rigidity is likely to cause them difficulties. If they must always have their steak done exactly medium rare when they go to a restaurant, the therapist can teach them, through social-skills training, how to be very specific in ordering and how to complain effectively if the order comes back wrong.

The Sociocultural Perspective

Predictably, sociocultural theorists have addressed themselves primarily to antisocial personality disorder. Most social scientists would agree that the injustices built into our society contribute their fair share to the development of criminal behavior. To what degree might the society also foster antisocial personality disorder? According to Gough (1948):

> There are very definite aspects of our cultural pattern which give [antisocial personalities] encouragement. In America we put great value on the acquisition of material gain, prestige, power, personal ascendance, and the competitive massing of goods. . . .
>
> We have very short memories about the origins of some of our great national fortunes, toward the holders of which we hold so much respect. At the other end,

of course, our machine civilization tends to level and strangle individuality, leaving large groups within our culture fearful, anxious, resentful and even occasionally openly hostile. In such an atmosphere [antisocial personality disorder] rises, grows and fattens. (pp. 359–366)

This critique summarizes the sociocultural position. While other theorists look to the individual psyche for the explanation of antisocial personality disorder, sociocultural theorists feel that these psychological processes are merely the products of large-scale social processes—processes that ensure the prosperity of certain social groups and the deprivation of others. Accordingly, they argue that psychologists should devote their efforts to changing the society rather than trying to change its victims (Holland, 1978).

Interesting to consider in this connection is the theory of **anomie,** offered by the sociologist Robert K. Merton to explain crime but possibly useful in explaining antisocial personality disorder as well. Merton claims that societies such as ours—societies in which material luxuries are highly valued and widely displayed but available only to certain groups—engender a state of anomie, or normlessness, in disadvantaged groups. These groups feel that since they cannot acquire the society's rewards by legitimate means, neither do the society's notions of what is legitimate apply to them. Consequently, according to Merton, they simply go after what they want without consulting any system of rules or values. Such normlessness is a characteristic feature of the antisocial personality, and since a disproportionate number of antisocial personalities come from impoverished backgrounds (McGarvey, Gabrielli, Beutler, et al., 1981), it is possible that this disorder is to some extent a product of the forces Merton describes.

More broadly, it could be argued that the values of modern society ("get it while you can," "don't get involved") encourage antisocial behavior patterns. As *DSM-IV* notes, people with some features of antisocial personality disorder—for example, the disregard for truth, though not the childhood delinquency—may achieve considerable success in public life. And the prominence of such people may breed an atmosphere in which antisocial behavior flourishes.

The Biological Perspective

As we have seen repeatedly, the swing of the pendulum in the early twentieth century toward seeing human behavior as the product of environmental influence has in some measure been reversed in the late twentieth century. With the rise of neuroscience research, we are returning, with empirical findings, to the pre-twentieth-century belief that much of human behavior is biologically based. Some of these findings have been quite dramatic. For example, in a study comparing MMPI scores of MZ and DZ twins—some raised together, some raised apart—it was found that the contribution of environment was small or negligible on all but two of the fourteen personality scales (Tellegen, Lykken, Bouchard, et al., 1988). The experimenters concluded that only 50 percent of measured personality difference among their subjects was due to environmental difference. The rest they attributed to genetic difference.

If biological factors are so powerful in forming the normal personality, presumably they are also involved in personality disorder. This is the possibility that neuroscience researchers are now investigating, with special attention to antisocial personality.

XYY and Other Genetic Factors A highly publicized discovery of the mid-1960s was that a certain percentage of violent criminals showed the rare XYY chromosomal abnormality. Almost every cell in the human body is equipped with twenty-three chromosomal pairs, one of which determines the sex of the individual. In the female, this sex-related pair is made up of two female (X) chromosomes; thus the female is an XX type. The male, in contrast, carries one female and one male (Y) chromosome and is therefore an XY type. In the 1960s, it was found that certain male criminals who had committed especially brutal crimes were XYY types—that is, they carried an extra male chromosome (P. A. Jacobs, Brunton, & Melville, 1965). Could it be that the extra Y chromosome produces some biochemical predisposition to violence—for example, an excess of testosterone, the hormone that some believe underlies "male aggressiveness"?

This discovery set off a flurry of chromosomal research on violent criminals. Such efforts were given further impetus when it was reported that Richard Speck, who murdered eight student nurses in Chicago one night in 1966, was an XYY type (Montague, 1968). In the end, however, these studies failed to prove the hypothesis that the XYY type was biochemically predisposed to violence. The XYY type has been found to be about fifteen times more common among male criminals than among males in general (Jarvik, Klodin, & Matsuyama, 1973). Yet the prevalence among male criminals is still very low: about 2 percent. Furthermore, most of the criminals who show the XYY configuration have not been convicted of *violent* crimes (Witkin, Mednick, Schulsinger, et al., 1976). Finally, most XYY types are not criminals but slightly mentally retarded, nonviolent people. The XYY research, in other words, has not yielded any solid answers as to what produces a criminal, let alone a violent criminal, and has probably received much more attention than it deserved (W. H. Reid, 1981).

Nevertheless, twin and adoption studies have produced evidence that heredity may be implicated in criminal behavior (Nigg & Goldsmith, 1994). Using the national birth and criminal registers, K. O. Christiansen (1968) studied all twins born in a specified area of Denmark between 1881 and 1910. Of 3,568 twin pairs born during that period, at least one member of 799 pairs later engaged in criminal activity. The concordance rate for monozygotic (identical) twins was 36 percent as compared with 12.5 percent for dizygotic (fraternal) twins. Thus the other member of a monozygotic pair was almost three times more likely to have engaged in criminal behavior than the other member of a dizygotic pair. A more recent study, combining the findings of twin studies in several countries, found the concordance rate for criminal behavior to be 52 percent in MZ twins versus 23 percent in DZ twins (Gottesman & Goldsmith, in press). The twin studies have been backed up, in some measure, by adoption studies showing that children of a criminal parent who are put up for adoption at birth are more likely to engage in criminal behavior in later life than are other matched adoptees (Crowe, 1975; Hutchings & Mednick, 1975). In this case, however, the relationship is small, and the vast majority of adoptees do not engage in criminal behavior no matter what their biological heritage.

The studies discussed so far did not distinguish between antisocial personalities and others who might engage in criminal activity. One important study did so, however. Using the Copenhagen adoption and psychiatric registers, along with police files, Schulsinger (1972) identified adopted infants who later met the criteria for diagnosis as psychopaths (antisocial personality disorder). He then examined the records of both the biological and adoptive relatives of the adoptee and found that biological relatives were four to five times more likely than adoptive relatives to meet the psychopathy criteria. Again, however, the percentage of biological relatives with psychopathy was small, indicating that although there is a genetic role, the environmental influence is also substantial.

Physiological Abnormalities We have already mentioned certain biological findings in relation to personality disorders. For example, schizophrenia seems to be more common among the relatives of paranoid personalities than in the population at large, and schizotypal personalities respond to the same medications as schizophrenics. And as we noted, it has been proposed that the emotional vulnerability of borderline personalities is due to disregulation of the limbic system. The focus of most of the research in this area has been on antisocial personality. If genes help to produce antisocial personality, what is the physiological means by which they produce it?

There is reason to believe that antisocial personalities have some defect in brain functioning (Gorenstein, 1982). In the first place, somewhere between 31 and 58 percent of all antisocial personalities show some form of EEG abnormality (Ellington, 1954), the most common being slow-wave activity, which is typical of the infant and the young child but not of the normal adult (Hare, 1970). This finding has led some researchers to propose that antisocial personality disorder may be the product of "cortical immaturity"—that is, delayed development of the cerebral cortex, the topmost layer of the brain and the seat of most of its "higher" functions (Chapter 16). If this is the case, then we might expect antisocial personalities to become better behaved with age; as the person grew older, the brain would finally mature, and consequently antisocial behavior would diminish. This does in fact seem to be true in many cases. Robins (1966), for example, found that one-third of a group of eighty-two diagnosed antisocial personalities showed marked behavioral improvements as they grew older, particularly between the ages of thirty and forty.

But if this cortical immaturity exists, what is the mental function that it impairs? According to one school of thought, it is the capacity for fear. Most of the abnormal slow-wave activity in antisocial personalities comes from the temporal lobe and the limbic system, two parts of the brain that are known to control memory and emotion. This finding suggests that the essential defect in antisocial personality disorder may be an inability to respond normally to fear-inducing stimuli, leading in turn to an inability to inhibit responses that will result in punishment. This suggestion may help to explain the resistance of antisocial personalities to passive avoidance learning—the fact that they can be punished again and again for the same offenses and still never learn how to avoid this consequence.

Evidence in support of "physiological fearlessness" was first provided by Lykken (1957). He subjected three groups—a group of college students, a group of nonsociopathic prisoners, and a group of sociopathic (i.e., antisocial) prisoners—to an ingeniously devised test involving the learning of correct responses to a series of twenty problems. The subjects responded by pressing levers on a board. For every correct press, there were three possible incorrect presses, one of which gave the subject a mild electric shock, while the other two simply turned on a red light. Lykken found that all three groups made approximately the same number of errors; in other words, there were no significant differences in intelligence. However, the nonsociopathic prisoners managed to avoid the "shock" errors better than the sociopathic prisoners, thus supporting the hypothesis that lack of anxiety renders the sociopath less adept at avoidance learning. Lykken's findings were later supported by Schachter and Latané (1964), who found that sociopathic prisoners did considerably better on Lykken's test when they had been injected with adrenaline, which promotes anxiety. It seems, then, that the antisocial personality lacks sufficient anxiety to learn—or bother to learn—how to avoid punishment, at least punishment in the form of physical discomfort.

Another finding that strengthens the physiological-fearlessness hypothesis is that the autonomic nervous system of the antisocial personality seems to operate at a lower level of arousal than that of the normal person. This finding is consistent with the discoveries of Lykken and of Schachter and Latané. In particular, it meshes neatly with the fact that injections of adrenaline, which the body naturally produces in a state of high autonomic arousal, improve the antisocial personality's performance in avoidance learning. According to Hare (1970), autonomic underarousal could explain a number of the antisocial personality's behavioral oddities. In the first place, as we indicated earlier, many antisocial personalities show an unshakable poise, even in situations that would prove extremely unnerving to anyone else (e.g., being interrogated by the police). Possibly the antisocial personality's autonomic nervous system is simply unable to achieve the degree of arousal necessary to produce fear. If so, this factor would in turn account for the antisocial personality's difficulties with avoidance learning. Finally, autonomic underarousal might also help to account for the impulsiveness of the antisocial personality. Quay (1965) has proposed that this impulsiveness is not so much passive—that is, a giving in to impulses—as it is active, a form of thrill seeking. If this is the case, the antisocial personality's quest for stimulation could be a function of the body's need to compensate for autonomic underarousal.

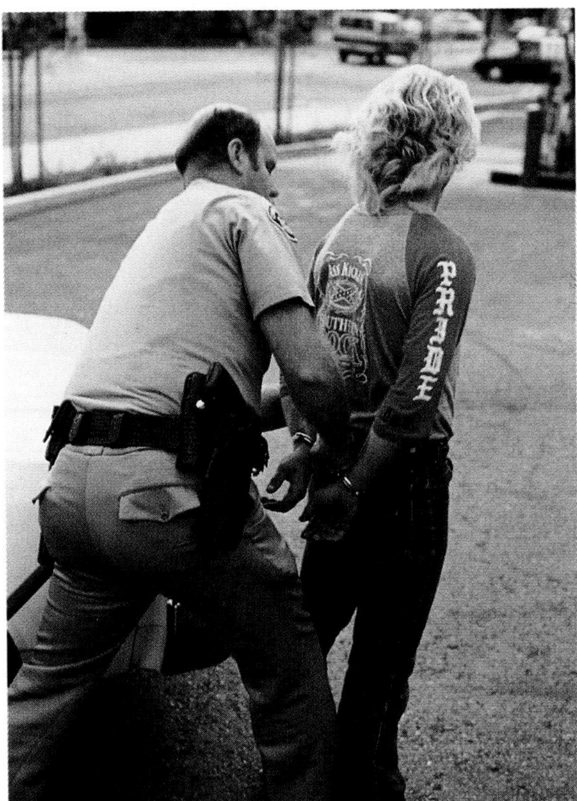

One physiological theory holds that antisocial personalities suffer from autonomic underarousal, which prevents them from fearing discovery and punishment. Another theory is that they are capable of fearing punishment but simply cannot switch their attention to cues for impending punishment as long as they are intent on rewards.

Some recent research has given rise to a different but perhaps complementary theory: that antisocial personalities have information-processing problems that make it hard for them to switch their attention from cues for reward to cues for punishment (C. M. Patterson & Newman, 1993). Contrary to the research that we have just discussed, Newman and his colleagues found that antisocial personalities are no less likely than other people to fear punishment—as long as that punishment is the focus of their attention (Newman, Kosson, & Patterson, 1992; Newman, Patterson, Howland, et al., 1990). But when their focus is on attaining rewards, they find it hard to redirect their attention to signals for avoiding punishment (Howland, Kosson, Patterson, et al., 1993; Kosson & Newman, 1989). On tests, and presumably in life, they will go on responding for rewards even when the rewards have not only stopped coming but been replaced by punishments. This "attentional rigidity" would explain their failure at passive avoidance learning.

So what physiological researchers now have is a cluster of interrelated findings: EEG abnormalities, behavioral improvements with age, poor performance in avoidance learning, improved performance with adrenaline injections, signs of autonomic underarousal, and problems in switching attention from rewards to punishments. Individually, each of these findings could be quarreled with. Taken together, however, they constitute an impressive argument that antisocial personality has some physiological foundation.

KEY TERMS

anomie (281)
antisocial behavior (270)
antisocial personality disorder (269)
avoidant personality disorder (266)
borderline personality disorder (267)
dependent personality disorder (266)
histrionic personality disorder (268)
impulse-control disorders (274)
narcissistic personality disorder (268)
noncontingent reinforcement (278)
obsessive-compulsive personality disorder (269)
paranoid personality disorder (265)
passive avoidance learning (274)
personality disorder (264)
schizoid personality disorder (266)
schizotypal personality disorder (266)

SUMMARY

- A personality disorder is a long-standing, pervasive, rigid pattern of thought, feeling, and behavior that impedes functioning and causes unhappiness for the person and, usually, the people around him or her. Because they are difficult to diagnose reliably and because their definition depends on the concept (opposed by some theorists) of stable traits, there is debate over the value of this diagnostic category. Nevertheless, it is useful as a description of people with a generally maladaptive "style." Personality disorders lie between neuroses and psychoses.
- Paranoid personality disorder is marked by suspicion of almost all people in almost all situations; it differs from paranoia and paranoid schizophrenia in that it is not severely disabling. In schizotypal personality disorder the person's speech, behavior, thinking, and/or perceptions are disturbed, but not enough to warrant a diagnosis of schizophrenia. In schizoid personality disorder, eccentricity is confined to social withdrawal. The individual seems unable to feel warmth or to form attachments.
- The essential feature of avoidant personality disorder is hypersensitivity to the possibility of rejection, humiliation, or shame; the result is a recoil from others and, typically, loneliness and regret. Dependent personality disorder is characterized by excessive dependence on others—turning over to another person responsibility for deciding the course of one's life. Fear of abandonment seems to underlie this passivity.
- Borderline personality disorder is distinguished by difficulty in controlling anger and other emotions; impulsive, often self-destructive behavior; distrust of others; problems forming a secure self-identity; and fear of being alone.
- The dominant feature of histrionic personality disorder is self-dramatization, often as a means to win attention and sympathy. Narcissistic personality disorder is characterized by an exaggerated sense of self-importance, often combined with an underlying sense of inferiority. Obsessive-compulsive personality disorder is defined by excessive preoccupation with trivial details, at the cost of spontaneity and effectiveness.
- The most reliably diagnosed and thoroughly researched of the personality disorders is antisocial personality disorder, which involves chronic indifference to and violation of the rights of others. In the late nineteenth century, those with antisocial personalities were called psychopaths, and their disorder was attributed to heredity. With the rise of sociology in the twentieth century, the syndrome was linked to social influences, and its victims were called sociopaths. Having swung from the biological to the environmental extreme, today the pendulum has settled in the middle.
- The *DSM-IV* criteria for diagnosing antisocial personality disorder include a history of illegal or socially disapproved behavior beginning at puberty or earlier and continuing into adulthood; failure to exercise responsibility; irritability and aggressiveness; reckless, impulsive behavior; and disregard for the truth. Of these five criteria, a history of antisocial behavior from adolescence into adulthood *must* be present for this diagnosis to be valid.
- Persons with antisocial personality disorder differ from normal people, including "normal" criminals, in that their behavior appears to lack purpose; they seem incapable of empathy and do not feel guilt or remorse for their actions; they seem immune to punishment; and they present a pleasant, convincing exterior.
- Young people may commit perverse and (increasingly) violent antisocial acts. But the *DSM-IV* classi-

fies juvenile delinquency as a conduct disorder, on the grounds that most youthful offenders do *not* go on to develop antisocial personalities as adults or even engage in "normal" antisocial behavior.

- Psychodynamic theorists trace personality disorders, which they call character disorders, to disturbances in the early parent-child relationship, leading to a weak ego. Antisocial personality disorder, in this view, is the product of poor superego development because of failure to identify with the same-sex parent in childhood, perhaps because the parent himself or herself is antisocial. People with personality disorders usually do not think that they have a problem, so do not seek treatment. When pushed into psychotherapy, either by a family member or (as is often the case with antisocial personalities) by social institutions such as prisons, most show little improvement.
- Behavioral theorists generally reject the concept of personality disorder because it implies the existence of stable personality traits—an assumption they do not endorse. Behaviorists focus on specific behaviors, which they see as the result of maladaptive modeling and reinforcement. In the case of antisocial behavior, violent models (including those on TV) and noncontingent reinforcement by parents (punishment that is not related to the child's behavior) may play a role. Behavioral therapy takes the form of learning new responses to problem situations.
- The cognitive perspective holds that personality disorders are products of distortions or exaggerations in the schemas that structure the information in our minds. The faulty beliefs are rigid and admit no exceptions. Cognitive therapy is directed at modifying, reinterpreting, or camouflaging the faulty schema.
- Sociocultural theorists are primarily concerned with antisocial personality disorder. Where others look into the person's psyche for explanations, these theorists examine social forces. According to the theory of anomie, or normlessness, when people are denied access to social rewards, they may conclude that social rules do not apply to them. Hence treating individuals will not reduce antisocial behavior; society itself must change.
- The biological perspective focuses on genetic and physiological factors that may contribute to antisocial and other personality disorders. Recent evidence—that antisocial personalities often have abnormal EEGs, that they are poor at avoidance learning but improve with adrenaline injections, that they show autonomic underarousal and attention rigidity—strongly suggests that this disorder has some physiological basis.

IN LOVING MEMORY OF
AMANDA ROSE RAMIREZ
BORN 10-16-76 & KILLED 7-23-88
ACROSS THE HIGHWAY FROM THIS LOCATION
BY A DRUNK DRIVER

12

SUBSTANCE-USE DISORDERS

forty-five year-old white male, who works as a construction foreman during his sober periods, completed eight years of education. . . . He started drinking at the age of eighteen. . . .

He described himself as a "spree" drinker, but his heavy-drinking episodes now last three to four weeks and occur about six times a year. During these drinking periods, according to his statement, he consumes at least a quart of whiskey, a gallon of wine, and one to three six-packs of beer per day. He has had loss of memory and times of extreme shakes and hallucinations on a "few" occasions. He has had so many arrests for public drunkenness that he cannot even estimate their number. He has also had one arrest for drunk driving. He reports that both of his brothers are also alcoholics. His father drank heavily for years but was dry for the year before his death.

On his first known admission five years ago, the patient denied that he had been drinking heavily and said he had only a few beers a day. He was brought to the hospital by his wife because he was talking to the television, hearing strange music, and seeing bugs and snakes. He was detoxified. On his next admission, two years ago, he said that he had not been working more than a day or two at a time and that his wife supported him by working as a manager at a local department store. . . . [After a few days in the hospital] he requested a long pass to "look for work," and when he was told that he wasn't ready to leave the hospital, he returned to his room, dressed and left.

A year later his wife brought him to the hospital because she had returned from work to find him unconscious on the floor. His heart was pounding furiously, and he was blood-red in color and gasping for breath. After sobering up in the hospital . . . he swore that he was "willing to do anything to get better."

Everyone was convinced, and eight days later he was given a one-day pass to visit his wife before entering the alcohol treatment program. He returned sober from the pass, but he must have brought a bottle with him, since the next morning he was intoxicated and unable to begin the treatment program. He left the hospital two days later against the advice of the staff. (Jellinek, 1946)

To many people the very word *drug* has connotations of danger. Yet most Americans do use some form of **psychoactive drug**—that is, a drug that alters one's psychological state—either occasionally or regularly. Most confine themselves to legal drugs such as alcohol, nicotine, and caffeine, which, precisely because they *are* legal, tend not to be looked upon as drugs. Yet, as can be seen in the case history above, legal drugs can damage people as severely as illegal drugs.

Psychoactive substances do not invariably cause harm. When they are prescribed by physicians, they can be very helpful indeed. In many societies, and in subcultures of our own society, they are an integral part of social and religious ritual. Nor is occasional recreational use, in small doses, necessarily the road to destruction. Certain drugs are an important source of harmless pleasure, as anyone knows who has ever enjoyed a cup of coffee in the morning or a beer at a ball game. It is when drug use becomes habitual and when it begins to erode the person's normal functioning—work, studies, relationships with others—that it is redefined as "abuse." As functioning continues to decline, and as use of and recovery from the drug come to occupy a major portion of the person's life, "abuse" is redefined as "dependence."

In the past few decades drugs have become a major focus of social concern, as evidenced by the recent proliferation of alcohol- and drug-treatment centers and of educational programs aimed at the prevention of abuse. Particularly in the eighties, with the appearance in the illegal drug market of "crack," a cheaper, more powerful, and highly addictive form of cocaine, social anxiety escalated feverishly. A nationwide anticrack campaign claimed billboards and television commercials. Efforts were made to mandate urine testing for holders of high-responsibility jobs in order to detect drug users. In 1986 drug abuse made the cover of *Newsweek* three times in five months. Yet in the early eighties cocaine use among high school students, the targets of the anticrack campaign, actually increased very little, if at all. Alcohol was then and is now America's number-one drug problem. And social alarm, though it may have contributed to prevention, has only just begun to spur the development of effective treatments for the abusers of any drug.

In this chapter we will first describe the common features of drug dependence. Then we will discuss alcohol and nicotine, the most easily available and widely used drugs in our society. Finally, we will examine other varieties of drugs: depressants, stimulants, hallucinogens, and marijuana. Theories as to the cause and treatment of abuse will also be covered.

Though our chapter will go drug by drug, it is important to keep in mind that in many cases drugs are not used individually. Some drug users like to combine effects, a common combination being marijuana and alcohol. Other drug users switch repeatedly from one drug to another. As a result, the current trend in drug-treatment centers is to deal with patients as people who seek *a* drug experience—any alteration in their state of consciousness—rather than to worry over whether they are abusing alcohol, heroin, or some other drug.

THE NATURE OF SUBSTANCE DEPENDENCE AND ABUSE

The discussion of drug abuse is hampered by the fact that neither the society nor the mental health profession has yet agreed on a clear and consistent terminology. For years it was customary to distinguish physiological and psychological need. Drug use that had altered the body's chemistry to the point where its "normal" state was the drugged state, so the body required the drug in order to feel normal, was called **addiction.** By contrast, the psychological dimension of drug abuse—the abuser's growing tendency to center his or her life on the drug—was often called **psychological dependence.** These definitions, however, were not accepted by all professionals. (Indeed, recent editions of the *DSM* reserve the term *dependence* specifically for conditions that involve addiction.) Furthermore, as methods for detecting "withdrawal symptoms" became more precise, researchers discovered that all psychoactive drugs had both physiological and psychological effects; the two could not be separated.

In response to these confusions, *DSM-IV* has placed both the physical and psychological manifestations of pathological drug use under two diagnostic categories: "substance dependence" and "substance abuse." Both problems are defined in terms of behavioral criteria. In other words, the problem lies not in the drug but in the way a person uses the drug. By itself, the fact that a person takes a drug—whether legal or not—does not necessarily indicate dependence or abuse. The drug may or may not be physiologically addictive. Substance use becomes abuse or dependence when the pattern of use causes the person problems.

There are seven criteria for **substance dependence;** fulfillment of any three qualifies the drug user for the diagnosis:

1 *Preoccupation with the drug.* A great deal of time is spent in activities necessary to obtain the substance (e.g., theft), in taking the substance (e.g., chain smoking), or in recovering from its effects.
2 *Unintentional overuse.* Problem users begin to find repeatedly that they have taken more of the drug than they intended.
3 *Tolerance.* As noted, habitual drug use alters the body chemistry. The body adjusts to the drug, so that the usual dose no longer produces the desired effect—a phenomenon called **tolerance.** Some alcoholics, for example, can drink a quart of whiskey a day without seeming intoxicated. As tolerance develops, the person requires larger and larger amounts of the drug in order to achieve the desired biochemical change.
4 *Withdrawal.* With prolonged use, the body eventually *requires* the drug in order to maintain stability. If the drug level is decreased, the person undergoes **withdrawal symptoms,** psychological and physical disruptions ranging from mild anxiety and tremors to acute psychosis and, in extreme cases, death. Consequently, the person often takes the drug in order to avoid or relieve withdrawal symptoms.
5 *Persistent desire or efforts to control drug use.* Many drug-dependent people try repeatedly to quit and repeatedly relapse. Drug dependence is a chronic disorder.
6 *The abandonment of important social, occupational, or recreational activities for the sake of drug use.* Many of life's major functions—work, friendship, marriage, child rearing—conflict with heavy drug use and may be given up as a result.
7 *Continued drug use despite serious drug-related problems.* Many people go on smoking despite emphysema or taking narcotics despite a long record of drug-related arrests. This is no longer recreational use.

DSM-IV also includes the diagnostic category of **substance abuse,** which is essentially a pattern of maladaptive drug use that has not progressed to full-blown dependence. According to *DSM-IV,* a person qualifies for this diagnosis if he or she shows any one of the following:

1 Recurrent drug-related failure to fulfill major role obligations (e.g., absenteeism from school or work, neglect of children).
2 Recurrent drug use in physically dangerous situations (e.g., drunk driving).
3 Drug-related legal problems (e.g., arrests for disorderly conduct).
4 Continued drug use despite social or interpersonal problems (e.g., marital quarrels) caused by the effects of the drug.

ALCOHOL DEPENDENCE

For thousands of years alcohol has been the traditional "high" of Western culture. And unlike most of the other drugs we will discuss in this chapter, it can be purchased legally in all but a few parts of the United States. For both of these reasons, alcohol is the most widely used of all the psychoactive drugs. In 1992, 26 percent of those between twelve and seventeen had had an alcoholic beverage during the previous month, as had 59 percent of those between eighteen and twenty-five (National Institute on Drug Abuse, 1992). In 1987, the average yearly alcohol consumption of adults in the United States was 2.3 gallons of distilled spirits *and* 3.4 gallons of wine *and* 34.4 gallons of beer (U.S. Bureau of the Census, 1990). Substantial as this may seem, it is, statistically, the normal rate of consumption. As for those who drink more, the National Institute on Alcohol Abuse and Alcoholism estimates that nearly 13 million people in the United States are either alcohol-abusing or alcohol-dependent (H. I. Kaplan & Sadock, 1991).

The Social Cost of Alcohol Problems

It is impossible to determine exactly how much damage is done to society at large as a result of alcohol dependence and abuse. Easier to measure is the amount of money it costs. It is estimated that alcohol-related problems cost the American economy more than $121 billion in 1990 (Institute of Medicine, 1990). Most of this economic loss is concentrated in three areas: decreased work productivity, health problems, and motor vehicle accidents.

The largest portion of this loss—about $70 billion—is due to decreased work productivity. Workers with drinking problems are slower and less efficient, lose time on the job, make hasty decisions, cause accidents, and lower the morale of their coworkers. Furthermore, they are more likely to become prematurely disabled and to die young.

As for their medical costs, more than $20 billion was spent in 1990 on medical treatment and support services for alcoholics (Rice et al., 1990). In one estimate, alcohol-dependent employees cost their companies the equivalent of 25 percent of their salaries (Alcoholism Council of Greater New York, 1987). Approximately 40 percent of all occupied beds in American hospitals are filled by people with ailments linked to alcohol consumption (Rice et al., 1990). And the ill effects of alcohol are not limited to the drinker if the drinker is pregnant. Babies born to mothers who drink during pregnancy run a substantial risk of having fetal alcohol syndrome, a pattern of damage involving bodily malformations, mental retardation, and delayed development (see Chapter 18).

Finally, $12 billion is lost annually in alcohol-related motor vehicle accidents (National Safety Council, 1992). Before we comment on the relationship between drinking and driving, it is necessary to clarify the matter of blood-alcohol levels. The effects of alcohol on the nervous system—and consequently on the drinker's behavior—are directly proportionate to the amount of alcohol in the bloodstream. This latter factor is called the **blood alcohol level,** which is expressed in terms of the amount of alcohol in relation to a specific volume of blood. Table 12.1 indicates the approximate relationship between alcohol intake and blood-alcohol level. Note that there is a sex difference. Women have less body fluid (but more fat) per pound of body weight. Therefore, if a 150-pound

Some of the social costs of alcohol abuse are beyond measurement. Five passengers died and more than 100 were injured when the driver of this New York City subway train drove it off the tracks in 1991. It was later determined that he had been intoxicated.

TABLE 12.1
RELATIONSHIPS AMONG SEX, WEIGHT, ORAL ALCOHOL CONSUMPTION, AND BLOOD ALCOHOL LEVEL

		Blood Alcohol Levels (mg/100 ml)					
Absolute Alcohol (ounces)	Beverage Intake*	Female (100 lb)	Male (100 lb)	Female (150 lb)	Male (150 lb)	Female (200 lb)	Male (200 lb)
½	1 oz spirits† 1 glass wine 1 can beer	0.045	0.037	0.03	0.025	0.022	0.019
1	2 oz spirits 2 glasses wine 2 cans beer	0.09	0.075	0.06	0.05	0.045	0.037
2	4 oz spirits 4 glasses wine 4 cans beer	0.18	0.15	0.12	0.10	0.09	0.07
3	6 oz spirits 6 glasses wine 6 cans beer	0.27	0.22	0.18	0.15	0.13	0.11
4	8 oz spirits 8 glasses wine 8 cans beer	0.36	0.30	0.24	0.20	0.18	0.15
5	10 oz spirits 10 glasses wine 10 cans beer	0.45	0.37	0.30	0.25	0.22	0.18

*In one hour.
†100 proof spirits.
SOURCE: Ray (1983).

woman and a 150-pound man have five drinks apiece, she will have a higher blood-alcohol level than he, and consequently will be more intoxicated.

In all states a person with a blood-alcohol level of 0.10 percent is considered by law to be intoxicated. As Table 12.2 indicates, a driver with a blood-alcohol level of 0.10 percent is less cautious, less alert, and slower to react than a nondrinking driver. A nighttime driver who has had several drinks is also laboring under a severe visual handicap, since it has been shown that visual recovery from glare slows down as blood-alcohol level increases (Sekuler & MacArthur, 1977).

The relationship between blood-alcohol level and motor vehicle accidents is all too clear. Alcohol is implicated in as many as half of all car accidents, and its involvement in fatal car accidents is even higher. A California study of 440 young men killed in motor vehicle accidents found that 81 percent of the bodies had drugs in the bloodstream, and of these, 70 percent had alcohol (Stinson & DeBakey, 1992; U.S. Department of Transportation, 1991). In one out of three fatal adult pedestrian accidents, the *pedestrian* has a blood-alcohol level above 0.10 percent. Thus the more

TABLE 12.2
BLOOD-ALCOHOL LEVEL: PHYSIOLOGICAL AND PSYCHOLOGICAL EFFECTS

Blood-Alcohol Level (%)	Effect
0.05	Lowered alertness; usually good feeling; release of inhibitions; impaired judgment
0.10	Less caution; impaired motor function
0.15	Large, consistent increases in reaction time
0.20	Marked depression in sensory and motor capability, decidedly intoxicated
0.25	Severe motor disturbance, staggering; sensory perceptions greatly impaired
0.30	Stuporous, but conscious—no comprehension of world around them
0.35	Equivalent to surgical anesthesia
0.40	Probable lethal dose

SOURCE: Adapted from Ray (1983).

you have had to drink—or the more the driver coming toward you has had to drink—the more likely you are to be injured or killed in a car accident.

Even if alcohol abusers don't drive, they can still cause serious social damage. Alcohol contributes to the incidence of physical assault and sexual offenses. One careful study of young offenders (Tinklenberg & Woodrow, 1974) found that alcohol use was involved in 30 percent of all the corroborated assaults in which tissue damage occurred and in 30 percent of the deaths. In the area of sexual offenses—pedophilia and forcible rape—alcohol use accounted for 90 percent of the drug-related sexual offenses. Impaired judgment also increases the likelihood of unprotected sex, with the possible consequences of pregnancy and sexually transmitted diseases—including AIDS.

The Personal Cost of Alcohol Dependence

The Immediate Effects of Alcohol Pharmacologically, alcohol is considered a depressant. It slows down and interferes with the transmission of electrical impulses in the higher brain centers, areas that control, organize, and inhibit some of our complex mental processes. And it is this release from control that helps people to relax, to stop worrying about what other people think of them, and to have a good time.

The initial effect of alcohol may be to stimulate rather than to depress. With a drink or two, people will often become more talkative, more active. By the time the blood-alcohol level reaches 0.03 to 0.06 percent, two types of effects occur. First, mood and social behavior change. Some people become depressed and remorseful; others become amorous or belligerent. The second effect is that judgment is impaired. Amorous types will begin making wanton remarks to strangers, belligerent types will start fights, and so forth. As the blood-alcohol level continues to rise, the depressant effect of alcohol becomes more obvious. People slow down, stumble and trip, and slur their words. Their judgment is further impaired, and they tend to engage in even more reckless behavior. "Depressive" drunks, for example, may begin loudly confessing their sins and failures.

For a long time it was believed that the "bad" behaviors associated with drinking, particularly sexual indiscretion and belligerence, resulted directly from the physiological effect of alcohol on the brain. Presumably alcohol impeded the brain's inhibition functions, and the "real person" came out. To quote the old Latin saying, *"In vino veritas"*—"In wine, truth." But experiments in which the behavior of people who have drunk alcohol is compared with the behavior of people who merely think they have drunk alcohol suggest that the disinhibiting effect has as much to do with expectations—learned beliefs about what alcohol does to people—as with biochemistry. Increased sexual arousal, in particular, is apparently due more to expectations than to chemical effects (Hull & Bond, 1986). Likewise it appears that beliefs about alcohol's unleashing of immoral and aggressive behavior do much to excuse and maintain such behavior (Critchlow, 1986). The context must also be taken into account—not just the drink but the fact that we are at a party or in a bar. Barrooms, as we know, are where brawls may occur. Therefore, for those inclined in that direction, the expectations associated with both the drink and the barroom may help produce brawling. Whatever their relative contributions, it appears that both alcohol and expectations about alcohol are implicated in the increased aggression of people who have been drinking (Bushman & Cooper, 1990).

The Long-Term Effects of Alcohol Abuse Because it can relieve tension, alcohol is often resorted to as a means of coping with, or at least enduring, life's problems. The ironic result is that alcohol abusers end up with more problems than they had before and fewer resources for dealing with them. Hence they drink more. Hence they have more problems—a classic vicious cycle. In the process, their mental acuteness is lost; memory, judgment, and the power to concentrate are all diminished. As their capabilities are eroded, so is their self-esteem. They neglect and alienate their friends and family. Often unable to work, alcohol abusers typically feel guilty toward their families, but at the same time they may take out their problems on the family. Child abuse, for example, is often connected with alcohol abuse. Alcohol also impairs sexual functioning and is one of the leading causes of impotence. Whether as cause or result of their drinking, alcohol abusers also have very high rates of other psychiatric disorders, especially antisocial personality disorder, depression, and anxiety disorders (H. E. Ross, Glaser, & Germanson, 1988; Roy, DeJong, Lamparski, et al., 1991).

As serious as the psychological consequences are the physiological effects. Habitual overuse of alcohol can cause stomach ulcers, hypertension, heart failure, cancer, and brain damage. Another common consequence is cirrhosis of the liver, which is now the ninth leading cause of death in the United States (National Institute on Alcohol

Abuse and Alcoholism, 1990). In addition, alcohol dependence often entails malnutrition. Alcohol is high in calories, which provide energy, but it is devoid of any known nutrient. Because alcohol-dependent people typically eat little and unselectively, their protein and vitamin intake tends to be dangerously insufficient. In extreme cases they may develop Korsakoff's psychosis (Chapter 16), a severe memory disorder thought to be caused by vitamin B deficiency.

An infrequent but terrifying complication of chronic alcohol dependence is **delirium tremens,** literally translated as "trembling delirium" and better known as the DTs. This severe reaction is actually a withdrawal symptom, occurring when the blood-alcohol level drops suddenly. Deprived of their needed dosage, patients with DTs tremble furiously, perspire heavily, become disoriented, and suffer nightmarish delusions. This condition usually lasts for three to six days, after which the patient may vow never to take another drink—a vow that in many cases is broken shortly after discharge from the treatment center.

In short, alcohol abuse is very damaging to health. Death rates are much higher for alcohol abusers than for nonabusers—two to four times higher in the case of men, three to seven times higher in the case of women (G. Edwards, 1989).

The Development of Alcohol Dependence

As we shall see later in this chapter, there is considerable confusion as to what type of person is likely to become alcohol-dependent. There is also considerable variability in *how* people become alcohol-dependent, but some common patterns have been noted. While some people develop abusive drinking patterns quite rapidly, most go through a long period of social drinking during which they gradually increase the quantity and frequency of their drinking and come to rely on the mood-altering effects of alcohol. As consumption increases, many people begin to experience "blackouts," periods of time in which, under the influence of alcohol, they remain conscious and carry on in a fairly normal fashion but of which they have no memory the following day. The alcoholic-to-be may also, in social situations, begin "sneaking drinks" (e.g., stopping at the bar on the way to the men's room) in order to keep ahead of the others without letting them know. Another serious danger sign is morning drinking, to get oneself "going." Eventually such people get drunk whenever they drink. They may also go on "benders," alcoholic binges lasting several days.

Whatever the pattern, most people headed for alcohol dependence eventually find that they are drunk at least two or three times a week and that they no longer have the ability not to drink. This "loss of control" over alcohol—as defined by the person's being unable to abstain, and habitually drinking more than he or she intended—ranks as a significant early warning sign. (Some alcoholics, however, remain "spree" drinkers, staying sober for long periods but then, often in response to stress, going on benders.) Jellinek (1946), who described many of these patterns, claimed that the total itinerary, from the beginning of heavy drinking to complete defeat by alcohol, took twelve to eighteen years, but for many people the route is shorter. The course of alcohol dependence has interesting parallels with the course of another devastating behavioral disorder, compulsive gambling (see the box on page 274).

Men are more prone than women to drinking problems—current estimates suggest that 9 percent of men suffer from alcohol abuse, compared with 1.5 percent of women (Robins, Helzer, Przybeck, et al., 1988)—and there are marked differences between the sexes in drinking patterns. First, women usually begin drinking later in their lives, experience their first intoxication later, develop dependence later, and come to facilities with shorter histories of drinking problems than do men. Women are more likely than men to cite a stressful event as precipitating the problem, and they are more likely than men to have a problem-drinking spouse or lover. Alcohol-dependent women are much more likely than their male counterparts to drink alone, but when women do drink with someone else, it is likely to be someone close to them. Conversely, men are more likely than women to drink in public places and with strangers. Women also drink large amounts less often, do less bender and morning drinking, and have shorter drinking bouts. Finally, women more frequently combine alcohol with other substances—tranquilizers, barbiturates, amphetamines, hypnotics, antidepressants, or nonprescription drugs (Gomberg, 1981). It is not clear whether these divergent drinking patterns have to do more with the social role differences or with biological differences between men and women.

PERSPECTIVES ON ALCOHOL DEPENDENCE

What causes alcohol dependence? As we shall see in the following section, there are many theories, but no one theory can yet be applied to all the different cases of dependence—the solitary woman drinking at home, the noisy man at the pinball machine, the Junior Chamber of Commerce Man of the Year, the derelict on the sidewalk. At this point the only trait that we know for certain is shared by all alcohol-dependent people is the need for alcohol. As with most kinds of abnormal behavior, multiple factors probably underly each case of alcohol dependence, and the importance of any one factor will vary from person to person.

The Psychodynamic Perspective

Meeting Emotional Needs with Drink Psychodynamic theorists view alcohol dependence as the symptom of an unconscious emotional conflict. Several theorists have attempted to identify that conflict.

The first is that the conflict has to do with unsatisfied dependency needs. This dependency, in turn, is thought to stem from oral fixation. In other words, people become alcohol-dependent in order to obtain oral gratification and to be cared for by others. There is some evidence that problem drinkers do in fact have more intense oral needs than other people. For example, they are much more likely than other people to be heavy cigarette smokers (Maletzky & Klotter, 1974). As for the dependency of problem drinkers, this theory is supported by a wealth of research data (e.g., McCord, McCord, & Gudeman, 1960) and is likely to receive the assent of anyone who has lived with an alcohol abuser. However, most of the evidence for dependency is retrospective, and prospective studies indicate that the problem drinker's dependency, or at least its overt expression, develops out of the drinking rather than vice versa (Vaillant & Milofsky, 1982). Psychodynamic theorists have also proposed that alcohol and other drugs are used to "medicate" strong, sometimes overpowering, feelings of shame, guilt, and self-loathing (Khantzian, 1981, Shaffer & Jones, 1989).

Another motivational theory related to the psychodynamic perspective is directly contrary to the dependency-needs hypothesis: David McClelland and his coworkers have proposed that what leads people to become dependent on alcohol is a drive for power. According to this view, people who feel that they lack control over themselves and their world can obtain from alcohol a renewed sense of confidence and mastery; hence they drink more and more. The aggressiveness commonly seen in problem drinkers—and interpreted by the dependency-need theorists as a defense against passivity—is viewed by this school as a direct expression of the power drive. Likewise, the tendency of problem drinkers to seek relationships with strong individuals is interpreted as an attempt to "borrow" strength from others, rather than as the expression of a desire to be cared for, as the dependency theory would have it. In a series of studies, McClelland and his colleagues have found a strong correlation between excessive drinking and the yearning for power. One finding was that the ingestion of alcohol leads to an increase in thoughts of winning personal victories over adversaries (McClelland, Davis, Kalin, et al., 1972).

Treatment Psychodynamic treatment for alcohol dependence aims less at the "symptom"—that is, the drinking—than at the underlying psychic cause, since according to psychodynamic theory, the symptom will not be relieved until the unconscious conflict is relieved. Insight-oriented psychodynamic therapy, however, has had poor success rates with alcoholism and is not a common form of treatment. When it is used, the therapist will often recommend that the patient also use some supplementary support system, such as Alcoholics Anonymous.

Group treatment programs based on McClelland's power theory have been implemented in some settings. In one program, alcoholics were given a thirty-five-hour intensive group course in power motivation training (Cutter, Boyatzis, & Clancy, 1977). The course included self-study, behavioral exercises, simulations, lectures, and discussions—all designed to help the group members learn alternative means for feeling in control of themselves and their world. For example, patients were taught how to resolve interpersonal conflicts, how to give and receive help, how to influence others, and how to relieve feelings of tension through yoga and meditation. In one study, problem drinkers who received this power motivation training in addition to standard hospital treatment showed a better improvement rate than those who received only the standard hospital treatment (McClelland, 1977).

The Behavioral Perspective

Psychological and Biochemical Rewards From the behavioral perspective, alcohol dependence is viewed as a powerful habit maintained by many antecedent cues and consequent reinforcers. Several suggestions have been offered as to what the primary reinforcer might be: social approval, ability to engage in relaxed social behavior, avoidance of physiological withdrawal symptoms, reduction

The behavioral perspective might explain teenage drinking in terms of the reduction of unpleasant states common to adolescents, such as shyness and insecurity, and the creation of such pleasant states as feelings of well-being and social acceptance.

of psychological tension. The last factor, tension reduction, was for years considered a prime suspect by behaviorists. According to this view, all of us have our share of troubles—anxiety, self-doubt, depression, guilt, annoyance. In the process of trying to reduce our psychological discomfort, some of us will take a drink, and if this works, then alcohol use becomes associated with the alleviation of psychological pain and is likely to be repeated. Eventually, of course, excessive drinking may itself create further psychological distress, especially guilt, which in turn will be alleviated by more drinking. Thus the vicious cycle begins.

The tension-reduction hypothesis has received some support from animal research. In a classic study (Conger, 1951), laboratory rats were given an electric shock whenever they came near their food dishes. As a result, the rats showed hesitation, vacillation, and other signs of inner conflict when they approached their food. When they were injected with alcohol, however, they went up to their food dishes with no signs of conflict. Unfortunately, however, other animal studies have not provided consistent support for the tension-reduction hypothesis.

Today, behavioral theories of alcohol dependence are generally based not so much on negative reinforcement, the reduction of unpleasant states, as on positive reinforcement, the creation of pleasant states. As neuroscience researchers have discovered, one of alcohol's effects on the central nervous system is a release of the neurotransmitters dopamine and norepinephrine and of endorphins, the body's "natural opiates." In a combination of learning theory and biochemical theory typical of contemporary psychology, it is these chemical rewards that many behaviorists now believe are the prime reinforcers of excessive drinking, though tension reduction and other kinds of maladaptive coping are thought to be involved as well.

Learning Not to Drink Early behavioral programs for alcoholism relied primarily on aversion conditioning: alcohol was paired with some unpleasant stimulus, usually electric shock or induced nausea. Such programs had some initial success but also a heavy relapse rate. Only 44 percent of subjects in one large program, for example, were found on follow-up to have remained abstinent (Lemere & Voegtlin, 1950).

The problem with such treatments, presumably, was that while they suppressed the behavior (drinking), they did nothing to alter the conditions that elicited and maintained it. Whatever the biochemical rewards of excessive drinking, compensation for poor coping skills, as noted, is probably involved as well. Under the influence of alcohol dependence, coping skills deteriorate further, at the same time that stresses (e.g., unemployment, marital conflicts) increase. The object of current behavioral programs is to remedy this broad adjustment problem. The alcoholism is still addressed directly. Patients are taught to identify cues and situations that lead to drinking, and through role playing and practicing they are taught alternative responses. But they are also taught new ways of dealing with life: how to solve problems and, by training in relaxation and social skills, how to cope with stress. Such programs have helped many people to stop drinking, but they are not clearly superior to other behavioral or nonbehavioral treatments (Sobell, Toneatto, & Sobell, 1990).

The Cognitive Perspective

Like the behaviorists, cognitive theorists view alcohol dependence as motivated and maintained both by negative reinforcement (tension reduction) and by positive reinforcement (attainment of desired goals). As usual, though, the cognitive theorists focus not on external reinforcers but on cognitive processes—expectations, self-evaluations, attributions—that they see as mediators of alcohol use.

Thinking about Drinking According to expectancy theory (Goldman, Brown, & Christiansen, 1987), people's expectations about the effects of alcohol play a critical role in whether they will use and abuse alcohol. Through modeling—the example of parents, peers, and people on television and in movies—children develop *alcohol expectancies*, beliefs about the effects of alcohol consumption. These expectancies congeal into a schema, which later, when the opportunity to drink arises, will determine how the person will use alcohol and also how he or she will act under its influence. According to research, the major positive expectancies that people hold about alcohol are that it transforms experiences in a positive way, that it enhances social and physical pleasure, that it enhances sexual performance, that it increases power and aggressiveness, that it facilitates social assertiveness, and that it reduces tension (S. A. Brown, Goldman, Inn, et al., 1980). People also hold certain negative expectancies about alcohol—specifically, that it impairs performance and encourages irresponsibility (Rohsenow, 1983)—but for many people who have problems with alcohol, the positive expectancies outweigh the negative, and so they drink, often to excess.

In support of this view, it has been shown that young adolescents' expectations about alcohol do significantly predict whether they will begin drinking, even when other known predictors—age, religious observance, parental drinking patterns—are controlled (Goldman, Brown, & Christiansen, 1987). Such expectations also predict whether they will go on to problem drinking (B. A. Christiansen, Smith, Roehling, et al., 1989; Stacy, Newcomb, & Bentler, 1991). It has been shown, in addition, that heavier drinkers do have stronger positive expectancies about alcohol than do light drinkers (S. A. Brown, Goldman, & Christiansen, 1985). Still, no research has as yet linked expectancies to actual drinking, only to self-reported drinking. Furthermore, while expectancy theory is persuasive on the subject of why people *begin* to drink, it is not as good at explaining why some of them go on to become alcohol-dependent. In the words of one researcher, "Expected consequences may play a greater part in influencing a teenager's first drink than in influencing an alcoholic's millionth drink" (Leigh, 1989, p. 370). By the millionth drink, it is the rare person who would still be nursing hopes of good times and enhanced sexual power.

A second cognitive theory, derived from social psychology, is the self-awareness model (Hull, 1987), which proposes that what makes alcohol reinforcing is its power to disrupt information processing and thereby reduce self-awareness. This is reinforcing in two ways. First, if being self-aware involves painful feelings, such as a sense of failure or guilt, then the suppression of self-awareness would be negatively reinforcing. Second, by reducing our self-awareness, alcohol may disinhibit us—permit us to flirt or tell somebody off—which would be positively reinforcing. Some research findings have supported this theory (Hull, 1987); others have not (Chassin, Mann, & Sher, 1988). As with expectancy theory, a problem with self-awareness theory is that it seems narrow. No one disputes that some drinking problems may stem from an effort to quell feelings of failure, but can this explain all drinking problems? Furthermore, the typical drinker proposed by this theory—reflective, self-focused, sensitive to criticism—is almost the opposite of what, according to empirical findings, the type of person most at risk for alcohol dependence tends to be like: aggressive, assertive, extroverted, and undercontrolled (M. C. Jones, 1968; McCord, McCord, & Gudeman, 1960).

A third cognitive theory, also derived from social psychology, is that alcohol dependence is a self-handicapping strategy (E. E. Jones & Berglas, 1978). According to this theory, the alcohol-dependent person, when placed in a situation likely to lead to failure, will drink in order to have an excuse for failing: "I'd have gotten that raise if it hadn't been for my drinking," or "I'd be able to pass this course if I didn't drink." Thus, by reasoning that the fault lies with the drinking and not with themselves, problem drinkers maintain a semblance of self-esteem. Research has established that people sometimes do use alcohol in this manner (Tucker, Vuchinich, & Sobell, 1981), though it has yet to be shown that self-handicapping actually *leads* to alcoholism. Note that the self-handicapping model has a connection with expectancy theory, for it depends on a widely held alcohol expectancy: that drinking impairs performance. The self-handicapping model is also related to self-awareness theory, in that both see alcoholism as rooted in feelings of failure. In self-awareness theory, however, problem drinkers feel that they have already failed; they drink in order to decrease their awareness of their failure. In the self-handicapping model, problem drinkers drink because they think they *may* fail, and they use alcohol not so much to numb their self-awareness as to control it by attribution, shifting the blame from themselves to the alcohol.

Cognitive Restructuring Cognitive treatments for alcoholism attack the cognitive variables presumably at fault. That is, they aim to change expectancies regarding drinking, to increase patients' sense of competence, and to teach them adaptive ways of coping with failure. This is done through a combination of cognitive restructuring and behavioral techniques. Such programs have had some success in preventing alcohol abuse and other substance abuse in adolescents (Botvin, Baker, Dusenbury, et al., 1990). Cognitive therapists (e.g., Marlatt & Gordon, 1985) have also paid special attention to relapse prevention, using cognitive restructuring to correct mistaken beliefs (e.g., that one lapse means defeat) and teaching the patient how to handle slips in such a way that they do not lead to total relapse. Some cognitive therapists have even guided patients through "planned relapses" in order to coach them to combat the defeatist thoughts that tend to follow slips. (For more on relapse-prevention treatment, see the discussion later in this chapter.)

TABLE 12.3
USE OF ALCOHOLIC BEVERAGES BY SEX, AGE, RACE, EDUCATION, AND INCOME, 1992

Question: Do you have occasion to use alcoholic beverages such as liquor, wine, or beer, or are you a total abstainer?

Category	Percent Answering Yes to Alcohol Use
National	65
Sex:	
Male	72
Female	57
Age:	
18–29	71
30–49	68
50 & older	56
65 & older	—
Race:	
White	66
Nonwhite	50
Education:	
College graduate	78
College incomplete	64
High school graduate	65
Not high school graduate	49
Income:	
$50,000 & over	80
$30,000–49,999	63
$20,000–29,999	64
Under $20,000	56

SOURCE: *Gallup Poll Monthly* (February 1992), p. 46. Reprinted with permission.

The Sociocultural Perspective

All groups in our society are not equally prone to alcohol abuse, so sociocultural factors are clearly involved. Statistics indicate that men are far more likely to abuse alcohol than women are. But more women are drinking than ever before. Some experts trace the rising rate of alcohol abuse among women to their entering the workforce and taking on high-pressure jobs formerly reserved for men. Others argue that the proportion of women with drinking problems hasn't risen but that more women are seeking help for alcohol abuse, rather than drinking in secret (Weisner & Schmidt, 1992).

In general, alcohol consumption rises sharply between ages eighteen and twenty-five but drops off after age thirty-five. Surprisingly perhaps, the more education a person has and the higher his or her income, the more likely that person will be to abuse alcohol. (See Table 12.3.) But these general data conceal racial and ethnic variations. The U.S. Department of Health and Human Services (1991) has reported that white teenagers and young adults are more likely to have alcohol-related problems than are blacks their age. But between ages thirty and thirty-nine, rates of alcohol abuse for black men rise rapidly, surpassing rates for white males. Interestingly, as African-American males' incomes rise, their rates of alcohol abuse fall; the reverse is true for white men. As for women, black women are far more likely to abstain from alcohol than are white women. The fact that income and gender override race indicates that the differences between whites and blacks are the result of different social conditions, not inherited genetic differences.

Within racial patterns there are ethnic patterns. Men of Irish extraction are more at risk than men of Italian extraction. Latino men (especially Mexican-American and Puerto Rican men in their thirties or older) have higher rates of alcohol abuse and dependency than either black or white males. Most Latino women either abstain or drink infrequently.

Charlie Parker (phenobarbital/heroin/ alcohol), died age 34

Billie Holiday (narcotics), died age 44

Hank Williams (alcohol), died age 29

Elvis Presley (barbiturates/alcohol), died age 43

Jimi Hendrix (multiple drug overdose), died age 27

Janis Joplin (heroin), died age 27

Substance dependence is a problem for people in most professions, but in popular music it can be said to be a tradition, or a plague. Various explanations for this phenomenon have been put forward: Musicians keep late hours; they work in nightclubs, where alcohol is all around them (and other drugs are often available as well); many of them grew up poor, and the poor are at greater risk for substance dependence. There is also the more romantic theory that drugs speed the mind to those inner chambers where musical genius dwells. But in fact, the habit is more likely to destroy talent than to nourish it. "Psychological infirmity is no more help to the artist than is a broken arm," writes musical historian James Collier (1978, p. 169). The musicians pictured here all had their careers shortened by substance dependence. Their average age at death was 34.

Native American men have the highest rate of alcohol abuse of all American racial and ethnic groups (U.S. Department of Health and Human Services, 1991). In fact, the American Indian Policy Review Commission declared alcohol abuse "the most severe and widespread health problem among Indians today" (Dorris, 1989). Alcohol is implicated in 40 percent of all Native American deaths, including accidents, liver disease, homicide, and suicide. Almost all crimes for which Native Americans are jailed or imprisoned are alcohol-related (Yetman, 1994).

Why should this be so? Alcoholic beverages were first introduced to Native Americans by European traders. Because they had not encountered alcohol before, Native Americans had no cultural norms defining its proper use. The traders were given to binge drinking and drunken brawls, and their behavior provided the model. Later, it seems, heavy drinking became a form of social protest for Native Americans, as well as an escape from a world in which their cultures, lands, and livelihoods were being destroyed (Dorris, 1989; Yetman, 1994). On most Native American reservations today, substandard living conditions, high rates of unemployment, and extreme poverty are still the norm, and rates of alcohol abuse remain high.

Another cultural correlate of alcohol abuse is religious affiliation. One religious group that seems particularly resistant to alcohol problems is, predictably, conservative Protestants, who have a notably high percentage of alcohol abstainers and a notably low percentage of heavy drinkers. There are also few alcohol abusers among Orthodox Jews, who drink wine but in controlled and primarily religious settings (C. R. Snyder, 1958). Catholic, Reform Jewish, and liberal Protestant groups all contain a fairly high proportion of alcohol users, with the Catholics leading the other groups in the percentage of heavy drinkers. In all religious groups, it appears that attendance at religious services correlates highly with abstinence.

Alcohol Abuse and the Young In recent years, alcohol consumption has been declining among Americans in general, but not among the young. America's children start drinking at a younger age, drink more often, and get drunk more often than most adults realize. By sixth grade, significant numbers of young people have at least tried alcohol, and the proportion of young drinkers increases with each grade. In one survey, 70 percent of high school seniors said they had tried alcohol, and 50 percent had used alcohol during the previous thirty days. Of those who had drunk recently, more than 60 percent had become intoxicated (Hansen, 1993).

The proportion of young people who drink regularly and drink heavily climbs during college. A 1994 survey found that almost half of all college students go in for binge drinking. (See the box on page 300.) Why, when adults are drinking less, are students drinking more? One answer is the "drug culture." For many people, this phrase conjures up images of the hippie pot parties of the 1960s or the crack houses in today's ghettos, but in fact it means something far more ordinary:

> You don't think of the Camel "Smooth" Character, "Spuds McKenzie" for "Bud Light," the "Schlitz Malt Liquor Bull," cigarettes "alive with pleasure," "Virginia Slims—you've come a long way baby," . . . "Miller Time," and "the night which belongs to Michelob." That's the drug culture. (Sterling, 1991, p. 627)

These images and slogans are so much a part of our environment that we hardly think about them—which makes their impact more insidious. Most of the drug ads, especially those for beer, associate drug use with success and happiness. They do not show young drinkers throwing up back at the dormitory or crashing their cars into telephone poles. They show them going on dates, wearing smart clothes, looking vivacious, sexy, and athletic. Parents often loudly condemn the use of illegal drugs but send a mixed message about alcohol abuse. "Don't drink and drive" can easily be in-

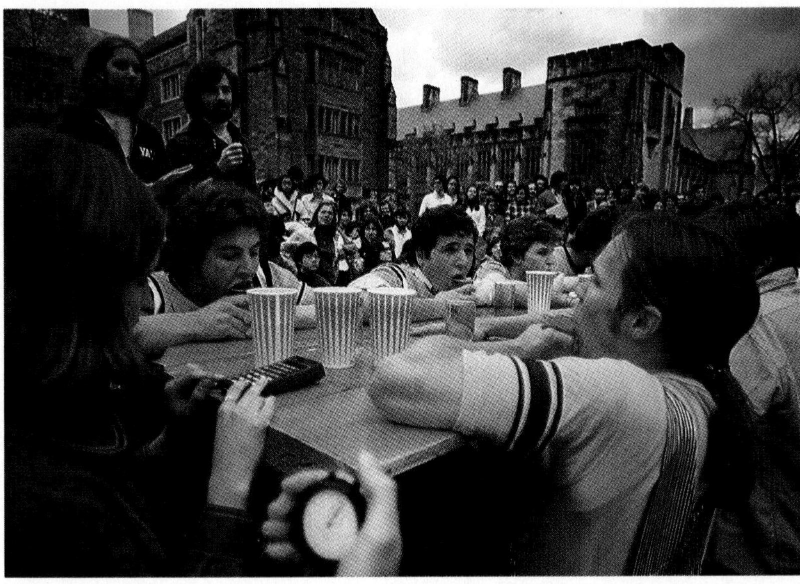

Though now acknowledged as a widespread and serious problem, binge drinking may have actually been encouraged by a collegiate culture that viewed drinking-as-sport. Here, students at a prestigious university participate in an annual beer-drinking contest.

BINGE DRINKING ON CAMPUS

Recently, National Public Radio reporter David Baron, researching a story about drinking among college students, went to a student party in Boston. Introduced to a freshman named Brian, he asked him how much he had had to drink. "Five or six pints of Guinness and then two or three beers, so far," Brian answered. "Are you expecting to have more?" Baron asked. "Yes, uh-huh," Brian replied.

In a recent nationwide survey of almost 18,000 college students, Henry Wechsler (1994) of the Harvard School of Public Health found that half the males and 40 percent of the females engaged in "binge drinking," defined as having five drinks in a row for men, four for women. The vast majority of these students saw nothing wrong with their behavior. Indeed, less than 1 percent felt they had an alcohol problem. Yet the binge drinkers were far more likely than their sober classmates to have been injured, to have gotten in trouble with the police, and to have missed classes because of alcohol. They were also seven times more likely to have had unprotected sex, ten times more likely to have driven after drinking, and eleven times more likely to have fallen behind in their schoolwork than nonbingers. Clearly, they had a problem, whether they thought so or not.

Beer busts on campus, and their destructive effects, are actually nothing new. The major revelation of the Wechsler survey was the degree to which campus alcohol abuse imposes hardships on *nonabusers,* the students who are trying to study while the party is going on. The survey found that at heavy-drinking schools nondrinkers and moderate drinkers were two to three times more likely to report physical assault, sexual harassment, destruction of their property, and interruption of their sleep and studies by drinkers. On some campuses students reported that from Thursday through Sunday the dormitory halls are loud with drunks, the bathrooms unusable. Female students claimed that they wake up Sunday after Sunday to find a strange man in their roommate's bed. (Often the man is strange to the roommate too.) To deal with such problems, certain colleges have now set up "substance-free" dorms. Others have stepped up controls on campus parties, banning kegs and sending out roving patrols of campus police to check on underage drinkers.

According to many experts, however, what is needed is not more rules but a change in student attitudes toward drinking. A recent study (Hansen, 1993) evaluated twelve different risk factors for alcohol use among young people: low self-esteem, poor coping skills, and the like. As it turned out, the factor that had the highest correlation with alcohol use was normative beliefs, namely, the belief "that alcohol use and abuse is prevalent and acceptable among young people" (Hansen, 1993, p. 57). In the past, programs to discourage high school students from abusing alcohol have tried *affective approaches:* stress management, confidence building, and other strategies for fostering emotional strength. Today, such programs are shifting to *social-influence approaches,* which place greater emphasis on changing attitudes and building resistance to peer pressure (Hansen, 1993).

That peer attitudes influence drinking is clear from the wide variations that the Wechsler survey found in different student bodies' drinking patterns. It was the small residential colleges and large universities of the northeastern and north central states that had the highest rates of binge drinking. The large regional or research universities in the South and West had lower rates. Women's colleges and black colleges also had fewer binge drinkers. These variations seem to indicate that the school subculture can encourage or discourage alcohol abuse, which in turn suggests that nonabusers might start trying to make their voices heard. Many people, and probably most young people, do not wish to be killjoys. But just as nonsmokers have begun objecting to secondary smoke, victims of the secondary effects of alcohol abuse should probably begin speaking out.

terpreted to mean "It's okay to get drunk, but don't drive." The message from peers is typically less mixed—indeed, decidedly pro-abuse—and according to recent research (Hansen, 1993), such attitudes are the primary risk factor for alcohol use.

The sociocultural perspective illuminates situational or environmental factors that play a role in alcohol abuse and dependency. But it does not explain why some people succumb to peer pressure while others do not, or why some young people who abuse alcohol in high school or college "outgrow" the problem, whereas some who abstain in their youth become dependent at a later time.

The Biological Perspective

A number of researchers and clinicians believe that the critical predisposing factors in alcohol dependency and abuse are genetically inherited physiological and biochemical anomalies. One type of genetic evidence comes from cross-cultural studies. It has been reported, for example, that Japanese, Koreans, and Taiwanese respond with obvious facial flushing and clear signs of intoxication after drinking amounts of alcohol that have no detectable effect on Caucasians (Harada, Agarwal, Goedde, et al., 1982; P. H. Wolff, 1972). Such ethnic differences have led some investigators to conclude that sensitivity to alcohol is related to genetic factors, possibly affecting the autonomic nervous system.

Goodwin and his coworkers have conducted an even more revealing study with a group of male adoptees (D. W. Goodwin, Schulsinger, Hermansen, et al., 1973). Each of the men in the index group had been separated in infancy from his biological parents, one of whom had been hospitalized at least once for alcohol dependence. Many more of the index children grew up to have drinking problems and to seek psychiatric treatment than did a matched control group of adoptees whose biological parents were not alcohol-dependent. However, the rate of drinking problems among the men in the index group was less than would be expected if their drinking pattern were due solely to genetic factors. Furthermore, in a companion study, the adopted-away daughters of alcohol-dependent parents showed no difference in their rate of drinking problems either from controls or from their nonadopted sisters (D. W. Goodwin, Schulsinger, Moller, et al., 1977). Still, the finding for the adopted sons clearly suggests some measure of genetic influence.

Additional support for the existence of a genetic factor comes from findings that the sons and brothers of severely alcohol-dependent men run a 25 to 50 percent risk of becoming alcohol-dependent themselves at some point in their lifetime, and that there is a 55 percent concordance rate for dependence in MZ twins compared with 28 percent for same-sex DZ twins (Hrubec & Omenn, 1981; Kaprio, Koskenvuo, Langinvainio, et al., 1987; Schuckit & Rayses, 1979). Again, however, genes are obviously not the only factor. As is clear from the fact that 45 percent of the MZ twins were discordant, environment plays its part. However, as suggested by the adoption studies of Goodwin and his colleagues, the genetic component appears to be stronger for men than for women. Twin studies have also suggested that the heritability of alcohol dependence is greater for men than for women. One research team, for example, selected a sample of twins in which one member of each pair was known to be alcohol-dependent or alcohol-abusing. Then the researchers determined whether the other member of each twin pair had problems with alcohol. In all, they compared eighty-five male MZ twin pairs with ninety-six male DZ twin pairs—and forty-four female MZ twin pairs with forty-three female DZ twin pairs—on rates of alcohol dependence and abuse (McGue, Pickens, & Svikis, 1992). They found higher concordance rates for alcohol dependence and abuse for male MZ (76.5 percent) than male DZ (53.6 percent) twins, but no difference in concordance rates for female MZ (38.6 percent) versus DZ (41.9 percent) twins.

Additional adoption studies by Cloninger and his colleagues have complicated the picture further (Bohman, Sigvardsson, & Cloninger, 1981; Cloninger, Bohman, & Sigvardsson, 1981). According to these researchers, a susceptibility to alcoholism is indeed inherited, but in two different ways. What this research group calls Type 1 susceptibility affects both men and women and follows the diathesis-stress model. That is, in order for the genetic susceptibility to lead to actual alcohol dependence, there must be some environmental stress—above all, the stresses associated with low socioeconomic status. Type 2 susceptibility is far more heritable—indeed, it seems to be independent of environmental influences—and is passed from father to son. In Type 2, it is very rare for either the mothers of alcohol-dependent sons or the daughters of alcohol-dependent fathers to be dependent themselves, whereas the heritability from father to son is about 90 percent. The two types also differ in their age at onset—Type 2 generally beginning in adolescence, Type 1 in adulthood—and they differ dramatically in severity. Type 1 is rarely associated with criminal behavior; these drinkers tend to be dependent, quiet-living people. By contrast, Type 2 alcohol-dependent men are impulsive and aggressive, prone to brawling, reckless driving, and other criminal behavior. They also seem to be significantly more prone to depression and suicide (Buydens-Branchey, Branchey, & Noumair, 1989). So it seems likely that there is more than one genetic factor involved in drinking problems and that at least one is sex-linked.

A final indicator of genetic heritability is the fact that experimenters have been able to breed rats with a taste for alcohol. The best known are the so-called P rats—alcohol-preferring rats—developed by Ting Kai Li and his associates (Li, Lumeng, McBride, et al., 1987; J. M. Murphy, Gatto, Waller, et al., 1986). While most rats find alcohol aversive, the P rats not only prefer alcohol solutions to water but will drink to intoxication, and they develop tolerance. They will also do tasks in order to gain access to alcohol. These rats do not meet the diagnostic criteria for alcohol dependence. For example, there is no evidence that they will give up normal behaviors such as grooming or social interaction in favor of alcohol. Nevertheless, as we just saw, they share a number of significant behaviors with alcohol-dependent human beings. And the fact that these behaviors were developed through selective breeding strongly suggests that genes are at work in human drinking problems as well.

The question of what the genetic variable might be—that is, what inherited organic abnormality might predispose a person to alcohol dependence—has been the focus of much biochemical and physiological research. No theory has yet been generally accepted, but researchers have come up with a few interesting leads. There is some evidence, for example, that what is inherited is an increased sensitivity to the reinforcing effects of alcohol. One of alcohol's effects is the enhancement of the brain's alpha waves, a phenomenon associated with feelings of relaxation and euphoria. EEG studies indicate that sons of alcohol-dependent parents experience greater alpha-wave enhancement than do sons of people without drinking problems (V. E. Pollock, Volavka, Goodwin, et al., 1983, 1988). Also, as noted earlier, sons of alcohol-dependent parents experience more of alcohol's tension-reducing effects than do sons of parents who are not alcohol-dependent (Finn & Pihl, 1987; Levenson, Oyama, & Meek, 1987). In other words, it may be that what places people at risk for alcohol dependence is a physiology especially sensitive to alcohol's effects.

Multimodal Treatments

The treatment of alcohol dependence begins with **detoxification**—that is, getting the alcohol out of the person's system and seeing him or her through the withdrawal symptoms. Detoxification can be done at home, under outpatient care, though it is often undertaken in the hospital. The patient is usually given a tranquilizer, such as Serax (oxazepam), for about a week to prevent the seizures that can sometimes follow a "cold-turkey" termination of chronically high alcohol consumption. At the same time, large amounts of vitamins and liquids are administered daily to counter nutritional deficiency and dehydration.

Through this process, the toxic effects of alcohol are eliminated from the system and the body is returned to a near-normal state. That, however, is only a prelude to the behavioral changes that are the major goal of alcohol rehabilitation—the effort to turn a person with a disrupted social, family, and professional life into an integrated, self-sustaining, coping member of society. This is no easy task. Since rehabilitation touches so many aspects of the alcohol-dependent person's life, the better-designed alcohol rehabilitation treatments are multimodal. In the very best programs, patients are provided with occupational therapy, to help them learn or relearn job skills; relaxation training, to teach them how to reduce tension without alcohol; group and individual therapy, to help them learn something about themselves and to show them how to relate to others without drinking; family and marital therapy, to resolve some of the problems at home that may have contributed to and/or resulted from their drinking; and job counseling, to get them back to work. These various forms of treatment are given concurrently, and most, if not all, patients participate in them daily. That, however, is the ideal scenario. In practice, most alcohol treatments, inpatient or outpatient, consist of group therapy twice a week plus educational films and Alcoholics Anonymous meetings (see below).

Sometimes hospitals treatment programs supply an additional deterrent to drinking, in the form of a drug called Antabuse. Antabuse (disulfiram) is a chemical that intereferes with the normal metabolic processing of alcohol for about two days after the medication is taken. When the Antabuse taker drinks alcolhol, a toxic byproduct of alcohol metabolism, acetaldehyde, accumulates in the bloodstream, causing flushing, increased heart rate, and intense nausea. Antabuse treatment is based on the assumption that it will help alcoholics to avoid impulsive drinking (Baekeland, Lundwall, Kissen, et al., 1971), since if they want to take a drink without becoming violently ill, they must stop taking the Antabuse at least two days in advance. The drug thereby provides artificial support for the patient's "will power." However, the support is artificial. Once out of the hospital, many alcoholics simply stop taking the drug. Nor is it clear that Antabuse is particularly effective for those who go on taking it. A national study comparing recovering drinkers who were prescribed Antabuse with controls who received a placebo found no difference in relapse rates between the two groups (Fuller et al., 1990).

One part of most successful rehabilitation programs is support groups. Ex-patients may meet one or more times a week for three to six months, or they may go on meeting indefinitely. This continued contact provides support, reminding people recovering from alcohol dependency that they need not battle their problem alone—that help is available. Furthermore, the follow-up meetings give them the opportunity to continue working on their problems and to learn additional interpersonal coping skills.

The most widely known of these regular meeting programs is Alcoholics Anonymous, better known as AA. The AA program started in the midthirties and has since spread around the world. AA operates on two basic tenets: (1) Once an al-

For thousands of alcohol-dependent people worldwide, Alcoholics Anonymous has been a valuable component of a multimodal treatment program.

coholic, always an alcoholic; and (2) an alcoholic can never go back to "normal" drinking. AA sees alcoholism as a lifelong problem; to combat it, the alcoholic must abstain completely from drink. For help in this difficult task, AA offers not just its regular meetings, at which members come together, usually several times a week, to air their problems, but also its famous "sponsor" system. New members are assigned a sponsor from among the regular members. If the new member has an overpowering urge to drink, he or she can call the sponsor, who will then give support over the phone or even come and stay with the new member until the crisis passes. Sponsors also help new members to begin the so-called Twelve Steps to recovery, which, while spiritual in focus, involve some very practical measures, such as self-examination, admission of fault, and making amends.

AA appears to have an extremely high dropout rate—as high as 80 percent (G. Edwards, Hensman, Hawker, et al., 1967). Of those who remain, AA claims that at least half manage to stop drinking. This claim has not yet been confirmed. However, one study (Cross, Morgan, Mooney, et al., 1990) suggests that long-term involvement in AA does keep people sober. In a follow-up assessment of 158 alcoholics who had been hospitalized for alcoholism treatment ten years earlier, it was found that the best predictor of abstinence and psychosocial stability was continued involvement in AA. Of those who were long-term members of AA, 72 percent were in remission; of those who had not just kept up with AA but sponsored other members, 91 percent were in remission. So AA does seem to be effective for those who commit themselves to the program.

The last decade has seen a tremendous growth in residential care for people who are alcohol-dependent. There are units in the Veterans Administration hospitals and in the psychiatric and general hospitals. In addition, the United States now has more than 400 private residential treatment facilities (Moore, 1985), some of them, such as the Betty Ford Center, highly visible. It is questionable, however, whether alcohol dependents really need to be hospitalized round the clock. Outpatient and day-hospital programs have also been expanding during the last decade, and several studies have found no difference in relapse rates between outpatient and inpatient programs (Alterman, McLellan, O'Brien, et al., 1994; McCrady et al., 1986; W. R. Miller & Hester, 1986). Partly because of such findings, and also because inpatient care costs five to ten times more than outpatient care (Alterman, McLellan, O'Brien, et al., 1994; Holder & Hallan, 1992), most insurance programs are now reluctant to pay for full hospitalization except in cases where the patient has clear medical or psychiatric problems beyond alcohol dependence. Follow-up studies indicate that of people who enter treatment, whether inpatient or outpatient, about 30 percent stop drinking permanently. Most of the others show improvements in their drinking pattern and in problem behaviors associated with drinking, but they will resume some level of drinking and will require ongoing care.

NICOTINE DEPENDENCE

Three out of every ten American adults are smokers (Toneatto, Sobell, Sobell, et al., 1991). Fewer people smoke than drink, but a much higher pro-

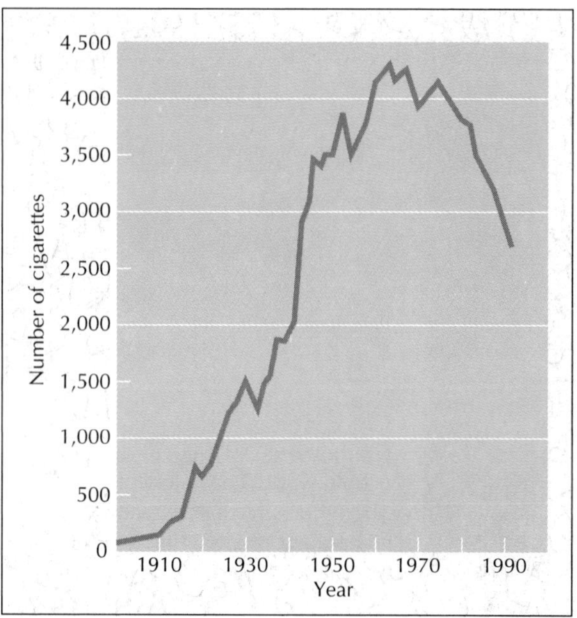

FIGURE 12.1 Cigarette consumption, per capita, in the United States, 1900–1991.

portion of smokers become dependent. As a result, nicotine dependence is the most common form of drug dependence in the United States. Yet discussions of psychoactive drugs often give little if any attention to nicotine, for of all the psychoactive drugs, it is the least destructive *psychologically*. Indeed, it appears to do no psychological damage whatsoever. The disorder "nicotine dependence," as defined by *DSM-IV*, refers primarily to those who want to stop smoking but cannot.

Tobacco contains nicotine, which has apparently paradoxical effects on the central nervous system. On the one hand, it stimulates the system by elevating the blood pressure and increasing the heart rate. At the same time, it has a calming effect. This effect is not just psychological—the product of the pleasure of indulging a habit. Animal studies have shown that injections of nicotine reduce aggression. In any case, nicotine does not seem to impair mental functioning. What it impairs is the smoker's health.

For generations, the use of nicotine products was considered a "vice," and children were warned that smoking would "stunt their growth." Not until 1964, in the famous "Surgeon General's Report" (U.S. Public Health Service, 1964), did the public receive compelling evidence that smoking is a major health hazard. Since 1964 further studies have confirmed this report. Current research shows that each year, more than 400,000 Americans die prematurely from tobacco-induced diseases, including lung cancer (136,000 deaths), coronary heart disease (115,000 deaths), and chronic obstructive lung disease, such as emphysema (60,000). Worldwide, about 2.5 *million* tobacco users die prematurely each year (Mintz, 1991).

Tobacco users are not the only ones who are harmed by smoking. In 1992 the Environmental Protection Agency reported that each year *second-hand smoke* causes 3,000 deaths from lung cancer, contributes to respiratory infections in babies (7,500 to 15,000 of whom require hospitalization), and triggers new cases of asthma in 8,000 to 26,000 young children (reported in Cowley, 1992a). Furthermore, congressional hearings held in the spring of 1994 revealed that tobacco companies not only suppressed research that showed smoking to be a health hazard but also halted research designed to isolate the addictive ingredients in cigarettes. Critics claim that the companies have deliberately raised the level of nicotine in their products to make them even more addicting. Tobacco company executives counter that the reason is to enhance taste (Hilts, 1994).

These findings have resulted in legislation banning cigarette advertisements from radio and television and requiring that each pack of cigarettes sold in this country carry an advertisement of its own potentially lethal effects. In recent years there has been a marked increase in antismoking legislation, with smoking now banned in most movie theaters, stores, and office buildings, as well as on public transportation systems. Current legislative proposals include limiting the amounts of nicotine and tar in cigarettes and enforcing stricter control over distribution (especially to young people).

The tobacco companies have vigorously opposed antismoking legislation, which they compare to Prohibition—the ban on alcohol that led to the growth of a black market. At the congressional hearings in 1994, the top executives of America's seven largest tobacco companies all testified that they did not believe cigarettes were addictive. But all said they would rather their own children did not smoke—prompting columnist Anna Quindlen (1994) to quip, "They were simply in the business of selling the stuff to other people's sons and daughters" (p. 23).

Nevertheless, the antismoking message has gotten through. The proportion of adult Americans who smoked dropped from 45 percent in 1954 to 28 percent in 1991. People who still use tobacco smoke fewer cigarettes than before (Hugick & Leonard, 1991). (See Figure 12.1.) And while many people are quitting, fewer are starting: the percentage of high school seniors who smoke daily dropped from 27 percent in 1975 to 19 percent in 1993 (L. D. Johnston, O'Malley, & Bachman, 1994).

Some, however, have taken up smokeless tobacco (chewing tobacco and snuff) instead. According to one survey, 9 percent of male high school seniors used smokeless tobacco during a sample thirty-day period in 1993 (L. D. Johnston, O'Malley, & Bachman, 1994). Many adolescents apparently believe that smokeless tobacco is safe, which is not the case. While it is not associated with lung cancer, it is associated with throat and mouth cancer.

Perspectives on Nicotine Dependence

Why tobacco should have such a firm hold over so many people is not at all clear. Explanations from various perspectives are similar to those advanced for alcohol dependence. Psychodynamic theorists generally regard smoking as another instance of oral fixation. Behavioral theorists see it as a learned habit maintained by a number of reinforcers—the stimulant effects of nicotine, the pleasure associated with inhaling and exhaling smoke, the experience of tension reduction in social situations, the enhanced image of oneself as "sophisticated," or perhaps all of these, the primary reinforcer varying from smoker to smoker (K. D. O'Leary & Wilson, 1975). Yet these reinforcers seem rather weak to maintain such a dangerous habit.

Is smoking, then, a physiological addiction? Yes. While this seemed obvious to many people, the research findings in favor of the addiction hypothesis were ambiguous. Furthermore, there was no evidence of tolerance; many people go on smoking a pack a day for decades. And the withdrawal symptoms experienced by those who stop smoking—irritability, anxiety, restlessness, difficulty in concentrating, decreased heart rate, craving for nicotine, overeating (White, 1991)—seem mild compared with those of addictions such as alcohol. Hence some people assumed that smoking was a case of psychological dependence rather than physiological addiction.

However, Schachter presented impressive evidence in support of the addiction hypothesis. In a number of studies, Schachter and his colleagues found that smoking does not calm smokers or elevate their mood, nor does it improve their performance over that of nonsmokers. On the other hand, *not* smoking, or an insufficient nicotine level in the bloodstream, causes smokers to perform considerably worse than nonsmokers. Schachter concluded that smokers get nothing out of smoking other than avoidance of the disruptive effect of withdrawal, and that it is for this reason—avoidance of withdrawal—that they smoke (Schacter, 1982).

In support of this conclusion, Schachter and his coworkers have good evidence that smokers regulate their nicotine levels in order to ensure that withdrawal symptoms do not occur. In one experiment, smokers increased their cigarette consumption when low-nicotine cigarettes were substituted for their regular, high-nicotine brands. In another experiment, a group of smokers were given vitamin C, which has the effect of lowering the nicotine level in the bloodstream. (Vitamin C acidifies the urine and so increases the rate at which nicotine is excreted.) Once again the subjects compensated by smoking more. Schachter suggests that this mechanism may explain why people smoke more when they are under stress. Stress, like vitamin C, acidifies the urine. Thus smokers under stress would have to increase their nicotine intake in order to maintain their usual nicotine level and thereby fend off withdrawal.

Treatment programs for smokers tend to report high relapse rates, and relapse is apparently even

Instruction in meditation can help smokers stay relaxed, feel less depressed, and remain focused on their determination to quit smoking.

more common for those who try to quit on their own: according to one survey, only 10 to 20 percent are still abstinent a year later (Lichtenstein & Glascow, 1992). Mark Twain summed it up neatly. He could stop smoking, he said, with great ease; he had done so hundreds of times. Many attempts to assess quitting on one's own and various treatment programs are under way. In one study, Gruder and colleagues randomly assign volunteers to a no-contact control group, a social-support condition, or a discussion condition (Gruder et al., 1993). All subjects were given a self-help manual and asked to watch a stop-smoking television program. No-contact subjects received no further assistance; social-support subjects were taught skills in seeking help from others and resisting temptations to backslide; discussion subjects were asked to attend group sessions, received supportive phone calls, and were monitored by unannounced home visits. Subjects were followed up at six, twelve, and twenty-four months, and considered abstinent if they had not smoked a cigarette during the preceding week. The researchers found that social support was the most effective in the short term (49 percent of the social-support subjects quit, compared with 17.4 percent of the self-help group). But the enhancement did not last. At twenty-four months, only 25.6 percent of the social-support subjects were still abstaining, compared with 18.2 percent of the self-help group.

Why are some people able to break the habit and others not? Recent research suggests that a number of different factors—motivational, cognitive, social—predict who, having quit smoking, will remain abstinent. Not surprisingly, the higher the person's motivation, the less likely a relapse (Marlatt, Curry, & Gordon, 1988), and it makes a difference whether the motivation is intrinsic (the person truly wants to stop smoking) or extrinsic (the person would happily go on smoking but wants to get the family off his or her back). Intrinsic motivation works better than extrinsic motivation (Curry, Wagner, & Grothaus, 1990). Two cognitive factors that predict continued abstinence are self-efficacy (M. E. Garcia, Schmitz, & Doerfler, 1990)—whether the person believes that he or she can actually succeed—and the use of coping mechanisms. Those who struggle actively with the desire to smoke—by talking to themselves, by calling up thoughts of emphysema and lung cancer, by substituting exercise or gum chewing—are most likely to conquer it (R. E. Bliss, Garvey, Heinold, et al., 1989). Another psychological factor that may affect nicotine dependence is depression. One study found that more than 50 percent of smokers who made repeated unsuccessful attempts to quit met the diagnostic criteria for major depressive disorder (Glassman, 1992). If indeed depression is a contributing problem, some smokers might be helped by antidepressant drugs or psychotherapy.

Finally, attempts to quit smoking are affected by the smoker's sociocultural environment. Cigarettes are one of the most heavily advertised consumer products on the market. Tobacco companies spend almost $4 billion a year to promote smoking in the United States alone (*Economist*, May 16, 1992). Often their ads are targeted at the groups that are the most likely to smoke and the least likely to quit—women, African-Americans and Latinos, youths, and the international market, especially Third World countries (Barry, 1991). Although it is difficult to prove cause and effect, the data suggest that advertising pays off. For example, smoking rates have declined more sharply for men than for women—not because fewer women quit smoking, but because more teenage girls and young women take up the habit (Fiore, Novotny, Pierce, et al., 1989). The fact that women are less likely than men to participate in sports, more likely than men to want to lose weight, and more inclined to view cigarettes as relaxing all contribute to this trend. (Waldron, Lye, & Brandon, 1991). Tobacco companies capitalize on "femininity" by featuring sexy young women in their ads and naming their cigarettes "thins," "lights," and "slims." But advertising also can be used to "sell" quitting. Smoking rates dropped twice as fast in California as in the nation as a whole after that state launched a media antismoking campaign (Cowley, 1992b).

The smoker's immediate environment also influences attempts to quit. People whose spouses and friends smoke are more likely to relapse than people who travel in smoke-free circles (G. D. Morgan, Ashenberg, & Fisher, 1988). Would-be quitters benefit more from spouses who support them with positive behaviors such as compliments and praise than with negative behaviors such as nagging (S. Cohen & Lichtenstein, 1990). Findings such as these should enable experts to design treatment programs more resistant to relapse.

OTHER PSYCHOACTIVE DRUGS

For the person in search of a potent psychoactive drug other than alcohol, a wide variety of drugs—depressants, stimulants, hallucinogens—can be equally destructive if they are used habitually. Most of these drugs are nothing new. Opium has been easing people's pain for almost 9,000 years. And until recently many of these drugs were sold

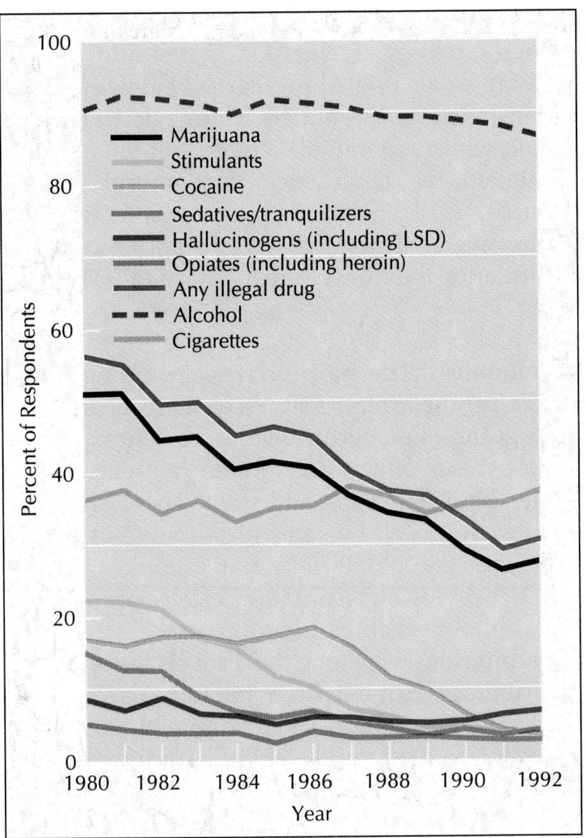

FIGURE 12.2 Trends in drug use among college students. Drug use declined during the 1980s but began to rise again around 1990. In contrast, alcohol and cigarette use remained fairly constant throughout this period.

legally over the counter in the United States. In the nineteenth century countless numbers of self-respecting women thought nothing of taking laudanum, a form of opium, to help them sleep. During the Civil War morphine was commonly administered as a cure for dysentery and other ailments, with the result that many soldiers returned from the war as morphine addicts. At the beginning of this century, the major ingredient in the best-selling cough syrups was a recently discovered miracle drug called heroin. But eventually controls began to be imposed. In 1914 Congress passed the Harrison Act, making the nonmedical use of the opiates illegal. Marijuana was made illegal in some states in 1937. Most of the drugs that we will discuss in the remainder of this chapter cannot be legally purchased for recreational purposes. They must be obtained either from a doctor or from illegal sources. Many people do obtain them, however. Figure 12.2 illustrates trends in drug use among college students. Prevalence rates for most drugs declined during the 1980s but began to increase again starting around 1990. In contrast, the use of legal drugs (alcohol and cigarettes) has remained fairly constant throughout this period.

Depressants

As we have seen in the case of alcohol, a **depressant** is a drug that acts on the central nervous system to reduce pain, tension, and anxiety, to relax and disinhibit, and to slow intellectual and motor reactivity. Along with alcohol, the major depressants are opiates, sedatives, and tranquilizers. All have a number of important effects in common: tolerance develops; withdrawal symptoms occur; and high dosages depress the functioning of vital systems, such as respiration, and thus may result in death.

Opiates The **opiates** are drugs that induce relaxation and reverie and provide relief from anxiety and pain. Included in this group are opium, the derivatives of opium, and chemically synthesized drugs that imitate certain effects of opium.

The grandfather of the opiates is **opium,** a chemically active substance derived from the opium poppy. Early in the nineteenth century, scientists succeeded in isolating one of the most powerful ingredients in opium. This new opiate, which they called **morphine** (after the Greek god of dreams, Morpheus), was soon widely used as an *analgesic,* or pain reliever. As the years passed, however, it became clear that morphine was dangerously addictive. So scientists went back to work, trying to find a pain reliever that would not cause addiction. In 1875 this research culminated in the discovery, by Heinrich Dreser (who also discovered aspirin), that a minor chemical change could transform morphine into a new miracle drug, **heroin,** much stronger than morphine and presumably nonaddictive. (This presumption was, of course, cruelly mistaken.)

The final entry in our list of opiates is **methadone,** a synthetic chemical developed by the Germans during World War II, when they were cut off from their opium supply. Methadone differs from other opiates in three important ways. First, it is effective when taken orally, so injection is not necessary. Second, it is longer-acting. Heroin, for example, takes effect immediately, and is active for only two to six hours. Methadone, by contrast, takes effect slowly—likewise, its effects taper off slowly—and it is active for twenty-four to thirty-six hours. Third, because of its slow onset and offset, methadone satisfies the craving for opiates without producing an equivalent euphoria, or "high." For this reason it is now used as a replacement drug in the treatment of heroin addicts.

Our discussion will focus on heroin, which is the most widely abused opiate in the United States. Through the early 1970s heroin use increased each year. In 1972–1973 there were an estimated 500,000 to 600,000 opiate abusers in the United States, most of them on heroin. Since then, the percentage of heroin users in the country seems to have remained constant.

Heroin is normally taken by injection, either directly beneath the skin ("skin-popping") or into a vein ("mainlining"). The immediate positive effects of mainlining heroin are twofold. First is the "rush," lasting five to fifteen minutes. As one addict described it, "Imagine that every cell in your body has a tongue and they are all licking honey" (Ray, 1983). The second effect is a simple state of satisfaction, euphoria, and well-being, in which all positive drives seem to be gratified and all negative feelings—guilt, tension, anxiety—disappear completely. As noted, this artificial paradise lasts only two to six hours, after which the heroin addict needs another injection.

Such are the positive effects. The negative effects are even more impressive. In the first place, not all people have the honey-licking experience. All users respond initially with nausea, and for some, this response outweighs the euphoric effects. Second, if heroin use becomes regular, both addiction and tolerance develop. As with alcohol and nicotine, people dependent on heroin must continue dosing themselves in order to avoid withdrawal symptoms, and as in alcoholism, this eventually requires larger and more frequent doses.

Third, should withdrawal take place, it can be a miserable experience. Withdrawal symptoms begin about four to six hours after the injection and vary in intensity according to the dosage regularly used. The first sign of withdrawal is anxiety. Then comes a period of physical wretchedness, something like a bad case of flu, which lasts one to five days. The symptoms generally include watering eyes, a runny nose, yawning, hot and cold flashes, tingling sensations, increased respiration and heart rate, profuse sweating, diarrhea and vomiting, headache, stomach cramps, aches and pains in other parts of the body, and possibly delirium and hallucinations as well—all this combined with an intense craving for the drug. Nevertheless, heroin withdrawal is not as devastating as some novels and movies have depicted it to be, particularly since in the hospital setting drugs are commonly used to relieve the symptoms.

Most people believe that repeated exposure to opiates automatically leads to long-term addiction. An alternative view is that drug use represents a means of adapting to major stresses in one's life; if these stresses are temporary, the addiction is likely to be also (B. Alexander & Hadaway, 1982). For instance, many soldiers became dependent on heroin while serving in Vietnam, but few of them continued the habit once they returned home (Bourne, 1974). Similarly, most people who are given opiates in the hospital do not become addicted after they have left the hospital (Melzack, 1988).

Barbiturates The **barbiturates,** including Nembutal (pentobarbital) and Seconal (secobarbital),* are a group of powerful *sedative,* or calming, drugs whose major effects are to alleviate tension and bring about relaxation and sleep. These drugs are legally prescribed by some physicians as sleeping pills. They are sold illegally on the street as "downers" to provide an alcohol-like experience without the alcohol taste, breath, or expense.

Barbiturates were long the drug of choice for suicide attempts. An overdose first induces sleep and then stops respiration. Furthermore, the overdose need not be made up solely of barbiturates. Both barbiturates and alcohol are depressants, so their combined impact is multiplied in what is called a **synergistic effect.** If a barbiturate is taken with alcohol, the effect is four times as great as that of either of the drugs taken alone (Combs, Hales, & Williams, 1980). The person who combines the two drugs runs the risk, intentionally or unintentionally, of becoming a suicide-overdose statistic. This was the cause of the well-publicized deaths of Judy Garland and Marilyn Monroe. Today, partly because of their danger, barbiturates are less widely prescribed, but, as noted, they are still sold illegally and continue to be implicated in many suicides.

The use of barbiturates by the young is generally recreational and sporadic. Among older people, barbiturate use typically begins as a way of relieving insomnia. As we shall see, however, barbiturates, along with other depressants, tend over time to aggravate rather than relieve sleeping problems. So the person takes more and more of the drug and eventually becomes addicted.

In their effects, which generally last from three to six hours, barbiturates are similar to alcohol. Like alcohol, they disinhibit, induce relaxation and mild euphoria, and impair judgment, speech, and

*Drugs have both a brand name (e.g., Valium) and a generic or chemical name (e.g., diazepam). While the brand name may have little or no relationship to the drug's chemical structure, it is usually better known than the chemical name. Therefore our discussion will generally use brand names.

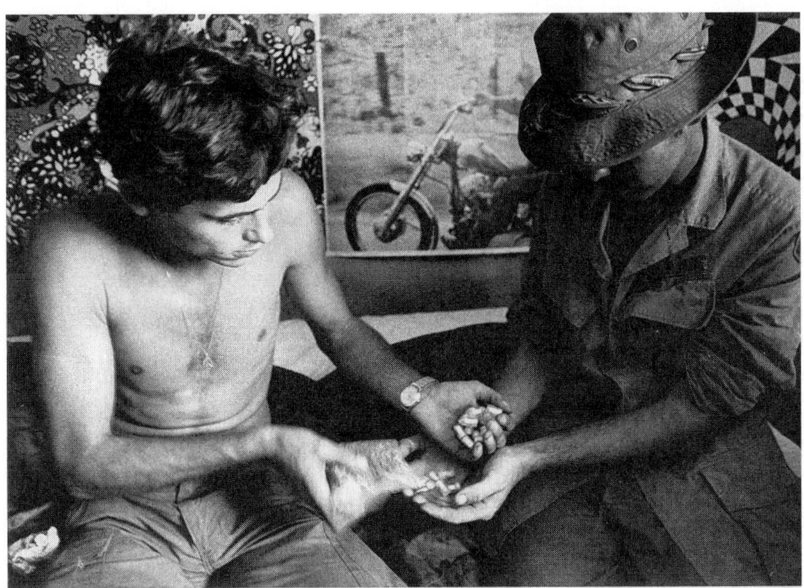

Heroin is highly addictive, but addiction to it may depend on the person's situation. Most military personnel who abused the drug in Vietnam gave it up once that extremely stressful experience was behind them.

motor coordination. Like alcohol-dependent people, barbiturate addicts will exhibit an unsteady gait, slurred speech, diminished intellectual functioning, and confusion. Again like alcohol, the barbiturates, though they are technically depressants, often have a stimulating effect, especially if they are taken with the expectation of "having some fun" rather than of getting to sleep (Wesson & Smith, 1971). Indeed, one of the major concerns of those who study barbiturates is the relationship between aggression and Seconal, a favored barbiturate of the young. For most people, however, the stimulating effect is only an early phase of barbiturate intoxication and wears off within a half hour. A final area of similarity between barbiturates and alcohol is the matter of withdrawal. Withdrawal from barbiturate addiction is similar to withdrawal from alcohol dependence and is equally unpleasant. Without medical supervision, either can result in death.

Tranquilizers and Nonbarbiturate Sedatives Within the last decade, the dangers associated with barbiturates have led to their widespread replacement, as a prescription sleeping medication, by such nonbarbiturate sedatives as Dalmane and Halcion. At the same time, **tranquilizers** (also called *anxiolytics*), such as Tranxene (chlorazepate), Librium (chlordiazepoxide), and Valium (diazepam), which have long been used in the treatment of anxiety disorders and stress-related physical disorders, are also prescribed for insomnia.

All these drugs have essentially the same problems as the barbiturates. They are habit-forming and they have serious side effects, including drowsiness, breathing difficulties, and impaired motor and intellectual functioning. The elderly are particularly vulnerable to the dangers of these drugs, for they are more likely to have disorders the drugs can aggravate—respiratory disorders and kidney and liver ailments (Institute of Medicine, 1991). Taken in high doses over a long period, these drugs can also create symptoms very close to those of major depression. Finally, like barbiturates, tranquilizers and nonbarbiturate sedatives have a synergistic effect in combination with other depressants, though the risk of accidental suicide is not as great.

As with barbiturates, dependence on nonbarbiturate sedatives often begins with a sleeping problem. The person takes the drug and initially obtains some relief. After about two weeks of continuous use, however, tolerance develops, and the usual dose no longer produces a good night's sleep. Yet at this point many people go on taking the drug, for two reasons. First, by this time their difficulties in sleeping may not only have returned; they may be worse than before. Prolonged drug use often creates what is called **drug-induced insomnia,** a pattern of fitful and disrupted slumber, without any deep sleep. Faced with this new problem, many users reason that if they needed pills before in order to sleep, now they *really* need them. Second, these drugs suppress *rapid-eye-movement (REM)* sleep, the stage of sleep in which dreams occur. If, after a week or two of drug-induced sleep, users try to sleep without the medication, they are likely to experience a *REM rebound*—a night of restless dreaming, nightmares, and extremely fitful sleep—after which they may go back to the drug simply to avoid a repetition of such a miserable night. (Dalmane is the only one of these drugs that suppresses REM sleep but does not produce a REM rebound, because it stays in the bloodstream for more than twenty-four hours. As a result of its prolonged effect, however, it produces daytime hangover and sedation effects.)

Thus although the drug soon loses its effectiveness against the original sleeping problem, the usual solution is not to abandon the drug but rather to take more of it. Once the person increases the dose to about two to three times the normal sleep-inducing dose, addiction begins to develop. And from that point on, the drug becomes a way of life.

Tranquilizers, of course, are taken not just for insomnia but for generalized anxiety—anxiety that is often the result of high-pressure jobs and an overstressful environment. Possibly for this reason, minor tranquilizers are among the most commonly prescribed drugs in this country, with more than 70 percent of the prescriptions written not by psychiatrists but by general-practice physicians—in other words, the family doctor (Clinthorne, Cisin, Balter, et al., 1986). While the majority of people who take tranquilizers develop no problems, many suffer side effects and some do become dependent (see Chapter 21).

Stimulants

The **stimulants** are a class of drugs whose major effect, as the name indicates, is to provide energy, alertness, and feelings of confidence. We have already discussed one widely used stimulant, nicotine. Another is caffeine. Far more powerful are the amphetamines, which can be obtained only by prescription or "on the street," and cocaine, which must be bought illegally.

Amphetamines The **amphetamines** are a group of synthetic stimulants—the most common are Benzedrine (amphetamine), Dexedrine (dextroamphetamine), and Methedrine (methamphetamine)—which reduce feelings of boredom or weariness. Suddenly users find themselves alert, confident, full of energy, and generally ready to take on the world. The amphetamines depress appetite—hence their use by people with weight problems. When taken in small doses for brief periods, they improve motor coordination—hence their use by professional athletes. And they inhibit sleepiness—hence their use by college students preparing for exams. Contrary to campus wisdom, however, they do not improve complex intellectual functioning (Tinklenberg, 1971a). The amphetamine user may experience a number of physical effects, including elevated blood pressure, racing heartbeat, fever, headache, tremor, and nausea. Psychologically, the user may feel restless, irritable, hostile, confused, anxious, or, briefly, euphoric (H. I. Kaplan & Sadock, 1991).

As long as they are taken irregularly and in low or moderate doses, amphetamines do not appear to pose any behavioral or psychological problems. As with most other psychoactive drugs, the problems arise from high doses and habitual use. Once use becomes habitual, tolerance develops, and accordingly higher doses become necessary. At the far end of the amphetamine-abuse spectrum are the "speed freaks," people who inject liquid amphetamine into their veins for periods of three to four days, during which they neither eat nor sleep but remain intensely active and euphoric to the point of mania. This heightened activity level can easily lead to paranoid and violent behavior.

Of special importance to the student of abnormal psychology is the resemblance between the effects of amphetamine abuse and the symptoms of paranoid schizophrenia (Chapter 14). Under the influence of heavy doses of amphetamines, people may express the same delusions of persecution that we see in the paranoid schizophrenic (Bell, 1973; S. H. Snyder, 1979). This amphetamine psychosis, the closest artificially induced counterpart to a "natural" psychosis, appears to be unrelated to any personality predispositions and is thus assumed to be the direct result of the drug. Accordingly, research is now in progress with both animals and human beings to determine whether paranoid schizophrenia may be caused by the same chemical changes that amphetamines induce in the brain. (This research will be discussed in Chapter 15.)

Cocaine Unlike the synthetic amphetamines, **cocaine** is a natural stimulant; it is the active ingredient in the coca plant. An "in" drug in the twenties, cocaine again became very fashionable in the seventies. Its popularity peaked in the mideighties at 5.8 million users and then declined to 1.3 million users in the United States by 1993 (preliminary estimates, National Institute on Drug Abuse, 1994). Until recently it was quite expensive, and consequently its regular users tended to be middle- and upper-class white-collar workers and executives. (It was also favored by entertainment celebrities, whose glamour attached itself to the drug.) But with the development of the variant form called crack cocaine, this drug is now within the

Readily available and cheap, crack has brought cocaine—once considered a drug for an overpaid young elite—within reach of just about everyone. As a result, thousands of lives have been devastated since the crack epidemic began in the 1980s.

buying power of people on weekly allowances. A vial of 0.1 gram of crack "rocks" may sell for as little as 50 cents.

In its classic form, cocaine is sold as a powder, which may be injected but is usually "snorted"—that is, the powder is inhaled into the nostrils, where it is absorbed into the bloodstream through the mucous membranes. A more elaborate procedure is "freebasing," in which the powder is heated with ether or some other agent—a process that "frees" its base, or active ingredients—and is then smoked. This method carries the psychoactive ingredients to the brain more quickly, and thereby delivers a more rapid high, than snorting or even injection.

Crack is a form of freebased cocaine that is sold in small chunks, or "rocks," which are smoked in a pipe. Because it is freebased, crack is exceptionally powerful, producing in seconds an intense rush, which wears off within twenty minutes. The rush produced by a snort of traditional cocaine does not take effect for about eight minutes, lasts about twenty minutes, and is milder than that of crack.

Cocaine intoxication is characterized by excitement, intense euphoria, impaired judgment, irritability, agitation, and impulsive sexual behavior. Physically, the user's blood pressure and heart rate increase. If a high dose is taken, seizures and cardiac arrest may result. Some people develop transient periods of paranoia from cocaine use, and those who do may be at higher risk for developing psychosis in the future (Satel & Edell, 1991).

As with amphetamines, tolerance develops with regular use of cocaine, and prolonged heavy use is followed by severe withdrawal symptoms. In a study of fourteen "binge" users, Gawin and Kleber (1986) charted the withdrawal symptoms in three distinct phases (Figure 12.3). The first phase, known to cocaine users as the "crash," begins horribly. Within a half hour of the final cocaine dose, the person experiences a mounting depression and agitation combined with an intense craving for the drug. These feelings then change to fatigue and an overwhelming sleepiness, which last several days. In the second, or "withdrawal" phase, the person returns to deceptively normal functioning, which then gives way to a fluctuating state of boredom and listlessness, mixed with anxiety. At this point, strong cocaine cravings return, and the person may begin another binge. If not, the withdrawal phase passes in anywhere from one to ten weeks. It is followed by phase 3, "extinction," in which the person regains normal functioning, though with occasional cocaine cravings, usually in response to some conditioned stimulus, such as seeing old cocaine-using friends. Such episodic cravings may recur indefinitely.

Caffeine When coffee was first introduced to Europe during the Renaissance, many people considered it dangerous because of its stimulating properties. But gradually, because of those very properties and also because people came to like its distinctive taste, the new import caught on. Today millions of people find it hard to get going in the morning without a cup of coffee. Coffee is also widely used in social rituals. When it is too early in the day to offer a person a drink, coffee is often brought out.

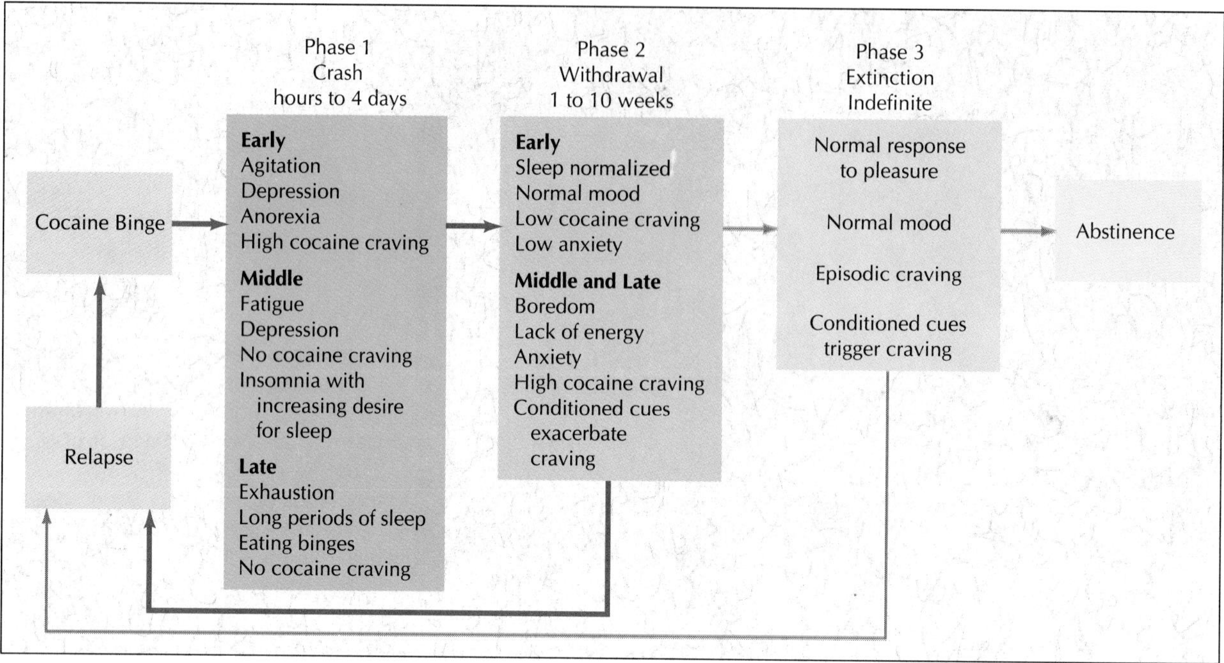

FIGURE 12.3 The three phases of cocaine withdrawal. As the symptom lists show, the craving for cocaine disappears in phase 1 only to reappear in phase 2 and then dissipate very gradually. The arrows at the bottom indicate the likelihood of relapse: strong in phase 2, moderate in phase 3. (Gawin & Kleber, 1986)

Coffee contains caffeine, a stimulant found also in tea, cola drinks, cocoa, and some other forms of chocolate. Like so many other psychoactive substances, caffeine is harmless in small amounts. But in excess—*DSM-IV* places the cutoff at 350 mg (about three cups of coffee or strong tea, or three glasses of cola)—it can cause intoxication, marked by nervousness, excitement, rambling thoughts, motor agitation, insomnia, muscle twitching, a flushed face, an irregular heartbeat, and an increased need to urinate: symptoms that many of us will recognize. Whether or not habitual caffeine users become intoxicated, they suffer withdrawal symptoms—irritability, moodiness, headache, fatigue—that can last a week if they are deprived of their usual dose (Hughes, Oliveto, Helzer, et al., 1992). The inclusion of caffeine on the list of substances that can be abused is controversial. *DSM-IV* includes a diagnosis of "intoxication" but does not recognize abuse, dependence, or withdrawal.

In the course of the health-food movement of the last twenty-five years, caffeine, along with sugar and saturated fats, has come under increasing suspicion. Food manufacturers, as usual, have been quick to respond. Caffeine-free soft drinks and sophisticated decaffeinated coffees are now widely available, and many people have switched to them.

Hallucinogens

The **hallucinogens** are a class of drugs that act on the central nervous system in such a way as to cause distortions in sensory perception—hence their name, which means "hallucination producing." Unlike the stimulants or depressants, they achieve their effect without substantial changes in level of arousal. Tolerance develops rapidly to most hallucinogens, but there is no evidence that they are physiologically addictive. There are many hallucinogens, including mescaline, psilocybin, PCP, and, best known of all, LSD, referred to by pharmacologists as lysergic acid diethylamide and by users as "acid." Despite this variety, rarely can any hallucinogen other than LSD or PCP be bought on the street.

LSD was originally synthesized by a Swiss chemist, Albert Hoffman, in 1938. Five years later, after working one morning with his new chemical, he had an interesting experience:

> Last Friday . . . I was forced to stop my work in the laboratory . . . and to go home, as I was seized by a peculiar restlessness associated with the sensation of mild dizziness. On arriving home, I lay down and sank into a kind of drunkenness which was not unpleasant and which was characterized by extreme

> activity of imagination. As I lay in a dazed condition with my eyes closed (I experienced daylight as disagreeably bright) there surged upon me an uninterrupted stream of fantastic images of extraordinary plasticity and vividness and accompanied by an intense, kaleidoscope-like play of colours. This condition gradually passed off after about two hours. (Hoffman, 1971, p. 23)

Hoffman guessed that this experience might have been due to his having ingested some of the new chemical on which he was working. So he purposely swallowed a small amount of LSD and found that he had indeed guessed correctly.

LSD and the other hallucinogens seem to work by interfering with the processing of information in the nervous system. That is their attraction and their danger. They can produce a kaleidoscope of colors and images. They can give the user a new way of seeing things. For example, they can produce changes in body image and alterations in time and space perception (H. I. Kaplan & Sadock, 1991). And they may open up new states of awareness, allowing the user to find out things about the self that were never imagined before. These are potentially attractive benefits. The problem arises with people who are unable to process or accept the new kinds of perceptions induced by hallucinogens. The person whose grasp on reality is not firm, who derives great support from the stability of the surrounding world, or who has emotional problems may suffer negative effects, possibly for years, from any of the hallucinogens.

The hallucinogens are most harmful when they produce a "bad trip," in which the user becomes terrified and disorganized in response to distorted perceptions. Such an experience is not quickly forgotten. For some people, the drug-induced disruption of their relationship with reality is so severe that they require some kind of long-term therapeutic assistance (Frosch, Robbins, & Stern, 1965). Also, a small percentage of regular LSD users suffer "flashbacks"—spontaneous recurrences, when not under the drug, of hallucinations and perceptual distortions that occurred under the drug—a phenomenon that may disrupt their functioning considerably. Flashbacks and other disruptions of visual processing can recur for as long as eight years after LSD use (H. D. Abraham, 1983; H. D. Abraham & Wolf, 1988). They are more likely to occur when the former LSD user is under stress, fatigued, or ill (H. I. Kaplan & Sadock, 1991).

PCP (phencyclidine), or "angel dust," is a hallucinogen that surfaced in the seventies and was widely used, since it was cheap, easily available, and often mixed with (or misrepresented as) other substances. The drug soon acquired a bad reputation. For one thing, overdoses were common and extremely toxic. In one large mental health facility in Washington, D.C., PCP poisoning accounted for one-third of inpatient admissions between 1974 and 1977, outstripping even alcoholism (Luisada, 1977). A more serious risk was PCP's behavioral toxicity, the tendency of users to harm themselves—through burns, falls, drowning, automobile accidents—and also to endanger others as a result of the paranoia and perceptual distortions produced by the drug. These problems discouraged many users, and PCP consumption has been declining steadily since the late seventies.

Marijuana and Hashish

Marijuana and hashish are often classified as hallucinogens, yet they deserve separate treatment. In the first place, their effects are considerably milder than those of the hallucinogens described above. For this reason, they are often referred to as "minor hallucinogens," while LSD, PCP, mescaline, and the others are called "major hallucinogens." Second, although the major hallucinogens may be widely used, the use of marijuana and hashish is far more common. More than one out of every two Americans between the ages of eighteen and twenty-five has tried marijuana (National Institute on Drug Abuse, 1989), and many, having tried it, become frequent users. Marijuana use among the young increased dramatically in the 1970s, peaked in 1979 and 1980, and has been declining slowly since then, but it is still America's most popular illicit drug.

Marijuana and hashish are both derived from cannabis, a hemp plant that grows, cultivated and wild, in many countries. Marijuana consists of the dried and crushed leaves of cannabis. Though it is usually rolled into a cigarette, or "joint," and smoked, it can also be eaten. Hashish, derived from the resin rather than the leaves of cannabis, is about five or six times stronger than marijuana. Like marijuana, it can be eaten, but it is usually smoked in a specially designed pipe.

The active ingredient is the same in both forms: THC (delta 9, tetrahydrocannabinol), which most researchers agree is not physiologically addictive. THC has two consistent physiological effects. The first is an accelerated heart rate. As the dose increases, so does the heart rate, which may go up to 140 to 150 beats per minute. The second change is a reddening of the whites of the eyes. Both effects disappear as the drug wears off.

The behavioral effects of marijuana have been studied in a variety of situations. The effects of a mild marijuana high on simple behaviors are either nil or minimal. The person can easily turn on the record player, dial a phone number, make a pot of coffee, and so forth. However, as the complexity of the task increases, as speed of response becomes more important, and as a more accurate sense of time and distance is required, the impairment of ability from a single-joint marijuana high becomes more apparent. It has been clearly established that driving under the influence of marijuana is dangerous (Hollister, 1988).

Having discussed the physiological and behavioral effects, we now come to the major reason for using marijuana and hashish—the psychological effects. These have been summarized by Tinklenberg (1975):

> Initial effects of cannabis at low doses usually include euphoria, heightening of subjective sensory experiences, alterations in time sense, and the induction of a relaxed, laissez-faire passivity. With moderate doses, these effects are intensified with impaired immediate memory function, disturbed thought patterns, lapses of attention, and a subjective feeling of unfamiliarity. (p. 4)

It should be noted that the latter group of reactions are generally not at all disturbing. The individual simply feels "spaced out"—a not unpleasant experience for most people under relaxed conditions. Many marijuana users report being totally absorbed in their drug experience while it is happening. During these episodes of total involvement, the person's perceptual, imaginative, and cognitive resources are completely engaged (Fabian & Fishkin, 1981).

There is also a negative side to marijuana: It can heighten unpleasant experiences. The drug may intensify an already frightened or depressed mood until the person experiences acute anxiety. This is most likely to happen to an inexperienced user who takes a large dose and is unprepared for its effects (Grinspoon, 1977). At high levels of THC intake, the effects and the dangers are similar to those of LSD. Some people experience sensory distortions, depersonalization, and changes in body image—all of which can result in a panic reaction and a fear of "going crazy." At this point, intervention by a professional or a trained lay therapist becomes necessary, and short-term psychotherapy may eventually be required. These severe reactions to the use of THC are the exception, however, not the rule, and they generally occur only at the higher dose levels.

Much less clear than the short-term effects of high doses of THC use are the long-term effects of low doses. Can regular use of marijuana or hashish cause psychological or physiological damage? This question has polarized scientists as well as generations (Maugh, 1982). For scientists there are four areas of specific concern.

The first has to do with the effect of prolonged heavy marijuana use on the blood levels of the male sex hormone, testosterone. There seems to be general agreement that regular marijuana use (about nine joints a week) for six or more months will result in a reduction of the testosterone level in the blood (L. L. Miller, 1975). The degree of testosterone reduction is directly related to the amount of marijuana smoked. But even the 40 percent reduction in testosterone reported in the original study of this problem (Kolodny, Masters, Kolodner, et al., 1974) does not seem to be enough to impair significantly the sexual activity of males *with established patterns of sexual activity*. Nevertheless, variations in sex-hormone level have a greater impact on the sexual activity of men who have not yet stabilized their patterns of sexual behavior. Therefore it is possible, though it has not been proved, that heavy chronic marijuana use by young sexually inactive men could result in impaired sexual functioning.

The second question is whether marijuana use suppresses immune reactions—the body's mechanisms for fighting off the invasion of foreign substances such as germs. The evidence is fairly solid that chronic marijuana smoking does in fact impair the functioning of one part of the immune system (L. L. Miller, 1975). However, this impairment has yet to show any recognizable clinical effect. Therefore, as with the testosterone problem, the significance of the immune response effect is unclear.

A third concern is the effect of marijuana smoke on the lungs. A report commissioned by the Institute of Medicine (1982) indicates that chronic marijuana use may injure the lungs. Since marijuana smoke contains about 50 percent more carcinogenic hydrocarbon than does tobacco smoke and since laboratory exposure of human lung cells to marijuana smoke produces changes that are characteristic of early cancer, health authorities are concerned that heavy, prolonged marijuana use could lead to lung cancer.

A fourth problem centers on the psychological effect of chronic marijuana use. Some professionals feel strongly that prolonged use of marijuana eventually results in impaired judgment, apathy, and—as with the more potent drugs—a focusing of one's existence on the drug experience. Related to this thinking is the argument that those who begin by smoking marijuana will go on to more dangerous drugs, such as heroin. However, a comparison of the figures on frequency of marijuana use and narcotics use will show that very few marijuana smokers make the transition to narcotics. As for general deficits that may result from prolonged use, the first study of long-term use among Americans found no cognitive effects after more than seven years of extremely heavy use (Schaeffer, Andrysiak, & Ungerleider, 1981). Intellectual functioning among these ten adults was above average and virtually identical with that shown in tests they had taken fifteen to twenty years previously. There *is* evidence that *amotivational syndrome*—apathy, loss of ambition, difficulty in concentrating—does exist among marijuana smokers, but there is some indication that it may be primarily an accentuation of preexisting behavior patterns (Maugh, 1982).

In sum, the issues are clear, but the answers aren't. Testosterone levels go down, but sexual activity may not. One immune response is suppressed, but there is no observable effect. The personality may be affected, but the evidence is incomplete. The only thing that we know for sure about long-term marijuana smoking is that it increases the likelihood of respiratory ailments. Much more data are needed before the marijuana issue can be reasonably settled.

PERSPECTIVES ON DRUG DEPENDENCE

As we mentioned earlier, the current trend in the study and rehabilitation of drug abusers is to consider these people as a group rather than to distinguish among them on the basis of the substances they are abusing. Hence the theoretical perspectives that we have discussed in relation to alcohol dependence generally apply to other drugs as well. The psychodynamic theorists would still point to dependency needs; the behaviorists, to reinforcement; and so on. In the following section we will examine briefly the biochemical research, personality theories, and social issues pertaining to drug abuse and the various current approaches to rehabilitation.

Drugs and Brain Chemistry

In the early seventies, scientists discovered that nerve cells in the brain have specific *opiate receptors*, sites to which opiates such as heroin and morphine attach themselves. The fit between the opiates and the receptors was so perfect that researchers suspected the brain must produce some natural substance that the receptors were intended to fit. This suspicion led in 1975 to the discovery of *enkephalins*, brain chemicals that are similar to morphine and that do indeed fit the opiate receptors (A. Goldstein, 1976). Several of these substances have been given the name *endorphins*, meaning "morphine within."

Endorphins may account for a number of mind-body phenomena that have puzzled scientists for many years. For one thing, they may underlie our natural control of pain and our natural experience of pleasure. It has long been known that stimulation of certain parts of the brain can produce pleasure and help control intractable pain. The stimulation seems to cause the brain to produce more endorphins. (If acupuncture controls pain—a

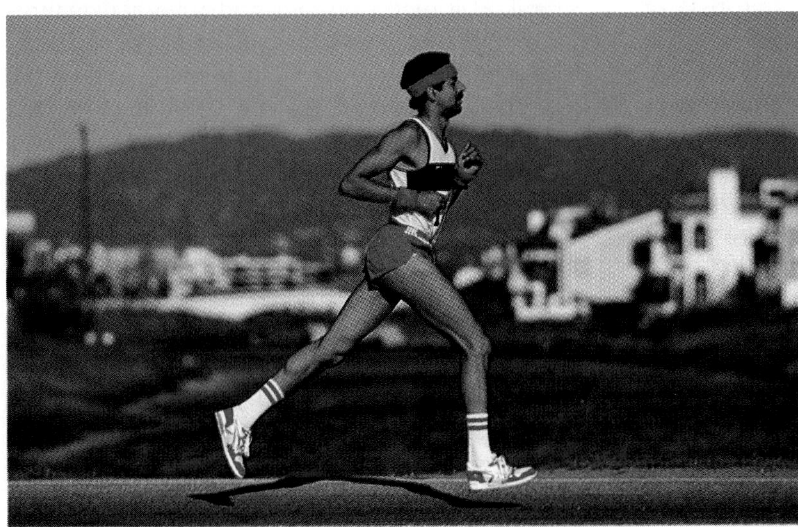

The "runner's high" is produced by the release of endorphins—natural brain chemicals that cause feelings of pleasure—in response to exertion. Morphine and other opiates produce the same biochemical reaction.

point that is still being debated—it may do so via the same mechanism.) Endorphins may also explain why placebo drugs can relieve pain. Possibly the person's expectation that the drug will relieve pain causes the brain to increase its production of endorphins, which then proceed to kill the pain.

More to the point of this chapter, endorphins may also explain physiological dependence on drugs. It is possible that when external opiates are taken, the brain ceases to produce internal opiates, or endorphins. The person thus becomes entirely dependent on external opiates for the relief of pain and the achievement of pleasure. Withdrawal symptoms, accordingly, occur during the time between the cessation of external opiate consumption and the resumption of internal opiate production.

Recently scientists have discovered that the opiate receptor sites can be occupied by substances that prevent both opiates and endorphins from attaching themselves to the receptors. One such opiate antagonist is naltrexone, which has been used in the treatment of opiate addiction. When a person on naltrexone takes an opiate, the opiate has no effect—it neither produces a rush nor reduces withdrawal symptoms. The hope is that the repeated experience of taking an opiate without any effect will eventually break the addiction.

A second important theory has to do with the neurotransmitter dopamine. According to this theory, most of the drugs of abuse, including alcohol, amphetamines, cocaine, and opiates, stimulate the dopamine-producing neurons in the median forebrain bundle, a complex neural pathway that connects the midbrain to the forebrain (Wise, 1988). This increased dopamine production is what creates the drug's positive effects (euphoria, stimulation) and thus, by reinforcement, the risk of addiction. Animal research has provided some support for this theory. Rats that have been trained to administer opiates, alcohol, and amphetamines to themselves will stop using these drugs if they are given a chemical that blocks the synthesis of dopamine. Presumably, once dopamine production is turned off, the drugs are no longer reinforcing. Such dopamine-suppressing chemicals can also block the stimulant effects of alcohol and amphetamines in human beings (J. Engel & Liljequist, 1983; Wise, 1988). If the implications of this research prove to be correct—that is, if a variety of addictive drugs all turn out to deliver their rewarding effects via dopamine—this means that one drug may satisfy the urge for a different drug. In turn, that might mean that people who have conquered an addiction to one drug, such as heroin, would be at risk for relapse from even occasional use of any other dopamine-mediated drug, such as alcohol, cocaine, or even caffeine.

Drugs and Personality Factors

Psychologists have long been intrigued by the question of what personality factors addicts may have in common, or, indeed, whether there are any common factors at all. There is some evidence that personality does in fact play a role in drug abuse. For example, the troops in Vietnam who habitually used heroin tended to drop the habit once they came home, but then many of them got hooked on another, more readily available drug: alcohol. In turn, many alcoholics who stop drinking begin "abusing" caffeine and nicotine by drinking coffee and smoking cigarettes to excess. Thus it seems that certain personality traits may lie behind the tendency toward drug abuse.

What might these traits be? Among those suggested by various studies are impulsive, sensation-seeking behavior; a nonconforming and antisocial personality; a feeling of alienation from society and a lack of respect for social values; a sense of heightened stress; hyperactivity, emotionality, and low frustration tolerance (J. R. Graham & Strenger, 1988; Tarter, 1988). Other similarities found among addicts are depressive tendencies, dependent behavior, and a focus on short-term goals at the expense of long-term ones. Many addicts have been found to have similar family backgrounds, including physical or sexual abuse in childhood and inconsistent parental behavior and expectations. And a great many addicts have a history of childhood antisocial behavior (P. E. Nathan, 1988; Tarter, 1988; Windle, 1990).

Still, as a report on the "addictive personality" by the National Academy of Sciences concludes, "There is no single unique personality entity that is a necessary and sufficient condition for substance use" (quoted in *New York Times*, January 18, 1983). Drugs affect people in different ways and serve different needs, so it is hard to predict whether a particular personality type will abuse a particular drug. Social factors are also important in the development of addiction. The drug must be readily available and its use promoted or at least tolerated by one's peers. According to the best evidence, the strongest predisposing factor for drug use in the case of adolescents is drug use by peers (Murray & Perry, 1985). Adolescents tend to smoke marijuana if their friends smoke marijuana. Drug use by parents also exerts an influence, but it is not as great an influence as that of peers (Murray & Perry, 1985).

For adolescents and young adults, drug use may be related to a period of confusion and transition in their lives. One study (Salzman & Lieff, 1974) of a group of young people who had discontinued heavy use of hallucinogens supports this notion. The subjects reported that they began using hallucinogens at a point when they were facing major life decisions—choosing a career, deciding whether to go to graduate school, and so forth. They discontinued their hallucinogen use when the transitions were finally made. For other young people, however, drug use may in fact predict a troubled adulthood. In a longitudinal study of drug use, more than a thousand subjects were assessed first at age fifteen or sixteen and then again at age twenty-five. It was found that, at least for this group, early drug use did correlate with later use of the same drug. It also correlated with increased delinquency, unemployment, divorce, abortion, and drug-related health problems (D. B. Kandel, Davies, Karus, et al., 1986).

Drugs and Society

The study just cited is only one of many studies showing that not just alcoholism but addiction to any drug is damaging to the society as well as to the individual. Work productivity declines, medical resources are wasted, and lives are lost in drug-related accidents. Out of the sports world in the seventies and eighties came a new drug controversy, over anabolic steroids. (See the box on page 318.)

In the 1980s, a new social problem was connected to drug use: the spread of AIDS. Injecting drugs intravenously is a primary way of contracting the AIDS virus, and female IV drug users may not only contract the virus but pass it on to their babies during pregnancy. Finally, there appears to be a clear correlation between the use of addictive drugs and involvement in crime. Heroin and cocaine addicts, for example, must come up with a substantial amount of money every day to support their habit. They are generally unemployable, and therefore, unless they are independently wealthy, they must steal: addicts are responsible for millions of dollars' worth of property crimes annually. A study of 354 narcotics addicts (Ball, Shaffer, & Nurco, 1983) found that the addicts were four to six times more likely to commit crimes when they were actively addicted than during periods of little or no drug use.

One often-suggested solution to the problem of addiction-related crime is to legalize the drugs and dispense them to addicts under medical supervision and at a nominal cost. Such a system was tried in Great Britain during the seventies and eighties. Opponents of this approach claim that it simply encourages addiction, and the apparent increase in the number of British addicts during the eighties seemed to support this argument. It was because of this increase that the British system was abandoned. However, defenders of legalization claim that it is the only reasonable way to prevent addicts from doing as much harm to society as they do to themselves.

Drug Rehabilitation

Most drug rehabilitation begins with withdrawal, which, though a painful experience, is nevertheless generally easier than the task that faces formerly drug-dependent people after withdrawal is completed: that of developing the skills and confidence to live a reasonably gratifying life in this society without drugs. As with alcohol dependence, so with other forms of drug dependence: the most ambitious treatments are multicomponent programs combining job-skills training with group, marital, and family therapy and training in relaxation, decision making, and general stress management. Several behavioral programs follow this comprehensive model (Grabowski, Stitzer, & Henningfield, 1984).

A more radical approach is that of the therapeutic residential community. The best-known of these was Synanon, a California group founded in the late fifties by a former AA member. Synanon based its rehabilitation program on two principles: (1) Once an addict, always an addict (note the resemblance to AA doctrine); and (2) the first step in learning new nondrug ways of coping with stress is to learn about oneself. In accordance with the second principle, an integral part of the rehabilitation program was regular attendance at intense, confrontational group-therapy sessions.

Though Synanon is now defunct, it served as the model for many surviving communities, such as Gateway House in Chicago and Phoenix House, Daytop Village, and Odyssey House in New York. As with AA, the dropout rates in such communities are reportedly high, and the rehabilitation rate among remaining members is hard to evaluate, for such groups do not always welcome scrutiny by scientific researchers.

The therapeutic communities treat drug abuse as an *adaptation* to stress and concentrate on providing coping skills. Another method of rehabilitation—methadone maintenance—focuses on *ex-*

ANABOLIC STEROIDS: NOT FOR ATHLETES ONLY

Anabolic steroids have stalked the fringe of sports for forty years, mostly in the shadows, illuminated for seconds by the sudden spotlight of breaking news:

- Chinese female swimmers test positive in 1994.
- NFL guard attempts suicide after flunking drug test in 1991.
- Canadian sprinter Ben Johnson stripped of Olympic medal and world record in 1988.
- College football star Brian Bosworth barred from the Orange Bowl in 1987.

But time moves on, and as once-celebrated names disappear from the media, steroids move back into the shadows, where as many as a million Americans take them every day, swallowing them and injecting them into their muscles. The majority of users are not elite athletes; they have moved on to more sophisticated drugs, harder to detect. The new converts to anabolic steroids are construction workers, cops, and lawyers, adding muscle to look good; and teenagers, bulking up to earn a spot on the team.

Vanity and glory were not the drugs' intent. Anabolic-androgenic steroids are a synthetic version of testosterone, the male hormone that occurs naturally in the body. Developed in the 1930s in Germany, they were used to help patients with wasting disorders to rebuild their bodies. Today their legitimate use is limited: they are prescribed primarily as androgens in treating men whose testes through accident or disease have lost the ability to produce testosterone.

But steroids' shadow life began early. Use by athletes was first confirmed when the success of Soviet weight lifters at the 1954 Vienna championships was traced to steroids. Within ten years, they were widely used in all strength areas of sports. Popularity spread quickly to professional and college football players, to runners and jumpers in track and field, to skiers and swimmers and cyclists and anybody else looking for extranatural help. Bodybuilders embraced them most; use throughout competitions became common. Their most celebrated star, Arnold Schwarzenegger, admitted to using them in 1972.

Sports' governing agencies moved first against steroids, mostly on the basis that they afforded an unfair advantage; they were banned in collegiate and Olympic competition in the mid-1970s. By 1991 Congress declared steroids a controlled substance, making illicit use and trafficking federal offenses.

The drugs' value was widely accepted within sports. They added lean muscle mass to athletes in training and helped them work harder and require less recovery time. But their worth outside sports has been debated; many medical and government officials insisted their impact was psychological. The debate hurt the establishment's credibility. Doctors and drug officials insisted that gains from steroids were limited, while athletes could watch Ben Johnson pumped up on steroids run the 100 at the Olympics in a time still unmatched six years later.

That credibility suffered even further with official claims of the drugs' risks. In women, certain effects of taking high levels of male hormone were predictable: acne, deepening voice, and proliferation of facial and body hair. Men may experience the paradoxical side effects of enlarged breasts and high-pitched voice. But doctors warned of heart attacks, strokes, and severe liver and kidney damage. While many of these in varying degrees were linked to steroid abuse, they were rare enough that few users knew anyone suffering serious side effects.

The problem has been that little solid research exists on the hazards of long-time, high-dose steroid use, and none is anticipated soon: no medical ethics board would risk a controlled study administering 100 times the therapeutic dose of steroids, the amount taken by many athletes.

While the best available knowledge contends that steroids are not killers, no one suggests they are safe. "You've got to look at the history of hormones and the ever-present possibility of delayed, adverse effects," says Gary Wadler, a trustee of the American College of Sports Medicine and clinical associate professor at Cornell University Medical College. "I have great concerns for what we're going to see 10 to 15 years down the road." Wadler draws comparisons with DES, a synthetic female hormone used to stabilize pregnancies in women who had repeated miscarriages; a generation later their daughters showed increased rates of vaginal cancer. High-dose use of the corticosteroid cortisone put patients fifteen years later at risk for hip fractures.

Other potential adverse medical effects of steroid abuse are reduction of HDL cholesterol (the beneficial kind) and increased total cholesterol, testicular shrinkage, decreased spermatogenesis, reduced testosterone production, benign and malignant liver tumors, liver chemistry abnormalities, alternations in tendons, and dependency syndrome, as well as the risk (from sharing needles) of AIDS and hepatitis. Among teenage users, premature closure of the growth plates in the long bones has been proved.

This last effect is particularly disturbing in light of the expansion of steroids from elite athletes to teenagers—not only jocks but kids trying to improve their appearance end up limiting their eventual height. According to Charles Yesalis, professor of health policy and administration and sports science at Penn State University, "Between 250,000 and 500,000 adolescents in the country have used or are currently using steroids." 38.3 percent of them began by fifteen or younger.

Add to all the other risks a wide range of possible behavioral changes, including increased irritability, aggressiveness, euphoria, sleeplessness, and recklessness. "Maybe one person of 20 will be very susceptible to these side effects," says Harrison Pope (Pope & Katz, 1990), who has studied the effects of anabolic steroids. "In rare cases, people on steroids have become homicidal, commited murders." The phenomenon occurs just often enough that it has its own name—"roid rage." Its existence, according to Pope and his research partner, David L. Katz, means these drugs post "a greater-than-expected public health problem, both for users and for society at large."

posure to opiates and attempts to break the link with withdrawal symptoms. As we have seen earlier in this chapter, methadone is a synthetic opiate, and like the other opiates, it is highly addictive. It does not produce the extreme euphoria of heroin, but it does satisfy the craving for heroin and prevent withdrawal symptoms. In short, what methadone maintenance programs do—at best—is switch people from dependence on heroin, in the form of three to four injections daily (with the attendant risk of AIDS), to dependence on methadone, in the form of one oral dose per day. This relieves them of their "doped" behavioral symptoms and also of the necessity of stealing to finance their drug habit. But while methadone maintenance may succeed in taking people off heroin, it does not prevent them from becoming dependent on alcohol, barbiturates, or other drugs.

Methadone maintenance programs have had substantial successes, particularly in terms of controlling the public health and public safety problems associated with drug abuse—notably, AIDS and crime. Nevertheless, there remain thousands of addicts whom we have not helped. At the same time that researchers are trying to develop better treatment programs, great efforts are being put into the *prevention* of drug abuse. Drug education is now common in the schools and the workplace. Television commercials show movie stars and sports heroes warning teenagers against drugs, and advertisements in buses and subways tell people who already have drug problems where they can go for help, what number they can call, before they become defeated.

Relapse Prevention

In the case of all substance-dependence disorders, behavioral improvements are usually temporary: estimates of relapse rates range from 50 to 90 percent (K. D. Brownell, 1986). Thus, the problem of relapse has become the major challenge of prevention and treatment programs. How we define *relapse*—as part of a process or as final outcome—has important implications for understanding behavior change. Kelly Brownell and his colleagues distinguish between a *lapse*, or slip, which they view as an event in the process of change, and a *relapse*, which may suggest instead a final outcome, a point of no return (K. D. Brownell, Marlatt, Lichtenstein, et al., 1986). The way the person views a slip, then—as a mistake to be learned from or as confirmation that the battle is lost—is a critical cognitive factor in efforts at recovery.

In keeping with this concept, it is important to understand relapse and its consequences in light of the stages of change that precede it. One model (Prochaska & DiClemente, 1984; Prochaska, DiClemente, & Norcross, 1992) proposes three stages in the process of changing addictive behavior: (1) decision and commitment, (2) the initial change, and (3) maintaining the change. If a relapse in the third stage is viewed as a step in incremental learning rather than as a failure, it can lead to new efforts to change—beginning at stage 1 and leading eventually to successful maintenance. This view is consistent with the finding of Stanley Schachter (1982) that permanent behavior change is more likely to occur after a person has dealt with several relapses. Researchers are now beginning to identify specific factors that lead to relapse. These fall into three categories: individual (intrapersonal), environmental (situational), and physiological.

In the first category, negative emotional states such as stress, anger, depression, and anxiety are among the strongest determinants of relapse, accounting for an estimated 30 percent of relapses across the substance-dependence disorders (C. Cummings, Gordon, & Marlatt, 1980). They also increase the likelihood that a single lapse, or slip, will lead to relapse rather than to renewed efforts to change. On the basis of such findings McAuliffe (1990) developed a program to help substance-dependent people head off negative emotional states by refining their coping skills. In McAuliffe's study 168 recovering heroin addicts were randomly assigned either to the usual aftercare treatment or to a specially designed relapse-prevention program involving two weekly meetings—one led by a professional counselor, one by a recovering addict—for six months. In the meetings the experimental subjects were taught strategies for dealing with former drug-using companions, with drug offers, and with job and family problems. They were also taught how to make new friends and develop drug-free recreational activities, as well as how to respond to slips. At a one-year follow-up, the subjects in the relapse-prevention program were significantly more likely to be completely abstinent or suffering only rare slips than those who had only the traditional aftercare.

Apart from negative emotional states, motivation and commitment are also key factors in the prediction of relapse (S. M. Hall, Havassy, & Wasserman, 1990). Bolstering motivation and also assessing motivation—does the person really want to quit, or has the boss delivered an ultimatum?—should become part of relapse-prevention programs in the future (S. M. Hall, Havassy, & Wasserman, 1991).

Apart from individual factors, environmental contingencies figure heavily in relapse risk. Possibly the key environmental factor is social support, its presence or absence. Relapses are often precipitated by interpersonal conflict—for example, family quarrels. Conversely, the recovering substance abuser can be greatly helped by encouragement from family, friends, and coworkers. Another source of social support is self-help groups such as Alcoholics Anonymous, SmokEnders, and Narcotics Anonymous, which offer the kind of understanding that only fellow sufferers can extend. At the same time, these groups teach their members how to cope with environmental contingencies. For example, two notorious predictors of lapses and relapses are exposure to the drug and social pressure from users (Shiffman, 1982). Alcoholics Anonymous and other self-help groups offer members advice on how to avoid or control such cues. This kind of contingency management can greatly increase a person's chances of remaining drug-free.

As for physiological factors, withdrawal cravings can lead swiftly to a slip, especially if they are combined with risk-laden individual and environmental factors. People who are angry or depressed, or who are spending the evening with old drinking buddies, will have a far harder time withstanding physiological pressures to return to the drug.

Researchers in substance dependence are now finding out more about how individual, environmental, and physiological factors interact during the course of recovery. They are also discovering that people trying to free themselves from drug dependence often benefit from learning new, "positive" addictions, such as physical exercise. People apparently need new sources of gratification if they are to maintain long-term behavior change. Although existing relapse rates are discouraging, this new focus on relapse prevention may eventually allow drug-treatment specialists to help thousands of previously unreachable people.

KEY TERMS

addiction (289)
amphetamines (310)
barbiturates (308)
blood-alcohol level (290)
cocaine (310)
delirium tremens (293)
depressant (307)
detoxification (302)
drug-induced insomnia (309)
hallucinogens (312)
heroin (307)
methadone (307)
morphine (307)
opiates (307)
opium (307)
psychoactive drug (288)
psychological dependence (289)
stimulants (310)
substance abuse (289)
substance dependence (289)
synergistic effect (308)
tolerance (289)
tranquilizers (309)
withdrawal symptoms (289)

SUMMARY

- Psychoactive drugs are substances used occasionally or regularly to alter one's psychological state. *DSM-IV* distinguishes between substance dependence and substance abuse. In either case, diagnosis depends on the user's behavior, not on the drug itself.
- A diagnosis of substance dependence requires that a person meet three of the following criteria: preoccupation with the drug; unintentional overuse; tolerance (progressively larger doses are needed to achieve the same effect); withdrawal symptoms when the drug is not used; persistent efforts to control use; abandonment of important social, occupational, or recreational activities that interfere with drug use; and continued use despite serious drug-related problems.
- A diagnosis of substance abuse requires that a person meet one of four criteria: recurrent, drug-related failure to meet social role obligations; recurrent use in dangerous situations (e.g., drunk driving); drug-related legal problems; continued use despite social or interpersonal problems.
- Alcohol, sanctioned in our society both by custom and by law, is one of the most widely abused drugs. The social and personal costs of alcohol abuse are enormous. A depressant, alcohol interferes with the higher brain centers, which control behavior. After one or two drinks a person may become talkative and happy; additional drinks cause changes in mood and behavior, and eventually stupor. Whether a person becomes amorous, aggressive, or sad when drinking heavily depends largely on his or her expectations. Long-term overuse of alcohol can cause heart disease, cirrhosis of the liver, and brain damage; withdrawal may cause DTs (trembling delirium) or even death.
- Alcohol dependence probably has multiple causes. Psychodynamic theory traditionally traced alcohol dependence to unmet emotional needs and oral fixa-

tion; another theory cites a drive for power. Recent research shows that a high proportion of alcohol abusers suffer from anxiety disorder and major depressive disorder, though which comes first is difficult to say. Psychodynamic therapies are directed at self-knowledge.

- Behaviorists argue that alcohol abuse and dependence are the result of conditioning. Traditional theories emphasized tension reduction (negative reinforcement); more recent theories emphasize pleasure seeking (positive reinforcement). Behavioral therapy teaches patients to recognize cues that lead to drinking and to develop alternate means of coping with life's problems.
- Cognitive theorists focus on positive expectations regarding alcohol; dulling painful self-awareness; and creating an excuse for anticipated failure. Cognitive therapies attempt to build confidence and to correct false beliefs.
- The sociocultural perspective stresses variations in rates of alcohol dependence among different segments of our society and the social conditions and cultural histories that help to explain these differences. Much research is devoted to reducing rates of alcohol use and abuse among young people.
- Neuroscience researchers study the genetic factors that might predispose individuals to alcohol dependence and the variable effects of alcohol on the brain. Multimodal treatment begins with detoxification, followed by a combination of occupational therapy, relaxation training, individual and group psychotherapy, job training, and support groups, such as Alcoholics Anonymous. Cure rates for all forms of treatment are still discouragingly low.
- Although fewer people smoke than drink today, a higher number of smokers become dependent. Nicotine is a paradoxical drug which both stimulates and calms users. Smoking exacts a high price in premature deaths from heart disease, lung cancer, and other respiratory disorders—not only in smokers but in the people (especially children) around them. Health warnings, social pressure, and legislation banning smoking in public places have led a significant number of smokers to quit; but advertising targeted at vulnerable groups encourages others to start.
- Other psychoactive drugs fall into three main categories: depressants, stimulants, and hallucinogens. The depressants include opiates (e.g., morphine and heroin), which induce relaxation, euphoria, and usually addiction; barbiturates (e.g., Nembutal and Seconal), which induce sleep but, combined with alcohol, may cause intentional or unintentional death; and tranquilizers (e.g., Valium and Librium), which reduce anxiety but may also lead to dependence. While most of these drugs have medical uses, all can be abused. Overuse of depressants leads to tolerance; withdrawal is extremely uncomfortable and often dangerous.
- The stimulants increase energy, alertness, and feelings of confidence. This category includes amphetamines (e.g., Benzedrine and Dexadrine), which in high doses may lead to induced psychosis; cocaine (and crack cocaine), which produces a rapid but short-lived "high"; and caffeine, which, used in excess, can cause sleeplessness, irritability, an irregular heartbeat, and other unpleasant symptoms. Regular or heavy use of amphetamines or cocaine leads to tolerance, addiction, and (if the person wishes to quit) withdrawal symptoms. Whether caffeine is addictive and leads to withdrawal symptoms is controversial.
- The hallucinogens cause distortions in sensory perception. While LSD may induce "bad trips" and "flashbacks," it does not appear to be addictive. PCP (angel dust) is a behavioral toxin that often induces risky and/or violent behavior. While usually classified as hallucinogens, marijuana and hashish are milder, producing euphoria, heightened sensory experiences, and a relaxed, timeless state. They can also heighten negative feelings and experiences. Research on the effects of marijuana on testosterone and sexual activity, the immune system, and personality has not produced consistent findings, but smoking marijuana does increase the incidence of respiratory ailments.
- Brain chemistry plays a special role in drug dependence. One theory holds that use of opiates decreases the production of endorphins, the brain's natural opiates, and thus creates a craving for external opiates; another holds that opiates and other addictive drugs increase the brain's production of dopamine, causing a surge of pleasure that the user seeks again. Drug abuse has been linked with a history of childhood antisocial behavior, but there is no single "addictive personality." The best predictor of drug use in adolescence is drug use by peers.
- Given the high cost of drugs, to society as well as to individual users, designing effective drug-rehabilitation programs is essential. Programs designed not only to help people stop using drugs but also to prevent relapse—by teaching strategies for resisting pressure from old drug-using friends and making new friends, boosting individual motivation, providing ongoing support groups, and introducing new "addictions," such as exercise—show promise.

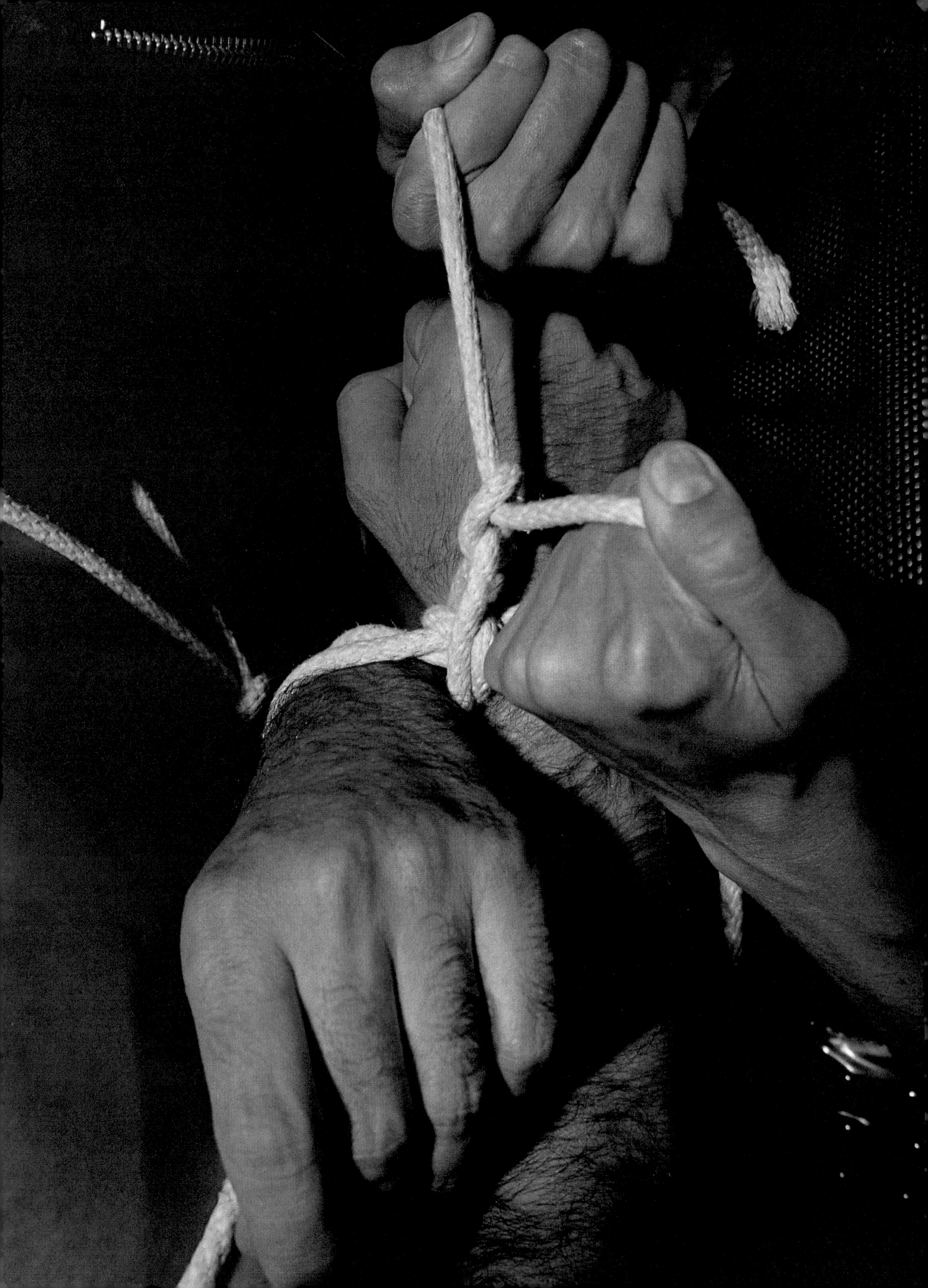

13

SEXUAL AND GENDER IDENTITY DISORDERS

r. and Ms. Albert are an attractive, gregarious couple, married for 15 years, who present in the midst of a crisis over their sexual problems. Mr. Albert, a successful restaurateur, is 38. Ms. Albert . . . is 35. She reports that throughout their marriage she has been extremely frustrated because sex has "always been hopeless for us." . . .

The difficulty is the husband's rapid ejaculation. Whenever any lovemaking is attempted, Mr. Albert becomes anxious, moves quickly toward intercourse, and reaches orgasm either immediately upon entering his wife's vagina or within one or two strokes. He then feels humiliated, recognizes his wife's dissatisfaction, and they both lapse into silent suffering. . . .

Mr. Albert has always been a perfectionist, priding himself on his ability to succeed at anything he sets his mind to. . . . His inability to control his ejaculation is a source of intense shame, and he finds himself unable to talk to his wife about his sexual "failures." Ms. Albert is highly sexual, easily aroused by foreplay, but has always felt that intercourse is the only "acceptable" way to reach orgasm. Intercourse with her husband has always been unsatisfying, and she holds him completely responsible for her sexual frustration. . . .

In other areas of their marriage, including rearing of their two children, managing the family restaurant, and socializing with friends, the Alberts are highly compatible. Despite these strong points, however, they are near separation because of . . . their mutual sexual disappointment. (Spitzer, Gibbon, Skodol, et al., 1989, pp. 229–230)

Like beauty, good sex is in the eye of the beholder. A sexual outlet that seems normal and healthy to one person may appear inadequate or even perverse to another. But while tastes are wide, life in society limits behavior. To begin with, people must cope with the needs of their sexual partners. Rapid ejaculation may be satisfactory for some men but not for the women they are having sex with, as the above case illustrates. Some sexual behaviors, such as rape and incest, violate the rights of others and accordingly are crimes. A number of sexual behaviors, while they involve no harm to others, nevertheless transgress social norms and are therefore considered psychological disorders—in the eyes of many people, shameful disorders. There are very few categories of abnormal behavior to which society attaches as much stigma as sexual disorders.

Most of this chapter will be devoted to discussing four categories of sexual behavior:

1 *Sexual dysfunction:* disruption of the sexual response cycle, or pain during intercourse.
2 *Paraphilias:* sexual desires or behaviors involving unusual sources of gratification.
3 *Gender identity disorder:* dissatisfaction with one's own biological sex and identification with the opposite sex.
4 *Incest and rape.*

Before discussing sexual behaviors, however, we must first look at our sexual norms and the extent to which they actually reflect our sexual makeup and behavior.

DEFINING SEXUAL DISORDERS

Compared with other cultures, Western culture has been sexually repressive. For example, while the ancient Greeks not only tolerated but actually glorified homosexuality, the Judeo-Christian tradition that supplanted classical thought has, for the most part, condemned same-sex relationships. Today, church doctrine on sexual morality has relaxed somewhat. Nevertheless, most present-day denominations still place restrictions on sexual activities that circumvent or replace *coitus,* or penile-vaginal intercourse, within the context of marriage.

Western sexual mores are derived not only from religious dogma but also from the writings of mental health experts. Two of the most influential early psychiatric works on sex, Richard von Krafft-Ebing's *Psychopathia Sexualis* (1886/1965a) and Havelock Ellis' *Studies in the Psychology of Sex* (1899–1928), condemned masturbation as a psychologically dangerous practice. In Krafft-Ebing's opinion, masturbation halted the development of normal erotic instincts, caused impotence in early heterosexual contacts, and thus led to homosexuality. Both Krafft-Ebing and Ellis regarded homosexuality as a form of psychopathology. In their view, and in Freud's too, the only genuinely healthy, mature, and normal sexual outlet was coitus. Succeeding generations of psychologists and psychiatrists concurred. In *DSM-II,* published in 1968, people whose sexual interests were "directed primarily toward objects other than people of the opposite sex [or] toward sexual acts not usually associated with coitus" were classified as suffering from sexual disorders.

This rather narrow definition of normal sexual behavior has served for many centuries to help guarantee the continuation of the human species and the survival of the family structure. However, there is little to indicate that human beings are programmed biologically to confine their sexual gratification to coitus. On the contrary, while the sex drive itself is inborn, the direction that it will take is, according to anthropological evidence, a result of socialization. For example, while Western culture considers the female breast an erotic object, many societies consider it sexually neutral. Likewise, while homosexuality is generally frowned on in our society, in other societies it is not only accepted but actually institutionalized as the proper sexual outlet for adolescent boys (Ford & Beach, 1951; Whitman, 1983).

As for freedom of sexual expression, an instructive contrast is provided by two small villages, one in Polynesia and one on an island off the coast of Ireland. In the Irish village of Inis Beag, a researcher (Messenger, 1971) who interviewed the inhabitants over nineteen months found that they had no apparent knowledge of tongue kissing, oral-genital contact, premarital coitus, or extramarital coitus. The idea of a man putting his mouth on the woman's breast, or the woman stimulating the man's penis with her hand, was also unheard of. Intercourse was considered a health risk and was achieved quickly, without removing underwear. Female orgasm was apparently unknown. By contrast, in the same year another researcher (Marshall, 1971) reported that on the Polynesian island of Mangaia, copulation was "a principal concern of the Mangaian of either sex" (p. 116). Mangaians began full-scale sexual activity at about thirteen years, after receiving detailed instruction from older "experts." Sexual technique and sexual anatomy were the object of passionate connoisseurship: "The average Mangaian youth has fully as detailed a knowledge . . . of the gross anatomy of the penis and vagina as does a European physician" (Marshall, 1971, p. 110). For males, the average rate of orgasm at age eighteen was three per night, seven nights a week; at age twenty-eight, two per night, five to six nights a week. Women had a higher rate, since the male's goal in intercourse was to bring the woman to orgasm several times before he himself reached climax. All Mangaian women were orgasmic. When told that many European and American women do not experience orgasm, Mangaians would typically ask whether this failing did not impair their health. In short, the definition of what is sexually normal and abnormal in Mangaia was almost the opposite of that in Inis Beag. These two cultures are extremes—perhaps the most sexually permissive and the most sexually repressive societies known to Western research. But they illustrate a crucial point: Human sexual behavior, viewed across cultures, is extremely variable.

The definition of sexual "normality" has always varied between cultures and across time. In ancient Greece, for example, male homosexuality was considered a normal adjunct to heterosexual marriage.

Within a culture, attitudes toward sexuality may change over time. Our own society is far more open about sex today than it was just a few decades ago, for example. Even in less tolerant times, however, sexual behavior does not necessarily conform to declared standards of sexual morality or normality. The famous Kinsey reports (Kinsey, Pomeroy, & Martin, 1948; Kinsey, Pomeroy, Martin, et al., 1953) revealed that many Americans had engaged in culturally prohibited sexual activities. More than 90 percent of the males Kinsey interviewed had masturbated; over 80 percent of the men and 50 percent of the women in his samples had participated in premarital sex; and oral sex was far from uncommon. In the fifties, these findings were very shocking to many people. Today, they would be considered unremarkable (Laumann, Micheal, Michaels, et al., 1994).

In part because of research, in part because of the general social climate, the 1960s and 1970s brought widespread questioning of traditional sexual morality in the United States. Prohibitions on such activities as premarital sex, masturbation, and oral-genital sex were relaxed. Homosexuality, too, has been reconsidered, not only by the public

Attitudes toward sexuality differ among cultures and vary over time within the same culture. In early twentieth-century America, for example, women's undergarments covered the body from breast to knee. Today, in contrast, highly erotic advertisements for revealing underwear can be seen on any street corner.

but also by the mental health establishment. In its early editions, the *DSM* listed homosexuality as a sexual disorder, along with pedophilia, fetishism, sadism, and so forth. Then in 1973 the board of trustees of the American Psychiatric Association voted to drop homosexuality per se from the list. The trustees' report described homosexuality as "a normal form of sexual life" (American Psychiatric Association, 1974). But they retained a category called "ego-dystonic homosexuality disorder" for individuals who *themselves* rejected their homosexuality and wanted to become exclusively heterosexual. Many psychologists, together with gay rights groups, objected to this category as well. In their view, homosexuals who rejected their sexual orientation did so because they had internalized negative stereotypes—stereotypes reinforced by psychiatric labeling, even in the milder form of "ego-dystonic homosexuality disorder." At the same time, more and more research was accumulating to show that there was no justification for regarding homosexuality as a pathological pattern. As these studies showed, homosexuals are no more prone to psychopathology than are matched groups of heterosexuals (Hooker, 1957; W. M. Paul, Gonsiorek, & Hotvedt, 1982; Saghir & Robins, 1969; Saghir, Robins, & Walbran, 1969). Moreover, there is no "typical" homosexual personality; homosexuals, both male and female, differ as much from one another in personality as do heterosexuals (Hooker, 1957; M. Wilson, 1984). In response to such findings, as well as the fact that "ego-dystonic" homosexuality was rarely diagnosed anyway, the APA in 1986 voted to drop homosexuality from the *DSM* altogether. Today, in *DSM-IV*'s listing of sexual disorders, there remains a residual category, "sexual disorder not otherwise specified," to cover problems not included in other categories, and one of the examples given is "persistent and marked distress about sexual orientation," but otherwise the manual makes no reference to homosexuality.

Nevertheless, the catalog of psychiatrically recognized sexual disorders remains a long one, and the list of sexual behaviors regarded as abnormal by society is even longer. The remainder of this chapter is devoted to these behaviors.

SEXUAL DYSFUNCTION

In the last three decades our society has seen two major upheavals in sexual attitudes. First came the "sexual revolution" of the sixties and seventies, with a new openness about sex and a new interest in sexual satisfaction—giving it and getting it. Sex manuals became best-sellers. Movies and television began showing explicit sex scenes. Popular magazines, even "family" publications such as *Reader's Digest,* began running articles on how to improve your love life.

Then, in the eighties, the fervor died down somewhat. In part, this was probably just the passing of a trend. (It is also possible that the trend was more in the media than in the population—see the box on page 328.) But a crucial factor was the rapidly spreading AIDS epidemic. "Casual sex" now lost its allure. Many people sought, instead, to settle down with one partner. Others opted for abstinence (Ingrassia, 1994). But for those having sex, the emphasis was now on safe sex, with sports and entertainment stars, not to speak of school health services, broadcasting the message.

The campaign for safe sex has not quelled the interest in good sex, however. Though more people are now confining their sex lives to a single relationship, the lesson of the sixties has not been forgotten: people still feel they have a right to sexual pleasure and are seeking to increase it. This concern with sexual gratification has had many beneficial effects. It has eased the flow of information about sex, increased sexual communication between partners, and dispelled anxiety over harmless sexual practices. At the same time, however, it has ushered in new forms of anxiety. Many sexually normal men and women now worry about the adequacy of their sexual "performance." The concern with gratification has also resulted in psychology's devoting considerable attention to sexual dysfunctions, disorders that prevent the person from having satisfactory sex.

Forms of Sexual Dysfunction

Sexual dysfunctions are disorders involving either a disruption of the sexual response cycle or pain during intercourse. The contemporary study of sexual dysfunction began, appropriately, in the sixties, with the work of William Masters and Virginia Johnson at the Reproductive Biology Foundation in St. Louis. When Masters and Johnson began their research, studies of sexuality were rare, and clinicians who dealt with sexual problems were rarer still. However, since the publication of Masters and Johnson's *Human Sexual Response* (1966) and *Human Sexual Inadequacy* (1970), the number of researchers, therapists, and journals specializing in sexuality has grown enormously. One result has been a more sophisticated understanding of sexual dysfunctions. In the past, any lack of sexual interest or arousal in males was called "impotence." Similarly, the pejorative label "frigidity" was applied to almost every female sexual complaint. Today psychologists recognize a variety of specific difficulties. In *DSM-IV* most of the sexual dysfunctions are grouped according to the phase in the sexual response cycle in which they occur.

Sexual Desire Disorders The first phase of normal sexual response, called the *desire phase,* involves interest in sexual activity. Disruptions of the desire phase include **hypoactive sexual desire disorder,** or lack of interest in sex, and **sexual aversion disorder,** in which the person is not just un-

The "sexual liberation" that seemed so desirable in the 1960s and 1970s has begun to seem dangerous and irresponsible in the age of AIDS. The cultural message now emphasizes good sex in the context of safer sex.

SEX IN AMERICA: MYTHS AND REALITY

From what Americans see in the movies, on television, and, above all, in advertising, a person might easily conclude that everyone else in the country has a vigorous, varied, even exotic sex life and that he or she is the only one home alone on Saturday night. But the findings of a sample of over 3,500 Americans, aged eighteen to fifty-nine, recently published under the title *Sex in America* (Michael, Gagnon, Laumann, et al., 1994), should offer comfort. The central findings of this study was that Americans are far more conservative sexually than has been thought.

Of those surveyed, only 56 percent of men and 29 percent of women had had more than four sexual partners since age eighteen. (One-fifth of men and almost one-third of women reported having had only one sexual partner since age eighteen.) Over a lifetime, the typical American male seems to have had six partners; the typical female, two. And however many partners they have had, most of them are faithful to the one they marry. Nearly 75 percent of married men and 85 percent of married women said they had never committed adultery.

Not only do most Americans have limited sexual histories; they also have less sex than might have been guessed. In terms of frequency, the population breaks down, roughly, into thirds. About one-third reported having sex twice a week or more often; another third, a few times a month; another third, a few times a year or not at all. And the people doing it most often (and most frequently reaching orgasm when they do it) are the married. Almost 40 percent of married people, as compared with 25 percent of the unmarried, said they have sex at least twice a week. Swinging singles are the exception, not the rule.

Nor were these the only signs of sexual restraint. According to the survey, homosexuality is rarer than is often claimed. Only 7.1 percent of men and 3.8 percent of women reported that they had ever had sex with someone of their own gender. (Only 2.7 percent of men and 1.3 percent of women said they had done so within the last year.) Masturbation was also less common than one might imagine. Only 63 percent of men and 42 percent of women said they had masturbated within the last year, and curiously, the people who masturbated the most were not those who were deprived of other outlets. On the contrary, they were the ones who were also having the most partnered sex.

Another finding was that American tastes in sex acts are far from kinky. In a list of fourteen acts, the one most often rated as very appealing by women (78 percent) and men (83 percent) was coitus. Next in line, in a near-tie for both men and women, were watching one's partner undress and receiving oral intercourse. Finally, the age at which Americans lose their virginity has dropped in the last few decades, but not by much: six months. For Americans born in the decade 1933–1942, the average age of deflowering was about eighteen. For those born twenty to thirty years later, it was about seventeen and a half.

While the survey exploded many popular notions, it confirmed others:

- Men are more likely than women to have sex on the mind. Among the respondents, 54 percent of men but only 19 percent of women said they thought about sex every day.
- There is such a thing as a pickup establishment. People who meet in bars are far more likely to end up in bed together before the month is out than people who meet at school or at work or even at a private party.
- There was a free-love boom in the sixties. The percentage of people who reported having had more than twenty sexual partners was significantly higher for the generation that came of age in the sixties.
- The AIDS crisis has caused people to be more careful. Of those who reported having had five or more sexual partners within the last year, three-quarters said they had changed their sexual behavior by having fewer partners, getting an HIV test, or using condoms more scrupulously.
- With aging, women have a harder time finding a sexual partner than men. By age fifty, 22 percent of women, as compared with 8 percent of men, have no sexual partner. (The good news is that women—and men—who have no sexual partners think less about sex and often report that they are happy and fulfilled without it.)

The survey also revealed interesting differences between ethnic and religious groups. For example, age at first intercourse varies along ethnic lines. Half of black males have lost their virginity by age fifteen, half of Hispanic males by about sixteen and a half, half of black females by about seventeen, and half of white and Hispanic females by about eighteen.

The methodology of the *Sex in America* survey has been highly praised. Unlike the Kinsey studies, which, conducted in less candid times, often had to rely on special groups, such as college fraternities, in order to find people willing to talk about their sex lives, this was a truly random sample, highly representative of the general population. And almost 80 percent of those contacted—in other words, not just the sexually talkative (and therefore, presumably, the sexually active)—agreed to participate. Nevertheless, any self-report survey is limited by what people choose to report, and obviously a survey of sexual behavior has greater problems in this regard. According to one of the researchers, Stuart Michaels, the subject on which distortion was most likely was homosexual behavior: "There is probably a lot more homosexual activity going on than we could get people to talk about," (quoted in Elmer-DeWitt, 1994).

interested in sex but disgusted or frightened by it and therefore actively avoids it. People with sexual aversion disorder often turn out to be victims of childhood molestation, incest, or rape. Their sexual impairment is, in a sense, a form of posttraumatic stress disorder.

Sexual Arousal Disorders In the second phase of the response cycle, called the *excitement phase,* feelings of sexual pleasure are normally accompanied by specific physiological changes. The tissues of the man's penis become congested with blood, producing an erection. Similar congestion causes the woman's genitals to swell, while the walls of the vagina secrete lubricant. The absence or weakness of excitement is called **male erectile disorder** in men, **female sexual arousal disorder** in women.

Orgasmic Disorders In the third, or *orgasm,* phase of sexual response, the peaking of sexual pleasure triggers rhythmic contractions of the muscles in the genital region and, in men, simultaneous ejaculation of semen from the penis. If the man ejaculates before, on, or shortly after penetration, robbing the couple of sexual satisfaction, this problem is called **premature ejaculation.** If, on the other hand, ejaculation is greatly delayed or does not occur at all, the condition is called **male orgasmic disorder.** The delay or absence of orgasm in women is called **female orgasmic disorder.**

Sexual Pain Disorders Two sexual dysfunctions do not fit into the response-cycle typology. One is **dyspareunia,** or pain during intercourse, which may occur in either sex, though it is usually a female complaint. The second is a female disorder, **vaginismus,** in which the muscles surrounding the entrance to the vagina undergo involuntary spasmodic contractions when attempts are made to insert the penis. These contractions make intercourse either impossible or painfully difficult.

In categorizing sexual problems, the *DSM* distinguishes between **lifelong dysfunction** (one that has existed, without relief, since the person's earliest sexual experiences) and **acquired dysfunction** (a dysfunction that develops after at least one episode of normal functioning). It also distinguishes between **generalized dysfunction,** a dysfunction that is present in all sexual situations at the time of diagnosis, and **situational dysfunction,** which, as the term indicates, is one that occurs only in certain situations or with certain partners. For example, a woman with a generalized orgasmic disorder never experiences orgasm. A woman with a situational orgasmic disorder reaches orgasm, say, when masturbating alone though not while having sex with a partner. (But see the box on page 330 for problems in defining situational orgasmic disorder in women.)

As for the prevalence of these syndromes, it is very hard to obtain data on the sexual desire disorders, because what some respondents consider normal in these matters others do not. Many people with desire disorders probably never come to the attention of a therapist. (Those who do usually come at the urging of their partners.) But more are seeking treatment, and these disorders, once considered rare and almost exclusively female, are now thought to be fairly common, in men as well as women (Rosen & Leiblum, 1989). The prevalence of arousal and orgasmic disorders is somewhat better known, because erections and orgasms are objective events and therefore more easily reported on. According to two reviews, one of twenty-two general-population surveys (S. G. Nathan, 1986) and the other of twenty-three community samples (Spector & Carey, 1990), 4 to 20 percent of men experience erectile disorder (no erection or weak erection). In men the prevalence of orgasmic disorder is 3 to 10 percent. In women, it is higher; 5 to 15 percent of women never have orgasms, while the proportion of women who experience orgasm during sex rarely or only "sometimes" is probably close to 30 percent. Finally, more than one-third of men have premature ejaculation. In all, sexual dysfunction is a common problem.

It is very important to note that according to *DSM-IV* no sexual dysfunction can be diagnosed without evidence that the person's condition "causes marked distress or interpersonal difficulty." In other words, if a person has no interest in sex or no arousal or no orgasm—or even vaginismus—and this does not cause unhappiness or disrupt a relationship, then the person does not have a sexual dysfunction. It should also be noted that the term *sexual dysfunction* applies only to problems that persist over time. Occasional episodes of "sexual failure" are normal. When an adult is tired, sick, upset, intoxicated, or simply distracted, sexual responsiveness may be dulled. Nor should the label of sexual dysfunction be applied to the common occurrence of premature ejaculation or fleeting erections or missing orgasms in young people who have not yet established a regular pattern of sexual activity and are so concerned with "doing it right" that they cannot fully enjoy sex. The myths that sex comes naturally and that a couple should be able to achieve mutual ecstasy under any and all conditions are frequent causes of sexual problems. Counseling of-

WHAT IS NORMAL SEXUAL RESPONSE IN A WOMAN?

One of the most common complaints women bring to sex therapists is a socially defined dysfunction: they reach orgasm not through intercourse but only through manual or oral stimulation of the clitoris or only when intercourse is combined with manual stimulation. The designation of this pattern as somehow less than normal is due in part to our society's moral strictures against masturbation; intercourse may be normal, but "touching" yourself (or being touched) is not. It is also reflected in an old Freudian distinction between "clitoral" and "vaginal" orgasms. According to Freud, only the woman who has "vaginal" orgasms is sexually normal and psychologically mature.

Many sex researchers feel that this definition of sexual normality is absurd. (It is also male-centered: because men reach orgasm through intercourse, therefore women should.) All orgasms, no matter how they are achieved, constitute the same physical process, and there is no evidence that women who require direct stimulation to achieve orgasm are any less healthy or mature than those who do not. Women who reach orgasm during intercourse receive indirect stimulation of the clitoris: their partner's pubis (the bony structure behind the penis) rubs against their genitals, and penile thrusting pulls the clitoral hood back and forth. Many, possibly most, women require the more intense, *direct* stimulation of the clitoris, but the physiological mechanism of the orgasm is identical in both instances.

To say that direct clitoral stimulation is less healthy or normal than indirect stimulation is, in the words of the psychologist Joseph LoPiccolo (1977), "to draw almost mystical distinctions between the male pubis and the male hand" (p. 1239). Thus, according to LoPiccolo:

> A woman who can have coital orgasm if she receives concurrent manual stimulation of her clitoris does not have secondary orgasmic dysfunction; she is normal. Similarly, a woman who regularly has orgasm during manual or oral stimulation . . . and who enjoys intercourse even though orgasm does not occur during coitus, is a candidate for reassurance about her normality rather than for sex therapy. (p. 1239)

As Helen Singer Kaplan (1974) points out, female sexual response, like most human traits, is extremely variable. Women reach orgasm from erotic fantasy alone, from brief foreplay, from coitus, from manual or oral stimulation of the clitoris without coitus, from coitus combined with manual stimulation, or from intense stimulation such as that provided by a vibrator. About 10 percent of women never experience orgasm, and although they may justifiably seek professional help if they are distressed by this, any pattern of response can serve as the foundation for a happy sexual relationship. Of course, women who are dissatisfied with their response pattern should seek sex therapy, for the pattern may well be changeable. But those who are satisfied sexually yet worry that they do not fit some definition of "normal" should save their money. There is no single normal pattern.

ten reveals that one episode of failure leads to another simply because the first episode created so much anxiety that sexual responsiveness is impaired on the next occasion. The second failure aggravates the anxiety, further undermining sexual performance, and so on, until a regular pattern of sexual failure is established. Furthermore, such anxiety is communicable: sexual anxiety is often found in both members of a couple. Vaginismus and lifelong erectile disorder, or premature ejaculation and female orgasmic disorder, are often seen together in couples.

PERSPECTIVES ON SEXUAL DYSFUNCTION

The Psychodynamic Perspective: Oedipal Conflict

As we saw in Chapter 2, Freud claimed that mature genital sexuality was the product of successful resolution of the Oedipus complex. Accordingly, classical psychodynamic theory tends to attribute sexual dysfunction to unresolved Oedipal conflicts. This line of thinking may be seen in the interpretation of impotence offered by Otto Fenichel (1945):

> Impotence is based on a persistence of an unconscious sensual attachment to the mother. Superficially no sexual attachment is completely attractive because the partner is never the mother; in a deeper layer, every sexual attachment has to be inhibited, because every partner represents the mother. (p. 170)

Similarly, psychoanalytic formulations of female orgasmic disorder tend to stress the role of continued penis envy.

Psychodynamic therapy has had some success with sexual dysfunction. In a review of sexually dysfunctional patients treated at one psychoanalytic institute, 77 percent of men with erectile disorder either improved or were cured after two years of psychoanalysis (O'Connor & Stern, 1972). The results with other forms of dysfunction were less impressive, however. Furthermore, even if the cure rate were 100 percent, the fact remains that only a tiny percentage of the millions of people who suffer from sexual dysfunction can afford two years of psychoanalysis.

For many years psychodynamic therapy was the only generally available form of treatment. Certain authorities who took other approaches (A. Ellis, 1962; Wolpe, 1958) argued that sexual dysfunction, instead of being analyzed as a symptom of underlying conflict, should be attacked directly, by altering either the behavior in question or the attitudes surrounding it. But this was a minority view. Then in 1970 came the publication of Masters and Johnson's *Human Sexual Inadequacy,* outlining a systematic, short-term approach to direct symptomatic treatment. This approach, described in the next section, revolutionized sex therapy.

The Behavioral and Cognitive Perspectives

Learned Anxiety and the Spectator Role Behavioral theories of sexual dysfunction have focused consistently on the role of early respondent conditioning in which sexual feelings are paired with shame, disgust, fear of discovery, and especially anxiety over possible failure, all of which then proceed to block sexual responsiveness (H. S. Kaplan, 1974; Wolpe, 1969). This is also the position of Masters and Johnson, though they do not associate themselves with behaviorism or with any other theoretical school. According to Masters and Johnson (1970), any one of a number of painful experiences can cause a person to worry that he or she will be unable to perform adequately—will not achieve erection, will reach orgasm too quickly or not quickly enough, or whatever. As a result of this anxiety, the worried partner assumes what Masters and Johnson call the **spectator role.** That is, instead of simply relaxing and experiencing pleasure, the person is constantly watching and judging his or her performance. And, with cruel irony, the performance is almost inevitably a failure because the person's tense and critical attitude blunts his or her responsiveness to sexual stimuli.

As for the factors that first trigger performance anxiety and lead to the adoption of the spectator role, Masters and Johnson (1970) point to several possibilities: religious and sociocultural taboos on sexual feelings, particularly in women; disturbance in the marriage; parental dominance of one or the other partner; overuse of alcohol; and, finally, early psychosexual trauma, which can range from molestation and rape to ordinary humiliation, such as the following:

> During the patient's first sexual episode the prostitute took the unsuspecting virginal male to a vacant field and suggested they have intercourse while she leaned against a stone fence. Since he had no concept of female anatomy, of where to insert the penis, he failed miserably in this sexually demanding opportunity. His graphic memory of the incident is of running away from a laughing woman.
>
> The second prostitute provided a condom and demanded its use. He had no concept of how to use the condom. While the prostitute was demonstrating the technique, he ejaculated. He dressed and again fled the scene in confusion. (p. 177)

Direct Symptomatic Treatment If sexual dysfunction stems from faulty learning, so that sexual arousal comes to be associated with anxiety, then presumably it may be curable through new learning that gradually breaks down and eliminates this association. This idea is the basis of Masters and Johnson's treatment strategy and of most behavioral sex therapies.

First the couple is retrained to experience sexual excitement without performance pressure. Training usually takes the form of "sensate focus" exercises. During the period devoted to these exercises, the couple observes a ban on sexual intercourse. Instead, the partners simply devote a certain amount of time each day to gentle stroking and caressing in the nude, according to instructions given by the therapist. Very gradually, the allowed sexual play is increased, but always without performance demands.*

The purpose of sensate focus exercises is not only to allow the partners to rediscover their natural sexual responses but also to improve their communication. In the course of the exercises, each provides the other with feedback—what feels good, what doesn't feel good. The sharing of such information, aside from its crucial value in allowing the partners to satisfy each other, also serves to deepen their commitment to and trust in each other, which may have been sorely damaged by years of unhappy sex.* After a period of sensate focus exercises, the couple is given more specific exercises, aimed directly at the disorder in question.

*When the person seeking therapy does not have a partner, or when the partner is unwilling, Masters and Johnson, together with other therapists, have sometimes provided surrogate partners. However, this practice is controversial. Indeed, it has been called prostitution. Furthermore, in the case of unwilling partners, the relationship is unlikely to benefit from what the willing partner learned with a surrogate.

*People who have experienced rape or incest without subsequent treatment usually will not be assigned sensate focus exercises. They are likely to respond with flashbacks or panic attacks. Such clients will usually be given therapy aimed at the sexual trauma before they can benefit from sensate focus therapy.

For premature ejaculation, many therapists prescribe the so-called start-stop technique (Semans, 1956). In this procedure the woman stimulates the man's penis until he feels ready to ejaculate, at which point he signals her to stop. Once the need to ejaculate subsides, she stimulates him again, until he once again signals her to stop. Repeated many times, this technique gradually increases the amount of stimulation required to trigger the ejaculation response, so that eventually the man can maintain an erection for a longer time. The "squeeze" technique, in which the woman squeezes the tip of the man's penis when he feels close to ejaculation, has a similar effect.

With erectile disorder, the therapist, to eliminate anxiety, may actually tell the patient to try *not* to have an erection while he and his partner are going through their sensate focus exercises. This technique of proscribing the behavior that the patient is trying to accomplish is called *paradoxical instruction.* Forbidden to have an erection, the patient may find himself sufficiently free of anxiety that he begins to respond to the sexual stimuli and thus has the "prohibited" erection. Once this happens, the therapist "permits" the couple, in very gradual stages, to proceed further and further toward intercourse, always with the warning that the techniques "work best" if the man can prevent himself from having an erection. In the end, intravaginal ejaculation is "allowed" only after it has already occurred, because the man could not stop himself (LoPiccolo & Lobitz, 1973). Unfortunately, this technique does not work as well as it used to, because most men who come into treatment for erectile failure have read about the technique and are no longer naive as to its paradoxical intention. They know that the release from performance anxiety is supposed to improve performance, and therefore they develop a "meta-anxiety," thinking to themselves, "Now that I'm relieved from anxiety, I should be getting an erection. So *where* is it?" (LoPiccolo, 1992). Another technique that is now being tried with erectile disorder involves the use of a vacuum device that draws blood into the penis and thus artificially causes an erection (L. A. Turner, Althof, Levine, et al., 1991).

The most effective treatment for lifelong orgasmic dysfunction in women (Andersen, 1983; LoPiccolo & Stock, 1986) begins with education on female sexual anatomy and self-exploration exercises designed to increase body awareness. Then the woman is taught techniques of self-stimulation, perhaps with the aid of an electric vibrator and/or erotic pictures and books. This approach is based on the belief that masturbation enables a woman to identify the "symptoms" of sexual excitation, to discover which techniques excite her, and to anticipate pleasure in sex. When she has achieved orgasm alone, the therapist recommends sensate exercises with her partner, gradually incorporating the "orgasm triggers" she used alone. She may be encouraged to use a vibrator while her partner is present and to engage in the fantasies that arouse her when she is masturbating. Teaching her partner what stimulates her is an essential element of this program. Treatment of women with situational orgasmic disorder is similar. For women with sexual aversion disorder, these procedures are often combined with systematic desensitization. As with male sexual problems, the goal is to remove the pressure to perform and to encourage instead the simple experience of pleasure.

Cognitive Psychology and Direct Treatment Masters and Johnson popularized the concept of direct treatment of sexual dysfunction: attacking the symptom itself, without extensive exploration of its psychic roots. At the same time, their concern is not just with the couple's sexual behavior, but also with the partners' thoughts about sex—and about each other. Throughout this therapy, the emphasis is on the *couple.* The first three days of treatment are devoted to extensive interviewing—the woman by a female therapist, the man by a male therapist, and then vice versa—leading to a roundtable meeting of the couple and the therapists. During the interviews the therapist explores the beliefs and experiences that may have led to the present dysfunction. Shame-ridden memories are discussed with comforting matter-of-factness; repressive attitudes are challenged outright; the person is encouraged to appreciate his or her sexuality. The roundtable meeting is designed to restore a sense of trusting collaboration between partners. Resentments, fears, and secret memories that may have blocked communication are aired. The partners are encouraged to provide each other with concrete feedback during their exercises and in future meetings with the therapists. Later therapists, experimenting with this approach, have found that the male-female therapist team is not essential—a single therapist, male or female, can accomplish the same goals (LoPiccolo, Heiman, Hogan, et al., 1985)—but that the focus on the couple is essential.

Following Masters and Johnson's lead, cognitive psychologists have further explored the mental processes underlying sexual response—for example, the development of attitudes that can block arousal. Wincze (1989) cites the case, not an unusual one, of a man who learned when he was young the difference between "good girls" and "bad girls." He knew that his wife was a "good girl," a respectable woman, but her desire for sex confused and inhibited him because it was "bad-girl" behavior. This man also believed that in order to approach his wife sexually he needed to be fully aroused; it did not occur to him that arousal might develop in the *course* of sexual intimacy. Between these two beliefs, this man and his wife, both in their thirties, had had intercourse only once in the seven months before they sought treatment (at the wife's urging).

Cognitive therapists have also developed treatments that aim directly at attitudes and beliefs hostile to sex. For women, common interferences include negative attitudes toward the body ("Does he think I'm fat?") and worries about the propriety of sexual expression ("If I act too eager, he won't respect me"). But thoughts need not be antisexual in order to interfere with sex. Worries about work or children can also block sexual responsiveness. Often cognitive therapists will urge patients to allow sexual stimuli into their lives, for example, by reading erotic literature or giving some time each day to sexual thoughts. Such techniques are not confined to strictly cognitive therapy. Almost all sex therapists try to attack negative cognitions. Conversely, cognitive therapy is often combined with other approaches, particularly behavioral "direct treatment."

Helen Singer Kaplan, a noted sex therapist, has devised a multifaceted treatment for sexual dysfunction that she calls psychosexual therapy.

Multifaceted Treatment

Some sex researchers are dissatisfied with the theory that sexual dysfunction is caused by faulty learning. As they point out, millions of sexually untroubled people have been exposed to learning of this sort. Many people, perhaps most, were taught that sex was dirty. For many people the first attempt at intercourse was painful and embarrassing, if indeed intercourse was achieved. And many people have unhappy marriages—yet their sexual functioning remains stubbornly normal. Obviously, the cause of sexual dysfunction involves more than bad experiences and repressive attitudes. Consequently, some sex therapists, while using the kind of direct treatment outlined above, combine it with an exploration of intrapsychic or relationship factors that may be causing sexual dysfunction, or at least helping to maintain it.

Kaplan: Remote Causes The sex therapists who came after Masters and Johnson have tended to probe psychological factors more systematically and more deeply. Helen Singer Kaplan (1974), for example, argues that sexual dysfunction is probably due to a combination of immediate and remote causes. *Immediate causes* are factors such as performance anxiety, overconcern about pleasing one's partner, poor technique, lack of communication between partners, and marital conflict—the sort of causes on which Masters and Johnson concentrate. Such factors, Kaplan claims, are potent stressors, but in most cases they are not enough to undermine sexual functioning unless they are combined with (or based on) *remote causes* of sexual dysfunction: intrapsychic conflicts that predispose the person to anxiety over sexual expression. These conflicts are essentially the same as those the psychodynamic theorists blame for sexual dysfunction: infantile needs, deep-seated guilt, and—above all—unresolved Oedipal struggles.

On the basis of this theory, Kaplan (1974, 1979) has devised a combined "direct" and psychodynamic treatment that she calls "psychosexual therapy." She agrees with other direct therapists that behavior should be the primary focus of treatment and that unconscious conflicts, even when they are obvious to the therapist, should be bypassed as long as the patient is responding to the direct treatment. However, in some instances the remote causes of sexual dysfunction prevent the patient from responding to therapy. In such cases, Kaplan argues, brief "insight" therapy is called for. Furthermore, in many instances the direct therapy itself brings to the surface psychological problems that the patient has been blocking through avoidance of normal sexual functioning. Indeed, it is extremely common for patients to progress well in direct therapy until they are just on the edge of reaching their goal, at which point they seem to experience a flood of anxiety and begin to resist treatment. Kaplan interprets this response as a last-ditch attempt to maintain psychological defenses against whatever conflict has been blocking sexual responsiveness. And she claims that at this point psychodynamic exploration and interpretation of the patient's conflict is necessary before one can resume direct therapy.

Systems Theory: The Function of the Dysfunction Other therapists confront the psychological components of sexual dysfunction via systems theory, the analysis of relationships as systems of interlocking needs (Chapter 3). According to this approach, sexual dysfunction, distressing though it may be to the couple, usually has an important function in the couple's total relationship—that is, it serves psychological purposes for both partners (Heiman, LoPiccolo, & LoPiccolo, 1981). Consider, for example, low sexual desire on the part of the man, a problem that is turning up more and more frequently in sex therapy (H. S. Kaplan, 1974; Schover & LoPiccolo, 1982; Spector & Carey, 1990). Low sexual desire often has a number of causes. If the relationship in question involves conflicts over power and control, with the woman tending to dominate, then the man's lack of interest in sex may be his way of preserving some area of control for himself. At the same time, the woman, though she may complain of the man's sexual indifference, may also be deriving benefits from it. By seeing him as weak, for example, she maintains power in the relationship.

According to systems therapists, such secret payoffs underlie many cases of sexual dysfunction and must be dealt with if the dysfunction is to be relieved. The therapist generally addresses the "function of the dysfunction" from the beginning of treatment, asking patients to describe the benefits they derive from the problem, warning them that they may feel considerable fear when the problem begins to lessen, analyzing this fear, once it appears, as the product of a shaken system, and helping them to devise a better system. Such analysis, like Kaplan's, is combined with direct treatment.

By now, direct treatment is over twenty-five years old, and it has achieved very respectable results. The average success rates of programs based on direct treatment, either alone or in combination with the psychological techniques described above, are highest for premature ejaculation (90 to 95 percent), and vaginismus (90 to 95 percent). Success rates are lower for other disorders, but they are still encouraging: orgasmic disorder, 70 to 95 percent; erectile disorder, 40 to 80 percent (D. R. Hogan, 1978; H. S. Kaplan, 1974; LoPiccolo & Hogan, 1979; Masters & Johnson, 1970).

The Biological Perspective

In 1970 Masters and Johnson asserted that 95 percent of erectile failures were psychological, not physiological or organic, in origin. Today researchers are not so sure (Krauss, 1983; LoPiccolo, 1992). In some cases, organic causes are known. Erectile disorder may be the result of diabetes, heart disease, kidney disease, or alcoholism. A variety of medical treatments—renal dialysis, tranquilizers, antidepressants, medications for hypertension—can also interfere with erection. Long-term use of oral contraceptives can reduce the female sex drive. Female dyspareunia may be caused by vaginal infections, ovarian cysts, or lacerations or scar tissue resulting from childbirth (Sarrel, 1977). Other organic factors—hormonal deficiencies, neurological impairment, neurotransmitter imbalances—are suspected contributors to sexual dysfunction. In any case, people seeking treatment for sexual dysfunction should first see a gynecologist or urologist to rule out treatable organic causes (Becker & Kavoussi, 1994).

In the 1970s and early 1980s, many sex researchers concentrated on developing diagnostic tools for differentiating between psychological and organic sexual dysfunction. They invented devices for measuring vasocongestion in the genital region; they devised tests of the sensory threshold in the genital area. Research on *nocturnal penile tumescence* (NPT) attracted a good deal of attention. Men have erections during rapid-eye-movement (REM) sleep, the stage of sleep associated with dreams. NPT research is based on the assumption that if a man has erections while he is asleep, but not during sexual encounters, his problem is primarily psychological in origin.

Today, however, researchers are questioning the very concept of differentiating the organic from the psychological cases (LoPiccolo, 1992). Rather, they believe that many (if not most) cases of sexual dysfunction involve *both* psychological and physiological factors. A mild organic impairment—perhaps one that cannot be detected by current techniques, or one not yet known to be associated with sexual functioning—may make a person vulnerable to sexual dysfunction. But whether that person actually experiences sexual difficulties may depend on psychological factors, learning, and/or sexual technique. This would help to explain, for example, why some people who have been taught that sex is sinful or who had humiliating early experiences with sex function normally, while others do not. Future research may show that some cases of sexual dysfunction are purely psychological in origin, some primarily organic, and many others the result of interacting organic and psychological factors.

Recently there has been considerable interest in the physical treatment of erectile disorders that seem to be organically based. One treatment involves the man's injecting a vascular dilation agent (either papaverine or phentolamine) into his penis when he wants an erection. The penis becomes erect within thirty minutes of the injection and remains erect for one to four hours. Many men have reported satisfaction with this method (L. A. Turner, Althof, Levine, et al., 1989), but there is some question about its long-term use, because a substantial number of patients develop nodules on their penises as a side effect (Althof, Turner, Levine, et al., 1987). Another physical treatment involves taking (by mouth) a drug called yohimbine, which has long had a reputation as an aphrodisiac. Yohimbine stimulates the secretion of norepinephrine and thereby increases the firing rate of nerve cells in the brain. Therefore it is possible that the drug corrects neurotransmission problems that are causing the erectile disorder. Yohimbine treatment is relatively new, has had mixed results, and needs to be studied further (Riley, Goodman, Kellett, et al., 1989; Sonda, Mazo, & Chancellor, 1990).

Finally, for men who do not benefit from medications or sex therapy, penile prosthesis is available. In one type, a semirigid rod is surgically inserted into the penis. This makes the penis permanently stiff enough for intercourse. At the same time the rod is bendable enough for the penis to look normal under clothing. In another type of prosthesis, a water-filled bag is surgically inserted into the abdomen and connected by tubes to inflatable cylinders that are inserted into the penis. When the man wants an erection, he pumps the bag, causing the water to flow into the penile cylinders and thus engorge the penis. Follow-ups on penile prosthesis recipients (Steege, Stout, & Culley, 1986; Tiefer, Pedersen, & Melman, 1988) indicate that while most of them, if they had to do it over again, would choose the prosthesis, primarily for the repair of their self-esteem, their sexual satisfaction was still not comparable to what they enjoyed before they developed erection problems.

PARAPHILIAS

The sexual revolution has expanded our definition of normal sexual behavior. Premarital sex, oral sex, homosexuality—behaviors that were spoken of in whispers, if at all, a generation ago—are now discussed casually by many people. This does not mean, however, that all barriers have fallen. According to *DSM-IV*—and, it is safe to assume, according to most members of our society—normal sexuality still consists of a nondestructive interplay between consenting adults.

A number of recognized sexual patterns deviate from this standard. These patterns are called **paraphilias** (from the Greek *para,* meaning "beside" or "amiss," and *philia,* meaning "love"). We shall discuss the following:

1 **Fetishism:** reliance on inanimate objects or on some body part (to the exclusion of the person as a whole) for sexual gratification.
2 **Transvestism:** sexual gratification through dressing in the clothes of the opposite sex.
3 **Exhibitionism:** sexual gratification through display of one's genitals to an involuntary observer.
4 **Voyeurism:** sexual gratification through clandestine observation of other people's sexual activities or sexual anatomy.
5 **Sadism:** sexual gratification through infliction of pain and/or humiliation on others.
6 **Masochism:** sexual gratification through pain and/or humiliation inflicted on oneself.
7 **Frotteurism:** sexual gratification through touching and rubbing against a nonconsenting person.
8 **Pedophilia:** child molesting—that is, sexual gratification, on the part of the adult, through sexual contact with children.

In all these patterns, what arouses the person is something other than what is commonly considered a normal sexual object or sexual activity. But a distinction must be drawn between those paraphilias that are essentially "victimless," such as fetishism and transvestism, and those, notably pedophilia, that cause psychological and/or physical damage. Other paraphilias fall between the two poles: they may or may not cause harm, depending on the circumstances.

It is important to note that most of these behaviors occur in mild, playful, or sublimated forms in what we call everyday life. Sexually explicit movies, videos, and television programs—magazine and billboard advertisements too—cater to what might be called normal voyeurism. It is only when the unusual object choice becomes the central focus and *sine qua non* of the person's arousal and gratification that the pattern is generally deemed abnormal by the society and by diagnosticians. Similarly, many people have fantasies involving sexual aggression, but it is only when these impulses are acted upon that they are labeled pathological.

According to *DSM-IV*, most of the paraphilias are all but exclusively male aberrations. The only exception is masochism, but even there the male-female ratio is 20 to 1. Some writers believe this is because female sexuality is repressed in the process of socialization, with the result that most women never develop truly normal or truly abnormal forms of sexual expression. It should be added, however, that data on the prevalence of the paraphilias generally often come from arrest records, and women are much less likely than men to be arrested, or even reported, for unconventional sexual behavior. Still, these facts do not account for the vastly greater numbers of male paraphiliacs. There seems to be a true difference between the sexes in this respect. Sociobiologists (e.g., G. D. Wilson, 1987) have proposed that natural selection breeds into males an instinctive desire to inseminate as many partners as possible and that this instinct makes men more responsive to a greater variety of sexual stimuli. Other researchers have suggested that the difference between the sexes in risk for paraphilias may be due to male-female differences in brain structure (Flor-Henry, 1987).

Fetishism

Fetishism is a good example of a "spectrum disorder," one that exists on a continuum ranging from normal to abnormal, with many variations in between. It is not unusual, of course, for people to concentrate sexual interest on some particular attribute of the opposite sex. Certain women consider the male buttocks to be particularly important, while many men are fascinated by large breasts. Other men prefer as sexual partners women who are stylishly dressed, and the sight of a pair of underpants held together with a safety pin can leave them discouraged sexually. In general, however, such people, despite their preferences, do not disregard the rest of the person and can respond to conventional sexual stimuli.

Further along the continuum we can place the following case, reported by Krafft-Ebing (1886/1965a):

> A lady told Dr. Gemy that in the bridal night and in the night following her husband contented himself with kissing her, and running his fingers through the wealth of her tresses. He then fell asleep. In the third night Mr. *X* produced an immense wig, with enormously long hair, and begged his wife to put it on. As soon as she had done so, he richly compensated her for his neglected marital duties. In the morning he showed again extreme tenderness, whilst he caressed the wig. When Mrs. *X* removed the wig she lost at once all charm for her husband. Mrs. *X* recognized this as a hobby, and readily yielded to the wishes of her husband, whom she loved dearly, and whose libido depended on the wearing of the wig. It was remarkable, however, that a wig had the desired effect only for a fortnight or three weeks at a time. It had to be made of thick, long hair, no matter of what colour. The result of this marriage was, after five years, two children, and a collection of seventy-two wigs. (pp. 157–158)

Mr. *X*'s "hobby" still falls in the middle of the continuum, for once the wig was present, he was interested in intercourse with his wife. In most cases of fetishism that come to the attention of diagnosticians, the person's fascination with a single body part or, more commonly, with some type of inanimate object has totally crowded out any interest in normal sexual interplay with another human being. Much of the person's life is occupied with collecting new examples of his favored object.

Common fetishistic objects are fur, women's stockings, women's shoes, women's gloves, and especially women's underpants, but more exotic fetishes have also been reported. Bergler (1947) cited the case of a man whose major source of sexual gratification was the sight of well-formed automobile exhaust pipes. The fetishist's sexual activity, typically, consists of fondling, kissing, and smelling the fetish and masturbating in the process.

Transvestism

Transvestism is similar to fetishism—indeed, *DSM-IV* calls it "transvestic fetishism"—in that it involves a fascination with inanimate objects. But transvestites go one step further and actually put on their fetish, which is the clothing of the opposite sex. Once cross-dressed, the transvestite typically masturbates privately or has heterosexual intercourse, though he may also enjoy appearing publicly in his costume.

Transvestites usually do not come into conflict

Cross-dressing is a feature of sexual patterns ranging from transvestism to homosexual "drag queens" to gender identity disorder, with no clear line separating one from the others.

with the law, and in recent years social attitudes toward transvestism have eased somewhat. Indeed, nightclubs featuring transvestite performers have become increasingly popular. Partly as a result of this social tolerance, there has been little psychological investigation of transvestism. However, some insight into the psychology of the transvestite has been provided by Bentler and his colleagues, who, with the help of a national transvestite organization, administered standardized personality tests to a large sample of male transvestites (Bentler & Prince, 1970; Bentler, Shearman, & Prince, 1970). These tests revealed what a number of clinicians had already suspected: that as a group, transvestites appear to be no more prone to psychological disturbance than the population at large. Not surprisingly, however, they tend to have marital problems. Most women, upon discovering their husbands' transvestism, are very distressed; many such marriages end in divorce. But some women will tolerate their husbands' transvestism and incorporate it into the sexual relationship, as in the following case:

> Curtis is a 29-year-old married contractor who has a secret. When he goes to work each morning he wears a pair of women's panties. He began cross-dressing as a young boy when he would sneak into his older sister's room and put on her panties or bra. Eventually, he stole some women's underwear from the girls locker room at school. He wore the panties while he masturbated. When Curtis left home and went to college he began wearing women's panties under his clothes every day and continued to use them to masturbate.
>
> He dated infrequently in college until he met Sally. She was kind and he enjoyed being with her. Curtis had his first sexual experience with a woman when he and Sally had sex one night during his junior year. As their relationship progressed, Curtis felt he could no longer hide his secret from her. One night he told Sally that he wore women's panties under his clothes. She seemed confused about why he needed to wear the panties, but was not very upset about the fact that he wore them. Tentatively, Curtis asked her if she would be willing to let him wear the panties while they were having sex. Sally nodded, and said, "I guess so, if that makes you happy." A year later they were married. During the first few years of their marriage Curtis continued to wear panties during sex. His wife periodically went shopping and brought home new panties for him as the old ones wore out. (Fauman, 1994, p. 295)

Transvestism is thought to be relatively rare, but the reported rarity may be due to lack of public exposure or public alarm. Many transvestites lead quiet, conventional lives, cross-dressing only in their bedrooms and never appearing on talk shows or in therapists' offices. Thus the pattern may be more common than is assumed.

The pattern may also be a less distinct phenomenon than is assumed. Because of the shared predilection for cross-dressing, transvestites are sometimes confused in the public mind with homosexual "drag queens." For many years it was thought that such confusion was unwarranted—that is, that the two patterns were totally separate, transvestites being predominantly heterosexual (Buckner, 1970). It now seems, however, that there is some overlap between the two categories, with some men starting out as heterosexual transvestites and eventually making the transition to homosexuality. The distinction between transvestism and gender identity disorder (see below) has also blurred somewhat in recent years, with a number of what seem to be transvestites deciding that in fact their problem is that they have been born with the wrong gender (V. Prince, 1978). In such cases, the diagnostic lines may be difficult to draw.

Exhibitionism

Exhibitionism and voyeurism are the two sex offenses most often reported to the police. They are usually treated harshly by the courts, on the assumption that if the offender is treated leniently, he will graduate to more serious sex crimes. Studies of sex offenders indicate that more than 10 percent of child molesters and 8 percent of rapists began as exhibitionists (Abel, Rouleau, & Cunningham-Rathner, 1984). But most exhibitionists are not dangerous; they do not attempt to have sexual contact with their victims.

Virtually all reported exhibitionists are male—a fact that is surely due in part to the reversed double standard. (Should a woman choose to undress regularly in front of a window, male observers are unlikely to report the matter to the police.) The typical exhibitionist is a young man, sexually inhibited and unhappily married (Blair & Lanyon, 1981; Mohr, Turner, & Jerry, 1964). Experiencing an irresistible impulse to exhibit himself, he will usually go to a public place such as a park, a movie theater, or a department store, or simply walk down a city street, and upon sighting the appropriate victim—typically a young woman, though sometimes a young girl—will show her his penis. The penis is usually, but not always, erect. The exhibitionist's gratification is derived from the woman's response, which is generally shock, fear, and revulsion, although exhibitionists also enjoy victims who show excitement. Observing the reaction, the exhibitionist experiences intense arousal, at which point he may ejaculate spontaneously or masturbate to ejaculation. In the usual case, however, he will go home and then masturbate while fantasizing about the event. (In some cases, the episode is not followed by ejaculation; the exhibitionist merely obtains psychic relief.) Although an encounter with an exhibitionist may involve no physical harm, it can be very upsetting for an adult and traumatic for a child.

In some cases, exhibitionism occurs as a symptom of a more pervasive disturbance, such as schizophrenia, epilepsy, senile brain deterioration, or mental retardation. But most exhibitionists turn out to be simply shy, submissive, immature men who have uncommonly puritanical attitudes about sex (Witzig, 1968), particularly about masturbation. Furthermore, they often experience feelings of social and sexual inferiority and serious doubts about their masculinity (Blair & Lanyon, 1981). Thus, it has been suggested, they display their genitals for shock value in a desperate effort to convince themselves of their masculine prowess (Blane & Roth, 1967; Christoffel, 1956), all the while arranging the circumstances so that the victim is unlikely to respond positively and thus make sexual demands on them. In the rare instance in which the victim shows indifference or scorn rather than the expected shock and dismay, the exhibitionist will generally be cheated of his sexual gratification. Indeed, it has been suggested that the best "cure" for exhibitionism would be to educate the public not to respond to it.

Voyeurism

An element of voyeurism, as of exhibitionism, is usually involved in normal sexual activity. In recent years, sexually oriented magazines and videos have provided more or less "acceptable" outlets for those people who derive pleasure from looking. The traditional definition of voyeurism distinguished true voyeurs—or "peeping Toms,"* as they are sometimes called—as those people for whom the pleasure of looking interferes with normal sexual interplay with another person. Actually, voyeurism often occurs alongside normal sexual interplay. Since this is the case, a realistic definition of voyeurism must take into account social sanctions against violating the privacy of others. In practice, then, a voyeur obtains gratification from watching strangers in violation of their sexual privacy. This usually means watching women who are undressing or couples engaged in sex play. The risk involved in watching strangers may be a desirable adjunct to the voyeur's pleasure. The danger of being discovered in his perch on the fire escape or balcony adds to the sexual thrill of the peeping, which usually leads to masturbation.

Like exhibitionism, voyeurism seems to provide a substitute gratification and a reassurance of power for otherwise sexually anxious and inhibited males. Voyeurs, like exhibitionists, are often withdrawn both socially and sexually, with little in their developmental histories to support the learning of more appropriate interpersonal skills. Again, like exhibitionists, most voyeurs are harm-

*The term is derived from English folklore. During Lady Godiva's nude ride through Coventry, to protest a raise in taxes, the only person who looked at her was a tailor named Tom, who, the story goes, was struck blind as a result.

less, but not all: 10 to 20 percent of them go on to rape the women they peep at.

Sadism and Masochism

There appears to be an element of aggression in even the most "natural" sexual activity. Human beings, like most other mammals, sometimes bite and scratch during intercourse, and aggressive sexual fantasies—of raping or of being raped—are not uncommon (Kinsey, 1953). Conversely, a sexual element often underlies aggression. Both men and women have reported becoming sexually excited at boxing matches and football games or while watching fires or executions—a fact that has led some theorists to propose that our society's preoccupation with violence may be sexually motivated.

In sadism and masochism, however, the element of physical and/or psychological cruelty—inflicting and being subjected to it, respectively—assumes a central role in sexual functioning. Both disorders are named for literary figures who publicized the sexual pleasures of cruelty. The term *sadism* is taken from the name of the Marquis de Sade (1740–1814), whose novels include numerous scenes featuring the torture of women for erotic purposes. Masochism is named for an Austrian novelist, Leopold von Sacher-Masoch (1836–1895), whose male characters tended to swoon with ecstasy when physically abused by women.

Individual patterns of sadism turn up primarily in men. The degree of cruelty may range from sticking a woman with a pin to gruesome acts of mutilation, numerous examples of which may be found in Krafft-Ebing's *Psychopathia Sexualis* (1886/1965a). Between these two extremes are sadists who bind, whip, bite, and cut their victims. For some, the mere sight of blood or the victim's cries of pain are sufficient to trigger ejaculation; for others, the act of cruelty merely intensifies arousal, which eventually leads to rape. Similarly, the masochist may need to suffer only a mild pain, such as spanking or verbal abuse, or may choose to be chained and whipped. And like the sadist, he or she may reach orgasm through the experience of pain alone, or the abuse stage may serve simply as "foreplay," leading eventually to intercourse. Masochists without sadistic partners usually have to resort to prostitutes, some of whom specialize in abusing clients. Sadists without partners may prey on prostitutes or other unwary women.

In many cases, however, sadists and masochists do have complementary partners, with whom they share a **sadomasochistic** relationship. In some of these pairings, one partner is always the sadist, the other always the masochist. Alternatively, both partners may enjoy both sadism and masochism, in which case they will switch between the two. According to a survey of male readers of a sadomasochistically oriented magazine (Moser & Levitt, 1987), most sadists and masochists are heterosexual, well educated, reasonably affluent, given to switching between sadism and masochism, and undisturbed by their specialized tastes. Other sadists and masochists are homosexuals; in fact, there is a substantial so-called S-and-M segment within the homosexual subculture. To serve sadomasochists, many underground newspapers carry advertisements by sadists and masochists seeking partners and stating their special requirements. Likewise, in many large American cities there are "sex shops" that specialize in selling sadomasochistic equipment.

In sadism and masochism, the line between normal and abnormal may be hard to draw. Just as

Jeffrey Dahmer (center) was one of the most notorious multiple murderers in U.S. history. His killings were sex-related, centering on sadistic abuse of and necrophilic sex with young men whom he abducted and drugged.

with the sexual dysfunctions *DSM-IV* requires evidence of distress or interpersonal difficulty, so with all the paraphilias one of the diagnostic criteria is that the person's sexual pattern has caused "clinically significant distress or impairment in social, occupational, or other important areas of functioning." By this standard, mutually consenting S-and-M partners who are satisfied with their sexual pattern and who show no disturbance in other aspects of their lives would not be candidates for diagnosis, though their behavior would probably be considered abnormal by most people.

Frotteurism

New in *DSM-IV* is a separate listing for frotteurism (from the French word *frotter,* "to rub"), in which the person obtains gratification by touching or rubbing against a nonconsenting person. Frotteurs usually operate in crowded places, such as buses or subways, where they are more likely to escape notice and arrest. Typically, the frotteur touches the person's breasts or genitals or rubs his own genitals against her thighs or buttocks. While he does this, he usually fantasizes about an exclusive and tender relationship with the person. Frotteurism tends to begin in adolescence, tapering off in early adulthood (American Psychiatric Association, 1994).

Pedophilia

Children, by definition, lack the knowledge and experience to consent to sexual relations. Thus pedophilia (from the Greek, meaning "love of children") involves a violation of the rights of the child, who may suffer serious psychological harm as a result. The pedophile may (in order of increasing rarity) covertly or overtly masturbate while caressing the child, stroke the child's genitals, masturbate between the child's thighs, have the child stimulate him manually or orally, or attempt intercourse. He may entice a group of children to participate in sexual activities and pose for pornographic pictures, using peer pressure to maintain secrecy (Burgess, Groth, & McCausland, 1981). Some pedophiles look for jobs or volunteer positions that involve extensive contact with children (Abel, Lawry, Karlstrom, et al., 1994).

An estimated 10 to 15 percent of children and adolescents have been sexually victimized by an adult at least once (Lanyon, 1986). Prepubescent children are more likely than older adolescents to be victimized, and girls twice as likely as boys. Although cases of female sexual abuse of children do turn up, they are rare: most pedophiles are male (Finkelhor, 1984). The stereotype of the child molester includes a number of myths, however. First, the typical pedophile is not a "dirty old man" who lives on the margins of society. In most cases he is an otherwise law-abiding citizen who may escape detection precisely because he does not appear disreputable. Although ranging in age from the teens to the seventies, most pedophiles are in their twenties, thirties, or forties. Many are also married or divorced, with children of their own. Second, most child molestation is not committed by strangers lurking about the schoolyard. The offender is usually acquainted with the victim and his or her family; indeed, many are related to the victim (Conte & Berliner, 1981), as we will see in our discussion of incest, below. Third, child molestation usually does not entail physical violence. Rather, the offender uses his authority as an adult to persuade the child to acquiesce (Finkelhor, 1979). Fourth, child molestation usually is not an isolated event but consists of repeated incidents with the same child. The molestation may begin when the child is quite young and recur continuously or at intervals over five or ten years before it is discovered or broken off (Finkelhor, 1979). A final interesting point about pedophilia is that it is usually accompanied by other paraphilias. In a survey of over 500 paraphiliacs, most of them pedophiles, half the respondents reported engaging in four or more paraphilias (Abel, Becker, Cunningham-Rathner, et al., 1988).

Several researchers feel that a distinction should be made between situational and preference molesters (Howells, 1981; Karpman, 1954). *Situational molesters* are people with more or less normal heterosexual histories who most of the time prefer adult sexual partners. Their child molesting is impulsive—it is usually a response to stress—and they view it with disgust. By contrast, *preference molesters,* people who actually prefer children as sexual partners, are generally not married, prefer male children, and do not view their behavior as abnormal. For these people, child molesting is a regular sexual outlet. Their contacts with children are planned, not impulsive or precipitated by stress. Whether or not they are preference molesters, pedophiles who specialize in male children have a much higher rate of recidivism, or repeat offenses (American Psychiatric Association, 1994). In the survey mentioned earlier (Abel, Becker, Cunningham-Rathner, et al., 1988), the pedophiles who preferred boys averaged about 150 victims; those who preferred girls averaged about 20 victims.

The causes of pedophilia seem to vary (Finkelhor & Araji, 1986). Sometimes it is associated with arrested psychological development: experiencing himself as a child, with childish emotional needs, the pedophile is most comfortable relating to children. Other pedophiles may be so isolated socially or so timid that they are unable to establish adult heterosexual relationships and turn to children as substitutes. In still other cases, an early experience of arousal with other children may become fixed in the person's mind. The pedophile may have been a victim of childhood molestation himself (de Young, 1982). In an attempt to restore his feeling of control, he reenacts his own victimization.

Children rarely report their victimization; they are afraid their parents will blame them. Molestation is generally discovered when an adult becomes suspicious, when the child tells an adult other than his or her parent, or when a physician sees signs of sexual abuse (Finkelhor, 1979). But children "tell" adults about their problem in indirect ways (Browne & Finkelhor, 1986). Most studies of child victims report varying degrees and combinations of sleep and eating disorders, fears and phobias, difficulties at school, and inappropriate sexual behavior. The effects do not go away when the abuse stops. Adults who were sexually exploited as children frequently exhibit depression, dissociative disorders, self-destructive behavior, feelings of being isolated and stigmatized, and distrust of others. They report problems relating to other adults of either sex, their parents, and even their children. Tragically, women who were sexually abused as children are more likely than other women to be physically abused by their husbands or other partners as adults (Finkelhor, 1984; J. L. Herman, 1981).

Some types of child abuse seem to do more psychological harm than others (Browne & Finkelhor, 1986). On the basis of clinical experience, Groth (1978) argued that if the abuse continues over a period of time, if it involves violence or penetration, or if the molester is closely related to the child, the risk of severe trauma is that much greater. According to MacFarlane (1978), any collusion or suggestion of collusion on the part of the child increases the risk. If the child cooperates to some degree, if he or she is older and aware of the taboo violation, or if the child's disclosure is met by parental anger or accusation, the psychological damage will be worse.

GENDER IDENTITY DISORDER

Whereas in the paraphilias the disturbance lies in the object of sexual interest, in **gender identity disorder** the problem is with the person's sense of his or her gender. People with this disorder, also called **transsexualism,** identify with the opposite sex—indeed, feel that they belong to that sex and that their own biological gender is simply a mistake. Typically cross-dressing on a regular basis, they do not feel the sexual arousal that transvestites feel in cross-sex clothing. Rather, they feel relaxed, "right." Indeed, they may feel as strange in the clothing of their own sex as others would feel cross-dressed (R. Green, 1971). By biological standards they are usually homosexual, but since they think of themselves as belonging to the opposite sex, in their minds they are heterosexual. Gender identity disorder is three to five times more common in males than in females (Zucker & Green, 1992).

The subjective reversal of gender usually dates from early childhood. In a thorough study of fourteen male transsexuals, Money and Primrose (1968) found that without exception all of these men had been branded as "sissies" in childhood and had presented a feminine rather than a masculine appearance. (The reversal is not true: only a minuscule proportion of "sissy" boys grow up to be transsexuals.) Not surprisingly, some researchers feel inborn hormonal differences are involved in gender identity disorder (Pillard & Weinrich, 1987).

There have been a few reported cases of transsexual "cures"—that is, of transsexuals reoriented toward their biological gender, usually through behavioral techniques—but in general, this pattern has proved resistant to therapy (Abramowitz, 1986). Some transsexuals are content to cross-dress and play the desired gender role. But a great many are deeply anguished at having been assigned the wrong gender and are very ashamed of their bodies. Such transsexuals typically see sex reassignment surgery as the only solution to their problems.

Sex Reassignment Surgery

The first "sex-change" operations were performed in the 1930s, but sex reassignment did not receive much attention until the highly publicized case of Christine Jorgensen, whose successful surgery was reported by Hamburger in 1953. In cases of male-to-female transsexualism, treatment begins with hormone injections to inhibit beard growth and stimulate breast development. Surgery involves the removal of the penis and testicles and the construction of a vagina, which (ideally) allows the person to experience orgasm through intercourse. In female-to-male sexual reassignment, treatment

Writer James Morris (left) had sex reassignment surgery and became Jan Morris (right) in the mid-1970s.

begins with hormone injections to lower the voice, promote beard growth, stop menstruation, and in some cases enlarge the clitoris. Surgery involves a mastectomy, removal of the ovaries and uterus, and closure of the vagina. In some cases an artificial penis is constructed of tissue taken from other parts of the body; in others, the urethra is rerouted through the enlarged clitoris. The penis thus created does not have erectile functioning itself, but an inflatable penile prosthesis is often implanted as part of the surgery.

By 1977 it was estimated that approximately 2,500 Americans had undergone sex reassignment surgery (Gagnon, 1977), and early reports were quite positive (Benjamin, 1966; Pauly, 1968). Then in 1979 a study of patients who had undergone surgery at Johns Hopkins University's Gender Identity Clinic, at that time one of the leading centers for gender reassignment, concluded that "sex reassignment confers no advantage in terms of social rehabilitation" (Meyer & Peter, 1979, p. 1015), and the clinic was closed the following year. That study has since been severely criticized on methodological grounds (Fleming et al., 1980). Indeed, many of the follow-up studies of surgically reassigned transsexuals have methodological problems, such as researcher bias—which is no surprise in view of the extremely controversial nature of this procedure. Despite the confusion over success rates, however, sex-change operations are still going on, at an estimated rate of 1,000 per year in the United States alone.

In a survey of follow-up studies with a total of 350 patients, 97 percent of female-to-male and 87 percent of male-to-female reassignments were judged satisfactory (R. Green & Fleming, 1990), though "satisfactory" was vaguely defined, often amounting to a statement by the patient that he or she did not regret the decision to have the surgery. Even if they do not regret the surgery, many reassigned transsexuals still report considerable unhappiness due to lack of a mate and lack of understanding from others, among other problems (Lindemalm, Körlin, & Uddenberg, 1986). Nearly all follow-up studies (e.g., Abramowitz, 1986) report some tragic outcomes—patients who commit suicide, patients who have psychotic breaks. On the other hand, many transsexuals predict tragic outcomes for themselves if they cannot obtain surgery. As the above percentages indicate, female-to-male reassignment, though rarer, is generally more successful than male-to-female. And as might be predicted, the patients most likely to have successful outcomes are those who before surgery had a reasonable degree of emotional stability, lived with some comfort in the desired gender role for at least a year, had a good understanding of the limitations of the surgery, and received psychotherapy directed at their gender problems (R. Green & Fleming, 1990).

INCEST AND RAPE

Incest and rape are not listed in the *DSM*. They are crimes, not symptoms of psychological disorder. Nevertheless, there are continuing questions about the psychological health of people who commit incest and rape, and there are often grave psychological consequences for the victims.

Incest

Incest, or sexual relations between family members, has been prohibited, in varying degrees, by virtually all human societies throughout their known histories. Explanations of this universal taboo range from the argument that it encouraged families to establish wider social contacts to the contention, supported by scientific studies, that inbreeding fosters genetic defects in offspring.

Despite the taboo, incest does occur. Alfred Kinsey (Kinsey, Pomeroy, & Martin, 1948; Kinsey, Pomeroy, Martin, et al., 1953) reported that only 3 percent of his sample had had incestuous relations. More recent studies indicate that the rate of incest in the general population is much higher: 7 to 17 percent (Finkelhor, 1980; Greenwald & Leitenberg, 1989; Hunt, 1974). One problem with studies of incest is that they are often based on clinical samples—that is, people who sought treatment. Diana Russell's household survey of women in the San Francisco area was an attempt to correct this bias. Russell (1986) found that 16 percent of women in her sample had been victims of incest at least once before age eighteen, 12 percent before age fourteen. Molestation by uncles was most common, followed by first cousins, fathers, and brothers. A quarter of the experiences were rated as "very severe sexual abuse" (actual or attempted intercourse, fellatio, cunnilingus, analingus, or anal intercourse), more than 40 percent as "severe sexual abuse" (genital contact without clothing). The age of victimization ranged from two years to seventeen. In most cases, the molester was at least twenty years older than the victim and lived under the same roof. Often (43 percent of cases) the incestuous assault was not repeated, but twenty-four of the women in the sample reported being molested by more than one relative.

Russell concludes that father-daughter incest is "the supreme betrayal": more than twice as many victims of fathers reported being extremely upset and suffering severe long-term effects as victims of all other incest perpetrators combined. Other researchers (Finkelhor, 1979) have also found that abuse by a father or stepfather is more damaging than any other form of abuse. What kind of man would assault his daughter? One who is promiscuous and unselective in his sexual partners? Research suggests not. Cavallin (1966) reports that the typical incestuous father confines his extramarital sexual contacts to his daughter, or perhaps to several daughters, beginning with the eldest. Far from being indiscriminately amoral, such fathers tend to be highly moralistic and devoutly attached to fundamentalist religious doctrines (Gebhard, Gagnon, Pomeroy, et al., 1965). Father-daughter incest tends to occur in connection with a troubled marriage. The man may abuse his wife (as well as his children) and then turn to the daughter sexually when the wife rejects his advances. The wife may pretend not to notice because she is afraid of her husband's violence. She is often isolated from other family members, due to chronic illness or infirmity. In many cases the victim assumes the caretaking role in the family, even acting as a surrogate wife. Some mothers blame their daughters for threatening to break up the family (Herman, 1981).

Not surprisingly, the impact on the daughter can be profound. The long-term effects reported by incest victims in the Russell survey were similar to those of nonincestuous child molestation: lowered self-esteem, self-blame, and self-hatred; a tendency to be vengeful or passive; emotional coldness and lack of responsiveness; negative feelings about physical closeness; and the belief that other people would think ill of them if the incest were known. Incest victims are also at higher risk for psychological disorders. As we saw in Chapter 8, most people with dissociative identity disorder report having been sexually abused as children by a member of the family (Coons & Milstein, 1986; Putnam, Guroff, Silberman, et al., 1986). Russell (1986) contrasts abuse of a child by a close relative with rape of an adult:

> An adult woman is more likely to have experienced trust in intimate relationships, to have a sense of who she is and what sex is before the traumatic attack. In contrast, children's capacity to trust can be shattered. Their sense of who they are and what sex is about is often totally or substantially shaped by the sexually abusive experience. (p. 157)

Predictably, incest bodes ill for adult sexual adjustment. In a survey of women with a childhood history of incest, 65 percent met *DSM-III* criteria for one or more sexual dysfunctions (J. L. Jackson, Calhoun, Amick, et al., 1990).

Rape

Rape, or sexual intercourse with a nonconsenting partner, is a common crime. About 100,000 rapes are reported to the police each year (Federal Bureau of Investigation, 1991), but national surveys suggest that the actual incidence of rape is some-

DATE RAPE

"Date rape" was described and documented in the fifties but it did not receive wide attention until the eighties, when, in the wake of contemporary feminism, it became a pressing issue on American college campuses. Date rape, like other rape, is very common, as even its perpetrators acknowledge, or used to acknowledge. In a survey conducted in the sixties, 26 percent of the college men interviewed admitted having attempted to force intercourse on a woman who was "fighting, kicking, screaming, pleading, etc." (Kanin, 1967, p. 429). More recently, a survey of 3,187 college women found that 54 percent had experienced some form of unwanted sexual contact and 15 percent had actually been raped (Koss, Gidycz, & Wisniewski, 1987).

While one might expect date rape to be less traumatic than an assault by a stranger, this is apparently not the case. A recent study found no differences between victims of stranger and acquaintance rape on measures of postassault depression, anxiety, relationship quality, or sexual adjustment (Koss, Dinero, Seibel, et al., 1988). According to another study, the psychological consequences for the victim of date rape are similar to those of incest and child molesting (S. Roth, Wayland, & Woolsey, 1988). This may be due in part to a factor already mentioned in the section on child molesting: the presumption of collusion on the part of the victim. Many studies have shown that rape victims tend to blame themselves for the rape, but victims of acquaintance rape seem to blame themselves more (Katz & Burt, 1986), and the public agrees with them. In a survey of undergraduates, both the men and the women blamed the rape victim more if she knew the rapist (Hodell, 1987).

This presumption of female responsibility is of course related to old "boys will be boys" attitudes: the idea that men are by nature sexually uncontrollable and that it is up to women, insofar as they are able (and even when they are not able), to set limits in a sexual encounter. As one might expect, it is the men who hold such attitudes who are most likely to commit date rape. In a review of research on sexually coercive men, Craig (1990) summarizes the pattern as follows: Sexually coercive men are more likely to have stereotyped ideas about sex roles, to view male-female relationships as fundamentally adversarial, to believe that women are responsible for preventing rape, and to endorse "rape myths"—for example, that women unconsciously want to be raped or that they set up the circumstances for rape and then blame the man. Coercive men are also more aggressive, more tolerant of aggression (they tend to have histories of family violence), more sexually experienced, less sexually satisfied, and, not surprisingly, more sexually aroused by the use of force.

where between six and fifteen times higher than this (Koss, 1993), for most rapes go unreported. In a survey of over 6,000 college students (Koss, Gidycz, & Wisniewski, 1987), 27.5 percent of the women reported experiencing and 7.7 percent of the men reported perpetrating an act that met the legal definition of rape (which includes attempted rape), though almost none of these crimes were reported. Another survey, this one of female rape victims, found that only 21 percent of stranger rapes and only 2 percent of acquaintance rapes had been reported (Koss, Dinero, Seibel, et al., 1988).

In dealing with rape, we are faced with the question of why a man who presumably could find a willing sexual partner, if only a prostitute, would force himself with violence on an unwilling woman. There seem to be several answers to this question. Some men apparently resort to rape because they cannot find—or feel they cannot find—a willing sex partner. Like the typical voyeur and exhibitionist, the rapist of this category is described as a timid, submissive male who has grave doubts about his masculinity and is so fearful of rejection that he cannot seek sexual gratification through more acceptable channels (M. Cohen & Seghorn, 1969). Other rapists are clearly antisocial personalities—people who simply seize whatever they want and are indifferent to the pain they inflict on others. In still other cases, the element of force may be a necessary prerequisite of sexual arousal, much as cruelty is for the sadist. (A new *DSM* category, "paraphilic rapism," was recently proposed to cover such rapists, but it was not adopted—a decision that involved some of the same political questions as "self-defeating personality disorder" and "sadistic personality disorder." See the box on pages 270–271.) In some instances, however, the rapist's motivation appears to be more aggressive than sexual. A significant proportion of rapists were victims of child abuse (Hartogs, 1951; Rada, 1978); for them, hurting and humiliating women is a form of revenge or "identification with the aggressor." But many rapists are no different psychologically from "normal" men. They have adequate sexual relationships and show no pattern of abnormality on tests of psychological functioning (Dean & de Bruyn-Kops, 1982).

This last finding suggests that many rapes are the result not of psychological disorders but of our cultural emphasis on sex and violence. To some extent, men in our culture are socialized to become sexual predators. A comparison of college undergraduates who admitted that they had forced a date to have intercourse ("date rape"—see the box on page 344) and undergraduates who had never done so found that the former were "sexually very active, successful, and aspiring," believed that rape was justified under certain circumstances (if the woman was "loose," a "pickup," or a "tease"), said their best friends would "definitely approve" of coercive tactics with certain women, and felt considerable pressure from their peers to engage in sexual exploits (Kanin, 1985). A more recent, integrative theory (Malamuth, Heavey, & Linz, 1993) highlights these same cognitive variables but claims that sexual aggression is best explained as a combination of three factors: motivation (sexual arousal via aggression, desire to dominate women), disinhibition (hostility toward women, attitudes supporting violence toward women, antisocial personality characteristics), and opportunity (sexual experience, situational factors).

With rape, as with pedophilia and incest, psychology must concern itself not only with the perpetrator but also with the victim. The psychological damage suffered by rape victims has already been discussed in Chapter 7. (See the box "Rape and Its Aftermath" on page 162). As we saw, rape victims are at risk for a number of psychological disorders, above all, sexual dysfunctions and posttraumatic stress disorder. At the same time, many women who report rape find that the search for justice leads to humiliation. Until recently, the laws in many states were designed to protect men from false accusations of rape, not to protect victims of rape. New York State, for example, required that there be a witness to the crime. (Needless to say, there rarely is.) More than 95 percent of rape cases reported to the police do not go to trial, either because identification of the rapist is uncertain or the evidence is insufficient (J. LoPiccolo, personal communication, 1986). So not only is justice not done, but the woman is left open to retaliation. If the case does go to court, the woman may feel that she, not the rapist, is on trial. Her way of dressing, her sexual history, her "reputation" may all be subject to skeptical scrutiny. If, to save her life, she submitted to the rape without a struggle, this may be used against her. The trial may thus be as traumatic as the rape.

Fortunately, these injustices are now receiving some attention. Counseling centers have been set up for rape victims. Police officers are being given special training for handling rape cases. (Some police departments have set up "rape squads" staffed with female officers.) And state laws dealing with rape are being revised. For example, New York State no longer requires a witness and does not permit the victim's sexual history (even with the defendant) to be brought into evidence unless it relates directly to the alleged crime.

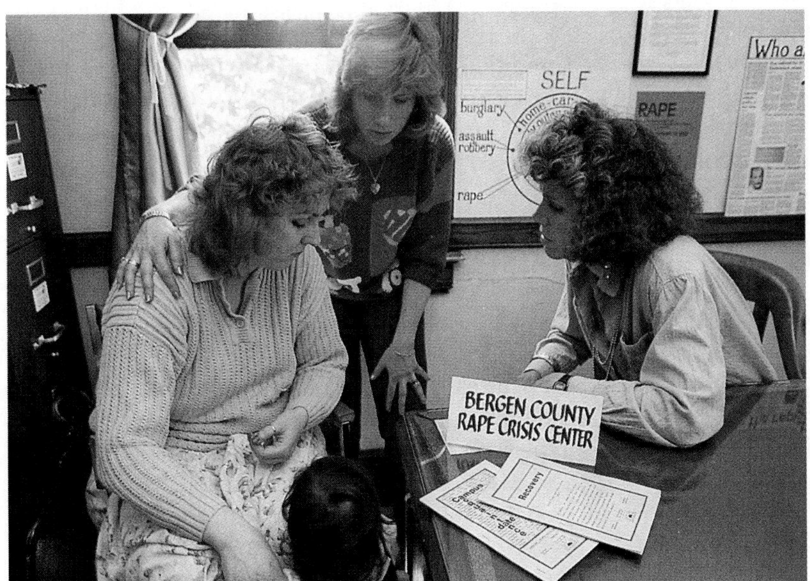

Rape is a crime that not only reflects psychological disorder in the perpetrator but also inflicts emotional damage on the victim, usually in the form of sexual dysfunctions and posttraumatic stress disorder. Effective counseling and fair treatment by the criminal-justice system can help the victim cope with the trauma.

PERSPECTIVES ON THE PARAPHILIAS AND GENDER IDENTITY DISORDER

The Psychodynamic Perspective

Oedipal Fixation According to Freudian theory, sexual disorders represent a continuation into adulthood of the diffuse sexual preoccupations of the child. In Freud's words, young children are "polymorphously perverse"—that is, their sexual pleasure has many sources: sucking, rubbing, defecating, "showing off" their sexual equipment, peeping at that of others. Furthermore, according to Freud, children are capable of any number of defensive maneuvers in attempting to deal with the castration anxiety and penis envy endemic to the Oedipal period. Thus, psychodynamic theorists generally consider paraphilias to be the result of fixation at a pregenital stage. And in general, with paraphilias as with sexual dysfunctions, it is the Oedipal stage, with its attendant castration anxiety, that is considered the major source of trouble.

Freud theorized that fetishism is a displacement of sexual interest to a safer object. Transvestism is seen as a denial of the mother's presumed castration. Dressed in the clothes of a woman but still equipped with a penis underneath, the transvestite can unconsciously convince himself that his mother did not suffer castration after all and that therefore he need not fear the same fate for himself (Nielson, 1960). Similarly, Fenichel (1945) interpreted sadism as an attempt, through cruelty and aggression, to take the part of the castrator rather than that of the castrated and thus to relieve anxiety. Indeed, castration anxiety is often seen as paramount in any paraphilia case that involves the avoidance of coitus. For the male who fears losing his penis, the thought of coming into contact with the supposedly maimed genitals of the woman and of watching his penis "disappear" inside her raises anxiety to an intolerable level. Hence he defends himself by redirecting his sexual impulses toward a safer outlet, such as a fetish, a child, or vicarious participation in the sexual activities of the neighbors.

Other psychodynamic interpretations of sexual disorders have stressed the person's inability to disentangle and control his or her basic id impulses. Thus sadism has been explained as a continuation of the child's confusion of sexual and aggressive impulses. Similarly, masochism may be seen as a redirection onto the self of aggressive impulses originally aimed at a powerful, threatening figure.

Group and Individual Therapy In individual psychotherapy or psychoanalysis, the procedure with paraphiliac patients follows traditional lines. The therapist interprets symbolic remarks, behaviors, and dreams in an attempt to bring the unconscious sexual conflict to the conscious level so that it can be confronted and "worked through." A variation on this technique—group therapy—has been employed as a substitute for imprisonment in the cases of some rapists, pedophiles, and other criminal offenders. The group technique has the advantage of placing the troubled person in a situation where he can take comfort from the knowledge that he is not "the only one"—a reassurance that can hasten his confrontation of his problem. In addition, group therapy saves costs.

Although successful treatment of paraphilias through group therapy, individual psychotherapy, and psychoanalysis has been reported (e.g., M. Cohen & Seghorn, 1969), such cases are the exceptions. Psychodynamic therapy for sex offenders has been found to be largely ineffective (Knopp, 1976). Such patients may have committed hundreds of offenses before they enter treatment, and when they do begin therapy, it is nearly always because they have been required to by the courts. Their motivation to stay out of jail, and hence their motivation to lie to the therapist—to claim that they are responding to treatment, thinking normal sexual thoughts, engaging in normal sexual acts—is often high. But their motivation to change may be very low. Having convinced a therapist (and perhaps themselves) that they are "cured," they often slip back into their old patterns.

The Behavioral Perspective

Conditioning The simplest behavioral interpretation of sexual deviations is that the deviation results from a respondent-conditioning process in which early sexual experiences, particularly masturbation, are paired with some unconventional stimulus, which then becomes the discriminative stimulus for arousal. For example, if a child experiences sexual arousal in connection with the help of a furry toy or a pair of women's underpants, this may lead to fetishism.

In the case of sadism and masochism, behavioral theorists have noted that sex, aggression, and the experience of pain all involve strong emotional and physiological arousal. Hence it has been proposed that the sadist and the masochist are simply persons who never learned to discriminate among the various types of arousal. Another learning theory of masochism is that the child may have been cuddled and loved by his parents only after being punished, with the result that physical affection and punishment became paired. Likewise, learning may play some role in the development of transvestism and gender identity disorder. The case histories of these people often reveal that they were reinforced by being given attention and being told that they were "cute" when they dressed up in their mothers' or sisters' clothes (Rekers & Lovaas, 1974). Recent behavioral theories of the paraphilias tend to stress cognitive factors as well as, or in preference to, direct conditioning. Albert Bandura (1986), for example, has argued that parents may knowingly or unknowingly model unconventional sexual behavior.

Unlearning Deviant Patterns New programs for the treatment of sex offenders take the complex nature of sexual behavior into account. A multifaceted approach combines elements of traditional psychotherapy with specific techniques for dealing with sexual issues. The goal is to change the patient's sexual arousal patterns, beliefs, and behavior (LoPiccolo, 1985).

Treatment begins with steps to bring deviant sexual behavior under temporary control. A man who drinks to reduce his inhibitions may be required to join Alcoholics Anonymous; a child molester is required to stop any job or recreational activities that bring him into contact with children; an incestuous father may be required to move out of his home temporarily.

Behavioral techniques are then used to eliminate deviant arousal. One such technique is called **stimulus satiation.** Suppose the patient is an exhibitionist who preys on young girls. He is asked to collect pictures of girls which arouse in him an urge to expose himself and to arrange them in order from the least to the most exciting. He is also told to collect "normal" sexual stimuli, such as erotic pictures from *Playboy*. Then he is instructed to take these materials home and masturbate while looking at the normal stimuli and to record his fantasies verbally with a tape recorder. Two minutes after he has ejaculated (or after ten minutes if he does not), he must switch to the deviant stimuli, begin masturbating again, and continue for fifty-five minutes. However, if he should become aroused again during this time, he switches his attention back to the normal pictures of adult women and ejaculates again while focused on normal sex. Therefore, he focuses on deviant stimuli only while he is not aroused and is not feeling any physical pleasure during masturbation of his nonerect penis. The patient is required to repeat this procedure three times a week for at least one month, moving from the stimuli that excite him least to those that stimulate him the most. His tapes are analyzed carefully. If his fantasies with normal stimuli are confined to such exhibitionist acts as looking at an adult woman and being looked at by her, he is encouraged to imagine physical contact with her. After ten to fifteen sessions, most sex offenders find the deviant stimuli boring or even aversive (LoPiccolo, 1985).

Stimulus satiation may be combined with other procedures. In **covert sensitization,** the patient is taught to indulge in a deviant fantasy until he is aroused and then to imagine the worst possible consequences—his wife finds him engaged in sex play with a child, he is arrested in front of his neighbors, the arrest makes headlines, his son attempts suicide, and so on. In **shame aversion therapy,** the patient is required to rehearse his paraphiliac behavior—to exhibit himself or, if he is a transvestite, to dress in female clothing—in the therapist's office, while the therapist and the patient's wife observe and comment. (This technique is so distressing that it is used only when other techniques seem to be failing.)

"Corrected" responses do not necessarily translate into normal behavior, however. Sex offenders often lack basic social and sexual skills. Treatment of unmarried offenders includes training in conversational skills, eye contact, empathy skills, listening skills, asking for a date, and making socially acceptable sexual advances. Married sex offenders often report that their sexual relationships with their wives are good or adequate, but further probing usually reveals that sex is infrequent and stereotyped, lacking in playful erotic activities. The partners are taught to do sensate exercises, communicate their desires, and explore new sexual experiences. Weekly therapy for at least six months is recommended for most sex offenders. Follow-up sessions every two weeks or once a month should continue for another year or year and a half. Thereafter the patient should be reassessed every six months for three to five years.

Even this refined, intensive, long-term therapy does not guarantee a cure, however. Recently, behavioral therapy for sex offenders has placed less emphasis on a comprehensive (and often elusive) cure than on simple relapse prevention, that is, teaching people how to prevent themselves from committing the offense again. Relapse prevention involves training patients to avoid situations that place them at risk, showing them how to interrupt thought chains that lead to the offense, and persuading them that having the impulse to commit the offense does not mean they must commit it—they can exert voluntary control through behavioral strategies. Reports on such programs indicate that they are successful in preventing relapses both in pedophiles and in rapists (Furby, Weinrott, & Blackshaw, 1989; W. L. Marshall & Pithers, 1994; Pithers & Cumming, 1989).

The Cognitive Perspective

Learning Deviant Attitudes As noted in the section on sexual dysfunction, the cognitive perspective holds that while we are born with a sex drive, the way that drive will be expressed depends on the attitudes we develop in childhood. A great deal of childhood sexual experimentation crosses "normal" boundaries. Children peep and display themselves, for example. If such behavior is reinforced—if, for example, a young boy's exhibiting himself to a girl is met with a reaction of pleasure or curiosity—this will foster attitudes ("Girls like this," "I can get attention this way") that lead to its adult repetition.

In our discussion of rape we already noted that rapists seem to have a number of characteristic attitudes and beliefs. For example, they often believe in sexual stereotypes and in adversarial male-female relationships. Other sex offenders also tend to "objectify" their victims, regarding them simply as potential sources of gratification rather than as human beings with feelings of their own (Abel, Gore, Holland, et al., 1989). Such beliefs are widespread in our society. According to cognitive theory, if they are combined with other predisposing factors—uncorrected childhood norm violation, lack of parental modeling of normative sexual values, poor self-esteem, poor social skills, and poor understanding of sexuality—they may well lead to sexual deviation (Malamuth, Heavey, & Linz, 1993; Wincze, 1989).

Combating Deviant Beliefs The cognitive treatment for paraphilias is essentially the same as that for sexual dysfunction: the procedure is to identify the deviation-supporting beliefs, challenge them, and replace them with more adaptive beliefs (W. D. Murphy, 1990). As usual, this cognitive restructuring is typically combined with behavioral therapy, just as behavioral therapy and most psychological therapies now incorporate cognitive techniques.

One mental process to which cognitive therapists have recently given great attention is objectification of the victim, for as long as sex offenders think in that way, they are likely to repeat the offense. (And at least in the case of pedophiles, the more they repeat the offense, the greater the degree of objectification [Abel, Gore, Holland, et al., 1989]—a vicious cycle.) Many programs for sex offenders now include "victim awareness" or "victim empathy" training, in which offenders are confronted with the emotional damage done to sex-offense victims. In one prison program rape victims were actually brought into group-therapy sessions with their attackers, and the victims told their side of the story—a confrontation that required considerable courage on the part of the victims (A. Freeman & Leaf, 1989). In other cases the offenders are asked to imagine what one of their victims was thinking during the assault (Wincze, 1989). They may also be assigned to read books, listen to audiotapes, and view videotapes in which victims of rape or child molesting describe their experience of the episode and its psychological consequences. The attackers often respond to these descriptions with great surprise, saying things like, "I didn't think it would hurt her [a six-year-old]; she had already been abused by someone else" (Hildebran & Pithers, 1989). Another technique is role reversal: the therapist takes the role of the offender while the offender takes the role of an authority figure and argues against the sexually aggressive belief system (Abel, Osborn, Anthony, et al., 1992).

The Biological Perspective

Since sexual arousal is controlled in part by the central nervous system, it is possible that paraphilias may be related to neurological disorders. A number of researchers have investigated this question, but without conclusive results (Blumer & Walker, 1975; Rada, 1978). Whatever its role in causation, however, there is no question (other than the ethical one) that biology can be employed in the treatment of sexual deviation. In various European countries, both castration and brain surgery have been used with dangerous sex offenders (usually rapists and pedophiles), this "treatment" usually being offered as an alternative to imprisonment. Another route is the administration of antiandrogen drugs, which decrease the level of testosterone, a hormone essential to male sexual functioning. Antiandrogen treatment is now widely used with chronic offenders in Europe and the United States, and it does seem to decrease arousal and thereby reduce recidivism (Bradford, 1990; Bradford & Pawlak, 1993). In a study of three chronic pedophiles, one of whom had averaged one offense weekly for forty years, all were able to control their behavior after antiandrogen treatment combined with psychotherapy (Wincze, Bansal, & Malamud, 1986). Antidepressants have also proved effective in treating paraphilias, particularly in cases involving shame and depression (Kafka & Pretky, 1992).

To assess arousal in such studies, and also to detect deviant (usually pedophile) attraction in men who have been arrested on sex-offense charges but deny any deviant pattern, a technique called *penile plethysmography* is often used. In penile plethysmography an apparatus attached to the penis measures erection while the subject is exposed to the presumed erotic stimulus via slides or films or audiotapes ("You are baby-sitting your neighbors' little girl for the evening" [Freund & Blanchard, 1989]). This technique seems to have some validity, though it is not foolproof (McConaghy, 1989). Many men are able to suppress deviant arousal in the laboratory, while others are sufficiently traumatized by being arrested on a sex charge that they temporarily lose their arousal capacity. Furthermore, the invasive nature and high cost of laboratory techniques makes them impractical for other purposes, such as screening job applicants. Recently, researchers have developed a noninvasive test, involving self-report and a few simple physiological measures, to screen people applying for positions that involve close contact with children (Abel, Lawry, Karlstrom, et al., 1994).

KEY TERMS

acquired dysfunction (329)
covert sensitization (347)
dyspareunia (329)
exhibitionism (335)
female orgasmic disorder (329)
female sexual arousal disorder (329)
fetishism (335)
frotteurism (335)
gender identity disorder (341)
generalized dysfunction (329)
hypoactive sexual desire disorder (327)
incest (343)
lifelong dysfunction (329)
male erectile disorder (329)
male orgasmic disorder (329)
masochism (335)
paraphilias (335)
pedophilia (335)
premature ejaculation (329)
rape (343)
sadism (335)
sadomasochistic (339)
sexual aversion disorder (327)
sexual dysfunctions (327)
shame aversion therapy (347)
situational dysfunction (329)
spectator role (331)
stimulus satiation (347)
transexualism (341)
transvestism (335)
vaginismus (329)
voyeurism (335)

SUMMARY

- Sexual disorders are among the most stigmatized abnormal behaviors in society. Western culture generally regards heterosexual relations as the only acceptable form of sexual activity and tends to view all other forms as abnormal. However, views of sexual activity vary greatly among different cultures and can change within a society over time.
- Sexual dysfunctions are disorders which, over a long period of time, disrupt the sexual response cycle or cause pain during intercourse. They are grouped according to the phase of the sexual response cycle in which they occur: hypoactive sexual desire disorder and sexual aversion disorder (desire phase); male erectile disorder and female sexual arousal disorder (excitement phase); and premature ejaculation and orgasmic disorder (orgasm phase). Other disorders, which don't disrupt a specific part of the cycle, include dyspareunia and vaginismus. Though data on the frequency of these disorders are limited, studies have shown that several types of sexual dysfunction are common.
- The psychodynamic perspective links sexual dysfunction to an unresolved Oedipal conflict among males and to penis envy among females.
- Masters and Johnson believe that sexual dysfunction results from performance anxiety, which causes the worried partner to become more of a spectator than a participant. The behavioral theory maintains that if sexual dysfunction results from learned anxiety, then the problem can be cured through new learning. Many types of direct symptomatic treatment, especially sensate focus exercises, are used to treat sexual dysfunctions through the behavioral method.
- Cognitive psychologists focus on attitudes and thoughts about sex that can block arousal. Therapists may combine direct treatment with an exploration of attitudes or problems in the relationship.
- The widely held belief that nearly all sexual dysfunctions are psychologically caused has recently been disputed, and researchers now believe that sexual dysfunction may result from a combination of organic *and* psychological factors. There are many treatments available for dysfunctions that are organic in origin.
- In the *paraphilias*, the person is aroused by something other than what is usually considered a normal sex-

ual object or activity. Males are much more likely than females to develop a paraphilia.

- In fetishism, inanimate objects or a body part is used for sexual gratification, generally replacing all interest in normal sexual activity.
- Transvestites seek sexual gratification by wearing clothing of the opposite gender, often at home. Many remain heterosexual, but transvestism often leads to marital problems if discovered by the spouse.
- Exhibitionists, almost always men, display their genitals to an involuntary observer. Exhibitionists receive gratification from the observer's response—often shock or fear.
- In voyeurism, the observation of other people's sexual activity or anatomy, unbeknownst to the subject, provides sexual gratification.
- Sadism and masochism—inflicting pain on others and subjecting oneself to pain, respectively—are sometimes difficult to classify as paraphilias, because in a consenting sadomasochistic couple there is generally no social or occupational distress or impairment.
- In frotteurism, a person obtains sexual gratification by touching or rubbing against a nonconsenting person.
- Pedophiles are adults who seek sexual gratification through sexual contact with children. Though pedophiles rarely cause physical harm to children, they can create severe emotional distress in their victims. Pedophilia has several causes, including arrested psychological development, social isolation, and childhood sexual abuse. Unfortunately, children rarely tell their parents that they have been abused.
- In gender identity disorder, or transsexualism, a person believes that he or she belongs to the opposite gender and that his or her own gender is a mistake. Such people are generally cross-dressers, and though biologically they tend to be homosexual, since they feel that they belong to the opposite sex, they believe that they are heterosexual. Some transsexuals elect to undergo sex reassignment surgery as a solution to their problem. This controversial surgery, through usually biologically successful, has no advantage regarding social rehabilitation. Patients with gender identity disorder are prone to psychotic episodes and suicide.
- Incest, sexual relations between family members, is a crime, not a psychological disorder, but it can have severe mental effects on the victim. Incest is most common between father and daughter, and the effects on the victim include low self-esteem, self-blame, self-hatred, and difficulties in sexual adjustment as adults.
- Rape, or forced sexual intercourse, is a common crime which is rarely reported. Studies indicate that some rapists are timid and shy, with doubts about their masculinity, while others are antisocial. Other rapists are motivated by aggression. Rape victims often suffer severe psychological distress and usually experience sexual dysfunctions and posttraumatic stress disorder.
- The psychodynamic perspective maintains that paraphilias result from Oedipal fixation and the associated castration anxiety. Psychodynamic therapy for paraphiliacs is often ineffective.
- Behavioral therapists believe that paraphilias are caused by respondent conditioning and the modeling of unconventional sexual behavior. Therapy involves removing the abnormal stimulus from the patient and then using a technique such as stimulus satiation, covert sensitization, or shame aversion therapy. Behavioral therapy for paraphilias has had some success.
- The cognitive perspective links paraphilias to attitudes developed in childhood. Offenders often "objectify" their victims. Therapy concentrates on identifying the deviation-supporting beliefs and replacing them. Therapists also try to increase the attacker's empathy for the victim.
- Neurological research on the causes of paraphilias has been inconclusive, but biological treatments, including antiandrogen drugs, seem to be effective.

PART FOUR

PSYCHOTIC AND COGNITIVE DISORDERS OF ADULTHOOD

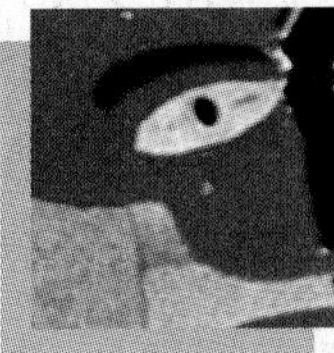

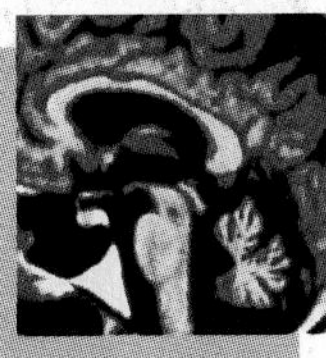

14

SCHIZOPHRENIA AND DELUSIONAL DISORDER

SCHIZOPHRENIA

- The Prevalence of Schizophrenia
- The History of the Diagnostic Category
- The Symptoms of Schizophrenia
- The Onset and Course of Schizophrenia
- The Subtypes of Schizophrenia
- The Dimensions of Schizophrenia
- Two Related Categories: Brief Psychotic Disorder and Schizophreniform Disorder

DELUSIONAL DISORDER

n his *Lectures on Clinical Psychiatry* (1904/1968), Emil Kraepelin (Chapter 1) describes the case of a woman he calls the "widow":

> The widow, aged thirty-five, . . . gives full information about her life in answer to our questions, knows where she is, can tell the date and the year, and gives proof of satisfactory school knowledge. . . . For many years she has heard voices, which insult her and cast suspicion on her chastity. They mention a number of names she knows, and tell her she will be stripped and abused. The voices are very distinct, and, in her opinion, they must be carried by a telescope or a machine from her home. Her thoughts are dictated to her; she is obliged to think them, and hears them repeated after her. She is interrupted in her work, and has all kinds of uncomfortable sensations in her body, to which something is "done." In particular, her "mother parts" are turned inside out, and people send a pain through her back, lay ice-water on her heart, squeeze her neck, injure her spine, and violate her. . . .
>
> The patient makes these extraordinary complaints without showing much emotion. She cries a little, but then describes her morbid experiences again with secret satisfaction and even with an erotic bias. She demands her discharge, but is easily consoled, and does not trouble at all about her position and her future. Her use of numerous strained and hardly intelligible phrases is very striking. She is ill-treated "flail-wise," "utterance-wise," "terror-wise"; she is "a picture of misery in angel's form," and "a defrauded mamma and housewife of sense of order." They have "altered her form of emotion." She is "persecuted by a secret insect from the District Office. . . ." Her former history shows that she has been ill for nearly ten years. (p. 157)

The "widow" offers a good illustration of psychosis. As we have noted previously, the **psychoses** are a class of psychological disorders in which reality contact—the capacity to perceive, process, and respond to environmental stimuli in an adaptive manner—is radically impaired, with the result that the person sometimes cannot meet even the most ordinary demands of life. The psychoses, then, are the most severe of all the psychological disorders. Most of the conditions that we have discussed in earlier chapters allow for some measure of adaptive functioning. Phobia, fetishism, substance dependence, posttraumatic stress disorder—people with these conditions can still, in many cases, look after themselves, earn a living, carry on a reasonable conversation, and so forth. Psychotics in the midst of an acute episode generally cannot. For this reason—and because their behavior is incomprehensible and disturbing to others—they are often hospitalized. There are three main groups of psychoses:

1 *The mood disorders,* characterized, as their name indicates, primarily by disturbances of *mood.* (But remember that not all mood disorders are psychotic.)
2 *Schizophrenia,* considered to be primarily a disturbance of *thought.*
3 *Delusional disorder,* in which the essential, and possibly the only, abnormality is a limited system of *delusions.*

Mood disorders have already been described in Chapter 10. The present chapter will focus on the two other main types of psychosis, schizophrenia and delusional disorder, with special emphasis on the former, as it is by far the more common. The purpose of this chapter is simply to describe these disorders. Theories as to cause and treatment will be discussed in Chapter 15.

SCHIZOPHRENIA

Schizophrenia is the label given to a group of psychoses in which deterioration of functioning is marked by severe distortion of thought, perception, and mood, by bizarre behavior, and by social withdrawal. Not all patients show all those symptoms. Indeed, it is possible that what we call schizophrenia is not a single disorder but a group of disorders, with different causes—a possibility that researchers are now investigating.

The Prevalence of Schizophrenia

Between 1 and 2 percent of people in the United States have had or will have a schizophrenic episode (Regier, Boyd, Burke, et al., 1988). Elsewhere, the rates are similar (American Psychiatric Association, 1994). For years it was thought that men and women were equally at risk, but recent studies have found that men are one and a half times more likely than women to develop schizophrenia (Iacono & Beiser, 1992a, 1992b). At present, there are about a million actively schizophrenic people in the country. Such people occupy about half the beds in U.S. mental hospitals (H. I. Kaplan & Sadock, 1991). Many other schizophrenics have been released from the hospital—either to smaller facilities or simply into the community. (It has been estimated that 10 to 13 percent of homeless people are schizophrenic [Fischer & Breakey, 1991].) But about half of those discharged for the first time return to the mental hospital within two years (H. I. Kaplan & Sadock, 1991). The estimated cost of schizophrenia to our society is greater than that of cancer (National Foundation for Brain Research, 1992). Clearly, this disorder constitutes an enormous public health problem.

The History of the Diagnostic Category

Though schizophrenia has probably been with us for thousands of years, it is only since the end of the nineteenth century that it has been recognized as a distinct disorder. The first identification of the disorder came in 1896, when Emil Kraepelin proposed that there were three major types of psychosis—manic-depressive psychosis, paranoia, and, finally, "dementia praecox," a syndrome marked by delusions, hallucinations, attention problems, and bizarre motor behavior. Kraepelin believed that dementia praecox normally began in adolescence and led to irreversible mental breakdown—hence his term for the disorder, which is Latin for "premature mental deterioration."

While Kraepelin's description of the disorder has lasted, the name he gave it was soon replaced. In 1911, the Swiss psychiatrist Eugen Bleuler, a highly influential teacher and writer, pointed out that "dementia praecox" was actually a poor description of the patients it was supposed to describe. In the first place, the disorder was not necessarily premature; many patients did not develop symptoms until well into their adult years. Second, most patients did not proceed to complete mental deterioration. Some remained the same year after year; others improved; others improved and relapsed. Bleuler (1911/1950) therefore proposed a new term:

> I call the dementia praecox "schizophrenia" from the Greek words *schizein*, meaning "to split," and *phren*, meaning "mind" because the "splitting" of the different psychic functions is one of its most important characteristics. For the sake of convenience, I use the word in the singular although it is apparent that the group includes several diseases. (p. 8)

Hence the term *schizophrenia*, which has since become the commonly accepted label. Because of its association with "splitting," many people misunderstand the term as designating multiple personality, or dissociative identity disorder (Chapter 8), but that is another syndrome altogether. What Bleuler was referring to was not a splitting of the personality into two or more distinct personalities but rather a split or disconsonance among different psychic *functions* within a single personality. In the mind of the schizophrenic, emotion, perception, and cognition cease to operate as an integral whole. Emotions may split off from perception, perception from reality. As Eugen Bleuler put it, "The personality loses its unity" (p. 9). A former schizophrenic quoted by Mendel (1976) described the experience more concretely: "The integrating mental picture in my personality was taken away and smashed to bits, leaving me like agitated hamburger distributed infinitely throughout the universe" (p. 8).

The Symptoms of Schizophrenia

DSM-IV lists five characteristic symptoms of schizophrenia: delusions, hallucinations, disorganized speech, disorganized or catatonic behavior, and "negative symptoms," meaning a reduction or loss of normal functions such as language or goal-directed behavior. If a person has shown two or more of those signs for at least a month and has been noticeably disturbed for at least six months, so that his or her normal functioning—relationships with others, performance at work or school—has deteriorated, the diagnosis is schizophrenia.

In the following section, for the sake of discussion, we will break down the symptoms of schizophrenia into separate categories. Keep in mind, however, that in reality they are not separate, for they influence one another. If a person's thought processes are derailed, this will affect mood; if mood is disturbed, this will affect behavior. And while all schizophrenics display some of these symptoms some of the time, no schizophrenic displays all of them all of the time. Indeed, some diagnosed schizophrenics often behave quite normally.

Disorders of Thought and Language

> I'm a doctor, you know. . . . I don't have a diploma, but I'm a doctor. I'm glad to be a mental patient, because it taught me how to be humble. I use Cover Girl creamy natural makeup. Oral Roberts has been here to visit me. . . . This place is where *Mad* magazine is published. The Nixons make Noxon metal polish. When I was a little girl, I used to sit and tell stories to myself. When I was older, I turned off the sound on the TV set and made up dialogue to go with the shows I watched. . . . I'm a week pregnant. I have schizophrenia—cancer of the nerves. My body is overcrowded with nerves. This is going to win me the Nobel Prize for medicine. I don't consider myself schizophrenic anymore. There's no such thing as

> schizophrenia, there's only mental telepathy. I once had a friend named Camilla Costello. She was Abbot and Costello's daughter. . . . I'm in the Pentecostal Church, but I'm thinking of changing my religion. I have a dog at home. I love instant oatmeal. When you have Jesus, you don't need a diet. Mick Jagger wants to marry me. I want to get out the revolving door. With Jesus Christ, anything is possible. I used to hit my mother. It was the hyperactivity from all the cookies I ate. I'm the personification of Casper the Friendly Ghost. I used to go outside asking the other kids to be my friend when I was little. California's the most beautiful state in the Union. I've been there once, by television. My name is Jack Warden, and I'm an actress. (quoted in S. Sheehan, 1982, pp. 72–73)

As one expert has written, "Perhaps the single most striking feature about schizophrenics is their peculiar use of language" (S. A. Shapiro, 1981, p. 64). That peculiarity is evident in the above quotation of a schizophrenic woman's attempt at conversation in a hospital ward. The disordered language of schizophrenics, with its odd associations and rapid changes of subject, is presumably a clue to their disordered thought processes. Some writers, in discussing the disorder, have tried to distinguish between disturbances of thought and disturbances of language, but such distinctions are possible only at a theoretical level. Language is nothing if not the expression of thought. Conversely, our primary clue to thought is language. The two functions, then, are interdependent, and for this reason we will consider them together. First, we will discuss disturbances in the content of schizophrenic thought, known as delusions, and then we will discuss abnormalities in the form schizophrenic thought takes.

Delusions A striking characteristic of schizophrenic thought is the presence of **delusions,** firmly held beliefs that have no basis in reality. Delusions may accompany a variety of psychological conditions—mania, depression, organic syndromes, drug overdose—but they are extremely common in schizophrenia (R. W. Butler & Braff, 1991), affecting three-quarters or more of hospitalized schizophrenic patients (Harrow, Carone, & Westermeyer, 1985; Lucas, Sansbury, & Collins, 1962).

Most schizophrenics do not seem to realize that other people find their delusional beliefs implausible (Harrow, Rattenbury, & Stoll, 1988). Nor will they abandon their delusions in the face of contradictory evidence—a point that was vividly demonstrated some years ago by the psychologist Milton Rokeach. In 1959 Rokeach had three men, each of whom claimed to be Jesus Christ, transferred to the same ward of a hospital in Ypsilanti, Michigan. For two years the "three Christs" lived together, sleeping in adjacent beds, sharing the same table in the dining hall, and working together in the hospital laundry room while Rokeach observed them. His purpose, as he explained it, was "to explore the processes by which their delusional systems of belief and their behavior might change if they were confronted with the ultimate contradiction conceivable for human beings: more than one person claiming the same identity" (Rokeach, 1964, p. 3). In other words, would any of them figure out that all three of them couldn't be Jesus? The following is an excerpt from one of their first encounters:

> "Well, I know your psychology," Clyde said, "and you are a knick-knacker, and in your Catholic church in North Bradley and in your education, and I know all of it—the whole thing. I know exactly what this fellow does. In my credit like I do from up above, that's the way it works."
>
> "As I was stating before I was interrupted," Leon went on, "it so happens that I was the first human spirit to be created with a glorified body before time existed."
>
> "Ah, well, he is just simply a creature, that's all," Joseph put in. "Man created by me when I created the world—nothing else."
>
> —*Did you create Clyde, too?* Rokeach asked.
>
> "Uh-huh. Him and a good many others."
>
> At this, Clyde laughed. (Rokeach, 1964, pp. 10–11)

After two years of continuous daily contact, each of the three men remained unmoved in his belief that he alone was Jesus Christ.

The content of schizophrenic delusions is as rich and diverse as the human imagination. However, most delusions fall into certain patterns:

1 *Delusions of persecution:* the belief that one is being plotted against, spied upon, threatened, interfered with, or otherwise mistreated, particularly by a number of parties joined in a conspiracy.
2 *Delusions of control* (also called *delusions of influence):* the belief that other people, forces, or perhaps extraterrestrial beings are controlling one's thoughts, feelings, and actions, often by means of electronic devices that send signals directly to the brain.
3 *Delusions of reference:* the belief that one is being referred to by events or stimuli that in fact have

nothing to do with one. For example, schizophrenics may think that their lives are being depicted on television or in news stories. (The case of Laura on page 370 illustrates delusions of reference.)

4 *Delusions of sin and guilt:* the belief that one has committed "the unpardonable sin" or inflicted great harm on others. Schizophrenics may claim, for example, that they have killed their children.

5 *Hypochondriacal delusions:* the unfounded belief that one is suffering from a hideous physical disease. The hypochondriacal delusions of schizophrenics differ from the fears seen in hypochondriasis (Chapter 8) in that they refer not to recognized diseases but to bizarre afflictions. While hypochondriacs may complain of brain tumors, for instance, schizophrenics will claim that their brains are full of mold or being carried away in pieces.

6 *Nihilistic delusions:* the belief that one or others or the whole world has ceased to exist. The patient may claim, for example, that he or she is a spirit returned from the dead.

7 *Delusions of grandeur:* the belief that one is an extremely famous and powerful person. Such delusions may crystallize into a stable delusional identity in which the person maintains that he or she is a renowned personage such as Joan of Arc, Napoleon, or God. (See the box on page 358.)

Finally, many schizophrenics complain that their thoughts are being tampered with in some way. Such delusions, related to delusions of control, include

1 *Thought broadcasting:* the belief that one's thoughts are being broadcast to the outside world, so that everyone can hear them.

2 *Thought insertion:* the belief that other people are inserting thoughts, especially obscene thoughts, into one's head.

3 *Thought withdrawal:* the belief that other people are removing thoughts from one's head.

These particular delusions seem to be highly specific to schizophrenia—in any case, they are not seen in people with psychotic mood disorders (Junginger, Barker, & Coe, 1992)—and they may represent an effort on the part of schizophrenics to explain to themselves the mental chaos that this disorder entails. Many schizophrenics, for example, experience what is called **blocking:** in the middle of talking about something, they suddenly fall silent, with no recollection whatsoever of what they were talking about. Such an experience, presumably, is as disturbing to a schizophrenic as it would be to anyone else, and one way to explain it is to say that someone is stealing the thoughts out of one's head. The box on page 359 explores the possibility that schizophrenic delusions may represent "normal" explanations for abnormal experiences.

Occasionally it is difficult for the diagnostician to distinguish between what is delusional and what is real. Kraft and Babigian (1972) report the case of a woman, Mrs. M., who appeared one day in a hospital emergency room complaining that she had needles in both arms. Upon questioning, the woman revealed that she had spent a total of nine years in psychiatric hospitals. Each of her eight hospitalizations had been precipitated by an episode of self-mutilation in which Mrs. M., obeying voices that told her that she was bad and should kill herself, had slashed her wrists, thighs, or abdomen. She also reported seven years of alcohol abuse. This history, along with the physical examination, which revealed no needle marks on her arms or any foreign bodies inside the arms, convinced the examining physicians that Mrs. M. was delusional. Still, they were thorough enough to order an x-ray, and they were very much surprised when it showed that the woman did indeed have a number of needles in both arms. Apparently, in a suicide attempt the year before, she had inserted several sewing needles in each arm, and they had remained undetected during three subsequent hospitalizations. It is probable that during these hospitalizations Mrs. M. reported the presence of the needles and that her reports were assumed to be delusional.

Loosening of associations As we saw earlier, it was for the quality of psychological "splitting"—a disconnection between different ideas or different mental functions—that Bleuler named the disorder in question schizophrenia. One of the clearest demonstrations of this splitting is the rambling, disjointed form or quality of schizophrenic speech. Normal speech tends to follow a single train of thought, with logical connections between ideas. By contrast, schizophrenic speech often shows a **loosening of associations.** Ideas jump from one track to another, one that is indirectly related, or to one that is completely unrelated, with the result that the person wanders further and further away from the topic. When the problem is severe, speech may become completely incoherent.

We do not know exactly what mental processes cause this confusion in speech, but it is likely that

NIJINSKY: DIARY OF A SCHIZOPHRENIC BREAK

In 1918, the Polish-Russian ballet dancer Vaslav Nijinsky, at that time the most famous male dancer in the world, began acting strangely. He threw his wife down a flight of stairs. He roamed the streets, telling people to go to church. He sat up late into the night, weeping and making drawings of staring eyes. He also began keeping a diary, in which he claimed that he was God and that his writings would save the world from war. In the following passage from the diary, he speaks alternately in his own voice and that of God (italics):

> *"Nijinsky has faults, but Nijinsky must be listened to because he speaks the words of God."* I am Nijinsky. *"I do not want Nijinsky to be hurt and therefore I will protect him. I am only afraid for him because he is afraid for himself. I know his strength. He is a good man. I am a good God. I do not like Nijinsky when he is bad."* I do not like God when he is bad. I am God, Nijinsky is God. *"He is a good man and not evil. People have not understood him and will not understand him if they think. If people listened to me for several weeks there would be great results. I hope that my teachings will be understood."* All that I write is necessary to mankind. (V. Nijinsky, 1936, p. 182)

Though delusional at times, Nijinsky at other times was well aware that something terrible was happening to him, as the diary reveals:

> I cry . . . I cannot restrain my tears, and they fall on my left hand and on my silken tie, but I cannot and do not want to hold them back. I feel that I am doomed. I do not want to go under. I do not know what I need, and I dislike to upset my people. If they are upset, I will die. (p. 31)

In early 1919, Nijinsky's wife persuaded him to consult Eugen Bleuler, the psychiatrist who eight years earlier had invented the term *schizophrenia.* That was Bleuler's diagnosis in this case. Bleuler gave the news to Nijinsky's wife, who then went into the waiting room to speak to Nijinsky. When Nijinsky saw her face, he said, "Femmka [little wife], you are bringing me my death warrant" (R. Nijinsky, 1934, p. 429). This was more or less true. Nijinsky, then twenty-nine years old, was institutionalized. He lived for thirty years more, occasionally violent but most of the time mute and withdrawn—a chronic schizophrenic.

Vaslav Nijinsky (1890–1950) is shown here in about 1922, when schizophrenia had already begun to impair his career as a brilliant dancer. The drawing of staring eyes was done by Nijinsky while he was in an asylum.

the problem lies in the mind's way of dealing with associations. Although language is the best mirror of thought processes, it is by no means an exact copy of thought. In communicating with one another, people make many mental associations both to the statements of those they are speaking to and to their own statements. Before speaking, however, the person "edits" these associations, selecting the ones that are most relevant to the topic and discarding the others. In the schizophrenic mind, this selection process seems to break down, so that the speaker follows his or her own private train of associations without any editing for relevance.

This does not mean that schizophrenics cannot give a straight answer to a direct question. Schizophrenics can make very common primary associations to a given stimulus about as easily as normal people. It is the more subtle secondary associations that many schizophrenics cannot make without becoming confused and incoherent. This phenomenon was illustrated in an experiment conducted by Cohen and his colleagues. A group of normal subjects and a group of schizophrenics were shown two colored disks and were asked to describe one of the colors in such a way that a listener who also had those two colors before him or

DELUSIONS: NORMAL EXPLANATIONS FOR ABNORMAL EXPERIENCES?

A woman is admitted to the hospital with her hands clasped over her ears; she believes that there are bees inside her skull. A middle-aged man tells the doctor that he is unable to eat anything at all; his stomach is always full, never empty. Clearly, these patients are delusional. According to Brendan Maher (1988; B.A. Maher & Spitzer, 1993), however, it is not their thinking processes that are abnormal but rather their perceptual experience. Both these patients were found, on autopsy, to have serious physical impairments—in the woman, a neurological disorder that may indeed have felt like bees in the brain; in the man, an abdominal disorder. In Maher's view, the same may be true of many other schizophrenic patients. The primary symptom is a sensory or motor impairment. The cognitive symptom, or delusion, is secondary—a sort of crude scientific theory that the person comes up with in order to explain his or her bizarre experience.

An experiment conducted at the University of Copenhagen (Nielsen, 1963) lends support to Maher's hypothesis. Normal adults engaged in a simple motor tracking task with a computer joystick while receiving feedback in the form of on-screen images of their hands. After several trials, the researchers secretly replaced the subjects' hand images with images of other hands, doing different things. They also introduced error into the subjects' performances. Later, the subjects were asked to explain their poor results. Here is a sample of their explanations:

> "It was done by magic."
>
> "I looked to see if there were electrodes on my hand, but I could not see any; they were there, but I was deceived about them."
>
> "My hand was controlled by an outside physical force—I don't know what it was, but I could feel it."
>
> (Nielsen, 1963)

These theories do not sound widely different from delusions.

A later study (Zimbardo, Andersen, & Kabat, 1981) suggests how readily even normal people will resort to irrational explanations for odd perceptual experiences. Normal subjects known to be highly susceptible to posthypnotic suggestion (suggestion while under hypnosis and acted on after hypnosis) were divided into three groups and hypnotized. The subjects in group *A* were given the suggestion that they would be partially deaf. Those in group *B* were given the same suggestion but were told, in addition, that they would not remember receiving this suggestion. The subjects in group *C* were told that they would scratch their ears, and they too were told that they would not recall being given this suggestion. Then the hypnotic spells were broken and the subjects were put to work on a problem-solving test, during which, eventually, they were given cues for their various posthypnotic suggestions. The subjects in group *A* remembered their partial deafness but were not distressed about it. They knew the reason, for they remembered being given the suggestion. The subjects in group *C* remembered scratching their ears, and in obedience to the hypnotist, they didn't recall why they had done so. This didn't upset them, however. Ear scratching apparently didn't seem to them odd enough to require explanation. But the subjects in group *B*, those who had become partially deaf and did not remember why, apparently did feel that a special explanation was needed, and they began to supply one. They said that the reason they had been unable to hear was that the investigators stood aloof from them, whispering, perhaps conspiring. In other words, they began having paranoid thoughts.

If delusions are "normal" explanations for abnormal experiences, why are delusional patients—for example, Rokeach's "three Christs"—so resistant to evidence that disproves their theories? According to Maher (1988), most people show vigorous resistance to information that challenges their cherished beliefs. Indeed, scientists are rarely willing to change their theories on the basis of new data alone but, rather, only in response to the pressure generated by competing theories (Popper, 1945). In the case of schizophrenics, "competing theories" may seem inadequate. As Maher (1988) puts it, schizophrenics "may not be ready to abandon their delusion for a naturalistic explanation for the good reason that their actual experiences are better explained by the delusional theory than by the naturalistic one" (p. 26).

Maher's hypothesis has itself been challenged by competing theories, basically stating that while delusional patients may be trying to explain odd perceptual experiences, they also show a bias toward unfounded explanations. In one experiment (Garety, Helmsley, & Wessely, 1991), a group of delusional patients were given various kinds of information and asked to draw inferences. Compared with normal people and also with nondelusional patients, the delusional patients required less information before reaching a conclusion. So it is possible that schizophrenics do have a primary cognitive disorder: a tendency to jump to conclusions, to account for their odd experiences.

This hectic scene of Mardi Gras in New Orleans conveys an idea of the bewildering sensory impressions that bombard schizophrenics, who lack the capacity for selective attention.

her could pick out the one being described. When the colors were quite dissimilar, the schizophrenics did about as well as the normal subjects. For example, when one color was red and the other a purple-blue and subjects were asked to describe the latter, responses were as follows:

> Normal Speaker 2: Purple.
>
> Normal Speaker 3: This is purple blue. . . .
>
> Schizophrenic Speaker 2: Purple.
>
> Schizophrenic Speaker 3: The bluer.
>
> (B. D. Cohen, Nachmani, & Rosenberg, 1974, p. 11)

In the next stage of the experiment, however, the two colors were quite similar, requiring that the speaker make subtle associations in order to describe the slight difference between the two. Faced with this task, the normal speakers managed to combine and refine their associations in such a way as to indicate which color they meant. The schizophrenics, on the other hand, began reeling off associations that, while quite vivid, failed to convey the appropriate information:

> Normal Speaker 2: My God, this is hard. They are both about the same, except that this one might be a little redder.
>
> Normal Speaker 3: They both are either the color of canned salmon or clay. This one here is the pinker one. . . .
>
> Schizophrenic Speaker 2: This is a stupid color of a shit ass bowl of salmon. Mix it with mayonnaise. Then it gets tasty. Leave it alone and puke all over the fuckin' place. Puke fish.
>
> Schizophrenic Speaker 3: Make-up. Pancake make-up. You put it on your face and they think guys run after you. Wait a second! I don't put it on my face and guys don't run after me. Girls put it on them.
>
> (B. D. Cohen, Nachmani, & Rosenberg, 1974, p. 11)

What is it that pushes schizophrenics off the track? Some experts believe that once schizophrenics make a given association, they cannot let go of it, as normal people can, and search for a more appropriate association. They get "stuck" on the first association, and the remainder of the response is "chained" off that first association, without any concern for relevance to the topic at hand. In other words, schizophrenics are at the mercy of their associative processes. In the examples just given, for instance, both of the schizophrenic speakers made a first association—one to salmon, one to pancake makeup—but then, instead of refining it in order to explain the difference between the two colors, they went off on trains of private associations to that first thought.

Like delusions, associative problems are seen in other psychoses besides schizophrenia, particularly in mania (Harrow, Grossman, Silverstein, et al., 1986). As recent studies have highlighted, however, manic thought disorder is of a different quality from schizophrenic thought disorder. Manic speech tends to combine things in an extravagant and often playful way; schizophrenic speech tends to be more radically confused, with different ideas melting into one another and losing their meanings (E. K. Daniels, Shenton, Holzman, et al., 1988). In one study, for example, a manic patient, after responding to a Rorschach card by saying that the design looked like a crab, was asked what made it look that way. The patient replied, "Cause I'm Cancer the crab maybe. My sign is cancer. My horoscope. And I'm thinking a lot about cancer, too. God forbid if anybody is dying of cancer. . . .

I wish it was me" (Soloway, Shenton, & Holzman, 1987, p. 19). By contrast, a schizophrenic patient's response to a Rorschach card was: "It's all in front. It's all freehand work. Freehand. Remember freehand? Once in a while we had to freehand. So I did that till I ended up here for down the rest. You get crabby. And it's more than aging gracefully. For strong people" (p. 20). The same, characteristic idiosyncrasies of speech—the manic playfulness, the schizophrenic confusion—often turn up in milder form in the relatives of manic and schizophrenic patients (Shenton, Soloway, Holzman, et al., 1989).

Poverty of content The result of loosened associations is that schizophrenic language may convey very little. Though the person may use many words, all grammatically correct, he or she nevertheless communicates poorly. This **poverty of content** may be seen in the following excerpt from a letter by a schizophrenic patient:

> Dear Mother,
>
> I am writing on paper. The pen which I am using is from a factory called "Perry & Co." This factory is in England. I assume this. Behind the name of Perry Co. the city of London is inscribed; but not the city. The city of London is in England. I know this from my school days. Then, I always liked geography. My last teacher in that subject was Professor August A. He was a man with black eyes. I also like black eyes. There are also blue and gray eyes and other sorts, too. I have heard it said that snakes have green eyes. All people have eyes. There are some, too, who are blind. These blind people are led about by a boy. It must be terrible not to be able to see. There are people who can't see and, in addition can't hear. I know some who hear too much. One can hear too much. (quoted in E. Bleuler, 1911/1950, p. 17)

Bleuler, who first published this letter, points out that the only common denominator of the ideas expressed in it is that they are all present in the patient's awareness: London—geography lesson—geography teacher—his black eyes—gray eyes —green snake eyes—human eyes—blind people—deaf people, and so on. The letter says much, and all very properly, but it conveys little, for it lacks any unifying principle beyond the irresistible linkage of associations.

Neologisms As we pointed out earlier, the confused speech of schizophrenics is generally interpreted as the product of confused thinking. However, some researchers (e.g., J. F. Fish, 1957; Kleist, 1960) have suggested that certain peculiarities of schizophrenic language may result not from radical thought disturbances but simply from an inability to retrieve commonly agreed-upon verbal symbols. That is, what schizophrenics have to say may be reasonable enough; they just can't find the right words with which to say it (Alpert, Clark, & Pouget, 1994).

This hypothesis might account for the rare appearance in schizophrenic speech of words and phrases not found in even the most comprehensive dictionary. These usages, called **neologisms** (literally "new words"), are sometimes formed by combining parts of two or more regular words. Or the neologism may involve the use of common words in a new way (Willerman & Cohen, 1990). In either case, what is interesting about neologisms is that while they are sometimes totally unintelligible, at other times they manage to communicate ideas quite clearly and vividly, as may be seen in the following transcript (possible intended meanings are indicated in brackets):

DR.: Sally, you're not eating supper tonight. What's the problem?

PT.: No, I had belly bad luck and brutal and outrageous. [I have stomach problems, and I don't feel good.] I gave all the work money. [I paid tokens for my meal.] Here, I work. Well, the difference is I work five days and when the word was [when I am told to work] but I had escapingly [I got out of some work]. I done it for Jones. He planned it and had me work and helped me work and all and had all the money. He's a tie-father [a relative]. Besides generation ties and generation hangages [relationships between family generations—the way generations hang together] . . . he gave love a lot. I fit in them generations since old-fashion time [since long ago]. I was raised in packs [with other people] . . . certain times I was, since I was in littlehood [since I was a little girl] . . . she said she concerned a Sally-twin [my twin sister]. She blamed a few people with minor words [she scolded people], but she done goodship [good things]. I've had to suffer so much. I done it United States long.

DR.: Sally, is there anything else you want to tell me before you go?

PT.: Well, I expect there's a lot of things, but I would know what they were, especially the unkind crimery [the bad things].

(R. Hagen, Florida State University, clinical files)

Clanging Another oddity sometimes found in the speech of schizophrenics (and, again, of manics as well) is **clanging**, the juxtaposition of words that have no relation to one another beyond the fact that they rhyme or sound alike. Clanging may be related to the associational problem discussed above. In this case, however, the basis for the associations is sound rather than sense. Hence clanging speech is often closer to nonsense verse than to rational communication.

The following is a transcript of a conversation between a doctor and a schizophrenic patient who was particularly adept at clanging. (About half of all his daily speech was rhymed.) As the transcript shows, clanging often involves neologisms:

DR.: How are things going today, Ernest?
PT.: Okay for a flump.
DR.: What is a flump?
PT.: A flump is a gump.
DR.: That doesn't make any sense.
PT.: Well, when you go to the next planet from the planet beyond the planet that landed on the danded and planded on the standed.
DR.: Wait a minute. I didn't follow any of that.
PT.: Well, when we was first bit on the slit on the rit and the man on the ran or the pan on the ban and the sand on the man and the pan on the ban on the can on the man on the fan on the pan. [All spoken very rhythmically, beginning slowly and building up to such a rapid pace that the words could no longer be understood.]
DR.: What's all that hitting your head for . . . and waving your arms?
PT.: That's to keep the boogers from eatin' the woogers.

(R. Hagen, Florida State University, clinical files)

Word salad In some cases, schizophrenic language seems to show a complete breakdown of the associational process, so it becomes impossible for the listener to trace any links between successive words and phrases. This extreme situation is illustrated in the following statement, made by the same patient whose clanging was quoted above:

> It's all over for a squab true tray and there ain't no music, there ain't no nothing besides my mother and my father who stand alone upon the Island of Capri where there is no ice, there is no nothing but changers, changers, changers. That comes like in first and last names, so that thing does. Well, it's my suitcase, sir. I've got to travel all the time to keep my energy alive. (R. Hagen, Florida State University, clinical files)

Appropriately, this type of speech, in which words and phrases are combined in what appears to be a completely disorganized fashion, is referred to as **word salad.** Unlike neologisms, word salad suggests no effort to communicate. Nor does it appear to reflect a train of tangential associations, as when associations are merely loosened. Nor are the words even connected on the basis of sound, as in clanging. Word salad, then, is the ultimate in schizophrenic splitting. Nothing is related to anything else, and therefore the message communicates nothing.

Disorders of Perception There is considerable evidence that schizophrenics perceive the world differently from other people. In the first place, schizophrenics consistently *report* perceptual abnormalities. In a comparative study of newly admitted schizophrenic and nonschizophrenic patients, Freedman and Chapman (1973) found that the schizophrenics reported a significantly greater number of changes in their perceptual functioning, including visual illusions, disturbingly acute auditory perception, inability to focus attention, difficulty in identifying people, and difficulty in understanding the speech of others. Schizophrenics have also reported olfactory changes, or changes in smell, complaining that their own body odor is more pronounced and more unpleasant, that other people smell stronger, and that objects have peculiar smells (H. I. Kaplan & Sadock, 1991). Among the many perceptual oddities involved in schizophrenia, two are of special concern: the breakdown of selective attention and the experience of hallucinations.

Breakdown of selective attention As we shall see in the next chapter, there is some dispute over what constitutes the *basic* pathology in schizophrenia—the main disturbance from which the other symptoms arise—but a number of experts believe that the answer has to do with attention (Nuechterlein & Dawson, 1984a, 1984b). Normal people, without thinking about it, exercise selective attention. That is, they decide what they want to focus on in the environment and then concentrate on that, with the result that sensory data from the thing they are interested in register forcibly in the mind while extraneous data (the sound of the air conditioner in the classroom, the earrings on the student in the front row) are confined to the edge of consciousness.

Schizophrenics seem unable to engage in this normal selection process—a fact that was noted by Kraepelin and Bleuler. Today, almost a century later, many researchers feel that the breakdown of selective attention underlies most of the other symptoms of schizophrenia. McGhie and Chapman (1961), two major proponents of this theory, ask us to imagine what would happen if the mind ceased to exercise selective attention:

> Consciousness would be flooded with an undifferentiated mass of incoming sensory data, transmitted

> from the environment via the sense organs. To this involuntary tide of impressions there would be added the diverse internal images, and their associations, which would no longer be coordinated with incoming information. Perception would revert to the passive and involuntary assimilative process of early childhood, and, if the incoming flood were to carry on unchecked, it would gradually sweep away the stable constructs of a former reality. (p. 105)

In consequence, the person would see an altered world, make odd associations, produce bizarre speech, experience inappropriate emotions—and, it is easy to imagine, work out strange beliefs and strange behavior patterns as a defense against the sensory overload. The result would be what we call schizophrenia. One patient of McGhie and Chapman (1961) testified to his attention problems in simple and poignant terms:

> My thoughts get all jumbled up. I start thinking or talking about something but I never get there. Instead I wander off in the wrong direction and get caught up with all sorts of different things that may be connected with the things I want to say but in a way I can't explain. People listening to me get more lost than I do. (p. 108)

Hallucinations Added to the perceptual problems of schizophrenics is the fact that many of them perceive things that are not there. Such perceptions, occurring in the absence of any appropriate external stimulus, are called **hallucinations.** About three-quarters of all newly hospitalized schizophrenics report hallucinations (Ludwig, 1986). Auditory hallucinations are apparently the most common, occurring in 70 percent of schizophrenic patients (Cleghorn, Franco, Szechtman, et al., 1992), and certain types of auditory hallucinations are especially characteristic of schizophrenia, notably the experience of hearing two or more voices conversing with one another or of hearing voices that keep a running commentary on the patient's thoughts or behavior. After auditory hallucinations, visual hallucinations are the most frequent, followed by hallucinations of the other senses (Ludwig, 1986).

Hallucinations are not entirely foreign to normal experience. Most of us are able, with varying degrees of vividness, to hear imagined voices, to form pictures "in the mind's eye," and even to recreate experiences of taste, touch, and smell in the absence of primary stimulation. But when we do so, we are aware (1) that we are controlling these sensory imaginings and (2) that they are products of the imagination rather than responses to actual external stimuli. Hallucinations, by contrast, are not conjured up at will; they occur spontaneously. Furthermore, while many schizophrenics recognize that the voices they hear are "only in my head," others are not sure whether their hallucinations are real or imagined (Frith & Done, 1988), and a fair percentage—presumably the more severely psychotic—are in fact convinced that their hallucinations are perceptions of objectively real events. (Schizophrenics also disagree on whether hallucinations are harmful or beneficial—see the box on page 364.)

Schizophrenics, then, may differ from normal people not in their imaginary experience but in their ability to differentiate between imaginary and actual experiences—that is, in reality discrimination. This hypothesis was supported by an experiment in which schizophrenics with hallucinations were exposed to two conditions. In one, they provided responses to cues (e.g., "Name a kind of dwelling that begins with *h*"). In the other, they were *given* responses to cues (e.g., "What is a type of footwear? A shoe"). A week later, all the

Schizophrenics who experience auditory hallucinations may be hearing their own voices speaking subvocally.

HALLUCINATIONS: TERROR OR COMFORT?

Most experts on schizophrenia now believe that hallucinations are at least partly the result of neurological dysfunction. Nevertheless, as we have seen repeatedly, patients don't just have symptoms. They also have reactions to symptoms, and if those reactions are positive—if the symptom serves some purpose in the person's life—they may feed the disorder.

This might be the case with some hallucinating psychotics. In a recent study, Miller and her colleagues interviewed fifty hallucinating patients about their attitudes toward their hallucinations. Surprisingly, more than half the subjects reported that hallucinating had some advantages. Many claimed that their hallucinations were soothing. In the words of one patient, "If I can keep it low, it's relaxing, like having a radio on" (L. J. Miller, O'Connor, & DiPasquale, 1993, p. 586). Others said that the hallucinations provided companionship ("I was lonely; I wanted some friends" [p. 586]), that they served protective functions ("I hallucinated shooting my dad instead of actually shooting him . . . I'm not in prison" [p. 586]), that they bolstered self-esteem, that they made it easier to get attention and disability payments, that they even helped with work ("When I do greeting cards, sometimes the voices make out the verses" [p. 586]). Ten out of the fifty patients said they would like to go on hallucinating as long as they could control the hallucinations.

At the same time, all but one of the patients also reported that their hallucinations had negative effects, preventing them from earning a living ("I've never been able to have a job because of this" [p. 587]), interfering with their activities ("The voices . . . try to help, but they may say do it in a different way than the boss" [p. 587]), upsetting them emotionally, damaging their social relationships and their self-esteem ("Every time I see the visions, they look so handsome; I feel worse about myself, since I'm uglier" [p. 587]), and also interfering with their sex lives ("It got in the way of sex; I feel like I'm on TV" [p. 587]). Two-thirds of the patients said that they would prefer not to hallucinate, even if they could make the hallucinations come and go at will.

So a clear majority of the patients wanted to be rid of their hallucinations, but a sizable minority did not, and the latter proved more resistant to treatment. The above interviews were conducted when the subjects entered the hospital for treatment. When they were released—after a mean stay of about two months—the researchers interviewed them again, to see if they were still hallucinating. Those who were had certain things in common. First, they were more likely to have olfactory hallucinations. (This is consistent with the finding that olfactory hallucinations may be associated with "pleasure centers" in the limbic structures of the brain [McLean, 1986].) Second, they were more likely to report that they could predict the onset of their hallucinations via some inner warning signal—a feature that probably makes hallucinations less threatening. Finally, those who were still hallucinating upon release tended to be the ones who, upon admission, had reported the most positive effects for their hallucinations. As the researchers point out, this last correlation does not prove a causal connection—that valuing one's hallucinations serves to perpetuate them—but it certainly raises the question.

responses were repeated back to them, and they were asked to say which ones they had provided and which had been given to them. Compared with normal subjects and also with nonhallucinating psychotics, the hallucinating schizophrenics had a harder time distinguishing between the memory of their own thoughts and the memory of information that came from the outside (Bentall, Baker, & Havers, 1991).

In the case of auditory hallucinations, it is possible that the voices are something more than imaginary. They may be the patient's own voice, speaking subvocally—that is, with activation of the larynx but with no audible sound. PET scans of schizophrenics taken while the subjects were having auditory hallucinations have shown a pattern of activity in the language regions of the brain that is similar to the activity seen in the brains of normal subjects speaking and listening to their own voices (Cleghorn, Franco, Szechtman, et al., 1992).

Disorders of Mood While schizophrenia is considered to be primarily a disturbance of thought, it often involves disturbances of mood as well. However, schizophrenic mood abnormalities have little in common with the psychotic mood disorders. As we saw in Chapter 10, the mood disorders involve either deep depression or manic elation, or an alternation between the two. In schizophrenia, what we see is a different pattern altogether,* or rather two patterns. One is a re-

*Some people, however, do have either a manic or a major depressive episode while showing the symptoms of schizophrenia. This intermediate syndrome is called **schizoaffective disorder** and has an intermediate prognosis. That is, schizoaffective patients fare somewhat better than schizophrenics, on the average, and somewhat worse than mood disorder patients (Harrow & Grossman, 1984).

duced emotional responsiveness, known either as **blunted affect** (when the patient shows little emotion) or **flat affect** (when the patient shows no emotion). In either case this reduction of emotion is often accompanied by **anhedonia,** a reduced experience of pleasure. The second major pattern of schizophrenic mood disturbance is **inappropriate affect,** the expression of emotions unsuitable to the situation. For example, the patient may giggle while relating a painful childhood memory or show anger when given a present. Usually, however, the inappropriateness is subtler. A number of studies have shown that schizophrenics tend to use the same gestures, show the same facial expression, and gaze at the listener in the same way regardless of whether the emotion they are describing is happy, sad, or angry. Furthermore, in all these situations their gestures, facial expression, and gaze tend to be similar to those that non-schizophrenic people use when describing something happy (Knight & Roff, 1985). So here again, the problem for schizophrenics seems to be one of differentiation. This is true even for those with blunted affect. Recent research suggests that such patients have difficulty only in expressing different emotions, not in feeling them (Berenbaum & Oltmanns, 1992; Kring, Kerr, Smith, et al., 1993).

Disorders of Motor Behavior The variety of unusual behaviors manifested by schizophrenics seems limited only by the boundaries of behavior itself. The following portrait of a schizophrenic ward shows a typical mix of behaviors that might be observed daily in hundreds of schizophrenic wards throughout the country:

> In the day room Lou stands hour after hour, never saying a word, just rubbing the palm of his hand around and around the top of his head. Jerry spends his day rubbing his hand against his stomach and running around a post at the same time. Helen paces back and forth, her head down, mumbling about enemies who are coming to get her, while Vic grimaces and giggles over in the corner. Virginia stands in the center of the day room vigorously slapping her hand against the fullness of her dress, making a rhythmical smacking sound which, because of its tireless repetition, goes unnoticed. Nick tears up magazines, puts bits of paper in his mouth, and then spits them out, while Bill sits immobile for hours, staring at the floor. Betty masturbates quietly on the couch, while Paul follows one of the young nurse's aides on her room check, hoping to get a chance to see up her dress as she leans over to smooth a bed. Geraldine is reading her Bible; Lillian is watching television; and Frank is hard at work scrubbing the floor. (R. Hagen, Florida State University, clinical files)

In some cases, such as the last three in this example, schizophrenic motor behavior appears perfectly normal. In other cases, such as those of Betty and Paul, it is merely inappropriate to the setting. However, certain repetitive motor behaviors, such as the head rubbing, dress smacking, and paper tearing in the above case, are clearly abnormal. The act of engaging in purposeless behaviors repetitively for hours is called **stereotypy.**

Schizophrenics sometimes show frenetically high levels of motor activity, running about, thrashing their arms, upsetting furniture, and generally expending a good deal of energy. Much more common, however, is the opposite: marked inactivity. In the extreme case, schizophrenics may lapse into a catatonic stupor, remaining mute and immobile for days on end. (Catatonic behavior will be discussed later in this chapter.)

Because social interaction is a hallmark of normal human existence, a great portion of the tragedy of schizophrenia is the inability to be involved with other people.

Social Withdrawal As we shall see, an early sign of schizophrenia is emotional detachment—a lack of attention to or interest in the goings-on of the external world. Preoccupied with their own thoughts, schizophrenics gradually withdraw from involvement with the environment. Above all, they withdraw from involvement with other people. Note that in spite of the wide range of behaviors taking place on the ward described above, there is one behavior that is strikingly absent: interpersonal interaction. Rarely do schizophrenic patients engage in small talk. Usually they act as if others did not exist (R. L. Morrison & Bellack, 1987).

Social withdrawal is particularly marked in the chronic schizophrenic, the type of patient in the ward described above. Chronic schizophrenics generally prefer greater interpersonal distance—that is, more space between themselves and the person standing or sitting next to them—than either nonschizophrenic patients or normal people (Duke & Mullins, 1973). When schizophrenics are obliged to interact with others, they operate under considerable handicaps. They are less adept than nonschizophrenics at picking up interpersonal cues—that is, at understanding what the other person is feeling or trying to do (Corrigan & Green, 1993). Many of them also have problems with gaze discrimination: they think other people are looking directly at them when this is not the case (Rosse, Kendrick, Wyatt, et al., 1994). Given these problems, it is no surprise that they recoil from social interaction.

The social withdrawal of schizophrenics is no doubt related to their attention problems as well. The mental havoc that presumably results from the attention deficit would make communication very difficult, and as we have seen, schizophrenics communicate poorly. Knowing that they are unlikely to make themselves understood—and knowing, furthermore, that people may treat them very curtly—schizophrenics may choose to focus on anything rather than on other people.

Other Symptoms In addition to displaying the symptoms described above, many schizophrenics show a *disturbance in the sense of self.* Though apparently preoccupied with themselves, they seem at the same time uncertain as to who they are, and they may dwell on this question. Another common schizophrenic symptom is *lack of volition.* Many patients lack the will to engage in any normal goal-directed behavior (putting on their clothes properly, completing a chore). Some lapse into complete inactivity. In others, activity is limited to the bizarre, purposeless motor behaviors described earlier.

Schizophrenics typically have little insight into their psychopathology. Mental disorganization, hallucinations, affective blunting, lack of volition—however much they labor under these burdens, they do not see them as signs of mental illness. Not surprisingly, those who do have some insight tend to lose it as the psychosis deepens (McEvoy, Schooler, Friedman, et al., 1993).

The Onset and Course of Schizophrenia

Onset Schizophrenia normally strikes during adolescence or early adulthood, and the timing of its appearance is related to other factors. One is sex. For men, the median age at onset is mid-twenties; for women, late twenties. In addition, an early onset tends to be a gradual onset (Haas & Sweeney, 1992), and early-onset cases, particularly those beginning in adolescence, have a worse prognosis (Eaton, Mortensen, Herrmann, et al., 1992).

Whatever the age at onset, schizophrenia, like some other disorders, seems to follow a regular course, or progression of stages, through time. The course of the disorder has traditionally been divided into three phases.

The Prodromal Phase In some cases, the onset of schizophrenia is very sudden. In a matter of days, a reasonably well-adjusted person is transformed into a hallucinating psychotic. In other cases, there is a slow, insidious deterioration of functioning that goes on for years before any clearly psychotic symptoms appear. This gradual downhill slide is known as the **prodromal phase.**

During the prodromal phase, incipient schizophrenics generally become withdrawn and socially isolated. Often they cease to care about their appearance or hygiene, forgetting to bathe, sleeping in their clothes, and so on. Performance in school or at work begins to deteriorate; the person shows up late, if at all, and seems careless and inattentive. At the same time, emotions begin to seem shallow and inappropriate. Eventually family and friends will note a change in the person. Sometimes, however, the disorder proceeds so gradually that it is not remarked upon until the person begins dressing in odd ways, collecting trash, talking to invisible companions, or engaging in some other unmistakably bizarre behavior. By this time the active phase has begun.

The Active Phase In the **active phase,** the patient

begins showing prominent psychotic symptoms—hallucinations, delusions, disorganized speech, severe withdrawal, and so forth. The symptoms outlined earlier in this chapter describe the active phase of schizophrenia. As we noted, however, no one patient is likely to show all those symptoms.

The Residual Phase Just as onset may occur almost overnight, so may recovery. Ordinarily, however, what recovery there is is gradual. In most patients, the active phase is followed by a **residual phase,** in which behavior is similar to that seen during the prodromal phase. Blunted or flat affect is especially common in this period. Speech may still ramble, hygiene may still be poor, and though outright hallucinations and delusions may have dissipated, the person may continue to have unusual perceptual experiences and odd ideas, claiming, for example, to be able to tell the future or to have other special powers. (In the words of one recovering schizophrenic, "I believe that I am psychic . . . but presently I believe that people can 'read my mind' only if they are in my immediate vicinity" [Bowden, 1993, p. 165].) In consequence, running a household or holding down a job is still difficult for most schizophrenics in the residual phase.

In some cases, the residual phase ends with a return to perfectly normal functioning, or "complete remission," as it is known in the psychiatric vocabulary. This outcome is not common, however. Many patients remain impaired to some degree, and many go on to have further psychotic (i.e., active-phase) episodes, with increasingly impaired functioning between episodes. An extensive long-term follow-up study of more than 1,000 schizophrenics by Manfred Bleuler (1978), the son of Eugen Bleuler, found that approximately 10 percent of the schizophrenics remained schizophrenic for the rest of their lives, 25 percent returned to and maintained normal functioning, and 50 to 65 percent alternated between the residual phase and a recurrence of an active phase. Other long-term studies have produced similar findings (Breier, Schreiber, Dyer, et al., 1991; Carone, Harrow, & Westermeyer, 1991; Ram, Bromet, Eaton, et al., 1992). As one might expect, relapses tend to be triggered by stressful life events (Ventura, Nuechterlein, Lukoff, et al., 1989).

Another sad truth revealed by longitudinal studies is that schizophrenics tend to die younger than other people. A ten-year follow-up of more than a thousand Swedish patients found that their overall mortality rate was double that of the general population, as a result of violent death, cardiovascular disorder, and, above all, suicide. The patients' suicide rate was ten times greater than that of the general population (Allebeck, 1989).

The Subtypes of Schizophrenia

Ever since the days of Kraepelin and Eugen Bleuler, schizophrenia has been divided into subtypes. Patients were described not merely as schizophrenic but as catatonic schizophrenics, paranoid schizophrenics, and so forth. These subtypes are often problematic for the diagnostician, for although they are based on behavioral signs, such signs may change over time. If, upon intake, a patient with other schizophrenic features claims that he is a famous person bedeviled by enemies, he will probably be classified as paranoid schizophrenic. But if, two weeks later, he no longer speaks of the enemies but will not move from his chair, should he be reclassified as a catatonic schizophrenic?

Despite the difficulties, subtype diagnoses may ultimately be of value. As we saw in Chapter 6, the process of sorting patients into relatively restrictive diagnostic groups is essential to research. Though at present we do not know whether different schizophrenic symptomatologies issue from different causes and call for different treatments, we can never find out unless we study groups of patients with similar symptomatologies. And this means sorting them into subtypes.

DSM-IV lists five subtypes. One of these, the "undifferentiated" type, is a miscellaneous category, used for patients who do not fit into any of the other categories or who fit into more than one. Many patients show aspects of more than one subtype or, if they begin by fitting into one subtype, drift toward a less differentiated symptom picture (T. H. McGlashan & Fenton, 1993). Therefore undifferentiated schizophrenia is a commonly employed diagnosis. A second category, the "residual" type, is for patients who have passed beyond the active phase. This leaves three categories that actually describe active-phase symptomatology: disorganized, catatonic, and paranoid schizophrenia.

Disorganized Schizophrenia What *DSM-IV* now calls **disorganized schizophrenia** has traditionally been known as *hebephrenic schizophrenia. Hebephrenic* comes from *hebe,* the Greek word for "youth," and the reference is to the childish behaviors typical of this subtype. Giggling wildly, making funny faces, and assuming absurd postures, the disorganized schizophrenic often resembles nothing so much as a normally silly seven-year-old trying to get a rise out of the older generation.

According to *DSM-IV,* three symptoms are especially characteristic of disorganized schizophrenia. First is a pronounced incoherence of speech; it is the disorganized schizophrenic who is most likely to produce neologisms, clang associations, and word salad. Second is mood disturbance, in the form of either flat affect or extreme silliness. Third is disorganized behavior, or lack of goal orientation—for example, a refusal to bathe or dress. Though these three signs may define the subtype, most disorganized schizophrenics run the gamut of schizophrenic symptomatology. Their motor behavior is strikingly odd. They may also experience hallucinations and delusions, though these are often confused and fragmentary, unlike the more coherent imaginings of the paranoid schizophrenic. Furthermore, most disorganized schizophrenics are severely withdrawn, utterly caught up in their own private worlds, and at times almost impervious to whatever is happening around them. With this wide array of bizarre characteristics, the disorganized schizophrenic, of all the varieties of the psychologically disturbed, is the one who best fits the popular stereotype of a "crazy" person.

The onset of disorganized schizophrenia is usually gradual and tends to occur at a relatively early age (Fenton & McGlashan, 1991a). The distinguishing mark of the onset—withdrawal into a realm of bizarre and childlike fantasies—is illustrated in the following case:

> Doris, Sam's wife, reported that she was bothered by his behavior at times but she attributed it to the pressure of business. . . . As Doris said, ". . . I was losing contact with him. It was as if he were drifting away from me. . . . Then he began to do scary and creepy things. I would wake up in the middle of the night and he would be gone. Once I found him sitting on the grass in the middle of the backyard at 4:00 A.M. and he didn't seem to know where he was or what was going on. . . ."
>
> About three weeks later, Sam was arrested at 3:00 A.M. in a small town about 40 miles from where he lived. The police report said that he was driving through town at nearly 85 miles an hour when he was stopped and that he told the arresting officers that he was trying to "get up escape velocity for a trip to Mars.". . .
>
> Some of the ideas Sam spoke about freely to doctors and fellow patients were extremely bizarre. At one time he was convinced he was Robin Hood, for example. He had not notified anyone of this sudden shift in his identity and it was discovered only [after] he leaped from a perch atop a door and landed on the back of an unsuspecting attendant who had just entered the room. (McNeil, 1970, p. 98)

Top: This painting was done by a young schizophrenic man in the early stages of the disorder. The sad, partially faceless woman alone in the desert suggests loss of identity and loss of meaning. *Bottom:* Another schizophrenic patient made this painting of the earth being split apart by lightning—perhaps the person's effort to picture his internal disintegration.

Do not assume, however, that the fantasy life of disorganized schizophrenics is fun. Along with Robin Hood, a number of grim horrors inhabit the private worlds of these patients. Enemies stalk them; voices accuse them of heinous crimes. McNeil (1970), who reported the case of Sam, has commented that the closest analogue of the disorganized schizophrenic's experience is the nightmare.

Catatonic Schizophrenia Once a common disorder but now quite rare (R. L. Morrison, 1991), **catatonic schizophrenia** has as its distinguishing feature a marked disturbance in motor behavior.

Sometimes this disturbance takes the form of **catatonic stupor,** or complete immobility, usually accompanied by **mutism,** the cessation of speech; the patient may remain in this condition for weeks. Some catatonics assume extremely bizarre postures during their stupors. They may also show *waxy flexibility,* a condition in which their limbs, like those of a rubber doll, can be "arranged" by another person and will remain in whatever position they are placed. However, catatonia is not limited to decreases in motor activity. Many catatonics alternate between periods of immobility and periods of frenzied motor activity, which may include violent behavior. In either form, catatonic schizophrenia often involves medical emergencies. When excited, patients may injure themselves or others; when stuporous, they must be prevented from starving.

Though catatonic immobility suggests passivity, it may in fact be quite "active." To hold for hours the bizarre postures that catatonics often assume requires an extraordinary expenditure of energy. Furthermore, while some patients assume waxy flexibility, others strenuously resist any effort on the part of others to move their limbs—a feature known as *catatonic rigidity.* Similarly, though catatonia seems to suggest extreme withdrawal, it is clear that many patients are well aware of what is going on around them. Some show **echolalia,** parroting what is said by others; some show **echopraxia,** imitating the movements of others. Finally, in many patients one sees what is called *catatonic negativism.* That is, they not only will refuse to do what is requested of them but will consistently do just the opposite, indicating that they understand very well the nature of the requests. This seeming willfulness has prompted certain experts to conceptualize catatonia as a defense against subjectively perceived threats (McNeil, 1970). On the other hand, the disorder may be neurologically based. In some catatonic patients there are signs of atrophy in the cerebellum, a part of the brain that is involved in movement, balance, and posture (Wilcox, 1993).

Paranoid Schizophrenia Though Kraepelin's term *dementia praecox* lasted only briefly, his descriptions of various aspects of the disorder continue to prove remarkably accurate. The following description of **paranoid schizophrenia,** written by Kraepelin (1902) nearly a century ago, dramatically captures the most prominent features of the disorder:

> The patients . . . divulge a *host of delusions,* almost entirely of persecution; people are watching them, intriguing against them, they are not wanted at home, former friends are talking about them and trying to injure their reputation. These delusions are changeable and soon become *fantastic.* The patients claim that some extreme punishment has been inflicted upon them, they have been shot down into the earth, have been transformed into spirits, and must undergo all sorts of torture. Their intestines have been removed by enemies and are being replaced a little at a time; their own heads have been removed, their throats occluded, and the blood no longer circulates. . . .
>
> *Hallucinations,* especially of hearing, are very prominent during this stage; fellow-men jeer at them, call them bastards, threaten them, accuse them of horrible crimes. . . .
>
> The *emotional attitude* soon changes and becomes more and more exalted. At the same time the delusions become less repressive and more expansive and fantastic. The patient, in spite of persecution, is happy and contented, extravagant and talkative, and boasts that he has been transformed into the Christ; others will ascend to heaven, have lived many lives, and traversed the universe. . . . The delusions may become most florid, foolish, and ridiculous. A patient may say that he is a star, that all light and darkness emanate from him; that he is the greatest inventor ever born, can create mountains, is endowed with all the attributes of God, can prophesy for coming ages, can talk to the people in Mars. (pp. 257–258)

The defining characteristics of paranoid schizophrenia are delusions and/or hallucinations of a relatively consistent nature, often related to the themes of persecution and grandeur. The delusions can range from a jumble of vague suspicions to an exquisitely worked-out system of imagined conspiracies. In either case, they are often accompanied by hallucinations—especially auditory hallucinations—supporting the delusional belief. When, in the classic case, the theme is persecution, it is often combined with the theme of grandeur. Thus, as Kraepelin notes, patients may claim immense power and wisdom. Or, in extreme cases, they may adopt a permanent delusional identity with some famous figure, such as Jesus Christ.*

*Stable delusional identities are apparently rare, however, and contrary to the popular stereotype, they are not necessarily of the magnitude of Christ or Napoleon. When Rokeach was planning the experiment described earlier in this chapter, he did a survey of all the state hospitals in Michigan in an effort to find two or more patients with the same delusional identity. It turned out that he had little to choose from:

> The replies revealed that of the 25,000 or so mental patients in the state hospitals of Michigan there were only a handful with delusional identities. There were no Napoleons or Caesars, no Khrushchevs or Eisenhowers. Two people claimed

(Continued on next page.)

Paranoid schizophrenia is far more common than either the disorganized or catatonic types. A 1974 survey of more than 8,000 hospitalized schizophrenics found that close to half were diagnosed as paranoid (Guggenheim & Babigian, 1974). Paranoid schizophrenics are also, in the main, more "normal" than other schizophrenics. They perform well on cognitive tests (M. E. Strauss, 1993). They have better records of premorbid adjustment, are more likely to be married, have a later onset, and show better long-term outcomes than do other kinds of schizophrenics (Fenton & McGlashan, 1991a; Kendler, McGuire, Gruenberg, et al., 1994; Nicholson & Neufeld, 1993).

Though the active phase of paranoid schizophrenia usually does not appear until after age twenty-five, it is typically preceded by years of fear and suspicion, leading to tense and fragile interpersonal relationships. The onset and development of a paranoid schizophrenic episode are illustrated in the following case of a forty-year-old woman:

> Laura started to complain [to her husband] about the neighbors. A woman who lived on the floor beneath them was knocking on the wall to irritate her. According to the husband, this woman had really knocked on the wall a few times; he had heard the noises. However, Laura became more and more concerned about it. . . . She started to feel that the neighbors were now recording everything she said; maybe they had hidden wires in the apartment. She started to feel "funny" sensations. There were many strange things happening, which she did not know how to explain; people were looking at her in a funny way in the street; in the butcher shop, the butcher had purposely served her last, although she was in the middle of the line. During the next few days she felt that people were planning to harm either her or her husband. In the neighborhood she saw a German woman whom she had not seen for several years. Now the woman had suddenly reappeared, probably to testify that the patient and her husband were involved in some sort of crime.
>
> Laura was distressed and agitated. She felt unjustly accused, because she had committed no crime. Maybe these people were really not after her, but after her husband. In the evening when she looked at television, it became obvious to her that the programs referred to her life. Often the people on the programs were just repeating what she had thought. They were stealing her ideas. She wanted to go to the police and report them. At this point the husband felt the patient could not be left alone. (Arieti, 1974a, pp. 165–166)

The Dimensions of Schizophrenia

The subtypes that we have just discussed (disorganized, catatonic, paranoid) are a classic way of looking at schizophrenia, but research has yet to prove that they are valid groupings—that is, that the schizophrenias they delineate are in fact different disorders, springing from different causes, requiring different treatments, and so forth. Accordingly, researchers have looked for other ways in which to organize information about schizophrenia. Today, discussions of this disorder are generally framed not according to subtypes but in terms of "dimensions." Like spatial dimensions (width, length), dimensions of schizophrenia are measures of *continuous* variation and are thus less exclusive than subtypes. With dimensions, patients are never "in" or "out"; they fall somewhere on the dimension. In practice, however, dimensions too tend to sort patients into groups. It is possible that their advantage over subtypes is simply that the groups they yield have so far proved more meaningful.

The three dimensions that have received the most attention are the process-reactive dimension, the positive-negative symptoms dimension, and the paranoid-nonparanoid dimension. Although they are based on different features of schizophrenia—for example, the process-reactive distinction has to do with the nature of onset, whereas the other two describe symptoms—in practice, the three dimensions overlap and may be identifying similar subgroups of schizophrenics.

The Process-Reactive or Good-Poor Premorbid Dimension As we noted, there is considerable variation in the onset of schizophrenia. Some patients go through an extended prodromal phase. Others go from normal functioning to full-blown psychosis almost overnight. This dimension of variation has traditionally been known as the **process-reactive dimension.** Those cases in which onset is gradual are called **process schizophrenia;** those in which onset is sudden and apparently precipitated by some traumatic event are called **reactive schizophrenia.**

(Continued from previous page.)

> to be members of the Ford family, but not the same person. We located one Tom Mix, one Cinderella, a member of the Morgan family, a Mrs. God, and an assortment of lesser known personages. (Rokeach, 1964, p. 36)

In addition, he located six Christs. Of these, however, only three were free of organic brain damage and consistently claimed that they were Christ. These three became the subjects of the study.

This dimension has a long history, beginning with Kraepelin and Bleuler. These two theorists believed that the onset of the psychoses was a clue to their cause. The biogenic psychoses, since they were the result of some abnormal physiological *process,* would presumably have a gradual onset. By contrast, the psychogenic psychoses, since they were *reactions* to traumatic experiences, would appear suddenly. Hence the terms *process* and *reactive.* Today many researchers view the process-reactive dimension more as a continuum than as a dichotomy. Indeed, some now avoid the terms *process* and *reactive* altogether and classify patients instead on the basis of *good versus poor premorbid adjustment*—that is, in terms of how well they were functioning before the onset of the active phase. Actually, the good-poor premorbid dimension is basically the same as the process-reactive dimension, minus the causal implications. To describe onset is to describe premorbid adjustment, and vice versa.

Although there is some disagreement over the usefulness of the process-reactive dimension, there is general agreement as to what the terms describe. The process (or poor-premorbid) case typically involves a long history of inadequate social, sexual, and occupational adjustment. Process schizophrenics typically did not belong to a group of friends in school, did not date regularly during adolescence, did not continue their education after high school, never held a job for longer than two years, and never married (Haas & Sweeney, 1992; H. I. Kaplan & Sadock, 1991). Furthermore, there appears to have been no precipitating event—no sudden stressor such as a divorce or a job change—immediately preceding the active phase. Rather, the history usually reveals a gradual eclipse of thoughts, interests, emotions, and activities, until the person becomes so withdrawn that he or she is hospitalized.

In contrast, histories of reactive (or good-premorbid) schizophrenics are apparently normal. The patient fit in at home and at school, had friends, dated, and got along well in general. The onset of the schizophrenic symptoms usually occurs after a clear precipitating event and is sudden and spectacular, often involving hallucinations and delusions. Such patients also tend to show extreme panic and confusion, for they are as horrified as everyone else over what has happened to them.

Premorbid adjustment has been useful in predicting which patients will recover and which will not (Gaebel & Pietzcker, 1987). Poor-premorbid schizophrenics are more likely to have longer hospitalizations and are less likely to be discharged than good-premorbid patients. It is this factor that allows the terms **chronic** and **acute** to be used, for all practical purposes, almost interchangeably with *poor premorbid* and *good premorbid* (or *process* and *reactive*). As the terms are generally defined, *chronic* refers to patients who have long-standing severe deficits. Often such patients are hospitalized for years. *Acute* usually refers to patients who are in the midst of the short-term active phase of their first schizophrenic episode.

The Positive-Negative Symptoms Dimension Of all the dimensions of schizophrenia, the one that has attracted the most research attention in recent years—and therefore the one that will be most important in our discussion of the possible causes of schizophrenia (Chapter 15)—is the positive-negative symptoms dimension. **Positive symptoms,** characterized by the presence of something that is normally absent, include hallucinations, delusions, bizarre or disorganized behavior, and positive thought disorder such as incoherence. **Negative symptoms,** characterized by the absence of something that is normally present, include poverty of speech, flat affect, withdrawal, apathy, and attentional impairment (Andreasen & Olsen, 1982; J. S. Strauss, Carpenter, & Bartko, 1974). The positive-negative symptoms dimension seems to parallel the good-poor premorbid dimension. Patients with negative symptoms are more likely to have had poor premorbid adjustment. And like poor-premorbid patients, they tend to have an earlier onset (Castle & Murray, 1993) and a worse prognosis (Fenton & McGlashan, 1994). Indeed, they are the ones most likely to have an "unremitting course"—that is, never to recover at all. Positive and negative symptoms also seem to be associated with different kinds of cognitive problems. Patients with negative symptoms do worse on tests involving the processing of visual stimuli. Patients with positive symptoms do worse on tests that require processing of auditory stimuli, especially language (M. Green & Walker, 1985; M. E. Strauss, 1993).

These findings have led to increased speculation that there may be two biologically distinct types of schizophrenia, of which the one with negative symptoms is more like Kraepelin's original dementia praecox. Some researchers (Crow, 1989; Crow, Cross, Johnstone, et al., 1982; Lenzenweger, Dworkin, & Wethington, 1989) have distinguished two such types. (See Table 14.1.) **Type I schizophrenia** is characterized by positive symptoms and tends to respond to medication. **Type II schizo-**

phrenia is characterized by negative symptoms (and associated with structural abnormalities in the brain) and according to some research does not respond as well to typical antipsychotic medication. As we will see in Chapter 15, the two types also seem to fit differently into the "dopamine hypothesis," the leading biochemical theory of schizophrenia.

Other research has linked sex differences to these dimensions of schizophrenia (Dworkin, 1990; Lewine, 1981). As we saw, male schizophrenics in general have an earlier onset. They are also more likely to be withdrawn and to exhibit negative symptoms; women are more likely to have affective and positive symptoms (Castle & Murray, 1993; J. M. Goldstein, Santangelo, Simpson, et al., 1990). In addition, men tend to have poorer premorbid adjustment and a worse prognosis (J. M. Goldstein, 1988). Finally, schizophrenic men are less likely to have a family history of schizophrenia than women (J. M. Goldstein, Faraone, Chen, et al., 1990) but are more likely to have had birth complications and to show brain abnormalities (Foerster, Lewis, Owen, et al., 1991; R. E. Gur, Mozley, Resnick, et al., 1991). These findings suggest that men and women may be differentially at risk for different types of schizophrenia, with men more susceptible to process, poor-premorbid, Type II schizophrenia and women more susceptible to reactive, good-premorbid, Type I schizophrenia.

While these categories sound very tidy and symmetrical, in fact they are not. Often a typical "Type I" characteristic will turn up in an otherwise "Type II" patient. Some schizophrenics show both positive and negative symptoms at the same time. Others initially show negative symptoms and then develop positive symptoms, or the reverse. In the latter case, the negative symptoms may be secondary. That is, they may develop as a *response* to the primary symptoms: under the pressure of frightening hallucinations (positive symptom), the patient withdraws socially, speaks little, and assumes a flat affect (negative symptoms). But it is very hard to determine whether negative symptoms are primary or secondary. All these problems must be taken into account in any theory that attempts to explain the mechanisms underlying positive and negative symptoms (Andreasen, 1989).

The Paranoid-Nonparanoid Dimension On the **paranoid-nonparanoid dimension** the criterion of classification is the presence (paranoid) or absence (nonparanoid) of delusions of persecution and/or grandeur. Although some studies have found the paranoid-nonparanoid dimension to be independent of the process-reactive dimension (e.g., Zigler & Levine, 1973), other studies have shown evidence of a relationship between the two (Fenton & McGlashan, 1991a). Buss (1966), for instance, points out that, in general, paranoid schizophrenics, like reactive schizophrenics, "are more intact intellectually, perform better in a variety of tasks, and have a higher level of maturity" (p. 230). And as we saw, they tend to have better premorbid adjustment, later onset, and better outcomes. Thus the paranoid-nonparanoid dimension, like the process-reactive, the good-poor premorbid, and the positive-negative symptoms, has had prognostic value and may aid in the development of theories as to the causes of schizophrenia.

TABLE 14.1
SUMMARY OF DIFFERENCES BETWEEN POSITIVE-SYMPTOM (TYPE I) AND NEGATIVE-SYMPTOM (TYPE II) SCHIZOPHRENIA

	Positive (Type I) Schizophrenia	Negative (Type II) Schizophrenia
Symptoms	Delusions Hallucinations Incoherence Bizarre behavior	Poverty of speech Flat affect Social withdrawal Apathy
Premorbid adjustment	Good	Poor
Onset	Tends to be later	Tends to be earlier
Prognosis	Good	Poor
Structural brain abnormalities	Absent	May be present
Drug response	Good	Poor
Sex distribution	More likely to be women	More likely to be men

Psychiatrist Herbert Meltzer, a strong advocate of obtaining the fully informed consent of schizophrenics who are recruited as research subjects, discusses issues of medication and consent with a patient.

Two Related Categories: Brief Psychotic Disorder and Schizophreniform Disorder

> A 17-year-old high-school junior was brought to the emergency room by her distraught mother. . . . Two days earlier the patient's father had been buried; he had died of a sudden myocardial infarction [heart attack] earlier in the week. The patient had become wildly agitated at the cemetery, screaming uncontrollably and needing to be restrained by relatives. She was inconsolable at home, sat rocking in a corner, and talked about a devil that had come to claim her soul. Before her father's death she was a "typical teenager, popular, and a very good student, but sometimes prone to overreacting." There was no previous psychiatric history. (Spitzer, Skodol, Gibbon, et al., 1981, p. 180)

What was the diagnosis in this patient's case? Since she was apparently out of touch with reality and also delusional, she might be called schizophrenic. However, in view of the shock she had received, her response might also seem normal—or at least different from the disorder that we call schizophrenia. Until recently, such cases—with rapid onset, short duration, a clear precipitating event, and no previous history of schizophrenic symptoms—were classified as "acute schizophrenic episode," a subtype of schizophrenia. Today they are specifically distinguished from schizophrenia. If the episode lasts for less than a month, it is called **brief psychotic disorder.** If it lasts for more than a month but less than six months, it is called **schizophreniform disorder.** If it lasts for more than six months, it is relabeled as schizophrenia. (The diagnoses of brief psychotic disorder and schizophreniform disorder no longer require a clear precipitating event, though such an event is often involved in such cases.)

Why these careful distinctions? Recall our discussion of the dimensions of schizophrenia. As we saw, researchers now suspect that there may be two kinds of schizophrenia, a good-premorbid, positive-symptom Type I and a poor-premorbid, negative-symptom Type II. Hence there is now a trend toward separating good-premorbid from poor-premorbid cases. Marking off brief psychotic disorder and schizophreniform disorder from schizophrenia is part of this trend. Both those lesser diagnoses are by definition good-premorbid, and brief psychotic disorder by definition involves positive symptoms.

It is important to note that during the active phase, neither brief psychotic disorder nor schizophreniform disorder need differ from schizophrenia in symptomatology. The primary criterion for differential diagnosis is the length of the episode. However, the course of the episode also tends to differ. Brief psychotic disorder is swift and complete not only in its onset but also in its resolution. After a brief psychotic disorder, the person is his or her "old self" again. With schizophreniform disorder, there may be a brief prodromal phase, and recovery is generally less complete, though more complete than in schizophrenia (Sautter, McDermott, & Garver, 1993).

In course, then, brief psychotic disorder, schizophreniform disorder, and schizophrenia are three points on a continuum. Possibly, they *are* the same disorder, differing only in severity. There are signs of a family resemblance between schizophreniform disorder and schizophrenia. On neuropsychological tests, schizophreniform patients show cognitive problems similar to those of chronic schizophrenics (Hoff, Riordan, O'Donnell, et al., 1992). Furthermore, rates of schizophreniform disorder are disproportionately high in relatives of schizophrenics, and vice versa (Kendler, McGuire, Gruenberg, et al., 1993). With brief psychotic disorder, on the other hand, recent findings do point to a difference in kind, rather than just in degree, from schizophrenia. For example, whereas men are one and a half times more vulnerable than women to schizophrenia, women are twice as vulnerable as men to brief psychotic disorder (Susser & Wanderling, 1994). Whether such contrasts reflect an important difference in cause remains to be seen.

DELUSIONAL DISORDER

Of the three major categories of psychosis, delusional disorder, sometimes called paranoia, is the most frequently portrayed in novels, movies, and television dramas. This type of psychosis is also the one most likely to involve violence to others. The reasons are made clear in the following case:

> Frank W., a thirty-two-year-old electrician, came to the clinic complaining of difficulties in his social life. Frank did his job competently. He seldom missed work and was never late. His co-workers found him quiet at times, but they noted nothing unusual about his behavior. The problem that brought him to the clinic was the threatened breakup of his current romance. Since his divorce five years earlier, Frank had dated five successive women. On each occasion, he had been more interested in the relationship than the woman had been, and each of the previous four relationships had ended in a serious heartbreak for him. When the most recent woman in his life began suggesting that they both date other people, Frank sought counseling.
>
> At first the therapist noted little out of the ordinary. Soon, however, it became apparent that Frank had a much more serious problem than his shaky romance. The therapist's suspicions were first aroused when he offered Frank a cup of coffee from the clinic "coffee station." Frank used a number of delaying tactics to avoid drinking his coffee until he had seen another person pour a cup of coffee from the same pot and take a drink of it. He was also wary of the one-way mirror in the counseling room, and he absolutely refused to allow the therapist to tape-record their sessions. Finally, after several sessions, Frank told the therapist about the people who regularly followed him to the clinic. Ultimately it came out that Frank was convinced that he was being pursued by a group of people bent on killing him. Through an elaborate system of safeguards, he had been able to thwart them so far, but much of his private life was devoted to these efforts at self-protection. Recently, he had begun planning strategies of reprisal. (R. Hagen, Florida State University, clinical files)

This patient's major symptom, a system of delusions, is something that we have already discussed under the heading "Paranoid Schizophrenia." In paranoid schizophrenia, however, the delusional system is simply one item in a cluster of abnormalities, all of which may function independently of one another. In **delusional disorder,** on the other hand, the delusional system is the fundamental abnormality. Indeed, in some cases, the delusional system is the *only* abnormality; in all other respects the person seems quite normal. Other patients may show some disturbances of mood, but only as a consequence of the delusional system. (For example, they may explode in anger at complete strangers, but only because they suspect those strangers of spying on them, flirting with their spouses, or whatever.) It is assumed, in other words, that if there were no delusions, there would be no abnormality. Furthermore, whatever other symptoms the person shows, they do not include the characteristic symptoms of schizophrenia, such as loosening of associations, incoherence, or thought broadcasting. Finally, unlike the delusions of the paranoid schizophrenic, the delusions seen in this disorder are not truly bizarre; they involve things that *could* happen. For example, the person may claim to be pursued by enemies, but not by enemies from outer space.

As for the content of the delusions, *DSM-IV* lists five specific categories. The classic type, just seen in the case of Frank, is the *persecutory type,* involving the belief that one is being threatened or maltreated by others. In the *grandiose type,* as the name indicates, the person believes that he or she is endowed with some extraordinary power or knowledge. In the *jealous type,* the delusion is that one's sexual partner is being unfaithful. In the *erotomanic type,* the victim believes that some person of high status—the president of the company or of the United States—is in love with him or her. Finally, the *somatic type* involves the false conviction

Jane H., a schizophrenic patient who suffers from auditory hallucinations, painted this picture while in an art therapy program in the hospital where she lives. Particularly striking are the decimated and defoliated trees and the distorted sizes of the objects.

that one is suffering from some physical abnormality or disorder.

With delusional disorder, differential diagnosis can be a problem. On one side it borders on paranoid schizophrenia, though genetic evidence indicates that there is a difference between the two patterns. (For example, the relatives of victims of delusional disorder are *not* at greater risk for schizophrenia than the general population [Kendler & Davis, 1981].) On the other side, delusional disorder borders on paranoid personality disorder (Chapter 11). According to *DSM-IV*, the difference here is that people with paranoid personality disorder are simply abnormally suspicious; they do not embrace actual delusions, beliefs that are patently false and indefensible. In addition, the suspicions of the paranoid personality are more realistic than psychotic delusions. For example, the belief that the coffee in a mental health clinic has been poisoned in anticipation of one's arrival is beyond the scope of the paranoid personality. Again, however, these distinctions are easier to make in a diagnostic manual than in actual diagnosis (H. I. Kaplan & Sadock, 1991). Furthermore, there are indications that delusional disorder is not altogether separate from paranoid personality. The rate of paranoid personality and of paranoid traits in general—suspiciousness, jealousy, secretiveness—is disproportionately high in the relatives of patients suffering from delusional disorder (Manschreck, 1992).

Delusional disorder differs from schizophrenia in striking more women than men and in having a later onset, between ages twenty-five and forty-five (Manschreck, 1992). It is also far less common. For schizophrenia, as we saw, the lifetime risk is 1 to 2 percent; for delusional disorder, it is 0.3 percent (H. I. Kaplan & Sadock, 1991). It is possible, of course, that many more cases exist. We have all probably encountered a few candidates for this diagnostic label: ignored geniuses, self-styled prophets, radio talk show callers who have a detailed scheme for solving the world's problems. Because such people tend, apart from their isolated delusional systems, to have relatively good contact with reality, many of them remain within the community and never see a therapist. Those who present themselves for treatment often do so not of their own volition but at the insistence of others.

KEY TERMS

active phase (366)
acute (371)
anhedonia (365)
blocking (357)
blunted affect (365)
brief psychotic disorder (373)
catatonic schizophrenia (368)
catatonic stupor (369)
chronic (371)
clanging (361)
delusional disorder (374)
delusions (356)
disorganized schizophrenia (367)
echolalia (369)
echopraxia (369)
flat affect (365)
hallucinations (363)
inappropriate affect (365)
loosening of associations (357)
mutism (369)
negative symptoms (371)
neologisms (361)
paranoid-nonparanoid dimension (372)
paranoid schizophrenia (369)
positive symptoms (371)
poverty of content (361)
process-reactive dimension (370)
process schizophrenia (370)
prodromal phase (366)
psychoses (354)
reactive schizophrenia (370)
residual phase (367)
schizoaffective disorder (364)
schizophrenia (354)
schizophreniform disorder (373)
stereotypy (365)
Type I schizophrenia (371)
Type II schizophrenia (371–372)
word salad (362)

SUMMARY

- Schizophrenia is the label given to a group of relatively common psychoses characterized by severe distortion of thought, bizarre behavior, and social withdrawal.
- *DSM-IV* identifies five characteristic symptoms of schizophrenia: delusions, hallucinations, disorganized speech, disorganized or catatonic behavior, and negative symptoms (a reduction in or loss of normal language and other functions). To be diagnosed with schizophrenia, a person must have shown two or more of these disturbances for at least a month and been functioning abnormally for at least six months.
- Disorders of thought and language include delusions and loosening of associations between concepts. Loosening of associations results in language marked by poverty of content, neologisms, clanging, or word salad.
- Disorders of perception produce a breakdown of selective attention, which some experts believe constitutes the basic pathology in schizophrenia. Hallucinations are often another perceptual problem for schizophrenics.
- Mood disorders in schizophrenia may take two forms: blunted or flat affect (reduced or absent emotional responsiveness) and inappropriate affect (emotional expression unsuited to the situation).
- Schizophrenics may display a wide variety of disorders of motor behavior, from merely inappropriate to bizarre.
- Social withdrawal is an early sign of schizophrenia, exacerbated by difficulty in maintaining appropriate interpersonal behavior.
- Schizophrenia usually first appears in adolescence or early adulthood. It follows a fairly regular course, involving three stages: (1) the prodromal phase, marked by a gradual social withdrawal and deterioration of functioning; (2) the active phase, marked by overt signs of psychosis; and (3) the residual phase, in which gross psychotic symptoms recede but functioning remains impaired. Some patients experience a complete remission, but most remain impaired to a greater or lesser degree.
- Schizophrenics may be classified into subtypes according to symptomatology. The three main subtypes are (1) disorganized schizophrenia, characterized by incoherent speech, mood disturbance (either flat affect or extreme silliness), and disorganized behavior; (2) catatonic schizophrenia, characterized by extremes of motor behavior (i.e., immobility or hyperactivity); and (3) paranoid schizophrenia, characterized by delusions and/or hallucinations of persecution and grandeur.
- Today classification of schizophrenics by symptomatology is considered less valid than classification along certain dimensions—an approach that allows for continuous variation in, rather than the mere presence or absence of, symptoms.
- One dimension is the process-reactive dimension, in which cases with a gradual onset (process, or poor-premorbid) are distinguished from those with a rapid onset precipitated by some traumatic event (reactive, or good-premorbid).
- A second dimension is the positive-negative symptoms dimension, distinguishing those with new and abnormal behaviors (positive symptoms), such as hallucinations, delusions, and bizarre behaviors, from those with abnormal "nonbehaviors" (negative symptoms), such as withdrawal, flat affect, and poverty of speech. This dimension is now the focus of considerable research, because its two patterns may represent two biologically distinct disorders: Type I schizophrenia (positive symptoms) and Type II schizophrenia (negative symptoms).
- Third is the paranoid-nonparanoid dimension, indicating the presence or absence of paranoid delusions.
- When symptoms of schizophrenia are short-lived,

and especially when their onset is precipitated by some psychological trauma, they are classified not as schizophrenia but as brief psychotic disorder (duration of less than a month) or schizophreniform disorder (duration of one to six months). These two disorders are on a continuum with schizophrenia (more than six months). They may all be the same disorder with different degrees of severity.

- Delusional disorder, another category of psychosis, resembles paranoid schizophrenia in that the most prominent symptom is a system of delusions. In delusional disorder, however, the delusions are the fundamental abnormality, from which any other abnormalities emanate, and in many cases they are the patient's only symptom. Furthermore, if the patient does have other symptoms, they do not include the characteristic symptoms of schizophrenia (e.g., loosening of associations and incoherence). The delusions are more plausible and less bizarre than those found in paranoid schizophrenia.

15

PERSPECTIVES ON SCHIZOPHRENIA

We have described the symptoms of schizophrenia and delusional disorder, but we have not yet raised the question of how these disorders arise. That question—causation—is the focus of most scientific writings on the psychoses, and it is the subject of our present chapter. Since schizophrenia has been much more thoroughly researched than delusional disorder, we will confine our discussion to theories of schizophrenia.

PROBLEMS IN THE STUDY OF SCHIZOPHRENIA

If schizophrenia is as widespread and debilitating as the last chapter claimed, why don't we appropriate the necessary funds, hire a team of researchers, and simply go to work until we have found both cause and cure? Unfortunately, it is not so easy. Schizophrenia is a slippery research problem. We do not know whether it is a single disorder or a group of disorders. Furthermore, it has many and varied symptoms, not all of which turn up in any single patient. Researchers have attacked the problem from many different directions, but only in recent years have they been able to arrive at any firm conclusions—and so far, only a few. A brief examination of the questions surrounding research in this area will show why.

What Is to Be Studied?

Historically, a nagging problem in schizophrenia research has been diagnostic disagreement. Researchers must learn from one another, each launching his or her work from findings produced by others. But this presupposes that everyone is talking about the same thing, and with schizophrenia, this has not always been the case.

As late as the sixties, agreement among professionals on the diagnosis of schizophrenia ranged from only 53 to 74 percent (A. T. Beck, Ward, Mendelson, et al., 1962; Sandifer, Pettus, & Quade, 1964), and agreement among professionals from different countries was even lower. What was called "schizophrenia" in New York was often called "depression" in London (J. E. Cooper, Kendell, Gurland, et al., 1972). The situation has since improved. There is still no laboratory test for schizophrenia, and as long as that is the case, interjudge reliability will never be 100 percent. But with the more stringent criteria laid down by recent editions of the *DSM*, the rate of diagnostic agreement has risen considerably.

A more serious problem today is disagreement over the primary pathology in schizophrenia—a matter that we touched upon in Chapter 14. Consider the analogy of a leg fracture. The fracture will produce pain, a bent leg, and also a limp. But of these three symptoms, only the first two are primary—direct results of the broken bone. The limp is a secondary symptom, a strategy that the person adopts in order to cope with the primary symptom of pain. Likewise in schizophrenia there is little doubt that among the recognized symptoms of the disorder, some are primary and others merely reactions to the primary symptoms. But which is which? Is social withdrawal the primary pathology, as some theorists believe, or do schizophrenics withdraw simply because their thought disorders make it difficult for them to communicate with others? Are delusions a primary symptom, or are they, as suggested earlier, merely the schizophrenic's way of explaining the chaos of his or her thoughts? Answering these questions is crucial to research on schizophrenia. Until we know what the basic disorder is, we stand little chance of discovering its cause.

Problems in Experimentation

The study of schizophrenia is also impeded by standard research problems. As we have seen throughout this book, the usual method of finding out the effect of a given set of conditions is to assign subjects at random either to be exposed to those conditions (experimental group) or not to be exposed to them (control group) and then to compare the results. But this method cannot be used for research into the causes of schizophrenia; we cannot subject people, for experimental purposes, to conditions that we think may cause schizophrenia.

The alternative, then, is to gather evidence ex post facto—that is, to compare groups of people who are already schizophrenic with groups of normal people on whatever variable we are interested in: socioeconomic background, size of brain ventricles, or whatever. But with this method, it is difficult to establish cause-and-effect relationships. Researchers may find—and they have found—that schizophrenia correlates with low socioeconomic status, but does this mean that the stresses of poverty contribute to schizophrenia? Or does it mean that people with schizophrenia, because they adapt so poorly, gravitate toward the lower socioeconomic strata?

Among the problems of conducting research on schizophrenia is the difficulty of separating the true causes of the disorder from the possible effects of such conditions as hospitalization and antipsychotic medication.

This chicken-and-egg problem is actually secondary. Prior to that is the question of whether there *is* a causal relationship between these two variables, or whether both are the result of an unidentified *third variable.* In research on schizophrenia there are two third variables that are notoriously difficult to control. Most of the schizophrenics available for research purposes are (1) hospitalized and (2) taking antipsychotic drugs. Consequently, any interesting differences that turn up between these subjects and nonhospitalized, nonmedicated controls may well be a function not of schizophrenia but of the medication or of the overcrowding, poor diet, difficult sleeping conditions, lack of exercise, and lack of privacy that are routine conditions of hospitalization (J. J. Blanchard & Neale, 1992).

Another vexing problem for schizophrenia researchers is finding what are called **differential deficits,** deficits that are specific to the disorder in question (as opposed to other disorders) and presumably central to it. Because schizophrenia has many debilitating symptoms, schizophrenics will have problems with many different kinds of tasks, but such problems do not necessarily tell us much about schizophrenia in particular (Chapman & Chapman, 1973, 1978). For example, if a researcher gave a group of schizophrenics a driving test, they would probably not do as well as controls, but that does not mean that bad driving is causally related to schizophrenia. In order to show a differential deficit in schizophrenia, research must be able to show that on two carefully constructed tasks, differing only in subtle ways, schizophrenics perform poorly on one and not on the other. Such findings are often very hard to produce, but the question of which deficits represent the central abnormality in schizophrenia causation cannot really be addressed without them.

PERSPECTIVES ON SCHIZOPHRENIA

With schizophrenia, as with all other disorders, the different perspectives stress different causes. It should be stated from the outset, however, that almost no one in the field believes that schizophrenia stems from a single cause. The disorder clearly has multiple sources, and one of them is already known. As we shall see, it is well established that genetic factors are partially, but not wholly, responsible for the development of schizophrenia. Consequently, most of today's researchers have adopted the so-called **diathesis-stress model,** which states that schizophrenia is due to the combination of a genetically inherited *diathesis,* or predisposition, and environmental *stress.* The various perspectives employ this model in keeping with their specialties, some focusing on the diathesis, others on the stress. But nowhere more than in the study of schizophrenia do researchers realize that they are working on a complex biological-environmental problem, one that requires a pooling of efforts across perspectives.

The Biological Perspective

One of the most exciting areas of abnormal psychology today is biological research in schizophrenia. For years, neuroscientists concentrated primarily on the schizophrenic diathesis: first, establishing its existence and then trying to discover what it actually consists of in biological terms. Today they are also investigating biological stressors that might activate that diathesis. A vast amount of work remains to be done, but the evidence accumulated so far has revolutionized our understanding of schizophrenia.

Genetic Studies The idea that schizophrenia might be passed from parent to child goes back at least as far as the eighteenth century. By the late nineteenth century, when biogenic theories were popular, the genetic hypothesis was endorsed by Kraepelin, Bleuler, and many other experts on schizophrenia. But it was not until about thirty years ago that researchers were able to design studies sophisticated enough to test the hypothesis scientifically. The evidence produced by these studies is extremely persuasive. In the words of David Rosenthal (1970), one of the foremost authorities on the genetics of abnormal behavior, "The issue must now be considered closed. Genetic factors do contribute appreciably and beyond any reasonable doubt to the development of schizophrenic illness" (pp. 131–132).

The studies leading up to this conclusion are—in order of chronology and sophistication—family, twin, and adoptive studies.

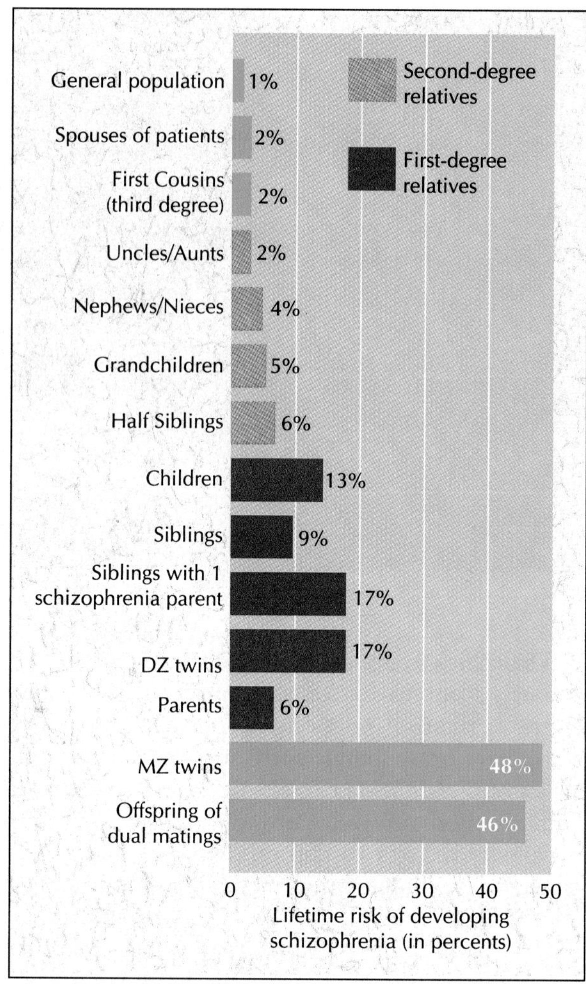

FIGURE 15.1 Lifetime risk of developing schizophrenia for the relatives of people with schizophrenia. The kinds of relatives are listed at the left. The children of a schizophrenic person have a 13 percent risk; the siblings of a schizophrenic, a 9 percent risk; and so on. These figures are averages of statistics compiled by family and twin studies in Europe between 1920 and 1987. (Gottesman, 1991)

Family studies The earliest studies of the genetics of schizophrenia were family studies. Their findings, together with those of more recent research, clearly indicate that the more closely one is related to a schizophrenic, the more likely one is to develop schizophrenia. Figure 15.1 shows the data published by Gottesman in 1991. As may be seen from this graph, children of one schizophrenic parent have a 13 percent chance, and children of two schizophrenic parents ("offspring of dual matings") a 46 percent chance of becoming schizophrenic, as compared with a prevalence of 1 to 2 percent in the general population—a striking differential. According to a recent review of family studies, a person with a schizophrenic first-degree relative is almost ten times likelier to develop schizophrenia than a person with no schizophrenia in the immediate family (Kendler & Diehl, 1993).

Yet family studies, no matter how striking or unanimous their findings, cannot be considered good tests of a genetic hypothesis, for the reason that we have discussed in earlier chapters: any psychological similarity between parent and child or sibling and sibling could be the product of a shared environment rather than of shared genes. If the child of a schizophrenic parent is thirteen times more likely to become schizophrenic than the child of a normal parent, this could be due to the fact that the child was raised by a schizophrenic.

The family studies, then, were only the beginning. Their major value was to spur researchers to design better studies—studies in which genetic and environmental variables could be separated.

Twin studies A great deal more precision on the question of genetics versus environment can be achieved in twin studies. As was pointed out in Chapter 4, these studies are based on the differ-

These quadruplets, the Genain sisters, were studied intensively for genetic causes of schizophrenia. All four had the disorder, with a wide range of severity.

ence between monozygotic (MZ) and dizygotic (DZ) twins in the degree of genetic similarity. Any pair of twins tend to share a highly similar environment. However, MZ twins, having developed from the same sperm and the same ovum, have 100 percent of their genes in common. DZ twins, like any pair of siblings, have only approximately 50 percent of their genes in common. Hence a wide disparity in concordance rates between MZ and DZ twins would seem to be a function of genetic factors alone.

In the case of schizophrenia, such a disparity in concordance rates does indeed exist. In twin studies conducted since 1960, the average concordance rate for schizophrenia in MZ twins is approximately 38 percent, almost three times greater than the 14 percent average concordance rate for DZ twins (Gottesman & Shields, 1982; Kendler & Robinette, 1983). As more recent studies have improved in research methodology, the concordance rates for both MZ and DZ twins have dropped, but proportionately. The MZ-DZ concordance ratios still lie between 3 to 1 and 5 to 1. Moreover, the MZ-DZ concordance difference tends to be greater when the index twin has more severe symptoms (Gottesman, 1991). It also varies depending on the nature of the index twin's symptoms. Recall the distinction (Chapter 14) between Type I schizophrenia, with positive symptoms (hallucinations, delusions, incoherence, disorganized behavior), and Type II schizophrenia, with negative symptoms (poverty of speech, withdrawal, flat affect). When the index twin has prominent negative symptoms, the MZ-DZ concordance difference is greater than when the index twin has prominent positive symptoms (Dworkin & Lenzenweger, 1984). This finding supports the validity of the Type I–Type II distinction and also the belief that Type II has a stronger genetic component.

Such data must be considered strong evidence for the genetic hypothesis. However, as we saw, twin studies too are subject to objections. To begin with, the researcher is dealing with a small sample. (There are not that many schizophrenic MZ twins in the world.) Second, as we saw, some researchers feel that MZ twins share not only a more similar genotype but also a more similar environment than DZ twins, in that the MZ twins are always the same sex, tend to be dressed alike, and so forth. Hence it is possible that here too the differential may be due to environment as well as genes.

In an effort to distinguish between genes and environment, several researchers have studied the offspring of MZ twins who are discordant for schizophrenia (Gottesman & Bertelsen, 1989; Kringlen & Cramer, 1989). The logic of these studies has to do with the fact that since MZ twins are genetically identical, they must transmit to their children the same genetic risk for schizophrenia regardless of whether they themselves are schizophrenic. So all the cousins have the same genetic risk. They do not all have the same environment, however. The children of the schizophrenic twin have the experience of being raised by a schizophrenic parent; the children of the other twin do not. Therefore, if both twins' children develop schizophrenia at approximately the same rate, this is very strong evidence for genetic transmission.

That is what these studies have found. In one study (Gottesman & Bertelsen, 1989) the risk for schizophrenia and schizophrenic-like disorders in the children of the schizophrenic twin was 16.8 percent; in the children of the nonschizophrenic twin, it was 17.4 percent. As might be expected, the differential was far greater in the children of discordant DZ twins, who have only half their genes in common. Using the same research design, the researchers found that the children of schizophrenic DZ twins were at a 17.4 percent risk; the children of their nonschizophrenic co-twins were at a 2.1 percent risk.

Again, this is good evidence for genetic transmission, and again, there is a problem with it: the samples are very small. As noted, schizophrenic MZ twins are rare. But these twin studies are backed up by another kind of research with far larger samples: adoption studies.

Adoption studies The subjects of adoption studies are children who were adopted away from their biological families in infancy and who thus have the genetic endowment of one family and the environmental history of another. If such a study could show that children who were born to schizophrenic mothers* but were adopted in infancy by psychologically normal families still developed schizophrenia at approximately the same rate as those children who were born of one schizophrenic parent and were not adopted away, then this again would be very strong evidence for the genetic hypothesis.

Such studies have been done, and such were the findings. In a pioneering study, Heston (1966) located forty-seven adoptees who had been born to hospitalized schizophrenic mothers. He also gathered a matched control group of fifty adoptees whose mothers were not schizophrenic. From a large variety of sources, mostly firsthand interviews, information was gathered on all these subjects. A file was then compiled on each subject, all identifying information was removed, and diagnoses were made by several independent psychiatrists. The results were that schizophrenia was found only in the children of schizophrenic mothers. The rate for schizophrenia among this group was 16.6 percent, very close to the 13 percent figure for children who are born of a schizophrenic parent and not adopted away.

Another study that has produced immensely influential findings was begun in 1963 in Denmark by David Rosenthal and his colleagues (Rosenthal, Wender, Kety, et al., 1968). The scope of this project is truly astounding. Through various central registries that have been maintained by the Danish government for some fifty years, the investigators identified 5,500 adoptees and 10,000 of their 11,000 biological parents. Then they identified all of those biological parents, called the *index parents*, who had at some time been admitted to a psychiatric hospital with a diagnosis of either schizophrenia or affective psychosis. The seventy-six adopted-away children of these parents (*index children*) were then matched with a control group of adopted children whose biological parents had no history of psychiatric hospitalization. Eventually, 19 percent of the index children versus 10 percent of the control children were diagnosed as having definite or possible schizophrenia (Gottesman & Shields, 1982). Perhaps of greater interest is the finding that 28 percent of the index children, compared with 10 percent of the control children, showed schizophrenic characteristics (Lowing, Mirsky, & Pereira, 1983).

Using the same Danish records, the same investigators (Kety, 1988; Kety, Rosenthal, Wender, et al., 1968, 1975) did another study from a slightly different perspective. In the same group of 5,500 adoptees from Copenhagen, 33 were identified as having psychiatric histories that warranted a diagnosis of schizophrenia. A matched control group of nonschizophrenic adoptees was selected from the same records. Then 463 biological and adoptive parents, siblings, and half-siblings were identified for both the index and control groups, and these relatives were interviewed to determine whether they had ever suffered from schizophrenia. As it turned out, the rate of schizophrenia in the biological relatives of the index cases was about double (21.4 percent) that in the biological relatives of the control cases (10.9 percent), whereas the rates of schizophrenia in the adoptive relatives of the index and control cases were about the same (5.4 versus 7.7 percent). Thus adopted children who later become schizophrenic are much more likely to have biological, rather than adoptive, relatives with schizophrenia. This finding, since confirmed (Kety, Wender, Jacobsen, et al., 1994), is persuasive evidence that there is a genetic component to schizophrenia.

Mode of transmission If there is a genetic component, where does the genetic abnormality lie? One viewpoint is that one or a few major genes are responsible for transmitting the risk, and some initial studies did succeed in linking schizophrenia to specific genes on this or that chromosome. But later studies have failed to support such connections (Kendler & Diehl, 1993). Consequently, many

*Studies of children of schizophrenic parents often limit their subjects to children of schizophrenic mothers, since paternity can never be established with absolute certainty.

EYE TRACKING AS A MARKER FOR SCHIZOPHRENIA

For researchers trying to locate the genetic bases of schizophrenia, a major problem is that the symptoms of this disorder are all complex behaviors, controlled by many genes, not to mention environmental influence. Social withdrawal, attention problems, odd perceptions—these experiences stand at a distant remove from the protein-coding functions of any single gene. To study the genetics of schizophrenia via family tendencies toward such symptoms is, in the words of one researcher, "like studying the genetics of color blindness through familial tendencies to run traffic lights" (Cromwell, 1993). A more profitable approach is to try to find in the schizophrenic population an unusual trait that may have a simpler and more direct link with genes. Such a trait, called a *genetic marker,* may be much less disabling than the main symptoms of schizophrenia—indeed, it may be utterly benign—but it could lead researchers to the genes that produce the disabling symptoms.

One of the hypothesized genetic markers for schizophrenia is an abnormality in what is called *smooth-pursuit eye tracking.* Most people can follow a moving object with their eyes in a smooth, continuous line while keeping their heads still. (Try this. Move your finger like a pendulum and track it with your eyes while keeping your head in a fixed position.) Many schizophrenics, however, cannot do this. Their eyes travel not in a smooth line but in a saccadic, or jerking, pattern (D. L. Levy, Holzman, Matthysse, et al., 1993)—a characteristic that is probably related to a specific neurological abnormality.

Schizophrenics with deviant eye tracking have other things in common too. Compared with schizophrenics who show normal eye tracking, they are more likely to have negative symptoms—flat affect, poverty of speech, anhedonia—and they do not perform as well on tasks controlled by the frontal lobes of the brain (Clementz, McDowell, & Zisook, 1994; Katsanis & Iacono, 1991). Furthermore, they are more likely to have relatives with poor eye tracking, and those relatives tend to show schizophrenic-like traits, such as odd social behavior (Clementz, Grove, Iacono, et al., 1992). Finally, people with schizotypal personality disorder (Chapter 11) are also unusually prone to deviant eye tracking, as are their relatives (Siever, Friedman, Moskowitz, et al., 1994). This is an important finding. As we shall see, children who have a genetic risk for schizophrenia but do not develop the disorder often show schizotypal personality disorder.

This suggests the existence of a specific subgroup of schizophrenics with a similar genetic abnormality, or pattern of abnormalities. It seems likely that the defect involves one major gene, a recessive gene, together with a number of less potent genes that can aggravate or mitigate the effect of the major gene (Iacono & Grove, 1993). Researchers are trying to locate a genetic marker for those schizophrenics with normal eye tracking.

researchers now suspect that schizophrenia is caused not by one gene but by a variety of genetic subtypes and that what they produce is not one disorder but a range of similar disorders that, for want of evidence, we now group in a single category. Researchers are now trying to identify "genetic markers," or simpler related traits, for these subtypes. (See the box above.)

Another view is that schizophrenia is the product not just of many genes but of their combination with environmental factors. Genetic and environmental disadvantage combine until a certain threshold is reached. Beyond that threshold, the person develops schizophrenia (McGue & Gottesman, 1989; Prescott & Gottesman, 1993). There is evidence for this view. For example, an adoption study that is still in progress (Tienari, 1991) has found that its adoptees' risk for schizophrenia correlates not only with the psychiatric history of their biological parents but also with the psychological functioning of their *adoptive* families. Not surprisingly, the latter correlation is strongest when the adoptee is the child of a schizophrenic mother and therefore genetically at risk. So this study, while supporting the role of genes, connects it back to the diathesis-stress model.

Genetic high-risk studies A vast number of studies have been conducted with children who have been born to schizophrenic parents and who have shown at least some symptoms of schizophrenia. These studies have revealed a wealth of information, but they are almost always contaminated by serious methodological problems. If, for example, you wanted to identify significant events in the background of a child who is now showing schizophrenic symptoms, your theoretical notions might well bias your attention toward certain details of the child's history. Furthermore, if you interview people who have known the child—parents, grandparents, and so forth—their recollection will undoubtedly be influenced by what they know of the child's present condition. In short, retrospective information is highly questionable.

The solution would be to conduct a *prospective* study—a longitudinal study—testing and interviewing a large random sample of children at regular intervals over a period of time. Then when some of these children developed schizophrenia, you would already have on file a reliable record of their physiological, psychological, and social histories and could begin searching for correlations. There is one problem with such a project, however. As we have seen, only 1 to 2 percent of the general population develops schizophrenia. Hence in order to end up with a reliable sample of schizophrenics, you would have to do longitudinal studies of thousands of children—a prohibitively expensive and time-consuming project.

In the early 1960s, Mednick and Schulsinger made a breakthrough in schizophrenia research by devising a longitudinal project that would resolve most of the problems outlined above (Mednick, 1970). Recognizing the impossibility of studying a random sample of normal children, the investigators turned to the **genetic high-risk design.** That is, they chose as their sample 200 children who, by virtue of being born of schizophrenic mothers, were already genetically vulnerable to schizophrenia. As we have seen, such children stand about a 13 percent chance of developing the disorder. Thus the investigators could predict that the number of eventual schizophrenics in their high-risk group would be large enough to permit meaningful comparisons with low-risk control children—children not born of schizophrenic mothers.

Mednick (1971) lists the following advantages of this research design over that of previous studies:

> 1 The children have not yet experienced the confounding effects of the schizophrenic life, such as hospitalization and drugs.
> 2 No one—teacher, relative, child or researcher—knows who will become schizophrenic, which eliminates much bias from testing and diagnosis.
> 3 Our information is current; we do not have to depend on anyone's recollection.
> 4 We have two built-in groups of controls for the children who become ill: the high-risk subjects who stay well and the low-risk subjects.
>
> (p. 80)

By 1989 the children in the project had reached a mean age of forty-two and were therefore past the major risk period for the onset of schizophrenia. (Remember that onset tends to occur in adolescence or early adulthood.) In the high-risk group, 16 percent had developed schizophrenia—approximately the expected figure—and another 26.5 percent had developed a *schizophrenic-spectrum* disorder, that is, a disorder related to schizophrenia. (In most cases, it was schizotypal personality disorder—see Chapter 11.) In the low-risk group, by contrast, only 2 percent had developed schizophrenia, and only 6 percent had developed a schizophrenic-spectrum disorder (Parnas, Cannon, Jacobsen, et al., 1993). The researchers list the factors that separate the high-risk children who developed schizophrenia from the high-risk and low-risk children who remained normal (T. D. Cannon, Mednick, Parnas, et al., 1993; J. M. Hollister, Mednick, Brennan, et al., 1994; Mednick & Silverton, 1988):

1 *Home life.* Their home lives were less stable, they had less satisfactory relationships with their parents, and their mothers were more likely to be irresponsible and antisocial.
2 *Institutionalization.* They spent more of their lives in institutions.
3 *School problems and criminal behavior.* They were more domineering, aggressive, and unmanageable in school, and they were more likely (as were their mothers) to have arrest records.
4 *Attention problems.* They showed less ANS habituation to the environment—that is, they had more difficulty "tuning out" incidental stimuli.
5 *Birth complications.* They were more likely to have experienced complications before or during birth, and those who had such complications were more likely to show brain atrophy.

This project has inspired many similar projects, and there is now intense activity in genetic high-risk research. Between the Mednick group and other research teams, the findings listed above have been confirmed and extended. A number of researchers have found a history of attention problems—for example, an inability to screen out repetitive stimuli, such as the ticking of a clock—in high-risk children who eventually become schizophrenic (J. M. Hollister, Mednick, Brennan, et al., 1994). Studies of home movies suggest that these children may also show characteristic motor behaviors and facial expressions. (See the box on page 387.) There is further evidence that these children's mothers are more disturbed—they developed schizophrenia at an earlier age, were more likely to have been hospitalized during the child's early years (Parnas, Teasdale, & Schulsinger, 1985), were more prone to childbirth-related psychosis, and had more unstable relationships with men (Mednick & Silverton, 1988). Finally, both the Mednick group and other groups have accumulated

PREDICTING SCHIZOPHRENIA FROM CHILDHOOD HOME MOVIES

In children who are genetically at risk for schizophrenia, is it possible to predict which ones will develop the disorder? One intriguing study made use of childhood home movies to explore this possibility (E. Walker & Lewine, 1990).

The experimenters collected home movies taken of four schizophrenic patients and their nonschizophrenic siblings when they were children. The films were then shown both to experienced clinicians and graduate students in clinical psychology. After each segment of film the viewers were asked to identify the preschizophrenic child, using their own criteria. How accurate were their judgments? Far better than chance. The total number of correct judgments was twenty-five out of thirty-two. A pilot study using only one patient's home movies also yielded a better-than-chance result: five out of seven correct judgments. In that case, not even the parents had been able to detect signs of the impending disorder. In fact, they had thought that the preschizophrenic child was the *least* likely of their children to later develop problems.

This experiment was the first to show that, given a genetic risk, it may be possible to identify preschizophrenic children on the basis of observation alone—and long before the onset of the disorder. The study also points to what the developmental precursors might be. High on the list of characteristics that the raters interpreted as preschizophrenic were atypical emotional and motor behavior: less responsiveness, less positive affect, less eye contact, and poorer physical coordination. In a later home-movies study, researchers found that fairly accurate predictions could be made on the basis of facial expressions. In the movies the children who later developed schizophrenia showed fewer expressions of joy and more expressions of negative affect (E. F. Walker, Grimes, Davis, et al., 1993).

These findings must be interpreted with caution. Social withdrawal and negative affect may be precursors not just of schizophrenia but of other disorders as well—depression, for example. Furthermore, the samples in these studies were small and not particularly representative of the schizophrenic population. It is middle- and upper-class families who tend to take movies of their children, and therefore it was from those classes that the samples were drawn. Still, childhood home movies may prove to be a rich source of information for researchers trying to identify and treat preschizophrenic children.

further evidence that prenatal or birth trauma, and particularly prenatal viral infection, is an important dividing line between high-risk children who develop schizophrenia and high-risk children who don't (T. D. Cannon, Mednick, Parnas, et al., 1993).

What do all these findings amount to? First, needless to say, they support the role of genetic inheritance. Second, the high rate of attention problems constitutes further support for the idea that attention deficits are a primary symptom of schizophrenia. Finally, and perhaps most important, the results of the high-risk studies offer suggestions as to the kinds of stress that may be especially likely to convert a schizophrenic diathesis into schizophrenia. Disrupted home lives, disabled mothers, institutionalization—these misfortunes may be the product of the genetic defect, but they also produce massive stress. As for prenatal and birth trauma, this is now a major concern to researchers trying to pinpoint the environmental pressures that may tip the balance in high-risk children.

Behavioral high-risk studies A second type of high-risk study uses the **behavioral high-risk design** (Chapter 5), which selects high-risk people not on the basis of genetics but on the basis of behavioral traits that are thought to be associated with the disorder in question. Using this design with schizophrenia has the advantage of yielding a more representative sample of future schizophrenics. (Only about 5 to 10 percent of schizophrenics have a schizophrenic parent. The genetic high-risk studies thus represent only a small portion of the schizophrenic population.) As we saw in Chapter 5, Loren and Jean Chapman and their colleagues have used the behavioral high-risk design to screen a large number of college students for those prone to perceptual abnormalities and magical thinking (J. J. Allen, Chapman, Chapman, et al., 1987; Chapman & Chapman, 1985). Their screening mechanism was a test called the Perceptual Aberration–Magical Ideation Scale, or Per-Mag Scale, in which the subjects respond true or false to such statements as "Sometimes I've had the feeling that I am united with an object near me" and "The hand motions that strangers make seem to influence me at times." Perceptual abnormalities and magical thinking seem to have a genetic basis (Grove, Lebow, Clementz, et al., 1991) and often turn up in the early histories of people diagnosed with schizophrenia. The Chapmans' goal is to discover whether this link holds up prospectively as

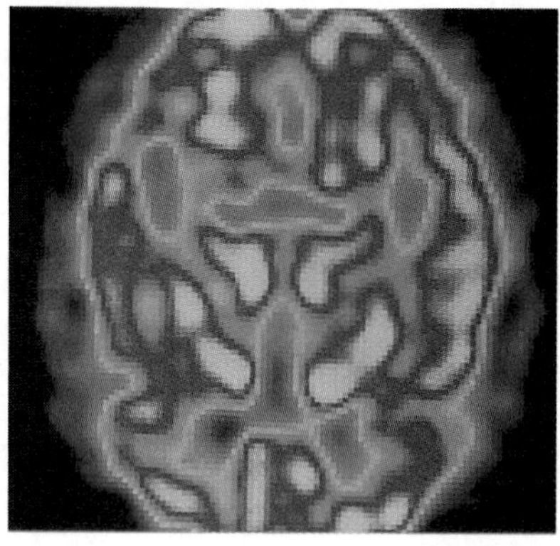
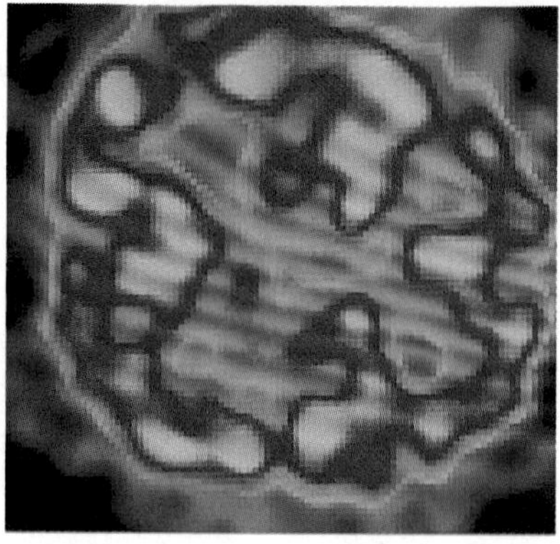

The PET scan at left shows brain activity in a normal person; the image at right shows the temporal lobe of a hallucinating schizophrenic. Normal brain metabolic activity produces a roughly symmetrical pattern in the yellow areas of the left and right cerebral hemispheres. In contrast, the visual areas (in yellow) of the schizophrenic are more active, possibly as a result of the hallucinations.

well as retrospectively, and their method is to track the psychiatric progress of people who score high on the Per-Mag Scale.

They have already produced interesting findings. In a ten-year follow-up, 10 of their 182 high-risk subjects had developed a full-blown psychosis, as compared with only 2 of their 153 low-risk subjects (Chapman, Chapman, Kwapil, et al., 1994). But for firmer results, we must await later follow-ups. The Chapmans' subjects are now only about thirty years old and are therefore still at risk for a first-time psychotic episode.

One potential problem with the Per-Mag Scale is that the people it selects are at risk not just for schizophrenia but for other psychoses as well. Still, researchers have been able to relate the cognitive idiosyncrasies measured by the scale to a wide range of schizophrenic characteristics. Compared with low Per-Mag scorers, high Per-Mag scorers show more hallucinations, delusions, and social withdrawal, more thought disorder and communication deviance, and more attention problems (J. J. Allen, Chapman, Chapman, et al., 1987; Lenzenweger, Cornblatt, & Putnick, 1991; Lenzenweger & Loranger, 1989b). They also have more first-degree relatives who have been treated for schizophrenia (Lenzenweger & Loranger, 1989a).

Brain Imaging Studies As we saw in Chapter 4, the study of the brain has been revolutionized in recent years by the development of new brain imaging technologies: PET, which measures brain functioning, and CT and MRI, which measure brain structure. Through these methods, researchers have been able to identify certain characteristic abnormalities in the brains of schizophrenics. To begin with, CT scans have shown that in chronic schizophrenics the brain ventricles—that is, the cavities containing the cerebrospinal fluid—tend to be enlarged (Raz, 1993) and that this particular sign is related to cognitive impairment (Golden, Moses, & Zelazowski, 1980), poor response to drug treatment (D. J. Luchins, Lewine, & Meltzer, 1983), poor premorbid adjustment (Weinberger, Cannon-Spoor, et al., 1980), and more negative than positive symptoms (R. E. Gur, Mozley, Shtasel, et al., 1994). It is also more likely to be found in male schizophrenics than in females (Flaum, Arndt, & Andreasen, 1990). These CT scan findings have been supported by postmortem analyses of schizophrenic brains (Bogerts, 1993) and by MRI studies (R. E. Gur & Pearlson, 1993). As noted, it is chronic patients who tend to show enlarged ventricles. Therefore it is possible that this abnormality is not so much a cause of schizophrenia as a result of the disorder—or a result of the cumulative effects of antipsychotic drugs. On the other hand, recent studies have reported similar abnormalities in first-episode schizophrenics (Degreef, Ashtari, Bogerts, et al., 1992).

If ventricles are enlarged, this suggests that the brain structures lying near those ventricles may also be affected. Brain imaging studies have found abnormalities in three specific systems: the frontal cortex, the temporal lobe–limbic structures, and the basal ganglia. Several PET scan studies have found that when schizophrenics are given brain metabolism tests while they are performing cognitive tasks requiring the problem-solving ability of the frontal lobe, many of them show abnormally low frontal-lobe activity (Andreason, Rezai, Alliger, et al., 1992; Wolkin, Sanfilipo, Wolf, et al., 1992). These patients tend to be those with negative symptoms. By contrast, patients with positive symptoms often show abnormalities in the temporal lobes or limbic structures (Bogerts, 1993; R. E. Gur & Pearlson, 1993). So positive symptoms and negative symptoms seem to stem from different parts of the brain—further evidence for the Type I–Type II theory. But, as usual, the picture is not simple. Both positive-symptom and negative-symptom patients show abnormalities in the basal ganglia (Siegel, Buchsbaum, Bunney, et al., 1993). Furthermore, some patients show abnormalities in the *connections* among all three of the brain systems in question. This may explain why so many patients have both positive and negative symptoms (Breier, Buchanan, Elkashef, et al., 1992; Buchsbaum, Haier, Potkin, et al., 1992).

Prenatal Brain Injury As we saw above, high-risk children who develop schizophrenia are likelier than those who don't to have suffered some prenatal or birth complication. Could this be a stressor that, at least for some people, helps to convert the genetic diathesis into schizophrenia? Several lines of evidence point to such a conclusion.

One involves MRI studies. The structure of the normal human brain is asymmetrical—a feature that develops in the second trimester (fourth through sixth months) of pregnancy. During that period, the frontal and temporal lobes become larger on the right than on the left, and other regions grow larger on the left than on the right. But in MRI scans many schizophrenic patients do not show this normal asymmetry (Bilder, Wu, Bogerts, et al., 1994)—which suggests that their brains may have suffered some trauma during the second trimester.

Other hints of early prenatal brain damage come from postmortem studies. We know that damage to fetal brain tissue leads to a tissue-repair response called gliosis, but this response occurs only in the third trimester, not before. Thus, when the brain shows structural abnormalities *without* evidence of gliosis, such changes may have occurred in the first or second trimester but not in the third. And that is what postmortem examinations of schizophrenic patients have shown: structural changes without gliosis (Bogerts, 1993). Other postmortem studies point specifically to the second trimester. During that period, neurons in the developing brain migrate from the walls of the ventricles to a temporary structure called the subplate in order, eventually, to form the association areas of the cerebral cortex. Those areas are responsible for our ability to make appropriate associations between things, a function that, as we saw in Chapter 14, is radically disrupted in schizophrenia. And postmortem examination of schizophrenic brains has shown evidence of some disruption in the neural migration that forms the association areas—a problem that could have occurred only in the second trimester (Akbarian, Bunney, Potkin, et al., 1993; Akbarian, Vinuela, Kim, et al., 1993).

Finally, twin studies have also found signs of problems during the second trimester. MZ twins have nearly identical fingerprints, with only minor variations. In MZ twins who are discordant for schizophrenia, however, fingerprint differences are greater than in normal MZ twins (Bracha, Torrey, Gottesman, et al., 1992). These twins, then, are abnormally different from each other in two ways: fingerprints and mental functioning. We know that fingerprints are established during the second trimester. So if both abnormalities were caused by the same prenatal disturbance, which is logical, that disturbance must have happened during the second trimester. (One theory about the nature of the prenatal disturbance is examined in the box on page 390.)

Biochemical Research: The Dopamine Hypothesis Some biochemical abnormality has long been suspected of causing schizophrenia. The biochemical theory that has attracted the most attention in the past three decades is the **dopamine hypothesis,** which posits that schizophrenia is associated with excess activity of those parts of the brain that use dopamine as a neurotransmitter. The major line of evidence for the dopamine hypothesis comes from research on the antipsychotic drugs (the phenothiazines and butyrophenones). These drugs have been dramatically effective in controlling schizophrenic symptoms. An interesting finding is that the antipsychotic drugs are most effective on symptoms such as thought disorder and withdrawal, are moderately effective on hallucinations, and are ineffective on neurotic symptoms such as anxiety (S. M. Paul, 1977). These drugs, in other words, seem to act on fundamental schizophrenic symptoms, and therefore many researchers feel that their chemical activity should provide a clue to the chemical activities underlying schizophrenia. The drugs work by blocking the brain's receptor sites for dopamine. That is, they reduce the activity of those parts of the brain that use dopamine to transmit neural impulses (Farde, Nordström, Wiesel, et al., 1992). Hence the dopamine hypothesis: that schizophrenia is connected to excess dopamine activity.

Another piece of evidence involves the stimulants amphetamine and methylphenidate, both of which are known to increase dopamine activity in the brain. As we saw in Chapter 12, amphetamines can produce psychotic states similar to schizophrenia, and so can methylphenidate (Bowers, 1987; S. H. Snyder, 1972). Furthermore, when these drugs are given to schizophrenic patients, the patients' symptomatology becomes more dramatic (Van Kammen, 1977). Here, then, we see another connection between schizophrenia and increased levels of dopamine activity. A final link has been

IS SCHIZOPHRENIA AN INFECTIOUS DISEASE? THE VIRAL HYPOTHESIS

Is schizophrenia caused, in part, by infection? Certainly not in the way that the common cold is, or the virus would have been discovered long ago. Yet certain research findings raise the possibility that to some degree, in some people, schizophrenia is due to viral infection.

First put forth by Torrey and Peterson in 1976, the *viral hypothesis* states that if infection is involved in schizophrenia, it cannot be the sole cause. It must interact with other causes, probably genetic abnormalities. Furthermore, such a virus could not be fast-acting, like the viruses that cause measles and chicken pox. It would have to be one of the "slow" viruses, which can remain latent within the body for years before any symptoms appear (Kirch, 1993). Slow viruses are known to be involved in other mental disorders, such as Jakob-Creutzfeldt disease, which involves progressive mental deterioration.

What is the evidence for the viral hypothesis? One well-established finding (Hare, Bulusu, & Adelstein, 1979; Torrey, Bowler, Rawlings, et al., 1993) is that people with schizophrenia are significantly more likely than other people—including people with "neurotic"-level disorders—to have been born in the winter. (See the accompanying graph.) Many viral infections show a peak incidence in the spring and winter months. So it is possible that the higher rate of schizophrenia in people who were winter babies is due to the fact that they were more likely to have been exposed to a virus in the late prenatal period (winter) or shortly after birth (spring).

Further support for the viral hypothesis comes from research on the relationship between schizophrenia and epidemics. One large-scale study followed up people who were exposed prenatally to the influenza epidemic that swept Helsinki, Finland, in 1957. As it turned out, those who were exposed in the second trimester were significantly more likely to have developed schizophrenia than either those who were not exposed or those who were exposed in the first or third trimester (Mednick, Machon, Huttunen, et al., 1988). Note how this finding connects with the suggestions of second-trimester brain damage that have been produced by other studies.

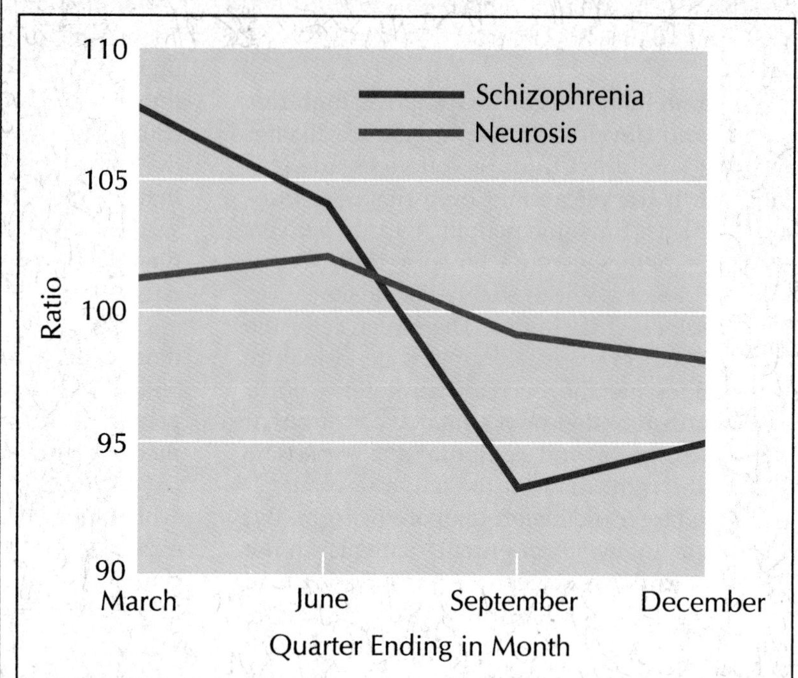

FIGURE 15.2 Schizophrenia and winter births: ratio of observed to expected numbers of births by quarter of the year for patients with a diagnosis of schizophrenia and neurosis and born between the years 1921 and 1960. A ratio of 100 means that the expected number of births occurred during that quarter. (Adapted from Hare, Belusu & Adelstein, 1979)

Further research on the relationship between schizophrenia and epidemics has shown conflicting results, however. Many studies have found a correlation (Takei, Sham, O' Callaghan, et al., 1994), but some have not (Susser, Lin, Brown, et al., 1994).

All the evidence for the viral hypothesis is circumstantial. If a virus is involved in schizophrenia, it has yet to be identified. Nevertheless, it is possible that for some people this is the stressor, or one of the stressors, that interacts with genetic vulnerability to produce schizophrenic symptoms.

provided by postmortem examinations. A number of postmortem studies have found increased brain dopamine and an increased number of dopamine receptors in the limbic structures of deceased schizophrenic patients (Kornhuber, Riederer, Reynolds, et al., 1989; Seeman & Niznik, 1990). Many of these patients, however, had been taking antipsychotic medication, and that may have caused the increase. PET scans of the brains of living schizophrenics who have not been taking antipsychotic drugs have produced inconsistent results. Some have shown an increased number of dopamine receptors in the limbic structures (Wong, Gjedde, Wagner, et al., 1986); some have not (Hietala, Syvälahti, Vuorio, et al., 1994).

This focus on dopamine has suggested a conceptual link between schizophrenia and Parkinson's disease (Chapter 16), an organic brain disorder that produces uncontrollable bodily tremors. Parkinson's disease is known to be caused, in part, by a deficiency of dopamine in certain parts of the brain, and drugs that increase dopamine levels are quite effective in reducing tremors in Parkinson's patients. However, these drugs can also produce schizophrenia-like symptoms (Celesia & Barr, 1970). Conversely, antipsychotic drugs often produce a Parkinson's-like movement disorder called tardive dyskinesia (discussed below) as a side effect.

Thus many lines of evidence converge to support the dopamine hypothesis. It is mostly indirect evidence, however. Other than the postmortem data and the PET scan findings, both of which have been challenged, we have no direct evidence that schizophrenics do in fact experience dopamine abnormalities (J. A. Lieberman & Koreen, 1993). And if they do, there are probably different patterns of abnormality (Davis, Kahn, Ko, et al., 1991). It is only Type I schizophrenics, those with positive symptoms, who seem to have excess dopamine activity in the limbic system (Andreasen, 1989). According to some studies, Type II schizophrenia is related to dopamine *underactivity* in the frontal lobe (Andreasen, 1989; Pickar, Breier, Hsiao, et al., 1990). Moreover, the dopamine underactivity in the frontal lobe may lead to the dopamine overactivity in the limbic structures (Breier, Davis, Buchanan, et al., 1993).

At the same time, there is some evidence *against* the dopamine hypothesis (Davis, Kahn, Ko, et al., 1991). There is also the confusing fact that the antipsychotic drugs, with their dopamine-blocking effect, relieve the symptoms not just of schizophrenia but of all the major psychoses: mania, depression, drug-induced psychoses, schizophreniform disorder, and so on (Donaldson, Gelenberg, & Baldessarini, 1983). In addition, schizophrenics who do respond to these drugs improve gradually over a period of about six weeks. Yet it takes only a few hours for the drugs to block dopamine receptors in the brain. If schizophrenia were merely the result of activity in these neural tracts, it should improve dramatically within a few hours (Pickar, 1988). Finally, clozapine, a new medication that works on many patients who do not respond to other antipsychotic drugs (Chapter 21), has only a weak effect on dopamine receptors. Its primary action is to block serotonin receptors. Many experts now believe that it is not dopamine alone but an interaction between dopamine and serotonin activity that underlies schizophrenic symptoms (Hsiao, Colison, Bartko, et al., 1993; R. S. Kahn, Davidson, Knott, et al., 1993). Whether or not this proves to be true, it seems likely that the biological explanation of schizophrenia, if it is ever arrived at, will be a highly complex one, involving a combination of biochemical imbalances—and different combinations both for different types of schizophrenia and for different phases of any single case of schizophrenia (Andreasen, 1989).

Chemotherapy Later in this chapter we will describe various forms of psychotherapy used with schizophrenics. The most common treatment for schizophrenia, however, is not psychotherapy but chemotherapy—drugs. Most schizophrenic patients are on a daily regimen of one of the phenothiazines, the antipsychotic drugs mentioned in the last section. And this is the only therapy that many patients receive.

Since their introduction in 1952, the antipsychotic drugs have revolutionized the study and treatment of schizophrenia. When they were first marketed, researchers had little idea of how they worked. But the fact that they did work, and so well, prompted research into their biochemical effects—research that has led so far to the dopamine hypothesis and may ultimately yield a comprehensive biochemical explanation of schizophrenia.

The impact of the antipsychotic medications on the treatment of schizophrenia has been even greater. These drugs, as noted above, are very effective. They reduce agitation, hallucinations, delusions, and indeed most of the major symptoms of schizophrenia (Lipton & Burnett, 1980). As a result, they have permitted us to "open up" our mental hospitals to some degree, releasing patients who would otherwise have spent long periods, if not the rest of their lives, in the hospital. In the twenty years after the introduction of antipsychotic drugs, the population of the state mental

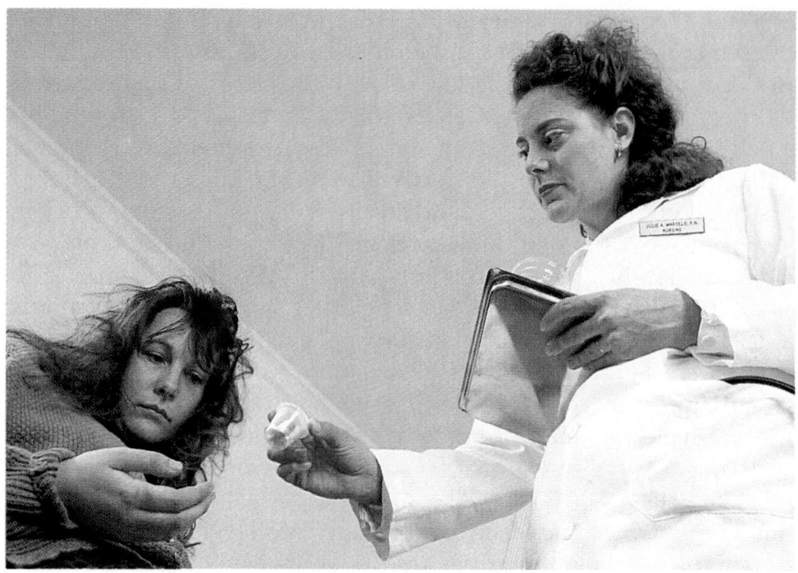

The antipsychotic drugs have wrought miracles in the treatment of schizophrenia, but at best they can only relieve the symptoms of the disorder; they cannot prevent or cure it.

hospitals was cut to less than half (Lipton & Burnett, 1980) and the length of hospitalization for a psychotic episode was reduced by about two-thirds. The drugs also help to prevent relapses. Patients who continue medication after release from the hospital have about a 32 percent chance of suffering a relapse within the year, compared with a 70 percent chance for patients who discontinue medication (Kane & Lieberman, 1987).

At the same time, there are good arguments against the antipsychotic drugs. To begin with, they can have debilitating side effects, the most serious being **tardive dyskinesia,** a muscle disorder that causes patients to grimace and smack their lips uncontrollably. Tardive dyskinesia usually appears in patients who have had more than six months of continuous treatment with antipsychotic drugs. The condition is very resistant to treatment, even after the drug is discontinued. Clozapine, the new antipsychotic medication mentioned above, does not seem to cause tardive dyskinesia, but it has other drawbacks. (See the box on clozapine in Chapter 21, page 550.)

However, the major criticism of the antipsychotic drugs is that they do not cure schizophrenia. Even with the medication, as we saw, a third of released patients relapse within the year. And even those who do not relapse to the point of rehospitalization often continue to require special care. In truth, the chances of a person's attaining full and permanent recovery after a schizophrenic episode have not been significantly increased by the advent of antipsychotic drugs (Kane & Marder, 1993). This does not mean that the drugs have no value. At the moment, we have no cure for schizophrenia, and no preventive measures. All we have are drugs that alleviate the symptoms. And once the symptoms are reduced, it may be possible for schizophrenics to benefit from other treatments—behavior therapy, for example. Just as with illnesses such as hypertension and diabetes, when cause and cure are unknown, we go on using symptom-relieving drugs while researchers continue to seek cause and cure.

The Cognitive Perspective

While neuroscience researchers concern themselves with both the diathesis and the stressor components of the diathesis-stress model, most cognitive theorists focus exclusively on the diathesis. As we know, a prominent symptom of schizophrenia is attention dysfunction. Remember the words of the patient quoted in Chapter 14: "My thoughts get all jumbled up. I start thinking or talking about something but I never get there." Since the time of Kraepelin and Bleuler, many researchers have suspected that this attention problem is the primary pathology in schizophrenia, with the other symptoms developing as results of the attention problem. And that, in brief, is the position of today's cognitive researchers. Cognitive theorists do not claim that attention deficits are the root cause of schizophrenia. In their view, the cause is biological. What they do claim, however, is that the psychological function most impaired by the biological abnormality is attention and that the attention problem in turn creates a predisposition to schizophrenia by making it hard for the person to cope with environmental stress (Nuechterlein & Dawson, 1984a, 1984b). Imagine, for example, a family with a highly charged, negative emotional atmosphere or a family in which the parents tend to give confusing messages. (As we shall see, these are two circumstances that, according to family theorists, may contribute to schizophrenia.) A child with normal cognitive skills would probably be able to navigate the emotional perils of such a family, but a child who had difficulty focusing attention (and hence, difficulty in solving problems) might well respond by becoming overaroused and disorganized—a condition that over time could develop into psychosis (Nuechterlein, Dawson, Gitlin, et al., 1992; W. Perry & Braff, 1994).

The goal of cognitive research in schizophrenia has been to determine the exact nature of the attention problems of schizophrenics and to relate these problems to other features of the disorder. Researchers have identified two distinct patterns, overattention and underattention.

Overattention In Chapter 14 we described the breakdown in selective attention that is seen in many schizophrenics. These patients "overattend" to the stimuli in their environment; they cannot focus on one thing and screen out the others. This phenomenon appears to be related to Type I, positive-symptom schizophrenia (e.g., Cornblatt, Lenzenweger, Dworkin, et al., 1985), and according to current cognitive theory, the positive symptoms of Type I patients—hallucinations, delusions, incoherent speech—are the product of their overattention (Braff & Geyer, 1990; W. Perry & Braff, 1994). The reason these patients are confused and disorganized is that their information-processing functions are overburdened, and their nervous systems overaroused, by stimuli that they cannot screen out (Dawson, Nuechterlein, & Schell, 1992). The reason their speech is full of irrelevant associations is that, unlike normal people, they cannot filter out such associations (B. A. Maher, 1983). Auditory hallucinations, according to this theory, would be explainable as traces of real sounds that the patient heard but could not eliminate from consciousness, and delusions would arise as the patient's effort to account for these and other bizarre perceptions (B. A. Maher & Spitzer, 1993).

Many studies have documented the poor selective attention and consequent distractibility of schizophrenics (Braff, 1993). In one experiment (Wielgus & Harvey, 1988) schizophrenic, manic, and normal subjects were fitted with headphones, and eight successive stories were read to them in one ear by a male voice. During four of the stories, however, a distraction was introduced: at the same time that the subjects heard the story from the male voice in one ear, they were told a different story by a female voice in the other ear. The subjects' task was to repeat back word for word the story that was being told to them by the male voice. As the poor-selective-attention hypothesis would predict, the schizophrenics did worse than the other subjects only when the distraction was introduced. The problem uncovered by this experiment is a good example of a differential deficit.

The inability of schizophrenics to filter out irrelevant stimuli has been documented in neurophysiological tests as well. In one experiment, schizophrenics were given the task of pressing a button when they heard a tone of a given frequency. Again, however, a distraction was introduced: on some trials, a tone of a different frequency was also sounded. As predicted, this distraction impaired the schizophrenics' performance more than the performance of the controls. Furthermore, the schizophrenics responded to the distracting tones with abnormally large brain waves of the kind that signal that the brain has focused its attention on an environmental stimulus. In other words, the schizophrenics, whatever their effort to focus on the target stimulus, were significantly distracted by the interfering stimulus (Grillon, Courchesne, Ameli, et al., 1990). Finally, it has also been shown that when an experiment is set up in such a way that picking up interfering stimuli *improves* performance, schizophrenics outperform nonschizophrenics (Beech, Powell, McWilliam, et al., 1989; M. Spitzer, Weisker, Winter, et al., 1994). Here again we have a differential deficit, and a remarkable one. When schizophrenics do better on a task than normal people, we are presumably tapping into something fundamental to schizophrenia (Braff, 1993).

As noted, this particular attention problem, the inability to screen out distractions, has been found to correlate with Type I, positive-symptom schizophrenia but not with Type II, negative-symptom schizophrenia (Cornblatt, Lenzenweger, Dworkin, et al., 1985; Wielgus & Harvey, 1988). The connection with Type I schizophrenia has also been demonstrated on a biochemical level. Type I, as we just saw, seems to be related to overactivity of dopamine transmission in subcortical areas of the brain. Following this lead, Swerdlow and his colleagues injected rats with dopamine in subcortical areas of the brain, thus creating the kind of dopamine overactivity that is presumed to underlie Type I schizophrenia. The rats responded by showing the kind of selective-attention problems seen in Type I schizophrenia. Furthermore, the attention problems of both Type I schizophrenics and dopamine-injected rats can be decreased by antipsychotic drugs that decrease dopamine activity (Swerdlow, Braff, Taaid, et al., 1994).

Underattention Whereas Type I schizophrenics seem to be overattentive, Type II schizophrenics appear to be underattentive to external stimuli. This fact has been repeatedly demonstrated in studies of the *orienting response,* a pattern of physiological changes (involving galvanic skin response, blood pressure, pupil dilation, heart rate, and brain waves) that is thought to indicate that the brain has allocated its central attentional resources to the perception and processing of a stimulus. In a review of such experiments, A. S. Bernstein (1987) found that 40 to 50 percent of schizophrenics, when presented with a stimulus of moderate intensity, failed to show a normal orienting response.

Another kind of study that has been used to measure underattention employs what is called the *backward-masking paradigm.* Here the subject is shown a visual stimulus, the so-called target stimulus, quickly or indistinctly. Then, after an interval, this is followed by a "masking stimulus," such as a picture of a grid. When the masking stimulus comes right after the target stimulus, it will "mask" the target stimulus. Not having had time to process the target stimulus before the intrusion of the masking stimulus, the subject will not register recognition of the target stimulus. But as the time interval between the presentation of the target stimulus and the masking stimulus is increased, the subject becomes more and more likely to remember the target stimulus. For many schizophrenics, however, the interval between the two has to be stretched far longer than for normal subjects before the target stimulus registers on the consciousness. In other words, these schizophrenics seem to have deficient perception of and responsiveness to environmental stimuli. And according to cognitive theorists, this underattention is what leads to such negative symptoms as flat affect and social withdrawal (Braff, 1993). This conclusion is quite logical. If a person's perception of the environment is dulled, he or she is not unlikely to become apathetic and withdrawn.

In keeping with this hypothesis, deficient orienting responses and poor performance on backward-masking tasks have both been found to correlate with negative symptoms such as blunted affect, withdrawal, and motor retardation, as well as with other factors in the Type II profile, such as poor premorbid adjustment and poor prognosis (A. S. Bernstein, 1987; Braff, 1993). They do not correlate with positive symptoms, however. Indeed, the orienting responses of positive-symptom schizophrenics are more likely to be abnormally high than abnormally low. Of course, these findings give further support to the Type I versus Type II hypothesis. There do in fact seem to be at least two distinct schizophrenic patterns, one marked by overattention and one by underattention.

Vulnerability If cognitive theorists are correct in claiming that biologically based attention problems create a vulnerability to schizophrenia, then these abnormalities should be present not just in active-phase schizophrenics but also in remitted (recovered) schizophrenics, in their biological relatives, and in people designated as being at risk for schizophrenia (Zubin & Spring, 1977). And they are. As we saw in our discussion of Mednick's high-risk children, one of the five characteristics separating those who developed schizophrenia from those who didn't was a history of selective-attention problems. Likewise, remitted schizophrenics, relatives of schizophrenics, children of schizophrenic parents, and people thought to be at risk for schizophrenia by virtue of showing schizophrenic-like personality features all show significantly high rates of selective-attention dysfunction (Braff, 1993; Lenzenweger, Cornblatt, & Putnick, 1991; Nuechterlein, 1985). Many remitted schizophrenics and high-risk people also show lowered orienting responses (Dawson, Nuechterlein, Schell, et al., 1994). For more solid confirmation of the attention-dysfunction hypothesis, we must await the outcomes of further longitudinal studies of high-risk children. But it seems clear already that if "preschizophrenic" people are to be treated, attention deficits are a logical target. Such treatments have been devised, but they are only in their earliest stages (M. F. Green, 1993; Liberman & Green, 1992).

Family Theories

The environmental stresses contributing to the development of schizophrenia may be biological—for example, prenatal brain injury—but it is likely that social factors are involved as well. Such environmental stressors have been the focus of the theories of schizophrenia coming from the other psychological perspectives.

The major concern has been trouble in the family. If, in Mednick's high-risk studies, one factor separating the high-risk children who developed schizophrenia from those who didn't was attention problems, another was an unstable family life. In that group, family disruption was probably due in part to genetic factors. The mothers of the high-risk children all had a history of schizophrenia, which does not bode well for parent-child interactions. But according to family theorists, psychological tensions in the home may also be a stress factor in schizophrenia, and not just for the children of schizophrenic mothers.

Expressed Emotion A popular early theory of schizophrenia was that of the *schizophrenogenic mother,* or schizophrenia-causing mother. According to Frieda Fromm-Reichman (1948), who put forth this theory, mothers who were cold, domineering, rejecting, and at the same time overprotective could induce schizophrenia in their children. In this scenario the father was at fault not so much for what he did as for what he didn't do—that is, interfere in the pernicious mother-child relationship. Fromm-Reichmann's theory was offered in a time when fewer mothers worked and parent-child relations were understood to be primarily mother-child relations. More recent research has implicated fathers as well, and also siblings, in the hostile atmosphere that seems to permeate the homes of many children who develop schizophrenia.

Today's family theorists are also less concerned with the personality traits of the family members than with what these people actually say to one another—something that is more easily measured. In a number of studies (e.g., Miklowitz, Goldstein, Doane, et al., 1989; Vaughan, Snyder, Jones, et al., 1984) families of hospitalized schizophrenics have been rated on **expressed emotion (EE)** toward the patient. In these studies, the EE rating was based on two factors—the level of criticism and the level of emotional overinvolvement—in the remarks made by a key relative (e.g., the father, the mother, the spouse) in an interview regarding the patient shortly after his or her admission. For example, the sister of a thirty-six-year-old schizophrenic patient remarked:

> To me that is a totally selfish illness.... Rachel could, if she really wanted to, pull herself out of it. But it's as though she wants to ... go into hospital. ... I feel that she should care enough about other people to keep herself well ... because it worries my father, it worries my family, it worries my brother, and it worries me. To me that is enough to try and keep yourself well. (Brewin, MacCarthy, Duda, et al., 1991, p. 552)

Nine months after a group of high-EE patients were discharged, they were followed up to see who had relapsed. Interestingly, of all the factors on which the patients varied, the family EE was the best single predictor of relapse: patients who lived with high-EE relatives were three to four times more likely to have been rehospitalized within nine months than patients who lived with low-EE relatives (Miklowitz, Goldstein, Doane, et al., 1989). So EE seems to influence relapse risk. In turn, EE is influenced by family members' attributions regarding the patient's condition. Logically, high-EE relatives tend to be those, like the woman quoted above, who hold the patient responsible for his or her condition (Brewin, MacCarthy, Duda, et al., 1991; Weisman, López, Karno, et al., 1993).

Some studies (e.g., G. Parker, Johnston, & Hayward, 1988) have failed to confirm the link between schizophrenia and high family EE. Still, many EE studies do suggest that a negative and emotionally charged family atmosphere may be related to both the onset and the course of schizophrenia. Other researchers feel that EE should be considered not as a contributor to the development of schizophrenia but specifically as a contributor to relapse—as a measure of the environmental stress that the remitted schizophrenic is exposed to when he or she returns home. In support of this idea, it has been shown that schizophrenics show higher autonomic arousal in the presence of high-EE relatives than in the presence of low-EE relatives (Tarrier, Barrowclough, Porceddu, et al., 1988).

Communication Deviance Some experts feel that the heart of the interpersonal disturbance lies in the matter of communications between parent and child. In a classic theory put forth in the fifties, Bateson and his coworkers proposed that schizophrenia might be the product of **double-bind communication,** a particular kind of no-win interchange illustrated in the following account:

> A young man who had fairly well recovered from an acute schizophrenic episode was visited in the hospital by his mother. He was glad to see her and impulsively put his arm around her shoulders, whereupon she stiffened. He withdrew his arm and she asked, "Don't you love me any more?" He then blushed, and she said, "Dear, you must not be so easily embarrassed and afraid of your feelings." The patient was able to stay with her only a few minutes more and following her departure he assaulted an aide. (Bateson, Jackson, Haley, et al., 1956, p. 251)

The double-bind situation, then, is one in which

the mother gives the child mutually contradictory messages (e.g., both rejection and affection in the case just cited), meanwhile implicitly forbidding the child to point out the contradiction. Whichever message the child acts upon, he or she is the loser. Bateson and his colleagues proposed that the type of mother most likely to engage in double-bind communication was one who found closeness with her child intolerable but who also found it intolerable to admit this to herself. Thus she would push the child away, but when the child withdrew, she would accuse the child of not loving her.

Like Fromm-Reichmann's notion of the schizophrenogenic mother, this theory, while less discussed today, helped to generate a line of more empirical research. That research has indeed shown that families of schizophrenics tend to have unusual communication patterns (Wynne, Singer, Bartko, et al., 1975). Their verbal exchanges are variously described as blurred, muddled, vague, fragmented, or incomplete (Hassan, 1974; J. M. Lewis, Rodnick, & Goldstein, 1981). Here, for example, is a recorded exchange between a schizophrenic woman and her parents:

DAUGHTER, complainingly: Nobody will listen to me. Everybody is trying to still me.
MOTHER: Nobody wants to kill you.
FATHER: If you're going to associate with intellectual people, you're going to have to remember that still is a noun and not a verb.

(Wynne & Singer, 1963, p. 195)

Many current studies describe this phenomenon in terms of **communication deviance (CD),** measured according to the number of deviant or idiosyncratic responses on a test such as the TAT or Rorschach. In one study, CD in parents proved a good predictor of whether their adolescent children would be diagnosed as schizophrenic fifteen years later (M. J. Goldstein, 1987). The finding (Miklowitz, Strachan, Goldstein, et al., 1986) that communication deviance seems to correlate with expressed emotion—relatives that are high-EE are also high-CD—has given added impetus to this line of research.

Yet, however well supported, these findings are still subject to the interpretation problems outlined at the beginning of our chapter. Given that schizophrenia in the child correlates with deviant communications in the family, there may still be no causal relationship between the two factors, for both may be the result of a third variable, such as a shared genetic defect (Miklowitz, Velligan, Goldstein, et al., 1991). Furthermore, even if there is a causal relationship between the two, we are faced with the chicken-and-egg problem: while disturbed family communications—and a negative emotional climate—may have fostered the child's disorder, it is equally possible that the child's disorder has fostered the high levels of CD and EE (M. J. Goldstein & Doane, 1985). That the families of schizophrenic patients tend to express painful emotions is no surprise. Indeed, in the case of EE, most researchers today view the correlation with schizophrenia simply as a broad interactive process, with the patient's symptoms causing the family to feel and vent negative emotions, which in turn exacerbate the patient's symptoms, thus creating a vicious cycle (Bellack & Mueser, 1993).

There is one further problem in evaluating the EE and CD findings. If the family setting is of major importance in the development of schizophrenia, why does one child in the family grow up schizophrenic while another turns out normally? It may be that the one who grows up schizophrenic was more vulnerable biologically to the emotional stress of a hostile family environment. But we do not know whether this is the case.

Despite these difficulties, most experts have not discarded the idea that the family may figure in the development of schizophrenia—only the claim that the family *alone* can engender the disorder. Again, the emphasis today is on diathesis and stress, and family hostility is still high on the list of stressors that could help to determine whether a schizophrenic diathesis is translated into schizophrenia.

Treatment for Families The findings regarding EE and CD have prompted the development of treatments for the families of schizophrenic patients. In one study, researchers spent several weeks with the families of eighteen schizophrenic patients, studying the family members' difficulties in dealing with the patient and with each other. Then the families were taught a step-by-step method of working out problems, from planning a dinner menu to coping with major crises. The families were also briefed on schizophrenia so that they would be less alarmed and distressed by the patient's symptoms. At a nine-month follow-up, only one patient from the eighteen experimental-group families had relapsed, compared with eight patients from eighteen families that had received no treatment. These results held through a two-year follow-up as well, so the gains seem to last (Falloon, Boyd, McGill, et al., 1985). In another study, high-EE families were counseled in how to make their interactions with the patient calmer and less negative. A year later, only 20 percent of the patients from these families had relapsed, compared with 41 percent of patients from high-EE families that had received no treatment (Hogarty, Anderson, Reiss, et al., 1986).

There have been other programs as well, each with different emphases, but according to a recent review, the most effective family treatments offer seven basic components: (1) a positive working relationship between therapist, patient, and family; (2) a stable, structured therapy format; (3) a focus on "here-and-now" problem solving, as opposed to dwelling on the past; (4) the use of behavioral techniques, such as breaking down goals into manageable steps; (5) the fostering of improved communications between family members; (6) the encouragement of respect for interpersonal boundaries between family members; and (7) the providing of information about schizophrenia, in order to reduce blame and guilt (Lam, 1991).

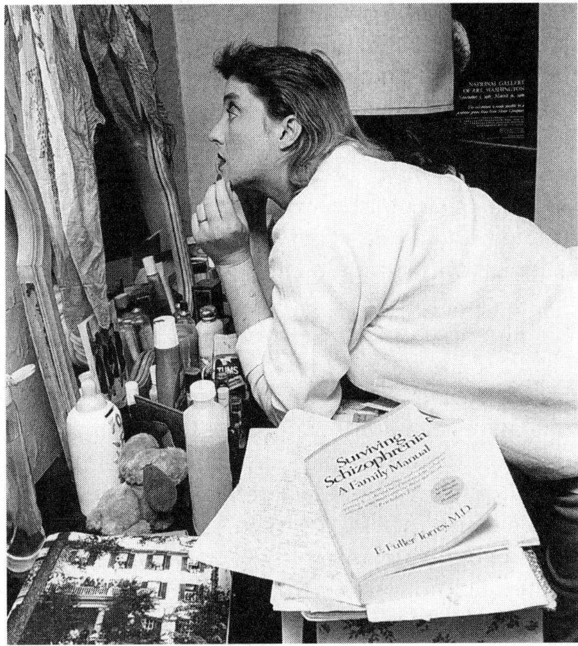

Patterns of communication within a family can influence the course of schizophrenia. Research has led to the development of effective treatments for the families of schizophrenic patients, such as the woman pictured here.

The Psychodynamic Perspective

Withdrawal from Intimacy Like Freud, most psychodynamic theorists have given far more attention to "neurotic"-level disorders than to psychoses such as schizophrenia. For those who have written about schizophrenia, however, the family is again the primary concern. The pioneering figure in this area was Harry Stack Sullivan (1962), who devoted much of his work to schizophrenia. Sullivan felt that the disorder originated in early childhood in a hostile, anxiety-ridden mother-child relationship. Scared off from intimacy by the terrors of this relationship, the child takes refuge in a private world of fantasy. This initiates a vicious cycle: the more the child withdraws, the less opportunity he or she has to develop the trust, confidence, and skills necessary for establishing bonds with others, and the fewer the bonds, the greater the anxiety. The spiral continues until, in early adulthood, the person is faced with a new and more taxing set of social demands—work, marriage, and so forth. In the face of these challenges, the person becomes so swamped with anxiety that he or she withdraws completely, closing down those mental faculties (e.g., communication, perception, reasoning) that are the bridge to the world of other people. This is the schizophrenic "break," though according to Sullivan and other psychodynamic writers it is only the culmination of a gradual disengagement from human relationships.

Psychodynamic Treatment for Schizophrenia Freud believed that psychoanalysis was of little use in the case of schizophrenia, and most of his followers have agreed. But Sullivan, together with his theory of schizophrenia, developed a treatment that adapted psychoanalysis to the special needs of schizophrenic patients. The crucial feature of this treatment is the patient-therapist relationship. In traditional psychodynamic treatment, the therapist tries to maintain considerable distance. With schizophrenics, on the other hand, the therapist takes an almost parental approach, offering interpretations only in a very gradual, gentle way and at the same time attempting to comfort these patients and help them with the practical details of living. In short, the therapist tries, belatedly, to offer these patients something like a decent parent-child relationship and thus to coax them out of their frightened withdrawal. For those schizophrenics who receive psychodynamic therapy—and they are a very small minority—this basic pattern still holds today (Arieti, 1974b), and it seems to benefit them (L. L. Glass, Katz, Schnitzer, et al., 1989), though like all other treatments it does not cure them.

The Humanistic-Existential Perspective

Schizophrenia and Alienation Those few humanistic-existential theorists who have put forth theories of schizophrenia have also implicated the family, but the family as representative of the ills of the culture. For example, R. D. Laing (1964), whose writings on schizophrenia were popular in the sixties, believed that the disorder sprang from a habitual mode of parent-child interaction that caused the child to doubt the legitimacy of his or her own feelings and perceptions—a process that Laing called **mystification.** In Laing's formulation, however, parents are not the only ones who mystify. Modern industrial societies are set up in such a way as to force people to adopt a false self. Everyone is alienated; schizophrenics are simply people who, in response to severe stress, find themselves unable to continue the masquerade. Their false selves crumble, and they retreat into their own minds—an experience that, in Laing's view, is not insanity but "hypersanity," the quest for a true self. From this it follows that the traditional power relationship between patient and therapist is a sham: the patient is more sane than the therapist, who is merely trying to restore the patient to the inauthentic values of the society. In his defense of the schizophrenic experience against the presumptions of psychiatry, Laing was supported by Thomas Szasz and other members of the *antipsychiatric movement,* whose ideas were also most prominent in the sixties. As we saw in Chapter 1, Szasz and other critics argued that "insanity" is simply a label that society uses to enforce compliance to its norms and to justify the removal of people who do not comply.

Milieu Therapy and Other Therapeutic Communities From a viewpoint such as Laing's, the ultimate treatment for all mental disorders would be a restructuring of society to eliminate distorted values and dehumanizing conditions. But since this is not likely to be undertaken, humanistic-existential therapists have concentrated on designing small communities aimed at fostering the personal growth of immediate members. Most of these communities offer one or another form of **milieu therapy,** which aims to help patients by placing them in a new, restorative environment, or milieu. A descendant of nineteenth-century moral therapy (Chapter 1), milieu therapy imposes as few restraints as possible on patients. Residents of the community are expected to take responsibility for their own behavior, to participate in their own rehabilitation and that of others, and to help in the making of decisions that affect the entire group. Some milieu programs have produced promising results (Artiss, 1962; Cumming & Cumming, 1962). Considerably more radical is the type of residential community first founded by Laing in London in 1965, under the name of Kingsley Hall, and since imitated by another community, Soteria House in San Jose, California. In these communities patients and staff are more or less equals, and in keeping with Laing's theories, psychotic behavior is treated as a valid experience—not a breakdown but potentially a breakthrough.

The humanistic-existential perspective has been valuable in insisting on the validity of the individual's experience, schizophrenic or otherwise, and in questioning such matters as the ethics of labeling and commitment, the effectiveness of traditional treatments, and the overall social significance of the disease model of mental illness. But

Humanistic-existential therapists have designed therapeutic communities offering milieu therapy to residents with schizophrenia and other disorders. The Bridge Over Troubled Waters program in Boston offers such help to teenagers in crisis.

in the wake of the neuroscience findings of the past few decades, Laing's view that schizophrenia is a "hypersanity" mislabeled as a medical condition has been largely superseded.

The Behavioral Perspective

Learned Nonresponsiveness The behaviorists too have offered environmental theories of schizophrenia. According to Ullmann and Krasner (1975), for example, schizophrenics are people who, because of a disturbed family life or other environmental misfortunes, have not learned to respond to the social stimuli to which most of us respond. As a result, they cease to attend to these stimuli and begin taking their behavioral cues from other, idiosyncratically chosen stimuli. In consequence, they tend to become objects of disciplinary action and social rejection, leading to feelings of alienation and to the belief that others are out to "get" them. Hence their behavior becomes even more bizarre. And if, as may happen, they are rewarded for bizarre responses—through attention, sympathy, or release from responsibilities—such responses are likely to become habitual.

There is some support for this hypothesis. It has been shown, for example, that like the learned behaviors of normal people, the "crazy" behaviors of schizophrenics are sometimes produced in situations where they will lead to rewards. But this does not prove that those behaviors originated through reinforcement. Today, in view of the neuroscience findings, most behaviorists use learning theory not to explain the development of schizophrenia—they too tend to believe that it develops in part from biological causes—but to reduce schizophrenic symptoms.

Relearning Normal Behavior Whatever the root cause of schizophrenic behavior, it may be that mental health settings inadvertently encourage such behavior by reinforcing "craziness" and not reinforcing adaptive responses. If so, then reversing that reinforcement pattern should lead to improvement. Such is the goal of the behavioral treatment of schizophrenia.

Direct reinforcement Many behavioral treatments are straightforward applications of the principles of operant conditioning. That is, they attempt to change behavior by changing the consequences of behavior. Let us look at a specific case:

> Mr. C.'s most obnoxious behaviors were: urinating and defecating on the floor, shouting, swearing, name-calling, begging cigarettes, demanding other things, striking at other patients. It . . . seemed evident that Mr. C.'s inappropriate conduct usually was followed by some kind of staff attention. Two procedures for eliminating Mr. C.'s disruptive behavior were [implemented]. 1. Social attention should no longer be given following inappropriate behavior. 2. Social attention and cigarettes . . . would be the consequence of socially acceptable behavior. (Sushinsky, 1970, p. 24)

Modest though it was, this treatment program proved effective. In two weeks, Mr. C.'s "obnoxious" behaviors disappeared. Furthermore, he was now striking up conversations and participating in rehabilitation therapy.

Procedures that involve the giving or withholding of tangible reinforcers are surrounded by a number of ethical and legal questions that are as yet unresolved. (These issues will be discussed in Chapter 22.) There is no question, however, that such procedures can change behavior. Researchers have succeeded in instituting or increasing speech in mute and near-mute patients through the use of such simple reinforcers as fruit, chocolate, and magazines (R. Baker, 1971; Thomson, Fraser, & McDougall, 1974).

The token economy Some hospitals have extended operant-conditioning procedures to entire wards, using a system called the token economy. In a **token economy** patients are given tokens or points or some other kind of generalized conditioned reinforcer in exchange for performing certain target behaviors, such as personal grooming, cleaning their rooms, or doing academic or vocational-training tasks. The patients can then exchange the tokens for any number of backup reinforcers, such as snacks, coffee, new clothes, or special privileges. The procedure is very much like that which operates outside the hospital: we earn money by performing specified tasks and then exchange this money for the privileges and goods that we want. (Token economies are described in more detail in Chapter 20.)

Social-skills training As we have seen, most schizophrenics are socially inept: they speak little to others, show emotions unconnected with the situation, and so forth. Needless to say, such social handicaps impede the schizophrenic's posthospitalization readjustment—his or her ability to make friends, to hold down a job, and in general to obtain those things that most of us associate with happi-

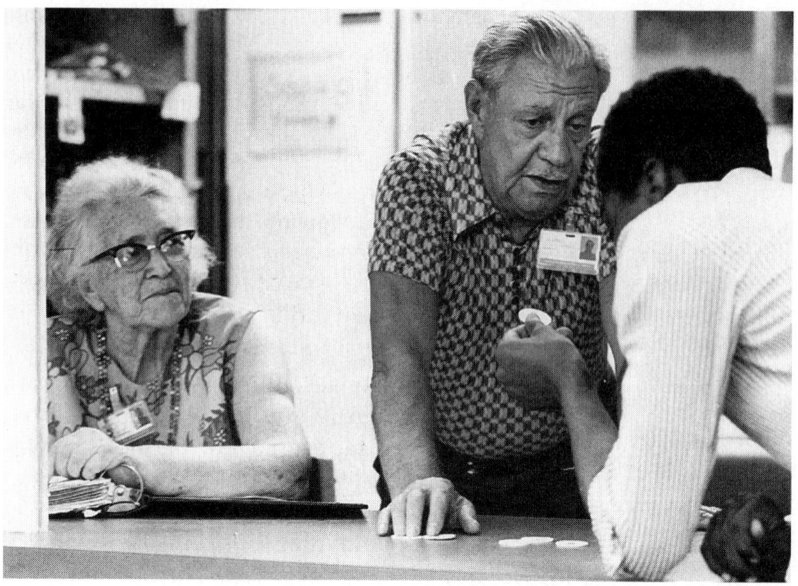

In exchange for keeping their rooms neat, grooming themselves, or performing other specified behaviors, these schizophrenic patients are receiving tokens as reinforcers. In turn, they can trade the tokens for specific privileges.

ness. To alleviate this problem, behavioral programs often include **social-skills training,** in which patients are taught conversation skills, eye contact, appropriate physical gestures, smiling, and improved intonation—generally those characteristics that make one attractive to others (Bellack & Mueser, 1993; Liberman, DeRisi, & Mueser, 1989).

At the other end of the spectrum are people who are indeed communicative but in the wrong way. They may be assaultive or destructive, particularly when frustrated. Such patients can also benefit from social-skills training. Through role playing, they can be taught to respond to frustrating situations by using appropriate verbal responses rather than physical aggression. This emphasis on problem solving has been widely adopted in social-skills training. One program, for example, involved the role playing of 200 interpersonal scenes, each devised to help the patients get through problems in interacting with family, friends, hospital personnel, or people in the community (Liberman, 1982a; Wallace & Liberman, 1985). In these role-playing sessions, appropriate behaviors are modeled, refined through coaching, and then rewarded with positive feedback.

How effective is behavioral treatment? One study (Wallace & Liberman, 1985) compared social-skills training with an alternative treatment, holistic health therapy. The patients in the social-skills program worked with a problem-solving model on how to receive, process, and give interpersonal communications. The holistic-therapy patients spent as many hours in treatment as the social-skills patients, but their time was devoted to jogging, meditation, yoga, group discussions of stress control, and the development of positive expectations. Both groups showed significant improvement in schizophrenic symptoms, and the improvements were approximately equal. Not surprisingly, the social-skills group showed better social skills, but it is still not known whether the social skills acquired in this or similar programs actually generalize to the patients' daily life (Halford & Hayes, 1991). If they do not, this may be the fault of their daily life. Implicit in social-skills training is the belief that the natural environment will reinforce the patients' improved skills, but most schizophrenics do not live in a natural environment. If they are not hospitalized, they tend to live in hostels with many other chronic psychiatric patients—an environment unlikely to reward normal sociability (Payne & Halford, 1990).

Insofar as schizophrenics are helped by behavioral therapy, they are simply helped, not cured. This is in keeping with the goal of most behavioral programs: enhanced functioning. Some behavioral programs have very modest objectives—for example, to help schizophrenic patients live happier and more useful lives within a hospital or some other protective setting. It is in the attainment of such goals that behaviorists may make their greatest contribution to the treatment of schizophrenia.

Unitary Theories: Diathesis and Stress

For a time, the breakthroughs in genetic research on schizophrenia seemed to cast doubt on environmental theories altogether. In the words of two researchers, the burden of proof was shifted "from showing that genes are important to showing that environment is important" (Gottesman & Shields, 1976, p. 367). But while the genetic findings are virtually incontrovertible, they are obviously not the whole story. As Seymour Kety (1970), one of the foremost genetic researchers, has pointed out, schizophrenia cannot be entirely controlled by genes, for if it were, the concordance rate for MZ twins would be 100 percent. Not only is it not 100 percent; as we saw, it is only 38 percent. Likewise, while having a schizophrenic first-degree relative increases one's risk of developing the disorder, it is by no means a necessary condition: 81 percent of people with schizophrenia have no schizophrenic parent or sibling (Gottesman, 1991).

Such are the findings that have led today's researchers to look for *both* genetic and environmental causes—in other words, to adopt the diathesis-stress model. But that model is not an answer; it is only a way of approaching the problem. Many questions remain. If there is a genetically inherited diathesis, what, exactly, is the genetic defect? And what is its primary expression? That is, what are the psychological functions that it directly impairs? Finally, there is the question that we have considered throughout this chapter: What are the stresses most likely to convert such a diathesis into schizophrenia? In an extensive review of the research, Mirsky and Duncan (1986) list the prime suspects: (1) feelings of clumsiness and a sense of being "different" as a result of attention deficits; (2) increased dependence on parents as a result of being impaired; (3) poor academic performance and poor coping skills, again as a result of the basic organic impairment; (4) stressful family interactions, including high expressed emotion; (5) communication deviance in the family, leading to difficulty in communicating with people outside the family and hence to increased isolation; and (6) frequent hospitalization of a parent or other family members. In view of later research, prenatal brain injury should probably be added to this list.

A number of studies (e.g., Nuechterlein, Dawson, Gitlin, et al., 1992) have shown that schizophrenic relapses tend to be preceded by an increase in stressful life events. But these events look more like triggering events than like fundamental causes. It is also possible that the difference lies less in raw numbers of stressful events than in the attitude toward such events. Problems that most of us would greet with mild worry arouse much more anxiety in schizophrenics. Again, this may be due to a primary attention deficit, impairing the person's coping abilities. It is only to people with a history of successful problem solving that problems seem solvable.

These studies of the effects of stressful life events on relapse are typical of current research on schizophrenia in that they not only assume diathesis-stress interaction but attempt to examine it. We have looked at other such studies in this chapter—notably Mednick's high-risk studies. Another example is the Bracha group's study of fingerprints in MZ twins discordant for schizophrenia; here the hypothesized cause is both environmental (prenatal brain injury) and genetic. The diathesis-stress model has also led researchers to ask what happens to people who inherit a genetic vulnerability to schizophrenia but do not develop schizophrenia. Some studies indicate that in such cases the genetic diathesis is often expressed as schizotypal personality disorder. As we noted, this syndrome was commonly seen in those of Mednick's high-risk children who did not develop schizophrenia.

The recent breakthroughs in the study of schizophrenia have been very exciting. Yet each new discovery has made the disorder seem more complicated. If the causes had proved to be wholly genetic or wholly environmental, research would have been far easier. But framed as a diathesis-stress interaction—and one that probably involves many different kinds of genetic diathesis, together with many kinds of stress—the disorder poses a highly intricate problem, one that will occupy researchers for many years to come.

KEY TERMS

behavioral high-risk design (387)
communication deviance (CD) (396)
diathesis-stress model (381)
differential deficits (381)
dopamine hypothesis (389)
double-bind communication (395)
expressed emotion (EE) (395)
genetic high-risk design (386)
milieu therapy (398)
mystification (398)
social-skills training (400)
tardive dyskinesia (392)
token economy (399)

SUMMARY

- Scientists have encountered several obstacles in trying to understand the causes of schizophrenia. Researchers don't know if schizophrenia is one disorder or a group of illnesses, and its wide range of symptoms makes research even harder. Misdiagnosis, while not as common as it was thirty years ago, still occurs, for there is no clear test for the disease.
- The difficulty of discriminating between primary symptoms and secondary symptoms adds to the problem of diagnosis. Additionally, the hospitalization and medication most schizophrenics receive could actually produce some of the unique features of schizophrenia. The difficulty in discovering differential deficits for schizophrenics further adds to the complexity of research.
- While there are many different perspectives on the causes of schizophrenia, most researchers incorporate the *diathesis-stress model*—the view that schizophrenia is caused by a combination of genetic inheritance and environmental stress.
- The biological perspective has convincingly indicated that genetic factors contribute to the development of schizophrenia. Genetic studies on schizophrenia in families, twins, and adopted children have produced very strong evidence for a genetic component of schizophrenia.
- Scientists have used deviant eye tracking, a trait unique to some schizophrenics, as a genetic marker when trying to find a genetic cause of schizophrenia.
- Results of a longitudinal study of children of schizophrenic mothers strongly support the role of genetic factors in schizophrenia.
- Some researchers are attempting to identify preschizophrenic behaviors by examining home movies taken of schizophrenics before they developed the illness. Results are inconclusive, but can offer useful information.
- Brain scans of schizophrenic sufferers have shown several abnormalities. These irregularities may be a result of the medication schizophrenics receive, but it is believed that they are a cause of the disease, as the findings also appear in first-episode schizophrenics.
- Another possible cause of the disorder is prenatal brain injury, specifically in the second trimester, when the brain undergoes important developmental stages. Studies showing that babies exposed to illnesses in their second trimester are more likely to develop schizophrenia than babies exposed in their first or third trimester or those not exposed to an illness prenatally have added support to this theory.
- The dopamine hypothesis, a theory based on biochemical research, states that schizophrenia is related to excess dopamine activity in the brain. The theory has been disputed by some researchers, and it is probable that a biological cause for the disorder will involve not one but many biochemical imbalances.
- Cognitive theorists believe that the primary problem in schizophrenia is a biologically based attention deficit, with other symptoms developing as a result of this problem. It is believed that Type I schizophrenia is related to overattention, the inability to screen out irrelevant stimuli. Type II schizophrenics, however, appear to be underattentive to external stimuli, as seen in their abnormal orienting responses. In support of these theories, researchers have found attention deficits in active and remitted schizophrenics, in their relatives, and in high-risk preschizophrenics.
- Family theorists propose that psychological tensions in the home may be a stress factor in causing schizophrenia. Studies on expressed emotion (based on levels of criticism and emotional overinvolvement) of close relatives of schizophrenics have shown that a negative and highly emotional family atmosphere may lead to the onset of, or a recurrence of, schizophrenia. Communication deviance in parents has proved a good predictor of schizophrenia in adolescents. Family theorists also emphasize the need to work with the families of patients to prevent recurrences of the disorder.
- The psychodynamic approach maintains that schizophrenia begins in early childhood with a hostile mother-child relationship. According to this theory, the child becomes afraid of intimacy and withdraws from the world. When the child reaches adulthood, he or she is overwhelmed by new stress and undergoes a schizophrenic "break." Psychodynamic treatment for the illness requires a close relationship between patient and therapist, as the therapist attempts to become a parental figure to the patient.
- The humanistic-existential viewpoint, as proposed by R. D. Laing, argues that schizophrenia arises from a parent-child relationship in which the child is forced to doubt the legitimacy of his or her own feelings and perceptions. According to this view, modern society forces people to adopt false selves, and schizophrenics are people who are unable to do so. Humanistic-existentialist treatment for the disorder centers on milieu therapy, which places patients in a restorative environment with few restraints and makes patients responsible for their own actions.
- The behavioral perspective sees schizophrenics as people who do not respond to normal social stimuli due to environmental factors. Behaviorists feel that schizophrenics may continue their abnormal behaviors if they are rewarded for them, and therefore treatment aims at changing the behaviors by reversing the

reinforcement. Patients are rewarded only for normal behaviors. Behavioral treatments include direct reinforcement, token economies, and social-skills training.

- Most researchers now recognize that environmental and genetic factors interact in the causation of schizophrenia. Hence many adopt the diathesis-stress model, which states that a predisposition to schizophrenia is inherited but that the disorder must be triggered by environmental stresses, such as poor coping skills and high expressed emotion and communication deviance within the family.

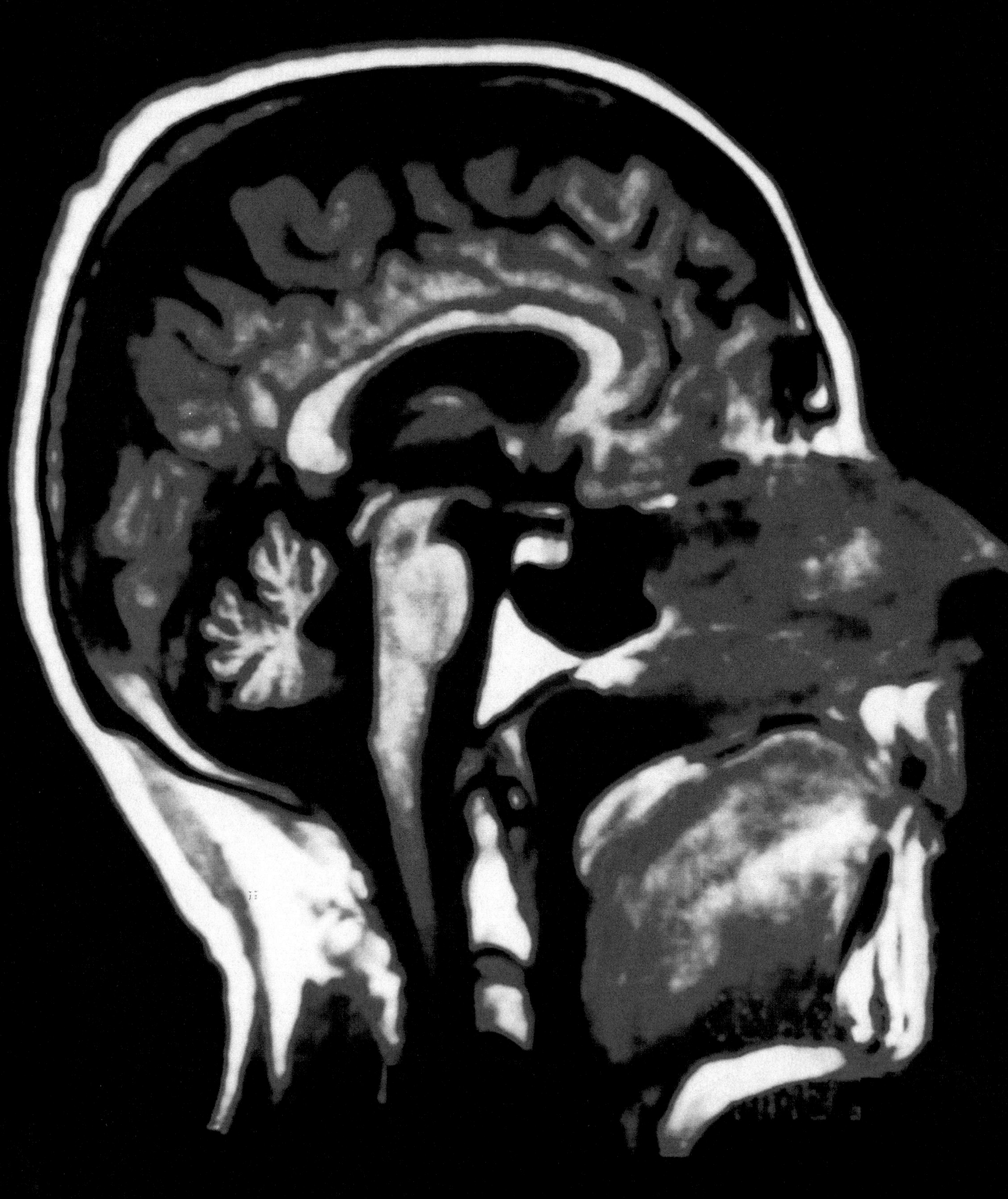

16

COGNITIVE DISORDERS OF ADULTHOOD

On Tuesday evening, April 24, 1973, I came home from teaching at about nine o'clock. . . . A meal had been left for me on the dining table, and I took along a newspaper to read. At the first bite, I choked and coughed, and my vision became hazy. It seemed to clear up in a few minutes, however, and I began reading the paper again. Very shortly I choked and coughed again. Although my vision was all right this time, the attack seemed worse, and I felt weak. When I tried to call for help, I couldn't. I knew what I wanted to say, but the words wouldn't come out. . . . At this point, I realized I had suffered a stroke. As a doctor I recognized the symptoms. . . .

Settled in the hospital, with an intravenous needle in my arm, I set about trying to communicate. Jane [the patient's wife] had a pad and pencil, and wrote down the alphabet on the pad. Nothing to it, I thought. I would simply point to the letters to form the words I wanted and she would write them down. I have no memory of what I wanted to say because it never got through. With utter confidence I pointed to each letter, and she wrote them down and showed it to me. It came out "aiu." . . . I could neither speak, read, nor write. . . .

Later that day, when I looked down at my feet, I couldn't even tell my right foot from my left. That puzzled me. When the nurse had put the intravenous needle into me and asked if I was right- or left-handed, I had raised my right hand, correctly. But when I looked down at my feet, I didn't know which was which. I knew I was improving, for I felt more alert. I glanced at *The New York Times,* but couldn't read it. . . .

Before long I was out of bed and in a wheel chair, sitting by the window looking over the river. I gradually learned to eat slowly so I wouldn't cough. I also indulged in one of my favorite vices—reading the racing form. Occasionally, to show confidence in my judgment, I made a small bet. But I discovered I couldn't add or subtract without great difficulty, and could rarely tell whether I had added two single digits correctly or not.

[After eight days, the patient was discharged from the hospital.] That was a glorious day. I started planning all the things I could do with the incredible amount of free time I was going to have. Chores I had put off, museums and galleries to visit, friends I had wanted to meet for lunch. It was not until several days later that I realized I simply couldn't do them. I didn't have the mental or physical strength, and I sank into a depression. (Dahlberg & Jaffe, 1977)

Most of the disorders that we have discussed in this book so far are thought to be either partly or largely psychogenic, the result of the person's relations to his or her experience and environment. By contrast, the **organic brain disorders,** as their name tells us, are by definition biogenic. They are directly traceable to the destruction of brain tissue or to biochemical imbalances in the brain, and they have a major effect on cognitive processes such as memory. This is not to say that these disorders are "purely" biological. The form an organic syndrome takes depends in part on psychosocial factors—above all, what sort of personality the person has and what his or her living situation is. Likewise, the treatment of organic brain disorders is psychological as well as medical. Rehabilitation programs typically involve not just physicians but psychologists, social workers, occupational therapists, physical therapists, and speech therapists.

The organic brain syndromes constitute a major health problem. At present they account for one-fourth of all first admissions to mental hospitals in the United States. In this chapter we will first examine the difficulties of diagnosing organic brain disorder. Then we will discuss the symptoms and the causes (those that are known) of the major syndromes.

PROBLEMS IN DIAGNOSIS

There are four major problems in the diagnosis of organic brain disorder: (1) deciding whether the disorder is in fact organic; (2) if it is, determining the cause of the brain pathology; (3) if the brain damage is localized (i.e., restricted to a specific area of the brain), determining the location; and (4) deciding how psychosocial factors influence the disorder symptoms and whether medical treatment or psychological therapy can modify them. None of these decisions is a simple matter.

Biogenic versus Psychogenic

Though the symptom picture varies from syndrome to syndrome, the most common signs of organic brain disorder are:

1. *Impairment of orientation.* The person may be unaware of his or her own body and surroundings, unable to tell who he or she is, what the date is, and so forth.
2. *Impairment of memory.* Memory loss is probably the most common symptom of organic brain disorder. The person may forget events of the distant past or, more typically, of the very recent past and may invent stories to fill in these memory gaps. The ability to learn and retain new information may also be disrupted.

3 *Impairment of other intellectual functions, such as comprehension and production of speech, calculation, and general knowledge.* The person may have difficulty speaking coherently, understanding the speech of others, reading, doing arithmetic, and the like. (See the opening case.)
4 *Impairment of judgment.* Patients often make inappropriate decisions—drive unsafely, give their money away to strangers, walk out of the house in their pajamas, and so on.
5 *Lability or shallowness of affect.* The person passes quickly and inappropriately from apathy to hostility or from laughing to weeping.
6 *Loss of mental and emotional resilience.* The person may function fairly well under ordinary circumstances but not when emotionally, mentally, or physically taxed.

The interesting thing about this list is how closely the symptoms of organic brain disorder resemble those of psychogenic disorders. Disorientation, impaired intellectual functioning, and inappropriate affect are well-recognized symptoms of schizophrenia, for example. Diagnosis in such cases may not be easy, at least initially. Furthermore, the symptoms of an organic disorder may be complicated by emotional disturbances developing *in response* to the organic impairment. Look again at the opening case. There the depression arrived once the patient went home from the hospital. But when the onset of organic brain disorder is more gradual, secondary emotional problems may be present long before the person gets to the hospital. When people find themselves taking the wrong bus, calling the wrong phone numbers, making embarrassing mistakes on the job, they tend to become anxious and depressed. So by the time they see a diagnostician, they may have *both* an organic and a psychogenic disorder.

Before the development of modern diagnostic techniques such as magnetic resonance imaging, or MRI (Chapter 4), it was exceedingly difficult to differentiate between organic and psychogenic disorders. Often it was not until the autopsy that a patient whose symptoms had been curiously resistant to several years of psychotherapy was found to have a brain tumor (Patton & Sheppard, 1956; Waggoner & Bagchi, 1954). Such was the case with composer George Gershwin. Young and seemingly healthy, Gershwin one day lost consciousness momentarily while conducting a concert of his works. In the months that followed, he began to act peculiarly. He was irritable and restless, and he had terrible headaches. At the urging of his family he entered a hospital for a complete physical examination and was declared "a perfect specimen of health" (Ewen, 1956, p. 298). He then began daily treatment with a psychotherapist, who decided that what Gershwin needed was rest and seclusion. The rest seemed to help, for about a month. Then Gershwin collapsed and went into a coma. He was rushed to a hospital, where exploratory surgery located an inoperable brain tumor. Gershwin died that same day, at the age of thirty-eight.

Before MRI and other sophisticated diagnostic techniques became available, brain disorders were even harder to diagnose than they are now. George Gershwin (1898–1937), composer of such classics as *An American in Paris* and *Porgy and Bess,* was thought to be mentally ill when he began behaving strangely. Exploratory surgery revealed a fatal brain tumor.

The reverse mistake—diagnosing a psychological problem as an organic disorder—also occurs, especially with elderly patients. Physicians may presume that an elderly patient is growing senile and diagnose dementia (an organic disorder) when in fact the person is suffering from depression brought on by the loss of a spouse, health problems, money problems, or any one of the many difficulties faced by older people (Gurland, Dean, Craw, et al., 1980). (See the box on page 408.)

The differential diagnosis of organic and psychological disturbances is crucial. Many organic disorders can be treated, but only if they are recognized for what they are. Misdiagnosis can be fatal. Sound practice calls for a diagnostician to rule

THE PROBLEMS OF AGING

When society idealizes "growing old gracefully," it asks a great deal of the aging person, for the over-sixty-five years often bring the most stressful changes of a person's life. Consider the changes that typically confront the elderly.

RETIREMENT

Many people look forward to the period of their lives when they will be free from the demands of the clock and the commuter train. And some do find their retirement years to be "golden"—particularly those who are healthy, happily married, financially comfortable, and well equipped with interests that they are eager to pursue. However, many others, cut off from the activity that has lent them an identity for a lifetime, feel bereft. Many miss their friends from the job and the camaraderie of the workplace.

POVERTY

People who have no money worries in their old age are a minority. While in general older people are better off today than their counterparts of the past, many still find that their pensions, social security checks, and savings do not allow them the comforts or even the necessities that they once took for granted. The deprivations may be subtle, such as not being able to buy one's grandchild a special graduation present, or they may be starkly obvious, such as hunger. In either case, the experience of having less money than one is accustomed to is stressful. Old women are more likely to be living in poverty than old men. Typically they have not worked as steadily as their husbands, have not earned as high salaries, and have accumulated fewer retirement benefits, but live longer.

LONELINESS

Many people in the over-sixty-five years must survive the death of a spouse, one of the most traumatic changes that a human being can suffer. The surviving partner may be ill equipped to live alone, and other choices—such as living with one's children—may be unattractive or unavailable. To compound the problem, the longer people live, the more likely they are to see their friends die one by one, leaving them more isolated every year.

PHYSICAL CHANGES

Older people must accept the unpleasant fact that in a society that overvalues the looks and concerns of youth, they no longer look young. Both men and women may be chagrined at their deepening wrinkles and sagging bodies. In addition, old people may begin to notice that their bodies just don't work as well as they used to. Eyes and ears are not as keen as they were. Worse still, more than 80 percent of people over sixty-five suffer from some form of chronic illness: heart disease, arthritis, problems with digestion and sleep, and so on.

An old man or woman may feel stress from every one of these sources. Add to these circumstances the generally negative attitude toward old people in our society—a society where even the fact of aging must be hidden under a euphemism ("senior citizens")—and it is hardly surprising that depression and anxiety are common among the aged.

And what becomes of old people who respond to such stresses with anxiety or depression? In some cases they may be labeled "senile" without showing real signs of organic brain pathology. It is easy for family members, nursing-home personnel, and even doctors and nurses to make this mistake. Consider the woman of eighty who seems sad and withdrawn, who complains about her health and reminisces about her past, who talks to herself because she has no other audience, who begins to neglect her appearance and hygiene because she has nowhere to go and no one to see, and whose memory doesn't seem what it used to be. Our reaction is too often to conclude that "Aunt Jane's mind is wandering" rather than "Aunt Jane is depressed." This error has sinister ramifications. For while depression is something that we can treat, senility is not. The senile are generally put away in nursing homes, where they are likely to deteriorate further.

Recent studies have found that psychotherapy is surprisingly effective for older people showing anxiety and depression (Smyer, Zarit, & Qualls, 1990). Such treatment should probably be considered more often. At the same time, it would be helpful to older people if their stage of life—like adolescence, for example—were recognized as one involving special stresses.

---

out organic factors before concluding that a disorder is psychological in origin. Diagnosticians can draw on a number of resources: direct observation of the patient, a detailed history of the onset and progress of the symptoms, interviews with the patient's family and physician. In addition, diagnosticians usually put the patient through a series of tests: neurological tests to assess reflexes, which may be faulty if there is damage to the nervous system; EEGs, brain CT scans, and chemical analyses of cerebrospinal fluids; and finally, neuropsychological tests, such as the Halstead-Reitan Battery and others that are specifically designed to detect organic impairment. Newer technologies such as MRI and PET (positron emission tomography) scans promise even better detection of brain pathology. Most of these tests are discussed in Chapters 4 and 6.

Specifying the Organic Impairment

If a man appears in an emergency room with a revolver in his hand and a bullet hole in his head, the physician on duty will have little difficulty determining the source, to say nothing of the presence, of organic brain damage. In most cases, however, it is even more difficult to specify the source of the organic impairment—tumor, poisoning, infection, "stroke," whatever—than to distinguish between psychogenic and biogenic pathologies. And like the psychogenic-biogenic distinction, the accurate identification of a biogenic disorder is essential, as it is on this decision that treatment is based. A physician does not wish to treat for a brain tumor only to discover that the patient actually has lead poisoning.

Several possible sources of confusion can make diagnosis difficult. In the first place, the symptoms of the various organic brain disorders overlap considerably. If it is determined that a patient's amnesia is biogenic, this condition could still be due to a number of possible brain pathologies, each requiring different treatment. Second, just as different organic pathologies may produce the same symptoms, so the same pathology may produce widely different symptoms, depending on its *location* in the brain. A brain tumor may cause a speech disorder in one patient, double vision in another, emotional lability in a third. Furthermore, the source of the brain pathology is only one of the many factors determining the patient's behavioral responses to the disease. The patient's age, general physical condition, prior intellectual achievements, premorbid personality, emotional stability, and social situation—as well as the nature, location, and extent of the brain damage—will affect the symptoms. A patient who is rigid and pessimistic or uninsured or alone in the world may respond to unwelcome symptoms with panic or total dejection. On the other hand, a patient who has money, family, and a resilient disposition may show a surprisingly moderate response, even to a severe impairment. From this bewildering array of variables the diagnostician must ferret out the single primary variable: the source of the brain pathology.

There is one final problem in determining the source of organic brain syndromes. As with so many of the psychogenic disorders, there are many organic brain disorders about which we know very little. Unfortunately, the better-understood syndromes are often the rarest, while many of the most common organic disorders remain somewhat baffling.

Specifying the Site of the Damage

We mentioned earlier the matter of determining the location of the brain damage. This is the third important problem in diagnosis. In the case of some disorders, such as the senile degenerative disorders, the problem may not apply, for the damage is usually diffused throughout the brain. But with many other disorders, such as "strokes" and brain tumors, damage may be restricted to one specific area, leaving the rest of the brain relatively unaffected. When this is the case it is essential to determine the site of the pathology, for treatment depends on this information. Obviously, a surgeon who is about to operate on a brain tumor needs to know where the tumor is. Such knowledge also guides rehabilitation. Therapists who know where the damage is can retrain patients to use the damaged parts or teach them to compensate by developing undamaged parts.

Physiological measures such as the EEG can sometimes give vague hints as to the location of the brain pathology. The patient's symptoms will provide further hints. As we saw in Chapter 4, certain areas of the brain are known to control certain behaviors. Using this knowledge, a neurologist may be able to determine the location of the damage on the basis of how the patient is acting and how he or she performs on neuropsychological tests. CT, PET, and MRI can also be used to pinpoint the site of the damage if the site is large enough.

Patterns of Disability: Aphasia, Apraxia, and Agnosia In some cases of organic brain disorder, the symptoms are *focal*, or restricted to a specific aspect of behavior. A common focal symptom is **aphasia,** or language impairment. The diagnosis of aphasia depends on fluency of speech, comprehension, and the ability to repeat phrases and sentences (J. L. Cummings, 1985). Patients with *fluent aphasia* produce streams of incoherent speech. Syllables are reversed, word order is jumbled, and so on. Patients with *nonfluent aphasia* have difficulty initiating speech and respond to questions with

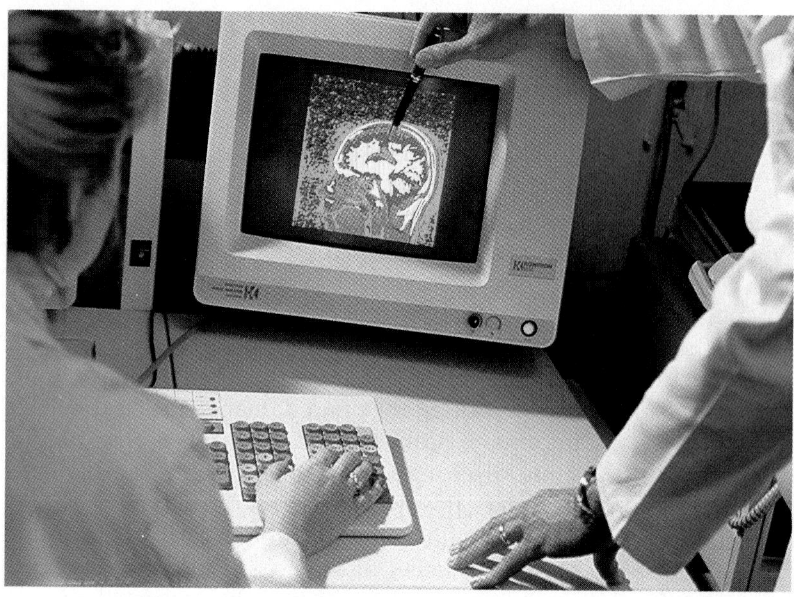

Computerized scans can help pinpoint the site of brain damage.

one-word answers, short phrases, and long pauses. Aphasia patients also differ in their ability to understand speech (ranging from good to poor) and their ability to repeat speech correctly (also ranging from good to poor).

When the patient is aphasic, the diagnostician can usually say with some precision where it is that the brain is injured. In most people language is controlled largely by the left hemisphere (Chapter 4). Aphasia is caused by damage to this hemisphere. Fluent aphasia is produced by injury closer to the rear of this hemisphere, nonfluent aphasia by injury closer to the front of the hemisphere. When damage is limited to the left frontal lobe, comprehension is usually preserved. When damage extends to the regions behind the frontal lobe, comprehension is impaired.

Another major class of disability is **apraxia,** impairment of the ability to perform voluntary movements. The patient may try to write with a pair of scissors, for example, or to light a match by striking the wrong end (Hécaen & Albert, 1978).

A third class of disability is **agnosia,** a disturbance in the ability to recognize familiar objects. In his book *The Man Who Mistook His Wife for a Hat and Other Clinical Tales* (1985), Oliver Sacks described the case of Dr. P., a professor of music, who had developed visual agnosia. Dr. P. often failed to recognize his students' faces, yet when they spoke, he knew immediately who they were. At the same time, he saw faces that didn't exist: he would pat the tops of fire hydrants as if they were the heads of children. An opthalmologist examined Dr. P. and, finding nothing wrong with his eyes, recommended that he see Sacks, a neurologist. Sacks found Dr. P. "a man of great cultivation and charm, who talked well and fluently, with imagination and humor" (p. 8). Gradually, however, it became clear that there was something seriously wrong with him. He was able to see but not to make sense of his perceptions. He could identify a cube, a dodecahedron, and other complex geometric forms, but when Sacks handed him a rose, he was baffled:

> "About six inches in length," he commented. "A convoluted red form with a linear green attachment."
>
> "Yes," I [Sacks] said encouragingly, "but what do you think it *is*, Dr. P.?"
>
> "Not easy to say." He seemed perplexed. . . .
>
> "Smell it," I suggested, and he again looked somewhat puzzled, as if I'd asked him to smell a higher symmetry. (p. 12)

When Sacks handed him a glove, he was again bewildered:

> "A continuous surface," he announced at last, "infolded on itself. It appears to have"—he hesitated—"five outpouchings, if this is the word." (p. 13)

On one occasion, as he was preparing to leave Sacks' office, Dr. P. reached for his wife's head and tried to lift it off, mistaking his wife for a hat. Interestingly, although Dr. P.'s visual sense was totally impaired, his musical sense remained intact. He was able to function in everyday life by composing eating songs, dressing songs, and bathing songs, which guided his actions. Dr. P.'s symptoms were due to organic pathology in the visual-processing region of the brain.

Dr. P. was an unusual patient in that his symptoms were so isolated and specific. Most patients show a combination of disabilities. Thus it is the rare case in which the diagnostician can accurately specify one spot, and one spot alone, in which the damage has occurred. Nevertheless, an educated guess must be made as to the site or sites.

In diagnosing an organic brain syndrome, the clinician classifies the syndrome according to its organic cause—trauma, infection, poisoning, or whatever. The one exception to this classification system is epilepsy, which, because its cause is in some cases unknown, is classified by its symptomatology. Our chapter will follow the same organizational plan.

ORGANIC BRAIN DISORDERS CLASSIFIED BY CAUSE

Cerebral Infection

Behavior disorders may result from infections that damage and destroy the neural tissue of the brain. There are four major categories of brain infection: cerebral abscess, encephalitis, meningitis, and neurosyphilis.

Cerebral Abscess A **cerebral abscess,** like an abscess in any other part of the body, is an infection that becomes encapsulated by connective tissue. Because it cannot drain and heal like an infection on the outside of the body, it simply continues to grow inside the body. Brain abscesses usually occur when an infection in some other part of the body travels to the brain or when a foreign object such as a piece of shrapnel enters the brain, introducing germs. With improved measures for preventing infection after injury, cerebral abscesses have become rare.

Encephalitis **Encephalitis** is a generic term meaning an inflammation of the brain. Infections which lead to encephalitis can be caused by viral or nonviral agents. One form, *epidemic encephalitis,* also known as "sleeping sickness," was widespread following World War I. Its most striking symptoms were profound lethargy and prolonged periods of sleep, often for days or even weeks at a time. In their periods of wakefulness, however, patients might become extremely hyperactive, irritable, and then breathless and unable to sleep. Other symptoms included convulsive seizures and delirium—a state of excitement and disorientation marked by incoherent speech, restless activity, and often hallucinations. Epidemic encephalitis often led to death. In those who survived—and especially in children, who were more susceptible—the disease often left an altered personality, in many cases a sociopathic personality.

The virus responsible for epidemic encephalitis, while still active in certain areas of Asia and Africa, is now virtually unknown in Europe and North America. However, there remain scores of viruses that can cause other types of encephalitis. Typically transmitted by such animals as mosquitoes, ticks, and horses, these viruses produce many of the same symptoms as epidemic encephalitis—lethargy, irritability, seizures—and often lead to death or, in those who survive, brain damage.

Encephalitis occurs as an infrequent consequence of many common illnesses, such as measles, mumps, and influenza. People infected with the Epstein-Barr or herpes simplex virus can develop encephalitis. Another common source of infection is organisms transmitted through insect bites. California and western equine encephalitis are mosquito-borne, while Rocky Mountain spotted fever is caused by a small microorganism carried by a tick. All three of these disorders are prevalent throughout the United States. Other common types of encephalitis are found only in specific regions, for instance, St. Louis encephalitis, which is mosquito-borne and generally found in southern states. Lyme disease, which is caused by a spirochete carried by a tick, can involve either encephalitis or meningitis.

Meningitis Another type of cerebral infection is **meningitis,** an acute inflammation of the *meninges,* the membranous covering of the brain and spinal cord. Meningitis may be caused by bacteria, viruses, protozoa, or fungi. As in cerebral abscess, these foreign bodies may be introduced into the brain either through an infection elsewhere in the body or by some outside agent entering the skull. Among the psychological symptoms usually observed in meningitis are drowsiness, confusion, irritability, inability to concentrate, memory defects, and sensory impairments. In milder cases the primary infection may be effectively eliminated, but residual effects such as motor and sensory impairments and, in infants, mental retardation are not uncommon.

Neurosyphilis **Neurosyphilis,** the deterioration of brain tissue as a result of syphilis, was once far more common than any of the forms of encephalitis. As we saw in Chapter 1, it was not until the late nineteenth century that the degenera-

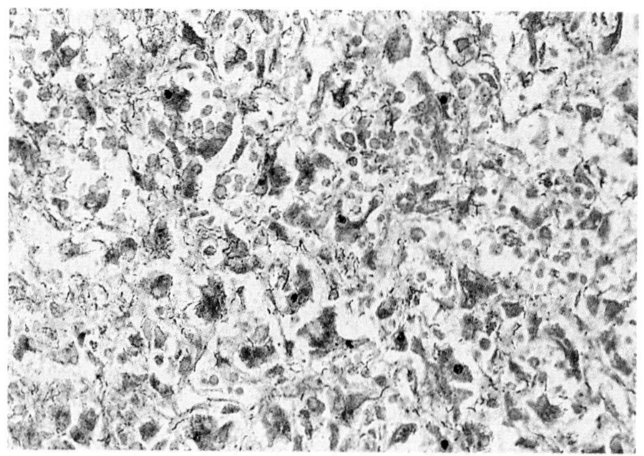

This light micrograph shows the spirochete bacterium *(Treponema pallidum)* that causes syphilis. In the late stages of untreated syphilis, deterioration of brain tissue produces the sloppiness, forgetfulness, and other characteristic symptoms of general paresis.

tive disorder called **general paresis** was finally linked to syphilis. Throughout the previous centuries syphilis had raged unchecked through Europe, taking a huge toll in infant mortality, blindness, madness, and death. Among its more famous victims were Henry VIII, and most of his many wives, and probably Christopher Columbus. Indeed, it is thought that the disease was introduced into Europe by Columbus' crew, who were apparently infected by the natives of the West Indies (Kemble, 1936).

Syphilis begins when a microorganism known as *Treponema pallidum* invades the victim's body, usually through the mucous membranes in the mouth or genital areas. (Transmission is almost always sexual.) In some cases, the infection is eliminated. If not, it spreads, and ten to thirty years later the damage begins to show in various forms of organ failure, including blindness and heart attack. In about 3 percent of untreated syphilitics, the infection also reaches the brain, causing general paresis.

The onset of general paresis is usually marked by a vague but pervasive slovenliness of behavior. Then a number of better-defined symptoms make their appearance, including tremors, slurring of speech, deterioration of handwriting, a shuffling gait, and, almost invariably, disturbances of vision. The personality too begins to deteriorate: patients become increasingly sloppy, indifferent, and forgetful. They may also show severe depression or a manic expansiveness. When the disease has progressed to this stage, the only possible treatment is custodial. Death soon follows.

Syphilis can be transmitted by a syphilitic mother to her unborn child, in which case the child may develop *juvenile paresis.* This involves the same symptoms as general paresis but usually appears between the ages of five and twenty.

With the development of such early detection procedures as the Wasserman test and with the advent of penicillin, the incidence of syphilis decreased dramatically in the late 1940s and the 1950s. Today general paresis accounts for less than 1 percent of all first admissions to mental hospitals in the United States.

Brain Trauma

More common than brain infection is **brain trauma,** or injury to brain tissue as a result of jarring, bruising, or cutting. With a prevalence of 200 per 100,000 population (Sorenson & Kraus, 1991), traumatic head injury is the leading cause of disability and death in children and young adults (National Institute of Neurological Disorders and Stroke, 1989). Two-thirds of victims are male, and the highest-risk age group is fifteen- to twenty-four-year-olds (Kraus, Black, Hessol, et al., 1984), though, as noted, children are also at risk, usually through falls (hence the laws requiring window guards in apartment buildings in many states). Indeed, falls are the second most common cause of head injury. The most common cause, accounting for over half of all serious head injuries, is automobile and motorcycle accidents. Many of these injuries could be prevented. It is estimated that the incidence of brain trauma could be reduced by one-fourth if all cars were equipped with air bags (Jagger, Vernberg, & Jones, 1987). It could also be reduced if people would not drive after drinking. More than half of all head-injury survivors have a documentable blood-alcohol level at the time of the accident (Sparedo & Gill, 1989).

A brain injury can have huge consequences. Every year, about 2,000 survivors lapse into a persistent vegetative state, and another 5,000 develop epilepsy (National Institute of Neurological Disorders and Stroke, 1989). These are the more serious cases; 80 percent of head injuries are classified as mild. But even in that group, more than three-quarters of victims show long-term disabilities. Almost all of them report verbal problems, and more than half have impaired memory (Sorenson & Kraus, 1991). Other persistent symptoms are fatigue, sleep disturbances, poor attention and concentration, slowed reactions, emotional ups and downs, and social and moral failures such as selfishness and callousness (Gronwall, Wrightson, & Waddell, 1990). In general, brain-injury survivors constitute a very troubled population, and a hidden one. They do not look disabled, and partly for that reason they often receive little understanding, let alone adequate treatment. But many of them are unable to live normal lives. One-third of brain-injured adults are unemployed six months after the injury (McMahan & Flowers, 1986), and they may remain so. They also have trouble sustaining marriages and friendships.

Brain trauma is subdivided into three categories, in order of increasing severity: concussion, contusion, and laceration.

Concussion In the case of a **concussion,** the blow to the head jars the brain, momentarily disrupting its functioning. The usual result is a temporary loss of consciousness, often lasting for only a few seconds or minutes, after which the person is typically unable to remember the events immediately preceding the injury. A familiar instance of concussion is a knockout in a boxing match. Concussions occur frequently too during football games (Figure 16.1), a problem we discuss in the box on page 414.

In general, the longer the person remains unconscious after the blow, the more severe the posttraumatic symptoms and the less likely it is that the victim will recover completely. In addition to experiencing headaches and dizziness, the person may display apathy, depression, irritability, and various cognitive problems (poor memory, poor concentration). In less severe cases, these symptoms disappear within the span of a few days to a few months, but in some cases, aftereffects may still be experienced months or even years later.

Contusion In a **contusion** the trauma is severe enough that the brain is not just jarred; it is actually bruised. The person typically lapses into a coma lasting for several hours or even days, and afterward may suffer convulsions and/or temporary speech loss. Furthermore, on awakening from the coma, contusion victims may fall into a state of disorientation called **traumatic delirium,** in which they may imagine, for example, that the hospital staff are enemies or kidnappers. These symptoms generally disappear within a week or so, but a very severe contusion or repeated contusions can result in permanent emotional instability and intellectual impairment. Again, the length of the period of unconsciousness is useful in predicting the severity and duration of the posttraumatic symptoms.

The effects of repeated head injuries, such as those suffered by boxers, can result in cumulative damage. The effects can be manifested years later, in *dementia pugilistica* (better known as the punch-drunk syndrome), which involves memory lapses, loss of coordination, dizziness, tremors, and other physical and psychological impairments. One study of a small sample of former prizefighters found that 87 percent exhibited abnormalities on at least two of four measures (Casson, Seigel, Sham, et al., 1984). Researchers have also found structural changes in the brains of former boxers, including abnormalities similar to those found in Alzheimer's

FIGURE 16.1 Anatomy of a concussion.

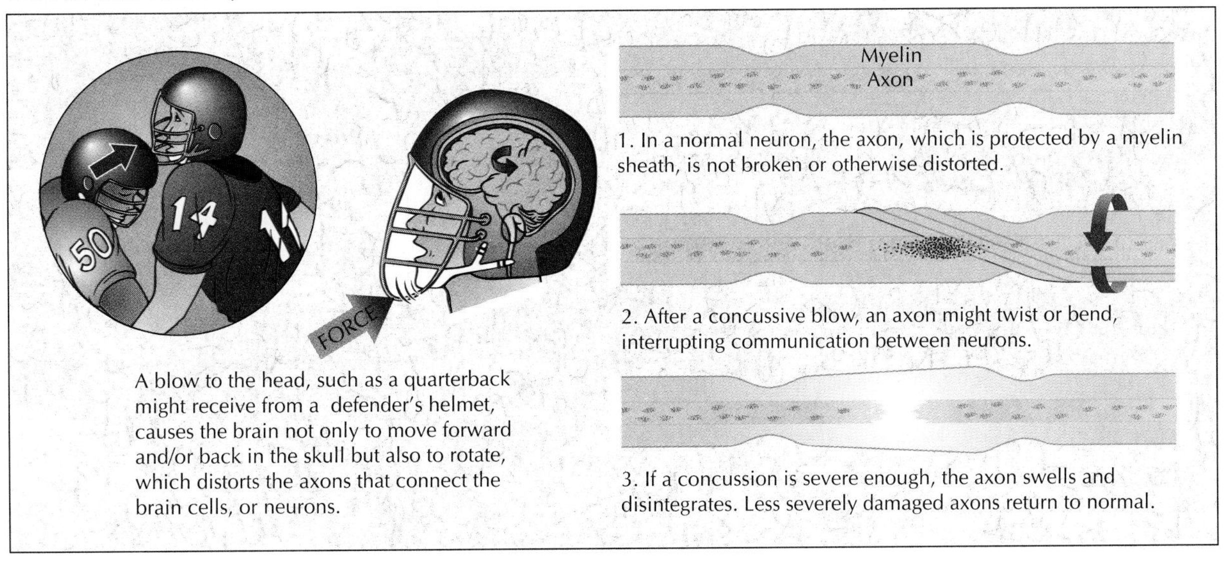

Myelin
Axon
1. In a normal neuron, the axon, which is protected by a myelin sheath, is not broken or otherwise distorted.
2. After a concussive blow, an axon might twist or bend, interrupting communication between neurons.
3. If a concussion is severe enough, the axon swells and disintegrates. Less severely damaged axons return to normal.
FORCE
A blow to the head, such as a quarterback might receive from a defender's helmet, causes the brain not only to move forward and/or back in the skull but also to rotate, which distorts the axons that connect the brain cells, or neurons.

CONCUSSIONS AND FOOTBALL: IF IT HURTS, RUB DIRT ON IT

In 1994 Merril Hoge, a running back for the Chicago Bears, was hit in the head during a preseason football game. When he came to the sidelines, the team trainer asked him if he knew where he was. "In Tampa Bay," Hoge answered. "How do you know that?" the trainer asked. "I can hear the ocean," Hoge replied (quoted in King, 1994, p. 92). In fact, they were in Kansas City, and the ocean Hoge heard was only in his head. He had suffered a concussion. Six weeks later, after a second concussion, he couldn't even recognize his wife. Hoge never played football again.

Head injuries are common on the football field. Between 1989 and 1993, according to data from the twenty-eight teams in the National Football League (NFL), 341 different players suffered 445 concussions (Farber, 1994). And while these men are paid handsomely for throwing themselves into harm's way, head injuries dog unprofessional football as well. Each season a quarter of a million high school football players suffer concussions (Farber, 1994). In 1991 Adrian Guitterez, a high school running back from Monte Vista, Colorado, ignored the symptoms of a concussion and died after he was tackled in a game two weeks later.

Most concussions, however, do not end lives or even careers. Still, according to many experts, repeated concussions pose a risk of long-term neurological damage. New York Jets wide receiver Al Toon, for example, suffered as many as thirteen concussions over the course of his eight-year career. He was finally forced to retire in 1992. Interviewed two years later, he reported that he was still chronically tired and irritable and that he couldn't watch his children on a carousel without becoming dizzy (Farber, 1994).

As concern over football head injuries has increased, so has awareness that these injuries are not always accidents—that defensive players sometimes engage in "head-hunting." That is, they aim for the head. For some players, aggression isn't just a means to a competitive end. Fred Stokes of the Los Angeles Rams, "one of the league's gentlemen" (King, 1994, p. 29) according to one sportswriter, describes his pursuit of a rival quarterback: "It sounds animalistic, but I got such a rush, I was slobbering. That's the game." Moreover, Stokes says, such bloodthirstiness is rewarded by his coaches. "At every level, the harder you hit, the more you get patted on the back" (quoted in King, 1994, p. 29).

Rough play is also rewarded by teammates. Few on-the-field player celebrations are more exuberant than those reserved for a hard hit on an opponent, regardless of whether the hit stopped him. Interestingly, the celebration itself often takes the form of teammates' butting each other in the head.

Football's machismo culture not only applauds the predator but also silences the victim. Having "bought into football's rub-dirt-on-it ethos," explains sportswriter Michael Farber, many players will refuse to be taken out of a game after a concussion. "If we get knocked in the head, it's embarrassing to come to the sideline and say 'Hey, my head's feeling funny,'" says San Francisco 49er quarterback Steve Young (quoted in Farber, 1994, p. 45). Players who play through pain are held up by commentators as an inspiration to their teammates.

Presumably, it is the job of the team medical staff to keep injured players off the field, but minor concussions can easily escape notice. In 1991, the Pittsburgh Steelers began conducting preseason neuropsychological tests on their players. By assessing a player before the season and again after a concussion, such tests measure the impact of the concussion. But so far the Steelers are the only NFL team to initiate such exams. "I don't think most athletes want to know the effect an injury has had . . . , and I don't think most pro or college teams want their athletes scrutinized that way," says Dr. James P. Kelly, director of the brain-injury program at the Chicago Rehabilitative Institute. "They're not in the business of identifying worrisome neurological problems" (quoted in Farber, 1994, p. 46).

Football wouldn't be football without hard contact, which will inevitably result in some injuries. But *Sports Illustrated* football writer Peter King (1994) has proposed a series of reforms that might make the game safer. One is harsh, personal punishment for "head-hunters." (Today, the team receives a 15-yard penalty. King believes the head-hunting player should also be penalized, by suspension from one game without pay.) King also suggests that the league add, for every game, an extra official whose sole responsibility would be to watch and protect the vulnerable quarterback. Finally, King says, players should wear more protective headgear, and teams that play on artificial surfaces should convert to softer, natural grass.

Even if such reforms are adopted, however, the NFL would still have to struggle to deliver in a reasonably safe fashion a product that is intrinsically violent.

disease (Lampert & Hardman, 1984). Indeed, head injury may be a risk factor for Alzheimer's disease, although research is not conclusive on this point (Graves, Larson, White, et al., 1994).

Laceration In a **laceration,** a foreign object, such as a bullet or a piece of metal, enters the skull and directly ruptures and destroys brain tissue. Laceration is the most serious form of brain trauma, though its effects depend on the site of the damage. Lacerations in certain areas of the brain result in death or extreme disability, while damage to other areas may have relatively minor consequences. Periodically the newspapers report a case in which a person who has been shot in the head simply waits for the external wounds to heal and then resumes normal functioning, going about his or her daily business with a bullet or two lodged in the brain. Such cases are rare, however. Normally, a cerebral laceration results in some form of physical impairment or personality change, whether major or minor.

The following classic case, reported in 1868, illustrates the subtle, variable, and unpredictable effects of cerebral laceration (see also Figure 16.2):

> Phineas P. Gage, age twenty-five and strong and healthy, was the popular foreman of a railroad excavation crew. While he was working at a site, an explosion drove a tamping iron into the left side of his face and up through his skull. Thrown onto his back by the force of the blast and by the entry of the rod, Gage convulsed, but he quickly regained speech and was placed in a cart, in which he rode in a sitting position for three-quarters of a mile to his hotel. He got out of the cart by himself and walked up a long flight of stairs to his room. Although bleeding profusely, he remained conscious during the doctor's ministrations.
>
> Soon afterward he appeared completely recovered physically, but his personality had undergone a radical change. The equilibrium between his intellectual faculties and his instincts seemed to have been destroyed. He was now inconsiderate, impatient, and obstinate, and yet at the same time capricious and

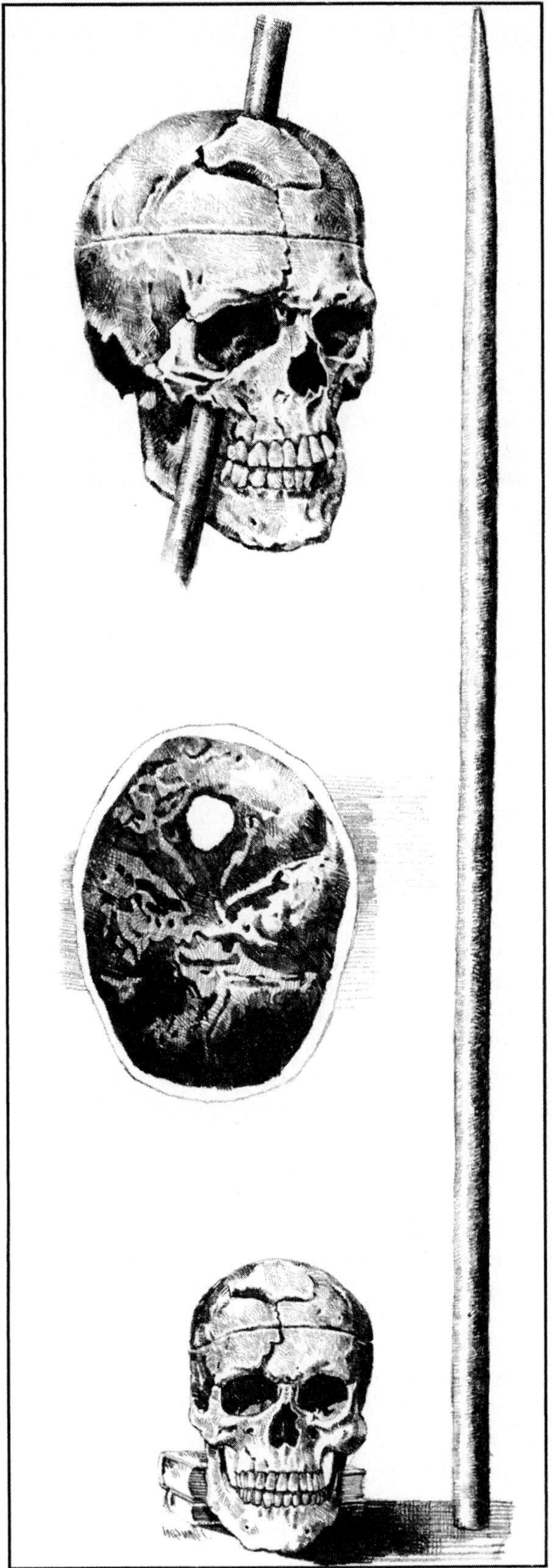

FIGURE 16.2 The cerebral laceration suffered by Phineas Gage is illustrated in these drawings, which are adapted from original sketches done by Dr. Harlow, the physician who attended Gage. The drawings show the relative sizes of the skull and the tamping iron that passed through it. The top drawing shows the position in which the iron lodged; it also shows the large section of the skull that was torn away and later replaced. The middle sketch, an upward view of the inside of the skull, shows the hole made by the iron, partially filled in by new bone deposit.

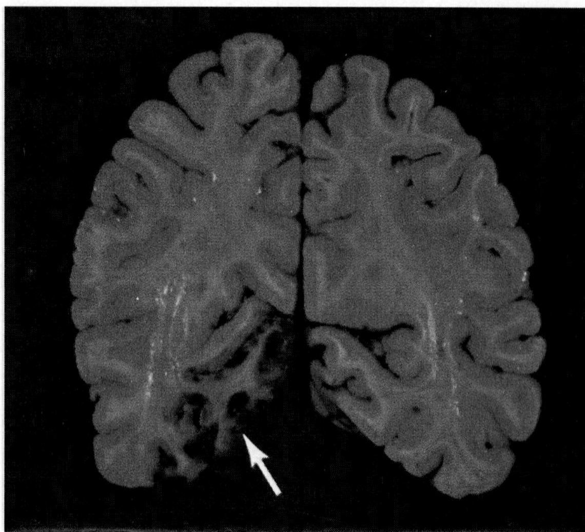

This brain section shows the atrophy of tissue *(arrow)* resulting from a cerebral hemorrhage.

vacillating. He also began indulging in the grossest profanity. The change in temperament was so extreme that his employers had to replace him. To his friends he was simply "no longer Gage." (adapted from J. Harlow, 1868, pp. 330–332, 339–340)

Cerebrovascular Accidents: Strokes

A third category of brain disorder includes those disorders due to a **cerebrovascular accident (CVA)**—better known as a **stroke**—in which blockage or breaking of the blood vessels in the brain results in injury to brain tissue. CVAs are common—indeed, they are the third leading cause of death in the United States. We have already seen an example of this disorder in the case at the opening of the chapter. In that instance, as in many, the occurrence of the CVA is marked by *stroke syndrome,* the acute onset of specific disabilities involving the central nervous system. The person wakes up from a nap or, as in our case, sits down to dinner, and suddenly he or she can no longer speak, understand speech, move the right side of the body, or perform some other CNS-controlled function. In some cases the stroke victim dies immediately or within days. In other cases the victim not only lives but does not show stroke syndrome. Many people apparently have what are called "silent strokes," small CVAs that occur in less critical regions of the brain and thus have a less noticeable effect on behavior, though the person may find that certain functions, such as memory, are gradually eroded. CVAs are found in 25 percent of routine autopsies, and many of these are silent strokes.

Infarction There are two broad categories of CVAs: infarction and hemorrhage. In **infarction** the supply of blood to the brain is somehow cut off, resulting in the death of brain tissue fed by that source. The two most common causes of infarction are thrombosis and embolism. In an **embolism** a ball of something such as fat, air, or clotted blood breaks off from the side of a blood vessel or in some other way enters the bloodstream and floats upward until it reaches a blood vessel too narrow to let it pass. At that point it blocks the vessel, cutting off the blood flow. In a **thrombosis** fatty material coating the inside of a blood vessel gradually builds up until it blocks the flow of blood in that vessel. Predictably, these two different causes produce different kinds of onset. When a CVA results from an embolism, onset is usually sudden, with dramatic symptoms: the person may collapse, suffer seizures, become paralyzed. In thrombosis, because the blockage is gradual, the onset is gradual.

Hemorrhage Aside from infarction, the other major category of CVA is cerebral **hemorrhage,** in which a blood vessel in the brain ruptures, causing blood to spill out into the brain tissue. When the hemorrhage occurs inside the brain, it is usually traceable to hypertension. When it occurs in the space around the brain, it is usually due to an aneurysm, or bulge in the wall of the blood vessel. Aneurysms may be as small as a pea or as large as a plum. They are common—they turn up in 2 percent of autopsied adults (Merritt, 1967)—and if they do not lead to hemorrhage, they may produce no symptoms whatsoever.

The Effects of a Stroke The aftereffects of a stroke depend on the nature of the stroke—infarction or hemorrhage, embolism or thrombosis, hemorrhage within or around the brain—together with the extent of the damage and, above all, the location of the damage. The most common effects are aphasia, agnosia, apraxia, and paralysis, usually of one limb or one half of the body (since a stroke occurs in one or the other brain hemisphere). These disabilities (whether they result from CVAs or from any other organic brain disorder) are almost invariably accompanied by some degree of emotional disturbance, partly organic and partly a psychological response to the new impairment. One common reaction is emotional lability: the patient may pass from laughing to weeping in an instant. Another response that is sometimes seen is a **catastrophic reaction** (K. Goldstein, 1948): suddenly unable to perform elementary tasks long since taken for granted—walking across a room, forming a sentence, reading a magazine—the patient reacts with disorganization and sometimes violent fury. Later, as a means of coping with the impairment, the patient may develop seemingly odd habits. To compensate for memory losses, for example, some people may make elaborate inventories of their belongings and may become very angry if something is moved from its proper place.

A catastrophic reaction is more frequently seen in patients who have damage in the left hemisphere. Those with right-hemisphere CVAs tend to show the opposite reaction: they minimize the problem, appear indifferent to it, and joke about it (Gainotti, 1972; Sackeim et al., 1982). Again, the response depends greatly on the premorbid personality. People with compulsive tendencies are generally intolerant of any reduction in their abilities and therefore may become very depressed after a stroke. Likewise, suspicious natures will be exacerbated by the sudden helplessness that accompanies a stroke. Such people may develop paranoid symptoms, accusing others of making fun of them, of stealing their belongings, and so forth. The symptomatology, then, is the result not just of a specific disorder in a specific part of the brain but of this disorder's *working on* a specific personality.

Half of first-stroke patients die within five years, usually from another stroke (Terént, 1993). This is a harsh statistic, but in fact it represents a medical victory. Stroke survival rates have almost doubled since the 1940s (Whisnant, 1993), and they are still improving. In those patients who survive, some of the behavioral symptoms may disappear spontaneously, while others can be remedied through rehabilitation. And as the disability is remedied, so in most cases is the attendant emotional disturbance. Some CVA patients recover completely, but most continue to labor under some form of impairment for the rest of their lives. In general, the younger the patient and the smaller the area of brain damage, the better the chance of recovery.

Risk Factors The clearest risk factor for CVAs is age. Between the ages of sixty and eighty, the risk increases almost eightfold. In people over seventy-five the rate of first stroke is almost twenty times that of the general population: 2,000 as opposed to 114 per 1,000 population (Terént, 1993). That is because the incidence of physical conditions that weaken the blood vessels—above all, hypertension, heart disease, and atherosclerosis, or thickening of the walls of the blood vessels—increases with age. Another risk factor is sex. Men are more vulnerable than women by a ratio of 1.3 to 1 (Kurtzke, 1980). The women's advantage is due in part to the fact that estrogen seems to protect against atherosclerosis, but even after menopause, when estrogen levels fall, women are still somewhat less susceptible to strokes, and hormone-replacement therapy may restore their former advantage. Other higher-risk groups are diabetics, people with a family history of strokes, and black people. African-Americans have twice the stroke risk of most other ethnic groups (Singleton & Johnson, 1993).

Those are the uncontrollable risk factors. In addition, there are several other conditions that make people vulnerable to this disorder. High cholesterol and obesity increase stroke risk; smoking almost doubles it; hypertension increases it anywhere from two to five times (Boysen, 1993). All these factors can be controlled.

Brain Tumors

Brain tumors are classified as either primary or metastatic. **Metastatic brain tumors** originate in some other part of the body and then metastasize, or spread, to the brain. Usually they develop from cancer of the lung, breast, stomach, or kidney and travel to the brain through the blood vessels. By contrast, **primary brain tumors,** as their name suggests, are tumors that originate in the brain. Some primary tumors are *intracerebral*—that is, they grow inside the brain. Others are *extracerebral,* growing outside the brain but inside the skull, often in the meninges. Intracranial tumors are more frequently seen in adults; extracranial tumors, in children. Brain tumors in general are common. Every year about 20,000 new primary brain tumors are diagnosed, and another 20,000 people are diagnosed as having metastatic brain tumors (G. Segal, 1991).

Although the actual cause of tumors has not yet been determined, their clinical course is clear. For some reason, a few cells begin to grow at an abnormally rapid rate, destroying the surrounding healthy brain tissue and resulting in a wide variety of psychological symptoms. In most cases, the first signs are subtle and insidious—headaches, seizures, visual problems, neglect of personal hygiene, indifference to previously valued activities, and failures of judgment and foresight. With the progressive destruction of brain tissue, the patient eventually develops at least one of the more obvious symptoms: abnormal reflexes; blunting of affect; disorientation in regard to time, place, and/or person; poor memory and concentration; double vision; and jerky motor coordination. The kind and severity of symptoms are directly related to the location of the tumor in the brain: the functions controlled by that section will probably be impaired earlier and more severely than other functions. However, as the tumor grows, pressing against other sections, their functioning too will be affected.

Any tumor that continues to grow, untreated, in the brain will eventually cause extreme physical distress (splitting headaches, vomiting, seizures), along with personality changes that may reach psychotic proportions. Just before death, the patient may become overtly psychotic and finally lapse into a coma.

Tumors can be removed surgically, and in many cases they are. However, since the surgery itself can cause additional brain damage, the physician may choose to avoid it. Surgeons are especially reluctant to operate on the language areas and on the major motor areas. In such cases, radiation treatment may be used, though this too can destroy brain tissue. In other cases, surgery and radiation are used in combination, both to remove the growth and to prevent future growths.

Degenerative Disorders

Degenerative disorders are syndromes characterized by a general deterioration of intellectual, emotional, and motor functioning as a result of progressive pathological change in the brain. As usual with organic brain disorders, symptoms vary depending on the site of the damage (J. L. Cummings & Benson, 1992). Disorders caused by deterioration of the cerebral cortex produce memory disturbances, impaired comprehension, naming difficulties, and environmental disorientation. Until the late stages of the disease, gait, posture, muscle tone, and reflexes are usually unimpaired. Alzheimer's disease is such a disorder. In disorders caused by deterioration of the subcortical regions of the brain (below the cerebral cortex), the usual symptoms are forgetfulness, difficulty in solving problems, mood swings, and motor disturbances. Huntington's chorea and Parkinson's disease are disorders of this type. Still other disorders are caused by vascular disease that affects both the cortical and subcortical regions of the brain. These disorders are characterized by abrupt onset, stepwise deterioration—that is, deterioration in a series of downward plateaus—and focal symptoms, such as aphasia. Vascular dementia is an example of this last category. Another degenerative brain disorder—and one that is becoming increasingly common—is AIDS dementia. (See the box on page 419).

Aging and Dementia Psychologists used to think that **dementia,** or severe mental deterioration, was a final stage of aging that would occur in everyone who lived long enough. Today we know that dementia is the result of degenerative brain disorders that affect only a small minority of the aged. Approximately 4 to 7 percent of people over sixty-five have definite signs of dementia. Prevalence rises with age, however: among people over eighty-five, about 30 percent show dementia (Kokmen, Beard, Offord, et al., 1989; Johansson & Zarit, 1991). Fortunately, even at such advanced ages, most people have little or no evidence of degenerative brain disorder—no pronounced loss of memory, impaired reasoning, or impaired judgment.

Almost all old people experience some psychological changes simply as a function of aging. Although the precise biological processes are still not clear, it seems that all behavior mediated by the central nervous system slows down as the body ages (Birren, 1974; Salthouse, 1985). Old people in general experience a slowing of motor reactions, a lessened capacity to process complex information, and decreased efficiency in memory and in the learning of new material. These changes are part of the *normal* process of aging; they are no more pathological than wrinkles or gray hair. By contrast, the degenerative diseases of late life, known collectively as **senile dementias,** are pathological; they are the direct result of a severe organic deterioration of the brain. Dementias account for more hospital admissions and for more inpatient hospital days than any other psychiatric disorder among elderly people (J. L. Cummings & Benson, 1992). The two most common senile dementias are Alzheimer's disease and vascular dementia.

The diagnosis of these two syndromes is a complicated matter. A host of treatable problems, including other illnesses, reactions to medication, and depression, can mimic the symptoms of senile dementia. Furthermore, Alzheimer's disease is sometimes difficult to distinguish from vascular dementia. The courses of the two disorders are different: vascular dementia involves a stepwise deterioration, whereas in Alzheimer's the deterioration is smooth and gradual. But usually, when the patient comes for diagnosis, most of the course is in the future, and there is considerable overlap between the symptoms of the two disorders. As yet, there is no sure medical test for Alzheimer's disease; the disorder cannot be diagnosed conclusively until postmortem examination. To make matters worse, more than one-third of all dementia patients have *both* Alzheimer's and vascular de-

AIDS DEMENTIA

Ted is a 32-year-old man who is a talented artist. He has been Human Immunodeficiency Virus (HIV)–positive for 8 years. Two of his close friends have died during the last year from active AIDS. Ted has had AIDS-related complex (ARC) with weight loss, fever, night sweats, fatigue, depression, and generalized lymphadenopathy for 2 years without other serious medical problems. Six months ago he developed [pneumonia], which was treated successfully. Three months ago his lover, Randy, noted that Ted was becoming forgetful and had difficulty concentrating on his artwork. Gradually, his memory impairment worsened and he began to have problems painting. He described the problem to Randy, "I can't seem to make the brush go where I want it to go. My hands don't work right." Ted complained of a constant headache and depression. He became increasingly confused and finally, in frustration, stopped trying to paint. The diagnosis is Dementia Due to HIV Disease. (Fauman, 1994, p. 63)

This condition, better known as *AIDS dementia,* develops in about 15 percent of all those diagnosed with AIDS (acquired immunodeficiency syndrome). Often it appears in the late stages of the disease, but it may also occur as an early symptom, as in the above case (McArthur, Hoover, Bacellar, et al., 1993).

AIDS dementia is often related to infections due to other agents, not the HIV virus. The damage to the brain seems to be diffuse rather than confined to a single area. Since there is as yet no cure for HIV, there is also no way to reverse the damage it does to the brain. Indeed, the dementia usually gets progressively worse over months or years.

The early symptoms of AIDS dementia sometimes go unnoticed or are mistaken for other problems, physiological or psychological. At first patients seem forgetful, apathetic, withdrawn, and either depressed or anxious or both. Later, they become confused, disoriented, and uncoordinated. At this point the disorder is likely to be recognized as an organic brain syndrome. In the final stages, the patient may go blind, have seizures, become mute, and lapse into a coma (Holland & Tross, 1985).

Treatment of AIDS dementia first requires that any CNS diseases that may be contributing to the problem be treated. (Some patients, in addition to having HIV, have infections that can be cleared up with medication.) Drugs such as antidepressants and tranquilizers may relieve some of the symptoms. But, above all, people with AIDS dementia need a safe and structured environment and the help of friends, family members, and health-care workers such as home health aides. The patient may use memory aids (a list of numbers by the phone, a note by the door as a reminder to turn the lights off, etc.) to cope with forgetfulness. Helpers may be needed to take over such tasks as driving, shopping, and preparing meals. In the final stages of the disorder, however, the patient will usually have to be moved to a hospice or nursing home.

---

mentia. A final source of confusion is one we mentioned earlier: the symptoms in any individual case of organic brain disorder have everything to do with the patient's premorbid personality and psychosocial history, the availability of outside supports, and any number of other intangible factors. This is particularly true of the senile dementias. Two patients with the same disorder may behave quite differently.

Alzheimer's Disease The most common form of dementia, and one of the most tragic, is **Alzheimer's disease.** Autopsies of patients with this disorder reveal both *neurofibrillary tangles* (twisted and distorted nerve fibers) and *senile plaques* (microscopic lesions in the neurons). Alzheimer's can occur as early as age forty, but its prevalence increases with age. It is estimated that in the United States, 4 to 5 percent of people over age sixty-five, and 20 percent over eighty-five, suffer from Alzheimer's (Johansson & Zarit, 1995).

The primary symptoms of Alzheimer's disease are cognitive deficits—particularly loss of memory for recent events. An Alzheimer's patient may be able to tell you the names of all the people in the office where she worked fifty years ago, and all their children's names, but not what she ate for breakfast this morning. As the disease worsens, there is loss of memory for distant events as well. The characteristic early signs of the disease are irritability and failure of concentration and memory, with mild difficulty in recalling names and words. Patients may also have problems with perception and spatial orientation.

The cognitive deficits of Alzheimer's patients create major difficulties for them and their families (Zarit, Orr, & Zarit, 1985). Usually, complex behaviors such as playing poker or balancing the checkbook are disrupted first, but eventually simple daily behaviors such as bathing and dressing also degenerate. Patients may also do things that are disturbing or simply stressful to their caregivers. They may ask the same question over and over again; they may confuse night and day. Some forget that they have turned on the bath water or lit the stove; some wander off and get lost; some become violent. As they weaken physically, they are likely to become bedridden. By this point, they may have little awareness of their surroundings. The rate of progression of the disease is highly variable. In some people, severe impairment and death occur between three and five years after onset, while other patients live fifteen years or more after onset.

Cause One of the "hottest" areas of recent neuroscience research has been the genetics of Alzheimer's disease. Family patterns strongly suggest that the disorder is controlled in part by genes, but in a complex way, involving not just one genetic abnormality but several (Hardy, 1993). The normal human cell contains twenty-three pairs of chromosomes, each of which has been numbered and partially "mapped" as to which genes it contains. The first breakthroughs in genetic research on Alzheimer's had to do with chromosome 21. It is a well-documented fact that almost all people with Down syndrome (Chapter 18), a disorder caused by the addition of an extra copy of chromosome 21, develop Alzheimer's disease if they live past age forty (Zigman, Schupf, Zigman, et al., 1992). So Alzheimer's researchers were alerted to the possible involvement of chromosome 21, and their interest was further piqued by the discovery that the production of amyloid, the substance at the core of the senile plaques found in the brains of Alzheimer's patients, is controlled by genes on chromosome 21 (Goldgaber, Lerman, et al., 1987). Finally, in 1987 researchers at Massachusetts General Hospital announced that they had found abnormalities on chromosome 21 in four families with a long history—145 cases—of Alzheimer's disease (St. George-Hyslop, et al., 1987).

But efforts to replicate those findings were only partly successful. Today, while it is accepted that chromosome 21 may be involved in some cases of Alzheimer's, interest has shifted to two other chromosomes: chromosome 14, which is associated with early-onset (before-age-sixty) cases, and chromosome 19, which is implicated in many late-onset cases. But this is not the end of the story. The Germans of the Volga region and their American descendants, who have a strong inherited pattern of Alzheimer's, do not seem to show abnormalities at any of the identified sites on chromosomes 21, 14, or 19. So other chromosomes are probably involved as well.

To account for this heterogeneity, researchers have proposed the so-called amyloid-cascade hypothesis (Hardy, 1993). According to this hypothesis, the key element in the onset of Alzheimer's disease is the buildup of toxic levels of one kind of amyloid, beta amyloid, in the brain, but this buildup can be caused by the breakdown of any one of several different regulatory mechanisms, each controlled by a different gene. Researchers have discovered, for example, that beta-amyloid accumulations (and a high risk for Alzheimer's) are linked to variations in a protein, ApoE (apolipoprotein E), that is controlled by genes on chromosome 19 (Corder, Saunders, Strittmatter, et al., 1993). That protein, however, is only one element in the long chain of reactions that, according to the cascade theory, constitute the brain's processing of beta amyloid. So ApoE is one link that can break, in which case the fault lies on chromosome 19. But other links, controlled by other genes, may also break.

This is not the only biochemical theory. It has been proposed, for example, that Alzheimer's—together with Parkinson's disease and Huntington's chorea, which will be discussed later—is the product of "excitotoxicity," whereby, in response to stress, certain "excitatory" neurotransmitters (those whose role is to facilitate communication among neurons) are released in abnormally high amounts, killing the adjacent neurons. One support for this theory is the link between head injury and Alzheimer's. As noted earlier, head injury seems to increase the risk for Alzheimer's. Furthermore, victims of dementia pugilistica, which results from repeated head injury, show tissue damage similar to that of Alzheimer's patients: neurofibrillary tangles and certain characteristic protein deposits. It is possible, therefore, that brain trauma contributes to some cases of Alzheimer's (R. Taylor, 1991), but not all, for many Alzheimer's patients have no significant history of head injury.

So Alzheimer's is one of those disorders, like schizophrenia, for which researchers have identified multiple contributing factors but no single cause. And as with schizophrenia, many researchers feel that in any given case the causes probably are multiple. Gatz and her colleagues, for example, have proposed a "threshold model" for Alzheimer's whereby genetic risk together with any combination of other risk factors—head injury, exposure to toxic substances, alcohol abuse, poor nutrition, even lack of mental stimulation—gradually brings the person closer to a threshold beyond which symptoms begin to appear (Gatz, Lowe, Berg, et al., 1994).

Treatment It is known that in Alzheimer's disease the production of the neurotransmitter acetylcholine is disrupted. Therfore, presumably, the symptoms might be relieved if levels of acetylcholine could be raised. Following this reasoning, researchers developed a drug, tacrine—its brand name is Cognex—that blocks acetylcholine reuptake. The first drug specifically approved for treating Alzheimer's patients, Cognex went on the market in the early 1990s amid a great blast of publicity. The results have been disappointing, however. Only 20 to 30 percent of patients on Cognex show any benefits. Furthermore, the benefits are modest and, in some cases, transient (Farlow, Gracon, Hershey, et al., 1992). Other drug regimens—estrogen replacement in older women, anti-inflammatory drugs and other drugs that inhibit the immune system—are apparently related to a decreased risk for Alzheimer's, but these findings are still speculative. Researchers are now very intent on finding drugs to control and prevent Alzheimer's, but a great deal of work remains to be done.

At present, then, there is no cure and little treatment for this widespread disease. Behavioral therapy techniques may suppress some symptoms. Tranquilizers may also be useful, though in some patients they make the symptoms worse. The most common treatment is custodial care, often in a nursing home. Still, many patients are able to remain at home with their families, especially if the families can rely on professional support services. The development of such services (see the box on page 422) is one of the most hopeful avenues in the treatment of Alzheimer's disease.

Vascular Dementia As we saw earlier, an infarction is a kind of stroke in which blood flow in the brain becomes blocked, resulting in damage to the area of the brain fed by the blood vessels in question. (The damaged area is called an *infarct.*) **Vascular dementia** is the cumulative effect of a number of small strokes of this kind, eventually impairing many of the brain's faculties. The physical signs of vascular dementia are blackouts, heart problems, kidney failure, hypertension, and retinal sclerosis (a scarring of the retina of the eye). Common psychological symptoms are language and memory defects, emotional lability, and depression. Psychosis may also develop, typically with delusions of persecution. As noted, some of these symptoms overlap those of Alzheimer's, making diagnosis difficult.

Vascular dementia is second only to Alzheimer's as a cause of acquired intellectual impairment in the elderly. It occurs in about 3 percent of people over sixty-five (J. L. Cummings, 1987). An estimated 53 percent of stroke patients also go on to develop vascular dementia. The major risk factor for the disorder is high blood pressure. Eighty percent of vascular dementia patients have a history of hypertension. Other risk factors are diabetes, obesity, and smoking. Better control of these problems may help in the prevention of vascular dementia, but as with Alzheimer's, there is no cure. Once the damage has occurred, decline is irreversible.

Alzheimer's disease and vascular dementia are cortical and mixed cortical-subcortical disorders, respectively; nearly all of their victims are elderly. The degenerative disorders to which we now turn—Huntington's chorea and Parkinson's disease—fall into the subcortical category; their vic-

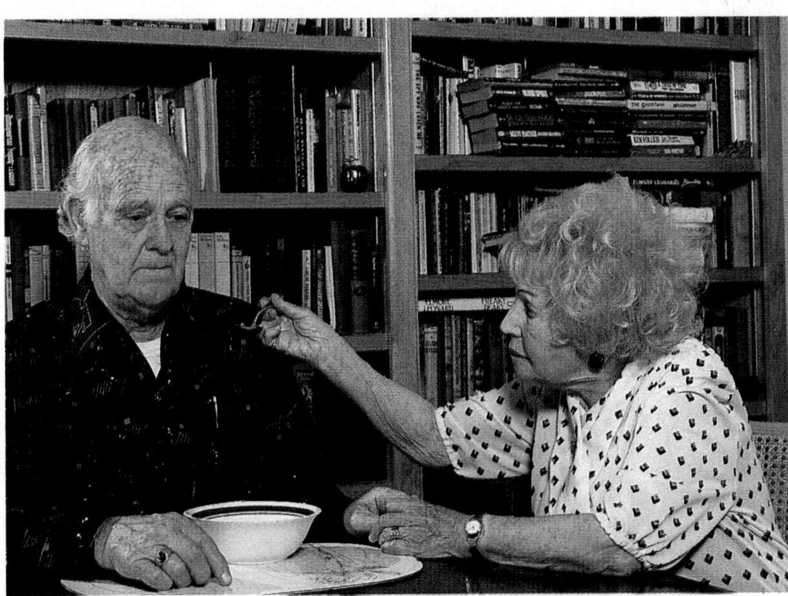

Alzheimer's is one of those degenerative disorders that inflicts ever-greater distress not only on the patient but also on those close to him or her—and often late in life, when it is harder to cope with a crisis.

CAREGIVERS: THE HIDDEN VICTIMS OF ALZHEIMER'S DISEASE

Caring for an Alzheimer's patient can be brutally taxing. What follows is the record of a typical day in the life of a young woman living with her husband, her seven-year-old son, and her grandmother, a dementia patient:

> The caregiver's day began at 5 A.M. when she got up and did light housekeeping chores. At 6, she prepared breakfast for her husband, and they had breakfast together. At 6:30, she woke her son up and began helping him get ready for school. From that time until 8, she either did chores or was with her son. At 8, she began the bathwater for her grandmother. Her grandmother got up at 8:15 and she asssisted her with her bath and then with dressing. At 8:45, she fixed breakfast for her grandmother and gave her medications. After breakfast, her grandmother sat in a rocker and watched television until about 10:15. During this time, she talked to an ornamental Santa Claus (it was a few days before Christmas), calling it by her great-grandson's name. The caregiver did not intervene and was not disturbed by this behavior. She was cleaning in the kitchen during this time. From 10:15 to 12, the caregiver did housekeeping chores and the patient followed her around. She asked repeatedly to go out and see Fred (her deceased husband). The caregiver made excuses why they could not go out, which satisfied the patient. She also gave the patient a snack during this period. At noon, the patient laid down on the couch and rested. The caregiver then did some laundry. Her grandmother called to her a few times during this period, and she would then go to her to tuck her in again.

The afternoon and evening followed the same pattern, except that the woman was now looking after her son as well as her grandmother and handling friction between the two. At one point,

> the patient became agitated because of the noise her great-grandson was making while playing, and she hit him on the head with a newspaper. The caregiver intervened, but the patient denied doing anything.

Finally, by 10:30 P.M., the woman got both the son and the grandmother into bed:

> From 11:10 to 11:20, the caregiver had a cup of tea and watched television. At 11:20, her husband came home, and she fixed him supper. They talked until 12:10 A.M. and then went to bed. At 2:00 A.M., her grandmother called for assistance to go to the bathroom, and then had difficulty going back to sleep. To calm her, the caregiver talked with her about Christmases they had spent together in the past when the caregiver was a child. At 2:30, they both went back to bed, and the caregiver slept until 5 A.M. (Zarit, 1992, pp. 3–15)

As noted, Alzheimer's patients may live for fifteen years or more after the onset of symptoms. Almost everyone agrees that the best situation for such patients is to remain with their families when possible, but this places a huge burden on the family. Even if patients are not agitated, as they often are, they still require constant supervision, and many of them sleep so little that they need something close to twenty-four-hour care.

In consequence, the family members suffer considerable stress (Gatz, Bengston, & Blum, 1991), and not just in the caregiving situation. They may have to give up their leisure activities and social lives; indeed, they may have to quit their jobs. (The woman in the above case did.) Or, if they go on working, they must struggle to divide their time between the requirements of the job and those of the patient, while their spare minutes are often spent arguing over the phone with other relatives over what should be done with the patient. Such a situation can lead to what researchers have called an "erosion of the self-concept" (Pearlin, Mullan, Semple, et al., 1990). The caregiver feels that he or she no longer has a self; it has been parceled out for use by others. Predictably, Alzheimer's caregivers are at higher-than-average risk for psychological disorders (Zarit, 1994). They also show lowered immune responses and are therefore more susceptible to physical disorders (Kiecolt-Glaser, Dura, Speicher, et al., 1991).

How can the caregivers be cared for? As soon as possible after the diagnosis of a degenerative brain disorder, the family members should meet with a professional who can advise them. This may be a psychologist, a social worker, or a representative of the Alzheimer's Association or another, similar organization. Such a professional can tell them what to expect as the disease progresses, teach them simple behavior-management techniques for coping with agitation, and direct them to services that can give them relief, such as adult day care and overnight respite care. (In the latter, the patient stays for short periods in a hospital or nursing home. This can free the family to take a vacation.) Legal and financial counseling is usually critical, so that families can plan how to manage the expense of caring for a dementia patient. And if there is conflict among the family members, as there typically is in this stressful situation, they can be referred for family counseling, which is often very effective for relatives of dementia patients (Mittelman, Ferris, Steinberg, et al., 1993; Whitlatch, Zarit, & von Eye, 1991).

Finally, caregivers can join a support group. As we will see in Chapter 20, support groups have been found to be very helpful to people with a wide range of problems—cancer patients, drug abusers, families of drug abusers, and so on. They can also be useful to families of dementia patients, providing them with tips, fellowship, and the kind of understanding that can come only from people in the same situation.

tims may be middle-aged or, in the case of Huntington's, young adults.

Huntington's Chorea **Huntington's chorea** is one of the very few neurological disorders definitely known to be transmitted genetically. It is passed on by a dominant gene from either parent to both male and female children. Forty to seventy cases of Huntington's chorea have been estimated to occur in every 1 million people (J. L. Cummings & Benson, 1992).

The primary site of the damage that causes Huntington's chorea is the basal ganglia, clusters of nerve-cell bodies located deep within the cerebral hemispheres and responsible primarily for posture, muscle tonus, and motor coordination. However, the first signs of the disease are not so much motor impairments as vague behavioral and emotional changes. In the typical case, the person becomes slovenly and rude, and his or her moods become unpredictable and inconsistent, running the gamut from obstinacy, passivity, and depression to inexplicable euphoria. Intellectual functions, particularly memory and judgment, are also disrupted. As the disease progresses, delusions, hallucinations, and suicidal tendencies commonly appear (Boll, Heaton, & Reitan, 1974).

In addition to developing these psychological problems, the patient will eventually begin to show the characteristic motor symptoms—an involuntary, spasmodic jerking of the limbs—to which the term *chorea* (from the Greek *choreia,* meaning "dance") refers. This sign appears to indicate irreversible brain damage (W. E. James, Mefford, & Kimbell, 1969). From then on, patients show increasingly bizarre behavior. They may spit, bark out words (often obscenities) explosively, walk with a jerky or shuffling gait, and smack their tongues and lips involuntarily. Eventually they lose control of bodily functions altogether. Death is the inevitable result, occurring, on average, fourteen years after onset.

Huntington's chorea is a genetic disorder, and the defective gene has been identified. There is now a test that can identify carriers, and it may eventually be possible, through genetic engineering, to treat them before symptoms develop.

Eugene O'Neill (1888–1953), widely regarded as the greatest American playwright, wrote *The Iceman Cometh* and *Long Day's Journey into Night.* His career ended abruptly when he was stricken with Parkinson's disease at age sixty. He lived five years more, increasingly incapacitated by tremors, depression, and hallucinations.

Parkinson's Disease First described in 1871 by James Parkinson (who suffered from it), **Parkinson's disease** also involves damage to the basal ganglia, particularly the region known as the substantia nigra. The cause of this condition is unknown, although it has been attributed to a variety of factors, including heredity, encephalitis, viruses, toxins, deficient brain metabolism, head trauma, and, as with Alzheimer's and Huntington's chorea, excitotoxicity. The illness occurs most frequently in people between the ages of fifty and seventy.

The primary symptom of Parkinson's is tremor, occurring at a rate of about four to eight movements per second. The tremors are usually present during rest periods, but tend to diminish or cease when the patient is sleeping. Interestingly, patients can often stop the tremors if someone orders them to do so, and for a short time they may even be able to perform motor activities requiring very fine muscular coordination. Such remissions are always temporary, however, and the patient once again lapses into the typical rhythmic jerking of arms, hands, jaws, and/or head.

Another highly characteristic sign of Parkinson's is an expressionless, masklike countenance, probably due to difficulties initiating movement and slowed motor responses. Parkinson's patients also tend to walk, when they *can* walk, with a distinctive slow, stiff gait, usually accompanied by a slight crouch.

Approximately 40 to 60 percent of Parkinson's disease patients also experience psychological disturbances. These include problems with memory, learning, judgment, and concentration, as well as apathy and social withdrawal. As many as half of Parkinson's patients also develop dementia. In more severe cases there may be highly systematized delusions and severe depression, including suicidal tendencies. However, it is difficult to determine whether these symptoms are due directly to the brain pathology or simply to patients' distress over their physical helplessness.

Parkinson's is unusual among degenerative disorders in that it can be treated with some success. The substantia nigra is involved in dopamine synthesis, so when this area degenerates in the course of Parkinson's, the patient's dopamine levels drop. Drugs that increase the amount of dopamine can in most cases control the tremor and other motor symptoms for several years, though they cannot cure the disease. Unfortunately, the beneficial effects of these medications decline with long-term use.

Delirium Delirium differs from the other organic brain disorders that we have described in that it remits quickly, leaving most patients unharmed. It is very dramatic, however. **Delirium** is a transient, global disorder of cognition and attention. Delirious patients are profoundly confused. Their thinking is disorganized, even dreamlike. In about half of all cases, hallucinations and delusions (usually of persecution) are present, and when they are, patients may harm themselves or others as they attempt to escape or fight the imagined enemy. Some patients are hyperalert, others lethargic and drowsy, and these disturbances extend to the sleep cycle. Patients are often drowsy during the day and awake and agitated at night. Emotional lability is common, running the gamut from apathy to the extremes of fear or rage. The onset of delirium is sudden, and its severity fluctuates during the course of the day. (Most patients are worse at night.) In the typical case, the delirium passes within a month, recovery is complete, and the patient is partially or totally amnesic for the whole episode.

Delirium is caused by a widespread disruption of cerebral metabolism and neurotransmission. It is a common condition in older people, and when it strikes the elderly, the cause is often intoxication from medication, even ordinary medication in prescribed doses. (Older people may respond to drugs very differently from the young.) Another common cause is surgery. Surgery produces delirium in 10 to 15 percent of older patients (Seymour, 1986), and certain kinds of surgery pose a far greater risk. (Heart surgery provokes delirium in 24 to 32 percent of older patients.) Other causes are withdrawal from alcohol or other drugs, head injury, sleep loss, malnutrition, and psychological stress, such as the death of a spouse or relocation to a nursing home.

A final common cause is physical illness, such as heart attack or pneumonia, of which delirium is often the main presenting symptom in the elderly. To quote one expert, "Acute confusion [delirium] is a far more common herald of the onset of physical illness in an older person than are, for example, fever, pain, or tachycardia" (Hodkinson, 1976). For this reason, it is very important that the delirium not be misdiagnosed. It is often mistaken for dementia, particularly in patients who already have dementia. (As with other organic brain disorders, these two can coexist in the same patient.) But if delirium is not recognized as such, the possibility of underlying physical illness will be ignored, perhaps with fatal results. The treatment of delirium is the removal of its cause—withdrawal of the intoxicating medication, treatment of the underlying physical illness, or whatever. Patients who are agitated may also be given sedatives (Lipowsky, 1989).

Nutritional Deficiency

Malnutrition—or, specifically, insufficient intake of one or more essential vitamins—can result in neurological damage and consequently in psychological disturbances. Two common syndromes in less industrialized nations are beriberi, due to thiamine deficiency, and pellagra, due to niacin deficiency, but improvements in diet have largely eliminated these conditions from the American population. More commonly seen in this country is Korsakoff's psychosis.

Korsakoff's Psychosis Victims of **Korsakoff's psychosis,** which is considered irreversible, invariably have a history of alcoholism. Alcoholics have notoriously bad diets, and it is generally agreed that the primary pathology in this disorder is due to a deficiency of vitamin B_1, or thiamine (Brion, 1969; Redlich & Freedman, 1966).

There are two classic behavioral signs of Korsakoff's psychosis, anterograde amnesia and confabulation. *Anterograde amnesia* is the inability to incorporate new memories, and *confabulation* is the tendency to fill in memory gaps with invented stories. In response to questioning, for example, patients may placidly offer a nonsensical account of why they are in the hospital, if indeed they admit

In an odd coincidence, both President George Bush and his wife, Barbara, developed the thyroid disorder known as Graves' disease. When their dog, Millie, began exhibiting some of the same symptoms, speculation arose (but was later discredited) that something in the White House water supply might have been responsible.

that the place is a hospital. Such patients usually seem calm and affable, while at the same time their total unawareness of the fantastic quality of their stories reveals a psychotic impairment of judgment. This impairment gradually spreads to other aspects of psychological functioning. In addition to having these memory deficits, many alcoholics experience a more generalized intellectual decline. Like the degenerative diseases discussed above, chronic alcoholism can lead to deficits in most cognitive abilities (J. L. Cummings & Benson, 1992).

Endocrine Disorders

The **endocrine glands** are responsible for the production of hormones. When released into the bloodstream, the hormones affect various bodily mechanisms, such as sexual functions, physical growth and development, and the availability of energy. Disturbances in the endocrine system, and particularly in the thyroid and adrenal glands, can give rise to a variety of psychological disorders.

Thyroid Syndromes Overactivity of the thyroid gland—a condition called *hyperthyroidism,* or *Graves' disease*—involves an excessive secretion of the hormone thyroxin, which gives rise to a variety of physical and psychological difficulties. Psychological symptoms accompanying the disorder may include severe apprehension and agitation, hallucinations, excessive motor activity, sweating, and other symptoms suggestive of anxiety. Former president George Bush and his wife, Barbara, both suffer from Graves' disease.

Opposite to hyperthyroidism in both cause and effect is *hypothyroidism,* sometimes referred to as *myxedema,* in which underactivity of the thyroid gland results in deficient production of thyroxin. Hypothyroidism may be due to iodine deficiency, a problem that has become much less common in the United States since the advent of iodized table salt. People suffering from hypothyroidism are frequently sluggish, have difficulties with memory and concentration, and appear to be lethargic and depressed. Again, however, symptomatology depends greatly on premorbid personality. The same is true of hyperthyroidism.

Adrenal Syndromes Chronic underactivity of the cortex, or outer layer, of the adrenal glands gives rise to *Addison's disease,* which involves both physical and psychological changes. Again, the psychological symptoms vary considerably according to the person's premorbid adjustment. Some patients just seem moderately depressed; others experience debilitating extremes of depression, anxiety, and irritability. Appropriate medication can relieve the symptoms of even a severe case of Addison's disease, restoring the person to normal functioning.

When the adrenal cortex is excessively active, several disorders may arise, one of which is *Cushing's syndrome.* This relatively rare disorder usually affects young women. Like the other endocrine disorders, Cushing's syndrome involves both physical symptoms—in this case, obesity and muscle weakness—and psychological difficulties, especially extreme emotional lability, with fluctuations in mood ranging from total indifference to violent hostility.

Toxic Disorders

Various plants, gases, drugs, and metals, when ingested or absorbed through the skin, can have a toxic, or poisonous, effect on the brain. Depending on the person, the toxic substance, and the amount ingested, the results of such brain poisoning range from temporary physical and emotional distress to psychosis and death. One sign that is almost always present in the toxic disorders is delirium.

Lead An especially tragic form of toxic brain disorder is lead poisoning. The excessive ingestion of lead causes a condition called **lead encephalopathy,** in which fluid accumulates in the brain, causing extreme pressure. Early symptoms include abdominal pains, constipation, facial pallor, and sometimes convulsions and bizarre behaviors such as hair pulling. In severe cases, the symptoms may be similar to those of psychosis, including hallucinations. The most common victims of lead poisoning are children, who may become mentally retarded as a result.

In recent years, consumer advocacy groups have identified a number of sources of lead contamination, including old lead-lined water pipes, lead-based paint on children's toys and furniture, old plaster walls, candles with lead-core wicks, certain electric tea kettles that release lead from soft solder joints when heated, pottery glazes from which foods that contain acetic acid (e.g., grape juice) can leach lead, exhaust from automobiles that burn leaded gasoline, and industrial pollution. As may be seen from this list, the issue of metal poisoning often involves a conflict between the needs of industry and the needs of the person.

Other Heavy-Metal Toxins The "industry versus the individual" conflict also crops up in two of the more common varieties of heavy-metal poisoning, mercury and manganese poisoning. Victims of these toxic disorders are usually those whose jobs bring them into close daily contact with mercury and manganese. However, other victims are simply unwitting citizens whose food or air has been contaminated by industrial wastes containing metallic toxins. One notorious source of such poisoning is fish taken from waters polluted by mercury wastes from nearby factories. In Japan, thousands of people have been permanently paralyzed and brain-damaged as a result of eating mercury-contaminated fish (Kurland, Faro, & Siedler, 1960).

Early signs of brain damage due to mercury poisoning are memory loss, irritability, and difficulty in concentration. As the disease progresses, the individual typically develops tunnel vision (i.e., loss of peripheral vision), faulty motor coordination, and difficulty in speaking and hearing. In extreme cases, these symptoms lead to paralysis, coma, and death. Manganese poisoning is manifested in motor and speech impairments, restlessness, and emotional instability. Some experts believe that the personality changes that accompany both types of poisoning are often simply pathological exaggerations of the individual's premorbid personality traits.

Psychoactive Drugs As we saw in Chapter 12, abuse of psychoactive drugs such as alcohol, opiates, and amphetamines can cause severe psychological disturbances. Other drugs have also been implicated in brain damage. In recent years, for example, the inhalation of aerosol gases and fumes of certain glues has become a popular "high" among adolescents. Unfortunately, the toxins in these gases and fumes tend to accumulate in the users' vital organs and can cause permanent damage not only to the liver and kidney but also to the brain, resulting in psychological deterioration and, in extreme cases, death.

Carbon Monoxide Carbon monoxide, an odorless, tasteless, and invisible gas usually inhaled with automobile exhaust fumes, combines with the hemoglobin in the blood in such a way as to prevent the blood from absorbing oxygen. The usual result of this process is a swift and rather painless death, which makes carbon monoxide inhalation a favored means of suicide. Patients who survive, however, suffer a number of psychological consequences, typically including apathy, confusion, and memory defects. While these symptoms may clear up within two years, some patients suffer permanent mental damage (Kolb, 1982).

THE EPILEPSIES

Approximately 0.6 percent of Americans suffer from the disease called epilepsy (Hauser & Hesdorfer, 1990). **Epilepsy,** actually, is a broad term covering a range of disorders. In all of them, however, the primary symptom is spontaneous seizures caused by a disruption of the electrical and physiological activity of the brain cells. This abnormal activity, which can usually be documented by an EEG recording, in turn disrupts the functions controlled by that part of the brain.

Causes of Epilepsy

Any condition that interferes with the brain's functioning, altering brain-wave patterns, can provoke epilepsy. This may happen at any time in life, beginning with prenatal life. People with severe seizures often have a history of trauma or anoxia (oxygen deprivation) at birth. But the most common cause is head injury (Meinardi & Pachlatko, 1991). This linkage is probably due in part to the fact that most cases of epilepsy have their onset

Glue sniffing offers a fast, cheap high to these street children in Lima, Peru, but it can cause lasting brain damage as well.

during childhood or adolescence—a period in which, as we noted earlier, there is a high risk for head injury. When epilepsy begins in middle age, a more likely cause is brain tumor; when it strikes in older age, it is often due to one of the cerebral vascular diseases that older people are prone to, such as stroke or cerebral arteriosclerosis (Annegers, 1993).

Cases such as these, in which the origin of the seizures can be identified, are known as **symptomatic epilepsy.** More common in the general population (Meinardi & Pachlatko, 1991), however, is **idiopathic epilepsy,** epilepsy in which the origin of the seizures is unknown. In many idiopathic cases, there is a family history of seizures, so genetic factors are probably involved (V. E. Anderson & Hauser, 1991).

Types of Seizures

There are two basic categories of seizures. The first is **partial seizures,** which originate in one part of the brain rather than in the brain as a whole. In a **simple partial seizure,** cognitive functioning remains intact. The person may experience sensory changes, such as stomach trouble or a strange smell, and/or motor symptoms on one side of the body. (For example, the fingers on one hand may start twitching.) Some people also report minor psychological changes, such as hearing a tune repeat itself again and again in their heads. But even in the midst of the seizure the person can still speak, understand speech, and think straight.

By contrast, a **complex partial seizure,** the most common form of seizure (Annegers, 1993), does interrupt cognitive functioning. Such attacks are often preceded by an *aura,* or warning, which the person may be able to describe only in vague terms (e.g., "a funny feeling"). Then, as the seizure begins, the person can no longer engage in purposeful activity and does not respond normally. What he or she does instead is highly variable. Some patients seem to fall into a stupor; others engage in *automatisms,* repetitive, purposeless movements such as fumbling with their clothes; others have been known to break into a run. But whatever the activity, the person is not thinking normally, nor can he or she speak coherently. Complex partial seizures usually last more than ten seconds, often for several minutes. They are sometimes called "temporal-lobe seizures" because they tend to arise in the temporal lobe, but they can originate in other parts of the brain as well.

While partial seizures begin and often remain in only one part of the brain, **generalized seizures,** the second major category of epileptic seizures, either involve the entire brain at the outset (primary generalized seizures) or soon spread from one part to the whole brain (secondary generalized seizures). Among the primary type are **absence seizures,** previously called *petit mal* ("little illness"). These attacks are usually seen in children rather than in adults. Absence seizures come without warning and typically last only a few seconds. During that period, children with these seizures seem to absent themselves from their surroundings. Their faces may take on a "spaced-out" look; they stop moving and speaking; if spoken to, they cannot respond. Then, as abruptly as it started, the seizure ends, whereupon some children are confused while others, unaware of what has happened, simply resume whatever they were doing before.

Feodor Dostoevsky, the Russian novelist, suffered from tonic-clonic seizures, as does the hero of his novel *The Idiot,* Prince Myshkin.

Tonic-clonic seizures, found in both children and adults, are another type of generalized seizure. Sometimes heralded by an aura, these attacks typically begin with a tonic, or rigid, extension of the arms and legs. This is followed by a clonic, or jerking, movement throughout the body. The jerking gradually diminishes until the attack ends, at which point the person usually feels confused and sleepy. People can bang their heads or otherwise harm themselves during a tonic-clonic seizure, so hard objects should be moved out of the way, if possible. The only other way bystanders can help people having such seizures is to move them onto their sides, so that if they vomit, the vomit will not back up into the air passages. (Contrary to popular wisdom, one should not put anything into their mouths to prevent them from swallowing their tongues; people cannot swallow their tongues.) Once known as *grand mal* ("great illness") seizures, tonic-clonic seizures are the most dramatic form of epileptic attack, and they are what most people think of when they think of epilepsy, though they are not the most common type.

Seizures starting in one part of the brain may spread to other parts. A simple partial seizure may develop into a complex partial seizure; a complex partial seizure, into a generalized tonic-clonic attack. In the latter case, the attack may look very much like a primary tonic-clonic seizure, but it is important for diagnosticians to distinguish between them, because each requires a different kind of drug.

Psychological Factors in Epilepsy

It is not just during seizures that the epilepsy disrupts the brain's functioning. Even between seizures, irregular brain waves often persist, interfering with concentration and learning. The most common complaint of people with epilepsy is that they have poor memories. This is no doubt due to the fact that most epilepsies involve the temporal lobes, and related structures, and these are the areas of the brain most related to memory. Despite these difficulties, however, many patients perform quite well in life, and some show great achievements. Julius Caesar, Fyodor Dostoyevsky, and Vincent van Gogh all reportedly suffered from epilepsy.

It was once thought that there was such a thing as an "epileptic personality." But in view of the fact that people with epilepsy have widely different kinds of seizures, beginning at different ages and occurring with different frequencies, there is little reason to believe that they would have similar personality traits. In any case, there are no data to support such a claim. People with epilepsy do share problems that other people do not face. Consider the following firsthand account of a tonic-clonic attack by the writer Margiad Evans:

> The food was on the table, the oil-stove lit. I picked up the coffee percolator to fill it. Just as I reached the sink and was standing in the doorway, I found I could not move, could not remember what I wanted to do. It seemed a long time that I stood there (actually perhaps a few seconds) saying to myself, "This is nothing. It will be all right in a moment and I shall remember *all the rest.*" Then I felt my head beginning to jerk backwards and my face to grimace. Then the percolator fell from my hand into the sink. But still some dogged part of me kept saying, "All this is really controllable." I was still conscious and felt violent gestures and spasms were shooting all over me, even till I felt my knees give and I fell down on the concrete floor. As I went, it shot through me, the astonishment: "As bad as this then?"
>
> The next thing I remember was the B______s' kitchen and Betty B______ . . . giving me tea and talking to me in the tone mothers use to little children coming out of nightmares. (quoted in B. Kaplan, 1964, pp. 346–347)

Such an experience, even if the person has had it many times, is nonetheless unsettling, and damaging to self-esteem. Therefore it is no surprise that people with epilepsy are more prone to anxiety and depression than the general population (Dodrill, 1992).

Treatment

Almost all people with diagnosed seizure disorders take antiepileptic drugs, most commonly Depakote, Dilatin, Tegretol, or phenobarbital. If used as prescribed, these drugs suppress seizures in about 80 percent of patients (Richens & Perucca, 1993). Many patients also report side effects—notably, slowed movements and a general feeling of being "drugged down." Antiepileptic medication is designed to alter the functioning of the nervous system so as to prevent seizures; if it also affects other behaviors, such as fully normal motor responses, that is not surprising. But side effects can often be reduced if the medication is taken correctly (Dodrill, 1993).

When drugs are not successful in controlling the seizures, surgery may be recommended. The most common type of surgery involves the removal of the focal epileptic area, the area where the attacks are known to originate. But this type of surgery can be done only when the area is focal: known and limited. (Thus the seizures must be partial rather than generalized.) Furthermore, the focal area must be one that can be removed without major damage to the person's mental faculties. Epilepsy surgery is becoming more common, but it is still performed on no more than perhaps one out of a hundred patients. Of these, 40 to 80 percent are seizure-free after surgery (J. Engel, Van Ness, Rasmussen, et al., 1993), and many report dramatic improvements in their lives as a result.

KEY TERMS

absence seizures (427)
agnosia (410)
Alzheimer's disease (419)
aphasia (409)
apraxia (410)
brain trauma (412)
brain tumors (417)
catastrophic reaction (416)
cerebral abscess (411)
cerebrovascular accident (CVA) (416)
complex partial seizure (427)
concussion (413)
contusion (413)
degenerative disorders (418)
delirium (424)
dementia (418)
embolism (416)
encephalitis (411)
endocrine glands (425)
epilepsy (426)
general paresis (412)
generalized seizures (427)
hemorrhage (416)
Huntington's chorea (423)
idiopathic epilepsy (427)
infarction (416)
Korsakoff's psychosis (424)
laceration (415)
lead encephalopathy (426)
meningitis (411)
metastatic brain tumors (417)
neurosyphilis (411)
organic brain disorders (406)
Parkinson's disease (423)
partial seizures (427)
primary brain tumors (417)
senile dementias (418)
simple partial seizure (427)
stroke (416)
symptomatic epilepsy (427)
thrombosis (416)
tonic-clonic seizures (428)
traumatic delirium (413)
vascular dementia (421)

SUMMARY

- Unlike most disorders discussed in this book, which have largely psychogenic causes, the organic brain disorders are directly caused by destruction of brain tissue or by biochemical imbalances in the brain.
- There are four main problems in diagnosing organic brain disorders: (1) Is the disorder in fact organic? (2) If so, what is causing the disorder? (3) What part of the brain is damaged? (4) How are psychosocial factors influencing symptoms, and can they be modified?
- There are six major symptoms of organic brain disorder: impairments of orientation, of memory, of general intellectual functions, and of judgment; emotional lability or shallowness; and loss of mental and emotional resilience. The similarity of many of these symptoms to those of psychogenic disorders makes a correct diagnosis very difficult. This difficulty in diagnosis increases with the age of the patient. Since the most stressful changes of a person's life generally occur after age sixty-five—such as retirement, poverty, loneliness, and physical change—depression and anxiety are very common among the elderly. However, these disorders are sometimes misdiagnosed as organic disorders, and vice versa.
- Often it is more difficult to diagnose a specific organic disorder than to distinguish between biogenic and psychogenic disorders. The symptoms of different biogenic disorders can be very similar, and the same disorder can produce different symptoms on the basis of its location in the brain. Other factors, including psychosocial conditions, can also affect the symptoms of the disorder. For some disorders, treatment depends on the location of damage in the brain. Physiological tests and a patient's symptoms and behaviors are used to isolate the damage.
- In some organic disorders, the symptoms are focal, that is, they are restricted to a certain aspect of be-

havior. Focal symptoms include aphasia, apraxia, and agnosia. If it is known which region of the brain controls the impaired behavior, the location of the injury can be determined.

- There are four main forms of cerebral infection. In a cerebral abscess, an infection becomes encapsulated within the brain. Encephalitis is an inflammation of the brain. Meningitis is an inflammation of the meninges, the covering of the brain and spinal cord. Neurosyphilis is the deterioration of brain tissue caused by the disease syphilis when it is untreated.
- Brain trauma, physical injury to brain tissue, is the leading cause of disability and death in children and young adults. There are several forms of brain trauma: concussion, contusion, and laceration. In a concussion, a blow to the head jars the brain, often causing a brief loss of consciousness. A contusion is a bruise on the brain tissue, generally resulting in a coma of several hours or days. In a laceration, a foreign object enters and destroys brain tissue. Consequences vary depending on the location of damage, ranging from a noninterruption of the patient's daily life to death.
- Cerebrovascular accidents (CVAs), or strokes, result from a blockage or break of a blood vessel in the brain. The two main types of strokes are infarction and hemorrhage. In an infarction, the brain's blood supply is cut off due to a thrombosis or an embolism. A hemorrhage occurs when a blood vessel in the brain ruptures. The effects of a stroke depend on the location and extent of the damage to the brain. There may be no noticeable effects or only slight effects such as tingling in a limb, or the results can be more serious, including paralysis and death. Risk of a stroke increases with age, because of the increased prevalence of conditions which weaken blood vessels.
- There are two types of brain tumors: metastatic tumors, which originate elsewhere in the body and spread to the brain, and primary tumors, which originate in the brain. Symptoms of brain tumors begin with headaches and visual problems, and the patient gradually develops abnormal reflexes, disorientation, and an inability to concentrate. If not treated with surgery or radiation, the patient will experience physical distress and personality changes and will die.
- Degenerative disorders are characterized by a general deterioration of intellectual, emotional, and motor functioning. Symptoms vary depending on the site of the damage. Degenerative disorders include Alzheimer's disease, Huntington's chorea, Parkinson's disease, and vascular dementia.
- AIDS dementia, a degenerative disorder sometimes seen in AIDS patients, is often related to infections due to other agents, not the HIV virus.
- Nearly all elderly people experience psychological changes as a function of aging. Generally, functions controlled by the central nervous system slow down as the body ages. A small percentage of the aged suffer from dementia, severe mental deterioration. The most common dementias experienced by the elderly are Alzheimer's disease and vascular dementia. Alzheimer's disease is characterized by a loss of memory for recent events and eventually loss of memory for long-past events. It is believed that Alzheimer's disease is at least partially controlled genetically, though it is probably a combination of circumstances that brings about the actual disease. Alzheimer's patients require almost constant care, which places a huge burden on the caregivers—often the patient's family. Vascular dementia is the cumulative effect of a number of small strokes. Its symptoms resemble those of Alzheimer's, and it is most common among the elderly, particularly those with high blood pressure.
- Huntington's chorea is a genetically transmitted degenerative disease involving damage to the brain's basal ganglia. Symptoms begin with mood changes and result in paralysis and death. Parkinson's disease, also resulting from damage to the basal ganglia, is characterized by tremors and slowed motor responses. Treatment with drugs can control symptoms but cannot cure the disease.
- Delirium is a transient, global disorder of cognition and attention. Delirious patients are confused and disoriented and may hallucinate. Deliriums generally subside within a month, resulting in a complete recovery.
- Malnutrition, specifically vitamin deficiency, can lead to neurological damage. Patients with Korsakoff's psychosis suffer from memory deficits. The disease is commonly associated with alcoholism.
- Disturbances in the endocrine system can produce many psychological problems. Thyroid syndromes, resulting from a malfunctioning thyroid gland, include hyperthyroidism and hypothyroidism. Abnormalities in the adrenal glands may give rise to Addison's disease and Cushing's syndrome.
- Toxic substances absorbed into the body may cause brain damage, ranging from temporary emotional distress to death. Toxic disorders almost always produce delirium. Lead and other heavy metals, some psychoactive drugs, and carbon monoxide all are toxic agents which may cause brain damage.
- The epilepsies are characterized by sudden seizures caused by a disruption of activity in brain cells. While in some cases the cause of epilepsy can be determined (usually a head injury or brain tumor), generally the origin of the seizures is unknown. There are two broad types of seizures: partial seizues, which start in only a portion of the brain, and generalized seizures, which involve the entire brain. The most common form, a complex partial seizure, interrupts cognitive functioning for up to several minutes. Between seizures, epileptics often complain of poor memories. Though the disease can interfere with concentration and learning, many epileptics are capable of leading productive lives. Most epileptics are treated with drugs which suppress seizures. If the drug treatment is unsuccessful, surgery can sometimes be performed to control the seizures.

PART FIVE

DEVELOPMENTAL DISORDERS

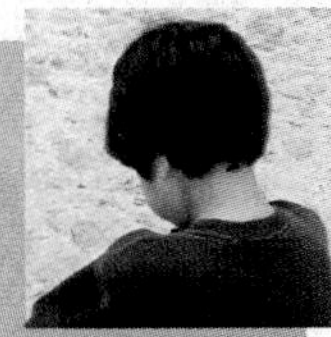

CHAPTER 17

DISORDERS OF CHILDHOOD AND ADOLESCENCE

CHAPTER 18

MENTAL RETARDATION AND AUTISM

17

DISORDERS OF CHILDHOOD AND ADOLESCENCE

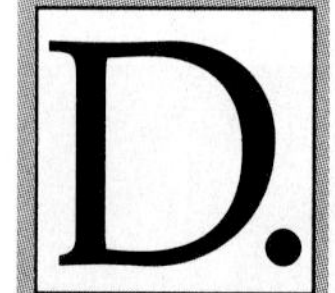

J., a five-year-old boy, was referred for treatment by his kindergarten teacher because, among other problems, he soiled his pants almost every day at school. Aside from the burden this placed on the teacher, it caused the child to be teased and excluded by the other children.

D.J.'s home situation was tense and chaotic. He was one of five children, ranging in age from nine years to six months. Both parents were employed full-time, the father working during the day and caring for the children at night, the mother taking the opposite shift. They were badly pressed financially and could not afford child care. During the interview with the parents, the mother appeared depressed. She complained of constant fatigue, and she said she had been plagued by crying spells since the birth of the last child. The father was merely angry over the school's "meddling." In his view, D.J.'s problem was minor and reflected his boredom with the school program.

The developmental history revealed that D.J. had never fully achieved bowel control. His early toilet training was disrupted by various upheavals in the family. (They moved several times; the father was laid off and then held several temporary jobs; two more babies were born.) Since that time the parents had tried various approaches to D.J.'s soiling—yelling, spanking, sitting the child on the toilet after meals, sometimes for as long as two hours—but to no avail. The parents claimed that in addition to soiling, D.J. was disobedient and aggressive at home. A medical examination revealed no organic problems. (K. Bierman, Pennsylvania State University, personal files)

The disorders of childhood and adolescence include a wide range of problems. Some, such as soiling in the above case, involve a failure to pass a developmental milestone "on time." Others, such as stuttering, involve a disruption of a developmentally acquired skill. Still others are simply psychological disorders that normally have their onset prior to adulthood (e.g., anorexia nervosa) or that afflict children as well as adults (e.g., depression).

Why must the disorders of childhood and adolescence be studied apart from adult disorders? To begin with, many of them have little counterpart in adult psychopathology. (Even when they do parallel adult disorders, and bear the same name, as in the case of depression, they manifest themselves differently in children.) But it is not just that children have different disorders; the entire phenomenon of psychological disturbance is different in children from what it is in adults. In the assessment of adult disorders, for example, age is a relatively unimportant matter, whereas it is crucial in the assessment of troubled children and adolescents. A two-year-old who assaults the new baby in the house is acting normally; a ten-year-old who does the same thing is not.

A second difference has to do with the question of what is normal. The period from infancy through adolescence involves so many rapid changes that the most stable of children may develop temporary psychological problems. It is often difficult for parents to decide when such problems require treatment. The lines between normal and abnormal are further blurred by the conflicting perceptions of parents, teachers, and doctors and by shifting cultural norms. Many parents and doctors today are fairly relaxed about masturbation, for example, but a few generations ago a child who masturbated was considered at risk for serious problems.

Third, the disorders of childhood and adolescence differ in course and outcome from adult psychological disorders. The less severe childhood disorders are often transitory. Children are more likely than adults, for example, to recover from phobias. This is partly because children change so rapidly and partly because they are so dependent on and responsive to their social environment.

Finally, unlike many troubled adults, most children do not think of themselves as having treatable psychological disorders. Even though they may be very upset by their problems, they do not ordinarily seek therapy. If they get it, they do so through the intervention of adults. Therefore it is important for adults to be able to recognize the disturbances that children are prone to.

We begin with general issues in childhood and adolescent psychopathology: the prevalence of the disorders, their classification and diagnosis, and their long-term consequences. Then we turn to the individual disorders. Finally, we will examine the various theories and treatments of these disorders.

ISSUES IN CHILDHOOD PSYCHOPATHOLOGY

Prevalence

We do not know exactly how many children and adolescents in the United States have serious psychological problems, but according to some estimates, one out of every four children has some form of disorder (Bergeron, Valla, & Breton, 1992; P. Cohen, Cohen, Kasen, et al., 1993), and one out of every five has a moderate or severe disorder (Brandenburg, Friedman, & Silver, 1990). When do the troubles begin? Are problems likely to surface at some ages rather than others? Surveys of mental health clinics show that admission rates begin to increase gradually at about age six or seven—a fact that is probably related to school entry. Problems that can be ignored or endured at home may not be tolerated in the classroom, and teachers, in general, are more prone than parents to conclude that a child needs treatment. Furthermore, starting school may itself be stressful enough to create or aggravate psychological problems. Until adolescence, psychological disturbance in general is more common in boys than in girls (M. Rutter, 1986)—a difference that is not yet clearly understood. In the case of some disorders, notably the disruptive disorders (see below), boys are as much as ten times more vulnerable. In adolescence, however, the girls dominate certain categories. Anorexia nervosa is primarily a girls' disorder, and teenage girls are more than twice as likely as boys to experience disorders of emotional distress (P. Cohen, Cohen, Kasen, et al., 1993).

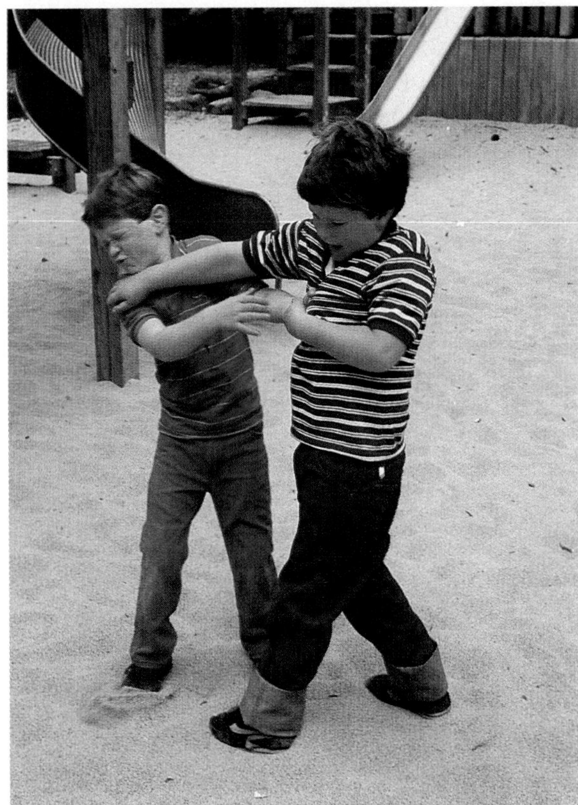

The diagnosis of a childhood psychlogical disorder depends not only on the kind of behavior involved but on the age of the child. An occasional outburst of aggression is normal in young children, but by adolescence such behavior may well be a sign of disorder.

Classification and Diagnosis

In *DSM-IV,* disorders of childhood and adolescence, like adult disorders, are classified by syndromes, with the hope that this will help to relate individual cases to other, similar cases. An alternative classification method involves grouping together those preadult problems that tend to occur together in the same children or the same age groups. This is called the *empirical method,* because it was developed by asking parents, teachers, and clinicians to fill out checklists describing the types of problems experienced by children at different ages.

Empirical studies indicate that there are four major categories of childhood and adolescent disorders. First are the disruptive behavior disorders, involving impulsive, aggressive, and other kinds of "acting-out" behaviors that are probably more bothersome to the people around the child than to the child. Second are the disorders of emotional distress; here the main problem is mental suffering, usually in the form of anxiety or depression. Third are the habit disorders, disruptions of daily physical habits such as eating, sleeping, and elimination. Fourth are the learning and communication disorders, involving difficulties with such skills as reading, writing, and speaking.

The empirical method is not inconsistent with *DSM-IV.* Indeed, most of the *DSM-IV* diagnostic categories can be grouped under these four headings, and that is how we have organized them in this chapter. Clinicians who treat children are wary of diagnostic labels, however. First, as we noted, children change rapidly. Second, they may not fit neatly into any one category. As was shown in the case of D.J., above, a child may have both a habit disorder (soiling) and a disruptive behavior disorder. Likewise, many children who are overanxious also have sleeping problems; many children who are depressed are also disruptive; and so on.

The Long-Term Consequences of Childhood Disorders

People who treat disturbed youngsters hope that by doing so they are not only relieving a childhood disorder but heading off an adult disorder. But do childhood disorders actually predict adult disorders? If so, can we, by treating the one, prevent the other?

The answer to the first question depends on what kind of predictability we are looking for. The clearest, and rarest, instance of predictability is *sta-*

bility, in which a childhood disorder simply persists into adulthood in the same or a similar form. One childhood problem that tends to remain stable is antisocial behavior. Antisocial behavior in adolescence is often followed by antisocial personality disorder in adulthood (Henggeler, 1988; Robins & Price, 1991).

Another type of predictability is *continuity of developmental adaptation.* In this case, the childhood problem handicaps later development not by persisting in the same form but instead by setting the child on a skewed developmental path, which then leads to other, later disorders that may bear little resemblance to the original one. For example, infants who develop avoidant or resistant relationships with their parents are prone to become highly oppositional at age two and highly disruptive at age three or four. In turn, disruptive behavior during the transition into the school years (ages five to seven) places a child at risk for more extreme behavioral problems and for learning disorders. In such a case, we cannot say that the learning disorder represents a continuation of the infant avoidance, but it does seem that the early problem may have established a maladaptive pattern of development, with the form of maladaptiveness changing over time.

A third kind of predictability has to do with an early disorder's creating *reactivity to particular stressors.* For example, a young child who becomes depressed upon losing a parent is not necessarily on the road to adult depression. Still, this early loss may make the person more reactive to later, similar losses (e.g., divorce) and thus render him or her more vulnerable to adult depression. In general, childhood disorders of emotional distress, such as depression or anxiety, are not stable—they tend to clear up—but they have some predictive value on the continuity-of-development and reactivity-to-stress scales, particularly if they involve poor peer relations (La Greca & Fetter, 1995; J. G. Parker & Asher, 1989). So if we consider the three kinds of

PREVENTING CHILDHOOD DISORDERS

Professionals who treat children with psychological disorders often express the wish that more could be done to prevent such problems. Yet it is hard to guard children against psychological disturbance as long as they are exposed to social conditions known to breed such problems. The following statistics document something close to an emergency in children's health care:

- One out of every four children under the age of six now lives in poverty, and the rate is increasing (Social Policy Report, 1992).
- About one-third of all first births in the United States are to teenage girls, and about half of all teenage mothers—indeed, two-thirds of unmarried teenage mothers—go on welfare within four years of the birth of the child (Carnegie Report, 1994).
- Of the 2.5 million Americans who are homeless, one-third are single mothers and young children (Bassuk & Roseberg, 1990). Homeless children have four times more health problems than the average for their age (Alperstein, Rapport, & Flanagan, 1988).
- Approximately 10 million children have no health insurance (Children's Defense Fund, 1991).
- The national commitment to preschool intervention remains precarious. Head Start and other programs must constantly struggle for funding.
- Between 1950 and 1990 the employment rate for American women with children under six rose from 12 to 60 percent (U.S. Department of Commerce, various years). So the majority of preschool children have mothers who work outside the home. Yet day care is still woefully inadequate—poorly funded, poorly staffed.
- Between 15 and 22 percent of children and adolescents have diagnosable mental disorders, and between one-quarter and half of them engage in behaviors (drug abuse, unprotected sex, delinquency, early withdrawal from school) that endanger their adjustment as adults (Weisberg, Caplan, & Harwood, 1991). Yet mental health care for such children is often unavailable. For lack of alternatives, children may be unjustifiably institutionalized, or their problems may be ignored until institutionalization becomes necessary.

In children, as in adults, some measure of psychological disturbance is no doubt due to heredity, but environment is also crucial, and as these statistics show, a large percentage of American children are being exposed, daily, to environmental conditions that foster psychological disorders. To prevent such disorders, those conditions—poverty; parental unemployment; teenage pregnancy; homelessness; inadequate day care, medical care, and mental health care—need to be alleviated. We also need to invest more in genetic counseling, prenatal care, and control of environmental toxins. Given current concerns about the federal budget deficit, it is unlikely that wide-ranging prevention programs will be forthcoming. Yet there is no doubt about the need for them.

The child with ADHD (attention deficit hyperactivity disorder) lives in a state of incessant, purposeless activity and finds it almost impossible to concentrate.

predictability together, the answer to our earlier question is yes, some childhood disorders do predict adult disorders, though often indirectly.

As for the second question—whether treatment can prevent childhood disorders from leading to adult disorders—the answer is that we don't know for sure. Clearly, treatment helps in the short term. Outcome studies have found psychotherapy to be about as successful with children as with adults (Casey & Berman, 1985; Weisz, Weiss, Alicke, et al., 1987), though it is more helpful for girls than for boys and less helpful with problems of social adjustment than with problems of other kinds. Children who receive psychotherapy do better than children who receive none, and all types of therapy—play and nonplay, individual and group, children only and children plus parents—seem equally effective. So some children and adolescents do respond well to treatment, which suggests that treating them will help to prevent adult disorders. (An even better scenario would be to prevent childhood disorders. See the box on page 436.)

DISRUPTIVE BEHAVIOR DISORDERS

The **disruptive behavior disorders** are characterized by poorly controlled, impulsive, acting-out behavior in situations where self-control is expected. The ability to control one's behavior depends on a number of skills developed over time. We don't expect hungry infants to show restraint—to wait patiently and refrain from crying. During the toddler and preschool years, however, expectations are raised. Children of this age are asked to learn to inhibit behavior on command ("Don't touch that electric outlet!") and to moderate their behavior in consideration of other people's feelings ("Don't take her toy—play with this one"). Such learning is slow and involves many lapses in the form of disobedience, aggression, and temper tantrums. Nevertheless, it proceeds. By the time they enter school, most children have developed the self-control skills necessary for compliant and organized behavior in the classroom and for responsive, nonaggressive interactions with peers. Those who have not developed these skills, who continue to be disruptive, impulsive, and aggressive, are at high risk for school adjustment difficulties, learning problems, and peer rejection. Among the disruptive behavior disorders listed by *DSM-IV,* the two most important are attention deficit hyperactivity disorder and conduct disorder.

Attention Deficit Hyperactivity Disorder

In almost every elementary school, there are a few children who cannot sit still, cannot finish a task, cannot wait their turn, cannot focus their attention for longer than a minute or two. A few decades ago researchers began to suspect that this pattern, characterized primarily by excess motor activity and short attention span, might be due to brain damage. It was known, for example, that certain kinds of brain infection produced restless motor activity. Furthermore, many of the children who manifested this pattern also showed "soft," or ambiguous, neurological signs that could suggest brain damage, and a small percentage of them showed definite signs of neurological impairment. On this evidence, the pattern was labeled "minimal brain dysfunction" (MBD). Still, no one could say exactly what the dysfunction was. Furthermore, there was (and still is) a strong trend away from labeling disorders according to cause when that cause was not definitely established. In time, therefore, the syndrome was given a new name, *hyperactivity,* which had to do with its symptoms rather than its presumed cause. Eventually, however, those who studied the disorder came to feel that the short attention span was as fundamental a symptom as the hyperactivity. Accordingly, the syndrome is now called **attention deficit hyperactivity disorder,** or **ADHD.**

Between 3 and 5 percent of elementary school children are said to have ADHD (Barkley, 1990), with boys outnumbering girls by about 9 to 1. So it is a common diagnosis. It is also a controversial one. Some experts believe that it is too readily applied to children whom parents and teachers find difficult to control.

We have already described the typical behavior of the ADHD child. Its most salient features are incessant restlessness and an extremely poor attention span, leading in turn to impulsive and disorganized behavior. These handicaps affect almost every area of the child's functioning. Even the most trivial human accomplishments—setting a table, playing a card game—depend on the ability to set goals, plan ahead, organize one's behavior, and postpone gratification. It is this ability that is most strikingly absent in the ADHD child. Thus the characteristic motor behavior of these children is often distinguished less by its excessiveness than by its haphazard quality. Most children are more physically active than adults, but their getting up and down and running back and forth is usually directed toward some goal. By contrast, the incessant activity of ADHD children seems purposeless and disorganized. Furthermore, a normal child can, if motivated, sit still and concentrate; an ADHD child has difficulty doing so.

This inability to focus and sustain attention has a ruinous effect on academic progress. Children with ADHD have great difficulty following instructions and finishing tasks. Often they cannot even remember what they set out to do. Consequently, however intelligent they are, they tend to have severe learning problems. They are also extremely disruptive in the classroom, making incessant demands for attention. (Typically, it is not until such children enter school that their problem is recognized. What parents can put up with, a teacher with twenty-five pupils and a lesson plan to complete usually cannot.) ADHD children also show poor social adjustment. They disrupt games, get into fights, refuse to play fair, and throw temper tantrums. Such behavior does not make them popular.

Not all ADHD children have all these symptoms, however. In some, the problem is much more one of inattention than hyperactivity; in others, the opposite. Accordingly, *DSM-IV* divides the syndrome into three subtypes: the *predominantly inattentive type,* the *predominantly hyperactive/impulsive type,* and the *combined type.* But most ADHD children are the combined type—that is, they have the full range of symptoms. Recent studies (Barkley, DuPaul, & McMurray, 1990; Biederman, Newcorn, & Sprich, 1991) have shown that children of the combined type are more likely than the other two types to have problems with other children, to engage in antisocial behavior, and to be placed in special-education classes. ADHD children also differ in the constancy of their symptoms. In some, the problem behaviors occur only at home or only at school, while the child shows adequate adjustment in the other setting. These situational ADHD children generally have less serious difficulties and a better prognosis than pervasive ADHD children, who show their symptoms in all settings.

As for general prognosis, a recent review of twenty outcome studies (R. Klein & Mannuzza, 1991) indicates that ADHD continues into adolescence, at which point it may branch out into the pattern of antisocial behavior known as conduct disorder (see the next section). According to teacher rating scales, 85 percent of children with conduct disorder also meet the criteria for ADHD (Pelham, Gnagy, Greenslade, et al., 1992). As for later adjustment, a study of young men who had had ADHD in childhood showed that, compared with controls, they had significantly higher rates of conduct or antisocial personality disorders (27 versus 8 percent), drug-use disorders (16 versus 3 percent), and full ADHD syndrome (31 versus 3 percent). Cognitive problems such as poor concentration tend to persist into adolescence, with predictable academic results: poor grades, expulsion, early withdrawal from school. It is not yet clear whether cognitive disabilities continue into adulthood, but the adult lives of former ADHD children are of course marked by their poor academic records (Barkley, 1990; R. Klein & Mannuzza, 1989).

Conduct Disorder

Cory [a ten-year-old boy] was referred to treatment by a school counselor. . . . At home, Cory constantly fights with his siblings. He steals personal possessions of all family members, swears, disobeys family rules, and refuses to participate in family activities. He has been caught on three occasions playing with matches and setting fires in his room. The fires have been with small pieces of paper, trash in his waste can, and books.

At school, Cory has been in fights with several of his peers in class. He reportedly threatens peers, runs around the classroom throwing crayons and pencils as if they were darts, spits, swears, and hits the teacher with various toys and supplies. Before coming for treatment, he was suspended from school for assaulting a classmate and choking him to the point that the child almost passed out. (Kazdin, 1988)

Some children seem indifferent to the rights of others. Rather than yield to anyone else, they will argue, threaten, cheat, steal. They may also go in for reckless behavior—setting fires, jumping off roofs—and for gratuitously cruel behavior. As they grow older, they graduate to the violation of major social norms. They are no longer just throwing blocks; they are committing assault and rape. At that point, usually in adolescence or preadolescence, they are given the diagnosis of **conduct disorder.**

The *DSM-IV* criteria for this diagnosis are grouped under four categories: aggression against people or animals (bullying, fighting, mugging, rape), destruction of property (vandalism, fire setting), deceitfulness or theft (lying, shoplifting, breaking and entering), and other serious violations of rules (absence from school, running away from home). If a person is under eighteen, has committed any three of these infractions (in any category) in the last year, and shows poor adjustment at home or at school, he or she qualifies for the diagnosis of conduct disorder.

Like ADHD, conduct disorder is one of the most common syndromes of childhood and adolescence, with an estimated prevalence of 4 to 16 percent in the under-eighteen population (P. Cohen, Cohen, Kasen, et al., 1993). And as with ADHD, boys greatly outnumber girls, by a ratio of anywhere from 4 to 1 to 12 to 1 (Kazdin, 1987; McMahon & Wells, 1989). The two sexes also show different symptom pictures, with the girls less prone to aggression. In boys, the most common symptoms are fighting, stealing, vandalism, and school problems. In girls, the predominant behaviors are lying, truancy, running away from home, drug use, and prostitution.

Age of onset seems to be very important in conduct disorder. Indeed, *DSM-IV* requires that diagnosticians specify whether a given case falls into the *childhood-onset type* (at least one symptom prior to age ten) or the *adolescent-onset type* (no symptoms before age ten). People of the childhood-onset type are usually male; they are more likely to be physically aggressive; they tend to have few, if any, friends. They are also more likely to graduate from conduct disorder to adult antisocial personality disorder. Teenagers with adolescent-onset conduct disorders are less aggressive, generally have friends—indeed, they may be valued gang members—and are less likely to become antisocial personalities as adults. (See the box on page 440.) The prognostic value of age of onset has been confirmed by many studies. Robins (1991), for example, tested a group of adults who had had pronounced conduct disorders as children to see if they met the criteria for antisocial personality disorder. The subjects who did meet the criteria constituted 48 percent of those whose symptoms began after age twelve, 53 percent of those whose symptoms appeared between six and twelve, and 71 percent of those whose symptoms surfaced before age six. But those children with conduct disorders who do not develop antisocial personality disorder are still more likely to become "ordinary" criminals. Some studies (e.g., McCord, 1979; Zoccolillo & Rogers, 1991) have found that 50 to 70 percent of juvenile offenders are arrested again as adults.

Whatever their future prospects, children with conduct disorders are cause for grave social concern. Whether in gangs or on their own, these children commit serious crimes. Over 16 percent of those arrested in the United States in 1992 for violent and property crimes were under eighteen (U.S. Department of Justice, 1993). Even more alarming is the fact that the rate of violent crime by juveniles increased by more than 25 percent between 1982 and 1992 (U.S. Department of Justice, 1993)—a rise that was probably due, however, not just to antisocial tendencies but to the increased availability of firearms.

Together, the disruptive behavior disorders, ADHD and conduct disorder, are the most predictive of childhood disorders, the ones most likely to be followed by adult maladjustment. This may be due to something inherent in these disorders, or it may be due to a third variable: the fact that many of these children—those with conduct disorders and those with aggressive forms of ADHD—tend to come from disorganized and unhappy families. However, the poor prognosis for the disruptive behavior disorders is also certainly due in part to the process described earlier: continuity of developmental adaptation. The behaviors involved in ADHD and conduct disorder cause immense disruptions in the lives of the children who have these disorders, damaging their academic

ANTISOCIAL ADOLESCENTS: ARE THERE TWO TYPES?

Most criminal offenders are teenagers. A graph that plots crime rate against age would produce a curve that rises sharply from age eleven, peaks at seventeen, and declines fairly steeply in the twenties. This pattern does not represent just a few adolescents who commit many offenses. Rather, it represents a tenfold increase in the number of young criminals. Arrest statistics do not even begin to tell the story of how prevalent delinquency is in adolescence. Using self-reports of deviant behavior, researchers have found that antisocial behavior appears to be a normal part of teenage life (Elliott, Ageton, Huizinga, et al, 1983). A study of over 1000 boys in New Zealand showed that between the ages of eleven and fifteen about one-third of the sample committed delinquent acts (Moffitt, 1991).

But the good news is that the steep decline in offenders in early adulthood means that for most delinquents, antisocial behavior is temporary and age-specific. T. E. Moffitt (1993) suggests that the pool of adolescent delinquents in society actually conceals two very distinct types of individuals: a very large group whose antisocial behavior is limited to adolescence, and a much smaller group that persists in antisocial behavior over the life course, from childhood through adulthood. According to Moffitt (1991), these two types may be indistinguishable during adolescence: her New Zealand study found that the two types did not differ in the variety of laws they broke, the frequency of delinquency, or the number of times they appeared in juvenile court. But a look at the *preadolescent* history of the offenders does offer a way to distinguish between the persistent and temporary types.

From early childhood, persistent types are marked by continuity in antisocial behavior, which may have its origins in disruptions in neuropsychological functions. The antisocial child's aggressive behavior tends to create situations that only reinforce the antisocial tendencies, especially in unsupportive environments. Options for learning prosocial behavior narrow until the persistent antisocial behavior becomes fixed. The behavior may take different forms at different ages: the child that bites and hits at age four may be shoplifting at age ten, stealing cars at sixteen, robbing people at twenty-two, and abusing a child at thirty. This behavior takes place in all kinds of situations—at home, at school, at work, in shops (Farrington, 1991). The more stable and continuous the antisocial behavior, the more extreme the forms it takes.

Various age groups of antisocial individuals show remarkably similar rates of prevalence in the population. This similarity leads Moffitt (1993) to believe that the same life-course-persistent individuals make up the categories of preschool boys who are "difficult to manage" (5 percent), elementary school boys with conduct disorder (4 to 9 percent), boys arrested as preteens (6 percent), convicted violent offenders among young adult males (3 to 6 percent), and men diagnosed with antisocial personality disorders (4 to 5 percent). Because antisocial behavior among these individuals begins long before police data banks track it, the relatively steep decline in antisocial behavior noted between ages seventeen and thirty would be mirrored by a steep incline from at least age seven to seventeen (Loeber, Stouthamer-Loeber, Van Kammen, et al., 1989).

The numerous individuals whose delinquency is limited to adolescence differ from the persistent types in many important ways. Most significantly, their behavior is marked by *discontinuity*—their delinquent behavior tends to begin abruptly and end just as quickly. Moreover, unlike their persistent peers, they are discriminating: the temporary delinquents behave antisocially only in situations where doing so seems rewarding to them; if prosocial behavior is more rewarding, they will engage in that. In other words, their antisocial behavior is adaptable and flexible rather than rigid and stable, as in the case of the persistent types.

The motivations of the two types are different as well. For life-persistent offenders, biological deficits combined with disadvantageous environmental factors produce antisocial behavior that is pathological and abnormal. By contrast, for the temporary types, delinquent behavior is normative. It is a group social phenomenon, not a matter of individual deviance. Moffitt (1993) believes that most delinquents start behaving antisocially in adolescence when they feel the gap between their physical maturity and the social maturity conferred by adulthood. Delinquent acts appear to be a way to gain adult power and status. The crimes of the temporary delinquents tend to be those that symbolize adult privilege or autonomy from parental control, such as vandalism, substance abuse, running away, theft; persistent offenders, on the other hand, are more likely to commit victim-oriented offenses, such as violence and fraud. As teenagers grow out of their maturity gap, most of them come to see that the negative consequences of their acts outweigh the rewards, and this realization gradually extinguishes the delinquent behavior.

Adolescent delinquency is ubiquitous, yet many teenagers remain nondelinquent. What accounts for that? According to Moffitt (1993), these individuals enter puberty late or have early access to adult roles, or they grow up in an environment that prevents them from learning about delinquent behavior, or they are shut out from peer networks for one reason or another.

Moffitt's theory of the two types of adolescent delinquents, if true, indicates that it is futile to study the peak period of delinquent activity in order to learn more about the antisocial individual who will go on to lead a life of crime. It is much more valuable to single out cases that begin in childhood, even infancy, and follow these antisocial individuals in longitudinal studies. Her theory also lends credibility to studying adolescent delinquency as a phenomenon in itself to learn more about what effects biological age, attitudes on maturity, and access to antisocial peer models have on nondelinquent teenagers.

performance, their social lives, their relationships with their families—in other words, all the critical areas of a child's existence. It is not easy to recover from such setbacks.

DISORDERS OF EMOTIONAL DISTRESS

In contrast to the acting-out involved in the disruptive behavior disorders, the disorders of emotional distress are "internalizing" disorders. The conflict is turned inward; the major victim is the child. Disorders of emotional distress are difficult to diagnose in the younger age groups, because children lack the verbal and conceptual skills to tell us what they are feeling. Their emotions have to be guessed at on the basis of their behavior. If a child refuses to go to school, for example, we may infer "school phobia"—and we may be wrong. School-avoidant children may not fear school; they may just find staying at home more rewarding (Kearney & Silverman, 1990). Nevertheless, in the absence of advanced verbal skills, children's behavior is still the best clue to their emotions.

The accurate assessment of anxiety and depression becomes far easier by adolescence, when children are capable of talking about their feelings. Indeed, the high prevalence of disorders of emotional distress in adolescents, relative to younger children, may be due simply to the fact that adolescents are capable of telling us about these problems. In any case, there is no doubt that both young children and adolescents experience severe emotional distress, in the form of both anxiety and depression.

Anxiety Disorders

The *DSM* used to have a separate list of "anxiety disorders of childhood and adolescence." Now all but one of these categories have been merged with adult anxiety syndromes, on the grounds that they are simply the childhood versions of those disorders—disorders which, indeed, generally begin prior to adulthood.

Separation Anxiety Disorder Separation anxiety—intense fear and distress upon being separated from parents (or other caretakers)—is seen in almost all children toward the end of the first year of life. It peaks at about twelve months and then gradually disappears. In some children, however, it does not disappear but persists well into the school years. Or, in the more typical pattern, it disappears on schedule and then reappears, at full intensity, some time later in childhood, usually after the child has undergone some kind of stress, such as the death of a pet or a move to a new school or new neighborhood. This condition, essentially a phobia of being parted from parents, is known as **separation anxiety disorder.** It is the one childhood anxiety syndrome that is still listed separately, under "disorders of childhood and adolescence."

In extreme cases, children with this disorder cannot be separated from their parents by so much as a wall and will shadow them from room to room. In most cases, however, all that the child asks is to be allowed to stay at home, with the parent in the house. But even with their parents present, children with this disorder may be haunted by fears of horrible things—kidnapping, automobile accidents, attacks by monsters—that may befall them or their parents if they are separated. They generally have sleeping problems as well, since sleep means separation, and consequently they may reappear night after night to crawl into bed with the parents. If banished from the parents' bedroom, they are likely to camp outside the door.

Children with this disorder are typically clinging and demanding, putting considerable strain on their parents. Parent-child conflicts, then, are common with separation anxiety disorder and of course exacerbate it, since the parents' annoyance makes the child all the more fearful of abandonment. In addition to experiencing family conflicts, these children also suffer in other areas. They may refuse to attend school, and consequently their academic progress comes to a halt. Furthermore, since they cannot go to school or to other children's houses, they make no friends or lose the friends they had.

The estimated prevalence of separation anxiety disorder is between 4 and 13 percent of children and adolescents (R. S. Benjamin, Costello, & Warren, 1990; Kashani & Orvaschel, 1990), with girls perhaps somewhat more vulnerable. By definition it appears before age eighteen, generally before puberty, and lasts for several years with fluctuating intensity. Indeed, it may last beyond age eighteen. Adults with separation anxiety disorder either refuse to move out of their childhood home or, if they succeed in establishing a new family, are as anxious about separating from their spouses and children as they formerly were about being parted from their parents.

Social phobia **Social phobia,** or fear of social or performance situations in which embarrassment may occur, has been discussed in Chapter 7. As we saw, it tends to have its onset in adolescence, but it may also begin in childhood, at which time it typically takes the form of a paralyzing fear of strangers—peers as well as adults. This disorder affects about 1.5 percent of children and adolescents (R. S. Benjamin, Costello, & Warren, 1990).

Like separation anxiety, fear of strangers is normal in very young children, beginning around eight months. But most children grow out of it by age two and a half. Older children may still be standoffish with people they don't know—averting their gaze, pretending not to hear questions, and so forth—but eventually they warm up to the new person and resume their normal behavior. Children with social phobia, on the other hand, do not warm up. When addressed by a stranger, they may be struck mute. When a new person enters the room, they will typically take refuge at the side of a familiar adult. When pushed into a situation with many new people, they will simply withdraw into a corner, blushing and tongue-tied, until rescued, or, depending on their age, they may burst into tears or even throw a tantrum.

Such children, unlike those with separation anxiety disorder, are often well adjusted at home and have normal relationships with their parents. But at school they are painfully withdrawn. This usually interferes with their academic progress, and of course it prevents them from making friends. Social phobia is possibly more painful for children than for adults, since children do not have the option of avoiding feared situations altogether. (Eventually, they are required to go to school.) Furthermore, they may not understand the source of their anxiety, and usually they do not know, as adult social phobics do, that it is excessive.

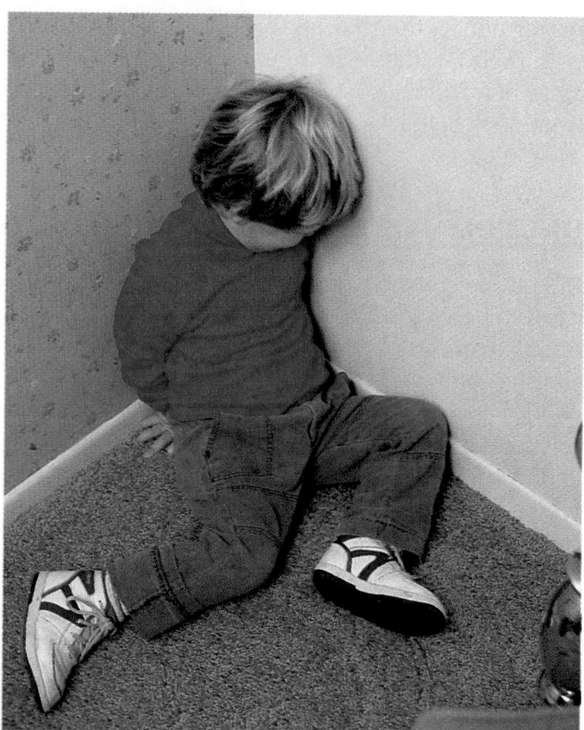

Though many adults find it hard to believe, even very young children can experience clinical depression.

Generalized Anxiety Disorder What was once called "overanxious disorder," a childhood syndrome, is now considered to be the childhood version of **generalized anxiety disorder.** Like social phobia, generalized anxiety disorder has already been described among the adult anxiety syndromes, but in the typical case it begins well before adulthood. (According to *DSM-IV,* most people with generalized anxiety disorder claim that they have been overanxious all their lives.) In children and adolescents, the disorder often takes the form of anticipatory anxiety about performance situations. Will they pass the test? Will they be picked for the baseball team? If so, will they get hurt playing ball?

As these worries suggest, such children tend to have severe doubts about their own capabilities—doubts that lead them to constant approval-seeking. This complex of worry and self-doubt may be the result of family dynamics. There is some evidence that children with generalized anxiety disorder tend to come from families where parental love is made conditional on consistently "good" behavior.

Whatever its cause, the pervasive anxiety of these children tends to breed failure. Anticipatory anxiety, because it robs behavior of its spontaneity, often creates the very problems that were anticipated. Terrified lest they fail the test or be excluded from a classmate's birthday party, overanxious children run a higher risk of failing and being excluded. Such failures tend to lead to further anxiety and further failure—the familiar vicious cycle (Eisen & Engler, 1995; Rapee & Barlow, 1991).

Childhood Depression

For years the fact that children suffer depression was overlooked—or, when it was pointed out, denied (Carlson & Garber, 1986). Still today, parents and teachers often fail to notice depression in children, even children who, when questioned, report severe depressive feelings, including suicidal thoughts (Rutter, Graham, Chadwick, et al., 1976).

Physicians too commonly fail to spot suicidal intent in young people (Slap, Vorters, Khalid, et al., 1992). By now, however, psychologists do recognize the existence of **childhood depression,** though there is disagreement as to its manifestations. According to some research, the symptoms are similar to those of adult depression: a sad or hopeless mood, a negative view of life, concentration problems, and so on (J. Mitchell, McCauley, Burke, et al., 1988; Prieto, Cole, & Tageson, 1992). But as developmental psychologists have pointed out, children express these symptoms differently from adults—by clinging to their parents, refusing to go to school, or expressing exaggerated fears (of their parents' death, for example). Older children may sulk, withdraw from family activities, and retreat to their rooms. They may have trouble in school, become slovenly, or engage in delinquent acts. In both children and adolescents, depression may appear as merely one symptom of another emotional disorder or of conduct disorder.

Still, clear-cut depressions are not rare in the underage population. Community surveys of children and adolescents have found the prevalence of clinical depression to be between 2 and 5 percent (P. Cohen, Cohen, Kasen, et al., 1993; Kashani, Carlson, Beck, et al., 1990; Lewinsohn, Hops, Roberts, et al., 1993). Adolescents may be somewhat more vulnerable than younger children. In preadolescent children, depression is more common in boys; in adolescents, it is more common in girls.

In school-age children in general, 1 percent are depressed enough to express clear suicidal thoughts (Larsson & Melin, 1992), but adolescents are more likely to contemplate, attempt, and complete a suicide. As we saw in Chapter 10, adolescent suicides have increased alarmingly in recent years. Follow-up studies of people diagnosed as depressed in childhood indicate that they are also at risk for mood disorders as adults. Therefore, they could probably benefit from early detection and treatment (Harrington, Fudge, Rutter, et al., 1990).

EATING DISORDERS

Since Freud's time, psychologists have interpreted eating as a crucial part of development, because children's feelings about eating are bound up with their feelings about those who feed and sustain them—their parents and others. For the same reason, experts tend to view eating disorders as a reflection of emotional conflicts. We will discuss two syndromes: anorexia nervosa and bulimia nervosa.

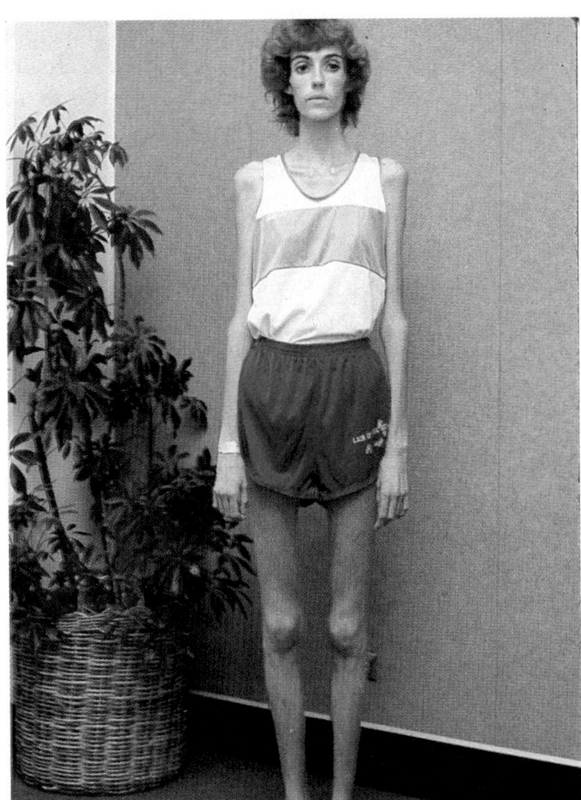

Anorexia nervosa might be seen as an extreme response to our culture's emphasis on slimness as the most important component of beauty.

Anorexia Nervosa

Defined as a severe restriction of food intake caused by a fear of gaining weight, **anorexia nervosa** is overwhelmingly a disease of adolescent girls and young women. From 85 to 95 percent of anorexics are female, and in most cases the onset is between ages twelve and eighteen, though it may also occur in prepuberty or as late as age thirty. Anorexia is a rare disorder, with annual incidence probably less than 1 in 100,000 population, but it is apparently becoming more common (American Psychiatric Association, 1994; A. R. Lucas, Beard, O'Fallon, et al., 1991). Unlike most psychological disorders, it is physically dangerous. About one-third of anorexics remain chronically ill, and an estimated 5 percent die (Steinhausen, 1994).

Predictably, the most dramatic physical sign of anorexia is emaciation. E. W. Bliss and Branch (1960) cite the case of a woman whose weight dropped from 180 to 60 pounds. Not all cases are that severe, however, and not all involve a *loss* of weight. The cutoff line in the *DSM-IV* criteria is a body weight less than 85 percent of what is normal for the patient's age and height, whether that condition is the result of the patient's losing weight or simply not gaining weight as she grew. Aside from low weight, the other criteria are an intense fear of becoming fat, an unrealistic body image, and, in girls, *amenorrhea,* or suspension of menstrual periods. All these symptoms must be present for the person to be diagnosed as anorexic.

In behavioral terms, the anorexic usually follows one of two patterns. In the *restricting type,* she simply refuses to eat (and perhaps overexercises as well). In the *binge-eating/purging type,* she eats, sometimes voraciously, but compensates by making herself vomit or by using laxatives or other purgatives. Some patients report that they are so repelled by food that they never experience normal sensations of hunger, but they are the exceptions. Most anorexics clearly have normal appetites, at least in the early stages of the disorder (Marrazzi & Luby, 1986). Indeed, they may become preoccupied with food, collecting cookbooks, preparing elaborate meals for others, and so forth.

Apart from low weight, fear of obesity is perhaps the most typical feature of anorexia. According to one expert, a better name for the disorder would be "weight phobia" (Crisp, 1984). Despite overwhelming evidence to the contrary—clawlike hands, skull-like faces, protruding ribs—anorexics insist that they are too fat and need to lose weight. This distorted body image, together with an iron determination to correct the supposed fatness, is critical to the development of the disorder. Some anorexic women have a history of obesity (Schlundt & Johnson, 1990), and anorexia often follows a period of dieting, as in the following case:

> At fifteen Alma had been healthy and well-developed, had menstruated at age twelve, was five feet six inches tall, and weighed one hundred twenty pounds. At that time her mother urged her to change to a school with higher academic standing, a change she resisted; her father suggested that she should watch her weight, an idea that she took up with great eagerness, and she began a rigid diet. She lost rapidly and her menses ceased. That she could be thin gave her a sense of pride, power, and accomplishment. She also began a frantic exercise program, would swim by the mile, play tennis for hours, or do calisthenics to the point of exhaustion. Whatever low point her weight reached, Alma feared that she might become "too fat" if she regained as little as an ounce. . . .
>
> When she came for consultation [at age twenty] she looked like a walking skeleton, scantily dressed in shorts and a halter, with her legs sticking out like broomsticks, every rib showing, and her shoulder blades standing up like little wings. . . . Alma insisted that she looked fine and that there was nothing wrong with being so skinny. (Bruch, 1978, pp. 1–2)

Because it so often occurs in adolescence, the point in development when secondary sexual characteristics emerge and when many people embark on sexual relationships, some experts interpret anorexia as a way of avoiding an adult sexual role and especially the possibility of pregnancy (Bruch, 1985). The fact that amenorrhea sometimes *precedes* the weight loss (Halmi, 1974) and therefore may be psychogenic rather than the result of malnutrition supports this hypothesis. But even if anorexia does not aim to suppress sexuality, that undoubtedly is its effect. Menstruation stops, the sex drive disappears, and breasts and hips shrink. Many anorexic women barely look female.

Another suspected cause of anorexia is family warfare, with self-starvation serving as a daughter's weapon against her parents. Few actions can bring parents to surrender as quickly as a child's refusal to eat. Clinicians often find disturbed relationships between parents and anorexic children, a connection that supports the family hypothesis. In one reported case, the patient confessed that she felt "full of my mother—I feel she is in me" (Bruch, 1978, p. 12). In starving herself, then, she was possibly laying siege to the "inner mother." But as with other disorders, disturbed family relationships may be the effect rather than the cause (Bemis, 1978). Families are not usually harmonious when one member is starving herself to death. Whatever the cause of anorexia, family therapy, as we shall see later in the chapter, is one of the most promising forms of treatment.

Bulimia Nervosa

The pattern of uncontrolled binge eating plus compensation that is shown by some anorexics is also a syndrome in itself, affecting nonanorexics. People with this disorder, called **bulimia nervosa,** regularly go on binges during which they consume extraordinary amounts of food, often sweet, high-calorie food—a whole cake, a quart of ice cream—until they are uncomfortably, even painfully, full. Then, in nine out of ten cases, they will make themselves vomit by sticking their fingers or some other instrument down the throat to stimulate the gag reflex. Some bulimics, instead of vomiting, use laxatives, diuretics (drugs that induce urination), or enemas. Still others do not purge themselves, but try to compensate by fasting or exercising.

Like anorexics, bulimics base their self-esteem in large measure on their body shape. (This is one of the diagnostic criteria.) Consequently, their binges are surrounded by shame. Most of them do their binge eating alone, in secret, and try to hide its traces from their families or roommates. Binges are often triggered by stress or unhappiness and followed by greater unhappiness. Bulimia can also have physical consequences—not only unstable weight but amenorrhea and rotted teeth. (Repeated vomiting overexposes the teeth to stomach acid.)

Bulimia resembles anorexia not just in symptomatology but in other ways as well: it usually has its onset in late adolescence or early adulthood; it tends to appear after or during a period of dieting; it is overwhelmingly a female disorder. In clinic and population samples, at least 90 percent of bulimics are female. But bulimia is far more common than anorexia, affecting 1 to 3 percent of adolescent girls and young women (Weltzing, Starzynski, Santelli, et al., 1993). The disorder tends to persist for several years, appearing and disappearing, but its long-term outcome is not yet known. For years a part of campus pathology, bulimia has only recently begun to be seriously studied. At this point, cognitive-behavioral treatment has been shown to be highly effective. One such program reduced binge-eating averages by 70 percent (Oesterhed, McKenna, & Gould, 1987).

ELIMINATION DISORDERS

Like eating, toilet training may be an arena of intense conflict for a child. Toilet training is one of the first points in development at which children have to comply with demands that run counter to their natural impulses. Sometimes these demands are extreme, for our society insists that children achieve control over elimination at an early age. When children fail to pass this developmental milestone, they are diagnosed as having either enuresis (lack of bladder control) or encopresis (lack of bowel control).

Enuresis

Enuresis usually is defined as a lack of bladder control past the age when such control is usual. In this country, most children achieve daytime control between the ages of two and three and nighttime control a year later, but many are much slower. Most children who fall behind in bladder control have trouble with nighttime control—bedwetting. Daytime wetting is much less common and may be the sign of a more serious psychological problem.

As for the age that separates normal "accidents" from enuresis, this varies with the clinician making the decision. *DSM-IV* specifies only a minimum age: no child under the age of five may be given this diagnosis. In addition, the child must be wetting his or her pants or bed at least twice a week or, if the frequency is less, must be suffering serious distress or impaired functioning (e.g., humiliations at school) as a result of the wetting. According to *DSM-IV,* the prevalence of enuresis at age five is 7 percent for boys and 3 percent for girls; at age ten, it is 3 percent for boys and 2 percent for girls.

Enuresis may be primary or secondary. Children with *primary enuresis* have never achieved bladder control; whenever they have to urinate, day or night, they wet themselves. Primary enuresis may last until middle childhood, and in rare cases it persists well beyond that point. (At age eighteen, the prevalence of enuresis is still 1 percent for males.) Some authorities have suggested that the condition may stem from organic, possibly genetic, abnormalities (Bakwin & Bakwin, 1972). By contrast, children with *secondary enuresis* achieve bladder control and then lose it, almost always as a result of stress. The birth of a baby brother or sister, with the insecurity this often provokes, is probably the most common cause. Whether treated or not, secondary enuresis is usually temporary.

Most enuretic children are not emotionally disturbed (Wagner, Smith, & Norris, 1988), and when the enuresis occurs in isolation—that is, not as part of a larger problem—it usually responds well to treatment. Treatment may be warranted, for enuresis can cause problems. Children who wet their pants are likely to be ridiculed by their schoolmates. They may also have problems with their parents, who typically begin to resent being awakened in the night to change wet sheets. Rejecting or ridiculing the child will only add to the child's problems. Reassurance is a better tactic. Another is to keep a clean set of sheets and nightclothes next to the child's bed. Even a six-year-old can be taught, when the bed is wet, to change pajamas, sheets, and rubber pad. This preserves the parents' peace and the child's self-respect. Bedwetting almost always clears up, but it may clear up slowly. Many normal children are still wetting their beds at age twelve, and, as noted, the causes may be organic. About three-quarters of enuretic children have a first-degree relative who was also enuretic, and the concordance rate is higher in MZ twins than in DZ twins (American Psychiatric Association, 1994).

Encopresis

When the elimination problem is lack of bowel control rather than of bladder control, the condition is called **encopresis.** Encopresis and enuresis may occur together—about one-quarter of encopretic children are also enuretic—and in some ways the two syndromes are alike. Encopresis too is classified as either primary (control is never achieved) or secondary (control is mastered and then lost). In the primary form, it too may have an organic basis. It too is more common in boys than in girls. Finally, even more than enuresis, encopresis can earn a child mockery from peers and wrath from parents, compounding whatever problems he or she has.

But encopresis is far rarer. Its prevalence—1 percent of five-year-olds (Doleys, 1989)—is one-fifth that of enuresis. And it is a more serious problem. It rarely appears in isolation; usually, it occurs as part of a larger disorder, such as a disruptive behavior disorder, or in the context of severe family problems. (We saw such family problems, together with the social disgrace attendant on encopresis, in the case of D.J. at the opening of the chapter.) A substantial percentage of encopretic children are abused children, though again this may be a result rather than, or as well as, a cause of the encopresis.

SLEEP DISORDERS

Probably the most common response to stress in early childhood is sleep disturbance, usually in the form of difficulties falling asleep or staying asleep. Such problems are endemic in children who are beginning school, and they generally clear up by themselves. About one-third of four- and five-year-olds—but only 15 percent of six-year-olds and 8 percent of ten-year-olds—wake up repeatedly during the night (Klackenberg, 1982).

Another common complaint is **nightmares,** which seem to occur more frequently in childhood than in the later years. Between 10 and 50 percent of children aged three to five have nightmares often enough to concern their parents (American Sleep Disorders Association, 1990). Less prevalent, but more disturbing, are **night terrors,** which occur in 1 to 6 percent of children and are very rare in adults (Thorpy & Glovinsky, 1987). Children having nightmares show no particular physiological arousal, and they may or may not be awakened by the dream. In any case, when they do wake up, they are usually able to describe the dream in detail—how big the monster was, what its cave looked like—and they soon calm down. By contrast, children in the throes of a night terror show intense physiological arousal (sweating, hyperventilation, racing heart) and wake up in a panic, screaming. They are very hard to comfort, and usually they cannot say what the problem is, nor can they describe any sort of dream. The next morning, they have no memory of the episode. Night terrors, then, are far more harrowing than nightmares. They are also timed differently, because they arise out of a different stage of sleep (slow-wave sleep) than do nightmares (REM sleep). Night terrors occur during the first few hours of sleep; nightmares, closer to morning (Bootzin, Manber, Perlis, et al., 1993; Mindell & Cashman, 1995).

Sleepwalking, or somnambulism, is another sleep disturbance that is much more common in the young. Less than 1 percent of adults sleepwalk,

Night terrors are a rare and puzzling sleep disorder. The child awakens in a state of complete panic, but has no memory of the incident the next day.

but between 15 and 30 percent of healthy children have at least one episode of sleepwalking, and 2 to 3 percent have frequent episodes (Thorpy & Glovinsky, 1987), with prevalence peaking at about age twelve. Children who sleepwalk typically fall asleep, and then, without waking up, they get out of bed an hour or two later and perform some complex action such as making a sandwich or even dressing and leaving the house. (They rarely go far, however.) Their eyes are open, and they do not bump into things. The episode may last anywhere from fifteen seconds to thirty minutes, after which the sleepwalker usually returns to bed (M. S. Aldrich, 1989). Contrary to popular belief, sleepwalkers are not acting out their dreams. Like night terrors, sleepwalking occurs during non-REM sleep, which is not a period of dreaming. Most experts do not regard sleepwalking in children as a serious problem. Generally, they advise parents to make sure the front door is locked and, if they find their children sleepwalking, not to wake them up—this often frightens them—but just to guide them back to bed (Barlin & Quaynum, 1986; Bootzin, Manber, Perlis, et al., 1993).

LEARNING DISORDERS

When a person's skill in reading, writing, or mathematics is substantially below what would be expected for his or her age, education, and intelligence, and when this interferes with the person's adjustment, academic or otherwise, the problem is said to be one of the three **learning disorders.** Children with *reading disorder* (also known as *dyslexia*) read slowly and with poor comprehension, and when reading aloud, they drop, substitute or distort words. Children with *disorder of written expression* typically have a number of writing problems: poor paragraph organization; faulty spelling, grammar, and punctuation; illegible handwriting. In *mathematics disorder,* the child may fail to understand concepts or to recognize symbols or to remember operations (e.g., to "carry" a number). In any case, the problem comes out wrong.

Anywhere from 5 to 15 percent of school-age children, the majority of them boys, are said to have learning disorders (H. G. Taylor, 1989), but prevalence figures are probably not very accurate, because clinicians disagree on the definition of this syndrome. Mentally retarded children and children with impaired vision or hearing are excluded from the category, but that still leaves an extremely heterogeneous group. As many as one-quarter of children with conduct disorders, ADHD, and depression also have diagnosable learning disorders (Durrant, 1994). Various medical conditions, such as lead poisoning and fetal alcohol syndrome, involve learning disorders. And though *DSM-IV* specifies that children whose school problems stem from lack of opportunity, poor teaching, and "cultural factors" should not receive this diagnosis, many of them undoubtedly do. At present, the diagnostic group probably runs the gamut from brain-damaged children to children with no quiet place to do their homework.

Though children with impaired vision and hearing are supposed to be excluded from the category, it is clear that many cases of learning disorder do involve distortions of visual and auditory perception. Indeed, disturbed visual perception is the most common problem of children in this category. Many have trouble focusing on lines of type on a page. Some cannot copy words from the blackboard correctly. Some cannot tell *mop* from *map,* or *N* from *M,* or a circle from a triangle.

As for problems of auditory perception, children with learning disorders often have to struggle to distinguish the sounds of different words or to make simple associations between the words they hear (Gelfand, Jenson, & Drew, 1982). Some may not be able to identify the sound of, for example, a car horn honking or a dog barking. When perceptual problems accompany a learning disorder, they usually occur in more than one system—visual, auditory, and haptic (touch and movement). It is the prevalence of such perceptual difficulties that has led many experts to believe that learning disorders are neurologically based.

Some children with learning disorders also show disturbances in memory and other cognitive functions. Many cannot recall from one day to the next what they have learned in school—a problem that is painfully frustrating to them and to their teachers. They may also have difficulties with sequential thinking and with organizing their thoughts. The cognitive aspects of learning disorders have been the subject of much research in recent years.

The memory lapses associated with learning disorders may be related to attention deficits. As noted, some children with learning disorders also have ADHD, but even those who don't often have short attention spans. While children with learning disorders do worse than normal children at recalling important information, they do better at recalling irrelevant information (Pelham & Ross, 1977; Tarver, Hallahan, Kauffman, et al., 1976). This suggests that their problem may lie not with remembering things but with paying attention to things that they will be expected to remember. Like other children, children with learning disorders get better at focusing attention as they grow older, but they lag two to four years behind. Some experts believe that learning disorders are fundamentally a problem of delayed development, and findings such as these support that theory.

Because children with learning disorders do poorly in school, they are often seen as failures by their teachers, parents, and peers. In consequence, they usually show low self-esteem by age nine (Wenar, 1983), a problem which then worsens with time and with further failures. (According to *DSM-IV*, their school dropout rate is 40 percent. They also tend to have employment problems as adults.) Children with learning disorders, especially girls, are usually less popular than other children with their peers, a disadvantage that is probably due to a number of factors. On the one hand, frustration and anxiety may cause these children to act in ways that alienate other people. On the other hand, their social success may be undermined by the same cognitive problems that impede their academic success. A child who can't remember the rules of a game tends to be left out of games.

The definitions, causes, and symptoms of learning disorders often merge confusingly. Children with the same symptoms may have different underlying disorders, and the same disorder may produce different symptoms in different children. Some people have attributed learning disorders to birth injuries; others, to genetic defects, dietary deficiencies, environmental problems, or poor teaching (P. I. Myers & Hammill, 1990; H. G. Taylor, 1989). It has also been suggested that learning disorders are only an extreme variation of normal development. In any case, the cause is not yet known, nor is it likely to be just one cause. Approaches to treatment are extremely varied, from diets and drugs (for children who also have ADHD) to special instructional techniques. The outlook for children with learning disorders is as variable as the conditions that gather under the umbrella term. It is hoped that future research will shed more light on this perplexing group of disorders.

COMMUNICATION DISORDERS

Delayed Speech and Other Gaps in Communication

Most children say their first words within a few months after their first birthday, and by eighteen to twenty-four months they put together two- and three-word sentences. A few months' delay in this schedule rarely signals a problem, but a prolonged delay is reason for worry. It may be an early sign of an organic disorder, such as deafness, autism (Chapter 18), or mental retardation, or it may stem from environmental causes.

In other cases, speech develops on time, but there are gaps in the child's communication skills. Some children have problems with *articulation:* they do not enunciate clearly, or they go on talking baby talk long after it is normally abandoned. Others have difficulties with *expressive language*—that is, with putting their thoughts into words—either because their vocabularies are limited or because they have a hard time formulating complete sentences. Both these patterns can cause a child to be treated "like a baby." The child may also become very frustrated when he or she is not understood. But both patterns tend to clear up by themselves during the grade school years.

More serious and typically more long-lasting are delays in *receptive language,* that is, in understanding the language of others. This type of disability can be disastrous for a child in school. Surrounded by fast-paced verbal messages that others are obviously understanding while he or she is not, the child may become overwhelmed with frustration. Special-education techniques are usually necessary for children with receptive language deficits.

Stuttering

Stuttering is the interruption of fluent speech through blocked, prolonged, or repeated words, syllables, or sounds. Hesitant speech is common in young children. Therefore, as with so many other childhood disorders, it often is difficult to decide when stuttering is a serious problem. Persistent stuttering occurs in about 1 percent of the population and in about four times as many boys as girls. It is most likely to appear between the ages of two and seven (with peak onset at around age five) and seldom appears after age eleven.

Many children outgrow stuttering as their motor skills and confidence increase. Even those who do not outgrow it completely eventually tend to stutter less or only in stressful situations. About 40 percent of stutterers are estimated to overcome the problem before they start school, and 80 percent overcome it by late adolescence. Even those who do not fully outgrow it stutter less, or only in stressful situations, as they grow older (Couture & Guitar, 1993).

Organic theories of stuttering are popular in some quarters. One hypothesis is that stuttering stems from a problem with the physical articulation of sounds in the mouth and larynx (Agnello, 1975; S. H. Kerr & Cooper, 1976). But many psychologists today think that stuttering is psychogenic. Stuttering may be created unwittingly by parents who become so alarmed at their children's mild speech hesitations that they make the children anxious about speaking (Levine & Ramirez, 1989). The children's anxiety further disturbs their speech, which in turn makes them more anxious, and so on, until a chronic problem has been created. Other theorists have proposed different scenarios, but almost all agree that anxiety is important in creating, maintaining, and aggravating stuttering.

PERSPECTIVES ON THE DISORDERS OF CHILDHOOD AND ADOLESCENCE

The Psychodynamic Perspective

Because of its emphasis on the childhood determinants of adult behavior, the psychodynamic perspective probably interests itself more than any other perspective in the disorders of childhood.

Conflict and Regression It may be said as a general rule that psychodynamic theorists interpret childhood developmental disorders as stemming from a conflict between, on the one hand, the child's sexual and aggressive impulses and, on the other hand, the prohibitions imposed by the parents and by the developing superego. For example, nightmares and night terrors may result when forbidden wishes, repressed during the waking hours, surface in the child's dreams. This process can then give rise to insomnia, with the child refusing to go to sleep for fear that the unacceptable desire will once again be reenacted in dreams.

In much the same way, encopresis can be interpreted as a disguised expression of hostility. A child who is caught in a power struggle with the parents over toilet training or anything else will need some release for aggressive feelings. To express them directly would arouse too much anxiety, so instead, he or she inflicts on the parents the annoyance of cleaning up dirty pants.

Enuresis, on the other hand, is usually interpreted as a sign of regression. As we saw earlier, secondary enuresis is often precipitated by the birth of a sibling. In such cases, according to psychodynamic theory, the wetting constitutes an envy-motivated regression to the new baby's level—a way of letting parents know that older children need as much attention as new babies. Even if the stressor is something altogether different, such as the death of a grandparent or the beginning of school, it is still interpretable as regression: a retreat to an earlier and less threatening stage of development.

Anorexia, too, is often viewed as regression by psychodynamic writers. As we saw earlier, anorexia has been interpreted as a strategy for avoiding adult sexuality. According to psychodynamic theorists, the young woman, unable to meet the demands of the mature genital stage, regresses to an earlier stage. Here, however, she is caught in a dilemma, for among very young children, according to Freudian theory, eating is associated with sexual pleasure; indeed, it may also be associated with pregnancy. (For lack of better information, many small children believe that women become pregnant via the mouth.) Hence the young woman, to avoid the disturbing sexual thoughts associated with food, refuses to eat (A. Freud, 1958; Szyrynski, 1973).

This classic psychodynamic interpretation has been challenged by ego psychologists who feel that anorexia has less to do with repressed instincts than with the adolescent's drive for autonomy. Bruch (1978), for example, sees anorexia as a "desperate struggle for a self-respecting identity" (p. 1) on the part of girls who for years have been dominated by their mothers. In childhood, these girls submit, becoming perfect, well-behaved daughters, but in adolescence they strike back by refusing to eat. This refusal constitutes both a rejection of the mother and a last-ditch attempt at self-determination. In effect, the girl is saying, "I will control my own life, even if it means starving to death." In support of this view, anorexic girls have repeatedly been described as shy, conscientious, and obedient prior to the onset of the disorder (Bruch, 1985; Goodsitt, 1985).

Play Therapy For children, as for adults, psychodynamic theorists feel that the best treatment is one that allows patients to bring to the surface and "work through" their unconscious conflicts. However, the specific procedures for achieving this result are tailored to the child's developmental level and therefore differ somewhat from adult psychotherapy.

A very popular technique is **play therapy.** Here, instead of asking young patients what the problem is, the therapist provides them with drawing materials and toys, on the assumption that whatever is troubling them will be expressed in their drawings and games. Typically the therapist's of-

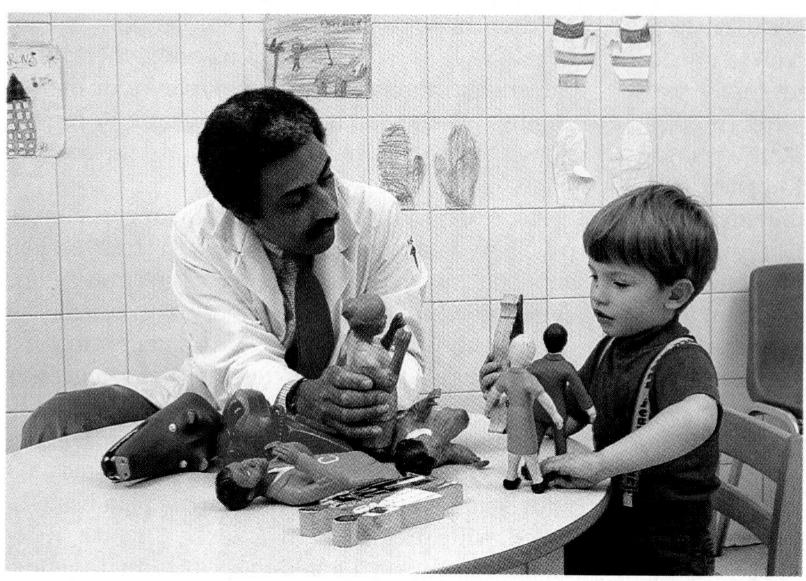

Very young children lack the ability to articulate what is troubling them. Through play therapy, they can express themselves nonverbally.

fice looks something like a small-scale nursery schoolroom, with blocks, crayons, and clay. Other essentials are toys for expressing aggression and dolls and puppets for play-acting family conflicts. Play therapy can be adapted to the theories of the therapist. As used by Anna Freud (1965), who was the best-known exponent of child psychoanalysis, it was closely modeled on adult psychoanalysis. The child was seen four to five times a week, and interpretations were an important part of the therapeutic exchange. For example, if a child commented, "You must see a lot of kids in this office," the therapist might respond, "Would you like to have me all to yourself?" Interpretations are geared to the child's level, however. Furthermore, the child is given more affection and support than an adult would receive in psychoanalysis. Less orthodox psychodynamic therapists will generally see the child once or twice a week and will place less emphasis on insight than on the venting of feelings.

Therapists treating children usually have a good deal of contact with parents. In some cases, the parents may be drawn in as "cotherapists," adopting at home techniques taught to them by the therapist. In other cases, all members of the family may be involved in therapy. Whatever the techniques used, the therapist's conversations with parents may help to resolve family conflicts that have been maintaining the child's problem.

While such methods are characteristic in general of psychodynamic treatment of children, the specific approach varies with the tastes of the therapist, the age of the child, and the nature of the problem. With an anorexic whose life is in danger, a highly directive approach may be used; with an enuretic child, a looser, less directive approach. In treating a preschooler, the therapist may have regular contact with the parents; in treating an adolescent at war with her parents, the therapist may limit conversations with the parents, so as not to forfeit the child's trust. In all cases, the technique will depend on the child's needs.

The Humanistic-Existential Perspective

Although humanistic and existential clinicians have written relatively little on the disorders of childhood, most of them, like the psychodynamic theorists, believe that adult disorders stem from childhood experience.

Denial of Self In explaining the evolution of psychological disorders, humanists and existentialists typically emphasize the loss of self-integrity in childhood. As we saw in Chapter 2, Rogers (1951) claimed that children deny aspects of their experience that are inconsistent with the values of their parents and other people whose approval they seek. Moustakas (1959) too argued that children's psychological difficulties are caused by a denial of the self. Laing (1965) carried this idea one step further with his concept of mystification (Chapter 15), in which the child comes to doubt the very legitimacy of his or her thoughts. (Remember, however, that Laing's theory has to do with schizophrenia, whereas Rogers and Moustakas are primarily concerned with nonpsychotic disorders.) Nevertheless, the humanistic-existential consensus is that psychological disorder takes root when the child, responding to the disapproval of others, begins to reject important parts of the self.

Play Therapy Like psychodynamic therapists, humanistic-existential therapists use play therapy, but their approach to it is somewhat different. Whereas psychodynamic therapists tend to regard play as the symbolic expression of unconscious conflicts which must then be worked through, humanistic therapists see the play itself as the therapy. If it helps young clients to express their feelings and to deal with their problems, then it has done its job. Accordingly, humanistic therapists generally do not offer interpretations. Axline (1969), following the guidelines of Rogers' client-centered therapy, argues that the therapist's role is simply to help children rediscover what they really feel and to provide a positive relationship within which they can obey their drive for self-actualization. Actually, many psychodynamic clinicians use play therapy in much the same way. In the treatment of children, there is considerable overlap between the two schools.

The Behavioral Perspective

With children, as with adults, behaviorists focus directly on the problem behavior. What situations elicit this behavior? What consequences maintain it? How can those antecedents and consequences be changed so that the behavior will change accordingly?

Inappropriate Learning From the behavioral point of view, childhood disorders usually stem from either inadequate learning or inappropriate learning. For example, inadequate learning—that is, a failure to learn relevant cues for performing desired behaviors—may play a role in primary enuresis: the child may never have learned to identify the physiological cues associated with a full bladder. In support of this idea, some researchers have found that enuresis can be successfully treated by teaching the child to recognize those cues (C. E. Walker, Milling, & Bonner, 1988). As for the development of problems through inappropriate learning—that is, the reinforcement of undesirable behavior—the behaviorist's prime example would be the conduct disorders. Children with conduct disorders often come from poor, violence-ridden neighborhoods, where being "tough" with others may be the quickest route to social prestige, especially within a gang. In addition, there is little doubt that modeling plays some role in the conduct disorders. Aside from the influence of gangs, parents may themselves be models of antisocial behavior, especially through indifferent and abusive treatment of the child.

In Chapters 3 and 7 we have already discussed the importance of avoidance learning—the reinforcement of avoidance behavior by the removal of an aversive stimulus such as anxiety—in the development of phobias. Behaviorists believe that this same mechanism—together with direct reinforcements associated with staying home (parental attention, home cooking, television)—may also explain separation anxiety disorder and social phobia.

Relearning To replace the child's maladaptive responses with adaptive behaviors, behavior therapists use the entire behavioral repertoire: reinforcement, extinction, punishment (usually in the form of the withdrawal of rewards), modeling, respondent conditioning, and so on. To begin with the simplest technique, respondent conditioning, a classic example is the treatment of nocturnal enuresis by means of the so-called Mowrer pad. This device, invented by the psychologist O. H. Mowrer, is a liquid-sensitive pad connected by a battery to an alarm. Any moisture on the pad sounds the alarm, awakening the child (Mowrer & Mowrer, 1938). Although theoretically the child should learn to awaken in anticipation of the alarm, many children learn instead to sleep throughout the night, neither awakening nor wetting.

In treating childhood anxiety disorders, behaviorists have used systematic desensitization (Wolpe, 1958). In this process, just as with adults, the child is taught to engage in relaxation or another response incompatible with anxiety while he or she is being gradually exposed to the feared stimuli, usually by imagining them at the therapist's request. A predecessor of this technique was Mary Cover Jones' famous desensitization of the boy Peter to his fear of furry animals by bringing a rabbit successively closer and closer to him while he was eating candy (Chapter 3).

Modeling has also proved very valuable in the treatment of phobias. The child watches the therapist or another person play with a dog, handle a snake, or deal in a relaxed manner with whatever it is that the child fears. Then, in successive steps, the child tries it, and the phobia gradually extinguishes (J. C. Masters, Brush, Hollon, et al., 1987; T. Rosenthal & Bandura, 1978).

Operant-conditioning programs have been successful in the treatment of ADHD. One classroom program, for example, combined extinction of problem behaviors, such as the distracting of one's schoolmates, with reinforcement of more positive behaviors, such as remaining seated long enough to finish a task (Patterson, 1965). Such operant techniques have proved as effective as drugs in controlling the disruptiveness of ADHD children (S. G. O'Leary & Pelham, 1978). Operant conditioning has also been used in the treatment of anorexia nervosa: when anorexic patients are hospitalized and their privileges are made contingent upon eating, they almost invariably gain weight. But once they are released from hospital treatment programs, they tend to relapse unless programs involving the family are also developed (Levendusky & Dooley, 1985). Parents, teachers, and other adults are a critical part of most behavioral programs.

One application of operant conditioning that has proved useful for certain behavior disorders is the token economy, a technique that we have discussed in relation to schizophrenia (Chapter 15). With children it is used just as with adults. Desirable behavior is rewarded with stars or points or some token that the child can save and later exchange for candy, a turn with a special toy, or some other coveted reward. Token systems have proved successful in institutions for delinquent children (Braukmann & Fixsen, 1975) and in schoolrooms (K. D. O'Leary, 1978).

The Cognitive Perspective

Negative Cognitions in Children Cognitive theorists argue that in children, as in adults, problem behaviors can stem from negative beliefs, faulty attributions, poor problem solving, and other cognitive factors. Depression offers a good example. Depression in a child is usually precipitated by some disruption in the life of the family, for example, parental separation. But according to cognitive theory, the real trigger is not the event but the cognitive factors that come into play around it. When parents separate, the children need to be reassured that this is for the best. Often, however, they get the opposite message, as one or the other parent succumbs to depression and by modeling depressive cognitive strategies—helplessness, hopelessness, self-blame—inadvertently teaches the child to adopt the same way of thinking. Many children of recently separated parents believe that they are responsible for the breakup. And, in general, depressed children tend to have at least one depressed parent.

Changing Children's Cognitions An important focus of cognitive therapy for depressed children is attributional retraining: teaching the child to make attributions that are less internal ("It wasn't my fault"), less stable ("It won't always be this way"), and less global ("Everything isn't bad"). Cognitive therapists will also teach depressed children—and often their parents as well—how to increase their activity levels, how to solve problems effectively, and how to improve their "affective communication," in other words, how to share their feelings. Social-skills training may also be used with a depressed child, though the choice of techniques depends on the child's age. Standard cognitive therapy is not appropriate for children under age seven or eight.

Cognitive therapy is now being used for a wide range of childhood disorders. In the early seventies Meichenbaum and Goodman (1971) pioneered cognitive therapy for ADHD children, the goal being to teach them to modify their impulsiveness through self-control skills and reflective problem solving. This was done by means of **self-instructional training,** whereby the person is taught to modify his or her "self-statements" before, during, and after a given action. The therapist models appropriate self-statements in the face of a task: defining the problem ("What do I have to do?"), focusing attention ("Keep working at it"), guiding performance ("Now I have to add the numbers in the right column and carry the first digit"), evaluating performance ("Did I do it right?"), correcting errors ("That's wrong—let's go back"), and rewarding oneself for good performance ("I did a good job"). Then the child attempts the task, using the same or similar self-statements as a guide.

Self-instructional training has now been used by many therapists working with ADHD children. A review of twenty-three studies (Abikoff, 1985) indicates that the method works well for specific tasks and for a while, though the child's newly learned skills do not generalize as widely as was hoped and can vanish if not carefully reinforced. The technique is still being experimented with, however, and has served as a model for similar therapies aimed at improving the reading, writing, penmanship, and arithmetic skills of children with learning disorders (Lloyd, Hallahan, Kauffman, et al., 1991).

The Interpersonal Perspective

The interpersonal perspective, as we saw in Chapter 3, sees the family as a miniature social system in which each member plays a critical role. According to family theory, a branch of the interpersonal perspective, a childhood disorder is a signal of a disturbance in this system. The child may have the symptoms, but it is the family that is "sick" (Haley, 1963; Satir, 1967).

Consider the case of one highly intelligent boy of fourteen who was referred for treatment because he was doing poorly in school. When the family was seen together, it soon became clear that there were problems between the mother and father. The mother repeatedly belittled the father, comparing him unfavorably to the son. The father in turn was gruff with his wife, and despite his apparent concern about his son's academic difficulties, he made it clear that he doubted the virility of any boy who spent too much time with books. The boy, then, was caught in a struggle between his parents. He wanted to do well in order to please his mother. Yet by succeeding academically, he would become a sissy in his father's eyes. Worse yet, he would give his mother one more reason to prefer him to his father, thus further straining the father-son relationship. Hence the boy's academic problems.

According to family therapists, such family psychopathology underlies many childhood disorders and must be dealt with if the child's problems are to be relieved. This is not to suggest that other therapists ignore family dynamics. (We have just seen how cognitive therapists implicate parent-child relations in childhood depression.) The difference is one of emphasis. Rather than concentrating on the present family interaction, a psychodynamic therapist handling the above case might search for deeper, earlier conflicts. (This case would lend itself to analysis of the Oedipal contest.) The behavioral therapist might emphasize the reinforcement patterns of the one-to-one relationship between father and child and between mother and child rather than exploring the complex triangular interaction among the three family members.

Anorexia is one disorder that has been treated successfully through family therapy. Minuchin and his colleagues, who have been working with anorexics for years, claim that these girls' families tend to share the same characteristics: overprotectiveness, rigidity, and a superficial "closeness" covering a good deal of unexpressed anger and resentment. The girl's anorexia, then, serves an important function for the family. It gives them a "safe" target for the expression of frustration and thus makes it possible for them to avoid open conflict over their true grievances. Since it performs this essential service, the anorexia is subtly and unwittingly encouraged by the family (Minuchin, Rosman, & Baker, 1978).

Thus in order to relieve the anorexia, the family problems must first be relieved. To this end, the researchers propose "family therapy lunch sessions." Minuchin (1974) describes one such session with a hospitalized anorexic teenager and her parents. First the therapist allows both parents to try to get their daughter to eat. Inevitably they fail, and the therapist points out to them why, in terms of intrafamily struggles, the child is responding in this way. Then the therapist, who interprets the girl's refusal to eat as a fight for independence within the family, tells the patient she has triumphed over the parents and can savor that triumph but to stay alive she must eat. After a time this strategy begins to work; the patient begins eating surreptitiously. Once the patient is released from the hospital, the parents are instructed to use behavior-modification techniques at home. The girl must eat enough to gain a certain amount of weight each week. If she falls short of the goal, she must remain in bed.

Approximately 85 percent of those on whom this method has been tried show a lasting recovery (Minuchin, Rosman, & Baker, 1978)—a far better outcome than other therapies have achieved. Family therapy is now widely used in the case of childhood disorders and has had some remarkable successes.

The Sociocultural Perspective

As is obvious from the evidence on child abuse (see the box on page 455), sociocultural factors such as poverty can place a child at risk for psychological disturbance. But can cultural patterns also determine the shape that a disorder will take? Weisz and his colleagues, pursuing this question, compared the records from mental health clinics in Thailand and the United States. These are two very different cultures. Americans place a high value on independence and open expression, whereas Thais, in keeping with Buddhist principles, value spontaneity less than the ability to maintain harmonious relations with others. And the American and Thai children in the Weisz team's sample conformed to these principles. The American children were more likely to have disorders of "undercontrolled behavior"—disruptiveness, fighting, temper tantrums—while the Thai children tended to have "overcontrolled-behavior" disorders such as anxiety, sleeping problems, and somatic complaints, particularly head-

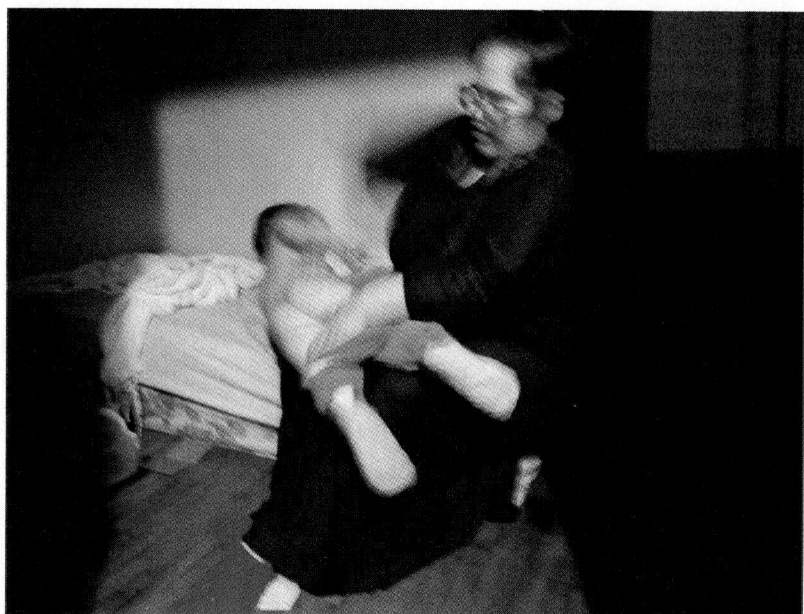

"I am sometimes afraid I might cross the fine line that separates abuse and discipline," says this woman. She and her husband attend parenting classes which teach them alternatives for discipline, such as time outs, using a timer, and notes on the walls reminding them that "children need nurturing like plants need water."

aches (Weisz, Suwanlert, Chaiyasit, et al., 1987b).

This sample, however, was limited to children who had used mental health clinics. To find out if the same principles applied to the general population, Weisz and his colleagues later interviewed parents of school-age children in the two countries (Weisz, Suwanlert, Chaiyasit, et al., 1987a, 1993). Now they found a slightly different pattern. Again problems of overcontrol—"sulks a lot," "has dizzy spells"—were more common in Thai children than in American children, but there was no difference in the incidence of undercontrol problems. Interestingly, though, the Thai children's undercontrol was more controlled than the American children's. They tended to show more subtle and indirect forms of acting-out—attention problems, cruelty to animals—whereas the American children used more direct forms, such as cruelty to other children. So the principle still applied: even when they are violating norms, children heed norms.

What this suggests with regard to childhood disorders is the same point that sociocultural theorists have repeatedly made regarding adult disorders: to find the cause (and the cure), we should look to the culture as well as to the individual. Particularly in the case of the conduct disorders, sociocultural theorists are impatient with purely psychological explanations. Parental unemployment, family disruption, inadequate schools, and subcultural approval of criminal acts have all been found to correlate with the incidence of conduct disorder (Gibbons, 1975). In addressing the disorder, therefore, the society should attend to those matters. Another factor that may well contribute to conduct disorder is the degree of violence in today's movies and on television. Children do imitate aggressive acts that they see on television (Liebert, Neale, & Davison, 1973), and horror movies have been implicated in a number of serious crimes committed by children (Chapter 11). For nearly 3 million children, exposure to violence happens in their own homes. Child abuse has been linked to a host of serious emotional problems in children (see the box on page 455).

Two other syndromes to which cultural norms probably contribute are anorexia and bulimia. As noted, it is young women who are most at risk for these disorders; likewise, it is young women who are subject to the most pervasive pressures to conform to cultural ideals of beauty, particularly of body shape. Those ideals, as reflected in magazine advertisements, have favored increasing thinness over the past few decades (Williamson, Kahn, Remington, et al., 1990), and it is in the past few decades that the reported incidence of anorexia and bulimia has increased, though this shift may reflect more awareness rather than more cases of the disorders. Very few experts would argue that anorexia and bulimia are wholly due to cultural influence, but it is worth noting that anorexia is far rarer among the Chinese (S. Lee & Chiu, 1989) and among American blacks (Dolan, 1991)—two groups that, in general, do not subscribe to the hyperthin female ideal—than it is among American whites.

CHILD ABUSE: CAUSES AND EFFECTS

Close to 3 million cases of child abuse are reported every year in the United States (Besharov, 1992), and the number of cases that are not reported is probably very high. For many reasons—the abusers' shame, the inability of small children to seek help outside the home, the reluctance of teachers and physicians to interfere with parents—child abuse is probably one of the most underreported of crimes.

THE CAUSES

Some researchers have emphasized the psychological causes of child abuse, some the social causes, but most agree that the problem is due to multiple, interlocking factors. One thing that is clear is that the majority of child abusers were themselves abused as children (Whipple & Webster-Stratton, 1991; Widom, 1991). So this behavior was modeled for them. Furthermore, many abused children suffer psychological damage (see below) and are therefore less able, as adults, to cope with their own children. Other factors that predispose parents to abuse their children are immaturity, rigidity, dependency, a sense of powerlessness, inappropriate expectations for parenthood, and, predictably, psychological disturbance (Azar & Twentyman, 1986; Ney, Fung, & Wickett, 1992). Abusing parents are rarely psychotic, but they are likely to show personality disorders and very likely to abuse alcohol or other drugs.

Apart from personal risk factors, there are obvious social factors, namely poverty and unemployment. "What often separates abusers from nonabusers is a job" (L. Steinberg & Meyer, 1995, p. 313). Some critics claim that child abuse is better reported among the poor because the poor have more contact with social agencies, but even this cannot account

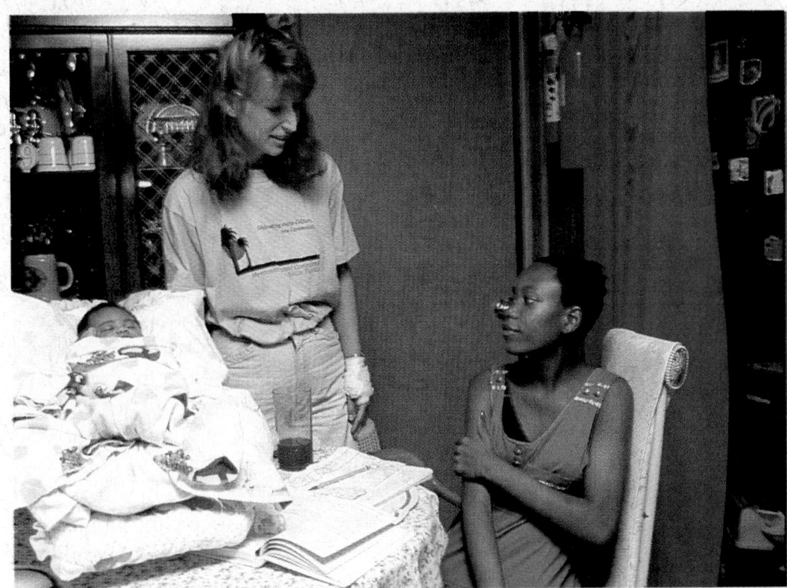

The thirteen-year-old single mother at right is participating in a program intended to help people in her high-risk situation avoid becoming abusive parents.

for the vastly increased risk of abuse in impoverished families. Children from families with an income of less than $15,000 are five times more likely to be maltreated than children from higher-income families (Sedlack, 1989). Poverty is a powerful stressor, and stress promotes aggression. Animal mothers under stress have been observed to attack their offspring, and human parents may do likewise (Williams, 1976). But poverty is not the only stressor that can push parents over the line. Marital discord contributes too. Families that are socially isolated and that are dominated by a male are also more likely to have abused children (Azar & Perlmutter, 1993).

Beyond socioeconomic pressures, large-scale cultural factors probably help to account for the high rate of child abuse in the United States. Ours is a violent society; it is also one that guards privacy heavily and considers individual family values more privileged than community values. Other societies have much lower rates of child abuse. In China it is rare for a child to be subjected to physical punishment (Kessen, 1979); in Sweden, it is illegal (that includes spankings).

THE EFFECTS

Even after it is reported, child abuse tends to be repeated (G. J. R. Williams, 1983), and the more often it happens, the greater the likelihood of irreversible effects, including death. According to the National Committee for the Prevention of Child Abuse, about 1,300 American children died of abuse in 1993 alone. As for those who survive frequent abuse, they are likely to suffer permanent gastrointestinal, orthopedic, and, above all, neurological injuries. Up to 30 percent of abused children show brain damage, which, by making it harder for them to do what their parents want from them, exposes them to further abuse—a cruel scenario. Repeated blows to the head can lead to mental retardation, cerebral palsy, and

(Continued)

CHILD ABUSE *(CONTINUED)*

other disorders (G. J. R. Williams, 1983).

Those are only the physical effects. The psychological effects can be equally profound. Young children who are abused are also more likely to show aggressiveness, impulsiveness, destructiveness, frequent temper tantrums, and low self-esteem (Alessandri, 1991; Kaufman & Cicchetti, 1989; Vondra, Barnett, & Cicchetti, 1990).—all of which, again, are likely to get on their parents' nerves, with predictable consequences. As teenagers, they are more prone to conduct disorders (Widom, 1989), and when they become adults, as we saw, they are more likely to abuse their children, thus continuing the cycle.

TREATMENT AND PREVENTION

All fifty states now prosecute child abusers, but neither legal nor preventative measures have curbed the problem. Studies by the National Center on Child Abuse and Neglect have led to the development of educational programs, which in turn have made teachers, physicians, and other professionals more watchful for signs of abuse and more likely to report them. There are now parents' support groups, including the Voluntary Intervention and Treatment Program (VITP) and Parents Anonymous, a self-help group. The courts have shown greater willingness to remove children from homes where they are likely to go on being victimized. In some cases, removal seems to be the only treatment. Ironically, abused children have fewer treatment opportunities than child abusers.

Prevention programs offer some hope. One program, aimed at poor, single teenage mothers—a group at high risk for child abuse—used visiting nurses as teachers, role models, and informal counselors. Before and after the children's birth, the nurses made regular home visits to the young mothers, teaching them about child development, encouraging them to form close ties to friends and family (thus preventing the social isolation that seems to foster abuse), and, above all, bolstering their self-esteem by emphasizing their capabilities. This apparently had an effect. After two years, only 4 percent of the mothers in the program had abused or neglected their children, as opposed to 20 percent of an untreated control group (Olds & Henderson, 1989).

The Biological Perspective

There have been a number of heated disputes between biogenic and psychogenic theorists in the area of childhood disorders. Biological causes have been proposed for encopresis and enuresis. (As noted, three-fourths of enuretic children have a first-degree relative who was also enuretic.) Likewise, it has been proposed that anorexia may be due to a disturbance in the biological hunger response. With anorexia, however, recent research points to both biological and psychological causes. The cerebrospinal fluid of severely underweight anorexics has been found to contain abnormally high levels of neuropeptide Y, a neurochemical that is known to signal the hunger response. Furthermore, when these anorexics regain their normal weight, their neuropeptide Y levels also return to normal. So it seems that anorexics *are* physiologically hungry—indeed, very hungry. However, psychological factors (such as fear of gaining weight) appear to override this physical need (Kaye, Berrettini, Gwirtsman, et al., 1990; Leibowitz, 1991).

Of all the disorders that we have discussed in this chapter, the one that seems most likely to have a biological basis is ADHD. As we saw earlier, the term *minimal brain dysfunction* is no longer widely used to describe this syndrome, and some researchers believe that ADHD is psychogenic. Nevertheless, the neuroscience perspective has contributed an effective drug treatment for the disorder. Most children with ADHD have a "paradoxical response" to stimulant drugs—above all, to amphetamines. Whereas amphetamines "speed up" normal people, so that they behave something like hyperactive children, the same drugs slow down hyperactive children, so that they behave more like normal people. Furthermore, stimulants work with both the inattentive types, increasing their powers of concentration, and the hyperactive types, reducing their fidgetiness and impulsiveness. One study found that about three-fourths of ADHD children who were put on stimulants showed dramatic improvements in attention span, social behavior, and self-control (DuPaul & Barkley, 1990).

A large percentage of children with ADHD are now on daily doses of amphetamines, usually either Dexedrine or Ritalin. Indeed, over 2 percent of the school population takes stimulant medication (Safer & Krager, 1988). Some experts have strongly objected to this. For one thing, the drugs may have adverse side effects, including weight loss, insomnia, and high blood pressure. Second, they do not actually cure the disorder. General behavior may improve, but academic performance usually does not (Barkley, 1989), and the prognosis for the child remains the same. No drug can compensate for the accumulated deficits in the child's problem-solving skills. Such skills must be taught after attention has been improved by medication, thus requiring a combination of approaches (DuPaul & Barkley, 1993). Third, if parents, schools, and physicians become accustomed to using drugs for "problem children," the possibilities for abuse are frightening. It is all too easy to imagine medication being administered to *all* problem children, including those whose disruptive behavior is a response to family conflicts or simply to a boring school program.

These objections are important, and it is generally agreed that drugs must be prescribed with great caution. And, as mentioned earlier, some behavioral programs have been as effective as drug therapy (Barkley, 1990). Nevertheless, since amphetamines do, in general, have beneficial effects on the adjustment of ADHD children, they are still widely used, often in conjunction with behavior therapy.

KEY TERMS

anorexia nervosa (443)
attention deficit hyperactivity disorder (ADHD) (438)
bulimia nervosa (444)
childhood depression (443)
conduct disorder (439)
disruptive behavior disorders (437)
encopresis (446)
enuresis (445)
generalized anxiety disorder (442)
learning disorders (447)
nightmares (446)
night terrors (446)
play therapy (449)
self-instructional training (452)
separation anxiety disorder (441)
sleepwalking (446)
social phobia (441)
stuttering (448)

SUMMARY

- The disorders of childhood and adolescence include a wide range of problems. Many of them have no parallel to adult disorders, and those that do (such as depression) may manifest themselves differently in children. Disorders of childhood are fairly common, become more prevalent with age, and are more common with boys up to adolescence.
- Empirical studies identify several general classes of childhood disorders: disruptive behavior disorders, involving impulsive, aggressive, acting-out behaviors; emotional distress disorders, such as anxiety and depression; habit disorders, the disruption of habits such as eating, sleeping, and elimination; and learning and communication disorders.
- Childhood disorders may affect adult adjustment. A disorder may simply persist into adulthood in a similar form, as in the case of antisocial behavior. Or a child's disorder may set him or her on a path that becomes a maladaptive pattern. Finally, childhood disturbances may create a reactivity to stressors, leaving the child at risk for problems later in life. Treatment (and prevention) of childhood disorders may help to prevent adult disorders.
- Two common disruptive behavior disorders are attention deficit hyperactivity disorder (ADHD) and conduct disorder. Children with ADHD lack the ability to focus their attention for more than a brief period and exhibit a variety of impulsive and disruptive behaviors. Some ADHD children show more inattentiveness, and some, more hyperactivity, but most of them combine the two.
- A preadolescent or adolescent child who persistently violates social norms—stealing, lying, running away from home, destroying property, and so on—is said to have a conduct disorder. The younger the age of onset, the more serious the problems, both in childhood and adulthood.
- Disorders of emotional distress are "internalizing" disorders: the child turns the conflict inward and becomes depressed or anxious. Children may suffer from many of the same anxiety disorders as adults, such as social phobias and generalized anxiety disorder; in addition, young children may experience separation anxiety disorder when having to part from their parents, however briefly. Depression in childhood may manifest itself like adult depression, or it may show up as problems at school, delinquency, or exaggerated fears.
- Habit disorders may appear with other childhood disorders, or they may occur alone. Eating disorders tend to be prompted by a distorted body image. They include anorexia nervosa, involving severely restricted food intake and substantial weight loss, and bulimia nervosa, a pattern of binge eating followed by induced vomiting or elimination. Elimination disorders include enuresis (lack of bladder control) and, more

rarely, encopresis (lack of bowel control). Among the sleep disorders are nightmares, night terrors, and sleepwalking.

- Learning disorders involve inadequate development of specific learning skills, such as reading, writing, or mathematics. Children with these problems may have abnormal visual or auditory perception or memory problems.
- Communication disorders include delayed speech and stuttering. Sometimes speech develops on time, but there are gaps in skills such as articulation, expressive language, and understanding others.
- The seven major perspectives on developmental disorders offer different interpretations and treatments. According to the psychodynamic perspective, disorders originate in a conflict between a child's impulses, on the one hand, and parents' prohibitions and the developing superego, on the other. Treatment aims at allowing the child to bring unconscious conflicts to the surface and deal with them.
- Humanistic-existential clinicians see disorders taking root when the child, responding to disapproval from others, begins to reject important parts of the self. Many use play therapy to allow the children to express their feelings and deal with their problems.
- Behaviorists focus on actual problem behaviors and the environmental variables that have conditioned them. They believe that children's behavioral problems usually stem from either inadequate or inappropriate learning. The behavioral treatment for both conduct and anxiety disorders makes use of the entire behavioral repertoire: reinforcement, extinction, withdrawal of rewards, modeling, respondent conditioning, and systematic desensitization.
- Cognitive theorists believe that some children's disorders may be caused by negative beliefs, faulty attributions, poor problem solving, and other cognitive factors. Cognitive therapy often focuses on teaching the child to make more positive and functional attributions. Self-instructional training may also be employed.
- The interpersonal perspective views the family as a miniature social system, in which each person plays a critical role. One branch of this perspective, family theory, holds that a child may manifest a disorder but it is the family that is "sick." Treatment involves an exploration of the interaction among all family members.
- From the sociocultural perspective, cultural patterns help determine the shape a disorder will take. Treatment and prevention entail tackling social problems, such as inadequate schools, poverty, family disruption, unemployment, and exposure to violence or unrealistic ideals of beauty.
- The biological perspective ascribes some developmental disorders to biological factors. Because ADHD has responded to medical treatment, it is assumed to be the developmental disorder most likely to have biological causes. Even so, there are strong arguments against using drugs to treat children's psychological disturbances.

18

MENTAL RETARDATION AND AUTISM

18

MENTAL RETARDATION AND AUTISM

Joan, a mildly retarded thirty-five-year-old woman, lived at home with her aging parents and her brother. In school she had been a "slow learner," and she finally dropped out of high school in her sophomore year. At the time of her evaluation, she had been employed as a factory worker for ten years, but she could never console herself for not having graduated from high school. Two years earlier she had started taking classes for a high school equivalency exam. When she arrived at the clinic, she had just taken the exam and failed it, scoring only 156 when the minimum passing score was 225.

Joan saw herself as "different" and stupid. All her shortcomings she saw clearly; all her good qualities she brushed aside. She was quite angry at her family. She felt they ignored her presence in family conversations and that they limited her independence. For example, they wouldn't let her go visit her cousin alone because they were afraid she would get lost. Above all, she blamed them for not allowing her to finish high school and for discouraging her high school equivalency studies. What she wanted most of all was to "finish high school like other people."

Aside from her anger at her family, Joan's most prominent emotion was depression. She had no friends and, other than needlepoint, no hobbies. She felt tired most of the day but had trouble sleeping at night. She also had a poor appetite and suffered crying bouts. She said she felt sad and lonely most of the time. (adapted from Reiss, 1985, pp. 173–174)

Mental retardation, the name we give to a condition of impaired intelligence and adaptive functioning, is not a single disorder with a single cause. It may be due to genetic abnormalities, to damage to the brain before or at birth, or—some experts believe—to deprivation in childhood. Its manifestations are as varied as its causes. Mentally retarded people in this country range from those who grow up, marry, and live on their own, going to work during the week and to the movies on Saturday night, to those who cannot learn, speak, or care for themselves in any way.

Although there are no absolute statistics on the prevalence of mental retardation, *DSM-IV* estimates that mental retardation affects approximately 1 percent of the U.S. population. However imprecise this estimate, it signifies an enormous problem for society.

In this chapter we will first discuss the definition and causes of mental retardation. Then we will describe a special syndrome, autism, that usually involves retardation. Finally, we will look at the social issues surrounding retardation and autism, together with methods of prevention and treatment.

MENTAL RETARDATION

As defined by the American Association on Mental Retardation (AAMR), **mental retardation** involves three components:

1 Significantly subaverage intellectual functioning

2 Related limitations in adaptive skills, such as communication, self-care, dealing with others, playing, and working

3 Onset before age eighteen (AAMR, 1992)

Several things should be noted about this definition. First, it requires that any person diagnosed as mentally retarded show serious deficits in *both* intellectual and adaptive functioning. A child who scores low on an IQ test but who functions well in his or her community is not a candidate for this diagnosis. Second, mental retardation by definition manifests itself in childhood, and it is by judging the child in comparison to his or her age-mates that the diagnosis is made. Finally, the AAMR definition says nothing about cause. In the majority of cases, mental retardation is due to some deficit or dysfunction of the nervous system, but in many cases the exact cause cannot be shown, and diagnosis does not depend on its being shown.

Levels of Retardation

Intelligence test scores have an approximately normal distribution, with 100 as the mean and 16 as the standard deviation (a measure of the dispersion of scores above and below the mean). In diagnosing mental retardation, the cutoff point between normal and "significantly subaverage intellectual functioning" is about two standard deviations below the mean—that is, an IQ of about 68 or 70. People whose scores fall below that line may be diagnosed as mentally retarded if their adaptive skills are also impaired. In addition, it has been traditional in the past few decades to specify the person's "level" of retardation: mild, moderate, severe, or profound. The following descriptions of these four levels are based on N. M. Robinson and Robinson (1976), Baroff (1974), and MacMillan (1982).

Mild Retardation (IQ 50–55 to 70) About 85 percent of all cases of retardation are classified as mild retardation—a condition that, because it is mild, is often not recognized until the person enters school. As young children, mildly retarded people develop more slowly and need help longer with

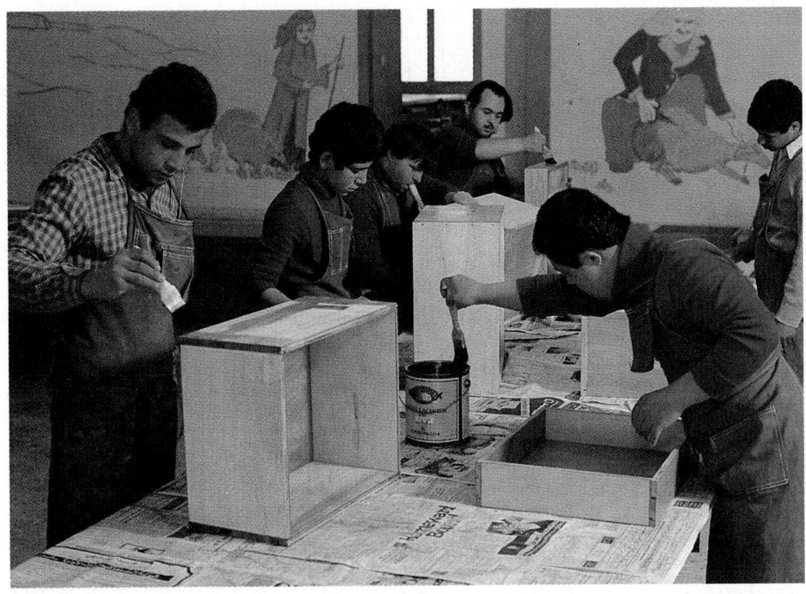

Roughly 85 percent of mentally retarded people have a mild form of the disorder. These mildly retarded men in Amman, Jordan are learning woodworking skills that will help them live productively and independently.

self-care tasks such as eating, dressing, and toilet training. By adolescence, mildly retarded people can function independently in most areas of life. They speak fluently, and can usually read easy material and do simple arithmetic. As adults, they may need someone who can act as an advisor, particularly with regard to money management. Most of them can hold a job and have friends; some can also marry and have children.

Moderate Retardation (IQ 35–40 to 50–55) Moderate retardation is usually evident by age two or three. By about age six, such children can feed themselves with cup and spoon, cooperate with dressing, begin toilet training, and use some words and recognize shapes. By adolescence, they have good self-care skills and can carry on simple conversations, read a few words, and do simple tasks. In the past, moderately retarded people were often institutionalized, but today many live in the community, in special residences or with their families.

Severe Retardation (IQ 20–25 to 35–40) Severely retarded people can learn some self-care skills and with proper training can perform jobs in a sheltered workshop or a daytime activity center. Training is especially valuable at the severely retarded level, since it can make the difference between institutionalization and a more productive and happy life in a family or residence group. Severely retarded people do, however, require considerable supervision. They can understand language, but many have trouble speaking, and their reading and number skills are not sufficient for normal living.

Profound Retardation (IQ below 20 or 25) Profoundly retarded people can carry out some self-care activities and can sometimes perform tasks in a daytime activity center, but they require extensive supervision and help. Language is a severe problem; they may understand a simple communication, but they have little or no ability to speak. Many profoundly retarded people remain institutionalized, usually because of severe behavior problems or multiple physical handicaps. Because of increased susceptibility to disease, people in this category often die in childhood or adolescence.

It should be added that these descriptions of the four levels of retardation are only broad generalizations. Even as generalizations, their value has been questioned. *DSM-IV* lists them, but the AAMR manual argues against these groups because they are based on IQ, which is only one measure of functioning. Furthermore, they assume more consistency between IQ scores and adaptive behavior than many people show. In sum, they give too much weight to IQ. The AAMR actually recommends that diagnosticians not apply the IQ criterion until deficits in adaptive behavior have been established. Two people with IQs of 60 may differ as much in their coping ability as two people with IQs of 100.

Genetic Factors in Retardation

In some cases, particularly the severest cases, mental retardation can be attributed to a specific biological factor. But the mechanism by which that factor produces retardation is seldom understood. We know, for example, that most people with

Down syndrome have an extra chromosome, but we do not know how that chromosome actually damages the nervous system. Furthermore, two people may have the same medical diagnosis yet be at very different levels of retardation. Finally, there is the problem of differential diagnosis. It is not always clear whether a diagnosis of retardation, autism, emotional disturbance, or learning disability is appropriate in any given case. All four conditions may result in generally impaired or deficient behavior and development, and the conditions are not mutually exclusive. Mental retardation and emotional disturbance, for example, may be present in the same person.

The AAMR manual lists more than 300 organic or genetic anomalies associated with retardation. We will discuss only a few of the more common and better-known syndromes.

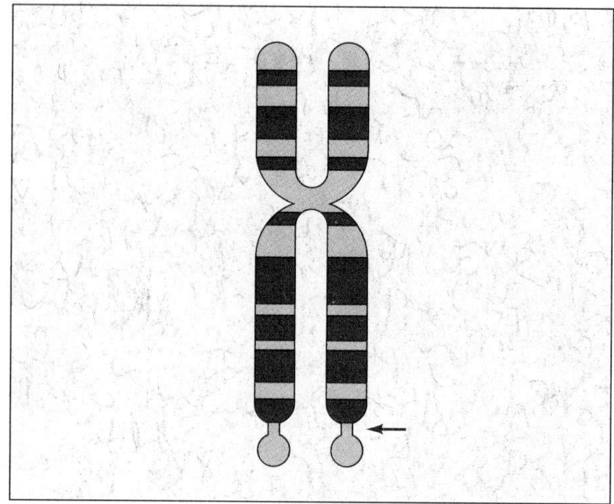

FIGURE 18.1 Schematic drawing of the fragile X chromosome. The arrow points to the fragile site. (Hagerman & McBogg, 1983)

Chromosomal Abnormalities Since the early twentieth century it has been known that certain forms of mental retardation are "X-linked"—that is, they are genetically inherited via the X chromosome, which also determines sex. But it was not until 1969 that H. A. Lubs, a researcher at the University of Miami School of Medicine, described the cause. In certain individuals, Lubs noted, the X chromosome shows a weak spot, where it appears to be bent or broken (Figure 18.1). This condition, which is called **fragile X syndrome** and occurs in about 1 out of every 870 births (Webb, Bundey, Thake, et al., 1986), is the most common genetic cause of mental retardation. People with fragile X syndrome have certain pronounced physical characteristics—large, prominent ears, an elongated face, and, in males, enlarged testicles. Many of them are hyperactive and may also show autistic characteristics: hand biting, limited speech, poor eye contact. (Accordingly, some are diagnosed as autistic.) In men, because they have only one X chromosome, this syndrome is more likely to have severe consequences; almost all males with fragile X experience some impairment to cognitive function, with the majority falling into the moderate-retardation category. In women, because there are two X chromosomes, with the possibility that a normal one may mask the effects of the abnormal one, the risk of mental retardation is less (Hagerman & McBogg, 1983).

Almost as common as fragile X syndrome is **Down syndrome,** which occurs in approximately 1 out of every 900 births (MacMillan, 1982). This condition is named after Langdon Down, the British physician who first described it in 1866. For many years, however, it was known as *mongolism,* the term coined by Down in reference to the slanting eyes and flat nose that characterize most people with this condition, making them look faintly like the Mongols of northeastern Asia. Other typical traits are a small, round head; an extra fold of skin on the upper eyelids; a small mouth with drooping corners; a thickened, protruding tongue; short, stubby fingers; poor muscle tone; and, in almost all cases, mental retardation. Most people with Down syndrome have IQs of 50 or less. They are also susceptible to serious cardiac and respiratory diseases, with the result that their life expectancy is shorter than average. With advances in medicine, however, a Down syndrome child who survives the first few months now has a good chance of living into adulthood.

While Down syndrome was described in the mid-nineteenth century, its genetic basis was not discovered until the mid-twentieth century. In 1959 the French geneticist Jerome Lejeune and his colleagues reported that people with Down syndrome almost always have an extra chromosome in pair 21, or **trisomy 21** (see Figure 18.2). This extra chromosome is thought to be caused by an error in cell division in the mother's ovum.

Together, fragile X and Down syndrome account for one-fourth of all cases of mental retardation, though their incidence—and that of the many other chromosomal abnormalities that can cause retardation—may eventually be reduced through genetic counseling. Since fragile X is inherited, those at risk are people with a family history of X-

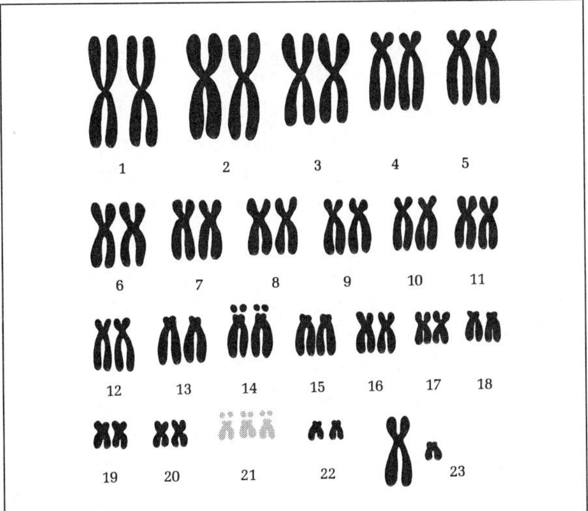

FIGURE 18.2 The chromosomes of a male child with Down syndrome. In most cases (as in this one), the presence of an extra chromosome in pair 21 causes the abnormality. More rarely, the trisomy occurs in the twenty-second pair.

linked retardation. As for Down syndrome, the risk is directly related to the mother's age: for women aged twenty-nine or under, the chances are about 1 in every 1,500 births, but for women over the age of forty-five, the chances are about 1 in 30 (MacMillan, 1982). In genetic counseling, high-risk prospective parents are advised as to the chances of an abnormal birth. If the woman is already pregnant, chromosomal abnormalities in the developing fetus can often be identified through a clinical procedure called **amniocentesis,** which involves extracting and analyzing a portion of the amniotic fluid in which the fetus is growing. Amniocentesis is now routinely recommended for pregnant women over thirty-five, to screen for Down syndrome. When the tests reveal abnormalities, many women choose to end the pregnancy.

Metabolic Disturbances Another form of genetic defect results in metabolic disturbances. One of the best known is **phenylketonuria (PKU),** which occurs in about 1 in every 13,000 to 20,000 live births (MacMillan, 1982). The cause of PKU appears to be a defective recessive gene, which leaves the child deficient in phenylalanine 4-hydroxylase, a liver enzyme that is needed to metabolize the amino acid phenylalanine. In consequence, phenylalaline and its derivatives accumulate in the body and eventually damage the developing central nervous system. The result is usually severe retardation, hyperactivity, and erratic and unpredictable behavior. Fortunately this disorder can be detected soon after birth. Most states now require that newborns be tested for PKU. A special low-phenylalanine diet from infancy to at least age six can often prevent or at least minimize neurological damage (MacMillan, 1982).

Another metabolic disorder is **Tay-Sachs disease.** This disorder, transmitted by a recessive gene, is a defect of lipid metabolism, due to the absence of the enzyme hexosominidase A in the brain tissues. It is usually detected between four and eight months and is confined largely to children of Eastern European Jewish ancestry. It is characterized by progressive deterioration to the point of complete immobility, with isolated episodes of convulsions. Tay-Sachs disease is untreatable. Even under intensive hospital care, only 17 percent of afflicted infants survive beyond four years, and death is virtually certain before the age of six (S. M. Aronson & Volk, 1965).

Environmental Factors in Retardation

Genes are one factor that can cause retardation. The other crucial influence on the developing brain is the environment, both prenatal—the environment of the uterus—and postnatal—the physical and social world surrounding the child in his or her early years.

Prenatal Environment

Congenital disorders Mental retardation can be caused by **congenital disorders,** disorders acquired during prenatal development but not transmitted genetically. Until recently, two common congenital causes of mental retardation were rubella (German measles) and syphilis, transmitted from the mother to the fetus. Children affected by congenital rubella may be born with various impairments, including brain lesions, which usually result in mental retardation. The earlier in her term the mother contracts the disease, the greater the risk to the fetus. Congenital syphilis, under certain circumstances, causes hydrocephalus, excessive cerebrospinal fluid, which results in retardation. Thanks to widespread immunization for rubella and premarital and prenatal blood tests for syphilis (which responds to penicillin), both these congenital diseases are now rare.

Thyroxine deficiency, a congenital hormonal imbalance, causes cretinism, a condition marked by serious mental retardation and physical disabili-

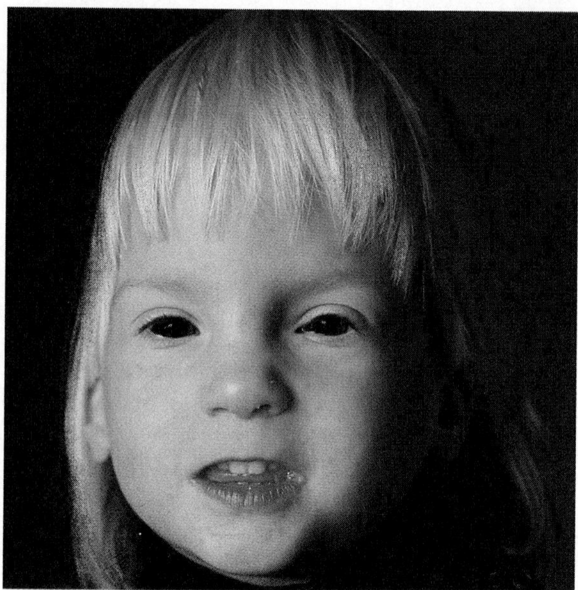

Babies born to drug-addicted mothers show a variety of ill effects, which often include low birth weight, irritability, and mental retardation. The child shown here displays the facial features typical of fetal alcohol syndrome, including a flattened bridge, missing indentation below the nose, and a barely formed upper lip.

ties. If a pregnant woman's diet lacks iodine—now widely available in iodized salt—or if the thyroid of the fetus is damaged during birth, thyroxine deficiency will result. Mental retardation can be prevented only if the deficiency is detected and treated with thyroid extract during the first year of the infant's life.

Drugs In the early sixties a new drug, thalidomide, was introduced in Europe and Canada to relieve morning sickness in pregnant women. Thalidomide did help with morning sickness; unfortunately, it had other effects as well. Many of the women who took the drug gave birth to mentally retarded babies with severely malformed limbs. Thalidomide was swiftly removed from the market, but it had far-reaching effects, and not just for the families of these unfortunate children. The thalidomide scandal helped to raise worldwide consciousness as to the potentially damaging effect that any drug taken during pregnancy can have on the developing fetus.

As many studies have shown, that includes alcohol. When a pregnant woman takes a drink, the alcohol enters the fetus' bloodstream almost immediately, slowing down the workings of the central nervous system (Landesman-Dwyer, 1981). Repeated exposure to this experience can damage the fetus. Even women who are only "social drinkers" are more likely than nondrinkers to have babies with birth defects (Oyellette et al., 1977). As for women who are alcoholic, their babies are at high risk for a complex of physical and behavioral defects known as **fetal alcohol syndrome,** or **FAS.** FAS involves distinctive facial characteristics (short eye slits, drooping eyelids, short nose, narrow upper lip), retarded physical growth, and, frequently, mental retardation (Streissguth, Landesman-Dwyer, Martin, et al., 1980). Approximately 1 out of every 750 babies born in the United States shows FAS (Landesman-Dwyer, 1981).

Illegal drugs have equally profound effects on the fetal brain, as has been seen in the increasing number of "crack babies"—babies prenatally addicted to cocaine—that have been born since crack cocaine entered the illegal drug market in the mid-1980s. These babies are likely to show retarded growth at birth (Hadeed & Siegel, 1989). Their brain development may also be affected. They tend to be either overexcited or depressed; they develop language more slowly (van Baar, 1990); they are less responsive to toys (Rodning, Beckwith, & Howard, 1989). The extent of retardation among crack-using mothers is not yet fully understood; more research is needed. There is no shortage of potential subjects. It has been estimated that 10 to 20 percent of urban U.S. babies are now exposed to cocaine before birth.

It should be added, however, that whatever damage these babies suffer is probably the result not just of prenatal environment but of a subtle interaction of prenatal and postnatal disadvantages. Cocaine-exposed babies tend to be born into families that are poor and unstable and that lack adequate health services (Mayes et al., 1992; Zuckerman & Frank, 1992). Their mothers are more likely to be clinically depressed (Hawley & Disney, 1992), not to mention cocaine-addicted, and therefore unlikely to offer the kind of stimulating interaction required for adequate brain development. In addition, such babies, because of the effects of the cocaine, are harder to care for—they are often overexcited or depressed—and this probably does not endear them to their mothers. In one study, substance-abusing women were observed with their babies at three months and then nine months after birth. In general, these women were less responsive to their babies' needs than were women who did not take drugs (Rodning, Beckwith, & Howard, 1992).

Malnutrition Another prenatal factor that can contribute to retardation is maternal malnutrition. A number of studies conducted in poorer countries have shown that women who are put on enriched diets during pregnancy tend to give birth to more alert babies than do women who are not given food supplements (Vuori et al., 1979). Many researchers suspect that such differences may have to do with *myelination*, the process whereby the developing nerves insulate themselves with a soft, white, fatty material called myelin, thereby increasing the speed and efficiency with which nerve impulses travel through the brain. Insufficient myelination, which is associated with fetal malnutrition, may thus slow down the workings of the brain (Davison & Dobbing, 1966). Again, however, malnutrition probably does not operate alone, for it is often seen in conjunction with other retardation-associated factors. Drug-addicted mothers, for example, also tend to suffer from malnutrition, thus placing their babies at a double risk.

Postnatal Environment

Toxins Various substances, if they enter the child's bloodstream during infancy or childhood, can cause neurological damage resulting in retardation. A sad example is the DPT vaccine, which is routinely given to children to protect them from diphtheria, pertussis, and tetanus. In a very small number of children, the pertussis component in the vaccine causes adverse reactions, including brain damage. DPT vaccination is thought to account for about fifty new cases of severe retardation per year.

A far higher risk of retardation is posed by lead poisoning (Chapter 16). Lead-based paint, though its use is now prohibited, is still to be found on the walls of older housing, particularly in low-income housing projects. If that paint is flaking and if the flakes, which have a sweet taste, are eaten by a child on a regular basis, lead deposits will accumulate in the tissues and interfere with brain-cell metabolism, resulting in permanent damage. Retardation due to lead poisoning is usually severe (Koch, 1971). Lead can affect children prenatally as well, if the mother is exposed to it. One study found that children with elevated lead levels in their umbilical-cord blood showed slower mental development through age two (Ballinger et al., 1987).

Physical trauma Another potential cause of mental retardation is trauma to the brain as a result of accidents or child abuse. Children who are repeatedly beaten may suffer irreversible brain damage. The brain can also be harmed during birth. If labor is rapid and the baby's head compresses and reexpands so quickly that it hemorrhages, or if labor is slow and delivery by forceps injures the brain, retardation can occur. Another birth hazard is hypoxia, or insufficient oxygenation of the baby's blood. If anesthesia is improperly administered, if the mother is hypertensive, if labor is prolonged, or if the umbilical cord ruptures, hypoxia can result, and even if it occurs only for a short period, it can cause mental retardation.

The effects of deprivation Lead-based paint, as we just saw, is more common in poor neighborhoods. So are malnutrition and drug abuse. Furthermore, children who are at organic risk for retardation are less likely to receive appropriate treatment if they are poor. These facts alone might account for the disproportionately high incidence of mental retardation among children from disadvantaged backgrounds. At the same time, it has been proposed that, in the absence of an identifiable physical cause, some cases of mild retardation may be due to the psychological handicaps of growing up in a deprived setting. According to this view, children who lack a stable home, proper parental care, intellectual stimulation, and adequate language models and who are exposed to low expectations for life advancement and feelings of hopelessness suffer a kind of mental impoverishment that is not organic but that is measurable with intelligence tests (Garber & McInerney, 1982). Such impoverishment is sometimes called *pseudo-retardation*, on the grounds that the primary disturbance is emotional, not intellectual. Although every aspect of poverty, including substandard housing, inferior education, and discrimination, can contribute to emotional disturbance and thus to impaired learning, it is the decreased level of stimulation—of varied sensory experiences, of verbal communication, of one-on-one, parent-child interaction—that is thought to be most closely associated with poor intellectual development.

This hypothesis stresses psychological, as opposed to organic, factors. However, a report recently issued by the Carnegie Corporation (1994) suggests that what begin as psychological factors *become* organic factors. As we saw in Chapter 9, the long-held distinction between mind and body has become increasingly blurred as advances in neuroscience have permitted researchers to observe the physical processes involved in "mental" events and vice versa. The research summarized by the Carnegie report constitutes a further stage in the collapse of the mind-body distinction. It also supports the concept of **brain plasticity**; that experiences can alter the structure and function of the brain. The research indicates that what infants learn, and don't learn, from their environments has a substantial effect on the physical development of their brains.

At birth, the formation of the neurons, or brain cells, is virtually complete. What is not finished is the *organization* of the neurons, the wiring up of one neuron to the next, via the synapses (Chapter 4), to create the brain's intricate structure. (A neuron may have up to 15,000 synapses.) Broadly speaking, the newborn brain consists of an immense tangle of neurons. Then, in the period after birth, this mass is "sculpted." Some neurons die; others remain. Those that remain develop synaptic connections to some cells and not to others. Through this process the brain develops the circuitry that will allow it to process environmental stimuli for the rest of its life.

What is most critical about this process is that it seems to occur very early. In the first few months after birth the number of synapses between neurons increases twentyfold, from 50 trillion to 1,000 trillion (Kolb, 1989). By the time children are walking, they may have developed most of the neural connections they will ever have. PET studies have shown that the biochemical patterns of a one-year-old's brain are qualitatively similar to those of a young adult's brain (Chugani, 1993). The second crucial point is that the formation of the neural synapses is heavily influenced by the environment, and this includes not only long-recognized biological factors such as nutrition but also psychological factors, above all, sensory experience. "The brain uses information about the outside world to design its architecture" (Carnegie Corporation, 1994, p. 8). A rich, stimulating, and benign sensory environment builds a more complex and efficient brain (Chugani, Phelps, & Mazziotta, 1987). A barren environment produces a less efficient brain. Furthermore, environmental stress seems to activate hormones that impede brain functioning (McEwen, 1992).

The consequences of these findings for disadvantaged children are grimly stated by the Carnegie report: "Studies of children raised in poor environments—both in this country and elsewhere—show that they have cognitive deficits of substantial magnitude by eighteen months of age" (Carnegie Corporation, 1994, p. 8). Those studies, so far, have consisted of observational and cognitive tests, but their findings seem to be on the verge of confirmation by brain scan technology. If they are confirmed, this will be bad news indeed, for such cognitive deficits, the report adds, may not be fully reversible. On the contrary, they may be cumulative. One study, for example, tracked the progress of two groups of inner-city children, one that had been exposed since early infancy to good nutrition, toys, and playmates versus a second group that had been raised in a less stimulating environment. By age twelve these factors had had a measurable impact on brain functioning, and by age fifteen the difference between the two groups was even greater (Campbell & Ramey, 1993).

Most of these findings are quite recent and difficult to apply definitively to mental retardation. "Cognitive deficits" are not necessarily retardation. Nevertheless, the research does suggest that children raised in poverty are at high risk.

Teenage mothers A factor that, in recent years, has placed the children of the poor at greater risk

An enriched sensory environment can stimulate the brain to function more efficiently. The lack of such stimulation may produce cognitive deficits that are not only irreversible but cumulative.

for developmental delays is the increase in teenage pregnancy. Among the industrialized nations, the United States now has one of the highest rates of adolescent pregnancy (Newberger, Melnicore, & Newberger, 1986)—twice as high as England's, seven times higher than that of the Netherlands. Every year, in this country, more than a million adolescent girls become pregnant, and half of these pregnancies go to term.

Children themselves, these girls are rarely equipped to raise children. To begin with, most of them are unmarried (Williams & Pratt, 1990) and therefore bear the burdens of parenthood alone—or oblige their own parents (or, frequently, their mothers) to share the burden. Furthermore, they are usually poor and, as a result of their premature motherhood, become poorer. Almost half of all teenage mothers—in the case of unmarried teenage mothers, three-quarters—go on welfare within four years of the birth of the child (Carnegie Corporation, 1994). In addition, teenage mothers, because they are caught up in the developmental struggles of adolescence, are unlikely to have the psychological stability, ego control, and attentiveness that underlie parental competence—a fact that has been borne out by observations of these girls in interaction with their children. According to a number of studies, adolescent mothers, compared with adult mothers, are less sensitive to their children's cues, less likely to interact with their children verbally, less likely to praise them, and more likely to criticize and punish them (Borkowski, Whitman, Passino, et al., 1992).

At the same time that they receive lesser care, the children of adolescent mothers suffer greater exposure to factors associated with developmental disabilities. Maternal use of drugs and alcohol, poor prenatal care, poor nutrition, low birth weight, maternal ignorance regarding child development, low maternal IQ—all these factors, known to predispose children to developmental delays, are more common with teenage motherhood. To take only the last factor, the average IQ of teen mothers who choose to raise their children has been estimated at 85 (Borkowski, Whitman, Passino, et al., 1992).

It should come as no surprise, therefore, that mild mental retardation turns up more frequently—according to one estimate, three times more frequently—in the children of adolescent mothers (Borkowski, Whitman, Passino, et al., 1992; Broman, Nichols, Shaughnessy, et al., 1987). To what extent is this attributable to the mother's age alone, as opposed to the problems so often seen in the lives of teen mothers, such as poverty, single parenthood, and interrupted education? In a study that controlled for those factors, the IQ differences between the children of teen mothers and those of adult mothers narrowed, with mean scores of 91 to 94 for the children of young teenagers, 95 to 98 for those of older teens, and 98 to 101 for those of adults (Belmont, Cohen, Dryfoos, et al., 1981). Nevertheless, those other disadvantages do tend to exist in the lives of teenage mothers, widening the gap between their children and those of adult mothers.

Institutionalization If, as has been proposed, mild retardation may be due in part to a nonstimulating environment, and particularly to a lack of stimulating interaction with parents, then an obvious test case would be institutionalized children. The pioneering work in this area was done by René Spitz (1945). Spitz found that children cared for in an institutional setting by professional nurses showed an average loss in developmental quotient from 124 to 72 within a year. In research done even earlier, Skeels and Dye (1938–1939) found that the IQs of thirteen mentally retarded children increased an average of 27.5 points over two years after they were moved from an overcrowded orphanage to living conditions in which they became the center of attention. They also found that twelve average to dull-normal children who remained at the orphanage decreased in IQ by an average of 26.2 points during the same two years.

There has been considerable debate over the meaning and methodology of both these studies. Nevertheless, more recent research has confirmed the negative impact of institutions. In comparisons of children reared at home and in institutions, those who lived at home, whether retarded or not, seemed to show improved mental development, especially in language, which seems to be a prime casualty of institutionalization (Dennis, 1973). On the other hand, much depends on the kind and quality of institutional care. Kibbutz children in Israel and children in well-staffed, high-quality residences seem to suffer little or no deprivation (Kohen-Raz, 1968; Moyles & Wolins, 1971).

Mental Retardation in Adults

Many mentally retarded people grow up to lead relatively happy and useful adult lives, but many others do not, for retardation involves an increased susceptibility both to further organic brain disorders and to emotional disturbance.

Down Syndrome and Alzheimer's disease In

years past, people with Down syndrome rarely lived beyond middle age, with the result that their aging process was little studied. Today, however, more and more people with this disorder are surviving into middle and even old age. One of the consequences of this development has been the discovery of a link between Down syndrome and Alzheimer's disease. In people with Down syndrome, furthermore, Alzheimer's strikes unusually early. To quote a recent review of research on this subject, "Virtually all adults with Down syndrome over 40 years of age have Alzheimer's disease" (Zigman, Schupf, Zigman, et al., 1992, p. 63). This is clearly the result of their abnormal genetic endowment, though the biochemistry of the connection is not yet fully understood.

In some respects, Alzheimer's in a person with Down syndrome is no different from Alzheimer's in other people, though because of Down-related behavioral deficits, it may be harder to diagnose. In general, the onset of Alzheimer's in people with Down syndrome is marked by behavioral regression. That is, the skills they have learned, often with great difficulty—gross motor skills, toileting, dressing and grooming, eating, speaking—begin to crumble, often necessitating their removal from home or from relatively open residential programs into more restricted living arrangements. Some will proceed to dementia. In any case, this is a cruel burden overlaid on an already difficult fate.

Mental Retardation and Depression Both Down syndrome patients and other mentally retarded people are at higher risk for emotional disturbance in adulthood. This includes mild disturbances such as social discomfort, low self-esteem, and hypersensitivity to criticism. In addition, mentally retarded adults are especially vulnerable to depression (A. H. Reid, 1972a, 1972b), a typical case being the one described at the opening of this chapter. When the person's IQ is over 50, the symptoms of emotional disturbance are much like those of people with normal intelligence. Depressed people with mild retardation report sadness, self-blame, and sleeping and eating problems, just like nonretarded depressed people. When IQ is lower, emotional disturbance is harder to detect, but there are now special scales for diagnosing psychopathology in mentally retarded people (e.g., Reiss, 1992; Reiss & Valenti-Hein, 1990).

Why are retarded people more subject to depression than the nonretarded? A likely reason is simply their social position (Reiss & Benson, 1985): the fact that many people avoid them, that they must watch others succeed where they themselves fail, that they cannot have the same privileges as others. The day when a retarded teenager sees his younger brother come home with a driver's license—something that he himself will never have—can be a bitter one, and the cumulative impact of these small, day-to-day sorrows can have serious emotional consequences.

Psychotherapy for the Mentally Retarded For years it was believed that mentally retarded people could not benefit from psychotherapy (Fine, 1965), because they lacked the intellectual sophistication to discuss their problems in psychodynamic terms. But with the development of less insight-oriented therapies, there are now many forms of psychological treatment that can help mentally retarded people: supportive psychotherapy (Fine, 1965), group psychotherapy (Szymanski & Rosefsky, 1980), assertiveness training and social-skills training (Matson & Adkins, 1980), self-instructional training (Benson, Johnson, & Miranti, 1984), and a modified form of Carl Rogers' client-centered therapy (Prouty, 1976).

Though these treatments are available and effective, most mentally retarded people do not get to make use of them. In many cases, the emotional difficulties of mentally retarded people are not even diagnosed—a problem that is due in part to "diagnostic overshadowing": because the intellectual deficit is so obvious, the emotional dysfunction is ignored (Reiss, Levitan, & Szysko, 1982). Another problem is that mentally retarded people with emotional disturbances fall through a crack in the service-delivery system—between agencies that serve mentally retarded people and those that serve the mentally ill. Recognizing this situation, researchers and clinicians are now trying to recast their thinking about mental retardation in terms of the "whole person." In recent years, several model mental health programs have been set up for the mentally retarded, but many more are needed.

AUTISM

Of all the conditions that involve mental retardation, one that deserves special attention, by virtue both of its fame and its severity, is autism. It has long been recognized that some children are profoundly disturbed, sometimes from earliest infancy. For years such children were often labeled schizophrenic, because their symptoms in some ways resembled those of adult schizophrenics. Then in 1943 the American psychiatrist Leo Kanner argued that within this group one could recognize a distinct syndrome, different from schizophrenia. Because its main symptom seemed to be the inability to relate to anyone outside of oneself, Kanner called the syndrome **early infantile autism,** from the Greek *autos,* "self." According to Kanner, autism was inborn and showed itself by age two and a half.

Today, as a result of Kanner's discovery, the diagnostic ground has shifted. The diagnosis of schizophrenia in childhood is now rare; most psychotic disorders in children are considered instances of autism. Prevalence figures vary, largely because there is a great deal of variation in symptoms and therefore considerable disagreement as to what should be called autism as opposed to "autistic-like" conditions. But a very thorough survey in Japan concluded that 16 to 20 out of every 10,000 preschool children qualify for the diagnosis of autism (Sugiyama & Abe, 1989). There is a marked sex difference: four out of five autistic children are male.

Despite the broad range of behaviors covered by the term *autism,* there are four symptoms that are almost invariably present: social isolation, cognitive impairment, language deficits, and stereotyped behavior.

The Symptoms of Autism

Social Isolation

> A beautiful, enigmatic child tiptoes into your waiting room, his gaze averted from you. Instead of a toy, he clutches a strange, dirty, dangling string which he twirls from time to time. When you start to examine him, he shrinks from your touch, particularly disturbed by your hands touching his head. He stares out the window instead of noticing you or your office. He seems alone, totally self-preoccupied. He is an autistic child. (Coleman, 1989, p. 1)

One striking abnormality common to all people diagnosed as autistic is impaired social behavior (Rapin, 1991; Waterhouse, 1994; Waterhouse, Wing, & Fein, 1989)—a problem implied, as we saw, in the very name of the syndrome. Many autistic children withdraw from all social contact into a state of what has been called "extreme autistic aloneness." As infants, they do not demand attention from others—a rare trait in a baby—and are difficult to hold and cuddle because they stiffen or go limp when they are picked up. The recoil from personal contact is even sharper in older children who may behave as though other people simply do not exist. As with other characteristics of autism, however, the degree of social isolation varies. Many autistic toddlers show an attachment to their mothers; they will cling to the mother and, when strangers are present, hover near her (Sigmund & Mundy, 1989). Furthermore, even when social isolation is extreme, this does not mean that the child shows no emotion. Autistic children may exhibit rage, panic, or inconsolable crying, but often in response to things that an observer cannot identify.

Partly on the basis of their social variability, Lorna Wing (Wing & Attwood, 1987; Wing & Gould, 1979) has proposed that autistic children can be subclassified into three types. In the *aloof* type, the child will rarely make a spontaneous social approach, except to get something he or she wants, and will reject approaches from others. In the *passive* type, the child again will not initiate contact, but he or she will respond if someone else makes the contact and structures the interaction. In the *active-but-odd* type, the child will approach others but in a peculiar, naive, or one-sided way. According to Wing and her colleagues, other characteristics of autistic children vary consistently with these "social types": aloof types move, play, and communicate in certain ways, passive types in other ways, and so on—a claim that has been at least partially validated (Castelloe & Dawson, 1993). It is possible that what we call autism is not one disorder but several. Subclassification schemes such as Wing's are an effort to make some sense out of the diversity of symptoms and, if different disorders are involved, to assemble the research groups necessary to find that out.

Mental Retardation Most autistic children are mentally retarded. About 70 percent have an IQ of less than 70. But autistic children differ from nonautistic mentally retarded children in the nature of their cognitive deficits. Autistic children do quite a bit better, for example, on tests of sensorimotor ability, such as finding hidden figures, than on tests of social understanding and language; nonautistic retarded children tend to perform more evenly on all such tests (Shah & Frith, 1983). When autistic children receive therapy to improve their social relationships, their mental retardation does *not* improve as well (M. Rutter, 1983). Therefore, autistic children's mental retardation is a primary cognitive problem, not merely a result of their social withdrawal.

Language Deficits More than half of all autistic children do not speak at all. Others babble, whine, scream, or show **echolalia**—that is, they simply echo what other people say. Some autistic children

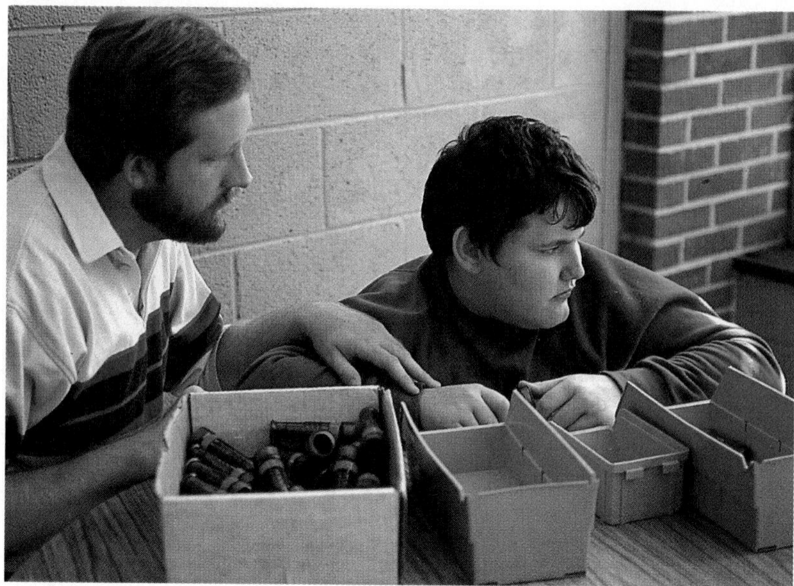

A therapist works with an autistic boy. Autistic children have distinctive cognitive deficits that are inherent in the disorder, not secondary to their extreme social withdrawal.

aimlessly repeat snatches of songs, television commercials, or other bits of overheard language. Those who do speak can communicate only in a limited way (Wetherby, 1986; Wing, 1981). Some use pronouns strangely, referring to themselves in the second person ("you") or third person ("he," "she"). Still others speak extremely literally. In essence, autistic children cannot communicate *reciprocally*, cannot engage in the usual give-and-take of conversation.

The severity of an autistic child's language problems is an excellent indicator of prognosis. Children most likely to benefit from treatment have developed some meaningful speech by the age of five (B. Fish, Shapiro, Campbell, et al., 1968; Goldfarb, 1963; Havelkova, 1968; M. Rutter & Lockyer, 1967). A child's intellectual development is another excellent indicator of his or her prognosis. Those autistic children who are not mentally retarded (about one-fourth of the autistic population) also tend to be those who have begun to speak meaningfully by age five and who adjust better as adults.

Stereotyped Behavior Many autistic children tend to repeat a limited number of movements endlessly, ritualistically, and without any clear goal. These self-stimulating movements—twirling, tiptoeing, hand flapping, rocking, tensing parts of the body—may involve the fine or gross muscles of the hands, face, trunk, arms, and legs. Left to themselves, most autistic children, especially those who are institutionalized, spend as much as 90 percent of their time in these bizarre forms of self-stimulation (Lovaas, Litrownik, & Mann, 1971).

Some of these repetitive movements cause physical harm. Head banging and hand biting are not uncommon. Autistic children have also been known to pull out their hair, bite off the ends of their fingers, and chew their shoulders down to the bone, often crying out in pain as they do so. The urge to perform these strange motor behaviors is apparently very strong. In one study autistic children who had not eaten in twenty-four hours and who were moving ritualistically either would not respond or delayed in responding to a sound that signaled that food was available (Lovaas, Koegel, & Schreibman, 1979; Lovaas, Litrownik, & Mann, 1971). When they were not repeating their stereotyped movements, however, the same children responded immediately to the same signal.

Nor are motor mannerisms the only area in which autistic children show an intense and narrow focus. They may have a favorite activity—tearing paper, spinning the wheels on a toy car—in which they will lose themselves for hours every day. With toys and other objects, they tend to interest themselves in the part rather than the whole—not the car, for example, but just the wheels. They are also likely to resist any change in their surroundings and routines. Toys must always be put in the same place on the same shelves. Breakfast must be an unvarying ritual of egg first, vitamin pill second, and then toast. If the child senses that any step has been skipped, he or she may respond with a tantrum. Clinicians have noted that many normal children, when they are about two and a half, insist on unvarying sameness in routines. They have suggested, therefore, that the development of autistic children may have stalled at this point.

The Case of Peter

All of these problems—the ritual behaviors, the self-absorption and bizarreness, the intellectual and social deficits—appear in the following case, reported by the child's mother:

> Peter nursed eagerly, sat and walked at the expected ages. Yet some of his behavior made us vaguely uneasy. . . .
>
> More troubling was the fact that Peter didn't look at us, or smile, and wouldn't play the games that seemed as much a part of babyhood as diapers. While he didn't cry, he rarely laughed, and when he did, it was at things that didn't seem funny to us. He didn't cuddle, but sat upright in my lap, even when I rocked him. But children differ and we were content to let Peter be himself. We thought it hilarious when my brother, visiting us when Peter was 8 months old, observed that "that kid has no social instincts, whatsoever." Although Peter was a first child, he was not isolated. I frequently put him in his playpen in front of the house, where the school children stopped to play with him as they passed. He ignored them too. . . .
>
> Peter's babbling had not turned into speech by the time he was three. His play was solitary and repetitious. He tore paper into long thin strips, bushel baskets of it every day. He spun the lids from my canning jars and became upset if we tried to divert him. Only rarely could I catch his eye, and then saw his focus change from me to the reflection in my glasses. It was like trying to pick up mercury with chopsticks.
>
> His adventures into our suburban neighborhood had been unhappy. He had disregarded the universal rule that sand is to be kept in sand-boxes, and the children themselves had punished him. He walked around a sad and solitary figure, always carrying a toy aeroplane, a toy he never played with. At that time, I had not heard the word that was to dominate our lives, to hover over every conversation, to sit through every meal beside us. That word was autism. (Eberhardy, 1967)

Peter's mother took him to various doctors and therapists, and finally he was sent to a special school, which apparently served him well.

> Peter chose his own vocation. He tunes pianos, giving them the same devotion that many teenage boys give to their cars. At present he needs help with transportation and arrangements. He does his own bookkeeping. He is happy in his work and happy to be home again. We have found a programme for him, where young adults with a history of emotional difficulties meet for recreation and group therapy. I'm sure this is a factor in his continuing improvement. (Eberhardy, 1967)

The only unrepresentative feature of this case is Peter's adult adjustment, which was atypically good. Some autistic children—5 to 17 percent, according to one review (Lotter, 1978)—improve enough by the time they are grown to hold down jobs and even live alone, though they are still aloof and still have language problems and poor social judgment. As for the remainder—that is, the vast majority of autistic children—most do improve with treatment but rarely enough to allow them to live outside a special residence when they reach adulthood, let alone on their own (DeMyer, Hingtgen, & Jackson, 1981).

Perspectives on Autism

Theories of autism have changed radically in the past few decades. Popular in the fifties and sixties was the psychodynamic view that autism was caused by cold, rejecting parents (e.g., Bettelheim, 1967)—a theory that, after adding grief and guilt to the lives of parents already coping with a difficult situation, has now been repudiated by research. Researchers are now focusing on brain dysfunction, investigating what organic factors may be involved, and the cognitive perspective, examining the consequences of the presumed organic flaw.

The Biological Perspective

Genetic research As we noted in Chapter 15, a great deal of sophisticated and productive research has been carried out on the genetics of schizophrenia. But so far there have been fewer genetic studies of autism, in part because it has been difficult to find large enough samples of twins. Researchers who scoured Great Britain, for example, found eleven pairs of monozygotic (MZ) twins and ten pairs of dizygotic (DZ) twins in which at least one twin was autistic (Folstein & Rutter, 1977). Of the MZ group, four of eleven were concordant. Of the DZ group, none were concordant. Even when a twin with an autistic MZ twin was *not* diagnosed as autistic, he or she was likely to be markedly impaired in language or cognition. The sample in this study was not large enough to support firm conclusions. Furthermore, several of the autistic children seemed to have suffered brain damage at birth, making it difficult for the researchers to say to what extent their impairment was inherited. Despite these drawbacks, however, the study suggests that autism has some genetic component, and this conclusion has been supported by family studies in Sweden and the United States showing an 8 percent incidence of autism in the extended families of autistic children (Coleman & Gillberg, 1985).

Whatever the genetic components involved, they are likely to differ with differing kinds of autism. One family study found that the autistic patients most likely to have autistic or retarded siblings were the most severely retarded ones (Baird & August, 1985). A more recent family study indicates that autistic patients at the other end of the spectrum—those who showed the best functioning—are the ones that tend to have a family history of mood disorder (DeLong, 1992).

Chromosome studies As was pointed out earlier, fragile X syndrome is associated not just with mental retardation but with autism. One study of autistic patients found that 16 percent of the males had fragile X syndrome (Blomquist, Bohman, Edvinsson, et al., 1985). Coming at the question from the opposite direction, another study (Hageman, Jackson, Levitas, et al., 1986) found that of fifty males with fragile X, 16 percent met the *DSM* criteria for autism and an additional 30 percent met the looser criteria for the residual state of autism. Moreover, some autistic symptoms were seen in almost all these men—hand flapping, hand biting, and other stereotyped motor behaviors in 88 percent; avoidance of eye contact in 90 percent; language delays with autistic peculiarities such as echolalia in 96 percent. In other words, there is a clear connection between autism and fragile X syndrome. Other chromosomal abnormalities, such as XYY syndrome, are also associated with autism, though none so strongly as fragile X.

Biochemical studies In autism, as in schizophrenia (Chapter 15), a major focus of research today is the role of neurotransmitters. It is now well established that many autistic children have abnormally high levels of serotonin and dopamine (M. Goldstein, Mahanand, Lee, et al., 1976; Hanley, Stahl, & Freedman, 1977; Takahashi, Kanai, & Miyamoto, 1976). Whatever their role in the development of autism, these two neurotransmitters may play a role in its treatment. When autistic children receive stimulants such as the amphetamines, which increase dopamine, their symptoms of hyperactivity, ritualistic behavior, and self-stimulation get worse (J. G. Young, Kavanagh, Anderson, et al., 1982). Dopamine-inhibiting drugs such as the phenothiazines mitigate many of the symptoms of autism, including self-mutilation and repetitive motions, although they are less effective with autism than with schizophrenia (Campbell, Anderson, Small, et al., 1982, P. F. Kernberg, 1979).

Congenital disorders and birth complications While genetic factors are implicated in many cases of autism, this does not rule out nongenetic factors. In 1981, for example, a study of the monthly distribution of autistic births showed a significant increase of such births during certain months of the year (March and August), a finding that suggests infectious causes (Bartlik, 1981). Two such causes have been established. In rare cases, the herpes simplex virus is involved in autism (Coleman, 1989). The other, far more common cause is congenital rubella, or German measles. After the last documented outbreak of rubella in the United States, which occurred in 1964, a group of researchers studied 243 children exposed prenatally to the virus. More than 7 percent of these children showed a full or partial autistic syndrome (Chess, Korn, & Fernandez, 1971). Other cases of autism may be connected to complications of pregnancy and birth, for the prevalence of such complications is higher in autistic children than in the general population (Kolvin, Ounsted, Humphrey, et al., 1971; Lotter, 1966; L. Taft & Goldfarb, 1964).

Such complications are not necessarily independent of genetic factors. Recall the situation with schizophrenia. As we saw in Chapter 15, Mednick's (1971) longitudinal study of children of schizophrenic parents showed that the pregnancies had involved more difficulties than normal and that the babies had had lower birth weights and more abnormalities than babies in a control group. Possibly, the genetic defect gives rise to birth problems. Alternatively, accidents at birth may exacerbate a genetic predisposition. In a study of identical seventeen-year-old triplet boys who had a mild form of autism, researchers found that although the boys were generally quite similar, the severity of their symptoms differed, in a manner consistent with their medical problems at birth and in early infancy (Burgoine & Wing, 1983). The triplet with the most severe symptoms had weighed the least at birth, had been slightly blue and needed oxygen, and had stayed longest (four and a half weeks) in an incubator. At the age of one year he had had pneumonia and again was in the hospital, this time for nearly a month. The triplet with the least severe symptoms had weighed the most at birth and had had the fewest problems after he was born. This study supports the hypothesis that birth complications and problems in infancy are implicated at least in the severity of autism.

Neurological research Most researchers today believe that, whatever its ultimate cause, autism results from a range of deficits in the brain. In the first place, most of the characteristic signs of autism—impaired language development, mental retardation, bizarre motor behavior, underreactivity and overreactivity to sensory input, responsiveness to touch and movement as opposed to auditory and visual stimuli—are related to the functioning of the central nervous system. Second, many autistic children, particularly as they enter adolescence, develop seizure disorders, which are known to originate in the central nervous system (Rapin, 1991). Third, neurological examinations of autistic children sometimes reveal abnormalities such as poor muscle tone, poor coordination, drooling, and hyperactivity.

A fourth line of evidence has to do with neurophysiology. Two general types of research have been conducted: *EEG* and *ERP* studies. Electroencephalograms of autistic people are difficult to obtain, for the test requires more cooperation than many such people can give. Nevertheless, many studies have reported EEGs of an abnormal nature in autistic people. ERP studies are concerned with event-related potential: how the brain waves of people show patterns of reaction to various sensory stimuli. ERP studies of autistic people have shown abnormalities of attention to both novel stimuli and language stimuli (Dunn, 1994).

Taken together, EEG and ERP studies show many patterns, from normal to abnormal, but the accumulated evidence strongly suggests a neurological impairment in autistic people.

Fifth, autopsies of autistic brains have revealed certain abnormalities in the cerebellum and in the limbic system, which is known to be involved in cognition, memory, emotion, and behavior. Specifically, the neurons in the limbic system appear to be smaller and more tightly packed. In some areas, their dendrites—the branching arms through which they receive signals from adjacent neurons—are shorter and less complex (Figure 18.3). Both these conditions are typical of earlier stages of prenatal brain maturation (Bauman & Kemper, 1994).

Another hopeful line of investigation has to do with MRI studies, but so far they have revealed little—basically, that autism does not involve gross structural abnormalities though in some cases it is associated with enlarged ventricles on the two sides of the brain (Minshew & Dombrowski, 1994). At this point the strongest evidence is that the basic deficit in autism is either in the limbic system or in the information-processing structures of the cerebral cortex, but closer study of those two areas awaits improvements in brain scan technology.

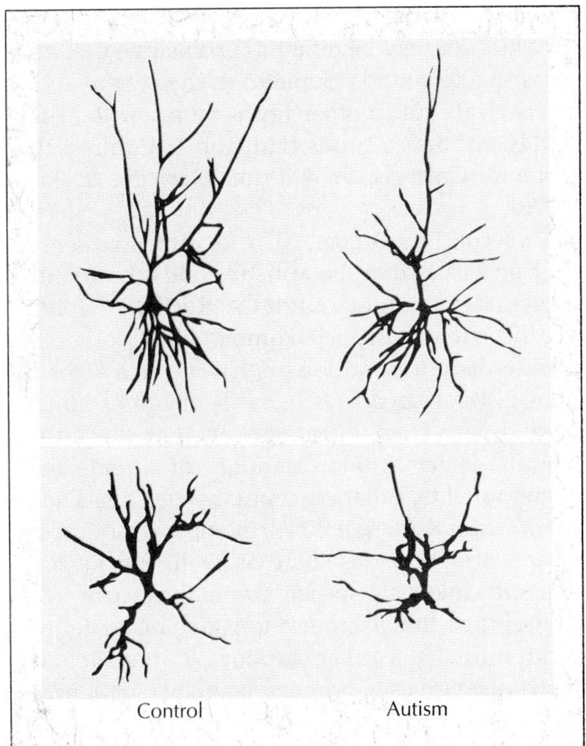

FIGURE 18.3 Photographic reproductions of neurons in autistic versus normal brains. In the upper pair, note the difference in the number of dendrites. In the lower pair, note the difference in dendrite length. (Adapted from Bauman & Kemper, 1994, p. 124)

The Cognitive Perspective No one denies that autistic children have problems affecting their capacity to imitate and comprehend, to be flexible and inventive, to form and apply rules, and to use information (Werry, 1979a)—in other words, to cope with the world. Cognitive theories hold that the cognitive problems of autistic children are primary and cause their social problems (M. Rutter, 1983).

Several theorists have tried to pinpoint the basic cognitive defect in autism. Some hold that the root problem lies in modulating and integrating input from different senses (Ornitz, 1974; Ornitz & Ritvo, 1968; Ritvo, 1976), and there is evidence for this position. It is known, for example, that autistic children may be either oversensitive or undersensitive to sounds. Sometimes they act as if they were deaf, but at other times they startle at relatively ordinary sounds (Hintgen & Coulter, 1967; Prior & Gajzago, 1974; Prior, Gajzago, & Knox, 1976).

A second argument, also focusing on sensory perception, is that the autistic child's basic defect is in understanding sounds (M. Rutter, 1968, 1971). In this view, autism is comparable to other language disorders, such as aphasia, the loss or impairment of speech as a result of brain damage, and differs from them only in that the autistic child's defective understanding of sounds is accompanied by other perceptual problems. The experimental evidence cited in the previous paragraph supports this view as well. Furthermore, autistic children's speech is retarded early in the progress of the disorder and is one of its defining symptoms. In further support of the idea that autism involves a primary language impairment is the pattern of cognitive abilities autistic children typically show. As we have said, they usually do far better on sensorimotor tasks, on visual motor tasks, and on rote memory than on verbal and conceptual tasks. Finally, one of the strongest arguments in favor of this hypothesis is that an autistic child's language ability is one of the best predictors of the child's chances of benefiting from treatment. A strange case in which improvement in language ability was accompanied by loss of another ability is described in the box on savant syndrome (page 477).

Another cognitive hypothesis is that autistic children are overselective in their attention (Lovaas, Koegel, & Schreibman, 1979). Because of a perceptual defect, they can process and respond to only one stimulus at a time, be it visual, tactile, or whatever. Experimental evidence to support this interpretation has come from tests of autistic children in finding hidden figures (Shah & Frith, 1983). They do well on such tests because they focus directly on each part and are not easily distracted by the overall picture. But they do not do well at deriving meaning from stimuli with several parts. This kind of impairment may well account for the social and intellectual retardation of the autistic child. According to Lovaas, children's intellectual and emotional development is based in large measure on the association of paired stimuli, through the process of respondent conditioning. Thus as children mentally pair their mother with food and cuddling, they come to love her. But if children process only the stimulus of the food or the cuddling and do not pair it with their mother's presence, they do not come to value her.

A final cognitive hypothesis is that the fundamental problem with autistic children is that they have no **theory of the mind**—that is, they cannot appreciate the existence of purely mental states, such as beliefs or desires, and therefore cannot predict or understand behavior based on such states. In one study, for example, autistic, normal, and retarded children were given the following task concerning two dolls, Sally and Anne (Baron-Cohen, Leslie, & Frith, 1985). Sally, they were shown, put her marble in her basket and left. While Sally was gone, Anne took the marble out of the basket and hid it. When Sally returned, the children were asked where Sally would look for the marble. Over 80 percent of both the normal and retarded children answered, "In the basket," but only 20 percent of the autistic children gave the obviously correct answer. It was not that they could not remember, but that they could not take another person's point of view. The lack of this critical skill undoubtedly contributes to the autistic child's social isolation.

Despite the popularity of the theory of the mind, one of its original proponents (Leslie, 1991) has noted that it raises a number of other questions. For example, is it just representations of the minds of other people or representations of *anything* that autistic children do not understand? In other words, it may be that all representations of complex or abstract or intangible things (like "democracy" or "love") are not properly developed in the autistic person's mind. Furthermore, why do autistic children vary in their success with theory-of-the-mind tasks? It may be that, as with so many other theories of autism, this explanation covers only some cases. Normal children develop a theory of the mind at around eighteen months; about 20 percent of cases of autism have their onset at that time. Fein and Waterhouse (1990) have suggested that the theory-of-the-mind explanation may apply to that subgroup—their development becomes abnormal at that point—but that it is less likely to apply to autistic children who show abnormal social development in their first year of life.

SOCIETY, MENTAL RETARDATION, AND AUTISM

Our society is designed for people with at least average coping skills, people who can park a car, pay a bill, fill out an income tax form. Most mentally retarded people cannot handle such tasks. Indeed,

SAVANT SYNDROME

In rare cases, a person with greatly diminished mental skills will show extraordinary proficiency in one isolated skill—a phenomenon known as **savant syndrome.** Until recently savant syndrome was thought to be associated with retardation, but it is likely that savants are actually autistic, not retarded. The abilities of savants are often so wildly exaggerated by the press that the phenomenon is often regarded with some skepticism. But scientists too have observed and described savants (e.g., Scheerer et al., 1945; Viscott, 1970).

How do these remarkable skills develop? Perhaps by way of compensation. Just as the blind may develop particularly keen hearing, so a child who is retarded in most skills may compensate by becoming "overproficient" in one salvaged skill. Alternatively, the source of savants' abilities may be purely biological. That is, one area of the brain may be rendered abnormally efficient by the same structural change that rendered the rest of the brain abnormally inefficient. Another possibility is that when such abilities appear in association with autism, they are produced by the intense concentration typical of autistic children. Whatever its source, the savant phenomenon makes an enigmatic disorder, autism, seem even more enigmatic.

In almost all reported cases, the skill in question is based on memory or calculation. There have been several reports of children who, if given a date, could say immediately what day of the week it fell on. Others can recite columns of numbers from the telephone book after one reading. Raymond (Dustin Hoffman), the hero of the movie *Rain Man,* was a "calculator savant." There have also been several reports of musical savants—not surprising, since music, like numbers, involves intricate systems. Some years ago an English psychiatrist, Lorna Selfe (1978), reported a truly unusual case—a drawing savant.

Nadia, the second of three children born to a Ukrainian couple living in England, was clearly abnormal from an early age. She did not speak, and she did not seem even to notice other people, with the exception of her mother and a few others. Most of her days were spent tearing paper into thin strips or performing some other ritualistic activity. Her diagnosis was autism.

When Nadia was three, her mother had to be hospitalized for several months. When the mother returned, the child was overjoyed. Inexplicably, she began to draw. What she drew was equally inexplicable—figures of astonishing beauty and sophistication. For the next three years Nadia produced drawing after drawing. She refused to use color; only a ballpoint pen would do. She would draw on any kind of paper she could find, including boxes. She would sketch with the utmost concentration, then sit back, survey the result, and wiggle her hands and knees with pleasure.

A rooster drawn by Nadia when she was about three and a half.

At the same time Nadia was being taken on the round of clinics and special schools. She was enrolled in several programs but made no progress. Then, around age six and a half, she began speaking and stopped drawing. At the time when this case was written up, Nadia was ten years old. She had acquired a small vocabulary, was responsive to a limited circle of people, and could even handle simple mathematics. When asked to draw a picture, she could produce one, but it had none of the genius of her earlier work. As mysteriously as it had appeared, her remarkable artistic talent had vanished.

most cannot care for themselves on their own. Some remain at home with their families, which is usually to their advantage, but many families cannot cope with a disabled member, and those that are willing are generally hard-pressed. Mentally retarded people need special schooling, special jobs (if they can hold jobs), special psychological supports. If the family cannot provide such things, should it be the responsibility of the society to do so? Our discussion of these social issues will focus on mental retardation in general, though the issues concern the autistic population as well.

Public Policy and Retardation

In the past twenty-five years there have been tremendous changes in the field of mental retardation. To begin with, parent groups—above all the Association for Retarded Citizens (ARC), founded in 1950—have vigorously lobbied federal and state governments and have obtained not only large increases in funding but also legislation guaranteeing the right of retarded people to a free education geared to their abilities. Second, these same parent organizations, along with other advocacy groups, have increasingly taken their grievances to the federal and state courts, whose decisions have substantially altered the treatment of retarded people in this country. Finally, the number of professionals in the field of mental retardation has expanded greatly, a reflection of the discovery that retarded people respond well to behavior therapy. This finding has generated a new mood of hope, attracting to the field a large number of young clinical psychologists. At the same time, several university-affiliated centers for training and research have been established to train these professionals and teach them to work in interdisciplinary teams.

This new activism has brought about sweeping changes in public policy toward retarded people. Whereas society once all but ignored the mentally handicapped, today certain principles have been established, which, though by no means fully implemented, are guiding public institutions toward the granting of full citizens' rights to retarded people. There are five basic principles:

1 *Free and appropriate education.* Public schools must create educational programs for retarded people so that they can learn with the maximum independence consistent with their abilities.
2 *Individualization.* Services should not be based on textbook descriptions of retarded people; they should be tailored to the person—what he or she needs and can do.
3 *Timely progress reviews.* Mentally retarded people, once placed in a given program, should not be left there indefinitely but should have their progress reviewed regularly, with at least one comprehensive annual evaluation.
4 *Community integration.* Services for mentally retarded people should be provided in the least restrictive environment consistent with the person's handicaps.
5 *Human rights.* The law should protect mentally retarded people from abuse in residential programs and facilitate lawsuits to obtain needed services. In keeping with this principle, the federal government has now established a protection and advocacy commission in each state to provide legal help for retarded people.

Some of the most important changes in recent years have been those under the heading "community integration." As recently as 1970, virtually all services for retarded people were segregated from services for the nonretarded. Children with mild and moderate retardation attended special-education classes separate from the classes of other children. People with severe and profound retardation were sent off to large institutions which, because they were outside the community, provided their own educational, medical, and psychological services. The effect of this segregation was to deprive mentally retarded people of any real participation in the life of the society. The principle of community integration holds that retarded people should be educated in the public schools, and when they get sick, they should go to the same hospitals as everyone else. They should be able to go to the same movie theaters, the same bowling alleys, the same restaurants as everybody else.

In some measure, this is now being achieved. Not only are mentally retarded children being educated in their local schools, but many in the mild-retardation category have been "mainstreamed"

Ideally, the "mainstreaming" of retarded children in regular public-school classrooms has educational and social benefits for the normal children as well as for the retarded ones.

into regular education classes. As for residential facilities, community planning has shifted from a model of institutional care to one of residence within the community.

Many mildly retarded adults with independent-living skills and jobs live in their own apartments, with no restraints at all. Other mildly retarded people live in a small group home called a *supported living arrangement (SLA),* where supervision is generally provided only in the evening. Many moderately retarded people, along with mildly retarded people who have behavioral or emotional problems, live in a *community living facility (CLF),* a small to medium-size residential center with round-the-clock supervision. For severely retarded people, the appropriate choice may be the *intermediate-care facility (ICF),* a nursing home located in a community setting and ideally providing close supervision. (Unfortunately, many ICFs have proved to offer less-than-ideal care in practice. Often they are little more than institutions located within the community.) Finally, the state institution, the most restrictive placement, is still the usual choice for profoundly retarded people.

As increasing numbers of SLAs, CLFs, and ICFs are being established, more and more mildly and moderately retarded people are being moved out of the state institutions and into these facilities. This is an extremely heartening development. Large institutions, as we have seen in previous chapters, can have damaging effects on the people they are supposed to care for, not only because so many of them offer dreary and even cruel living conditions but, in a subtler sense, because they do not allow patients to use the skills they have. Those skills, consequently, tend to disappear. The great virtue of the residential alternatives for retarded people is that they challenge residents to use and develop their coping abilities.

Supporting the Family

When a child is diagnosed as mentally retarded or autistic, the parents usually suffer terrible grief. In the past, the diagnosis was usually accompanied by a recommendation that the child be institutionalized. Today, even in the case of profoundly retarded children, the recommendation is likely to be the opposite: that the parents try to care for the child at home. If they do so, however, they need supportive training and counseling (Dunst, Johanson, Trivette, et al., 1991).

Retarded children, of course, have many of the same needs as normal children. They need to be fed, to be loved and held, to be given structure and discipline. Like normal children, they need to interact with other children and with adults in order to develop social skills, and they must be encouraged to be as independent as possible. But retarded children also have special needs. They may be physically handicapped. They are often teased or shunned by other children. They learn more slowly. In recent years, efforts have been made to teach parents simple behavioral techniques for dealing with these problems (Baroff, 1974). Through reinforcement, parents can help their retarded child develop speech. Through shaping, they can help the child master complex behaviors such as self-feeding and using the toilet. Such home training not only increases the child's skills; it also tightens the parent-child bond by making the parents feel that they can actually do something concrete to help the child.

The retarded adolescent presents additional concerns to family and community. Parents must walk a narrow line between the child's need for independence and his or her lack of maturity. They must help the child to deal with physical changes, with sexual feelings, with threats to self-esteem (an especially difficult task if the child is aware of being "different"), and with a peer group that is outgrowing him or her. The extent to which these problems become an issue depends, of course, on the level of retardation. They are of greatest concern for parents of mildly and moderately retarded teenagers.

As the adolescent nears adulthood, family and community must consider carefully the extent to which he or she will be able to live independently. Although parents may be confident of their ability to provide for a young retarded child, they become uneasy when they think about the stresses and demands placed on the retarded adult. One of the most complex issues is that of sex and marriage.

Historically, attitudes toward the mentally retarded person's sexual development have favored complete desexualization, physically and emotionally (Perske, 1973). Relationships between retarded men and women were discouraged, and involuntary sterilization was common. Today a more humane approach is taken. The trend is toward the belief that retarded people, like normal people, have a right to sexual development and that they can be taught sexual behavior appropriate to their level of functioning. In keeping with this trend, state laws prohibiting marriage for the retarded and permitting sterilization without consent are being challenged, and some have been repealed. But as of 1983, fifteen states still had statutes authorizing compulsory sterilization of the mentally retarded (Drew, Logan, & Hardman, 1988). Programs exist to teach retarded young adults "dating skills," and studies have shown that with some assistance from families or social agencies, many mildly retarded people are able to marry and maintain themselves as functioning units in society (Floor, Baxter, Rosen, et al., 1975).

Employment

New federal and state laws provide that retarded people must have opportunities for useful employment, whether or not in the types of jobs nonretarded people hold. In practice, this means that whatever their residential placement, retarded people must be offered planned daytime programs. In the case of severely and profoundly retarded people, such daytime activities may be very simple, but many mildly retarded people and some moderately retarded people do hold paying jobs, some in ordinary work environments, others in special work centers, called **sheltered workshops,** tailored to their needs.

It has long been assumed that retarded people belong to America's socioeconomic surplus population—that most of them either can't or don't want to work or, if they do work, that they are the first to lose their jobs when the payroll is being cut. But this is no longer the case. Many, if not most, retarded people do want to work (P. Friedman, 1976). Furthermore, when properly placed, they make good employees and consequently are not necessarily the first to be fired when jobs become scarce (Halpern, 1973). Interestingly, research also indicates that when they are fired, it is often not because of a failure to do the job but because of a lack of social skills. Greenspan and Shoultz (1981) cite the following example:

> This incident involved a mildly mentally retarded woman who worked as a chambermaid in a large hotel. She was under considerable pressure to clean a certain number of rooms per day and was frustrated, therefore, when guests would sleep late. Her way of coping with this dilemma was to bang on a guest's door and say, "All right, get your fucking ass out of bed." Not surprisingly, this behavior was reported and the client was fired. (pp. 32–33)

The problem, in other words, was not a lack of attention to the job she was assigned to do, but a failure to appreciate the subtle social rules surrounding that job. The obvious conclusion is that vocational training for retarded people must cover social skills as well as vocational skills—and training programs now tend to include them.

PREVENTION, EDUCATION, AND TREATMENT

One of the most significant developments in the field of mental retardation is the idea that treatment can make a decisive difference in the lives of mentally retarded people. Whereas early detection of chromosomal and congenital abnormalities is available to help couples at risk and expectant parents, who may then seek counseling about the pregnancy, the new hope in the therapeutic community is to improve the quality of life of mentally retarded children and adults.

Prevention

A major breakthrough in the prevention of mental retardation has been the advent of genetic analysis and counseling. Couples at risk for abnormal births can be identified, informed of the risk, and advised how to proceed. The gene for Tay-Sachs disease, for example, occurs in about one of every thirty people of Eastern European Jewish descent. If one carrier marries another, their chances of having a child with the disease are one in four. A simple blood test can identify carriers, who can then get advice from a genetic counselor. Genetic analysis can also identify abnormalities in the developing fetus. If fragile X, Down syndrome, or another abnormality is detected, the parents may choose to terminate the pregnancy.

Early Intervention

When a child already has a condition that could lead to retardation, early intervention can do much to minimize its effects. We have already described several medical procedures that fall under this heading, including low-phenylalanine diets for PKU children and thyroid treatments for infants with missing or damaged thyroid glands. There are also psychological therapies. In infant stimulation therapy, for example, babies who are mentally handicapped—for example, Down syndrome children—are played with intensively several hours a day to stimulate their language acquisition, problem-solving skills, and achievement motivation. Infant stimulation programs capitalize on the extraordinary flexibility of the very young brain. Parents do most of the teaching, aided and guided by a special-education teacher, a physical therapist, a speech/language therapist, a social worker, an occupational therapist, and other child development specialists who observe the child periodically at home or at school and who suggest

Early intervention can help mentally retarded children achieve the fullest possible range of development. Such intensive programs are time-consuming and expensive, however, and cutbacks in government funding have meant that relatively few children have been able to benefit from them.

and demonstrate activities to be added to the child's regimen (Brody, 1982a).

The key to these children's development is the amount of stimulation, exercise, and encouragement they receive as they strive to master the skills that come more easily to nonretarded youngsters. Infant stimulation activities may be as simple as mothers talking to and making eye contact with their babies. Mothers can aid the babies' fine-motor coordination by providing pegs and other objects for them to play with. They can sharpen the babies' perception by exposing them to different sounds, colors, and tastes. They can encourage use of the long muscles, helping the babies sit up and lift their heads. (Down syndrome children are often strikingly "loose jointed" and have poor muscle tone.) Activities and equipment become more sophisticated as the child progresses. Many "graduates" of early intervention programs are able to feed and dress themselves, talk fluently, and participate in most children's activities. Some have learned to read and have acquired other academic skills (Pines, 1982a).

In recent years, infant stimulation programs have been expanded to include children whose only apparent risk factor is poverty. If it is true, as the research assembled by the Carnegie report suggests, that the conditions associated with poverty can lead to mild retardation, could helping poor families early lessen the risk? This has been the goal of family-support programs instituted in various American cities in the 1980s and 1990s. In one such program, called Avance, that serves 2,000 Mexican-American families yearly in and around San Antonio, Texas, parents are given special help with their infants for two years. In weekly classes and monthly home visits, the mothers are trained in how to interact with their babies. During the second year of the program, the mothers are also given academic and vocational training—courses in English as a second language, preparation for high school equivalency exams, and the like. Evaluations of Avance have shown that at the end of the program and also at a one-year follow-up, mothers who have been in the program are more affectionate and positive with their children, encourage the children's speech more, and provide a more stimulating environment than mothers who have received no special services (D. Johnson, Walker, & Rodriguez, 1993).

Avance is considered a model program. The Carnegie report calls for an expansion of such services and also for a broad range of other reforms—promotion of family planning; inclusion of child development courses in high school curricula; improvement of prenatal-care services, parental-leave benefits, and child-care facilities—to help break the link between poverty and developmental delay.

Education

For many years mentally retarded children were essentially excluded from the public school system. Then, in the early seventies, decisions in a number of class-action suits required that local school systems provide special education for retarded children. Finally, in 1975, this requirement became effective nationwide when Congress passed Public Law 94–142, guaranteeing to every citizen under the age of twenty-one a free public education appropriate to his or her needs. New programs—and lawsuits—soon followed.

P.L. 94–142 has been responsible for a great increase in special-education programs since the late seventies. These programs are carefully tailored to the person, in keeping with the requirement that public education be "appropriate" to each child's needs. Typically, the school system will have what is called an individualized education program (IEP). The school holds a multidisciplinary conference to identify the handicaps of children requesting special education and to review the progress of those already receiving such services. The committee then formulates, in writing, an IEP for each child, and the appropriate services are provided.

The new law has stimulated some highly innovative thinking. One concept, for example, is the "cascade system." Nine educational programs, beginning with a regular classroom in a regular school and ending with a hospital setting, are designed to accommodate individual needs and to provide for progression from one level to another. Upward mobility is the goal, and it is to be achieved by constant periodic evaluation, so that assignment to a particular cascade level does not become a life sentence. Many retarded children, as noted, have been mainstreamed into regular classes. (They are usually given modified tasks.) Other children may spend part of the school day in the regular class and part in a special class. Children who need more help and guidance may attend a special day school or live in a residential school. At all levels, the emphasis is on individual programs tailored to each child's needs and modified continuously as the child develops.

Such programs, however, are by no means the norm. Though P.L. 94–142 mandates special education for all handicapped children, Congress has not provided full funding for the implementation of the law, and many communities have been unable or unwilling to find the necessary funds. Some school districts have raised local taxes to pay for special education, but others are still taking their time about putting the law into practice. Furthermore, recent court decisions have raised some questions regarding the extent of the services that school systems must provide. A case in point is *Board of Education of the Hendrick Hudson School District v. Rowley,* involving a deaf girl whose request for a sign-language interpreter as part of her IEP was rejected by the school district. Deciding in favor of the school district, the U.S. Supreme Court ruled that while P.L. 94–142 requires that handicapped children be given a "basic floor of opportunity" in the education system, it does not specify the *level* of education to be provided. In other words, beyond a certain point it is up to the school district to determine how special the special-education program will be. The *Rowley* decision, combined with current economic pressures, suggests that full implementation of P.L. 94–142 will be a long and gradual process, with a number of lawsuits along the way.

In the case of autistic children, designing an appropriate education program may be a harder task, because of these children's special disabilities. Their need for an unvarying routine is not easy to meet in a classroom, even a special classroom, and their ritualistic movements may leave little room in their attentional field for what the teacher is trying to say. Furthermore, as noted earlier, they tend not to respond to social reinforcement (e.g., the teacher's approval), which is the usual form of classroom reinforcement. Finally, the overselective attention of autistic children tends to sabotage the kind of association making that is essential to learning. When a teacher points to the letter *D* on the blackboard and makes the sound of *D,* it is hoped that the students will make a mental connection between the two. But autistic children, because of their hyperconcentration, are more likely to attend to only one of the stimuli. This overselective attention also makes the generalization of learning difficult for autistic children. Should they learn to make the connection between the visual stimulus of the letter *D* and the auditory stimulus of its sound, they may still be unable to carry this lesson over when the letter *D* appears in a book rather than on a blackboard or indeed when it is written on a blackboard in a different color of chalk from the one in which they originally saw it written. Nevertheless, educators have maneuvered around these barriers to produce some effective teaching methods for autistic students (Newsome, Carr, & Rincover, 1974).

Self-Instructional Training

Many mentally retarded people have been helped to get through tasks and difficulties by means of *self-instructional training* (Chapter 19), a cognitive-behavioral therapy that teaches people to control their actions by controlling what they say to themselves before, during, and after the action. One group of researchers (Rusch et al., 1985), for example, reported on the use of self-instructional training with two mentally retarded women who had jobs as kitchen helpers in a university dormitory. Both these women enjoyed their jobs, but both had received feedback that they were doing certain things wrong. Specifically, they were forgetting to wipe the counters and to check and restock supplies. So they were taught to make a series of statements to themselves on the job: first a question ("What does the supervisor want me to do?"), then an answer to that question ("I am supposed to wipe the counters, check the supplies, and restock the supplies"), then a performance-guiding statement ("Okay, I need to wipe the counter," etc.), then a self-reinforcement ("I did that right"). The statements, together with the accompanying actions, were first modeled for the women by a therapist. Then the women copied the therapist's performance, first saying the statements out loud, then whispering them, then instructing themselves covertly, without speaking. Both women improved and kept their jobs.

Variations on self-instructional training have been used to teach mentally retarded children to do arithmetic problems (M. B. Johnston, Whitman, & Johnston, 1980), to help mentally retarded mothers to handle their babies (Tymchuk, Andron, & Rahbar, 1988), to teach dating skills to mentally retarded adults (Muesser, Valenti-Hein, & Yarnold, 1987), and to teach a mentally retarded janitor to control his anger on the job (Benson, 1986). Not surprisingly, in all these reports, the subjects have been in the mild-retardation category. The technique seems simple, but it is often just such simple skills—knowing what to do when a baby has a fever, knowing not to yell at one's boss—that mentally retarded people need in order to remain in normalizing situations (a mother-child relationship, a job) rather than be relegated to the fringes of society.

Behavior Therapy

Of all the services for retarded people, almost none has generated more enthusiasm than the application of learning principles to training and behavior management. Behavioral techniques are being used extensively and with good success in the home, in schools and workshops, in institutional settings, and with both children and adults. They can be taught to parents, teachers, therapists, and hospital staffs, and they can be used for a variety of purposes.

The three basic techniques of behavior therapy are shaping (reinforcing successive approximations of desirable behavior), chaining (teaching the person to finish the task and then gradually expanding the number of steps required to finish), and stimulus control (teaching that a behavior should occur in some situations but not in others). These methods have proved successful in the training of retarded people in many areas, including verbal behaviors, academic skills, classroom social behaviors (e.g., sitting and talking only at the appropriate time), self-care behaviors, social skills, and work habits such as promptness and task completion. In early childhood, one of the most important applications has been language acquisition (Grabowski & Thompson, 1977). Research into patterns of language acquisition by both normal and retarded children has yielded information that has allowed for the construction of step-by-step behavioral sequences to teach both speech and comprehension among the mentally retarded. Another area in which behavior therapy has been useful is the counseling of parents of retarded children. With relatively brief training, parents can employ behavior therapy to teach their children toileting, dressing, social skills, and even academic subjects.

In daytime adult programs, behavior therapists have been able to teach retarded people the skills necessary for holding a job. Token economies have been especially successful in vocational training programs, improving job performance rates (Rusch & Mithaug, 1980) and on-the-job social behavior (Eilbracht & Thompson, 1977) and inculcating work habits such as arriving on time, punching in and out, and taking breaks and lunch periods at the right times.

For more severely retarded people, especially those confined to institutions, behavior therapy is considered one of the most appropriate and effective techniques (Grabowski & Thompson, 1977; Matson & Andrasik, 1982). It has been used in teaching self-help skills (L. S. Watson & Uzzell, 1981) and in decreasing hyperactivity (Alabiso, 1975) and self-destructive behavior (Favell, 1982). The results, for both patients and staff, can be startling. Incontinence, for example, is a persistent problem in institutions for the severely retarded. Cleaning up not only consumes most of the staff's time but makes assignment to these wards undesirable, so patients receive little friendly attention from the staff. Furthermore, patients who are incontinent generally cannot leave the ward. Toilet training not only improves patients' hygiene and promotes positive interactions with the staff but opens new worlds; toilet-trained people can go out of the ward to other parts of the building or onto the grounds for outdoor recreation (McCartney & Holden, 1981).

In programs for autistic children, roughly the same behavioral techniques are used to build adaptive behaviors, while extinction and punishment are used to suppress maladaptive behaviors.

In the latter case, effectiveness seems to depend greatly on what behavior is being eliminated. For example, self-mutilating responses such as head banging will eventually extinguish if social attention is withdrawn when the head banging occurs. In one case, however, it took nearly eight days and 1,800 head bangs before the response dropped out (Simmons & Lovaas, 1969). Another problem with extinction procedures is that some behaviors seem to be maintained by internal rather than external rewards, in which case withdrawing social attention or food will have little if any effect. For example, autistic children's ritualistic motor behaviors—which, as we have seen, they will prefer over food even when they are hungry—are highly resistant to extinction through the withdrawal of food or attention (Reuter, Walsh, Buck, et al., 1974), apparently because they satisfy an internal need for stimulation (Litrownik, 1969).

Procedures for developing appropriate responses in autistic children have first and foremost focused on conquering these children's insensitivity to social reinforcement. To learn from others, autistic children must regard others as important. The therapist can often bring the child to value other people through respondent conditioning, by pairing praise (social reinforcement) with primary positive reinforcers such as food or with primary negative reinforcers such as pain relief (Lovaas, Schaeffer, & Simmons, 1965). Next, through shaping and modeling—with the use of social reinforcement as well as direct reinforcers such as food—the child is taught new responses such as toileting, speaking, and playing with other children (Lovaas, Berberich, Perloff, et al., 1966; M. M. Wolf, Risley, & Mees, 1964). Once having learned these basic skills, the child can be placed in a group learning situation (Koegel & Rincover, 1974) and thus will be able to learn by observing others.

For therapeutic changes to be maintained, the environment must support them. Follow-up reports indicate that responses learned in the treatment laboratory often do not generalize to the school or the home (Koegel & Rincover, 1977; Nordquist & Wahler, 1973). And some children, especially those who are returned to institutions after their treatment, relapse completely. There is no question that institutions foster such relapses, since in many institutional settings patients are expected to act in an inappropriate fashion and no rewards are given for acting otherwise. For example, one therapist who was visiting an institution decided to look up a child with whom he had worked with considerable success. He found her crouched in a corner, flapping her hand and making bizarre sounds. As soon as she saw the therapist, she got up, walked over, and said, "Hi, how are you?" She continued to talk and act appropriately while the therapist was there. After he left, she presumably returned to her hand flapping.

Attempts to get around this problem have involved keeping the child at home and directing treatment efforts at the parents as well as at the child. The parents are actually trained to act as behavioral therapists. Such home therapy can apparently be very successful (Lovaas, Koegel, Simmons, et al., 1973). Once the parents see the child improving as a result of their efforts, they are likely to try even harder, with the result that the child will make further gains.

Most behavior therapists have no illusion that they are transforming autistic children into normal children (Margolies, 1977). Rather, their aim is to provide these children with enough adaptive responses so that they can graduate from custodial care to a more useful and fulfilling existence, albeit in a "special" class. Critics of behavioral therapy for autistic children have claimed that its products are no better than performing robots (Bettelheim, 1967), and in some instances this seems to be the case. For example, one autistic child, when asked, "What did you have for breakfast?" would tell you that she had had "eggs, toast, jelly, juice, and milk" even on days when she had had no breakfast at all. In short, she had no understanding of the concept; she was simply responding with a programmed answer. In many other instances, however, behavioral treatment has resulted in the development of responses that are spontaneous as well as appropriate. Substantial gains have been made in eliminating self-mutilating and bizarre motor behavior and developing language, self-help, and social skills (Lovaas, Koegel, Simmons, et al., 1973).

Controversial Treatments for Autism

Apart from those just discussed, other therapies are being tried, with mixed results and sometimes in the face of vigorous opposition.

Punishment in Behavior Therapy As we saw, behavior therapy with autistic children is often impeded by the fact that extinction may not suffice to eliminate harmful behaviors. In that case, the therapist may resort to punishment, usually in the form of spankings or, in cases of extreme self-destructive behavior, electric shock. Ivar Lovaas (1970) has conducted research on the use of electric shock in treating autistic children, and as he

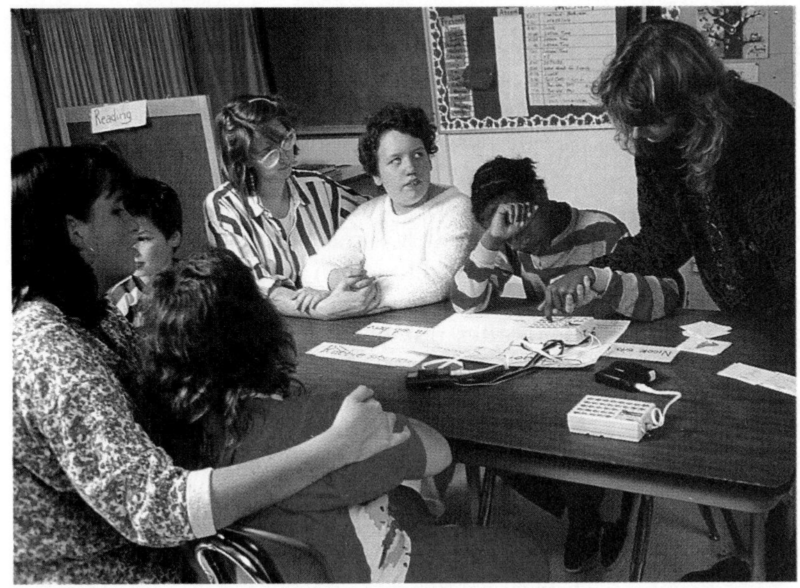

Facilitated communication, in which autistic people are helped to express themselves with the use of keyboards, has generated both hope and controversy. Is the speech pathologist helping the children communicate their own ideas or unconsciously conveying ideas through them?

points out, it is extremely effective in eliminating self-mutilating behavior. "Seemingly independently of how badly the child is mutilating himself or how long he has been doing so, we can essentially remove the self-destructive behavior within the first minute" (p. 38). Many experts object strongly to the use of punishment with disturbed children. In response, Lovaas argues that disturbed children are more likely to respond to therapy when they are treated like people—that is, rewarded, punished, and generally held responsible for their behavior—rather than like patients. Lovaas has also pointed out that if self-destructive behavior is *not* eliminated by some kind of treatment, the child may spend long periods of time tied down in restraints, which is a punishment in itself and which makes it impossible for the child to participate in any other kind of therapy.

Facilitated Communication A new treatment approach that generated some excitement in the early 1990s is based on *facilitated communication (FC)*. Originally developed for cerebral palsy patients, FC enables people with motor and speech problems to communicate by typing letters on a keyboard or pointing to letters on a letter board with a "facilitator" helping to guide their hands. In 1990 Biklen reported that in using FC with autistic patients he had discovered unexpected literacy in these people. One patient produced the message "MY MOTHER FEELS IM STUPID BECAUSE IH CANT USE MY VOICE PROPERLY"; another, "CAN I COME AGAIN" (Biklen, 1990, p. 296). In addition, Biklen wrote, several of these subjects showed advanced cognitive skills. "They chose to converse about concepts. Each of them . . . had thought about the issues we discussed. Also, they had chosen to speak about their feelings" (p. 312). These claims, raising the possibility that beneath their communication problems autistic people were leading, in secret, rich and reasonable mental lives, created much hope and publicity. However, a number of experimental studies (e.g., S. Moore, Donovan, Hudson, et al., 1993) have failed to replicate Biklen's results. One such report concluded that the sophisticated responses of Biklen's subjects were reactions to the demand characteristics of the facilitators—that the facilitators were "putting words into their client's hands" (Eberlin, McConnachie, Ibel, et al., 1993). In response to such skepticism, Biklen (1992) has argued that the reason experimental procedures cannot replicate his results is that the cold laboratory atmosphere of experimental research destroys the subjects' trust and thus quells their desire to communicate.

Auditory Training In the 1940s Dr. Alfred A. Tomatis, a French physician conducting research on hearing loss, found that as his patients' hearing improved, so did their emotional stability and cognitive functioning. Tomatis' hearing therapy was later adapted by one of his students, Guy Bernard. Bernard created a program called Auditory Training in which, for an hour a day, over ten days, patients would be hooked up to a training machine that, by playing them specially selected music, would reeducate their hearing and consequently their behavior. In 1982 Bernard published a book, *Hearing Is Behaving*, in which he claimed to have successfully treated 1,850 cases of dyslexia, 228 cases of depression, and 48 cases of autism through Auditory Training. Still, this technique did not receive wide public attention until 1991, when Annabel Stehli published a book, *The Sound of a Miracle,* describing her daughter Georgiana's autism cure via Auditory Training. There is now a large Auditory Training center in Portland, Oregon. Through the Georgiana Foundation, set up by the Stehli family, this therapy is also being disseminated elsewhere. At present its promoters no longer claim that it operates by changing hearing patterns, but rather that it retrains patients' attention and thereby may affect the structure of the left brain, which controls language and speech.

While Auditory Training has won support from some autism experts (Rimland, 1991), many others are skeptical, for its effectiveness has never been validated by controlled studies. At present there is no way of knowing whether the cures described by the Portland center are not due to the placebo effect, which is known to increase when, as with Auditory Training, elaborate equipment and substantial fees are involved. It is also possible that the reported results are due not to the Auditory Training but to the mandatory "aftercare" therapy that follows it—or indeed to other circumstances in the patients' lives. (As Annabel Stehli wrote revealingly in *The Sound of a Miracle* [1991], "In addition to Auditory Training, faith and miracles, behavior modification helped Georgie more than anything else.") Until controlled studies are conducted, these other factors cannot be ruled out, and therefore the benefits of Auditory Training remain entirely conjectural (Amos, 1993).

Megavitamin Therapy Another "fringe" treatment involves giving autistic children high doses of vitamins. In the early 1970s Rimland (1973, 1974) reported good results from high doses of vitamin B_6. Then investigators in France (e.g., Martineau, Barthélémy, Garreau, et al., 1985) claimed their autistic subjects improved when put on high doses of B_6 and magnesium. It was later discovered, however, that high doses of B_6 could damage the nerves in hands and feet (Bendrich & Cohen, 1990). On the other hand, doses low enough to ensure against side effects seemed to have no influence on subjects' behavior (Tolbert, Haigler, Waits, et al., 1993). Some autistic people—and some other mentally retarded people—are still receiving megavitamin therapy, but it remains controversial.

Drug Treatments In view of the fact that autistic people show abnormally high levels of serotonin, it was hoped that they might be helped by serotonin-reducing drugs. One such drug, fenfluramine, was given to two autistic boys, a three-year-old and a five-year-old, for three months. Both improved noticeably in their speech, social behavior, and IQ scores (the three-year-old's IQ nearly doubled). When the drug treatment was stopped, these gains held for at least six weeks but then, after three months, began diminishing (Geller, Ritvo, Freeman, et al., 1982). Such results raised hopes, but only briefly, for later studies found fenfluramine far less effective, at the same time that several autistic children died while receiving the drug.

The causes of autism are still being energetically sought, but many parents of autistic children now distrust confidently asserted theories, not to mention the "miracle cures" so enthusiastically reported by the press. For years these parents lived under the shadow of Bruno Bettelheim's widely accepted theory that they themselves had caused their children's autism. That view has now been discredited, but it has been succeeded by others. To quote a paper published by one parent organization:

> Over the last decade alone we have seen the eclipse of Barry Kaufmann's *Son-Rise,* a made-for-TV movie suggesting that you could love your child out of his or her autism. We have seen sensitivity training for parents and teachers of autistic children which was somehow dependent on dolphin research. We have seen "holding therapy" designed to forge a "mother-infant bond" which some mothers supposedly forgot to do at their child's birth. We have seen megavitamin therapy, B_6 therapy, magnesium therapy, special diets, and untold other variations on this theme, all supposed to alleviate various symptoms and behaviors of autism and produce a happier child. . . . Various drug therapies arrive with much fanfare, as did fenfluramine, only to have later studies question or negate the original findings. All of these treatments produce an initial rush of participants who claim varying degrees of success, yet it is instructive to note, five or ten years after the initial excitement has died down, how few are still claiming success. (Amos, 1993, p. 10)

Research on autism continues, but parents today tend to greet its findings with less hope and less gullibility.

KEY TERMS

amniocentesis (465)
brain plasticity (467)
congenital disorders (465)
Down syndrome (464)
early infantile autism (471)
echolalia (471)
fetal alcohol syndrome (FAS) (466)
fragile X syndrome (464)
mental retardation (462)
phenylketonuria (PKU) (465)
savant syndrome (477)
sheltered workshops (480)
Tay-Sachs disease (465)
theory of the mind (476)
trisomy 21 (464)

SUMMARY

- Mental retardation, which affects about 1 percent of the U.S. population, is defined as involving significantly subaverage intellectual functioning (below an IQ of 70), related limitation in adaptive skills, and onset before age eighteen. Four levels of retardation are generally recognized: mild, moderate, severe, and profound.
- About 85 percent of people diagnosed as retarded fall into the category of mild retardation. As adults they can often lead relatively independent lives. Moderately retarded people can learn to care for themselves but do not become independent. Severely and profoundly retarded people require considerable supervision.
- Many organic or genetic anomalies are associated with retardation, including chromosomal abnormalities, such as fragile X syndrome and Down syndrome, and metabolic disturbances, such as phenylketonuria.
- Environmental factors also contribute to retardation. In the prenatal environment, congenital disorders (such as rubella), drugs (such as cocaine and alcohol), and maternal malnutrition can cause retardation. In the postnatal environment, important causal factors include reactions to toxins, physical trauma, and the psychological handicaps of growing up in a deprived setting. The latter may cause, or at least foster, cultural-familial retardation, a condition for which children of teenage mothers are especially at risk. Research suggests that what begins as psychological factors may become organic factors through effects on the developing brain. Institutionalization can also have profound effects on intellectual functioning.
- As adults, mentally retarded people are susceptible to other organic brain disorders (such as Alzheimer's disease) and emotional disturbance. Many forms of psychological treatment can help the mentally retarded, if they can find access to the treatment.
- Autism, normally recognizable in early childhood, is a profound disturbance with four basic symptoms: social isolation, cognitive impairments, language deficits, and stereotyped, ritualistic behavior. Many autistic children insist on preserving the sameness of their environment. Only a small percentage make a good adjustment as adults.
- Autism may have a genetic component; it has been associated with fragile X syndrome. It almost certainly has a biochemical component, for many autistic children show abnormally high levels of serotonin and dopamine. Congenital disorders and complications in pregnancy and birth are closely associated with autism. Neurological studies suggest that the basic deficit in autism lies in the limbic system or in the information-processing structures of the cerebral cortex.
- Cognitive researchers argue that cognitive abnormalities are the primary problem in autism. Some identify the essential dysfunction as an inability to integrate input from the different senses; others as overselective attention; still others as basically a language disorder. Yet another hypothesis is that autistic children have no "theory of the mind."
- Opportunities for mentally retarded people have expanded greatly in recent years. Five principles have been established: (1) Mentally retarded people are entitled to free and appropriate education; (2) services for them should be individualized; (3) progress should be evaluated regularly; (4) their lives should be integrated into the community, not segregated from it; and (5) the law should protect them from abuse and deprivation.
- Parents today are normally urged to try to care for a mentally retarded child at home, though they need support in order to handle the problems involved. In the child's early years, parents can use behavioral techniques to teach self-care, self-discipline, and academic skills. In adulthood, some mentally retarded people may be able to live on their own or to marry. Many also work, either in ordinary jobs or in sheltered workshops.
- Efforts are being made to prevent mental retardation (such as through genetic counseling and improved prenatal care) and to minimize the effect of retardation when it occurs (e.g., through infant stimulation programs). The education of mentally retarded children has been upgraded, but educating autistic children is difficult, because of their overselective attention and other cognitive problems.
- Self-instructional training has been successful in helping mentally retarded people. Behavior therapy has helped both mentally retarded and autistic children. Other, more controversial approaches to treating autism include the use of punishment in behavior therapy, facilitated communication (communicating by keyboard), auditory training, megavitamin therapy, and drug treatments.

PART SIX

THERAPIES AND LEGAL ISSUES

CHAPTER 19
INDIVIDUAL PSYCHOTHERAPY

CHAPTER 20
GROUP, FAMILY, AND COMMUNITY THERAPY

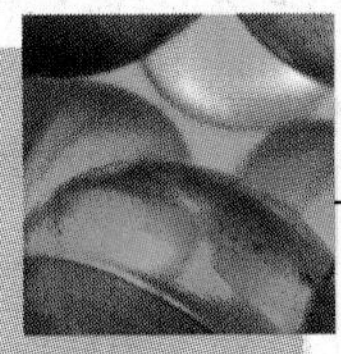

CHAPTER 21
BIOLOGICAL THERAPY

CHAPTER 22
LEGAL ISSUES IN ABNORMAL PSYCHOLOGY

19

INDIVIDUAL PSYCHOTHERAPY

Centuries ago, when people had spells of depression or problems within their families, they might have gone to a relative or perhaps a priest and received some sympathy and a dose of conventional wisdom. Today, while many people still take their problems to friends, relatives, members of the clergy, or even hairdressers, many others turn to professional counselors.

A succinct but comprehensive definition of **psychotherapy** has been offered by Lewis Wolberg (1977):

> Psychotherapy is the treatment, by psychological means, of problems of an emotional nature in which a trained person deliberately establishes a professional relationship with the patient with the object of (1) removing, modifying, or retarding existing symptoms, (2) mediating disturbed patterns of behavior, and (3) promoting positive personality growth and development. (p. 3)

Psychotherapy often includes the same kind of comfort and advice that we get from our friends, but it differs in that it involves a formal relationship in which a client pays for a professional service. In addition, some forms of psychotherapy aspire to the level of science. That is, they claim to be based upon, and aim to contribute to, empirically verifiable laws of behavior—a goal undreamed of by our friends and relatives.

In a book on psychotherapy, Michael J. Mahoney (1991) poses three fundamental questions: Can people change? Can people help other people change? And are some forms of help better than others? The answer to the first and second questions, as we've seen in the preceding chapters, is yes, in some cases. The third question will be examined later in this chapter.

Although individual psychotherapy is an important treatment for emotional problems, it is not the only form of treatment, nor is it necessarily the best. In recent years, many people have turned to psychological self-help books. (Regarding their effectiveness, see the box on page 493.) There are also various group treatments and biological treatments, such as drugs, that may be used instead of, or in addition to, individual psychotherapy. We will discuss these in Chapters 20 and 21, respectively.

THE DIVERSITY OF PSYCHOTHERAPIES

Though it is possible to give a one-sentence definition of *psychotherapy,* this term actually encom-

The value of self-help books is highly variable. Not many of them can take the place of a qualified therapist.

passes a great variety of techniques, ranging from dream analysis to reading assignments to instructions for talking back to rude waiters. Therapists differ in their professional training, in their conception of the therapist's role, and in their personal styles. The result is a large assortment of therapeutic approaches.

Two differences deserve special attention. The first has to do with the basic approach to bringing about change in the client's behavior. London (1964) divides psychotherapy into two categories: insight therapy and action therapy. **Insight therapy** is based on the theory that behavior problems arise when people fail to understand the motives underlying their actions, and especially when they refuse to confront conflicts between different motives. Accordingly, the goal of insight therapy, as the name indicates, is to increase patients' awareness of why they do what they do, the assumption being that once they understand their behavior, they will be able to control it better. In **action therapy,** on the other hand, there is little or no discussion of motives. The therapist focuses directly on the patient's problem behavior and attempts to correct it by teaching the patient new skills.

We have already seen numerous examples of both of these kinds of therapy. Psychodynamic therapy, humanistic-existential therapy, and even cognitive therapy, in their classic forms, are insight therapies, differing only in the kinds of insights at which they aim. Behavioral therapy, on the other hand, is generally action therapy, and cognitive therapy, as currently practiced, is generally a com-

SELF-HELP BOOKS: DO THEY WORK?

The last twenty years have seen an explosion of psychological self-help books, many by the same experts whose research is cited in this textbook: Lewisohn and his colleagues, on depression (*Control Your Depression*, 1979); Wolpe, on phobias (*Our Useless Fears*, 1981); Brownell, on obesity (*The Partnership Diet Program*, 1980); and so on. At the end of the 1980s it was estimated that 2,000 new self-help books were appearing every year (Doheny, 1988). Today, the figure is probably higher, and it is being supplemented by audiotapes and computerized treatments.

The potential advantages of self-help books over psychotherapy are obvious. They are far cheaper, and they reach people who want to avoid seeing a therapist. Furthermore, some evaluations (Gould & Clum, 1993; Scogin, Bynum, Stephens, et al., 1990) have found them as effective as therapist-administered treatments, particularly for skills deficits, such as assertiveness, and for anxiety and depression. (They apparently do not work as well with habit problems such as smoking, drinking, and obesity.)

But there is a problem with these evaluations, and that is that the studies involved do not replicate the conditions under which self-help books are ordinarily used. First, the subjects in these studies are professionally diagnosed before being given the book. Second, their progress is checked on by the experimenters, thus motivating the subjects to make progress.

For ordinary users of self-help books, the situation is different. There is no one to diagnose them, with the result, for example, that depressed people may waste valuable time trying to lift their spirits with relaxation exercises. Furthermore, book users have no one to monitor their progress, and consequently they are less likely to complete the prescribed treatment. The dropout rate for book users is high even in monitored studies (Rosen, 1987). In real life, it is no doubt much higher, and for good reasons. All forms of psychological treatment are full of lulls and snags and periods of no improvement. People in therapist-administered treatment are motivated to overcome these discouragements. The therapist is there to help them do so. Also, they have invested a lot of money; they want some return on it. But people with self-help books have spent only a few dollars. If they get bored or find they're not improving, they can just put the book down. Nothing is lost; no one will care.

Unfortunately, someone does care: the dropouts, who, despite the fact that they themselves chose not to finish the program, may feel much more hopeless about their condition. Rosen (1987), discussing this problem, cites a study comparing three therapies—self-administered treatment, minimal therapist contact, and therapist-administered treatment—for premature ejaculation. Of the six couples in the first group, not one completed the program. "One can imagine," Rosen writes, "how tension would have developed in these couples, especially if they were unaware that all other couples [in the self-administered treatment group] had been equally unsuccessful" (p. 47).

It is possible that the best use of self-help books is in a group setting, with a professional available to diagnose the book users and monitor their progress. As for people using such books on their own, they should not become discouraged or angry with themselves if they don't improve. They should simply look for a live therapist.

bination of action and insight. As we shall see later in this chapter, there is a growing trend toward integration of the action and insight schools, with adherents of each school now willing to learn from the successes of the other. Nevertheless, as a matter of emphasis, the difference between the two approaches is still valid.

Another important distinction concerns the scientific status of psychotherapy. Many therapists regard psychotherapy as an applied science, in which one can achieve a predicted result by controlling a certain number of variables. In the words of Gordon Paul (1969a), such therapists ask themselves, "What treatment, by whom, is most effective for this individual, with that specific problem, under which set of circumstances?" (p. 62). This question is answered according to scientific evidence accumulated from past treatments, and the results of the present treatment, once it is completed, are added to that body of evidence, in the effort to refine our scientific understanding of human behavior. By contrast, other therapists feel that because of the complex interactions between therapist and patient, psychotherapy can never be—nor should it be—wholly scientific. According to this latter group, psychological treatment is not just a science but also an "art"—something that depends as much on empathy and intuition as on empirical analysis. Behaviorists and cognitive therapists generally regard therapy more as an applied science, while psychodynamic and humanistic-existential therapists are likely to see it somewhat more as an art. Most see it as both; they simply emphasize one side or the other.

Curiously, such differences of emphasis between therapists apply even when the therapists are taking their patients through what is roughly the same process. Wiser and Goldfried (1993), using audiotapes and transcripts of treatment sessions with cognitive-behavioral therapists and psychodynamic-interpersonal therapists, compared the extent and intensity of the patients' emotional experience in the two kinds of therapy. They found no difference. But when they asked the therapists to say which portions of the session they thought contributed most to the patients' improvement, serious differences emerged. The psychodynamic-interpersonal therapists chose the segments that were high in emotional content, whereas the cognitive-behavioral therapists stressed those that were low in emotional content.

Beyond these differences among psychotherapists, there are also broad areas of agreement. Therapists of all persuasions tend to agree that a crucial factor in determining whether therapy will succeed or fail is the relationship between the therapist and the patient—the so-called therapeutic alliance or therapeutic bond. When the patient perceives the therapist as an ally in the process of change, the chances of change are that much greater—in all types of therapy (Beutler, Machado, & Neufeldt, 1994; Orlinsky, Grawe, & Parks, 1994). Most therapists also agree that increased self-examination and trying out new experiences both contribute to therapeutic change (Mahoney, 1991).

Since World War II the field of psychotherapy has expanded at an astounding rate. One indication of this growth is the increase in the number of clinical psychology programs accredited by the American Psychological Association. In 1947, there were 29 such programs (R. R. Sears, 1947); in 1962, 60 (S. Ross, 1962); in 1993, 175 (American Psychological Association, 1993). In other words, there are six times as many accredited programs than there were a half-century ago. With this growth has come the kind of diversification we have mentioned. Today there are well over 200 varieties of psychotherapy, each with its own program for solving human problems.

As psychotherapy has diversified, it has changed in other ways as well. For one thing, it has become much more popular. Approximately 5 percent of the population makes at least one voluntary mental health visit in a given year (Horgan, 1985). That is one of every twenty people; obviously, psychotherapy is no longer the private preserve of the "crazy." Consequently, the stigma attached to psychological treatment has greatly diminished. Though we still do not find political candidates discussing their therapy, ordinary citizens are increasingly willing to consult a therapist, and to tell their friends that they do.

As the stigma of psychological treatment has diminished, so has its mystique. With each new therapeutic school challenging the others, the actual methods employed by different schools have been placed more and more squarely before the public. And this exposure has resulted in a good deal of critical questioning. Today the assessment of therapy—does it work? if so, how? is it cost-effective?—is receiving unprecedented emphasis. Many of these challenges come not just from the public but also from the third-party payers who pick up a good part of this country's psychological treatment bill: insurance companies, industrial health plans, and the government.

Whoever the challenger, today's therapists must justify their techniques. The clinical psychology division of the American Psychological Association has now set up a special task force to identify, for each psychological disorder, which treatments have been empirically validated as successful in at least two independent outcome studies. There have also been many recent studies—we examine some below—measuring the *relative* effectiveness of different therapies for the same disorder. This demand for accountability is one of the most important trends in psychology today. In general, the field is becoming less concerned with high-level theoretical disputes and more concerned with practical results. In the process, it is becoming more realistic. The title of Martin Seligman's recent book on psychotherapy, *What You Can Change & What You Can't* (1994), strikes a typically sober note. "Much of successful living consists of learning to make the best of a bad situation," Seligman writes (p. 5). Though therapists may disagree on which bad situations can be changed and which can't, sweeping claims are less often heard today, and all claimants are asked for proof.

In earlier chapters, we discussed a number of specific individual treatments. In this chapter, we will pull together those threads and summarize each perspective's general approach to treatment. This is possible despite the diversity described above. No matter how eclectic the therapist, he or she has still been trained according to one or another of the major theoretical perspectives. Practices may vary, but within each perspective the principles of treatment are unified, and it is these principles that we will now describe.

THE PSYCHODYNAMIC APPROACH TO TREATMENT

Though **psychoanalysis,** as practiced by Freud, is rarely used today, it is nevertheless the grandfa-

This is Freud's office in Vienna, with the famous couch on which his patients reclined while he analyzed them. Freud's chair was at the head of the couch, out of the patient's view. The comforts of the couch (note the pillows and coverlets) and the removal of the analyst from the patient's line of sight were intended to free the patient from inhibition in discussing intimate matters.

ther of all psychodynamic therapies. Therefore we will give this technique first consideration and then discuss its modern variants.

Freudian Psychoanalysis

Freud's experience with his patients led him to conclude that the source of "neurosis" was anxiety experienced by the ego when unconscious material threatened to break through into the conscious mind. To deal with this threat, the ego might use a number of defense mechanisms, the most important of which was repression—the pushing back of the impulse into the unconscious. Repression weakened the ego, however. Furthermore, some anxiety remained, forcing its victims into various self-defeating postures. Thus, according to Freud, the proper treatment for neurosis was to coax the unconscious material out into consciousness so that the patient could at last confront it. Once acknowledged and "worked through," this material would lose its power to terrorize the ego. Self-defeating defenses could accordingly be abandoned, and the ego would then be free to devote itself to more constructive pursuits. As Freud succinctly put it, "Where id was, there shall ego be."

It is on this theory that the techniques of psychoanalysis are founded. In the first place, because the trouble is thought to be within the client's psyche, which the analyst is helping the client to explore, psychoanalysis is strictly a one-on-one client-analyst relationship. The client often lies on a couch, the better to relax, thus loosening the restraints on the unconscious, and the analyst typically sits outside the client's field of vision. What the client then does is talk—usually for fifty minutes a day, three to four days a week, over a period of several years. The client may talk about his or her childhood, since it is there that the roots of the problem presumably lie, but present difficulties are also discussed. The analyst remains silent much of the time, so as not to derail the client's inner journey. When the analyst does speak, it is generally to *interpret* the client's remarks—that is, to point out their possible connection with unconscious material. This dialogue between client and therapist turns on four basic techniques: free association, dream interpretation, analysis of resistance, and analysis of transference.

Free Association Freud's primary route to the unconscious was **free association,** whereby the client simply verbalizes whatever thoughts come to mind, in whatever order they occur, taking care not to censor them either for logic or for propriety. The rationale is that the unconscious has its own logic and that if clients report their thoughts exactly as they occur, the connective threads between verbalizations and unconscious impulses will be revealed. When such connections do become clear, the analyst points them out.

Dream Interpretation A second important tunnel to the unconscious is **dream interpretation.** Freud believed that in sleep, the ego's defenses were lowered, allowing unconscious material to surface. But defenses are never completely abandoned, and therefore even in dreams repressed impulses reveal themselves only in symbolic fashion. Beneath the dream's **manifest content,** or surface meaning, lies its **latent content,** or unconscious understory. For example, one patient, a new mother who was up at all hours of the night tending to her baby, reported to her analyst a dream in which she gave

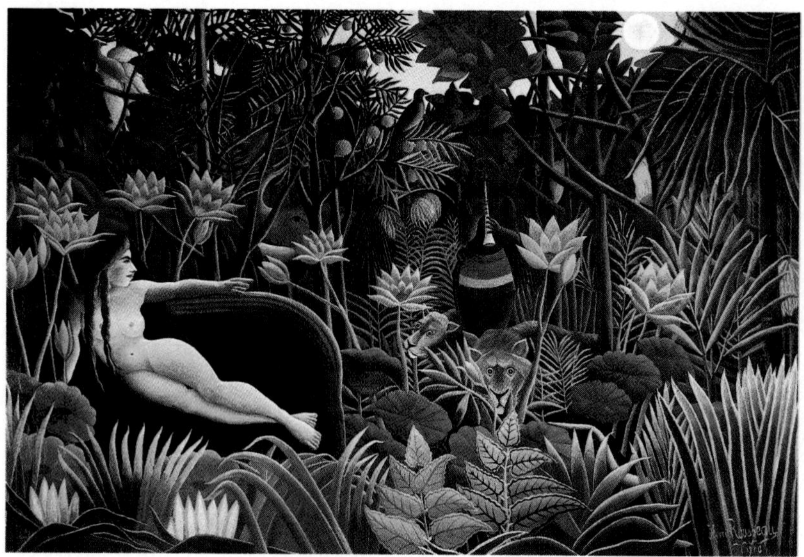

This painting by Henri Rousseau is titled *The Dream.* Psychoanalytic methods encourage the patient to report his or her dreams and then to free-associate to the dream material. In light of the patient's associations, the analyst interprets the dream, revealing its latent content, which will presumably center on unconscious conflicts.

birth to identical twin boys, one of whom then died. According to the analyst, the latent content of this dream was that the woman, while she loved her new son, also wished him dead for destroying her peace of mind. However, the ego's defenses against this aggressive id impulse were still in partial operation during the dream. So the ego and the id "compromised," multiplying the baby into two identical babies and killing only one (I. Mohacsy, personal communication, 1975).

This is a simplified example, for dream interpretation normally involves free association. After the dream is reported, the analyst asks the patient to free-associate to its contents, and the resulting associations are taken as clues to the meaning of the dream.

Analysis of Resistance As clients are guided toward the unwelcome knowledge of their unconscious motivations, they may begin to show **resistance,** using various defenses to avoid confronting the painful material. They may change the subject, make jokes, pick a fight with the analyst; they may even begin missing appointments. It is then the analyst's job to point out the resistance and, if possible, to interpret it—that is, to suggest what the patient is trying not to find out.

Analysis of Transference As psychoanalysis progresses, with the client revealing his or her secret life to the analyst, the relationship between the two partners becomes understandably complex. In his own practice, Freud noted that while he tried to remain steadfastly neutral, many of his patients began responding to him with very passionate emotions—sometimes with a childlike love and dependency, at other times with bitter hostility and rebellion. Freud interpreted this phenomenon as a **transference** onto him of his clients' childhood feelings toward important people in their lives—above all, their feelings toward their parents.

Transference is an essential component of psychoanalysis. In fact, traditional analysts maintain that in order for the therapeutic process to be successful, clients must go through a stage, called *transference neurosis,* of reenacting with the analyst their childhood conflicts with their parents, for it is these repressed conflicts that are typically undermining their adult relationships. The belief is that once these central emotions are brought out, clients have reached the core of the neurosis, which, with the analyst's help, they can then confront, evaluate realistically, and thereby overcome. This is a prime example of what psychoanalysts mean by the term "working through."

Modern Psychodynamic Therapy

Most of today's psychodynamic therapists, though they may retain the Freudian vocabulary, practice a considerably modified form of psychoanalysis, often based not only on Freud's theory but also on the theories of his followers. Like Freud and his descendants, their primary concern is with the unconscious and its effects on behavior, and their goal is to increase the patient's insight into unconscious motivations. But they depart from orthodox psychoanalytic techniques in several important respects. First, they generally take a more active part in the therapy session, dealing with the client face to face (the couch is seldom used) and speaking, directing, and advising much more extensively than Freud would have considered appropriate. Second, while the client's past history is by no means ignored, modern psychodynamic therapists generally pay more attention to the client's present life, especially his or her personal relationships. Finally, most psychodynamic treatment today is briefer and less intensive than orthodox psychoanalysis. Therapist and client typically meet once or twice a week for anywhere from a few months to a few years. This broad category of therapy is probably the most common form of psychological treatment in the United States. We will examine one approach, that of the ego psychologists.

Ego Psychology We pointed out in Chapter 2 that a major revision of Freudian theory was that of the ego psychologists, a loosely formed group including, among others, Heinz Hartmann and Erik Erikson. The basic contention of **ego psychology** is that ego is at least as important as id in controlling human behavior. As we have seen, Freud's conceptualization of the psyche was one in which the ego, borrowing its energy from the id, merely served as a sort of reality-oriented mediator of the id's sexual and aggressive strivings. In contrast, the ego psychologists argue that the ego has substantial energy of its own and that its functions—memory, judgment, perception, problem solving, planning—serve constructive purposes independent of id strivings. A second fundamental premise of ego psychology is the critical importance of interpersonal relationships, especially the mother-child relationship. As we saw, Erikson advanced his theory of psychosocial development—development through interaction with others—as a revision of Freud's theory of psychosexual development.

The contributions of the ego psychologists have been more theoretical than practical. In therapy, they tend to use Freudian methods—interpretation of dreams, analysis of resistance and of transference—but to adapt them to ego-based concerns. Like most other modern psychodynamic therapists, they tend to be active in the therapy hour, trying to help patients cope with their present world, especially their relationships with others, rather than concentrating on the inner psyche. In general, ego psychologists stress the present as opposed to the past, the development of identity as opposed to the replay of childhood experience. They regard the therapy situation as the home base from which the client may venture out to new experiments in living—and not just as a setting for reexperiencing the formative events of childhood.

Psychodynamic Therapy: Pros and Cons

In the entire field of psychology there is perhaps no issue more controversial than the value of psychodynamic treatment. The psychiatric literature contains many testimonials to the insights and personality changes achieved through psychoanalysis. From other quarters, however, psychodynamic therapy has been strongly criticized.

A common objection is that psychodynamic therapy is based on a theory that is difficult to validate scientifically. As we saw in Chapter 2, empirical studies have in fact supported a number of psychodynamic principles (and not supported others) in the past few decades. Nevertheless, it remains true that most psychodynamic and especially psychoanalytic writing rests more on intuition and personal judgment than on scientific measures.

A second criticism has to do with the multiplicity of psychodynamic theories. Almost all psychodynamic theorists would agree that a successful therapy depends on the attainment of insight. But insight into what? In fact, patients develop insights according to the theory that their therapist espouses. And this makes the central mechanism of psychodynamic therapy look less like insight—a confrontation with something that is truly there—than a form of persuasion, in which the patient is won over to the therapist's belief system (London, 1964).

This charge is basically unanswerable. (And it applies to all therapies, though it is a special problem with the insight therapies.) At the same time, recent research has shown that psychodynamic methods do in fact lead patients to discover important things about themselves; that central interpersonal conflicts can be reliably identified in psychodynamic therapy (Luborsky, Crits-Christoph, & Mellon, 1986); that when they are, patients become more involved in the therapy session and more expressive (Silberschatz, Fretter, & Curtis, 1986); and that the more accurate the therapist's interpretations at such moments, the more likely the patient is to improve (Crits-Christoph, Cooper, & Luborsky, 1988; Piper, Joyce, McCallum, et al., 1993). Conceivably, the specific insights may depend on the therapist's training, but something like insight does seem to occur, and to have therapeutic effects. Interestingly, however, psychodynamic therapy may "work" even if the patient's insight into his or her problems is imperfect. In 1952 the Menninger Foundation initiated an intensive study of forty-two psychodynamic-therapy patients (Wallerstein, 1989). Following these people for thirty years, long after they had left therapy, the researchers were surprised to find that many of the patients were able, through treatment, to make positive changes in their lives even though they had not achieved a comparable degree of insight into their problems. Furthermore, the changes lasted. This suggests that other mechanisms in therapy—for example, direct attempts to change, together with the patient's effort to please the therapist—may be as important as insight.

A third criticism of psychodynamic therapy is that it is "elitist," since, by its very nature, it seems to exclude a large number of patients. Some are barred purely on financial grounds. Though more and more health plans are now including some coverage for psychotherapy, psychodynamic treatment, because it tends to take longer than other therapies, is rarely paid for in full, or even in large part, by health plans. Also, psychodynamic therapy is generally limited to people with "neurotic" disorders and long-standing personality disorders, thus leaving out vast numbers of psychotics. Finally, because psychodynamic therapy is such a highly verbal enterprise, it tends to work best for those who are articulate and well educated (Luborsky & Spence, 1978). Indeed, the patients most likely to benefit from this kind of therapy—as from any verbal therapy—are the so-called YAVIS patients: young, attractive, verbal, intelligent, and successful (Schofield, 1964). In other words, those who tend to succeed at psychodynamic therapy are those who tend to succeed at most things in life.

The fact that most psychodynamic therapy today is briefer than traditional psychoanalysis is in part a response to the financial objection. Even shorter therapies—treatments of fifteen or twenty sessions—are now being developed and evaluated. But the "elitist" charge is arguably irrelevant. If psychodynamic therapy works for neurotics and not for psychotics, that is only one of the many ways in which it is better to be neurotic than psychotic. Furthermore, *most* therapies work for some disorders and not for others. As for the socioeconomic factor, the answer is not to chide psychodynamic therapy for favoring well-educated patients but to develop effective treatments for that larger segment of the population that, while less verbal, is equally prone to psychological disorders.

THE HUMANISTIC-EXISTENTIAL APPROACH TO TREATMENT

While humanistic and existential therapists are highly individualistic in their techniques, they share the common objective of helping patients to become more truly "themselves"—to seek meaning from life and then to make deliberate choices in order to live more meaningfully. In keeping with this goal, humanistic-existential treatment differs from other psychotherapies in that it maximizes clients' sense of freedom, discourages them from engaging in deterministic thinking (e.g., "passing the buck" to a stern father, an insensitive spouse, a dreary job), turns them face-front toward the future, and asks them to "become"—to choose their own destiny. This approach further differs from other treatment philosophies in that it places greater emphasis on intimacy in the client-therapist relationship, with the therapist attempting to enter the client's phenomenological world and the client constantly drawing strength from that new partnership.

Client-Centered Therapy

The best-known and most popular humanistic therapy is **client-centered therapy,** designed by Carl Rogers (1951). The fundamental principle of this treatment approach, which we have already outlined in Chapter 2, is that human beings are innately good and innately motivated to actualize their potential. Self-actualization, however, may be impeded by *conditions of worth,* values that people learn from their families and friends. To be loved by these others, the person screens out large portions of his or her experience, thus blocking the unfolding of the self. According to Rogers, the only way to solve this problem is to eliminate unrealistic conditions of worth, and client-centered therapy is a means to that end. As its name indicates, the treatment is focused directly on the client's individual personality, not on any system of theories or laws regarding human behavior in general. Indeed, the therapist tries to see the world through the client's eyes, so that the client will come to see his or her experience of reality as a thing of value.

The therapist's ability to do this depends on two basic factors. The first is *unconditional positive regard.* In contrast to the limiting conditions of worth, the therapist offers unlimited acceptance, hoping by this means to induce clients to accept the totality of their experience.

Second, the therapist must "hear" the client, which means resonating to what the client is communicating. Most people, according to Rogers (1980), have scant experience of being "heard":

> I have had the fantasy of a prisoner in a dungeon, tapping out day after day a Morse code message, "Does anybody hear me? Is anybody there?" And finally one day he hears some faint tappings which spell out "Yes." By that one simple response he is released from his loneliness; he has become a human being again. There are many, many people living in private dungeons today, people who give no evidence of it whatsoever on the outside, where you have to listen very

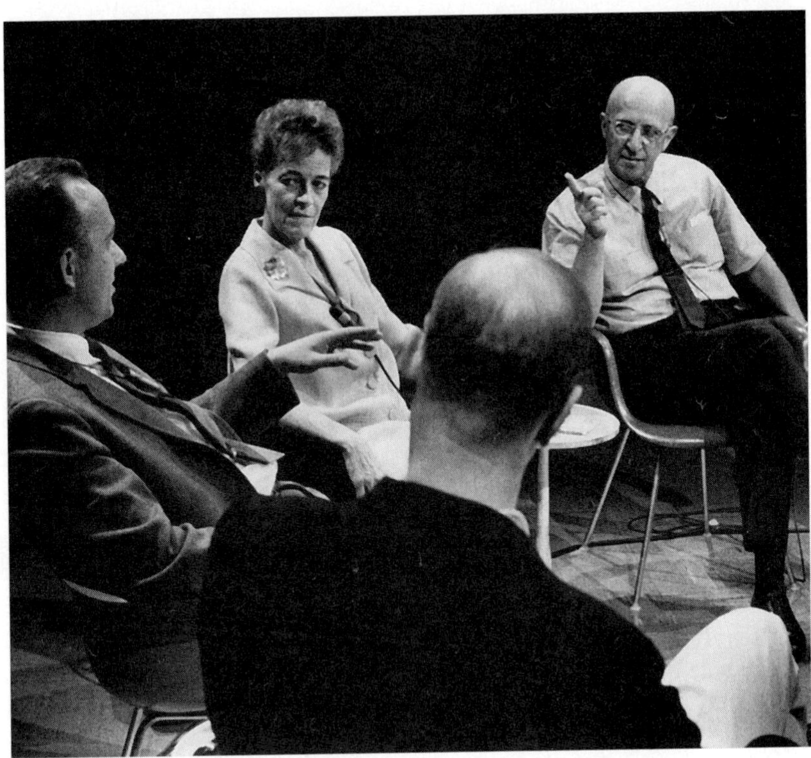

Carl Rogers, at right, conducts a group therapy session. In client-centered therapy, the therapist's goal is to offer the client empathy, intuitive understanding, and unconditional positive regard.

> sharply to hear the faint messages from the dungeon. (p. 10)

Therapists, once they hear the client, "mirror" back the message—that is, they state the feelings that they are picking up. This process allows clients to clarify their feelings and, since the feelings are mirrored back to them without any disapproval, to accept their inner experience.

The touchstones of client-centered therapy, then, are empathy and intuition. While the psychodynamic therapist will, to some extent, remain outside the client's experience, so as to be able to interpret it, the Rogerian therapist tries to close the gap between therapist and client and "be with" the client as fully as possible.

Existential Therapy

While humanistic and existential psychology both stress freedom, they understand it differently. The humanists see freedom as liberation from limiting conditions of worth—something that the human personality is always working toward and that, once achieved, will automatically lead to self-actualization. The existentialists, on the other hand, see freedom as a constant struggle, something that people may actually wish to avoid and that, once embraced, still entails considerable anguish. The goal of existential therapy, however, is to set the patient on this hard road. As popularized by such figures as Viktor Frankl and Rollo May (Chapter 2), existential therapy encourages patients to take responsibility for their symptoms as something that they themselves have chosen and aims to show them that they are free—indeed, almost obligated—to choose better ways of coping, ways that will give meaning to their lives.

Perhaps the most important source of meaning, as existential therapists see it, is honest, respectful personal relationships, and in their strictly *phenomenological approach* (Chapter 2) to the patient, they try to provide a model. Many of them begin therapy by "bracketing" their theoretical assumptions—that is, stating these assumptions and then laying them aside as completely as possible. Then, presumably, they can truly enter into the patient's phenomenological universe and see the world as the patient sees it. Existentialists also tend to be less empathically warm than the humanists. In their view, therapy is a sort of heroic partnership, therapist and client together facing the facts of life in a world where human values, because of social constraints, are hard to locate and harder still to pursue.

Gestalt Therapy

The founder of **Gestalt therapy,** Frederick (Fritz) Perls (1893–1970) was trained as a Freudian psy-

Fritz Perls, the founder of Gestalt therapy, believed that when clients act out their conflicts and confront their feelings, they learn to control them rather than being controlled by them.

choanalyst, but he eventually repudiated large portions of Freudian theory. Thus Gestalt therapy (Perls, 1970; Perls, Hefferline, & Goodman, 1951) is both an outgrowth of and a departure from psychoanalysis. On the Freudian side, Perls adhered to the theory that psychological disturbance is the result of unresolved childhood conflicts that had to be located and worked through. But Perls' handling of childhood conflicts was decidedly un-Freudian—and far more humanistic-existential—in that all these matters were brought to bear solely on the present, the *now,* in which clients had to choose what they would become and whether they would allow their past to control their future.

Accordingly, Gestalt-therapy clients are asked to reenact their conflicts in the consulting room. If, for example, the client is still disturbed, at age forty, over the way his father treated him when he was ten, the therapist will assume the role of the father and have the client act out the conflict—reopen the quarrel and perhaps this time close it as well. Clients are also encouraged to "act out" as violently as they need to—to yell, weep, kick the chair, and so on. In this way, Perls argued, clients could confront their feelings, learn to control them, and thereby begin living more spontaneous and honest lives.

Gestalt therapy peaked in the sixties and seventies and is less popular today. However, it left a deep imprint on the group-therapy movement (Chapter 20), and recently it has had a rebirth of sorts in *experiential therapy,* a new movement combining elements of Gestalt and client-centered therapy. Experiential therapy is as insistent as Gestalt on the curative effects of expressing emotion—as opposed to the psychodynamic emphasis on analyzing emotion—and it is equally concerned with the patient's here and now: the present, not the past. On the other hand, it aims to be more scientific than other emotion-centered therapies. Experiential therapists have produced detailed manuals for conducting treatment (Beutler, Engle, Mohr, et al., 1991) and have worked out specific techniques for teaching therapists to help their clients express emotion (L. S. Greenberg, Elliott, & Lietaer, 1994; L. S. Greenberg & Goldman, 1988).

Humanistic-Existential Therapy: Pros and Cons

Not just Gestalt therapy but most forms of humanistic-existential treatment had their greatest vogue during the 1960s, when their philosophy converged with the political sentiments of the time. Today they have a smaller, though faithful, following. Client-centered therapy remains popular, in part because of its simplicity. Client-centered therapists do not have to interpret obscure symbols, as in psychodynamic therapy, or implement highly precise treatment techniques, as in behavior therapy. What they must do is be empathic and warm—surely an appealing style of therapy to most people.

As an insight therapy, humanistic-existential treatment is credited with many of the same virtues as psychodynamic treatment—that it deals with the person as a whole rather than with fragments of behavior, that it goes to the root of the patient's problem, and that it leads to genuine self-knowledge. Furthermore, humanistic-existential therapists claim that they offer their patients a sense of hope that no deterministic psychology, whether behavioral or psychodynamic, can offer. These therapists also deserve credit for showing the maximum possible respect for the patient's point of view.

If humanistic-existential therapy has many of the same strengths as psychodynamic therapy, it is also subject to the same criticisms, the criticisms of insight therapy as a whole: that the treatment is long and costly, that it is appropriate only for "neurotic" disorders, and that it benefits only a certain sector of the population—the YAVIS patients described above. Finally, like psychodynamic therapy, humanistic-existential therapy has been faulted for being unscientific and therefore hard to evaluate empirically.

To this final charge the existentialists reply that the scientific standards being invoked are those of natural science, which they regard as inadequate for the study and treatment of human beings. Other humanistic-existential therapists have responded to the "unscientific" charge by becoming more scientific. The experiential therapists, as we saw, have evolved precise, testable techniques. As for Rogers and his followers, they have been subjecting their theory and therapy to scientific testing for decades. Their major research tool has been the Q-sort, a personality test that measures the subject's self-image and "ideal self." Research with the Q-sort (Rogers, 1959; Rogers & Dymond, 1954) has supported Rogers' argument that patients seeking therapy tend to have an unrealistically low self-image and unrealistically high ideals, together with his claim that client-centered therapy helps to close that gap. Client-centered therapists have also tried to identify the qualities that make a therapist more effective. Rogers, for example, was among the first to tape-record his therapy sessions in an attempt to analyze the therapeutic process. This practice led to a great surge in research on therapy—all forms of therapy—and many of the results have supported Rogers' claims. In particular, the therapist's warmth, empathy, and "congruence," or intuitive abilities, have all been frequently associated with successful therapeutic outcomes (Beutler, Machado, & Neufeldt, 1994; Orlinsky, Grawe, & Parks, 1994).

Despite such research efforts, humanistic-existential therapy is likely to remain a less than perfectly mapped territory. Humanistic-existential therapists, in general, concern themselves with helping clients, not with generating data. As for the existentialists, they are at least as committed to philosophy and morality as to what most psychologists understand by the term *science.*

THE BEHAVIORAL APPROACH TO TREATMENT

Like the techniques of psychodynamic therapy, those of behavior therapy have already been examined to some degree in earlier chapters. And in Chapter 3 we discussed in detail the principles on which behavior therapy is based. The most fundamental of these principles is that all behavior, whether psychotic, "neurotic," or normal, is governed by the same laws. Consequently the goal of therapy is to use those laws—learning and other experimentally derived principles—to teach people with behavioral problems the skills they need in order to enhance their functioning. The behaviorists, then, do not regard behavior as a symptom—a signpost pointing to the true target, an underlying conflict. For them, the behavior itself is the target, and they aim at it directly.

What this means is that behaviorists place considerably less emphasis on a person's past than do psychodynamic therapists. They do not ignore the client's history; they recognize that current functioning is based in part on past learning. However, they point out that maladaptive behavior is maintained not by past conditions but by current conditions, which may be very different from the circumstances that originally produced the behavior. (This is one reason for behaviorists' skepticism regarding the curative power of insight into the past.) Consequently, treatment emphasizes the conditions that elicit and reinforce the problem behavior in the present.

Another consequence of the behavior therapists' direct approach is that they focus less on the inner life than other therapists do. Again, they do not ignore this aspect of experience. However strict the empiricism of the early behaviorists, modern behaviorism has been so influenced by the cognitive school that there is now almost no behavioral therapist who does not take self-defeating thoughts into account in treatment. Nevertheless, the behaviorists' approach to the client's thoughts differs substantially from that of insight therapists. While the latter tend to regard thoughts as elusive clues to deep-seated conflicts, the behaviorists consider these internal events relatively accessible and tend to take them at face value. To them, cognitions are simply covert responses, subject to the same laws of learning as overt responses and therefore equally open to change (e.g., Wolpe, 1978).

Just as the behaviorists' goal is pragmatic—the building of skills—so is their therapeutic manner. While insight therapists aim at creating a special emotional climate in which patients can discover their own truths, the behaviorists devote the therapeutic hour to giving instructions, analyzing goals, implementing strategies, modeling appropriate behaviors, and providing reinforcement for goal attainment. Behavior therapists also are supportive, but they generally regard the establishment of a sympathetic client-therapist relationship as a first step to the remaining, essential steps of behavioral or cognitive retraining. The "therapeutic bond," in other words, is not central to behavior therapy in the same way that it is to the insight therapies.

Behavioral treatments tend to be multicomponent "packages." Still, these complex treatment programs are based on relatively few and simple principles. When the primary goal is a change in overt behavior, treatment usually takes the form of operant conditioning. When the primary goal is a change in emotion (i.e., in the patient's attraction or aversion to certain stimuli), treatment generally centers on respondent conditioning. When the primary goal is a change in cognition, the therapist will tend to use the recently developed techniques of cognitive restructuring. Actually, many treatments have all three of these goals—hence the multicomponent approach. But for the sake of clarity, we will consider each principle separately.

Operant Conditioning

Operant conditioning, as we have seen, is learning via consequences. Under certain stimulus conditions, we produce a certain response, and the fact that this response is followed by positive or negative consequences provides an incentive for us to repeat or avoid that same response when next we are faced with those same stimulus conditions. Operant behavior, then, involves three components: (1) the stimulus or cue for a certain response, (2) the response, and (3) the consequences. Behavior therapists have found that by altering any of these components, they can change maladaptive patterns of behavior.

Contingency Management The manipulation of the consequences of a response in order to change the frequency of that response is called **contingency management.** Throughout earlier chapters, we have seen applications of this simple rewards-and-punishments technique. An interesting recent example involved forty participants in a six-month behavioral program for cocaine dependence (Higgins, Budney, Bickel, et al., 1994). All the subjects had to have their urine tested for cocaine traces three times a week. After the test, half simply received their test results. The other half received rewards as well as results: every time their urine was "clean," they were given a voucher that could be used to buy articles in local stores. For the first three months, the vouchers increased in value with each consecutive clean test. In the second three months, the vouchers were replaced by state lottery tickets. Both rewards worked very well. In the rewards group, 75 percent of the subjects completed the whole six-month program, as compared with 40 percent of the no-rewards group. Furthermore, the average length of continuous cocaine abstinence, as documented by the urine tests, was twice as long for the rewards group as for the no-rewards group. Clearly, behavior can be changed by managing its contingencies.

Stimulus Control Behaviorists have found that operant behavior is controlled not only by the events that follow it but also by those that precede it. Our environment is filled with "cues for reinforcement," which, without thinking about it, we are constantly obeying. For many people, finishing a meal is a cue for smoking. For others, sitting down in front of the television is a cue for snacking. And just as behavior can be changed by controlling its consequences, it can be changed by controlling its cues—a procedure known as stimulus control.

In **stimulus control** one establishes a highly predictable relationship between a given stimulus and a given response by eliminating all other stimuli associated with that response and all other responses associated with that stimulus. The object is to create a situation in which that stimulus, and no other, will automatically elicit that response, and no other. If this object is attained, then the frequency of the response can be controlled by controlling the frequency of exposure to the stimulus.

A good example of stimulus control is behavioral treatment for insomnia. Insomniacs often use their beds at night for many activities besides sleeping—reading, television watching, telephone conversations, and so forth. The bed must therefore be reestablished as a cue only for sleeping. In one treatment program, the instructions to the patients are as follows:

> **1** Lie down intending to go to sleep *only* when you are sleepy.
> **2** Do not use your bed for anything except sleep; that is, do not read, watch television, eat, or worry in bed. Sexual activity is the only exception to this rule. . . .
> **3** If you find yourself unable to fall asleep, get up and go into another room. Stay up as long as you wish and then return to the bedroom to sleep. Although we do not want you to watch the clock, we want you to get out of bed if you do not fall asleep immediately. Remember the goal is to associate your bed with falling asleep *quickly!* If you are in bed more than about 10 minutes without falling asleep and have not gotten up, you are not following this instruction.
> **4** If you still cannot fall asleep, repeat Step 3. Do this as often as is necessary throughout the night.
> **5** Set your alarm and get up at the same time every morning irrespective of how much sleep you got during the night. This will help your body acquire a consistent sleep rhythm.
> **6** Do not nap during the day.
>
> (Bootzin, Epstein, & Wood, 1991)

In a number of evaluations, stimulus-control instructions such as these have been found to be the most effective treatment for chronic insomnia (Lacks & Morin, 1992).

Respondent Conditioning and Extinction

The operant-conditioning techniques that we have just discussed are aimed at changing behavior directly. The respondent-conditioning techniques that we will now describe are aimed at changing emotion—the degree to which we like, dislike, or fear certain stimuli—and thereby at changing behavior. As we saw in Chapter 3, respondent conditioning is a type of learning in which a previously neutral stimulus comes to elicit a response similar to that elicited by another stimulus with which it has been paired. All human beings, every day of their lives, are subject to respondent conditioning, sometimes with unfortunate results, so that they develop fears and desires that interfere with their functioning. When this happens, the maladaptive response can be therapeutically *unlearned,* either by removing the stimuli that reinforce it (extinction) or by pairing it with incompatible positive or negative stimuli. Among the many techniques that employ these principles, we shall discuss four: systematic desensitization, flooding, aversion therapy, and covert sensitization.

"Now relax.... Just like last week, I'm going to hold the cape up for the count of 10. ... When you start getting angry, I'll put it down."

This cartoon both lampoons and summarizes the technique of systematic desensitization: learning to maintain a state of relaxation during exposure to increasingly anxiety-producing stimuli.

Systematic Desensitization First named and developed as a formal treatment procedure by Joseph Wolpe (1958), **systematic desensitization** is based on the premise that if a response antagonistic to anxiety (such as relaxation) can be made to occur in the presence of anxiety-provoking stimuli, the bond between these stimuli and anxiety will be weakened and the anxiety will extinguish. Systematic desensitization involves three steps. In the first step, the client is given relaxation training, usually via Jacobson's progressive-relaxation method (Chapter 9). In the second step, therapist and client construct a **hierarchy of fears**—that is, a list of anxiety-producing situations in the order of their increasing horror to the client. The following, for example, is the hierarchy of fears (in this case going from most to least frightening) established for a patient who was plagued by fears of dying:

1 Seeing a dead man in a coffin.
2 Being at a burial.
3 Seeing a burial assemblage from a distance.
4 Reading the obituary notice of a young person who died of a heart attack.
5 Driving past a cemetery (the nearer, the worse).
6 Seeing a funeral (the nearer, the worse).
7 Passing a funeral home (the nearer, the worse).
8 Reading the obituary notice of an old person.
9 Being inside a hospital.
10 Seeing a hospital.
11 Seeing an ambulance.

(Wolpe & Wolpe, 1981, p. 54)

Once the relaxation response and the hierarchy of fears have both been established, then the two can be combined in the third step, the actual desensitization. In some cases, the desensitization is conducted **in vivo**—that is, the client practices relaxing while actually confronting the feared stimuli in the flesh. Most desensitization, however, takes place in the consulting office and relies on imagery. Clients are asked to relax and then to imagine themselves experiencing, one by one, the anxiety-producing stimuli listed in their hierarchies, starting with the least frightening and moving upward. When the client arrives at an item that undoes the relaxation response, he or she is asked to stop imagining the scene, rest, reestablish the relaxation, and then try the scene again. (If this doesn't work, intermediate scenes may have to be inserted into the hierarchy.) Depending on the severity of the problem, treatment generally takes about ten to thirty sessions (Wolpe, 1976), with a few in vivo sessions at the end to make sure that the relaxation response carries over from the imagined situation to the real one.

Systematic desensitization has proved effective with a wide variety of problems, notably phobias, recurrent nightmares, and complex interpersonal problems involving various fears—of social and sexual intimacy, aggressive behavior, social disapproval, rejection, and authority figures (e.g., Kazdin & Wilson, 1978). In a review of seventy-five articles describing the use of systematic desensitization with approximately a thousand patients, Gordon Paul (1969b) concluded, "For the first time in the history of psychological treatments, a specific therapeutic package reliably produced measurable benefits for clients across a broad range of problems in which anxiety was of fundamental importance" (p. 159). In all, this has proved a remarkably versatile and successful treatment.

Flooding **Flooding** might be described as a cold-turkey extinction therapy. Unlike the gradual exposure paired with relaxation that constitutes systematic desensitization, flooding involves prolonged exposure to the feared stimulus—or, if that is not possible, then to vivid representations of the stimulus—in a situation that does not permit avoidance (Levis, 1985). Like systematic desensitization, the technique depends on the therapist's first finding out exactly what it is that the client most fears.

Flooding has proved to be particularly useful in the elimination of obsessive-compulsive rituals (Rachman & Hodgson, 1980). As we saw in Chapter 7, obsessive-compulsive rituals usually have to do with one of two themes: contamination and checking. When the fear is contamination, flooding involves having clients actually "contaminate" themselves by touching and handling dirt or whatever substance they are trying to avoid, all the while barring them from carrying out their anxiety-alleviating rituals (in this case, usually hand washing)—a technique called *response prevention.* The hoped-for result is that they will realize that the thing they fear actually poses no real threat. Flooding with response prevention can apparently produce therapeutic change faster than systematic desensitization, but it is harder for patients to tolerate (Gelder, 1991).

Aversion Therapy As we have seen in earlier chapters, **aversion therapy,** whereby a maladaptive response is paired with an aversive stimulus such as electric shock or a nausea-producing drug, has been used in the treatment of various disorders, notably paraphilias and substance dependence. Such therapy, particularly when it involves electric shock, seems extremely harsh to many people, including many clinicians, and therefore it is used very sparingly today. Nevertheless, a number of clients consider it far preferable to the behavior they are trying to eradicate. Furthermore, the mere fact that it seems to work in cases where other therapies do not is a strong argument for its use. As we saw in Chapter 18, electric shock has succeeded, where all other techniques have failed, in eliminating self-mutilation in autistic children—something that is a prerequisite for any real treatment of such children (Bucher & Lovaas, 1968).

A gentler version of aversion therapy is **covert sensitization,** whereby instead of encountering the aversive stimulus, the person simply imagines it. Clients are asked to conjure up in their minds the image of an extremely painful or revolting stimulus, along with a visualization of the behavior that they are trying to eliminate (Cautela, 1966, 1967). For example, a therapist treating a problem drinker might ask the client to imagine having a pleasurable first and second drink at a party, then becoming progressively more drunk, then insulting people, then vomiting on the rug, and so forth.

Such therapy, like other forms of aversion therapy, is almost never used alone. Rather, it is simply one component of a multicomponent treatment.

Multicomponent Treatment

Not just aversion therapy but almost all forms of behavior therapy are generally administered as part of multicomponent treatment. A psychological disorder typically has many facets, and as the person comes to live with the disorder, it develops more facets. Problem drinkers, for example, do not just have problems with drinking. Whether as cause or result of the drinking, they have problems with their marriages, their children, their jobs, their social skills, their expectations and self-esteem. The best treatments for substance dependence address all these difficulties, via different techniques. Recall, for example, the voucher program for cocaine abusers described earlier in this chapter (Higgins, Budney, Bickel, et al., 1994). As we saw, the vouchers worked well, but their primary purpose was simply to keep the participants in the program, where, at the same time, they were receiving relationship counseling, instructions on avoiding cues for drug use, various kinds of skills training (drug refusal, problem solving, assertiveness), employment counseling, and help in developing new recreational activities. In such programs, the hope is that each kind of therapeutic change will bolster the others and thus, in a holistic fashion, free the person from the disorder.

Behavior Therapy: Pros and Cons

A commonly voiced criticism of behavior therapy is that it is superficial. Because it does not dwell on the patient's past and does not have insight as a primary goal, it seems shallow to those who feel that therapy should lead to greater self-acceptance and self-understanding. This is a criticism that cannot really be answered. Though many behavior therapists believe in the value of self-understanding, they also feel that it is too vague and grandiose an ideal to serve as a treatment goal. The goal of behavior therapy is simply to provide people with the skills they need in order to deal more effectively with life. If this leads to self-understanding, so much the better. But patients looking for treatment that is specifically aimed at self-understanding must look elsewhere.

A more serious version of the "superficiality" charge is the claim that behavior therapy can do patients harm by addressing only their symptoms and ignoring the "underlying cause." In such a case, the patient might be relieved of the symptom only to be faced, later, with another and possibly worse symptom because the underlying conflict has not been dealt with. This phenomenon, called "symptom substitution" by the critics of behavior therapy, has been largely disconfirmed. Usually, symptom relief leads to more general improvement rather than to symptom substitution (Bandura, Blanchard, & Ritter, 1969; Sloane, Staples, Cristol, et al., 1975).

Other critics of behavior therapy argue that it denies individual freedom—that behavior therapists move in and take control of the patient's behavior, manipulating it according to their own values. Actually, all psychotherapies involve some control on the part of the therapist, whether that control is directed toward insight or self-actualization or reconditioning. Likewise, in all therapies the therapist's values play an important part. Indeed, in this respect the only important difference between behavior therapy and the insight therapies is that in the latter the therapist's values are often implicit, whereas the clear spelling out of treatment goals in behavior therapy tends to make the therapist's values clearer from the start.

How well does behavior therapy do in achieving its goal of behavior change? According to the evidence, quite well. We have already discussed the effectiveness of individual treatment methods. In general, behavior therapy has a good record in treating anxiety and phobias (Emmelkamp, 1994), insomnia (Lacks & Morin, 1992), obesity (K. D. Brownell & Wadden, 1992), alcohol dependence (P. E. Nathan, Marlatt, & Loberg, 1978), and other problems (Kazdin & Wilson, 1978). For depression, both cognitive therapy and traditional behavioral therapy have been shown to be effective, in about equal measure (Agency for Health Care Policy and Research, 1993).

Aside from the fact that it often works, behavior therapy has other advantages as well. It tends to be faster and less expensive than other therapies. Its techniques can be taught to paraprofessionals and nonprofessionals, so therapy can be extended beyond the consulting room to hospital wards, classrooms, and homes. Finally, because behavior therapy is precise in its goals and techniques, it can be reported, discussed, and evaluated with precision.

THE COGNITIVE APPROACH TO TREATMENT

A number of behavior-therapy techniques depend in part on cognitive processes. For example, both systematic desensitization and covert sensitization use mental imagery. But if cognitive processes play some part in traditional behavior therapy, in **cognitive therapy** they are the main focus of attention. As we saw in Chapter 3, the central tenet of the cognitive perspective is that cognitions, or thoughts, are the most important causes of behavior; it is our thoughts, more than any external stimuli, that elicit, reward, and punish our actions and thereby control them. Hence if we wish to change a pattern of behavior, we must change the pattern of thoughts underlying it. To this end, cognitive theorists have developed a variety of techniques to increase coping skills, to develop problem solving, and to change the ways clients perceive and interpret their worlds. These techniques and the broader therapy in which they are applied are called **cognitive restructuring.**

Self-Instructional Training

A straightforward version of cognitive restructuring is *self-instructional training,* which we have already discussed as a treatment for retarded people

(Chapter 18). Developed by Donald Meichenbaum and his colleagues (Meichenbaum, 1975, 1977; Meichenbaum & Cameron, 1973; Meichenbaum & Goodman, 1971), this technique concentrates on "self-talk," the things that people say to themselves before, during, and after their actions. The object is to change the pattern of self-talk in such a way that instead of defeating the person, it helps him or her to cope with threatening situations.

In self-instructional training, therapists will model "cognitive coping exercises." First, they will voice defeating self-sentences, so as to alert clients to the kinds of thoughts that trigger and reinforce maladaptive behavior. Then they will "answer back" with more constructive self-talk, thus showing clients how they can combat self-defeating thoughts. Once the therapist has modeled this sequence, the client imitates it. For example, a person with a fear of driving a car might say, "This is so dangerous. The minute I'm out of the driveway I could be killed. Wouldn't it be better just to stay home? But wait . . . millions of people drive cars every day without having accidents. And can't I be in control of my own safety by driving defensively? If I don't try, I'll end up stuck at home forever, and never get to go where I want to go. I'll just do my best and I'll be fine!" Finally, clients are asked to practice pairing the behavior with self-talk and reinforcement through graduated performance assignments (driving farther from home each time, or driving on busier roads, supporting each successful assignment with appropriate self-talk). Self-instructional training is a practical treatment aimed at straightforward problem solving, and as such, it is the most "behavioral" of the cognitive therapies. It does not require that the client understand or develop "insight" into his or her cognitive dysfunctions.

Rational-Emotive Therapy

Other kinds of cognitive therapy call on the client to identify and analyze self-defeating cognitions as well as to revise them. Perhaps the oldest such treatment is **rational-emotive therapy,** developed by Albert Ellis (1962, 1993). Ellis' basic contention is that emotional disturbances are the result not of objective events in people's lives but of the irrational beliefs that guide their interpretations of those events. For example, it is not failure that causes depression but rather failure filtered through the belief that one should be, at all times and in all situations, utterly thoroughly competent, adequate, and intelligent. Likewise, it is not threatening situations that generate anxiety but rather threatening situations interpreted according to the irrational belief that if something is frightening, one should be very upset about it.

To combat such beliefs, Ellis and his followers point out in blunt terms the irrationality of the client's thinking, model more realistic evaluations of the client's situation (e.g., "So what if your mother didn't love you. That's *her* problem!"), instruct the client to monitor and correct his or her thoughts, rehearse the client in appraising situations realistically, and give homework assignments so that new ways of interpreting experience can be strengthened.

Adults who, as children, were intimidated by demands for perfection, may be helped, by cognitive therapy, to experience the pleasure of learning to play an instrument.

Beck's Cognitive Therapy

Similar in theory if not in tone is the version of cognitive therapy developed by Aaron Beck (1976). Like Ellis, Beck holds that emotional disorders are caused primarily by irrational thoughts. We have already described Beck's interpretation and treatment of depression in Chapter 10. In his view, this disturbance is the result of a "cognitive triad" of (1) self-devaluation, (2) a negative view of life experiences, and (3) a pessimistic view of the future. To change such cognitions, Beck adopts a less didactic and more Socratic approach than Ellis, questioning patients in such a way that they themselves gradually discover the inappropriateness of their thoughts.

Constructivist Cognitive Therapy

A slightly different version of cognitive therapy has been proposed by Michael J. Mahoney (1991). He calls this **constructivist cognitive therapy,** as opposed to the Beck and Ellis approaches, which he calls "rationalist." For Mahoney, rationalist cognitive therapy depends too much on conscious, rational, verbal analysis and does not take sufficient account of emotion and other seemingly irrational components of behavior. According to Mahoney, people begin in childhood to *construct* their worlds, out of their experience: their actions and the feedback they receive from those actions. If the cognitive patterns developed in this way are self-defeating, then constructivist cognitive therapy is a chance to construct new patterns. Self-exploration is an important part of the process. Among the techniques Mahoney recommends are writing (stories, poetry, journals, letters not to be mailed), observing oneself sitting in front of a mirror, and speaking in a "stream-of-consciousness" manner in the therapeutic setting. These techniques all aim at helping the client understand his or her characteristic way of viewing the world, in the hope of changing that view for the better.

Common Strategies in Cognitive Therapy

The common element in all cognitive therapy is an attempt to identify and to alter the pattern of thought that is causing a client's maladaptive behavior. Cognitive therapists have devised a number of useful strategies aimed at identifying faulty cognitions and replacing them with more realistic ones. In **hypothesis testing,** clients are urged to test their assumptions in the real world. A depressed woman, for example, who insists that her friends no longer want anything to do with her might be urged to call a few friends on the phone and suggest a get-together. Did the friends refuse to talk to her? Did they all refuse her invitation?

In **reattribution training,** the client is helped to change distorted ideas of cause and effect and to attribute events to their causes in a realistic manner. In one reported case, for example, a lawyer facing a trial with the belief that a loss would be entirely his fault was asked by his therapist to estimate the relative importance of the factors that influence the outcome of a trial (jury composition, nature of the offense, appearance of the plaintiff and defendant, length of trial, competence of the judge and the opposing lawyer, and so on). He was thus able to realize that the verdict would be affected by many circumstances, several of them beyond his control (Bedrosian & Beck, 1980).

In the technique known as **decatastrophizing,** the client is asked to consider what would actually happen if his or her worst fear were realized. A client with a social phobia, for example, might say that he can't go to a party because he would feel foolish and no one would talk to him and he would have a terrible time. "And what if that happened?" the therapist might ask. What is the *worst possible* result? That the client would leave the party early, without having spoken to anyone? And would that be a catastrophe, or would it simply be embarrassing? Questions like these help clients realize that their fears are exaggerated.

Cognitive Therapy: Pros and Cons

Cognitive therapists, like behaviorists, have emphasized the practical value of their approach: their techniques can be described forthrightly and applied by any clinician—or even in some cases used by the person seeking help without the intervention of a therapist. (Anyone, for example, can use Meichenbaum's "self-talk" technique.) Moreover, cognitive therapy works, at least for some disorders. Its most notable success thus far has been in the treatment of depression; cognitive therapy has been found to be at least as effective as drugs in treating acute depression and seems to be more effective than drugs in reducing the likelihood of further depressive episodes (Hollon & Beck, 1994). Cognitive therapy has also proved helpful with panic disorder (Michelson & Marchione, 1991), substance dependence, and some personality disorders (A. T. Beck & Freeman, 1990). Another advantage of cognitive therapy is that there are manuals describing how to administer and evaluate it. Beck and his colleagues, for example, have developed a detailed manual for the administration of cognitive therapy for depressives (A. T. Beck, Rush, Shaw, et al., 1979). The manual has made it possible to train many therapists in this technique as well as to conduct large-scale outcome studies.

One major objection to the cognitive approach is that life is not always rational and that simply recognizing that one's view of life is based on "irrational" assumptions—as Ellis would have it—is not enough to produce therapeutic change. Sometimes dysfunctional thoughts persist, despite the client's best attempts to brand them as irrational and self-defeating. A second objection is that there are times when changing one's way of thinking about the world may not be appropriate or right. As Mahoney (1991) writes, "When the Roman slave Epictetus (A.D. 60–138) wrote his famous manual for how to be happy as a slave, he did not consider the possibility of social action against the practice of slavery" (p. 115). With certain realities of life—a poor work situation, an abusive marriage—changing one's view of the situation may not be the whole answer.

A final point about cognitive therapy, though not necessarily a shortcoming, is that we don't really know how it works (Whisman, 1993). With depressed patients, for example, does cognitive therapy actually reduce the frequency of their negative thoughts, or does it just teach them a new set of skills for dealing with such thoughts (Barber & DeRubeis, 1989)? It is possible that cognitive therapy's successes with depression actually have little to do with cognitive change. Perhaps the improvement in mood is due instead to the satisfaction of mastering therapeutic tasks or simply to the increase in pleasurable activities. Cognitive changes occur in cognitive therapy, but do they come before or after the changes in emotion and behavior? Preliminary studies indicate that they come before (Whisman, 1993), but these results are tentative. Cognitive therapy is the newest of the major treatment strategies, and more research is needed before we will understand its mechanisms.

EFFECTIVENESS: WHAT WORKS BEST?

In recent years many comprehensive reviews of psychotherapy outcome studies have appeared, and the results indicate that, on the average, people who receive psychotherapy do better than about 80 percent of those who receive no treatment (M. J. Lambert, Shapiro, & Bergin, 1986). Furthermore, the effects of psychotherapy have been shown to be as powerful as, or more powerful than, drug treatment (M. J. Lambert & Bergin, 1994). In other words, psychotherapy, in general, works. It also works quickly. In an analysis of thirty years of outcome research involving over 2,000 patients, Howard and his coworkers found that after two months of once-a-week psychotherapy 50 percent of patients were substantially improved. The improvement rates then tapered off. After six months 75 percent had improved; after a year, about 80 percent, as shown in Figure 19.1 (Howard, Kopta, Krause, et al., 1986).

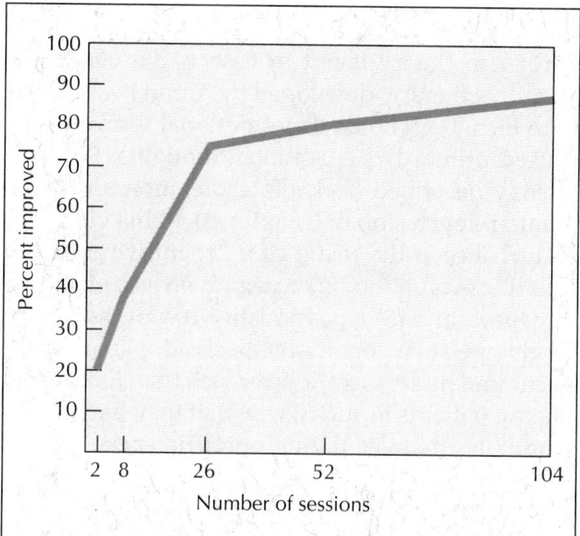

FIGURE 19.1 Relation of number of psychotherapy sessions to percentage of patients improved, as measured by objective ratings at termination of therapy. (Adapted from Howard, Kopta, Krause, et al., 1986)

Do some psychotherapies work better than others? This is an issue that has been hotly debated for almost a half-century. The controversy began in 1952, when the behaviorist Hans Eysenck published a review of psychotherapy outcome studies in which he concluded that the improvement rate for patients who underwent psychodynamic therapy was approximately the same as for people who received no formal treatment at all but simply "waited out" the problem. According to Eysenck, about two-thirds of "neurotics" got better within two years whether they were treated or not. In other words, the patients who underwent psychodynamic therapy could have stayed home and saved their money. In Eysenck's view, the only kind of treatment that worked was behavioral therapy.

Eysenck's article stimulated a good deal of bitter discussion, along with much research aimed at

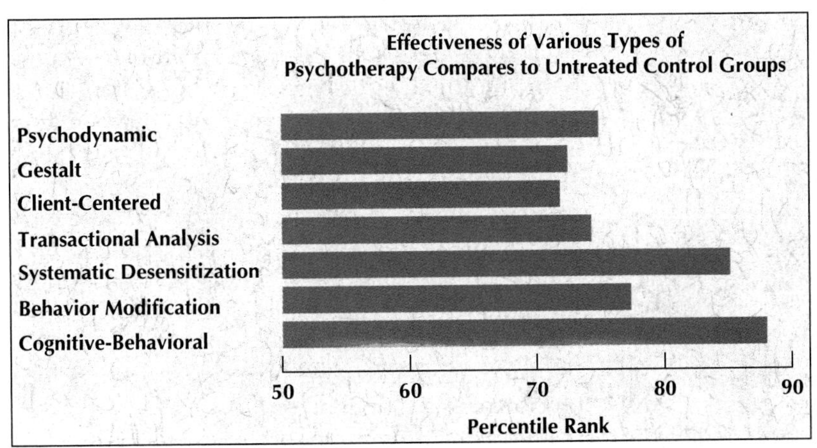

FIGURE 19.2 Is psychotherapy effective? Researchers who reviewed 475 studies think the answer is yes. The bars indicate the percentile rank that the average treated client attained on outcome measures when compared with control subjects. Thus the average client receiving psychodynamic therapy scored more favorably on outcome measures than 75 percent of the untreated controls. (Adapted from M. L. Smith, Glass, & Miller, 1980)

checking his conclusions. The findings, for the most part, have not supported his claims. For one thing, spontaneous remission (i.e., recovery without treatment) is apparently not as common as he judged it to be. In a review of seventeen studies of untreated "neurotics," Bergin and Lambert (1978) found that the median rate of spontaneous remission was 43 percent, considerably lower than Eysenck's figure of 66 percent. Second and more important is the finding, reported by two comprehensive reviews of psychotherapy outcome studies (Luborsky, Singer, & Luborsky, 1975; M. L. Smith, Glass, & Miller, 1980), that psychodynamic therapy *does* result in greater improvement than no treatment and that in fact psychodynamic, behavioral, and humanistic-existential therapies are approximately equal in effectiveness, with a slight edge to the behavioral. (See Figure 19.2.)

The case is by no means closed, however, for many people question the methodological adequacy of the psychodynamic outcome studies included in the two reviews just cited. In most of these studies the patient's improvement was measured not by any objective yardstick, such as testing or behavioral observation, but by the therapist's overall impression, which in turn was based in part on the patient's self-report—both extremely indirect and bias-prone measures. Yet the same finding of equivalent effectiveness, at least for psychodynamic and behavioral therapies, emerged from a methodologically excellent study undertaken at the Temple University Outpatient Clinic (Sloane, Staples, Cristol, et al., 1975). In this study "neurotic" patients seeking treatment at the clinic were matched for age, sex, and severity of problem, then randomly assigned to three different conditions: behavior therapy (mostly systematic desensitization), short-term psychodynamic therapy, or a waiting list. After four months the subjects' improvement was measured via psychological tests, reports from the patients' close associates, and interviews of the patients by blind independent raters—raters who were not involved in treating the subjects and did not know which experimental condition they had been assigned to. The results showed that of those on the waiting list, 48 percent had improved; of those in *either* the psychodynamic or behavioral treatment group, 80 percent had improved. Again a tie.

One of the most ambitious comparative studies of recent years has been the National Institute of Mental Health study of three different treatments for depression (Elkin, Shea, Watkins, et al., 1989). This study compared interpersonal psychotherapy (a structured version of psychodynamic therapy in which core interpersonal problems are identified and alternative ways of responding are explored), cognitive-behavior therapy, and treatment with a standard antidepressant drug, Tofranil (imipramine). The study found that patients given any of the three treatments did better than a placebo-plus-clinical-management control group. Patients who received the drug treatment had a slight edge, but none of the three treatments was significantly better than the others.

A serious problem in evaluating outcome studies is the possibility of bias caused by a researcher's commitment to a particular theoretical approach. For example, in an evaluation of treatments for depression, therapies preferred by the evaluator tended to achieve better results than the therapies with which they were compared (L. A. Robinson, Berman, & Neimeyer, 1990). Robinson and his colleagues (1990) found that the greater effectiveness of behavioral and cognitive treatments over general "talk" therapy disappeared when the evaluation was limited to studies in which the researcher had no allegiance. Clearly, cross-treatment com-

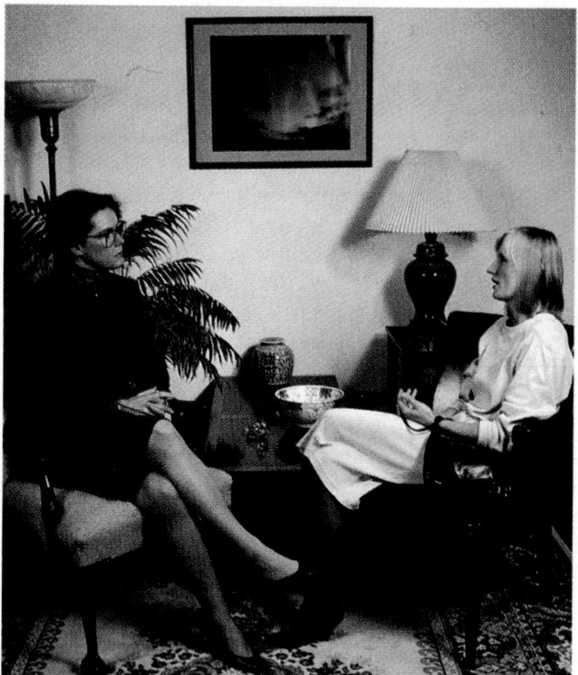

A solid rapport between therapist and client—a situation in which the client feels understood, supported, and helped—overrides most considerations of which psychological theory or school of thought the therapist adheres to.

parisons should be collaborative efforts among researchers of different persuasions.

In sum, because of the hazards of making comparisons between studies with different methodologies, we are not yet able to say with certainty which treatments work better than others. The different therapies need to be much more thoroughly evaluated—a process that is well under way in the behavioral and cognitive camps but is only beginning in the psychodynamic and humanistic therapies.

INTEGRATION AND ECLECTICISM

In the history of all disciplines, periods of differentiation and competition between theoretical schools are followed by periods of integration, in which different theories mingle, make truces, and learn from one another. Psychology is now in a period of integration (Beutler, 1983; Garfield, 1980; Goldfried, 1980; Orlinsky & Howard, 1987). This development is due in part to the research just discussed. With the provisional finding that all the psychotherapies work, and may work equally well, adherents of different approaches have become less defensive. Today, writings on treatment tend to emphasize not the differences among the psychotherapies but their similarities, together with the therapeutic importance of these shared qualities: the provision of support, the giving of information, the raising of hopes. J. D. Frank (1961, 1983) has proposed that a central ingredient of all psychotherapies is merely the hope that the therapist gives the patient, which combats demoralization. In support of this suggestion is the finding that many patients experience some relief from their problems after just an initial interview (Howard, Kopta, Krause, et al., 1986). (See the box on choosing a therapist, page 511).

With the recognition of common ground has come a tendency to enlarge that common ground by trading ideas across perspectives. Already some years ago it was found that most therapists regarded themselves not as adherents of a specific perspective but as "eclectic" practitioners (Garfield & Kurtz, 1977), choosing the techniques that served them best from whatever source. Today there is even a *Journal of Psychotherapy Integration.*

In 1984 a behaviorist, H. Arkowitz, and a psychoanalyst, S. B. Messer, published a book titled *Psychoanalytic Therapy and Behavior Therapy: Is Integration Possible?* Possible or not, it is being tried. Behaviorism has been profoundly affected by cognitive theory and accordingly has become more and more interested in "mental events." In turn, cognitive theory, in the hands of people such as Mahoney (1991, 1993), with his constructivist cognitive therapy, is now showing greater concern with mental events that lie *outside awareness.* This is a concept that would sound familiar to Freud, as would certain of Mahoney's techniques—for example, stream-of-consciousness self-exploration—for penetrating to those hidden events.

Conversely, psychodynamic therapists have become more interested in promoting direct behavior change. As with the behaviorists, this shift came originally from within the school—from ego psychology, with its emphasis on the active, adaptive functions of the ego. But today there is a conscious willingness in many quarters to incorporate into psychodynamic therapy the strengths of behaviorism. Wachtel (1977), for example, has suggested that the ideal therapy might involve, first, a psychodynamic "working through" of the patient's problem, with the goal of insight, and then a behavioral treatment aimed at changing the maladaptive behaviors involved in that problem. As we have seen, this is the basic design of many current therapies for sexual dysfunction (Chapter 13). Recently, a cognitive explanation of the psychodynamic phenomenon of transference was put

HOW TO CHOOSE A THERAPIST

If at some point in your life you experience emotional problems like those described in this book—serious depression, for example, or alcohol dependence—you may want to consult a professional therapist. But how do you find one?

If you have friends who have had a good experience in therapy, ask them for the name of their therapist. Your college health service should also be able to recommend a therapist; indeed, the health service may itself administer short-term psychotherapy. Other sources to turn to are your family doctor, your school's department of psychology or social work, or, if you belong to a religious congregation, your minister or rabbi. If none of these can help, call a local hospital and ask for a referral for psychological treatment. The hospital will usually be able to provide the name of a psychiatrist, psychologist, social worker, or psychiatric nurse.

Once you have a name, call and ask for a consultation—a single office visit in which you describe the problem and ask for a treatment recommendation. At the consultation, the therapist will ask you about yourself and why you think you need treatment. If the therapist offers to treat you, you should then ask some questions on your own. What are the therapist's qualifications: an M.D. or a Ph.D.? a degree in social work or nursing? a state license? (In some states, it is legal for anyone, regardless of training, to set up shop as a "therapist.") You should also find out, in general, what kind of treatment the therapist offers. How often will you meet, and what will the format be? Is the therapist committed to any particular theory? What will the fee be?

Most important of all should be your own feeling about the therapist. Were your questions answered fully? Were you treated with respect? Did the therapist listen carefully to what you said? Is this a person you want to spend many hours with, discussing intimate parts of your life? Remember that a consultation carries absolutely no obligation. If the therapist seems bored or condescending or in any way wrong for you, pay the fee for the consultation and get another name. Even if you are feeling very miserable and needy, as is the case with most people seeking psychotherapy, it is not a good idea to start treatment with someone you do not like.

Once you begin therapy, you should not stop evaluating the therapist. Keep in mind that *you* are the purchaser of a service. If at some point you feel that the therapy is not going well, that you are getting worse or that your treatment is not appropriately addressing your concerns, let your therapist know. If he or she cannot resolve the situation or explain it in a way that you are comfortable with, you are perfectly free to leave treatment. If the therapist ignores your complaints or reacts with annoyance, you are well advised to go elsewhere.

forward (Westen, 1988). In this view, a client's distorted view of the therapist (the transference phenomenon) is an illustration of his or her "interpersonal schema," or characteristic way of interpreting other people's actions.

The integrative trend is seen not just in therapy but in the highest reaches of theory. For example, Kohut's *self psychology* (Chapter 2), one of the most influential recent advances in psychodynamic thought, is not distant from humanistic psychology. In his idea that the crux of personality development is empathy between parent and child and in his consequent belief that therapists seeking to strengthen the patient's self should stress empathy over interpretation, Kohut was undoubtedly influenced by Rogers (E. Kahn, 1985).

This does not mean that the different perspectives have lost their distinctiveness. For one thing, many practitioners want no part of integration. And as for those to whom it appeals, behaviorists may become more introspective and psychodynamic therapists more practical without forsaking the methods in which they were trained. But the differences are blurring somewhat. Action and insight, art and science, are crossing over—a process that makes textbook definitions harder to frame but that probably is helping patients.

KEY TERMS

action therapy (492)
aversion therapy (504)
client-centered therapy (498)
cognitive restructuring (505)
cognitive therapy (505)
constructivist cognitive therapy (507)
contingency management (502)
covert sensitization (504)
decatastrophizing (507)
dream interpretation (495)
ego psychology (497)
flooding (504)
free association (495)
Gestalt therapy (499)
hierarchy of fears (503)
hypothesis testing (507)
in vivo (503)
insight therapy (492)
latent content (495)
manifest content (495)
psychoanalysis (494)
psychotherapy (492)
rational-emotive therapy (506)
reattribution training (507)
resistance (496)
stimulus control (502)
systematic desensitization (503)
transference (496)

SUMMARY

- In psychotherapy—the psychological treatment of emotional problems—the therapist establishes a professional relationship with the patient to (1) remove or modify symptoms, (2) mediate disturbed patterns of behavior, and (3) promote positive personality growth.
- Therapists differ in their approaches. Insight therapy tries to help clients understand the motives for their behavior so that they can change or control it; action therapy focuses on the problem behavior itself, in an attempt to correct it. Some therapists see psychotherapy as an applied science, whereas others regard it as both a science and an art.
- All psychodynamic therapy is based to some extent on Freudian psychoanalytic theory. In psychoanalysis, the patient talks, and the analyst interprets possible connections with unconscious material. The process relies on free association, dream interpretation, and analysis of resistance and transference.
- Most psychodynamic therapists today practice a modified form of psychoanalysis that includes neo-Freudian approaches. Ego psychology, for example, stresses the importance of interpersonal relationships and of the ego as a source of energy.
- Critics of psychodynamic therapies say that these treatments cannot be validated scientifically, involve too many theories, and are elitist and expensive. Supporters counter that psychodynamic methods do lead to insight and self-discovery and that briefer treatment today makes it more affordable.
- Humanistic and existential therapies share the goal of helping clients to make choices that will add meaning to their lives. Rogers' client-centered therapy uses empathy and positive regard to remove unrealistic conditions of worth that impede self-actualization. Existential therapy stresses the acceptance and exercise of freedom through the phenomenological approach. Gestalt therapy helps patients to reenact unresolved conflicts, confront their feelings, and learn to control them. Experiential therapy is also emotion-centered but aims to be more scientific in its techniques.
- Humanistic-existential therapies, like psychodynamic therapies, are criticized as being long and costly and difficult to validate by scientific measures. Supporters praise them for their simplicity and warmth and the value they place on the patient.
- Behavior therapy uses the principles of learning to help patients change maladaptive behavior, including self-defeating thoughts as well as inappropriate actions. Operant-conditioning techniques (such as contingency management and stimulus control) are used when the goal is to change overt behavior. Respondent-conditioning and extinction techniques (systematic desensitization, flooding, and aversion therapy) are used when the aim is to change emotional responses. Most forms of behavior therapy are administered as part of multicomponent treatment.
- Behavior therapy is effective in teaching people better skills to deal with life and is often less expensive and faster than insight therapies. It is criticized for denying the client's freedom and uniqueness and for being superficial.
- Cognitive therapy is based on the idea that to change a pattern of maladaptive behavior it is necessary to change the pattern of thoughts that maintains it. In self-instructional training, the client is taught to engage in more constructive self-talk. Rational-emotive therapy is aimed at identifying irrational assumptions that guide clients' interpretations of events and thus their behavior. Aaron Beck's cognitive therapy holds that emotional disorders are caused primarily by irrational negative thoughts. Constructivist cognitive therapy uses self-exploration to gradually reveal new ways of thinking and feeling. Common strategies in cognitive therapy include hypothesis testing, reattribution training, and decatastrophizing.
- Although cognitive therapy is accessible and often effective, it is sometimes criticized for not recognizing that life can be irrational and that changing one's thinking is not always an appropriate response.
- The value of different therapies and of psychotherapy itself has been long debated. Recent studies show that people who receive psychotherapy do better than 80 percent of those who receive no treatment. In his review of therapy effectiveness, Eysenck concluded that

only behavioral techniques brought clear results, but other studies have suggested that psychodynamic, behavioral, and humanistic-existential therapies are roughly equally effective. Very recent studies indicate that a cognitive therapy is as effective as or more effective than drug therapy for acute episodes of depression.

- Psychotherapies are now in a period of integration: as ideas are traded across perspectives, therapists are becoming more eclectic.

20

GROUP, FAMILY, AND COMMUNITY THERAPY

In Chapter 19 we discussed individual psychotherapy, in which therapist and client meet alone to discuss the client's problem. This is the traditional therapy for nonpsychotic clients. But other kinds of treatment are often used in addition to, or in place of, individual therapy. One is biological treatment—drugs, for example. (This will be the subject of the next chapter.) Another is treatment in a group setting. The patients may be a "naturally occurring" group, such as a couple or a family or the residents of a single hospital ward. Or they may be a collection of people trying to cope with the same problem (e.g., alcohol dependence, depression, child abuse). Alternatively, the group members may have no connection with one another beyond the fact that they have been brought together by the same therapist. Different though they are, all group therapies have one thing in common: The client is treated within a social context—an approach that, as we shall see, many therapists feel is the most logical.

In this chapter we will discuss the various forms of group therapy. Then we will describe the psychological services offered by a larger group, the social community.

GROUP THERAPY

One of the most significant changes in psychological treatment in the past thirty years has been the **group-therapy** movement. Treatment in groups has the obvious advantage of saving time and money. Instead of seeing only one client per hour, the therapist can handle perhaps eight or ten. This means that each client pays less. It also means that more people, in absolute terms, can receive help—an important advantage in a society where mental health professionals are in short supply.

However, cost efficiency alone does not account for the rise of group therapy. Rather, the popularity of this type of treatment is due primarily to the current belief that many psychological difficulties are basically interpersonal difficulties—problems in dealing with other people—and that consequently these difficulties must be worked out with other people. What, specifically, does group treatment have to offer? Irvin Yalom (1985) has listed eleven factors that help to promote therapeutic change in this type of treatment:

1 *Hope.* Like most other kinds of therapy, group therapy instills in clients the hope that they can change, and this has great therapeutic value.

2 *Universality.* Clients often enter therapy believing that they are "unique in their wretchedness" (Yalom, 1985, p. 7)—that no one else could possibly have feelings as painful and frightening as theirs. In the group they make the comforting discovery that such problems are relatively common.

3 *Information.* From the group leader the clients can acquire information about psychological disturbance in general and their problem in particular. They may also pick up valuable information (tips, coping mechanisms) from other clients.

4 *Social support.* Group members help one another with advice, encouragement, and sympathy. In the process, the givers learn that they have something to offer their fellow human beings, while the receivers learn that they are not alone. This exchange of social support is perhaps the chief virtue of group therapy.

5 *Corrective recapitulation of the primary family group.* The group is like a family, with leaders representing parents and other members representing siblings. Thus the group, as a sort of new family, may help to heal wounds produced by the client's original family.

6 *Development of social skills.* Corrective feedback from other group members may help to correct flaws in the client's interpersonal behavior (e.g., a sarcastic tone of voice, a condescending manner).

7 *Imitative behavior.* The group leader and other members of the group may serve as useful models for new kinds of behavior.

8 *Interpersonal learning.* By interacting with the group, clients may gain insight into themselves and revise their ideas of the kinds of relationships they want to have. Furthermore, the group may serve as a social laboratory in which to try out new "selves" and new kinds of relationships.

9 *Group cohesiveness.* The sense of belongingness and intimacy that develops within the group as a whole may give clients both comfort and courage.

10 *Catharsis.* Within the protective atmosphere of the group, members may feel free to express emotions that they have been bottling up, to the detriment of their behavior, for years.

11 *Existential factors.* Clients learn from sharing their experiences that life is often unfair and that although the support of others can be very helpful, they must make their own decisions.

Not all these factors are unique to group therapy. Information is conveyed, hope instilled, behavior modeled, and catharsis achieved in indi-

The social support that members can provide one another is one of the main factors in the effectiveness of group therapy.

vidual therapy as well. Furthermore, not all these factors will be equally important in every form of group therapy. Nevertheless, this list shows the mechanisms by which group therapy in general operates. And in the following section, it will help us differentiate among modes of group treatment.

Psychodynamic Approaches to Group Treatment

In psychodynamic theory, as we have seen, childhood conflicts are seen as the most important cause of psychological disturbance, and insight into these conflicts is considered the key to therapeutic change. Hence, not surprisingly, psychodynamic group therapy stresses items 5 and 8 of Yalom's list—corrective recapitulation of the family group and interpersonal learning. Within the group context, therapy operates in much the same way as individual psychodynamic therapy and uses many of the same techniques, such as analysis of resistance and transference. The therapist pays close attention to what group members say and do, looking always for clues to unconscious motives and pointing to them via interpretation. For example, a client who shows extreme sensitivity to criticism, seeing other group members' neutral remarks as hostile, may be led to see that his misperception is related to his having had an overly critical parent. In effect, he is still waging a childhood battle. Or if a group member consistently falls silent when the group raises certain topics, the therapist might suggest to her the possibility that she has conflicts attached to those issues. Although the main focus is on the group members' interactions, the therapist may also observe a client's pattern of associations (as in free association in the individual setting). For example, a woman who consistently brings up her father when other group members are talking about romantic relationships might be giving a clue as to the source of her problems with men.

Whatever the therapist's observations, the goal is always to offer clients insights into how their emotional past is still affecting them in the present. In some cases, psychodynamic therapists recommend the use of group and individual therapy in combination so that the issues raised in each can be dealt with in the other (Caligor, Fieldsteel, & Brok, 1984).

Psychodrama A specialized form of psychoanalytically oriented group therapy is psychodrama, developed in the 1920s by J. L. Moreno, a Viennese psychiatrist. Participants in **psychodrama** act out their emotional conflicts in company with other group members, often on an actual stage. If a male member of the group is terrified of women, for example, he may be put on the stage with a female member of the group, playing his mother, and be asked to act out a childhood scene with her. If necessary, other members may enter the play as his father, his brothers, or his sisters. Presumably the sources of the client's fear of women will emerge in the family drama.

Since Moreno's time, this pattern has been varied in a number of ways (Olsson, 1989; Starr, 1977; Yablonsky, 1976). Three common techniques are *role reversal,* in which actors switch parts; the *double technique,* in which the therapist gets up on the

Using the technique of psychodrama, members of a theater troupe in Massachusetts have been working with imprisoned sex offenders to improvise plays that help the prisoners acknowledge the connection between their crimes and the sexual abuse most of them suffered as children.

stage and acts out a client's part at the same time that the client does; and *mirroring,* in which group members portray one another on the stage. In each case, the goal is to show clients how they actually behave and why. The usefulness of this technique has not been lost on therapists of other persuasions. As we shall see, several kinds of therapy involve role playing (Kipper, 1981).

Behavioral and Cognitive Approaches to Group Treatment

Most behavioral group therapy is directed toward a very specific goal. In consequence, behavioral groups are less likely than other kinds of groups to depend heavily on *group process,* the sum of the interactions within the group, as the major mechanism of change. This does not mean that the group format serves no purpose in behavioral group therapy—only that its importance varies. At one end of the continuum, groups of clients may be brought together to undergo relaxation training or systematic desensitization in the same place at the same time. Here the group format is simply a convenience, aimed at saving the therapist's time and the client's money. Further along the continuum, there are many kinds of special-purpose groups—for example, groups to stop smoking or to lose weight—in which group interactions play a more important role. While exercises administered by the group leader constitute the major therapeutic tool, social support from group members serves as a valuable source of reinforcement. At the far end of the continuum is social-skills training, where the group format is of great importance, since the clients use one another to rehearse the interpersonal skills that they are learning. Thus the dependence on group interaction ranges from small to great. It should be added, however, that the kinds of therapy that behaviorists do in groups could be (and are) done, without much change of technique, in individual counseling as well. This could not be said of most psychodynamic and humanistic groups.

In general, behavioral groups concentrate on items 3, 6, and 7 of Yalom's list: information, development of social skill, and imitative behavior. We shall describe social-skills training, which combines these three elements and which, as we just saw, makes greater use of group interaction than do other behavioral group therapies.

Social-Skills Training and Assertiveness Training **Social-skills training,** mentioned in earlier chapters, is based on the premise that many behavior problems are due not (or not only) to deep-rooted emotional conflicts but to a lack of expertise in dealing with certain interpersonal situations—giving and receiving criticism, accepting and offering compliments, approaching members of the opposite sex, and so forth. In social-skills training, useful responses to such situations are taught through what is called **behavioral rehearsal,** in which the therapist tells clients how to perform the target behavior, demonstrates the behavior for them, and then has them practice the behavior repeatedly in little skits that simulate the situations they find troubling. Critical to behavioral rehearsal is modeling, or imitative learning. In social skills training as in other learning situations, the wish to be like the model is probably a prime motivator of imitative behavior.

Social-skills training may be conducted on either an individual or a group basis. When it is conducted in groups, the participants are people with similar interpersonal problems, and the training focuses on those particular problems. With a group of juvenile delinquents, for example, the therapist would concentrate on how to respond to authority figures, how to react to aggression, how to act in a job interview, and so forth (Sarason, 1976). With schizophrenics, as we saw in Chapter 15, social-skills training concentrates on pulling the patients out of negative-symptom withdrawal. Typically, the patients will be rehearsed in grooming and hygiene, social conversation, family communications, self-directed recreation, money management, and job finding—skills that will speed their release from the hospital and reduce their risk of relapse (A. S. Bellack, Morrison, Wixted, et al., 1990; Liberman, Kopelowicz, & Young, 1994).

One form of social-skills training that has become popular in recent years is **assertiveness training.** Assertiveness is often defined as the ability to stand up for one's rights without violating other people's rights. It is somewhat broader than that, however. It can perhaps best be characterized as a style of behavior based on the assumption that one's own feelings and opinions *count.* Andrew Salter (1949), one of the earliest therapists to discuss assertiveness, drew up for his clients a list of rules that nicely summarize an assertive approach to life. They are as follows: (1) Verbally express your feelings; that is, let people know when you are happy, sad, determined, angry, and so forth. (2) Show your emotions nonverbally. If you are happy, smile and look happy; if angry, scowl. (3) When you disagree with someone, contradict that person. Do not sit quietly. (4) Use the pronoun "I" as much as possible. (5) Express agreement when praised. (6) Improvise; live for the moment.

Such an agenda, if followed relentlessly, might produce overbearing behavior. However, as an antidote to anxious passivity, it is quite useful. As assertiveness training has developed in the hands of later therapists, it has incorporated several of Salter's rules.

In group assertiveness training, clients discuss their individual problems with assertiveness and then, under the therapist's guidance, role-play more assertive responses in those situations. In the following dialogue, for example, "Sally" is rehearsing a more forthright way of dealing with her boss. "Louis," a group member who has problems being a boss, has volunteered to play the boss:

LOUIS: What were you hired for? (speaks in a good firm voice)

SALLY: Typist. Now I'm doing record keeping, have no lunch hour. I'm answering phones all day (complaining tone of voice).

LOUIS: What do you want?

SALLY: I really can't handle all this work you pile on me (voice is cracking and she is close to tears).

[THERAPIST]: What did you want? What are your goals?

SALLY: I want him to know there's too much work for one person. We need an extra person.

[THERAPIST]: Did you tell him that?

(Fodor, 1980, p. 530)

In many cases, the therapist will first model the assertive response. In all cases, the client's role playing is followed by feedback from the therapist and the other group members. Then it is practiced again and again until the client feels comfortable with it. In addition, clients are usually given "homework" assignments. (For example, someone who is overly aggressive may be "assigned" to make a complaint at a restaurant in a firm but not insulting manner.) Problems encountered while carrying out these tasks will be brought back to the group session, and especially troubling situations will be re-rehearsed.

The major therapeutic tools in this kind of treatment are modeling, rehearsal, and reinforcement. However, assertiveness training is also an extinction therapy: clients learn that no catastrophe will ensue if they express their feelings and prevent people from taking advantage of them. In addition, most assertiveness training involves some cognitive therapy. Clients are asked to discuss and reexamine their fear of rejection, their sense that it is "wrong" to complain, their tendency to define themselves in terms of others' approval, and other assertiveness-squelching attitudes and emotions.

Cognitive Group Therapy While in behavioral groups cognitive principles influence treatment, in other groups they are the basis of treatment. It is with depressed patients that cognitive group therapy has most often been used (Beutler, Engle, Mohr, et al., 1991; Yost, Beutler, Corbishley, et al., 1986), typically according to Beck's principles for individual therapy (Chapter 10). The group members are asked to identify the thoughts that trigger their depressive emotions. Then these thoughts are analyzed by the therapist and the other group members, and new, less destructive thoughts are offered in their place. So such groups stress Yalom's item 3, information—specifically, information about how cognitions influence emotions—and item 7, imitative behavior, in this case the client's imitation of the less negative thoughts proposed by the therapist and the rest of the group. But item 2, universality, also comes into play (as it does in behavioral group therapy too). Watching others struggle with self-defeating thoughts, each patient, it is hoped, will feel less uniquely at a loss.

Humanistic Approaches to Group Treatment

Of all the theoretical schools, it is the humanistic perspective that has interested itself most intensively in the unique possibilities of group therapy, as opposed to individual therapy. And it is this perspective that has contributed most to the group-therapy movement. (Conversely, the rise of group therapy helped to disseminate the principles of humanistic psychology.) In humanistic groups, more than in any other kind, it is the *group* experience that is foremost. To return to Yalom's list, the emphasis is on items 4 and 8, social support and interpersonal learning. The major therapeutic gains are expected to come from the clients' (1) learning intimacy and cooperation by virtue of being part of a mutually supportive group and (2) finding out about themselves by interacting candidly with others. In addition, many humanistic groups also stress Yalom's item 10, emotional catharsis, on the assumption that this is both therapeutic for the client and conducive to intimacy within the group.

Encounter Groups and Gestalt Groups One of the earliest forms of humanistic group therapy was the **encounter group,** originating in such human-potential centers as California's Esalen Institute in the sixties and involving touching exercises, yelling, weeping, and other unrestrained shows of emotion. Another important tributary of humanistic group treatment was Gestalt therapy. As we saw in Chapter 19, Gestalt therapy offers clients the opportunity to finish their "unfinished business"—to dredge up unresolved emotional conflicts, act them out, and take responsibility for the feelings involved. Such therapy has been conducted not only in individual counseling but also in groups, where participants help one another work through their emotional crises. While similar to the early encounter groups in encouraging catharsis, Gestalt groups differ in their concern with the clients' past histories. (Encounter groups generally confine discussion to the "here and now.") With time and cross-fertilization, however, the distinctions have blurred. Today's descendants of the early encounter groups and Gestalt groups are often called *experiential groups* (see the discussion of experiential therapy in Chapter 19) because they focus on the clients' experiencing and expressing emotion.

The central goals of humanistically oriented group therapy are, predictably, personal growth—that is, understanding of and experimentation with one's own behavior—and increased openness and honesty in personal relations. Note that the emphasis is positive rather than negative, as is typical of humanistic psychology. The group mem-

The encounter group has often been derided as a form of self-indulgence. Yet many of the techniques developed for these groups during the 1960s are still used in humanistically oriented group therapy.

bers are there not to become less sick but to become more well. Indeed, hundreds of people join groups not because they feel they are psychologically disturbed but simply because they find their lives lacking in intensity or intimacy.

During a typical session, group members may talk about the problems they encounter in their outside lives, but the emphasis usually shifts to the members' reactions to one another, which they are encouraged to express with complete candor. Love, anger, warmth, suspicion—whatever a member feels toward another member he or she is free to voice. And the other member is free to respond in kind, so that both can gain practice in expressing their emotions honestly, achieve some insight into how they affect other people, and eventually learn how to work out interpersonal conflicts with patience, tolerance, and sympathy.

During such interchanges, the group leader (sometimes called the "facilitator") straddles a fence between directing and participating. On the one hand, the leader is fair game for the other participants; he or she is not to be the "expert," as in other therapies. On the other hand, the leader must also make sure that each person is allowed a fair say and that no member is scapegoated by the group (E. Aronson, 1972).

Such are the basic themes of the humanistic group, but they are subject to hundreds of variations. Some groups are conducted as marathons, lasting as long as an entire weekend, with only short breaks, if any, for sleep. This has been called the "pressure cooker" approach to therapeutic change. Presumably, by exposing clients to one another for hours on end, without distractions or interruptions, the marathon creates a continual buildup of emotional intensity and thus hastens the process of self-revelation. There are numerous other techniques as well. Some groups are conducted in the nude, others in swimming pools. Some use "warming-up" exercises, such as *eyeball-to-eyeball,* in which participants pair off and stare into each other's eyes for a minute or more, or *blind mill,* in which participants close their eyes and wander around the room, communicating only by touch. Such maneuvers are designed to jolt participants out of the polite conventions of normal social intercourse and force them to interact more spontaneously.

An interesting recent variant is the **large community group,** which, in contrast to the usual 10-person gathering, includes anywhere from 50 to 2,000 people, under several leaders. Community groups will typically convene for one long session, perhaps a weekend, perhaps one or two weeks, breaking up regularly into smaller groups during the course of the session. Client-centered therapists have been in the forefront of the community group movement (e.g., Bozarth, 1981), but the format has been tried by group leaders of many persuasions. One popular example is Marriage Encounter, an organization that convenes large groups of married couples for a single weekend devoted to improving communication and increasing intimacy within the marriage. Marriage Encounter has now reached approximately 1.5 million couples worldwide.

Peer Self-Help Groups

An important trend of the past few decades is the increase in **peer self-help groups**—that is, groups of people who share a special problem and meet to discuss that problem without the help of mental health professionals. We have already examined one such group, the one from which most of the others are descended—Alcoholics Anonymous (Chapter 12). When AA was founded in the 1930s, the idea that people with similar problems could obtain from one another as much help as they could obtain from experts was a novel one. Today it is much more widely accepted, and self-help groups have been organized to deal with hundreds of problems. There are groups for dieters, stutterers, drug addicts, former mental patients, dialysis patients, cancer patients, families of cancer patients, spouses of alcoholics, children of alcoholics, parents of hyperactive children, single parents, widows, widowers, and so forth. It has been estimated that 3.7 percent of American adults, or more than 6 million people, are currently in self-help groups (M. K. Jacobs & Goodman, 1989).

More than anything else, these are social-support groups (Yalom's item 4). AA, for example, uses social support, along with other techniques, to help members to overcome a specific behavioral problem. In other groups, social support is itself the primary goal, along with the important secondary goal of giving members an opportunity to air their problems. A group of mastectomy patients, for example, may discuss everything from problems with buying clothes to postoperative sexual inhibitions to fear of death. The group may not actually *solve* these problems for any member, but it can offer her encouragement, a sympathetic ear, and the knowledge that she is not alone. For almost anyone with a serious problem, such support may be very helpful, but for people without

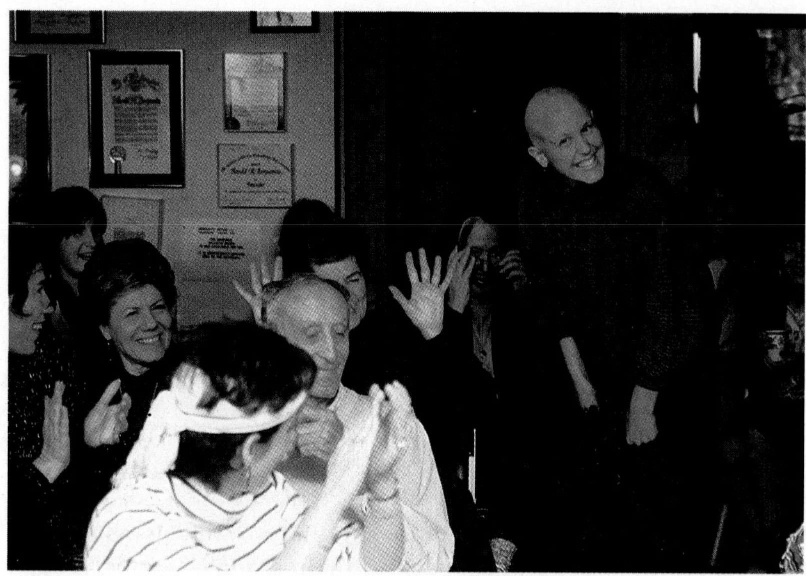

Peer self-help groups enable people with cancer or some other problem in common to give one another support and advice.

other sources of social support (e.g., the single, the widowed, the elderly) it can be absolutely crucial. In both kinds of groups, the goal-directed type and the pure emotional-support type, the assumption is that no one can help you or understand you better than someone who has been through what you have been through.

This assumption may be correct to some degree, for in many instances self-help groups have apparently brought about therapeutic gains as great as those of professional mental health services. This fact is all the more remarkable when we consider that such groups have developed at a time when professional mental health services have become considerably more varied, sophisticated, and available (Stuart, 1977). It is hard to tell, however, whether the success rates claimed by self-help groups are accurate, for most of the evaluation studies of these groups have been methodologically flawed (e.g., lacking in controls for placebo effect or evaluator bias). Nevertheless, self-help groups are undoubtedly the best bargain in the therapy market, and they probably reach many people who would not seek professional help.

Other groups that are not, strictly speaking, peer self-help groups—groups that have professional leaders—may nevertheless owe their successes largely to peer self-help. As we saw in Chapter 9, group therapy for breast cancer and skin cancer patients (Fawzy, Fawzy, Hyun, et al., 1993; Spiegel, Bloom, Kraemer, et al., 1989) has had astonishing successes, clearly lengthening the group members' lives.

Evaluation

What group therapy *may* offer clients has already been detailed in Yalom's list. Does it in fact offer these things? And if so, do they produce beneficial changes in behavior? Systematic reviews of group-therapy outcome literature (Bednar & Kaul, 1978, 1994; Kaul & Bednar, 1986) conclude that group therapy in general results in more improvement than either no treatment or placebo treatment (i.e., treatment in which the client's problem merely receives attention) and that some of the improvements do persist over time. Several qualifications must be added, however. First, the improvements were usually in attitude and self-concept but not necessarily in behavior. Second, the methodology of many of the studies reviewed was poor. Particularly in the early studies, the rating was often done by the therapist and client, not by a blind, independent rater, and it was done primarily on the basis of the client's self-report, not on the basis of observed behavior. Third, group therapy is far too vast and heterogeneous a field to be summed up in a single evaluation. Any general verdict that embraces everything from social-skills training to Gestalt marathons cannot be very meaningful.

Outcome studies of specific forms of group therapy present a mixed picture. The results from social-skills training and assertiveness training are very good (Bellack, Morrison, Wixted, et al., 1990; Benton & Schroeder, 1990). Outcome studies of humanistic groups are less encouraging. Some follow-up studies have reported heartfelt endorsement (e.g., Bozarth, 1981). At the same time, many people have raised questions about the usefulness of such groups. Do the skills learned in the group actually generalize to the client's outside life? If so, are they really adaptive to life outside the group? (The extreme bluntness encouraged in encounter groups, for example, might be a handicap in normal social intercourse.) Finally, what are the chances that intense encountering will be actually harmful to more vulnerable group members?

A partial answer to these questions was provided by a comprehensive study of the long-term effects of seventeen encounter groups (Lieberman, Yalom, & Miks, 1973). The group participants were 206 college students. Fifteen of the groups were conducted by experienced group leaders. Two had no leader, but simply followed tape-recorded instructions. Each of the groups met for a total of thirty hours. The orientations varied—some were psychoanalytic, some used Gestalt, some used other approaches. The groups varied with the preferences of the leaders. Before entering the group, immediately after leaving the group, and then several months later, the participants filled out extensive self-report questionnaires. On the basis of their answers, 33 percent were classified as having undergone positive change, 38 percent no change, and 16 percent negative change as a result of their group experience. In other words, only one-third benefited, and for every two who showed positive results, one suffered negative results. Furthermore, half of the negative-change subjects (8 percent of the total) had to be rated as "casualties"—people who as a direct result of the group experience became more psychologically distressed than before and remained so eight months after the termination of the group. In all, this is not a good showing, compared with other kinds of therapy. Later studies have found somewhat better results (R. E. Kaplan, 1982), but in some the rate of negative change remains high (M. E. Lester & Doherty, 1983).

The results of these studies also suggest how encounter groups might be improved. It seems that leaders who devote more time to explaining and interpreting what is happening in the group, and who stress "caring" over confrontation, produce better results (Lieberman, Yalom, & Miks, 1973). It is also clear that encounter groups are not for everyone. People who are experiencing serious psychological distress should probably avoid them, and group leaders should be better trained to identify such people and refer them to other kinds of treatment.

Not just encounter groups but also other kinds of groups seem to work better with some types of patients than with others. In a recent study (Beutler, Engle, Mohr, et al., 1991), depressed patients were assigned to three different treatment conditions: experiential group therapy, cognitive group therapy, or support/self-directed therapy. (In the last condition, patients were given a list of books to read and had regular telephone consultations with a paraprofessional.) All three treatments worked well, and about equally well. But those patients who saw themselves as primarily responsible for their problems did best in the self-directed therapy, whereas those who felt that their problems were due to factors outside their control did best in the cognitive group therapy. Also, those patients who were most defensive or resistant had better success in self-directed therapy; those who were least defensive had better success in the cognitive groups. These results make sense. (For example, more defensive patients and patients who felt more responsible for their lives *would* do best without a therapist pressuring them.) But this kind of evaluation—not just which treatments work best but which work best for whom—had seldom been done before and represents a new level of sophistication in outcome studies.

FAMILY AND MARITAL THERAPY

Approaches to Family Therapy

Although **family therapy** originated in the 1950s, it has become popular only in the past twenty-five years or so. In 1962, there were only three professional journals devoted to family therapy; in 1990, there were nineteen published in the United States and seventeen published abroad (Sluzki, 1991). Family treatment is now a thriving field.

What all family therapies have in common, regardless of their theoretical orientation, is the assumption that while one member of the family may have symptoms, the disturbance lies not merely in the symptomatic person but in the family unit as a whole. The family is seen as a system in which the whole is more than the sum of its parts.

There are a variety of approaches to family therapy. One is the **communications,** or *strategic,* **approach** (Haley, 1976; Satir, 1967; Watzlawick, Beavin, & Jackson, 1967), which developed as an extension of the double-bind theory of schizophrenia. As we saw in Chapter 15, the double-bind

In family therapy, only one person may have symptoms, but the entire family is treated as a system in disarray.

theory holds that an important cause of schizophrenia is childhood exposure to mutually contradictory messages from parents. According to communications theorists, such messages contribute not just to schizophrenia but to most forms of family disturbance. In family therapy, communications-minded therapists try to pinpoint contradictory messages, show the message givers what they are communicating, and indicate how this message undercuts the one they claim to be sending. In general the therapist's effort is to prod family members into telling one another what they actually feel and what kind of relationship they really want.

Often, in order to shake up a faulty communication system, the therapist will use a technique know as **paradoxical intention** (Shoham-Salomon & Rosenthal, 1987). That is, the therapist will instruct the family members to engage in whatever maladaptive pattern of behavior they are already engaging in. For example, if a father is constantly interrupting his daughter, the therapist will tell the father that in the next session he is to interrupt the daughter every time she begins to speak. This stratagem has a way of upsetting the maladaptive pattern and thus forcing patients to find other, and perhaps more useful, ways of dealing with their problems.

A second approach to family therapy is **structural family therapy,** in which a therapist analyzes the family unit as a set of interlocking roles (Minuchin & Fishman, 1981). Like any group, family members create roles for one another: the disciplinarian, the scapegoat, the one who needs looking after, the one who is expected to take care of everyone else, and so on. These roles satisfy certain needs; furthermore, each member must go on enacting his or her role in order for the others to continue in their roles. Consequently, any effort on the part of an individual member to step out of an accustomed role will meet with resistance from the rest of the family. According to adherents of structural family therapy, such roles are the key to family disturbance. Indeed, some therapists contend that the reason one family member becomes "sick" is that the family role system requires a sick member (Minuchin, 1974). Structural family therapy thus concentrates on analyzing roles, along with the psychological purposes they serve, and encouraging members to fashion more comfortable and flexible roles for themselves.

Other family therapies are offsprings of the major psychological perspectives. There are psychodynamic, humanistic, and behavioral family therapies—but as yet no cognitive family therapy per se, though cognitive techniques have been adopted by some therapists. Since the mid-1980s, there has been a resurgence of psychodynamic family therapy, based on the idea that problems in current relationships are caused by unconscious impulses, defenses against them, and old expectations that need to be changed (Nichols & Schwartz, 1991). Transference relationships with the therapist are seen as revealing problems within the family or, alternatively, problems within the parents' families of origin. The techniques of psychodynamic family therapy are similar to those of individual therapy: listening and interpretation.

Behavioral family therapy has been primarily of two kinds. One involves training parents of conduct-disordered children to interact with their children in ways that decrease antisocial and increase prosocial acts (G. E. Miller & Prinz, 1990). In this type of therapy, parents are taught not to reinforce bad behavior by simply giving in when the child annoys them for long enough. They are also shown how to administer effective rewards and punishments. Such treatments are generally quite successful (Kazdin, 1987). The other common form of behavioral family therapy is treatment to lower EE (expressed emotion) in the families of schizophrenic patients. As we saw in Chapter 15, this therapy, in which family members are taught how to solve problems in a calmer, less abrasive manner, has significantly lowered the relapse rates of the schizophrenic patients involved (Falloon, Boyd, McGill, et al., 1982, 1985; Halford & Hayes, 1991).

Approaches to Marital Therapy

Marital therapy—also called *couples therapy* (because it is also used for unmarried heterosexual couples and for homosexual couples)—follows essentially the same lines as family therapy. Troubled marriages almost invariably involve communications problems. Indeed, in some cases, communication has broken down altogether. Thus the establishment of an honest dialogue between the two partners is of top priority in almost all marital therapy. However, roles too are of great concern to marital therapists. Many marriages have a designated "strong" partner and a designated "weak" partner. Others will have a dogged, responsible partner and a naughty, "spoiled" partner. As in family therapy, such roles and the needs they fulfill will be analyzed, and the partners will be urged to try out more honest and satisfying ways of relating to each other.

A relatively recent entry into the field of family and marital counseling is behavior therapy. One behavioral view of family and marital distress is that it is the result of *coercion* (Patterson & Hops, 1972)—that is, the reciprocal use of aversive stimuli—to influence the other person's behavior. The opposite of coercion is *reciprocity*, the mutual use of positive reinforcement to influence the other person's behavior. In coercive marriages, for example, spouses get each other to do things by means of complaints, accusations, and the like. In reciprocal marriages, on the other hand, spouses get what they want out of each other by selectively reinforcing desirable behavior with compliments, thanks, and more tangible rewards. Through the use of contingency contracting, behavioral rehearsal, and other techniques, behavior therapists try to teach families and married couples how to convert from coercion to reciprocity and also how to improve their skills for solving problems and settling conflicts (J. F. Alexander, Holtzworth-Munroe, & Jameson, 1994; Emmelkamp, van Linden, van den Heuvell, et al., 1988).

Some marital therapists have begun to adopt cognitive as well as behavioral techniques into marital therapy. The hope is that teaching partners communication skills may help them identify cognitive distortions that affect their understanding of each other. For example, a wife may find that comments she thought were neutral ("Did you pick up the things at the dry cleaner's?") are interpreted by the husband as highly critical ("Why are you always so lazy and forgetful?"). When couples are taught "expressive communication skills"—how to verbalize their feelings effectively—such misunderstandings can be brought into the open. Another important cognitive technique is teaching partners problem-solving skills: how to identify a problem, think of possible solutions, discuss the pros and cons without emotional overreaction, and so on (N. S. Jacobson & Holtzworth-Munroe, 1986). Cognitive restructuring is also sometimes used in marital therapies and has been found to be useful (Baucom & Epstein, 1990). Whether cognitive restructuring can be effective when spouses use physical violence is discussed in the box on pages 526–527.

A more recent entry into marital counseling is humanistic therapy, in the form of *emotionally focused marital therapy*. This kind of treatment, an offshoot of experiential therapy—and developed by the same researchers (L. S. Greenberg & Johnson, 1988)—aims at getting the partners to experience and express their emotions toward one another and, in particular, to tell one another what kind of relationship they truly want.

Just as group therapy is seen as having certain advantages over individual therapy, so some have suggested that multiple-family and multiple-couple groups may achieve more than therapy with a single family or a single couple. Marriage Encounter, as we have seen, has a multiple-couple format. Multiple-family therapy, though less common, has also been tried. One of the first experiments with this technique was a remarkable project conducted by Murray Bowen in the late 1950s. Bowen had the families of a number of schizophrenics move into the hospital with their schizophrenic members. During their stay the families all participated in joint-therapy sessions, in which

MARITAL VIOLENCE: IS TREATMENT EFFECTIVE?

The brutal murder of Nicole Brown Simpson and her friend, Ronald L. Goldman, and the subsequent arrest of her ex-husband, former football star O. J. Simpson, focused national attention on marital violence in the United States. FBI statistics show that about three out of ten female homicide victims, or 1,400 women each year, are killed by their husbands or partners. Indeed, women are more likely to be killed by "loved ones" than by any other category of individual (Gelles, Lackner, & Wolfner, 1994).

These homicides are only part of the story. Domestic violence occurs in about one out of four American families. Each year some 2 million women are abused by their husbands, ex-husbands, or boyfriends.

Historically, our society has treated wife battering as a private family matter. Indeed, Nicole Brown Simpson had called the police eight times, claiming her husband had beaten her. Simpson had been arrested and pleaded "no contest" to charges that he had beaten and threatened to kill his wife on New Year's day, 1989. He was sentenced to probation, fined $700, and required to perform community service and seek psychological counseling. Simpson's lenient treatment was not due to his celebrity. "It doesn't have to be O. J. Simpson," says Rita Smith, coordinator of the National Coalition against Domestic Violence. "It could be Joe Jones in Iowa. The system makes all kinds of concessions in these cases" (Lewin, 1994, p. 21).

How should society deal with violent spouses? One strategy is to arrest the batterer (nearly always the man). Traditionally, police rarely intervened in marital violence because officers did not view the crime as serious or because victims refused to press charges. At least fifteen states now require police to make arrests in cases of serious domestic violence. But whether arrest is effective in preventing recurrences of spouse abuse is questionable. Studies comparing the impact of different forms of police intervention—separating the spouses, police counseling, and arrest—found arrest to be the most effective. But a recent review conducted by the National Research Council (A. J. Reiss & Roth, 1993) concluded that the impact was relatively small and arrest usually did not serve as a deterrent to repeat marital violence.

Another possible answer is shelters for battered women. Each year more than 300,000 women and children seek emergency help at some 1,200 shelters (A. J. Reiss & Roth, 1993). In addition to temporary housing, shelters provide a variety of services including help finding employment and housing, day care, educational training in parenting, budgeting, and support groups.

Psychological intervention in marital violence usually takes the form of group therapy provided separately for batterers and their victims. Group therapy for victims, nearly all of whom are women, often takes place in shelters and typically focuses on the issues of safety, effective use of police and legal protection, and practical advice in achieving self-sufficiency. Therapy also addresses such psychological issues as feelings of powerlessness and misplaced responsibility for being abused. Many abused women believe that they provoked abuse from their men. Falling into the "Beauty and the Beast syndrome," they are convinced that if they had been better wives or lovers, the "monster" who abuses them would become a "prince."

Many women say that the support they received from other battered women was the most important factor in helping them to achieve self-sufficiency and overcome feelings of isolation and powerlessness (A. J. Reiss & Roth, 1993). The catch is that women may be at greatest risk when they sever ties to the abuser. The man may attempt to reestablish control by escalating the violence, stalking and threatening his former partner.

Group therapy for abusers typically emphasizes cognitive restructuring, anger management, and alternatives to violence. Typically, men who batter "blame the victim": they deny that they have done anything wrong and/or claim that they were provoked, says Evan Stark, codirector of the Domestic Violence Training Program (Ingrassia & Beck, 1994, p. 30). Often these men have failed to measure up to material and

each family had its turn being the focus of therapy while the others observed. Bowen (1976) claims that the experiment was extremely valuable not only in teaching the families that their miseries were not unique (Yalom's item 2, universality) but also in giving them the opportunity to try out one another's solutions to interpersonal problems. Others have since used this type of therapy with many kinds of dysfunctional families and have reported positive results, though the technique has not yet been systematically evaluated (Strelnick, 1977).

Evaluation

Marital and family therapies appear to be generally successful—more so, in some cases, than individual therapy. A thorough review of research in this area found that out of thirty studies comparing family or marital therapy to individual or group treatment of the "identified patient" (i.e., the symptomatic member of the family), twenty-two—or 73 percent—found marital or family therapy to be superior (Gurman & Kniskern, 1978). More recent reviews (Hazelrigg, Cooper, & Borcultural standards of manhood (they may be unemployed or underemployed) and lack skills in verbal assertiveness and problem solving (Gelles, Lackner, & Wolfner, 1994). In therapy, the men are expected to take responsibility for violence, whether or not there was any provocation or participation by their partners. They are taught to recognize extramarital sources of frustration as well as internal signals of rage and to manage their anger more constructively.

Group therapy for batterers can be effective. At the Domestic Abuse Project in Minneapolis, two out of three men who underwent therapy had not battered their partners eighteen months after completing treatment. But most abusive men avoid treatment. Only half of the men who register at the Abuse Project, usually under court mandate, ever show up, and only half of those who start therapy complete the program (Ingrassia & Beck, 1994).

Furthermore, researchers have identified a group of batterers who may be beyond the reach of therapy. In one study (Gottman, Jacobson, Rushe, et al., in press) researchers observed sixty couples who had experienced mild to severe levels of violence. In the first session the couples were interviewed and asked to complete questionnaires. In the second session a number of physiological measures were taken during a fifteen-minute interaction that was videotaped and coded. Eighty percent of the husbands showed increased heart rate during the first five minutes of the interaction. But 20 percent showed *decreased* heart rate during the same period, even though they were more belligerent and contemptuous toward their wives than were the other men. If marital interactions produce anger, which in turn leads to violence, heart rate should increase. This suggests that for some men, expressing hostility may have a paradoxical effect or reflect other mechanisms, such as an attempt to control the spouse. Clearly, anger management would not be therapeutic for these men.

Although anger management isn't right for everyone, group therapy has been effective. In some cases, the partners are seen together, either as a single couple or in a group. Couples therapy emphasizes that although anger and conflict are normal elements of family life, violence is never justified. Typically the program includes education about the causes and consequences of violence (both legal and psychological), anger management, conflict containment (such as time out and behavioral contracts), communication and problem-solving techniques, stress management, and discussion of issues related to power and control within the family (Feldman, 1994).

Although to date there are few studies evaluating the outcome of these treatments, most suggest that groups for batterers and couples therapy are better than no treatment at all. But therapy does not end violence in many cases; nor does it eliminate more subtle psychological forms of abuse (Feldman, 1994).

Although there are some grounds for optimism in the treatment outcome literature, the therapeutic approach to spouse abuse has been criticized. Sociologists Richard Gelles and Murray Straus (1988) argue that marital violence is not just an individual problem but also a social problem. The idea that a man is "king of his castle" (or should be) and that how he treats "his wife" (his property) is his business still runs strong in our culture. The sports subculture, in particular, emphasizes that it is a "man's world" and that a woman's place is on the sidelines, cheering men on. Marital violence, argue feminist theorists (L. E. A. Walker, 1989), is a reflection of gender inequality and is better understood as a technique of control and dominance than as an expression of anger. Couples therapy implies that marital violence is a shared problem and may even encourage women to "adjust" to an intolerable situation. Feminist theorists tend to support increased use of police intervention and shelters for women.

Most researchers and therapists agree that therapy can be effective only if the victims of marital violence can be guaranteed safety. But many question the appropriateness of therapy for family violence at all. Should we as a society be trying to save such marriages or, where violence occurs, should the intervention be a legal one?

duin, 1987; Shadish, Montgomery, Wilson, et al., 1993) found that family therapy of various kinds was more effective than no treatment or other control conditions when measured by either family interactions or behavior ratings.

In view of the good showings for behavioral marital therapy in particular, the scope of this treatment is now being broadened. Prompted by evidence that depression is often related to marital warfare, some therapists have begun using behavioral marital therapy in cases where either the husband or the wife is depressed. Recent outcome studies indicate that, compared with individual cognitive therapy, this treatment is as effective in reducing depression and more effective in reducing marital discord (Beach, Whisman, & O'Leary, 1994).

One problem in evaluating family and marital therapies is that research on the outcome of therapy is uneven: we know more about the outcome of some kinds of therapy than we do about others. Just as with individual therapy, the behavioral approaches to family and marital therapy have been the most thoroughly researched. An interesting exception to this rule is a study comparing behavioral marital therapy with a psychodynamic insight-oriented approach. The study found that both approaches resulted in significant immediate improvement and no differences at a six-month follow-up. At a four-year follow-up, however, the insight-oriented-therapy couples had maintained their improvement better than those receiving the behavioral-therapy treatment and had significantly fewer divorces (D. K. Snyder & Wills, 1989; D. K. Snyder, Wills, & Grady-Fletcher, 1991).

INSTITUTIONAL CARE AND COMMUNITY-BASED SERVICES

The State Institution

As we saw in Chapter 1, one of the fruits of the Enlightenment was the widespread development of large hospitals for the mentally disturbed. Most of these hospitals, both in the United States and elsewhere, were built in relatively isolated rural or suburban areas. There were a number of reasons for this decision. First, it was thought that patients would recover sooner if they were removed from the stresses of community life and allowed to repose in the fresh country air. A second reason was economy; land was far less expensive in the countryside. Furthermore, until fairly recently, most of these state mental hospitals had large farms attached to them, where the patients, as part of their "therapy," worked to produce their own food. A final reason for transferring these patients to remote locations was that no one wanted to see them. Mental patients were considered unsightly and dangerous—an attitude that is still widely held today.

Whatever the causes, the isolation of the large state mental hospitals did not contribute to their effectiveness. Very few competent professionals were willing to take poorly paid jobs in remote areas, and as a result, staffing became a serious problem. (It was not uncommon to find hospitals with over a thousand patients and only one or two psychologists or psychiatrists on the staff.) The consequence, of course, was that care was custodial rather than remedial. Moreover, the very fact that patients were removed from their communities proved counterproductive. Families, friends, and jobs give people a sense of identity, provide an incentive to be "normal," and can often be mobilized to aid in psychological treatment. Isolation from their communities cuts patients off from these informal therapeutic benefits. Finally, the remoteness of the mental hospitals made it impossible for patients to engage in any kind of *partial* treatment. It was all or nothing—hospitalization or no treatment. Consequently, thousands of patients who might have benefited from less drastic intervention were hospitalized, with all the damaging effects that psychiatric hospitalization involves—the loss of one's moorings in reality, the temptation to fall into the "sick" role, the social stigma, the loss of self-esteem.

The problems of public hospitalization led to a search for alternatives to hospitalization and the development of services for patients within the community. These will be discussed later in this chapter. But there also have been attempts to develop improved therapeutic environments within some institutions.

This is a typical state hospital—a large, barracks-like building in an isolated location. Today, the trend is away from housing large numbers of patients in such institutions, and the number of hospitalized patients has shrunk considerably in the past thirty years.

Therapeutic Environments within Institutions

Some private hospitals and a few public institutions have sought to offer their residents not just custodial care but also effective treatment. One effort has been to turn the particular features of the institution itself into a kind of therapy—to make the *entire environment* within the hospital therapeutic. In a **therapeutic environment,** the hospital setting is arranged in such a way that all the patient's interactions with the environment will serve some therapeutic purpose.

Psychodynamic Therapeutic Environments One of the earliest therapeutic communities was a residence for juvenile delinquents established by Aichhorn (1935) in Vienna at the end of World War I. In several respects this residence was markedly different from other juvenile facilities of that and the present day. First, the purpose of the program was treatment rather than simply custody. Second, the institutional environment was manipulated for therapeutic purposes. (For example, boys were assigned to living cottages according to the type and severity of their psychological problems.) Third, the staff made every attempt to create a warm, accepting environment for the residents. Fourth, aggressive behavior was permitted, even encouraged, unless there was a possibility of serious harm to one of the residents. The idea was to create an environment that would repair early damage to the psyche and strengthen the ego and superego. Aichhorn's school has long since closed its doors, but it engendered a number of like-minded institutions both in Europe and in the United States. One of the best-known was Fritz Redl's Pioneer School for delinquent boys, which opened in Detroit in 1946.

The assumption behind most of these psychodynamic facilities was that since their patients (usually either delinquent or psychotic children) did not benefit greatly from intensive individual therapy, the best treatment would be reeducation through identification with an adult. Obviously, this approach requires an extremely high ratio of staff to patients. Such an arrangement is extremely expensive and cannot accommodate many patients. (Pioneer School, for example, never housed more than five boys.) For this reason and others, strictly psychodynamic facilities are now rare, though many therapeutic residences still use psychodynamic techniques in individual counseling.

Behavioral Therapeutic Environments Many times in this book we have presented evidence for the power of systematic reinforcement to change specific behaviors. Such evidence has encouraged behavioral therapists to expand their reinforcement programs. If rewards can change a patient's manner of eating or speaking, why not structure that patient's environment so that in *all* areas of his or her life appropriate behavior is reinforced and inappropriate behavior extinguished? The result has been the token economy.

As we have seen in earlier chapters, a **token economy** is an institutional program in which various behaviors are rewarded with tangible conditioned reinforcers, or tokens, that patients can then use to "buy" backup reinforcers. In the typical token-economy ward, there is a board listing various desirable behaviors and their token rewards. There is also a canteen where patients can exchange their tokens for backup reinforcer. Some institutions even have department store catalogs from which patients can order their rewards. In many cases, however, tokens are spent not on tangible rewards but on privileges—television time, telephone time, overnight passes, and so forth.

The token system has a number of advantages. For example, tokens can be given for small gradations of improvement in a behavior and gradually accumulated toward a desired reinforcer. They also constitute visible proof of improvement and are resistant to satiation, since they can be exchanged for a variety of rewards. They can be dispensed by staff members at any time (unlike other kinds of rewards). And they get around the problem of differences in individual tastes—patients can exchange them for whatever they like.

Finally, a token economy simulates life in the outside world—at least to some extent—as other kinds of therapeutic environments do not. The behaviors that token economies attempt to increase are those that people most need (and that chronic patients most lack) in order to make their way in normal society—work skills, social skills, grooming and hygiene. Like our society, the token economy offers reinforcement for such behaviors.

But directors of token economies do not just wait around for patients to develop the behaviors that are slated for token rewards. Most token economies are part of multifaceted programs, involving social-skills training and other kinds of behavioral interventions, as well as token reinforcement. (See the box on pages 531–532).

Humanistic-Existential Therapeutic Environments The humanistic-existential perspective's contribution to the idea of the therapeutic environment is milieu therapy, also called the therapeutic community. Milieu therapy arose in the 1940s and 1950s (e.g., M. Jones, 1953) as a reaction to the type of custodial care typically offered to chronic patients: care that tended to reinforce withdrawal, and hence chronic hospitalization, since withdrawn behaviors posed fewer problems for the staff. In a sense, the emergence of milieu therapy was a case of history repeating itself. Just as moral therapy (Chapter 1) developed in the nineteenth century as an antidote to custodial neglect, so milieu therapy, based on many of the same principles as moral therapy, developed in the twentieth century as a solution to the same problem.

As we saw in Chapter 15, **milieu therapy** is essentially an institutional environment designed to maximize the independence, self-respect, and activity level of severely disturbed patients. One of the most distinctive qualities of milieu therapy is its democratic nature. Everyone in the community is valued as a therapeutic agent: the patients for one another, the staff for the patients, and the patients for the staff. The atmosphere is warm, open, and, above all, busy, involving the patients in occupational therapy, recreational activities, self-governmental meetings, and other projects.

The major use of milieu therapy has been in residences for schizophrenics. However, other kinds of programs have also been affected by the principles underlying milieu therapy. Particularly influential has been the idea that disturbed people, if given the opportunity, can run their own lives and that the experience of doing so may have a powerful healing effect. The patient-administered wards that now exist in some mental hospitals and the self-governing halfway houses that have been established for former mental patients in numerous communities are both products of this idea.

Evaluation *Do* therapeutic environments achieve their goal of enabling patients to transfer new skills to life outside the institution? With regard to psychodynamic programs this is hard to say, for the number of patients is small and the outcome data consist mainly of case histories (e.g., Bettelheim, 1967). Milieu programs too are small and generally are not subjected to systematic evaluation. Yet there has been at least one careful outcome study of milieu therapy. G. L. Paul and Lentz (1977) conducted a long-term comparative study of the effectiveness of three programs for chronic mental patients: custodial care, milieu therapy, and a multifaceted behavioral program involving a token economy. (See the box on pages 531–532.) The experimenters found that milieu therapy was superior to custodial care both in changing in-hospital behavior and in getting patients discharged and that the token economy surpassed the milieu program on both scores. This is by no means the only evidence for the effectiveness of the token economy. There is a vast literature on this treatment strategy, including several comprehensive reviews (e.g., Kazdin, 1985; G. L. Paul & Menditto, 1992). In general, these studies support the conclusions of Paul and Lentz: token economies—and above all, token economies in conjunction with other forms of behavior therapy—are capable of producing extensive changes in behavior. This is true for hospitalized mental patients as well as for retarded people (e.g., Welch & Gist, 1974), juvenile delinquents (e.g., Kirigin, Braukmann, Atwater, et al., 1982), and even ordinary children in their classrooms (e.g., K. D. O'Leary, 1978).

But what happens once the patients leave the token economy? Most outcome studies have not done extensive follow-up. Those that have are not heartening. In general, it appears that generalization does *not* occur automatically to any significant extent. When the tokens disappear, so do the improvements in behavior. This has persuaded many therapists that instead of merely hoping for generalization, they must program it into the treatment (Stokes & Osnes, 1989). In some programs, patients are gradually weaned from tokens to "real-world" reinforcers (praise, extra privileges) before they are discharged from the hospital. In other programs, patients are taught to reinforce themselves for appropriate behavior. The aim of most programs is to use the token economy to help develop skills that will be reinforced naturally in the social world outside the hospital—social and communication skills, anger management, and so on. In the best-run programs, generalization training is part of a comprehensive aftercare program. Even so, many patients will need to remain in the aftercare program.

The Exodus to the Community

The disadvantages of large state mental hospitals were recognized by the twentieth century, but the alternatives were few. How was society to cope with large numbers of disturbed people who were not able to cope on their own? Despite reports of inadequate treatment and inadequate and even squalid living conditions, the system continued more or less unchanged until the mid-1950s. Then, the first effective antipsychotic drugs were introduced into American mental hospitals. Under the influence of these drugs, many patients became calmer—calm enough, it seemed, to reenter society. Around the same time, evidence of the damaging effects of hospitalization began to accumu-

SOLVING THE "CHRONIC PROBLEM": THE PAUL AND LENTZ STUDY

Of all the psychologically disturbed, those who receive perhaps the least attention are chronic psychotic patients. These are essentially forgotten people; no one knows how to solve their problems, and many have ceased to care. For this reason, among others, the Paul and Lentz (1977) comparative study of treatments for chronic patients, already briefly described in this chapter, is of great importance. Gordon Paul first became interested in the "chronic problem" in the mid-1960s, while working as a consultant to the state mental hospitals of Illinois. These hospitals, like state institutions throughout the country, had back wards filled with chronic schizophrenics—people who had stagnated there for years and would presumably continue to do so until they died. Could such patients, given appropriate treatment, return to some kind of independent life in the community? If so, what *was* the appropriate treatment? These were the questions that Paul set out to answer.

With the help of his colleagues at the University of Illinois, Paul selected three groups of twenty-eight patients each, matched for age, sex, and other variables. One group, the control group, remained in custodial care at the state hospital. The remaining two groups were transferred to adjacent units of a new mental health center, where one embarked on a program of milieu therapy and the other entered a token-economy-based program of behavior therapy—the two treatment strategies that research suggested might hold some promise for chronic patients. Each program was to run for three years, with the goal of releasing its patients to relatively independent living (e.g., at home or with a foster family). The object of the study was to see which of the treatment conditions did best at achieving this goal.

The original plan was to use typical chronic patients. However, by the time the study began, the deinstitutionalization movement was under way, with the result that there were no "typical" chronics left in the state hospitals. All patients who could meet minimal standards had been transferred to community shelter-care programs. Hence the pool from which Paul drew his subjects consisted of only the most dysfunctional patients. Just how dysfunctional they were became clear in the first week of the program. At any given movement, fully 90 percent of the patients were behaving bizarrely. Some were mute; others screamed for hours on end. Many were incontinent. Worse yet, some smeared their feces on the walls or threw them at the staff. At meals it was the rare patient who used silverware, and some habitually buried their faces in their food. Physical assaults were not uncommon. At the first meeting of the behavioral group, a staff member narrowly escaped being stabbed by a naked patient armed with a knife that she had stolen from the kitchen. The experimenters had their work cut out for them.

How were the programs designed? The hospital program consisted of typical custodial care: patients were treated like sick people, given high doses of antipsychotic medication, and essentially left to their own devices. (Though formal therapy was offered, it occupied less than 5 percent of the patients' waking hours.) Nothing much was either given to them or expected of them.

This was precisely the environment that the experimental programs aimed to avoid. In both the milieu and the behavioral units, subjects were treated as "residents," not patients. Appropriate behavior was expected of them, and they spent 85 percent of their waking hours learning, in formal treatment situations, how to produce it. In return, they received prompt, courteous, and friendly attention from the staff.

Similar in these respects, the two experimental programs differed sharply in other respects. The milieu program was organized around the principles outlined in Chapter 15. The major emphasis was on the residents' assuming responsibility, at both an individual and a group level. The unit was organized as a community, with an executive council elected from among the residents. The community in turn was divided into three living groups. Both the living groups and the executive council had wide decision-making powers. (It was the residents, for example, who decided how to punish assaultive behavior.) And though some of their rulings were unwise, the staff honored them all the same, on the theory that residents would learn from their mistakes.

Another matter emphasized in the milieu program was clear, plentiful, and positive communication. This was the staff's major tool for influencing the residents' behavior. To elicit appropriate behavior, staff members communicated positive expectations (e.g., "I know you'll remember to comb your hair tomorrow, Charlie"). To maintain appropriate behavior, they responded to it with praise. As for inappropriate behavior, it was never ignored. On the contrary, staff members were instructed to remain with the offending resident, providing negative feedback for the behavior in question and voicing expectations of more appropriate behavior.

(Continued)

SOLVING THE "CHRONIC PROBLEM" *(CONTINUED)*

While the milieu program relied on trust and encouragement as the two major rehabilitative forces, the behavioral program relied on operant conditioning. Appropriate behavior was elicited through prompting, verbal instruction, modeling, and shaping. When it appeared, it was systematically reinforced with praise and tokens. Inappropriate behavior, on the other hand, was generally ignored. (In addition, of course, it resulted in failure to earn tokens.) This operant-conditioning program embraced every conceivable aspect of the residents' lives. Before breakfast, for example, the residents underwent an "appearance check." If they met the eleven criteria for good appearance—proper use of makeup; clean fingernails; hair combed; teeth brushed; all appropriate clothing on; clothing buttoned, zipped, tucked; clothing clean and neat; body clean; no odor; shaven; hair cut appropriately—they were given a token and praised. If not, they were given no token and were told what to do in order to earn the token next time. Likewise, there were specific criteria for appropriate bedmaking, bathing, mealtime behavior, classroom participation, and social behavior during free periods, and tokens were accordingly given or withheld. (If the behavior was still being shaped, the resident did not have to meet all the criteria—only those that he or she had already met plus one.)

The earning of these tokens was serious business, for they were used to purchase not only luxuries such as candy or magazines but also necessities such as meals. Breakfast cost three tokens, lunch six tokens, dinner five, and those who did not have the price of admission were turned away. If residents missed enough consecutive meals to pose a health problem, they were eventually given a free meal—the so-called medical meal. This consisted of all the elements of the regular meal pureed together in a blender and dyed purple-gray—a nutritious but unappetizing mush. As this example illustrates, life in the behavioral unit was not soft.

How the subjects progressed in the three programs is documented by voluminous observational notes. (In the experimental programs, each resident's behavior was observed and recorded at least once every hour of every day!) The notes tell an interesting story. At the end of the first seven months, the behavioral subjects and, to a somewhat lesser extent, the milieu subjects had made substantial improvements, enough to qualify most of them for release to shelter-care facilities. However, the goal of the program was not shelter care but independent living. So the treatment continued—and began to encounter difficulties. The major problem was that the frequency of assaults, both on staff and on other patients, steadily increased, especially in the milieu unit. (At one point, the milieu unit was averaging *320* assaults per week.) This, of course, interfered with treatment. Though the program was extended to four and a half years, at the end of that time the average improvement in the behavioral unit was roughly the same as at the end of the first seven months, while in the milieu unit it was somewhat inferior to what it had been at the end of the first seven months.

This does not mean that the treatments failed. On the contrary, the improvements were still substantial enough so that the behavioral unit was able to release 98 percent of its residents and the milieu program 71 percent of its residents, compared with 45 percent for the hospital program. (Of these, only five residents—three behavioral and two milieu—were able to take up independent living; the rest went to shelter-care facilities.) And after eighteen months of follow-up and aftercare, only two of the seventy-four release patients, both behavioral, had to be rehospitalized. This study, then, definitely benefited its subjects. Furthermore, it is of great value as a piece of careful research, establishing two important principles. First, even the most dysfunctional chronic patients, with the longest histories of hospitalization (Paul's subjects averaged seventeen years apiece), can, with appropriate treatment, improve sufficiently to be released from the hospital. Second, the most useful treatment for this purpose is apparently a behavioral token economy.

It would be encouraging to report that public hospitals have taken the Paul and Lentz study to heart and developed effective token economies for their seriously disturbed patients. Unfortunately, this is not the case. A 1986 survey of 152 Veterans Administration (VA) medical centers found that only ten had programs similar to the one developed by Paul and Lentz; these programs served only 1.01 percent of all psychiatric patients treated in the VA system (Boudewyns, Fry, & Nightingale, 1986). Among the reasons suggested for the scarcity of these programs are (1) pressures to reduce the amount of time each patient stays in the hospital, and consequently the amount of inpatient services; and (2) the reliance of the token economy on the services of nurses' aides, who are among the most poorly paid employees and thus often resist the imposition of additional duties. As long as these conditions prevail, the lessons learned by the Paul and Lentz study are likely to remain theoretical.

late (Goffman, 1961; Scheff, 1966). It soon became conventional wisdom that hospitalization was bad; patients should be treated within their communities. And with the new drugs, releasing patients into the community now seemed possible. Finally, many state officials thought that it would be less expensive to treat patients in the community than to maintain them in mental hospitals.

Thus the exodus from the hospitals began. Starting in the late 1950s, mental institutions discharged more and more patients every year. Not only acute patients but also chronic patients—people who had spent the better part of their lives in mental hospitals—were given supplies of pills and either sent home or placed in community facilities. Throughout the country, the resident population of the mental hospitals dwindled. With fewer patients to serve, many of the hospitals were either closed or converted into other kinds of mental health facilities. In 1970, there were 525,000 beds for psychiatric patients in American mental health facilities. By 1986, the number had dropped to 268,000—half as many (C. A. Kiesler, 1993).

Of course, most of the newly released patients still required some kind of treatment. Furthermore, if other people were to be saved from hospitalization, alternative services had to be created. Thus, while the mental hospitals were gradually emptying, mental health professionals devoted their energies to developing psychological services within the communities. Perhaps the most important of these was a totally new kind of service known as the **community mental health center**.

Fountain House, in New York City, was one of the first community mental health centers, providing alternatives to full-time, indefinite hospitalization.

The Community Mental Health Center

In 1963, as part of President Kennedy's drive for a "bold new approach" to mental illness, Congress passed the Community Mental Health Centers Act. The law provided for the establishment of one mental health center for every 50,000 people. In these centers, anyone, rich or poor, from the center's catchment area, or area of geographical coverage, would receive the psychological services he or she required without having to leave the community. Furthermore, the centers were to implement programs for the prevention of mental disturbance; to educate other community workers, such as teachers, clergy, and police, in the principles of preventive mental health; to train professionals and nonprofessionals to work in the centers; and, finally, to carry out research. In this section we will describe how some of these services are provided.

Outpatient Services The outpatient service, the first place to which the disturbed person turns for help, is the most heavily used service of the community mental health center. Partly because the community mental health centers have offered such services and partly because of the mounting popularity of psychotherapy, the use of outpatient counseling has risen dramatically in the last few decades. In the twenty years from 1955 to 1975, for example, outpatient care increased twelvefold (C. A. Kiesler, 1982a). Between 1980 and 1985, an estimated 23 million people in the United States—that is, about 10 percent of the population at that time—made 326 million outpatient visits to professionals and volunteers for mental health problems (Narrow, Regier, Rae, et al., 1993).

The goal of outpatient care is to provide help without disrupting the patient's normal routine. People can receive psychotherapy once or twice a week without leaving their families (indeed, their families can be brought into the therapy) and without abandoning their schooling, their work, their friends, their turf—all the things that give them a sense of identity. Furthermore, the services are convenient and available, only a short trip away. And many community mental health centers have additional, satellite operations, such as storefront offices and traveling teams, that attempt to bring help even closer. Thus people with problems can receive therapy and still be home in time for dinner—a fact that encourages them to see their problems as natural and solvable rather than hideous and extreme.

Another goal of the community mental health center's outpatient services was the provision of aftercare (e.g., weekly therapy or perhaps just monthly checkups) for people who have been discharged from the hospital—a crucial matter that we have already touched upon. In the community center, it was thought, patients could be treated by the same people who had treated them in the hospital—people who remembered their names and their problems. In some community mental health centers, that is in fact what happens. In most others, however, such ideal aftercare never went beyond the stage of hopeful planning. Because of tightened public budgets, the number of centers set up fell short of the need, and those that were provided had to curtail their services. Aftercare was a common casualty of such cutbacks. Consequently, despite the success of the community mental health centers in other respects, the provision of truly adequate aftercare services is something that in most communities remains to be done.

Inpatient Services While effective outpatient services can reduce the need for hospitalization, some patients still have to be hospitalized, either because they pose a threat to themselves and others or because they lack family or other resources to support them in their difficulties. In such cases, the community mental health center provides hospitalization, usually in a general hospital in the community. Because these facilities are readily and quickly available, because family and friends can easily visit, and because (in some cases) coordinated aftercare can be provided, it is hoped that this system of hospitalization can speed up the patient's release. Furthermore, in many centers patients can receive partial hospitalization through the innovative systems of the day hospital and the night hospital. In the **day hospital,** patients are hospitalized only on a nine-to-five basis. During the day they take part in the hospital's therapeutic activities; then at night they return home to their families, their friends, their poker games, and so on. In the **night hospital,** the system is the opposite. From nine to five, patients go to work or to school; then in the evening they return to the hospital. In both cases, the emphasis is once again on preserving the patients' normal lives, so that they will not fall into the role of the chronic patient.

Day hospitals, first introduced at the Menninger Clinic in 1949 and now numbering over a thousand nationwide, seem to be particularly successful (L. R. Greene, 1981; Straw, 1982). Needless to say, they are more cost-effective than full-time hospitalization. Furthermore, because they ease the burden on the family, they can be the crucial deciding factor between the family's retaining the patient at home and their throwing up their hands and turning the patient over to an institution. Finally, day hospitals seem to be helpful in preventing full-time rehospitalization. In one study, a group of chronic schizophrenics, upon release from full-time hospitalization, were randomly assigned either to drug treatment alone or to drug treatment combined with day hospitalization as aftercare. Of the ten day hospitals involved, six were more effective than drug treatment alone in preventing rehospitalization. Interestingly, those six were low-cost centers that focused primarily on offering a "sustained nonthreatening environment" and favored occupational therapy over psychotherapy (Lin, Caffey, Klett, et al., 1979).

Emergency Services Before the advent of the community mental health center, emergency psychological services were virtually nonexistent. The public mental hospitals, as we have seen, were usually miles away from major population centers, and even communities that were rich in mental health services generally provided such services only during ordinary work hours and almost never on weekends or holidays. People who did not time their psychological emergencies to fit this schedule usually either spent the night in jail, sat for hours in an emergency room, or weathered the crisis alone.

To solve this problem, many community mental health centers have established various kinds of emergency services. In some cases a satellite storefront clinic will remain open at night for emergencies. Here the troubled person can come for an informal talk (and possibly a tranquilizer) and make an appointment to go to the regular outpatient clinic in the morning. Other community centers provide teams of mental health workers to serve in the emergency rooms of the community's general hospitals so that acute psychological problems can be given the same swift attention as acute physical problems. In addition to filling the obvious need for emergency psychological services, the presence of these mental health professionals in hospital emergency rooms has had the beneficial side effect of sensitizing the rest of the emergency room staff to the psychological condition of people who have been involved in automobile accidents, fires, rape, and other threatening situations. In this way the psychological trauma can be dealt with at the same time as the physical trauma, thus minimizing posttraumatic stress disorders.

In other communities, the mental health center runs a twenty-four-hour service for police referrals. Until recently, for example, the Chicago police, in handling people who obviously needed psychological supervision—usually they were seriously disturbed people, with psychotic symptoms, who lived alone and had no social supports—referred them to the state hospital. With the establishment of an emergency service at the community mental health center, the policy changed and severely distressed people were taken to the community center. In a two-year follow-up comparing the patients referred to the state hospital in the three months before the establishment of the emergency service with the patients referred to the community mental health center in the three months after the establishment of the emergency service, researchers found that the latter group had fewer subsequent hospital admissions and spent fewer total days in the hospital (Sheridan & Teplin, 1981).

Consultation A chronic problem in the delivery of psychological services is that there are simply not enough mental health workers to go around. One solution to this problem is consultation, whereby mental health professionals, instead of working with specific cases themselves, advise other types of professionals—physicians, teachers, police, clergy, and the like—on how to deal with the psychologically troubled people they encounter in the course of their work. For example, if a teacher is having great difficulty with a particular child, the school could ask a psychologist from the community mental health center to observe the child in question during a class hour and then to advise the teacher, and perhaps other teachers at the same time, on how to deal with the problem. This type of consulting service is being given increasing attention by community mental health centers, not only because it saves professional time but also because it allows behavior problems to be handled at the moment and in the context in which they occur.

A good example of the usefulness of the consultation approach was a program in which a group of New York City police officers were trained by mental health professionals in how to intervene in family quarrels (Bard, 1970). Family quarrels are a major source of assaults and homicides. Domestic quarrels are dangerous not only for the family members involved but also for the police officers called in to handle them. Hence New York City's innovative consultation program. In one precinct, eighteen police officers received 160 hours of training—including lectures, demonstrations, and behavioral rehearsal—in how to intervene effectively in family quarrels. These trained officers then worked as family-crisis intervention teams in that precinct. In contrast to police officers in a neighboring district, who witnessed and suffered the same amount of violence normally involved in such calls, the trained team members were able to decrease the number of assaults on family members, did not themselves suffer a single assault, and did not witness a single family homicide in 1,388 family-crisis calls. The spectacular success of this program has led to the adoption of similar programs by police departments all over the United States and offers strong support for the effectiveness of providing consultation services to other human service agencies.

Halfway Houses

Another type of community service that has proliferated in recent years is the halfway house, a service closely related to the partial-hospitalization programs offered by many community mental health centers. A **halfway house** is a residence for people (e.g., ex-drug addicts or newly released mental patients) who no longer require institutionalization but still need some support in readjusting to community life. In the halfway house these people live together, talk out their difficulties, and relearn appropriate social skills.

The best halfway houses are small residences, with perhaps fifteen to twenty acute patients (M. S. Cannon, 1975). There may be a psychologist or psychiatrist who visits regularly, but the live-in staff usually consists of a paraprofessional, such as a graduate student in psychology, who advises the residents on practical problems—how to enforce house rules, how to do the grocery shopping—and acts as an informal counselor. Many halfway houses set up stores, janitorial services, and other moneymaking enterprises that support the members and at the same time train them to support themselves on their own once they leave the house. For many people, these residences appear far preferable to a cold-turkey return to the community. Early reports indicate that small halfway houses do a good job of reducing the chances of rehospitalization. For chronic patients who have

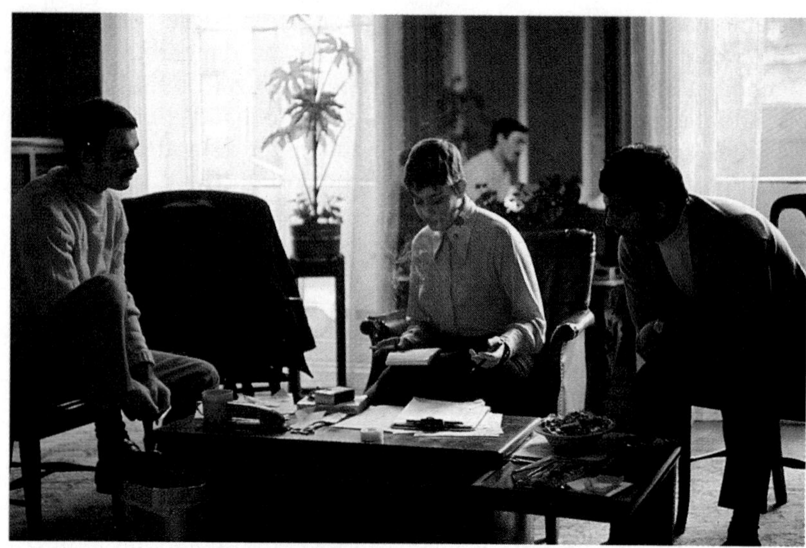

Daytop Village is a halfway house for recovering drug addicts who do not require hospitalization but are not yet ready for completely independent living.

lived in smaller halfway houses, the recidivism rate after one year of independent living (i.e., one year after leaving the halfway house) is estimated at 20 percent (M. S. Cannon, 1975), whereas the recidivism rate for chronic patients in general after one year on their own is about 40 to 50 percent (Rog & Rausch, 1975). A recent study of posthospital psychiatric halfway-house stays found that a 120-day benefit package that allowed for halfway-house care reduced recidivism rates from 79 to 29 percent and reduced the average yearly hospital stay from eighty-three days to eighteen days (Coursey, Ward-Alexander, & Katz, 1990).

Long-Term-Care Facilities

Closer to hospitalization are **long-term-care facilities,** which, while they resemble halfway houses in being smaller than hospitals and located in the community, differ in that they are not a bridge between the institution and independent living. Their purpose, as their name indicates, is long-term care, for patients who presumably will never, or not soon, achieve independent living.

There are several kinds of long-term-care facilities, but by far the most common is the nursing home (Bootzin, Shadish, & McSweeny, 1989). A high percentage of the residents of this country's intermediate-care nursing homes (i.e., nursing homes without intensive medical supervision) are not old people but former mental patients. Indeed, the decrease in psychiatric inpatient care in American hospitals during the past few decades has been offset in some measure by the increase in the nursing-home population, whether for reasons of old age or mental disturbance or both (Gatz & Snyder, 1992). Thus, despite a national emphasis on deinstitutionalization, a large proportion of funds for mental health continues to be spent on custodial care.

Alternatives to Hospitalization

Day hospitals, night hospitals, and halfway houses are all attempts to cut down on the amount of time that the patient spends in the hospital. But the fact is that most acute patients do not need hospitalization at all. As we saw earlier, the experience of psychiatric hospitalization can actually harm them, whereas all it usually offers by way of help is medication, the opportunity to consult a mental health professional, and a chance to rest for a few weeks, after which the person is typically discharged. Couldn't we offer patients these things without hospitalizing them? A number of innovative programs have attempted to do just that.

In one program, operating out of southwest Denver, patients seeking hospitalization are sent instead to one of six participating families in the community, who house the patients as their guests for a small fee. If the families encounter problems, psychiatric nurses are available to them on a twenty-four-hour basis. Patients requiring a day or two of close supervision are sent to an "intensive observation" apartment, staffed by a psychology student and his or her spouse. Here the patient can receive rapid tranquilization, if it is necessary, and is looked after around the clock. As a last resort, hospital beds are available, but they are rarely used. Within a few weeks most patients are back home, with no record of psychiatric hospitalization (Polak, 1978).

A second, more experimental program was part of a study that took place in Madison, Wisconsin (Test & Stein, 1978). Patients seeking psychiatric hospitalization were randomly assigned either to brief hospitalization (the median stay was seventeen days), with typical aftercare, or to a community treatment service not involving hospitalization. In the later service the staff helped the patients find an acceptable community residence if staying at home was not feasible, and they showed them how to find jobs or places in sheltered workshops if they were unemployed. They also created an individually tailored treatment program for each patient, based on an assessment of what coping skills that particular patient was lacking. Treatment took place *in vivo*—that is, in the patients' homes, places of work, and neighborhood haunts. For fourteen months the staff maintained daily contact with the patients, calling them, dropping by, offering suggestions, and in general actively helping them make their way in the community. At the end of the fourteen-month experimental period and again upon follow-up one and a half years later, the community treatment patients showed better adjustment (e.g., fewer days unemployed) than the hospitalized patients. Upon two-year follow-up, however, the advantage of the community treatment program began to narrow. This finding suggests that community treatment, if it is to be successful, must maintain active involvement with patients long after their crises have passed.

Such an effort was made in a third experimental program, Tucson's Treatment Network Team, organized to serve chronic mental patients who live in the community. Such patients, when they need help, are often extremely unwilling to go to the hospital—indeed, to any traditional kind of mental health facility—and many of them are also uninterested in traditional kinds of help. Yet they still need some assistance. Hence the Treatment Network Team, which assigns its members to individual patients and trains them to place the patients in settings consistent with their needs. Through these representatives, who stay in close touch with them, the patients can then receive whatever services they need—medication, crisis intervention, family counseling, informal advice—when and where they need them. A study of the program found that this flexible service-delivery approach did increase patient participation and that the patients who participated improved substantially more than those who received typical hospital and outpatient care (Santiago, McCall-Perez, & Bachrach, 1985).

Hot Lines

As we saw earlier, some community mental health centers have devoted considerable energy to providing emergency psychological services. But face-to-face emergency counseling is simply one part of a whole new trend toward crisis intervention, the handling of severe emotional stress on the spot. Another innovation in this area has been the development of telephone **hot lines**—that is, round-the-clock telephone services whereby people who are in trouble can call and receive immediate comfort and advice, usually from trained but nonprofessional volunteers. The prototype was the suicide-prevention hot line, the most famous of which is the Los Angeles Suicide Prevention Center, established by Shneidman and Farberow in 1958. That service has since spawned many other varieties of hot lines—numbers for people with drinking, gambling, or drug problems, for rape victims, for child-abusing parents, for troubled teenagers. There are even so-called Dial-a-Shoulder numbers, at which volunteers take calls from people who simply need a kindly ear to listen to their troubles. But the most influential services have been those for drug problems, teenage problems, and suicide prevention. Since 1960, more than 180 suicide-prevention and 600 youth and/or drug hot lines have been established in the United States (Trowell, 1979).

Aside from providing a kindly ear, a major function of hot-line volunteers is to give callers information on community services where they can obtain help and to try to induce them to use these services. In some cases, the volunteer can make an appointment for the caller then and there. Not all hot-line conversations are unqualified successes, however. Indeed, volunteers on suicide hot lines often have no idea, once they have hung up the phone, whether the caller will keep the clinic appointment he or she has just made or swallow a bottle of pills. As we saw in Chapter 10, recent studies suggest that suicide hot lines do not substantially decrease suicide rates (Shaffer, Garland, Fisher, et al., 1990), though other kinds of hot lines may be more effective.

Prevention

In psychology there are three levels of prevention: **primary prevention,** the goal of which is to prevent disorders from developing; **secondary prevention,** which aims at early detection and early treatment, so that minor disorders do not become major ones; and **tertiary prevention,** which attempts to minimize the damage, to both the victim and the society, of a major disorder.

Among the services dispensed by community mental health centers, we have already seen many instances of preventive effort. Halfway houses, day hospitals, night hospitals, and experimental noninstitutional treatments are all instances of tertiary prevention, just as hot lines and outpatient services are attempts at secondary prevention. But a frequent criticism of community mental health centers is that they have not exerted themselves to engage in primary prevention—that is, to attack community problems that breed psychological disturbance, such as racism, poverty, and drug use (Holden, 1972).

This is a tall order. However, the National Mental Health Association (Long, 1986) has outlined four specific areas as having immediate potential for preventing psychological disorders. First is the provision of family-planning and prenatal-care services, along with information on health and parenting, to ensure that babies are healthy and wanted. Second is the prevention of teenage pregnancies, through sex education, contraception and health services, and counseling on responsible decision making. Third is the promotion of academic mastery and psychosocial skills in the early grades by bringing mental health strategies into the schools. A final need is the extension of support, information, and training to people in stressful situations, such as families with an alcoholic or schizophrenic member. The idea is to create a healthier society, one with fewer built-in stresses—or stresses that seem unmanageable—for we know that whatever the biological correlates of psychological disorder, stress still makes a great difference.

Evaluation

It is difficult to evaluate the community services described in this section. Those services that exist have unquestionably made psychological help more widely and quickly available to the population at large, and this is their great advantage over mental hospitals. The hospitals see people only after they have reached the breaking point; community centers can help people long before they reach that point. Furthermore, for those who do have to be hospitalized, community-based services such as day hospitals, night hospitals, and halfway houses are demonstrably effective in preventing recurrence, as we have seen.

The major criticism of community services is not that what they are doing is wrong but that they are not doing enough. As we just saw, they have barely begun the job of primary prevention, and even in secondary and tertiary prevention a huge amount remains to be done. The innovative services that we described above—the courses for police, the day hospitals and night hospitals—are typical only of the better-funded, better-staffed, and more carefully thought-out programs. Such programs are still comparatively rare. Many community mental health centers offer only the old, standard services, such as psychotherapy and short-term hospitalization. The same is true of emergency care. A large percentage of psychiatric emergencies still end up in general hospitals without specialized psychiatric staff or separate psychiatric inpatient facilities, for no such services are available (Hendryx & Bootzin, 1986). Similarly, the halfway houses that we have described are the smaller, better-run ones, whereas many of what are called halfway houses are actually large "sheltercare" facilities where patients may get nothing more than the same custodial treatment that they received in the hospital. Indeed, some of the so-called halfway houses are merely seedy hotels where patients see a social worker for perhaps a few minutes a week and spend the rest of their time in front of a television. In the extreme case, some patients released to "community care" simply roam the streets and sleep on doorsteps. The community, in other words, can be as neglectful as the mental hospital (See the box on page 539.)

Because of the continuing inadequacy of community services, the move toward deinstitutionalization has been slowed and in some ways reversed. There is now considerable evidence that hospitalization, when necessary, should be brief (P. Braun, Kochansky, Shapiro, et al., 1981; Caton, 1982; Straw, 1982)—perhaps two to three weeks—and that experimental alternatives such as day hospitals and halfway houses are preferable. But these facts have only partially been acted upon. It is true, as stated earlier, that the population of the state mental hospitals has been greatly reduced. So has the average length of hospitalization. Even in settings where, traditionally, most patients were lifetime residents (e.g., state and county mental hospitals, VA psychiatric hospitals), the average length of stay is now less than three months. And in general hospitals, which account for most psychiatric admissions, the average length of stay is less than twelve days (C. A. Kiesler, 1982b). At the

THE HOMELESS AND MENTALLY ILL

Shifting the care of chronic mental patients from state hospitals to the community is called deinstitutionalization, but many city dwellers call it "dumping." In cities across the country, hundreds of thousands of patients considered capable of functioning on medication outside the institution have been released. Of the million or so homeless people nationwide, approximately one-third are thought to be suffering from mental disorders, most of them from schizophrenia (Goleman, 1986a, 1986b; Rossi, 1990). A study of homeless men recruited from the lines of a southwestern city soup kitchen and tested on the MMPI found that half showed evidence of either severe alcoholism or severe psychopathology (M. W. Kahn, Hannah, Hinkin, et al., 1987). Community services in every city are insufficiently staffed and funded to see that the mentally ill are housed, put to work, or looked after.

Where do they live? Some are placed in inexpensive single-room-occupancy (SRO) "hotels"—often warrens of tiny, filthy rooms. Community services to the chronic mentally ill may consist of a welfare check and occasional visits by a social worker dispensing tranquilizers. Otherwise, they are typically on their own, sitting in their rooms or drifting through the streets. When they die, they are rarely missed.

Still worse, some of the mentally ill have no housing at all, since they lack the money even for the cheapest flophouse. Many have essentially no income and are dependent on city shelters and soup kitchens. Some spend their days wandering from neighborhood to neighborhood; others travel around one or a few blocks. They sleep where they can—if not in shelters, then in doorways, in parks, in subways and train stations. They carry their belongings in shopping bags or roll grocery carts along the sidewalks.

For people with homes and jobs, it can be difficult to understand that the mentally ill "street person," ragged and dirty, once had a normal life. In 1991, the composer and writer Elizabeth Swados told such a story, describing the descent of her brother Lincoln Swados into schizophrenia and eventually life on the street. The Swados family was privileged, and Lincoln grew up intelligent and talented. But he was eccentric, and he often misbehaved at school. When he went away to college, he broke down. As Swados (1991) describes it:

> He never made it through his freshman year at Syracuse. . . . Lincoln promised to write, but he never did. Several months later, my father received an almost book-length letter from my brother describing himself as in a helplessly disoriented state. He was unable to go to classes, unable to leave his room. The voices in his head were directing him to do too many different things. My father showed the letter to several psychiatrists, who recommended that Lincoln be hospitalized immediately. (p. 18)

Released from the hospital after lengthy treatment, Lincoln again deteriorated. In a suicidal period, he tried to kill himself by jumping in front of a subway train. This resulted in the amputation of his right arm and leg. Then, disabled physically as well as mentally, Lincoln Swados went to live on the Lower East Side of New York, a poor and dangerous neighborhood. Repeatedly rejecting the efforts of family and friends to help him (not answering the door when they came to see him, for example), Swados sank further into mental and physical illness. His sister eventually found him dead in the middle of a shabby apartment that had become "the stinking hovel of a madman." He was forty-six.

Compared with many schizophrenics, Lincoln Swados was fortunate—he had financial resources and a family that tried to help him. Given his fate, it is easier to understand how others with serious disorders end up on the street, penniless and in desperate need of care.

The deinstitutionalization movement of the past quarter-century sought to release many mentally ill people from hospitals. Often, however, government funding has not followed the released patients into the community. As a result, adequate programs do not exist for the treatment and supervision of the thousands of homeless mentally ill people who now roam the streets of American cities.

same time, the number of mental hospital admissions has not only not decreased but has actually *increased* since the advent of deinstitutionalization (C. A. Kiesler, 1982b). Between 1980 and 1985 there was a very substantial increase in inpatient treatment within *private* psychiatric hospitals (C. A. Kiesler & Simpkins, 1991). A particularly alarming part of that trend is a substantial increase in private inpatient treatment for children and adolescents, who may be much better served by outpatient treatment that permits them to live with their families. In children's residential treatment centers, the number of inpatient admissions increased fivefold between 1980 and 1985 (C. A. Kiesler, 1993).

In 1991 law enforcement officials in several states began to investigate private psychiatric hospitals following accusations that they were admitting patients who did not need inpatient treatment, giving them inappropriate diagnoses, keeping them in the hospital longer than necessary, and abruptly discharging them the day their insurance coverage expired (P. Kerr, 1991). The concern was that large chains of for-profit hospitals were more concerned with collecting patients' insurance money than with providing appropriate care. Interestingly, about half of all private for-profit psychiatric hospitals are owned by chains, and only four corporations own 59 percent of all such hospitals (Bickman & Dokecki, 1989).

The primary reason for the scarcity of innovative intermediate services, services other than hospitalization, is simply lack of funds. Already in the 1970s, funding for the community mental health centers was being cut back. Then in 1981 the Community Mental Health Centers Act was replaced by block grants to the states, so the community centers were forced to rely on state budgets and third-party reimbursers such as Medicaid. In recent years this has meant pressure to reduce expenditures—in other words, to reduce services. So while people are still being discharged from mental hospitals as quickly as possible, the community services that were supposed to take responsibility for these people after discharge often do not exist. Hence the "revolving door" syndrome, mentioned earlier: whatever gains the person has made in the hospital are lost in the community, and the person is readmitted. In sum, while there is little doubt that comprehensive community-based care is an excellent idea, it is still far from a reality.

KEY TERMS

assertiveness training (519)
behavioral rehearsal (518)
communications approach (523)
community mental health center (533)
day hospital (534)
encounter group (520)
family therapy (523)
group therapy (516)
halfway house (535)
hot lines (537)
large community group (521)
long-term-care facilities (536)
marital therapy (525)
milieu therapy (530)
night hospital (534)
paradoxical intention (524)
peer self-help groups (521)
primary prevention (538)
psychodrama (517)
secondary prevention (538)
social-skills training (518)
structural family therapy (524)
tertiary prevention (538)
therapeutic environment (529)
token economy (529)

SUMMARY

- Group therapy has become a popular method of treatment in the past thirty years. The idea behind group therapy is that many psychological difficulties are basically interpersonal and are best treated in an interpersonal context. The benefits of group therapy, according to Irvin Yalom, are (1) hope, (2) universality, (3) information, (4) social support, (5) corrective recapitulation of the primary family group, (6) development of social skills, (7) imitative behavior, (8) interpersonal learning, (9) group cohesiveness, (10) catharsis, and (11) existential factors.
- The psychodynamic approach emphasizes items 5 and 8 on Yalom's list. Psychodynamic group therapy is similar to individual therapy, as the therapist searches for unconscious motives for the group members' actions. Psychodrama, in which clients act out their emotional conflicts with other group members, is also used in psychoanalytic group therapy.
- Behavioral therapy is generally directed toward a specific goal, and therefore group behavior therapy is very similar to individual behavior therapy. Behavioral group therapy is often done as a convenience, to save the therapist time and the client money. But behavioral group therapy does have some distinct uses. Behaviorists focus on items 3, 6, and 7 on Yalom's list, as they emphasize social-skills training. In social-skills training, the therapist tells the clients how to perform a desired behavior, and the clients then practice the behavior in a series of skits. The client's wish to imitate the therapist is an important factor in social-skills training.
- In cognitive group therapy, group members identify

the thoughts that trigger their depressive emotions. These thoughts are then analyzed by the therapist and the group members, who suggest alternative, less destructive ways of thinking. Cognitive therapy stresses items 3 and 7 on Yalom's list.

- The humanistic approach focuses on group therapy more than on individual treatment, emphasizing the group experience as a necessary part of rehabilitation. Items 4 and 8 on Yalom's list are stressed, as clients are expected to learn intimacy and cooperation through the group. Humanistic group therapy centers around experiential groups, which force the client to experience and express emotion. Personal growth, especially increased openness and honesty, is the goal of humanistic treatment.
- Peer self-help groups are groups of people with the same problem who meet regularly to provide social support for each other and to attempt to overcome the problem.
- Studies on the effectiveness of group therapy have yielded mixed results. While group therapy generally results in more improvement in a patient than no therapy or placebo therapy, studies of humanistic groups have shown that they are often ineffective and sometimes harmful.
- The main principle behind family therapy is that although only one family member may be showing distress of symptoms, the entire family may be having difficulties. The family is seen as more than the sum of its members.
- There are several types of family therapies. In the communications approach, the therapist points out the contradictory messages family members are giving each other. The therapist's goal is to lead the way for family members to tell each other how they really feel. Structural family therapists try to analyze the role each family member has within the family. They then encourage each person to mold his or her role to personal desires. There are also family therapies based on each of the major psychological perspectives, including psychodynamic, humanistic, and behavioral approaches.
- The main goal in most marital therapy is the establishment of an honest dialogue between the two partners. As in family therapy, the roles of both partners are examined. The psychological perspectives generally associated with marital therapy are behavioral, in which couples are taught to switch from coercive to reciprocal relationships; cognitive, which emphasizes communication skills; and humanistic, in which therapy attempts to make the partners experience and express their emotions toward each other.
- Traditionally, mental patients were placed in large, understaffed, isolated hospitals far from their families and friends. Patients in these state hospitals received little direct care, and their isolation from society reduced their chances for recovery.
- Some mental hospitals have begun to improve the care given to patients by turning the entire hospital into a therapeutic environment. There are psychodynamic, behavioral, and humanistic-existential approaches to creating a therapeutic environment. The psychodynamic approach emphasizes reeducation of delinquent children through identification with adults. The behavioral approach uses token economies to reinforce all appropriate behaviors and extinguish all negative behaviors. The humanistic approach, which centers around milieu therapy, maintains that patients can run their own lives within the hospital and that the chance to do this may advance their recovery. Studies have shown that token economies are the most effective form of therapeutic environment in terms of changing behaviors and getting patients discharged. However, research has shown that the behavioral changes do not always last after the patient is discharged from the hospital.
- Beginning in the late 1950s, with the development of antipsychotic drugs and the realization that large mental hospitals were often detrimental to their patients, huge numbers of mentally ill people were released from hospitals into the community. These former patients were then treated in community mental health centers.
- Community mental health centers, first organized in 1963, allow anyone to receive psychological treatment without leaving his or her community. The centers also run many mental health–related programs. The outpatient service provides psychotherapy to patients without disrupting their normal lives and, in some centers, provides aftercare to people recently discharged from mental hospitals. The community centers also provide inpatient hospitalization for more seriously ill patients. Hospitalization can take three forms: complete, day, and night hospitalizations.
- Community mental health centers also provide emergency psychological services to patients with acute psychological problems.
- Halfway houses are residences for groups of recovering mental patients who no longer need institutionalization but still require some support in readjusting to their community. Halfway houses are usually led by a paraprofessional who advises residents and acts as a counselor.
- Long-term-care facilities, such as nursing homes, provide extended care for patients who will never be able to live independently.
- Research has shown that many acute psychological patients do not need hospitalization and that hospitalization may actually be damaging. As an alternative, the patient may live with a family in the community who will provide care.
- Hot lines were developed as an attempt to handle severe emotional stress immediately. Callers can receive instant comfort and advice from trained volunteers.
- Community mental health centers have served to make psychological help more widely available, yet many problems remain to be solved. The centers are still not doing enough to help the psychologically disturbed.

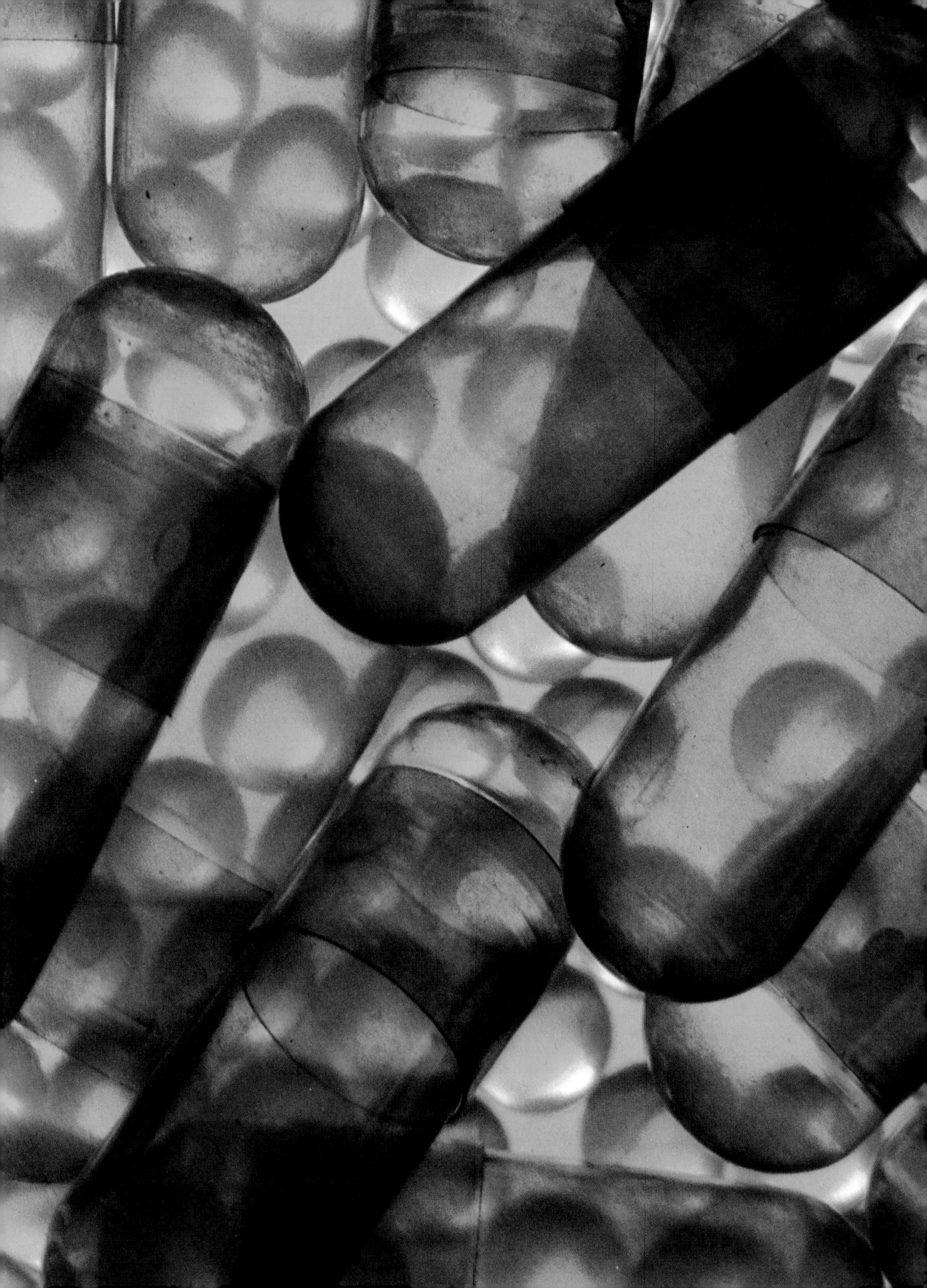

21

BIOLOGICAL THERAPY

Tess was the oldest of ten children born to an alcoholic father and a brow-beaten mother living in a public housing project. In her childhood she was beaten, sexually abused, and otherwise neglected. When she was twelve, her father died, whereupon her mother sank into a depression from which she never recovered. Tess took over the care of her younger brothers and sisters and managed to get them and herself through school. At seventeen, she married an older man—an abusive alcoholic, like her father—largely to provide a home base for her younger siblings, but once they were launched, the marriage collapsed. She then lurched from one affair to the next, always with married men who treated her badly. By the time she came for treatment, she had given up hope on her love life. She had a good job, as an administrator with a large corporation, but she was now faced with union negotiations before which she felt helpless. She had crying fits, couldn't eat, couldn't sleep, couldn't concentrate. She felt guilty and worthless. She wished she were dead. She seemed headed for the same chronic depression that had claimed her mother.

After trying various other treatments, the doctor prescribed Prozac. Within a few weeks, Tess appeared altogether different, full of energy and authority. She said she had never known before what it was like not to be depressed. She was eating and sleeping well. She was dating. She handled the union negotiations deftly. Not only was she free of the symptoms of her former depression, but her personality seemed changed. She was no longer drawn to tragedy. The friends with whom she used to sit and complain about life now seemed to her boring and depressing: "It is as if they are under the influence of a harmful chemical and I am all right—as if I had been in a drugged state all those years and now I am clearheaded." Her masochism was gone. She radiated hopefulness and confidence. "People on the sidewalk ask me for directions!" she said. They never had before. (adapted from P. D. Kramer, 1993, pp. 1–9)

Perhaps the most important trend in abnormal psychology in the last decade has been the rise of biological theory and biological therapy. It is now generally acknowledged that a vulnerability to schizophrenia can be genetically transmitted and that biochemical abnormalities, whether genetic or not, are implicated in both schizophrenia and depression. Such findings have led, in turn, to intense scrutiny of the neurotransmitters, whose complicated operations and interrelations seem to be the most likely seat of many abnormalities. Biological research is addressing itself not just to psychoses but also to the entire range of psychological disorders—generalized anxiety disorder, panic disorder, obsessive-compulsive disorder—together with personality disorders, alcohol dependence, and of course the stress-related physical disorders. Every year, new drugs come onto the market, and even when they fail to have the effects hoped for, or when their good effects are accompanied by bad side effects, their results still advance our knowledge of brain chemistry and thus lead to sounder theories and improved treatments, biological and psychological. Neuroscience research is now one of the best-funded, most active, and most exciting areas of abnormal psychology.

Since drugs are by far the most common form of biological treatment, drug therapy will occupy most of this chapter. However, we will also consider two more limited biological treatments: electroconvulsive therapy and psychosurgery.

DRUGS

Most of the advances in neuroscience are taking place in **psychopharmacology,** the study of the drug treatment of psychological disorders. Drugs are an extremely common mode of psychological treatment, for disorders ranging from schizophrenia to transient anxiety. At the same time, as we shall see, drug treatment has many problems: inadequate results, side effects, and the continuing question of whether it is wise to treat symptoms without addressing the cause.

We will discuss five main categories of drugs used for treating abnormal behavior (see Table 21.1): antianxiety drugs, hypnotics, antipsychotic drugs, antidepressant drugs, and antimanic drugs.

Antianxiety Drugs

As their name indicates, **antianxiety drugs,** also called *minor tranquilizers,* are taken to reduce anxiety. The most popular antianxiety drugs are the benzodiazepines—particularly Valium (diazepam), Xanax (alprazolam), Ativan (lorazepam), Tranxene (chlorazepate), and Librium (chlordiazepoxide hydrochloride)—and they are very popular indeed. In 1989 American pharmacies filled over 52 million prescriptions for the antianxiety benzodiazepines (Shader, Greenblatt, & Balter, 1991)—that is, one prescription for one out of every five men, women, and children in the United States. For a number of years, Valium was the most widely prescribed drug in the world. This wide use of antianxiety medications is often assumed to be a plague of modern life. As it happens, the percentage of people using drugs to con-

TABLE 21.1
MAJOR PSYCHOTHERAPEUTIC DRUGS

Category	Chemical Structure or Psychopharmacologic Action	Generic Name	Trade Name
Antipsychotic drugs (also called major tranquilizers or neuroleptics)	Phenothiazines		
	Aliphatic	Chlorpromazine	Thorazine
	Piperidine	Thioridazine	Mellaril
	Piperazine	Trifluoperazine	Stelazine
		Fluphenazine	Prolixine
	Thioxanthenes		
	Aliphatic	Chlorprothixene	Taractan
	Piperazine	Thiothixene	Navane
	Butyrophenones	Haloperidol	Haldol
	Dibenzoxazepines	Loxapine	Loxitane
	Dibenzodiazephines	Clozapine	Clozaril
	Dihydroindolines	Molindone	Moban
	Rauwolfia alkaloids	Reserpine	Sandril
	Benzoquinolines	Tetrabenazine	
Antidepressant drugs	Tricyclic antidepressants (TCAs)		
	Tertiary amines	Amitriptyline	Elavil
		Imipramine	Tofranil
		Doxepin	Sinequan
	Secondary amines	Desipramine	Norpramin
		Nortriptyline	Pamelor
		Protriptyline	Vivactil
	Monoamine oxidase (MAO) inhibitors	Phenelzine	Nardil
		Tranylcypromine	Parnate
		Pargyline	Eutonyl
		Isocarboxazid	Marplan
	Selective serotonin reuptake inhibitors (SSRIs)	Fluoxetine	Prozac
		Paroxetine	Paxil
		Sertraline	Zoloft
Antimanic drugs		Lithium	Eskalith
		Carbamazepine	Tegretol
Antianxiety drugs	Benzodiazepines	Chlordiazepoxide	Librium
		Diazepam	Valium
		Chlorazepate	Tranxene
		Oxazepam	Serax
		Lorazepam	Ativan
		Alprazolam	Xanax
	Propanediol carbamates	Meprobamate	Miltown
	Azaspirodecanediones	Buspirone	BuSpar
Hypnotics	Benzodiazepines	Flurazepam	Dalmane
		Triazolam	Halcion
		Temazepam	Restoril
		Quazepam	Doral
	Imidazopyridines	Zolpidem	Ambien
	Barbiturates	Phenobarbital	Luminal
		Secobarbital	Seconal

Antidepressants and other drugs have greatly benefited many patients, though the possibility of undesirable side effects means that they must be used with care. This woman says that Prozac helps her to cope with the stresses of work and family.

trol anxiety and insomnia has remained relatively stable over the past hundred years. The drugs themselves have changed—whereas people in the 1990s use benzodiazepines, people in the 1890s used bromides and opium-based compounds—but the use of drugs for these purposes was as widespread in the late nineteenth century as it is now (Woods, Katz, & Winger, 1987).

In most cases, antianxiety drugs are prescribed by family doctors for people who are not in psychological treatment but are simply going though a hard time in their lives. Indeed, half the users of such drugs are people who are medically ill; the drug is prescribed to control the patient's emotional reactions to the illness (Uhlenhuth, Balter, Mellinger, et al., 1983). However, antianxiety drugs are also often used in conjunction with psychological treatment, particularly for anxiety disorders, stress-related physical disorders, and withdrawal from alcohol and other drugs.

Side Effects and Withdrawal Benzodiazepines are CNS depressants; they slow down the workings of the central nervous system, and in doing so, they can create disturbing side effects. A common problem is daytime sedation, in the form of fatigue, drowsiness, and impaired motor coordination. (Benzodiazepines are often implicated in falls in the elderly and also in automobile and industrial accidents.) These drugs may also interfere with memory particularly for events that occur after taking the drug. Finally, benzodiazepines may aggravate physical disorders involving respiration, such as congestive heart failure or sleep apnea, a disorder in which breathing repeatedly stops for ten seconds or more during the night (Chapter 9). All these side effects are dose-dependent: the higher the dose, the greater the likelihood of problems. (Therefore physicians try to prescribe the lowest effective dose.) The risk of side effects is also multiplied if benzodiazepines are taken in combination with other central nervous system depressants, especially alcohol. Like barbiturates, benzodiazepines, when combined with alcohol, have a synergistic effect: each multiplies the other's power, placing the person at risk for an overdose. As we saw in Chapter 12, this process can result in death when the combination is barbiturates and alcohol. With the combination of benzodiazepines and alcohol, death is rare, but it can happen. For example, if a person with severe sleep apnea went to bed with both alcohol and benzodiazepines in his or her system, death could result.

Apart from side effects, a major drawback of benzodiazepines is the difficulty of withdrawal. Part of the reason for this is that when a benzodiazepine is taken in large doses, termination of the drug is often followed by *rebound* (Chapter 12): the symptoms return with redoubled force. Thus the person is likely to start taking the drug again—in larger and larger doses, because of tolerance—in order to suppress the now-magnified symptoms. This has been a problem with Xanax. Xanax is very effective in the treatment of panic attacks (Shader & Greenblatt, 1993), but when it is withdrawn, 90 percent of patients relapse, many of them experiencing worse panic attacks than they had before (Michelson & Marchione, 1991).

The difficulty of withdrawal is related to whether a drug is short-acting or long-acting—

that is, how quickly it is absorbed into the bloodstream and how long it stays there. Long-acting benzodiazepines, such as Valium and Tranxene, tend to accumulate in the body over time, so the longer the person takes the drug, the higher the dose he or she is getting. By contrast, short-acting benzodiazepines, such as Xanax and Ativan, are usually eliminated from the system in less than eight hours. As a result, going "cold turkey" with a short-acting benzodiazepine is more likely to result in rebound and other withdrawal symptoms (Rickels, Schweizer, Case, et al., 1990). The long-acting benzodiazepines, however abruptly terminated, naturally eliminate themselves from the system bit by bit, with less disturbing effects.

But even with long-acting benzodiazepines, and even with a therapeutically tapered withdrawal, discontinuing these drugs is very hard for long-time users—that is, people who have taken the drug daily for over a year. In a study of sixty-three benzodiazepine-dependent patients going through a gradual termination, only 63 percent of those on long-acting drugs—and worse, only 58 percent of those on short-acting drugs—were able to achieve a drug-free state (Schweizer, Rickels, Case, et al., 1990). For panic disorder patients, the figures are even less encouraging. In a recent study, only one-fourth of panic disorder patients who had participated in a gradual benzodiazepine withdrawal program were drug-free at a three-month follow-up, though when the patients received cognitive-behavioral therapy in conjunction with the drug taper, their success rate tripled (Otto, Pollack, Sachs, et al., 1993).

Because of these problems with benzodiazepines, physicians have tried using other drugs to treat anxiety disorders. Antidepressants (see below) are often effective for panic disorder, obsessive-compulsive disorder, and generalized anxiety disorder (Rosenbaum & Gelenberg, 1991). Another alternative is BuSpar (buspirone), a recently introduced nonbenzodiazepine. BuSpar does not interact with alcohol and seems to be more selective in its effects on anxiety, though it is ineffective with panic disorder and only sometimes effective for generalized anxiety (Rosenbaum & Gelenberg, 1991).

The most common criticism of antianxiety drugs, however, is not that they don't work well enough but that, by working as well as they do, they may invite people to avoid solving their problems. As Freud pointed out, anxiety is a *signal*. By taking antianxiety drugs, we suppress the signal, but we do not solve the problem. Indeed, the problem may become more serious as a result of our ignoring it. Taking antianxiety drugs, then, is something like turning off a fire alarm because we can't stand the noise.

Even when drugs are used in conjunction with psychotherapy, there is some question as to their usefulness. Learning, as psychologists have discovered, is state-dependent (Ho, Richard, & Chute, 1978; Overton, 1966). What we learn in a given biological or psychological state does not fully generalize to other states. Thus if, while taking antianxiety medication, we learn new skills for dealing with stress, this does not mean that these skills will necessarily survive the withdrawal of the medication.

Hypnotics

Until recently the most widely used **hypnotics,** or sleeping pills—Dalmane (flurazepam), Halcion (triazolam), and Restoril (temazepam)—were also benzodiazepines, with all the same problems as the antianxiety benzodiazepines: daytime sedation, memory loss, synergistic effect with alcohol, high rebound rate upon withdrawal. Like the benzodiazepine antianxiety drugs, the benzodiazepine hypnotics differ in their effects depending on whether they are short- or long-acting. Dalmane, because it is long-acting, produces more daytime grogginess but less rebound. Halcion, because it is short-acting, has the opposite profile: it causes less grogginess but it can involve severe rebound—not just insomnia but acute daytime anxiety, sometimes escalating to panic attacks. Restoril is intermediate between short- and long-acting, but it does not reach its peak effectiveness until more than an hour after it is taken. Therefore Restoril is generally prescribed when the sleep problem consists of waking during the night; Halcion, when the problem is *falling* asleep. Dalmane is often avoided because of the daytime grogginess, but it is resorted to if the patient doesn't respond to the other drugs.

All the benzodiazepine hypnotics have the additional disadvantage that they alter the "architecture" of sleep—our passage through the various stages of sleep in the course of the night. In particular, they all suppress REM sleep, with the result, in some cases, that the patient will experience *REM rebound*—restless sleep, nightmares—when he or she tries to go to bed without taking the drug. And in most cases, withdrawal from the drug means a return to insomnia.

Because of these drawbacks, and because benzodiazepines are often diverted onto the illegal drug market, efforts have been made to stem their

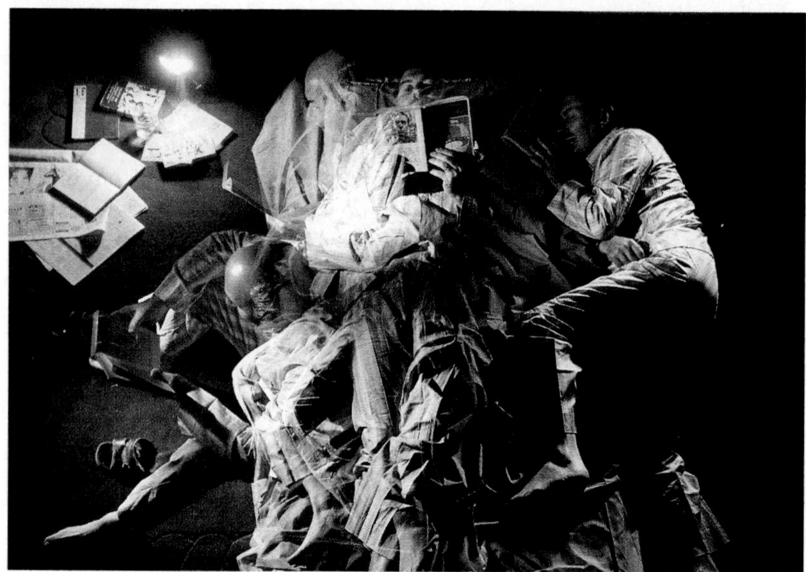

This multiple-exposure image conveys some of the frustration and exhaustion of insomnia. Treatment of this condition with hypnotic drugs is tricky, because withdrawal from "sleeping pills" can involve the return of insomnia along with the onset of other symptoms.

use. Some drugs have been removed from the market. (Halcion's side effects and rebound potential have caused it to be banned in Britain.) In other cases, laws have been changed to make these drugs harder to prescribe. In New York State, for example, benzodiazepines can be obtained only through "triplicate prescription." For every prescription, there must be three copies: the physician keeps one, the pharmacy retains the second, and a third is sent to the state regulatory agency. This cumbersome procedure, with its implication of supervision, was intended to discourage physicians from prescribing benzodiazepines, and it has done so. But while the number of benzodiazepine prescriptions has diminished, the number of prescriptions for barbiturates, which are generally more dangerous, has increased (Shader, Greenblatt, & Balter, 1991). Apparently, when people cannot sleep, drugs are what they turn to, though behavioral therapy has proved more effective than medication for severe insomnia (Chapter 9).

An encouraging recent development has been the introduction of Ambien (zolpidem), a hypnotic that is not a benzodiazepine. Ambien is short-acting and is absorbed very quickly. Therefore it is useful primarily for sleep-onset disorders. Most crucial, however, is the fact that it has far fewer side effects than the benzodiazepines. It does not have a synergistic effect with alcohol; it does not alter the architecture of sleep; it does not produce rebound or severe withdrawal. As a result, it is now very popular. In 1994, less than a year after its approval by the FDA, Ambien became the most frequently prescribed hypnotic in the United States.

Antipsychotic Drugs

As their name indicates, the **antipsychotic drugs** (also called *major tranquilizers* or *neuroleptics*) are used to relieve symptoms of psychosis—confusion, withdrawal, hallucinations, delusions, and so forth. The most common antipsychotic drugs are the phenothiazines, which we have already discussed briefly in Chapter 15. As with so many other drugs, the therapeutic use of the phenothiazines was discovered by accident. Phenothiazine, the nucleus of this group of compounds, was first synthesized in 1883 by a German research chemist and was used to treat infections of the digestive system in animals. That the drug also had psychoactive properties was not understood until sixty years later, when the antihistamines, which also have a phenothiazine base, were discovered. Antihistamines, it was found, not only helped to relieve colds and allergies (their major use today) but also had tranquilizing effects. This discovery prompted chemists to look again at the other phenothiazines. In 1950 a French drug company produced a new phenothiazine derivative called chlorpromazine, advertised as a potent tranquilizer. Four years later chlorpromazine was marketed in the United States under the trade name Thorazine. It was an overnight success. Within eight months of its appearance, it had been used by approximately 2 million patients (*Hospital and Community Psychiatry*, 1976). Today, though there are some antipsychotic drugs that are not phenothiazines—for example, Haldol (butyrophenone haloperidol)—many psychotic patients in the United States take either Thorazine or one of the other phenothiazines, such as Stelazine (trifluoperazine), Prolixin (fluphenazine), or Mellaril (thioridazine), on a daily basis.

In general, antipsychotic drugs are quite effective at reducing schizophrenic symptoms (Shader, 1994). As a result, they have radically altered the conditions under which schizophrenics live. Patients who would have been in straitjackets thirty years ago are now free to roam hospital grounds. And many patients are sufficiently calm and functional to be released altogether, though they must go on taking the medication. At the same time, these drugs have had an enormous impact on schizophrenia research. It was the effort to find out how the phenothiazines worked that led biochemical researchers to the dopamine hypothesis, which at this point seems the most promising theory as to the organic basis of schizophrenia (Chapter 15).

Side Effects Antipsychotic drugs have their drawbacks too. In producing calm, they often produce fatigue and apathy as well. Overmedication can reduce the patient to a "zombielike" state. Capitalizing on this effect, some hospitals have been known to use high doses of Thorazine for "patient management"—that is, to control patients who are making trouble. (Such high doses usually tranquilize patients to the point where they can barely move for several days.) On the other hand, too low a dose will not have the desired effect of suppressing psychotic symptoms. Other side effects—constipation, blurred vision, dry mouth, muscle rigidity, and tremors—can sometimes be reduced by additional drugs. This cat's cradle of different effects makes the prescribing of antipsychotic medication something of an art. With any given patient, a number of different dosages and different combinations of drugs may have to be tried before an appropriate drug program is decided upon, and then the patient's response to the drugs must be carefully monitored so that adjustments can be made.

One serious side effect of antipsychotic drugs has so far proved resistant to treatment. That is tardive dyskinesia (described in Chapter 15), a muscle disorder in which patients grimace and smack their lips uncontrollably. Tardive dyskinesia usually appears in patients over forty after at least six months of continuous treatment with antipsychotic drugs. Unlike other side effects, it does not disappear when the drug is discontinued. On the contrary, it usually surfaces when the drug dosage is reduced or when the drug is withdrawn altogether. The prevalence of tardive dyskinesia in schizophrenics maintained on antipsychotic drugs is estimated to be 20 to 30 percent (Gelenberg, 1991). A newer antipsychotic medication, clozapine, is less likely to cause tardive dyskinesia, but there are other problems associated with this drug (see the box on page 550).

Finally, it should be stressed that antipsychotic drugs alone cannot solve the problem of schizophrenia. Patients who are released from the hospital under the calming influence of antipsychotic drugs usually make only a marginal adjustment to life on the outside. And once outside, they often

Some schizophrenics credit clozapine with giving them a chance at a normal life. These patients, in their thirties, held a prom to make up for the one they had missed because of their illness fifteen years before.

CLOZAPINE: A CONTROVERSIAL ANTIPSYCHOTIC DRUG

While most psychotic patients are helped by drugs such as the phenothiazines, most is not all. As many as 25 percent of schizophrenic patients are treatment-resistant—that is, unresponsive to traditional antipsychotic medication. For these patients, a new drug, clozapine, was introduced in the United States in 1990 under the brand name Clozaril. Actually, clozapine was not a new drug. It was discovered in the 1970s, but when it was tried out experimentally, about 2 percent of the subjects came down with a potentially fatal blood disorder, agranulocytosis (Baldessarini & Frankenberg, 1991). That ended plans to market clozapine. But then years passed, and no new antipsychotic drugs were developed. Clozapine was given a second look.

New studies showed once again that clozapine did help schizophrenics who were otherwise treatment-resistant (Kane, Honigfeld, Singer, et al., 1988). Therefore it seemed valuable enough to put on the market as long as patients were carefully monitored for signs of agranulocytosis. In 1990 a drug company won FDA approval to sell clozapine as a "package" including instructions and equipment for weekly blood sampling. But these extra safety features made the drug extraordinarily expensive—about $9,000 a year per patient—so eventually the blood-monitoring package was dropped.

Clozapine, then, is a risky drug. On the other hand, early reports indicate that it is quite effective (P. J. Perry, Miller, Arndt, et al., 1991; Pickar, Owen, Litman, et al., 1992). One study of thirty-eight formerly treatment-resistant schizophrenics found that after a year on clozapine, the subjects' rehospitalization rate dropped by 83 percent. Furthermore, over half these patients could now go to work or to school (Meltzer, Burnett, Bastani, et al., 1990). Apart from the danger of agranulocytosis, clozapine has fewer side effects than the phenothiazines. Most important, it does not seem to cause tardive dyskinesia. Therefore, in the absence of safer drugs, it does offer hope to patients not helped by the phenothiazines. And it may encourage researchers to develop other drugs that have its virtues without its hazards.

stop taking the drugs, in which case they may have to be readmitted, only to be released and readmitted again. Thus although antipsychotic drugs have definitely reduced the number of chronically hospitalized schizophrenics, it has been argued that they have merely replaced long-term institutionalization with "revolving door" admission. This outcome, however, is not the fault of the medication—no one ever claimed that the antipsychotic drugs cured schizophrenia—but rather of the society's failure to provide community services for released patients, a problem that we discussed in Chapter 20.

Antidepressant and Antimanic Drugs

Antidepressant drugs, as the name indicates, are used to elevate mood in depressed patients. The first important class of antidepressants to gain a wide following was the **MAO inhibitors,** including phenelzine (Nardil) and tranylcypromine (Parnate). The name of this class of drugs was based on the belief that they interfered with the action of the enzyme monoamine oxidase (MAO). The MAO enzyme serves to degrade certain neurotransmitters, including norepinephrine and serotonin, in the nervous system. As we saw in Chapter 10, deficiencies of both norepinephrine and serotonin have been implicated in depression. By blocking the action of MAO, the MAO inhibitors presumably correct this deficiency. However, it has never been satisfactorily established that the MAO inhibitors work by inhibiting MAO and increasing norepinephrine and serotonin. More to the point, these drugs can have adverse effects on the brain, the liver, and the cardiovascular system, and when combined with certain other drugs or foods—especially foods prepared by fermentation (e.g., beer, wine, some varieties of cheese—can result in severe illness and even death.

Because of these risks, the MAO inhibitors were gradually replaced by another class of antidepressants, the **tricyclics,** so named for their three-ringed molecular structure. Commonly used tricyclics are Tofranil (imipramine), Elavil (amitriptyline), and Sinequan (doxepin). The tricyclics seem to have the same effect that the MAO inhibitors were thought to produce—an increase in norepinephrine and serotonin—but by a different means: they block the reabsorption of these neurotransmitters by the nerve cells. They, too, have some unpleasant side effects, similar to those of the antipsychotic drugs: drowsiness, blurred vision, constipation, dry mouth. But presumably because tricyclics are taken in smaller doses than antipsychotic drugs, these side effects are milder, and they do not include tardive dyskinesia. Another disadvantage is that the tricyclics do not begin to take effect for about two to four weeks—which, to a severely depressed person, is a long time to wait for relief. Still, these drugs have proved successful with many patients.

The tricyclics are now being gradually displaced by a newer class of antidepressants, the **selective serotonin reuptake inhibitors,** or **SSRIs.** Like the tricyclics, the SSRIs work by blocking neurotransmitter reuptake, but they zero in on only one neurotransmitter, serotonin (hence their name). For reasons that are not yet understood, this makes the SSRIs effective for many patients who do not respond to other antidepressants or who have abandoned other antidepressants because of unpleasant side effects.

There are several SSRIs on the market—Paxil (paroxetine) and Zoloft (sertraline) are two of the newer ones—but by far the most popular has been Prozac (fluoxetine). Introduced in 1987, it soon became America's most widely prescribed antidepressant. By the end of 1993, more than 10 million people in the United States had been given prescriptions for Prozac (Barondes, 1994). Prozac too, like the other SSRIs, can have side effects—primarily headache, upset stomach, and anxiety. Furthermore, in a small number of cases it seems to produce an extreme "behavioral toxicity": manic agitation, violence, suicidal thoughts, even suicide. Finally, determining the correct dose is a delicate procedure. Prozac's *half-life*—the amount of time it stays in the system—is very long: seven days (Agency for Health Care Policy and Research, 1993). Thus patients who are taking the drug daily are gradually increasing its level in the bloodstream, a process which can lead to overdose. Unfortunately, the symptoms of a Prozac overdose resemble the symptoms of depression, so there is a danger, when the signs of overdose appear, that the patient will *increase* the dose, thinking that what is needed is simply more of the drug (Cain, 1992).

Despite these complications, Prozac has proved extremely effective in combating depression, and it seems to work well with obsessive-compulsive patients also. What is remarkable about the drug, however, is that it sometimes does far more than eliminate symptoms. In certain reported cases, such as that of Tess, cited at the opening of this chapter, the drug seems actually to transform the personality. Patients who all their lives have suffered from fear of rejection, low self-esteem, and social awkwardness are, like Tess, suddenly confident, decisive, full of energy and hope. This ability to make people "better than well" was the subject of Peter Kramer's 1993 book *Listening to Prozac,* which in turn boosted the drug's popularity. As

The notion that Prozac—or any other drug—can magically "change your personality" is largely a flight of journalistic fancy. Yet Prozac does seem able to alter certain long-standing negative characteristics, making insecure and depressed people feel more confident and optimistic.

Kramer points out, Prozac's apparent power to alter long-standing personality characteristics raises the possibility that what we think of as "personality"—our core characteristics as human beings—may be more biologically based than we have imagined. (See the box on page 552.)

While there are many competing drugs in the antidepressant market, the field of **antimanic drugs** is dominated by one medication, **lithium.** Lithium is administered as lithium carbonate, a natural mineral salt that has no known physiological function (Berger, 1978). Yet for some reason this simple salt is capable of ending swiftly and effectively about 70 percent of all manic episodes. In some cases, it also terminates depressive episodes, particularly in bipolar patients. At the moment, the great virtue of lithium is preventive: when taken regularly, in maintenance doses, it is generally effective in eliminating or at least diminishing mood swings in bipolar disorder (Prien & Gelenberg, 1989). It is not easy, however, to determine what

PROZAC: THE UNANSWERED QUESTIONS

Within two years of its appearance, Prozac was being sold at a rate of 650,000 prescriptions per month. It appeared on the cover of *Newsweek;* it was profiled on *Nightline* and the *Today* show. It was a celebrity. Then, as often happens with celebrities, the wave of enthusiasm was followed by a wave of skepticism. A team of researchers from Harvard Medical School reported on six patients who began showing suicidal behavior under the influence of Prozac (Teicher, Glod, & Cole, 1990). There were also reports of patients who became violent toward others. Joseph Wesbecker, an unemployed printer with known mental problems but no history of violence, invaded the printing plant where he had worked, shot twenty people—eight of them died—and then turned the gun on himself. An autopsy revealed therapeutic doses of Prozac in his blood.]

Such cases were few and inconclusive. Suicidal behavior is not uncommon in depressed patients. As for Wesbecker, there were other medications besides Prozac in his blood. Nevertheless, the media seized on the reports of Prozac's dangers as eagerly as, before, they had bannered its virtues. Talk shows featured Prozac "survivors." The Scientologists began a campaign against the drug. Macy's refused to hire a Santa Claus who was taking Prozac.

Today, both the "miracle-cure" claims and the backlash have receded. Prozac enjoys a large and steady popularity. Nevertheless, there are many unanswered questions about the drug. To begin with, researchers still know very little about how it works. Clearly it blocks the reuptake of serotonin, but why does this reduce depression, relieve anxiety, and improve self-esteem? And are those three effects the results of Prozac's attacking one biochemical abnormality or three separate ones (Barondes, 1994)?

Another question is whether, once people are "cured" by Prozac, they can go off the drug. Consider the case of Tess, summarized at the opening of this chapter. Tess's case was described by Peter Kramer, her physician, in his 1993 book *Listening to Prozac,* and as he adds, her recovery was not permanent. After nine months on Prozac she went off the drug, and for a while she seemed to do fine without it. Then, after another few months, Kramer got a call from Tess, asking for a new prescription. She was not depressed, she said. She simply wasn't herself—that self being the new one, confident and charismatic, that Prozac had created for her. Kramer gave her the prescription, but as he points out, the administration of drugs to people who are not suffering from psychological disorders but simply want to be happier and more effective raises serious ethical problems. If people are taking Prozac just to feel good, how does that differ from the sale of "street drugs," which is illegal? And if people using Prozac are more effective in daily life—do business better, are more persuasive and attractive—then what is the social fairness of giving this advantage to some people and not to others? Should insurance companies pay for this "cosmetic psychopharmacology"? Should a national health program?

Prozac also raises philosophical questions. If the drug can actually transform personality, how do we square this with our belief in a consistent, "core" self? And how do we reconcile such transformations with notions of free will and responsibility—or even with our belief in the effects of experience on human character? A biochemical agent that can radically alter personality suggests that personality may be biochemical to begin with.

Finally, Prozac poses a challenge to what has been called the "tragic sense of life"—the idea that human wisdom involves a recognition of life's built-in defeats as well as its portion of happiness. Much of Western philosophy and art is based on this belief. Should we now regard the knowledge of life's darkness as a temporary discomfort that humankind had to suffer until it was rescued by biochemical research? In sum, is Prozac an answer, or is it a blindfold? Considering the case of Tess, Kramer (1993) wonders

> whether the medication had not ironed out too many character-giving wrinkles, like an overly aggressive plastic surgery. . . . I found it astonishing that a pill could do in a matter of days what psychiatrists hope, and often fail, to accomplish by other means over a course of years: to restore to a person robbed of it in childhood the capacity to play. Yes, there remained a disquieting element to this restoration. Were I scripting the story, I might have made Tess's metamorphosis more gradual, more humanly comprehensible, more in sync with the ordinary rhythm of growth. I might even have preferred if her play as an adult had been, for continuity's sake, more suffused with the memory of melancholy. But medicines do not work just as we wish. (pp. 12, 21)

the maintenance dose is, since for most patients the effective dosage is close to the toxic dosage, and a toxic dose can cause convulsions, delirium, and in rare cases, death. An overdose is generally preceded by clear warning signs, such as nausea, alerting the patient to discontinue the drug. Still, because of its potential dangers, patients who take lithium must have regular blood tests to monitor the level of the drug in their systems. Another problem with lithium is that when people have taken the drug for more than two years, stopping the medication often results in a new manic episode within two to three months (Suppes, Baldessarini, Faedda, et al., 1991).

Because of the risks associated with lithium, researchers have been trying to develop other drugs for mania. An anticonvulsant medication, Tegretol (carbamazepine), has been found to be effective for about a third of manic patients (Small, Klapper, Milstein, et al., 1991).

Drug Therapy versus Psychotherapy

The recent successes of psychopharmacology have created a sometimes bitter controversy within the field of psychological treatment. Certain advocates of drug therapy speak as if drugs were on their way to making behavioral and insight therapies obsolete. In the words of psychiatrist Paul Wender, one day "every disease is going to be [seen as] a chemical or an electrical disease" (quoted in Gelman, 1990, p. 42). Indeed, some experts believe that personality itself may come to be seen as a biological phenomenon. As Peter Kramer (1993) puts it, "When one pill at breakfast makes you a new person, . . . it is difficult to resist the suggestion, the visceral certainty, that who people are is largely biologically determined" (p. 18).

To many psychotherapists—people who have spent their careers treating psychological disturbance as part of the deepest problems of living—such statements seem naive and presumptuous. An editorial in the *Journal of the American Psychoanalytic Association* called attention to the dangers of "the recent and forceful biologization of everything from cigar smoking to love (a deficiency of phenylalanine treatable by chocolate in the absence of the loved person)" (T. Shapiro, 1989a). Some experts also fear that psychotherapists may be becoming like internists, "managing" depression, for example, the way internists manage hypertension, by prescribing drugs and monitoring their effects, while the root cause of the depression goes unexplored. As noted earlier, to suppress symptoms is not necessarily the wisest course. By definition, symptoms are symptoms *of* something.

On the side of the drug-therapy advocates, it must be said that the root cause of some depressions may in fact be biochemical—that biochemical imbalance is what the symptoms are signaling and what the drugs are correcting. Furthermore, as we have seen, in some cases they correct it very efficiently. Drug treatment for certain disorders is now so widely regarded as effective that *not* to prescribe drugs for these disorders can be viewed as malpractice. (In a celebrated case, a doctor suffering from bipolar disorder sued a Maryland hospital for treating his illness with psychotherapy rather than drugs. The case was settled out of court.)

Does drug therapy in fact work better than psychotherapy? Most of the research on this question has to do with depression. One large-scale review of outcome studies concluded that both biological and psychological therapies are effective treatments for depression, though the most effective treatment was a combination of the two (Free & Oei, 1989). The Agency for Health Care Policy and Research (1993) recently conducted a review of the literature on the treatment of depression and came to four conclusions. First, about half of depressed outpatients show marked improvement from medication. Second, the most appropriate patients for medication are those who have the most severe symptoms, plus recurrent episodes and a family history of depression. Third, psychotherapy—particularly cognitive, behavioral, and interpersonal—is effective for mild to moderate depression. Fourth, combined treatment should be considered for more severe depressions and for those that have not improved with psychotherapy or drug therapy alone. While these recommendations have been criticized for overstating the effectiveness of medication, in a sense they are nothing new, for they repeat a long-held principle: that the treatment of choice depends on severity. Ever since the introduction of the phenothiazines in the 1950s, it has been widely believed that in general the most severely disturbed patients needed drugs, while the less severely disturbed needed psychotherapy. It should be added, however, that this principle is now being challenged. Some researchers (e.g., Hollon, DeRubeis, Evans, et al., 1992) have found that the most severe depressions are as likely to yield to cognitive therapy as to drug therapy. As for the idea that the least severe depressions are those that require psychotherapy, much of the controversy surrounding Prozac has to do with its challenge to that point. Sensitivity to criticism, low self-esteem, fear of rejection: these mild, nagging problems, which have for so long been thought the province of psychotherapy, not drugs, are exactly what Prozac seems to relieve—a fact that, in the words of one expert, is causing "a rethinking of fundamental assumptions in psychiatry" (Barondes, 1994, p. 1102).

One fairly consistent finding is that drug therapy, when it is discontinued, is more likely than psychotherapy to be followed by relapse. In a study of medication *versus* cognitive therapy for depression, it was found that the two worked equally well during the acute phase of the depression but that once the treatment ended, the patients in the medication group were more likely to have subsequent depressions (Hollon, Shelton, &

Loosen, 1991). Likewise, a study comparing cognitive-behavioral therapy with drug therapy for panic attacks found that both methods were equally effective at controlling symptoms but that the cognitive-behavioral patients had a much lower relapse rate (Michelson & Marchione, 1991). One of the drugs in this study was Xanax, which, as we saw, appears to have a relapse rate of 90 percent in the treatment of panic disorder—a very poor showing.

It may be that the wave of the future is combined treatment. Even if, in some cases, there is a clear biochemical abnormality, and one that can be corrected biochemically, the patient is still left with the damage that has been done to his or her life by the disorder. People who for five or ten years have not been able to leave home without checking the locks twenty times, or not been able to leave home at all, have almost invariably developed, in *response* to these circumstances, a wide range of painful attitudes and feelings about themselves and the world. They may also have wrecked marriages, strained family relations, and few friends. While the drug may help to relieve the symptoms of the disorder, psychotherapy may be needed to repair the results of the disorder.

Furthermore, a psychological disorder is never *just* biochemical. Recall the discussion of the mind-body problem in Chapter 9. All mental events are both biochemical and psychological. Drug therapy and psychotherapy are two different ways of approaching them. With gradual adjustments, the two therapies may be able to work together. While the defenders of psychotherapy often feel called upon to protect psychology against the incursions of biology, Freud, who was certainly a defender of psychotherapy, repeatedly predicted that its cause would ultimately be served by biological research. "Let the biologists go as far as they can," he said, "and let us go as far as we can—one day the two will meet" (quoted in Gelman, 1990, p. 42).

ELECTROCONVULSIVE THERAPY

For reasons that are not completely understood, electric shock, when applied to the brain under controlled circumstances, seems to help in relieving severe depression. This type of treatment, known as **electroconvulsive therapy (ECT),** involves administering to the patient a shock of approximately 70 to 130 volts, thus inducing a convulsion similar to an epileptic seizure. Typically, therapy involves about nine or ten such treatments, spaced over a period of several weeks, though the total may be much lower or higher.

This technique was first discovered in the thirties (Bini, 1938). Since that time it has become clear that, like antidepressants, the shock affects the levels of norepinephrine and serotonin in the brain, but theories as to its exact mode of operation are as various and incomplete as those regarding the antidepressants. At present all we know is that electric shock apparently *does* work, and quite well, for many seriously depressed patients (Abrams, 1992; American Psychiatric Association, 1990).

Like other biological treatments, ECT has its complications. The most common side effect is memory dysfunction, both anterograde (the capacity to learn new material) and retrograde (the capacity to recall material learned before the treatment). Research indicates that in the great majority of cases, anterograde memory gradually improves after treatment (Squire & Slater, 1978). As for retrograde memory, there is generally a marked loss one week after treatment, with nearly complete recovery within seven months after treatment. In many cases, however, some subtle memory losses, particularly for events occurring within the year preceding hospitalization, will persist beyond seven months (Squire, Slater, & Miller, 1981). And in very rare cases (e.g., Roueché, 1974), such persisting losses are not subtle but comprehensive and debilitating. The probability of memory dysfunction is less if ECT is confined to only one hemisphere of the brain (Squire & Slater, 1978), the one having less to do with language functions—as we saw in Chapter 4, this is usually the right hemisphere—and this approach has proved as effective as bilateral shock (Horne, Pettinati, Sugerman et al., 1985).

Another problem with ECT is that although the treatment is painless (the patient is anesthetized before the shock is administered), many patients are very frightened of it. And in some cases, ward personnel have made use of this fear, again for "patient management," telling patients that if they don't cooperate, they will have to be recommended for an ECT series.

These problems have made ECT a controversial issue over the years. Defenders of ECT point out that many studies have found it highly effective—more effective, in fact, than antidepressants (National Institute of Mental Health, 1985). Furthermore, unlike antidepressants, it works relatively quickly—an important advantage with suicidally depressed patients. On the other hand, ECT has vociferous critics, who consider it yet another form

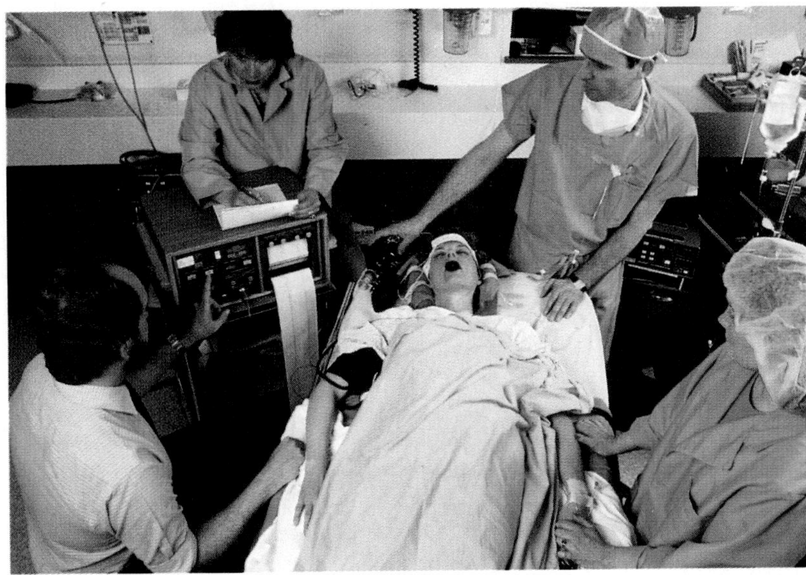

Electroconvulsive therapy is a controversial treatment with potentially serious side effects, but it has been shown to help many severely depressed people.

of psychiatric assault on mental patients. In support of this view, the voters of Berkeley, California, in 1982 passed a referendum making the administration of ECT a misdemeanor punishable by a fine of up to $500 and six months in jail. While the ban was later reversed by the courts, the fact that the voters passed it indicates the strength of opposition to this treatment.

Though the controversy over ECT is not settled, it has had its impact on practice. State legislatures have established legal safeguards against the abuse of ECT, and in general the technique is being used less frequently than it was in the sixties and seventies. At the same time, a 1990 report of the American Psychiatric Association concluded that ECT *was* an effective treatment for serious depressions and should be used, particularly in cases where other treatments, such as antidepressants, have failed.

PSYCHOSURGERY

Severely disturbed patients who do not respond to other treatments may be recommended for **psychosurgery,** surgery aimed at reducing abnormal behavior in the absence of any signs of organic brain pathology. In 1935, two Portuguese physicians, Egas Moniz and Almeida Lima, developed what is called the **prefrontal lobotomy.** In this surgical procedure an instrument is inserted into the frontal lobe and rotated, thus destroying a substantial portion of brain tissue. The theory behind this technique was that in extremely disturbed patients, activity in the frontal lobe was intensifying emotional impulses originating in lower parts of the brain, especially the thalamus and hypothalamus. Presumably, if some of the connections between the frontal lobe and these lower regions could be severed, behavior would improve. This was the goal of the operation.

In the 1940s and early 1950s thousands of lobotomies were performed, and some patients undoubtedly benefited from them. Others, however, emerged from surgery in a vegetative state, in which they remained permanently; others were hostile, childlike, lethargic, or generally devoid of affect; some suffered recurring convulsions; some died (Redlich & Freedman, 1966). It was therefore with considerable relief that mental health professionals welcomed the phenothiazines in the 1950s as a safer method of calming the severely disturbed. Lobotomy is now resorted to only very rarely.

In recent years, however, researchers have developed more refined psychosurgical techniques—techniques that destroy less brain tissue and therefore produce fewer and milder side effects. One procedure, called **cingulotomy,** involves inserting an electrode into the cingulate gyrus, a ridge of brain tissue lying above the corpus callosum (Chapter 4). The electrode is then heated, creating a small lesion. The principle here is basically the same as that in lobotomy: to disrupt pathways leading from the emotion centers of the thalamus and hypothalamus to the frontal lobe and thus to reduce the expression of emotion. Cingulotomy has proved effective for severe obsessive-compulsive patients who have not responded to other treatments (Jenike, Baer, Martuza, et al., 1991). In another procedure, called **stereotactic subcaudate tractotomy,** a small localized area of the brain is destroyed by radioactive particles inserted through small ceramic rods. The site varies with the nature of the disturbance. For depressed patients, it is the frontal lobe; for aggressive patients, it is the amygdala, a structure in the lower part of the brain.

Psychosurgery has been found to be effective with severe depression—and also with intractable pain (Bartlett, Bridges, & Kelly, 1981). Nevertheless, it is still extremely controversial, and even in its newer, more conservative forms, it is used only when other treatments have failed. Its defenders claim that the benefits are substantial and the side effects relatively mild. Other observers doubt both claims and feel that the public should be very wary of such radical and irreversible treatments. In particular, many writers, including many psychosurgeons, feel that surgical procedures for controlling aggression should be regarded with the gravest suspicion, as procedures that could easily be abused (Valenstein, 1987).

EVALUATION

We have already discussed the major objections to drug therapy: by suppressing symptoms, it invites patient and therapist to ignore the cause, and possibly as a result, it tends to have higher relapse rates than psychotherapy. Another problem that should not be minimized is side effects. Many patients would rather go without treatment than endure the range of side effects—jitteriness, grogginess, dizziness, headache, constipation, dry mouth, blurred vision, sexual dysfunction, insomnia, weight gain—that accompany some medications. Another consideration is cost. Though it is often argued that drugs are less expensive than psychotherapy, that is not true if the drugs, unlike the psychotherapy, must be administered over a long period. Several years' worth of daily medication costs far more than twelve sessions of psychotherapy, for example.

But perhaps the crucial consideration is the relative effectiveness of drugs and psychotherapy. This will depend on the problem that the patient has and on the individual patient. In general, however, there is very little evidence that any psychological procedure is as effective as antipsychotic medication in controlling psychotic symptoms, and this is a strong argument for its use. Drugs are certainly preferable to straitjackets, and there is no question that antipsychotic medication has introduced a calmer atmosphere into modern mental hospitals.

In other cases drug therapy can make nondrug therapy possible. And as we have seen in the case of depression, the best treatment may be a combination of the two. One reason for this, according to Klerman (1986), is that each therapy bolsters the other, the drugs making the patient willing and able to engage in psychotherapy, and the psychotherapy increasing the patient's motivation to take the drugs and building on their positive effects. Unfortunately, however, many patients, particularly those in institutions, receive *only* drugs. Drug therapy requires fewer employee hours than psychotherapy. Consequently, when budgets are cut back, it is the psychotherapy that is eliminated, not the drugs. And it is arguable that by calming the patients, drugs have encouraged such cutbacks, as well as made the need for better treatments seem less urgent.

As for ECT, its risks, in the form of memory loss, have already been discussed, but these risks are less serious in the newer, one-hemisphere technique. Meanwhile, ECT is apparently an effective treatment for severe depression that has not responded to other forms of treatment.

In psychosurgery, even the newer forms, the risks are far graver, but they must still be weighed against the patient's problem. If, for example, a man is subject to uncontrollable fits of violence, so that he must be kept locked in solitary confinement, is he better or worse off if surgery eliminates his rage attacks but leaves him sexually impotent? On the one hand, it can be said that the surgery has enabled him to function in *some* capacity. On the other hand, it can be argued that his physicians should have gone on looking for some other, less risky treatment. Psychosurgery is a treatment of last resort, but even as a last resort, it will undoubtedly remain controversial.

KEY TERMS

antianxiety drugs (544)
antidepressant drugs (550)
antimanic drugs (551)
antipsychotic drugs (548)
cingulotomy (555)
electroconvulsive therapy (ECT) (554)
hypnotics (547)
lithium (551)
MAO inhibitors (550)
prefrontal lobotomy (555)
psychopharmacology (544)
psychosurgery (555)
selective serotonin reuptake inhibitors (SSRIs) (551)
stereotactic subcaudate tractotomy (556)
tricyclics (550)

SUMMARY

- Of all the biological treatment used for abnormal behavior, the most common is drug therapy. Five main categories of drugs are used: antianxiety drugs, hypnotics, antipsychotic drugs, antidepressant drugs, and antimanic drugs.
- Antianxiety drugs, or minor tranquilizers, such as Valium, Xanax, Ativan, Tranxene, and Librium, are taken to reduce anxiety. They are very widely used both for anxiety conditions and to relieve stress related to illness and medical treatment. Antianxiety drugs have side effects, principally daytime sedation, interference with memory, and aggravation of respiratory disorders. These drugs act synergistically with alcohol. They may also produce a rebound effect: when the patient stops taking the drug, the symptoms return with added force. Withdrawal from benzodiazepines is usually more difficult with short-acting drugs than long-acting ones. Use of antianxiety drugs may lead a person to avoid confronting the sources of his or her anxiety.
- Hypnotics are sleeping pills; the most commonly used are Dalmane, Halcion, and Restoril. Their side effects are similar to those of the antianxiety drugs. Their effects also differ depending on whether they are short- or long-acting. Ambien, an new nonbenzodiazepine hypnotic, relieves insomnia with fewer undesirable side effects.
- Antipsychotic drugs, or major tranquilizers, are used to relieve the symptoms of psychosis—hallucinations, delusions, confusion, and withdrawal. The most common antipsychotic drugs are the phenothiazines, such as Thorazine, and they are widely used by schizophrenic patients. Although they often have good results in reducing schizophrenic symptoms, they do not cure the disorder, and they have a number of serious side effects. The most serious of these is tardive dyskinesia, a muscle disorder that is still incurable.
- Antidepressant drugs elevate mood in depressed patients. Among these are MAO inhibitors (Nardil, Parnate) and tricyclics (Tofranil, Elavil, Sinequan). These drugs too, although generally effective, have a number of side effects. The tricyclics are being replaced by SSRIs, especially Prozac, which is now the most widely prescribed antidepressant in the United States.
- Lithium is the dominant antimanic drug. It is used in the treatment of mania and bipolar disorder and is effective for most manic episodes. Overdoses of the drug are toxic, however, and it must be taken with care.
- Outcome research on drug therapy versus psychotherapy suggests that both types of treatment are effective for various conditions and especially for various degrees of depression. In many cases, the best treatment is both biological and psychological.
- Electroconvulsive therapy (ECT) is used in serious cases of depression, especially when other treatments have failed. It involves administering a brief electric shock to the brain. ECT is sometimes associated with memory dysfunction.
- Psychosurgery is surgery aimed at reducing abnormal behavior in the absence of any signs of organic brain pathology. In an operation called prefrontal lobotomy, brain tissue is destroyed in an effort to calm the behavior of extremely disturbed patients. Lobotomies are rarely performed today. Less destructive techniques are cingulotomy and stereotactic subcaudate tractotomy. Psychosurgery is controversial and is used only when other treatments have failed.

22

LEGAL ISSUES IN ABNORMAL PSYCHOLOGY

According to Lorena Bobbitt, a twenty-four-year-old manicurist living in Manassas, Virginia, she was asleep on the night of June 23, 1993, when her husband, John Bobbitt, came home drunk and raped her. He then passed out, and she went into the kitchen. There, as she later testified, she began having flashbacks of the many instances of rape and other abuse she had suffered at her husband's hands. Then her eye lighted on a 12-inch carving knife. That, she said, was the last thing she remembered until she "came to" later in her car, some distance from home. In one hand she was holding the carving knife; in the other, two-thirds of her husband's penis. She threw the severed organ into some underbrush. (It was later retrieved and surgically reattached.) Lorena Bobbitt was arrested on the charge of malicious wounding, a crime for which she could have been imprisoned for twenty years.

It seemed a clear-cut case. No one, not even Lorena Bobbitt, contested that she had cut off her husband's penis. According to the prosecution, she did so out of hatred and revenge, and knew what she was doing. Indeed, a friend of hers testified that, some time before, Lorena Bobbitt had said that she would cut off her husband's penis if she ever caught him cheating on her. But according to Virginia law, a person accused of a crime may be held blameless if "his mind has become so impaired by disease that he is totally deprived of mental power to control or restrain his act" (Margolick, 1994a). At the trial three expert witnesses, a psychiatrist and two forensic psychologists, testified that despite the mental stress Lorena Bobbitt was under, her actions were nevertheless purposeful and goal-oriented. As one of them put it, "She came to the conclusion that the penis was at fault, and that she was going to remove the source of all her problems" (in Margolick, 1994c). At the same time, another psychiatrist claimed that Lorena Bobbitt was not just under mental stress at the time of the crime; after the rape, she suffered a brief reactive psychosis (Chapter 14), during which she could not summon any defense against her wish to retaliate. She succumbed to an "irresistible impulse"—grounds, in Virginia, for acquittal. This was the explanation that the jury eventually accepted. Amid mixed cries of jubilation and disgust from a nation that had watched this trial intently, Lorena Bobbitt was acquitted on the grounds of temporary insanity.

This case is a typical illustration of the overlap between mental health and the law. By now, the issues generated by that overlap are very familiar to the public. When we read newspaper accounts of bizarre crimes, we take it for granted that a psychiatrist or psychologist will be called on to make judgments about the defendant's sanity and possibly to give "expert testimony" at the trial. In other widely publicized court cases—such as the 1975 case of Kenneth Donaldson, who sued officials of the state of Florida for wrongfully keeping him in a mental institution for fourteen years—the public saw the mental health system itself on trial.

The Lorena Bobbitt case was a notorious example of the kinds of controversies that arise when issues of mental health and the law intersect. Despite the prosecution's contention that she cut off her husband's penis out of anger and a desire for revenge, the jury agreed with Mrs. Bobbitt's defense that she had been temporarily insane.

These court cases are only the most obvious examples of the fact that decisions about people's mental health have important legal implications. For one thing, people who are judged to be insane may be relieved of legal responsibility for crimes that they commit. For another thing, if they are institutionalized for their own or for society's protection, such people may also be relieved of many of their constitutional rights.

Mental health law, the branch of law that deals with such matters, has been changing at a rapid pace. In recent years nearly all states have substantially revised their laws regarding the commitment and treatment of the psychologically disturbed (La Fond & Durham, 1992), and more changes can be expected. These new laws are attempting to settle what are essentially three issues:

1 *Psychological disturbance and criminal law.* Can psychologically disturbed people be held guilty of breaking the law? Can such people be given a fair trial? If they are not tried or are acquitted by reason of insanity, what should the state then do with them?
2 *Civil commitment.* Under what circumstances can people who have committed no crime but appear to be severely disturbed be involuntarily institutionalized by the state?
3 *Patients' rights.* Once a person is institutionalized, what are his or her rights concerning living conditions, psychological treatment, and so forth?

Most of this chapter will be devoted to an examination of these three issues. Then, in a final section, we will address the larger issue of the power of the mental health profession—how that power is used and how, in recent years, it has been challenged.

PSYCHOLOGICAL DISTURBANCE AND CRIMINAL LAW

Abnormal behavior, as we saw in Chapter 1, can be defined as a violation of the society's norms. Many social norms, however, are not just standards of behavior but legal requirements. Hence abnormal behavior may also be illegal behavior, ranging from drug abuse to murder. Most people agree that when deeply disturbed people commit such crimes, they should not be treated in the same way as ordinary lawbreakers. But how they *should* be treated is a matter of great controversy.

The Insanity Defense

Though psychologists may question the concept of free will, criminal law does not. The business of criminal law is to fix blame for and to penalize socially intolerable conduct. For the law to carry out these functions, it must assume that human beings freely choose their actions. (If they didn't, how could we justifiably blame them?) Thus when a court pronounces someone guilty, it is making both a judgment of fact *and* a moral judgment: the defendant not only committed the crime but is also morally responsible for it and can therefore be punished for it.

Nevertheless, the law does acknowledge that certain people may commit crimes not out of free choice but because mental disturbance has somehow deprived them of free choice. For such people, there is what is known in legal terms as the **insanity defense,** whereby the defendant admits to having committed the crime but nevertheless pleads not guilty, stating that because of mental disturbance he or she was not morally responsible at the time of the crime. Though guilty in fact, the defendant claims to be innocent in moral terms, and therefore exempt from punishment.

The insanity defense, then, is intended to protect the mentally disturbed from the penalties that we impose on the mentally sound. At the same time, it serves to protect the moral prestige of the law (Meehl, 1991). By making exceptions of people who cannot be held responsible for their actions, the insanity defense implies that every other defendant does have the capacity to choose "between good and evil."

Legal Tests of Insanity If the defendant pleads insanity, how is the jury to decide whether that plea is justifiable? What, in other words, is the legal test of insanity? This question has haunted the courts for many years and has been answered in a variety of ways.

For the purpose of modern law, the first important ruling on this matter was the so-called irresistible-impulse decision, handed down by an Ohio court in 1834. According to this test, defendants are acquitted if, as a result of mental illness, they could not *resist* the impulse to do wrong. The main problem with this test is obvious: How is the jury to distinguish between resistible and irresistible impulses? (From the point of view of psychoanalytic or behavioral theory, *is* there any difference?) But as we shall see, this distinction may be no more difficult to draw than the distinctions required by other tests of insanity (LaFave & Scott, 1972).

Historically, the second important test is the so-called M'Naghten rule, handed down by an English court in 1843. The defendant in this case, Daniel M'Naghten, claimed that he had been commanded by the voice of God to kill the English prime minister, Sir Robert Peel; he then killed Peel's secretary by mistake. In acquitting M'Naghten, the court ruled that defendants are legally insane and therefore not criminally responsible if, as a result of a "disease of the mind" and consequent impairment of reason, they either (1) did not know what they were doing or (2) did not know that what they were doing was wrong. (Hence the commonly heard question "Did the defendant know right from wrong?") Thus while the irresistible-impulse test stresses the whole matter of self-control, the M'Naghten test singles out one aspect of self-control, cognition, and makes the test of insanity rest on that.

Critics of this test (e.g., Bromberg, 1965; Weihofen, 1957) argue that cognitive activity cannot be separated from emotion or from any other mental activity; the mind is an integrated whole, not a collection of separate compartments. Legal scholars have responded that while the mind may be integrated, it is not an undifferentiated blob; almost all psychological theories recognize the existence of distinguishable mental processes. Furthermore, the M'Naghten rule has the virtue of limiting the insanity defense to those people who are perceived by the public as truly "insane." All of us have difficulty, in varying degrees, with resisting impulses, but very few of us commit misdeeds because we do not know what we are doing or because we do not know that they are wrong. By reserving the insanity defense for people who *are* in this extreme situation and who therefore cannot reasonably be expected to comply with the law, the M'Naghten test, in the eyes of some legal scholars (e.g., Livermore & Meehl, 1967), serves the purpose of excusing the truly excusable and preserving the moral authority of the law.

A third test, known as the Durham test, states that the defendant is not criminally responsible "if his unlawful act was the product of mental disease or mental defect." As is obvious from the wording, this test forces the jury to rely on expert testimony, for how is a jury of ordinary citizens to determine whether the defendant has a mental disease or defect? But in American courts people are supposed to be tried by their peers, not by the mental health profession. Actually, the rules preceding the Durham test also involve this problem. How can a jury decide whether the defendant was under the sway of an irresistible impulse or knew right from wrong? But the Durham test, because of its wording, more or less *requires* expert judgment, and for this reason it has been replaced in most jurisdictions that had adopted it.

The most recent formulation of the insanity defense is that adopted by the American Law Institute (ALI) in its Model Penal Code of 1962:

> **1** A person is not responsible for criminal conduct if at the time of such conduct as a result of mental disease or defect he lacks substantial capacity either to appreciate the criminality of his conduct or to conform his conduct to the requirements of law.
>
> **2** As used in the Article [of the code], the terms "mental disease or defect" do not include an abnormality manifested only by repeated criminal or otherwise antisocial conduct (sec. 4.01).

Many legal scholars feel that the ALI test is the best that can be hoped for. To a degree it incorporates the irresistible-impulse criterion ("conform his conduct to the requirements of law") and the M'Naghten criterion ("appreciate the criminality of his conduct") and the Durham criterion ("as a result of mental disease or defect"). At the same time, however, it states these criteria in broader terms and adds the phrase "substantial capacity." The result is a test that *can* be applied without expert knowledge. In effect, the ALI rule asks the jury, "Can the defendant be justly blamed for his or her misbehavior?" In the opinion of many legal scholars, this is the question that should be asked—and of the jury, not of the mental health profession. The ALI test has been adopted by many of the states. Other states are still using the M'-Naghten test, with or without a supplemental irresistible-impulse test. Only New Hampshire uses the Durham test. In 1984 Congress adopted an insanity test for federal courts that is similar to the M'Naghten test (Steadman, McGreevy, Morrissey, et al., 1993).

After all this discussion, it must be added that according to recent research the verbal formula used to define legal insanity has little practical significance. In any given case, the verdict will usually be the same under any of the insanity tests now in use (Steadman, McGreevy, Morrissey, et al., 1993).

A New Verdict—Guilty but Mentally Ill Several scholars have expressed concern that as the concept of mental illness has expanded from encompassing only the grossly psychotic to embracing what is potentially a very substantial fraction of the population, many defendants may escape responsibility for their crimes. This situation may weaken the deterrent effect of criminal law (Berns, 1994). The deterrent effect is not compromised when an obviously psychotic person is found not guilty by reason of insanity, but when someone who appears to be "sane" is found to lack criminal responsibility, the authority of criminal law may seem to be diminished. (See the box on page 564.) A case often cited in this regard is that of John Hinckley, who in 1982 was acquitted on grounds of insanity after he tried to assassinate President Ronald Reagan. Hinckley claimed that he did this in order to "gain [the] love and respect" of the movie actress Jodie Foster, whom he had never met.

The successful use of the insanity defense by John W. Hinckley, Jr., following his attempt to assassinate President Ronald Reagan set off a storm of controversy. The uproar obscured the fact that very few defendants are found not guilty by reason of insanity.

Hinckley's trial focused not on whether he had committed the assassination attempt—clearly he had—but on his sanity at the time. The jury was presented with vast amounts of conflicting evidence from expert witnesses called by both sides. The defense witnesses portrayed Hinckley as driven by a delusion of achieving a "magical union" with Jodie Foster and as suffering from a severe form of schizophrenia, as well as numerous other mental problems. The psychiatrists called by the prosecution testified that Hinckley made a conscious choice to shoot Reagan and had no "compelling drive" to do so. They depicted Hinckley as selfish and manipulative and suffering from only some minor personality disorders.

The jury's verdict of not guilty by reason of insanity stunned the courtroom, including the judge and Hinckley himself, who had fully expected conviction. Law professor Charles Nesson (1982) expressed the feelings of many when he wrote, "For anyone who experiences life as a struggle to act responsibly in the face of various temptations to let go, the Hinckley verdict is demoralizing, an example of someone who let himself go and who has been exonerated because of it" (p. A19).

This concern has led to consideration of a new verdict of "guilty but mentally ill" to serve as an intermediate between "guilty" and "not guilty by reason of insanity." It would be appropriate in cases in which the defendant knew what he or she was doing and that it was wrong but nonetheless had some form of mental illness. A defendant convicted by this verdict would serve time and receive treatment within the penal system. Michigan was the first state to adopt the "guilty but mentally ill" verdict (in 1975); about a dozen states have since followed suit. It appears, however, that this new verdict has not reduced the number of insanity acquittals (Steadman, McGreevy, Morrissey, et al., 1993).

Procedural Aspects of the Insanity Defense The John Hinckley case stirred interest in two procedural aspects of the insanity defense. First, whose responsibility is it to prove the defendant's insanity (or sanity)? Second, if the defendant is acquitted, how do we determine whether he or she should be committed to a mental hospital or released back into the community?

As a general rule, the prosecution must prove beyond a reasonable doubt all elements of a criminal offense—including both the physical act and the requisite mental state, which in a murder case is the intent to kill (LaFave & Scott, 1972). When defendants raise the insanity defense, must they prove that they were insane at the time of the crime, or must the prosecution instead prove that they were sane?

Before the *Hinckley* verdict, a majority of states placed the burden on the prosecution to prove sanity, and prove it beyond a reasonable doubt, once the defense had presented some evidence, such as psychiatric testimony, suggesting insanity. This is the rule under which Hinckley was tried. But in 1984, partly because of the outcome of that case, the federal rules were changed to place the burden of proving insanity on the defendant, and about three-quarters of the states now do so as well. This shift has substantially reduced the number of insanity acquittals, which are now more likely to involve people with serious mental illnesses, such as

CAN JUSTICE SURVIVE THE SOCIAL SCIENCES?

In his 1980 book *Psychology and Law: Can Justice Survive the Social Sciences,* psychologist Daniel Robinson wrote:

> By none of the historical scientific standards does psychiatric or psychological testimony qualify as "evidence," since such testimony does not confine itself to publicly verifiable facts. . . . The inclusion of [psychological] "experts" places jurors in the position of diagnosticians once they accept the testimony of "experts" as evidence. The real effect is to put justice at the mercy of theory and the courts at the mercy of a professional community in which an anarchy of speculation is the rule and an informed consensus the exception. This part of justice cannot survive the social sciences. (p. 63)

We have already seen this "anarchy of speculation" in the case of Lorena Bobbitt, with one psychological professional saying one thing, a second the opposite. At about the same time that experts were disagreeing in Virginia about Bobbitt, other experts were disagreeing in California at the trials of Lyle and Erik Menendez. In August 1989, the Menendez brothers—Lyle aged 21, Erik 18—killed their parents, Jose and Mary Louise Menendez, with shotguns after a family argument. They later lied to the police, claiming that they were out that night and were horrified when they returned and came upon their parents' bodies, riddled with bullets. But eventually Erik confessed the crime to a psychologist, and the psychologist went to the police.

At their separate trials, which took place in 1993–1994, the Menendez brothers no longer denied that they had killed their parents. What they said was that they had done so in order to prevent their father from killing *them.* Both brothers claimed that their father had subjected them to years of sexual abuse. (Erik's accounts of being raped and sodomized reduced many in the courtroom to tears.) Lyle said that when he confronted his father with these facts, Jose Menendez threatened the boys' lives; Lyle and Erik then bought shotguns and made their preemptive strike. They killed their mother as well as their father, they said, because they felt that without her husband she would not be able to function and would be suicidal.

The attorneys for the Menendez brothers did not use the insanity defense. Rather, in an innovative step, they employed an argument that had been used earlier for battered wives: that the crime was committed in self-defense. If the brothers exaggerated their father's threat to their lives, this was the result of the abuse they had suffered; as the defense's expert psychological witnesses testified, abused children may distort reality and misperceive threats. Meanwhile, as usual, other expert witnesses maintained the exact opposite: that the Menendez brothers were quite sane and had killed their parents in order to inherit their money. (The estate was valued at $14 million.) In support of this position, Erik's taped confession made no reference to sexual abuse or to fear of the father.

Like the Bobbitt trial, this case was part of the dispute Daniel Robinson described above: the claims of law versus the claims of the social sciences. Over the years psychology and sociology have made known the emotional damage that people may suffer from various kinds of abuse. Today, abuse and victimization in general have become subjects of near-obsessive concern in the mass culture, as television talk shows demonstrate. In any case, they were the main subjects of the Bobbitt and Menendez trials, and the chief defense strategy was to arouse compassion. One of Lorena Bobbitt's lawyers, in his summation, appealed directly to the women of the jury: "This lady is ill, this lady has been stripped of all dignity, done in by the man she loved. She needs your help" (Margolick, 1994b). Leslie Abramson, Erik Menendez's lawyer, made essentially the same appeal: "Human beings are very sensitive creatures, and they suffer terribly when they are treated badly" (Mydans, 1993). In both cases, the defense was conducted as if the question before the court was not whether the defendants were criminals but whether they were victims. With the Menendez brothers the court could not decide on either score. Both juries deadlocked.

What worries many observers is that the current wave of interest in victimization may breed a "no-fault sentimentality" incompatible with the premise of personal responsibility at the core of the criminal justice system (W. Goodman, 1994). As television journalist Barbara Walters commented in the wake of the Bobbitt and Menendez verdicts, "Everybody has a psychological background." To sort out those whose backgrounds *should* excuse them from criminal responsibility, psychologist Paul E. Meehl (1991) has proposed that criminal statutes be revised to include a list of specific psychiatric diagnoses that would have to be established in order for an insanity defense to succeed. These include major affective disorder, paranoid and catatonic schizophrenia, coarse brain syndrome, and psychomotor epilepsy. Meehl continues:

> Nothing else goes, so you can't plead not guilty by reason of mental illness on the grounds that you had a battle-ax mother or a pick-pocket uncle or a poverty-stricken childhood, or whatever. . . . The point is that mere intensity of motivation, of whatever character and origin, is not an excuse for predatory conduct. (p. 488)

In order for an insanity defense to succeed, then, a defendant would have to be conspicuously "crazy." All the rest of us would be held responsible for criminal behavior, thereby preserving the moral seriousness of the law.

schizophrenia or major mood disorders (Steadman, McGreevy, Morrissey, et al., 1993).

What is to be done with defendants who are acquitted by reason of insanity? Prior to the 1970s, they were usually subjected to long-term confinement in a mental hospital, often a high-security hospital with the physical appearance of a prison. Then, in the 1970s, the field of mental health law was swept by a wave of reform, drawing on the antiestablishment politics of the 1960s. Law after law was changed, almost always in the direction of protecting civil rights, and this included laws governing defendants acquitted on the grounds of insanity. In many states, such acquittals were no longer automatically followed by commitment. The person might be placed briefly in a mental health facility for evaluation, but prolonged hospitalization was permitted only under standards of ordinary civil commitment ("Commitment Following," 1981). As we will see later, these standards typically require a finding that the person is *currently* mentally ill and dangerous. Since a great deal of time may have elapsed between the commission of the offense and the acquittal, the defendant's mental condition may have changed. Thus, under the new rules of the 1970s, it was entirely possible that a defendant might not meet commitment criteria at the postacquittal commitment hearing.

This possibility alarmed many people, including a majority of U.S. Supreme Court justices, and in *Jones v. United States* (1983) the Court ruled that it *is* permissible to commit insanity acquittees automatically. The acquittees could then be hospitalized until they proved themselves either no longer mentally ill or no longer dangerous. Further, the Court ruled that they could be hospitalized for longer than they could have been imprisoned had they been convicted. The year of this decision is significant: 1983, a year after the *Hinckley* verdict. In the wake of the Hinckley trial, a majority of states also tightened up postacquittal procedures so as to make release more difficult (Steadman, McGreevy, Morrissey, et al., 1993).

Lyle (left) and Erik Menendez enter a courtroom soon after their arrest for killing their parents in 1989. Expert psychological witnesses gave contradictory testimony at their trial, some asserting that the brothers had committed cold-blooded murder to gain a sizable inheritance, others that they had acted in self-defense against their father's abuse.

Criticism of the Insanity Defense In the abstract, it seems only fair to provide an insanity defense for people who violate the law as a result of psychological disturbance. In reality, however, the insanity defense poses very thorny problems, both practical and moral.

For one thing, how can a jury accurately determine whether the case conforms to the court's definition of insanity? To rule on a person's sanity is to arrive at a subjective judgment that is extremely difficult to make. Furthermore, it is important to note that the jury is required to make a *retrospective* judgment. The question is not the defendant's current mental state, which the jury might at least guess at by observing his or her courtroom behavior, but the defendant's mental state at the time of the crime.

In most cases, the jury must rely on testimony of psychological professionals, but this is no solution. In the first place, psychiatrists and psychologists have as much difficulty with retrospective diagnoses as other people. Second, they often produce diametrically opposed diagnoses, thus producing a "battle of the shrinks" in the courtroom (Meehl, 1991). Often even experts who are called by the same side will contradict one another. A third problem we have already mentioned: the opinions of expert witnesses are at best only partially relevant in criminal proceedings. The court is there not to make a scientific judgment but to make a legal judgment—whether the defendant should be held legally responsible for the crime. This is a judgment that only the jury, not the mental health profession, is empowered to make. But because the jury has so little concrete information to go on, that judgment may be wrong.

A second criticism of the insanity defense, based on a totally different point of view, is that of Thomas Szasz (1963). According to Szasz, the problem with the insanity defense is not that it is difficult for the jury to evaluate but that the special circumstance that it attempts to deal with—insanity—does not exist. As we saw in Chapter 1, Szasz claims that mental illness is a myth perpetuated by an arrogant profession. In his opinion, all behavior is of a purposeful and therefore responsible nature. If people act in socially offensive or hostile ways, they do so because they *mean* to. To label them "insane" is to deny their behavior any meaning or value and thus, by extension, to deny that there is any conflict between the individual and society. Szasz proposes that the courts get out of the business of judging people on their intentions and judge them instead on their behavior. If a person has committed hostile and dangerous acts, Szasz (1977) argues, "he should be punished, not treated—in jail, not in a hospital" (p. 135).

Szasz's stance brings us to the third major criticism of the insanity defense: that those who successfully plead it sometimes end up in a worse situation than if they had been convicted of their crimes. As we pointed out earlier, people who are found not guilty by reason of insanity are usually not set free like others who are acquitted of crimes. Rather, they are often committed to mental hospitals and are kept there until such time as experts testify that they are no longer dangerous. Such testimony is usually very long in coming; indeed, it may never come. Thus, while people convicted of crimes are deprived of their liberty for a specific period of time—after which, by law, they are free—many people acquitted by reason of insanity are given **indeterminate sentences,** sentences with no limit. They could languish for the rest of their lives in a mental hospital before a staff member decided that they were no longer dangerous.

These considerations, among others, have led to widespread criticism of the insanity defense, and not just by extremists such as Szasz. Three states—Idaho, Montana, and Utah—actually abolished the insanity defense in the early 1980s. It remains to be seen if the courts will decide that such a defense is in fact constitutionally required. It should be added that, statistically speaking, the insanity defense is much less important than other questions linking law and psychology. Because it is sometimes involved in especially notorious cases, such as those of Bobbitt and Hinckley, and because it touches on the elemental question of free will, the insanity defense receives a great deal of public attention. Yet it is invoked in less than 1 percent of felony cases, and it is successful in less than one-quarter of the cases in which it is raised (Steadman, McGreevy, Morrissey, et al., 1993).

Competency to Stand Trial

The number of people confined in mental hospitals as a result of successful insanity pleas is small in comparison with the number who are there because they are judged mentally unfit even to be tried (American Bar Association, 1989). In most states, defendants, in order to stand trial, must understand the nature of the proceedings against them and must be able to assist counsel in their own defense. When a defendant does not meet these requirements, the trial is delayed, and the person is sent to a mental health facility in hope of restoring competency. As with the insanity defense, the purpose is to protect the defendant and at the same time to preserve the court's reputation for justice. The courts would not inspire public trust if they tried people who were obviously out of touch with reality.

Incompetency to stand trial must not be confused with legal insanity. The insanity defense has to do with the defendant's mental state *at the time of the crime;* competency to stand trial has to do with the defendant's mental state *at the time of the trial.* Furthermore, while the insanity defense concerns moral responsibility for crime, competency to stand trial is merely a question of ability to understand the charges and to confer fairly reasonably with one's attorney. Thus a person who is judged competent to stand trial can still successfully assert an insanity defense. Even people diagnosed as psychotic may be competent to stand trial; many are lucid enough to meet the competency requirements (Roesch & Golding, 1980).

Incompetency, then, is a limited concept. The rule is often applied in a loose fashion, however. Both prosecutors and defense attorneys have been accused of abusing the competency issue (American Bar Association, 1989). Prosecutors who fear that their cases are too weak can use it to keep the defendant incarcerated, thus accomplishing the same purpose that would be gained by a conviction. On the other hand, defense attorneys may use the competency proceedings in order to delay the trial, either in the hope that some of the prosecutor's witnesses may become unavailable to testify or simply in order to convince the defendant that they are doing all they can.

For the defendants, the consequences used to be grave. Once ruled incompetent, they were often denied bail, cut off from their jobs, friends, family, and other social supports, and confined in a hospital for the criminally insane, when in fact they might never have committed the crimes they were charged with. They often remained in the hospital for years, since there was often no means of restoring their competency (Morris & Meloy, 1993). However, this particular abuse was ruled unconstitutional by the U.S. Supreme Court in the case of *Jackson v. Indiana (1972)*. The defendant in this case was a mentally retarded deaf-mute who had been charged with robbery. Judged incompetent to stand trial, he was being held in a state hospital indefinitely, since there was no way to render him competent to stand trial. The Court ruled that when a person is detained solely on the grounds of incompetency to stand trial, the detention can last only as long as it takes to determine whether the defendant is likely to become competent to stand trial in the foreseeable future. If the likelihood is poor or nil, the defendant must be either released or committed to an institution according to the state's ordinary civil commitment procedures. (Civil commitment will be discussed below.)

Competency and Antipsychotic Medication One controversy surrounding the competency issue has to do with antipsychotic drugs. If defendants fulfill the competency requirements only when under the influence of antipsychotic drugs, are they in fact competent to stand trial? On the one hand, it seems almost unfair not to try such patients if the drugs render them lucid enough to be tried. On the other hand, these drugs, as we have seen, often render people groggy and passive—surely an inappropriate state in which to attend one's own trial. Furthermore, antipsychotic medication might well affect the defendant's chances of successfully pleading the insanity defense. The "crazier" the defendant seems during the trial, the more likely it is that the jury will accept the insanity plea. But whatever crazy behavior the defendant normally exhibits may well be reduced by the medication. Should we then allow defendants to undergo trial without medication, so that the jury can see them in their "true" state? But even if this were the most direct route to justice (which is questionable), many defendants could not be tried because they would not be competent to stand trial without the medication. This catch-22 has not yet been fully resolved, but in *Riggins v. Nevada* (1992) the Supreme Court ruled that people being tried for a crime could not be *forced* to take psychotropic (mind-affecting) medication unless the trial court specifically found this necessary to a fair trial.

CIVIL COMMITMENT

Criminal commitment accounts for only a small percentage of those committed involuntarily to our mental hospitals. The remainder are there as a result of **civil commitment.** That is, they have been committed not because they were charged with a crime but because the state decided that they were disturbed enough to require hospitalization. About 55 percent of admissions to public mental hospitals are involuntary (Brakel, 1985). Because it does not involve interesting crimes, civil commitment receives far less public attention than criminal commitment, yet the legal questions it involves are equally difficult and directly affect far more people.

Procedures for Commitment

The U.S. Constitution provides that the government may not deprive a person of life, liberty, or property without "due process of law." Involuntary commitment to a mental hospital is clearly a deprivation of liberty. What in the way of "due process," or legal procedures, is required before a person may be subjected to involuntary commitment? This is a question that the Supreme Court has not fully considered. Many lower courts have addressed it, but the answers they have given vary from jurisdiction to jurisdiction.

A useful way to approach the problem is to consider the rights that a defendant has in a criminal trial and then to ask whether a person faced with the possibility of involuntary civil commitment should have the same rights. Among other things, the following are guaranteed to persons accused of serious crimes: (1) a jury trial, (2) the assistance of counsel, (3) a right not to be compelled to incriminate themselves, and (4) the requirement that guilt be proved "beyond a reasonable doubt." Should these rights also apply to involuntary civil commitment?

The Right to a Jury Trial Today states typically require a formal judicial hearing before commitment (though the hearing may follow a brief period of emergency commitment). In fifteen states the defendant has a right to have a jury at such a hearing. Other states make no provision for a jury; the decision is rendered by the judge or a lower judicial officer.

The argument against a jury trial is that juries are expensive and time-consuming and furthermore that it is not in the best interests of mentally distressed people to have their psychological condition formally debated before a jury. The argument for a jury trial is that, distressed or otherwise, these people stand to lose their liberty, and that in a matter so serious, the judgment must come from the citizenry, just as in a criminal trial, for this is the best protection against oppression. (Keep in mind that many civil libertarians do feel that involuntary mental patients are akin to prisoners.) However, since the Supreme Court has ruled that jury trials are not required in juvenile cases, it is unlikely that the Court will require them in commitment cases (Brakel, 1985).

The Right to the Assistance of Counsel A central feature of the wave of reform in mental health law in the 1970s was the provision of court-appointed lawyers for people faced with involuntary-commitment proceedings. Prior to the 1970s, commitments were often made on physicians' certifications alone, with little due process (Turkheimer & Parry, 1992). Now, in almost all jurisdictions, people facing involuntary-commitment proceedings are provided with lawyers to protect their rights, but there is still considerable disagreement about what lawyers are supposed to do for their clients at such hearings (Leavitt & Maykuth, 1989).

In criminal trials, defense attorneys have a clear role: they are the adversaries of the prosecutor, and they are supposed to do everything they legally can to get their clients acquitted. It is not their job to worry about the legal question of the defendant's guilt or innocence. Should lawyers at commitment hearings behave in the same way—that is, as advocates for their clients' wishes? Or should they act instead as "guardians," pursuing their clients' best interests as they, the lawyers, see them? If we assume that some people are too disturbed to know what their best interests are, then lawyers who take the advocate role run the risk of acting against their clients' best interests. If, on the other hand, they take the guardian role, they may well act in direct opposition to the clients' wishes, deferring instead to the judgment of expert witnesses who claim hospitalization is necessary. Apparently most lawyers at commitment hearings do precisely that (Turkheimer & Perry, 1992)—a practice that is bitterly criticized by those who feel that clients should be allowed to decide what their best interests are.

The Right against Self-Incrimination Defendants at criminal trials have the right to remain silent, and their silence may not be used against them. The prosecutor is not even allowed to comment on their silence to the jury (Israel & LaFave, 1975). Should the same rule apply at a commitment hearing? Some people would say yes, that people threatened with commitment should have the same protections as those threatened with imprisonment, for they have as much, if not more, to lose. Others would say that since silence may be a symptom of serious mental disturbance, it is inappropriate to exclude it from the evidence. Should psychiatrists, for example, be barred from testifying that their diagnosis of psychotic depression is based in part on the patient's muteness? Like the matter of a jury, protection against self-incrimination has been variously interpreted by the states.

The Standard of Proof Finally, in a criminal trial a jury can convict only if the prosecution has proved guilt "beyond a reasonable doubt." The degree of certainty is called the **standard of proof.** The *beyond-a-reasonable-doubt* standard is a very high one—perhaps a 90 to 95 percent certainty. Should this requirement also apply to commitment hearings? There are other possibilities. In most civil proceedings (e.g., lawsuits), the standard of proof is the *preponderance of evidence*—in other words, "more likely than not," or at least 51 percent certainty (A. A. Stone, 1975). A third possibility is the far lower standard of proof used in medical diagnosis, where any evidence whatsoever—theoretically even a 5 to 10 percent certainty—may lead to diagnosis of illness. Which of these standards should apply in the case of involuntary commitment?

To answer this question, we must consider the seriousness of two possible errors: (1) a **false positive,** or an unjustified commitment, and (2) a **false negative,** or a failure to commit when commitment is in fact justified and necessary.* In a criminal trial, a false positive—that is, the conviction of an innocent person—is considered a far more serious error than a false negative—that is, the acquittal of a guilty person. In the famous words of the eighteenth-century English jurist William Blackstone, "It is better that ten guilty persons escape than one innocent suffer." Hence the extremely high standard of proof in criminal trials: "When in doubt, acquit."

In a civil proceeding, a false positive (the complainant's unjustifiably winning the lawsuit) is considered approximately as serious as a false neg-

*These terms are taken from the medical diagnostic vocabulary. A *false positive* is an incorrect diagnosis of illness; a *true positive,* a correct diagnosis of illness; a *false negative,* an incorrect diagnosis of no illness; a *true negative,* a correct diagnosis of no illness.

Advances in DNA testing have made possible the correction of a number of "false positives"—the conviction and imprisonment of innocent persons. Kerry Kotler (center, flanked by his attorneys) served eleven years in prison for rape before a comparison of the DNA in his blood with the DNA in a sample of semen used as evidence in his trial showed that he could not have committed the crime.

ative (the complainant's unjustifiably losing the lawsuit). Therefore the standard of proof falls in the middle: 51 percent certainty. In medical diagnosis, on the other hand, a false positive (a false diagnosis of illness) is considered a negligible error compared with the extremely serious mistake of a false negative (a false diagnosis of no illness). Imagine, for example, that a person is being tested for cancer and the physician finds only a few slightly suspicious cell changes. If the diagnosis is a false positive, this fact will emerge in the course of further testing, and the diagnosis will be changed, with no harm done. But a false-negative diagnosis may well eliminate the chance of the cancer's being treated at an early and perhaps curable stage. In other words, a great deal of harm will have been done. Hence the extremely low standard of proof in medicine: "When in doubt, diagnose illness."

Which standard we should apply at a commitment hearing depends on what we see as the purpose of commitment. Generally the law recognizes two justifications for involuntary commitment: the good of the patient and the good of society. At first glance, it would seem that when commitment is undertaken for the good of society (i.e., to protect people from harm by the patient), the criminal standard of proof should be used, since the issue in both cases is the same: public safety versus individual liberty. By the same token, it would seem that when commitment is sought for the good of the patient (e.g., so that he or she can be treated), the medical standard of proof should be applied.

Critics of civil commitment (e.g., Ennis & Emery, 1978) argue, however, that the medical standard should never be used, since commitment cases, no matter what their stated purpose, are not analogous to medical diagnosis. According to these writers, so-called good-of-the-patient commitments are often undertaken more for the sake of others—usually, the patient's family—than for the sake of the patient. Moreover, unlike medical diagnosis, a diagnosis to commit cannot be disproved, deprives the patient of liberty, stigmatizes the patient, and does not necessarily lead to treatment. For these reasons, among others, critics of commitment insist that no matter what the reason for commitment, the beyond-a-reasonable-doubt standard should be used. It should be added that in general, civil libertarians are extremely skeptical of procedures that are purportedly "for the good of the patient." Their skepticism extends beyond the lowered standard of proof to the nonjury hearing, the "guardian" lawyer, and the lack of protection against self-incrimination. In their opinion, an expressed attitude of concern for patients assumes that they are "guilty" and leads directly to a violation of their civil rights. If these people are threatened with loss of liberty as a result of socially offensive behavior, then they are in the same position as alleged criminals and should be accorded the same rights.

Unlike the other three procedural questions we have discussed, the standard of proof at commitment hearings *has* been dealt with by the Supreme Court. In the case of *Addington v. Texas* (1979) the defendant was a man whose mother had filed a petition to have him committed. The commitment was approved by a Texas court according to the preponderance-of-evidence standard. The defendant then appealed the decision, arguing that the need for hospitalization should be proved "beyond a reasonable doubt." The Supreme Court quickly rejected the preponderance-of-evidence standard (and by implication any less stringent standard) because of the liberty interest at stake. Yet the Court also rejected the criminal beyond-a-reasonable-doubt standard, for several reasons. The Court observed that unlike the wrongfully convicted criminal defendant, who would languish in prison until his sentence had been served, the wrongfully civilly committed person would probably be discharged, as doctors would recognize that hospitalization was unwarranted. Thus the false-positive error is less serious in the civil context than in the criminal context because of the greater opportunity to correct the error. The consequences of a false-negative error were also seen as different in the two contexts. A truly guilty criminal defendant benefits from a wrongful acquittal, whereas a truly mentally ill person who is not ordered to get treatment suffers from the absence of the needed treatment.

The Court thus used some of the notions underlying the medical decision rule as grounds for rejecting the beyond-a-reasonable-doubt standard. The Court adopted an intermediate standard of proof, called *clear and convincing evidence,* as the proper standard for commitment hearings. It corresponds to approximately "75 percent sure," higher than the ordinary civil standard but lower than the criminal one. This decision is to some extent a victory for the proponents of the criminal standard, in that it at least rules out the civil and medical standards and moves the required degree of certainty that much closer to the criminal standard. Nevertheless, it remains to be seen how jurors and judicial officers will interpret this standard of proof.

Standards for Commitment

So far we have dealt only with the procedures for commitment; we must now consider the *standards* for commitment. What must be proved in order to justify involuntary commitment?

Until the early 1970s, mental illness alone, or mental illness and "need for treatment," were sufficient grounds for involuntary commitment in many states. Then came the reform movement of the 1970s. Not just the general public but also judges and legislators read Szasz's *Myth of Mental Illness* (1961), and also Erving Goffman's *Asylums* (1961) and R. D. Laing's writings—all of them critical of the concept of mental illness and, above all, of involuntary hospitalization. As a result, there was a trend throughout the 1970s toward changing laws in such a way as to require evidence not just of mental illness but also of dangerousness to self and others as grounds for involuntary commitment (La Fond & Durham, 1992; McHugh, 1992).

The Definition of Dangerousness But how do we define dangerousness? Should it be confined to the threat of physical harm to oneself or others? What about emotional harm, such as schizophrenic parents may inflict on their children? What about economic harm, such as people in a manic episode may bring down upon their families by spending their life savings on foolish business ventures? What about harm to property? Various courts and legislatures have taken different positions on this matter, but some states do consider a threat of harm to property sufficient for commitment (La Fond & Durham, 1992).

The Determination of Dangerousness Whatever the definition of dangerousness, determining it is an extremely difficult matter. To say that someone is dangerous is to predict future behavior. The rarer an event, the harder it is to predict accurately. Hence if dangerousness is defined as homicide or suicide, both of which are rare events, the prediction of dangerousness will inevitably involve many unjustified commitments as well as justified ones. Consider, for example, the following hypothetical case:

> A man with classic paranoia exhibits in a clinical interview a fixed belief that his wife is attempting to poison him. He calmly states that on release he will be forced to kill her in self-defense. The experts agree that his condition is untreatable. Assume that statistical data indicate an eighty percent probability that homicide will occur. (Livermore, Malmquist, & Meehl, 1968)

What should the court do? Instinctively, it would seem correct to "play it safe" and commit the patient. (See the box on page 571). However, as the authors of this case point out, even accepting an 80 percent probability of homicide as sufficient to commit means committing twenty nonhomicidal people for every eighty homicidal ones.

Perhaps society could accept such a ratio. But the fact is that an 80 percent probability is unrealistically high. Despite public alarm over violence, murder is statistically rare: in any year, only 1 person in 10,000 in the United States commits homicide (Department of Justice, 1993), and mental patients without arrest records are no more likely than the general public to commit murder (Mon-

THE LIMITS OF CONFIDENTIALITY

On October 27, 1969, a student at the University of California at Berkeley named Prosenjit Poddar killed a young woman named Tatiana Tarasoff. Two months earlier, Poddar had told his therapist that he intended to commit the crime. Although the therapist then notified the police—who detained Poddar briefly but released him upon finding him "rational"—neither Tatiana Tarasoff nor her family was informed of Poddar's threat. After the murder, the young woman's parents brought suit against the therapist and the university that employed him, charging that they should have been warned about the man's intentions. The California Supreme Court agreed, holding that "when a therapist determines . . . that a patient presents a serious danger of violence to another, he incurs an obligation to use reasonable care to protect the intended victim against such danger" (*Tarasoff v. Regents of California,* 1976).

In effect, this ruling meant that psychotherapists have obligations to the society at large that override their obligations to their own patients. Traditionally, the relationship between therapist and patient has been considered privileged: information supplied by the patient is held in strict confidence by the therapist. According to this ruling, however, the therapist must divulge such information if the patient is "dangerous"; the police and the family of the threatened victim must be warned. As the court stated in its opinion, "the protective privilege ends where the public peril begins."

But where does the public peril begin? The prediction of dangerousness is an uncertain (if not impossible) task. As a dissenting opinion in this case pointed out, psychotherapists find it difficult enough to diagnose mental illness itself, without also having to predict whether a patient will or will not be dangerous at some time in the future.

The *Tarasoff* decision was widely denounced by mental health professionals. The psychiatrist Alan Stone (1976), for example, wrote that "the imposition of a duty to protect, which may take the form of a duty to warn threatened third parties, will imperil the therapeutic alliance and destroy the patient's expectation of confidentiality, thereby thwarting effective treatment and ultimately reducing the public safety" (p. 368). Under circumstances of reduced confidentiality, a patient who felt a compulsion to do violence might well be reluctant to confide it to a therapist. Potentially dangerous patients might be unwilling to seek therapy at all, for fear that the police would ultimately deal with them. On the other side, therapists, to avoid lawsuits, would be encouraged to report all threats of violence to potential victims and to the police—or even to seek the commitment of "dangerous" patients to avoid possible harm to others and to themselves.

In fact, the impact of the *Tarasoff* decision has not been noticeably negative (Appelbaum, 1994). According to surveys of psychotherapists, it has not seriously affected the way they handle threats, for they were accustomed to taking some protective measures already, simply on ethical grounds (Gouelber, Bowers, & Blitch, 1985). As law professor David Wexler (1981) has pointed out, *Tarasoff* could even have a positive impact on treatment. Since 80 to 90 percent of people threatened by patients in therapy are family members or lovers (J. MacDonald, 1967), the prospective victim could be encouraged to participate in "conjoint," or family, therapy with the patient. Direct discussion of the patient's anger and the potential victim's role in precipitating violence might serve to reduce the likelihood of such violence. Despite these potential benefits, however, many therapists still view the *Tarasoff* decision as threatening to the therapeutic process (Appelbaum & Gutheil, 1991).

ahan, 1981). Further, very few patients threatened with commitment will calmly state in a clinical interview that they intend to commit murder upon release. In many cases, for example, the evidence for possible future homicide is simply a report from a family member that in the past the patient has threatened homicide, perhaps in a moment of extreme anger. In such a case, the probability of homicide would be very low—probably less than 1 percent. Is this a ratio that society can accept? If in criminal law it is better that ten guilty people go free than that one innocent person suffer, how can we say that in cases of civil commitment it is better for ninety-nine harmless people to be locked up than for one dangerous person to go free?

In addition to the rarity of dangerous behavior, several other factors tend to swell the number of false positives in predictions of dangerousness (Monahan, 1976). These factors include:

1 *Lack of corrective feedback.* Since patients who are judged to be dangerous are institutionalized, there is no opportunity to find out whether they would in fact have been dangerous if released.
2 *Differential consequences to the predictor.* False negatives (people who are released and turn out to be dangerous) create very bad publicity. False positives (people who are committed when in fact they are harmless) do not.
3 *Unreliability of the criterion.* The only hard evi-

dence for a prediction of dangerousness is the patient's past record of *detected* violence, which may be unrepresentative. Knowing this, clinicians may tend to "play it safe."

4 *Powerlessness of the subject.* Until recently, people erroneously committed on the grounds of dangerousness had little power to oppose this decision.

All of these factors encourage mental health professionals to err in the direction of overpredicting dangerousness. Do they in fact do so? Studies of predictions of dangerousness have yielded far more false positives than false negatives (Grisso, 1991). But such studies may have inherent limitations, for they are based on predictions from an institutional context applied to a real-world context. In most of these studies, mental health professionals were asked to predict the likelihood of dangerous behavior in patients about to be released from institutions. Since there is considerable evidence that human behavior is situation-specific, changing as we move from classroom to work to home, it is no surprise that predictions of real-world behavior based on institutional behavior have turned out to have poor validity (Monahan & Steadman, 1994).

Furthermore, this is not actually the kind of prediction that is made at commitment hearings. At such hearings, mental health professionals are called upon to predict real-world behavior on the basis of reports of the patient's prior real-world behavior and of interviews with the patient. But we have little means of determining the validity of such predictions. It is not feasible to have mental health professionals evaluate the dangerousness of a large number of people threatened with commitment and then release all those people and keep track of them to find out whether they bore out the predictions made for them. The knowledge to be gained from such an experiment would not justify the hazard to society.

Recent research has provided clear evidence that there is a connection between mental illness and dangerousness: mental patients experiencing psychotic symptoms do commit violent acts at a rate several times higher than that of the general population. But this higher risk exists only during the presence of psychotic symptoms, and in any event it is modest compared with other risk factors such as drug or alcohol abuse (Monahan, 1992). Violent acts associated with mental illness clearly account for only a tiny portion of the violence in our society. Accordingly, some experts seriously question the wisdom of tying commitment criteria to predictions of dangerousness.

The "Thank-You" Proposition What, then, *should* the courts use as a basis for commitment decisions? In place of dangerousness, A. A. Stone (1975) has offered the "thank-you" proposition. It runs as follows: If a person is suffering from mental illness, if a treatment is available to relieve that illness, and if the patient refuses treatment on grossly irrational grounds (e.g., "Don't come near me—I'm radioactive"), then the involuntary commitment for the sake of providing that treatment is justified. After the treatment is provided, the patient will be grateful that his or her wishes were disregarded, just as children who are required to go to school are grateful, as adults, that education was forced on them. Stone's proposition has been criticized on the grounds that most involuntarily treated patients do *not* in fact become grateful for their treatment (Ennis & Emery, 1978). Research on this issue has yielded mixed results (L. Roth, 1979). Nevertheless, the proposition does at least have the virtue of stressing the patient's welfare—a matter that is not prominently featured in the dangerousness rule. Critics of involuntary commitment would respond that many wrongs have been inflicted on patients because of someone's judgment of what is in the patient's best interest. A version of Stone's proposition was adopted by the American Psychiatric Association in its model commitment law in 1983 (Stromberg & Stone, 1983).

Expert Testimony in Civil Commitment Whatever the standard for involuntary commitment, whether dangerousness or the expectation of gratitude, expert testimony will continue to be called for. As we saw earlier, many legal scholars feel that criminal courts rely too much on the opinions of mental health professionals. The same problem exists at commitment hearings. To say what mental health professionals should and should not rule upon in commitment cases requires certain fine distinctions, but they are distinctions that must be made. At commitment hearings psychologists and psychiatrists may be asked, "How dangerous is this patient?" Though they may have only limited ability to respond to this question, it is still not an improper question to put to them. However, expert witnesses are frequently asked not only how dangerous patients are but whether they are *too dangerous to be released,* and this is not a proper question for the expert witness to answer. How dangerous a person must be in order to be deprived of his or her freedom is not a mental health question but a legal and moral question. It involves weighing the person's interest in liberty against the society's interest in public safety, and the weighing of these competing interests is the business not of the mental health profession but of the court (Morse, 1978). Similarly, if involuntary commitment is sought on the basis of the thank-you proposition, the proper question for the expert witness would be "What is the probability that the patient will later be grateful for having been treated involuntarily?" or at a minimum, "How effective is the treatment likely to be?" How high that probability must be in order to justify involuntary treatment is again a legal and moral issue that only the courts or the legislatures can decide.

Making Commitment Easier During the 1970s, as we saw, nearly all states tightened their standards for civil commitment. Then in the 1980s several states decided they had gone too far, and they amended their laws so as to make commitment easier. For example, threats to engage in violent conduct would not have qualified a person for commitment under a typical 1970s statute. But in the 1980s some state legislatures determined that such threats alone did justify commitment. In other states danger to property was insufficient for commitment in the 1970s but was added to commitment criteria in the 1980s (La Fond & Durham, 1992).

Despite the controversies that commitment criteria often generate, most research reveals little long-term effect of changes in commitment criteria on the type or number of persons committed (Appelbaum, 1994). Here, as in the case with the definition of insanity in the criminal law, decisions seem to be made intuitively, with official definitions and standards having only a small effect.

The Case against Involuntary Commitment Just as some people have argued against the insanity plea, some argue that civil commitment itself should be abolished (Morse, 1982; Szasz, 1963). They maintain that people who engage in criminal activity should be dealt with by the criminal justice system; those who do not should simply be left alone. "Disturbed" people who truly were dangerous would ultimately find themselves subject to the criminal justice system. This, the proponents argue, would be a benefit—both because of the greater procedural safeguards of the criminal process (trial by jury, etc.) and because of the fixed sentences of the criminal system (in contrast to the indeterminate "sentences" of the mental health system).

Those who argue that there should be *no* involuntary commitment are in the minority, however. Proponents of commitment find flaws in the argument for abolition, at least insofar as it relies on a comparison between commitment and imprisonment. Although the criminal justice system would seem to offer more protection to individual rights, the widespread practice of plea bargaining often acts to negate these legal safeguards (Brooks, 1974). Any procedural protections a defendant has may mean little in a system in which over 90 percent of all defendants plead guilty (Alschuler, 1979) in exchange for a reduced sentence. The distinction between fixed sentences for criminal defendants and indeterminate "sentences" for those involuntarily committed is also not completely compelling. Modern commitment statutes often put limits on involuntary commitment, though these limits are usually subject to extension through further judicial review (Brakel, 1985).

Nevertheless, the argument against involuntary commitment has gained a certain measure of support, particularly among civil libertarians. In their view, innocent people should never be confined in institutions against their will, no matter how "crazy" their behavior in some eyes or how convincingly it can be argued that they need therapy.

PATIENTS' RIGHTS

Until recently, people who were deprived of their liberty on the grounds that they were mentally ill and dangerous were usually deprived of most of their other civil rights as well. Once institutionalized, they were largely at the mercy of the institution, which decided for them what privileges and duties they should have and what treatments, if any, they should undergo (Appelbaum, 1994). Today there is a strong trend toward guaranteeing patients certain basic rights, especially the right to treatment, the right to refuse certain types of treatment, and the right to decent living conditions.

The Right to Treatment

For decades the need for treatment has served as a justification, explicit or implicit, for involuntary commitment. However, it was not until the 1960s that the courts suggested that involuntary mental patients had a constitutional *right* to treatment. And it was not until the following decade that this right was spelled out, by an Alabama federal court in the case of *Wyatt v. Stickney* (1972), which has already been discussed briefly in Chapter 18. In this case, the state of Alabama was accused of failure to provide adequate treatment for those confined in its hospitals for the mentally disabled and retarded. As it turned out, treatment was not all that these hospitals failed to provide. In the two institutions where the case originated, conditions were shocking. The wards were filthy, dark, and chaotic. The food was barely edible. (The state at that time spent less than fifty cents a day on food for each patient.) As for treatment, both of the institutions had well over a thousand patients for every psychologist. Needless to say, no treatment was being given under these conditions. As one expert witness put it, these were neither treatment facilities nor even facilities for "care" or "custody," since these words imply safekeeping. Rather, they were storage facilities.

In deciding the case against the state, the court ruled that it was a violation of due process to deny people their liberty on the grounds that they needed treatment and then to provide no treatment. The court went on to state that all Alabama mental institutions must provide (1) an individualized treatment program for each patient, (2) skilled staff in sufficient numbers to administer such treatment, and (3) a humane psychological and physical environment. This decision, then, established the right to treatment, at least in Alabama. Although binding only in Alabama, the *Wyatt* decision has influenced mental health procedures across the country. Several states have passed revised mental health codes that incorporate most aspects of the *Wyatt* decision.

The next major case to touch upon the right-to-treatment issue was the highly publicized case of *O'Connor v. Donaldson* (1975), mentioned earlier. Kenneth Donaldson had been institutionalized involuntarily in 1957 on the petition of his father. The father claimed that Donaldson had delusions that people were poisoning his food. This testimony, along with the fact that Donaldson had been institutionalized for three months thirteen years earlier, led the judge to conclude that Donaldson should be committed. He was sent to a Florida state mental hospital, and there he remained for fourteen years. During this time he was given no treatment that could realistically be expected to cure or improve his "condition." He petitioned repeatedly for his release. Finally, under threat of a lawsuit, the hospital authorities discharged him. He then sued them for damages and ultimately settled for $20,000. The Supreme Court ruled that "a finding of mental illness alone cannot justify a State's locking a person up against his will and keeping him indefinitely in simple custodial confinement."

Though it has been hailed as a victory for right-to-treatment advocates, the *Donaldson* ruling, strictly speaking, has to do with the right to liberty rather than the right to treatment. (And even on the right to liberty it is somewhat vague. For example, if a person is found to be dangerous as well as mentally ill, can he or she then be subjected to simple custodial confinement?) However, it does at least lend indirect support to the view that involuntary patients have a constitutional right to treatment (Ennis & Emery, 1978).

The Supreme Court did not directly address the right-to-treatment issue until the case of *Youngberg v. Romeo* (1982). The lawsuit had been initiated on behalf of Nicholas Romeo, a resident of a state institution for the retarded in Pennsylvania. Romeo had been injured on numerous occasions, both by himself and by other residents. On several occasions he was placed in physical restraints to prevent harm to himself and others. The Supreme Court held that involuntarily committed mentally retarded people—and presumably mentally ill people as well—have a constitutional right to "conditions of reasonable care and safety, reasonably non-restrictive confinement conditions, and such training as may be required by these interests." The Court emphasized, however, that treatment decisions made by professionals are "presumptively valid" and that courts should not second-guess the judgment of professionals responsible for the care of patients. Thus this decision provides a subtle shift in emphasis from absolute patient rights to support for decisions made by mental health professionals.

The Court did not decide whether there is a constitutional right to treatment per se, apart from any impact such treatment may have on safety and freedom from restraints. This is a question that remains to be addressed in a future Supreme Court decision.

The Right to Refuse Treatment

If mental patients have a right to treatment, do they also have a right to refuse treatment? This question was addressed in a 1990 case involving a man, Walter Harper, serving a prison sentence for robbery in the state of Washington. Harper was sometimes violent—a condition the prison doctors said was due to manic-depressive illness. At times, Harper took the antipsychotic medication the doctors prescribed for him. At other times, he refused. The prison had a policy whereby medication could be administered over a prisoner's objection if a panel consisting of a psychiatrist, a psychologist, and a prison administrator held a hearing and determined that the prisoner was likely, without the medication, to do serious harm to himself or others as a result of mental illness. Harper claimed that this procedure was not sufficient to protect his constitutional rights in light of the recognized health risks involved in antipsychotic drugs. He therefore sued the state of Washington, arguing that medication over his objection should not be permitted unless a *judge* determined it was necessary.

Harper's suit ultimately reached the Supreme Court (*Washington v. Harper,* 1990), which upheld the constitutionality of the prison's policy on the grounds that decisions regarding the necessity of medication should be made by doctors, not judges. So again, as in the Romeo case, the Court affirmed the "presumptive validity" of treatment decisions made by mental health professionals.

It remains to be seen how this decision will affect lower courts, which generally take a more limited view of the authority of doctors. In any case, the right to refuse treatment is still an open question. We have already discussed one possible solution: Stone's thank-you proposition, which states that if treatment is refused on irrational grounds, it should be administered involuntarily, for the patient's own good. However, Stone's proposition seems to assume that treatment will be effective and that it will not have harmful side effects—a very unsafe assumption. As we have seen in earlier chapters, the history of psychological treatment is replete with unpleasant surprises. When iproniazid was introduced as a treatment for depression, no one knew that it caused liver damage. When chlorpromazine was put on the market, no one knew that it could cause tardive dyskinesia. (In the case of Walter Harper, the risk of tardive dyskinesia was the primary grounds for refusal of treatment.) Thus there is no reason to assume that when patients refuse treatment, they are refusing something that will truly work for their good. Furthermore, as civil rights advocates have pointed out, to deprive mental patients of any control over treatment is to make them vulnerable to a wide range of abuses.

But what if a patient's refusal does in fact seem grossly irrational? Or what if it is not grossly irrational but nevertheless infringes on the rights of others? Assume that a depressed suicidal woman, involuntarily hospitalized, refuses electroconvulsive therapy (ECT), insisting instead on antidepressant drugs, which may not be as effective. Should the hospital assign one of its staff members to watch over the patient day and night to make sure she doesn't commit suicide? If so, what about the rights of the other patients, who are then deprived of that staff member's services? One might answer at this point that since the woman made the choice, she should not be given special treatment; if she commits suicide, that is her decision. But surely the hospital has the duty to prevent suicides on its premises, particularly since it cannot be therapeutic for other patients to watch people kill themselves (A. A. Stone, 1975). Should the patient be coerced into receiving a particular treatment because less elaborate security measures would then be required?

State statutes and regulations regarding the right to refuse treatment vary considerably (Reisner, 1985), but the general rule is that involuntary patients may be required to undergo "routine" treatment, which may include psychotropic medication—a rule that will no doubt be strengthened by the Supreme Court's decision in the Harper case. More controversial forms of treatment, such as ECT, are usually regulated more closely, and consent from the patient or next of kin or, in some states, a court order may be required.

The Right to a Humane Environment

As we saw above, the decision in the case of *Wyatt v. Stickney* affirmed not only the right to treatment but also the right to a humane environment. What the court meant by a humane environment is spelled out in the decision. The following is only a partial list of the minimum requirements:

1 Patients have a right to privacy and dignity.
2 An opportunity must exist for voluntary religious worship on a nondiscriminatory basis.
3 Dietary menus must be satisfying and nutritionally adequate to provide the recommended daily dietary allowances. Nutritionally adequate meals must not be withheld as punishment.
4 Within multipatient sleeping rooms, screens or curtains must be provided to ensure privacy. Each patient must be furnished with a comfortable bed, a closet or locker for personal belongings, a chair, and a bedside table.
5 Toilets must be installed in separate stalls to ensure privacy. If a central bathing area is provided, showers must be separated by curtains to ensure privacy.
6 Patients have a right to wear their own clothes

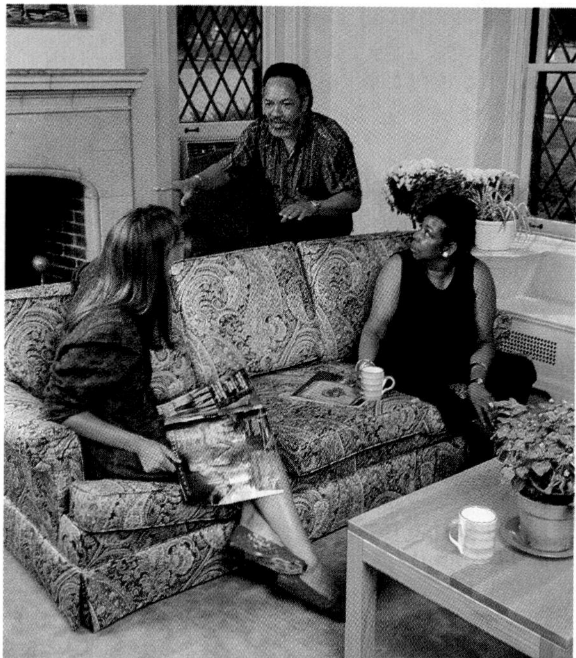

Modern mental institutions like the Westchester Division of New York Hospital–Cornell Medical Center, pictured here, provide the human environment that is now widely recognized as a right of mental patients.

and to keep and use their own personal possessions.*

7 Patients have the same rights to visitation and telephone communications as patients at other public hospitals.*

8 Patients have an unrestricted right to send and receive mail.*

9 Patients have a right to regular physical exercise several times a week as well as a right to be out of doors at regular and frequent intervals.

10 An opportunity must exist for interaction with members of the opposite sex (*Wyatt v. Stickney*, 1972, pp. 379–383). (Apropos of this last right, see the box on page 577.)

In addition, the *Wyatt* decision addressed the matter of work requirements imposed on institutionalized patients. For years mental institutions have used patients as a supplementary work force. Throughout the country mental patients clear tables, wash dishes, scrub floors, feed other patients, and otherwise help to maintain the institutions in which they live. For their work they often receive some reward—perhaps a small allowance or special privileges—but this reward in no way approximates the compensation that would be expected for such work in the outside world. The *Wyatt* ruling declared this practice unconstitutional. The court ruled that patients may not be required to do any work aimed at maintaining the institution in which they live. If, however, they *volunteer* for such work, they must be given at least minimum-wage compensation for it. The point is that involuntary patients, by definition, do not ask to be committed to an institution. If the society chooses to commit them and then compels them to work without pay, their position is essentially that of slaves. (Indeed, this practice has been referred to as "institutional peonage.") Subsequent rulings by other courts have reaffirmed the *Wyatt* position on this matter. And though in many states mental patients are still assigned unpaid jobs in the hospital kitchen or laundry, the practice may well be on its way out.

*The asterisks indicate rights that may be abridged if, in the judgment of a mental health professional, their exercise is detrimental to the patient's safety or welfare.

Behavior Therapy and Patients' Rights

Almost every issue raised in this chapter is the subject of intense debate between those concerned primarily with the constitutional rights of mental patients and those concerned primarily with what they consider the "best interests" of such patients. The issue of a humane environment is no exception. On the one hand, it seems indisputable that if a society confines people to mental hospitals against their will, either to protect itself or to help them, then the people in question should be free from forced labor and should be provided with simple amenities that the rest of us take for granted—a comfortable bed, nourishing meals, privacy in the bathroom, and so forth. To treat them otherwise would seem quite improper. On the other hand, the guarantee of these rights may directly conflict with a mode of therapy that has proved most effective with long-term institutionalized patients: behavior therapy.

As we saw in earlier chapters, behavioral techniques for chronic patients tend to be contingency management techniques, the most widespread and useful being the token economy. The principle on which these techniques work is that patients are given reinforcers as rewards for socially desirable behaviors. In many cases, however, these reinforcers are the very same items and activities that such decisions as *Wyatt* have affirmed are absolute rights. If patients have an absolute right to stall showers or to curtains around their beds, you cannot offer them these things in return for making their beds

SEX, LIVES, AND MENTAL PATIENTS: THE HOSPITAL'S DILEMMA IN THE AGE OF AIDS

The Supreme Court's decision in *Wyatt v. Stickney* (1972) stipulates that mental patients have the right to interact with the opposite sex. How far should interaction go? Before the AIDS epidemic, little was said about this question, nor was it felt that anything needed to be said. Now and then, a hospitalized patient would be found to be pregnant or to have a sexually transmitted disease—usually curable—and these problems were handled somehow. But as long as patients conducted their sex lives in private, hospitals had little incentive (or, many thought, legal or ethical justification) to prevent consensual sexual contact between patients. Especially in state mental hospitals, where patients were often shut in for years, sometimes decades, efforts to prevent sexual behavior in private have often been thought cruel.

But that was before AIDS. What now? Are hospitalized mental patients competent to accept the risk of HIV infection? If the hospital knows a particular patient to be HIV-infected, should the staff warn the other patients? Or just warn them about AIDS and make condoms available?

The problem with these approaches is that they assume that the patients are competent to assess the risks of HIV infection and act appropriately if properly informed. Recent court cases strongly suggest that for most patients, this assumption is unfounded. While there are only a few cases that explicitly address the competence of mentally disabled people to consent to sex, two recent decisions, one from Idaho and one from the state of Washington, require a high degree of understanding before the legal standard for competence is satisfied. The Idaho case, *State v. Soura* (1990), involved a mentally retarded woman (IQ of 71) living with her husband. She had sexual relations with another man, who was then charged with and convicted of rape on the grounds that the woman was not competent to consent. The Supreme Court of Idaho upheld the conviction, explaining that even though the woman was competent to engage in marital sex, she was not competent to engage in extramarital sex, because the former is safe while the latter is dangerous. One of the dangers mentioned was AIDS. The Washington case, *State v. Summers* (1993), involved a mentally ill woman living in a group home. She too was found incompetent to consent to sex. The conviction of her sex partner was upheld on the grounds that although she "had a basic understanding of the mechanical act of sexual intercourse," she did not understand its "nature and consequences," including the risk of AIDS.

The issue of sex between mental patients remains virtually undiscussed (Perlin, 1993–1994), but in view of these decisions, it will have to be addressed soon. If mental hospitals are to maintain conditions of reasonable safety for their patients, they will probably have to take measures to limit the sexual opportunities of their HIV-positive patients.

or completing a reading program. They are entitled to them no matter what they do. A related problem arises with the ban on compulsory labor. Many token economies have used institution-maintaining work as a target response that earns reinforcers. If such work must be compensated by the minimum wage, then institutions may prefer to hire nonpatient labor rather than encourage patients to acquire work skills. In sum, "patients' rights" may make contingency management within institutions more difficult (Wexler, 1981).

Another aspect of behavior therapy that is now being carefully restricted is the use of aversive techniques. As we saw in Chapter 19, aversive techniques are not widely used either inside or outside institutions, but in extreme cases therapists have used hand slapping and even electric shock to suppress severely self-injurious behavior. Such practices are coming under increasing legal regulation. In the *Wyatt* decision, for example, the court ruled that electric shock could be used only "in extraordinary circumstances to prevent self-mutilation leading to repeated and possibly permanent physical damage to the resident and only after alternative techniques have failed" (*Wyatt v. Stickney*, 1972, pp. 400–401).

To the dismay of many behavior therapists, the courts have tended to regard time-out as a punishment procedure requiring extensive regulation. As we saw in Chapter 19, time-out is technically an extinction technique, not punishment. It does not involve the application of aversive stimuli; it removes the patient from the presence of reinforcing stimuli. But perhaps out of fear that patients will simply be locked up in time-out rooms indefinitely, like prisoners in solitary confinement, the courts have severely limited the use of time-out, and some have prohibited it altogether. Behavior therapists have shown that time-out procedures are often the most effective and least intrusive procedures available to deal with violent behavior. If time-out is prohibited, the alternatives are often physical restraints or large doses of sedatives. The *Romeo* case, described earlier, however, suggests that therapists will be given considerable latitude in using emergency management procedures. It has been suggested (Wexler, 1982) that if time-out procedures are used only to prevent or interrupt seriously dangerous or destructive behaviors, they will continue to be allowed. The use of time-out in nonemergency situations is still being debated.

Many behavior therapists feel that their techniques have been unfairly singled out by the courts. To some extent this may be true. In the last decade there have been a couple of notorious cases in which mental patients have been cruelly abused in programs masquerading as behavioral aversion therapy. In one case, mentally ill prisoners at the Iowa Security Medical Facility were punished for minor rule violations by injections of apomorphine, a drug that induces continuous vomiting for about fifteen minutes (*Knecht v. Gillman*, 1973). The supposed justification for this program was that an aversion to antisocial behavior was being conditioned. However, the rule infractions that resulted in this treatment—failure to get out of bed, giving cigarettes against orders, talking, swearing, lying—are not serious antisocial actions that threaten society. What the hospital administrators were in fact doing was using a cruel punishment to terrify mental patients into cooperating with rules. Such procedures do not constitute behavior therapy; behaviorists find them as appalling as anyone else would. Nevertheless, because this and other abusive programs have been "justified" by their administrators as applications of behavioral psychology, the courts have cast an extremely suspicious eye on behavioral techniques in general.

There are other reasons for the emphasis on behavior therapy in the recent patients' rights decisions. First, because many behavioral techniques are still relatively new, they have come under close scrutiny (G. L. Paul & Lentz, 1977). Second, behavior therapy is highly specific and concrete. It is far easier to weigh the dangers of a procedure in which identifiable actions are taken and concrete things are given or withheld than it is to evaluate a process such as insight therapy. Finally, while much less intrusive than medication, electroconvulsive therapy, or psychosurgery, behavior therapy may cause patients distress. They may have to do things that are difficult for them, or they may be deprived of something that they want, or in rare cases they may actually experience physical pain. This makes behavior therapy easier to criticize, no matter how positive its results. By contrast, psychodynamic therapy may be of no help to chronic patients, but it is hard to say how such therapy could cause them pain either.

If in fact the courts severely limit behavior therapy for institutionalized patients, they may be working against these patients' best interests. As we saw in Chapter 20, there is good evidence that at least with chronic schizophrenics, a token economy in combination with individualized behavioral programs results in a greater increase in adaptive behavior, a greater decrease in bizarre and violent behavior, and a higher rate of release than either of the other two treatments available to such patients, milieu therapy and traditional custodial care (G. L. Paul & Lentz, 1977).

Could contingency management procedures be modified in such a way as to conform to decisions such as *Wyatt?* For example, instead of making breakfast contingent upon bedmaking, you might provide a very plain breakfast noncontingently and then offer a fancy breakfast as a reward for bedmaking (Wexler, 1981). It remains to be seen, however, whether chronic patients would appreciate such gradations. Often it is primary reinforcers—breakfast, not enhancements of breakfast—that are most effective with chronic mental patients.

Another possibility is that the superior effectiveness of behavior therapy, at least with chronic patients, will eventually encourage the courts to ease some restrictions. So far the courts have been concerned primarily with the adequacy of treatment. When they start to focus on the results of treatment—establishing the right to *effective* treatment—the courts may find that previous patients' rights decisions have severely restricted the effective treatments. Should this happen, some of those restrictions may have to be eased.

POWER AND THE MENTAL HEALTH PROFESSION

The thrust of most of the recent court decisions discussed in this chapter is the same: to limit the power of the mental health profession. Yet the power of psychological professionals is still immense. To begin with, it is the mental health profession that declares, in the form of the *DSM*, which among the countless variations of human behavior are abnormal. This is a momentous decision—and one that psychologists and psychiatrists have a questionable right to make. Many homosexuals, for example, find it bitter to recall that in 1973 the American Psychiatric Association *voted* on the normality of their sexual preference. Presumably, if a condition were severe enough to be labeled abnormal, it should not require a vote.

Whether or not mental health professionals are qualified to make such decisions, they do in fact make them, and the decisions carry tremendous weight. The very word *abnormal,* as used in psychology, implies a need for change. Thus, included in the power to decide what behavior is abnormal is the power to decide who and what needs changing in our society. Again, do mental health professionals have the right to make this decision? Many people feel that the major cause of psychological disturbance in our society is not individual genes or parent-child relationships but poverty. What is the probability that mental health professionals—who are largely middle-class people of middle to high income—will be especially sensitive to this problem?

Finally, as we have seen, psychological professionals are often the ones who determine whether people identified as mentally disturbed should be institutionalized and whether those who are currently institutionalized should be released. It is hard to imagine a one-to-one relationship in our society that involves greater power than this, for what situation in our society involves a greater loss of power than involuntary commitment?

The powers held by the mental health profession are now being disputed. Numerous groups—women, ethnic minorities, the poor—have asked why a professional class traditionally made up largely of affluent white males should be given such broad authority. It has been argued that the mental health profession suffers from a tradition of paternalism that permits a handful of "experts" to determine the fate of a large part of the rest of the population. Just as the consumer movement has demanded of the automobile industry that cars be equipped with safety devices and of food manufacturers that harmful chemicals be removed from packaged foods, so a "consumer" movement has made demands on the mental health profession. In this case, the demands have been for a sharing of information between professionals and laypeople, so that those who need therapy can give it their *informed consent.* This implies, of course, the right to say no and the right to question the therapist. Patients for whom ECT is recommended should be told that their memory may be impaired by the procedure; those for whom drugs are prescribed should be told about side effects. Alternative treatments—and alternatives to treatment—should be discussed. When information is shared in this way, power is diffused and abuses are less likely.

KEY TERMS

civil commitment (567)
false negative (568)
false positive (568)
indeterminate sentences (566)
insanity defense (561)
standard of proof (568)

SUMMARY

- Mental health law deals with both the legal responsibility and the constitutional rights of those people judged to be mentally disturbed. These rapidly changing laws address three major issues: psychological disturbance and criminal responsibility, involuntary civil commitment, and patients' rights.
- Abnormal behavior may also be illegal behavior. The insanity defense is designed to protect those who are not morally responsible for committing crimes because of mental disturbance. The test of insanity is based on the irresistible-impulse decision of 1834; the M'Naghten rule, handed down by a British court in 1843; and the Durham test. The American Law Institute's formulation of the insanity defense places the burden of deciding a defendant's moral responsibility on the jury rather than on mental health professionals.
- After the Hinckley case, several states adopted a new verdict of "guilty but mentally ill" to serve as an intermediate between "guilty" and "not guilty by reason of insanity." The Hinckley case was also largely responsible for shifting the burden of proof in insanity cases from the prosecution to the defense.
- There are three major criticisms of the insanity defense. First, the jury is asked to make a judgment that is both subjective and retrospective and that often relies on conflicting testimony. A second criticism based on the views of Thomas Szasz, contends that what a jury is asked to judge—insanity—does not exist and that courts should judge people solely on their behavior, not on their intentions. Third, for those who successfully plead insanity, commitment to a mental hospital is in essence an indeterminate sentence, having no limit.
- Competency is another legal issue in criminal trials. Defendants must be judged mentally competent to stand trial; that is, they must understand the nature of the proceedings against them and be able to assist counsel in their own defense.

- One controversy surrounding competency is whether incompetent defendants should be detained in jail. Another is whether defendants are competent who only fulfill the competency requirement when under the influence of antipsychotic drugs.
- Involuntary civil commitment to a mental hospital raises serious legal questions. The Supreme Court has failed to establish specific legal procedures necessary before a person may be involuntarily committed, and lower courts have differed on the issue. As a result, a person faced with involuntary civil commitment may not have the same legal rights that a criminal defendant has.
- The Supreme Court has held that a person cannot be involuntarily committed to a mental institution without "clear and convincing" evidence that he or she is committable. Typically, statutes require that to be committable, a person must be found mentally ill and dangerous. "Dangerous" behavior, however, is open to interpretation, and predictions of such behavior are shaky at best.
- One possible standard for involuntary commitment is the "thank-you" proposition, which states that patients should be involuntarily committed and treated if it is likely that they will benefit from such treatment. Whatever the standard for commitment, distinctions must be made between mental health questions, which psychologists and psychiatrists are qualified to answer, and legal and moral questions, which should be left to the courts.
- The third major issue in mental health law is patients' rights, including the right to treatment, the right to refuse treatment, and the right to decent living conditions. These rights may conflict with some techniques used in behavior therapy: legally guaranteed rights and amenities can no longer be withheld to reinforce desired behavior. Also, it is now questionable whether certain behavioral techniques are legal.
- The mental health profession has the power to determine what is "normal" and whether people judged to be abnormal should be institutionalized. Court decisions limiting this power and challenges from numerous advocate groups indicate that the relationship between the mental health profession and society is in transition.

GLOSSARY

ABAB design An experimental research design that seeks to confirm a treatment effect by showing that behavior changes systematically with alternate conditions of no treatment (A) and treatment (B). **5**

absence seizures Brief generalized epileptic seizures during which patients, usually children, seem to absent themselves from their surroundings. **16**

acquired dysfunction A sexual dysfunction that develops after at least one episode of normal functioning. **13**

acquired immune deficiency syndrome (AIDS) A disease caused by the human immunodeficiency virus (HIV), which attacks the immune system, making patients susceptible to infection. **9**

acrophobia The fear of high places. **7**

action therapy The approach to psychotherapy that focuses on correcting problem behaviors by teaching the patient new skills. **19**

active phase The second stage of schizophrenia, during which the patient begins showing prominent psychotic symptoms. **14**

acute Referring to patients who are in the midst of the short-term active phase of their first schizophrenic episode. *Cf.* **chronic. 14.**

addiction A physiological dependence on a drug in which the drug use has altered the body's chemistry to the point where its "normal state" is the drugged state. **12**

agitated depression A form of depression characterized by incessant activity and restlessness. **10**

agnosia A disturbance in the ability to recognize familiar objects. **16**

agoraphobia A complication of panic disorder characterized by fear of being in any situation from which escape might be difficult and in which help would be unavailable in the event of panic symptoms. **7**

alternating personality A form of dissociative identity disorder in which two identities alternate with each other, each having amnesia for the thoughts and actions of the other. **8**

Alzheimer's disease An organic brain disorder characterized by cognitive deficits such as failure of concentration and memory. The disease can occur as early as age forty, but its prevalence increases with age. **16**

amnesia The partial or total forgetting of past experiences. It can be associated with organic brain syndromes or with psychological stress. **8**

amniocentesis A clinical procedure that can identify abnormal chromosomes in a developing fetus. **18**

amphetamines A group of synthetic stimulants—the most common of which are Benzedrine, Dexedrine, and Methedrine—which reduce feelings of boredom or weariness. **12**

anal stage In psychodynamic theory, the second stage of psychosocial development, in which the child's focus is on the pleasurable feelings of retaining and expelling the feces; occurs in the second year of life. **2**

analogue experiments Experimental situations that attempt to reproduce, under controlled conditions, the essential features of naturally occurring psychopathology or its treatment. **5**

anhedonia A mood abnormality among schizophrenics in which the person's experience of pleasure is reduced. Often experienced by people during major depressive episodes, the inability to enjoy accustomed activities leads to a lack of interest in those activities. **10, 14**

anomie Merton's term for a feeling of normlessness that exists in disadvantaged groups. Such a feeling may contribute to the development of antisocial personalities found in some members of such groups. **11**

anorexia nervosa Chronic failure to eat for fear of gaining weight. Occurring usually among adolescent girls and young women, the disorder results in severe malnutrition, semistarvation, and sometimes death. **17**

antianxiety drugs Drugs used to reduce tension and anxiety. They are used by normal people during times of stress and by people undergoing psychological treatment for anxiety disorders, stress-related physical disorders, and withdrawal from alcohol and other drugs. Also called *minor tranquilizers.* **21**

antidepressant drugs Drugs used to elevate mood in depressed patients. **21**

antimanic drugs Drugs, principally lithium, used to prevent and treat manic episodes. **21**

antipsychotic drugs Drugs used to relieve symptoms such as confusion, withdrawal, hallucinations, and delusions in psychotic patients. Also called *major tranquilizers* or *neuroleptics.* **21**

antisocial behavior Behavior that violates the rights of others; usually associated with antisocial personality. **11**

antisocial personality disorder A disorder marked by chronic indifference to and violation of the rights of others. **11**

anxiety A state of fear and apprehension that affects many areas of functioning and that involves three basic components: subjective reports of tension and dread, behavioral inhibitions and impairments, and certain physiological responses. **2, 7**

anxiety disorders Disturbances characterized either by manifest anxiety or by behavior patterns aimed at warding off anxiety. **7**

aphasias Language impairments generally attributable to damage in the left hemisphere of the brain. **16**

apraxia Impairment of the ability to perform voluntary movements. **16**

assertiveness training A form of social-skills training in which clients are taught how to assert themselves properly with other people and thus avoid being either passive or overaggressive. **20**

asthma A respiratory disorder in which the body's air passageways narrow, causing coughing, wheezing, and shortness of breath. The condition is usually associated with allergies or organic problems, but some cases may be related to stress. **9**

attention deficit hyperactivity disorder (ADHD) A childhood disorder characterized by incessant restlessness and an extremely poor attention span, leading to impulsive and disorganized behavior. **17**

attribution One form of cognitive appraisal concerning beliefs about the causes of life events; how people explain events to themselves will affect their emotional state. **3**

autism *See* **early infantile autism.**

autonomic nervous system (ANS) That part of the nervous system which governs the smooth muscles, the heart muscle, the glands, and the viscera and controls their functions, including physiological responses to emotion. It has two divisions, the sympathetic and parasympathetic. **4**

aversion therapy A respondent-conditioning technique in which a patient's maladaptive response is paired with an aversive stimulus such as an electric shock or a nausea-producing drug; often used in the behavioral treatment of paraphilias and substance dependence. **19**

avoidant personality disorder A disorder in which the individual withdraws from social contact out of fear of rejection. **11**

barbiturates A group of powerful sedative drugs used to alleviate tension and bring about relaxation and sleep. **12**

basic anxiety Horney's term for a pervasive view of the world as impersonal and cold that results from a failed parent–child relationship, and leads to one of three "neurotic trends": moving away (shy, withdrawn behavior), moving toward (dependent, needy behavior), or moving against (hostile, aggressive behavior). **2**

behavior genetics A subfield of psychology that is concerned with determining the extent to which behavior, including abnormal behavior, is influenced by genetics. **4**

behavior therapy A method of treatment for specific problems that uses the principles of learning theory. **3**

behavioral high-risk design A research design in which high-risk subjects are selected on the basis of behavioral traits thought to be associated with the disorder in question. **15**

behavioral perspective A theoretical approach which departs from psychodynamic theory in viewing all behavior as a result of learning. **3**

behavioral rehearsal A method of social-skills training in which the therapist tells clients how to perform the target behavior, models the behavior for them, and then has them practice the behavior in skits that simulate the situations they find troubling. **20**

biofeedback training A technique by which subjects, with the help of various machines, can monitor and control their own biological processes such as pulse, blood pressure, and brain waves. **9**

biogenic A term used to describe abnormal behavior that results from some malfunction within the body. According to biogenic theory, mental disturbance is due to organic disorders. **1**

biological perspective A theory of abnormal behavior that concentrates on the physical aspects of a disorder in an effort to understand its characteristics. **1**

bipolar disorder A mood disorder involving both manic and depressive episodes. **10**

blocking A condition sometimes experienced by schizophrenics in which the person falls silent in the midst of talking, with no recollection of what he or she was talking about. **14**

blood alcohol level The amount of alcohol in the bloodstream, expressed in terms of the number of milligrams of alcohol per 100 ml of blood. **12**

blunted affect A mood abnormality among schizophrenics in which the person shows little emotion. **14**

body dysmorphic disorder A preoccupation with an imagined or grossly exaggerated defect in one's appearance. **8**

borderline personality disorder A disorder marked by an unstable sense of self, distrust, impulsive and self-destructive behavior, and difficulty in controlling anger and other emotions. **11**

brain plasticity The brain's ability, during infancy, to be altered by environmental stimulation. **18**

brain trauma Injury to brain tissue as a result of jarring, bruising, or cutting. **16**

brain tumors Abnormal growths within the brain, classified as either **primary** or **metastatic. 16**

brief psychotic disorder A condition in which a person with no history of schizophrenic symptoms has an episode of such symptoms that is marked by rapid onset, a clear precipitating event, and a duration of less than a month. **14**

bulimia nervosa Excessive overeating or uncontrolled binge eating followed by self-induced vomiting. **17**

case-control design A research design in which *cases,* people diagnosed as having a mental disorder, are compared with *controls,* people who have not been diagnosed as having the disorder. **5**

case study A research design that focuses on a single individual for description and analysis. **5**

castration anxiety In psychodynamic theory, the male child's fear that his penis will be cut off as punishment for his sexual desire of his mother. **2**

catastrophic reaction An emotional disturbance sometimes accompanying organic brain disorder in which the person, bewildered by his or her inability to perform elementary tasks, responds with disorganization and sometimes violent fury. **16**

catatonic schizophrenia A form of schizophrenia characterized by a marked disturbance in motor behavior: decreases in motion, complete immobility, cessation of speech, or alternating periods of immobility and extreme agitation. **14**

catatonic stupor An extreme form of withdrawal in which the individual retreats into a completely immobile state, showing a total lack of responsiveness to stimulation. **14**

catecholamine hypothesis The biochemical theory that increased levels of the neurotransmitter norepinephrine produce mania, while decreased levels produce depression. **10**

central nervous system (CNS) That part of the nervous system made up of the brain and spinal cord. **4**

cerebral abscess A brain infection that becomes encapsulated by connective tissue. **16**

cerebrovascular accident (CVA) A blockage of or break in the blood vessels in the brain, resulting in injury to brain tissue. Commonly called *stroke.* **16**

childhood depression A disorder of emotional distress with symptoms similar to those of adult depression (sadness, hopelessness, etc.) but expressed differently by children (e.g., by clinging to their parents) and by adolescents (e.g., by engaging in delinquent acts). **17**

chromosomes Threadlike structures in all the cells of the body that carry genes in a linear order. **4**

chronic Referring to schizophrenics who have long-standing severe deficits. *Cf.* **acute. 14**

cingulotomy A psychosurgical procedure for patients with severe obsessive-compulsive disorder in which an electrode is inserted into the cingulate gyrus of the brain and heated to create a small lesion. **21**

circadian rhythm disorders Disruptions in sleep cycles that occur when people try to sleep at times that are inconsistent with circadian rhythms, the cycles dictated by their "biological clocks." **9**

civil commitment The commitment of a person to a mental institution because the state has decided that he or she is disturbed enough to require hospitalization. **22**

clanging A characteristic speech pattern of schizophrenics in which words are used together because they rhyme or sound similar, without regard to logic. **14**

claustrophobia The fear of enclosed places. **7**

client-centered therapy A therapeutic procedure developed by Rogers in which the therapist provides a safe environment for the patient by mirroring the patient's own perceptions and offering unconditional positive regard, thus releasing the patient from the necessity of defending his or her unrealistic self-image. **2, 7, 19**

clinical evidence Observations of patients in therapy. **2**

clinical psychologist A Ph.D. or Psy.D. who spent four to six years in graduate school and completed a one-year clinical internship. Clinical psychology programs emphasize training in psychological assessment and therapeutic intervention, as well as research. **1**

cocaine A natural stimulant, made from the coca plant, that produces feelings of euphoria and omnipotence. **12**

coconscious In dissociative identity disorder, the term used to refer to a subordinate personality that is fully aware of the dominant personality's thoughts and actions. **8**

cognition The act of knowing, including mental processes such as emotion, thought, expectation, and interpretation. **3**

cognitive appraisal According to cognitive behaviorists, the process by which a person evaluates a stimulus in accordance with his or her memories, beliefs, and expectations before responding. It accounts for the wide variation in responses to the same stimulus. **3**

cognitive behaviorism The school of behaviorism that proposes that the study of cognitive events should be incorporated into behavioral research. **3**

cognitive perspective The view of abnormal behavior as the product of mental processing of environmental stimuli (cognition). **3**

cognitive restructuring A variety of cognitive therapy techniques that help clients increase coping skills, develop problem solving, and change the way they perceive and interpret their worlds. **19**

cognitive therapy A method of treatment that focuses primarily on cognitive processes, or thoughts, seeing them as the most important causes of behavior. To change a behavior pattern, patients are encouraged to change the pattern of thoughts underlying it. **19**

collective unconscious According to Jung, a repository of archetypes, or symbols, expressive of universal human experiences that each individual's mind contains in addition to the personal unconscious. **2**

communication deviance (CD) A measurement of parental deviant or idiosyncratic test responses; used to predict the potential for their children's future schizophrenic behaviors. **15**

communications approach An approach to family therapy in which family members are encouraged to tell one another what they actually feel and what kind of relationship they really want. Also called *strategic approach.* **20**

community mental health center A facility designed to provide a variety of psychological services for everyone within a specified area. **20**

comorbidity A condition in which a patient meets the criteria for more than one *DSM-IV* Axis I disorders. **6, 10**

complex partial seizure A partial epileptic seizure in which cognitive functioning is interrupted. **16**

compulsion An action that a person feels compelled to repeat again and again in a stereotyped fashion, though he or she has no conscious desire to do so. **7**

computerized tomography (CT) A technique for mapping brain structure in which X-rays are passed through cross-sections of the brain, measuring the density of the tissue in each section. **4**

concordant A genetic term that means sharing the same disorder. **4**

concussion A head injury caused by a blow to the head that jars the brain and momentarily disrupts its functioning. **16**

conditioned reflex A basic mechanism of learning whereby if a neutral stimulus is paired with a nonneutral stimulus, the organism will eventually respond to the neutral stimulus as it does to the nonneutral stimulus. **3**

conditioned reinforcers Stimuli or needs that one learns to respond to by associating them with primary reinforcers. Also called *secondary reinforcers.* **3**

conditioned response A simple response is a neutral stimulus that is the result of repeatedly pairing the neutral stimulus with a nonneutral stimulus that would have naturally elicited the response. **3**

conditioned stimulus The neutral stimulus that elicits a particular response as a result of repeated pairings with a nonneutral or unconditioned stimulus that naturally elicits that response. **3**

conditions of worth According to Rogers, the values incorporated by the child that dictate which of his or her self-experiences are "good" and which are "bad." **2**

conduct disorder A childhood disorder in which a preadolescent or an adolescent persistently violates social norms through aggression against people or animals, destruction of property, deceitfulness or theft, and/or other serious violations of rules. **17**

confounding In a research study, a phenomenon that occurs when two or more causal factors are operating on the same thing simultaneously, interfering with accurate measurement of the causal role of either factor. **5**

congenital disorders Disorders acquired during prenatal development but not transmitted genetically. **18**

constructivist cognitive therapy Mahoney's approach to cognitive therapy, which sees emotional disturbances as reflections of people's imperfect attempts to adapt and develop. Through self-exploration, clients are helped to construct more functional patterns. **19**

contingency In operant conditioning, a perceived association between action and consequence which, once learned, directs behavior: an individual will repeat a behavior or cease it in order to obtain or avoid the consequence. **3**

contingency management An operant-conditioning technique in which the consequences of a response are manipulated in order to change the frequency of that response. **19**

continuity hypothesis The theory that pathological depression and normal sadness are two points on a continuum of mood reactions. **10**

control The third objective of the scientific method: the ability to influence behavior through treatment and preventive strategies. **5**

control techniques The three methods by which the independent variable in an experiment can be controlled: manipulating, holding conditions constant, and balancing. **5**

contusion A head injury in which the brain is shifted out of its normal position and pressed against one side of the skull, thus bruising the neural tissue. **16**

conversion disorder The loss or impairment of some motor or sensory function for which there is no organic cause. Formerly known as "hysteria" or "hysterical neurosis." **8**

correlational research designs Research studies that seek to find the relationships between subjects' characteristics and their performance. Such studies effectively meet two of the objectives of the scientific method—description and prediction—but the results of correlational studies should not be used to make causal interferences. **5**

co-twins A term used by genetic researchers to refer to the twins of the index cases in a study. **4**

covariation of events The first condition to be met before causality can be demonstrated: Two events must vary together; when one changes, the other must also change. **5**

covert sensitization A behavioral technique in which the effect of a stimulus is changed by pairing an imagined stimulus with imagined dire consequences. **13, 19**

cultural-familial retardation Retardation thought to have been caused, or at least fostered, by the individual's home environment. It is believed to be related to the effects of poverty. **18**

cyclothymic disorder A chronic mood disorder in which, for years, the person goes no longer than a few months without a phase of hypomanic or depressive behavior. **10**

day hospital A partial-hospitalization system in which the patients are hospitalized on a nine-to-five basis and then return home for the night. **20**

decatastrophizing A strategy used in cognitive therapy whereby clients are helped to realize that their fears are exaggerated by being asked to consider what would actually happen if their worst fears were realized. **19**

defense mechanism Any psychic stratagem that reduces anxiety by concealing the source of anxiety from the self and the world. **2**

degenerative disorders Organic brain syndromes characterized by a general deterioration of intellectual, emotional, and motor functioning as a result of progressive pathological change in the brain. **16**

delirium A global disorder of cognition and attention that begins suddenly and remits quickly, leaving most patients unharmed. Symptoms include confusion, hallucinations, and emotional lability. **16**

delirium tremens A severe withdrawal symptom experienced by alcoholics when their blood alcohol level drops suddenly. Known as the DTs, the condition consists of severe trembling, heavy perspiring, feeling disoriented, and experiencing delusions. **12**

delusional disorder A psychosis in which the delusional system is the basic or even the only abnormality, and in all other respects the person seems quite normal. **14**

delusions Irrational beliefs that a person will defend with great vigor despite overwhelming evidence that they have no basis in reality. Delusions are among the most common schizophrenic thought disorders. **14**

demand characteristics A methodological problem in which a subject's response is strongly determined by the expectations of the subject or the researchers. **5**

dementia Severe mental deterioration. **16**

denial A defense mechanism in which the person refuses to acknowledge the existence of an external source of anxiety. **2**

dependent personality disorder A disorder marked by extreme dependence on others. **11**

dependent variable In a research study, the factor (in psychology, a particular behavior) that will be affected by the experimenter's manipulation of the independent variable, and whose changes the researcher wishes to measure. **5**

depersonalization disorder A disruption of personal identity that is characterized by a sense of strangeness or unreality in oneself, e.g., feeling that one is viewing oneself from the outside or is functioning like a robot. **8**

depressant A drug that acts on the central nervous system to reduce pain, tension, and anxiety, to relax and disinhibit, and to slow intellectual and motor reactivity. **12**

depression An emotional state characterized by the exaggeration of negative feelings. The person becomes inactive and dejected and thinks nothing is worthwhile. **10**

depth interview A psychodynamic assessment method in which subjects are encouraged to talk about their childhood and about their current lives as candidly as possible. **6**

depth hypothesis Freud's view that almost all mental activity takes place unconsciously. **2**

derealization A feeling of strangeness about the world. Other people, and the self, seem robotic, dead, or somehow unreal. **8**

description (1) The first objective of the scientific method: the procedure by which events and their relationships are defined, classified, cataloged, or categorized. (2) The first goal of psychological assessment: the rendering of an accurate portrait of personality, cognitive functioning, mood, and behavior. **5, 6**

descriptive validity The degree to which an assessment device provides significant information about the current behavior of the people being assessed. **6**

detoxification A medical treatment for alcoholism that consists of getting the alcohol out of the alcoholic's system and seeing him or her through the withdrawal symptoms. **12**

dexamethasone suppression test (DST) A laboratory test used to identify people suffering from endogenous depression. In depressed individuals, dexamethasone suppresses cortisol secretion for at least twenty-four hours. Cortisol secretion of individuals with endogenous depression returns to high levels within twenty-four hours despite administration of dexamethasone. **10**

diagnosis The classification and labeling of a patient's problem within one of a set of recognized categories of abnormal behavior. **6**

diathesis A constitutional predisposition toward a disorder. **4**

diathesis-stress model The belief that certain genes or gene combinations may lead to a diathesis, or predisposition, toward a disorder and that if this is combined with certain kinds of environmental stress, abnormal behavior will result. In schizophrenia research, an approach which holds that a predisposition to schizophrenia is inherited but that the disorder must be triggered by environmental stresses. **4, 15**

differential deficits Deficits that are specific to the disorder in question (as opposed to other disorders) and that are presumably central to it. **15**

disaster syndrome A pattern of response to severe physical trauma involving three stages—shock, suggestibility, and recovery. **7**

discrimination The process of learning to distinguish among similar stimuli and to respond only to the appropriate one. **3**

disorganized schizophrenia A form of schizophrenia characterized by pronounced incoherence of speech, childlike disturbed affect, such as giggling wildly and assuming absurd postures, and disorganized behavior, or lack of goal orientation. Also called *hebephrenic schizophrenia.* **14**

displacement A defense mechanism that involves the transfer of emotion from an unacceptable object to a safer one. **2**

disruptive behavior disorders Childhood disorders characterized by poorly controlled, impulsive, acting-out behavior in situations where self-control is expected. **17**

dissociative amnesia Memory loss without any apparent physiological cause, as a response to psychological stress. Dissociative amnesia tends to be anterograde, blotting out a period of time after the precipitating stress. **8**

dissociative disorders Disorders resulting from the splitting off of some psychological function—such as identity or memory—from the rest of the conscious mind. **8**

dissociative fugue A condition related to amnesia in which a person not only forgets most or all of their past but also takes a sudden, unexpected trip away from home. **8**

dissociative identity disorder A condition in which the personality breaks apart into two or more distinct personalities, each well integrated and well developed, which then take turns controlling the person's behavior. Also known as *multiple personality.* **8**

dizygotic (DZ) twins Twins who develop from two eggs fertilized by two different sperm and who have only approximately 50 percent of their genes in common. Also called *fraternal twins.* **4**

dopamine hypothesis The theory that schizophrenia is associated with excess activity of those parts of the brain that use dopamine as a neurotransmitter. **15**

double-bind communication The situation in which a mother gives mutually contradictory messages to her child while implicitly forbidding the child to point out the contradiction; believed by some to be a causative agent in schizophrenia. **15**

double-blind A procedure in scientific research that seeks to minimize the influence of subjects' and experimenters' expectations. Both the subject and the experimenter are unaware of what treatment is being administered, that is, whether they are in the experimental group or the control group. **5**

Down syndrome A form of mental retardation caused by an extra chromosome. Individuals with this condition usually have IQs of 50 or less and distinctive physical characteristics, such as an extra fold of skin on the upper eyelid, a flat nose, and poor muscle tone. **18**

dream interpretation A psychoanalytic technique in which patients report their dreams as accurately as possible and the therapist explores with the patient the elements of the dreams as symbols of unconscious wishes and conflicts. **7, 19**

drug-induced insomnia A pattern of disrupted slumber without any deep sleep; created by prolonged use of sedatives. **12**

DSM-IV The most recent revision of the *Diagnostic and Statistical Manual,* the handbook that classifies the symptoms and types of mental disorders. **6**

dyspareunia A sexual dysfunction characterized by pain during intercourse. **13**

dysthymic disorder A chronic mood disorder involving a mild, persistent depression. Symptoms are similar to those of a major depressive episode, but they are not as severe or as numerous. **10**

early infantile autism A disorder in children in which the primary symptom, apparent from infancy, is the inability to relate to anyone outside of oneself. **18**

echolalia A speech deficit, characteristic of autistic children and some catatonic schizophrenics, in which the child aimlessly repeats what other people say. **14, 18**

echopraxia Imitation of the movements of others; sometimes manifested by catatonic schizophrenics. **14**

ego According to Freud, the psychic component that mediates between the id and the forces that restrict the id's satisfactions. **2**

ego ideal In Freudian theory, the composite picture of values and moral ideals held by the superego. **2**

ego identity Erikson's belief that the ego does more than just assimilate values of a parent, that it goes on to form an integrated, unique, and autonomous "self." **2**

ego psychology A post-Freudian school of thought which emphasizes less deterministic and less biologically oriented psychology and which holds that the ego has its own energy and autonomous functions apart from the id. **2, 19**

Electra complex A facet of Freud's phallic stage of psychosexual development (analogous to the Oedipus complex in boys) in which a girl observes that she has been born without a penis and experiences penis envy; her sexual interest is thus oriented toward her father: if she can seduce him, then—at least vicariously—she can obtain the desired organ. **2**

electroconvulsive therapy (ECT) The administering of an electric shock to a patient, thus inducing a convulsion; used in the treatment of serious depression. **21**

electroencephalography (EEG) A brain test in which electrodes, attached to the head with tape, pick up electrical activity within the brain and measure it in oscillating patterns known as brain waves. **4, 6**

electromyogram (EMG) A polygraph recording of the changes in the electrical activity of muscles. **6**

elimination of plausible alternative causes The third condition to be met before causality can be demonstrated: The proposed causal relationship can be accepted only after other likely causes have been ruled out. **5**

embolism The obstruction of a blood vessel by a ball of a substance such as fat, air, or clotted blood, thus cutting off the blood supply; a common cause of infarction. **16**

encephalitis Any acute infection of the brain. **16**

encopresis A lack of bowel control past the age when such control is normally achieved. **17**

encounter group A humanistic form of group therapy that emphasizes personal growth and increased openness and honesty in personal relations by means of free and candid expression within the group. **20**

endocrine glands Glands responsible for the production of hormones that, when released into the bloodstream, affect various bodily mechanisms such as physical growth and development. **16**

endocrine system The system of endocrine, or ductless, glands—such as the hypothalamus and the pituitary—that is closely integrated with the central nervous system and is responsible for the production of hormones. **4**

endogenous In depression, the term used to describe patients whose symptoms are primarily physical. **10**

enuresis A lack of bladder control past the age when such control is normally achieved. Children with *primary enuresis* have never achieved bladder control. Those with *secondary enuresis* have lost the control they once had. **17**

epidemiology The study of the frequency and distribution of disorders within specific populations. **5**

epilepsy A generic term for a variety of organic disorders characterized by irregularly occurring disturbances in consciousness in the form of seizures or convulsions. The seizures seem to be caused by a disruption in the electrical and physiochemical activity of the discharging cells of the brain. **16**

essential hypertension Chronically high blood pressure for which no organic cause can be found. **9**

exhibitionism Sexual gratification through displaying one's genitals to an involuntary observer. **13**

exorcism The practice of expelling evil spirits from a person believed to be possessed by such demons. **7**

experimenter effects A methodological problem in which researchers inadvertently influence the subjects' responses or perceive the subjects' behavior in terms of their own biases. **5**

explicit memories Memories we are aware of, which may disappear in amnesia. *Cf.* **implicit memories. 8**

expressed emotion (EE) A measurement of key relatives' level of criticism and emotional overinvolvement, used in determining the family type of a hospitalized schizophrenic. **15**

external validity The degree to which research results can be generalized, or applied, to different populations, settings, and conditions. **5**

extinction A process in which a conditioned response is reduced to its preconditioned level. Previously reinforced responses are no longer reinforced. **3**

false negative In commitment hearings, a failure to commit a person when commitment is justified and necessary. **22**

false positive In commitment hearings, an unjustified commitment. **22**

family therapy A form of group therapy in which the members of a family are seen together on the assumption that the disturbance lies not only in the symptomatic individual but in the family unit as a whole. Goals include more honest communications and more flexible roles within the family. **20**

feedback A process in which information is returned to a system in order to regulate that system. **9**

female orgasmic disorder A recurrent, lengthy delay or absence of orgasm in a woman. **13**

female sexual arousal disorder In women, the absence or weakness of the physiological changes or feelings of sexual excitement that normally occur in the arousal phase of sexual response. **13**

fetal alcohol syndrome (FAS) A complex of physical and behavioral defects found in many children of alcoholic women. The defects include distinctive facial characteristics, retarded physical growth, and, frequently, mental retardation. **18**

fetishism Sexual gratification via inanimate objects or some part of the partner's body to the exclusion of the person as a whole. **13**

fixation A pathological process in which a person experiences anxiety at a certain stage of development and fails to progress beyond that stage. **2**

flat affect A mood abnormality among schizophrenics in which the person shows no emotion. **14**

flooding A respondent-conditioning technique in which extinction of fear is achieved by prolonged exposure to the feared stimulus in a situation that does not permit avoidance. **19**

fragile X syndrome A condition in which an individual's X chromosome shows a weak spot; the most common genetic cause of mental retardation. **18**

free association A psychoanalytic technique in which the patient verbalizes whatever thoughts come to mind, without structuring or censoring the remarks. **1, 7, 19**

frotteurism Sexual gratification through touching and rubbing against a nonconsenting person. **13**

functional analysis An assessment interview as conducted by a behaviorist, which involves a systematic dissection of the person's complaint: precisely what the problem behavior is, how it developed, what the person has done to try to combat it, and—most important—the changes in the environment that precede, accompany, and follow the behavior. **6**

galvanic skin response (GSR) A polygraphic recording of the changes in the electrical resistance of the skin, an indication of sweat gland activity. There is an intimate relationship between emotion and physiological functioning; when a person's anxiety level rises, so may the activity of the sweat glands. **6**

gender identity disorder A condition in which people identify with the opposite sex so completely that they feel that they belong to that sex and that their own biological gender is simply a mistake. Also called *transsexualism.* **13**

general paresis A final stage of syphilis, involving the gradual and irreversible breakdown of physical and mental functioning. **1, 16**

generalizability The ability of research results to be applied to different populations, settings, and conditions. **5**

generalization The process by which an organism, conditioned to respond in a certain way to a particular stimulus, will respond to other, similar stimuli in the same way. **3**

generalized anxiety disorder A chronic state of diffuse anxiety characterized by excessive worry, over a period of at least six months, about several life circumstances (most often family, money, work, and health). **7, 17**

generalized dysfunction A sexual dysfunction that occurs in all sexual situations. **13**

generalized seizures Epileptic seizures that either involve the entire brain at the outset (primary) or soon spread from one part to the whole brain (secondary). *Cf.* **partial seizure. 16**

genes The units of heredity on a chromosome that carry the instructions, inherited from the parents at conception, about the proteins that the body should produce. The proteins, in turn, determine the hereditary characteristics of the person—height, hair and eye color, and so on. **4**

genetic high-risk design A research design in which high-risk subjects are selected on the basis of genetic factors associated with the disorder in question. **15**

genital stage According to Freud, the final phase of mature sexuality, by which he meant heterosexual genital mating. **2**

genotype The unique combination of genes which represents one's biological inheritance from one's parents. **4**

Gestalt therapy Perls' humanistic existential form of therapy in which the patients act out past conflicts with the therapist in order to confront their feelings, take responsibility for them, and learn to control them. **19**

glove anesthesia A form of conversion disorder in which the individual reports a numbness in his or her hand from the tips of the fingers to a clear cutoff point at the wrist. **1**

group therapy Treatment of up to eight or ten clients at a time by a single therapist. **20**

habituation A learning mechanism whereby repeated exposure to a stimulus results in the lessening of an organism's response to the stimulus. **3**

halfway house A residence for people who no longer require institutionalization but who still need some support in readjusting to community life. **20**

hallucinations Sensory perceptions that occur in the absence of any appropriate external stimulus. **14**

hallucinogens A class of drugs that act on the central nervous system in such a way as to cause distortions in sensory perception. **12**

health psychology A research discipline that focuses on the relationship between mental and physical health. Also called *behavioral medicine.* **9**

helplessness-hopelessness syndrome A thought process characteristic of deeply depressed persons in which they regard their condition as irreversible, believing that they are both unable to help themselves and unlikely to be helped by external forces. **10**

hemorrhage A cerebrovascular accident in which a blood vessel in the brain ruptures, causing blood to spill out into the brain tissue. **16**

heroin An addictive opiate derived from morphine. **12**

hierarchy of fears In systematic desensitization, a list of anxiety-producing situations in the order of their increasing horror to the client. **19**

hierarchy of needs Maslow's concept of a series of needs that must be satisfied one by one in the process of development before the adult can begin to pursue self-actualization. **2**

high-risk design A form of longitudinal research that involves the study of people who have a high probability of developing a disorder. **5**

histrionic personality disorder A disorder involving the exaggerated display of emotion. **11**

hormones Chemical messengers that are released directly into the bloodstream by the endocrine glands and that affect sexual functioning, physical growth and development, and emotional responses. **4**

hot lines Round-the-clock telephone services that people in trouble can call to receive immediate comfort and advice from trained volunteers. **20**

human immunodeficiency virus (HIV) The virus that attacks and breaks down the human immune system and causes AIDS. It is transmitted by blood, semen, vaginal secretions, or breast milk of an infected person through unsafe sex, the sharing of hypodermic needles, a contaminated blood transfusion, or to a child in the womb of an infected mother. **9**

humanistic-existential perspective A diverse approach to abnormal psychology whose proponents generally agree that behavior is both willed and purposive and that human beings choose their lives and therefore are responsible for their lives. **2**

humors In Hippocrates' view, the four vital fluids possessed by humans: phlegm, blood, black bile, and yellow bile. The balance of these humors in each individual was thought to influence personality. **1**

Huntington's chorea A fatal organic brain disorder which is transmitted genetically. Symptoms include spasmodic jerking of the limbs, bizarre behavior, and mental deterioration. **16**

hypertension Chronic elevation of blood pressure due to constriction of the arteries; a stress-related physical disorder. Also called *high blood pressure.* **9**

hypnosis An artificially induced trance, or sleeplike state, in which the subject is highly susceptible to suggestion. **1**

hypnotics Drugs used to induce sleep. Also called *sleeping pills.* **21**

hypoactive sexual desire disorder A chronic lack of interest in sex. **13**

hypochondriasis A disorder in which a person converts anxiety into a chronic fear of disease. The fear is maintained by the constant misinterpretation of physical signs and sensations as abnormal. **8**

hypomanic episode A briefer and less severe version of a manic episode. **10**

hypothesis A tentative explanation for behavior that attempts to answer the questions "How?" and "Why?" Scientific research often begins with a hypothesis. **5**

hypothesis testing A strategy used in cognitive therapy whereby clients are urged to test their assumptions in the real world. **19**

hysteria A psychogenic disorder that mimics a biogenic disorder. **8**

id According to Freud, the basic psychic structure, consisting of primitive biological drives toward sex and aggression. **2**

identification In psychodynamic theory, the incorporation of the same-sex parent's values, standards, sexual orientation, and mannerisms as part of the development of the superego. As a defense mechanism, attaching oneself psychologically to a group in order to diminish personal anxieties. **2**

idiographic research Research built on the individual, such as the *case study.* **5**

idiopathic epilepsy A convulsive disorder for which there is no known cause. **16**

immune system The body's system of defense against infectious disease and cancer. **9**

implicit memories Memories that a person with amnesia cannot call into conscious awareness but that still affect his or her behavior. *Cf.* **explicit memories. 8**

impulse-control disorders Patterns of impulsive behavior that seem to exist not as part of another major syndrome, but independently. Their essential feature is the inability to resist the impulse to act in ways harmful to oneself or to others. **11**

inappropriate affect A mood abnormality among schizophrenics in which the person's emotional responses seem unsuitable to the situation. **14**

incest Sexual relations between family members. **13**

incidence The number of new cases of a disorder reported during a specific time period. **5**

independent variable In a research study, a factor that has been determined before the experiment and may be manipulated by the experimenters in order to measure its effect. **5**

indeterminate sentences Periods of incarceration with no limit, often given to those defendants acquitted by reason of insanity. **22**

index case In genetic family studies, the individual in the family who has the diagnosed case of the disorder being studied. Also called *proband case.* **4**

individual response specificity The principle that people seem to have characteristic patterns of autonomic nervous system response which carry over from one kind of stress to another. **9**

infarction A cerebrovascular accident in which the supply of blood to the brain is cut off, resulting in the death of brain tissue fed by that source. **16**

insanity defense A legal plea in which the defendant admits to having committed the crime but pleads not guilty, stating that because of mental disturbance he or she was not morally responsible at the time of the crime. **22**

insight therapy The approach to psychotherapy that focuses on increasing patients' awareness of the motives underlying their actions so that, by understanding their behavior, they will be able to control it better. **19**

insomnia The chronic inability to sleep. The condition can stem from both physical and psychological factors. **9**

intellectualization A defense mechanism in which a person avoids unacceptable feelings by repressing them and replacing them with an abstract, intellectual analysis of the problem.

intelligence quotient (IQ) The subject's final score on an adult version of the Stanford-Binet Intelligence scale, a test which measures a child's ability to perform a range of intellectual tasks. IQ tests play an important part in the diagnosis of mental retardation and brain damage. **6**

intelligence tests Psychological assessment techniques effective in predicting success in school but questionable as a valid measure of intelligence. **6**

interjudge reliability A criterion for judging the reliability of a psychological test: the test should yield the same results when scored or interpreted by different judges. **6**

internal consistency A criterion for judging the reliability of a psychological test: different parts of the test should yield the same result. **6**

internal validity The extent to which the results of an experiment can be confidently attributed to the effects of the independent variable. **5**

interpersonal perspective A theoretical approach within psychodynamic theory that is devoted to analyzing behavior as a function of people's relationships with others. **3**

interpretation Freud's primary tool for revealing hidden, intrapsychic motives; it involves going beyond observing surface behavior to uncover its latent content. **2**

interview An assessment method consisting of a face-to-face conversation between subject and examiner. **6**

in vivo desensitization A variation on the systematic-desensitization technique that involves leading patients through their hierarchy of fears not just in their imaginations, but in real life. **7, 19**

isolation A defense mechanism that separates feelings from the events to which they are attached. The feelings are repressed, and the events are viewed without emotion. **2**

Korsakoff's psychosis An irreversible nutritional deficiency due to vitamin B_1 deficiency associated with alcoholism; characterized by anterograde amnesia and confabulation. **16**

la belle indifférence A response often seen in conversion disorder in which the person does not seem at all disturbed by his or her disability. **8**

laceration The most serious form of brain trauma, in which a foreign object, such as a bullet or piece of metal, enters the skull and directly ruptures and destroys brain tissue. **16**

large community group A variant of humanistically oriented group therapy in which 50 to 2,000 people convene with several leaders for sessions lasting from one weekend to two weeks. **20**

latency The dormancy of a particular behavior or response. **2**

latent content In psychoanalytic theory, the true, unconscious meaning of a dream or other human behavior. *Cf.* **manifest content. 2, 19**

lateralization The differences in structure and function between the right and the left hemispheres of the brain. **4**

law of effect Thorndike's formulation of the importance of reward in the learning process which states that responses that lead to satisfying consequences are strengthened and therefore are likely to be repeated, while responses with unsatisfying consequences are weakened and therefore unlikely to be repeated. **3**

lead encephalopathy A toxic disorder due to excessive ingestion of lead, which causes fluid to accumulate in the brain and results in extraordinary intracranial pressure. **16**

learned helplessness In behavioral theory, the depressive's inability to initiate adaptive responses, possibly due to a helplessness conditioned by earlier, inescapable trauma. **10**

learning The process whereby behavior changes in response to the environment. **3**

learning disorders Three conditions characterized by reading, writing, or mathematical skills that are substantially below what would be expected for the person's age, education, and intelligence, and by a resulting interference with the person's adjustment. The three conditions are reading disorder (dyslexia), disorder of written expression, and mathematics disorder. **17**

libido Freud's term for a basic sexual drive which he saw as the major source of psychic energy. **2**

lifelong dysfunction A sexual dysfunction that has existed, without relief, since the person's earliest sexual experiences. **13**

lithium A mood-altering drug used to control manic episodes. **21**

logotherapy Frankl's technique for dealing with the spiritual aspect of psychopathology, in which the therapist confronts patients with their responsibility for their existence and their obligation to pursue the values inherent in life. **2**

long-term-care facilities Facilities within a community that are designed to meet the needs of patients, who presumably will never, or not soon, achieve independent living. **20**

longitudinal studies Scientific research designs in which a group of subjects is studied several different times over an extended period of time. Also called *prospective studies.* **5**

loosening of associations The rambling, disjointed quality that is characteristic of schizophrenic speech. **14**

magnetic resonance imaging (MRI) The use of magnetic fields to produce a highly precise picture of the brain. **4**

major depressive disorder A condition characterized by one or more major depressive episodes with no intervening periods of mania. **10**

major depressive episode An extended period of intense depression that usually begins and ends gradually and causes a radical change in most aspects of the individual's functioning. **10**

male erectile disorder In the second phase of sexual arousal, a failure of the tissues in a man's penis to become congested with blood. **13**

male orgasmic disorder A recurrent, lengthy delay or absence of ejaculation and orgasm in a man. **13**

malingering The conscious faking of disease symptoms in order to avoid responsibility. **8**

mania An emotional state characterized by the exaggeration of positive feelings. The person becomes feverishly active and excited and feels capable of accomplishing anything. **10**

manic episode An extended period of intense mania that usually begins and ends suddenly and causes a radical change in an individual's social functioning. **10**

manifest content In psychoanalytic theory, the surface meaning of a dream or other human behavior as seen and reported by the individual. (*Cf.* **latent content.**) **2, 19**

MAO inhibitors The first important class of antidepressants. Although named on the assumption that they block the action of monoamine oxidase, their mechanism has not been established. **21**

marital therapy A form of group therapy in which both partners are seen in an attempt to pinpoint their role expectations and communication patterns. Goals include an honest dialogue and more satisfying ways of relating within the relationship. Also called *couples therapy.* **20**

masculine protest According to Adler, the unwarranted belief that men are superior to women. **2**

masochism Sexual gratification through pain and/or humiliation inflicted on oneself. **13**

medical model The conceptualization of psychological abnormality as a group of diseases analogous to physical diseases. **1**

meningitis A brain infection involving an acute inflammation of the meninges and characterized by drowsiness, confusion, irritability, and sensory impairments. **16**

mental retardation A condition that is characterized by subaverage intellectual functioning, by serious deficits in adaptive skills, and by onset before age eighteen. **18**

metastatic brain tumors Brain tumors that originate in some other part of the body and then metastasize, or spread, to the brain. **16**

methadone A synthetic opiate that satisfies the craving for narcotics but does not produce narcotic euphoria. **12**

migraine headache A severe form of chronic headache that is usually localized on one side of the head, is sometimes preceded by perceptual distortion, and is typically accompanied by other symptoms such as nausea or confusion; a stress-related disorder. **9**

milieu therapy A residential-community therapy in which patients take responsibility for their behavior, participate in their rehabilitation and that of others, and help in making decisions that affect the community, thereby maximizing their independence, self-respect, and activity level. **15, 20**

mind-body problem The issue of the relationship between the psychic and somatic aspects of human functioning. **9**

Minnesota Multiphasic Personality Inventory-2 (MMPI-2) The most widely used self-report personality inventory, the purpose of which is to simplify differential diagnosis by comparing self-descriptive statements endorsed by new patients to statements endorsed by groups of people already diagnosed with a particular condition. **6**

mixed episode An episode in which a patient meets the diagnostic criteria for both a manic episode and a major depressive episode (for example, exhibiting manic grandiosity and hyperactivity, yet weeping and threatening suicide at the same time). **10**

modeling In behavioral theory, the learning of a new behavior by imitating another person performing that behavior. **3**

monozygotic (MZ) twins Twins who develop from a single fertilized egg and have exactly the same genotype. They are always of the same sex, have the same eye color and blood type, and so on. Also called *identical twins.* **4**

mood disorders Emotional conditions in which feelings of depression or mania become so extreme and prolonged that the person's life is completely disrupted. Also called *affective disorders.* **10**

moral therapy A nineteenth-century approach to treatment that involved providing an environment in which the mentally ill would be treated humanely and could discuss their difficulties, live in peace, and engage in some useful employment. **1**

morphine An addictive depressant derived from opium. **12**

multiple-baseline design An experimental research design in which treatment is introduced at different intervals across subjects, behaviors, or situations. **5**

muscle-contraction headaches Ordinary headaches. Also called *tension headaches.* **9**

mutism The cessation of speech; often a characteristic of catatonic schizophrenia. **14**

mystification Laing's term for a habitual mode of interaction between parent and child that causes the child to doubt the legitimacy of his or her own thoughts, feelings, and perceptions. **15**

narcissistic personality disorder A disorder characterized by a grandiose sense of self-importance, often combined with periodic feelings of inferiority. **11**

natural group designs Research designed to investigate whether systematic differences exist between existing, "natural" groups: for example, people who have been divorced and people who have remained married; people who have been assaulted and people who have not. **5**

negative feedback Feedback in which the turning on of one component of a system leads to the turning off of another component, in order to regulate the system. **9**

negative reinforcement A conditioning procedure in which a response is followed by the removal of an aversive event or stimulus, thereby promoting the response. **3**

negative symptoms In schizophrenia, the absence of something that is normally present, including poverty of speech, flat affect, withdrawal, apathy, and attentional impairment. **14**

neologisms A schizophrenic speech pattern in which new words are formed by combining parts of two or more regular words or in which common words are used in a unique fashion. **14**

nervous system The vast electrochemical conducting network that extends from the brain through the rest of the body and carries information, in the form of electrical impulses, from the brain to the rest of the body and back to the brain. **4**

neurons The cells of the nervous system, which connect motor and receptor cells and transmit information throughout the body. **4**

neuroses Conditions in which maladaptive behaviors serve as a protection against a source of unconscious anxiety. **2**

neurosyphilis The deterioration of brain tissue as a result of syphilis. **16**

neurotransmitters One of a group of chemicals that facilitate the transmission of electrical impulses between nerve endings in the brain. **4**

night hospital A partial-hospitalization system in which the patients go to work or school from nine to five and then return to the hospital for the night. **20**

nightmare A frightening dream which does not cause physiological arousal and does not necessarily awaken the dreamer. During early childhood, nightmares are distinguished from *night terrors,* which are both more physically arousing and more harrowing. **13**

night terror A harrowing variety of bad dream experienced by children, who show extreme autonomic arousal and violent movements during the dream and are confused, disoriented, and upset when awakened. **13**

noncontingent reinforcement Arbitrary responses to behavior.

Among parents and children, it occurs when the nature of the parents' responses to the child's behavior is not related to whether the child's behavior is prosocial or antisocial. **11**

norms The rules in any society that define "right" and "wrong." Norms guide most of our actions and are an important standard for defining abnormality. **1**

null hypothesis The assumption that the independent variable had no effect on the differences between experimental groups. **5**

obesity An excessive amount of fat on the body. Each culture sets its own standard for ideal body weight, so what is considered obese in one culture may be desirable in another. **9**

object relations In psychodynamic terminology, "objects" are the people to whom one is attached by strong emotional ties. According to object-relations theorists, the most powerful determinant of psychological development is the child's interaction with the primary caregiver, the child's chief object. **2**

obsession A thought or an image that keeps unwillingly intruding into a person's consciousness, though the person may consider it senseless or even unpleasant. **7**

obsessive-compulsive disorder Involuntary dwelling on an unwelcome thought *(obsession)* and/or involuntary repetition of an unnecessary action *(compulsion)*. **7**

obsessive-compulsive personality disorder A disorder marked by excessive preoccupation with trivial details, at the cost of both spontaneity and effectiveness. **11**

Oedipus complex According to Freud, the desire that all male children have during the phallic stage to do away with the parent of the same sex in order to take sexual possession of the parent of the opposite sex; a crucial stage of development which determines the child's future sexual adjustment. **2**

operant behavior In behavioral theory, a class of complex behavior in which an organism acts upon the environment in order to achieve a desired result. All operant behavior is the result of conditioning. (*Cf.* **respondent behavior.**) **3**

operant conditioning The process by which an organism learns to associate certain consequences with certain actions it has taken. Also called *instrumental conditioning*. **3**

operational definitions The definition of concepts involved in a hypothesis in terms of operations that can be observed and measured, so that the hypothesis can be tested. **5**

opiates A class of drugs that induce relaxation and reverie and provide relief from anxiety and pain. **12**

opium A depressant derived from the opium poppy. **12**

oral stage In psychodynamic theory, the first stage of psychosocial development, in which the mouth is the primary focus of libidinal impulses and pleasure; occurs in the first year of life. **2**

organic brain disorders Behavioral problems that are directly traceable to the destruction of brain tissue or to biochemical imbalance in the brain. **16**

oscillations The rhythmic back-and-forth cycles of the various systems of the body—for example, breathing, heartbeat, blood pressure, temperature, digestion, sleep, menstruation, and the production of hormones, neurotransmitters, and immune cells. **9**

panic attack An attack of almost unbearable anxiety, beginning suddenly and unexpectedly and usually lasting several minutes though possibly continuing for hours. **7**

panic disorder A disorder characterized by recurrent panic attacks followed by psychological or behavioral problems. **7**

paradoxical intention (1) In existential therapy, a technique in which patients are asked to indulge or exaggerate their symptoms in order to prove to patients that they can control their symptoms. (2) In family therapy, a technique in which a family member is told to engage deliberately in his or her maladaptive pattern of behavior on the theory that this will disrupt the pattern and force the patient to find a better way of dealing with problems. **7, 20**

paranoid-nonparanoid dimension The classification of schizophrenics according to the presence (paranoid) or absence (nonparanoid) of delusions of persecution and/or grandeur. **14**

paranoid personality disorder A disorder defined by suspiciousness in almost all situations and with almost all people. **11**

paranoid schizophrenia A form of schizophrenia characterized by consistent delusions and/or hallucinations, often related to themes of persecution and grandeur. **14**

paraphilias Sexual patterns—such as fetishism, transvestism, etc.—that deviate from the standard of normal sexuality as consisting of a nondestructive interplay between consenting adults. **13**

parasympathetic division The division of the autonomic nervous system that decreases physical arousal and is usually dominant under less emotional conditions. It regulates breathing, heart rate, blood pressure, stomach and intestinal activity, and elimination. (*Cf.* **sympathetic division.**) **4**

Parkinson's disease An organic brain disorder involving damage to the basal ganglia. Symptoms include tremors, a masklike countenance, stiff gait, and psychological disturbances such as a general mental deficit and social withdrawal. **16**

partial seizure An epileptic seizure that originates in one part of the brain rather than in the brain as a whole. May be either **simple** or **complex.** *Cf.* **generalized seizures. 16**

passive avoidance learning Learning to stop making certain behavioral responses to stimuli when those responses will result in punishment. **11**

pedophilia Child molesting—that is, sexual gratification, on the part of an adult, through sexual contact with children. **13**

peer self-help groups Groups of people who share a special problem and meet to discuss that problem without the help or guidance of a mental health professional. **20**

penis envy In psychodynamic theory, the female child's feeling that she has been born unequipped with a penis because of her sexual desire toward her father; female counterpart of castration anxiety. **2**

perceptual conscious In Freudian theory, the surface level of the mind's consciousness, which consists of the narrow range of mental events of which the person is aware at any given instant. **2**

peripheral nervous system The network of nerve fibers that leads from the central nervous system to all parts of the body and carries out the commands of the CNS. It has two branches: the somatic nervous system and the autonomic nervous system. **4**

person variables A person's stable traits. Adherents of the psychometric approach hold that personality issues mainly from person variables. **6**

personality disorder An enduring pattern of inner experience and behavior that deviates markedly from the expectations of the individual's culture, is pervasive and inflexible, has an onset in adolescence or early adulthood, is stable over time, and leads to distress or impairment. **11**

phallic stage In psychodynamic theory, the third stage of psychosocial development, in which pleasure is derived from masturbation, the stroking and handling of the genitals; occurs from the third to the fifth or sixth year of life. **2**

phenomenological approach A therapeutic procedure in which the therapist attempts to see the patient's world from the vantage point of the patient's own internal frame of reference. **2**

phenotype The unique combination of observable characteristics that results from the combination of a person's genotype with the environment. **4**

phenylketonuria (PKU) A genetic defect caused by a deficiency in a liver enzyme, phenylalanine 4-hydroxylase, which results in severe retardation, hyperactivity, and erratic behavior. **18**

phobia An intense and persistent fear of some object or situation which, as the person realizes, actually poses no real threat; accompanied by avoidance of the phobic stimulus. **7**

placebo control group In a research study, a group of subjects given a treatment designed to affect only their expectations of change, thus minimizing the effects of expectations of subjects and experimenters. **5**

play therapy A psychodynamic technique in which the therapist provides young patients with drawing materials and toys, rather than asking them questions, on the assumption that whatever is troubling them will be expressed in their drawings and games. **17**

pleasure principle In Freudian theory, the tendency of the id to devote itself exclusively to the immediate reduction of tension. **2**

polygenic Referring to a trait that is the product of the interaction of many genes. **4**

polygraph A recording device equipped with sensors which, when attached to the body, can pick up subtle physiological changes in the form of electrical impulses. The changes are recorded on a moving roll of paper. **6**

polysomnography The all-night employment of a variety of measures including EEG, EMG, and respiration invaluable for measuring sleep. **6**

positive regard As defined by Rogers, people's need for affection and approval from those most important to them, particularly parents. **2**

positive reinforcement A situation in which a response is followed by a positive event or stimulus, thereby increasing the probability that the response will be repeated. **3**

positive symptoms In schizophrenia, the presence of something that is normally absent, including hallucinations, delusions, bizarre behavior, and incoherent thought patterns. **14**

positron emission tomography (PET) A means of examining the brain. The patient is injected with a radioactively labeled sugar solution, and the path of the radioactive particles through the brain is traced. **4**

posttraumatic stress disorder A severe psychological reaction to intensely traumatic events, including assault, rape, natural disasters, and wartime combat. Victims may reexperience the traumatic event in recollections or in nightmares, show diminished responsiveness to their present surroundings, and suffer physical symptoms and intense irritability. Generally appearing shortly after the trauma, the symptoms usually disappear within six months, but some may last for years. **7**

poverty of content A characteristic of schizophrenic speech in which words are used correctly but communication is poor. **14**

preconscious The level of the unconscious that contains all materials that are normally unconscious but can still be easily retrieved. **2**

prediction (1) The second objective of the scientific method: the ability to predict the relationship between events. (2) The second goal of psychological assessment: the development of hypotheses about future behavior, treatment, and statistical likelihoods. **5, 6**

predictive validity The degree to which a test's findings are consistent with the subject's future performance. **6**

prefrontal lobotomy A psychosurgical procedure for severely disturbed patients in which some of the connections between the frontal lobe and the lower parts of the brain are severed; very rarely performed today. **21**

premature ejaculation A sexual disorder in which the rapidity of ejaculation interferes with the couple's enjoyment. **13**

premorbid adjustment The level of functioning that was normal for a person before the onset of a disorder. **10**

prevalence The percentage of a population that has a particular disorder at a particular time. **5**

primary brain tumors Tumors that originate either within the brain or outside the brain but inside the skull. **16**

primary gain In conversion disorder, the relief from anxiety that is experienced by the person as a result of the conversion symptom, which blocks the person's awareness of internal conflict. **8**

primary prevention The first level of prevention of psychological disorder, the goal of which is to prevent disorders from developing. **20**

primary reinforcer A stimulus or need that one responds to instinctively, without learning. **3**

process-reactive dimension The classification of schizophrenics according to whether the onset of symptoms is gradual (process) or abrupt and precipitated by some traumatic event (reactive). **14**

process schizophrenia Schizophrenia in which onset is gradual. **14**

prodromal phase The initial stage of schizophrenia, during which the person generally becomes withdrawn and socially isolated. **14**

prognosis The prediction of the course of a patient's illness. **6**

projection A defense mechanism whereby unacceptable id impulses are first repressed and then attributed to others. **2**

projective personality tests Assessment techniques used to draw out, indirectly, individuals' true conflicts and motives by presenting them with ambiguous stimuli and allowing them to project their private selves into their responses. **6**

psychiatric social worker Someone who has earned an M.S.W. (master of social work), with special courses and training in psychological counseling. **1**

psychiatrist An M.D. who specializes in diagnosing and treating mental disorders. Because of their medical degree, psychiatrists can also prescribe psychoactive drugs. **1**

psychoactive drug A drug that alters one's psychological state. **12**

psychoanalysis The psychodynamic therapy method that relies heavily on the techniques of free association, dream interpretation, and analysis of resistance and transference. The aim is to give patients insight into their unconscious conflicts, impulses, and motives. **1, 2, 19**

psychoanalyst Someone who has had postgraduate training at a psychoanalytic institute and has undergone psychoanalysis him- or herself. (Most psychoanalysts are psychiatrists, but other mental health professionals may undertake this training.) **1**

psychodrama A psychoanalytically oriented form of group therapy in which members act out their emotional conflicts together, often on a stage. Through role-taking, clients are encouraged to reveal the roots of the problems, which can then be discussed with the group. **20**

psychodynamic perspective A school of thought united by a common concern with the dynamics, or interaction, of forces lying deep within the mind. Almost all psychodynamic theorists agree on three basic principles: much human behavior is determined by intrapsychic forces; such forces generally operate unconsciously; and the form taken by these forces is deeply affected by developmental factors, especially by family relationships. **2**

psychogenic theory The theory that psychological disturbance is due primarily not to organic dysfunction but to emotional stress. **1**

psychological assessment The collection, organization, and interpretation of information about a person and his or her situation. **6**

psychological dependence The nonphysiological dimension of drug abuse, characterized by the abuser's growing tendency to center his or her life on the drug. **12**

psychological test An assessment technique in which the subject is presented with a series of stimuli to which he or she is asked to respond. **6**

psychometric approach A method of psychological testing that aims at locating and measuring stable underlying traits. **6**

psychoneuroimmunology (PNI) The subspecialty of health medicine that studies the interaction between psychological factors and the immune system, mediated by the central nervous system. **9**

psychopathology Abnormal psychology. **1**

psychopharmacology The study of the drug treatment of psychological disorders. **21**

psychophysiological disorders Physical disorders that are influenced by emotional factors and that are also scientifically traceable to a clear organic cause. Also called *psychosomatic disorders.* **9**

psychoses. *See* **psychosis.**

psychosexual development Freud's theory that personality development takes place in a series of stages, in each of which the child's central motivation is to gratify the drive for pleasure in a different zone of the body. **2**

psychosis A condition of ego collapse in which adaptive functioning is drastically curtailed. **2, 14**

psychosocial development Erikson's theory of personality development, consisting of a series of chronological stages extending from birth to death. **2**

psychosurgery Surgery aimed at reducing abnormal behavior in the absence of any signs of organic brain pathology. **21**

psychotherapy The psychological treatment of emotional problems, in which the therapist aims to establish a relationship with the patient in order to remove or modify symptoms, mediate disturbed patterns of behavior, and promote positive personality growth. **19**

punishment The process in which an organism, in order to avoid (or, less often, obtain) a consequence, stops performing a behavior. **3**

random assignment A balancing control technique that involves assigning subjects randomly to the different groups in the experiment. **5**

random sample A sample in which every element of a population has an equal likelihood of being included. **5**

rape Sexual intercourse with a nonconsenting partner. **13**

rational-emotive therapy Ellis' approach to cognitive therapy, which sees emotional disturbances as the result of irrational beliefs that guide people's interpretation of events. Clients are helped to appraise their situations realistically and develop new ways of interpreting experience. **19**

rationalization A defense mechanism in which a person offers socially acceptable reasons for something that he or she has actually done for unconscious and unacceptable reasons. **2**

reaction formation A defense mechanism in which a person represses feelings that are arousing anxiety and then vehemently professes the exact opposite of those feelings. **2**

reactive In depression, the term used to describe patients whose symptoms are primarily emotional and cognitive. **10**

reactive schizophrenia Schizophrenia in which onset is sudden and apparently precipitated by some traumatic event. **14**

reality principle In Freudian theory, the way in which the ego seeks safe and effective means of gratifying the desires of the id. **2**

reattribution training A strategy used in cognitive therapy whereby the client is helped to change distorted ideas of cause and effect and to attribute events to their causes in a realistic manner. **19**

receptors Special proteins on the surface of neurons that bind with neurotransmitters squirted into the synapse from the dendrites of adjoining neurons. Molecules in the neurotransmitter fit into the receptor like a key into a lock. **4**

regression A defense mechanism that involves the return to an earlier, less threatening developmental stage that one has already passed through. **2**

reinforcement The process by which behavior is increased or maintained by rewarding consequences. Operant conditioning depends on reinforcement: most people would not go to work if it weren't for the paycheck. **3**

relaxation training A technique that behaviorists have used in stress-relief programs in which the subject alternately tenses, then relaxes, groups of muscles. The goal is to teach the patient to distinguish between tension and relaxation and ultimately achieve the latter. **9**

reliability (1) In the scientific method, the degree to which a description remains stable over time and under different testing conditions. (2) The degree to which a measurement device yields consistent results under varying conditions. **5, 6**

representativeness The degree to which a research sample's characteristics match those of the population under study. **5**

repression A defense mechanism in which unacceptable id impulses are pushed down into the unconscious and thereby rendered unable to disturb the person consciously. **2**

residual phase The third phase of schizophrenia, during which behavior is similar to that seen during the prodromal phase. **14**

resistance In psychoanalytic theory, a defense mechanism used by the patient to avoid confronting certain memories and impulses. The patient may argue with the therapist, change the subject, miss appointments, and so on. **7, 19**

respondent behavior In behavioral theory, that behavior which is elicited by specific stimuli, both unlearned and conditioned. (*Cf.* **operant behavior.**) **3**

respondent conditioning The process of learning a conditioned response. Also called *classical conditioning.* **3**

response sets Test-taking attitudes that lead subjects to distort their responses, often unconsciously. **6**

retarded depression A type of depression in which there is little spontaneous motor activity. Movement is slow and deliberate, with a minimum number of gestures and little verbalization. **10**

reuptake A process by which, after crossing the synapse and binding with receptors, a neurotransmitter is broken down into its constituent amino acids and reincorporated into the axon terminal. **4**

Rorschach Psychodiagnostic Inkblot Test The most well known projective personality test, in which subjects are asked to interpret ten cards, each showing a symmetrical inkblot design. **6**

sadism Sexual gratification through infliction of pain and/or humiliation on others. **13**

sadomasochistic The term applied to sexual partners in which either a sadist and a masochist pair up to satisfy their complementary needs, or both partners enjoy both sadism and masochism and switch between the two. **13**

savant syndrome A disorder in which a person with greatly diminished mental skill shows extraordinary proficiency in one isolated skill. **18**

schema An organized structure of information about a particular domain in life; it is stored in the mind and helps a person to organize and process newly learned information. **3**

schizoaffective disorder A syndrome intermediate between schizophrenia and the mood disorders in which individuals suffer a manic or a depressive episode while showing the symptoms of schizophrenia. **14**

schizoid personality disorder A disorder marked by social withdrawal and isolation. **11**

schizophrenia A group of psychoses marked by severe distortion of thought, perception, and mood, by bizarre behavior, and by social withdrawal. **14**

schizophreniform disorder A disorder in which a person with no history of schizophrenic symptoms has an episode of such symptoms that is marked by rapid onset, with or without a precipitating event, and a duration of one to six months. **14**

schizotypal personality disorder A disorder marked by odd speech, behavior, thinking, and/or perception. **11**

seasonal affective disorder (SAD) A mood disorder characterized by depression that occurs only during the winter. **10**

secondary gain In conversion disorder, the "benefit" of being excused from responsibilities and attracting sympathy and attention, which accrue to the person as a result of the conversion symptom. **8**

secondary prevention The second level of prevention of psychological disorder, the goal of which is to detect and treat disorders at an early stage, so that minor disorders do not develop into major ones. **20**

selective attention. An adaptive mechanism by which human beings take in and process only some of the information bombarding their senses at any given moment. **3**

selective serotonin reuptake inhibitors (SSRIs) A class of antidepressants that work by blocking the reuptake of the neurotransmitter serotonin. **21**

self-actualization According to Rogers, the process of exploring and fulfilling one's potential. **2**

self-help groups Groups of people who share a special problem and meet to discuss that problem without the help of mental health professionals. **20**

self-instructional training A cognitive therapy technique that teaches people to control their behavior by controlling what they say to themselves before, during, and after their actions. **17**

self psychology Kohut's view, based on his work with narcissistic personality patients, that the development of the self depends on the child's receiving from the parents confirmation of his or her sense of "greatness" and sense of calmness and infallibility. Thus, empathy in treatment is more effective than interpretation in strengthening the patient's self. **2**

self-report personality inventories Psychological tests which, unlike projective tests such as the Rorschach and TAT, ask the subjects direct questions about themselves. **6**

senile dementias The pathological degenerative diseases of later life resulting from a severe organic deterioration of the brain. **16**

separation anxiety disorder A childhood disorder characterized by intense fear and distress upon being separated from parents or other caretakers. **17**

separation-individuation The four-stage process, outlined by Mahler, by which the infant separates psychologically from the mother. Beginning at five months of age, the infant undergoes differentiation (distinguishing between his or her own and the mother's bodies), practicing (physically escaping from the mother), rapprochement (alternatively pushing away and clinging to the mother), and object constancy (internalizing the image of the mother and consolidating his or her own personality). **2**

sexual aversion disorder Active avoidance of sex as a result of feelings of disgust or fear about it. **73**

sexual dysfunctions Disorders involving either a disruption of the sexual response cycle or pain during intercourse. **13**

shame aversion therapy A behavioral technique in which deviant sexual arousal is eliminated by having the patient perform a deviant act in the therapist's office while the therapist observes and comments. **13**

shaping A type of operant conditioning, often used with children, whereby the subject is reinforced for successive approximations of target behavior. **3**

sheltered workshops Special work centers designed to meet the needs of the retarded people who are employed in them. **18**

simple partial seizure A partial epileptic seizure in which cognitive functioning remains intact. **16**

single-case experiment A research design that focuses on behavior change in one person but, unlike the *case study*, methodically varies the conditions surrounding the person's behavior and monitors the behavior under the changing conditions. **5**

situational dysfunction A sexual dysfunction that occurs only in certain situations or with certain partners. **13**

situational variables The environmental stimuli that precede and follow any given action by a person. **6**

sleepwalking A dissociative disorder in which the person walks and performs some complex action while asleep. It is much more common in children than in adults. Also called *somnambulism.*

social phobia A phobic disorder in which the person's anxiety is aroused by one or more social situations and is related to the person's fear of being humiliated or criticized. In childhood, this disorder typically takes the form of a paralyzing fear of strangers—peers as well as adults. **7, 17**

social-skills training A behavioral therapy that teaches depressed or schizophrenic people basic techniques for engaging in satisfying interactions with others. **10, 15, 20**

sociocultural perspective The theory that abnormal behavior is the product of broad social forces and conditions such as poverty, urbanization, and inequality. **3**

somatic nervous system That part of the peripheral nervous system that senses and acts on the external world, relaying to the brain information picked up by the sense organs and transmitting the brain's messages to the skeletal muscles, which move the body. **4**

somatization disorder A syndrome characterized by numerous and recurrent physical complaints, persisting for several years, for which no medical basis can be found. **8**

somatoform disorders Conditions in which psychological conflicts take on a somatic or physical form. These disorders include hypochondriasis, somatization disorder, and conversion disorder. **8**

specific phobia A phobic disorder with a particular stimulus, such as heights, enclosed places, injury, or a certain type of animal. **7**

spectator role A sexual dysfunction in which a person is constantly watching and judging his or her sexual performance and is not able to relax and experience pleasure. This worry often causes the much-feared failure, because the tension blunts response to sexual stimuli. **13**

standard of proof In commitment hearings, the degree of certainty required in order to commit someone to a mental institution. There must be "clear and convincing evidence" that the person is mentally ill and dangerous. **22**

statistical inference A technique used by researchers to try to determine whether differences between experimental groups are due to the independent variable. It begins by assuming the *null hypothesis* and then using probability theory to determine the likelihood of having obtained the experimental results if the independent variable had had no effect. If the likelihood is small, the result is judged to be statistically significant and the independent variable is assumed to have had an effect. **5**

stereotactic subcaudate tractotomy A psychosurgical technique for severely depressed or aggressive patients in which a small, localized area of the brain is destroyed by radioactive particles inserted through small ceramic rods. **21**

stereotypy The act of engaging in purposeless behaviors repetitively for hours, sometimes manifested by schizophrenics. **14**

stimulants A class of drugs that provide energy, alertness, and feelings of confidence. **12**

stimulus control An operant-conditioning technique in which a predictable relationship is established between a given stimulus and a given response by eliminating all other stimuli associated with that response and all other responses associated with that stimulus. **19**

stimulus satiation A behavioral technique in which the attractiveness of a stimulus is reduced by providing an overabundance of it. **13**

stimulus specificity The principle that different kinds of stress produce different kinds of physiological response. **9**

stress Variously defined as environmental stimulus of the body, as the body's response to the demands of the environment, and as the interaction between an environmental stimulus and the body's appraisal of it. **9**

stroke *See* **cerebrovascular accident.**

structural family therapy A therapeutic approach in which family members are encouraged to fashion more comfortable and flexible roles for themselves within the family unit. **20**

structural hypothesis Freud's belief that the mind can be divided into three broad forces: the id, the ego, and the superego. **2**

stuttering The interruption of fluent speech through blocked, prolonged, or repeated words, syllables, or sounds. **17**

sublimation A defense mechanism in which sexual or aggressive energy is transformed and expressed in more socially acceptable forms. **2**

substance abuse A pattern of maladaptive drug use that has not progressed to full-blown dependence. It is determined by the appearance of any one of the following symptoms: recurrent drug-related failure to fulfill major role obligations (e.g., absenteeism from school or work, neglect of children); recurrent drug use in physically dangerous situations (e.g., drunk driving); drug-related legal problems; and continued drug use despite social or interpersonal problems caused by the effects of the drug. *Cf.* **substance dependence. 12**

substance dependence The diagnostic category to which a drug user is assigned who fulfills any three of these seven criteria: preoccupation with the drug; unintentional overuse; tolerance; withdrawal; persistent desire or efforts to control drug use; the abandonment of important social, occupational, or recreational activities for the sake of drug use; and continued drug use despite serious drug-related problems. *Cf.* **substance abuse. 12**

superego According to Freud, the part of the mind that represents the moral standards of the society and parents, as internalized by the child. **2**

sympathetic division The division of the autonomic nervous system which becomes dominant in times of stress and which heightens the body's arousal, causing blood pressure, heart rate, perspiration, and adrenaline to increase, pupils to dilate, and salivation and digestive functions to diminish. (*Cf.* **parasympathetic division.**) **4**

symptomatic epilepsy The label applied to convulsions that are a function of brain damage caused by pathologies such as neurosyphilis, alcohol or drug intoxication, tumors, encephalitis, trauma, or strokes. **16**

synapse The gap between two neurons across which nerve impulses pass. **4**

syndrome The distinct cluster of symptoms that tend to occur in a particular disease. **1**

synergistic effect The combined impact of two drugs, which is greater than the effect of either drug when taken alone. **12**

systematic desensitization A behavior therapy technique in which the patient, while in a relaxed state, imagines his or her anxiety-provoking stimuli or is presented with the actual stimuli. Progressing from the least to the most feared situations, the patient learns to remain relaxed—a response that should carry over to real-life situations. **7, 19**

systems theories Perspectives that view abnormal behavior as the product of habitual relationship patterns, usually within the family. An approach to understanding sexual dysfunction that is based on the analysis of relationships as systems of interlocking needs. The theory holds that sexual dysfunction, although distressing to a couple, has a function in their overall relationship. **3, 13**

tardive dyskinesia A muscle disorder that causes uncontrollable grimacing and lip smacking; caused by antipsychotic drugs. **15**

Tay-Sachs disease A genetic disorder of lipid metabolism marked by the absence of the enzyme hexosominidase A in brain tissues; causes mental retardation, muscular deterioration, convulsions, and death before the age of six. **18**

tertiary prevention The third level of prevention of psychological disorder, the goal of which is to minimize the damage, to both the victim and society, of a major disorder. **20**

test-retest reliability A criterion for judging the reliability of a psychological test: the test should yield the same results when administered to the same person at different times. **6**

Thematic Apperception Test (TAT) A frequently used projective personality test in which the subject is presented with a series of pictures showing one, two, or three people doing something. The scenes are ambiguous enough to allow for a variety of interpretations, yet they nudge the subject in the direction of certain kinds of associations, unlike the Rorschach test. For example, a picture of a man in a business suit might tap a subject's feelings about his or her father. **6**

theory of the mind The ability, lacking in autistic children, to appreciate the existence of purely mental states, such as beliefs or desires, and to predict or understand behavior based on such states. **18**

therapeutic environment The arrangement of an institutional environment in such a way that all the patient's interactions with that environment will serve some therapeutic purpose. **20**

third-variable problem In scientific research, an alternative factor, not considered by the researchers, that may be causing the covariation of the two factors being investigated. **5**

thrombosis The obstruction of a blood vessel by a buildup of fatty material coating the inside of the vessel, thus blocking the flow of blood; a common cause of infarction. **16**

time-order relationship The second condition to be met before causality can be demonstrated: The presumed cause must occur before the presumed effect. **5**

token economy A behavior modification procedure, based on operant-conditioning principles, in which patients are given a conditioned reinforcer such as tokens for performing target behaviors. The patients can exchange the tokens for backup reinforcers such as snacks or special privileges. **15, 20**

tolerance The physiological condition in which the usual dosage of a drug no longer produces the desired effect. **12**

tonic-clonic seizures Generalized epileptic seizures that typically begin with a tonic, or rigid, extension of the arms and legs, followed by a clonic, or jerking, movement throughout the body. **16**

traits Stable underlying characteristics that presumably exist in differing degrees in everyone. **6**

tranquilizers A group of drugs that produce mild calm and relaxation. They can be addictive and have side effects. Among the most popular are Tranxene, Librium, and Valium. **12**

transference In psychoanalytic theory, the process by which patients identify the therapist with important people in their lives, usually with their parents, and project onto the therapist their relationship with those people. **7, 19**

transsexualism *See* **gender identity disorder.**

transvestism Sexual gratification through dressing in the clothes of the opposite sex. **13**

traumatic delirium The state of disorientation that a patient suffering from a brain contusion may experience upon awakening from the coma. **16**

trichotillomania The compulsive pulling out of one's own hair. **7**

tricyclics A class of drugs widely used to treat depression, which generally work by blocking the reuptake of the neurotransmitter norepinephrine by the presynaptic neuron. **10, 21**

trisomy 21 A condition in which there is an extra chromosome in pair 21 in the human cell; the genetic basis of Down syndrome. **18**

Type A A personality characterized by pressure to achieve, impatience, high standards of self-evaluation, and hostility. **9**

Type I schizophrenia A dimension of schizophrenia characterized by positive symptoms. **14**

Type II schizophrenia A dimension of schizophrenia characterized by negative symptoms. **14**

unconditioned response A natural, unlearned response to a stimulus. **3**

unconditioned stimulus A stimulus that elicits a natural or unconditioned response. **3**

unconscious In Freudian theory, the level of the mind consciousness that contains all memories not readily available to the perceptual conscious, because they have been either forgotten or repressed. **2**

understanding The fourth objective of the scientific method: the identification of the cause or causes of a phenomenon. **5**

undoing A defense mechanism in which a person engages in a ritual behavior or thought in order to cancel out an unacceptable impulse. **2**

vaginismus A sexual dysfunction in which the muscles surrounding the entrance to the vagina undergo involuntary spasmodic contractions, making intercourse either impossible or painfully difficult. **13**

validity The degree to which a description or test measures what it is supposed to measure. **5, 6**

valuing process Rogers' theory that people judge experiences as self-enhancing or not enhancing. Self-enhancing experiences are sought after, and negative experiences are avoided. **2**

vascular dementia The impairment of many of the brain's faculties as the cumulative result of many infarctions. **16**

voyeurism Sexual gratification through clandestine observation of other people's sexual activities or sexual anatomy. **13**

will-to-meaning In Frankl's existential philosophy, the struggle of human beings to find some reason for their troubled, complicated, and finite existence. **2**

withdrawal symptoms Temporary psychological and physiological disturbances resulting from the body's attempt to readjust to the absence of a drug. **12**

word salad A schizophrenic speech pattern in which words and phrases are combined in a disorganized fashion, seemingly devoid of logic, meaning, and even associational links. **14**

REFERENCES

Abel, G. G., Becker, J. V., Cunningham-Rathner, J., Mittelman, M., et al. (1988). Multiple paraphilic diagnoses among sex offenders. *Bulletin of the American Academy of Psychiatry and the Law, 16,* 153–168.

Abel, G. G., Gore, D. K., Holland, C. L., Camp, N., Becker, J. V., & Rathner, J. (1989). The measurement of cognitive distortions in child molesters. *Annals of Sex Research, 2,* 135–153.

Abel, G. G., Lawry, A. S., Karlstrom, K., Osborn, C. A., & Gillespie, C. F. (1994). Screening tests for pedophilia. *Criminal Justice and Behavior, 21,* 115–131.

Abel, G. G., Osborn, C., Anthony, D., & Gardos, P. (1992). Current treatment of paraphiliacs. In J. Bancroft, C. Davis, & H. Ruppel (Eds.), *Annual Review of Sex Research,* 255–290.

Abel, G. G., Rouleau, J., & Cunningham-Rathner, J. (1984). Sexually aggressive behavior. In W. Curran, A. L. McGarry, & S. A. Shah (Eds.), *Modern legal psychiatry and psychology.* Philadelphia: Davis.

Abikoff, H. (1985). Efficacy of cognitive training interventions in hyperactive children: A critical review. Special Issue: Attention deficit disorder: Issues in assessment and intervention. *Clinical Psychology Review, 5,* 479–512.

Abraham, H. D. (1983). Visual phenomenology of the LSD flashback. *Archives of General Psychiatry, 40,* 518–520.

Abraham, H. D., & Wolf, E. (1988). Visual function in past users of LSD: Psychophysical findings. *Journal of Abnormal Psychology, 97,* 443–447.

Abraham, K. (1948). Notes on psychoanalytic investigation and treatment of manic-depressive insanity and applied conditions. In *Selected papers of Karl Abraham, M.D.* (D. Bryan & A. Strachey, Trans.). London: Hogarth Press. (Original work published 1911)

Abraham, K. (1948). The first pregenital stage of the libido. In *Selected papers of Karl Abraham, M.D.* (D. Bryan & A. Strachey, Trans.). London: Hogarth Press. (Original work published 1916)

Abramowitz, S. I. (1986). Psychosocial outcomes of sex reassignment surgery. *Journal of Consulting and Clinical Psychology, 54,* 183–189.

Abrams, R. (1992). *Electroconvulsive therapy* (2nd ed). New York: Oxford University Press.

Abramson, L. Y., Alloy, L. B., & Metalsky, G. I. (1994). Hopelessness depression. In G. Buchanan & M. E. P. Seligman (Eds.), *Explanatory style.* Hillsdale, NJ: Erlbaum.

Abramson, L. Y., Metalsky, G. I., & Alloy, L. B. (1989). Hopelessness depression: A theory-based subtype of depression. *Psychological Review. 96:*358–372.

Abramson, L. Y., Seligman, M. E. P., & Teasdale, J. D. (1978). Learned helplessness in humans: Critique and reformulation. *Journal of Abnormal Psychology, 96,* 358–372.

Addington v. Texas, 99 S.Ct. 1804 (1979).

Adler, A. (1988). The child's inner life and sense of community. *Individual Psychology, 44,* 417–423. (Original work published 1917)

Agency for Health Care Policy and Research. (1993). *Depression in primary care: Treatment of major depression* Rockville, MD: Author. (DHHS, AHCPR Publication No. 93–0551).

Aggleton, J. P. (1992). *The amygdala: Neurobiological aspects of emotion, memory, and mental dysfunction.* New York: Wiley-Liss.

Agnello, J. G. (1975). Voice onset and voice termination features of stutters. In L. M. Webster & L. C. Furst (Eds.), *Vocal tract dynamics and dysfluency.* New York: Speech and Hearing Institute.

Aichhorn, A. (1935). *Wayward youth.* London: Putnam.

Akbarian, S., Bunney, W. E., Potkin, S. G., Wigal, S. B., Hagman, J. O., Sandman, C. A., & Jones, E. G. (1993). Altered distribution of nicotinamide-adenine dinucleotide phosphate-diaphorase cells in frontal lobe of schizophrenics implies disturbances of cortical development. *Archives of General Psychiatry, 50,* 169–177.

Akbarian, S., Vinuela, A., Kim, J. J., Potkin, S. G., Bunney, W. E., Jr., & Jones, E. G. (1993). Distorted distribution of nicotinamide-adenine dinucleotide phosphate-diaphorase neurons in temporal lobe of schizophrenics implies anomalous cortical development. *Archives of General Psychiatry, 50,* 178–187.

Akiskal, H. S. (1983). Dysthymic disorder: Psychopathology of proposed chronic depressive subtypes. *American Journal of Psychiatry, 140,* 11–20.

Alabiso, F. (1975). Operant control of attention behavior: A treatment for hyperactivity. *Behavior Therapy, 6,* 39–42.

Alcoholism Council of Greater New York. (1987). *Some facts of alcoholism in industry.* New York: Author.

Aldrich, C. K. (1986). The clouded crystal ball: A 35-year follow-up of psychiatrists' predictions. *American Journal of Psychiatry, 143,* 45–49.

Aldrich, M. S. (1989). Cardinal manifestations of sleep disorders. In M. H. Kryger, T. Roth, & W. C. Dement (Eds.), *Principles and practice of sleep medicine* (pp. 351–357). Philadelphia: Saunders.

Alessandri, S. (1991). Play and social behavior in maltreated preschoolers. *Development and Psychopathology, 3,* 191–205.

Alexander, A. B. (1981). Asthma. In S. N. Haynes & L. Gannon (Eds.), *Psychosomatic disorders: A psychophysiological approach to etiology and treatment.* New York: Praeger.

Alexander, B. K., & Hadaway, P. F. (1982). Opiate addiction: The case for an adaptive orientation. *Psychological Bulletin, 92,* 367–381.

Alexander, F. (1939). Emotional factors in essential hypertension. *Psychosomatic Medicine, 1,* 153–216.

Alexander, J. F., Holtzworth-Munroe, & Jameson, P. (1994). The process and outcome of marital and family therapy: Research review and evaluation. In A. E. Bergin, & S. L. Garfield (Eds.), *Handbook of psychotherapy and behavior change* (4th ed., pp. 595–630). New York: Wiley.

Allderidge, P. (1979). Hospitals, madhouses and asylums: Cycles in the care of the insane. *British Journal of Psychiatry, 134,* 321–334.

Allderidge, P. (1985). Bedlam: Fact or fantasy? In W. F. Bynum, R. Porter, & M. Shepherd (Eds.), *The anatomy of madness: Essays in the history of psychiatry* (Vol. 2). New York: Tavistock.

Allebeck, P. (1989). Schizophrenia: A life-shortening disease. *Schizophrenia Bulletin, 15,* 81–89.

Allen, J. J., Chapman, L. J., Chapman, J., Vuchetich, J. P., & Frost, L. A. (1987). Prediction of psychoticlike symptoms in hypothetically psychosis-prone college students. *Journal of Abnormal Psychology, 96,* 83–88.

Allen, M. G. (1976). Twin studies of affective illness. *Archives of General Psychiatry, 33,* 1476–1478.

Allgood-Merten, B., Lewinsohn, P. M., & Hops, H. (1990). Sex differences and adolescent depression. *Journal of Abnormal Psychology, 99,* 55–63.

Alloy, L. B., & Abramson, L. Y. (1979). The judgment of contingency in depressed and nondepressed students: Sadder but wiser? *Journal of Experimental Psychology: General, 108,* 441–485.

Alloy, L. B., & Abramson, L. Y. (1988). Depressive realism: Four theoretical perspectives. In L. B. Alloy (Ed.), *Cognitive processes in depression* (pp. 223–265). New York: Guilford Press.

Alloy, L. B., Abramson, L. Y., & Viscusi, D. (1981). Induced mood and the illusion of control. *Journal of Personality and Social Psychology, 41,* 1129–1140.

Alloy, L. B., Abramson, L. Y., Whitehouse, W. G., Teraspulsky, L., & Hogan, M. (1994). *Prospective incidence of unipolar depressive disorders: Cognitive diathesis-stress prediction.* Paper presented at the meeting of the American Psychopathological Association, March 3–5, 1994, New York.

Alloy, L. B., & Clements, C. M. (1992). Illusion of control: Invulnerability to negative affect and depressive symptoms after laboratory and natural stressors. *Journal of Abnormal Psychology, 101,* 234–245.

Alloy, L. B., Clements, C. M., & Kolden, G. (1985). The cognitive diathesis-stress theories of depression: Therapeutic implications. In S. Reiss & R. R. Bootzin (Eds.), *Theoretical issues in behavior therapy* (pp. 379–410). New York: Academic Press.

Alloy, L. B., Just, N., & Panzarella, C. (1994). *Attributional style, life events and variability of depressive symptoms: A prospective behavioral high-risk paradigm.* Unpublished manuscript, Temple University, Philadelphia.

Alloy, L. B., Kelly, K. A., Mineka, S., & Clements, C. M. (1990). Comorbidity of anxiety and depressive disorders: A helplessness-hopelessness perspective. In J. D. Maser & R. C. R. Cloninger (Eds.), *Comorbidity of mood and anxiety disorders* (pp. 499–543). Washington, DC: American Psychiatric Press.

Alloy, L. B., Lipman, A. J., & Abramson, L. Y. (1992). Attributional style as a vulnerability factor for depression: Validation by past history of mood disorders. *Cognitive Therapy and Research, 16,* 391–407.

Allport, G. W. (1961). *Pattern and growth in personality.* New York: Holt, Rinehart and Winston.

Alperstein, G., Rapport, C., & Flanagan, J. (1988). Health problems of homeless children in New York City. *American Journal of Public Health, 78,* 1231–1233.

Alpert, M., Clark, A., & Pouget, E. R. (1994). The syntactic role of pauses in the speech of schizophrenic patients with alogia. *Journal of Abnormal Psychology, 103,* 750–757.

Alschuler, R. (1979). Plea bargaining and its history. *Law and Society Review, 13,* 211–245.

Alterman, A. I., O'Brien, C. P., McLellan, A. T., August, D. S., et al. (1994). Effectiveness and costs of inpatient versus day hospital cocaine rehabilitation. *Journal of Nervous and Mental Disease, 182,* 157–163.

Althof, S. E., Turner, L. A., Levine, S. B., Risen, C., Kursh, E. D., Bodner, D., & Resnick, M. (1987). Intracavernosal injection in the treatment of impotence: A prospective study of sexual, psychological, and marital functioning. *Journal of Sex and Marital Therapy, 13*(3), 155–167.

American Association on Mental Retardation. (1992). *Mental retardation: Definition, classification, and systems of support* (9th ed.).

American Cancer Society. (1994). *Cancer facts and figures—1993,* New York: Author.

American Psychiatric Association. (1980). *Diagnostic and statistical manual of mental disorders (DSM-III)* (3rd ed.). Washington, DC: Author.

American Psychiatric Association. (1987). *Diagnostic and statistical manual of mental disorders (DSM-III-R)* (3rd ed. rev.). Washington, DC: Author.

American Psychiatric Association. (1990). *The practice of electroconvulsive therapy: Recommendations for treatment, training, and privileging.* Washington, DC: Author.

American Psychiatric Association. (1994). *Diagnostic and statistical manual of mental disorders* (4th ed.). Washington, DC: Author.

American Psychiatric Association membership upholds decision of trustees bid to drop homosexuality from list of mental disorders. (1974, April 9). *The New York Times,* p. 12.

American Psychological Association. (1993). APA-accredited doctoral programs in professional psychology: 1993. *American Psychologist, 12,* 1260–1270.

American Sleep Disorder Association. (1990). *The international classification of sleep disorders: Diagnostic and coding manual.* Rochester, MN: Diagnostic Classification Steering Committee.

Amos, P. (Ed.). (1993). *Auditory training as autism therapy: A preliminary review.* Autism Support and Advocacy in Pennsylvania.

Anastasi, A. (1982). *Psychological testing* (5th ed.). New York: Macmillan.

Anderson, B. L. (1983). Primary orgasmic dysfunction: Diagnostic considerations and review of treatment. *Psychological Bulletin, 93,* 105–136.

Anderson, B. L., Kiecolt-Glaser, J. K., & Glaser, R. (1994). A biobehavioral model of cancer stress and disease course. *American Psychologist, 49,* 389–404.

Anderson, J. C. (1994). Epidemiological issues. In Ollendick, T. H., King, N. J., & Yule, W. (Eds.), *International handbook of phobic and anxiety disorders in children and adolescents* (pp. 43–65). New York: Plenum Press.

Anderson, V. E., & Hauser, W. A. (1991). Genetics. In M. Dam & L. Gram (Eds.), *Comprehensive epileptology* (pp. 57–76). New York: Raven Press.

Andreasen, N. C. (1987). Creativity and mental illness: Prevalence rates in writers and their first-degree relatives. *American Journal of Psychiatry, 144,* 1288–1292.

Andreasen, N. C. (1989). Neural mechanisms of negative symptoms. *British Journal of Psychiatry, 155,* 93–98.

Andreasen, N. C., McDonald-Scott, P., Grove, W. M., Keller, M. B., Shapiro, R. W., & Hirschfeld, R. (1982). Assessment of reliability in multicenter collaborative research with a videotape approach. *American Journal of Psychiatry, 139,* 876–882.

Andreasen, N. C., & Olsen, S. (1982). Negative v. positive schizophrenia: Definition and validation. *Archives of General Psychiatry, 39,* 789–794.

Andreasen, N. C., Rezai, K., Alliger, R., Swayze, V. W., II, Flaum, M., Kirchner, P., Cohen, G., & O'Leary, D. S. (1992). Hypofrontality in neuroleptic-naive patients and in patients with chronic schizophrenia: Assessment with Xenon 133 single-photon emission computed tomography and the Tower of London. *Archives of General Psychiatry, 49,* 943–958.

Andrews, J. A., & Lewinsohn, P. M. (1992). Suicidal attempts among older adolescents: Prevalence and co-occurrence with psychiatric disorders. *Journal of the American Academy of Child and Adolescent Psychiatry, 31,* 655–662.

Annegers, J. F. (1993). The epidemiology of epilepsy. In E. Wyllie (Ed.), *The treatment of epilepsy: Principles and practice* (pp. 157–164). Philadelphia: Lea & Febiger.

Appelbaum, P. A. (1994). *Almost a revolution: Mental health law and the limits of change.* New York: Oxford University Press.

Appelbaum, P. A., & Gutheil, T. G. (1991). *Clinical handbook of psychiatry and the law* (2nd ed.). Baltimore: Williams & Wilkins.

Arieti, S. (1974a). *Interpretation of schizophrenia.* New York: Basic Books.

Arieti, S. (1974b). An overview of schizophrenia from a predominantly psychological approach. *American Journal of Psychiatry, 131*(3), 241–249.

Aring, C. D. (1974). The Gheel experience: Eternal spirit of the chainless mind! *Journal of the American Medical Association, 203,* 998–1001.

Arkowitz, H., & Messer, S. B. (Eds.). (1984). *Psychoanalytic therapy and behavior therapy: Is integration possible?* New York: Plenum Press.

Aronson, E. (1972). *The social animal.* San Francisco: Freeman.

Aronson, S. M., & Volk, B. W. (1965). The nervous system sphingolipodoses. In C. H. Carter (Ed.), *Medical aspects of mental retardation.* Springfield, IL: Charles C Thomas.

Aronson, T. A., Carasiti, I., McBane, D., & Whitaker-Azmitia, P. (1989). Biological correlates of lactate sensitivity in panic disorder. *Biological Psychiatry, 26,* 463–477.

Arrindell, W. A., Emmelkamp, P. M. G., Monsma, A., & Brilman, E. (1983). The role of perceived parental rearing practices in the etiology of phobic disorders: A controlled study. *British Journal of Psychiatry, 143,* 183–187.

Artiss, K. L. (1962). *Milieu therapy in schizophrenia.* New York: Grune & Stratton.

Axline, V. M. (1969). *Play therapy* (rev. ed.). New York: Ballantine.

Azar, S. T., & Pearlmutter, R. (1993). Physical abuse and neglect. In R. T. Ammerman, C. G. Last, & M. Hersen

(Eds.), *Handbook of prescriptive treatments for children and adolescents* (pp. 367–382). Boston: Allyn and Bacon.

Azar, S. T., & Twentyman, C. T. (1986). Cognitive-behavioral perspectives on the assessment and treatment of child abuse. *Advances in cognitive-behavioral research* (Vol. 5, pp. 237–267). New York: Academic Press.

Baekeland, F., Lundwall, L., Kissin, B., & Shanahan, T. (1971). Correlates of outcome in disulfiram treatment of alcoholism. *Journal of Nervous and Mental Disease, 153*(1), 1–9.

Baer, L., & Jenike, M. A. (1992). Personality disorders in obsessive compulsive disorder. *Psychiatric Clinics of North America, 15,* 803–812.

Baird, T. D., & August, G. J. (1985). Familial heterogeneity in infantile autism. *Journal of Autism and Developmental Disorders, 15,* 315–321.

Baker, B., & Merskey, H. (1982). Parental representations of hypochondriacal patients from a psychiatric hospital. *British Journal of Psychiatry, 141,* 233–238.

Baker, R. (1971). The use of operant conditioning to reinstate speech in mute schizophrenics. *Behaviour Research and Therapy, 9,* 329–336.

Bakwin, H., & Bakwin, R. M. (1972). *Behavior disorders in children.* Philadelphia: Saunders.

Baldessarini, R. J., & Frankenburg, F. R. (1991). Clozapine—a novel antipsychotic agent. *New England Journal of Medicine, 324,* 746.

Ball, J. C., Shaffer, J. W., & Nurco, D. N. (1983). Day to day criminality of heroin addicts in Baltimore: A study in the continuity of offense rates. *Drug and Alcohol Dependence, 12,* 119–142.

Bandura, A. (1976). Social learning analysis of aggression. In E. Ribes-Inesta & A. Bandura (Eds.), *Analysis of delinquency and aggression.* Hillsdale, NJ: Erlbaum.

Bandura, A. (1977). Self-efficacy: Toward a unifying theory of behavioral change. *Psychological Review, 84,* 191–215.

Bandura, A. (1982). Self-efficacy mechanism in human agency. *American Psychologist, 37,* 122–147.

Bandura, A. (1986). *Social foundations of thought and action.* Englewood Cliffs, NJ: Prentice-Hall.

Bandura, A., Taylor, C. B., & Williams, S. L. (1985). Catecholamine secretion as a function of perceived coping self-efficacy. *Journal of Consulting and Clinical Psychology, 53,* 406–414.

Bandura, A., & Walters, R. (1963). *Social learning and personality development.* New York: Holt, Rinehart and Winston.

Barber, J. P., & DeRubeis, R. J. (1989). On second thought: Where the action is in cognitive therapy for depression. *Cognitive Therapy and Research, 13,* 441–457.

Bard, M. (1970). *Training police as specialists in family crisis intervention.* Washington, DC: U.S. Government Printing Office.

Barkley, R. A. (1989). Attention-deficit hyperactivity disorder. In E. J. Mash & R. A. Barkley (Eds.), *Treatment of childhood disorders.* New York: Guilford Press.

Barkley, R. A. (1990). *Attention-deficit hyperactivity disorder: A handbook for diagnosis and treatment.* New York: Guilford Press.

Barkley, R. A., DuPaul, G. J., & McMurray, M. B. (1990). A comprehensive evaluation of attention-deficit disorder with and without hyperactivity defined by research criteria. *Journal of Consulting and Clinical Psychology, 58,* 775–789.

Barlow, D. H. (1988). *Anxiety and its disorders.* New York: Guilford Press.

Barnett, P. A., & Gotlib, I. H. (1990). Cognitive vulnerability to depressive symptoms among men and women. *Cognitive Therapy and Research, 14,* 47–61.

Baroff, G. S. (1974). *Mental retardation: Nature, cause, and management.* Washington, DC: Hemisphere.

Baron-Cohen, S., Leslie, A. M., & Frith, U. (1985). Does the autistic child have a "theory of mind"? *Cognition, 21,* 37–46.

Barondes, S. H. (1994). Thinking about Prozac. *Science, 263,* 1102–1103.

Barr, L. C., Goodman, W. K., Price, L. H., McDougle, C. J., & Charney, D. S. (1992). The serotonin hypothesis of obsessive compulsive disorder: Implications of pharmacologic challenge studies. *Journal of Clinical Psychiatry, 53,* 17–28.

Barrett, J. E., Barrett, J. A., Oxman, T. E., & Gerber, P. D. (1988). The prevalence of psychiatric disorders in a primary care practice. *Archives of General Psychiatry, 45,* 1100–1106.

Barry, M. (1991). The influence of the U.S. tobacco industry on the health, economy, and environment of developing countries. *New England Journal of Medicine, 342,* 917–920.

Barsky, A. J. (1992a). Amplification, somatization, and the somatoform disorders. *Psychosomatics, 33,* 28–34.

Barsky, A. J. (1992b). Hypochondriasis and obsessive compulsive disorder. *Psychiatric Clinics of North America, 15,* 791–801.

Barsky, A. J., Wyshak, G., & Klerman, G. (1990). The somatosensory amplification scale and its relationship to hypochondriasis. *Journal of Psychiatric Research, 24,* 328–334.

Bartlett, J., Bridges, P., & Kelly, D. (1981). Contemporary indications for psychosurgery. *British Journal of Psychiatry, 138,* 507–511.

Bartlik, B. D. (1981). Monthly variation in births of autistic children in North Carolina. *Journal of the American Medical Women's Association, 36,* 363–368.

Bartrop, R. W., Luckhurst, E., Lazarus, L., Kiloh, L. G., & Penny, R. (1977). Depressed lymphocyte function after bereavement. *Lancet,* 834–836.

Bass, E., & Davis, L. (1988). *The courage to heal.* New York: Harper & Row.

Bateson, G., Jackson, D., Haley, J., & Weakland, J. (1956). Toward a theory of schizophrenia. *Behavioral Science, 1,* 251–264.

Baucom, D. H., & Epstein, N. (1990). *Cognitive behavioral marital therapy.* New York: Brunner/Mazel.

Bauer, M. S., Calabrese, J., Dunner, D. L., Post, R., Whybrow, P. C., Gyulai, L., Tay, L. K., Younkin, S. R., Bynum, D., Lavori, P., & Price, R. A. (1994). Multisite data reanalysis of the validity of rapid cycling as a course modifier for bipolar disorder in *DSM-IV. American Journal of Psychiatry, 151,* 506–515.

Bauer, M. S., & Whybrow, P. C. (1990). Rapid cycling bipolar affective disorder: II. Treatment of refractory rapid cycling with high-dose levothyroxine: A preliminary study. *Archives of General Psychiatry, 47,* 435–440.

Baxter, L. R., Phelps, M. E., Mazziotta, S. C., et al. (1987). Local cerebral glucose metabolic rates in obsessive-compulsive disorder. *Archives of General Psychiatry, 44,* 211–218.

Beach, S. R. H., Whisman, M. A., & O'Leary, K. D. (1994). Marital therapy for depression: Theoretical foundation, current status, and future directions. *Behavior Therapy, 25,* 345–371.

Beck, A. T. (1963). Thinking and depression: I. Idiosyncratic content and cognitive distortion. *Archives of General Psychiatry, 9,* 324–333.

Beck, A. T. (1967). *Depression: Clinical, experimental, and theoretical aspects.* New York: Harper & Row.

Beck, A. T. (1976). *Cognitive therapy and the emotional disorders.* New York: International Universities Press.

Beck, A. T. (1987). Cognitive models of depression. *Journal of Cognitive Psychotherapy, 1,* 5–37.

Beck, A. T. (1988). Cognitive approaches to panic disorder: Theory and therapy. In S. Rachman & J. D. Maser (Eds.), *Panic: Psychological perspectives.* Hillsdale, NJ: Erlbaum.

Beck, A. T., Brown, G., Berchick, R. J., Stewart, B. L., & Steer, R. A. (1990). Relationship between hopelessness and ultimate suicide: A replication with psychiatric outpatients. *American Journal of Psychiatry, 147,* 190–195.

Beck, A. T., Emery, G., & Greenberg, R. L. (1985). *Anxiety disorders and phobias: A cognitive perspective.* New York: Basic Books.

Beck, A. T., Freeman, A., Pretzer, J., Davis, D., Fleming, B., Ottaviani, R., Beck, J., Simon, K. M., Padesky, C., Meyer, J., & Trexler, L. (1990). *Cognitive therapy of personality disorders.* New York: Guilford Press.

Beck, A. T., Rush, A. J., Shaw, B. F., & Emery, G. (1979). *Cognitive theory of depression.* New York: Guilford Press.

Beck, A. T., Steer, R. A., Kovacs, M., & Garrison, B. (1985). Hopelessness and eventual suicide: A 10-year prospective study of patients hospitalized with suicidal ideation. *American Journal of Psychiatry, 142,* 559–563.

Beck, A. T., Ward, C. H., Mendelson, M., Mock, J., & Erbaugh, J. (1962). Reliability of psychiatric diagnoses: 2. A study of consistency of clinical judgments and ratings. *American Journal of Psychiatry, 119,* 351–357.

Beck, A. T., Weissman, A., Lester, D., & Trexler, L. (1974). The measurement of pessimism: The hopelessness scale. *Journal of Consulting and Clinical Psychology, 42,* 861–865.

Beck, S. J. (1961). *Rorschach's test: I. Basic processes* (3rd ed.). New York: Grune & Stratton.

Becker, J. V., & Kavoussi, R. J. (1994). Sexual and gender identity disorders. In *The American Psychiatric Press textbook of psychiatry.* Washington, DC: American Psychiatric Press.

Becker, J. V., Skinner, L. J., & Abel, G. G. (1983). Sequelae of sexual assault: The survivor's perspective. In J. G. Green & I. R. Stuart (Eds.), *The sexual aggressor.* New York: Van Nostrand.

Becker, J. V., Skinner, L. J., Abel, G. G., & Cichon, J. (1986). Level of postassault sexual functioning in rape and incest victims. *Archives of Sexual Behavior, 15,* 37–49.

Bednar, R. L., & Kaul, T. J. (1978). Experimental group research: Current perspectives. In S. L. Garfield & A. E. Bergin (Eds.), *Handbook of psychotherapy and behavior change: An empirical analysis* (2nd ed.). New York: Wiley.

Bednar, R. L., & Kaul, T. (1994). Experiential group research. In A. E. Bergin & S. L. Garfield (Eds.), *Handbook of psychotherapy and behavior change* (4th ed., pp. 630–663. New York: Wiley.

Bedrosian, R. C., & Beck, A. T. (1980). Principles of cognitive therapy. In M. J. Mahoney (Ed.), *Psychotherapy process: Current issues and future directions.* New York: Plenum Press.

Beech, A., Powell, T., McWilliam, J., & Claridge, G. (1989). Evidence of reduced "cognitive inhibition" in schizophrenia. *British Journal of Clinical Psychology, 28,* 109–116.

Bell, D. S. (1973). The experimental reproduction of amphetamine psychosis. *Archives of General Psychiatry, 39*(1), 35–40.

Bellack, A. S., Morrison, R. L., Wixted, J. T., & Mueser, K. T. (1990). An analysis of social competence in schizophrenia. *British Journal of Psychiatry, 56,* 809–818.

Bellack, A. S., & Mueser, K. T. (1993). Psychosocial treatment for schizophrenia. *Schizophrenia Bulletin, 19,* 317–336.

Bellak, I. (1954). *The Thematic Apperception Test and the Children's Thematic Apperception Test in clinical use.* New York: Grune & Stratton.

Bellinger, D., Leviton, A., Waternaux, C., Needleman, H., & Rabinowitz, M. (1987). Longitudinal analyses of prenatal and postnatal lead exposure and early cognitive development. *New England Journal of Medicine, 316,* 1037–1043.

Belmont, L., Cohen, P., Dryfoos, J., et al. (1981). Maternal age and children's intelligence. In K. G. Scott, T. Field, & E. G. Robertson (Eds.), *Teenage parents and their offspring* (pp. 177–197). New York: Grune & Stratton.

Belsher, G., & Costello, C. G. (1988). Relapse after recovery from unipolar depression; A critical review. *Psychological Bulletin, 104,* 84–96.

Belsher, G., & Costello, C. G. (1991). Do confidants of depressed women provide less social support than confidants of nondepressed women? *Journal of Abnormal Psychology, 100,* 516–525.

Bemporad, J. R. (1988). Psychodynamic models of depression and mania. In A. Georgotas and R. Cancro (Eds.), *Depression and mania.* New York: Elsevier Science.

Benca, R. M., Obermeyer, W. H., Thisted, R. A., & Gillin, J. C. (1992). Sleep and psychiatric disorders: A meta-analysis. *Archives of General Psychiatry, 49,* 651–668.

Bender, L. (1938). A visual motor gestalt test and its clinical use. *Research Monograph of the American Orthopsychiatric Association, 3,* xi, 176.

Bendich, A., & Cohen, M. (1990). Vitamin B_6 safety issues. *Annals of the New York Academy of Science, 585,* 321–337.

Benjamin, H. (1966). *The transsexual phenomenon.* New York: Julian Press.

Benjamin, R. S., Costello, E. J., & Warren, M. (1990). Anxiety disorders in a pediatric sample. *Journal of Anxiety Disorders, 4,* 293–316.

Benson, B. A. (1986). Anger management training. *Psychiatric Aspects of Mental Retardation Reviews, 5*(10), 51–55.

Benson, B. A., Johnson, C., & Miranti, S. V. (1984). *Effects of anger management training with mentally retarded adults.* Paper presented at the 17th annual Gatlinburg Conference on Research in Mental Retardation and Developmental Disabilities.

Bentall, R. P., Baker, G. A., & Havers, S. (1991). Reality monitoring and psychotic hallucinations. *British Journal of Clinical Psychology, 30,* 213–222.

Bentler, P. M., & Prince, C. (1970). Psychiatric symptomology in transvestites. *Journal of Clinical Psychology, 26*(4), 434–455.

Bentler, P. M., Shearman, R. W., & Prince, C. (1970). Personality characteristics of male transvestites. *Journal of Clinical Psychology, 26,* 287–291.

Benton, M. K., & Schroeder, H. E. (1990). Social skills training with schizophrenics: A metaanalytic evaluation. *Journal of Consulting and Clinical Psychology, 58,* 741–747.

Berenbaum, H., & Oltmanns, T. F. (1992). Emotional experience and expression in schizophrenia and depression. *Journal of Abnormal Psychology, 101,* 37–44.

Berger, P. A. (1978). Medical treatment of mental illness. *Science, 200,* 974–981.

Bergeron, L., Valla, J. P., & Breton, J. J. (1992). Pilot study for the Quebec child mental health survey: Part I. Measurement of prevalence estimates among six to fourteen year olds. *Canadian Journal of Psychiatry, 37,* 374–380.

Bergin, A. E., & Lambert, M. J. (1978). The evaluation of therapeutic outcomes. In S. L. Garfield & A. E. Bergin (Eds.), *Handbook of psychotherapy and behavior change: An empirical analysis* (2nd ed.). New York: Wiley.

Bergler, E. (1947). Analysis of an unusual case of fetishism. *Bulletin of the Menninger Clinic, 2,* 67–75.

Berlin, R. M., & Qayyum, U. (1986). Sleepwalking: Diagnosis and treatment through the life cycle. *Psychosomatics, 27,* 755–781.

Berman, A. L. (1988). Fictional depiction of suicide in television films and imitation effects. *American Journal of Psychiatry, 145,* 982–986.

Berns, W. (1994). Getting away with murder. *Commentary, 97*(4), 25–29.

Bernstein, A. S. (1987). Orienting response research in schizophrenia: Where we have come and where we might go. *Schizophrenia Bulletin, 13,* 623–641.

Bernston, G. G., Cacioppo, J. T., & Quigley, K. S. (1991). Autonomic determinism: Modes of autonomic control, the doctrine of autonomic space and laws of autonomic constraint. *Psychological Review, 98,* 459–487.

Berrios, D. C., Hearst, N., Coates, T. J., Stall, R., Hudes, E. S., Turner, H., Eversly, R., & Catania, J. (1993). HIV antibody testing among those at risk for infection: The national AIDS behavioral surveys. *Journal of the American Medical Association, 270,* 1576–1580.

Bettelheim, B. (1967). *The empty fortress.* New York: Free Press.

Beutler, L. (1983). *Eclectic psychotherapy: A systematic approach.* New York: Pergamon Press.

Beutler, L. E., Engle, D., Mohr, D., Daldrup, R. J., Bergan, J., Meredith, K., & Merry, W. (1991). Predictors of differential response to cognitive, experiential, and self-directed psychotherapeutic procedures. *Journal of Consulting and Clinical Psychology, 59,* 333–340.

Beutler, L. E., Machado, P. P. P., & Neufeldt, S. A. (1994). Therapist variables. In A. E. Bergin & S. L. Garfield (Eds.), *Handbook of psychotherapy and behavior change* (4th ed., pp. 229–269). New York: Wiley.

Bickman, L., & Dokecki, P. R. (1989). Public and private responsibility for mental health services. *American Psychologist, 44,* 1133–1137.

Biederman, J., Newcorn, J., & Sprich, S. (1991). Comorbidity of attention deficit hyperactivity disorder with conduct, depressive, anxiety, and other disorders. *American Journal of Psychiatry, 148,* 564–577.

Biklen, D. (1990). Communication unbound: Autism and praxis. *Harvard Educational Review, 60,* 291–314.

Biklen, D. (1992). Autism orthodoxy versus free speech: A reply to Cummins and Prior. *Harvard Educational Review, 62,* 242–256.

Bilder, R. M., Wu, H., Bogerts, B., Degreef, G., Ashtari, M., Alvir, J. M. J., Snyder, P. J., & Lieberman, J. A. (1994). Absence of regional hemispheric volume asymmetries in first-episode schizophrenia. *American Journal of Psychiatry, 151,* 1437–1447.

Bini, L. (1938). Experimental researches on epileptic attacks induced by the electric current. *American Journal of Psychiatry* (Suppl. 94), 172–183.

Birnbaum, K. (1914). *Die psychopathischen verbrecker* (2nd ed.). Leipzig: Thieme.

Birren, J. E. (1974). Translations in gerontology—from lab to life: Psychophysiology and speed of response. *American Psychologist, 29,* 808–815.

Blair, C. D., & Lanyon, R. I. (1981). Exhibitionism: Etiology and treatment. *Psychological Bulletin, 89*(3), 439–463.

Blanchard, E. B., & Andraski, F. (1985). *Management of chronic headaches: A psychological approach.* New York: Pergamon Press.

Blanchard, J. J., & Neale, J. M. (1992). Medication effects: Conceptual and methodological issues in schizophrenia research. *Clinical Psychology Review, 12,* 345–361.

Blane, L., & Roth, R. H. (1967). Voyeurism and exhibitionism. *Perceptual and Motor Skills, 24,* 391–400.

Blaney, P. H. (1986). Affect and memory: A review. *Psychological Bulletin, 99,* 229–246.

Blashfield, R. K. (1973). An evaluation of the *DSM-II* classification of schizophrenia as a nomenclature. *Journal of Abnormal Psychology, 82,* 382–389.

Blashfield, R. K., & Draguns, J. G. (1976). Evaluative criteria for psychiatric classification. *Journal of Abnormal Psychology, 85,* 140–150.

Blatt, S. J., & Homann, E. (1992). Parent-child interaction in the etiology of dependent and self-critical depression. *Clinical Psychology Review, 12,* 47–91.

Blazer, D. G., Kessler, R. C., McGonagle, K. A., & Swartz, M. S. (1994). The prevalence and distribution of major depression in a national community sample: The national comorbidity survey. *American Journal of Psychiatry, 151,* 979–986.

Bleuler, E. (1950). *Dementia praecox or the group of schizophrenias* (J. Zinkin, Trans.). New York: International Universities Press. (Original work published 1911)

Bleuler, M. E. (1978). The long term course of schizophrenic psychoses. In L. C. Wynne, R. L. Cromwell, & S. Matthyse (Eds.), *The nature of schizophrenia: New approaches to research and treatment.* New York: Wiley.

Bliss, E. L. (1984). A symptom profile of patients with multiple personalities—with MMPI results. *Journal of Nervous and Mental Disease, 172,* 197–202.

Bliss, E. L. (1986). *Multiple personality, allied disorders, and hypnosis.* New York: Oxford University Press.

Bliss, E. W., & Branch, C. H. (1960). *Anorexia nervosa: Its history, psychology, and biology.* New York: Hoeber Medical Book.

Bliss, R. E., Garvey, A. J., Heinold, J. W., & Hitchcock, J. L. (1989). The influence of situation and coping on relapse crisis outcomes after smoking cessation. *Journal of Consulting and Clinical Psychology, 57,* 443–449.

Blumer, D., & Walker, A. E. (1975). The neural basis of sexual behavior. In D. F. Benson & D. Blumer (Eds.), *Psychiatric aspects of neurological disease.* New York: Grune & Stratton.

Bockoven, J. S. (1963). *Moral treatment in American psychiatry.* New York: Springer.

Bogen, J. E., Fisher, E. D., & Vogel, P. J. (1965). Cerebral commissarotomy: A second case report. *Journal of the American Medical Association, 194,* 1328–1329.

Bogerts, B. (1993). Recent advances in the neuropathology of schizophrenia. *Schizophrenia Bulletin, 19,* 431–445.

Bohman, M., Cloninger, C. R., von Knorring, A., & Sigvardsson, S. (1984). An adoption study of somatoform disorders: III. Cross-fostering analysis and genetic relationship to alcoholism and criminality. *Archives of General Psychiatry, 41,* 872–878.

Bohman, M., Sigvardsson, S., & Cloninger, C. R. (1981). Maternal inheritance of alcohol abuse: Cross-fostering analysis of adopted women. *Archives of General Psychiatry, 38,* 965–970.

Boll, T. J., Heaton, R., & Reitan, R. M. (1974). Neuropsychological and emotional correlates of Huntington's chorea. *Journal of Nervous and Mental Disease, 158,* 61–69.

Boon, S., & Draijer, N. (1993). Multiple personality disorder in the Netherlands: A clinical investigation of 71 patients. *American Journal of Psychiatry, 150,* 489–494.

Booth-Kewley, S., & Friedman, H. S. (1987). Psychological predictors of heart disease: A quantitative review. *Psychological Bulletin, 101,* 343–362.

Bootzin, R. R. (1975). *Behavior modification and therapy: An introduction.* Cambridge, MA: Winthrop Press.

Bootzin, R. R., Epstein, D., & Wood, J. M. (1991). Stimulus control instructions. In P. Hauri (Ed.), *Case studies in insomnia.* New York: Plenum Press.

Bootzin, R. R., Manber, R., Perlis, M. L., Salvio, M., & Wyatt, J. K. (1993). Sleep disorders. In P. B. Sutker & H. E. Adams (Eds.), *Comprehensive handbook of psychopathology* (2nd ed., pp. 531–561). New York: Plenum Press.

Bootzin, R. R., & Max, D. (1980). Learning and behavioral theories. In I. L. Kutash & L. B. Schlesinger (Eds.), *Handbook on stress and anxiety.* San Francisco: Jossey-Bass.

Bootzin, R. R., & Perlis, M. L. (1992). Nonpharmacological treatments for insomnia. *Journal of Clinical Psychiatry.*

Bootzin, R. R., Shadish, W. R., & McSweeny, A. J. (1989). Longitudinal outcomes of nursing home care for severely mentally ill patients. *Journal of Social Issues, 45,* 31–48.

Borkovec, T. D., Lane, T. W., & VanOot, P. H. (1981). Phenomenology of sleep among insomniacs and good sleepers: Wakefulness experience when cortically asleep. *Journal of Abnormal Psychology, 90,* 607–609.

Borkowski, J. G., Whitman, T. L., Passino, A. W., Rellinger, E. A., Sommer, K., Keogh, D., & Weed, K. (1992). Unraveling the "new morbidity": Adolescent parenting and developmental delays. In N. W. Bray (Ed.), *International review of research in mental retardation* (Vol. 18, pp. 159–196). San Diego, CA: Academic Press.

Borkowski, J. G., Whitman, T. L., Passino, A. W., et al. (1993, Spring). Personal adjustment during pregnancy and adolescent parenting. *Adolescence, 28,* 97–122.

Boss, M. (1976). Flight from death—mere survival: And flight into death—suicide. In B. B. Wolman & H. H. Krauss (Eds.), *Between survival and suicide.* New York: Gardner Press.

Botvin, G. J., Baker, E., Dusenbury, L., Tortu, S., & Botvin, E. M. (1990). Preventing adolescent drug abuse through a multimodal cognitive-behavioral approach: Results of a 3-year study. *Journal of Consulting and Clinical Psychology, 58,* 437–446.

Bouchard, T. J., Jr., Lykken, D. T., McGue, M., Segal, N. L., et al. (1990). Sources of human psychological differences: The Minnesota study of twins reared apart. *Science, 250,* 223–250.

Bourne, P. G. (1974). *Addiction.* New York: Academic Press.

Bovjberg, D. H., Redd, W. H., Maier, L. A., Holland, J. C., Lesko, L. M., Niedzwiecki, D., Rubin, S. C., &

Hakes, T. B. (1990). Anticipatory immune suppression and nausea in women receiving cyclic chemotherapy for ovarian cancer. *Journal of Consulting and Clinical Psychology, 58,* 153–157.

Bowden, W. D. (1993). First person account: The onset of paranoia. *Schizophrenia Bulletin, 19,* 165–167.

Bowen, M. (1976). Principles and techniques of multiple family therapy. In P. J. Guerin (Ed.), *Family therapy: Theory and practice.* New York: Gardner Press.

Bower, G. H. (1981). Mood and memory. *American Psychologist, 36,* 129–148.

Bowers, M. B. (1987). The role of drugs in the production of schizophreniform psychosis and related disorders. In H. Meltzer (Ed.), *Psychopharmacology: Third generation of progress* (pp. 819–823). New York: Raven Press.

Bowman, M. L. (1989). Testing individual differences in ancient China. *American Psychologist, 44,* 576–578.

Boyd, J. H., Rae, D. S., Thompson, J. W., Burns, B. J., Bourdon, K., Locke, B. Z., & Regier, D. A. (1990). Phobia: Prevalence and risk factors. *Social Psychiatry and Psychiatric Epidemiology, 25,* 314–323.

Boysen, G. (1993). Prevention of stroke. In J. P. Whisnant (Ed.), *Stroke, populations, cohorts, and clinical trials.* Boston: Butterworth-Heinemann.

Bozarth, J. D. (1981). The person-centered approach in the large community group. In G. M. Gazda (Ed.), *Innovations to group psychotherapy* (2nd ed.). Springfield, IL: Charles C Thomas.

Bracha, H. S., Torrey, E. F., Gottesman, I. I., Bigelow, L. B., & Cunniff, C. (1992). Second-trimester markers of fetal size in schizophrenia: A study of monozygotic twins. *American Journal of Psychiatry, 149,* 1355–1361.

Bradford, J. M. W. (1990). The antiandrogen and hormonal treatment of sex offenders. In W. L. Marshall, D. R. Laws, & H. E. Barbaree (Eds.), *Handbook of sexual assault* (pp. 297–310). New York: Plenum Press.

Bradford, J. M. W., & Pawlak, A. (1993). Double-blind placebo crossover study of cyproterone acetate in the treatment of paraphilias. *Archives of Sexual Behavior, 22,* 383–402.

Brady, J. V. (1958). Ulcers in "executive" monkeys. *Scientific American, 199,* 95–100.

Braff, D. L. (1993). Information processing and attention dysfunctions in schizophrenia. *Schizophrenia Bulletin, 19,* 233–259.

Braff, D. L., & Geyer, M. A. (1990). Sensorimotor gating and schizophrenia: Human and animal model studies. *Archives of General Psychiatry, 47,* 181–188.

Braginsky, B. M., Braginsky, D. D., & Ring, K. (1969). *Methods of madness: The mental hospital as a last resort.* New York: Holt, Rinehart and Winston.

Brakel, S. J. (1985). Involuntary institutionalization. In S. J. Brakel, J. Parry, & B. A. Weiner (Eds.), *The mentally disabled and the law* (3rd ed.). Chicago: American Bar Foundation.

Brandenburg, N. A., Friedman, R. M., & Silver, S. E. (1990). The epidemiology of childhood psychiatric disorders: Prevalence findings from recent studies. *Journal of the American Academy of Child and Adolescent Psychiatry, 29,* 76–83.

Brantley, P. J., & Garrett, V. D. (1993). Psychobiological approaches to health and disease. In P. B. Sutker & H. E. Adams (Eds.), *Comprehensive handbook of psychopathology* (2nd ed., pp. 647–670). New York: Plenum Press.

Brantley, P. J., & Jones, G. N. (1993). Daily stress and stress-related disorders. *Annals of Behavioral Medicine, 15,* 17–25.

Braukmann, C. J., & Fixsen, D. L. (1975). Behavior modification with delinquents. In M. Hersen, R. M. Eisler, & P. M. Miller (Eds.), *Progress in behavior modification* (Vol. 1). New York: Academic Press.

Braun, B. G., & Sachs, R. G. (1985). The development of multiple personality disorder: Predisposing, precipitating, and perpetuating factors. In R. P. Kluft (Ed.), *Childhood antecedents of multiple personality* (pp. 37–64). Washington, DC: American Psychiatric Press.

Braun, P., Kochansky, G., Shapiro, R., Greenberg, S., Gudeman, J. E., Johnson, S., & Shore, M. R. (1981). Overview: Deinstitutionalization of psychiatric patients, a critical review of outcome studies. *American Journal of Psychiatry, 138,* 736–749.

Bray, G. A. (1984). The role of weight control in health promotion and disease prevention. In J. D. Matarazzo, S. M. Weiss, J. A. Herd, N. E. Miller, (Eds.), *Behavioral health: A handbook of health enhancement and disease prevention* (pp. 632–656). New York: Wiley.

Breier, A., Buchanan, R. W., Elkashef, A., Munson, R. C., Kirkpatrick, B., & Gellad, F. (1992). Brain morphology and schizophrenia: A magnetic resonance imaging study of limbic, prefrontal cortex, and caudate structures. *Archives of General Psychiatry, 49,* 921–926.

Breier, A., Davis, O. R., Buchanan, R. W., Moricle, L. A., & Munson, R. C. (1993). Effects of metabolic perturbation on plasma homovanillic acid in schizophrenia: Relationship to prefrontal cortex volume. *Archives of General Psychiatry, 50,* 541–550.

Breier, A., Schreiber, J. L., Dyer, J., & Pickar, D. (1991). National Institute of Mental Health longitudinal study of chronic schizophrenia. *Archives of General Psychiatry, 48,* 239–246.

Brent, D. A., Perper, J. A., Goldstein, C. E., Kolko, D. J., Allan, M. J., Allman, C. J., & Zelenak, J. P. (1988). Risk factors for adolescent suicide: A comparison of adolescent suicide victims with suicidal in-patients. *Archives of General Psychiatry, 45,* 581–588.

Brewin, C. R., MacCarthy, B., Duda, K., & Vaughn, C. E. (1991). Attribution and expressed emotion in the relatives of patients with schizophrenia. *Journal of Abnormal Psychology, 100,* 546–554.

Brion, S. (1969). Korsakoff's syndrome: Clinico-anatomical and physiopathological considerations. In G. A. Talland & N. C. Waugh (Eds.), *The pathology of memory.* New York: Academic Press.

Brodaty, H., Peters, K., Boyce, P., Hickie, I., Parker, G., Mitchell, P., & Wilhelm, K. (1991). Age and depression. *Journal of Affective Disorders, 23,* 137–149.

Brody, J. E. (1982a, December 22). Personal health. *The New York Times,* p. C6.

Broman, S., Nichols, P. L., Shaugnessy, P., & Kennedy, W., et al. (1987). *Retardation in young children.* Hillsdale, NJ: Erlbaum.

Bromberg, W. (1965). *Crime and the mind.* New York: Macmillan.

Bron, B., Strack, M., & Rudolph, G. (1991). Childhood experiences of loss and suicide attempts: Significance in depressive states of major depressed and dysthymic or adjustment disordered patients. *Journal of Affective Disorders, 23,* 165–172.

Brooks, A. (1974). *Law psychiatry and the mental health system.* Boston: Little, Brown.

Brooks-Gunn, J. (1988). Antecedents and consequences of variations in girls' maturational timing. *Journal of Adolescent Health Care, 9,* 365–373.

Brown, G. W. (1979). The social etiology of depression—London studies. In R. A. Depue (Ed.), *The psychobiology of the depressive disorders.* New York: Academic Press.

Brown, G. W., Harris, T. O., & Hepworth, C. (1994). Life events and endogenous depression: A puzzle reexamined. *Archives of General Psychiatry, 51,* 525–534.

Brown, H. N., & Vaillant, G. E. (1981). Hypochondriasis. *Archives of Internal Medicine, 141,* 723–726.

Brown, L. T., & Weiner, E. E. (1979). *Introduction to psychology.* Boston: Winthrop Press.

Brown, S. A., Goldman, M. S., & Christiansen, B. A. (1985). Do alcohol expectancies mediate drinking patterns of adults? *Journal of Consulting and Clinical Psychology, 53,* 512–519.

Brown, S. A., Goldman, M. S., Inn, A., & Anderson, L. R. (1980). Expectations of reinforcement from alcohol: Their domain and relation to drinking patterns. *Journal of Consulting and Clinical Psychology, 48,* 419–426.

Browne, A., & Finkelhor, D. (1986). Impact of child sexual abuse: A review of the research. *Psychological Bulletin, 99,* 66–77.

Brownell, H. H., Simpson, T. L., Bihrle, A. M., Potter, H. H., & Gardner, H. (1990) Appreciation of metaphoric alternative word meanings by left and right brain-damaged patients. *Neuropsychologia, 28,* 375–384.

Brownell, K. D. (1986). Public health approaches to obesity and its management. *Annual Review of Public Health, 7,* 521–533.

Brownell, K. D. (1993). Whether obesity should be treated. *Health Psychology, 12,* 339–341.

Brownell, K. D., & Wadden, T. A. (1992). Etiology and treatment of obesity: Understanding a serious, prevalent, and refractory disorder. *Journal of Consulting and Clinical Psychology, 60,* 505–517.

Bruce, M. L., & Kim, K. M. (1992). Differences in the effects of divorce on major depression in men and women. *American Journal of Psychiatry, 149,* 914–917.

Bruch, H. (1978). *The golden cage: The enigma of anorexia nervosa.* Cambridge, MA: Harvard University Press.

Bruch, H. (1985). Four decades of eating disorders. In D. M. Garner & P. E. Garfinkel (Eds.), *Handbook of psychotherapy for anorexia and bulimia.* New York: Guilford Press.

Bryant, R. A., & McConkey, K. M. (1989). Visual conversion disorder: A case analysis of the influence of visual information. *Journal of Abnormal Psychology, 98,* 326–329.

Bucher, B., & Lovaas, O. I. (1968). Use of aversive stimulation in behavior modification. In M. R. Jones (Ed.), *Miami symposium on the prediction of behavior, 1967: Aversive stimulation.* Coral Gables, FL: University of Miami Press.

Buchsbaum, M. S., Haier, R. J., Potkin, S. G., Nuechterlein, K. H., Bracha, S., Katz, M., Lohr, J., Wu, J., Lottenberg, S., Jerabeck, P. A., Trenary, M., Tafalla, R., Reynolds, C., & Bunney, W. E., Jr. (1992). Frontostriatal disorder of cerebral metabolism in never-medicated schizophrenics. *Archives of General Psychiatry, 49,* 935–942.

Buckner, H. T. (1970). The transvestic career path. *Psychiatry, 33*(3), 381–389.

Burgess, A. W., Groth, A. N., & McCausland, M. P. (1981). Child sex initiation rings. *American Journal of Orthopsychiatry, 51,* 110–119.

Burgoine, E., & Wing, L. (1983). Identical triplets with Asperger's syndrome. *British Journal of Psychiatry, 143,* 261–265.

Burke, K. C., Burke, J. D., Jr., Regier, D. A., & Rae, D. S. (1990). Age at onset of selected mental disorders in five community populations. *Archives of General Psychiatry, 47,* 511–518.

Burke, K. C., Burke, J. D., Roe, D. S., & Regier, D. A. (1991). Comparing age at onset of major depression and other psychiatric disorders by birth cohorts in five U.S. community populations. *Archives of General Psychiatry, 48,* 789–795.

Burnam, M. A., Stein, J. A., Golding, J. M., Siegel, J. M., Sorenson, S. B., Forsythe, A. B., & Telles, C. A. (1988). Sexual assault and mental disorders in a community population. *Journal of Consulting and Clinical Psychology, 56,* 843–850.

Bushman, B. J., & Cooper, H. M. (1990). Effects of alcohol on human aggression: An integrative research review. *Psychological Bulletin, 107,* 341–354.

Buss, A. H. (1966). *Psychopathology.* New York: Wiley.

Buss, A. H. (1980). *Self-consciousness and social anxiety.* San Francisco: Freeman.

Buss, A. H. (1986). A theory of shyness. In W. H. Jones, J. M. Cheek, & S. R. Briggs (Eds.), *Shyness: Perspectives on research and treatment* (pp. 39–46). New York: Plenum Press.

Butcher, J. N. (1978). Present status of computerized MMPI reporting devices. In O. Buros (Ed.), *Eighth mental measurements yearbook.* Highland Park, NJ: Gryphon Press.

Butcher, J. N. (1990). *MMPI-2 in psychological treatment.* New York: Oxford University Press.

Butler, J., O'Halloran, A., & Leonard, B. E. (1992). The Galway study of panic disorder: II. Changes in some peripheral markers of noradrenergic and serotonergic function in *DSM-III-R* panic disorder. *Journal of Affective Disorders, 26,* 89–100.

Butler, R. W., & Braff, D. L. (1991). Delusions: A review and integration. *Schizophrenia Bulletin, 17,* 633–647.

Buydens-Branchey, L., Branchey, M. H., & Noumair, D. (1989). Age of alcoholism onset: I. Relationship to psychopathology. *Archives of General Psychiatry, 46,* 225–230.

Buysse, D. J., & Kupfer, D. J. (1993). Sleep disorders in depressive disorders. In J. J. Mann & D. J. Kupfer (Eds.), *Biology of depressive disorders: Part A. A systems perspective* (pp. 123–154). New York: Plenum.

Cain, J. W. (1992). Poor response to fluoxetine: Underlying depression, serotonergic overstimulation, or a "therapeutic window"? *Journal of Clinical Psychiatry, 53,* 272–277.

Caligor, J., Fieldsteel, N. D., & Brok, A. J. (1984). *Individual and group therapy: Combining psychoanalytic treatments.* New York: Basic Books.

Campbell, F., & Ramey, C. T. (1994). Effect of early intervention on intellectual and academic achievement: A follow-up study of children from low-income families. *Child Development, 65,* 684–698.

Campbell, M., Anderson, L. T., Small, A. M., Perry, R., Green, W. H., & Caplan, R. (1982). The effects of haloperidol on learning and behavior in autistic children. *Journal of Autism and Developmental Disorders, 12,* 167–175.

Cannon, M. S. (1975). The halfway house as an alternative to hospitalization. In Zusman & E. Bertsch (Eds.), *The future role of the state hospital.* Lexington, MA: Lexington Books.

Cannon, T. D., & Mednick, S. A. (1993). The schizophrenia high-risk project in Copenhagen: Three decades of progress. *Acta Psychiatrica Scandinavica,* (Suppl. 370), 33–47.

Cannon, T. D., Mednick, S. A., Parnas, J., Schulsinger, F., Praestholm, J., & Vestergaard, A. (1993). Developmental brain abnormalities in the offspring of schizophrenic mothers: I. Contributions of genetic and perinatal factors. *Archives of General Psychiatry, 50,* 551–564.

Cannon, W. B. (1936). *Bodily changes in pain, hunger, fear and rage.* New York: Appleton-Century.

Cantor, N., & Genero, N. (1986). Psychiatric diagnosis and natural categorization: A close analogy. In T. Millon & G. L. Klerman (Eds.), *Contemporary directions in psychopathology: Toward the* DSM-IV (pp. 233–256). New York: Guilford Press.

Cantwell, D. P. (1982). Childhood depression: A review of current research. In B. B. Lahey & A. E. Kazdin (Eds.), *Advances in clinical child psychology.* New York: Plenum Press.

Carey, G., & Gottesman, I. I. (1981). Twin and family studies of anxiety, phobic and obsessive disorders. In D. F. Klein & J. G. Rabkin (Eds.), *Anxiety: New research and changing concepts.* New York: Raven Press.

Carlson, G. A., & Garber, J. (1986). Developmental issues in the classification of depression in children. In M. Rutter, C. Izard, & P. Read (Eds.), *Depression in young people: Issues and perspectives.* New York: Guilford Press.

Carnegie Corporation of New York. (1994). *Starting points: Meeting the Needs of Our Youngest Children* (Report of the Carnegie Task Force on Meeting the Needs of Young Children).

Carone, B. J., Harrow, M., & Westermeyer, J. F. (1991). Posthospital course and outcome in schizophrenia. *Archives of General Psychiatry, 48,* 247–253.

Carr, E. G., & Durand, V. M. (1985). The social-communicative basis of severe behavior problems in children. In S. Reiss & R. R. Bootzin (Eds.), *Theoretical issues in behavior therapy.* New York: Academic Press.

Carroll, B. J., et al. (1981). A specific laboratory test for the diagnosis of melancholia. *Archives of General Psychiatry, 38,* 15–22.

Carroll, E. M., Rueger, D. B., Foy, D. W., & Donahoe, C. P., Jr. (1985). Vietnam combat veterans with posttraumatic stress disorder: Analysis of marital and cohabitating adjustment. *Journal of Abnormal Psychology, 94,* 329–337.

Carson, R. C. (1969). *Interaction concepts of personality.* Chicago: Aldine.

Carstensen, L. L., & Fisher, J. E. (1991). Treatment applications for psychological and behavioral problems of the elderly in nursing homes. In P. A. Wisocki (Ed.), *Handbook of clinical behavior therapy with the elderly client.* New York: Plenum Press.

Cartwright, S. A. (1981). Report on the diseases and physical peculiarities of the Negro race. In A. L. Caplan, H. T. Englehardt, Jr., & J. J. McCartney (Eds.), *Concepts of health and disease: Interdisciplinary perspectives* (pp. 305–326). Reading MA: Addison-Wesley. (Original work published 1851)

Casson, I. R., Seigel, O., Sham, R., Campbell, E. A., Tarlau, M., & DiDomenico, A. (1984). Brain damage in modern boxers. *Journal of the American Medical Association, 251,* 2663–2667.

Castelloe, P., & Dawson, G. (1993). Subclassification of children with autism and pervasive developmental disorder: A questionnaire based on Wing's subgrouping scheme. *Journal of Autism and Developmental Disorders, 23.*

Castle, D. J., & Murray, R. M. (1993). The epidemiology of late-onset schizophrenia. *Schizophrenia Bulletin, 19,* 691–700.

Cavallin, H. (1966). Incestuous fathers: A clinical report. *American Journal of Psychiatry, 122*(10), 1132–1138.

Celesia, G. G., & Barr, A. N. (1970). Psychosis and other psychiatric manifestations of levodopa therapy. *Archives of Neurology, 23,* 193–200.

Chapman, L. J., & Chapman, J. P. (1969). Illusory correlation as an obstacle to the use of valid psychodiagnostic signs. *Journal of Abnormal Psychology, 74,* 271–287.

Chapman, L. J., & Chapman, J. P. (1973). *Disordered thought in schizophrenia.* New York: Appleton-Century-Crofts.

Chapman, L. J., & Chapman, J. P. (1978). The measurement of differential deficit. *Journal of Psychiatry Research, 14,* 303–311.

Chapman, L. J., & Chapman, J. P. (1985). Psychosis proneness. In M. Alpert (Ed.), *Controversies in schizophrenia* (pp. 157–172). New York: Guilford Press.

Chapman, L. J., & Chapman, J. P. (1987). The search for symptom predictive of schizophrenia. *Schizophrenia Bulletin, 13,* 497–503.

Chapman, L. J., Chapman, J. P., Kwapil, T. R., Eckblad, M., & Zinser, M. C. (1994). Putatively psychosis-prone subjects 10 years later. *Journal of Abnormal Psychology, 103,* 171–183.

Charcot, J., & Marie, P. (1892). On hystero-epilepsy. In D. H. Tuke (Ed.), *A dictionary of psychological medicine* (Vol. 1). Philadelphia: Blakiston.

Chassin, L., Mann, L. M., & Sher, K. J. (1988). Self-awareness theory, family history of alcoholism, and adolescent alcohol involvement. *Journal of Abnormal Psychology, 97,* 206–217.

Chess, S., Korn, S. J., & Fernandez, P. B. (1971). *Psychiatric disorders of children with congenital rubella.* New York: Brunner/Mazel.

Children's Defense Fund. (1991). *The state of America's children.*

Chodorow, N. (1978). *The reproduction of mothering: Psychoanalysis and the sociology of gender.* Berkeley: University of California Press.

Christenson, G. A., Pyle, R. I., & Mitchell, J. E. (1991). Estimated lifetime prevalence of trichotillomania in college students. *Journal of Clinical Psychology, 52,* 415–417.

Christiansen, B. A., Smith, G. T., Roehling, P. V., & Goldman, M. S. (1989). Using alcohol expectancies to predict adolescent drinking behavior after one year. *Journal of Consulting and Clinical Psychology, 57,* 93–99.

Christiansen, K. O. (1968). Threshold of tolerance in various population groups illustrated by results from the Danish criminologic twin study. In A. V. S. de Reuck & R. Porter (Eds.), *The mentally abnormal offender.* Boston: Little, Brown.

Christoffel, H. (1956). Male genital exhibitionism. In S. Lorand & M. Bolint (Eds.), *Perversions: Psychodynamics and therapy.* New York: Random House.

Chugani, H. (1993). Positron emission tomography scanning in newborns. *Clinics in Perinatology, 20*(2), 398.

Chugani, H., Phelps, M. E., & Mazziotta, J. C. (1987). Positron emission tomography study of human brain functional development. *Annals of Neurology,* 22(4), 495.

Clark, D. M. (1988). A cognitive model of panic attacks. In S. Rachman & J. D. Maser (Eds.), *Panic: Psychological perspectives.* Hillsdale, NJ: Erlbaum.

Clark, D. M. (1991, September 23–25). *Cognitive therapy for panic disorder.* Paper presented at the NIH Consensus Development Conference on the Treatment of Panic Disorders, Bethesda, MD.

Clark, D. M., Gelder, M., Salkovskis, P. M., & Anastasiades, P. (1991). *Cognitive mediation of lactate-induced panic.* Paper presented at the annual conference of the American Psychiatric Association, New Orleans.

Clark, D. M., Salkovskis, P. M., & Chalkley, A. J. (1985). Respiratory control as a treatment for panic attacks. *Journal of Behavior Therapy and Experimental Psychiatry, 16,* 23–30.

Clark, D. M., Salkovskis, P. M., Gelder, M., Koehler, C., Martin, M., Anastasiades, P., Hackmann, A., Middleton, H., & Jeavons, A. (1988). Tests of a cognitive theory of panic. In I. Hand & H. V. Wittchen (Eds.), *Panic and phobias 2.* Berlin: Springer-Verlag.

Clarkin, J. F., Marziali, E., & Monroe-Blum, H. (1991). Group and family treatments for borderline personality disorder. *Hospital and Community Psychiatry, 42,* 1038–1043.

Cleckley, H. M. (1976). *The mask of sanity.* St. Louis: Mosby.

Cleghorn, J. M., Franco, S., Szechtman, B., Kaplan, R. D., Szechtman, H., Brown, G. M., Nahmias, C., & Garnett, E. S. (1992). Toward a brain map of auditory hallucinations. *American Journal of Psychiatry, 149,* 1062–1069.

Clementz, B. A., Grove, W. M., Iacono, W. G., & Sweeney, J. A. (1992) Smooth-pursuit eye movement dysfunction and liability for schizophrenia: Implications for genetic modelling. *Journal of Abnormal Psychology, 101,* 117–129.

Clementz, B. A., McDowell, J. E., & Zisook, S. (1994). Saccadic system functioning among schizophrenia patients and their first-degree biological relatives. *Journal of Abnormal Psychology, 103,* 277–287.

Clinthorne, J. K., Cisin, I. H., Balter, M. B., Mellinger, G. D., & Uhlenhuth, E. H. (1986). Changes in popular attitudes and beliefs about tranquilizers: 1970–1979. *Archives of General Psychiatry, 43,* 527–532.

Cloninger, C. R., Bohman, M., & Sigvardsson, S. (1981). Inheritance of alcohol abuse: Cross-fostering analysis of adopted men. *Archives of General Psychiatry, 38,* 861–868.

Cloninger, C. R., Sigvardsson, S., von Knorring, A., & Bohman, M. (1984). An adoption study of somatoform disorders: II. Identification of two discrete somatoform disorders. *Archives of General Psychiatry, 41,* 863–871.

Clum, G. A., & Knowles, S. L. (1991). Why do some people with panic disorders become avoidant? A review. *Clinical Psychology Review, 11,* 295–313.

Cohen, B. D., Nachmani, G., & Rosenberg, S. (1974). Referent communication disturbances in acute schizophrenia. *Journal of Abnormal Psychology, 83*(1), 1–13.

Cohen, M., & Seghorn, T. (1969). Sociometric study of the sex offender. *Journal of Abnormal Psychology, 74,* 249–255.

Cohen, P., Cohen, J., Kasen, S., Velez, C. N., Hartmark, C., Johnson, J., Rojas, M., Brook, J., Streuning, E. L. (1993). An epidemiological study of disorders in late childhood and adolescence: I. Age- and gender-specific prevalence. *Journal of Child Psychology and Psychiatry and Allied Disciplines, 34,* 851–867.

Cohen, S., & Lichtenstein, E. (1990). Partner behaviors that support quitting smoking. *Journal of Consulting and Clinical Psychology, 58,* 304–309.

Cohen, S., Tyrrell, D. A. J., & Smith, A. P. (1991). Psychological stress and susceptibility to the common cold. *New England Journal of Medicine, 325,* 606–612.

Cohen, S., & Williamson, G. M. (1991). Stress and infectious disease in humans. *Psychological Bulletin, 109,* 5–24.

Cohen, S., & Wills, T. A. (1985). Stress, social support, and the buffering hypothesis. *Psychological Bulletin, 98,* 310–357.

Coleman, M. (1989). Medical evaluation of individuals with an autistic disorder. *Forum Medicum.*

Coleman, M., & Gillberg, C. (1985). *The biology of the autistic syndromes.* New York: Praeger.

Combs, B. J., Hales, D. R., & Williams, B. K. (1980). *An invitation to health: Your personal responsibility.* Menlo Park, CA: Benjamin/Cummings.

Commitment following an insanity acquittal. (1981). *Harvard Law Review, 94,* 604–625.

Conger, J. J. (1951). The effects of alcohol on conflict behavior in the albino rat. *Quarterly Journal of Studies on Alcohol, 12,* 1–29.

Conte, J. R., & Berliner, L. (1981). Sexual abuse of children: Implications for practice. *Social Casework, 62,* 601–606.

Cook, M., Mineka, S., Wolkenstein, B., & Laitsch, K. (1985). Observational conditioning of snake fear in unrelated rhesus monkeys. *Journal of Abnormal Psychology, 94,* 591–610.

Cools, J., Schotte, D. E., & McNally, R. J. (1992). Emotional arousal and overeating in restrained eaters. *Journals of Abnormal Psychology, 101,* 348–351.

Coons, P. M. (1986). Treatment progress in 20 patients with multiple personality disorder. *Journal of Nervous and Mental Disease, 174,* 715–721.

Coons, P. M. (1991). Iatrogenesis and malingering of multiple personality disorder in the forensic evaluation of homicide defendants. *Psychiatric Clinics of North America, 14,* 757–768.

Coons, P. M., & Milstein, V. (1986). Psychosexual disturbances in multiple personality: Characteristics, etiology, and treatment. *Journal of Clinical Psychiatry, 47,* 106–110.

Coons, P. M., & Milstein, V. (1992). Amnesia: A clinical investigation of 25 cases. *Dissociation, 5,* 73–79.

Cooper, J. E., Kendell, R. E., Gurland, B. J., Sharp, L., Copeland, J. R. M., & Simon, R. (1972). *Psychiatric diagnosis in New York and London: A comparative study of mental hospital admissions.* New York: Oxford University Press.

Corder, E. H., Saunders, A. M., Strittmatter, W. J., Schmechel, D. E., Gaskell, P. C., Small, G. W., Roses, A. D., Haines, J. L., & Pericak-Vance, M. A. (1993). Gene dose of apolipoprotein E type 4 allele and the risk of Alzheimer's disease in late onset families. *Science, 261,* 921–924.

Cornblatt, B. A., Lenzenweger, M. F., Dworkin, R. H., & Erlenmeyer-Kimling, L. (1985). Positive and negative schizophrenic symptoms, attention, and information processing. *Schizophrenia Bulletin, 11,* 397–408.

Corrigan, P. W., & Green, M. F. (1993). Schizophrenic patients' sensitivity to social cues: The role of abstraction. *American Journal of Psychiatry, 150,* 589–594.

Coryell, W. (1980). A blind family history study of Briquet's syndrome: Further validation of the diagnosis. *Archives of General Psychiatry, 37,* 1266–1269.

Coryell, W., Akiskal, H. S., Leon, A. C., Winokur, G., Maser, J. D., Mueller, T. I., & Keller, M. B. (1994). The time course of nonchronic major depressive disorder: Uniformity across episodes and samples. *Archives of General Psychiatry, 51,* 405–410.

Coryell, W., Scheftner, W., Keller, M., Endicott, J., Maser, J., & Klerman, G. L. (1993). The enduring psychosocial consequences of mania and depression. *American Journal of Psychiatry, 150,* 720–727.

Costa, E., & Guidotti, A. (1985). Endogenous ligands for benzodiazepine recognition sites. *Biochemical Pharmacology, 34,* 3399–3403.

Costa, P. T., & Widiger, T. A. (Eds.). (1994). *Personality disorders and the five-factor model of personality.* Washington, DC; American Psychological Association.

Costello, C. G. (1982). Fears and phobias in women: A community study. *Journal of Abnormal Psychology, 91,* 280–286.

Coursey, R. D., Ward-Alexander, L., & Katz, B. (1990). Cost-effectiveness of providing insurance benefits for posthospital psychiatric halfway house stays. *American Psychologist, 45,* 1118–1126.

Couture, E. G., & Guitar, B. E. (1993). Treatment efficacy research in stuttering. *Journal of Fluency Disorders, 18,* 253–387.

Cowley, G. (1992a, June 29). Poison at home and at work. *Newsweek,* p. 54.

Cowley, G. (1992b, April 6). A quit-now drive that worked. *Newsweek,* p. 54.

Coyne, J. C. (1976a). Depression and the response of others. *Journal of Abnormal Psychology, 85,* 186–193.

Coyne, J. C. (1976b). Toward an interactional description of depression. *Psychiatry, 39,* 14–27.

Coyne, J. C. (1994). Self-reported distress: Analog or ersatz depression? *Psychological Bulletin, 116,* 29–45.

Craig, M. E. (1990). Coercive sexuality in dating relationships: A situational model. *Clinical Psychology Review, 10,* 395–423.

Craighead, L. W., & Agras, W. S. (1991). Mechanisms of action in cognitive-behavioral and pharmacological interventions for obesity and bulimia nervosa. *Journal of Consulting and Clinical Psychology, 59,* 115–125.

Craske, M. G. (1991). Phobic fear and panic attacks: The same emotional states triggered by different cues? *Clinical Psychology Review, 11,* 599–620.

Craske, M. G., & Barlow, D. H. (1988). A review of the relationship between panic and avoidance. *Clinical Psychology Review, 8,* 667–685.

Crisp, A. H. (1984). The psychopathology of anorexia nervosa: Getting the "heat" out of the system. In A. J. Stunkard & E. Stellar (Eds.), *Eating and its disorders.* New York: Raven Press.

Crits-Christoph, P., Cooper, A., & Luborsky, L. (1988). The accuracy of therapists' interpretations and the outcome of dynamic psychotherapy. *Journal of Consulting and Clinical Psychology, 56,* 490–495.

Cromwell, R. L. (1993). Searching for the origins of schizophrenia. *Psychological Science, 4,* 276–279.

Cross, G. M., Morgan, C. W., Mooney, A. J., Martin, C. A., & Rafter, J. A. (1990). Alcoholism treatment: A ten-year follow-up study. *Alcoholism: Clinical and Experimental Research, 14,* 169–173.

Crow, T. J. (1989). A current view of the Type II syndrome: Age of onset, intellectual impairment, and the meaning of structural changes in the brain. *British Journal of Psychiatry, 155,* 15–20.

Crow, T. J., Cross, A. J., Johnstone, E. C., & Owen, F. (1982). Two syndromes in schizophrenia and their pathogenesis. In F. A. Henn & H. A. Nasrallah (Eds.), *Schizophrenia as a brain disease.* New York: Oxford University Press.

Crowe, R. (1975). An adoptive study of psychopathy: Preliminary results from arrest records and psychiatric hospital records. In R. Fieve, D. Rosenthal, & H. Brill (Eds.), *Genetic research in psychiatry.* Baltimore: Johns Hopkins University Press.

Crowe, R. R. (1991). Genetic studies of anxiety disorders. In M. T. Tsuang, K. S. Kendler, & M. T. Lyons (Eds.), *Genetic issues in psychosocial epidemiology.* (pp. 175–190). New Brunswick, NJ: Rutgers University Press.

Crowe, R. R., Noyes, R., Jr., Pauls, D. L., et al. (1983). A family study of panic disorder. *Archives of General Psychiatry, 40,* 1065–1069.

Cumming, J., & Cumming, E. (1962). *Ego and milieu.* New York: Atherton.

Cummings, C., Gordon, J. R., & Marlatt, G. A. (1980). Relapse: Prevention and prediction. In W. R. Miller (Ed.), *The addictive disorders: Treatment of alcoholism, drug abuse, smoking, and obesity.* New York: Pergamon Press.

Cummings, J. L. (1985). *Clinical neuropsychiatry.* Orlando, FL: Grune & Stratton.

Cummings, J. L. (1987). Multi-infarct: Diagnosis and management. *Psychosomatics, 28,* 117–126.

Cummings, J. L., & Benson, D. F. (1992). *Dementia: A clinical approach* (2nd ed.). Boston: Butterworths.

Curry, S., Wagner, E. H., & Grothaus, L. C. (1990). Intrinsic and extrinsic motivation for smoking cessation. *Journal of Consulting and Clinical Psychology, 58,* 310–316.

Curtiss, S. R. (1977). *Genie: A psycholinguistic study of a modern-day "wild child."* New York: Academic Press.

Custer, R. L., & Custer, R. F. (1978). *Characteristics of the recovering compulsive gambler: A survey of 150 members of Gamblers Anonymous.* Paper presented at the fourth annual Conference on Gambling, Reno, NV.

Cutter, H. S. G., Boyatzis, R. E., & Clancy, D. D. (1977). Effectiveness of power motivation training in rehabilitating alcoholics. *Journal of Studies on Alcohol, 38,* 131–141.

Czeisler, C. A., Kronauer, R. E., Allen, J. S., Duffy, J. F., Jewett, M. E., Brown, E. N., & Ronda, J. M. (1989). Bright light induction of strong (type 0) resetting of the human circadian pacemaker. *Science, 244,* 1328–1333.

Czeisler, C. A., Richardson, G. S., Coleman, R. M., Zimmerman, J. C., Moore-Ede, M. C., Dement, W. C., & Weitzman, E. D. (1981). Chronotherapy: Resetting the circadian clocks of patients with delayed sleep phase insomnia. *Sleep, 4,* 1–21.

Dain, N. (1964). *Concepts of sanity in the United States, 1789–1895.* New Brunswick, NJ: Rutgers University Press.

Dana, R. H. (1982). *A human science model for personality assessment with projective techniques.* Springfield, IL: Charles C Thomas.

Daniels, D., & Plomin, R. (1985). Origins of individual differences in infant shyness. *Developmental Psychology, 21,* 118–121.

Daniels, E. K., Shenton, M. E., Holzman, P. S., Benowitz, L. I., Coleman, M., Levin, S., & Levine, D. (1988). Patterns of thought disorder associated with right cortical damage, schizophrenia, and mania. *American Journal of Psychiatry, 145,* 944–949.

Datel, W. E., & Gengerelli, J. A. (1955). Reliability of Rorschach interpretations. *Journal of Projective Techniques, 19,* 372–381.

Davey, G. C. L. (in press). Preparedness and phobias: Specific evolved associations or a generalized expectancy bias? *Behavioral and Brain Sciences.*

Davidson, A., & Dobbing, J. (1966). Myelination as a vulnerable period in brain development. *British Medical Bulletin, 22,* 40–44.

Davidson, J. R. T., & Foa, E. B. (1991). Diagnostic issues in post-traumatic stress disorder: Considerations for the *DSM-IV. Journal of Abnormal Psychology.*

Davidson, J. R. T., Hughes, D., Blazer, D. G., & George, L. K. (1991). Posttraumatic stress disorder in the community: An epidemiological study. *Psychological Medicine, 21,* 713–721.

Davidson, J. R. T., Smith, R. D., & Kudler, H. S. (1989). Familial psychiatric illness in chronic posttraumatic stress disorder. *Comprehensive Psychiatry, 30,* 339–345.

Davidson, R. J. (1992). Emotion and affective style: Hemispheric substrates. *Psychological Science, 3,* 39–43.

Davidson, R. J., & Fox, N. A. (1989). Frontal brain asymmetry predicts infants' response to maternal separation. *Journal of Abnormal Psychology, 98,* 127–131.

Davis, K. L., Kahn, R. S., Ko, G., & Davidson, M. (1991). Dopamine in schizophrenia: Review and reconceptualization. *American Journal of Psychiatry, 148,* 1474–1486.

Dawes, R. M., Faust, D., & Meehl, P. E. (1989). Clinical versus actuarial judgment. *Science, 243,* 1668–1674.

Dawson, M. E., Nuechterlein, K. H., & Schell, A. M. (1992). Electrodermal anomalies in recent-onset schizophrenia: Relationships to symptoms and prognosis. *Schizophrenia Bulletin, 18,* 295–311.

Dawson, M. E., Neuchterlein, K. H., Schell, A. M., Gitlin, M., & Ventura, J. (1994). Autonomic abnormalities in schizophrenia: State or trait indicators? *Archives of General Psychiatry, 51,* 813–824.

Dean, C. W., & de Bruyn-Kops, E. (1982). *The crime and consequences of rape.* Springfield, IL: Charles C Thomas.

Degreef, G., Ashtari, M., Bogerts, B., Bilder, R. M., Jody, D. N., Alvir, J. M. J., & Lieberman, J. A. (1992). Volumes of ventricular system subdivisions measured from magnetic resonance images in first-episode schizophrenic patients. *Archives of General Psychiatry, 49,* 531–537.

DeCastillo, J. (1970). The influence of language upon symptomatology in foreign-born patients. *American Journal of Psychiatry, 127,* 242–244.

Delgado, P. L., Charney, D. S., Price, L. H., Aghajanian, G. K., Landis, H., & Heninger, G. R. (1990). Serotonin function and the mechanism of antidepressant action: Reversal of antidepressant-induced remission by rapid depletion of plasma tryptophan. *Archives of General Psychiatry, 47,* 411–418.

Delgado, P. L., Price, L. H., Heninger, G. R., & Charney, D. S. (1992). Neurochemistry. In E. S. Paykel (Ed.), *Handbook of affective disorders,* (2nd ed., pp. 219–254). New York: Guilford Press.

Delong, R. G. (1992). Autism, amnesia hippocampus and learning. *Neuroscience and Biobehavioral Review, 16,* 63–70.

DeLongis, A. D., Coyne, J. C., Dakof, G., Folkman, S., & Lazarus, R. S. (1982). Relationship of daily hassles, uplifts, and major life events to health status. *Health Psychology, 1,* 119–136.

DeMyer, M. K., Hingtgen, J. N., & Jackson, R. K. (1981). Infantile autism reviewed: A decade of research. *Schizophrenia Bulletin, 7,* 388–451.

Dennis, W. (1973). *Children of the Créche.* New York: Appleton-Century-Crofts.

Depue, R. A., & Monroe, S. M. (1978). The unipolar-bipolar distinction in the depressive disorders. *Psychological Bulletin, 85,* 1001–1029.

Derry, P. A., & Kuiper, N. A. (1981). Schematic processing and self-reference in clinical depression. *Journal of Abnormal Psychology, 90,* 286–297.

Deutsch, A. (1949). *The mentally ill in America* (2nd ed.). New York and London: Columbia University Press.

de Wilde, E. J., Kienhorst, I. C. W. M., Diekstra, R. F. W., & Wolters, W. H. G. (1992). The relationship between adolescent suicidal behavior and life events in childhood and adolescence. *American Journal of Psychiatry, 149,* 45–51.

de Young, M. (1982). *Sexual victimization of children.* Jefferson, NC: MacFarland.

Di Cara, L., & Miller, N. (1968). Instrumental learning of vasomotor responses by rats: Learning to respond differentially in the two ears. *Science, 159,* 1485–1486.

Dittmar, H., & Bates, B. (1987). Humanistic approaches to the understanding of treatment of anorexia nervosa. *Journal of Adolescence, 10,* 57–69.

Dobson, K. S. (1989). A meta-analysis of the efficacy of cognitive therapy for depression. *Journal of Consulting and Clinical Psychology, 57,* 414–419.

Dodrill, C. B. (1992). Neuropsychological aspects of epilepsy. *Psychiatric Clinics of North America, 15,* 383–394.

Dodrill, C. B. (1993). Neuropsychology. In J. Laidlaw, A. Richens, & D. Chadwick (Eds.), *A textbook of epilepsy* (pp. 459–473). Edinburgh: Churchill Livingstone.

Dohrenwend, B. S., & Dohrenwend, B. P. (1981). Hypotheses about stress processes linking social class to various types of psychopathology. *American Journal of Community Psychology, 9,* 146–159.

Dolan, B. (1991). Cross-cultural aspects of anorexia nervosa and bulimia: A review. *International Journal of Eating Disorders, 10,* 67–79.

Doleys, D. M. (1989). Enuresis and encopresis. In T. H. Ollendick & M. Hersen (Eds.), *Handbook of child psychopathology* (2nd ed.). New York: Plenum.

Donaldson, S. R., Gelenberg, A. J., & Baldessarini, R. J. (1983). The pharmacologic treatment of schizophrenia: A progress report. *Schizophrenia Bulletin, 9,* 504–527.

Dorris, M. A. (1989). *The broken cord.* New York: Harper & Row.

Drake, R. E., & Vaillant, G. E. (1985). A validity study of axis II of *DSM-III. American Journal of Psychiatry, 142,* 553–558.

Drew, C. J., Logan, D. R., & Hardman, M. L. (1988). *Mental retardation: A life cycle approach* (4th ed.). Columbus, OH: Merrill.

DSM. See entries under **American Psychiatric Association.**

Duke, M. P., & Mullins, M. C. (1973). Preferred interpersonal distance as a function of locus of control orientation in chronic schizophrenics, non-schizophrenic patients, and normals. *Journal of Consulting and Clinical Psychology, 41*(2), 230–234.

Dunbar, H. F. (1935). *Emotions and bodily changes.* New York: Columbia University Press.

Dunham, H. W. (1965). *Community and schizophrenia: An epidemiological analysis.* Detroit: Wayne State University Press.

Dunn, M. (1994). Neurophysiologic observations in autism. In M. L. Bauman & T. L. Kempner (Eds.), *The neurobiology of autism.* Baltimore: Johns Hopkins University Press.

Dunst, C. J., Johanson, C., Trivette, C. M., & Hamby, D. (1991), October–November). Family-oriented early intervention policies and practices: Family-centered or not? *Exceptional Children.*

DuPaul, G. J., & Barkley, R. A. (1990). Medication therapy. In R. A. Barkley (Ed.), *Attention-deficit hyperactivity disorder: A handbook for diagnosis and treatment* (pp. 573–612). New York: Guilford Press.

DuPaul, G. J., & Barkley, R. A. (1993). Behavioral contributions to pharmacotherapy: The utility of behavioral methodology in medication treatment of children with attention-deficit hyperactivity disorder. *Behavior Therapy, 24,* 47–65.

Durkheim, E. (1951). *Suicide* (J. A. Spaulding & G. Simpson, Trans.). Glencoe, IL: Free Press. (Original work published 1897)

Durrant, J. E. (1994). A decade of research on learning disabilities: A report card on the state of the literature. *Journal of Learning Disabilities, 27,* 25–33.

Dworkin, R. H. (1990). Patterns of six differences in negative symptoms and social functioning consistent with separate dimensions of schizophrenic psychopathology. *American Journal of Psychiatry, 147,* 347–349.

Dworkin, R. H., & Lenzenweger, M. F. (1984). Symptoms and the genetics of schizophrenia: Implications for diagnosis. *American Journal of Psychiatry, 141,* 1541–1546.

Dyer, K., Christian, W. P., & Luce, S. C. (1982). The role of response delay in improving the discrimination performance of autistic children. *Journal of Applied Behavior Analysis, 15,* 231–240.

Eagly, A. H., Makhijani, M. G., & Klonsky, B. G. (1992). Gender and the evaluation of leaders: A meta-analysis. *Psychological Bulletin, 111,* 3–22.

Eames, P. (1992). Hysteria following brain injury. *Journal of Neurology, Neurosurgery, and Psychiatry, 55,* 1046–1053.

Eaton, W. W., Kessler, R. C., Wittchen, H. U., & Magee, W. J. (1994). Panic and panic disorder in the United States. *American Journal of Psychiatry, 151,* 413–420.

Eaton, W. W., & Keyl, P. M. (1990). Risk factors for the onset of diagnostic interview schedule/*DSM-III* agoraphobia in a prospective, population-based study. *Archives of General Psychiatry, 47,* 819–824.

Eaton, W. W., Mortensen, P. B., Herrman, H., Freeman, H., Bilder, W., Burgess, P., & Wooff, K. (1992). Long-term course of hospitalization for schizophrenia: Part I. Risk for rehospitalization. *Schizophrenia Bulletin, 18,* 217–228.

Eberhardy, F. (1967). The view from "the couch." *Journal of Child's Psychology and Psychiatry, 8,* 257–263.

Eberlin, M., McConnachie, G., Ibel, S., & Volpe, L. (1993). Facilitated communication: A failure to replicate the phenomenon. *Journal of Autism and Developmental Disorders, 23.*

Edwards, G. (1989). As the years go rolling by: Drinking problems in the time dimension. *British Journal of Psychiatry, 154,* 18–26.

Edwards, G., Hensman, C., Hawker, A., & Williamson, V. (1967). Alcoholics Anonymous: The anatomy of a self-help group. *Social Psychiatry, 1,* 195–204.

Egeland, J. A., Gerhard, D. S., Pauls, D. L., Sussex, J. N., Kidd, K. K., Allen, C. R., Hostetter, A. M., & Housman, D. E. (1987). Bipolar affective disorders linked to DNA markers on chromosome 11. *Nature, 325,* 783–787.

Egeland, J. A., & Hostetter, A. M. (1983). Amish study: I. Affective disorders among the Amish. *American Journal of Psychiatry, 140,* 56–61.

Egeland, J. A., & Sussex, J. N. (1985). Suicide and family loading for affective disorders. *Journal of the American Medical Association, 254,* 915–918.

Ehlers, C. L., Frank, E., & Kupfer, D. J. (1988). Social zeitgebers and biological rhythms. A unified approach to understanding the etiology of depression. *Archives of General Psychiatry, 45,* 948–952.

Eich, E. (1986). Paper presented at the convention of the American Psychological Association, Washington, DC.

Eilbracht, A., & Thompson, T. (1977). Behavioral intervention in a sheltered work activity setting for retarded adults. In T. Thompson & J. Grabowski (Eds.), *Behavior modification of the mentally retarded* (2nd ed.). New York: Oxford University Press.

Eisen, A. R., & Engler, L. B. (1995). Chronic anxiety. In A. R. Eisen, C. A. Kearney, & C. E. Schaefer (Eds.), *Clinical handbook of anxiety disorders in children and adolescents.* Northvale, NJ: Aronson.

Elkin, I., Shea, T., Watkins, J. T., Imber, S. D., Sotsky, S. M., Collins, J. F., Glass, D. R., Pilkonis, P. A., Leber, W. R., Docherty, J. P., Fiester, S. J., & Parloff, M. B. (1989). National Institute of Mental Health treatment of depression collaborative research program. *Archives of General Psychiatry, 46,* 971–982.

Ellington, R. J. (1954). Incidence of EEG abnormality among patients with mental disorders of apparently nonorganic origin: A criminal review. *American Journal of Psychiatry, 3,* 263–275.

Elliott, D. S., Ageton, S. S., Huizinga, D., Knowles, B. A., & Canter, R. J. (1983). *The prevalence and incidence of delinquent behavior: 1976–1980* (National Youth Survey Report No. 26). Boulder, CO: Behavioral Research Institute.

Ellis, A. (1962). *Reason and emotion in psychotherapy.* New York: Lyle Stuart.

Ellis, A. (1977). The treatment of a psychopath with rational therapy. In S. J. Morse & R. I. Watson (Eds.), *Psychotherapies: A comparative casebook.* New York: Holt, Rinehart and Winston.

Ellis, A. (1980). An overview of the clinical theory of rational-emotive therapy. In R. Grieger & J. Boyd (Eds.), *Rational-emotive therapy: A skills-based approach.* New York: Van Nostrand Reinhold.

Ellis, A. (1993). Reflections on rational-emotive therapy. *Journal of Consulting and Clinical Psychology, 61,* 199–201.

Ellis, H. (1899–1928). *Studies in the psychology of sex* (7 vols.). Philadelphia: Davis.

Elmer-De Witt, P. (1994, October 17). Now for the truth about Americans and sex. *Time.*

Emmelkamp, P. M. G. (1994). Behavior therapy with adults. In A. E. Bergin & S. L. Garfield (Eds.), *Handbook of psychotherapy and behavior change* (4th ed., pp. 379–427). New York: Wiley.

Emmelkamp, P. M. G., van Linden, G., van den Heuvell, C., Ruphan, M., Sanderman, R. Scholing, A., & Stroink, F. (1988). Cognitive and behavioral interventions: A comparative evaluation with clinically distressed couples. *Journal of Family Psychology, 1,* 365–377.

Engel, B. T. (1960). Stimulus-response and individual-response specificity. *Archives of General Psychiatry, 2,* 305–313.

Engel, B. T., & Bickford, A. F. (1961). Response specificity: Stimulus response and individual response specificity in essential hypertension. *Archives of General Psychiatry, 5,* 478–489.

Engel, J., & Liljequist, S. (1983). The involvement of different neurotransmitters in mediating stimulatory and sedative effects of ethanol. In L. A. Pohorecky & J. Brick (Eds.), *Stress and alcohol use* (pp. 153–169). New York: Elsevier.

Engel, J., Van Ness, P. C., Rasmussen, T. B., Ojemann, L. M. (1993). Outcome with respect to epileptic seizures. In J. Engel, Jr. (Ed.), *Surgical treatment of the epilepsies* (2nd ed., pp. 609–621). New York: Raven Press.

Engle-Friedman, M., Baker, E. A., & Bootzin, R. R. (1985). Reports of wakefulness during EEG identified states of sleep. *Sleep Research, 14,* 121.

Ennis, B. J., & Emery, R. D. (1978). *The rights of mental patients.* New York: Avon.

Epstein, S. (1983). The stability of confusion: A reply to Mischel and Peake. *Psychological Review, 90,* 179–184.

Erdelyi, M. H. (1985). *Psychoanalysis: Freud's cognitive view.* New York: Freeman.

Erdelyi, M. H., & Goldberg, B. (1979). Let's not sweep repression under the rug: Toward a cognitive psychology of repression. In J. F. Kihlstrom & F. J. Evans (Eds.), *Functional disorders of memory.* Hillsdale, NJ: Erlbaum.

Erikson, K. T. (1976). *Everything in its path: Destruction of community in the Buffalo Creek flood.* New York: Simon & Schuster.

Escobar, J. I., Burnam, M. A., Karno, M., Forsythe, A., & Golding, J. M. (1987). Somatization in the community. *Archives of General Psychiatry, 44,* 713–718.

Escobar, J. I., & Canino, G. (1989). Unexplained physical complaints: Psychopathology and epidemiological correlates. *British Journal of Psychiatry, 154,* 24–27.

Esterling, B., Antoni, M., Kuman, M., & Schneiderman, N. (1990). Emotional repression, stress disclosure responses, and Epstein-Barr viral capsid antigen titers. *Psychosomatic Medicine, 52,* 397–410.

Evans, D. L., Folds, J. D., Petitto, J. M., Golden, R. N., Pedersen, C. A., Corrigan, M., Gilmore, J. H., Silva, S. G., Quade, D., & Ozer, H. (1992). Circulating natural killer cell phenotypes in men and women with major depression: Relation to cytotoxic activity and severity of depression. *Archives of General Psychiatry, 49,* 388–395.

Evans, M. D., Hollon, S. D, DeRubeis, R. J., Piasecki, J. M., Grove, W. M., Garvey, M. J., & Tuason, V. B. (1992). Differential relapse following cognitive therapy and pharmacotherapy for depression. *Archives of General Psychiatry, 49,* 802–808.

Ewen, D. (1956). *Journey to greatness: The life and music of George Gershwin.* New York: Holt, Rinehart and Winston.

Exner, J. E. (1978). *The Rorschach: A comprehensive system* (Vol. 1). New York: Wiley.

Exner, J. E. (1982). *The Rorschach: A comprehensive system* (Vol. 2). New York: Wiley.

Exner, J. E. (1986). *The Rorschach: A comprehensive system* (Vol. 3). New York: Wiley.

Eysenck, H. J. (1952). The effects of psychotherapy: An evaluation. *Journal of Consulting Psychology, 16,* 319–324.

Eysenck, H. J. (Ed.). (1967). *The biological basis of personality.* Springfield, IL: Charles C Thomas.

Fabian, W. D., Jr., & Fishkin, S. M. (1981). A replicated study of self-reported changes in psychological absorption with marijuana intoxication. *Journal of Abnormal Psychology, 90,* 546–553.

Fahy, T. A. (1988). The diagnosis of multiple personality disorder: A critical review. *British Journal of Psychiatry, 153,* 597–606.

Fairbank, J. A., Schlenger, W. E., Caddell, J. M., & Woods, M. G. (1993). Post-traumatic stress disorder. In P. B. Sutker & H. E. Adams (Eds.), *Comprehensive handbook of psychopathology* (2nd ed., pp. 145–165). New York: Plenum Press.

Falkner, B., Kushner, H., Onesti, G., & Angelakos, E. T. (1981). Cardiovascular characteristics in adolescents who develop essential hypertension. *Hypertension, 3,* 521–527.

Falloon, I. R. H., Boyd, J. L., McGill, C. W., et al. (1982). Family management in prevention of exacerbation of schizophrenia: A controlled study. *New England Journal of Medicine, 306*(24), 1437–1440.

Falloon, I. R. H., Boyd, J. L., McGill, C. W., Williamson, M., Razani, J., Moss, H. B., Gilderman, A. M., & Simpson, G. M. (1985). Family management in the prevention of morbidity of schizophrenia. *Archives of General Psychiatry, 42,* 887–896.

Faraone, S. V., Kremen, W. S., & Tsuang, M. T. (1990). Genetic transmission of major affective disorders: Quantitative models and linkage analyses. *Psychological Bulletin, 108,* 109–127.

Farberow, N. L., & Litman, R. E. (1970). *A comprehensive suicide prevention program. Suicide Prevention Center of Los Angeles, 1958–1969* (Unpublished final report, DHEW NIMH Grants No. MH 14946 and MH 00128). Los Angeles.

Farde, L., Nordström, A. L., Wiesel, F. A., Pauli, S., Halldin, C., & Sedvall, G. (1992). Positron emission tomographic analysis of central D1 and D2 dopamine receptor occupancy in patients treated with classical neuroleptics and clozapine: Relation to extrapyramidal side effects. *Archives of General Psychiatry, 49,* 538–544.

Farlow, M., Gracon, S. I., Hershey, L. A., Lewis, K. W., Sadowsky, C. H., & Dolan-Ureno, J. (1992). A controlled trial of tacrine in Alzheimer's disease. *Journal of the American Medical Association, 268,* 2523–2529.

Farrington, D. P. (1991). Antisocial personality from childhood to adulthood. *Psychologist, 4,* 389–394.

Fauman, M. A. (1994). *Study guide to* DSM-IV. Washington, DC: American Psychiatric Press.

Fava, G. A., Grandi, S., Rafanelli, C., & Canestrari, R. (1992). Prodromal symptoms in panic disorder with agoraphobia: A replication study. *Journal of Affective Disorders, 26,* 85–88.

Favell, J. E. (1982). The treatment of self-injurious behavior. *Behavior Therapy, 13,* 529–554.

Fawzy, F. L., Fawzy, N. W., Hyun, C. S., Elashoff, R., Guthrie, D., Fahey, J. L., & Morton, D. L. (1993). Malignant melanoma: Effects of an early structured psychiatric intervention, coping, and affective state on recurrence and survival 6 years later. *Archives of General Psychiatry, 50,* 681–689.

Federal Bureau of Investigation. (1991) *Uniform crime reports.* Washington, DC: U.S. Department of Justice.

Fein, D., & Waterhouse, L. (1990). Social cognition in infantile autism. *Forum Medicum.*

Feldman, C. M. (1994). *The etiology and treatment of domestic violence between adult partners.* Unpublished manuscript. University of Arizona, Tucson.

Feldman-Summers, S., & Pope, K. S. (1994). The experience of "forgetting" childhood abuse: A national survey of psychologists. *Journal of Consulting and Clinical Psychology, 62,* 636–639.

Fenichel, O. (1945). *The psychoanalytic theory of neurosis.* New York: Norton.

Fensterheim, H., and Baer, J. (1975). *Don't say yes when you want to say no.* New York: McKay.

Fenton, W. S., & McGlashan, T. H. (1991a). Natural history of schizophrenia subtypes: I. Longitudinal study of paranoid, hebephrenic, and undifferentiated schizophrenia. *Archives of General Psychiatry, 48,* 969–977.

Fenton, W. S., & McGlashan, T. H. (1994). Antecedents, symptom progression, and long-term outcome of the deficit syndrome in schizophrenia. *American Journal of Psychiatry, 151,* 351–356.

Ferster, C. B. (1965). Classification of behavioral pathology. In L. Krasner & L. P. Ullmann (Eds.), *Research in behavioral modification.* New York: Holt, Rinehart and Winston.

Ferster, C. B. (1973). A functional analysis of depression. *American Psychologist, 28,* 857–870.

Figley, C. R. (1979). *Combat as disaster: Treating combat veterans as survivors.* Paper presented at the annual meeting of the American Psychiatric Association, Chicago.

Finch, J. R., Smith, J. P., & Pokorny, A. D. (1970, May). *Vehicular studies.* Paper presented at meetings of the American Psychiatric Association.

Fine, R. H. (1965). Psychotherapy with the mentally retarded adolescent. *Current Psychiatric Therapies, 5,* 58–66.

Finkelhor, D. (1980). Sex among siblings: A survey on prevalence, variety, and effects. *Archives of Sexual Behavior, 9,* 171–194.

Finkelhor, D. (1984). *Child sexual abuse: New theory and research.* New York: Free Press.

Finkelhor, D., & Araji, S. (1986). Explanations of pedophilia: A four factor model. *The Journal of Sex Research, 22,* 145–161.

Finn, P. R., & Pihl, R. O. (1987). Men at high risk for alcoholism: The effect of alcohol on cardiovascular response to unavoidable shock. *Journal of Abnormal Psychology, 96,* 230–236.

Firoe, M. C., Novotny, T. E., Pierce, J. P., Hatziandreu, E. J., Patel, K. M., & Davis, R. M. (1989). Trends in cigarette smoking in the United States: The changing influence of gender and race. *Journal of the American Medical Association, 261,* 49–55.

Fischer, P. J., & Breakey, W. R. (1991). The epidemiology of alcohol, drug, and mental disorders among homeless persons. *American Psychologist, 46,* 1115–1128.

Fish, B., Shapiro, T., Campbell, M., et al. (1968). A classification of schizophrenic children under five years. *American Journal of Psychiatry, 124,* 109–117.

Fish, J. F. (1957). The classification of schizophrenia. *Journal of Mental Science, 103,* 443–465.

Fisher, S., & Greenberg, R. P. (1977). *The scientific credibility of Freud's theories and therapy.* New York: Basic Books.

Flaskerud, J. H. (1987). AIDS: Neuropsychiatric complications. *Journal of Psychosocial Nursing, 25*(12), 17–20.

Floor, L., Baxter, D., Rosen, M., & Zisfein, L. (1975). A survey of marriages among previously institutionalized retardates. *Mental Retardation, 13,* 33–37.

Flor-Henry, P. (1987). Cerebral aspects of sexual deviation. In G. D. Wilson (Ed.), *Variant sexuality: Research and theory.* Baltimore: Johns Hopkins University Press.

Flor-Henry, P., Fromm-Auch, D., Tapper, M., & Schopflocher, D. (1981). A neuropsychological study of the stable syndrome of hysteria. *Biological Psychiatry, 16,* 601–626.

Foa, E. B. (1988). What cognitions differentiate panic disorder from other anxiety disorders? In I. Hard & H. Wittchen (Eds.), *Panic and Phobias 2.* New York: Springer-Verlag.

Foa, E. B., Steketee, G., & Rothbaum, B. O. (1989). Behavioral/cognitive conceptualization of post-traumatic stress disorder. *Behavior Therapy, 20,* 155–176.

Fodor, I. G. (1980). The treatment of communication problems with assertiveness training. In A. Goldstein & E. B. Foa (Eds.), *Handbook of behavioral interventions: A clinical guide.* New York: Wiley.

Foerster, A., Lewis, S. W., Owen, M. J., & Murray, R. M. (1991). Low birth weight and a family history of schizophrenia predict poor premorbid functioning in psychosis. *Schizophrenia Research, 5,* 13–20.

Folkman, S., Lazarus, R., Dunkel-Schetter, C., DeLongis, A., & Gruen, R. (1986). The dynamics of a stressful encounter: Cognitive appraisal, coping, and encounter outcomes. *Journal of Personality and Social Psychology, 50,* 992–1003.

Folks, D. G., Ford, C. V., & Regan, W. M. (1984). Conversion symptoms in a general hospital. *Psychosomatics, 25,* 285–295.

Folstein, S., & Rutter, M. (1977). Genetic influences and infantile autism. *Nature, 265,* 726–728.

Ford, C. S., & Beach, F. A. (1951). *Patterns of sexual behavior.* New York: Ace.

Forsyth, R. P. (1974). Mechanisms of the cardiovascular responses to environmental stressors. In P. A. Obrist, A. H. Black, J. Brener, & L. U. Di Cara (Eds.), *Cardiovascular psychophysiology: Current issues in response mechanisms, biofeedback and methodology.* Hawthorne, NY: Aldine.

Foy, D. W., Resnick, H. S., Sipprelle, R. C., & Carroll, E. M. (1987). Premilitary, military, and postmilitary factors in the development of combat-related stress disorders. *Behavior Therapist, 10,* 3–9.

Frances, A. J., Widiger, T. A., & Pincus, H. A. (1989). The development of *DSM-IV. Archives of General Psychiatry, 46,* 373–375.

Frank, E., Anderson, B., Reynolds, C. F., III, Ritenour, A., & Kupfer, D. J. (1994). Life events and the research diagnostic criteria endogenous subtype. *Archives of General Psychiatry, 51,* 519–524.

Frank, E., Kupfer, D. J., Perel, T. M., Cornes, C. L., Jarrett, D. J., Mallinger, A., Thase, M. E., McEachran, A. B., & Grochocinski, V. J. (1990). Three-year outcomes for maintenance therapies in recurrent depression. *Archives of General Psychiatry, 47,* 1093–1099.

Frank, E., Kupfer, D. J., Wagner, E. F., McEachran, A. B., & Cornes, C. L. (1991). Efficacy of interpersonal psychotherapy as a maintenance treatment of recurrent depression: Contributing factors. *Archives of General Psychiatry, 48,* 1053–1059.

Frank, G. (1966). *The Boston strangler.* New York: New American Library.

Frank, J. D. (1961). *Persuasion and healing: A comparative study of psychotherapy.* Baltimore: Johns Hopkins University Press.

Frank, J. D. (1983). The placebo in psychotherapy. *Behavioral and Brain Sciences, 6,* 291–292.

Frankel, F. H. (1990). Hypnotizability and dissociation. *American Journal of Psychiatry, 147,* 823–829.

Frankl, V. E. (1962). *Man's search for meaning.* Boston: Beacon Press.

Frankl, V. E. (1975a). Paradoxical intention and dereflection. *Psychotherapy: Theory, Research, and Practice, 12,* 226–237.

Frankl, V. E. (1975b). *The unconscious god: Psychotherapy and theology.* New York: Simon & Schuster.

Fredrikson, M. (1990). Cardiovascular responses to behavioral stress and hypertension: A meta-analytic review. *Annals of Behavioral Medicine, 12,* 30–39.

Free, M. L., & Oei, T. P. S. (1989). Biological and psychological processes in the treatment and maintenance of depression. *Clinical Psychology Review, 9,* 653–688.

Freedman, B., & Chapman, L. J. (1973). Early subjective experience in schizophrenic episodes. *Journal of Abnormal Psychology, 82*(1), 46–59.

Freeman, A., & Leaf, R. (1989). Cognitive therapy applied to personality disorders. In A. Freeman, K. Simon, L. Beutler, & H. Arkowitz (Eds.), *Comprehensive handbook of cognitive therapy.* New York: Plenum Press.

Freeman, H. (1989). Relationship of schizophrenia to the environment. *British Journal of Psychiatry, 155,* 90–99.

Freeman, M. B., Leary, T. F., Ossorio, A. G., & Coffey, H. S. (1951). The interpersonal dimension of personality. *Journal of Personality, 20,* 143–161.

French, S. A., & Jeffrey, R. W. (1994). Consequences of dieting to lose weight: Effects on physical and mental health. *Health Psychology, 13,* 195–212.

Freud, A. (1946). *The ego and mechanisms of defense.* New York: International Universities Press.

Freud, A. (1958). Adolescence. *Psychoanalytic Study of the Child, 13,* 255–278.

Freud, A. (1965). *Normality and pathology: Assessment of development.* New York: International Universities Press.

Freud, S. (1953). Three essays on sexuality. In J. Strachey (Ed.), *The standard edition of the complete psychological works of Sigmund Freud* (Vol. 3). London: Hogarth Press. (Original work published 1905)

Freud, S. (1953). The questioning of lay analysis. In J. Strachey (Ed.), *The standard edition of the complete psychological works of Sigmund Freud* (Vol. 20). London: Hogarth Press. (Original work published 1926)

Freud, S. (1957). Mourning and melancholia. In J. Rickman (Ed.), *A general selection from the works of Sigmund Freud.* Garden City, NY: Doubleday. (Original work published 1917)

Freud, S. (1962). Studies on hysteria. In J. Strachey (Ed.), *The standard edition of the complete psychological works of Sigmund Freud* (Vol. 2). London: Hogarth Press. (Original work published 1895)

Freud, S. (1962). Analysis of a phobia in a five-year-old boy. In J. Strachey (Ed.), *The standard edition of the complete psychological works of Sigmund Freud* (Vol. 10). London: Hogarth Press. (Original work published 1909)

Freud, S. (1974). Femininity. In J. Strachey (Ed.), *The standard edition of the complete psychological works of Sigmund Freud* (Vol. 22). London: Hogarth Press. (Original work published 1932)

Freund, K., & Blanchard, R. (1989). Phallometric diagnosis of pedophilia. *Journal of Consulting and Clinical Psychology, 57,* 100–105.

Friedman, M., & Rosenman, R. H. (1974). *Type A behavior and your heart.* New York: Knopf.

Friedman, M., Thoresen, C. E., Gill, J. J., Powell, L. H., Ulmer, D., Thompson, L., Price, V. A., Rabin, D. D., Breall, W. S., Dixon, T., Levy, R., & Bourg, E. (1984). Alteration of Type A behavior and reduction in cardiac recurrences in postmyocardial infarction patients. *American Heart Journal, 108,* 237–248.

Friedman, P. (1976). Overview of the institutional labor problem: The nature and extent of institutional labor in the United States. In M. Kindred, J. Cohen, D. Penrod, & T. Shaffer (Eds.), *The mentally retarded citizen and the law: President's Committee on Mental Retardation.* New York: Free Press.

Frith, C. D., & Done, D. J. (1988). Towards a neuropsychology of schizophrenia. *British Journal of Psychiatry, 153,* 437–443.

Fromm, Erich. (1980). *Greatness and limitations of Freud's thought.* New York: Harper & Row.

Frosch, W. A., Robbins, E. S., & Stern, M. (1965). Untoward reactions to lysergic acid diethylamide (LSD) resulting in hospitalization. *New England Journal of Medicine, 273*(23), 1236.

Furby, L., Weinrott, M. R., & Blackshaw, L. (1989). Sex offender recidivism: A review. *Psychological Bulletin,* 105(1), 3–30.

Fuster, J. M. (1989). *The prefrontal cortex* (2nd ed.). New York: Raven Press.

Fyer, A. J., Liebowitz, M. R., & Klein, D. F. (1990). Treatment trials, comorbidity, and syndromal complexity. In J. D. Maser and C. R. Cloninger (Eds.), *Comorbidity of mood and anxiety disorders.* Washington, DC: American Psychiatric Press.

Fyer, A. J., Mannuzza, S., Gallops, M. S., Martin, L. Y., Aaronson, C., Gorman, J. M., Liebowitz, M. R., & Klein, D. F. (1990). Familial transmission of simple phobias and fears. *Archives of General Psychiatry, 47,* 252–256.

Fyer, M. R. (1990). Phobia. In M. E. Thase, B. A. Edelstein, & M. Hersen (Eds.), *Handbook of outpatient treatment of adults: Nonpsychotic mental disorders* (pp. 161–175). New York: Plenum Press.

Gaebel, W., & Pietzcker, A. (1987). Prospective study of course of illness in schizophrenia. *Schizophrenia Bulletin, 13,* 307–316.

Gagnon, J. H. (1977). *Human sexualities.* Chicago: Scott, Foresman.

Gainotti, G. (1972). Emotional behavior and hemispheric side of the lesion. *Cortex, 8,* 41–55.

Garber, H. L., & McInerney, M. (1982). Sociobehavioral factors in mental retardation. In P. T. Legelka & H. G. Prehm (Eds.), *Mental retardation: From categories to people.* Columbus, OH: Charles E. Merrill.

Garcia, M. E., Schmitz, J. M., & Doerfler, L. A. (1990). A fine-grained analysis of the role of self-efficacy in self-initiated attempts to quit smoking. *Journal of Consulting and Clinical Psychology, 58,* 317–322.

Gardner, H., & Hatch, T. (1989). Multiple intelligences go to school: Educational implications of the theory of multiple intelligences. *Educational Research, 18*(8), 6.

Garety, P. A., Hemsley, D. R., & Wessely, S. (1991). Reasoning in deluded schizophrenic and paranoid patients: Biases in performance on a probabilistic inference task. *Journal of Nervous and Mental Disease, 179,* 194–201.

Garfield, S. L. (1980). *Psychotherapy: An elective approach.* New York: Wiley.

Garfield, S. L., & Kurtz, R. (1977). A study of eclectic views. *Journal of Consulting and Clinical Psychology, 45,* 78–83.

Garfinkel, B. D., Froese, A., & Hood, J. (1982). Suicide attempts in children and adolescents. *American Journal of Psychiatry, 139,* 1257–1261.

Garland, A. F., & Zigler, E. (1993). Adolescent suicide prevention: Current research and social policy implications. *American Psychologist, 48,* 169–182.

Gatz, M., Bengtson, V. L., & Blum, M. J. (1990). Caregiving families. In J. E. Birren & K. W. Schaie (Eds.), *Handbook of the psychology of aging* (3rd ed., pp. 405–426). New York: Academic Press.

Gatz, M., Lowe, B., Berg, S., Mortimer, J., & Pedersen, N. (1994). Dementia: Not just a search for the gene. *Gerontologist, 34,* 251–255.

Gatz, M., & Snyder, M. A. (1992). The mental health system and older adults in the 1990s. *American Psychologist, 47,* 741–751.

Gawin, F. H., & Kleber, H. D. (1986). Abstinence symptomatology and psychiatric diagnosis in cocaine abusers. *Archives of General Psychiatry, 43,* 107–113.

Gazzaniga, M. S. (1972). One brain—two minds? *American Scientist, 60,* 311–317.

Gebbard, P. H., Gagnon, J. H., Pomeroy, W. B., & Christenson, C. V. (1965). *Sex offenders.* New York: Harper & Row.

Gelder, M. (1991). Psychological treatment for anxiety disorders: Adjustment disorder with anxious mood, generalized anxiety disorders, panic disorder, agoraphobia, and avoidant personality disorder. In W. Coryell & G. Winokur (Eds.), *The clinical management of anxiety disorders* (pp. 10–27). New York: Oxford University Press.

Gelenberg, A. J. (1991). Psychoses. In A. J. Gelenberg, E. L. Bassuk, & S. C. Schoonover (Eds.), *The practitioner's guide to psychoactive drugs* (3rd ed., pp. 125–218). New York: Plenum Press.

Gelfand, D. M., Jenson, W. R., & Drew, C. J. (1982). *Understanding child behavior disorders.* New York: Holt, Rinehart and Winston.

Gelles, R. J., Lackner, R., & Wolfner, G. D. (1994). *Violence Update, 4*(12), 1–10 passim.

Gelles, R. J., & Straus, M. (1988). *Intimate violence.* New York: Simon & Schuster.

Gelman, D. (1990, March 26). Drugs vs. the couch. *Newsweek,* pp. 42–43.

Gibbons, D. C. (1975). *Delinquent behavior.* Englewood Cliffs, NJ: Prentice-Hall.

Giles, D. E., Biggs, M. E., Rush, A. J., & Roffwarg, H. P. (1988). Risk factors in families of unipolar depression: I. Psychiatric illness and reduced REM latency. *Journal of Affective Disorders, 14,* 51–59.

Gill, M., McKeon, P., & Humphries, P. (1988). Linkage analysis of manic depression in an Irish family using H-ras 1 and INS DNA markers. *Journal of Medical Genetics, 25,* 634–635.

Gilligan, C. (1982). *In a different voice.* Cambridge, MA: Harvard University Press.

Giorgi, A. (1970). *Psychology as a human science: A phenomenologically based approach.* New York: Harper & Row.

Girgus. J. S., Nolen-Hoeksema. S. Paul. G., & Spears, H. (1991, April). *Does participation in feminine or masculine activities predict sex differences in adolescent depression?* Paper presented at the meeting of the Eastern Psychological Association, New York.

Glaser, R., Pearson, G. R., Bonneau, R. H., Esterling, B. A., Atkinson, C., & Kiecolt-Glaser, J. K. (1993). Stress and the memory T-cell response to the Epstein-Barr virus in healthy medical students. *Health Psychology, 12,* 435–442.

Glass, L. L., Katz, H. M., Schnitzer, R. D., Knapp, P. H., Frank, A. F., & Gunderson, J. G. (1989). Psychotherapy of schizophrenia: An empirical investigation of the relationship of process to outcome. *American Journal of Psychiatry, 146,* 603–608.

Glassman, A. H. (1993). Cigarette smoking: Implications for psychiatric illness. *American Journal of Psychiatry, 150,* 546–553.

Goffman, E. (1959a). The moral career of the mental patient. *Psychiatry: Journal for the Study of Interpersonal Processes, 22,* 123–131.

Goffman, E. (1961). *Asylums: Essays on the social situation of mental patients and other inmates.* New York: Doubleday.

Goldberg, D. P., & Bridges, K. (1988). Somatic presentations of psychiatric illness in primary care settings. *Journal of Psychosomatic Research, 32,* 137–144.

Goldblatt, M., & Munitz, H. (1976). Behavioral treatment of hysterical leg paralysis. *Journal of Behavior Therapy and Experimental Psychiatry, 7*(3), 259–263.

Golden, C. J., Moses, J. A., Jr., & Zelazowski, R. (1980). Cerebral ventricular size and neuropsychological impairment in young chronic schizophrenics. *Archives of General Psychiatry, 37,* 619–626.

Goldfarb, W. (1963). Self-awareness in schizophrenic children. *Archives of General Psychiatry, 8,* 47–60.

Goldfried, M. R. (1980). Psychotherapy as coping skills training. In M. J. Mahoney (Ed.), *Psychotherapy process: Current issues and future directions.* New York: Plenum Press.

Golding, J. M., Smith, R., Jr., & Kashner, M. (1991). Does somatization disorder occur in men? *Archives of General Psychiatry, 48,* 231–235.

Goldman, M. S., Brown, S. A., & Christiansen, B. A. (1987). Expectancy theory: Thinking about drinking. In H. T. Blane & K. E. Leonard (Eds.), *Psychological theories of drinking and alcoholism* (pp. 181–226). New York: Guilford Press.

Goldstein, A. (1976). Opioid peptides (endorphins) in pituitary and brain. *Science, 193,* 1081–1086.

Goldstein, J. M. (1988). Gender differences in the course of schizophrenia. *American Journal of Psychiatry, 145,* 684–689.

Goldstein, J. M., Faraone, S. V., Chen, W. J., Tolomiczencko, G. S., & Tsuang, M. T. (1990). Sex differences in the familial transmission of schizophrenia. *British Journal of Psychiatry, 156,* 819–826.

Goldstein, J. M., Santangelo, S. L., Simpson, J. C., & Tsuang, M. T. (1990). The role of gender in identifying subtypes of schizophrenia: A latent class analytic approach. *Schizophrenia Bulletin, 16,* 263–275.

Goldstein, K. (1948). *Aftereffects of brain injuries in war: Their evaluation and treatment.* New York: Grune & Stratton.

Goldstein, M., Mahanand, D., Lee, J., et al. (1976). Dopamine-β-hydroxylase and endogenous total 5-hydroxindole levels in autistic patients and controls. In M. Coleman (Ed.), *The autistic syndrome* (pp. 57–63). Amsterdam: North-Holland.

Goldstein, M. J. (1987). Family interaction patterns that antedate the onset of schizophrenia and related disorders: A further analysis of data from a longitudinal prospective study. In K. Hahlweg & M. J. Goldstein (Eds.), *Understanding major mental disorder: The contribution of family interaction research* (pp. 11–32). New York: Family Process Press.

Goldstein, M. J., & Doane, J. A. (1985). Interventions with families and the course of schizophrenia. In M. Alpert (Ed.), *Controversies in schizophrenia* (pp. 381–397). New York: Guilford Press.

Goldstein, R. B., Black, D. W., Nasrallah, A., & Winokur, G. (1991). The prediction of suicide: Sensitivity, specificity, and predictive value of a multivariate model applied to suicide among 1906 patients with affective disorders. *Archives of General Psychiatry, 48,* 418–422.

Goleman, D. (1986a, November 11). For mentally ill on the street, a new approach shines. *The New York Times,* pp. C1, C3.

Goleman, D. (1986b, November 4). To expert eyes, city streets are open mental wards. *The New York Times,* pp. C1, C3.

Goodkin, K., Blaney, N. T., Feasler, D., Fletcher, M. A., Baum, M. K., Mantero-Atienza, E., Klimas, N. G., Millon, C., Szapocznik, J., & Eisdorfer, C. (1992). Active coping style is associated with natural killer cell cytotoxicity in asymptomatic HIV-1 seropositive homosexual men. *Journal of Psychosomatic Research, 36,* 635–650.

Goodman, A. (1992). Empathy and inquiry: Integrating empathic mirroring in an interpersonal framework. *Contemporary Psychoanalysis, 28,* 631–646.

Goodman, W. (1994, March 28). *When even victimizers say they are victims. The New York Times,* p. C14.

Goodsitt, A. (1985). Self-psychology and the treatment of anorexia nervosa. In D. M. Garner & P. E. Garfinkel (Eds.), *Handbook of psychotherapy for anorexia nervosa and bulima* (pp. 55–82). New York: Guilford Press.

Goodwin, D. W., Schulsinger, F., Hermansen, L., Guze, S. B., & Winokur, G. (1973). Alcohol problems in adoptees raised apart from alcoholic biological parents. *Archives of General Psychiatry, 28,* 238–243.

Goodwin, D. W., Schulsinger, F., Moller, N., Mednick, S., & Guze, S. (1977). Psychopathology in adopted and nonadopted daughters of alcoholics. *Archives of General Psychiatry, 34,* 1005–1009.

Goodwin, F. K., & Jamison, K. R. (1990). *Manic-depressive illness.* New York: Oxford University Press.

Goodyer, I. M. (1992). Depression in childhood and adolescence. In E. S. Paykel (Ed.), *Handbook of affective disorders* (2nd ed., pp. 585–600). New York: Guilford Press.

Gorenstein, E. E. (1982). Frontal lobe functions in psychopaths. *Journal of Abnormal Psychology, 91,* 368–379.

Gorman, J. M., Liebowitz, M. R., Fyer, A. J., & Stein, J. (1989). A neuroanatomical hypothesis for panic disorder. *American Journal of Psychiatry, 146,* 148–161.

Gotlib, I. H., & Robinson, L. A. (1982). Responses to depressed individuals: Discrepancies between self-report and observer rated behavior. *Journal of Abnormal Psychology, 91,* 231–240.

Gottesman, I. I. (1991). *Schizophrenia genesis: The origins of madness.* New York: Freeman.

Gottesman, I. I., & Bertelsen, A. (1989). Confirming unexpressed genotypes for schizophrenia. *Archives of General Psychiatry, 46,* 867–872.

Gottesman, I. I., & Goldsmith, H. H. (in press). Developmental psychopathology of antisocial behavior: Inserting genes into its ontogenesis and epigenesis. In C. Nelson (Ed.), *Threats to optimal development: Integrating biological, social, and psychological risk factors* (Vol. 27). Hillsdale, NJ: Erlbaum.

Gottesman, I. I., & Shields, J. (1976). A critical review of recent adoption, twin and family studies of schizophrenia: Behavioral genetics perspectives. *Schizophrenia Bulletin, 2*(3), 360–398.

Gottesman, I. I., & Shields, J. (1982). *Schizophrenia: The epigenetic puzzle.* New York: Cambridge University Press.

Gottman, J. M. (1979). *Marital interaction: Experimental investigations.* New York: Academic Press.

Gottman, J. M., Jacobson, N. S., Rushe, R. H., Short, J. W., Babcock, J., La Taillade, J. J., & Waltz, J. (in press). The relationship between heart rate reactivity, emotionally aggressive behavior and general violence in batterers. *Journal of Family Psychology.*

Gough, H. C. (1948). A sociological theory of psychopathy. *American Journal of Sociology, 53,* 359–366.

Gould, M. S., Shaffer, D., Fisher, P., Kleinman, M., & Morishima, A. (1992). The clinical prediction of adolescent suicide. In R. W. Maris, A. L. Berman, J. T. Maltsberger, & R. I. Yufit (Eds.), *Assessment and prediction of suicide* (pp. 130–143). New York: Guilford Press.

Gould, R., Miller, B. L., Goldberg, M. A., & Benson, D. F. (1986). The validity of hysterical signs and symptoms. *Journal of Nervous and Mental Disease, 174,* 593–597.

Gove, W., & Herb, T. (1974). Stress and mental illness among the young: A comparison of the sexes. *Social Forces, 53,* 256–265.

Gove, W. R. (1982). The current status of the labelling theory of mental illness. In W. R. Gove (Ed.), *Deviance and mental illness.* Beverly Hills, CA: Sage.

Grabowski, J., Stitzer, M. L., & Henningfield, J. E. (1984). *Behavioral intervention techniques in drug abuse treatment.* Rockville, MD: National Institute on Drug Abuse.

Grabowski, J., & Thompson, T. (1977). Development and maintenance of a behavior modification program for behaviorally retarded institutionalized men. In T. Thompson & J. Grabowski (Eds.), *Behavior modification of the mentally retarded* (2nd ed.). New York: Oxford University Press.

Graham, D. T. (1967). Health, disease, and the mind-body problem: Linguistic parallelism. *Psychosomatic Medicine, 39,* 52–71.

Graham, J. R. (1990). *MMPI-2: Assessing personality and psychopathology.* New York: Oxford University Press.

Graham, J. R., & Strenger, V. E. (1988). MMPI characteristics of alcoholics: A review. *Journal of Consulting and Clinical Psychology, 56,* 197–205.

Graves, A. B., Larson, E. B., White, L. R., Teng, E. L., & Homma, A. (1994). Opportunities and challenges in international collaborative epidemiologic research of dementia and its subtypes: Studies between Japan and the U.S. *International Psychogeriatrics, 6,* 209–224.

Green, B. L., Lindy, J. D., Grace, M. C., Gleser, G. C., Leonard, A. C., Korol, M., & Winget, C. (1990). Buffalo Creek survivors in the second decade: Stability of stress symptoms. *American Journal of Orthopsychiatry, 60,* 43–54.

Green, M. F. (1993). Cognitive remediation in schizophrenia: Is it time yet? *American Journal of Psychiatry, 150,* 178–187.

Green, M. F., & Walker, E. (1985). Neuropsychological performance and positive and negative symptoms in schizophrenia. *Journal of Abnormal Psychology, 94,* 460–469.

Green, R., & Fleming, D. T. (1990). Transsexual surgery follow-up: Status in the 1990s. *Annual Review of Sex Research, 1,* 163–174.

Greenberg, G. (1977). The family interactional perspective: A study and examination of the work of Don D. Jackson. *Family Process, 16,* 385–412.

Greenberg, L. S., Elliott, R., & Lietaer, G. (1994). Research on experiential psychotherapies. In A. E. Bergin and S. L. Garfield (Eds.), *Handbook of psychotherapy and behavior change* (4th ed., pp. 509–539). New York: Wiley.

Greenberg, L. S., & Goldman, R. L. (1988). Training in experiential therapy. *Journal of Consulting and Clinical Psychology, 56,* 696–702.

Greenberg, L. S., & Johnson, S. M. (1988). *Emotionally focused therapy for couples.* New York: Guilford Press.

Greenspan, S., & Shoultz, B. (1981). Why mentally retarded adults lose their jobs: Social competence as a factor in work adjustment. *Applied Research in Mental Retardation, 2,* 22–38.

Greenwald, E., & Leitenberg, H. (1989). Long-term effects of sexual experiences with siblings and nonsiblings during childhood. *ASB, 18,* 389–400.

Greer, S. (1964). Study of parental loss in neurotics and sociopaths. *Archives of General Psychiatry, 11,* 177–180.

Grey, A. L. (1988). Sullivan's contribution to psychoanalysis: An overview. *Contemporary Psychoanalysis, 24,* 548–576.

Griffin, D. E., & Johnson, R. T. (1990). Encephalitis, myelitis, and neuritis. In G. L. Mandell, R. G. Douglas, Jr., & J. E. Bennett (Eds.), *Principles and practice of infectious disease* (3rd ed., pp. 726–769). New York: Churchill Livingstone.

Grinspoon, L. (1977). *Marihuana reconsidered* (2nd ed.). Cambridge, MA: Harvard University Press.

Grisso, T. (1991). Clinical assessments for legal decision making. In S. A. Shah & B. D. Sales (Eds.), *Law and mental health: Major developments and research needs.* Rockville, MD: National Institute of Mental Health.

Gronwall, D., Wrightson, P., & Waddell, P. (1990). *Head injury: The facts. A guide for families and care-givers.* New York: Oxford University Press.

Groth, N. A. (1978). Guidelines for assessment and management of the offender. In A. Burgess, N. Groth, S. Holmstrom, & S. Sgroi (Eds.), *Sexual assault of children and adolescents* (pp. 25–42). Lexington, MA: Lexington Books.

Grove, W. M., Eckert, Heston, et al. (1990). Heritability of substance abuse and antisocial behavior: A study of monozygotic twins reared apart. *Biological Psychiatry, 27,* 1293–1304.

Grove, W. M., Lebow, B. S., Clementz, B. A., Cerri, A., Medus, C., & Iacono, W. G. (1991). Familial prevalence and coaggregation of schizotype indicators: A multitrait family study. *Journal of Abnormal Psychology, 100,* 115–121.

Gruder, C. L., Mermelstein, R. J., Kirkendol, S., & Hedeker, D. (1993). Effects of social support and relapse prevention training as adjuncts to a televised smoking cessation intervention. *Journal of Consulting and Clinical Psychology, 61,* 113–120.

Guggenheim, F. G., & Babigian, H. M. (1974). Catatonic schizophrenia—epidemiology and clinical course—7-year register study of 798 cases. *Journal of Nervous and Mental Disease, 158*(4), 291–305.

Gunderson, J. G. (1992). Diagnostic controversies. In A. Tasman & M. B. Riba (Eds.), *Review of psychiatry* (Vol. 11, pp. 9–24). Washington, DC: American Psychiatric Press.

Gunderson, J. G., & Elliott, G. R. (1985). The interface between borderline personality disorder and affective disorder. *American Journal of Psychiatry, 142,* 277–287.

Gunderson, J. G., & Phillips, K. A. (1991). A current view of the interspace between borderline personality disorder and depression. *American Journal of Psychiatry, 148,* 967–975.

Gur, R. C. (1982). Measurement and imaging of regional brain function: Implications for neuropsychiatry. In J. Gruzelier & P. Flor-Henry (Eds.), *Hemispheric asymmetries of function in psychopathology* (Vol. 2, pp. 589–616). New York: Elsevier/North-Holland.

Gur, R. E., Mozley, P. D., Resnick, S. M., Shtasel, D., Kohn, M., Zimmerman, R., Herman, G., Atlas, S., Grossman, R., Erwin, R., & Gur, R. C. (1991). Magnetic resonance imaging in schizophrenia: I. Volumetric analysis of brain and cerebrospinal fluid. *Archives of General Psychiatry, 48,* 407–412.

Gur, R. E., Mozley, P. D., Shtasel, D. L., Cannon, T. D., Gallacher, F., Turetsky, B., Grossman, R., & Gur, R. C. (1994). Clinical subtypes of schizophrenia: Differences in brain and CSF volume. *American Journal of Psychiatry, 151,* 343–350.

Gur, R. E., & Pearlson, G. D. (1993). Neuroimaging in schizophrenia research. *Schizophrenia Bulletin, 19,* 337–353.

Gurland, B., Dean, L., Craw, P., & Golden, R. (1980). The epidemiology of depression and delirium in the elderly: The use of multiple indicators of these conditions. In J. O. Cole & J. E. Barrett (Eds.), *Psychopathology in the aged.* New York: Raven Press.

Gurman, A. S., & Kniskern, D. P. (1978). Research on marital and family therapy: Progress, perspective, and prospect. In S. L. Garfield & A. E. Bergin (Eds.), *Handbook of psychotherapy and behavior change: An empirical analysis* (2nd ed.). New York: Wiley.

Gutmann, M. C., & Benson, H. (1971). Interaction of environmental factors and systemic arterial blood pressure: A review. *Medicine, 50,* 543–553.

Guy, B. (1982). *Audition egale comportement.* Sainte Ruffine, France: Maisonneuve.

Guze, S. B., Cloninger, C. R., Martin, R. L., & Clayton, P. J. (1986). A follow-up and family study of Briquet's syndrome. *British Journal of Psychiatry, 149,* 17–23.

Guze, S. B., Woodruff, R. A., & Clayton, P. J. (1971). A study of conversion symptoms in psychiatric outpatients. *American Journal of Psychiatry, 128,* 135–138.

Haaga, D. A. F., Dyck, M. J., & Ernst, D. (1991). Empirical status of cognitive theory of depression. *Psychological Bulletin, 110,* 215–236.

Haas, G. L., & Sweeney, J. A. (1992). Premorbid and onset features of first-episode schizophrenia. *Schizophrenia Bulletin, 18,* 373–386.

Hadeed, A., & Seigel, S. (1989). Maternal cocaine use during pregnancy: Effect on the newborn infant. *Pediatrics, 84,* 205–210.

Hagerman, R. J., & McBogg, P. M. (1983). *The fragile X syndrome: Diagnosis, biochemistry, and intervention.* Dillon, Co: Spectra.

Haley, J. (1963). *Strategies of psychotherapy.* New York: Grune & Stratton.

Haley, J. (1976). *Problem-solving therapy.* San Francisco: Jossey-Bass.

Halford, W. K., & Hayes, R. (1991). Psychological rehabilitation of chronic schizophrenic patients: Recent findings on social skills training and family psychoeducation. *Clinical Psychology Review, 11,* 23–44.

Hall, E. T. (1976). *Beyond culture: Into the cultural unconscious.* Garden City, NY: Anchor Press.

Hall, S. M., Havassy, B. E., & Wasserman, D. A. (1990). Commitment to abstinence and acute stress in relapse to alcohol, opiates, and nicotine. *Journal of Consulting and Clinical Psychology, 58,* 175–181.

Hall, S. M., Havassy, B. E., & Wasserman, D. A. (1991). Effects of commitment to abstinence, positive moods, stress, and coping on relapse to cocaine use. *Journal of Consulting and Clinical Psychology, 59,* 526–532.

Halmi, K. A. (1974). Anorexia nervosa: Demographic and clinical features in 94 cases. *Journal of Psychosomatic Medicine, 36,* 18–25.

Halper, J. P., Brown, R. P., Sweeney, J. A., Kocsis, J. H., Peters, A., & Mann, J. J. (1988). Blunted β-adrenergic responsivity of peripheral blood mononuclear cells in endogenous depression. *Archives of General Psychiatry, 45,* 241–244.

Halpern, A. (1973). General unemployment and vocational opportunities for EMR individuals. *American Journal of Mental Deficiency, 78,* 123–127.

Hammen, C. (1991). Generation of stress in the course of unipolar depression. *Journal of Abnormal Psychology, 100,* 555–561.

Hammen, C., Adrian, C., & Hiroto, D. (1988). A longitudinal test of the attributional vulnerability model in children at risk for depression. *British Journal of Clinical Psychology, 27,* 37–46.

Hanley, H. G., Stahl, S. M., & Freedman, D. X. (1977). Hyperserotonemia and amine metabolites in autistic and retarded children. *Archives of General Psychiatry, 34,* 521–531.

Hansen, W. B. (1993). School-based alcohol prevention programs. *Alcohol, Health & Research World, 17*(1), 54–60.

Harada, S., Agarwal, D., Goedde, H., Takagi, S., & Ishikawa, B. (1982). Possible protective role against alcoholism for aldehyde dehydrogenase isozyme deficiency in Japan. *Lancet, 2,* 827.

Harburg, E. (1978). Skin color, ethnicity and blood pressure in Detroit blacks. *American Journal of Public Health, 68,* 1177–1183.

Hardy, J. (1993, November). Genetic mistakes point the way for Alzheimer's disease. *Journal of NIH Research, 5,* 46–49.

Hare, E., Bulusu, L., & Adelstein, A. (1979). Schizophrenia and season of birth. *Population Trends, 17,* 9.

Hare, R. D. (1970). *Psychopathy: Theory and research.* New York: Wiley.

Hare, R. D., Hart, S. D., & Harpur, T. J. (1991). Psychopathy and the *DSM-IV* criteria for antisocial personality disorder. *Journal of Abnormal Psychology, 100,* 391–398.

Harkavy-Friedman, J. M., Asnis, G. M., Boeck, M., & DiFiore, J. (1987). Prevalence of specific suicidal behaviors in a high school sample. *American Journal of Psychiatry, 144,* 1203–1206.

Harlage, S., Howard, K., & Ostrov, E. (1984). The mental health professional and the normal adolescent. In D. Offer, E. Ostrov, & K. I. Howard (Eds.), *Patterns of adolescent self-image.* San Francisco: Jossey-Bass.

Harlow, J. (1868). Recovery from the passage of an iron bar through the head. *Publication of the Massachusetts Medical Society, 2,* 327–340.

Harrington, R. (1993). Similarities and dissimilarities between child and adult disorders: The case of depression. In C. G. Costello (Ed.), *Basic issues in psychopathology* (pp. 103–124). New York: Guilford Press.

Harrington, R., Fudge, H., Rutter, M., Pickels, A., & Hill, J. (1990). Adult outcomes of childhood and adolescent depression. *Archives of General Psychiatry, 47,* 465–473.

Harris, T. O., Brown, G. W., & Bifulco, A. T. (1990). Depression and situational helplessness/mastery in a sample selected to study childhood parental loss. *Journal of Affective Disorders, 20,* 27–41.

Harrow, M., Carone, B. J., & Westermeyer, J. (1985). The course of psychosis in early phases of schizophrenia. *American Journal of Psychiatry, 142,* 702–707.

Harrow, M., & Grossman, L. S. (1984). Outcome in schizoaffective disorders: A critical review and reevaluation of the literature. *Schizophrenia Bulletin, 10,* 87–108.

Harrow, M., Grossman, L. S., Silverstein, M. L., Meltzer, H. Y., & Kettering, R. L. (1986). A longitudinal study of thought disorder in manic patients. *Archives of General Psychiatry, 43,* 781–785.

Harrow, M., Rattenbury, F., & Stoll, F. (1988). Schizophrenic delusions: An analysis of their persistence, of related premorbid ideas, and of three major dimensions. In T. F. Oltmanns & B. A. Maher (Eds.), *Delusional beliefs* (pp. 184–211). New York: Wiley.

Hartlage, S., Alloy, L. B., Vázquez, C., & Dykman, B. (1993). Automatic and effortful processing in depression. *Psychological Bulletin, 113,* 247–278.

Hartmann, H. (1939). *Ego psychology and the problem of adaptation.* New York: International Universities Press.

Hartogs, R. (1951). Discipline in the early life of sex-delinquents and sex-criminals. *New Child, 9,* 167–173.

Hassan, S. A. (1974). Transactional and contextual invalidation between the parents of disturbed families: A comparative study. *Family Process, 13,* 53–76.

Hathaway, S. R., & McKinley, J. C. (1940). A multiphasic personality schedule (Minnesota): 1. Construction of the schedule. *Journal of Psychology, 10,* 249–254.

Hathaway, S. R., & McKinley, J. C. (1943). *Minnesota Multiphasic Personality Inventory: Manual.* New York: Psychological Corporation.

Hathaway, S. R., & McKinley, J. D. (1989). *Manual for administration and scoring MMPI-2.* Minneapolis: University of Minnesota Press.

Hauser, W. A., & Hesdorfer, D. C. (1990). *Epilepsy: Frequency, causes, and consequences.* New York: Demos.

Havelkova, M. (1968). Follow-up study of 71 children diagnosed as psychotic in pre-school age. *American Journal of Orthopsychiatry, 38,* 846–857.

Hawton, K., & Fagg, J. (1988). Suicide, and other causes of death, following attempted suicide. *British Journal of Psychiatry, 152,* 359–366.

Hayman, C. R., Stewart, W. F., Lewis, F. R., & Grant, M. (1968). Sexual assault on women and children in the District of Columbia. *Public Health Reports, 83,* 12–20.

Hazelrigg, M. D., Cooper, H. M., & Borduin, C. M. (1987). Evaluating the effectiveness of family therapies: An integrative review and analysis. *Psychological Bulletin, 101,* 428–442.

Heatherton, T. F., Herman, C. P., & Polivy, J. (1991). Effects of physical threat and ego threat on eating behavior. *Journal of Personality and Social Psychology, 60,* 138–143.

Hécaen, H., & Albert, M. C. (1978). *Human neuropsychology.* New York: Wiley.

Heiman, J. R., LoPiccolo, L., & LoPiccolo, J. (1981). The treatment of sexual dysfunction. In A. Gurma & D. Kniskern (Eds.), *Handbook of family therapy.* New York: Brunner/Mazel.

Hellige, J. B. (1993). *Hemispheric asymmetry: What's right and what's left.* Cambridge, MA: Harvard University Press.

Helmes, E., & Reddon, J. R. (1993). A perspective on developments in assessing psychopathology: A critical review of the MMPI and MMPI-2. *Psychological Bulletin, 113,* 453–471.

Helzer, J. E., Brockington, I. F., & Kendell, R. E. (1981). Predictive validity of *DSM-III* and Feigner definitions of schizophrenia. *Archives of General Psychiatry, 38,* 791–797.

Helzer, J. E., Robins, L., & McEvoy, L. (1987). Post-traumatic stress disorder in the general population. *New England Journal of Medicine, 317,* 1630–1634.

Hendryx, M., & Bootzin, R. R. (1986). Psychiatric episodes in general hospitals without psychiatric units. *Hospital and Community Psychiatry, 37,* 1025–1029.

Henggeler, S. (1988). *Delinquency in adolescence.* Newbury Park, CA: Sage.

Heninger, G. R. (1990). A biologic perspective on comorbidity of major depressive disorder and panic disorder. In J. D. Maser & C. R. Cloninger (Eds.), *Comorbidity of mood and anxiety disorders.* Washington, DC: American Psychiatric Press.

Heninger, G. R., Charney, D. S., & Price, L. H. (1988). α_2-adrenergic receptor sensitivity in depression: The plasma MHPG, behavioral, and cardiovascular response to yohimbine. *Archives of General Psychiatry, 45,* 718–726.

Henninger, P. (1992). Conditional handedness: Handedness changes in multiple personality disordered subject reflect shift in hemispheric dominance. *Consciousness and Cognition, 1,* 265–287.

Henriques, J. B., & Davidson, R. J. (1990). Regional brain electrical asymmetries discriminate between previously depressed and healthy control subjects. *Journal of Abnormal Psychology, 99,* 22–31.

Henriques, J. B., & Davidson, R. J. (1991). Left frontal hypoactivation in depression. *Journal of Abnormal Psychology, 100,* 535–545.

Henry, W. P., Schacht, T. E., & Strupp, H. H. (1990). Patient and therapist introject, interpersonal process, and differential psychotherapy outcome. *Journal of Consulting and Clinical Psychology, 58,* 768–774.

Herman, C. P., & Mack, D. (1975). Restrained and unrestrained eating. *Journal of Personality, 43,* 647–660.

Herman, J. L. (1981). *Father-daughter incest.* Cambridge, MA: Harvard University Press.

Herman, J. L., Perry, J. C., & van der Kolk, B. A. (1989). Childhood trauma in borderline personality disorder. *American Journal of Psychiatry, 146,* 490–495.

Hernandez-Peon, R., Chavez-Ibarra, G., & Aguilar-Figueroa, E. (1963). Somatic evoked potentials in one case of hysterical anaesthesia. *Electroencephalography and Clinical Neurophysiology, 15,* 889–892.

Hersen, M., & Barlow, D. H. (1976). *Single case experimental designs: Strategies for studying behavior change.* New York: Pergamon Press.

Hersen, M., & Turner, S. M. (1984). *DSM-III* and behavior therapy. In S. M. Turner & M. Hersen (Eds.), *Adult psychopathology and diagnosis.* New York: Wiley.

Heston, L. L. (1966). Psychiatric disorders in foster home reared children of schizophrenic mothers. *British Journal of Psychiatry, 112,* 819–825.

Hibbs, E. D. (1993). Psychosocial treatment research with children and adolescents: Methodological issues. *Psychopharmacology Bulletin, 29,* 27–33.

Hietala, J., Syvälahti, E., Vuorio, K., Nagren, K., Lehikoinen, P., Ruotsalainen, U., Rakkolainen, V., Lehtinen, V., & Wegelius, U. (1994). Striatal D2 dopamine receptor characteristics in neuroleptic-naive schizophrenic patients studied with positron emission tomography. *Archives of General Psychiatry, 51,* 116–123.

Higgins, S. T., Budney, A. J., Bickel, W. K., Foerg, F. E., Donham, R., & Badger, G. J. (1994). Incentives improve outcome in outpatient behavioral treatment of cocaine dependence. *Archives of General Psychiatry, 51,* 568–576.

Hildebran, D., & Pithers, W. D. (1989). Enhancing offender empathy for sexual abuse victims. In D. R. Laws (Ed.), *Relapse prevention with sex offenders* (pp. 236–243). New York: Guilford Press.

Hilts, P. J. (1994, April 15). Tobacco chiefs say cigarettes aren't addictive. *The New York Times,* p. A1.

Hintgen, J. N., & Coulter, S. K. (1967). Auditory control of operant behaviour in mute autistic children. *Perceptual and Motor Skills, 25,* 561–565.

Hiroto, D. J., & Seligman, M. E. P. (1975). Generality of learned helplessness in man. *Journal of Personality and Social Psychology, 31,* 311–327.

Hirsch, B. J., & Rapkin, B. D. (1987). The transition to junior high school: A longitudinal study of self-esteem, psychological symptomatology, school life, and social support. *Child Development, 58,* 1235–1243.

Ho, B. T., Richard, D. W., & Chute, D. L. (Eds.). (1978). *Drug discrimination and state dependent learning.* New York: Academic Press.

Hodell, M. (1987). *Who blames whom: Men's and women's attitudes toward rape survivors.* Paper presented at the meeting of the American Psychological Association, New York.

Hodgkinson, S., Sherrington, R., Gurling, H., Marchbanks, R., Reeders, S., Mallet, J., McInnis, M., Petursson, H., & Brynjolfsson, J. (1987). Molecular genetic evidence for heterogeneity in manic depression. *Nature, 325,* 805–806.

Hodkinson, H. M. (1976). *Common symptoms of disease in the elderly.* Oxford: Blackwell.

Hoehn-Saric, R. (1982). Neurotransmitters in anxiety. *Archives of General Psychiatry, 39,* 735–742.

Hoff, A. L., Riordan, H., O'Donnell, D. W., Morris, L., & DeLisi, L. E. (1992). Neuropsychological functioning of first-episode schizophreniform patients. *American Journal of Psychiatry, 149,* 898–903.

Hoffman, A. (1971). LSD discoverer disputes "chance" factor in finding. *Psychiatric News, 6*(8), 23–26.

Hogarty, G. E., Anderson, C. M., Reiss, D. J., Kornblith, S. J., Greenwald, D. P., Javna, C. D., & Madonia, M. J. (1986). Family psychoeducation, social skills training, and maintenance chemotherapy in the aftercare treatment of schizophrenia: I. One-year effects of a controlled study on relapse and expressed emotion. *Archives of General Psychiatry, 43,* 633–642.

Hokanson, J. E., Rubert, M. P., Welker, R. A., Hollander, G. R., & Hedeen, C. (1989). Interpersonal concomitants and antecedents of depression among college students. *Journal of Abnormal Psychology, 98,* 209–217.

Holahan, C. J., & Moos, R. H. (1991). Life stressors, personal and social resources, and depression: A 4-year structural model. *Journal of Abnormal Psychology, 100,* 31–38.

Holden, C. (1972). Nader on mental health centers: A movement that got bogged down. *Science, 177,* 413–415.

Holland, J. G. (1978). Behaviorism: Part of the problem or part of the solution? *Journal of Applied Behavior Analysis, 11,* 163–174.

Holland, J. G., & Tross, S. (1985). The psychosocial and neuropsychiatric sequelae of the acquired immunodeficiency syndrome and related disorders. *Annals of Internal Medicine, 103,* 760–764.

Hollingshead, A. B., & Redlich, F. C. (1958). *Social class and mental illness.* New York: Wiley.

Hollister, J. M., Mednick, S. A., Brennan, P., & Cannon, T. D. (1994). Impaired autonomic nervous system habituation in those at genetic risk for schizophrenia. *Archives of General Psychiatry, 51,* 552–558.

Hollon, S. D., & Beck, A. T. (1994). Cognitive and cognitive-behavioral therapies. In A. E. Bergin &

S. L. Garfield (Eds.), *Handbook of psychotherapy and behavior change* (4th ed., pp. 428–466). New York: Wiley.

Hollon, S. D., DeRubeis, R. J., Evans, M. D., Wiemer, M. J., Garvey, M. J., Grove, W. M., & Tuason, V. B. (1992). Cognitive therapy and pharmacotherapy for depression: Singly and in combination. *Archives of General Psychiatry, 49,* 774–781.

Hollon, S. D., Shelton, R. C., & Davis, D. D. (1993). Cognitive therapy for depression: Conceptual issues and clinical efficacy. *Journal of Consulting and Clinical Psychology, 61,* 270–275.

Hollon, S. D., Shelton, R. C., & Loosen, P. T. (1991). Cognitive therapy and psychopharmacotherapy for depression. *Journal of Consulting and Clinical Psychology, 59,* 88–99.

Holmes, D. S. (1978). Projection as a defense mechanism. *Psychological Bulletin, 85,* 677–688.

Holmes, T. H., & Rahe, R. H. (1967). The social readjustment rating scale. *Journal of Psychosomatic Research, 11,* 213–218.

Holsboer, F. (1992). The hypothalamic-pituitary-adrenocortical system. In E. S. Paykel (Ed.), *Handbook of affective disorders* (2nd ed., pp. 267–288). New York: Guilford Press.

Hooker, E. (1957). The adjustment of the male overt homosexual. *Journal of Projective Techniques, 21*(1), 18–31.

Hooley, J. M., & Teasdale, J. D. (1989). Predictors of relapse in unipolar depressives: Expressed emotion, marital distress, and perceived criticism. *Journal of Abnormal Psychology, 98,* 229–235.

Horgan, C. M. (1985). Specialty and general ambulatory mental health services. *Archives of General Psychiatry, 42,* 565–572.

Horne, R. L., Pettinati, M. M., Sugerman, A., & Varga, E. (1985). Comparing bilateral to unilateral electroconvulsive therapy in a randomized study of EEG monitoring. *Archives of General Psychiatry, 42,* 1087–1092.

Horney, K. (1937). *The neurotic personality of our time.* New York: Norton.

Horney, K. (1939). *New ways in psychoanalysis.* New York: Norton.

Horney, K. (1967). *Feminine psychology* (H. Kelman, Ed.). New York: Norton.

Horowitz, L. M., & Vitkus, J. (1986). The interpersonal basis of psychiatric symptoms. *Clinical Psychology Review, 6,* 443–469.

Hough, M. S. (1990). Narrative comprehension in adults with right and left hemisphere brain damage: Theme organization. *Brain and Language, 38,* 253–277.

Hovens, J. E., Falger, P. R. J., Op den Velde, W., Schouten, E. G. W., de Groen, J. H. M., & van Duijn, H. (1992). Occurrence of current post traumatic stress disorder among Dutch World War II resistance veterans according to the SCID. *Journal of Anxiety Disorders, 6,* 147–157.

Howard, K. I. (1962). The convergent and discriminant validation of ipsative ratings from three projective instruments. *Journal of Clinical Psychology, 18,* 183–188.

Howard, K. I., Kopta, S. M., Krause, M. S., & Orlinsky, D. E. (1986). The dose-effect relationship in psychotherapy. *American Psychologist, 41,* 159–164.

Howells, K. (1981). Some meanings of children for pedophiles. In M. Cook & G. Wilson (Eds.), *Love and attraction* (pp. 57–82). London: Pergamon Press.

Howland, E. W., Kosson, D. S., Patterson, C. M., & Newmay, J. P. (1993). Altering a dominant response: Performance of psychopaths and low socialization college students on a cued reaction time task. *Journal of Abnormal Psychology, 102,* 379–387.

Hoyer, G., & Lund, E. (1993). Suicide among women related to number of children in marriage. *Archives of General Psychiatry, 50,* 134–137.

Hrubec, Z., & Omenn, G. S. (1981). Evidence of genetic predisposition to alcoholic cirrhosis and psychosis: Twin concordances for alcoholism and its biological end points by zygosity among male veterans. *Alcoholism: Clinical and Experimental Research, 5,* 207–215.

Hsiao, J. K., Colison, J., Bartko, J. J., Doran, A. R., Konicki, P. E., Potter, W. Z., & Pickar, D. (1993). Monoamine neurotransmitter interactions in drug-free and neuroleptic-treated schizophrenics. *Archives of General Psychiatry, 50,* 606–614.

Hughes, J. R., Oliveto, A. H., Helzer, J. E., Higgins, S. T., & Bickel, W. K. (1992). Should caffeine abuse, dependence, or withdrawal be added to *DSM-IV* and *ICD-10? American Journal of Psychiatry, 149,* 33–40.

Hugick, L., & Leonard, J. (1991, December). Despite increasing hostility, one in four Americans still smokes. *Gallup Poll Monthly,* pp. 2–9.

Hull, J. G. (1987). Self-awareness model. In H. T. Blane & K. E. Leonard (Eds.), *Psychological theories of drinking and alcoholism* (pp. 272–304). New York: Guilford Press.

Hull, J. G., & Bond, C. F., Jr. (1986). Social and behavioral consequences of alcohol consumption and expectancy: A meta-analysis. *Psychological Bulletin, 99,* 347–360.

Hunt, M. (1979). *Sexual behavior in the 1970s.* Chicago: Playboy Press.

Hutchings, B., & Mednick, S. A. (1975). Registered criminality in the adoptive and biological parents of registered male criminal adoptees. In R. R. Fieve, D. Rosenthal, & H. Brill (Eds.), *Genetic research in psychiatry.* Baltimore: Johns Hopkins University Press.

Iacono, W. G., & Beiser, M. (1992a). Are males more likely than females to develop schizophrenia? *American Journal of Psychiatry, 149,* 1070–1074.

Iacono, W. G., & Beiser, M. (1992b). Where are the women in the first-episode studies of schizophrenia? *Schizophrenia Bulletin, 18,* 471–480.

Iacono, W. G., & Grove, W. M. (1993). Schizophrenia revisited: Toward an integrative genetic model. *Psychological Science, 4,* 273–276.

Iezzi, A., & Adams, H. E. (1993). Somatoform and factitious disorders. In P. B. Sutker & H. E. Adams (Eds.), *Comprehensive handbook of psychopathology* (2nd ed.). New York: Plenum Press.

Ingram, R. E. (1990). Self-focused attention in clinical disorders: Review and a conceptual model. *Psychological Bulletin, 107,* 156–176.

Ingrassia, M., & Beck, M. (1994, July 4). Patterns of abuse. *Newsweek,* p. 26.

Insel, T. R., Zahn, T., & Murphy, D. L. (1985). Obsessive-compulsive disorder: An anxiety disorder? In A. H. Tuma & J. D. Maser (Eds.), *Anxiety and the anxiety disorders.* Hillsdale, NJ: Erlbaum.

Institute of Medicine. (1982). *Marijuana and health.* Washington, DC: National Academy Press.

Isaacs, W., Thomas, J., & Goldiamond, I. (1960). Application of operant conditioning to reinstate verbal behavior in psychotics. *Journal of Speech and Hearing Disorders, 25,* 8–12.

Isometsa, E. T., Henriksson, M. E., Aro, H. M., Heikkinen, M. E., Kuoppasalmi, K. I., & Lonnqvist, J. K. (1994). Suicide in major depression. *American Journal of Psychiatry, 151,* 530–536.

Israel, J. H., & LaFave, W. F. (1975). *Criminal procedure* (2nd ed.). St. Paul, MN: West.

Jackson v. Indiana, 92 S.Ct. 1845 (1972).

Jackson, D. N., & Messick, S. (1961). Acquiescence and desirability as response determinants on the MMPI. *Education and Psychological Measurement, 21,* 771–790.

Jackson, J. L., Calhoun, K. S., Amick, A. E., Maddover, H. M., & Habif, V. L. (1990). Young adult women who report childhood intrafamilial sexual abuse: Subsequent adjustment. *Archives of Sexual Behavior, 19,* 211–221.

Jacobs, M. K., & Goodman, G. (1989). Psychology and self-help groups: Predictions on a partnership. *American Psychologist, 44,* 536–545.

Jacobs, P. A., Brunton, M., & Melville, M. M. (1965). Aggressive behavior, mental subnormality, and the XYY male. *Nature, 208,* 1351–1352.

Jacobson, E. (1938). *Progressive relaxation.* Chicago: University of Chicago Press.

Jacobson, N. S., & Holtzworth-Munroe, A. (1986). Marital therapy: A social learning–cognitive perspective. In N. S. Jacobson & A. S. Gurman (Eds.), *Clinical handbook of marital therapy.* New York: Guilford Press.

Jagger, J., Vernberg, K., & Jones, J. A. (1987). Airbags: Reducing the toll of brain trauma. *Neurosurgery, 20*(5), 815–817.

James, L., Singer, A., Zurynski, Y., Gordon, E., Kraiuhin, C., Harris, A., Howson, A., & Meares, R. (1987). Evoked response potentials and regional cerebral blood flow in somatization disorder. *Psychotherapy and Psychosomatics, 47,* 190–196.

James, W. E., Mefford, R. B., & Kimbell, I. (1969). Early signs of Huntington's chorea. *Diseases of the Nervous System, 30,* 556–559.

Jamison, K. R. (1992). *Touched with fire: Manic-depressive illness and the artistic temperament.* New York: Free Press.

Jampala, V. C., Sierles, F. S., & Taylor, M. A. (1986). Consumers' views of *DSM-III:* Attitudes and practices of U.S. psychiatrists and 1984 graduating psychiatric residents. *American Journal of Psychiatry, 143,* 148–153.

Janet, P. (1929). *The major symptoms of hysteria.* New York: Macmillan.

Jarvik, L. F., Klodin, V., & Matsuyama, S. S. (1973). Human aggression and the extra Y chromosome: Fact or fantasy? *American Psychologist, 28*(8), 674–682.

Jellinek, E. M. (1946). *Phases in the drinking history of alcoholics.* New Haven, CT: Hillhouse Press.

Jenike, M. A., Baer, L., Ballantine, T., Martuza, R. L., Tynes, S., Giriunas, I., Buttolph, L., & Cassem, N. H. (1991). Cingulotomy for refractory obsessive-compulsive disorder: A long-term follow-up of 33 patients. *Archives of General Psychiatry, 48,* 548–555.

Johansson, B., & Zarit, S. H. (1991). Dementia and cognitive impairment in the oldest old: A comparison of two rating methods. *International Psychogeriatrics, 3,* 29–38.

Johansson, B., & Zarit, S. H. (1995). Prevalence and incidence of dementia in the oldest old: A longitudinal study of a population-based sample of 84–90-year-olds in Sweden. *International Journal of Geriatric Psychology, 10.*

Johnson, D., Walker, T., & Rodriquez, G. (1993, March). *Teaching low-income mothers to teach their children.* Paper presented at the biennial meeting of the Society for Research in Child Development, New Orleans.

Johnson, S. M., Wahl, G., Martin, S., & Johansson, S. (1973). How deviant is the normal child? A behavioral analysis of the preschool child and his family. In R. D. Rubin, J. P. Brady, & J. D. Henderson (Eds.), *Advances in behavior therapy* (Vol. 4). New York: Academic Press.

Johnston, M. B., Whitman, T. L., & Johnson, M. (1980). Teaching addition and subtraction to mentally retarded children: A self-instruction program. *Applied Research in Mental Retardation, 1,* 141–160.

Jones v. United States, 103 S.Ct. 3043 (1983).

Jones, E. (1963). Rationalization in everyday life. In *Papers on psychoanalysis.* New York: Wood.

Jones, E. E., & Berglas, S. (1978). Control of attributions about the self through self-handicapping strategies: The appeal of alcohol and the role of unachievement. *Personality and Social Psychology Bulletin, 4,* 200–206.

Jones, M. (1953). *The therapeutic community: A new treatment method in psychiatry.* New York: Basic Books.

Jones, M. C. (1924). A laboratory study of fear: The case of Peter. *Pedagogical Seminary, 31,* 308–315.

Jones, M. C. (1968). Personality correlates and antecedents of drinking patterns in adult males. *Journal of Consulting and Clinical Psychology, 32,* 2–12.

Jones, M. M. (1980). Conversion reaction: Anachronism or evolutionary form? A review of the neurologic, behavioral, and psychoanalytic literature. *Psychological Bulletin, 87,* 427–441.

Jung, C. G. (1935). Fundamental psychological conceptions. In M. Barker & M. Game (Eds.), *A report of five lectures.* London: Institute of Medical Psychology.

Junginger, J., Barker, S., & Coe, D. (1992). Mood theme and bizarreness of delusions in schizophrenia and mood psychosis. *Journal of Abnormal Psychology, 101,* 287–292.

Kafka, M. P., & Pretky, R. (1992). Fluoxetine treatment of nonparaphilic sexual addictions and paraphilias in men. *Journal of Clinical Psychiatry, 53,* 351–358.

Kahn, E. (1985). Heinz Kohut and Carl Rogers: A timely comparison. *American Psychologist, 40,* 893–904.

Kahn, M. W., Hannah, M., Hinkin, C., Montgomery, C., & Pitz, D. (1987). Psychopathology on the streets: Psychological measurement of the homeless. *Professional Psychology.*

Kahn, R. S., Davidson, M., Knott, P., Stern, R. G., Apter, S., & Davis, K. L. (1993). Effect of neuroleptic medication on cerebrospinal fluid monoamine metabolite concentrations in schizophrenia: Serotonin-dopamine interactions as a target for treatment. *Archives of General Psychiatry, 50,* 599–605.

Kamarck, T., & Jennings, J. R. (1991). Biobehavioral factors in sudden cardiac death. *Psychological Bulletin, 109,* 42–75.

Kandel, D. B., Davies, M., Karus, D., & Yamaguchi, K. (1986). The consequences in young adulthood of adolescent drug involvement. *Archives of General Psychiatry, 43,* 746–754.

Kane, J., Honigfeld, G., Singer, J., Meltzer, H., & Clozaril Collaborative Study Group. (1988). Clozapine for the treatment-resistant schizophrenic: A double-blind comparison with chlorpromazine. *Archives of General Psychiatry, 45,* 789–797.

Kane, J. M., & Lieberman, J. (1987). Maintenance pharmacotherapy in schizophrenia. In H. Y. Meltzer (Ed.), *Psychopharmacology, the third generation of progress: The emergence of molecular biology and biological psychiatry* (pp. 1103–1109). New York: Raven Press.

Kane, J. M., & Marder, S. R. (1993). Psychopharmacologic treatment of schizophrenia. *Schizophrenia Bulletin, 19,* 287–302.

Kanfer, F. H., & Hagerman, S. M. (1985). Behavior therapy and the information-processing paradigm. In S. Reiss & R. R. Bootzin (Eds.), *Theoretical issues in behavior therapy.* New York: Academic Press.

Kanin, E. J. (1967). An examination of sexual aggression as a response to sexual frustration. *Journal of Marriage and the Family, 24,* 428–433.

Kanin, E. J. (1985). Date rapists: Differential sexual socialization and relative deprivation. *Archives of Sexual Behavior, 14,* 219–231.

Kanner, A. D., Coyne, J. C., Schaeffer, C., & Lazarus, R. S. (1981). Comparison of two modes of stress measurement: Daily hassles and uplifts versus major life events. *Journal of Behavioral Medicine, 4,* 1–39.

Kanner, L. (1943). Autistic disturbances of effective content. *Nervous Child, 2,* 217–240.

Kaplan, B. (Ed.). (1964). *The inner world of mental illness.* New York: Harper & Row.

Kaplan, H. I., & Sadock, B. J. (1991). *Synopsis of psychiatry: Behavioral sciences, clinical psychiatry* (6th ed.). Baltimore: Williams & Wilkins.

Kaplan, H. S. (1974). *The new sex therapy: Active treatment of sexual dysfunctions.* New York: Brunner/Mazel, in cooperation with Quadrangle/New York Times Book Co.

Kaplan, H. S. (1979). *Disorder of sexual desire.* New York: Brunner/Mazel.

Kaplan, M. (1983, July). A woman's view of *DSM-III. American Psychologist,* 786–792.

Kaplan, R. E. (1982). The dynamics of injury in encounter groups: Power, splitting, and the mismanagement of resistance. *International Journal of Group Psychotherapy, 32,* 163–187.

Kaprio, J., Koskenvuo, M., Langinvainio, H., Romanov, K., Sarna, S., & Rose, R. J. (1987). Genetic influences on use and abuse of alcohol: A study of 5638 adult Finnish twin brothers. *Alcoholism: Clinical and Experimental Research, 11,* 349–356.

Karno, M., Golding, J. M., Sorenson, S. B., & Burnam, M. A. (1988). The epidemiology of obsessive-compulsive disorder in five U.S. communities. *Archives of General Psychiatry, 45,* 1094–1099.

Karpman, (1954). *The sexual offender and his offenses.* New York: Julian Press.

Kashani, J. H., Carlson, G. A., Beck, N. C., et al. (1990). Depression, depressive symptoms, and depressed mood among a community sample of adolescents. *American Journal of Psychiatry, 144,* 931–934.

Kashani, J. H., & Orvaschel, H. (1990). A community study of anxiety in children and adolescents. *American Journal of Psychiatry, 147,* 313–318.

Kass, D. J., Silver, F. M., & Abrams, G. M. (1972). Behavioral group treatment of hysteria. *Archives of General Psychiatry, 26,* 42–50.

Kaszniak, A. W., Nussbaum, P. D., Berren, M. R., & Santiago, J. (1988). Amnesia as a consequence of male rape: A case report. *Journal of Abnormal Psychology, 97,* 100–104.

Katon, W. (1989). *Panic disorder in the medical setting.* Washington, DC: U.S. Government Printing Office.

Katon, W., Lin, E., Von Korff, M., Russo, J., Lipscomb, P., & Bush, T. (1991). Somatization: A spectrum of severity. *American Journal of Psychiatry, 148,* 34–40.

Katon, W., & Roy-Byrne, P. P. (1991). Mixed anxiety and depression. *Journal of Abnormal Psychology, 100,* 337–345.

Katsanis, J., & Iacono, W. G. (1991). Clinical, neuropsychological, and brain structural correlates of smooth-pursuit eye-tracking performance in chronic schizophrenia. *Journal of Abnormal Psychology, 100,* 526–534.

Katz, B., & Burt, M. (1986). *Effects of familiarity with the rapist on post rape recovery.* Paper presented at the meeting of the American Psychological Association, Washington, DC.

Kaufman, J., & Cicchetti, D. (1989). The effects of maltreatment on school-age children's socioemotional development. *Developmental Psychology, 25,* 516–524.

Kaul, T. J., & Bednar, R. L. (1986). Experiential group research: Results, questions, and suggestions. In S. L. Garfield & A. E. Bergin (Eds.), *Handbook of psychotherapy and behavior change: An evaluative analysis* (3rd ed.). New York: Wiley.

Kaye, W. H., Berrettini, W., Gwirtsman, H., & George, D. T. (1990). Altered cerebrospinal fluid neuropeptide Y and peptide YY immunoreactivity in anorexia and bulimia nervosa. *Archives of General Psychiatry, 47,* 548–556.

Kazdin, A. E. (1978). Methodological and interpretive problems of single-case experimental designs. *Journal of Consulting and Clinical Psychology, 46,* 629–642.

Kazdin, A. E. (1980). *Research design in clinical psychology.* New York: Harper & Row.

Kazdin, A. E. (1985). The token economy. In R. Turner & L. M. Asher (Eds.), *Evaluating behavior therapy outcome* (pp. 225–253). New York: Spring.

Kazdin, A. E. (1987). Treatment of antisocial behavior in children: Current status and future directions. *Psychological Bulletin, 102,* 187–203.

Kazdin, A. E. (1988). Conduct disorder. In M. Hersen & C. G. Last (Eds.), *Child behavior therapy casebook* (pp. 229–330). New York: Plenum Press.

Kazdin, A. E., & Rogers, T. (1978). On paradigms and recycled ideologies: Analogue research revisited. *Cognitive Therapy and Research, 2,* 105–117.

Kazdin, A. E., & Wilson, G. T. (1978). *Evaluation of behavior therapy: Issues, evidence and research strategies.* Cambridge, MA: Ballinger.

Kearney, C. A., & Silverman, W. K. (1990). A preliminary analysis of a functional model of assessment and treatment for school refusal behavior. *Behavior Modification, 14,* 344–360.

Keith-Spiegel, P., & Spiegel, D. (1967). Affective states of patients immediately preceding suicide. *Journal of Psychiatric Research, 5,* 89–93.

Keller, M. B., Lavori, P. W., Mueller, T. I., Endicott, J., Coryell, W., Hirschfeld, R. M. A., & Shea, T. (1992). Time to recovery, chronicity, and levels of psychopathology in major depression. *Archives of General Psychiatry, 49,* 809–816.

Kellner, R. (1985). Functional somatic symptoms and hypochondriasis: A survey of empirical studies. *Archives of General Psychiatry, 42,* 821–833.

Kellner, R. (1990). Somatization. *Journal of Nervous and Mental Disease, 178,* 150–160.

Kellner, R. (1992). Diagnosis and treatment of hypochondriacal syndromes. *Psychosomatics, 33,* 278–289.

Kelly, J. A., & Drabman, R. S. (1977). The modification of socially detrimental behavior. *Journal of Behavior Therapy and Experimental Psychiatry, 8,* 101–104.

Kelly, J. A., & Murphy, D. A. (1992). Psychological interventions with AIDS and HIV: Prevention and treatment. *Journal of Consulting and Clinical Psychology, 60,* 576–585.

Kemp, S. (1990). *Medieval psychology.* New York: Greenwood Press.

Kendall, P. C. (1992). Healthy thinking. *Behavior Therapy, 23,* 1–11.

Kendall, P. C., & Hollon, S. D. (Eds.). (1981). *Assessment strategies for cognitive-behavioral interventions.* New York: Academic Press.

Kendler, K. S., & Davis, K. L. (1981). The genetics and biochemistry of paranoid schizophrenia and other paranoid psychoses. *Schizophrenia Bulletin, 7,* 689–709.

Kendler, K. S., Diehl, S. R. (1993). The genetics of schizophrenia: A current, genetic-epidemiological perspective. *Schizophrenia Bulletin, 19,* 261–285.

Kendler, K. S., Kessler, R. C., Neale, M. C., Heath, A. C., & Eaves, L. J. (1993). The prediction of major depression in women: Toward an integrated etiologic model. *American Journal of Psychiatry, 150,* 1139–1148.

Kendler, K. S., McGuire, M., Gruenberg, A. M., Spellman, M., O'Hare, A., & Walsh, D. (1993). The Roscommon family study: II. The risk of nonschizophrenic nonaffective psychoses in relatives. *Archives of General Psychiatry, 50,* 645–652.

Kendler, K. S., McGuire, M., Gruenberg, A. M., & Walsh, D. (1994). Outcome and family study of the subtypes of schizophrenia in the west of Ireland. *American Journal Of Psychiatry, 151,* 849–856.

Kendler, K. S., Neale, M. C., Kessler, R. C., Heath, A. C., & Eaves, L. J. (1992a). Childhood parental loss and adult psychopathology in women: A twin study perspective. *Archives of General Psychiatry, 49,* 109–116.

Kendler, K. S., Neale, M. C., Kessler, R. C., Heath, A. C., & Eaves, L. J. (1992b). A population-based twin study of major depression in women: The impact of varying definitions of illness. *Archives of General Psychiatry, 49,* 257–266.

Kendler, K. S., Neale, M. C., Kessler, R. C., Heath, A. C., & Eaves, L. J. (1993). A longitudinal twin study of 1-year prevalence of major depression in women. *Archives of General Psychiatry, 50,* 843–852.

Kendler, K. S., & Robinette, C. D. (1983). Schizophrenia in the National Academy of Sciences' National Research Council twin registry: A 16-year update. *American Journal of Psychiatry, 140,* 1551–1563.

Kenrick, D. T., & Funder, D. C. (1988). Profiting from controversy: Lessons from the person-situation debate. *American Psychologist, 43,* 23–34.

Kernberg, O. F. (1975). *Borderline conditions and pathological narcissism.* New York: Aronson.

Kernberg, P. F. (1979). Childhood schizophrenia and autism: A selective review. In L. Bellak (Ed.), *Disorders of the schizophrenic syndrome.* New York: Basic Books.

Kerr, P. (1991, October 22). Chain of mental hospitals faces inquiry in 4 states. *The New York Times,* p. A1.

Kerr, S. H., & Cooper, E. B. (1976). *Phonatory adjustment times in stutterers and nonstutterers.* Unpublished manuscript.

Kessler, R. C., Foster, C., Joseph, J., Ostrow, D., Wortman, C., Phair, J., & Chmiel, J. (1991). Stressful life events and symptom onset in HIV infection. *American Journal of Psychiatry, 148,* 733–738.

Kessler, R. C., McGonagle, K. A., Zhao, S., Nelson, C. B., Hughes, M., Eshleman, S., Wittchen, H. U., & Kendler, K. S. (1994). Lifetime and 12-month prevalence of *DSM-III-R* psychiatric disorders in the United States: Results from the National Comorbidity Study. *Archives of General Psychiatry, 51,* 8–19.

Kety, S. S. (1988). Schizophrenic illness in the families of schizophrenic adoptees: Findings from the Danish national sample. *Schizophrenia Bulletin, 14,* 217–222.

Kety, S. S., Rosenthal, D., Wender, P. H., & Schulsinger, F. (1968). The types and prevalence of mental illness in the biological and adoptive families of adopted schizophrenics. In D. Rosenthal & S. S. Kety (Eds.), *The transmission of schizophrenia.* Oxford: Pergamon Press.

Kety, S. S., Rosenthal, D., Wender, P. H., Schulsinger, F., & Jacobsen, B. (1975). Mental illness in the biological and adoptive families of adopted individuals who have become schizophrenic: A preliminary report based upon psychiatric interviews. In R. Fieve, D. Rosenthal, & H. Brill (Eds.), *Genetic research in psychiatry.* Baltimore: Johns Hopkins University Press.

Kety, S. S., Wender, P. H., Jacobsen, B., Ingraham, L. J., Jansson, L., Faber, B., & Kinney, D. K. (1994). Mental illness in the biological and adoptive relatives of schizophrenic adoptees: Replication of the Copenhagen study in the rest of Denmark. *Archives of General Psychiatry, 51,* 442–455.

Khanna, S., & Mukherjee, D. (1992). Checkers and washers: Valid subtypes of obsessive compulsive disorder. *Psychopathology, 25,* 283–288.

Kiecolt-Glaser, J. K., Dura, J. R., Speicher, C. E., Trask, O. J., & Glaser, R. (1991). Spousal caregivers of dementia victims: Longitudinal changes in immunity and health. *Psychosomatic Medicine, 53,* 345–362.

Kiecolt-Glaser, J. K., Fisher, L., Ogrocki, P., Stout, J. C., Speicher, C. E., & Glaser, R. (1987). Marital quality, marital disruption, and immune function. *Psychosomatic Medicine, 46,* 7–14.

Kiecolt-Glaser, J. K., & Glaser, R. (1991). Stress and immune function in humans. In R. Ader, D. Felten, & N. Cohen (Eds.), *Psychoneuroimmunology II* (pp. 849–867). San Diego, CA: Academic Press.

Kiecolt-Glaser, J. K., Glaser, R., Williger, D., Stout, J., Messick, G., Sheppard, S., Ricker, D., Romisher, S. C., Briner, W., Bonnell, G., & Donnerberg, R. (1985). Psychosocial enhancement of immunocompetence in a geriatric population. *Health Psychology, 4,* 25–41.

Kiecolt-Glaser, J. K., Malarkey, W. B., Chee, M., Newton, T., Cacioppo, J. T., Mao, H., & Glaser, R. (1993). Negative behavior during marital conflict is associated with immunological down-regulation. *Psychosomatic Medicine, 55,* 395–409.

Kiesler, C. A. (1982a). Mental hospitals and alternative care. *American Psychologist, 37,* 349–360.

Kiesler, C. A. (1982b). Public and professional myths about mental hospitalization. *American Psychologist, 37,* 1323–1339.

Kiesler, C. A. (1993). Mental health policy and the psychiatric inpatient care of children. *Applied & Preventive Psychology, 2,* 91–99.

Kiesler, C. A., & Simpkins, C. (1991). The de facto national system of psychiatric inpatient care: Piecing together the national puzzle. *American Psychologist, 46,* 579–584.

Kiesler, D. J. (1983). The 1982 interpersonal circle: A taxonomy for complementarity in human transactions. *Psychological Review, 90,* 185–214.

Kiesler, D. J. (1992). Interpersonal circle inventories: Pantheoretical applications to psychotherapy research and practice. *Journal of Psychotherapy Integration, 2,* 77–99.

Kihlstrom, J. F. (1987). The cognitive unconscious. *Science, 237,* 1445–1452.

Kihlstrom, J. F. (1990). The psychological unconscious. In L. Pervin (Ed.), *Handbook of personality: Theory and research* (pp. 445–464). New York: Guilford Press.

Kihlstrom, J. F., Barnhardt, T. M., & Tataryn, D. J. (1991). Implicit perception. In R. F. Bornstein & T. S. Pittman (Eds.), *Perception without awareness.* New York: Guilford Press.

Kihlstrom, J. F., Glisky, M. L., & Angiulo, M. J. (1994). Dissociative tendencies and dissociative disorders. *Journal of Abnormal Psychology, 103,* 117–124.

Kihlstrom, J. F., Tataryn, D. J., & Hoyt, I. P. (1993). Dissociative disorders. In P. B. Sutker & H. E. Adams (Eds.), *Comprehensive handbook of psychopathology* (2nd ed.). New York: Plenum Press.

Kilpatrick, D. G., Saunders, B., Amick-McMullen, A., Best, C., Veronen, L., & Resnick, H. (1989). Victim and crime factors associated with the development of posttraumatic stress disorder. *Behavior Therapy, 20,* 199–214.

King, J. A., Campbell, D., & Edwards, E. (1993). Differential development of the stress response in congenital learned helplessness. *International Journal of Developmental Neuroscience, 11,* 435–442.

Kinsey, A. C., Pomeroy, W. B., & Martin, C. E. (1948). *Sexual behavior in the human male.* Philadelphia: Saunders.

Kinsey, A. C., Pomeroy, W. B., Martin, C. E., & Gebhard, P. H. (1953). *Sexual behavior in the human female.* Philadelphia: Saunders.

Kipper, D. A. (1981). Behavior simulation interventions in group psychotherapy. In G. M. Gazda (Ed.), *Innovations to group psychotherapy* (2nd ed.). Springfield, IL: Charles C Thomas.

Kirch, D. G. (1993). Infection and autoimmunity as etiologic factors in schizophrenia: A review and reappraisal. *Schizophrenia Bulletin, 19,* 355–370.

Klackenberg, G. (1982). Sleep behavior studied longitudinally: Data from 4–16 years on duration, night-awakening and bed-sharing. *Acta Paediatrica Scandinavica, 71,* 501–506.

Klajner, R., Herman, C. P., Polivy, J., & Chhabra, R. (1981). Human obesity, dieting, and anticipatory salivation. *Physiology and Behavior, 27,* 195–198.

Klein, D. N., Taylor, E. B., Dickstein, S., & Harding, K. (1988). The early-late onset distinction in *DSM-III-R* dysthymia. *Journal of Affective Disorders, 14,* 25–33.

Klein, R., & Mannuzza, S. (1991). Long-term outcome of hyperactive children: A review. Special Section: Longitudinal research. *Journal of the American Academy of Child and Adolescent Psychiatry, 30,* 383–387.

Kleist, K. (1960). Schizophrenic symptoms and cerebral pathology. *Journal of Mental Science, 106,* 246–253.

Klerman, G. L. (1986). Drugs and psychotherapy. In S. L. Garfield & A. E. Bergin (Eds.), *Handbook of psychotherapy and behavior change: An evaluative analysis* (3rd ed.). New York: Wiley.

Klerman, G. L. (1988). The current age of youthful melancholia. *British Journal of Psychiatry, 152,* 4–14.

Klerman, G. L. (1990). Approaches to the phenomena of comorbidity. In J. D. Maser & C. R. Cloninger (Eds.), *Comorbidity of mood and anxiety disorders.* Washington, DC: American Psychiatric Press.

Klerman, G. L., Lavori, P. W., Rice, J., Reich, T., Endicott, J., Andreasen, N. C., Keller, M. B., &

Hirschfeld, R. M. A. (1985). Birth cohort trends in rates of major depressive disorder among relatives of patients with affective disorder. *Archives of General Psychiatry, 42,* 689–693.

Kling, M. A., Kellner, C. H., Post, R. M., Cowdry, R. W., Gardner, D. L., Coppola, R., Putnam, F. W., Gold, P. W. (1987). Neuroendocrine effects of limbic activation by electrical, spontaneous, and pharmacological modes: Relevance to the pathophysiology of affective dysregulation in psychiatric disorders. *Progress in Neuropsychopharmacology and Biological Psychiatry, 11,* 459–481.

Kluft, R. P. (1984b). Treatment of multiple personality disorder: A study of 33 cases. *Psychiatric Clinics of North America, 7,* 9–29.

Kluft, R. P. (1986). Personality unification in multiple personality disorder: A follow-up study. In B. G. Braun (Ed.), *Treatment of multiple personality disorder.* Washington, DC: American Psychiatric Press.

Kluft, R. P. (1987). An update on multiple personality disorder. *Hospital and Community Psychiatry, 38,* 363–373.

Kluft, R. P. (1988). Dissociative disorders. In J. A. Talbott, R. E. Hales, & S. C. Yudofsky (Eds.), *The American Psychiatric Press textbook of psychiatry* (pp. 557–586). Washington, DC: American Psychiatry Press.

Kluft, R. P. (1991). Clinical presentations of multiple personality disorder. *Psychiatric Clinics of North America, 14,* 605–629.

Knecht v. Gillman (1973).

Knight, R. A., & Roff, J. D. (1985). Affectivity in schizophrenia. In M. Alpert (Ed.), *Controversies in schizophrenia* (pp. 280–313). New York: Guilford Press.

Knopp, F. H. (1976). *Instead of prisons.* Syracuse, NY: Safer Society Press.

Koch, R. (1971). Prenatal factors in causation (general). In R. Koch & J. C. Dobson (Eds.), *The mentally retarded child and his family.* New York: Brunner/Mazel.

Koegel, R. L., & Rincover, A. (1974). Treatment of psychotic children in a classroom environment: I. Learning in a large group. *Journal of Applied Behavior Analysis, 7,* 45–59.

Koegel, R. L., & Rincover, A. (1977). Research on the difference between generalization and maintenance in extra-therapy responding. *Journal of Applied Behavior Analysis, 10,* 1–12.

Kohen-Raz, R. (1968). Mental and motor development of kibbutz, institutionalized, and home-reared infants in Israel. *Child Development, 39,* 489–504.

Kohlenberg, R. J. (1973). Behavioristic approach to multiple personality: A case study. *Behavior Therapy, 4,* 137–140.

Kohut, H. (1966). Forms and transformations of narcissism. *Journal of the American Psychoanalytic Association, 14,* 243–272.

Kohut, H. (1972). Thoughts on narcissism and narcissistic rage. *Psychoanalytic Study of the Child, 27,* 360–400.

Kohut, H. (1977). *The restoration of the self.* New York: International Universities Press.

Kohut, H., & Wolf, E. S. (1978). The disorders of the self and their treatment: An outline. *International Journal of Psychoanalysis, 59,* 413–425.

Kokmen, K., Beard, C. M., Offord, K. P., & Kurland, L. T. (1989). Prevalence of medically diagnosed dementia in a defined United States population. *Neurology, 39,* 773–776.

Kolb, B. (1989). Brain development, plasticity, and behavior. *American Psychologist, 44,* 1203–1212.

Kolb, L. C. (1982). *Modern clinical psychiatry* (10th ed.). Philadelphia: Saunders.

Kolodny, R. C., Masters, W. H., Kolodner, R. M., & Gelson, T. (1974). Depression of plasma testosterone levels after chronic intensive marihuana use. *New England Journal of Medicine, 290*(16), 872–874.

Kolvin, I., Ounsted, C., Humphrey, M., & McMay, A. (1971). The phenomenology of childhood psychoses. *British Journal of Psychiatry, 118,* 385–395.

Kornhuber, J., Riederer, P., Reynolds, G. P., Beckmann, H., Jellinger, K., & Gabriel, E. (1989). 3H-spiperone binding in post-mortem brains from schizophrenic patients: Relationship to neuroleptic drug treatment, abnormal movements, and positive symptoms. *Journal of Neural Transmission, 75,* 1–10.

Koss, M. P. (1988). Hidden rape: Sexual aggression and victimization in a national sample of students in higher education. In A. W. Burgess (Ed.), *Rape and sexual assault* (Vol. 2, pp. 3–26). New York: Garland.

Koss, M. P. (1993). Rape: Scope, impact, interventions, and public policy responses. *American Psychologist, 48,* 1062–1069.

Koss, M. P., Dinero, T. E., Seibel, C. A., & Cox, S. L. (1988). Stranger and acquaintance rape: Are there differences in the victim's experience? *Psychology of Women Quarterly, 12,* 1–24.

Koss, M. P., Gidycz, C. A., & Wisniewski, N. (1987). The scope of rape: Incidence and prevalence of sexual aggression and victimization in a national sample of higher education students. *Journal of Consulting and Clinical Psychology, 55,* 162–170.

Koss, M. P., & Harvey, M. R. (1991). *The rape victim: Clinical and community interventions.* Newbury Park, CA: Sage.

Koss, M. P., Woodruff, W. J., & Koss, P. (1991). Criminal victimization among primary care medical patients: Prevalence, incidence, and physician usage. *Behavioral Sciences and the Law, 9,* 85–96.

Kosson, D. S., & Newman, J. P. (1989). Socialization and attentional deficits under focusing and divided attention conditions. *Journal of Personality and Social Psychology, 57,* 87–99.

Kraepelin, E. (1902). *Clinical psychiatry: A textbook for physicians* (A. Diffendorf, Trans.). New York: Macmillan.

Kraepelin, E. (1968). *Lectures on clinical psychiatry* (T. P. Johnstone, Trans.). New York: Hafner. (Original work published 1904)

Kraepelin, E. (1923). *Textbook of psychiatry.* New York: Macmillan. (Original work published 1883)

Krafft-Ebing, R. von. (1900). *Textbook of psychiatry.* (Original work published 1879)

Krafft-Ebing, R. von. (1965a). *Psychopathia sexualis* (F. S. Klaf, Trans.). New York: Bell. (Original work published 1886)

Krafft-Ebing, R. von. (1965b). *Texts of psychiatry.* New York: Bell. (Original work published 1886)

Kraft, D. P., & Babigian, H. (1972). Somatic delusion or self-mutilation in a schizophrenic woman: A psychiatric emergency room case report. *American Journal of Psychiatry, 128*(7), 127–129.

Kramer, P. D. (1993). *Listening to Prozac.* New York: Viking.

Kraus, J. F., Black, M., Hessol, N., Ley, P., Rokaw, W., Sullivan, C., Bowers, S., Knowlton, S., & Marshall, L. (1984). The incidence of acute brain injury and serious impairment in a defined population. *American Journal of Epidemiology, 119*(2), 186–201.

Krauss, D. (1983). The physiologic basis of male sexual dysfunction. *Hospital Practice, 2,* 193–222.

Kring, A. M., Kerr, S. L., Smith, D. A., & Neale, J. M. (1993). Flat affect in schizophrenia does not reflect diminished subjective experience of emotion. *Journal of Abnormal Psychology, 102,* 507–517.

Kringlen, E., & Cramer, G. (1989). Offspring of monozygotic twins discordant for schizophrenia. *Archives of General Psychiatry, 46,* 873–877.

Kroll, J. (1988). *The challenge of the borderline patient.* New York: Norton.

Kuiper, N. A., Olinger, L. J., & MacDonald, M. R. (1988). Depressive schemata and the processing of personal and social information. In L. B. Alloy (Ed.), *Cognitive processes in depression.* New York: Guilford Press.

Kupfer, D. J., Frank, E., Carpenter, L. L., Neiswanger, K. (1989). Family history in recurrent depression. *Journal of Affective Disorders, 17,* 113–119.

Kurland, L. T., Faro, S. N., & Siedler, H. (1960). Minamata disease. The outbreak of neurologic disorder in Minamata, Japan, and its relationship to the ingestion of seafood contaminated by mercuric compounds. *World Neurology, 1,* 370–395.

Lacks, P., & Morin, C. M. (1992). Recent advances in the assessment and treatment of insomnia. *Journal of Consulting and Clinical Psychology, 60,* 586–594.

Lader, M., & Sartorius, N. (1968). Anxiety in patients with hysterical conversion symptoms. *Journal of Neurology, Neurosurgery, and Psychiatry, 31,* 490–495.

LaFave, W. F., & Scott, A. (1972). *Criminal law.* St. Paul, MN: West.

La Fond, J. Q., & Durham, M. L. (1992). *Back to the asylum.* New York: Oxford.

LaForge, R., & Suczek, R. F. (1955). The interpersonal dimension of personality: III. An interpersonal check list. *Journal of Personality, 24,* 94–112.

La Greca, A. M., & Fetter, M. (1995). Peer relations. In A. R. Eisen, C. A. Kearney, & C. E. Schaefer (Eds.), *Clinical handbook of anxiety disorders in children and adolescents.* Northvale, NJ: Aronson.

Laing, R. D. (1964). Is schizophrenia a disease? *International Journal of Social Psychiatry, 10,* 184–193.

Laing, R. D. (1965). Mystification, confusion and conflict. In I. Boszormenyi-Nagy & J. L. Framo (Eds.), *Intensive family therapy.* New York: Hoeber Medical Division, Harper & Row.

Laing, R. D. (1967). *The politics of experience.* New York: Pantheon.

Laing, R. D. (1979, July 20). Round the bend. *New Statesman.*

Lambert, M. J., & Bergin, A. E. (1994). The effectiveness of psychotherapy. In A. E. Bergin & S. L. Garfield (Eds.), *Handbook of psychotherapy and behavior change* (4th ed., pp. 143–189). New York: Wiley.

Lambert, M. J., Shapiro, D. A., & Bergin, A. E. (1986). The effectiveness of psychotherapy. In S. L. Garfield & A. E. Bergin (Eds.), *Handbook of psychotherapy and behavior change: An evaluative analysis* (3rd ed.). New York: Wiley.

Lampert, P. W., & Hardman, J. M. (1984). Morphological changes in brains of boxers. *Journal of the American Medical Association, 251,* 2676–2679.

Lampley, D. A., & Rust, J. O. (1986). Validation of the Kaufman Battery for Children with a sample of preschool children. *Psychology in Schools, 23*(2), 131–137.

Landesman-Dwyer, S. (1981). Drinking during pregnancy: Effects on human development [Monograph]. *Alcohol and Health, 4.*

Lane, R. D., & Jennings, J. R. (in press). Hemispheric asymmetry, autonomic asymmetry and the problem of sudden cardiac death. In R. J. Davidson & K. Hugdahl (Eds.), *Brain Asymmetry.* Cambridge, MA: M.I.T. Press.

Lanyon, R. I. (1986). Theory and treatment in child molestation. *Journal of Counseling and Clinical Psychology, 54,* 176–182.

LaPerriere, A. R., Antoni, M. H., Schneiderman, N., Ironson, G., Klimas, N., Caralis, P., & Fletcher, M. A. (1990). Exercise intervention attenuates emotional distress and natural killer cell decrements following notification of positive serologic status for HIV-1. *Biofeedback and Self-Regulation, 15,* 229–242.

Larsson, B., & Melin, L. (1992). Prevalence and short-term stability of depressive symptoms in school children. *Acta Psychiatrica Scandinavica 85,* 17–22.

Laufer, R. S., Brett, E., & Gallops, M. S. (1985). Symptom pattern associated with post-traumatic stress disorder among Vietnam veterans exposed to war trauma. *American Journal of Psychiatry, 142,* 1304–1311.

Laumann, E., Michael, R., Michaels, S., & Gagnon, J. (1994). *The social organization of sexuality.* Chicago: University of Chicago Press.

Lazarus, R. S. (1980). The stress and coping paradigm. In C. Eisdorfer, D. Cohen, & A. Kleinman (Eds.), *Conceptual models for psychopathology.* New York: Spectrum.

Lazarus, R. S., Kanner, A., & Folkman, S. (1980). Emotions: A cognitive-phenomenological approach. In R. Plutchik & H. Kellerman (Eds.), *Theories of emotion.* New York: Academic Press.

Leary, T. F. (1957). *The interpersonal diagnosis of personality.* New York: Ronald.

Leavitt, N., & Maykuth, P. L. (1989). Conformance to attorney performance standards: Advocacy behavior in a maximum security prison hospital. *Law and Human Behavior, 13,* 217–230.

LeDoux, J. E. (1986). The neurobiology of emotion. In J. E. LeDoux and W. Hirst (Eds.), *Mind and behavior: Dialogues in cognitive neuroscience.* Cambridge, MA: Cambridge University Press.

Lee, A. S., & Murray, R. M. (1988). The long-term outcome of Maudsley depressives. *British Journal of Psychiatry, 153,* 741–751.

Lee, G. P., Loring, D. W., Meader, K. J., & Brooks, B. B. (1990). Hemispheric specialization for emotional expression: A reexamination of results from intracarotid administration of sodium amobarbital. *Brain and Cognition, 12,* 267–280.

Lee, S., & Chiu, H. F. (1989). Anorexia nervosa in Hong Kong—Why not more in Chinese? *British Journal of Psychiatry, 154,* 683–688.

Leenaars, A. A., & Wenckstern, S. (1991). The school-age child and adolescent. In A. A. Leenaars (Ed.), *Life span perspectives of suicide: Timeliness in the suicide process.* New York: Plenum Press.

Leibowitz, S. F. (1991). Brain neuropeptide Y: An integrator of endocrine, metabolic, and behavioral processes. *Brain Research Bulletin, 27,* 333–337.

Leigh, B. C. (1989). In search of the seven dwarves: Issues of measurement and meaning in alcohol expectancy research. *Psychological Bulletin, 105,* 361–373.

Lelliott, P., Marks, I., McNamee, G., & Tobeña, A. (1989). Onset of panic disorder with agoraphobia. *Archives of General Psychiatry, 46,* 1000–1004.

Lemere, F., & Voegtlin, W. (1950). An evaluation of the aversion treatment of alcoholism. *Quarterly Journal of Studies on Alcohol, 11,* 199–204.

Lenane, M. C., Swedo, S. E., Leonard, H., et al. (1990). Psychiatric disorders in first degree relatives of children and adolescents with obsessive-compulsive disorders. *Journal of the American Academy of Child and Adolescent Psychiatry, 29,* 407–412.

Lenneberg, E. H. (1967). *Biological foundations of language.* New York: Wiley.

Lenzenweger, M. F., Cornblatt, B. A., & Putnick, M. (1991). Schizotypy and sustained attention. *Journal of Abnormal Psychology, 100,* 84–89.

Lenzenweger, M. F., Dworkin, R. H., & Wethington, E. (1989). Models of positive and negative symptoms in schizophrenia: An empirical evaluation of latent structures. *Journal of Abnormal Psychology, 98,* 62–70.

Lenzenweger, M. F., & Loranger, A. W. (1989a). Detection of familial schizophrenia using a psychometric measure of schizotypy. *Archives of General Psychiatry, 46,* 902–907.

Lenzenweger, M. F., & Loranger, A. W. (1989b). Psychosis proneness and clinical psychopathology: Examination of the correlates of schizotypy. *Journal of Abnormal Psychology, 98,* 3–8.

Leon, G. R. (1977). Anxiety neurosis: The case of Richard Benson. *Case histories in deviant behavior* (2nd ed.). Boston: Holbrook Press.

Lesage, A. D., Boyer, R., Grunberg, F., Vanier, C., Morissette, R., Menard-Buteau, C., & Loyer, M. (1994). Suicide and mental disorders: A case-control study of young men. *American Journal of Psychiatry, 151,* 1063–1068.

LeShan, L. (1966a). An emotional life-history pattern associated with neoplastic disease. *Annals of New York Academy of Sciences, 125,* 780–793.

LeShan, L. (1966b). In E. M. Weyer & H. Hutchins (Eds.), *Psychophysiological aspects of cancer* (pp. 780–793). New York: New York Academy of Sciences.

Leslie, A. M. (1991). The theory of mind impairment in autism: Evidence for a modular mechanism of development? In. A. Whiten (Ed.), *Natural theories of mind: Evolution, development and simulation of everyday mindreading.* Oxford: Blackwell.

Lester, D., & Murell, M. E. (1980). The influence of gun control laws on suicidal behavior. *American Journal of Psychiatry, 137,* 121–122.

Lester, M. E., & Doherty, W. J. (1983). Couples' long-term evaluations of their marriage encounter experience. *Journal of Marital and Family Therapy, 9,* 183–188.

Levendusky, P. G., & Dooley, C. P. (1985). An inpatient model for the treatment of anorexia nervosa. In S. Emmett (Ed.), *Eating disorders: Research, theory, and treatment* (pp. 211–233). New York: Brunner/Mazel.

Levenson, R. W., Oyama, O. N., & Meek, P. S. (1987). Greater reinforcement from alcohol for those at risk: Parental risk, personality risk, and sex. *Journal of Abnormal Psychology, 96,* 242–253.

Levine, F. M., & Ramirez, R. (1989). Contingent negative practice as a home-based treatment of tics and stuttering. In C. E. Schaefer and J. M. Briesmeister (Eds.), *Handbook of parent training: Parents as co-therapists for children's behavior problems.* New York: Wiley.

Levis, D. J. (1985). Implosive theory: A comprehensive extension of conditioning theory of fear/anxiety to psychology. In S. Reiss & R. R. Bootzin (Eds.), *Theoretical issues in behavior therapy.* New York: Academic Press.

Levy, D. L., Holzman, P. S., Matthysse, S., & Mendell, N. R. (1993). Eye tracking dysfunction and schizophrenia: A critical perspective. *Schizophrenia Bulletin, 19,* 461–536.

Levy, R., & Behrman, J. (1970). Clinical and laboratory notes: Cortical evoked responses in hysterical hemianaesthesia. *Electroencephalography and Clinical Neurophysiology, 29,* 400–402.

Levy, R., & Mushin, J. (1973). The somatosensory evoked response in patients with hysterical anaesthesia. *Journal of Psychosomatic Research, 17,* 81–84.

Lewin, T. (1994, June 19). The Simpson case: The syndrome. *The New York Times,* sec. 1, p. 21.

Lewine, R. R. J. (1981). Sex differences in schizophrenia: Timing or subtypes? *Psychological Bulletin, 90,* 432–444.

Lewinsohn, P. M. (1974). Clinical and theoretical aspects of depression. In K. S. Calhoun, H. E. Adams, & K. M. Mitchell (Eds.), *Innovative treatment methods of psychopathology.* New York: Wiley.

Lewinsohn, P. M., Hoberman, H. M., & Rosenbaum, M. (1988). A prospective study of risk factors for unipolar depression. *Journal of Abnormal Psychology, 97,* 251–264.

Lewinsohn, P. M., Hoberman, H., Teri, L., & Hautzinger, M. (1985). An integrative theory of depression. In S. Reiss & R. R. Bootzin (Eds.), *Theoretical issues in behavior therapy* (pp. 331–359). New York: Academic Press.

Lewinsohn, P. M., Hops, H., Roberts, R. E., Seely, J. R., & Andrews, J. A. (1993). Adolescent psychopathology: I. Prevalence and incidence of depression and other *DSM-III-R* disorders in high school students. *Journal of Abnormal Psychology, 102,* 133–144.

Lewinsohn, P. M., Mischel, W., Chaplin, W., & Barton, R. (1980). Social competence and depression: The role of illusory self-perceptions. *Journal of Abnormal Psychology, 89,* 203–212.

Lewinsohn, P. M., Roberts, R. E., Seeley, J. R., Rohde, P., Gotlib, I. H., & Hops, H. (1994). Adolescent psychopathology: II. Psychosocial risk factors for depression. *Journal of Abnormal Psychology, 103,* 302–315.

Lewinsohn, P. M., Rohde, P., Seeley, J. R., & Fischer, S. A. (1993). Age-cohort changes in the lifetime occurrence of depression and other mental disorders. *Journal of Abnormal Psychology, 102,* 110–120.

Lewinsohn, P. M., Sullivan, J. M., & Grosscup, S. J. (1980). Changing reinforcing events: An approach to the treatment of depression. *Psychotherapy: Theory, Research, and Practice, 17,* 322–334.

Lewis, D. O., & Bard, J. S. (1991). Multiple personality and forensic issues. *Psychiatric Clinics of North America, 14,* 741–756.

Lewis, J. M., Rodnick, E. H., & Goldstein, M. J. (1981). Intrafamilial interactive behavior, parental communication deviance, and risk for schizophrenia. *Journal of Abnormal Psychology, 90,* 448–457.

Ley, R. (1988a). Panic attacks during relaxation and relaxation-induced anxiety: A hyperventilation interpretation. *Journal of Behavior Therapy and Experimental Psychiatry, 19,* 305–316.

Ley, R. (1988b). Panic attacks during sleep: A hyperventilation-probability model. *Journal of Behavior Therapy and Experimental Psychiatry, 19,* 181–192.

Li, T., Lumeng, L., McBride, W. J., & Murphy, J. M. (1987). Alcoholism: Is it a model for the study of mood or consummatory behavior? *Annals of the New York Academy of Science, 499,* 239–249.

Liberman, R. P. (1982a). Assessment of social skills. *Schizophrenia Bulletin, 8,* 62–81.

Liberman, R. P., DeRisi, W. J., & Mueser, K. T. (1989). *Social skills training with psychiatric patients.* New York: Pergamon Press.

Liberman, R. P., & Eckman, T. (1981). Behavior therapy vs. insight-oriented therapy for repeated suicide attemptors. *Archives of General Psychiatry, 38,* 1126–1130.

Liberman, R. P., & Green, M. F. (1992). Whither cognitive-behavioral therapy for schizophrenia? *Schizophrenia Bulletin, 18,* 27–35.

Liberman, R. P., Kopelowicz, A., & Young, A. S. (1994). Biobehavioral treatment and rehabilitation of schizophrenia. *Behavior Therapy, 25,* 89–107.

Lichtenstein, E., & Glasgow, R. E. (1992). Smoking cessation: What have we learned over the past decade? *Journal of Consulting and Clinical Psychology, 60,* 518–527.

Liebenluft, E., & Wehr, T. A. (1992). Is sleep deprivation useful in the treatment of depression? *American Journal of Psychiatry, 149,* 159–168.

Lieberman, J. A., & Koreen, A. R. (1993). Neurochemistry and neuroendocrinology of schizophrenia: A selective review. *Schizophrenia Bulletin, 19,* 371–429.

Lieberman, M. A., Yalom, I. D., & Miks, M. B. (1973). *Encounter groups: First facts.* New York: Basic Books.

Liebert, R. M., Neale, J. M., & Davison, E. S. (1973). *The early window.* Elmsford, NY: Pergamon Press.

Liebowitz, M. R., Gorman, J. M., Fyer, A. J., & Klein, D. F. (1985). Social phobia: Review of a neglected anxiety disorder. *Archives of General Psychiatry, 42,* 729–736.

Lilienfeld, S. O. (1992). The association between antisocial personality and somatization disorders: A review and integration of theoretical models. *Clinical Psychology Review, 12,* 641–662.

Lin, M. W., Caffey, E. M., Klett, C. J., Hogarty, G. E., & Lamb, H. R. (1979). Day treatment and psychotropic drugs in the aftercare of schizophrenic patients. *Archives of General Psychiatry, 36,* 1055–1066.

Lindemalm, G., Körlin, D., & Uddenberg, N. (1986). Long-term follow-up of "sex change" in 13 male-to-female transsexuals. *Archives of Sexual Behavior, 15,* 182–210.

Lindemann, J. E., & Matarazzo, J. D. (1990). Assessment of adult intelligence. In G. Goldstein & M. Hersen (Eds.), *Handbook of psychological assessment* (2nd ed.). New York: Pergamon Press.

Lindzey, G., Hall, C. S., & Manosevitz, M. (1973). *Theories of personality: Primary sources and research* (2nd ed.). New York: Wiley.

Linehan, M. M. (1987). Dialectical behavior therapy for borderline personality disorder. *Bulletin of the Menninger Clinic, 41*(3), 261–276.

Linehan, M. M., Heard, H. L., & Armstrong, H. E. (1993). Naturalistic follow-up of a behavioral treatment for chronically parasuicidal borderline patients. *Archives of General Psychiatry, 50,* 971–974.

Lion, J. R. (1981). A comparison between *DSM-III* and *DSM-II* personality disorders. In J. R. Lion (Ed.), *Personality disorders: Diagnosis and management* (2nd ed.). Baltimore: Williams & Wilkins.

Lipowsky, Z. J. (1989). Delirium in the elderly patient. *New England Journal of Medicine, 320,* 578–582.

Lipton, M. A., & Burnett, G. B. (1980). Pharmacological treatment of schizophrenia. In L. Bellak (Ed.), *Disorders of the schizophrenic syndrome.* New York: Basic Books.

Litrownik, A. J. (1969). *The relationship of self-stimulatory behavior in autistic children to the intensity and complexity of environmental stimulation.* Unpublished master's thesis, University of Illinois, Champaign-Urbana.

Little, K. B., & Shneidman, E. S. (1954). The validity of MMPI interpretations. *Journal of Consulting Psychology, 18,* 425–428.

Little, K. B., & Shneidman, E. S. (1959). Congruencies among interpretations of psychological test and anamnestic data. *Psychological Monographs, 73*(6, Whole No. 476).

Livermore, J. M., Malmquist, C. P., & Meehl, P. E. (1968). On the justifications for civil commitment. *University of Pennsylvania Law Review, 117,* 75–96.

Livermore, J. M., & Meehl, P. E. (1967). The virtues of M'Naghten. *Minnesota Law Review, 51,* 789–856.

Lloyd, J. W., Hallahan, D. P., Kauffman, J. M., & Keller, C. E. (1991). Academic problems. In R. J. Morris & T. R. Kratochwill (Eds.), *The practice of child therapy* (2nd ed.). Elmsford, NY: Pergamon Press.

Loeber, R., & Dishion, T. (1983). Early predictors of male delinquency: A review. *Psychological Bulletin, 94,* 68–99.

Loeber, R., Stouthamer-Loeber, M., Van Kammen, W., & Farrington, D. P. (1989). Development of a new measure of self-reported antisocial behavior for young children: Prevalence and reliability. In M. Klein (Ed.), *Cross-national research in self-reported crime and delinquency* (pp. 203–226). Boston: Kluwer-Nijhoff.

Loewenstein, R. J. (1991). Psychogenic amnesia and psychogenic fugue: A comprehensive review. *Annual Review of Psychiatry, 10,* 223–247.

Loewenstein, R. J., & Ross, D. R. (1992). Multiple personality and psychoanalysis: An introduction. *Psychoanalytic Inquiry, 12,* 3–48.

Loftus, E. F. (1993). The reality of repressed memories. *American Psychologist, 48,* 518–537.

London, P. (1964). *The modes and morals of psychotherapy.* New York: Holt, Rinehart and Winston.

Long, B. B. (1986). The prevention of mental-emotional disabilities: A report from a National Health Association Commission. *American Psychologist, 41,* 825–829.

Lopez, S. R. (1988). The empirical basis of ethnocultural and linguistic bias in mental health evaluations of Hispanics. *American Psychologist, 43,* 1095–1097.

Lopez, S. R. (1989). Patient variable biases in clinical judgment: Conceptual overview and methodological considerations. *Psychological Bulletin, 106,* 184–203.

Lopez, S. R., Hernandez, P. (1986). How culture is considered in evaluations of psychopathology. *Journal of Nervous and Mental Disease, 176,* 598–606.

LoPiccolo, J. (1977). Direct treatment of sexual dysfunction in the couple. In J. Money & H. Musaph (Eds.), *Handbook of sexology.* Amsterdam: Excerpta Medica.

LoPiccolo, J. (1992). Post-modern sex therapy for erectile failure. In R. C. Rosen & S. R. Leiblum (Eds.), *Erectile failure: Assessment and treatment.* New York: Guilford Press.

LoPiccolo, J., Heiman, J. R., Hogan, D. R., & Roberts, C. W. (1985). Effectiveness of single therapists versus cotherapy teams in sex therapy. *Journal of Consulting and Clinical Psychology, 53,* 287–294.

LoPiccolo, J., & Hogan, P. (1979). Multidimensional behavioral treatment of sexual dysfunction. In O. Pomerleau & J. P. Brady (Eds.), *Behavioral medicine: Theory and practice.* Baltimore: Williams & Wilkins.

LoPiccolo, J., & Lobitz, W. C. (1973). Behavior therapy of sexual dysfunction. In L. A. Hammerlynck, L. C. Handy, & E. J. Mash (Eds.), *Behavior change: Methodology, concepts and practice.* Champaign, IL: Research Press.

LoPiccolo, J., & Stock, W. E. (1986). Treatment of sexual dysfunction. *Journal of Consulting and Clinical Psychology, 54,* 158–167.

Lotter, V. (1966). Epidemiology of autistic conditions in young children: I. Prevalence. *Social Psychiatry, 1*(3), 124–137.

Lovaas, O. I. (1977). *The autistic child.* New York: Halsted.

Lovaas, O. I. (1987). Behavioral treatment and normal educational and intellectual functioning in young autistic children. *Journal of Consulting and Clinical Psychology, 55,* 3–9.

Lovaas, O. I., Berberich, J. P., Perloff, B. F., & Schaeffer, B. (1966). Acquisition of imitative speech in schizophrenic children. *Science, 151,* 705–707.

Lovaas, O. I., Koegel, R. L., & Schreibman, L. (1979). Stimulus overselectivity in autism: A review of research. *Psychological Bulletin, 86,* 1236–1254.

Lovaas, O. I., Koegel, R. L., Simmons, J., & Long, J. (1973). Some generalization and follow up measures on autistic children in behavior therapy. *Journal of Applied Behaviour Analysis, 6,* 131–166.

Lovaas, O. I., Litrownik, A., & Mann, R. (1971). Response latencies to auditory stimuli in autistic children engaged in self-stimulatory behavior. *Behaviour Research and Therapy, 2,* 39–49.

Lovaas, O. I., Schaeffer, B., & Simmons, J. Q. (1965). Building social behavior in autistic children by use of electric shock. *Journal of Experimental Research in Personality, 1,* 99–109.

Lowing, P. A., Mirsky, A. F., Pereira, R. (1983). The inheritance of schizophrenia spectrum disorders: A reanalysis of the Danish adoptee study data. *American Journal of Psychiatry, 140,* 1167–1171.

Lubin, B., Larsen, R. M., & Matarazzo, J. D. (1984). Patterns of psychological test usage in the United States: 1935–1982. *American Psychologist, 39,* 451–454.

Luborsky, L., Barber, J. P., & Crits-Christoph, P. (1990). Theory-based research for understanding the process of dynamic psychotherapy. *Journal of Consulting and Clinical Psychology, 58,* 281–287.

Luborsky, L., Crits-Christoph, P., & Mellon, J. (1986). Advent of objective measures of the transference concept. *Journal of Consulting and Clinical Psychology, 54,* 39–47.

Luborsky, L., Crits-Christoph, P., Mintz, J., & Auerbach, A. (1988). *Who will benefit from psychotherapy? Predicting therapeutic outcomes.* New York: Basic Books.

Luborsky, L., Singer, B., & Luborsky, L. (1975). Comparative studies of psychotherapies: Is it true that everyone has won and all must have prizes? *Archives of General Psychiatry, 32,* 995–1008.

Luborsky, L., & Spence, D. P. (1978). Quantitative research on psychoanalytic therapy. In S. L. Garfield & A. E. Bergin (Eds.), *Handbook of psychotherapy and behavior change: An empirical analysis* (2nd ed.). New York: Wiley.

Lucas, A. R., Beard, C. M., O'Fallon, W. M., & Kurlan, L. T. (1991). Fifty year trends in the incidence of anorexia nervosa in Rochester, Minnesota: A population-based study. *American Journal of Psychiatry, 148,* 917–922.

Lucas, C., Sansbury, P., & Collins, J. G. (1962). A social and clinical study of delusions in schizophrenia. *Journal of Mental Health, 108,* 747–758.

Luchins, A. S. (1993). Social control doctrines of mental illness and the medical profession in nineteenth-century America. *Journal of the History of the Behavioral Sciences, 29,* 29–47.

Luchins, D. J., Lewine, R. J., & Meltzer, H. Y. (1983). Lateral ventricular size in the psychoses: Relation to psychopathology and therapeutic and adverse response to medication. *Schizophrenia Bulletin, 9,* 518–522.

Ludwig, A. M. (1986). *Principles of clinical psychiatry.* New York: Free Press.

Luepnitz, R. R., Randolph, D. L., & Gutsch, K. W. (1982). Race and socioeconomic status as confounding variables in the accurate diagnosis of alcoholism. *Journal of Clinical Psychology, 38,* 665–669.

Luisada, P. V. (1977, August). *The PCP psychosis: A hidden epidemic.* Paper presented at the Sixth World Congress of Psychiatry, Honolulu, HI.

Luparello, T. J., McFadden, E. R., Lyons, H. A., & Bleecker, E. R. (1971). Psychologic factors and bronchial asthma. *New York State Journal of Medicine, 71,* 2161–2165.

Lykken, D. I. (1957). A study of anxiety in the sociopathic personality. *Journal of Abnormal and Social Psychology, 55*(1), 6–10.

Lynch, J. J. (1977). *The broken heart: The medical consequences of loneliness.* New York: Basic Books.

Lyness, S. A. (1993). Predictors of differences between Type A and B individuals in heart rate and blood pressure reactivity. *Psychological Bulletin, 114,* 266–295.

Lyon, L. S. (1985). Facilitating telephone number recall in a case of psychogenic amnesia. *Journal of Behavior Therapy and Experimental Psychiatry, 16,* 147–149.

MacDonald, J. (1967). Homicidal threats. *American Journal of Psychiatry, 124,* 475.

MacFarlane, K. (1978). Sexual abuse of children. In J. R. Chapman & M. Gates (Eds.), *The victimization of women* (pp. 81–109). Beverly Hills, CA: Sage.

MacLean, P. D. (1986). Culminating developments in the evolution of the limbic system: The thalamocingulate division. In B. K. Doane & K. E. Livingston (Eds.), *The limbic system: Functional organization and clinical disorders.* New York: Raven Press.

MacMahon, S., Peto, R., Cutter, J., Collins, R., Sorlie, P., Neaton, J., Abbott, R., Godwin, J., Dyer, A., & Stamler, J. (1990). Blood pressure, stroke, and coronary heart disease. *Lancet, 335,* 765–774.

MacMillan, D. L. (1982). *Mental retardation in school and society* (2nd ed.). Boston: Little, Brown.

Maher, B. A. (1983). A tentative theory of schizophrenic utterance. In B. A. Maher & W. B. Maher (Eds.), *Progress in experimental personality research: Vol. 12, Psychopathology* (pp. 1–52). New York: Academic Press.

Maher, B. A. (1988). Anomalous experience and delusional thinking: The logic of explanations. In T. F. Oltmanns & B. A. Maher (Eds.), *Delusional beliefs* (pp. 15–33). New York: Wiley.

Maher, B. A., & Maher, W. B. (1979). Psychopathology. In E. Hearst (Ed.), *The first century of experimental psychology.* Hillsdale, NJ: Erlbaum.

Maher, B. A., & Maher, W. B. (1985). Psychopathology: II. From the eighteenth century to modern times. In G. A. Kimble & K. Schlesinger (Eds.), *Topics in the history of psychology* (Vol. 2). Hillsdale, NJ: Erlbaum.

Maher, B. A., & Spitzer, M. (1993). Delusions. In P. B. Sutker & H. E. Adams (Eds.), *Comprehensive handbook of psychopathology* (2nd ed., pp. 263–293). New York: Plenum Press.

Maher, W. B., & Maher, B. A. (1985). Psychopathology: I. From ancient times to the eighteenth century. In G. A. Kimble & K. Schlesinger (Eds.), *Topics in the history of psychology* (Vol. 2). Hillsdale, NJ: Erlbaum.

Mahler, M. S., Pine, F., & Bergman, A. (1975). *The psychological birth of the human infant.* New York: Basic Books.

Mahoney, M. J. (1991). *Human change process: The scientific foundations of psychotherapy.* New York: Basic Books.

Mahoney, M. J. (1993). Introduction to special section: Theoretical developments in the cognitive psychotherapies. *Journal of Consulting and Clinical Psychology, 61,* 187–193.

Malamuth, N. M., Heavey, C. L., & Linz, D. (1993). Predicting mens's antisocial behavior against women: The interaction model of sexual aggression. In C. C. Nagayama Hall, R. Hirschman, J. Graham, & M. Zaragoza (Eds.), *Sexual aggression: Issues and etiology, assessment and treatment* (pp. 63–97). Washington, DC: Taylor Francis.

Maletzky, B. M., & Klotter, J. (1974). Smoking and alcoholism. *American Journal of Psychiatry, 131*(4), 445–447.

Malmo, R. B., & Shagass, C. (1949). Physiologic study of symptom mechanisms in psychiatric patients under stress. *Psychosomatic Medicine, 11,* 25–29.

Mann, J. J., McBride, A., Brown, R. P., Linnoila, M., Leon, A. C., DeMeo, M., Mieczkowski, T., Myers, J. E., & Stanley, M. (1992). Relationship between central and peripheral serotonin indexes in depressed and suicidal psychiatric inpatients. *Archives of General Psychiatry, 49,* 442–446.

Manschreck, T. C. (1992). Delusional disorders: Clinical concepts and diagnostic strategies. *Psychiatric Annals, 22,* 241–251.

Marcos L. R., Alpert M., Urcuyo, L., & Kesselman, M. (1973). The language barrier in evaluating Spanish-American patients. *Archives of General Psychiatry, 29,* 655–659.

Marcus, D. K., & Nardone, M. E. (1992). Depression and interpersonal rejection. *Clinical Psychology Review, 12,* 433–449.

Margolick, D. (1994a, January 16). Does Mrs. Bobbitt count as another battered wife? *The New York Times,* p. E5.

Margolick, D. (1994b, January 21). Malicious or insane? Now the jury decides in mutilation case; was Lorena Bobbitt fending off more abuse or avenging herself? *The New York Times,* p. A8.

Margolick, D. (1994c, January 19). Psychiatrist says years of abuse led woman to cut husband. *The New York Times,* p. A9.

Margolies, A. (1977). Behavioral approaches to the treatment of early infantile autism: A review. *Psychological Bulletin, 84,* 249–264.

Maris, R. W. (1992). The relation of nonfatal suicide attempts to completed suicides. In R. W. Maris, A. L. Berman, J. T. Maltsberger, & R. I. Yufit (Eds.), *Assessment and prediction of suicide* (pp. 362–380). New York: Guilford Press.

Marlatt, G. A., Curry, S., & Gordon, J. R. (1988). A longitudinal analysis of unaided smoking cessation. *Journal of Consulting and Clinical Psychology, 56,* 715–720.

Marlatt, G. A., & Gordon, J. R. (1985). *Relapse prevention: Maintenance strategies in addictive behavior change.* New York: Guilford Press.

Marmer, S. S. (1991). Multiple personality disorder: A psychoanalytic perspective. *Psychiatric Clinics of North America, 14,* 677–693.

Marrazzi, M. A., & Luby, E. D. (1986). An auto-addiction model of chronic anorexia nervosa. *International Journal of Eating Disorders, 5,* 191–208.

Marsden, C. D. (1986). Hysteria—a neurologist's view. *Psychological Medicine, 16,* 277–288.

Marshall, D. S. (1971). Sexual behavior on Mangaia. In D. S. Marshall & R. C. Suggs (Eds.), *Human sexual behavior.* New York: Basic Books.

Marshall, W. L., & Pithers, W. D. (1994). A reconsideration of treatment outcome with sex offenders. *Criminal Justice and Behavior, 21,* 10–27.

Martineau, J., Barthélémy, C., Garreau, B., & Lelord, G. (1985). Vitamin B_6, magnesium, and combined B_6-Mg: Therapeutic effects of childhood autism. *Biological Psychiatry, 20,* 467–473.

Marttunen, M. J., Aro, H. M., Henriksson, M. M., & Lönnqvist, J. K. (1991). Mental disorders in adolescent suicide: *DSM-III-R* Axes I and II diagnoses in suicides among 13- to 19-year-olds in Finland. *Archives of General Psychiatry, 48,* 834–839.

Masling, J. M. (1960). The influence of situational and interpersonal variables in projective testing. *Psychological Bulletin, 57,* 65–85.

Maslow, A. H. (1987). *Motivation and personality* (3rd ed.). New York: Harper & Row.

Masserman, J. H. (1961). *Principles of dynamic psychiatry* (2nd ed.). Philadelphia: Saunders.

Masters, J. C., Brush, T. G., Hollon, S. D., & Rimm, D. C. (1987). *Behavior Therapy* (3rd ed.). New York: Harcourt Brace Jovanovich.

Masters, W. H., & Johnson, V. E. (1966). *Human sexual response.* Boston: Little, Brown.

Masters, W. H., & Johnson, V. E. (1970). *Human sexual inadequacy.* Boston: Little, Brown.

Matarazzo, J. D. (1972). *Wechsler's measurement and appraisal of adult intelligence* (5th ed.). Baltimore: Williams & Wilkins.

Matarazzo, J. D. (1990). Psychological assessment versus psychological testing. *American Psychologist, 45,* 999–1017.

Mathews, A., Richards, A., & Eysenck, M. (1989). Interpretation of homophones related to threat in anxiety states. *Journal of Abnormal Psychology, 98,* 31–34.

Matson, J. L., & Andrasik, F. (1982). *Treatment issues and innovations in mental retardation.* New York: Plenum Press.

Matson, J. L., Marchetti, A., & Adkins, J. A. (1980). Comparison of operant—and independence—training procedures for mentally retarded adults. *American Journal of Mental Deficiency, 84,* 487–492.

Matthews, K. A. (1988). Coronary heart disease and Type A behaviors: Update on and alternative to the Booth-Kewley and Friedman (1987) quantitative review. *Psychological Bulletin, 104,* 373–380.

Maugh, T. H. (1982). Marijuana "justifies serious concern." *Science, 215,* 1488–1489.

May, R. (1958). Contributions of existential psychotherapy. In R. May, E. Angel, & H. F. Ellenberger (Eds.), *Existence: A new dimension in psychiatry and psychology.* New York: Basic Books.

May, R. (1959). *The discovery of being: Writings in existential psychology* (p. 37). New York: Norton.

May, R. (1961). Existential bases of psychotherapy. In R. May (Ed.), *Existential psychology.* New York: Random House.

May, R. (1990). Will, decision, and responsibility. *Review of Existential Psychology and Psychiatry, 20,* 269–278.

McArthur, J. C., Hoover, D. R., Bacellar, H., Miller, E. N., Cohen, B. A., Becker, J. T., Graham, N. M. H., McArthur, J. H., Selnes, O. A., Jacobson, L. P., Visscher, B. R., Concha, M., & Saah, A. (1993). Dementia in AIDS patients: Incidence and risk factors. *Neurology, 43,* 2245–2252.

McAuliffe, W. E. (1990). A randomized controlled trial of recovery training and self-help for opioid addicts in New England and Hong Kong. *Journal of Psychoactive Drugs, 22,* 197–209.

McCartney, J. R., & Holden, J. C. (1981). Toilet training for the mentally retarded. In J. L. Matson & J. R. McCartney (Eds.), *Handbook of behavior modification with the mentally retarded.* New York: Plenum Press.

McClelland, D. C. (1977). The impact of power motivation training on alcoholics. *Journal of Studies on Alcohol, 38,* 142–144.

McClelland, D. C., Davis, W. N., Kalin, R., & Wanner, E. (1972). *The drinking man.* New York: Free Press.

McConaghy, N. (1989). Validity and ethics of penile circumference measures of sexual arousal: A critical review. *Archives of Sexual Behavior, 18,* 357–369.

McCord, W., & McCord, J. (1964). *The psychopath: An essay on the criminal mind.* New York: Van Nostrand.

McCord, W., McCord, J., & Gudeman, J. (1960). *Origins of alcoholism.* Stanford, CA: Stanford University Press.

McCrady, B. S., Longabaugh, R., Fink, E., Stout, R., Beattie, M., & Ruggieri-Authelet, A. (1986). Cost effectiveness of alcoholism treatment in partial hospital versus inpatient settings after brief inpatient treatment: 12-month outcomes. *Journal of Consulting and Clinical Psychology, 54,* 708–713.

McEvoy, J. P., Schooler, N. R., Friedman, E., Steingard, S., & Allen, M. (1993). Use of psychopathology vignettes by patients with schizophrenia or schizoaffective disorder and by mental health professionals to judge patients' insight. *American Journal of Psychiatry, 150,* 1649–1653.

McEwen, B. S. (1992). *Hormones and brain development.* Address to the American Health Foundation, Washington, DC.

McFarlane, A. C. (1986). Posttraumatic morbidity of a disaster. *Journal of Nervous and Mental Disease, 174,* 4–14.

McFarlane, A. C. (1988). The aetiology of post-traumatic stress disorders following a natural disaster. *British Journal of Psychiatry, 152,* 116–121.

McFarlane, A. C. (1989). The aetiology of post-traumatic morbidity: Predisposing, precipitating and perpetuating factors. *British Journal of Psychiatry, 154,* 221–228.

McGarvey, B., Gabrielli, W. F., Beutler, P. M., & Mednick, S. (1981). Rearing social class, education, and criminality: A multiple indicator model. *Journal of Abnormal Psychology, 90,* 354–364.

McGeer, P. L., Eccles, J. C., & McGeer, E. G. (1987). *Molecular neurobiology of the mammalian brain* (2nd ed.). New York: Plenum Press.

McGhie, A., & Chapman, J. (1961). Disorders of attention and perception in early schizophrenia. *British Journal of Medical Psychology, 34,* 103–116.

McGlashan, T. H., & Fenton, W. S. (1993). Subtype progression and pathophysiologic deterioration in early schizophrenia. *Schizophrenia Bulletin, 19,* 71–83.

McGue, M., & Gottesman, I. I. (1989). Genetic linkage in schizophrenia: Perspectives from genetic epidemiology. *Schizophrenia Bulletin, 15,* 453–464.

McGue, M., Pickens, R. W., & Svikis, D. S. (1992). Sex and age effects on the inheritance of alcohol problems: A twin study. *Journal of Abnormal Psychology, 101,* 3–17.

McHugh, P. R. (1992) Psychiatric misadventures. *The American scholar, 61*(4), 497–510.

McMahan, B. T., & Flowers, S. M. (1986). The high cost of a bump on the head. *Business and Health, 3*(7), 47–48.

McMahon, R. J., & Wells, K. C. (1989). Conduct disorders. In E. J. Mash & R. A. Barkley (Eds.), *Treatment of childhood disorders* (pp. 73–132). New York: Guilford Press.

McNally, R. J. (1987). Preparedness and phobias: A review. *Psychological Bulletin, 101,* 283–303.

McNally, R. J., Kaspi, S. P., Riemann, B. C., Zeitlin, S. B. (1990). Selective processing of threat cues in posttraumatic stress disorder. *Journal of Abnormal Psychology, 99,* 398–402.

McNally, R. J., Riemann, B. C., Kim, E. (1990). Selective processing of threat cues in panic disorder. *Behaviour Research and Therapy, 28,* 407–412.

McNeal, E. T., & Cimbolic, P. (1986). Antidepressants and biochemical theories of depression. *Psychological Bulletin, 99,* 361–374.

McNeil, E. B. (1970). *The psychoses.* Englewood Cliffs, NJ: Prentice-Hall.

McReynolds, P. (1975). Historical antecedents of personality assessment. In P. McReynolds (Ed.), *Advances in psychological assessment* (Vol. 3). San Francisco: Jossey-Bass.

McReynolds, P. (1989). Diagnosis and clinical assessment: Current status and major issues. *Annual Review of Psychology, 40,* 83–108.

Mechanic, D. (1962). The concept of illness behavior *Journal of Chronic Diseases, 15,* 189–194.

Mednick, S. A. (1970). Breakdown in individuals at high risk for schizophrenia: Possible predispositional perinatal factors. *Mental Hygiene, 54,* 50–63.

Mednick, S. A. (1971). Birth defects and schizophrenia. *Psychology Today, 4,* 48–50.

Mednick, S. A., Machon, R. A., Huttunen, M. O., & Bonett, D. (1988). Adult schizophrenia following prenatal exposure to an influenza epidemic. *Archives of General Psychiatry, 45,* 189–192.

Mednick, S. A., & Silverton, L. (1988). High-risk studies of the etiology of schizophrenia. In H. A. Nasrallah, M. T. Tsuang, & J. C. Simpson (Eds.), *Handbook of schizophrenia: Vol. 3. Nosology, epidemiology, and genetics of schizophrenia.* (pp. 543–562). New York: Elsevier.

Meehl, P. E. (1991). The insanity defense. In C. A. Anderson & K. Gunderson (Eds.), *Paul E. Meehl: Selected philosophical and methodological papers.* Minneapolis: University of Minnesota Press.

Meesters, Y., Jansen, J. H. C., Beersma, D. G. M., Bouhuys, A. L., & van den Hoofdakker, R. H. (1993). Early light treatment can prevent an emerging winter depression from developing into a full-blown depression. *Journal of Affective Disorders, 29,* 41–47.

Meichenbaum, D. H. (1975). Self-instructional methods. In F. H. Kanfer & A. P. Goldstein (Eds.), *Helping people change: A textbook of methods.* New York: Pergamon Press.

Meichenbaum, D. H. (Ed.). (1977). *Cognitive behavior modification: An integrative approach.* New York: Plenum Press.

Meichenbaum, D. H., & Cameron, R. (1973). Training schizophrenics to talk to themselves: A means of developing attentional controls. *Behavior Therapy, 4,* 515–534.

Meichenbaum, D. H., & Goodman, J. (1971). Training impulsive children to talk to themselves: A means of developing self control. *Journal of Abnormal Psychology, 77,* 115–126.

Meichenbaum, D. H., & Jaremko, M. E. (Eds.). (1983). *Stress reduction and prevention.* New York: Plenum Press.

Meinardi, H., & Pachlatko, C. (1991). Special centers for epilepsy. In M. Dam & L. Gram (Eds.), *Comprehensive epileptology* (pp. 769–779). New York: Raven Press.

Mellsop, G., Varghere, F., Joshua, S., et al. (1982). The reliability of axis II of *DSM-III*. *American Journal of Psychiatry, 139,* 1360–1361.

Meltzer, H. Y., Burnett, S., Bastani, B., & Ramirez, L. F. (1990). Effects of six months of clozapine treatment on the quality of life of chronic schizophrenic patients. *Hospital and Community Psychiatry, 41*(8), 892–897.

Melzack, R. (1988). The tragedy of needless pain: A call for social action. In R. Dubner, R. G. F. Gebhart, & M. R. Bond (Eds.), *Proceedings for the Fifth World Congress on Pain.* New York: Elsevier.

Mendel, W. M. (1976). *Schizophrenia: The experience and its treatment.* San Francisco: Jossey-Bass.

Mendlewicz, J., & Rainer, J. D. (1977). Adoption study supporting genetic transmission in manic-depressive illness. *Nature, 168,* 327–329.

Merckelbach, H., DeRuiter, C., Van Den Hout, M. A., & Hoekstra, R. (1989). Conditioning experiences and phobias. *Behaviour Research and Therapy, 27,* 657–662.

Merikangus, K. R. (1990). Comorbidity for anxiety and depression: Review of family and genetic studies. In J. D. Maser & C. R. Cloninger (Eds.), *Comorbidity of mood and anxiety disorders.* Washington, DC: American Psychiatric Press.

Merritt, H. H. (1967). *A textbook of neurology* (4th ed.). Philadelphia: Lea & Febiger.

Merskey, H. (1992). The manufacture of personalities: The production of multiple personality disorder. *British Journal of Psychiatry, 160,* 327–340.

Messer, S. B., & Winokur, M. (1984). Ways of knowing and visions of reality in psychoanalytic therapy and behavior therapy. In H. Arkowitz & S. B. Messer (Eds.), *Psychoanalytic therapy and behavior therapy: Is integration possible?* New York: Plenum Press.

Mesulam, M. (1981). Dissociative states with abnormal temporal lobe EEG: Multiple personality and the illusion of possession. *Archives of Neurology, 38,* 176–181.

Metalsky, G. I., Joiner, T. E., Jr., Hardin, T. S., & Abramson, L. Y. (1993). Depressive reactions to failure in a naturalistic setting: A test of the hopelessness and self-esteem theories of depression. *Journal of Abnormal Psychology, 102,* 101–109.

Meyer, J. K., & Peter, D. J. (1979). Sex reassignment: Follow-up. *Archives of General Psychiatry, 36,* 1010–1015.

Meyerowitz, B. E. (1980). Psychosocial correlates of breast cancer and its treatments. *Psychological Bulletin, 87,* 108–131.

Mezzich, J. E., Fabrega, H., Coffman, G. A., & Haley, R. (1989). *DSM-III* disorders in a large sample of psychiatric patients: Frequency and specificity of diagnoses. *American Journal of Psychiatry, 146,* 212–219.

Michael, R. T., Gagnon, J. H., Laumann, E. O., & Kolata, G. (1994). *Sex in America: A definitive survey.* Boston: Little, Brown.

Michelson, L. K., & Marchione, K. (1991). Behavioral, cognitive, and pharmacological treatments of panic disorder with agoraphobia: Critique and synthesis. *Journal of Consulting and Clinical Psychology, 59,* 100–114.

Miklowitz, D. J., Goldstein, M. J., Doane, J. A., Nuechterlein, K. H., Strachan, A. M., Snyder, K. S., & Magana-Amato, A. (1989). Is expressed emotion an index of a transactional process? I. Parents' affective style. *Family Process, 22,* 153–167.

Miklowitz, D. J., Strachan, A. M., Goldstein, M. J., Doane, J. A., Snyder, K. S., Hogarty, G. E., & Falloon, I. R. H. (1986). Expressed emotion and communication deviance in the families of schizophrenics. *Journal of Abnormal Psychology, 95,* 60–66.

Miklowitz, D. J., Velligan, D. I., Goldstein, M. J., Nuechterlein, K. H., & Gitlin, M. J. (1991). Communication deviance in families of schizophrenic and manic patients. *Journal of Abnormal Psychology, 100,* 163–173.

Mikulincer, M., & Solomon, Z. (1988). Attributional style and combat-related posttraumatic stress disorder. *Journal of Abnormal Psychology,* 97, 308–313.

Miller, E. (1987). Hysteria: Its nature and explanation. *British Journal of Clinical Psychology, 26,* 163–173.

Miller, G. (1956). The magical number seven, plus or minus two: Some limits of our capacity for processing information. *Psychological Review, 63,* 81–97.

Miller, G. E., & Prinz, R. J. (1990). Enhancement of social learning family interventions for childhood conduct disorder. *Psychological Bulletin, 108,* 291–307.

Miller, H. L., Coombs, D. W., & Leeper, J. D. (1984). An analysis of the effects of suicide prevention facilities on suicide rates in the United States. *American Journal of Public Health, 74,* 340–343.

Miller, L. J., O'Connor, E., & DiPasquale, T. (1993). Patients' attitudes toward hallucinations. *American Journal of Psychiatry, 150,* 584–588.

Miller, L. L. (Ed.). (1975). *Marihuana: Current research.* New York: Academic Press.

Miller, N. E. (1969). Learning of visceral and glandular responses. *Science, 163,* 434–445.

Miller, N. E. (1972). Comments on strategy and tactics of research. In A. E. Bergin & H. H. Strupp (Eds.), *Changing frontiers in the science of psychotherapy.* New York: Aldine-Atherton.

Miller, N. S., Mahler, J. C., & Gold, M. S. (1991). Suicide risk associated with drug and alcohol dependence. *Journal of Addictive Diseases, 10,* 49–61.

Miller, S. D., & Triggiano, P. J. (1992). The psychophysiological investigation of multiple personality disorder: Review and update. *American Journal of Clinical Hypnosis, 35,* 47–61.

Miller, W. R., & Hester, R. K. (1986). Inpatient alcoholism treatment: Who benefits? *American Psychologist, 41,* 794–805.

Millon, T. (1969). *Modern psychopathology.* Philadelphia: Saunders.

Millon, T. (1981). *Disorders of personality.* New York: Wiley.

Millon, T. (1985a). The MCMI provides a good assessment of *DSM-III* disorders: The MCMI-II will prove even better. *Journal of Personality Assessment, 49,* 379–391.

Millon, T. (1985b). *Millon Clinical Multiaxial Inventory: Second edition* (MCMI-II). Minneapolis: National Computer Systems.

Millon, T. (1987). *Manual for the MCMI-II.* Minneapolis: National Computer Systems.

Mindell, J. A., & Cashman, L. (1995). Sleep disorders. In A. R. Eisen, C. A. Kearney, & C. E. Schaefer (Eds.), *Clinical handbook of anxiety disorders in children and adolescents.* Northvale, NJ: Aronson.

Mindus, P., & Jenike, M. A. (1992). Neurosurgical treatment of malignant obsessive compulsive disorder. *Psychiatric Clinics of North America, 15,* 921–938.

Mineka, S., Davidson, M., Cook, M., & Keir, R. (1984). Observational conditioning of snake fear in rhesus monkeys. *Journal of Abnormal Psychology, 93,* 355–374.

Minshew, N. J., & Dombrowski, S. M. (1994). In vivo neuroanatomy of autism: Neuroimaging studies. In M. L. Bauman & T. L. Kemper (Eds.), *The neurobiology of autism.* Baltimore: Johns Hopkins University Press.

Mintz, M. (1991, May). Tobacco roads: Delivering death to the third world. *Progressive, 55,* 24–29.

Minuchin, S. (1972). Structural family therapy. In G. Caplan (Ed.), *American handbook of psychiatry* (Vol. 2). New York: Basic Books.

Minuchin, S. (1974). *Families and family therapy.* Cambridge, MA: Harvard University Press.

Minuchin, S., & Fishman, H. C. (1981). *Family therapy techniques.* Cambridge, MA: Harvard University Press.

Minuchin, S., Rosman, B. L., & Baker, L. (1978). *Psychosomatic families: Anorexia nervosa in context.* Cambridge, MA: Harvard University Press.

Mirsky, A. F., & Duncan, C. C. (1986). Etiology and expression of schizophrenia: Neurobiological and psychosocial factors. *Annual Review of Psychology, 37,* 291–319.

Mischel, W. (1968). *Personality and assessment.* New York: Wiley.

Mischel, W. (1973). Toward a cognitive social learning reconceptualization of personality. *Psychological Review, 80,* 252–283.

Mischel, W. (1979). On the interface of cognition and personality: Beyond the person-situation debate. *American Psychologist, 34,* 740–754.

Mischel, W., & Peake, P. K. (1982). Beyond deja vu in the search for cross-situational consistency. *Psychological Review, 89,* 730–755.

Mitchell, J., McCauley, E., Burke, P. M., & Moss, S. J. (1988). Phenomenology of depression in children and adolescents. *Journal of the American Academy of Child and Adolescent Psychiatry, 27,* 12–20.

Mittelman, M., Ferris, S. H., Steinberg, G., Shulman, E., Mackell, J. A., Ambinder, A., & Cohen, J. (1993). An intervention that delays institutionalization of Alzheimer's disease patients: Treatment of spouse-caregivers. *Gerontologist, 33,* 730–740.

Moffitt, T. E. (1991). *Juvenile delinquency: Seed of a career in violent crime, just sowing wild oats—or both?* Paper presented at the Science and Public Policy Seminars of the Federation of Behavioral, Psychological, and Cognitive Sciences, Washington, DC.

Moffitt, T. E. (1993). Adolescence-limited and life-course-persistent antisocial behavior: A developmental taxonomy. *Psychological Review, 100,* 674–701.

Mogg, K., Mathews, A., & Weinman, J. (1989). Selective processing of threat cues in anxiety states: A replication. *Behaviour Research and Therapy 27,* 317–320.

Mohr, J. W., Turner, R. E., & Jerry, M. B. (1964). *Pedophilia and exhibitionism.* Toronto: University of Toronto Press.

Monahan, J. (1976). The prevention of violence. In J. Monahan (Ed.), *Community mental health and the criminal justice system.* New York: Pergamon Press.

Monahan, J. (1981). *The clinical prediction of violent behavior.* Rockville, MD: National Institute of Mental Health.

Monahan, J. (1992). Mental disorder and violent behavior. *American Psychologist, 47,* 511–521.

Monahan, J., & Steadman, H. (1994). Toward a rejuvenation of risk assessment research. In J. Monahan & H. Steadman (Eds.), *Violence and mental disorder: Developments in risk assessment.* Chicago: University of Chicago Press.

Money, J., & Primrose, C. (1968). Sexual dimorphism and dissociation in the psychology of male transsexuals. *Journal of Nervous and Mental Disease, 147,* 472–486.

Monroe, S. M., & Simons, A. D. (1991). Diathesis-stress theories in the context of life stress research: Implications for the depressive disorders. *Psychological Bulletin, 110,* 406–425.

Montague, A. (1968). Chromosomes and crime. *Psychology Today, 2*(5), 43–49.

Moore, J. (1985). *Roads to recovery.* New York: Guilford Press.

Moore, S., Donovan, B., Hudson, A., Dykstra, J., & Lawrence, J. (1993). Brief report: Evaluation of eight case studies of facilitated communication. *Journal of Autism and Developmental Disorders, 23.*

Mora, G. (1980). Mind-body concepts in the Middle Ages: Part II. The Moslem influence, the great theological systems and cultural attitudes toward the mentally ill in the late Middle Ages. *Journal of the History of the Behavioral Sciences, 16,* 58–72.

Moran, E. (1970). Varieties of pathological gambling. *British Journal of Psychiatry, 116,* 593–597.

Moreau, D. L., Weissman, M., & Warner, V. (1989). Panic disorder in children at high risk for depression. *American Journal of Psychiatry, 146,* 1059–1060.

Morey, L. (1988). The categorical representation of personality disorder: A cluster analysis of *DSM-III-R* personality features. *Journal of American Psychology, 97,* 314–321.

Morey, L. C. (1991). *The Personality Assessment Inventory Professional Manual.* Odessa, FL: Psychological Assessment Resources, Inc.

Morgan, G. D., Ashenberg, Z. S., & Fisher, E. B., Jr. (1988). Abstinence from smoking and the social environment. *Journal of Consulting and Clinical Psychology, 56,* 298–301.

Morley, J. E., & Krahn, D. D. (1987). Endocrinology for the psychiatrist. In C. B. Nemeroff & P. T. Loosen (Eds.), *Handbook of clinical psychoneuroendocrinology* (pp. 3–37). New York: Guilford Press.

Morris, G. H., & Meloy, J. R. (1993). Out of mind? Out of sight: The uncivil commitment of permanently incompetent criminal defendants. *University of California Davis Law Review, 27,* 1–23.

Morrison, J. (1989). Childhood sexual histories of women with somatization disorder. *American Journal of Psychiatry, 146,* 239–241.

Morrison, R. L. (1991). Schizophrenia. In M. Hersen & S. M. Turner (Eds.), *Adult psychopathology and diagnosis* (2nd ed., pp. 149–169). New York: Wiley.

Morrison, R. L., & Bellack, A. S. (1987). Social functioning of schizophrenic patients: Clinical and research issues. *Schizophrenia Bulletin, 13,* 715–725.

Morse, S. J. (1978). Law and mental health professionals: The limits of expertise. *Professional Psychology, 9,* 389–399.

Morse, S. J. (1982). A preference for liberty: The case against the involuntary commitment of the mentally disordered. *California Law Review, 70,* 55–106.

Moser, C., & Levitt, E. E. (1987). An exploratory-descriptive study of a sadomasochistically oriented sample. *Journal of Sex Research, 23*(3), 322–337.

Mosley, T. H., Jr., Penizen, D. B., Johnson, C. A., et al. (1991). Time-series analysis of stress and headache. *Cephalalgia, 11,* 306–307.

Moustakas, C. E. (1959). *Psychotherapy with children.* New York: Harper & Row.

Moustakas, C. E. (1961). *Loneliness.* New York: Prentice-Hall.

Moustakas, C. E. (1972). *Loneliness and love.* Englewood Cliffs, NJ: Prentice-Hall.

Moustakas, C. E. (1975). *The touch of loneliness.* Englewood Cliffs, NJ: Prentice-Hall.

Mowrer, O. H. (1948). Learning theory and the neurotic paradox. *American Journal of Orthopsychiatry, 18,* 571–610.

Mowrer, O. H., & Mowrer, W. M. (1938). Enuresis: A method for its study and treatment. *American Journal of Orthopsychiatry, 8,* 436–459.

Moyles, E. W., & Wolins, M. (1971). Group care and intellectual development. *Developmental Psychology, 4,* 370–380.

Muesser, K. T., Valenti-Hein, D., & Yarnold, P. R. (1987). Dating-skills groups for the developmentally disabled. *Behavior Modification, 11*(2), 200–228.

Murphy, E., Lindesay, J., & Grundy, E. (1986). 60 years of suicide in England and Wales: A cohort study. *Archives of General Psychiatry, 43,* 969–976.

Murphy, G. E., & Wetzel, R. D. (1980). Suicide risk by birth cohort in the United States, 1949 to 1974. *Archives of General Psychiatry, 37,* 519–523.

Murphy, J. M., Gatto, G. J., Waller, M. B., McBride, W. J., Lumeng, L., & Li, T.-K. (1986). Effects of scheduled access on ethanol intake by the alcohol-preferring P line of rats. *Alcohol, 3,* 331–336.

Murphy, W. D. (1990). Assessment and modification of cognitive distortions in sex offenders. In W. L. Marshall, D. R. Laws, & H. E. Barbaree (Eds.), *The handbook of sexual assault: Issues, theories, and treatment of the offender* (pp. 331–342). New York: Plenum.

Murray, D. M., & Perry, C. L. (1985). The prevention of adolescent drug abuse: Implications of etiological, developmental, behavioral, and environmental models. In C. L. Jones and R. J. Battjes (Eds.), *Etiology of drug abuse: Implications for treatment* (DHHS Publication No. ADM 85-1335, pp. 236–255). Washington, DC: U.S. Government Printing Office.

Mydans, S. (1993, December 20). *The New York Times,* p. A11.

Myers, J. K., & Bean, L. L. (1968). *A decade later: A follow-up of social class and mental illness.* New York: Wiley.

Myers, P. I., & Hammill, D. D. (1990). *Learning disabilities: Basic concepts, assessment practices, and instructional strategies* (4th ed.). Austin, TX: Pro-Ed.

Narrow, W. E., Regier, D. A., Rae, D. S., Manderscheid, R. W., & Locke, B. Z. (1993). Use of services by persons with mental and addictive disorders. *Archives of General Psychiatry, 50,* 95–107.

Nasby, W., & Kihlstrom, J. F. (1986). Cognitive assessment of personality and psychopathology. In R. E. Ingram (Ed.), *Information processing approaches to clinical psychology.* New York: Academic Press.

Nathan, P. E. (1988). The addictive personality is the behavior of the addict. *Journal of Consulting and Clinical Psychology, 56,* 183–188.

Nathan, P. E., Marlatt, G. A., & Loberg, T. (Eds.). (1978). *Alcoholism: New directions in behavioral research and treatment.* New York: Plenum Press.

Nathan, S. G. (1986). The epidemiology of the *DSM-III* psychosexual dysfunctions. *Journal of Sex and Marital Therapy, 12,* 267–281.

National Center for Education Statistics. (1989). *Digest of education statistics.* Washington, DC: U.S. Department of Education. Office of Education Research and Improvement.

National Foundation for Brain Research. (1992). *The care of disorders of the brain.* Washington, DC: Author.

National Institute of Mental Health. (1985). *Electroconvulsive therapy: Consensus development conference statement.* Bethesda, MD: Office of Medical Applications of Research.

National Institute on Alcohol Abuse and Alcoholism. (1990). *Seventh special report to the U.S. Congress on alcohol and health from the secretary of health and human services.* U.S. Department of Health and Human Services.

National Institute on Drug Abuse. (1989). *1988 National Household Survey on Drug Abuse.* Rockville, MD: Author.

National Institute on Drug Abuse. (1992). *National Household Survey on Drug Abuse: Population estimates 1992.* Rockville, MD: Author.

National Institute on Drug Abuse. (1994). *National Household Survey on Drug Abuse: Population estimates 1994.* Rockville, MD: Author.

Neal, A. M., & Turner, S. M. (1991). Anxiety disorders research with African Americans: Current status. *Psychological Bulletin, 109,* 400–410.

Needles, D. J., & Abramson, L. Y. (1990). Positive life events, attributional style, and hopefulness: Testing a model of recovery from depression. *Journal of Abnormal Psychology, 99,* 156–165.

Nelles, W. B., & Barlow, D. H. (1988). Do children panic? *Clinical Psychology Review, 8,* 359–372.

Nemeroff, C. B., Krishnan, R. R., Reed, D., Leder, R., Beam, C., & Dunnick, N. R. (1992). Adrenal gland enlargement in major depression: A computed tomographic study. *Archives of General Psychiatry, 49,* 384–387.

Nesson, C. (1982, July 1). A needed verdict: Guilty but insane. *The New York Times,* p. A19.

Neugebauer, R. (1978). Treatment of the mentally ill in medieval and early modern England: A reappraisal. *Journal of the History of the Behavioral Sciences, 14,* 158–169.

Newberger, C. M., Melnicore, L. H., & Newberger, E. H. (1986). *The American family at crisis: Implications for children* (Vol. 16, No. 12). Chicago: Year Book Medical.

Newman, J. P., Kosson, D. S., & Patterson, C. M. (1992). Delay of gratification in psychopathic and nonpsychopathic offenders. *Journal of Abnormal Psychology, 101,* 630–636.

Newman, J. P., Patterson, C. M., Howland, E. W., & Nichols, S. L. (1990). Passive avoidance in psychopaths: The effects of reward. *Personality and Individual Differences, 11,* 1101–1114.

Newsome, C. D., Carr, E. A., & Rincover, A. (1974, April). *Identifying and using sensory reinforcers.* Paper presented at the meeting of the Western Psychological Association, San Francisco.

Ney, P. G., Fung, T., & Wickett, A. R. (1992). Causes of child abuse and neglect. *Canadian Journal of Psychiatry, 37,* 401–405.

Nezworski, T., & Wood, J. M. (1995). Narcissism in the comprehensive Rorschach system: An empirical review. *Clinical Psychology: Science and Practice.*

Nichols, M. P., & Schwartz, R. C. (1991). *Family therapy: Concepts and methods* (2nd ed.). Boston: Allyn and Bacon.

Nicholson, I. R., & Neufeld, R. W. J. (1993). Classification of the schizophrenias according to symptomatology: A two-factor model. *Journal of Abnormal Psychology, 102,* 259–270.

Nicolosi, A., Molinari, S., Musicco, M., Saracco, A., Ziliani, N., & Lazzarin, A. (1991). Positive modification of injecting behavior among intravenous heroin users from Milan and northern Italy, 1987–1989. *British Journal of Addiction, 86,* 91–102.

Nielsen, T. I. (1963). Volition: A new experimental approach. *Scandinavian Journal of Psychology, 4,* 225–230.

Nielson, P. E. (1960). A study in transsexualism. *Psychiatric Quarterly, 34,* 203–235.

Nietzel, M. T., & Harris, M. J. (1990). Relationship of dependency and achievement/autonomy to depression. *Clinical Psychology Review, 10,* 279–297.

Nigg, J. T., & Goldsmith, H. H. (1994). Genetics of personality disorders: Perspectives from personality and psychopathology research. *Psychological Bulletin, 115,* 346–380.

Nijinsky, R. (1936). *Nijinsky.* New York: Simon & Schuster.

Nijinsky, V. (1936). *The diary of Vaslav Nijinsky* (R. Nijinsky, Ed.). New York: Simon & Schuster.

Nisbett, R. E. (1968). Taste, deprivation, and weight determinants of eating behavior. *Journal of Personality and Social Psychology, 10,* 107–116.

Nisbett, R. E., & Ross, L. (1980). *Human inference: Strategies and shortcomings of social judgment.* Englewood Cliffs, NJ: Prentice-Hall.

Nisbett, R. E., & Wilson, T. D. (1977). Telling more than we can know: Verbal reports on mental processes. *Psychological Review, 84,* 231–259.

Nolen-Hoeksema, S. (1987). Sex differences in unipolar depression: Evidence and theory. *Psychological Bulletin, 101,* 259–282.

Nolen-Hoeksema, S. (1991). Responses to depression and their effects on the duration of depressive episodes. *Journal of Abnormal Psychology, 100,* 569–582.

Nolen-Hoeksema, S., & Girgus, J. S. (1994). The emergence of gender differences in depression during adolescence. *Psychological Bulletin, 115,* 424–443.

Nolen-Hoeksema, S., Girgus, J. S. & Seligman, M. E. P. (1992). Predictors and consequences of childhood depressive symptoms: A 5-year longitudinal study. *Journal of Abnormal Psychology, 101,* 405–422.

Nordquist, V. M., & Wahler, R. G. (1973). Naturalistic treatment of an autistic child. *Journal of Applied Behavior Analysis, 6,* 79–87.

Nordström, P., & Asberg, M. (1992). Suicide risk and serotonin. *International Clinical Psychopharmacology, 6,* 12–21.

Norris, F. H. (1992). Epidemiology of trauma: Frequency and impact of different potentially traumatic events on different demographic groups. *Journal of Consulting and Clinical Psychology, 60,* 409–418.

Noyes, R., Jr., Clarkson, C., Crowe, R. R., Yates, W. R., & McChesney, C. M. (1987). A family study of generalized anxiety disorder. *American Journal of Psychiatry, 144,* 1019–1024.

Noyes, R., Jr., Woodman, C., Garvey, M. J., Cook, B. L., Suelzer, M., Clancy, J., & Anderson, D. J. (1992). Generalized anxiety disorder vs. panic disorder: Distinguishing characteristics and patterns of comorbidity. *Journal of Nervous and Mental Disease, 180,* 369–379.

Nuechterlein, K. H. (1985). Converging evidence for vigilance deficit as a vulnerability indicator for schizophrenic disorders. In M. Alpert (Ed.)., *Controversies in schizophrenia* (pp. 175–198). New York: Guilford Press.

Nuechterlein, K. H., & Dawson, M. E. (1984a). A heuristic vulnerability/stress model of schizophrenic episodes. *Schizophrenia Bulletin, 10,* 300–312.

Nuechterlein, K. H., & Dawson, M. E. (1984b). Information processing and attentional functioning in the developmental course of schizophrenic disorders. *Schizophrenia Bulletin, 10,* 160–203.

Nuechterlein, K. H., Dawson, M. E., Gitlin, M., Ventura, J., Goldstein, M. J., Snyder, K. S., Yee, C. M., & Mintz, J. (1992). Developmental processes in schizophrenic disorders: Longitudinal studies of vulnerability and stress. *Schizophrenia Bulletin, 18,* 387–425.

Nunes, D. (1975, September 15). The anguish behind the three faces of Eve. *New York Post,* pp. 4, 26.

Nunnally, J. (1978). *Psychometric theory* (2nd ed.). New York: McGraw-Hill.

O'Connor v. Donaldson, 95 S.Ct. 2486 (1975).

O'Connor, J. F., & Stern, L. O. (1972). Results of treatment in functional sexual disorders. *New York State Journal of Medicine, 72*(15), 1927–1934.

Oesterhed, J. D., McKenna, M. S., & Gould, N. B. (1987). Group psychotherapy for bulimia: A critical review. *International Journal of Group Psychotherapy, 37,* 163–184.

Olds, D., Henderson, C. (1989). The prevention of child maltreatment. In D. Cicchetti & V. Carlson (Eds.), *Child maltreatment* (pp. 722–763). New York: Cambridge University Press.

O'Leary, K. D. (1978). The operant and social psychology of token systems. In A. C. Catania & T. A. Brigham (Eds.), *Handbook of applied behavior analysis: Social and instructional processes.* New York: Irvington.

O'Leary, K. D., & Wilson, G. T. (1975). *Behavior therapy—application and outcome.* Englewood Cliffs, NJ: Prentice-Hall.

O'Leary, S. G., & Pelham, W. E. (1978). Behavior therapy and withdrawal of stimulant medication in hyperactive children. *Pediatrics, 61,* 211–217.

Olsson, P. A. (1989). Psychodrama and group therapy approaches to alexithymia. In D. A. Halperin (Ed.), *Group psychodynamics: New paradigms and new perspectives.* Chicago: Year Book Medical.

Oltman, J., & Friedman, S. (1967). Parental deprivation in psychiatric conditions. *Distribution of the Nervous System, 28,* 298–303.

Olton, D. S., & Noonberg, A. R. (1980). *Biofeedback: Clinical applications in behavioral medicine.* Englewood Cliffs, NJ: Prentice-Hall.

Oren, D. A., & Rosenthal, N. E. (1992). Seasonal affective disorders. In E. S. Paykel (Ed.), *Handbook of affective disorders* (2nd ed., pp. 551–568). New York: Guilford Press.

Orlinsky, D. E., Grawe, K., & Parks, B. K. (1994). Process and outcome in psychotherapy—noch einmal. In A. E. Bergin & S. L. Garfield (Eds.), *Handbook of psychotherapy and behavior change* (4th ed., pps. 270–376). New York: Wiley.

Orlinsky, D. E., & Howard, K. I. (1987). A generic model of psychotherapy. *Journal of Integrative and Eclectic Psychotherapy, 6,* 6–27.

Ornitz, E. M. (1974). The modulation of sensory input and motor output in autistic children. *Journal of Autism and Childhood Schizophrenia, 4,* 197–215.

Ornitz, E. M., & Ritvo, E. R. (1968). Perceptual inconstancy in early infantile autism. *Archives of General Psychiatry, 18,* 76–98.

Osgood, C., Luria, Z., Jeans, R., & Smith S. (1976). The three faces of Evelyn: A case report. *Journal of Abnormal Psychology, 85,* 247–286.

Otto, M. W., Pollack, M. H., Sachs, G. S., Reiter, S. R., Meltzer-Brody, S., & Rosenbaum, J. F. (1993). Discontinuation of benzodiazepine treatment: Efficacy of cognitive-behavioral therapy for patients with panic disorder. *American Journal of Psychiatry, 150,* 1485–1490.

Overholser, J., Evans, S., & Spirito, A. (1990). Sex differences and their relevance to primary prevention of adolescent suicide. *Death Studies, 14,* 391–402.

Overton, D. A. (1966). State-dependent learning produced by depressant and atropine-like drugs. *Psychopharmacologia, 10,* 6–31.

Palmer, T. (1984). Treatment and the role of classification: Review of basics. *Crime and Delinquency, 30,* 245–267.

Parker, G. (1979). Reported parental characteristics of agoraphobics and social phobics. *British Journal of Psychiatry, 135,* 550–560.

Parker, G. (1992). Early environment. In E. S. Paykel (Ed.), *Handbook of affective disorders* (2nd ed., pp. 171–184). New York: Guilford Press.

Parker, G., & Lipscombe, P. (1980). The relevance of early parental experiences to adult dependency, hypochondriasis and utilization of primary physicians. *British Journal of Medical Psychology, 53,* 355–363.

Parker, J. G., & Asher, S. R. (1987). Peer relations and later personal adjustment: Are low-accepted children at risk? *Psychological Bulletin, 102,* 357–389.

Parnas, J., Cannon, T. D., Jacobsen, B., Schulsinger, H., Schulsinger, F., & Mednick, S. A. (1993). Lifetime *DSM-III-R* diagnostic outcomes in the offspring of schizophrenic mothers: Results from the Copenhagen high-risk study. *Archives of General Psychiatry, 50,* 707–714.

Parnas, J., Teasdale, T. W., & Schulsinger, H. (1985). Institutional rearing and diagnostic outcome in children of schizophrenic mothers: A prospective high-risk study. *Archives of General Psychiatry, 42,* 762–769.

Parry, G., & Brewin, C. R. (1988). Cognitive style and depression: Symptom-related, event-related or independent provoking factor? *British Journal of Clinical Psychology, 27,* 23–35.

Patterson, C. M., & Newman, J. P. (1993). Reflectivity and learning from aversive events: Toward a psychological mechanism for the syndromes of disinhibition. *Psychological Review, 100,* 716–736.

Patterson, G. R. (1982). *A social learning approach: Vol. 3. Coercive family processes.* Eugene, OR: Castilia.

Patterson, G. R., & Hops, H. (1972). Coercion: A game for two: Intervention techniques for marital conflict. In R. Ulrich & P. Mountjoy (Eds.), *The experimental analysis of social behavior.* New York: Appleton-Century-Crofts.

Patton, R. B., & Sheppard, J. A. (1956). Intercranial tumors found at autopsy in mental patients. *American Journal of Psychiatry, 113,* 319–324.

Paul, G. L. (1969a). Outcome of systematic desensitization: I. Background procedures and uncontrolled reports of individual treatment. In C. M. Franks (Ed.), *Behavior therapy: Appraisal and status.* New York: McGraw-Hill.

Paul, G. L. (1969b). Outcome of systematic desensitization: II. Controlled investigation of individual treatment technique variations and current status. In C. M.

Franks (Ed.), *Behavior therapy: Appraisal and status.* New York: McGraw-Hill.

Paul, G. L., & Lentz, R. J. (1977). *Psychosocial treatment of chronic mental patients: Milieu versus social-learning programs.* Cambridge, MA: Harvard University Press.

Paul, G. L., & Menditto, A. A. (1992). Effectiveness of inpatient treatment programs for mentally ill adults in public psychiatric facilities. *Applied & Preventive Psychology, 1,* 41–63.

Paul, S. M. (1977). Movement, mood and madness: A biological model of schizophrenia. In J. D. Maser & M. E. P. Seligman (Eds.), *Psychopathology: Experimental Models.* San Francisco: W. H. Freeman.

Paul, W. M., Gonsiorek, J. C., & Hotvedt, M. E. (Eds.). (1982). *Homosexuality.* Beverly Hills, CA: Sage.

Pauls, D. L. (1990). Tourette syndrome and obsessive-compulsive disorder: Familial relationships. In M. A. Jenike, L. Baer, & W. E. Minichiello (Eds.), *Obsessive-compulsive disorders: Theory and management.* (2nd ed, pp. 149–153). Chicago: Mosby-Yearbook Medical.

Pauly, I. B. (1968). The current status of the change of sex operation. *Journal of Nervous and Mental Disease, 147,* 460–471.

Paykel, E. S. (1979a). Life stress. In L. D. Hankoff & B. Einsidler (Eds.), *Suicide: Theory and clinical aspects.* Littleton, MA: PSG.

Paykel, E. S. (1979b). Recent life events in the development of the depressive disorders. In R. A. Depue (Ed.), *The psychobiology of the depressive disorders.* New York: Academic Press.

Paykel, E. S., & Cooper, Z. (1992). Life events and social stress. In E. S. Paykel (Ed.), *Handbook of affective disorders.* (2nd ed., pp. 149–170). New York: Guilford Press.

Payne, P., & Halford, W. K. (1990). Generalization of social skills training with schizophrenic patients living in the community. *Behaviourial Psychotherapy, 18,* 49–64.

Pearlin, L. I., Mullan, J. T., Semple, S. J., & Skaff, M. M. (1990). Caregiving and the stress process: An overview of concepts and their measures. *Gerontologist, 30,* 583–594.

Peck, C. P. (1986). A public mental health issue. Risk-taking behavior and compulsive gambling. *American Psychologist, 41,* 461–465.

Pelham, W. E., Gnagy, E. M., Greenslade, K. E., & Milich, R. (1992). Teacher ratings of *DSM-III-R* symptoms for the disruptive behavior disorders. *Journal of the American Academy of Child and Adolescent Psychiatry, 31,* 210–218.

Pelham, W. E., & Ross, A. O. (1977). Selective attention in children with reading problems: A developmental study of incidental learning. *Journal of Abnormal Child Psychology, 5,* 1–8.

Pennebaker, J. W. (1990). *Opening up: The healing power of confiding in others.* New York: Morrow.

Pennebaker, J. W. (1993). Putting stress into words: Health, linguistic and therapeutic implications. *Behavior Research and Therapy, 31,* 539–548.

Pennebaker, J. W., Kiecolt-Glaser, J., & Glaser, R. (1988). Disclosure of traumas and immune function: Health implications for psychotherapy. *Journal of Consulting and Clinical Psychology, 56,* 239–245.

Pennebaker, J. W., & Watson, D. (1991). The psychology of somatic symptoms. In L. J. Kirmayer & J. M. Robbins (Eds.), *Current concepts of somatization: Research and clinical perspectives* (pp. 21–35). Washington, DC: American Psychiatric Press.

Perlin, M. L. (1993–1994). Hospitalized patients and the right to sexual interaction: Beyond the last frontier? *NYU Review of Law and Social Change, 20,* 517–547.

Perls, F. S. (1970). Four lectures. In J. Fagan & I. L. Shepherd (Eds.), *Gestalt therapy now: Therapy, techniques, applications.* Palo Alto, CA: Science and Behavior Books.

Perls, F. S., Hefferline, R. F., & Goodman, P. (1951). *Gestalt therapy: Excitement and growth in the human personality.* New York: Julian Press.

Perry, P. J., Miller, D. D., Arndt, S. V., & Cadoret, R. J. (1991). Clozapine and norclozapine plasma concentrations and clinical response of treatment-refractory schizophrenic patients. *American Journal of Psychiatry, 148,* 231–235.

Perry, S., Frances, A., & Clarkin, J. (1990). *A* DSM-III-R *casebook of treatment selection.* New York: Brunner/Mazel.

Perry, W., & Braff, D. L. (1994). Information-processing deficits and thought disorder in schizophrenia. *American Journal of Psychiatry, 151,* 363–367.

Perske, R. (1973). About sexual development. *Mental Retardation, 11,* 6–8.

Peterson, C., Semmel, A., von Baeyer, C., Abramson, L. Y., Metalsky, G. I., & Seligman, M. E. P. (1982). The attributional style questionnaire. *Cognitive Therapy and Research, 6,* 287–299.

Peterson, G. (1991). Children coping with trauma: Diagnosis of "dissociation identity disorder." *Dissociation, 4,* 152–164.

Phillips, K. A. (1991). Body dysmorphic disorder: The distress of imagined ugliness. *American Journal of Psychiatry, 148,* 1138–1149.

Phillips, K. A., McElroy, S. L., Keck, P. E., Jr., Pope, H. G., Jr., & Hudson, J. I. (1993). Body dysmorphic disorder: 30 cases of imagined ugliness. *American Journal of Psychiatry, 150,* 302–308.

Pickar, D. (1988). Perspectives on a time-dependent model of neuroleptic action. *Schizophrenia Bulletin, 14,* 255–265.

Pickar, D., Breier, A., Hsiao, J. K., Doran, A. R., Wolkowitz, O. M., Pato, C. N., Konicki, P. E., & Potter, W. Z. (1990). Cerebrospinal fluid and plasma monoamine metabolites and their relation to psychosis: Implications for regional brain dysfunction in schizophrenia. *Archives of General Psychiatry, 47,* 641–648.

Pickar, D., Owen, A. R., Litman, R. E., Konicki, P. E., Gutierrez, R., & Rapaport, M. H. (1992). Clinical and biologic response to clozapine in patients with schizophrenia: Crossover comparison with fluphenazine. *Archives of General Psychiatry, 49,* 345–353.

Pillard, R. C., & Weinrich, J. D. (1987). The periodic table model of the gender transpositions: Part I. A theory based on masculinization and defeminization of the brain. *Journal of Sex Research, 23*(4), 425–454.

Pilowsky, I. (1990). The concept of abnormal illness behavior. *Psychosomatics, 31,* 207–213.

Pinel, P. (1967). *A treatise on insanity* (D. D. Davis, Trans.). New York: Hafner. (Original work published 1801)

Pines, M. (1982a, June). Infant-stim. It's changing the lives of handicapped kids. *Psychology Today,* pp. 48–52.

Pines, M. (1982b, April 16). Recession is linked to far-reaching psychological harm. *The New York Times,* p. C1.

Piper, W. E., Joyce, A. S., McCallum, M., & Azim, H. F. A. (1993). Concentration and correspondence of transference interpretations in short-term psychotherapy. *Journal of Consulting and Clinical Psychology, 61,* 586–595.

Pithers, W. D., & Cumming, G. F. (1989). *Can relapse be prevented? Initial outcome data from the Vermont treatment program for sexual aggressors.* New York: Guilford Press.

Pitman, R. K. (1988). Post-traumatic stress disorder, conditioning, and network theory. *Psychiatric Annals, 18,* 182–189.

Pitman, R. K. (1989). Editorial: Post-traumatic stress disorder, hormones, and memory. *Biological Psychiatry, 26,* 221–223.

Pitman, R. K., Green, R. C., Jenike, M. A., et al. (1987). Clinical comparison of Tourette syndrome and obsessive-compulsive disorder. *American Journal of Psychiatry, 144,* 1166–1171.

Pitman, R. K., Orr, S. P., Forgue, D. F., Altman, B., de Jong, J. B., & Herz, L. R. (1990). Psychophysiologic responses to combat imagery of Vietnam veterans with posttraumatic stress disorder versus other anxiety disorders. *Journal of Abnormal Psychology, 99,* 49–54.

Plomin, R., & Daniels, D. (1986). Genetics and shyness. In W. H. Jones, J. M. Cheek, & S. R. Briggs (Eds.), *Shyness: Perspectives on research and treatment* (pp. 63–90). New York: Plenum Press.

Plomin, R., & Rende, R. (1991). Human behavioral genetics. *Annual Review of Psychology, 42,* 161–190.

Polak, P. R. (1978). A comprehensive system of alternatives to psychiatric hospitalization. In L. I. Stein & M. A. Test (Eds.), *Alternatives to mental hospital treatment.* New York: Plenum Press.

Polivy, J., & Herman, C. P. (1985). Dieting and binging: A causal analysis. *American Psychologist, 40,* 193–201.

Pollard, C. A., Pollard, H. J., & Corn, K. J. (1989). Panic onset and major events in the lives of agoraphobics: A test of contiguity. *Journal of Abnormal Psychology, 98,* 318–321.

Pollock, V. E., Volavka, J., Goodwin, D. W., Gabrielli, W. F., Mednick, S. A., Knop, J., & Schulsinger, F. (1988). Pattern reversal visual evoked potentials after alcohol administration among men at risk for alcoholism. *Psychiatry Research, 26,* 191–202.

Pollock, V. E., Volavka, J., Goodwin, D. W., Mednick, S. A., Gabrielli, W. F., Knop, J., & Schulsinger, F. (1983). The EEG after alcohol administration in men at risk for alcoholism. *Archives of General Psychiatry, 40,* 857–861.

Pope, H. G., & Katz, D. L. (1990). *Journal of Clinical Psychology, 51.*

Popper, K. (1945).*The open society and its enemies.* London: Routledge, Kegan Paul.

Prange, A. J., Jr., Lipton, M. A., Nemeroff, C. B., & Wilson, I. C. (1977). Minireview—the role of hormones in depression. *Life Sciences, 20,* 1305–1318.

Prange, A. J., Jr., Wilson, I. C., Lynn, C. W., Lacoe, B. A., & Stikeleather, R. A. (1974). L-Tryptophan in mania—contribution to a permissive hypothesis of affective disorders. *Archives of General Psychiatry, 30,* 56–62.

Prescott, C. A., & Gottesman, I. I. (1993). Genetically mediated vulnerability to schizophrenia. *Psychiatric Clinics of North America, 16,* 245–267.

Preu, P. W. (1944). The concept of the psychopathic personality. In J. McV. Hunt (Ed.), *Personality and the behavior disorders* (Vol. 2). New York: Ronald Press.

Price, C., & Cuellar, I. (1981). Effects of language and related variables on the expression of psychopathology of Mexican Americans. *Hispanic Journal of Behavioral Sciences, 3,* 145–160.

Price, J., & Hess, N. C. (1979). *Australian and New Zealand Journal of Psychiatry, 13,* 63–66.

Price, R. A., Kidd, K. K., & Weissman, M. M. (1987). Early onset (under age 30 years) and panic disorder as markers for etiologic homogeneity in major depression. *Archives of General Psychiatry, 44,* 434–440.

Price, R. H. (1978). *Abnormal behavior: Perspectives in conflict* (2nd ed.). New York: Holt, Rinehart and Winston.

Prien, R. F., & Gelenberg, A. J. (1989). Alternatives to lithium for preventive treatment of bipolar disorder. *American Journal of Psychiatry, 146,* 840–848.

Prieto, S. L., Cole, D. A., & Tageson, C. W. (1992). Depressive self-schemas in clinic and nonclinic children. *Cognitive Therapy and Research, 16,* 521–534.

Prince, M. (1905). *The dissociation of personality.* New York: Longman.

Prince, V. (1978). Transsexuals and pseudotranssexuals. *Archives of Sexual Behavior, 7*(4), 263–272.

Prior, M., & Gajzago, C. (1974, August 1). Early signs of autism. *Medical Journal of Australia.*

Prior, M., Gajzago, C., & Knox, D. (1976). An epidemiological study of autistic and psychotic children in the four eastern states of Australia. *Australian and New Zealand Journal of Psychiatry, 10*(2), 173–184.

Prochaska, J. O., & DiClemente, C. C. (1984). *The transtheoretical approach: Crossing traditional boundaries of therapy.* Homewood, IL: Dow Jones/Irwin.

Prochaska, J. O., DiClemente, C. C., & Norcross, J. C. (1992). In search of how people change: Applications to addictive behaviors. *American Psychologist, 47,* 1102–1114.

Prouty, G. (1976). Pre-therapy—a method of treating preexpressive psychotic and retarded patients. *Psychotherapy: Theory, Research, and Practice, 13,* 290–294.

Putnam, F. W. (1984). The psychophysiologic investigation of multiple personality disorder: A review. *Psychiatric Clinics of North America, 7,* 31–39.

Putnam, F. W. (1989). *Diagnosis and treatment of multiple personality disorder.* New York: Guilford Press.

Putnam, F. W. (1991a). Dissociative disorders in children and adolescents: A developmental perspective. *Psychiatric Clinics of North America, 14,* 519–531.

Putnam, F. W. (1991b). Recent research on multiple personality disorder. *Psychiatric Clinics of North America, 14,* 489–501.

Putnam, F. W., Guroff, J. J., Silberman, E. K., Barban, L., & Post, R. M. (1986). The clinical phenomenology of multiple personality disorder: Review of 100 recent cases. *Journal of Clinical Psychiatry, 47,* 285–293.

Putnam, F. W., & Loewenstein, R. J. (1993). Treatment of multiple personality disorder: A survey of current practices. *American Journal of Psychiatry, 150,* 1048–1052.

Quindlen, A. (1994, April 30). Public and private: Second-stage smoke. *The New York Times,* p. 23.

Rabkin, J. G., Williams, J. B., Remien, R. H., Goetz, R., Kertzner, R., & Gorman (1991). Depression, distress, lymphocyte subsets, and human immunodeficiency virus symptoms on two occasions in HIV-positive homosexual men. *Archives of General Psychiatry, 48,* 111–119.

Rachman, S., Levitt, K., & Lopatka, C. (1987). Panic: The links between cognitions and bodily symptoms—I. *Behaviour Research and Therapy, 25,* 411–423.

Rachman, S., Lopatka, C., & Levitt, K. (1988). Experimental analyses of panic—II. Panic patients. *Behaviour Research and Therapy, 26,* 33–40.

Rachman, S. J., & Hodgson, R. J. (1980). *Obsessions and compulsions.* Englewood Cliffs, NJ: Prentice-Hall.

Rada, R. T. (1978). Psychological factors in rapist behavior. In R. T. Rada (Ed.), *Clinical aspects of the rapist.* New York: Grune & Stratton.

Ragland, D. R., & Brand, R. J. (1988). Type A behavior and mortality from coronary heart disease. *New England Journal of Medicine, 318,* 65–69.

Raiche, M. E. (1994). Visualizing the mind. *Scientific American, 270*(4), 58–64.

Raker, J. W., Wallace, A. F., & Raymer, J. F. (1956). *Emergency medical care in disasters* (Disaster Study No. 6). Washington, DC: National Academy of Sciences. (National Resources Council Publication No. 457)

Ram, R., Bromet, E. J., Eaton, W. W., Pato, C., & Schwartz, J. E. (1992). The natural course of schizophrenia: A review of first-admission studies. *Schizophrenia Bulletin, 18,* 185–207.

Rapaport, D., Gill, M., & Schaefer, R. (1968). *Diagnostic psychological testing.* New York: International Universities Press.

Rapee, R. M., & Barlow, D. H. (Eds.). (1991). *Chronic anxiety: Generalized anxiety disorder and mixed anxiety-depression.* New York: Guilford Press.

Rapee, R. M., & Barlow, D. H. (1993). Generalized anxiety disorder, panic disorder, and the phobias. In P. B. Sutker & H. E. Adams (Eds.). *Comprehensive handbook of psychopathology* (2nd ed., pp. 109–127). New York: Plenum Press.

Rapin, I. (1991). Autistic children: Diagnosis and clinical features. *Pediatrics, 87* (Suppl.), 751–760.

Raskin, N. H., Hosobuchi, Y., & Lamb, S A. (1987). Headache may arise from perturbation of brain. *Headache, 27,* 416–420.

Rasmussen, S. A., & Eisen, J. L. (1992). The epidemiology and clinical features of obsessive compulsive disorder. *Psychiatric Clinics of North America, 15,* 743–758.

Ray, O. S. (1983). *Drugs, society, and human behavior.* St. Louis, MO: Mosby.

Raz, S. (1993). Structural cerebral pathology in schizophrenia: Regional or diffuse? *Journal of Abnormal Psychology, 102,* 445–452.

Redlich, F. C., & Freedman, D. X. (1966). *The theory and practice of psychiatry.* New York: Basic Books.

Redmond, D. E. (1977). Alterations in the function of the nucleus locus coeruleus: A possible model for studies of anxiety. In I. Hanin & E. Usdin (Eds.), *Animal models in psychiatry and neurology.* New York: Pergamon Press.

Redmond, D. E. (1979). New and old evidence for the involvement of a brain norepinephrine system in anxiety. In W. E. Fann, I. Karacan, A. D. Pokorny, et al. (Eds.), *Phenomenology and treatment of anxiety.* New York: SP Medical & Scientific Books.

Reed, G. (1988). *The psychology of anomalous experience* (rev. ed.). Buffalo, NY: Prometheus.

Reed, P. (1987). Spirituality and well-being in terminally ill hospitalized adults. *Research in Nursing and Health, 10,* 335–344.

Regier, D. A., Boyd, J. H., Burke, J. D., Jr., Rae, D. S., Myers, J. K., Kramer, M., Robins, L. N., George, L. K., Karno, M., & Locke, B. Z. (1988). One-month prevalence of mental disorders in the United States. *Archives of General Psychiatry, 45,* 977–986.

Reich, J., & Yates, W. (1988). Family history of psychiatric disorders in social phobia. *Comprehensive Psychiatry, 2,* 72–75.

Reid, A. H. (1972a). Psychoses in adult mental defectives: I. Manic depressive psychoses. *British Journal of Psychiatry, 120,* 205–212.

Reid, A. H. (1972b). Psychoses in adult mental defectives: II. Schizophrenic and paranoid psychoses. *British Journal of Psychiatry, 120,* 213–218.

Reid, W. H. (1981). The antisocial personality and related symptoms. In J. R. Lion (Ed.), *Personality disorders: Diagnosis and management* (2nd ed.). Baltimore: Williams & Wilkins.

Reisner, R. (1985). *Law and the mental health system.* St. Paul, MN: West.

Reiss, A. J., Jr., & Roth, J. A. (Eds.). (1993). *Understanding and preventing violence.* Washington, DC: National Academy Press.

Reiss, S. (1985). The mentally retarded, emotionally disturbed adult. In M. Sigman (Ed.), *Children with emotional disorders and developmental disabilities.* New York: Grune & Stratton.

Reiss, S. (1992). Assessment of psychopathology in persons with mental retardation. In J. L. Matson & R. P. Barrett (Eds.), *Psychopathology and mental retardation.* New York: Grune & Stratton.

Reiss, S., & Benson, B. A. (1985). Psychosocial correlates of depression in mentally retarded adults: I. Minimal social support and stigmatization. *American Journal of Medical Deficiency, 89,* 331–337.

Reiss, S., Levitan, G. W., & Szysko, J. (1982). Emotional disturbance and mental retardation: Diagnostic overshadowing. *American Journal of Mental Deficiency, 86*(6), 567–574.

Reiss, S., Peterson, R. A., Gursky, D. M., & McNally, R. J. (1986). Anxiety sensitivity, anxiety frequency, and the prediction of fearfulness. *Behaviour Research and Therapy, 24,* 1–8.

Reiss, S., & Valenti-Hein, D. (1990). *Reiss scales for children's dual diagnosis test manual.* Worthington, OH: International Diagnostic Systems.

Rekers, G. A., & Lovaas, O. I. (1974). Behavioral treatment of deviant sex-role behaviors in a male child. *Journal of Applied Behavior Analysis, 7,* 173–190.

Ribeiro, S. C. M., Tandon, R., Grunhaus, L., & Greden, J. F. (1993). The DST as a predictor of outcome in depression: A meta-analysis. *American Journal of Psychiatry, 150,* 1618–1629.

Rich, C. L., Warsradt, M. D., Nemiroff, R. A., Fowler, R. C., & Young, D. (1991). Suicide, stressors, and the life cycle. *American Journal of Psychiatry, 148,* 534–527.

Richards, R. L., Kinney, D. K., Lunde, I., et al. (1988). Creativity in manic-depressives, cyclothymes, their normal relatives and control subjects. *Journal of Abnormal Psychology, 97,* pp. 281–288.

Richens, A., & Perucca, E. (1993). Clinical pharmacology and medical treatment. In J. Laidlaw, A. Richens, & D. Chadwick (Eds.), *A textbook of epilepsy* (pp. 495–559). Edinburgh: Churchill Livingstone.

Rickels, K., Schweizer, E., Case, W. G., & Greenblatt, D. J. (1990). Long-term therapeutic use of benzodiazepines: I. Effects of abrupt discontinuation. *Archives of General Psychiatry, 47,* 899–907.

Riddle, M. A., Schaill, L., King, R., et al. (1990). Obsessive compulsive disorder in children and adolescents: Phenomenology and family history. *Journal of the American Academy of Child and Adolescent Psychiatry, 29,* 766–772.

Riether, A. M., & Stoudemire, A. (1988). Psychogenic fugue states: A review. *Southern Medical Journal, 81,* 568–571.

Riggins v. Nevada, 112 S. Ct. 1810 (1992).

Riggs, D. S., Dancu, C. V., Gershuny, B. S., Greenberg, D., & Foa, E. B. (1992). Anger and post-traumatic stress disorder in female crime victims. *Journal of Traumatic Stress, 5,* 613–625.

Riggs, D. S., Foa, E. B., Rothbaum, B. O., & Murdock, T. (1991). Post-traumatic stress disorder following rape and non-sexual assault: A predictive model. Unpublished manuscript.

Riley, A. J., Goodman, R. E., Kellett, J. M., Orr, R. (1989). Double blind trial of yohimbine hydrochloride in the treatment of erection inadequacy. *Sexual and Marital Therapy, 4*(1), 17–26.

Rimland, B. (1973). High-dosage levels of certain vitamins in the treatment of children with severe mental disorders. In D. Hawkins & L. Pauling (Eds.), *Orthomolecular psychiatry.* San Francisco: Freeman.

Rimland, B. (1974). An orthomolecular study of psychotic children. *Orthomolecular Psychiatry, 3,* 371–377.

Rimland, B. (1991, Winter). Update: Sound sensitivity/auditory training. *Autism Research Review International, 5.*

Ritvo, E. R. (Ed.). (1976). *Autism: Diagnosis, current research, and management.* New York: Spectrum.

Roberts, J. E., & Monroe, S. M. (1994). A multidimensional model of self-esteem in depression. *Clinical Psychology Review, 14,* 161–181.

Robins, L. N. (1966). *Deviant children grow up.* Baltimore: Williams & Wilkins.

Robins, L. N. (1979). Follow-up studies. In H. C. Quay & J. S. Werry (Eds.), *Psychopathological disorders of childhood* (2nd ed.). New York: Wiley.

Robins, L. N. (1991). Conduct disorder. *Journal of Child Psychology and Psychiatry and Allied Disciplines, 32,* 193–212.

Robins, L. N., Helzer, J. E., Croughan, J., & Ratcliff, K. S. (1981). National Institute of Mental Health diagnostic interview schedule. *Archives of General Psychiatry, 38,* 381–389.

Robins, L. N., Helzer, J. E., Przybeck, T. R., & Regier, D. A. (1988). Alcohol disorders in the community: A report from the Epidemiologic Catchment area. In R. M. Rose and J. Barrett (Eds.), *Alcoholism: Origins and outcome* (pp. 15–28). New York: Raven Press.

Robins, L. N., Helzer, J. E., Weissman, M. M., Orvaschel, H., Gruenberg, E., Burke, J. D., & Regier, D. A. (1984). Lifetime prevalence of specific psychiatric disorders in three sites. *Archives of General Psychiatry, 41,* 949–958.

Robins, L. N., & Price, R. K. (1991). Adult disorders predicted by childhood conduct problems: Results from the NIMH epidemiologic catchment area project. *Psychiatry, 54,* 116–132.

Robins, L. N., Tipp, J., & Przybeck, T. (1991). Antisocial personality. In L. N. Robins & D. A. Regier (Eds.), *Psychiatric disorders in America* (pp. 258–290). New York: Free Press.

Robinson, D. N. (1980). *Law and psychology: Can justice survive the social sciences?* New York: Oxford.

Robinson, L. A., Berman, J. S., & Neimeyer, R. A. (1990). Psychotherapy for the treatment of depression: A comprehensive review of controlled outcome research. *Psychological Bulletin, 108,* 30–49.

Robinson, N. M., & Robinson, H. B. (1976). *The mentally retarded child, a psychological approach* (2nd ed.). New York: McGraw-Hill.

Rodin, G., & Voshort, K. (1986). Depression in the medically ill: An overview. *American Journal of Psychiatry, 143,* 696–705.

Rodin, J. (1977a). Bidirectional influences of emotionality, stimulus responsivity and metabolic events in obesity. In J. D. Maser & M. E. P. Seligman (Eds.), *Psychopathology: Experimental models.* San Francisco: Freeman.

Rodin, J. (1977b). Research on eating behavior and obesity: Where does it fit in personality and social psychology? *Personality and Social Psychology Bulletin, 3,* 335–355.

Rodin, J. (1981). Current status of the internal-external hypothesis for obesity: What went wrong? *American Psychologist, 36,* 361–372.

Rodin, J., & Salovey, P. (1989). Health psychology. *Annual Review of Psychology, 40,* 533–579.

Rodning, C., Beckwith, L., & Howard, J. (1992). Quality of attachments and home environments in children prenatally exposed to PCP and cocaine. *Development and Psychopathology, 3,* 351–366.

Roesch, R., & Golding, S. L. (1980). *Competency to stand trial.* Urbana: University of Illinois Press.

Rog, D. J., & Rausch, H. L. (1975). The psychiatric halfway house: How is it measuring up? *Community Mental Health Journal, 11,* 155–162.

Rogers, C. R. (1951). *Client-centered therapy: Its current practice, implications and theory.* Boston: Houghton Mifflin.

Rogers, C. R. (1955). Persons or science? A philosophical question. *American Psychologist, 10,* 267–278.

Rogers, C. R. (1959). A theory of therapy, personality, and interpersonal relationships, as developed in the client-centered framework. In S. Koch (Ed.), *Psychology: A study of a science* (Vol. 3). New York: Basic Books.

Rogers, C. R. (1980). *A way of being.* Boston: Houghton Mifflin.

Rogers, C. R., & Dymond, R. F. (Eds.)., (1954). *Psychotherapy and personality change: Coordinated studies in the client-centered approach.* Chicago: University of Chicago Press.

Rohde, P., Lewinsohn, P. M., & Seeley, J. R. (1990). Are people changed by the experience of having an episode of depression? A further test of the scar hypothesis. *Journal of Abnormal Psychology, 99,* 264–271.

Rohsenow, D. J. (1983). Drinking habits and expectancies about alcohol's effects for self versus others. *Journal of Consulting and Clinical Psychology, 51,* 752–756.

Rokeach, M. (1964). *The three Christs of Ypsilanti.* New York: Random House.

Rorschach, H. (1942). *Psychodiagnostics: A diagnostic test based on perception.* New York: Grune & Stratton.

Rose, R. J., & Chesney, M. A. (1986). Cardiovascular stress reactivity: A behavioral-genetic perspective. *Behavior Therapy, 17,* 314–323.

Rosen, G. M. (1987). Self-help treatment books and the commercialization of psychotherapy. *American Psychologist, 42,* 46–51.

Rosen, R. C., & Leiblum, S. R. (1989). Assessment and treatment of desire disorders. In S. R. Leiblum & R. C. Rosen (Eds.), *Principles and practice of sex therapy* (2nd ed., pp. 19–50). New York: Guilford Press.

Rosenbaum, J. F., & Gelenberg, A. J. (1991). Anxiety. In A. J. Gelenberg, E. L. Bassuk, & S. C. Schoonover (Eds.), *The practitioner's guide to psychoactive drugs* (3rd ed.). New York: Plenum Press.

Rosenblatt, A. (1984). Concepts of the asylum in the care of the mentally ill. *Hospital and Community Psychiatry, 35,* 244–250.

Rosenhan, D. L. (1973). On being sane in insane places. *Science, 179,* 250–258.

Rosenhan, D. L. (1975). The contextual nature of psychiatric diagnosis. *Journal of Abnormal Psychology, 84,* 442–452.

Rosenman, R. H., Brand, R. J., Jenkins, C. D., Friedman, M., Straus, R., & Wurm, M. (1975). Coronary heart disease in the Western Collaborative Group study: Final follow-up experience of 8½ years. *Journal of the American Medical Association, 8,* 872–877.

Rosenthal, D. (1970). *Genetic theory and abnormal behavior.* New York: McGraw-Hill.

Rosenthal, D., Wender, P. H., Kety, S. S., Schulsinger, F., Welner, J., & Ostergaard, L. (1968). Schizophrenics' offspring reared in adoptive homes. In D. Rosenthal & S. S. Kety (Eds.). *The transmission of schizophrenia.* Oxford: Pergamon Press.

Rosenthal, T., & Bandura, A. (1978). Psychological modeling: Theory and practice. In. S. L. Garfield & A. E. Bergin (Eds.), *Handbook of psychotherapy and behavior change: An empirical analysis* (2nd ed.). New York: Wiley.

Ross, C. A. (1991). Epidemiology of multiple personality disorder and dissociation. *Psychiatric Clinics of North America, 14,* 503–517.

Ross, C. A., Joshi, S., & Currie, R. (1991). Dissociative experiences in the general population: A factor analysis. *Hospital and Community Psychiatry, 42,* 297–301.

Ross, C. A., Miller, S. D., Reagor, P., Bjornson, L., Fraser, G. A., & Anderson, G. (1990). Structured interview data on 102 cases of multiple personality disorder from four centers. *American Journal of Psychiatry, 147,* 596–601.

Ross, H. E., Glaser, F. B., & Germanson, T. (1988). The prevalence of psychiatric disorders in patients with alcohol and other drug problems. *Archives of General Psychiatry, 45,* 1023–1031.

Ross, S. (1962). APA approved doctoral programs in clinical and in counseling psychology, 1962. *American Psychologist, 17,* 501–502.

Rosse, R. B., Kendrick, K., Wyatt, R. J., Isaac, A., & Deutsch, S. I. (1994). Gaze discrimination in patients with schizophrenia: Preliminary report. *American Journal of Psychiatry, 151,* 919–921.

Roth, L. (1979). A commitment law for patients, doctors, and lawyers. *American Journal of Psychiatry, 136,* 1121–1127.

Roth, S., Wayland, K., & Woolsey, M. (1988). Victimization history and victim-assailant relationship as factors in recovery from sexual trauma. In J. White (Chair), *Sexual aggression correlates, causes, and consequences.* Symposium conducted at the meeting of the Southeastern Psychological Association, New Orleans.

Rothbaum, B. O., Foa, E. B., Murdock, T., Riggs, D., & Walsh, W. (1990). *Post-traumatic stress disorder following rape.* Unpublished manuscript.

Rothbaum, B. O., Foa, E. B., Riggs, D. S., Murdock, T., & Walsh, W. (1992). A prospective examination of post-traumatic stress disorder in rape victims. *Journal of Traumatic Stress, 5,* 455–475.

Rotheram-Borus, M. J., Koopman C., & Haignere, C. (1991). Reducing HIV sexual risk behaviors among runaway adolescents. *Journal of the American Medical Association, 266,* 1237–1241.

Roueché, B. (1974, September 9). Annals of medicine: As empty as Eve. *The New Yorker,* pp. 84–100.

Roy, A. (1992). Genetics, biology, and suicide in the family. In R. W. Maris, A. L. Berman, J. T. Maltsberger, & R. I. Yufit (Eds.), *Assessment and prediction of suicide* (pp. 574–588). New York: Guilford Press.

Roy, A., Adinoff, B., Roehrich, L., Lamparski, D., Custer, R., Lorenz, V., Barbaccia, M., Guidotti, A., Costa, E., & Linnoila, M. (1988). Pathological gambling: A psychobiological study. *Archives of General Psychiatry, 45,* 369–373.

Roy, A., DeJong, J., Lamparski, D., Adinoff, B., George, T., Moore, V., Garnett, D., Kerich, M., & Linnoila, M. (1991). Mental disorders among alcoholics: Relationship to age of onset and cerebrospinal fluid neuropeptides. *Archives of General Psychiatry, 48,* 423–427.

Roy, A., DeJong, J., & Linnoila, M. (1989b). Extraversion in pathological gamblers: Correlates with indexes of noradrenergic function. *Archives of General Psychiatry, 46,* 679–681.

Rude, S. S., & Burnham, B. L. (1993). Do interpersonal and achievement vulnerabilities interact with congruent events to predict depression? Comparison of DEQ, SAS, DAS, and combined scales. *Cognitive Therapy and Research, 17,* 531–548.

Ruderman, A. J. (1986). Dietary restraint: A theoretical and empirical review. *Psychological Bulletin, 99,* 247–262.

Ruderman, A. J., & Wilson, G. T. (1979). Weight, restraint, cognitions, and counterregulation. *Behaviour Research and Therapy, 17,* 581–590.

Ruedrich, S. L., Chu, C., & Wadle, C. V. (1985). The amytal interview in the treatment of psychogenic amnesia. *Hospital and Community Psychiatry, 36,* 1045–1046.

Rusch, F. R., & Mithaug, D. E. (1980). *Vocational training for mentally retarded adults: A behavior analytic approach.* Champaign, IL: Research Press.

Rush, A. J., & Weissenburger, J. E. (1994). Melancholic symptom features and *DSM-IV. American Journal of Psychiatry, 151,* 489–498.

Russell, D. E. H. (1986). *The secret trauma: Incest in the lives of girls and women.* New York: Basic Books.

Rutenfanz, J., Haider, M., & Koller, M. (1985). Occupational health measures for nightworkers and shiftworkers. In S. Folkard & T. W. Monk (Eds.), *Hours of work: Temporal factors in work scheduling* (pp. 199–210). New York: Wiley.

Rutter, M. (1968). Concepts of autism: A review of research. *Journal of Child Psychology and Psychiatry, 9,* 1–25.

Rutter, M. (1971). The description and classification of infantile autism. In D. W. Churchill, G. D. Alpern, & M. K. DeMyer (Eds.), *Infantile autism.* Springfield, IL: Charles C Thomas.

Rutter, M. (1983). Cognitive deficits in the pathogenesis of autism. *Journal of Child Psychology and Psychiatry, 24,* 513–531.

Rutter, M. (1986). Child psychiatry: Looking 30 years ahead. *Journal of Child Psychology and Psychiatry, 27,* 803–840.

Rutter, M., & Lockyer, L. (1967). A five to fifteen year follow-up of infantile psychosis: I. Description of sample. *British Journal of Psychiatry, 113,* 1169–1182.

Sackeim, H. A., & Devanand, D. P. (1991). Dissociative disorders. In M. Hersen & S. M. Turner (Eds.), *Adult psychopathology and diagnosis* (2nd ed., pp. 279–322). New York: Wiley.

Sackeim, H. A., et al. (1982). Hemispheric asymmetry in the expression of positive and negative emotions: Neurologic evidence. *Archives of Neurology, 39,* 210–218.

Sacks, O. (1985). *The man who mistook his wife for a hat and other clinical tales.* New York: Summit Books.

Sadowski, C., & Kelley, M. L. (1993). Social problem solving in suicidal adolescents. *Journal of Consulting and Clinical Psychology, 61,* 121–127.

Safer, D. J., & Krager, J. M. (1988). A survey of medication treatment for hyperactive/inattentive students. *Journal of the American Medical Association, 260,* 2256–2258.

Safran, J. D. (1990a). Towards a refinement of cognitive therapy in light of interpersonal theory: I. Theory. *Clinical Psychology Review, 10,* 87–105.

Safran, J. D. (1990b). Towards a refinement of cognitive therapy in light of interpersonal theory: II. Practice. *Clinical Psychology Review, 10,* 107–121.

Saghir, M. T., & Robins, E. (1969). Homosexuality: I. Sexual behavior of the female homosexual. *Archives of General Psychiatry, 20,* 192–201.

Saghir, M. T., Robins, E., & Walbran, B. (1969). Homosexuality: II. Sexual behavior of the male homosexual. *Archives of General Psychiatry, 21,* 219–229.

St. George-Hyslop, P. H., et al. (1987). The genetic defect causing familial Alzheimer's disease maps on chromosome 21. *Science, 235,* 885–889.

Salkovskis, P. M., & Clark, D. M. (in press). Cognitive therapy for panic disorder. *Journal of Cognitive Psychotherapy.*

Salkovskis, P. M., & Warwick, H. M. C. (1986). Morbid preoccupations, health anxiety and reassurance: A cognitive-behavioural approach to hypochondriasis. *Behaviour Research and Therapy, 24,* 597–602.

Salter, A. (1949). *Conditioned reflex therapy.* New York: Farrar, Strauss.

Salthouse, T. A. (1985). Speed of behavior and its implications for cognition. In J. E. Birren & K. W. Scale (Eds.), *Handbook for the psychology of aging.* Englewood Cliffs, NJ: Prentice-Hall.

Salzman, C., & Lieff, J. (1974). Interviews with hallucinogenic drug discontinuers. *Journal of Psychedelic Drugs, 6*(3), 329–332.

Samson, J. A., Mirin, S. M., Hauser, S. T., Fenton, B. T., & Schildkraut, J. J. (1992). Learned helplessness and urinary MHPG levels in unipolar depression. *American Journal of Psychiatry, 149,* 806–809.

Sanderson, W. C., Rapee, R. M., & Barlow, D. H. (1989). The influence of an illusion of control on panic attacks induced via inhalation of 5.5% carbon dioxide-enriched air. *Archives of General Psychiatry, 46,* 157–162.

Sandifer, M. G., Jr., Pettus, C., & Quade, D. (1964). A study of psychiatric diagnosis. *Journal of Nervous and Mental Disease, 139,* 350–356.

Santiago, J. M., McCall-Perez, F., & Bachrach, L. J. (1985). Integrated services for chronic mental patients: Theoretical perspective and experimental results. *General Hospital Psychiatry, 7,* 309–315.

Sarason, I. G. (1976). A modeling and informational approach to delinquency. In E. Ribes-Inesta & A. Bandura (Eds.), *Analysis of delinquency and aggression.* Hillsdale, NJ: Erlbaum.

Sarrel, P. (1977). Biological aspects of sexual functioning. In R. Gemene & C. C. Wheeler (Eds.), *Progress in sexology* (pp. 227–244). New York: Plenum Press.

Satel, S. L., & Edell, W. S. (1991). Cocaine-induced paranoia and psychosis proneness. *American Journal of Psychiatry, 148,* 1708–1711.

Satir, V. (1967). *Conjoint family therapy* (rev. ed.). Palo Alto, CA: Science and Behavior Books.

Saunders, B. (1992). The imaginary companion experience in multiple personality disorder. *Dissociation, 5,* 159–162.

Sautter, F., McDermott, B., Garver, D. (1993). The course of *DSM-III-R* schizophreniform disorder. *Journal of Clinical Psychology, 49,* 339–344.

Saxena, S., & Prasad, K. (1989). *DSM-III* subclassifications of dissociative disorders applied to psychiatric outpatients in India. *American Journal of Psychiatry, 146,* 261–262.

Schachter, S. (1971). Eat, eat. *Psychology Today, 4*(11), 44–47, 78–79.

Schachter, S. (1982). Recidivism and self-cure of smoking and obesity. *American Psychologist, 37,* 436–444.

Schachter, S., & Gross, L. (1968). Manipulated time and eating behavior. *Journal of Personality and Social Psychology, 10,* 98–106.

Schachter, S., & Latané, B. (1964). Crime, cognition, and the autonomic nervous system. In D. Levine (Ed.), *Nebraska Symposium on Motivation* (Vol. 12, pp. 211–273). Lincoln: University of Nebraska Press.

Schacter, D. L. (1986a). Amnesia and crime: How much do we really know? *American Psychologist, 41,* 286–295.

Schacter, D. L. (1986b). On the relation between genuine and simulated amnesia. *Behavioral Sciences and the Law, 4,* 47–64.

Schacter, D. L. (1987). Implicit memory: History and current status. *Journal of Experimental Psychology: Learning, Memory, and Cognition, 13,* 501–518.

Schacter, D. L., Wang, P. L., Tulving, E., & Freedman, M. (1982). Functional retrograde amnesia: A quantitative case study. *Neuropsychologia, 20,* 523–532.

Schatzber, A. F., & Rothschild, A. J. (1992). Psychotic (delusional) major depression: Should it be included as a distinct syndrome in *DSM-IV? American Journal of Psychiatry, 149,* 733–745.

Scheff, T. J. (1966). *Being mentally ill: A sociological theory.* Chicago: Aldine.

Scheff, T. J. (1975). *Labeling madness.* Englewood Cliffs, NJ: Prentice-Hall.

Scheiffelin, E. (1984). *The cultural analysis of depressive affect: An example from New Guinea.* Unpublished manuscript, University of Pennsylvania, Philadelphia.

Schenk, L., & Bear, D. (1981). Multiple personality and related dissociative phenomena in patients with temporal lobe epilepsy. *American Journal of Psychiatry, 138,* 1311–1316.

Schildkraut, J. (1965). The catecholamine hypothesis of affective disorders: A review of supporting evidence. *American Journal of Psychiatry, 122,* 509–522.

Schildkraut, J. J. (1972). Neuropharmacological studies of mood disorders. In J. Zubin & F. A. Freyhan (Eds.), *Disorders of mood.* Baltimore: Johns Hopkins University Press.

Schlenger, W. E., Kulka, R. A., Fairbank, J. A., Hough, R. L., Jordan, B. K., Marmar, C. R., & Weiss, D. S. (1992). The prevalence of post-traumatic stress disorder in the Vietnam generation: A multimethod, multisource assessment of psychiatric disorder. *Journal of Traumatic Stress, 5,* 333–363.

Schlundt, D. G., & Johnson, W. G. (1990). *Eating disorders: Assessment and treatment.* Boston: Allyn and Bacon.

Schmeck, H. M., Jr. (1982, September 7). The biology of fear and anxiety: Evidence points to chemical triggers. *The New York Times,* p. C7.

Schneier, F. R. (1991). Social phobia. *Psychiatric Annals, 21,* 349–353.

Schofield, W. (1964). *Psychotherapy, the purchase of friendship.* Englewood Cliffs, NJ: Prentice-Hall.

Schover, L. R., & LoPiccolo, J. (1982). Treatment effectiveness for dysfunctions of sexual desire. *Journal of Sex and Marital Therapy, 8*(3), 179–197.

Schreiber, F. (1974). *Sybil.* New York: Warner.

Schuckit, M. A., & Rayses, V. (1979). Ethanol ingestion: Differences in blood acetaldehyde concentrations in relatives of alcoholics and controls. *Science, 203,* 54–55.

Schulenberg, J., Bachman, J. G., O'Malley, P. M., & Johnston, L. D. (1994). High school educational success and subsequent substance use: A panel analysis following adolescents into young adulthood. *Journal of Health and Social Behavior, 35,* 45–62.

Schulsinger, F. (1972). Psychopathy: Heredity and environment. *International Journal of Mental Health, 1,* 190–206.

Schulz, S. C., Schulz, P. M., & Wilson, W. H. (1988). Medication treatment of schizotypal personality disorder. *Journal of Personality Disorders, 2,* 1–13.

Schwartz, G. E. (1977). Psychosomatic disorders and biofeedback: A psychobiological model of disregulation. In J. D. Maser & M. E. P. Seligman (Eds.), *Psychopathology: Experimental models.* San Francisco: Freeman.

Schwartz, G. E. (1978). Psychobiological foundations of psychotherapy and behavior change. In S. L. Garfield & A. E. Bergin (Eds.), *Handbook of psychotherapy and behavior change.* New York: Wiley.

Schwartz, G. E., Weinberger, D. A., & Singer, J. A. (1981). Cardiovascular differentiation of happiness, sadness, anger, and fear following imagery and exercise. *Psychosomatic Medicine, 43,* 343–364.

Schwartz, R. M., & Gottman, J. M. (1976). Toward a task analysis of assertive behavior. *Journal of Consulting and Clinical Psychology, 44,* 910–920.

Schwarz, J. R. (1981). *The Hillside strangler: A murderer's mind.* New York: New American Library.

Schweizer, E., Rickels, K., Case, W. G., & Greenblatt, D. J. (1990). Long-term therapeutic use of benzodiazepines: II. Effects of gradual taper. *Archives of General Psychiatry, 47,* 908–916.

Scull, A. (1993). *The most solitary of afflictions: Madness and society in Britain, 1700–1900.* New Haven, CT: Yale University Press.

Sears, M. R. (1991). Epidemiological trends in bronchial asthma. In M. A. Kaliner, P. J. Barnes, & C. G. A. Persson (Eds.), *Asthma: Its pathology and treatment* (pp. 1–49). New York: Marcel Dekker.

Sears, R. R. (1947). Clinical training facilities: 1947. *American Psychologist, 2,* 199–205.

Sedgwick, P. (1982). Antipsychiatry from the sixties to the eighties. In W. R. Gove (Ed.), *Deviance and mental illness.* Beverly Hills, CA: Sage.

Sedlack, A. (1989). *National incidence of child abuse and neglect.* Paper presented at the biennial meeting of the Society for Research in Child Development, Kansas City, MO.

Seeman, P., & Niznik, H. B. (1990). Dopamine receptors and transporters in Parkinson's disease and schizophrenia. *Federation of Associated Society of Experimental Biology, 4,* 2737–2744.

Segal, G. (1991). *A primer on brain tumors* (5th ed.). Des Plains, IL: American Brain Tumor Association.

Segal, N. L. (1984, July–August). The nature vs. nurture laboratory. *Twins,* 56–67.

Segal, Z. V. (1988). Appraisal of the self-schema construct in cognitive models of depression. *Psychological Bulletin, 103,* 147–162.

Segal, Z. V., & Muran, J. C. (1993). A cognitive perspective on self-representation in depression. In Z. V. Segal & S. J. Blatt (Eds.), *The self in emotional distress: Cognitive and psychodynamic perspectives* (pp. 131–163). New York: Guilford Press.

Segal, Z. V., Shaw, B. F., Vella, D. D., & Katz, R. (1992). Cognitive and life stress predictors of relapse in remitted unipolar depressed patients: Test of the congruency hypothesis. *Journal of Abnormal Psychology, 101,* 20–30.

Sekuler, R., & MacArthur, R. D. (1977). Alcohol retards visual recovery from glare by hampering target acquisition. *Nature, 270,* 428–429.

Selfe, L. (1978). *Nadia: A case of extraordinary drawing ability in an autistic child.* New York: Academic Press.

Seligman, M. E. P. (1971). Phobias and preparedness. *Behavior Therapy, 2,* 307–320.

Seligman, M. E. P. (1975). *Helplessness: On depression, development, and death.* San Francisco: Freeman.

Seligman, M. E. P. (1988). Research in clinical psychology: Why is there so much depression today? *G. Stanley Hall Lecture Series, 9,* 79–96.

Seligman, M. E. P. (1994). *What you can change & what you can't.* New York: Knopf.

Selling, L. S. (1940). *Men against madness.* New York: Greenberg.

Selye, H. (1956). *The stress of life.* New York: McGraw-Hill.

Selye, H. (1974). *Stress without distress.* Philadelphia: Lippincott.

Selye, H. (1976). *Stress in health and disease.* Woburn, MA: Butterworths.

Semans, J. H. (1956). Premature ejaculation: A new approach. *Southern Medical Journal, 49,* 353–357.

Shader, R. I. (Ed.) (1994). *Manual of psychiatric therapeutics* (2nd ed.). Boston: Little, Brown.

Shader, R. I., & Greenblatt, D. J. (1993). Use of benzodiazepines in anxiety disorders. *New England Journal of Medicine, 328,* 1398–1405.

Shader, R. I., Greenblatt, D. J., & Balter, M. B. (1991). Appropriate use and regulatory control of benzodiazepines. *Journal of Clinical Pharmacology, 31,* 781–784.

Shadish, W. R., Montgomery, L. M., Wilson, P., Wilson, R. R., Bright, I., & Okwumabua, T. (1993). *Journal of Consulting and Clinical Psychology, 61,* 992–1002.

Shaffer, D., Garland, A., Fisher, P., et al. (1990). Suicide crisis centers: A critical reappraisal with specific reference to the prevention of youth suicide. In F. E. Goldsten, C. M. Heinecke, R. S. Pynoos, & J. Yager (Eds.), *Prevention of mental health disturbance in childhood* (pp. 135–166). Washington DC: American Psychiatric Association.

Shaffer, D., Garland, A., Vieland, V., et al. (1991). The impact of curriculum-based suicide prevention programs for teenagers. *Journal of the American Academy of Child and Adolescent Psychiatry, 30,* 588–596.

Shah, A., & Frith, U. (1983). An islet of ability in autistic children: A research note. *Journal of Child Psychology and Psychiatry, 24,* 613–620.

Shapiro, D., & Goldstein, I. B. (1982). Biobehavioral perspectives on hypertension. *Journal of Consulting and Clinical Psychology,* 841–858.

Shapiro, S. A. (1981). *Contemporary theories of schizophrenia.* New York: McGraw-Hill.

Shapiro, T. (1989a). Our changing science. *Journal of the American Psychoanalytic Association, 37,* 3–6.

Shapiro, T. (1989b). Psychoanalytic classification and empiricism with borderline personality disorder as a model. *Journal of Consulting and Clinical Psychology, 57,* 187–194.

Shea, M. T., Elkin, I., Imber, S. D., Sotsky, S. M., Watkins, J. T., Collins, J. F., Pilkonis, P. A., Beckham, E., Glass, D. R., Dolan, R. T., &

Parloff, M. B. (1992). Course of depressive symptoms over follow-up. *Archives of General Psychiatry, 49,* 782–787.

Sheehan, S. (1982). *Is there no place on earth for me?* Boston: Houghton Mifflin.

Shenton, M. E., Soloway, M. R., Holzman, P. S., Coleman, M., & Gale, H. J. (1989). Thought disorder in the relatives of psychotic patients. *Archives of General Psychiatry, 46,* 897–901.

Sheridan, E. P., & Teplin, L. A. (1981). Police-referred psychiatric emergencies: Advantages of community treatment. *Journal of Community Psychology, 9,* 140–147.

Shiffman, S. (1982). Relapse following smoking cessation: A situational analysis. *Journal of Consulting and Clinical Psychology, 50,* 71–86.

Shilony, E., & Grossman, F. K. (1993). Depersonalization as a defense mechanism in survivors of trauma. *Journal of Traumatic Stress, 6,* 119–128.

Shipko, S. (1982). Alexithymia and somatization. *Psychotherapy and Psychosomatics, 37,* 193–201.

Shneidman, E. S. (1992). A conspectus of the suicidal scenario. In R. W. Maris, A. L. Berman, J. T. Maltsberger, & R. I. Yufit (Eds.), *Assessment and prediction of suicide* (pp. 50–64). New York: Guilford Press.

Shneidman, E. S., & Farberow N. L. (1957). *Clues to suicide.* New York: Blakiston.

Shneidman, E. S., & Farberow, N. L. (1970). Attempted and completed suicide. In E. S. Shneidman, N. L. Farberow, & R. E. Litman (Eds.), *The psychology of suicide.* New York: Science House.

Shoham-Salomon, V., & Rosenthal, R. (1987). Paradoxical interventions: A meta-analysis. *Journal of Consulting and Clinical Psychology, 55,* 22–28.

Shore, J., Tatum, E., & Vollmer, W. (1986). Psychiatric reactions to disaster: The Mount St. Helens experience. *American Journal of Psychiatry, 143,* 590–595.

Shrout, P. E., Link, B. G., Dohrenwend, B. P., Skodol, A. E., Stueve, A., & Mirotznik, J. (1989). Characterizing life events as risk factors for depression: The role of fateful loss events. *Journal of Abnormal Psychology, 98,* 460–467.

Siegel, B. V., Buchsbaum, M. S., Bunney, W. E., Jr., Gottschalk, L. A., Haier, R. J., Lohr, J. B., Lottenberg, S., Najafi, A., Nuechterlein, K. H., Potkin, S. G., & Wu, J. C. (1993). Cortical-striatal-thalamic circuits and brain glucose metabolic activity in 70 unmedicated male schizophrenic patients. *American Journal of Psychiatry, 150,* 1325–1336.

Siever, L. J., & Davis, K. L. (1991). A psychobiological perspective on personality disorders. *American Journal of Psychiatry, 148,* 1647–1658.

Siever, L. J., Friedman, L., Moskowitz, J., Mitropoulou, V., Keefe, R., Roitman, S. L., Merhige, D., Trestman, R., Silverman, J., & Mohs, R. (1994). Eye movement impairment and schizotypal psychopathology. *American Journal of Psychiatry, 151,* 1209–1215.

Silberschatz, G., Fretter, P. B., & Curtis, J. T. (1986). How do interpretations influence the process of psychotherapy? *Journal of Consulting and Clinical Psychology, 54,* 646–652.

Silver, R. L., & Wortman, C. B. (1980). Coping with undesirable life events. In J. Garber & M. E. P. Seligman (Eds.), *Human helplessness: Theory and applications.* New York: Academic Press.

Silverman, W. K., & Eisen, A. R. (1993). Overanxious disorder. In R. T. Ammerman & M. Hersen (Eds.), *Handbook of behavior therapy with children and adults: A developmental and longitudinal perspective* (pp. 189–201). Needham, MA: Allyn and Bacon.

Sim, J. P., & Romney, D. M. (1990). The relationship between a circumplex model of interpersonal behavior and personality disorders. *Journal of Personality Disorders, 4,* 329–341.

Simeon, D., & Hollander, E. (1993). Depersonalization disorder. *Psychiatric Annals, 23,* 382–388.

Simmons, J. Q., & Lovaas, O. I. (1969). Use of pain and punishment as treatment techniques with childhood schizophrenics. *American Journal of Psychotherapy, 23,* 23–36.

Simon, G. E. (1991). Somatization and psychiatric disorders. In L. J. Kirmayer & J. M. Robbins (Eds.), *Current concepts of somatization: Research and clinical perspectives.* (pp. 37–62). Washington, DC: American Psychiatric Press.

Singleton, L., & Johnson, K. A. (1993). *The black health library guide to stroke.* New York: Holt.

Sizemore, C. C., & Pittillo, E. S. (1977). *I'm Eve.* Garden City, NY: Doubleday.

Skeels, H. M., & Dye, H. B. (1938–1939). A study of the effects of differential stimulation on mentally retarded children. *AAMD Proceedings, 44,* 114–136.

Skinner, B. F. (1965). *Science and human behavior.* New York: Free Press.

Skinner, B. F. (1990). Can psychology be a science of mind? *American Psychologist, 45,* 1206–1210.

Sklar, L. S., & Anisman, H. (1979). Stress and coping factors influence tumor growth. *Science, 205,* 513–515.

Sklar, L. S., & Anisman, H. (1981). Stress and cancer. *Psychological Bulletin, 89,* 369–406.

Slap, G. B., Vorters, D. F., Khalid, N., Margulies, S. R., et al. (1992). Adolescent suicide attempters: Do physicians recognize them? *Journal of Adolescent Health, 13,* 286–292.

Sloane, R. B., Staples, F. R., Cristol, A. H., Yorkston, N. J., & Whipple, K. (1975). *Psychoanalysis versus behavior therapy.* Cambridge, MA: Harvard University Press.

Sluzki, C. E. (1991). Foreword. In M. P. Nichols & R. C. Schwartz, *Family therapy: Concepts and methods* (2nd ed., pp ix–x). Boston: Allyn and Bacon.

Small, J. G., Klapper, M. H., Milstein, V., Kellams, J. J., Miller, M. J., Marhenke, J. D., & Small, I. F. (1991). Carbamazepine compared with lithium in the treatment of mania. *Archives of General Psychiatry, 48,* 915–921.

Smith, E. M., North, C. S., McColl, R. E., & Shea, J. M. (1990). Acute postdisaster psychiatric disorders: Identification of persons at risk. *American Journal of Psychiatry, 147,* 202–206.

Smith, G. R., Monson, R. A., & Ray, D. C. (1986a). Patients with multiple unexplained symptoms. *Archives of Internal Medicine, 146,* 69–72.

Smith, G. R., Monson, R. A., & Ray, D. C. (1986b). Psychiatric consultation in somatization disorder. *New England Journal of Medicine, 314,* 1407–1413.

Smith, M. L., Glass, G. V., & Miller, T. J. (1980). *The benefits of psychotherapy.* Baltimore: Johns Hopkins University Press.

Smith T. W. (1992). Hostility and health: Current status of a psychosomatic hypothesis. *Health Psychology, 11,* 139–150.

Smyer, M. A., Zarit, S. H., & Qualls, S. H. (1990). Psychological interventions with the aging individual. In J. E. Birren & K. W. Schaie (Eds.), *Handbook of the psychology of aging* (3rd ed., pp. 375–404). New York: Academic Press.

Snyder, C. R. (1958). *Alcohol and the Jews.* New York: Free Press.

Snyder, D. K., & Wills, R. M. (1989). Behavioral versus insight-oriented marital therapy: Effects on individual and interspousal functioning. *Journal of Consulting and Clinical Psychology, 57,* 39–46.

Snyder, D. K., Wills, R. M., & Grady-Fletcher, A. (1991). Long-term effectiveness of behavioral versus insight-oriented marital therapy: A 4-year follow-up study. *Journal of Consulting and Clinical Psychology, 59,* 138–141.

Snyder, J. J. (1977). Reinforcement and analysis of interaction in problem and nonproblem families. *Journal of Abnormal Psychology, 86,* 528–535.

Snyder, S. H. (1972). Catecholamines in the brain as mediators of amphetamine psychosis. *Archives of General Psychiatry, 27,* 169–179.

Snyder, S. H. (1979). The true speed trip: Schizophrenia. In D. Goleman & R. J. Davidson (Eds.), *Consciousness: Brain, states of awareness, and mysticism.* New York: Harper & Row.

Snyder, S. H. (1980). *Biological aspects of mental disorder.* New York: Oxford University Press.

Sobell, L. C., Toneatto, A., & Sobell, M. B. (1990). Behavior therapy (alcohol and other substance abuse). In A. S. Bellack & M. Hersen (Eds.), *Handbook of comparative treatments for adult disorders* (pp. 479–505). New York: Wiley.

Solomon, Z., Mikulincer, M., & Benbenishty, R. (1989a). Combat stress reaction: Clinical manifestations and correlates. *Military Psychology, 1,* 35–47.

Solomon, Z., Mikulincer, M., & Benbenishty, R. (1989b). Locus of control and combat-related post-trauma stress disorder: The intervening role of battle intensity, threat appraisal and coping. *British Journal of Clinical Psychology, 28,* 131–144.

Solomon, Z., Mikulincer, M., & Flum, H. (1988). Negative life events, coping responses, and combat-related psychopathology: A prospective study. *Journal of Abnormal Psychology, 97,* 302–307.

Soloway, M. R., Shenton, M. E., & Holzman, P. S. (1987). Comparative studies of thought disorders: I. Mania and schizophrenia. *Archives of General Psychiatry, 44,* 13–20.

Sonda, L. P., Mazo, R., & Chancellor, M. B. (1990). The role of yohimbine for the treatment of erectile impotence. *Journal of Sex and Marital Therapy,* 16, 15–21.

Sorenson, S., & Kraus, J. F. (1991). Occurrence, severity, and outcome of brain injury. *Journal of Head Trauma Rehabilitation, 6,* 1–10.

Sotsky, S. M., Glass, D. R., Shea, M. T., Pilkonis, P. A., Collins, J. F., Watkins, J. T., Imber, S. D., Leber, W. R., Moyer, J., & Oliver, M. E. (1991). Patient predictors of response to psychotherapy and pharmacotherapy: Findings in the NIMH Treatment of Depression Collaborative Research Program. *American Journal of Psychiatry, 148,* 997–1008.

Spangler, D. L., Simons, A. D., Monroe, S. M., & Thase, M. E. (1993). Evaluating the hopelessness model of depression: Diathesis-stress and symptom components. *Journal of Abnormal Psychology, 102,* 592–600.

Spanos, N. P. (1994). Multiple identity enactments and multiple person disorder: A sociocognitive perspective. *Psychological Bulletin, 116,* 143–165.

Spanos, N. P., Weekes, J. R., & Bertrand, L. D. (1985). Multiple personality: A social psychological perspective. *Journal of Abnormal Psychology, 94,* 362–376.

Spector, I. P., & Carey, M. P. (1990). Incidence and prevalence of the sexual dysfunctions: A critical review of the empirical literature. *Archives of Sexual Behavior, 19,* 389–408.

Spiegel, D. (1984). Multiple personality as a post-traumatic stress disorder. *Psychiatric Clinics of North America, 7,* 101–110.

Spiegel, D., Bloom, J. R., Kraemer, H. C., & Gottheil, E. (1989). Effect of psychosocial treatment on survival of patients with metastatic breast cancer. *Lancet,* 888–891.

Spirito, A., Brown, L., Overholser, J., & Fritz, G. (1989). Attempted suicide in adolescence: A review and critique of the literature. *Clinical Psychology Review, 9,* 335–363.

Spirito, A., Overholser, J. C., & Stark, L. J. (1989). Common problems and coping strategies: II. Findings with adolescent suicide attempters. *Journal of Abnormal Child Psychology, 17,* 213–221.

Spitz, R. A. (1945). Hospitalism: An inquiry into the genesis of psychiatric conditions in early childhood. *Psychoanalytic Study of the Child, 1,* 53–74.

Spitzer, M., Weisker, I., Winter, M., Maier, S., Hermle, L., & Maher, B. A. (1994). Semantic and phonological priming in schizophrenia. *Journal of Abnormal Psychology, 103,* 485–494.

Spitzer, R. L. (1976). More on pseudoscience in science and the case for psychiatric diagnosis: A critique of D. L. Rosenhan's "On being sane in insane places" and "The contextual nature of psychiatric diagnosis." *Archives of General Psychiatry, 33,* 459–470.

Spitzer, R. L., & Fleiss, J. L. (1974). A reanalysis of the reliability of psychiatric diagnosis. *British Journal of Psychiatry, 125,* 341–347.

Spitzer, R. L., Gibbon, M., Skodol, A. E., Williams, J. B. W., & First, M. B. (Eds.). (1989). DSM-III-R *casebook: A learning companion and statis-*

tical manual of mental disorders (3rd ed. rev.). Washington, DC: American Psychiatric Press.

Spitzer, R. L., Skodol, A. E., Gibbon, M., & Williams, J. B. W. (1981). DSM-III *casebook: A learning companion to the diagnostic and statistical manual of mental disorders* (3rd ed.). Washington, DC: American Psychiatric Press.

Spitzer, R. L., Skodol, A. E., Gibbon, M., & Williams, J. B. W. (1983). *Psychopathology: A case book.* New York: McGraw-Hill.

Squire, L. R., & Slater, P. C. (1978). Bilateral and unilateral ECT: Effects on verbal and nonverbal memory. *American Journal of Psychiatry, 135,* 1316–1320.

Squire, L. R., Slater, P. C., & Miller, P. L. (1981). Retrograde amnesia and bilateral electroconvulsive therapy. *Archives of General Psychiatry, 38,* 89–95.

Stacy, A. W., Newcomb, M. D., & Bentler, P. M. (1991). Cognitive motivation and drug use: A 9-year longitudinal study. *Journal of Abnormal Psychology, 100,* 502–515.

Starr, A. (1977). *Psychodrama: Rehearsal for living.* Chicago: Nelson-Hall.

State v. Soura, 796 P.2d 109 (Idaho 1990).

State v. Summers, 853 P.2d 953 (Wash. App. 1993).

Steadman, H., McGreevy, M. A., Morrissey, J. P., et al. (1993). *Before and after Hinckley: Evaluating insanity defense reform.* New York: Guilford Press.

Steckel, W. (1943). *The interpretation of dreams.* New York: Liveright.

Steege, J. F., Stout, A. L., & Culley, C. C. (1986). Patient satisfaction in Scott and Small-Carrion penile implant recipients: A study of 52 patients. *Archives of Sexual Behavior, 15*(5), 393–399.

Stehli, A. (1991). *The sound of a miracle: A child's triumph over autism.* New York: Doubleday.

Steinberg, L., & Meyer, R. (1995). *Childhood.* New York: McGraw-Hill.

Steinhausen, H. C. (1994). Anorexia and bulimia nervosa. In M. Rutter, E. Taylor, & L. Hersov (Eds.), *Child and adolescent psychiatry.* Oxford: Blackwell Scientific Publications.

Steketee, G. (1990). Personality traits and disorders in obsessive-compulsives. *Journal of Anxiety Disorders, 4,* 351–364.

Steptoe, A. (1984). Psychophysiological processes in disease. In A. Steptoe & A. Mathews (Eds.), *Health care and human behavior.* New York: Academic Press.

Sterling, E. E. (1991, August 1). What should we do about drugs? *Vital Speeches of the Day, 57,* 626–632.

Stinson, F. S., & DeBakey, S. F. (1992). Alcohol-related mortality in the United States 1979–1988. *British Journal of Addiction, 87,* 777–783.

Stokes, T. F., & Osnes, P. G. (1989). An operant pursuit of generalization. *Behavior Therapy, 20,* 337–355.

Stone, A. A. (1975). *Mental health and law: A system in transition.* Rockville, MD: National Institute of Mental Health.

Stone, A. A. (1976). The *Tarasoff* decision: Suing psychotherapists to safeguard society. *Harvard Law Review, 90,* 358.

Stone, A. A. (1992). Development of cold symptoms following experimental rhinovirus infection is related to prior stressful life events. *Behavioral Medicine, 18,* 115–120.

Stone, A. A., Bovbjerg, D. M., Neale, J. M., & Napoli, A. (1992). Development of cold symptoms following experimental rhinovirus infection is related to prior stressful life events. *Behavioral Medicine, 18,* 115–120.

Stone, A. A., Valdimarsdottir, H. B., Katkin, E. S., Burns, J., & Cox, D. S. (1993). Effects of mental stressors on mitogen-induced lymphocyte responses in the laboratory. *Psychology and Health, 8,* 269–284.

Strauss, J. S., Carpenter, W. T., & Bartko, J. J. (1974). The diagnosis and understanding of schizophrenia: II. Speculations on the processes that underlie schizophrenic symptoms and signs. *Schizophrenia Bulletin, 11,* 61–76.

Strauss, M. E. (1993). Relations of symptoms to cognitive deficits in schizophrenia. *Schizophrenia Bulletin, 19,* 215–231.

Straw, R. B. (1982). *Meta-analysis of deinstitutionalization in mental health.* Unpublished doctoral dissertation, Northwestern University, Evanston, IL.

Streissguth, A. P., Landesman-Dwyer, S., Martin, D. C., & Smith, D. M. (1980). Teratogenic effects of alcohol in humans and laboratory animals. *Science, 209,* 353–361.

Strelnick, A. H. (1977). Multiple family therapy: A review of the literature. *Family Process, 16,* 307–325.

Stricker, G. (1983). Some issues in psychodynamic treatment of the depressed patient. *Professional Psychology: Research and Practice, 14,* 209–217.

Strober, M., Morrell, W., Burroughs, J., Lampert, C., Danforth, H., & Freeman, R. (1988). A family study of bipolar I disorder in adolescence: Early onset of symptoms linked to increased familial loading and lithium resistance. *Journal of Affective Disorders, 15,* 255–268.

Stromberg, C. D., & Stone, A. A. (1983). A model state law on civil commitment of the mentally ill. *Harvard Journal on Legislation, 20,* 275–396.

Stroop, J. R. (1935). Studies of interference in serial verbal reactions. *Journal of Experimental Psychology, 18,* 643–661.

Stuart, R. B. (1977). Self-help group approach to self-management. In R. B. Stuart (Ed.), *Behavioral self-management: Strategies, techniques and outcome.* New York: Brunner/Mazel.

Stunkard, A. J., Fernstrom, M. H., Price, R. A., Frank, E., & Kupfer, D. J. (1990). Direction of weight change in recurrent depression: Consistency across episodes. *Archives of General Psychiatry, 47,* 857–860.

Stunkard, A. J., & Koch, C. (1964). The interpretation of gastric motility: I. Apparent bias in the reports of hunger by obese persons. *Archives of General Psychiatry, 11,* 74–82.

Sturgis, E. T. (1993). Obsessive-compulsive disorders. In P. B. Sutker & H. E. Adams (Eds.), *Comprehensive handbook of psychopathology* (2nd ed., pp. 129–144). New York: Plenum Press.

Sugiyama, T., & Abe, T. (1989). The prevalence of autism in Nagoya, Japan: A total population study. *Journal of Autism and Developmental Disorders, 19,* 87–96.

Sullivan, H. S. (1940). Conceptions of modern psychiatry. *Psychiatry, 3,* 1–117.

Sullivan, H. S. (1953). *The interpersonal theory of psychiatry.* New York: Norton.

Sullivan, H. S. (1962). *Schizophrenia as a human process.* New York: Norton.

Suomi, S. J. (1982). Relevance of animal models for clinical psychology. In P. C. Kendall & J. N. Butcher (Eds.), *Handbook of research methods in clinical psychology.* New York: Wiley.

Suppes, T., Baldessarini, R. J., Faedda, G. L., & Tohen, M. (1991). Risk of recurrence following discontinuation of lithium treatment in bipolar disorder. *Archives of General Psychiatry, 48,* 1082–1088.

Sushinsky, L. (1970). An illustration of a behavioral therapy intervention with nursing staff in a therapeutic role. *Journal of Psychiatric Nursing and Mental Health Services, 8*(5), 24–26.

Susser, E., Lin, S. P., Brown, A. S., Lumey, L. H., & Erlenmeyer-Kimling, L. (1994). No relation between risk of schizophrenia and prenatal exposure to influenza in Holland. *American Journal of Psychiatry, 151,* 922–924.

Susser, E., & Wanderling, J. (1994). Epidemiology of nonaffective acute remitting psychosis vs. schizophrenia: Sex and sociocultural setting. *Archives of General Psychiatry, 51,* 294–301.

Swados, E. (1991, August 18). The story of a street person. *The New York Times Magazine,* pp. 16–18.

Swann, W. B., Jr., Wenzlaff, R. M., Krull, D. S., & Pelham, B. W. (1992). Allure of negative feedback: Self-verification strivings among depressed persons. *Journal of Abnormal Psychology, 101,* 293–306.

Swartz, M., Blazer, D., George, L., & Landerman, R. (1986). Somatization disorder in a community population. *American Journal of Psychiatry, 143,* 1403–1408.

Swedo, S. E., Leonard, H. L., & Rapoport, J. L. (1992). Childhood-onset obsessive compulsive disorder. *Psychiatric Clinics of North America, 15,* 767–775.

Sweeney, P. D., Anderson, K., & Bailey, S. (1986). Attributional style in depression: A meta-analytic review. *Journal of Personality and Social Psychology, 50,* 974–991.

Swerdlow, N. R., Braff, D. L., Taaid, N., & Geyer, M. A. (1994). Assessing the validity of an animal model of deficient sensorimotor gating in schizophrenic patients. *Archives of General Psychiatry, 51,* 139–154.

Szasz, T. S. (1961). *The myth of mental illness.* New York: Harper & Row.

Szasz, T. S. (1963). *Law, liberty, and psychiatry.* New York: Macmillan.

Szasz, T. S. (1971). The sane slave. *American Journal of Psychotherapy, 25,* 228–239.

Szasz, T. S. (1977). *Psychiatric slavery.* New York: Free Press.

Szyrynski, V. (1973). Anorexia nervosa and psychotherapy. *American Journal of Psychotherapy, 27,* 492–505.

Taft, L., & Goldfarb, W. (1964). Prenatal and perinatal factors in childhood schizophrenia. *Developmental Medicine and Child Neurology, 6*(1), 32–43.

Takahashi, S., Kanai, H., & Miyamoto, Y. (1976). Reassessment of elevated serotonin levels in blood platelets in early infantile autism. *Journal of Autism and Childhood Schizophrenia, 6*(31), 7–26.

Takei, N., Sham, P., O'Callaghan, E., Murray, G. K., Glover, G., & Murray, R. M. (1994). Prenatal exposure to influenza and the development of schizophrenia: Is the effect confined to females? *American Journal of Psychiatry, 151,* 117–119.

Tarasoff v. Regents of California, 17 Cal. 3d 425, 131 Cal. Rptr. 14 (1976).

Tarrier, N., Barrowclough, C., Porceddu, K., et al. (1988). The assessment of psychophysiological reactivity to the expressed emotion of the relatives of schizophrenic patients. *British Journal of Psychiatry, 152,* 618–624.

Tarter, R. E. (1988). Are there inherited behavioral traits that predispose to substance abuse? *Journal of Consulting and Clinical Psychology, 56,* 189–196.

Tarver, S. G., Hallahan, D. P., Kauffman, J. M., & Ball, D. W. (1976). Verbal rehearsal and selective attention in children with learning disabilities: A developmental lag. *Journal of Experimental Child Psychology, 22,* 375–385.

Taylor, C. B., & Arnow, B. (1988). *The nature and treatment of anxiety disorders:* New York: Free Press.

Taylor, H. G. (1989). Learning disabilities. In E. J. Mash & R. A. Barkley (Eds.), *Treatment of childhood disorders.* New York: Guilford Press.

Taylor, S., & McLean, P. (1993). Outcome profiles in the treatment of unipolar depression. *Behaviour Research and Therapy, 31,* 325–330.

Teicher, M. H., Glod, C., & Cole, J. O. (1990). Emergence of intense suicidal preoccupation during fluoxetine treatment. *American Journal of Psychiatry, 147,* 207–210.

Telch, M. J., Brouillard, M., Telch, C. F., Agras, W. S., & Taylor, C. B. (1989). Role of cognitive appraisal in panic-related avoidance. *Behaviour Research and Therapy, 27,* 373–383.

Telch, M. J., Lucas, J. A., & Nelson, P. (1989). Nonclinical panic in college students: An investigation of prevalence and symptomatology. *Journal of Abnormal Psychology, 98,* 300–306.

Tellegen, A., Lykken, D. T., Bouchard, T. J., Wilcox, K. J., Segal, N. L., & Rich, S. (1988). Personality similarity in twins reared apart and together. *Journal of Personality and Social Psychology, 54,* 1031–1039.

Tennant, C. (1988). Parental loss in childhood: Its effect in adult life. *Archives of General Psychiatry, 45,* 1045–1050.

Terént, A. (1993). Stroke mortality. In J. P. Whisnant (Ed.), *Stroke, populations, cohorts, and clinical trials* (pp. 37–58). Boston: Butterworth-Heinemann.

Terr, L. (1994). *Unchained memories: True stories of traumatic memories, lost and found.* New York: Basic Books.

Test, M. A., & Stein, L. I. (1978). Training in community living: Research design and results. In L. I. Stein & M. A. Test (Eds.), *Alternatives to mental hospital treatment.* New York: Plenum Press.

Thase, M. E., Frank, E., & Kupfer, D. J. (1985). Biological processes in major depression. In E. E. Beckham & W. R. Leber (Eds.), *Handbook of depression* (pp. 816–913). Homewood, IL: Dorsey Press.

Thase, M. E., Simons, A. D., Cahalano, J., McGoory, J., & Harden, T. (1991). Severity of depression and response to cognitive behavior therapy. *American Journal of Psychiatry, 148,* 784–789.

Thigpen, C. H., & Cleckley, H. (1957). *The three faces of Eve.* New York: McGraw-Hill.

Thompson, J. K., Jarvie, G. J., Lahey, B. B., & Cureton, K. J. (1982). Exercise and obesity: Etiology, physiology, and intervention. *Psychological Bulletin, 91,* 55–79.

Thomson, N., Fraser, D., & McDougall, A. (1974). The reinstatement of speech in near-mute chronic schizophrenics by instructions, imitative prompts and reinforcement. *Journal of Behavior Therapy and Experimental Psychiatry, 5,* 83–89.

Thorpy, M., & Glovinsky, P. (1987). Parasomnias. *Psychiatric Clinics of North America, 10,* 623–639.

Tiefer, L., Pedersen, B., & Melman, A. (1988). Psychosocial follow-up of penile prosthesis implant patients and partners. *Journal of Sex and Marital Therapy, 14,* 184–201.

Tienari, P. (1991). Interaction between genetic vulnerability and family environment: The Finnish adoptive family study of schizophrenia. *Acta Psychiatrica Scandinavica, 84,* 460–465.

Tinklenberg, J. R. (1971a). A clinical view of the amphetamines. *American Family Physician,* (5), 82–86.

Tinklenberg, J. R. (1974). What a physician should know about marihuana. *Rational Drug Therapy* (American Pharmacology and Experimental Therapeutics).

Tinklenberg, J. R., & Woodrow, K. M. (1974). Drug use among youthful assaultive and sexual offenders. *The Association for Research in Nervous and Mental Disease: Aggression, 52,* 209–224.

Tolbert, L., Haigler, T., Waits, M. M., & Dennis, T. (1993). Brief report: Lack of response in an autistic population to a low dose clinical trial of pyridoxine plus magnesium. *Journal of Autism and Developmental Disorders, 23.*

Tolman, E. C. (1948). Cognitive maps in rats and men. *Psychological Review, 55,* 189–208.

Tolman, E. C., & Honzig, C. H. (1930). "Insight" in rats. *University of California Publications in Psychology, 4,* 215–232.

Tomarken, A. J., Mineka, S., & Cook, M. (1989). Fear-relevant selective associations and covariation bias. *Journal of Abnormal Psychology, 98,* 381–394.

Toneatto, T., Sobell, L. C., Sobell, M. B., & Leo, G. I. (1991). Psychoactive substance use disorder (alcohol). In M. Hersen & S. M. Turner (Eds.), *Adult psychopathology and diagnosis* (2nd ed., pp. 84–109). New York: Wiley.

Torgersen, S. (1983). Genetic factors in anxiety disorders. *Archives of General Psychiatry, 40,* 1085–1089.

Torgersen, S. (1986b). Genetics of somatoform disorders. *Archives of General Psychiatry, 43,* 502–505.

Torrey, E. F., Bowler, A. E., Rawlings, R., & Terrazas, A. (1993). Seasonality of schizophrenia and stillbirths. *Schizophrenia Bulletin, 19,* 557–562.

Torrey, E. F., & Peterson, M. R. (1976). The viral hypothesis of schizophrenia. *Schizophrenia Bulletin, 2,* 136–145.

Trowell, I. (1979). Telephone services. In L. D. Hankoff & B. Einsidler (Eds.), *Suicide: Theory and clinical aspects.* Littleton, MA: PSG.

Tucker, J. A., Vuchinich, R. E., & Sobell, M. B. (1981). Alcohol consumption as a self-handicapping strategy. *Journal of Abnormal Psychology, 90,* 220–230.

Turkat, I. D., & Levin, R. A. (1984). Formulation of personality disorders. In H. E. Adams & P. B. Sutker (Eds.), *Comprehensive handbook of psychopathology.* New York: Plenum Press.

Turkheimer, E., & Parry, C. D. H. (1992). Why the gap? Practice and policy in civil commitment hearings. *American Psychologist, 47,* 646–655.

Turner, L. A., Althof, S. E., Levine, S. B., Bodner, D. R., Kursh, E. D., & Resnick, M. I. (1991). External vacuum devices in the treatment of erectile dysfunction: A one-year study of sexual and psychosocial impact. *Journal of Sex and Marital Therapy, 17,* 81–93.

Turner, L. A., Althof, S. E., Levine, S. B., Risen, C. B., Bodner, D. R., Kursh, E. D., & Resnick, M. I. (1989). Self-injection of papaverine and phentolamine in the treatment of psychogenic impotence. *Journal of Sex and Marital Therapy, 15,* 163–176.

Turner, S. M., & Beidel, D. C. (1989). Social phobia: Clinical syndrome, diagnosis, and comorbidity. *Clinical Psychology Review, 9,* 3–18.

Turner, S. M., Beidel, D. C., Dancu, C. V., & Keys, D. J. (1986). Psychopathology of social phobia and comparison to avoidant personality disorder. *Journal of Abnormal Psychology, 95,* 389–394.

Turner, S. M., Jacob, R. G., & Morrison, R. (1985). Somatoform and factitious disorders. In H. E. Adams & P. Sutker (Eds.), *Comprehensive handbook of psychopathology* (pp. 307–345). New York: Plenum Press.

Tymchuk, A. J., Andron, L., & Rahbar, B. (1988). Effective decision-making/problem-solving training with mothers who have mental retardation. *American Journal on Mental Retardation, 92*(6), 510–516.

Uhde, T. W., Tancer, M. E., Black, B., & Brown, T. M. (1991). Phenomenology and neurobiology of social phobia: Comparison with panic disorder. *Journal of Clinical Psychiatry, 52,* 31–40.

Uhlenhuth, E. H., Balter, M. B., Mellinger, G. D., Cisin, I. H., & Clinthorne, J. (1983). Symptom checklist syndromes in the general population. *Archives of General Psychiatry, 40,* 1167–1173.

Ullmann, L. P., & Krasner, L. (Eds.). (1965). *Case studies in behavior modification.* New York: Holt, Rinehart and Winston.

Ullmann, L. P., & Krasner, L. (1975). *A psychological approach to abnormal behavior* (2nd ed.). Englewood Cliffs, NJ: Prentice-Hall.

U.S. Bureau of the Census. (1990). *Statistical abstract of the United States* (110th ed.). Washington, DC: U.S. Government Printing Office.

U.S. Department of Health and Human Services. (1991). *Health status of minorities and low-income groups.* Hyattsville, MD.

U.S. Department of Justice, Federal Bureau of Investigation (1993). *Crime in the United States, 1992.* Washington DC: U.S. Government Printing Office.

U.S. Public Health Service. (1964). *Smoking and health* (Report of the Advisory Committee to the Surgeon General of the Public Health Service). Washington, DC: Department of Health, Education, and Welfare.

Vaillant, G. E., & Milofsky, E. S. (1982). The etiology of alcoholism: A prospective view point. *American Psychologist, 37,* 494–503.

Valenstein, E. S. (1987). *Great and desperate cures: The rise and decline of psychosurgery.* New York: Basic Books.

Vanderlinden, J., Van Dyck, R., Vandereycken, W., & Vertommen, H. (1991). Dissociative experiences in the general population in the Netherlands and Belgium: A study with the dissociative questionnaire (DIS-Q). *Dissociation, 4,* 180–184.

Van Italli, J. B. (1985). Health implications of overweight and obesity in the United States. *Annals of Internal Medicine, 103,* 983–988.

Van Kammen, D. P. (1977). Y-Aminobutyric acid (Gaba) and the dopamine hypothesis of schizophrenia. *American Journal of Psychiatry, 134,* 138–143.

Vaughn, C. E., Snyder, K., Jones, S., Freeman, W. B., & Falloon, I. R. H. (1984). Family factors in schizophrenic relapse: A replication in California of British research on expressed emotion. *Archives of General Psychiatry, 41,* 1169–1177.

Velten, E. (1968). A laboratory task for the induction of mood states. *Behaviour Research and Therapy, 6,* 473–482.

Ventura, J., Nuechterlein, K. H., Lukoff, D., & Hardesty, J. P. (1989). A prospective study of stressful life events and schizophrenic relapse. *Journal of Abnormal Psychology, 98,* 407–411.

Vernon, P. (1941). Psychological effects of air raids. *Journal of Abnormal and Social Psychology, 36,* 457–476.

Visintainer, M. A., Volpicelli, J. R., & Seligman, M. E. P. (1982). Tumor rejection in rats after inescapable or escapable shock. *Science, 216*(23), 437–439.

Visser, S., & Bouman, T. K. (1992). Cognitive-behavioural approaches in the treatment of hypochondriasis: Six single case cross-over studies. *Behaviour Research and Therapy, 30,* 301–306.

Vitkus, J., & Horowitz, L. M. (1987). The poor social performance of lonely people: Lacking a skill or adopting a role? *Journal of Personality and Social Psychiatry, 57,* 1266–1273.

Vondra, J., Barnett, D., & Cicchetti, D. (1990). Self-concept, motivation and competence among preschoolers from maltreating and comparison families. *Child Abuse and Neglect, 14,* 525–540.

Vrendenberg, K., Flett, G. L., & Krames, L. (1993). Analog versus clinical depression: A clinical reappraisal. *Psychological Bulletin, 113,* 327–344.

Vuori, L., Christiansen, N., Clement, J., Mora, J., Wagner, M., & Herrara, M. (1979). Nutritional supplementation and the outcome of pregnancy: II. Visual habituation at 15 days. *Journal of Clinical Nutrition, 32,* 463–469.

Wachtel, P. L. (1973). Psychodynamics, behavior therapy, and the implacable experimenter: An inquiry into the consistency of personality. *Journal of Abnormal Psychology, 82,* 324–334.

Wachtel, P. L. (1977). *Psychoanalysis and behavior therapy: Toward an integration.* New York: Basic Books.

Waggoner, R. W., & Bagchi, B. K. (1954). Initial masking of organic brain changes by psychic symptoms. *American Journal of Psychiatry, 110,* 904–910.

Wagner, W. G., Smith, D., & Norris, W. R. (1988). The psychological adjustment of enuretic children: A comparison of two types. *Journal of Pediatric Psychology, 13,* 33–38.

Wakefield, H., & Underwager, R. (1992). Recovered memories of alleged sexual abuse: Lawsuits against parents. *Behavioral Sciences and the Law, 10,* 483–507.

Wakefield, J. C. (1992). The concept of mental disorder. *American Psychologist, 47,* 373–388.

Waldinger, R. J., & Gunderson, J. G. (1987). *Effective psychotherapy with borderline patients: Case studies.* New York: Macmillan.

Waldron, I., Lye, D., & Brandon, A. (1991). Gender differences in teenage smoking. *Women and Health, 17,*(2), 65–90.

Walker, C. E., Milling, L., & Bonner, B. (1988). Incontinence disorders: Enuresis and encopresis. In D. Routh (Ed.), *Handbook of pediatric psychology.* New York: Guilford Press.

Walker, E. F., Grimes, K. E., Davis, D. M., & Smith, A. J. (1993). Childhood precursors of schizophrenia: Facial expressions of emotion. *American Journal of Psychiatry, 150,* 1654–1660.

Walker, E. F., & Lewine, R. J. (1990). Prediction of adult-onset schizophrenia from childhood home movies of the patients. *American Journal of Psychiatry, 147,* 1052–1056.

Walker, L. E. A. (1989). Psychology and violence against women. *American Psychologist, 44,* 695–702.

Wallace, C. J., & Liberman, R. P. (1985). Social skills training for patients with schizophrenia: A controlled clinical trial. *Psychiatry Research, 15,* 239–247.

Wallerstein, R. S. (1989). The psychotherapy research project of the Menninger Foundation: An overview. *Journal of Consulting and Clinical Psychology, 57,* 195–205.

Wardle, J. (1980). Dietary restraint and binge eating. *Behavioral Analysis and Modification, 4,* 201–209.

Warwick, H. M. C., & Marks, I. M. (1988). Behavioural treatment of illness phobia and hypochondriasis: A pilot study of 17 cases. *British Journal of Psychiatry, 152,* 239–241.

Warwick, H. M. C., & Salkovskis, P. M. (1990). Hypochondriasis. *Behaviour Research and Therapy, 28,* 105–117.

Washington v. Harper, 110 S.Ct. 1028 (1990).

Waterhouse, L. (1994). Severity of impairment in autistic spectrum disorders. In S. H. Broman & J. Grafman (Eds.), *Atypical cognitive deficits in developmental disorders: Implications for brain function* (pp. 159–182). Hillsdale, NJ: Erlbaum.

Waterhouse, L., Wing, L., & Fein, D. (1989). Reevaluating the syndrome of autism in the light of empirical research. In G. Dawson & S. Segalowitz (Eds.), *Autism: Perspectives on diagnosis, nature and treatment* (pp. 263–281). New York: Guilford Press.

Watkins, M. J. (1990). Mediationism and the obfuscation of memory. *American Psychologist, 45,* 328–335.

Watson, J. B. (1913). Psychology as the behaviorist views it. *Psychological Review, 20,* 158–177.

Watson, J. B., & Rayner, R. (1920). Conditioning emotional responses. *Journal of Experimental Psychology, 3,* 1–14.

Watson, L. S., & Uzzell, R. (1981). Teaching self-help skills to the mentally retarded. In J. L. Matson & J. R. McCartney (Eds.), *Handbook of behavior modification with the mentally retarded.* New York: Plenum Press.

Watzlawick, P., Beavin, J., & Jackson, D. (1967). *Pragmatics of human communication: A study of interaction patterns, pathologies, and paradoxes.* New York: Norton.

Webb, L. J., Gold, R. S., Johnstone, E. E., & DiClemente, C. C. (1981). Accuracy of *DSM-III* diagnoses following a training program. *American Journal of Psychiatry, 138,* 376–378.

Webb, T., Bundey, S., Thake, A., & Todd, J. (1986). Population incidence and segregation ratios on the Martin Bell syndrome. *American Journal of Medical Genetics, 23,* 573–580.

Wechsler, D. (1958). *The measurement and appraisal of adult intelligence* (4th ed.). Baltimore: Williams & Wilkins.

Wechsler, H., Davenport, A., Dowdall, G., Moeykens, B., & Castillo, S. (1994). Health and behavioral consequences of binge drinking in college: A national survey of students at 140 campuses. *Journal of the American Medical Association, 272,* 1672–1677.

Wehr, T. A. (1990). Effects of wakefulness and sleep on depression and mania. In J. Montplaisir & R. Godbout (Eds.), *Sleep and biological rhythyms: Basic mechanisms and applications to psychiatry* (pp. 42–86). New York: Oxford University Press.

Weihofen, H. (1957). *The urge to punish.* London: Gollancz.

Weinberger, D. R. (1987). Implications of normal brain development for the pathogenesis of schizophrenia. *Archives of General Psychiatry, 44,* 660–669.

Weinberger, D. R., Cannon-Spoor, et al. (1980). Poor premorbid adjustment and CT scan abnormalities in chronic schizophrenia. *American Journal of Psychiatry, 137,* 1410–1413.

Weiner, B., Frieze, L., Kukla, A., Reed, L., Rest, S., & Rosenbaum, R. M. (1971). *Perceiving the causes of success and failure.* New York: General Learning Press.

Weiner, D. B. (1979). The apprenticeship of Philippe Pinel: A new document, "Observations of Citizen Pussin on the insane." *American Journal of Psychiatry, 136,* 1128–1134.

Weiner, H. (1994). The revolution in stress theory and research. In R. P. Liberman & J. Yager (Eds.), *Stress in Psychiatric Disorders* (pp. 1–36). New York: Springer.

Weishaar, M. E., & Beck, A. T. (1992). Clinical and cognitive predictors of suicide. In R. W. Maris, A. L. Berman, J. T. Maltsberger, & R. I. Yufit (Eds.), *Assessment and prediction of suicide* (pp. 467–483). New York: Guilford Press.

Weisman, A., López, S. R., Karno, M., & Jenkins, J. (1993). An attributional analysis of expressed emotion in Mexican-American families with schizophrenia. *Journal of Abnormal Psychology, 102,* 601–606.

Weiss, D. S., Marmar, C. R., Schlenger, W. E., Fairbank, J. A., Jordan, B. K., Hough, R. L., & Kulka, R. A. (1992). The prevalence of lifetime and partial posttraumatic stress disorder in Vietnam theater veterans. *Journal of Traumatic Stress, 5,* 365–376.

Weiss, J. M. (1977). Psychosomatic disorders. In J. D. Maser & M. E. P. Seligman (Eds.), *Psychopathology: Experimental models.* San Francisco: Freeman.

Weiss, J. M. (1982, August). *A model for neurochemical study of depression.* Paper presented at the annual meeting of the American Psychological Association, Washington, DC.

Weiss, J. M., Glazer, H. I., & Pohorecky, L. A. (1976). Coping behavior and neurochemical changes: An alternative explanation for the original "learned helplessness" experiments. In G. Serban & A. Kling (Eds.), *Animal models of human psychobiology.* New York: Plenum Press.

Weissberg, R. P., Caplan, M., & Harwood, R. L. (1991). Promoting competent young people in competence-enhancing environments: A systems-based perspective on primary prevention. *Journal of Consulting and Clinical Psychology, 59,* 830–841

Weissman, M. M. (1990). Evidence for comorbidity of anxiety and depression: Family and genetic studies of children. In J. D. Maser & C. R. Cloninger (Eds.), *Comorbidity of mood and anxiety disorders.* Washington, DC: American Psychiatric Press.

Weissman, M. M., Warner, V., Wickramaratne, P., & Prusoff, B. A. (1988). Early-onset major depression in parents and their children. *Journal of Affective Disorders, 15,* 269–277.

Weisz, J. R., Suwanlert, S., Chaiyasit, W., & Walter, B. (1987a). Epidemiology of behavioral and emotional problems among Thai and American children: Parent reports for ages 6–11. *Journal of the American Academy of Child and Adolescent Psychiatry, 26,* 890–897.

Weisz, J. R., Suwanlert, S., Chaiyasit, W., & Walter, B. (1987b). Over- and undercontrolled referral problems among children and adolescents from Thailand and the United States: The *Wat* and *Wai* of cultural differences. *Journal of Consulting and Clinical Psychology, 55,* 719–726.

Weisz, J. R., Suwanlert, S., Chaiyasit, W., Weiss, B., Achenbach, T. M., & Eastman, K. I. (1993). Behavioral and emotional problems among Thai and American adolescents: Parent reports for ages 12–16. *Journal of Abnormal Psychology, 102,* 395–403.

Weisz, J. R., Weiss, B., Alicke, M. D., & Klotz, M. L. (1987). Effectiveness of psychotherapy with children and adolescents: A meta-analysis for clinicians. *Journal of Consulting and Clinical Psychology, 55,* 542–549.

Wekstein, L. (1979). *Handbook of suicidology: Principles, problems, and practice.* New York: Brunner/Mazel.

Welch, M. W., & Gist, J. W. (1974). *The open token economy system: A handbook for a behavioral approach to rehabilitation.* Springfield, IL: Charles C Thomas.

Wells, K. B., Golding, J. M., & Burnam, M. A. (1989). Chronic medical conditions in a sample of the general population with anxiety, affective, and substance use disorders. *American Journal of Psychiatry, 146,* 1440–1446.

Wells, K. B., Stewart, A., Hays, R. D., Burnam, A., Rogers, W., Daniels, M., Berry, S., Greenfield, S., & Ware, J. (1989). The functioning and well-being of depressed patients: Results from the Medical Outcomes Study. *Journal of the American Medical Association, 262,* 914–919.

Weltzin, T. E., Starzynski, J., Santelli, R., & Kaye, W. H. (1993). Anorexia and bulimia nervosa. In R. T. Ammerman, C. G. Last, & M. Hersen (Eds.), *Handbook of prescriptive treatments for children and adolescents* (pp. 214–239). Boston: Allyn and Bacon.

Wenar, C. (1983). *Psychopathology from infancy through adolescence: A developmental approach.* New York: Random House.

Werry, J. S. (1979a). The childhood psychoses. In H. C. Quay & J. S. Werry (Eds.), *Psychopathological disorders of childhood* (2nd ed.). New York: Wiley.

Wesson, D. R., & Smith, D. E. (1971, December 15). *Barbiturate use as an intoxicant: A San Francisco perspective.* Testimony presented at the subcommittee to investigate juvenile delinquency.

Westen, D. (1988). Transference and information processing. *Clinical Psychology Review, 8,* 161–179.

Wetherby, A. M. (1986). Ontogeny of communicative functions in autism. *Journal of Autism and Developmental Disorders, 16,* 295–316.

Wexler, D. B. (1981). *Mental health law: Major issues.* New York: Plenum Press.

Wexler, D. B. (1982). Seclusion and restraint: Lessons from law, psychiatry, and psychology. *International Journal of Law and Psychiatry, 5,* 285–294.

Whipple, E., & Webster-Stratton, C. (1991). The role of parental stress in physically abusive families. *Child Abuse and Neglect, 15,* 279–291.

Whisman, M. A. (1993). Mediators and moderators of change in cognitive therapy of depression. *Psychological Bulletin, 114,* 248–265.

Whisnant, J. P. (1993). Natural history of transient ischemic attack and ischemic stroke. In J. P. Whisnant (Ed.), *Stroke, populations, cohorts, and clinical trials* (pp. 135–153). Boston: Butterworth-Heinemann.

Whitam, F. L. (1983). Culturally invariable properties of male homosexuality: Tentative conclusions from cross-cultural research. *Archives of Sexual Behavior, 11,* 11–22.

White, J. (1991). *Drug dependence.* Englewood Cliffs, NJ: Prentice-Hall.

Whitlatch, C. J., Zarit, S. H., & von Eye, A. (1991). Efficacy of interventions with caregivers: A reanalysis. *Gerontologist, 31,* 9–14.

Whitlock, F. A. (1967). The aetiology of hysteria. *Acta Psychiatrica Scandinavica, 43,* 144–162.

Whybrow, P. C., Akiskal, H. S., & McKinney, W. T., Jr. (1984). *Mood disorders: Toward a new psychobiology.* New York: Plenum Press.

Widiger, T. A. (in press). Deletion of self-defeating and sadistic personality disorder diagnoses. In W. J. Livesley (Ed.), *The* DSM-IV *personality disorders.* New York: Guilford Press.

Widiger, T. A., & Costa, P. T. (1994). Personality and personality disorders. *Journal of Abnormal Psychology, 103,* 78–91.

Widiger, T. A., & Trull, T. J. (1991). Diagnosis and clinical assessment. *Annual Review of Psychology, 41,* 109–135.

Widom, C. (1989). The cycle of violence. *Science, 244,* 160–166.

Wielgus, M. S., & Harvey, P. D. (1988). Dichotic listening and recall in schizophrenia and mania. *Schizophrenia Bulletin, 14,* 689–700.

Wilcox, J. A. (1993). Structural brain abnormalities in catatonia. *Biological Psychiatry, 27,* 61–64.

Wihelmsen, L. (1988). Coronary heart disease: Epidemiology of smoking and intervention studies of smoking. *American Heart Journal, 115,* 242–249.

Willerman, L., & Cohen, D. B. (1990). *Psychopathology.* New York: McGraw-Hill.

Williams, G. J. R. (1983). Child abuse. In C. E. Walker & M. C. Roberts (Eds.), *Handbook of clinical child psychology* (pp. 1219–1248). New York: Wiley.

Williams, L. B., & Pratt, W. F. (1990). *Wanted and unwanted childbearing in the United States: 1973–88* (data from the National Survey of Family Growth; advance data from *Vital and Health Statistics, 189*). Hyattsville, MD: National Center for Health Statistics.

Williams, L. M. (1994). Recall of childhood trauma: A prospective study of women's memories of child sexual abuse. *Journal of Consulting and Clinical Psychology.*

Williamson, D. F., Kahn, H. S., Remington, P. L., & Anda, R. F. (1990). The 10-year incidence of overweight and weight gain in U.S. adults. *Archives of Internal Medicine, 150,* 665–672.

Wilson, G. D. (1987). An ethological approach to sexual deviation. In G. D. Wilson (Ed.), *Variant sexuality: Research and theory.* Baltimore: Johns Hopkins University Press.

Wilson, M. (1984). Female homosexuals' need for dominance and endurance. *Psychological Reports, 55,* 79–82.

Wincze, J. P. (1989). Assessment and treatment of atypical sexual behavior. In S. R. Leiblum & R. C. Rosen (Eds.), *Principles and practice of sex therapy*. New York: Guilford Press.

Wincze, J. P., Bansal, S., & Malamud, M. (1986). Effects of medroxyprogesterone acetate on subjective arousal, arousal to erotic stimulation, and nocturnal penile tumescence in male sex offenders. *Archives of Sexual Behavior, 15*(4), 293–305.

Windle, M. (1990). A longitudinal study of antisocial behaviors in early adolescence as predictors of late adolescent substance use: Gender and ethnic group differences. *Journal of Abnormal Psychology, 99*, 86–91.

Wing, L. (1981). Language, social, and cognitive impairments in autism and severe mental retardation. *Journal of Autism and Developmental Disorders, 11*, 31–44.

Wing, L., & Attwood, A. (1987). Syndromes of autism and atypical development. In D. J. Cohen & A. Donnelan (Eds.), *Handbook of autism* (pp. 3–17). New York: Wiley.

Wing, L., & Gould, J. (1979). Severe impairments of social interaction and associated abnormalities in children: Epidemiology and classification. *Journal of Autism and Developmental Disorders, 9*, 11–29.

Winokur, G., Coryell, W., Endicott, J., & Akiskal, H. (1993). Further distinctions between manic-depressive illness (bipolar disorder) and primary depressive disorder (unipolar depression). *American Journal of Psychiatry, 150*, 1176–1181.

Wirz-Justice, A., Graw, P., Kräuchi, K., Jochum, A., Arendt, J., Fisch, H. U., Buddeberg, C., & Poldinger, W. (1993). Light therapy in seasonal affective disorder is independent of time of day or circadian phase. *Archives of General Psychiatry, 50*, 929–937.

Wise, R. A. (1988). The neurobiology of craving: Implications for the understanding and treatment of addiction. *Journal of Abnormal Psychology, 97*, 118–132.

Wiser, S., & Goldfried, M. R. (1993). Comparative study of emotional experiencing in psychodynamic-interpersonal and cognitive-behavioral therapies. *Journal of Consulting and Clinical Psychology, 61*, 892–895.

Witzig, J. S. (1968). The group treatment of male exhibitionists. *American Journal of Psychiatry, 25*, 75–81.

Wolberg, L. R. (1977). *The technique of psychotherapy*. New York: Grune & Stratton.

Wolf, M. M., Risley, T., & Mees, M. L. (1964). Application of operant conditioning procedures to the behavior problems of an autistic child. *Behaviour Research and Therapy, 1*, 305–313.

Wolf, S., & Wolff, H. G. (1947). *Human gastric functions*. New York: Oxford University Press.

Wolkin, A., Sanfilipo, M., Wolf, A. P., Angrist, B., Brodie, J. D., & Rotrosen, J. (1992). Negative symptoms and hypofrontality in chronic schizophrenia. *Archives of General Psychiatry, 49*, 959–965.

Wolpe, J. (1958). *Psychotherapy by reciprocal inhibition*. Stanford, CA: Stanford University Press.

Wolpe, J. (1969). *The practice of behavior therapy*. New York: Pergamon Press.

Wolpe, J. (1973). *The practice of behavior therapy* (2nd ed.). New York: Pergamon Press.

Wolpe, J. (1976). *Theme and variations: A behavior therapy casebook*. Elmsford, NY: Pergamon Press.

Wolpe, J. (1978). Cognition and causation in human behavior and its therapy. *American Psychologist, 33*, 437–446.

Wolpe, J., & Rachman, S. (1960). Psychoanalytic evidence: A critique of psychoanalytic technique based on Freud's case of Little Hans. *Journal of Nervous and Mental Disease, 130*, 135–147.

Wolpe, J., & Rowan, V. C. (1988). Panic disorder: A product of classical conditioning. *Behaviour Research and Therapy, 26*, 441–450.

Wolpe, J., & Wolpe, D. (1981). *Our useless fears*. Boston: Houghton Mifflin.

Wong, D. F., Gjedde, A., Wagner, H. N., Jr., Tune, L. E., Dannals, R. F., Pearlsson, G. D., Links, J. M., Tamminga, C. A., Broussolle, E. P., Ravert, H. T., Wilson, A. A., Toung, J. K. T., Malat, J., Williams, F. A., O'Touma, L. A., Snyder, S. H., Kuhar, M. J., & Gjedde, A. (1986). Positron emission tomography reveals elevated D2 dopamine receptors in drug-naive schizophrenics. *Science, 234*, 1558–1563.

Woods, J. H., Katz, J. L., & Winger, G. (1987). Abuse liability of benzodiazepines. *Pharmacological Reviews, 39*, 251–413.

Woolson, A. M., & Swanson, M. G. (1972). The second time around: Psychotherapy with the "hysterical woman." *Psychotherapy: Theory, Research, and Practice, 9*, 168–173.

Wright, L. (1994). *Remembering Satan*. New York: Knopf.

Wyatt v. Stickney, (1972).

Wynne, L. C., & Singer, M. T. (1963). Thought disorder and family relations of schizophrenics: I. A research strategy. *Archives of General Psychiatry, 9*, 191–198.

Wynne, L. C., Singer, M. T., Bartko, J. J., & Toohey, M. L. (1975). Schizophrenics and their families: Recent research on parental communication. In J. M. Tanner (Ed.), *Psychiatric research: The widening perspective*. New York: International Universities Press.

Yablonsky, L. (1976). *Psychodrama: Resolving emotional problems through role-playing*. New York: Basic Books.

Yalom, I. D. (1985). *The theory and practice of group psychotherapy* (3rd ed.). New York: Basic Books.

Yeaton, W. H., & Sechrest, L. (1981). Critical dimensions in the choice and maintenance of successful treatments: Strength, integrity, and effectiveness. *Journal of Consulting and Clinical Psychology, 49*, 156–167.

Yetman, N. R. (1994). Race and ethnic inequality. In C. Calhoun & G. Ritzer (Eds.), *Social problems*. New York: McGraw-Hill/Primis.

Yost, E., Beutler, L. E., Corbishley, M. A., & Allender, J. R. (1986). *Group cognitive therapy: A treatment approach for depressed older adults*. New York: Pergamon Press.

Young, J. G., Kavanagh, M. E., Anderson, G. M., Shaywitz, B. A., & Cohen, D. J. (1982). Clinical neurochemistry of autism and associated disorders. *Journal of Autism and Developmental Disorders, 12*, 147–165.

Young, T. J. (1985). Adolescent suicide: The clinical manifestation of alienation. *High School Journal, 69,* 55–60.

Youngberg v. Romeo, 102 S.Ct. 2452, 2462, 2463 (1982).

Zarit, S. H. (1992). Concepts and measures in family caregiving research. In B. Bauer (Ed.), *Conceptual and methodological issues in family caregiver research* (pp. 1–19). Toronto, Canada: University of Toronto Press.

Zarit, S. H. (1994). Research perspectives on family caregiving. In M. Cantor (Ed.), *Family caregiving: Agenda for the future* (pp. 9–24). San Francisco: American Society on Aging.

Zarit, S. H., Orr, N. K., & Zarit, J. M. (1985). *The hidden victims of Alzheimer's disease: Families under stress.* New York: New York University Press.

Zax, M., & Stricker, G. (1963). *Patterns of psychopathology: Case studies in behavioral dysfunction.* New York and London: Macmillan.

Zigler, E., & Levine, J. (1973). Premorbid adjustment and paranoid-nonparanoid status in schizophrenia: A further investigation. *Journal of Abnormal Psychology, 82*(2), 189–199.

Zigler, E., & Phillips, L. (1961). Psychiatric diagnosis and symptomatology. *Journal of Abnormal and Social Psychology, 63,* 69–75.

Zigman, W. M., Schupf, N., Zigman, A., et al. (1993). Aging and Alzheimer disease in people with mental retardation. *International Review of Research in Mental Retardation, 19,* 63.

Zilboorg, G., & Henry, G. W. (1941). *A history of medical psychology.* New York: Norton.

Zimbardo, P. G., Andersen, S. M., & Kabat, L. G. (1981). Induced hearing deficit generates experimental paranoia. *Science, 212,* 1529–1531.

Zinborg, R. E., Barlow, D. H., Liebowitz, M., Street, L., Broadhead, E., Katon, W., Roy-Byrne, P., Lepine, J. P., Teherani, M., Richards, J., Brantley, P. J., & Kraemer, H. (1994). The *DSM-IV* field trial for mixed anxiety-depression. *American Journal of Psychiatry, 151,* 1153–1162.

Zoccolillo, M., & Rogers, K. (1991). Characteristics and outcome of hospitalized adolescent girls with conduct disorder. *Journal of the American Academy of Child and Adolescent Psychiatry, 30,* 973–981.

Zohar, J., & Zohar-Kadouch, R. C. (1991). Is there a specific role for serotonin in obsessive compulsive disorder? In S. Brown & H. M. van Praag (Eds.), *Clinical and experimental psychiatry* (Monograph No. 4, pp. 161–182). New York: Brunner/Mazel.

Zubin, J., & Spring, B. (1977). Vulnerability—new view of schizophrenia. *Journal of Abnormal Psychology, 86,* 103–126.

Zucker, K. J., & Green, R. (1992). Psychosexual disorders in children and adolescents. *Journal of Child Psychology and Psychiatry, 33,* 107–151.

CREDITS AND ACKNOWLEDGMENTS

McGraw-Hill thanks the copyright holders for making it possible to include the following copyrighted material in this publication:

CHAPTER 1
Text: *Page 15:* Allderidge, P. (1979). Hospitals, madhouses and asylums: Cycles in the care of the insane. *British Journal of Psychiatry, 134,* 327. Reprinted by permission.

CHAPTER 2
Text: *Page 35 (in box):* Erdelyi, M. H., & Goldberg, B. (1979). Let's not sweep repression under the rug: Toward a cognitive psychology of repression. In J. F. Kihlstrom & F. J. Evans (Eds.), *Functional disorders of memory.* Reprinted by permission of Lawrence Erlbaum Associates, Inc., and the authors. / *Page 47:* May, R. (1961). Existential bases of psychotherapy. In R. May (Ed.), *Existential psychology.* Reprinted by permission of McGraw-Hill, Inc. / Figures: *Page 38, Fig. 2.1:* Erikson, E. H. (1950). *Childhood and society.* Copyright 1950, © 1953 by W. W. Norton & Company, Inc., renewed 1978, 1991 by Erik H. Erikson. Adapted by permission of W. W. Norton & Company, Inc.

CHAPTER 5
Text: *Page 102:* Miller, N. E. (1972). Comments on strategy and tactics of research. In A. E. Bergin & H. H. Strupp (Eds.), *Changing frontiers in the science of psychotherapy* (Aldine-Atherton), 348. Reprinted by permission of the author. / *Page 107(in box):* Curtiss, S. R. (1977). *Genie: A psycholinguistic study of a modern-day "wild child,"* 5–6. Reprinted by permission of Academic Press and the author. / Figures: *Page 114, Fig. 5.2:* Kelly, J. A. & Drabman, R. S. (1977). The modification of socially detrimental behavior. *Journal of Behavior Therapy and Experimental Psychiatry, 8,* 101–104. Copyright 1977 Pergamon Press. Reprinted by permission of Elsevier Science, Ltd., Pergamon Imprint, The Boulevard, Langford Lane, Kidlington OX5 1GB, UK. / *Page 115, Fig. 5.3:* Dyer, K., Christian, W. P., & Luce, S. C. (1982). The role of response delay in improving the discrimination performance of autistic children. *Journal of Applied Behavior Analysis, 15,* 231–240. Copyright © 1982 the Journal of Applied Behavior Analysis. Reprinted by permission of the Journal of Applied Behavior Analysis and the authors.

CHAPTER 6
Text: *Page 123:* Spitzer, R. L. (1976). More on pseudoscience in science and the case for psychiatric diagnosis: A critique of D. L. Rosenhan's "On being sane in insane places" and "The contextual nature of psychiatric diagnosis." *Archives of General Psychiatry,* 469. Copyright © 1976, American Medical Association. Reprinted by permission. / *Pages 123, 125, 143:* American Psychiatric Association. (1994). *Diagnostic and statistical manual of mental disorders,* fourth edition. Reprinted by permission of American Psychiatric Association, Washington, DC. / *Page 124 (in box):* Rosenhan, D. L. (1973). "On being sane in insane places," *Science, 179.* Copyright © 1973 American Association for the Advancement of Science. Abstracted with permission from Science and the author. *Page 143:* Del Castillo, J. (1970). The influence of language upon symptomalogy in foreign-born patients. *American Journal of Psychiatry, 127* (August), 161. Reprinted by permission of the American Psychiatric Association. / Figures: *Page 132, Fig. 6.1:* Simulated items similar to those in the Wechsler Adult Scales for Adults and Children. Copyright 1949, 1955, 1974, 1981, 1991 by

The Psychological Corporation. Reprinted by permission. All rights reserved. / *Page 135, Fig. 6.3:* Simulated items similar to those in the Thematic Apperception Test (TAT). Copyright © 1943 by the President and Fellows of Harvard College, © 1971 by Henry A. Murray. / *Page 138, Fig. 6.4:* Bender, L. (1938). A visual motor gestalt test and its clinical use. *Research Monographs of the American Orthopsychiatric Association, 3,* xi, 176. Reprinted by permission.

CHAPTER 7

Text: *Page 150:* Leon, G. R. (1977). *Case histories in deviant behavior,* second edition, 113–188. Copyright © 1977 by Allyn & Bacon, Inc. Reprinted by permission. / *Page 154–155:* Kaplan, H. I., & Sadock, B. J. (1991). *Synopsis of psychiatry: Behavioral sciences, clinical psychiatry,* sixth edition, 401–402. Published by Williams & Wilkins. Reprinted by permission of the publisher and the author. / *Page 156:* Rachman, S. J., & Hodgson, R. J. (1980). *Obsessions and compulsions,* 66–67. Reprinted by permission of Prentice Hall, Inc. / *Page 160:* Erikson, K. T. (1976). *Everything in its path: Destruction of community in the Buffalo Creek flood.* Copyright © 1976 by Kai T. Erikson. Reprinted by permission of Simon & Schuster, Inc. / *Page 161:* American Psychiatric Association (1994). *Diagnostic and statistical manual of mental disorders,* fourth edition. Reprinted by permission of American Psychiatric Association, Washington, DC. / *Page 162 (in box):* Becker, J. V., Skinner, L. J., & Abel, G. G. (1983). *Sequelae of sexual assault: The survivor's perspective.* In J. G. Green and I. R. Stuart (Eds.), *The sexual aggressor,* 252–253. Copyright © 1983. Reprinted by permission of Van Nostrand Reinhold. / Figures: *Page 167, Fig. 7.1:* Clark, D. M. (1986). A cognitive approach to panic. *Behavior Research and Therapy, 24,* 463. Reprinted by permission of Elsevier Science Ltd., Pergamon Imprint, The Boulevard, Langford Lane, Kidlington OX5 1GB, UK.

CHAPTER 8

Text: *Page 176:* Lyon, L. S. (1985). Facilitating telephone number recall in a case of psychogenic amnesia. *Journal of Behavior Therapy and Experimental Psychiatry, 16,* 147–149. Adapted by permission of Elsevier Science Ltd., Pergamon Imprint, The Boulevard, Langford Lane, Kidlington OX5 1GB, UK. / *Page 176:* Bryant, R. A., & McConkey, K. M. (1989). Visual conversion disorder: A case analysis of the influence of visual information. *Journal of Abnormal Psychology, 98,* 326–329. Adapted by permission of the American Psychological Association. / *Page 179:* Masserman, J. H. (1961). *Principles of Dynamic Psychiatry,* second edition, 35–37. Adapted by permission of W. B. Saunders Company. / *Page 180 (in box):* Kihlstrom, J. F., Tataryn, D. J., & Hoyt, I. P. Dissociative disorders. In P. B. Sutker & H. E. Adams (Eds.), *Comprehensive handbook of psychopathology,* second edition. Abstracted by permission of Plenum Publishing Corp. and J. F. Kihlstrom. / *Page 182:* Nunes, D. (1975). The anguish behind the three faces of Eve. *New York Post* (September 15). Reprinted from the Washington Post. / *Page 185 (in box):* Loftus, E. F. (1993). The reality of repressed memories. *American Psychologist, 48,* 532. Reprinted by permission of the American Psychological Association and the author. / *Page 187:* Spitzer, R. L., Skodol, A. E., Gibbon, M., & Williams, J. B. W. (1981). *DSM-III casebook: A learning companion to the diagnostic and statistical manual of mental disorders, third edition,* 112–113. Reprinted by permission of American Psychiatric Press. / *Page 190:* Schwarz, J. R. (1981). *The Hillside Strangler: A Murderer's Mind,* 139–140, 142–143. © 1981 Ted Schwarz. Reprinted by permission of Doubleday, a division of Bantam Doubleday Dell Publishing Group, Inc. / *Pages 196, 197:* Goldblatt, M., & Munitz, H. (1976). Behavioral treatment of hysterical leg paralysis. *Journal of Behavior Therapy and Experimental Psychiatry, 7, (3),* 259–263. Adapted with permission from Elsevier Science Ltd., Pergamon Imprint, The Boulevard, Langford Lane, Kidlington OX5 1GB, UK.

CHAPTER 9

Text: *Page 206:* American Psychiatric Association. (1994). *Diagnostic and statistical manual of mental disorders,* fourth edition. Reprinted by permission of American Psychiatric Association, Washington, DC. / *Page 209 (in box):* Kanner, A. D., Coyne, J. C., Schaeffer, C., & Lazarus, R. S. (1981). Comparison of two modes of stress measurement: Daily hassles and uplifts versus major life events. *Journal of Behavioral Medicine, 4,* 1–39. Reprinted by permission of Plenum Publishing Corporation and A. D. Kanner. / Figures: *Page 228, Figs. 9.1 & 9.2:* Cohen, S., & Williamson, G. M. (1991). Stress and infectious disease in humans. *Psychological Bulletin, 109,* 8. Copyright 1991 by the American Psychological Association. Adapted by permission of the American Psychological Association and the authors.

CHAPTER 10

Text: *Pages 232, 234:* Spitzer, R. L., Skodol, A. E., Gibbon, M., & Williams, J. B. W. (1983). *Psychopathology: A case book, 118, 115.* Copyright 1983. Reprinted by permission of McGraw-Hill, Inc. / *Page 237:* Kolb, L. C. (1982). *Modern clinical psychiatry,* 10th edition, 376–377. Reprinted by permission of W. B. Saunders Company. / *Page 245:* Shneidman, E. S. (1992). A conspectus of the suicidal scenario. In R. W. Maris, A. L. Berman, J. T. Maltsberger, & R. I. Yufit (Eds.), *Assessment and predication of suicide,* 51–52. Reprinted by permission of The Guilford Press. / Table: *Page 242, Table 10.1:* Alloy, L. B., Kelly, K. A., Mineka, S., & Clements, C. M. (1990). Comorbidity of anxiety and depression disorders: A helplessness-hopelessness perspective. In J. D. Maser & C. R. Cloninger (Eds.), *Comorbidity of mood and anxiety disorders,* 507. Copyright 1990 American Psychiatric Press, Inc., Washington, DC. Reprinted by permission. Includes data from Garber, J., Miller, S. M., & Abramson, L. Y. (1980). On the distinction between anxiety states and depression: Perceived control certainty, and probability of goal attainment. In J. Garber & M. E. P. Seligman (Eds.), *Human helplessness: Theory and applications* (New York: Academic Press).

CHAPTER 11

Text: *Page 264:* Perry, S., Frances, A., & Clarkin, J. (1990). *A DSM-III-R Casebook of treatment selection,* 324–326. Copyright © 1990 by Brunner/Mazel, Inc. Reprinted by permission of Brunner/Mazel Inc., and J. Clarkin. / *Page 264:* American Psychiatric Association (1994). *Diagnostic and statistical manual of mental disorders,* fourth edition, 342–345. Reprinted by permission of American Psychiatric Association, Washington, DC. / *Page 267:* Spitzer, R. L., Gibbon, M., Skodol, A. E., et al. (Eds.). (1989). Mental disorders in adults. In *DSM-III-R casebook: A learning companion to the diagnostic and statistical manual of mental disorders, third edition revised,* 123–124. Reprinted by permission of American Psychiatric Press, Inc. / *Pages 273, 275, 276:* Cleckley, H. M. (1976). *The mask of sanity,* 342, 46–55. Reprinted by permission of Emily S. Cleckley, Publisher, Augusta, Georgia. / *Pages 278, 279:* Frank, G. (1966). *The Boston strangler,* 316. Copyright © 1966 by Gerold Frank. Reprinted by permission of Dutton Signet, a Division of Penguin Books USA Inc., and the William Morris Agency. / *Pages 280–281:* Gough, H. C. (1948). A sociological theory of psychotherapy. *American Journal of Sociology,* 53, 359–366. Reprinted by permission of University of Chicago Press.

CHAPTER 12

Text: *Page 288:* Jellinek, E. M. (1946). *Phases in the drinking history of alcoholics.* Reprinted by permission of Rutgers Center of Alcohol Studies, New Brunswick, NJ. / *Page 289:* American Psychiatric Association (1994). *Diagnostic and statistical manual of mental disorders,* fourth edition. Reprinted by permission of American Psychiatric Association, Washington, DC. / *Pages 312, 313:* Hoffman, A. (1971). LSD discoverer disputes "chance" factor in finding. *Psychiatric News, 6(8),* 23. Reprinted by permission of American Psychiatric Press. / *Page 314:* Tinklenberg, J. R. (1974). What a physician should know about marijuana. *Rational Drug Therapy, 4.* Reprinted by permission of W. B. Saunders Company. / Tables: *Page 291, Tables 12.1 & 12.2:* Ray, O. S., & Ksir, C. J. (1993). *Drugs, society and human behavior, 6th edition.* Adapted by permission of Mosby-Year Book, Inc., St. Louis.

/ *Page 297, Table 12.3:* Gallup Poll News Service (1992). *Gallup Poll Monthly* (February), 46. Reprinted by permission. / Figures: *Page 304, Fig. 12.1:* Hugick, L., & Leonard, J. (1991). Despite increasing hostility, one in four Americans still smokes. *Gallup Poll Monthly* (December). Reprinted by permission of Gallup Poll News Service. / *Page 312, Fig. 12.3:* Gawin, F. H., & Kleber, H. D. (1986). Abstinence symptomatology and psychiatric diagnosis in cocaine abusers. *Archives of General Psychiatry, 43,* 107–113. © 1986, American Medical Association. Reprinted by permission.

CHAPTER 13

Text: *Page 324:* Spitzer, R. L., Gibbon, M., Skodol, A. E., et al., (1989). *DSM-III-R casebook: A learning companion to the diagnostic and statistical manual of mental disorders, third edition revised.* Reprinted by permission of American Psychiatric Press. / *Page 330 (in box):* LoPiccolo, J. (1977). Direct treatment of sexual dysfunction in the couple. In J. Money & H. Musaph (Eds.), *Handbook of sexology,* 1239, Elsevier, Amsterdam. Reprinted by permission of the editors. *Page 331:* Masters, W. H., & Johnson, B. E. (1970). *Human sexual inadequacy.* St. Louis: Masters & Johnson Institute. / *Page 337:* Fauman, M. A. (1994). *Study guide to DSM-IV,* 295. Reprinted by permission of American Psychiatric Press. / *Page 343:* Russell, D. E. H. (1986). *The secret trauma: Incest in the lives of girls and women, 157.* Copyright © 1988 by Diane E. H. Russell. Reprinted by permission of BasicBooks, Inc., a Division of HarperCollins Publishers.

CHAPTER 14

Text: *Pages 355–356:* Sheehan, S. (1982). *Is there no place on earth for me?,* 72–73. Copyright © 1982 by Susan Sheehan. This material originally appeared in slightly different form in *The New Yorker,* Spring 1981. Reprinted by permission of Houghton Mifflin Company and Lescher & Lescher, Ltd. All rights reserved. / *Page 356:* Rokeach, M. (1964). *The three Christs of Ypsilanti,* 10–11. Copyright © 1964. Reprinted by permission of Random House, Inc. / *Page 358 (in box):* Nijinsky, V. (1936). *The diary of Vaslav Nijinsky* (R. Nijinsky, Ed.). Copyright 1936, 1964. Reprinted by permission of Simon & Schuster. / *Page 359 (in box):* Nielsen, T. I. (1963). Volition: A new experimental approach. *Scandinavian Journal of Psychology, 4,* 225–230. Reprinted by permission of Scandinavian University Press, Oslo. / *Page 360:* Cohen, B. D., Nachmani, G., & Rosenberg, S. (1974). Referent communication disturbances in acute schizophrenia. *Journal of Abnormal Psychology, 83,* (1), 11. Reprinted by permission of American Psychological Association. / *Pages 360–361:* Soloway, M. R., Shenton, M. E., & Holzman, P. S. (1987). Comparative studies of thought disorders, I: Mania and schizophrenia. *Archives of General Psychiatry, 44,* 13–20. © 1987, American Medical Association. Reprinted by permission of the American Medical Association. / *Pages 355, 361:* Bleuler, E. (1950). *Dementia praecox or the group of schizophrenia,* trans. J. Zinkin. Copyright 1950 by International Universities Press, Inc. Reprinted by permission. / *Pages 361, 362, 365, 374:* Hagen, R. (n.d.). Unpublished case examples from the clinical files of Dr. Richard Hagen, Florida University, Tallahassee, Florida. Reprinted by permission of Dr. Richard Hagen. / *Pages 362–363:* McGhie, A., & Chapman, J. (1961). Disorders of attention and perception in early schizophrenia. *British Journal of Medical Psychology,* 34, 105, 108. Reprinted by permission of British Psychological Society. / *Page 364 (in box):* Miller, L. J., O'Connor, E., & DiPasquale, T. (1993). Patients' attitudes toward hallucinations. *American Journal of Psychiatry, 150,* 587. Reprinted with permission of the American Psychiatric Association. / *Page 368:* McNeil, E. B. (1970). *The psychoses,* 98. Reprinted by permission of Prentice Hall, Inc. / *Page 370:* Arieti, S. (1974). *The interpretation of schizophrenia,* second edition, 165–166. Copyright © 1955 by Robert Brunner. Copyright © 1974 by Silvano Arieti. Reprinted by permission of BasicBooks, a division of HarperCollins Publishers, Inc. / *Page 373:* Spitzer, R. L., Skodol, A. E., Gibbon, M., and Williams, J. B. W. (1981). *DSM-III casebook: A learning companion to the diagnostic and statistical manual of mental disorders, third edition,* 180. Reprinted by permission of American Psychiatric Press.

CHAPTER 15

Text: *Page 386:* Mednick, S. A. (1971). Birth defects and schizophrenia. *Psychology Today, 4,* 80. Copyright 1971 by Sussex Publishers, Inc. Reprinted by permission. / *Page 395:* Brewin, C. R., MacCarthy, B., Duda, K., & Vaughn, C. E. (1991). Attribution and expressed emotion in the relatives of patients with schizophrenia. *Journal of Abnormal Psychology, 100,* 552. Reprinted by permission of Journal of Abnormal Psychology. / *Page 395:* Bateson, G., Jackson, D., Haley, J., & Weakland, J. (1956). Toward a theory of schizophrenia. *Behavioral Science, 1,* 251. Reprinted by permission of the publisher. / *Page 399:* Sushinsky, L. (1970). An illustration of a behavioral therapy intervention with nursing staff in a therapeutic role. *Journal of Psychiatric Nursing and Mental Health Services, 8*(5). Reprinted by permission of Slack, Inc. / Figures: *Page 390, Fig. 15.2:* Hare, E., Bulusu, L., & Adelstein, A. (1979). Schizophrenia and season of birth. *Population Trends, 17.* Adapted by permission of Office of Population Services & Surveys, London. © British Crown copyright.

CHAPTER 16

Text: *Page 406:* Dahlberg, C. C., & Jaffe, J. (1977). *Stroke: A doctor's personal story of his recovery.* Reprinted by permission of W. W. Norton & Company, Inc. / *Page 419 (in box):* Fauman, M. A. (1994). *Study guide to DSM-IV,* 63. Reprinted by permission of American Psychiatric Association. / *Page 422 (in box):* Zarit, S. H. (1992). *The hidden victims of Alzheimer's disease: Families under stress,* 3–15. Reprinted by permission of New York University Press. / *Page 428:* Evans, M. (1953). *A ray of darkness.* New York: Roy Publishers. Reprinted in Kaplan, B. (Ed.). 1964. *The inner world of mental illness.* New York: HarperCollins Publishers. / Figures: *Page 413, Fig. 16.1:* Farber, M. (1994). The worst case. *Sports Illustrated* (December). Illustration by Paragraphics; consultation by Daniel S. Casper, M.D., Ph.D., and Technical Medical Animation Corp. Adapted by permission.

CHAPTER 17

Text: *Page 434:* Bierman, K. (n.d.). Unpublished case examples from the clinical files of Dr. K. Bierman, Pennsylvania State University, State College, Pennsylvania. Reprinted by permission of K. Bierman. / *Pages 438–439:* Kazdin, A. E. (1988). Conduct disorder. In M. Hersen & C. G. Last (Eds.), *Child behavior therapy casebook.* Reprinted by permission of Plenum Press. / *Page 444:* Bruch, H. (1978). *The golden cage: The enigma of anorexia nervosa,* 1–2. Copyright © 1978 by Harvard University Press. Reprinted by permission of Harvard University Press.

CHAPTER 18

Text: *Page 462:* Reiss, S. (1985). The mentally retarded, emotionally disturbed adult. In M. Sigman (Ed.), *Children with emotional disorders and developmental disabilities.* Copyright © 1985 by Allyn & Bacon. Adapted by permission. / *Page 471:* Coleman, M. (1989). *Medical evaluation of individuals with an autistic disorder.* Forum Medicum. / *Page 473:* Eberhardy, F. (1967). The view from the "couch." *Journal of Child Psychology & Psychiatry, 8,* 257–263. Reprinted by permission. / *Page 477 (in box):* Selfe, L. (1978). *Nadia: A case of extraordinary drawing ability in an autistic child.* Reprinted by permission of Academic Press Ltd., London. / *Page 480:* Greenspan, S., & Shoultz, B. (1981). Why mentally retarded adults lose their jobs: Social competence as a factor in work adjustment. *Research in Developmental Disabilities, 2,* 32–33. Copyright © 1981 by Elsevier Science Ltd., Pergamon Imprint, The Boulevard, Langford Lane, Kidlington OX5 1GB, UK. Reprinted by permission. / *Page 486:* Amos, P. (Ed.), (1993). Auditory training as autism therapy: A preliminary review, 10. Newsletter excerpt reprinted by permission of Autism Support & Advocacy in PA, Amore, PA. / Figures: *Page 464, Fig. 18.1:* Hagerman, R. J. & McBogg, P. M. (1983). *The fragile x syndrome: Diagnosis, biochemistry, and intervention.* Reprinted by permission of Spectra Publishing. / *Page 475, Fig. 18.3:* Bauman, M. D., & Kemper, T. L. (1994).

In vivo neuroanatomy of autism: Neuroimaging studies. In M. D. Bauman & T. L. Kemper, (Eds.), *The neurobiology of autism,* 124. Adapted by permission of Johns Hopkins University Press.

CHAPTER 19

Page 492: Wolfberg, L. R. (1977). *The technique of psychotherapy,* 3. Reprinted by permission of Grune & Stratton, a division of W. B. Saunders Company, and the author. / *Page 502:* Bootzin, R. R., Epstein, D., & Wood, J. M. (1991). Stimulus control instructions. In P. Hauri (Ed.), *Case studies in insomnia.* Reprinted by permission of Plenum Press. / *Page 503:* Wolpe, J., and Wolpe, D. (1981). *Our useless fears,* 54. Reprinted by permission of Houghton Mifflin Co. and the author. / Figures: *Fig. 9.1, Page 508:* Howard, K. I., Kopta, S. M., Krause, M. S., & Orlinsky, D. E. (1986). The dose-effect relationship in psychotherapy. *American Psychologist, 41,* 159–164. Reprinted by permission of American Psychological Association and Dr. Kenneth Howard, Northwestern University. / *Page 509, Fig. 19.2:* Smith, M. L., Glass, G. V., and Miller, T. J. (1980). *The benefits of psychotherapy.* Adapted by permission of Johns Hopkins University Press.

CHAPTER 20

Text: *Page 519:* Fodor, I. G. (1980). The treatment of communication problems with assertiveness training. In A. Goldstein & E. B. Foa (Eds.), *Handbook of behavioral interventions: A clinical guide,* 530. Reprinted by permission of John Wiley & Sons. / *Page 539 (in box):* Swados, E. (1991). The story of a street person. *New York Times Magazine* (August 18), 18. Copyright 1991 by The New York Times Company. Reprinted by permission.

CHAPTER 21

Text: *Pages 544, 552 (in box), 553:* Kramer, P. (1993). *Listening to Prozac,* 1–9, 12, 21, 18. Copyright © 1993 by Peter D. Kramer. Adapted and reprinted by permission of Viking Penguin, a division of Penguin Books USA Inc.

CHAPTER 22

Text: *Page 562:* Model Penal Code. (1962), sec. 4.01. Copyright © 1962 by the American Law Institute, Philadelphia, PA. Reprinted by permission of the American Law Institute. / *Page 564 (in box):* Robinson, D. N. (1980). *Law and Psychology: Can justice survive the social sciences?,* 63. Reprinted by permission of Oxford University Press. / *Page 570:* Livermore, J. M., Malmquist, C. P., & Meehl, P. E. (1968). On the justifications for civil commitment. *University of Pennsylvania Law Review, 117,* 75–96. Reprinted by permission.

PHOTO CREDITS

CHAPTER 1

2: R. Flynt/Image Works; *5:* Renato Rotolo/Gamma-Liaison; *9:* Bettmann; *12:* Scala/Art Resource; *13:* Diputación de Valencia; *15:* Bettmann; *17:* Belzeaux/Photo Researchers; *19:* Culver; *21:* National Library of Medicine.

CHAPTER 2

24: Erich Hartmann/Magnum; *26:* Archiv/Photo Researchers; *28:* Lynne J. Weinstein/Woodfin Camp; *31:* The Photo Works/Photo Researchers; *32:* Ed Malitsky/Picture Cube; *36:* Top, Karsh/Woodfin Camp; *bottom,*National Library of Medicine/Mark Marten/Photo Researchers; *38:* Joel Gordon; *39:* Manuscripts and Archives, Yale University Library; *40:* Yves Tanguy. *Mama, Papa is Wounded! [Maman, papa est blessé].* Oil on canvas. 36 1/4" x 28 3/4". 1927. Collection, The Museum of Modern Art, New York. Purchase.; *44:* Ted Polumbaum; *46:* David Young-Wolff/PhotoEdit.

CHAPTER 3

52: David Young-Wolff/PhotoEdit; *55: Top,* Culver; *bottom left,* The Ferdinand Hamburger, Jr. Archives/The Johns Hopkins University; *bottom right,* Teachers College, Columbia University; *56:* Joe McNally; *60: Top,* Joe McNally; *bottom,* Martha Cooper/Peter Arnold; *63:* N. Rowan/Image Works; *67:* Dean Abramson/Stock, Boston; *70:* Tony Freeman/PhotoEdit; *73:* Kirk Condyles/Impact Visuals.

CHAPTER 4

78: Howard Sochurek/Stock Market; *81:* Will McIntyre/Photo Researchers; *82:* Bob Sacha; *85:* CNRI/Science Photo Library/Photo Researchers; *87:* Joel Gordon; *90: Top and bottom,* Dr. Nancy C. Andreasen/Science Photo Library/Photo Researchers; *91:* A. Glauberman/Photo Researchers; *94:* John Ficara/Woodfin Camp.

CHAPTER 5

98: Randy Duchaine/Stock Market; *102:* Chuck Savage/Stock Market; *104:* Erich Hartmann/Magnum; *106:* Springer/Bettmann; *111:* Donna De Cesare/Impact Visuals; *112: Left and right,* Matthew McVay/Saba.

CHAPTER 6

118: Fundació Joan Miró, Barcelona; *120:* Bettmann; *127:* Alan Carey/Image Works; *130:* Goldberg/Monkmeyer; *131:* Dan McCoy/Rainbow; *132:* Reproduced by permission of The Psychological Corporation, New York; *134:* Simulated items similar to those in the Weschler Intelligence Scales for Adults and Children. Copyright 1949, 1955, 1974, 1981, 1991 by the Psychological Corporation. Reproduced by permission. All rights reserved.; *140:* Jeff Greenberg/Picture Cube.

CHAPTER 7

148: John Spragens Jr./Photo Researchers; *152:* Arthur Tress/Photo Researchers; *154:* Dion Ogust/Image Works; *156:* Collins/Monkmeyer; *159:* Jeffrey D. Smith/Woodfin Camp; *160:* Kennerly/Gamma-Liaison; *163:* Mimi Forsyth/Monkmeyer; *165:* Nubar Alexanian/Stock, Boston.

CHAPTER 8

174: Frieman/Photo Researchers; *177:* Bettmann; *181:* Lois Bernstein/Gamma-Liaison; *184:* AP/Wide World; *186:* Courtesy of Dr. Bennett Braun; *189:* Philippe Plailly/Science Photo Library/Photo Researchers; *190:* Susan Ragan/UPI/Bettmann; *192:* UPI/Bettmann; *194:* Gerry Goodstein/Hartman Theatre Company; *199:* Mary Evans Picture Library/Photo Researchers.

CHAPTER 9
204: M. Dwyer/Stock, Boston; *207:* Brian Brake/Photo Researchers; *211:* Steve Liss/Time; *215:* Bernstein/Gamma-Liaison; *216:* George Cruikshank: *The Head-Ache,* 1819. 8¼ x 10", colored etching. Philadelphia Museum of Art: SmithKline Beckman Corporation Fund; *217:* Art Resource; *222:* Alon Reininger/Woodfin Camp; *226:* Tony Freeman/Photo Edit.

CHAPTER 10
230: Cecile Brunswick/Peter Arnold; *233:* Alex Hesler/Bettmann; *238: Left,* Sylvia Beach Collection/Photo Researchers; *right,* Bettmann; *241:* Joel Gordon; *244:* Goldberg/Monkmeyer; *247:* Brian Masck/The Muskegon Chronicle; *250:* Renee Lynn/Photo Researchers; *255:* David Strickler/Picture Cube; *257:* Erik Hill/Anchorage Daily News; *259:* Stephen Frisch/Stock, Boston.

CHAPTER 11
262: Wayne Miles/Gamma-Liaison; *267:* Arlene Collins/Monkmeyer; *269:* Drawing by H. Martin; © 1975 The New Yorker Magazine, Inc.; *272:* Bettmann; *273:* © 1994 Donna Ferrato/Domestic Abuse Awarenes Project, NYC from the book "Living With the Enemy" (Aperture); *276:* The Leader/Sipa Press; *279:* A. Ramey/Woodfin Camp; *283:* Hans Halberstadt/Photo Researchers.

CHAPTER 12
286: Bob Daemmrich/Image Works; *290:* Joyce George/Reuters/Bettmann; *295:* Richard Hutchings/Photo Researchers; *298: Top left, center, right,* Bettmann; *bottom left, center,* UPI/Bettmann; *bottom right,* Elliot Landy/Magnum; *299:* Robert E. Murowchick/Photo Researchers; *303:* Hank Morgan/Photo Researchers; *305:* Lester Sloan/Woodfin Camp & Assoc.; *309:* Jeff Taylor/UPI/Bettmann; *311:* James Prince/Photo Researchers; *315:* Larry Brownstein/Rainbow.

CHAPTER 13
322: Douglas Mason/Woodfin Camp; *325:* The Metropoitan Museum of Art, Rogers Fund, 1941; (41.162.101) Photographic Services; *326: Left,* Bettmann; *right,* Birgit Pohl; *327:* Susan Van Etten/Picture Cube; *333:* Theo Westenberger/Gamma-Liaison; *337:* Susan Leaviges/Photo Researchers; *339:* Reuters/Bettmann; *342: Left and right,* UPI/Bettmann; *345:* Sidney/Monkmeyer.

CHAPTER 14
352: From *Art as Healing,* by Edward Adamson. Reproduced by permission of Coventure, Ltd., London/Boston; *358: Top,* Bettmann; *bottom,* From "The Diary of Vaslav Nijinsky", edited by Romila Nijinsky, Simon & Shuster, NY, 1936; *360:* John M. Roberts/Stock Market; *363:* Mary Ellen Mark Library; *365:* Erich Roth/Picture Cube; *368:* National Institute for Mental Health; *373:* Bulvony/Time Life Photo Lab; *375:* Courtesy of Camarillo State Hospital.

CHAPTER 15
378: Chris Steele-Perkins/Magnum; *381:* Rick Rickman/Matrix; *383:* Courtesy of Dr. Allan F. Mirsky, National Institute of Mental Health, Bethesda, MD; *388: Left and right,* Tim Beddow/Science Photo Library/Photo Researchers; *392:* Michael Newman/Photo Edit; *397:* John Anderson/Impact Visuals; *398:* Nubar Alexanian/Stock, Boston; *400:* Joel Gordon.

CHAPTER 16
404: Scott Camazine/Photo Researchers; *407:* Bettmann; *410:* Richard Pasley/Gamma-Liaison; *412:* Astrid & Hans Frider-Michler/Science Photo Library/Photo Researchers; *416:* California Medical Publications; *421:* Bill Aron/Photo Edit; *423:* UPI/Bettmann; *425: Top,* UPI/Bettmann; *bottom,* Bettmann; *427:* F. Savariau/Gamma-Liaison.

CHAPTER 17
432: Bob Daemmrich/The Image Works; *435:* Ken Gaghan/Jeroboam; *437:* José Asel/Aurora; *442:* Lew Merrim/Monkmeyer; *443:* William Thompson/Picture Cube; *446:* Dan McCoy/Rainbow; *450:* Heron/Monkmeyer; *454:* Stormi Greener/*The Star Tribune,* Minneapolis; *455:* Dorothy Littell/Stock, Boston.

CHAPTER 18
460: M. Greenlar/Image Works; *463:* Bill Lyons/Photo Researchers; *466:* George Steinmetz/National Geographic Society; *468:* Jacques Charlas/Stock, Boston; *472:* Will & Deni McIntyre/Photo Researchers; *478:* Conclin/Monkmeyer; *481:* Paul Conklin/Monkmeyer; *485:* Alan Carey/Image Works.

CHAPTER 19
490: Ed Lallo/Gamma-Liaison; *492:* Dion Ogust/Image Works; *495:* Edmund Engelman; *496:* Rousseau, Henri. *The Dream.* 1910. Oil on canvas, 6'8 ½" x 9'9 ½". The Museum of Modern Art, New York. Gift of Nelson A. Rockefeller. Photograph © 1995 The Museum of Modern Art, New York; *499:* Life Magazine/Time Warner Inc.; *500:* Hugh L. Wilkerson; *503: The Far Side,* © 1987 Universal Press Syndicate. Reprinted with permission.; *506:* John Bova/Photo Researchers; *510:* James Prince/Photo Researchers.

CHAPTER 20
514: Bob Daemmrich/Stock, Boston; *517:* James Wilson/Woodfin Camp; *518:* Steve Liss/Time Magazine; *520:* Paul Fusco/Magnum; *522:* Paul Fusco/Magnum; *524:* Bob Daemmrich/Stock, Boston; *528:* Paul Fusco/Magnum; *533:* Freda Leinwand/Monkmeyer; *536:* Hap Stewart/Jeroboam; *539:* Eunice Harris/Photo Researchers.

CHAPTER 21
542: Charlotte Raymond/Science Source/Photo Researchers; *546:* Seth Resnick/Stock, Boston; *548:* Oscar Burriel/Latin Stock/Science Photo Library/Photo Researchers; *549:* Lynn Johnson/Black Star; *551:* Photo by MYKO; *555:* James Wilson/Woodfin Camp.

CHAPTER 22
558: Paul Conclin/Photo Edit; *560:* Pool photo/Gamma-Liaison; *563:* AP/Wide World; *565:* John Barr/Gamma-Liaison; *569:* Renato Rotolo/Gamma-Liaison; *576:* Sandor ACS/Courtesy of New York Hospital - Cornell University Medical Center, Westchester Division.

NAME INDEX

Note: Page numbers followed by *n.* indicate material in footnotes.

SUBJECT INDEX

Note: Page numbers followed by *n.* indicate material in footnotes.